STRATEGIC MANAGEMENT

A MANAGERIAL PERSPECTIVE

SECOND EDITION

L. J. BOURGEOIS, III
University of Virginia
Darden Graduate School of Business

IRENE M. DUHAIME
Georgia State University

J. L. STIMPERT
Colorado College

STRATEGIC MANAGEMENT

A MANAGERIAL PERSPECTIVE

SECOND EDITION

L. J. BOURGEOIS, III
University of Virginia
Darden Graduate School of Business

IRENE M. DUHAIME
Georgia State University

J. L. STIMPERT
Colorado College

The Dryden Press

HARCOURT BRACE COLLEGE PUBLISHERS

Fort Worth Philadelphia San Diego New York Orlando Austin San Antonio
Toronto Montreal London Sydney Tokyo

Publisher: George Provol
Acquisitions Editor: John R. Weimeister
Developmental Editor: Jennifer Sheetz Langer
Executive Marketing Strategist: Lisé Johnson
Project Editor: John Haakenson
Production Manager: Anne Dunigan
Art Director: Carol Kincaid
Electronic Publishing Coordinators: Kathi Embry / Ellie Moore
Permissions Editor: Adele Krause

ISBN:0-03-022373-3
Library of Congress Catalog Card Number: 98-73693

Address for Editorial Correspondence:
The Dryden Press
301 Commerce Street, Suite 3700
Fort Worth, Texas 76102.

Address for Orders:
The Dryden Press
6277 Sea Harbor Drive
Orlando, Florida 32887-6777
1-800-782-4479 (in Florida).

Website address:
http://www.hbcollege.com

(Copyright Acknowledgements begin on page CR-1, which constitutes a continuation of this copyright page.)

Printed in the United States of America.

8 9 0 1 2 3 4 5 6 7 032 9 8 7 6 5 4 3 2 1

The Dryden Press
Harcourt Brace College Publishers

to Lionel and Claire – L.J.B.
to Walter and to Irene and the memory of Jim – I.M.D.
to Lesley – J.L.S.

The Dryden Press Series in Management

Anthony, Perrewé, and Kacmar
Strategic Human Resource Management
Second Edition

Bereman, Lengnick-Hall, Mark
Compensation Decision Making: A Computer-Based Approach
Second Edition

Bergmann, Scarpello, and Hills
Compensation Decision Making
Second Edition

Boone and Kurtz
Contemporary Business
Ninth Edition

Bourgeois, Duhaime and Stimpert
Strategic Management: A Managerial Perspective
Second Edition

Bracker, Montanari, and Morgan
Cases in Strategic Management

Brechner
Contemporary Mathematics for Business and Consumers

Calvasina and Barton
Chopstick Company: A Business Simulation

Costin
Readings in Total Quality Management

Costin
Managing in the Global Economy: The European Union

Costin
Economic Reform in Latin America

Costin
Management Development and Training: A TQM Approach

Costin
Readings in Strategy and Strategic Management

Czinkota, Ronkainen, and Moffett
International Business
Fifth Edition

Czinkota, Ronkainen, Moffett, and Moynihan
Global Business
Second Edition

Daft
Leadership

Daft
Management
Fourth Edition

Daft and Marcic
Understanding Management
Second Edition

DeSimone and Harris
Human Resource Development
Second Edition

Foegen
Business Plan Guidebook
Revised Edition

Gatewood and Feild
Human Resource Selection
Fourth Edition

Gold
Exploring Organizational Behavior: Readings, Cases, Experiences

Greenhaus and Callanan
Career Management
Second Edition

Higgins and Vincze
Strategic Management: Text and Cases
Fifth Edition

Hodgetts
Modern Human Relations at Work
Seventh Edition

Hodgetts and Kroeck
Personnel and Human Resource Management

Hodgetts and Kuratko
Effective Small Business Management
Sixth Edition

Holley and Jennings
The Labor Relations Process
Sixth Edition

Holt
International Management: Text and Cases

Jauch and Coltrin
The Managerial Experience: Cases and Exercises
Sixth Edition

Kindler and Ginsburg
Strategic & Interpersonal Skill Building

Kirkpatrick and Lewis
Effective Supervision: Preparing for the 21st Century

Kuratko and Hodgetts
Entrepreneurship: A Contemporary Approach
Fourth Edition

Kuratko and Welsch
Entrepreneurial Strategy: Text and Cases

Lengnick-Hall, Cynthia, and Hartman
Experiencing Quality

Lewis
Io Enterprises Simulation

Long and Arnold
The Power of Environmental Partnerships

Morgan
Managing for Success

Oddou and Derr
Managing Internationally: A Personal Journey

Ryan, Eckert, and Ray
Small Business: An Entrepreneur's Plan
Fourth Edition

Sandburg
Career Design Software

Vecchio
Organizational Behavior
Third Edition

Walton
Corporate Encounters: Law, Ethics, and the Business Environment

Weiss
Business Ethics: A Stakeholder and Issues Management Approach
Second Edition

Zikmund
Business Research Methods
Fifth Edition

Preface

Our vision in writing this book is to offer a strategy text that will introduce students to the field of strategic management and excite them about the dynamic nature of the business world. Today's business students are tomorrow's business leaders, so it's appropriate that the most distinctive feature of the book is its emphasis on general managers. The text builds on recent developments in the management research literature and Peter Senge's book, *The Fifth Discipline*, to highlight the important role of managers in the formulation and implementation of strategy. The text's organizing framework suggests that managers' mental models — their beliefs and understandings — influence strategic decision making. The text then examines how managers' decisions and their firms' resulting strategies can lead to the development of unique resources and capabilities that can be the source of sustained competitive advantage and high performance.

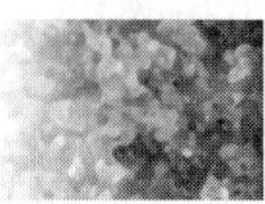

What's Unique about This Book

Three key themes are emphasized throughout the text and further reinforced in the cases:

- First, this book places managers at center stage by focusing on *how managerial thinking influences strategy formulation and implementation*. Because managers make the decisions that form the basis of strategies, the only way to understand and fully appreciate the strategy formulation and implementation processes is to examine the thinking that causes managers to make a particular set of decisions rather than some other set of decisions. The text draws on the latest concepts and theories from management practice and academic research to examine managerial thinking and decision making.
- The text also emphasizes *the importance of change and the need to think dynamically about strategic management*. Strategies that are effective today will almost certainly be ineffective in the future because companies do not enjoy the luxury of competing in static worlds. Demographic changes produce new customer needs and wants, while the emergence of new technologies leads to the development of new products and services, so firms' industry environments are constantly changing. One entire chapter of the text (Chapter 5) is devoted to exploring the ongoing evolution of industry environments.
- Finally, the book underscores *the importance of organizational learning*. Knowledge resides in organizations in the heads of managers and employees, in routines and standard operating procedures, and in the equipment and technologies that are employed. As the business world becomes increasingly knowledge-intensive, the ability to learn, store, retrieve, and exploit new knowledge and information will become a key source of competitive advantage. The book therefore examines how managers can mobilize the knowledge residing in employees and in organizational capabilities and processes to develop and maintain competitive advantage.

Text Chapters Deal with Many Real-World Phenomena

Discussion is included on topics such as the problems associated with price competition, the use of litigation as a competitive weapon, the unique challenges of service businesses, and the limitations of boards of directors.

THE SECOND EDITION CONTAINS ELEVEN NEW CASES

These field-based cases have strengthened our coverage of global issues and not-for-profit organizations. Several cases now feature women protagonists to better reflect the diversity in today's business environments. We want to discuss a variety of business situations in diverse industries. Therefore new industries are included in this text such as publishing, botanical gardens, and financial services.

AN OVERVIEW OF THE TEXT

The text begins by introducing a model of strategic management that appears in all subsequent chapters. As noted above, the model highlights the importance of managers' mental models — their beliefs and understandings — and how these mental models influence strategic decision making and the development of firm-specific capabilities that can be the source of competitive advantage and high firm performance. Chapter 2 builds on research on managerial and organizational cognition, highlighting the role of general managers in strategy formulation and implementation and emphasizing the importance of expertise and flexibility in managerial thinking. The third chapter defines the concept of competitive advantage and incorporates resource-based theory to describe the processes by which firms develop and sustain competitive advantage.

The analysis of industries is the focus of Chapters 4 and 5. Chapter 4 describes SWOT Analysis and the Five Forces Model, two well-known techniques or tools for analyzing industries. Chapter 5 builds on the work of Hamel and Prahalad, Bourgeois and Eisenhardt, and D'Aveni to develop a dynamic model that explains how industries evolve over time, focusing specifically on the role played by entrepreneurs and the responses of incumbent firms' managers.

Chapter 6 is devoted to the topic of business definition or how managers position their firms in their competitive environments. The chapter builds on academic research and the popular management literature, which emphasizes the importance of organizational identity, strategic intent, vision, and purpose. Many actual business examples are presented to emphasize the importance of effective business definition and the need for continuous redefinition to respond to or anticipate changes in firms' competitive environments.

Business strategy is the central topic of Chapters 7 and 8. Chapter 7 introduces the concept of generic strategies. In addition to describing the generic strategies of cost leadership, differentiation, and focus, the chapter also addresses a number of real-world business issues, including the hazards of competing on the basis of price and, in particular, the dangers of price wars. The chapter also takes up the problem of "commoditization" or the tendency for differentiated products to lose their distinctiveness. The challenges that store-brand or generic products pose to the major consumer products companies such as Procter & Gamble are also described. Chapter 8 builds on the life cycle concept to describe the unique challenges faced by firms in emerging and mature industry environments. The chapter also compares and contrasts the challenges faced by manufacturing and service firms and focuses on the special challenges facing the managers of service firms.

Chapter 9 examines corporate strategy and diversification. The chapter describes why firms diversify and the different types of diversification strategies. The chapter focuses extensively on the synergies that corporate strategies should achieve while also describing the difficulties managers encounter as they seek to achieve synergies. The last half of the chapter examines the relationship between diversification and performance, while also suggesting the kinds of managerial expertise that are needed to manage corporate strategy and diversification effectively.

Organizational structure is covered in Chapter 10. The chapter emphasizes that the objective of organizational structure is to effectively implement strategies. The chapter also defines organizational structure broadly to incorporate not just hierarchy and organizational forms (i.e., the organizational chart), but also to include standard operating procedures, routines, systems (especially organizational information systems), and culture. The chapter concludes by examining a range of new issues that are likely to influence how firms are organized in the future and also discusses some of the organizational innovations that many firms are currently adopting.

Chapters 11 and 12 focus on the problems of organizational responsiveness and the management of strategic change. Chapter 11 describes both boards of directors and strategic planning processes and discusses some of the controversies surrounding both management mechanisms. The chapter notes their limitations and weaknesses while also highlighting steps many managers and firms are taking to improve their effectiveness. Chapter 12 examines the challenges of organizational change and the central role managers play in "managing" the strategic change process. The chapter begins by describing some of the reasons why managers often fail to respond effectively to changes in their firms' business environments. It concludes by suggesting some ways to make managers more responsive and more effective "change agents."

"Learning" Strategic Management

The word that best summarizes our beliefs about education and teaching is ***encounter***. Encounter not only captures the importance of coming into contact with ideas, objects, and persons, but it also implies engagement or a deeper involvement that will produce some lasting impact or meaning. When we encounter ideas, we figuratively grasp them, struggle with them, and learn from them. Encounter, then, is the essence of education, and any educational experience should offer students and faculty alike the opportunity to be exposed to new ideas, concepts, theories, to struggle with them, and to learn.

Today's business environments are incredibly dynamic, exciting, and increasingly global – qualities that make them inherently interesting and invite encounter. The pace of change in the business world guarantees that new customer needs and wants, new technologies, new products and services, and whole new companies and industries will continuously enter the competitive landscape. Furthermore, the influence of business enterprise is pervasive. No profession, no aspect of our culture, and few parts of our lives are free from the influence of business and commercial activity. Few forces in our society have the same potential for improving the quality of our personal lives and the larger communities in which we live and work.

Encounter is most likely to occur when students can apply concepts and theories to actual business problems. As a result, the chapters and cases of this book seek to bring text material to life by offering many examples to illustrate and reinforce important concepts. All chapters contain "Management Focus" capsules that describe business issues that have challenged or currently challenge managers, elaborate on companies' specific competitive dilemmas, or introduce tools and ways of thinking that managers have employed in different business situations. All chapters begin by identifying a set of learning objectives and each chapter concludes with a list of summary points. The text aims to be comprehensive, yet attempts to explain key points as succinctly and clearly as possible.

In keeping with this emphasis on managers, nearly all of the book's cases are based on field research, written with direct input from company executives and managers. The cases are based on well-known companies, including Marriott Corporation, Dollar General Stores, Hewlett-Packard, Walt Disney Productions, Yamaha Corporation, and Bacardi. Ten cases are enhanced by videotaped classroom presentations by or interviews with the companies' chief executives or other senior officers.

The concept of mental models, which is emphasized throughout the text, is not simply an important management concept. While the text focuses on the importance of managers' mental models and their influence on strategic decision making, the cases encourage students to focus on the development of their own mental models. Students should examine their beliefs about industry environments, the importance of business definition and positioning, how firms and businesses should compete, the appropriate size and diversity of firms, and how organizations should be structured. While the text emphasizes the importance of expertise and flexibility in managerial thinking, students are also encouraged to think about their own beliefs and understandings and the importance of adapting these beliefs and understandings as they move into, and advance through, their business careers.

In fact, we believe the best way for students to encounter and learn from the material presented in this book is to assume the role of manager. As the text introduces topics and describes concepts, frameworks, and models, students are encouraged to ask how they would respond to various business issues and problems. While reading through the chapters, apply concepts introduced in the text to contemporary business situations and use the various frameworks and models to analyze actual firms and industries and the cases included in the book.

The very fast pace of change which characterizes most business environments ensures that the future will be very different than the present, as new customer demands and technologies emerge, new products and services are developed, new firms appear on the scene, and whole new industries are created. Thus, our overall objective is not to predict the future, but — through encounter with the ideas and concepts presented in this book — to help students develop ways of thinking and learning that will make them effective business leaders throughout their careers. We eagerly await the contributions of our readers to the exciting world of business.

The Ancillary Package

Instructor's manual The second edition is accompanied by a complete instructor's manual designed to provide in-depth assistance to the instructor. This guide, written by the text authors, provides teaching suggestions, outlines and overviews of the chapters, case teaching notes, and possible group projects.

Ancillary cases Four of the cases have short follow-on cases which present the students with unfolding challenges as they were encountered by the general managers in the "A" cases. The follow-on cases are included in the Instructor's Manual.

Test bank *Strategic Management* comes with a comprehensive test bank written by Robert Fleming of Delta State University, with multiple choice, short answer, and essay questions covering every chapter of the book.

Computerized test bank All the questions in the printed test bank are available on computer diskette in PC and Macintosh compatible forms. For PC users, Dryden offers DOS and Windows versions of the test bank.

Lecture presentation software in Microsoft PowerPoint Interactive lecture software, created by William Coon of Washington University in St. Louis, is available to assist instructors with their lecture preparation. Slides present key concepts with exhibits from the text to highlight important topics.

Darden Cases To order additional copies of cases from The Darden Case Collection, send an email to dardencases@virginia.edu or telephone 1.800.246.3367. For a complete listing of the Case Collection along with case abstracts, please visit the web site http://www.darden.virginia.edu/case/bib/.

ACKNOWLEDGMENTS

No intellectual effort is ever an individual product, and authorship of this textbook is certainly no exception to this rule. We have attempted to write an outstanding textbook on strategic management, but our efforts build on a solid foundation laid by our mentors and on many contributions and insights from our associates, faculty colleagues, and students. Every page of this textbook reflects their teaching and wisdom.

A special thanks is also due to our schools and professional colleagues for providing us with the time and support for writing this text. A number of individuals deserve special recognition for their contributions to this textbook. A special thanks to several Darden colleagues who contributed cases, including John Colley (Bacova Guild), Alex Horniman (Big Sky and Public Communications Department at New York Telephone), Lynn Isabella (Astral Records and Grupo Bacardi de Mexico), Bob Landel (Public Communications Department at New York Telephone), Andrea Larson (Women's World Banking), Jeanne Liedtka (Iran Office Automation, Copeland/Bain, Charlottesville-Albemarle Legal Aid Society, New York Botanical Garden, and Disney: The Arrival of Eisner and Wells), John Rosenblum (Copeland/Bain), and Elliott Weiss (Southwest Airlines). Thanks also go to former Darden colleagues Bill Fulmer (Walt Disney Productions and Marriott) and Paul McKinnon (Bennett Association), as well as to Jeff Barach of Tulane University (Alaska Gold Mine). Thanks to Cal Tate of Darden Communications Services for his help in developing the videos that accompany this book. Mike Wasserman, a colleague at George Mason University, has been a constant supporter of this project and has provided many ideas and much enthusiasm.

We also extend a special thanks to those who reviewed this second edition of the text and offered many suggestions for improvement. We especially thank

Cynthia Lengnick-Hall, Wichita State University; Donald Bergh, Penn State University; Elizabeth Fitzgerald, Kennesaw State University; Loren Gustafson, Seattle Pacific University; Alan Hoffman, Bentley College; and Yolanda Sarason, University of New Mexico. We also appreciate the support and enthusiasm of our colleagues at The Dryden Press. John Weimeister brought us together as collaborators, Jennifer Sheetz Langer saw us through a thousand questions involved in the publication of the text, our production staff who designed and produced this text, and Lisé Johnson who developed a marketing campaign for bringing this text to the marketplace. Last, but certainly not least, we owe much to our families for their encouragement and support.

L. J. Bourgeois III	Irene M. Duhaime	J. L. Stimpert
Charlottesville	Atlanta	Colorado Springs

About The Authors

L. J. "Jay" Bourgeois III received his Ph.D. from the University of Washington in 1978, where he wrote an A.T. Kearney Award-winning dissertation about strategic decision making in firms facing volatile environments. Prior to his doctoral work, he was employed as a financial analyst in the corporate planning department of Castle & Cooke Foods, and held several assignments in the firm's Latin American operations.

Professor Bourgeois has taught at the University of Washington, the University of Pittsburgh, McGill University, and Stanford Business School, and has been teaching strategy at the University of Virginia's Darden Graduate School of Business since 1986. He has published over two dozen articles and chapters in various management journals and books. He has served on the review boards of the *Academy of Management Journal* and *Strategic Management Journal*, was associate editor of *Management Science*, and was chair of the Business Policy and Strategy Division of the Academy of Management in 1989-1990.

Professor Bourgeois teaches in several executive programs, including TEP, Darden's senior executive program, and provides strategy consulting for a variety of North and South American, European, Asian, and Australian corporations. He lives with his wife, Maggie, and their three children in Charlottesville, Virginia, where he plays jazz guitar and bikes long distances for relaxation.

Irene M. Duhaime received her Ph.D. from the University of Pittsburgh in 1981. Her dissertation on corporate divestment won the General Electric Award for Outstanding Research in Strategic Management. Before entering the doctoral program, she was responsible for cash management and short-term investments at New England Mutual Life Insurance Company and was an investment officer at Pittsburgh National Bank.

Professor Duhaime has taught at the University of Pittsburgh, the University of Illinois at Urbana-Champaign, and the University of Memphis, where she was Associate Dean for six years. She now holds the Carl R. Zwerner Chair in Family-Owned Enterprises at Georgia State University, where she teaches strategic management, family business, and entrepreneurship. Her research on diversification, acquisition, divestment, and turnaround has been published in the leading management journals, including the *Academy of Management Journal*, the *Academy of Management Review*, and *Strategic Management Journal*. Her research and teaching interests have spanned the range from large diversified corporations to small entrepreneurial firms and family businesses. As Associate Dean at the University of Memphis, she served as judge for *The Memphis Business Journal's* Small Business and Entrepreneur of the Year awards program for three years and worked closely with the local business community.

Professor Duhaime has served in a variety of leadership roles in the Academy of Management, including Book Review Editor of the *Academy of Management Review* and chair of the Business Policy and Strategy Division in 1993-1994. She lives with her husband, Walter, in Atlanta; she enjoys music, reading, discovering new restaurants, and weekend exploration of the South Carolina beach.

J. L. "Larry" Stimpert received his B.A. in economics from Illinois Wesleyan University and his M.B.A. in finance from Columbia University. Prior to entering the academic field, he worked in the railroad industry and served in various marketing, forecasting, and economic analysis positions at the Southern Railway Company and the Norfolk Southern Corporation. Later, he worked as a manager of marketing and pricing for the Chicago and North Western Transportation Company. Professor Stimpert received his Ph.D. in business administration from the University of Illinois where he was recognized for the quality of his teaching while still a graduate student.

Professor Stimpert's research interests focus on top managers and their influence on strategic decision making and firm strategies. He has written on many strategy issues, including managerial responses to environmental change and organizational decline, business definition and organizational identity, the management of corporate strategy and diversification, company strategies following deregulation, and corporate governance. His articles have appeared in the *Academy of Management Journal*, the *Academy of Management Review*, the *Journal of Management Studies*, and the *Strategic Management Journal*, and he has also authored chapters of several edited books. He is a member of the Academy of Management and the Strategic Management Society.

Professor Stimpert currently teaches management and business courses at Colorado College. Previously, he served on the faculty and taught strategic management courses at Michigan State University. He lives with his wife, Lesley, in Colorado, where he enjoys hiking, backpacking, and skiing as well as reading and playing the piano.

Contents in Brief

TABLE OF CONTENTS

CHAPTER 11: ORGANIZATIONAL RESPONSIVENESS: THE ROLE OF BOARD GOVERNANCE AND STRATEGIC PLANNING 287

CHAPTER 12: THE MANAGEMENT OF STRATEGIC CHANGE 313

Cases in Strategic Management

PART 1

CONCEPTS

Chapter 1

Introduction: A Model of Strategic Management, and an Overview of the Text

Chapter Objectives

This first chapter seeks to introduce students to the field of strategic management and to provide an overview of the book. Its specific objectives are to:

- Describe the dynamic characteristics of the business environments in which general managers must formulate and implement strategies.
- Define the concept of strategy.
- Describe how the study of strategic management is unique and what makes strategy and strategic management "strategic."
- Define and illustrate the concept of mental models.
- Describe how managerial thinking influences strategic decision making and firm performance outcomes.
- Provide a model of strategic management that will serve as an organizing framework for this book.

The chapter begins by considering some of the key characteristics or features of today's business environments.

The Competitive Landscape of the Last Decade of the Twentieth Century

The end of this decade is almost certainly one of the most exciting times in history to be preparing for a career in business. An incredibly rapid rate of technological innovation, significant shifts in the demographic characteristics of the consumer population, and considerable economic growth among newly industrialized nations and developing countries have combined to produce a vibrant competitive landscape that not only offers opportunities for entrepreneurs but also poses considerable risks for established firms.

In such an economic landscape, companies like Apple Computer, founded by two entrepreneurs working in a garage, can so successfully exploit new technologies to develop products that meet previously unknown consumer needs that the business becomes one of the largest companies in the world in less than a decade. That same company, which so fundamentally changed the computer industry, has now been overshadowed by technological and other industry developments that Apple itself set in motion two decades ago. Whether Apple can continue to maintain market relevance in the years ahead will depend on the success its managers achieve in crafting and implementing new strategies.

The challenges of this dynamic competitive landscape are likely to become only more formidable in the years ahead as several factors continue to exert their influence on the business world. Here, a number of these factors are reviewed:

THE COMPETITIVE LANDSCAPE IS CHARACTERIZED BY A RAPID RATE OF CHANGE

Although business environments have probably always changed faster than managers would prefer, consumer demographics, tastes and preferences, the nature of products and services, and the technologies businesses use to provide products and services are now changing more rapidly than ever before. In some rapidly changing markets, such as personal computers, companies face product life cycles as short as four months. In fact, management scholars have coined new terms, including *high-velocity environments*[1] and *hypercompetition*,[2] to describe the dynamics of these rapidly changing competitive environments.

Rapidly changing business environments require company managers to anticipate and/or respond quickly to both changing customer preferences and the moves of their competitors in order to introduce the "right" products and services on a timely basis. Far different from the economic ideal of market equilibrium, many industry environments appear to be in a permanent state of disequilibrium in which demand and supply do not stabilize because technological innovation and changing consumer wants and needs encourage the rapid introduction of new products and services. Consider how this rapid rate of change has affected some of the largest and most successful companies in the business world:

- IBM has now come to represent a classic example of a company caught off guard by changes in its industry. Long dominant in its traditional mainframe computer markets, IBM was able to respond quite quickly to the development of personal computer systems. In fact, IBM's ability to develop its own personal computers and its solid reputation among its mainframe business customers almost certainly played a very important role in encouraging businesses to adopt personal computer technology.

  By the 1990s, however, "clone" manufacturers had flooded the market with low-cost personal computers that rivaled or exceeded the technical capabilities of IBM's PC products. As a result, personal computers became a commodity product in which price was apparently the only characteristic distinguishing one company's products from any other company's. IBM seemed unable to respond effectively to this new wave of competition, leading industry observers to conclude that IBM's top managers still maintained a "mainframe mentality" and did not understand how to compete effectively in what had become a commodity market. Almost overnight, IBM was forced to lay off hundreds of thousands of employees, see its stock lose half its value, and replace its CEO with an industry outsider, Lou Gerstner.

  Now Compaq and Dell set the standards for makers of personal computers, while firms like Sun Microsystems, America Online, Netscape, and Yahoo! have been at the forefront of companies rushing to develop and exploit growing interest in the Internet. To date, these companies have been very successful at anticipating and responding to the rapid rate of change in the computer industry, but can they stay vigilant and avoid IBM-like periods of stagnation?

- Sears, Roebuck and Company offers another example of how a once seemingly invincible company can be buffeted by industry change. By the 1920s, Sears had been so successful that it had become the largest retailer in the world. In fact, Sears was so large during the 1920s and 1930s that its sales revenues represented 1 percent of the gross national product of the United States. In the 1970s, "the world's largest store" built the world's tallest skyscraper for its headquarters in Chicago, and began a program of diversification into financial services and real estate. Already owning the Allstate Insurance Company, Sears went on to acquire the investment banking company Dean Witter Reynolds, and the Coldwell Banker real estate firm. The company also launched its own Discover credit card.

  As Sears was building a portfolio of retailing and financial businesses, however, its core merchandising operations lost ground to competitors, including a retailing upstart from Arkansas called Wal-Mart, Kmart, and many specialty retailers, such as the Limited, Gap, Best Buy, and Home Depot. By the early 1990s, the sales of Wal-Mart and Kmart exceeded the sales of Sears' merchandise unit. In spite of its importance in retailing history, such well-known brand names as Kenmore, Craftsman, and Die-Hard, and many other significant assets and resources, Sears seemed to be lost and to have no consistent strategy for its merchandising operations.

  In response, the company turned to an unlikely source for help, hiring Al Martinez, CEO of the exclusive Saks Fifth Avenue department store chain. Under Martinez's leadership, Sears' sales have grown, profit margins have improved, and the company seems to have engineered a turnaround. Yet, Sears will probably never regain its once-dominant position in the home appliance market; that has been lost to companies like Best Buy and Circuit City. And Sears will continue to be pressured by both specialty retailers and high-end department stores and by discounters, including Wal-Mart, Kmart, and Dollar General.

THE TRADITIONAL BOUNDARIES AROUND MARKETS, NATIONS, AND COMPANIES ARE BEING REDRAWN

Not so long ago, savings and loans, commercial banks, investment banking firms, insurance companies, and mutual funds all competed in their own distinct and specialized markets, and a typical consumer might have had a checking account with a local bank, a home mortgage from a savings and loan, a life insurance policy from an insurance company, and an account with a broker who represented a major investment banking company. Today, with deregulation in the financial arena, firms that once enjoyed a sort of friendly competition in their own distinct market niches now compete vigorously against one another in a single "financial services industry" so that consumers can have savings and checking accounts, home equity loans, insurance policies, and investment services provided by a single company. The State Farm Insurance Company has recently announced plans to open its own bank,[3] and similar moves can be expected by other participants in the new financial services industry.

A similar disintegration of boundaries is occurring among firms in industries as diverse as entertainment, telecommunications, cable television, publishing, and software. In just the last few years, Disney has acquired ABC, Time Warner has acquired Turner Broadcasting, Viacom has acquired Paramount Communications and Blockbuster Video, and Microsoft has made investments in TCI. Most of these companies are headed by visionary leaders and managers, and the strategies devised by Michael Eisner, Gerald Levin, Sumner Redstone, Bill Gates, and John Malone will create and shape the new industry that is now emerging.

Another important development of the last decade is that nearly all firms in the United States are now realizing that they compete in global markets against an array of foreign competitors. Though a few major U.S. companies, such as Boeing, Caterpillar, and the Kellogg Company, have long been global or international companies, more and more companies—even many small businesses—have concluded that their future success depends on the extent to which they can develop and maintain a global scope and presence.

Managers are also rethinking their firms' operations and structures and concluding that many activities, which they have long believed to be essential, actually contribute little or nothing to their success or their ability to compete. Such analyses have led many companies to "re-engineer" their operations, and a growing number of companies are now outsourcing many activities that they once deemed essential.

Nike offers an excellent example of how traditional boundaries around companies, industries, and nations are shifting and becoming more flexible and permeable. As recently as the early 1970s, when someone mentioned athletic shoes or sneakers, the prototypical product that came to mind was a pair of classic "Chuck Taylor" Converse All Stars, which came in either black or white and high- or low-top versions. Nike, of course, completely revolutionized this industry. By emphasizing athletic performance, style, and product marketing, while also turning to foreign companies to manufacture virtually all its shoes, Nike reinvented the athletic shoe industry, and, today, the Nike "swoosh" logo is the second most widely recognized trademark (after the Coca-Cola label) in the world. Nike enjoys a remarkable reputation even though the company doesn't manufacture any of its own shoes or athletic apparel. Later, in Chapter 8, we'll see how an athletic shoe and apparel company can enjoy so much success without manufacturing any of the products it sells.

Societies Are Becoming More Fragmented

Traditional boundaries separating customer groups, companies, industries, and even nations are also evaporating, yet this trend is not necessarily leading to more homogeneous cultures and societies. In fact, evidence suggests that societies are fragmenting and that fewer and fewer common characteristics unite individuals who live in the same country or even in the same community. This will pose unique challenges for companies as they seek to design new products and services and attempt to market these products and services to potential customers.

A recent *Wall Street Journal* article described the dilemma facing General Mills as it seeks to market its cereals and other food products to an increasingly heterogeneous customer base here in the United States. The article noted that twenty years ago, commercial advertisements that appeared on network television could be expected to reach 95 percent of the television viewing audience. Today, however, with the proliferation of cable television channels, General Mills can expect its network television commercials to reach only 50 percent of all television viewers.[4] As cable television, the Internet, and other media further erode network television's market share, General Mills and other consumer products companies will have to develop new means for reaching their target customers.

MANAGEMENT FOCUS

THE GLOBALIZATION OF BUSINESS ACTIVITY

One of the most significant forces shaping the business world today is the globalization of business activity. Some companies based in other countries have always been major players in international business, but most U.S. companies have had the luxury of focusing on a very large domestic market while largely ignoring global business opportunities. Although U.S. companies are responsible for 25 percent of the world's output of goods and services, the U.S. share of total exports is less than 12 percent.[1]

The picture could look very different in another decade as many factors combine to stimulate globalization. Industrialized and newly industrialized nations have concluded a number of agreements aimed at reducing tariffs and trade barriers. Many companies have also found that their domestic markets are now saturated and that the only way to maintain sales growth is to seek out new selling opportunities in international markets. Furthermore, many managers are now turning to outsourcing—the practice of acquiring raw materials, products, and services from other companies—as a way to lower their companies' costs. They have found that their companies can gain competitive advantage by focusing on marketing and distributing while turning to foreign producers for the manufacture of their products. Finally, a rising standard of living in many newly industrialized countries is allowing consumers the opportunity to afford products and services that were once out of reach. Managers are now scrambling to capitalize on these emerging markets.

While the international arena offers firms many new opportunities to increase sales and profits, it also entails some significant challenges and risks. Language, cultural and business practices, and political and legal environments can differ greatly across national borders. Practices that are perfectly acceptable in one country can be taboo in another country. McDonald's decision to enter India meant that its menu had to change drastically in order to accommodate the culture of a country in which cattle are revered. While managers of companies operating in the United States can lay off employees easily, many other countries have legal restrictions that forbid companies from laying off or dismissing employees. Ignoring these differences across nations can have disastrous consequences for companies' global strategies.

The decision to engage in international business activities also requires managers to augment their firms' operational and structural capabilities. Probably the easiest way to begin operating in international markets is to export products to foreign countries. At the other extreme, companies can establish subsidiary companies in foreign countries that will manufacture products, provide services, and direct local marketing activities. If the exporting route is taken, managers must still create marketing strategies, develop relationships with foreign distributors, and establish lines of credit. Other market entry strategies, especially the establishment of foreign subsidiaries, can require elaborate organizational structures to effectively coordinate national and international business operations. Chapter 10 examines the special organizational requirements of global or international companies.

Almost all managers find that international business operations require individual and organizational learning in order to be successful. Managers have to become familiar with the cultures and business practices of foreign markets. In developing marketing strategies, managers must determine which product and service attributes "travel"—that is, which attributes work in many or all countries—and which must be tailored to the cultures and practices of specific countries. They also have to learn how to manage international business operations and develop, primarily through trial and error learning, appropriate structures for coordinating these operations. International business transactions also require sophisticated accounting, banking, and other financial skills. Almost all managers find that the move from operating at the domestic level to competing in the international arena requires a quantum leap in knowledge and capabilities. ■

[1]Hill, C. W. L. 1997. *International Business: Competing in the Global Marketplace.* 2nd ed. Chicago: Irwin.

Companies Must Now Be Very Responsive to Institutional Investors

The early 1930s saw growing concern that the ownership of large corporations had become so diffused that stockholders exercised almost no control over the managers of the firms they owned.[5] Since that time, however, a profound shift has occurred and today, mutual funds, such as Fidelity and Vanguard, retirement plans, such as TIAA-CREF and Calpers, and other institutional investors hold over 50 percent of the outstanding shares traded on the major stock exchanges. Exhibit 1.1 illustrates the growing significance of institutional investors as corporate owners. In his analysis of our "post-capitalist" society, Peter Drucker concluded that this shift toward a greater concentration of corporate ownership will have a profound influence on how managers respond to both their short- and long-term tasks and priorities.[6]

Institutional investors have already flexed their muscle and have begun to make more demands on companies to maintain consistently high levels of performance. Low-performing firms now face considerable criticism from their institutional owners. Over the last decade, many well-known but low-performing companies, including GM, IBM, Apple Computer, Kodak, and American Express, replaced their chief executives because of pressure for change from their institutional owners.

Products and Services Are Increasingly Knowledge-Intensive

Traditionally, the largest cost component of most products or services has been the direct costs of raw materials or the labor required to assemble products and

Exhibit 1.1

The Growth of Institutional Ownership of U.S. Corporations

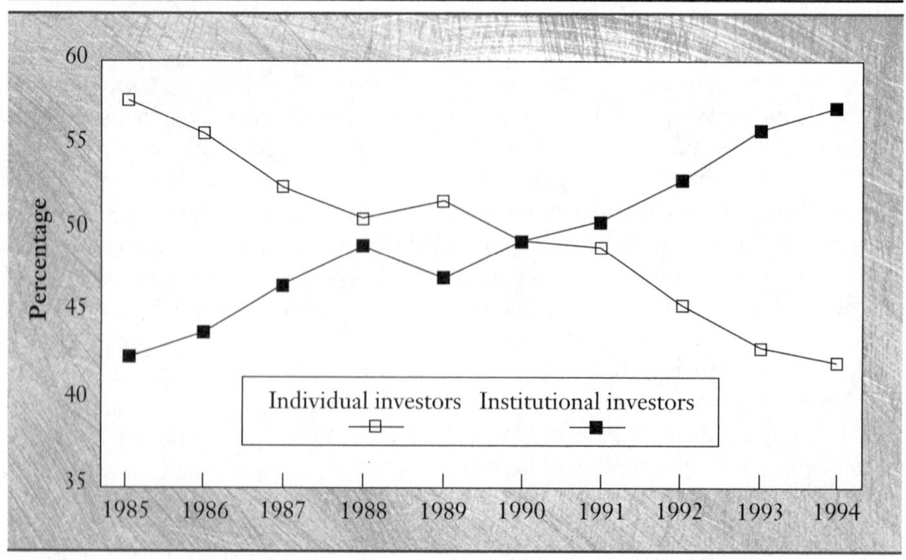

Source: Michael Useem. 1996. *Investor Capitalism: How Money Managers Are Changing the Face of Corporate America.* New York: Basic Books.

deliver services. Today, however, the importance of raw materials and labor has become almost trivial in most manufactured products. For example, it's uncommon for labor to represent more than 15 to 25 percent of the total costs of most products.

Now, the knowledge embedded in most products and services as well as the knowledge required to develop, produce, and provide products and services represents a growing proportion of total cost. In fact, these "knowledge costs" have largely supplanted the importance of traditional labor and material costs. Consider some examples: The largest component of the cost of a microprocessor is not raw material cost—silica sand, an inexpensive commodity, is the raw material in the microprocessors that power today's personal computers; instead, the major component of cost is the technological knowledge embedded in microprocessors as well as the knowledge embedded in the highly specialized equipment required to transform a commodity like silica sand into finished semiconductors.

The materials used to make computer disks are likewise commodities, and blank disks are produced and sold very inexpensively. On the other hand, consumers will pay high prices to buy the latest software packages—not because of the cost of raw materials required to make the computer disks, but because of the value of the knowledge and intellectual content contained in the software on those disks. Even for products like the automobile, in which raw materials and direct labor costs remain a relatively high proportion of total costs, the increasing use of highly technological components as well as computer-aided design and manufacturing techniques have greatly increased the value of the intellectual content of automobiles being produced today.

A Shift Has Occurred in the Relative Importance of "Fixed" versus "Human" Capital

One final trend that will be highlighted here is the growing importance of human capital. Evaluations of companies' internal operations have focused on configurations of fixed assets and emphasized the capacity and efficiency of plant and equipment. The important lesson from the remarkable renaissance of U.S. manufacturing companies over the last decade, however, is that advantage depends to a great extent on "socially complex resources," such as leadership, organizational culture, reputation, and an organization's own internal processes. The effectiveness of internal organizational processes, in which individuals interact with each other and with fixed assets, depends on the knowledge of employees, and such organizational knowledge and learning is largely a function of individual "learning by doing." The growing importance of human capital has many implications, including a much more important role for human resource management in the recruitment, training, motivation, and retention of human capital.

Consequences and Implications

At no time in the history of business enterprise have managers had an easy task, but the factors just outlined, which characterize the current economic landscape, do seem to pose unique challenges that greatly complicate the task of strategic management. Especially compelling is the need for managers to anticipate and be responsive to industry change and disequilibrium so that their companies can remain viable and vibrant. Unfortunately, it is becoming clear that many traditional management principles are either not particularly helpful or totally inadequate for meeting these challenges.

Competitive forces are relentless, and many once "excellent" companies that were doing everything "right" are now declining or failing. Perhaps the most vivid illustration is provided by a review of the many "excellent companies" profiled in Peters and Waterman's book, *In Search of Excellence: Lessons from America's Best-Run Companies;* many of these companies have since suffered through periods of declining fortunes.[7] Data General, Digital Equipment, IBM, Eastman Kodak, Delta Air Lines, McDonald's, Kmart, and Wang Laboratories are just a few of Peters and Waterman's "excellent companies" that have since faced periods of decline. Some of these firms have been able to come back strongly, some will probably never be strong or dominant companies again, while the fate of many others is yet to be determined.

The Field of Strategy: A Unique Focus on the Management of Firms and Businesses

This book seeks to improve your understanding of how managers formulate and implement strategies that lead to sustained *competitive advantage—the reason some firms enjoy higher levels of performance than their rivals.* For most of the students reading this text, the strategic management class you're now beginning is a final capstone course in your business studies. Many business programs expect that the strategy course will provide students with an overview or "big picture" of how other courses in accounting, finance, marketing, and operations tie together.

Beyond offering students an integrative capstone experience, however, this text aims to introduce students to exciting developments in the field of strategic management, a field that has enjoyed considerable theoretical and empirical research over the last few decades. In fact, the field of strategic management has become one of the most vibrant areas of business research, and a considerable body of strategic management theory now exists. As a result, this text seeks to do much more than integrate the material covered in previous business courses. A major aim of the text is to introduce you to concepts, ideas, and theories that will stimulate your thinking about the important roles of general managers, those who have broad responsibilities for the strategic management of entire firms or of the business units of multibusiness firms.

One of the most distinguishing features of a course on strategic management is its unique focus or level of analysis. Review quickly the courses you have completed in your business programs. As illustrated in Exhibit 1.2, the economics courses you have taken focus on "macro" level —or outside the company—issues. For example, macroeconomics courses examine employment, price levels, and the growth of the national and international economies. A primary focus of microeconomics courses is on industries and the nature of competition in various industry environments. On the other hand, most business courses, especially those courses you have taken in your major or your area of concentration, have been at more "micro"—or inside the firm—levels of analysis. For example, the focus of most finance courses is on firms' investment projects and how those projects will be financed. The aim of most marketing courses is to understand the promotion of products or portfolios of products. Similarly, the focus of most organizational behavior courses is on the motivation and job performance of individuals.

EXHIBIT 1.2

Strategy's Level of Analysis Is Unique

Field of Study	*Level of Analysis*
• Macroeconomics	• The economy
• Microeconomics	• Industries and markets
• Strategy	• Firms and businesses
• Finance	• Investment projects
• Marketing	• Products and services
• Organizational behavior	• Individuals
• Operations management	• Plants

Strategic management, in contrast, is one of the few courses that focuses specifically on the management of firms and businesses. At the same time, strategists cannot make decisions in isolation, but must necessarily integrate information from across the broader industry and market levels of analysis while also considering the important roles played by functional departments and individuals within their own firms and businesses. As a result, the task of general managers is not only important and demanding, but it is also a knowledge-intensive job in which managers use information and knowledge gleaned from experience and other sources to make key—strategic—decisions.

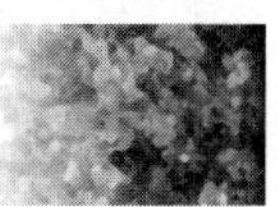

Strategy: A Pattern in a Stream of Decisions

The decisions managers make are critical to the success of their firms, and *the overall objective of this text is to understand managerial decision making and how managers' decisions affect the performance of firms and businesses.* The decisions managers make are so important because they are the raw material or basis of strategies. In fact, throughout this book, strategy will be defined as *"a pattern in a stream of decisions."*[8] In other words, strategies emerge over time as decisions accumulate to form coherent recognizable patterns of action.

This definition of strategy is quite different from the conventional view of strategy as a "grand plan" that emerges after careful and insightful analyses of competitive environments and organizational capabilities. The problem with the "grand plan" view of strategy is that it does not reflect how strategies are actually formulated and implemented in most organizations. Typically, strategies do not emerge from a corporate headquarters as comprehensive statements of objectives and action plans for achieving those objectives. Although strategies do sometimes result from a formal planning process, most strategies emerge in a piecemeal fashion—as managers make decisions in response to a competitor's move, or on a pending situation or crisis, or in anticipation of future changes in the business environment.

"UNREALIZED STRATEGIES" AND THE "EMERGENT" NATURE OF BUSINESS STRATEGIES

Two organizational realities exert a great deal of influence on the strategy formulation and implementation processes in business firms. First, many intended plans do not get implemented; they become "unrealized strategies." [9] Many factors are responsible for plans becoming "unrealized strategies." Sometimes the plans are simply poorly conceived or inappropriate; this fact becomes widely recognized and no action is taken. This possibility is illustrated in the accompanying Management Focus, "Two Views of Senior Management 'Grand Plans.'"

Other times, problems will arise that prevent implementation—circumstances may change and what was seen as a good idea becomes less attractive, a necessary political coalition may not materialize, or key resources that are essential to the implementation of the plan may not be forthcoming. And often, the crush of dealing with day-to-day issues and crises prevents managers from implementing even the best-laid plans. One noted academic and management consultant summarized this tendency by stating that "in most American companies the urgent has driven out the important." [10]

Second, it's important to understand and acknowledge that many strategies *emerge* without ever being part of a formal plan.[11] Because of the rapid pace of change that characterizes most business environments, new issues arise frequently and quite unexpectedly (i.e., a competitor will lower prices, a competitor's new marketing strategy negatively impacts a company's sales and threatens its market share position, new products with better features are introduced by competitors, new technologies are developed, or totally new competitors enter the market). Managers not only have to identify these new issues as they go about performing their routine, day-to-day activities, but they must also respond quickly to these issues if their companies are to avoid negative consequences. In short, managers must make complex decisions quickly and with very little information or very little time to engage in any formal planning activities. In the process of making these almost spontaneous decisions, new strategies "emerge" as patterns develop in streams of decision making. According to Andrew Grove, chief executive officer of Intel, "people formulate strategy with their fingertips. Day in and day out they respond to things, by virtue of the products they promote, the price concessions they make, the distribution channels they choose." [12]

Therefore, a more accurate depiction of the strategy formulation and implementation process is suggested by Exhibit 1.3. The "intended strategy" portion of Exhibit 1.3 represents those plans or initiatives that managers *intend* for their firms to pursue. Note also the box labeled "unrealized strategy"; this represents decisions that are not implemented for any of the reasons described earlier. The key point of the illustration, however, is to demonstrate that "realized strategy" is a product, not just of plans or intentions, but of decisions made in response to emergent issues.

In summary, strategies are rarely the product of a grand plan or formal planning process. The strategies pursued by most companies include some elements from a formal planning process, but many aspects of company strategies are conceived "in real time" as managers wrestle with issues that emerge from ongoing day-to-day business activities. The decisions made by managers accumulate and, over time, reveal patterns that are recognized as coherent strategies.

MANAGEMENT FOCUS

TWO VIEWS OF SENIOR MANAGEMENT "GRAND PLANS"

A short paragraph that appeared in *The Wall Street Journal* noted that many top managers felt that their middle managers were spending too much time and energy "fighting fires and resolving operational issues" while ignoring or failing to execute "the boss's grand plan." A short time later, the newspaper published a follow-up letter suggesting that "much 'grand' thinking at the top is not." The short paragraph and the follow-up letter from *The Wall Street Journal* are reprinted here:

February 9, 1988—TOP MANAGERS fret they're leading a balky horse. Learning International, a training company, says the executives grumble that the middle managers below them focus too much on fighting fires and resolving operational issues and not enough on the boss's grand plan.

February 26, 1988—In your Labor Letter column of Feb. 9, I see that executives complain of foot dragging by middle managers who "focus too much on fighting fires and resolving operational issues and not enough time on the boss's grand plan." Before we do too much hand-wringing over top management's plight, let's consider some other points of view.

In my professional experience with corporate strategy and planning matters, there are usually three basic deficiencies in the "boss's grand plan" that make middle managers' tepid responses entirely understandable: process, content and follow-through.

First, the chief executive officer's brainchild is too often only his or, at best, the result of negotiations among senior executives and consultants whose knowledge of business units begins and ends with "the numbers." More, their products either become top secret or are poorly communicated to the operating level. When a general manager is no more than polite to an executive scheme that he had no hand in building, no one should be surprised.

As to content, let's face it, much "grand" thinking at the top is not. Many otherwise respectable managements permit themselves the delusion that they are providing "vision" when they are merely projecting today's business ahead in time. Sorry, but summing business units' annual plans and pushing them out as far as the spreadsheet will go doesn't make it as valid strategy. Unit people know that. Genuinely creative thinking about business configurations that can deliver competitive advantage, say, a decade hence is quite rare at the top and often unhealthy below.

Finally, if there is anyone left who understands what a true plan is, it must be the unit manager who lives or dies by the one sanctified in the last budget (planning) cycle. Plans make resource, time, accountability and contingency requirements explicit. So-called "strategic plans" are usually far less demanding of their authors. Concepts, policy pronouncements and performance targets decreed by the front office are fine as far as they go, but they are by no means plans that either obligate executive performance or provide a tool for measuring it. Again not surprisingly, corporate's grand "plans" would play better at the front, as it were, if the generals at headquarters themselves faced live ammo.

None of this is to deny that America's middle-management ranks have their share of blockheads. But if the greater number of good operators is preoccupied with fighting fires, it is precisely because of constraints imposed by action, or inaction, from above. Even when invited to "strategize" by executive levels, operating heads are most often being offered responsibility without control, and that is not a game played with much heart.

The view from this vantage point is that senior managements typically have set themselves far too low a standard for their strategic planning work. The people who actually run the businesses in corporate portfolios—middle managers—recognize poor quality when they see it and aren't likely to risk serious time or treasure on direction they regard as superficial or wrongheaded. When the troops won't follow or fight, they must want leadership, in both senses. ■

M. R. Eigerman, Vice President,
Strategy Management
Semcor

EXHIBIT 1.3

Strategy Formulation as a Product of Intended and Emergent Processes

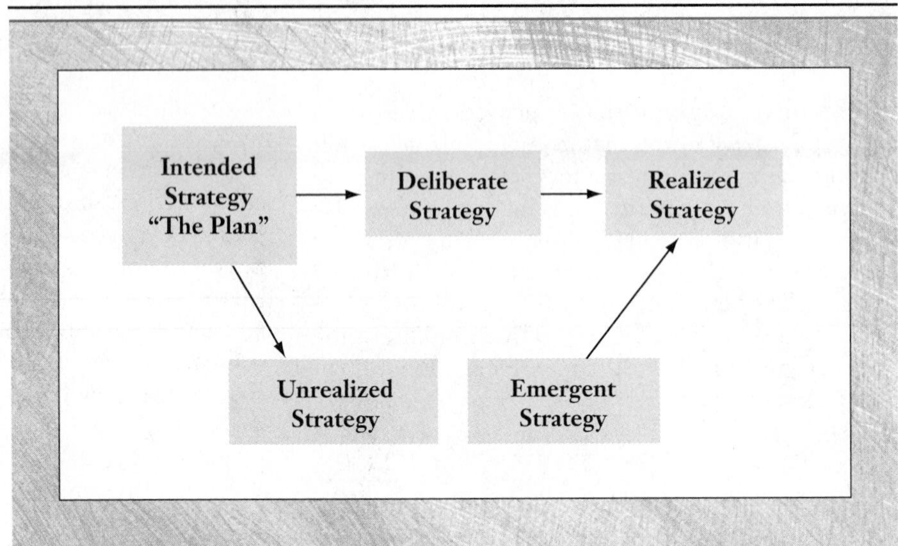

SOURCE: H. Mintzberg, 1978. Patterns in strategy formation. *Management Science* 24:934–948, p. 945.

SOME ILLUSTRATIONS

The emergent nature of most company strategies was illustrated in an article that examined Honda's success at entering the U.S. motorcycle market in the 1960s and 1970s.[13] The article first summarized a study prepared by the Boston Consulting Group (BCG) that attributed Honda's success to a formal strategic planning process that sought to achieve production economies through market share leadership. The article then contrasted the BCG study with accounts by Honda's own managers that described how its successful entry into the U.S. motorcycle market was really a process of learning from trial and error. In the words of one Honda manager:

> In truth, we had no strategy other than the idea of seeing if we could sell something in the United States. It was a new frontier, a new challenge, and it fit the "success against all odds" culture that Mr. Honda had cultivated.[14]

The key idea that the article sought to emphasize was that:

> consultants, academics, and executives express a preference for oversimplifications of reality and cognitively linear explanations of events. To be sure, they have always acknowledged that the "human factor" must be taken into account. But extensive reading of strategy cases at business schools, consultants' reports, [and] strategic planning documents, as well as the coverage of the popular press, reveals a widespread tendency to overlook the process through which organizations experiment, adapt, and learn. We tend to impute coherence and purposive rationality to events when the opposite may be closer to the truth. How an organization deals with miscalculation, mistakes, and serendipitous events *outside its field of vision is often crucial to success over time.*[15]

Another example of the emergent nature of strategy is provided by the recent strategy formulation activities at General Mills' cereal business. Several years ago,

EXHIBIT 1.4

Strategy Formulation Activities at General Mills' Cereal Business

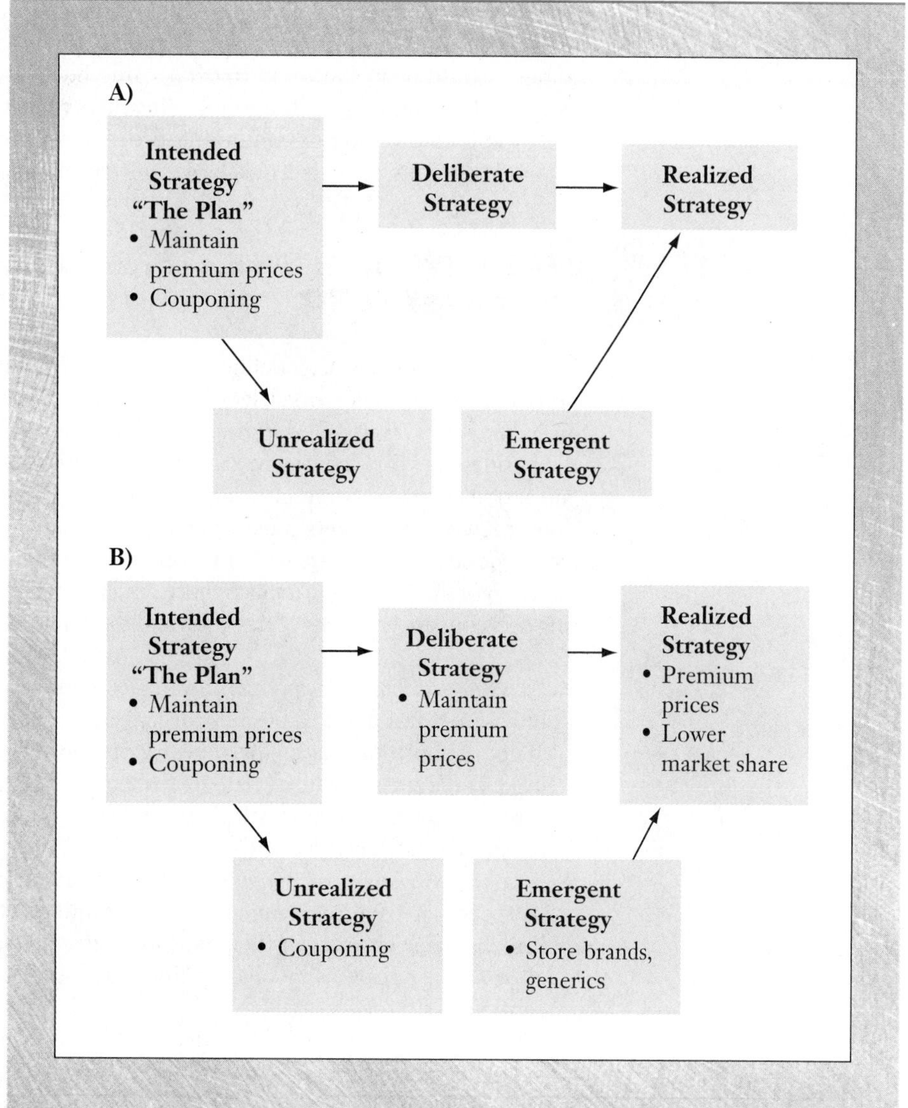

SOURCE: Adapted from H. Mintzberg, 1978. Patterns in strategy formation. *Management Science* 24:934–948, p. 945.

as illustrated by part A of Exhibit 1.4, General Mills announced an "intended strategy" of maintaining premium pricing for its cereal products while using couponing to promote its cereals and attract additional customer interest.

As shown in part B of the exhibit, General Mills deliberately pursued its strategy of maintaining premium prices, but its strategy of using couponing became an unrealized strategy as the company found that a mere 2 percent of all its coupons were redeemed by customers. Furthermore, as also illustrated in part B of the exhibit, the company faced an emerging source of competition from a new player in the ready-to-eat breakfast cereal industry—store brand cereals. As a result, the "realized strategy" at General Mills was to maintain premium prices, while also losing market share to store brands.

In response, General Mills announced in 1995 a new "intended strategy." The two key components of this new intended strategy were (1) to attract customers, not with coupons, but with lower prices, and (2) to reformulate products so that customers would perceive them to offer value beyond what the store brands could provide. The General Mills example illustrates that strategy formulation and reformulation is an ongoing or continuous process in which managers anticipate and/or respond to events in their firms' larger environments.

What Makes Strategic Management "Strategic"?

Now that strategy has been defined and the strategy formulation and implementation processes have been described, let's consider what makes strategic management "strategic." The terms *strategy* and *strategic* are used frequently—perhaps too frequently—in the business world. One way to clarify these terms is to distinguish between decisions and actions that are "strategic" and those that are more "tactical." Every day, several times each day, managers must make a variety of decisions. Some of these decisions will respond to routine issues, while others have the potential to affect the health or direction of the business in a much more fundamental way. These critical, direction-setting decisions are the focus of this book and they are "strategic" for at least three reasons:

1. *Strategic decisions are important.* Strategic decisions and strategic management not only shape and define a business organization, but they also have the potential to affect the bottom-line financial health of a business and even the survival of the organization. As a result, strategic management is a fundamentally important activity; how managers respond to important issues can affect the health and prosperity of their firms and businesses in the short run as well as the long run.
2. *Strategic decisions involve significant reallocations of resources.* Strategic decisions have the potential to change the purpose and direction of a firm and, therefore, lead to major changes in the definition, scale, and scope of the business. Nearly all strategic decisions involve significant allocations or reallocations of organizational resources.

   For example, firms will often decide that they must target a different set of customers, offer a new line of products or services, or employ new technologies. GM's decision to create its Saturn division was made in response to a view that the company needed to target buyers of Japanese cars by offering a new product line that would employ new manufacturing and marketing methods. This decision required a significant reallocation of resources to the new Saturn division away from GM's other car lines. Similarly, decisions to acquire a new business or to divest an existing business will almost always alter the scale or scope of any firm. All these decisions involve major commitments or reallocations of organizational resources.
3. *Strategic decisions tend to involve more than one functional department.* Finally, strategic decisions are rarely focused on a "marketing problem" or a "manufacturing problem." Instead, strategic decision making usually cuts across functional departments, involving marketing *and* manufacturing and, possibly, finance, research and development, and engineering. Strategic decision making

thus requires the attention of general managers and chief executive officers who must often mediate interdepartmental or interdivisional disagreements and rivalries.

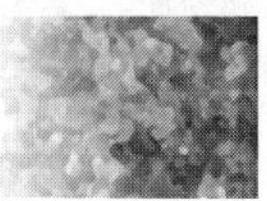

Managerial Thinking: A New Perspective on Strategic Management

By focusing on managerial decision making, this text departs from traditional approaches to the study of strategic management. Almost all previous strategy texts have focused on economic or structural explanations for firm performance. According to this perspective, firm performance is largely a function of industry structure. In other words, firms operating in less competitive industries will enjoy higher performance than firms operating in highly competitive environments.

The underlying thesis of this book, however, is that the task of strategic management is both structural *and managerial*. This book does not argue that structure is unimportant—in fact, two chapters are devoted to developing ways to analyze and understand industry structure. However, we begin with the premise that managers and managerial decision making are fundamentally important to the success of business organizations. This text, therefore, places general managers at the heart of strategic management. It builds on theories and recent research studies that seek to understand how managerial thinking—managers' attitudes, beliefs, and understandings—influence strategic decision making.

At the heart of our emphasis on managerial thinking is the concept of *mental models*, which Peter Senge has defined as "deeply ingrained assumptions, generalizations, or even pictures or images that influence how we understand the world and how we take action."[16] Mental models are simplified understandings or representations of the phenomena we encounter. Mental models tell us what is and is not important to us, what we like and do not like, what we should and should not notice. Mental models include our understandings of how things work and what we expect to happen next. When we encounter something novel, our minds quickly construct new mental models to help us understand this new phenomenon.

Managerial thinking—contained in managers' mental models—influences strategic decision making and the actions firms take. Managers' mental models of the situations they encounter determine whether a particular strategic issue or situation will be noticed, how it will be interpreted and understood, and how they should respond to the situation. The study of mental models thus helps to explain why some managers notice important business issues while other managers do not, why some managers correctly interpret these issues while others do not, and why some managers respond appropriately to these issues while others do not. As a result, the linkages among business environments, managerial thinking, and strategic decision making are keys to understanding performance differences across firms and how competitive advantage is developed.

Exhibit 1.5 illustrates this managerial thinking perspective on strategy. As seen in Exhibit 1.5, managers' mental models influence decision making. These decisions are the basis of strategies. Strategies, in turn, influence business and firm performance outcomes. These performance outcomes provide important feedback to managers that will either reinforce existing mental models (most likely when performance outcomes are positive) or suggest to managers that they need to change their beliefs or understandings about the decisions and strategies that lead to high

EXHIBIT 1.5

The Relationships among Managers' Mental Models, Decision Making, Strategies, and Performance Outcomes

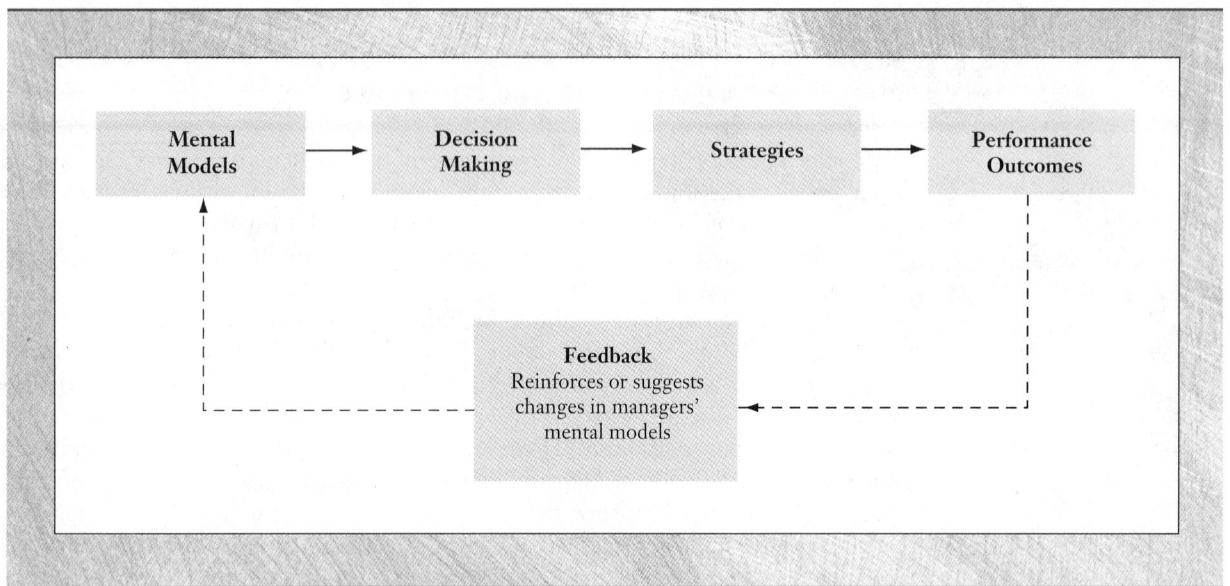

performance (most likely when performance falls short of managers' aspirations or expectations). The exhibit shows that mental models not only influence the choice of strategies but that their success or failure provides managers with feedback that can lead to subsequent changes in mental models. By this ongoing process, individual managers, and their organizations, learn.

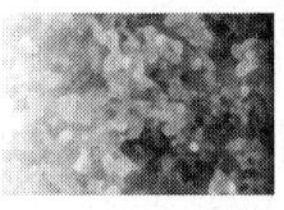

A Model of Strategic Management: The Mental Models and Strategic Decisions That Will Be Studied in This Text

Exhibit 1.6 expands on Exhibit 1.5, illustrating a model of strategic management that provides the organizing framework for this book. Like the framework shown in Exhibit 1.5, the model portrayed in Exhibit 1.6 builds on the assumption that general managers' mental models—their beliefs and understandings—influence decisions and shape strategies that, in turn, influence performance outcomes and determine whether their firms enjoy a competitive advantage. As in Exhibit 1.5, performance outcomes provide important feedback to managers that will either reinforce existing beliefs or suggest to managers that they need to change their beliefs and understandings.

Another way to depict and think about this model is illustrated in Exhibit 1.7. It places managers' mental models at the center of the diagram. Managers' mental models or beliefs influence decisions about their firms' definitions, business strategies, corporate strategies, and structures. One advantage of this depiction of our model of strategic management is that it explicitly shows the firm operating in an industry or competitive environment determined by the intersection of customers, products and services, and technologies.

EXHIBIT 1.6

The Book's Model of Strategic Management: The Mental Models and Strategic Decisions Studied in This Text and Their Influence on Performance and Competitive Advantage

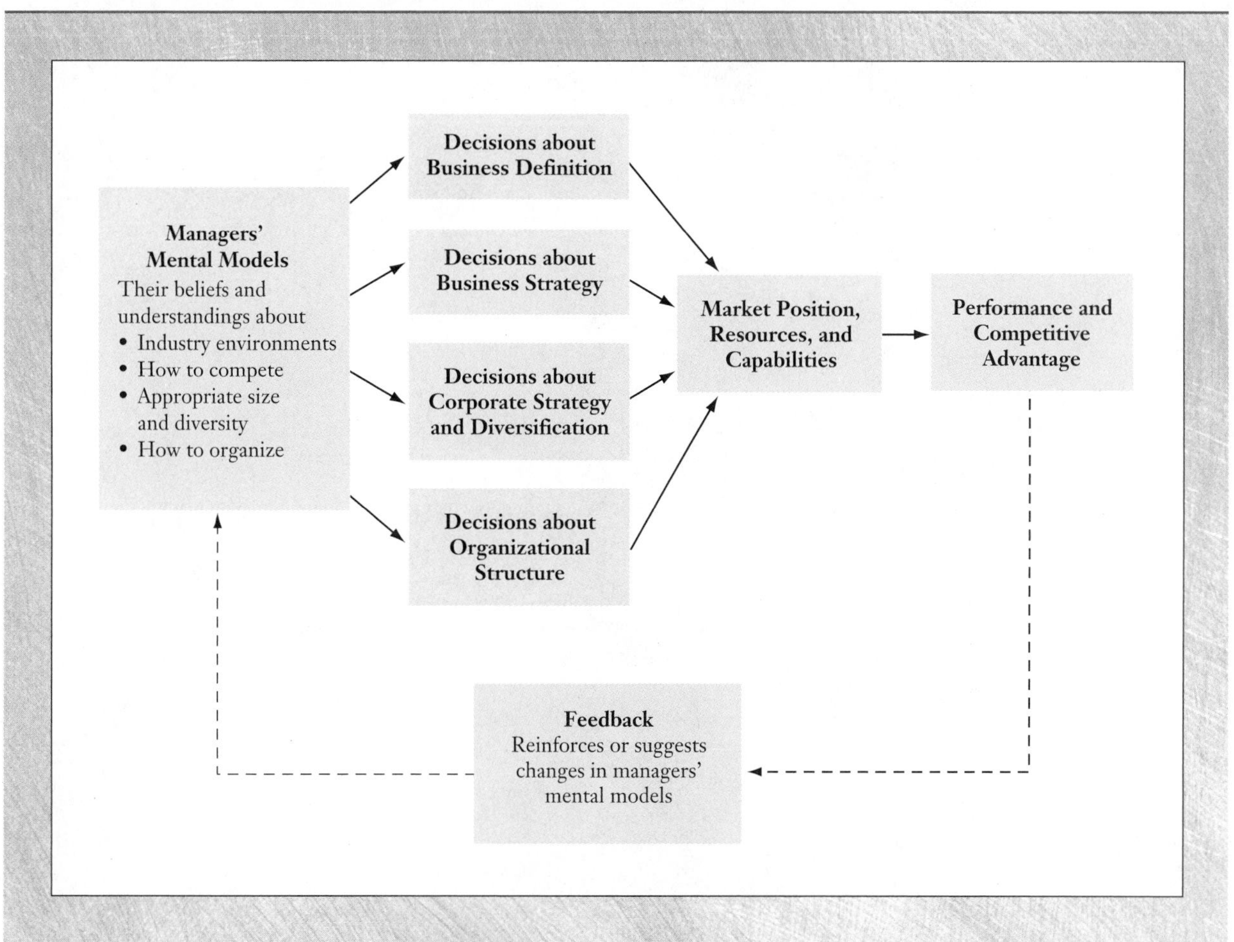

As suggested in Exhibits 1.6 and 1.7, this book focuses on four important types of mental models and decisions:

1. *Mental models about industry environments and how these beliefs influence decisions about business definition and positioning.* Industries are the competitive environments in which firms interact with customers, rivals, suppliers, and other stakeholders. Thus, managers must develop mental models about the nature of competition in their industries. Chapter 4 will describe two well-known frameworks that are useful for analyzing industry structure, and Chapter 5 will suggest a more dynamic framework that can be helpful for anticipating how industries will evolve over time.

   Managers' beliefs and understandings of their industries are important as they seek to define or position their firms and businesses in these ever-changing competitive environments. Chapter 6 takes up the challenges of business definition and positioning. Chapter 6 also emphasizes the need for managers to

EXHIBIT 1.7

Another Way to Depict the Book's Model of Strategic Management

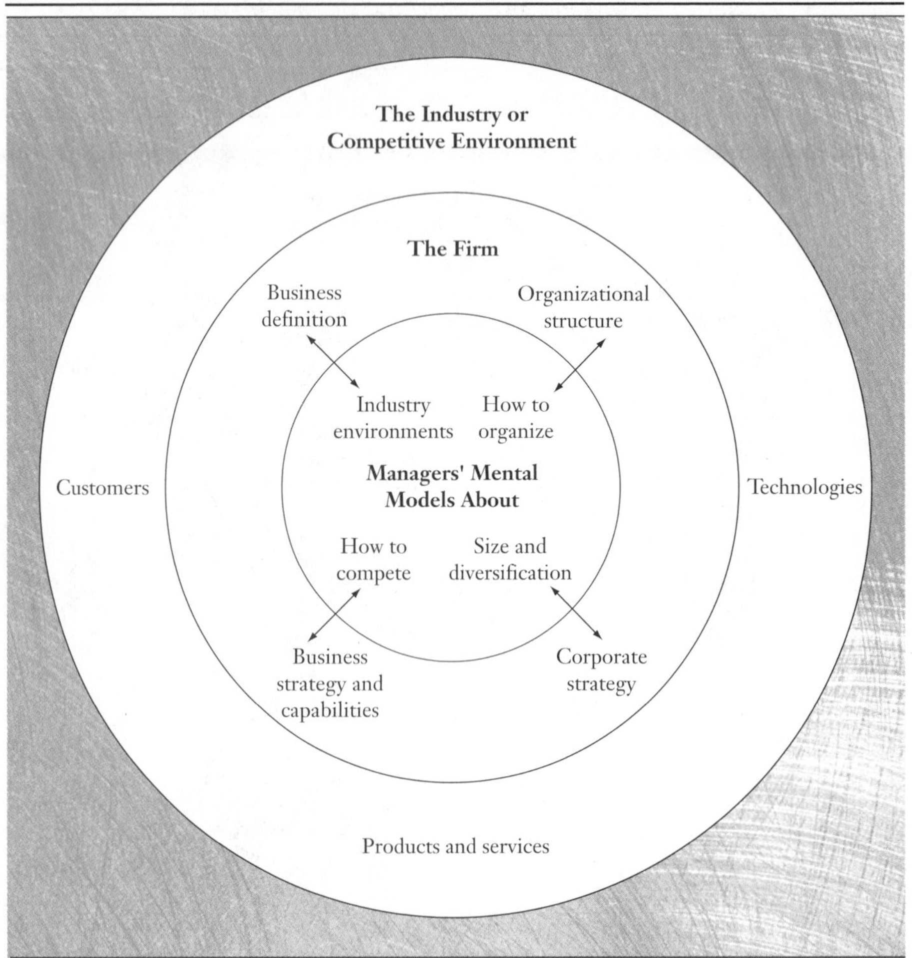

anticipate how demographic changes and technological innovations will create future arenas of opportunities so that they can proactively position their firms to enjoy "first-mover" and other advantages.

2. *Beliefs about how to compete and how these mental models influence decisions about business strategy*. Managers' beliefs about how to compete in their firms' industries will influence decisions that become the basis of their firms' strategies. Of course, business strategies will also be influenced by decisions about business definition. For example, Rolex enjoys a very distinctive yet narrow business definition in the high end of the wristwatch market. Because of its distinctive position, Rolex will pursue business strategies that are very different from those of Timex, Swatch, or Seiko—all of which compete for much broader segments of the wristwatch market.

   The text takes up the subject of business strategy in Chapters 7 and 8. Chapter 7 describes several different types of business strategies. Chapter 8 builds on this foundation by examining the appropriateness and effectiveness of various business strategies in different industry contexts, including emerging industries, more mature industry environments, and service industries.

3. *Beliefs about the appropriate scale and scope of the business enterprise, beliefs about how firms' businesses are related, and beliefs about how diversification should be managed and how these mental models influence decisions about corporate strategy.* A third group of mental models that are crucial to the success of firms involves managers' beliefs about the appropriate scale (i.e., size) and scope (i.e., breadth and diversity of product offerings) of their firms. Many firms, even many small firms, are diversified, multibusiness firms—that is, they have more than one main business and compete in different markets or industries. Managers' beliefs about how these businesses are related to each other and how diversification should be managed are also critically important mental models. These beliefs, in turn, influence decisions about corporate strategy, including decisions about vertical integration, diversification, and mergers and acquisitions. These topics are considered in Chapter 9.

   The issues of scale and scope are of interest to managers of all types of businesses, not just managers of large companies. Nearly all large companies are quite diversified, but many small businesses also operate in diverse markets. For example, a small accounting firm would be expected to do audit and tax work, but many small CPA firms also provide consulting services to their clients, advising them on computer purchases and accounting software.
4. *Beliefs about how to organize and how these mental models influence decisions about organizational structure.* A fourth group of mental models that will be explored in this book includes managers' beliefs about how their firms should be organized. These mental models influence managers' decisions about the structures they employ in their organizations to implement strategies and to coordinate human resources and information flows. Like effective definitions and business and corporate strategies, effective structures can also be a source of competitive advantage. Chapter 10 describes the various components of organizational structure, assesses the value of these components, and describes a number of companies that have achieved great success by adopting innovative structures.

We begin, however, with a close look at general managers and the task of building competitive advantage. Before examining the various components of the model illustrated in Exhibits 1.6 and 1.7, Chapter 2 considers the importance of general managers. Chapter 2 focuses specifically on how managers' mental models influence strategic decisions and craft strategies that lead to competitive advantage, the reason why some firms consistently enjoy high performance relative to their rivals. The chapter will explore the sources of mental models while also noting some of the biases, limitations, and weaknesses associated with managerial thinking.

Chapter 3 provides a detailed introduction to the concept of competitive advantage, focusing specifically on the factors associated with its creation and maintenance. The chapter will emphasize that competitive advantage results from *asymmetry: high-performing firms either occupy unique positions in their industries, or they develop and possess unique capabilities that cannot be easily duplicated by their rivals.*

The book concludes with a look at the problem of organizational responsiveness. The last two chapters of the book return to the topics introduced at the beginning of this first chapter—the rapid pace of industry change, and the need for managers to anticipate and respond to these changes if their firms are to remain viable and enjoy high levels of performance. Chapter 11 examines strengths and limitations of boards of directors and strategic planning processes, and Chapter 12 explores some of the reasons why managers fail to respond to changes in their industry environments while also suggesting some ways to make managers more responsive.

Three Key Themes

This chapter suggests three key themes that will be emphasized throughout this book:

Managers and Managerial Thinking

The decisions that form the basis of strategies are made by managers, so to understand company strategies, we must understand the thinking that causes managers to make a particular set of decisions rather than some other set of decisions. The importance of managers will therefore be emphasized throughout the book. We will focus on how managers develop the beliefs and understandings that influence the decisions they make, how managers come to acquire new beliefs and understandings, and the inherent problems and weaknesses associated with managerial thinking and decision making.

Change and the Need to Think Dynamically About Strategic Management

Strategies that are effective today will almost certainly be ineffective in the future because, as suggested by the opening section of this chapter, companies do not enjoy the luxury of competing in static worlds. Thus, the book will emphasize the importance of thinking dynamically about strategic management. All business organizations face the challenge of developing and maintaining a competitive advantage while also anticipating or responding to changes in their industry environments. Managers who choose to ignore changes in their industry environments risk seeing their firms blindsided by new customer wants and needs, new products and services, and new developments in technology. Decline or organizational failure are the price their firms must pay for this lack of diligence.

The Importance of Organizational Learning

Knowledge resides in organizations in the heads of managers and employees, in routines and standard operating procedures, and in the equipment and technologies that are employed. As the business world becomes increasingly knowledge-intensive, the ability to learn, store, retrieve, and exploit new knowledge and information will become a key source of sustained competitive advantage.

A Look Ahead

In the chapters to come, we will see that the model of strategic management illustrated in Exhibits 1.6 and 1.7 provides compelling explanations for many contemporary business situations. Take, for example, the erratic performance of two of the world's largest companies, General Motors (GM) and IBM, over the last two decades. In each case, we can find convincing evidence that the managers of these two companies failed to keep pace with rapidly changing business environments. As a consequence, both companies' business definitions became dated, and both companies failed to develop the organizational capabilities that would allow them to enjoy a competitive advantage over their rivals.

- The 1980s saw General Motors' market share drop from over 50 percent of the domestic automobile market to just over 30 percent as consumers rejected GM's product offerings in favor of Japanese models featuring superior quality. During this same time, Japanese manufacturers enjoyed significant advantages in production efficiency and quality over GM and the other U.S. automobile producers. Later, the Japanese producers opened state-of-the-art factories in the United States while much of the existing U.S. domestic automobile capacity lay idle or was closed down.

  Clearly many factors are to blame for GM's fall. Its cars became "dated." It fell behind technologically and lost a competitive advantage in manufacturing. Its internal structures had become ossified. Yet, primary responsibility for GM's decline must be placed on its managers, whose mental models failed to anticipate or respond quickly to profound changes in the automobile industry. Evidence suggests that executives at all the Big Three companies—GM, Ford, and Chrysler—shared a "Detroit mind," possessing mental models that failed to notice and correctly understand the tenacity with which the Japanese manufacturers were attacking the worldwide automobile market.[17] As a result, the Japanese manufacturers have come to dominate that market, producing more automobiles than the Big Three combined.
- Similarly, IBM's managers did not anticipate, and more recently could not accept, the dramatic pace at which computer use switched from centralized, mainframe computing to distributed computing and personal computers. Again, many factors are responsible for IBM's decline, but the major problem was almost certainly the thinking of IBM's top executives, who were unprepared to accept the shift away from mainframe to personal computing. Their "mainframe mentality" resulted in an inability to respond to changing industry conditions and also prevented the company from building the necessary internal capabilities, including the marketing and manufacturing infrastructure that would support IBM's competitive position in the personal computer market.

For both GM and IBM, the model of business performance illustrated in Exhibits 1.6 and 1.7 suggests that managers, specifically their mental models, failed to anticipate or keep pace with changes in the industry, thus leaving the firms unprepared to maintain or develop a competitive advantage in the new industry environments in which they found themselves. As a consequence, these firms lacked vision, uncertainty prevailed, new strategic initiatives failed to receive sufficient resources, talented employees became dissatisfied and left, and morale problems developed among those employees who stayed. The cost of such failures in managerial thinking is staggering. At the height of their downturns, GM and IBM reported billions of dollars in restructuring charges. Plants have been closed, and both companies laid off hundreds of thousands of employees. IBM saw its share price fall from over $100 to less than $40 in a relatively short period of time.

The three themes of this book—the central role of managerial thinking, the rapid rate of industry change, and the importance of organizational learning—are all prominent in the stories of decline at General Motors and IBM. These two examples vividly illustrate that changes in managerial thinking are fundamental to firm success because managers usually cannot recommend strategic changes without first changing their own mental models. It's not that mental models are the only thing that must change in order to renew a sleepy organization, but a change in mental models is often a necessary prerequisite to organizational change and renewal.

Unfortunately, GM and IBM are not isolated incidents. Similar patterns are observed almost daily, and this book will point out many examples in which managerial thinking failed to keep pace with changes in the business environment. On the other hand, we have many exemplary companies that have enjoyed and maintained consistently high levels of performance in spite of significant changes in their industry environments or fierce competition from their rivals.

- Gillette is one of many companies that has enjoyed a sustained competitive advantage in its industry—*due largely to the belief of the company's top managers that innovation and renewal are essential to its success.* Long a leading manufacturer in the "wet-shaving" industry, Gillette saw a serious threat to its position in the early 1970s when Bic, the French maker of cheap ballpoint pens, introduced the plastic disposable razor. By the mid-1970s, sales of plastic disposable razors had grown to 60 percent of the wet-shave market, eroding Gillette's dominant position in the industry. Gillette fought back, however, introducing its own plastic disposable razor, but also developing the highly successful Sensor. So effective was the Sensor that Gillette immediately began winning back market share from the manufacturers of disposables. Gillette's profits and its runaway stock price reflect its success.

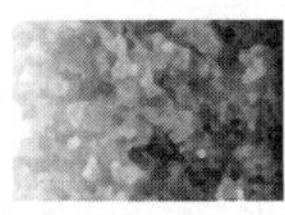

Conclusion

This introductory chapter has had many aims and objectives. It began by reviewing some of the most important characteristics of today's business environments. The chapter then introduced you to the field of strategic management. It defined strategy as "a pattern in a stream of decisions,"[18] and described the "emergent" nature of the strategy formulation and implementation processes. The chapter then introduced the model of strategic management that will serve as the organizing framework for this book.

Being able to think strategically, to evaluate business environments, to understand the content, formulation, and implementation of business and corporate strategies, and to appreciate how your position in a particular functional department is an integral part of the larger company mission—all are skills that should significantly enhance your potential for making meaningful contributions at the firms where you work. Furthermore, in many "high involvement" companies today, responsibility for decision making has been widely distributed so that employees at all levels must think strategically, and decisions made only from a manager's functional point of view will be far too parochial.

Because of its focus on firms and businesses, you're likely to find that you can quickly identify with many of the concepts, issues, and topics introduced in this book. Firms and businesses are the focus of most articles and news stories found in the business press, and you cannot read *The Wall Street Journal* or other business periodicals without being confronted by many issues that will be covered in this book or any course in strategic management. In fact, you are strongly encouraged to make *The Wall Street Journal* and *Business Week*, *Fortune*, or *Forbes* a complementary part of your strategic management education. News stories in these business publications offer you a "real-time" laboratory for studying strategic management concepts and topics.

Although this book offers many business examples and addresses many contemporary issues, no book can possibly begin to anticipate the issues you will confront in the years ahead. As a result, your primary objective should be to use this material to help you *develop ways of thinking and learning* that will make you an effective business leader throughout your career. This ability to think creatively and insightfully, when combined with hard work, should make you a successful manager in the years ahead.

Key Points

- The context of strategic management is dynamic. The business world at the end of the twentieth century is the scene of profound changes. These changes present managers with extraordinary opportunities, but also pose significant challenges as managers must navigate their firms and businesses through turbulent industry environments.
- Strategy's focus or level of analysis is unique. Economics courses tend to focus on the economy or industry, while most business courses in functional areas, such as finance, marketing, operations management, and organizational behavior, tend to focus on more "micro" levels of analysis. Strategy is one of the few courses in most business schools that focuses on the overall management of firms and businesses.
- Most textbooks on strategic management emphasize the importance of industry structure as a primary influence on firm performance. According to this view, firm performance is a function of operating in attractive industries. In contrast, this book adds an emphasis on the critical role of general managers and strategic thinking in understanding industry environments, defining or positioning businesses in their competitive arenas, developing and maintaining capabilities, and developing organizational structures and other coordinating mechanisms.
- The book focuses on managers' mental models. Mental models are simplified representations of the phenomena we encounter; these models contain our attitudes, beliefs, and understandings about these phenomena.
- The book is organized around a model of strategic management that emphasizes the importance of:
  - Managers' mental models about industry environments and how those beliefs influence decisions about business definition and positioning.
  - Managers' mental models about how businesses should compete and how those beliefs influence decisions about business strategy.
  - Managers' mental models about (1) the appropriate scale and scope of their firms, (2) how their firms' businesses are related, and (3) how diversification should be managed and how those beliefs influence decisions about corporate strategy.
  - Managers' mental models about how to organize and how those beliefs influence decisions about organizational structure.

Review and Discussion Questions

1. *Describe the key characteristics of the current competitive landscape. What are the consequences or implications of this competitive environment for managers and their firms?*
2. *What makes the study of strategy unique? What makes strategic management "strategic"?*
3. *What is meant by the concepts of managerial thinking and mental models? Why are the concepts of managerial thinking and mental models central to the study of strategic managment?*
4. *Distinguish between "structural" and "managerial" approaches to the study of strategic management.*
5. *Distinguish between intended and emergent strategies. Why do so many intended strategies become unrealized strategies? What does the emergent nature of business strategies imply about the job of general managers?*

Suggestions for Further Reading

Drucker, P. F. 1993. *Post-Capitalist Society*. New York: HarperBusiness.
Mintzberg, H. 1978. Patterns in strategy formation. *Management Science*, 25: 934-948.
Pascale, R. T. 1984. Perspectives on strategy: The real story behind Honda's success. *California Management Review*, 26(3): 47-72.
Senge, P. M. 1990. *The Fifth Discipline: The Act and Practice of the Learning Organization*. New York: Doubleday/Currency.

Endnotes

1. Bourgeois, L. J., III, and K. M. Eisenhardt, 1988. Strategic decision processes in high-velocity environments: Four cases in the microcomputer industry. *Management Science* 34:816-835.
2. D'Aveni, R. 1994. *Hypercompetition*. New York: Free Press.
3. *The Wall Street Journal*, 1997. State Farm to apply with thrift regulator to open savings bank. April 30; C18.
4. Helliker, K. 1997. A new mix: Old-fashioned PR gives General Mills advertising bargains. *The Wall Street Journal*, March 20; A1, A6.
5. Bearle, A. A., and G. Means, 1932. *The Modern Corporation and Private Society*. New York: Macmillan.
6. Drucker, P. F. 1993. *Post-Capitalist Society*. New York: HarperBusiness.
7. Peters, T. J., and R.H. Waterman, Jr. 1982. *In Search of Excellence: Lessons from America's Best-Run Companies*. New York: Harper & Row.
8. Mintzberg, H. 1978. Patterns in strategy formation. *Management Science* 24:934-948.
9. Ibid, p. 935.
10. Henkoff, R. 1990. How to plan for 1995. *Fortune*, December 31; 70-77.
11. Mintzberg, H. 1978. Patterns in strategy formation. *Management Science* 24:934-948.
12. Henkoff, R. 1990. How to plan for 1995. *Fortune*, December 31; 70-77.
13. Pascale, R. T. 1984. Perspectives on strategy: The real story behind Honda's success. *California Management Review* 26(3): 47-72.
14. Ibid, p. 54.
15. Ibid, p. 57, emphasis in original.
16. Senge, P. M. 1990. *The Fifth Discipline: The Art and Practice of the Learning Organization*. New York: Doubleday/Currency.
17. Yates, B. 1983. *The Decline and Fall of the American Automobile Industry*. New York: Empire Books.
18. Mintzberg, H. 1978. Patterns in strategy formation. *Management Science* 24:934-948.

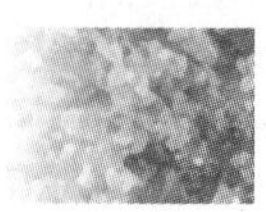

CHAPTER 2

GENERAL MANAGERS AND THE STRATEGIC MANAGEMENT OF BUSINESS FIRMS

CHAPTER OBJECTIVES

This chapter takes up the study of managers and their role in strategic decision making that was introduced in Chapter 1. The specific objectives of this chapter are to:

- Describe the nature of managerial decision making.
- Develop an understanding of the sources of managerial thinking and demonstrate how mental models reflect learning and expertise.
- Describe and illustrate some of the problems associated with mental models.
- Describe the qualities of effective managers and leaders.
- Describe the practical usefulness of understanding how mental models influence decision making.
- Illustrate (in the Appendix) two techniques for assessing or "mapping" managers' mental models.

CHARACTERISTICS OF MANAGERIAL DECISION MAKING

The stories reported daily in *The Wall Street Journal* and other business publications may give the impression that managerial decision making is a highly rational process in which managers assess their industry environments, consider their firms' strengths and weaknesses, and then make carefully considered decisions based on thoughtful analysis of all relevant data. In fact, as emphasized in the first chapter, managerial decision making is typically anything but a rational and well-informed "grand plan," and many of the most important strategic decisions are made under a number of limitations:

- *Executives often lack adequate information when making important decisions.* Even the best-informed executives must often make important decisions with less than adequate data. A perfect illustration of this point is provided in a statement made by Thomas J. Watson, the founder of IBM, in 1948: "I think there is a world market for about five computers." This anecdote illustrates how a business can be built successfully even though its managers may lack accurate or adequate data, but a lack of accurate data can also contribute to management mistakes. AT&T once owned the rights to cellular telephone technology but estimated that less than one million customers would be using cellular telephones by the year 2000. It therefore sold the rights to cellular telephone technology. Demand has, of course, significantly exceeded earlier forecasts, and today, over 50 million people in the United States use cellular telephones. AT&T decided that it needed to get back into the cellular telephone business and paid $12 billion to acquire McCaw Cellular Communications—a company using the very same technology AT&T once owned!

A lack of information also explains the disappointment of Quaker Oats over its acquisition of the beverage company, Snapple. Quaker, already the owner of Gatorade, which continues to enjoy double-digit sales growth, acquired Snapple in 1994 for $1.7 billion, betting that Snapple's "new age" line of beverages already popular on the east and west coasts would continue to grow in popularity among health-conscious consumers. It didn't quite work out that way. Snapple's sales volume fell by 20 percent after its acquisition by Quaker, and the company is estimated to have lost more than $100 million on Snapple due to the high costs of distribution and promotion.[1] No doubt Quaker's executives were expecting that Snapple would replicate the success of Gatorade, and they could not foresee that Snapple's early success might be nothing more than a passing fad. Less than three years after its purchase for $1.7 billion, Quaker sold Snapple for a mere $300 million, taking a $1.4 billion charge against its earnings.

- In addition, *managers—like all individuals—tend to give greater attention to information that confirms their views while discounting data and other information that would discredit their beliefs*. As a result, managers—like the Quaker executives—will often base their decisions on optimistic or unrealistic forecasts even though the available evidence would warrant more modest expectations. Furthermore, once individuals psychologically commit themselves to a particular course of action, it is very difficult to get them to change even when they are confronted with considerable evidence that they have made a wrong decision. This tendency to commit psychologically to a particular course of action has been used to explain a variety of management and policy mistakes, including the growing involvement of the United States in the Vietnam War, the Watergate fiasco, and bidding wars in which acquiring companies end up paying too much for their acquired businesses.
- Even worse, *top executives are often insulated from and out of touch with reality*, surrounded by other managers who rarely want the task of telling their superiors that things aren't as good as they seem. As a result, "bad news" tends to travel up through a company's ranks very slowly, leaving many top managers poorly informed about the very problems for which they need the most information.[2]
- *The explosive growth of information technology and information flows has not been accompanied by a corresponding growth in the ability of managers to process this information*. Few companies have modified their internal structures to take advantage of the availability of information or the opportunities afforded by information technology. As a result, the availability of data often hinders rather than helps managers as they wrestle with important decisions or immediate problems—in fact, the availability of data often results in an "information overload" that overwhelms many managers.

The Role of Managerial Thinking and Decision Making

Given these characteristics or factors that complicate decision making, it's a wonder that managers are able to make any decisions at all. Yet, every day, managers at all levels are making a multitude of tactical and strategic decisions that shape strategies and determine performance outcomes. Chapter 1 introduced the concept of mental models—managers' assumptions, beliefs, and understandings—that guide and influence decision making. Chapter 1 emphasized that mental models tell us what is and is not important, what we do and do not like, what we should and should not notice, and how things function or work. These beliefs and understandings influence the decisions we make. In the business world, these decisions are the basis of strategies that, in turn, influence performance and determine whether firms enjoy a competitive advantage over their rivals.

Exhibit 2.1 illustrates the model of strategic management introduced in Chapter 1. As seen in the exhibit, managers' mental models influence different types of decisions that determine firm performance outcomes. These performance outcomes provide important feedback to managers that will either reinforce existing mental models (most likely when performance outcomes are positive) or suggest to managers that they need to change their beliefs or understandings about the decisions and strategies that lead to high performance.

The aim of this chapter is to help you develop a better understanding of the concept of mental models. This section examines more closely how mental models influence decision making. Subsequent sections examine the sources of mental models as well as the biases, limitations, and weaknesses that are inherent in mental models. The chapter concludes by describing some of the qualities of effective managers and leaders and the practical usefulness of understanding the concept of mental models. Finally, the Appendix to this chapter describes two methods for assessing or "mapping" mental models.

As noted in Chapter 1, we have mental models about a vast array of phenomena, including people, hobbies, classes, music, sports, business, politics, and religion, and our minds are able to construct new mental models very quickly when we encounter new or novel phenomena. Because mental models are cognitive representations—i.e., "models"—of the phenomena we encounter, they may be more or less complete. For example, for some phenomena—a favorite hobby or sport, for example—an individual's mental models might be very complete, including understandings of the key features as well as more peripheral aspects of the hobby. For other less well-understood phenomena, mental models might contain only very cursory or superficial understandings.

The power of mental models is that they allow us to function in a complex world. For example, a key use of mental models is to filter information and focus attention. We are bombarded by stimuli—far more than any individual could possibly comprehend or process, but only a few of these stimuli receive our attention. Why? Because our mental models focus our attention on those stimuli that are considered most important and relevant. One way to think about this is to recall those many times in your life when, after you've just learned the meaning of a new word, you then hear the word used—often within a short period of time. It is not that the word has never been used around you before; you've just never "heard" the word because you've never had a mental model to focus your attention on it.

EXHIBIT 2.1

The Mental Models and Strategic Decisions Studied in This Text and Their Influence on Performance and Competitive Advantage

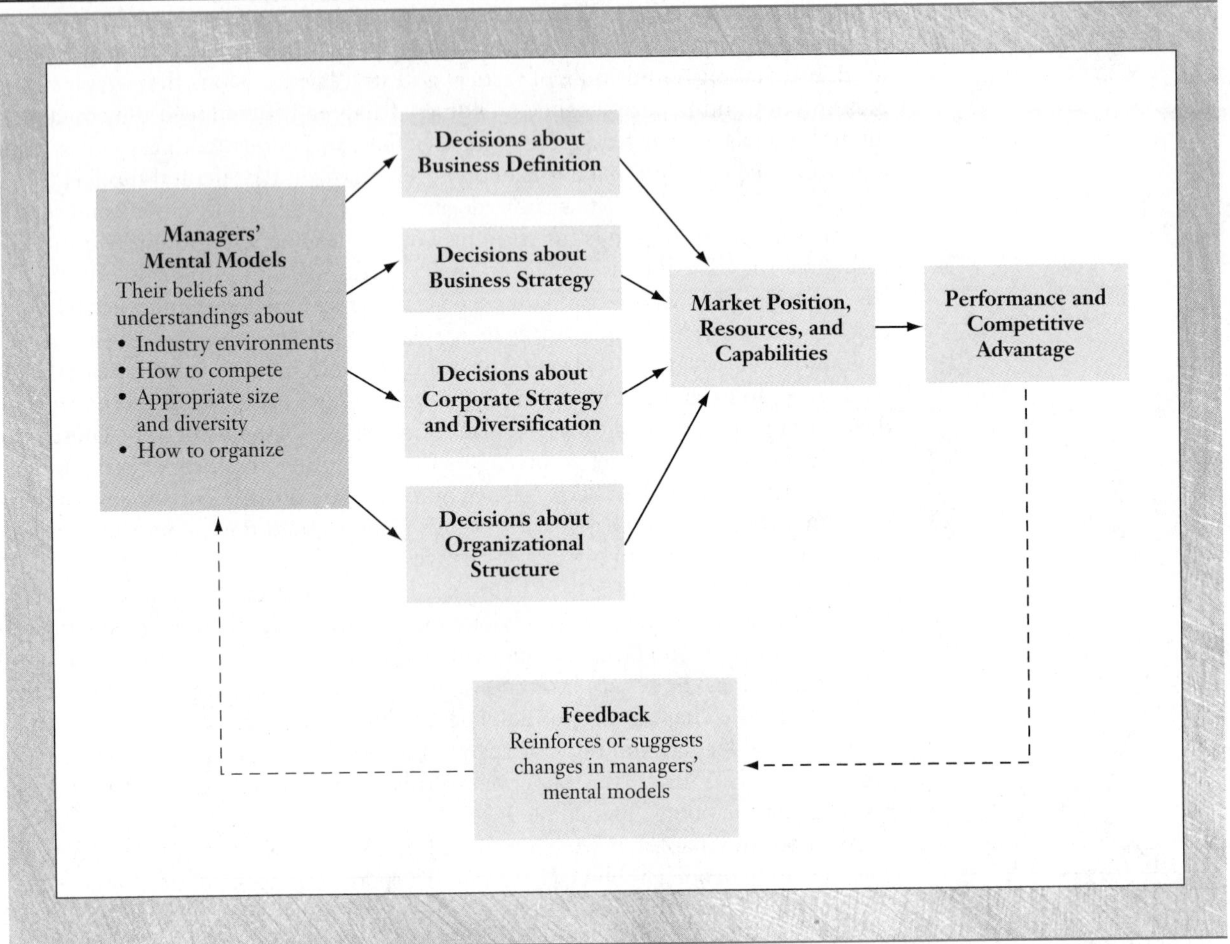

Mental models contain our attitudes, beliefs, and understandings, but they also influence our responses to the stimuli we notice. For example, being a smart shopper who values a good bargain, your mental models might focus your attention on an advertisement containing the word "sale." Reading farther, however, you might notice that the advertisement is for a sale at an exclusive department store, say, Neiman Marcus, and you might have another mental model or belief that everything at that department store is overpriced and that anyone who shops there pays too much, even for sale items. Based on these mental models, you would then decide not to go to the sale.

Similarly, many of us hold the following very simple understanding about the weather: "red sky at night, sailor's delight." As a result, we might observe a beautiful sunset and decide that the next day would be perfect for a hiking trip or a round of golf. In this example, a simple understanding of cause and effect about the weather is used as a basis for scheduling the next day's activities.

Like all individuals, managers use mental models to filter what would otherwise be an overwhelming amount of information and stimuli they receive from interactions with their environments. They can then focus their attention on those aspects of their environments that they deem most important. Their mental models further aid them as they attempt to interpret the information and stimuli on which they choose to focus. Following this interpretation process, managers' mental models then influence the decisions they make. Thus, managers' mental models exert a powerful influence on strategic decision making. And, even after decisions have been made and action is taken, managers' mental models monitor the outcomes of their decisions. Such monitoring of performance outcomes provides managers with feedback from which they can "learn" about the effectiveness of their decisions.

Just how powerful is the influence of mental models? Consider the opinion of Thomas Watson, Jr., the legendary former chief executive of IBM, on the importance of mental models:

> [an organization like IBM] . . . owes its resiliency not to its form of organization or administrative skills, but to the power of what we call beliefs and the appeal those beliefs have for its people. . . . In other words the basic philosophy, spirit and drive of an organization have far more to do with its relative achievements than do technological and economic resources, organizational structure, innovation and timing.[3]

Two Harvard Business School professors who have studied the influence of managerial beliefs on decision making concluded that managers' mental models provide them with

> a shared commitment to a vision of their organization's distinctive competence, the risks they are willing to take, and the degree of self-sufficiency they desire. As a result, these beliefs are themselves a powerful constraint on the options the executives will consider and the decisions they make.[4]

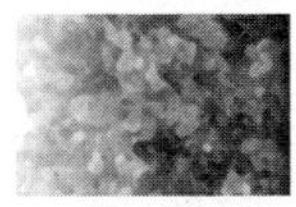

THE NATURE AND TYPES OF MENTAL MODELS

Though mental models are inherently unobservable, individuals can "map" or otherwise make explicit their own thinking or the thinking of other individuals. For example, if you were asked to distinguish between a good class and a bad class, you would have no trouble identifying a set of characteristics that would distinguish between the two. Psychologists call this type of thinking *categorical knowledge* because it is the knowledge individuals use to distinguish between and among categories of people, objects, and other phenomena (i.e., "good class" and "bad class"). One way business executives use categorical knowledge on a daily basis is to distinguish firms that are competitors from those firms that they do not consider competitors. Stock analysts also use categorical knowledge whenever they analyze companies and sort their stocks into "buy," "sell," or "hold" recommendations.

Another type of mental model describes understandings of *causality*. Individuals have causal beliefs about all kinds of phenomena. As with categorical knowledge, managers of business firms have causal beliefs about a wide array of phenomena. For example, many executives believe that advertising leads to higher sales revenues. Likewise, many executives believe that R&D spending leads to innovative products or more efficient production processes. Exhibit 2.2 illustrates the causal reasoning embedded in a well-known proverb as well as in these managerial beliefs.

EXHIBIT 2.2

Maps of Some Simple Causal Beliefs

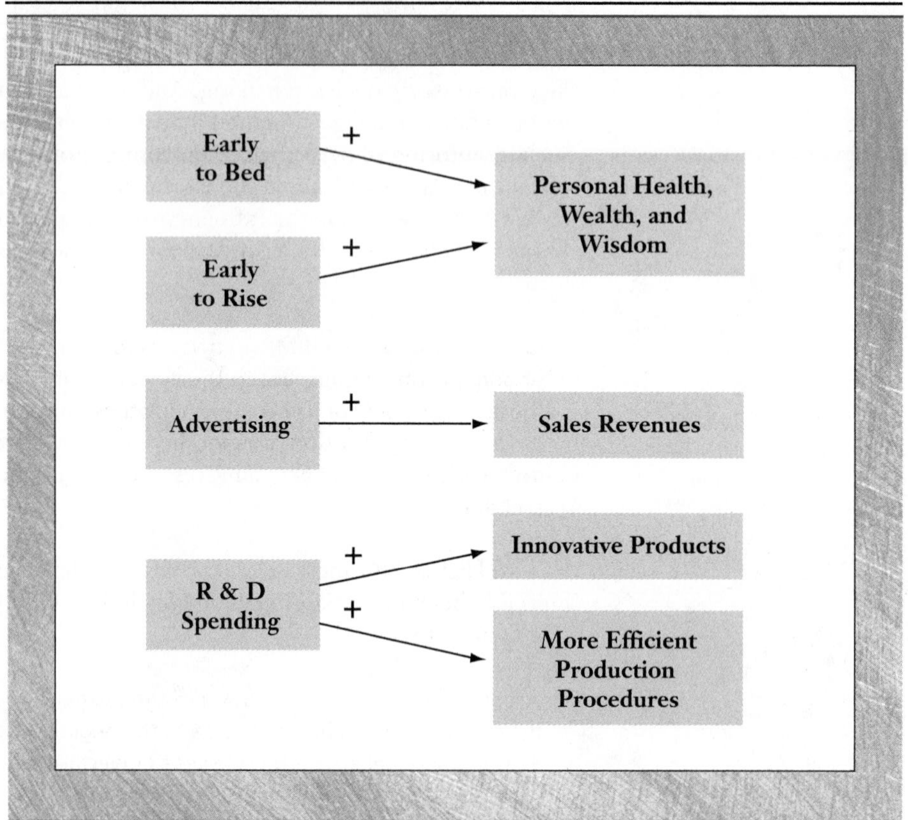

Like all mental models, categorical knowledge and beliefs and understandings of causality can change over time. For example, two decades ago, quality was rarely mentioned by business executives, and few stories about quality appeared in the business press. Today, most top executives and much of the business community have come to adopt a new causal belief that quality can have a very significant positive impact on the image of a company's products or services, which, in turn, can lead to higher sales and market share.[5]

The Sources of Managerial Thinking

How are managers' mental models developed and how do managers come to hold certain beliefs and understandings? At least three sources of managerial thinking have been identified:

Experience and Trial-and-Error Learning

First, experience is a major source of thinking. In fact, much of what is contained in our mental models is a product of trial-and-error learning. Many children have touched a hot stove and learned that the resulting burn is quite painful. Later on, we acquire interpersonal skills, study habits, hobbies, clothing and recreational preferences, and a multitude of other beliefs and understandings based on trial-and-error learning.

Managers learn all the time from their decisions and from the impacts of their decisions and strategies on the performance of their companies. In fact, firm performance provides managers with a good deal of feedback about the effectiveness of their decision making and strategies. A vivid example of this trial-and-error learning is provided by Sunbeam's former CEO, Albert Dunlap. Throughout his career as a chief executive, Mr. Dunlap has aggressively cut costs, divested unprofitable business units, and laid off thousands of employees. Before he became CEO at Sunbeam, in his previous job as the CEO of Scott Paper Company, Mr. Dunlap laid off 11,200 employees—one third of Scott Paper's workforce. As a result, Scott's operating margins improved significantly and shareholders gained as Scott's stock price appreciated and the company was sold to Kimberly-Clark.

It's not surprising, then, that within four months of becoming Sunbeam's CEO, "Chainsaw Al" announced that the company would lay off 6,000 employees—50 percent of its workforce—and sell or consolidate 18 of its 26 factories.[6] At Sunbeam, Mr. Dunlap was merely reusing a mental model that he has found to be so effective at the other companies where he has worked. And, the improvement in Sunbeam's performance that occurred in early 1997 probably reinforced Mr. Dunlap's mental model about how to turn around low-performing companies.[7] As Sunbeam developed new problems in 1998, however, the company's directors quickly lost confidence in Mr. Dunlap's leadership and he was treated to a taste of his own medicine when the board summarily fired him.

Another example of how learning from experience has reinforced an executive's mental models is provided by Stephen M. Wolf, currently CEO of US Airways. Throughout his career at several different airlines, Mr. Wolf has aggressively sought to cut costs. First, as CEO of Republic Airlines during the mid-1980s, he won employee concessions worth $100 million. Later, as president of Flying Tiger, he won concessions worth $50 million. During the late 1980s and early 1990s, as CEO of United Airlines, Wolf persuaded employees to reduce wages and benefits by $4.9 billion in exchange for employee ownership of the airline. Now, at US Airways, Mr. Wolf is again using this same "formula" to cut costs and improve the performance of the company.[8]

After enjoying tremendous success from sales of its minivans in the 1980s, Chrysler Corporation's executives sought to determine what made this vehicle so extraordinarily popular among consumers. In focus groups, minivan buyers consistently mentioned that minivans offered so much interior space for a vehicle that is not much larger than a passenger car. In fact, Chrysler minivans have a very high ratio of interior space to exterior size. In attempting to "learn" from the success of its minivans, Chrysler introduced its line of LH cars featuring "cab forward design," which aims to give buyers much more interior space than competing cars of comparable size.

It's also important to note that managers can learn the wrong lessons from their experiences, leading to inaccuracies in their mental models or to superstitious beliefs. For example, in the automobile industry, executives at General Motors, Ford, and Chrysler may have felt that they were invulnerable to competition from Japanese producers after successfully battling attempts in the 1950s and 1960s by foreign producers to gain significant shares of the U.S. market.

Imitation

Imitation also provides raw material for mental models. Many of our attitudes, beliefs, and understandings come from observing and then adopting the attitudes, beliefs, and understandings of others. For example, college students who desire to be "cool" might observe other very cool students sporting tattoos and might quickly develop a belief that they, too, will be cool if they acquire a tattoo. Likewise, such sports as snowboarding and in-line skating become popular through rapid imitation.

Similarly, company managers might observe other companies adopting a particular strategy. If they conclude that this strategy leads to positive performance outcomes, they will probably develop a belief in the efficacy of that strategy. For example, General Electric has long sought to have each of its many businesses occupy the number one or number two position in the various industries in which they compete. In the years since the widely admired and high-performing General Electric Company adopted this strategy, many other firms have copied or imitated the same management strategy.

One weakness of imitation is that strategies based on or copied from other firms are necessarily less distinctive or unique than innovative strategies. The next chapter and Chapter 5 discuss in more detail the weaknesses and risks of basing strategies on imitation. For now, we'll simply argue that because competitive advantage results from uniqueness, imitation is less likely to contribute to the development of competitive advantage than independent learning or creativity would be.

Creativity

Creativity and imagination can provide the raw material for new thinking or the development of totally new mental models containing new beliefs and understandings. Unfortunately, creative processes are not well understood and we don't really know why some individuals are more creative than others, nor do we really know what triggers a creative insight. Rollo May's remarkable little book, *The Courage to Create*, suggests some of the characteristics of the creative process.[9] For example, May concluded that creative insights occur suddenly, that they are particularly vivid, and that they usually provide the individual with a sense of certainty about the appropriateness of the insight.

Furthermore, May found that creative insights tend to run counter to the beliefs that individuals have held or maintained in the past; new mental models resulting from these insights are different from or run counter to old beliefs and understandings. They also tend to follow long periods of hard work on a particular problem or question. Frequently, they occur during a period of rest during which the unconscious mind has an opportunity to work through the problem or question.[10] In any event, this creative encounter represents an "ah-ha" experience in which an individual comes to a new belief or understanding about a particular phenomenon.

Regardless of what triggers this creative insight, the ability to see the world in a new way is a gift or talent vitally important to the success of business organizations that must continually renew themselves due to changes in their industries. Unfortunately, creativity and insight are not always or widely appreciated by others. For example, the suggestion by Copernicus, and later proof offered by Galileo, that we live in a heliocentric universe—that the earth revolves around the sun and not the other way around—was not well received.

In a more recent example from the business world, computers had existed for at least three decades—primarily the domain of scientists and engineers—before Apple Computer's founders concluded that computing power should be accessible to the general public. In fact, the genius of Apple's founders, Jobs and Wozniak, was to see that the development of microprocessors could be exploited to place a great deal of computing power into a relatively small box *and* to see that this development could equip a whole new segment of the population with "personal" computers. Their innovation has, of course, changed the computer industry and everyday life in our society in profound ways.

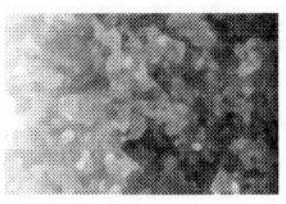

Problems Associated with Managerial Thinking

Incompleteness and Inaccuracies

One key characteristic of mental models is that they are representations of phenomena. Because they are only representations, mental models are necessarily incomplete and do not fully embody or portray all the aspects or characteristics of the phenomena they model. Thus, mental models can be more or less accurate or complete. Therefore, interpretations of stimuli based on mental models can be more or less correct and the decisions that follow from these interpretations can be more or less appropriate.

Timeliness and the Difficulty Associated with Altering Mental Models

As emphasized in Chapter 1, environments can change so that previous attitudes, beliefs, and understandings can become obsolete. In fact, a major challenge for people, like business managers, who must function in rapidly changing environments is to keep their mental models aligned with the pace of changes in their industries. If this updating of mental models does not occur, then new or novel issues may be interpreted using dated or obsolete understandings. This can lead to incorrect interpretations of the issues and poor decision making. Organizational decline and even failure can result.

The experience of U.S. railroad companies provides an illustration of how once accurate beliefs can become increasingly inaccurate as the business environment changes. Before the development of a national highway system, the railroads had a virtual monopoly on most freight transportation. An analysis of corporate documents has suggested that most railroad executives held a fairly reasonable belief, given their monopoly position, that charging customers higher rates would lead to higher performance. Yet, this same analysis has also suggested that most railroad executives continued to hold this belief long after a new national highway system had allowed trucks to become a major presence in intercity freight transportation. They simply failed to grasp that ever higher freight rates would only divert more and more freight traffic to the emerging trucking businesses.[11]

Not only do managers face the constant challenge of altering their thinking in order to keep pace with changes in the environments in which their companies must compete, but the cognitive processes that are required to change attitudes, beliefs, and understandings are prone to failure. Much evidence suggests that we are often reluctant to change our mental models even when confronted by overwhelming evidence that change would be in our best interest. Examples from history demonstrate both the difficulty of changing mental models and the strategic consequences resulting from a failure of individuals' mental models to keep pace with a changing environment.

Bruce Catton, the eloquent Civil War author, argued that a war that would totally destroy the South was inevitable when the leaders of the Confederacy could not come to accept new understandings.

> The war had begun in the flame and darkness of the Carolina marshes, and fire and night as a result had begun to rise around the notion that one kind of man may own another kind. Even at the final minute of the eleventh hour *the men who dominated the Confederate government did not understand this, and it was their lack of understanding that had brought them to the end of the tether.*[12]

Edith Hamilton concluded that this lack of responsiveness to change helps to explain the decline of the Roman Empire:

> Rome had . . . accomplished marvels; she had made the framework for a new world. A mightier task by far remained: to keep pace intellectually and spiritually with the enormous material advance . . .
>
> All that men were able to do when confronted with difficulties such as never had been known before, was to look to the past, which always seems so good, so comprehensible, and try to apply to the baffling present the solutions of a life that was outgrown.
>
> The final reason for Rome's defeat was the failure of mind and spirit to rise to a new and great opportunity, to meet the challenge of new and great events.[13]

Though Hamilton was writing about the decline of Roman civilization, she just as easily could have been writing about the challenges facing the managers who must guide their firms through changing business environments. Business executives often find it very difficult to alter their mental models. Writing on the importance of mental models, Peter Senge concluded that one reason executives find it so difficult to change or alter their beliefs is their "taken-for-granted" nature:

> The problems with mental models lie not in whether they are right or wrong—by definition, all models are simplifications. The problems with mental models arise when the models are tacit—when they exist below the level of awareness. The Detroit automakers didn't say, "We have a *mental model* that all people care about is styling." They said, "All people *care* about is styling." Because they remained unaware of their mental models, the models remained unexamined. Because they were unexamined, the models remained unchanged. As the world changed, a gap widened between Detroit's mental models and reality, leading to increasingly counterproductive actions.[14]

All these examples suggest that beliefs and understandings that have been developed over long periods of time are unlikely to be easily shaken, even when individuals are confronted by widespread disconfirming evidence.[15] The incompleteness of mental models and the challenge of keeping pace with changes in the larger environments in which we live and work are further complicated by a number of social-psychological factors, including *groupthink* and *escalation of commitment*.

Social-psychological factors: groupthink and escalation

Two additional problems or pathologies are also likely to contribute to the tendency for managers' mental models to be inflexible. One is the danger of *groupthink*, in which intragroup pressures enforce a uniformity of thinking on group members.[16] As a result of the groupthink phenomenon, a top management team or other group will explicitly or implicitly limit its consideration of fundamental assumptions, causal factors, and likely outcomes. Furthermore, groups that fall victim to the groupthink phenomenon will often intentionally disregard information that would serve to disconfirm their predetermined opinions or chosen courses of action.

A related phenomenon is *escalation of commitment*, in which managers continue to pursue a particular course of action or strategy even though performance outcomes and other sources of feedback indicate that the strategy is inappropriate.[17] Research suggests that escalation is often due to individuals or managers attempting to appear consistent rather than waffling in their decision making. Managers will also continue in a particular course of action or strategy in order to justify or reinforce past decisions. What is remarkable about research on the escalation of commitment phenomenon is the degree to which subjects will persist in pursuing a particular strategy in spite of disconfirming or negative feedback. This research certainly suggests that individual and organizational learning is not always a straightforward, rational process!

Cognitive biases

Thinking and learning are also impaired by a number of *cognitive biases*. These biases undermine rational thinking so that decisions are often made more on the basis of hope than evidence. Research demonstrates, for example, that individuals often make decisions on the basis of very little information or in spite of evidence that supports a different decision. For example, a large percentage of the population buys lottery tickets, and, week after week, many people are convinced that they have at least a reasonably good chance of buying a "winner," even though statistically they have a much better chance of being struck by lightning or even drowning in the bathtub. People have a remarkable tendency to trust their "hunches" and "gut feelings" more than objective evidence would suggest they should.

Many different types of cognitive biases exist and it's probably useful to focus on some examples of these biases in order to dispel notions that individuals—even highly trained and experienced managers—are coolly rational thinkers. Consider, for example, the maps shown in Exhibit 2.3. These maps illustrate that people often make use of very simple beliefs about the position of objects or places. For example, most individuals assume that because California is west of Nevada, then Los Angeles will be west of Reno, but as map A in Exhibit 2.3 demonstrates, this is not the case. Similarly, most individuals assume that because South America is south of North America, then Miami, a city on the eastern seaboard of North America, will be east of Lima, Peru, a city in western South America. As map B in Exhibit 2.3 shows, however, this is not the case, and the "simple" beliefs or representations that most people hold are not accurate.[18]

Another factor that can lead to biases or inaccuracies in beliefs or understandings is the social context of thinking. A story told by sociologist Erving Goffman illustrates how socialization influences thinking.[19] According to the story, a young boy, whose grandfather owned a baseball team, was asked by his teacher, "What is one

EXHIBIT 2.3

Examples of Biases in Thinking about Places

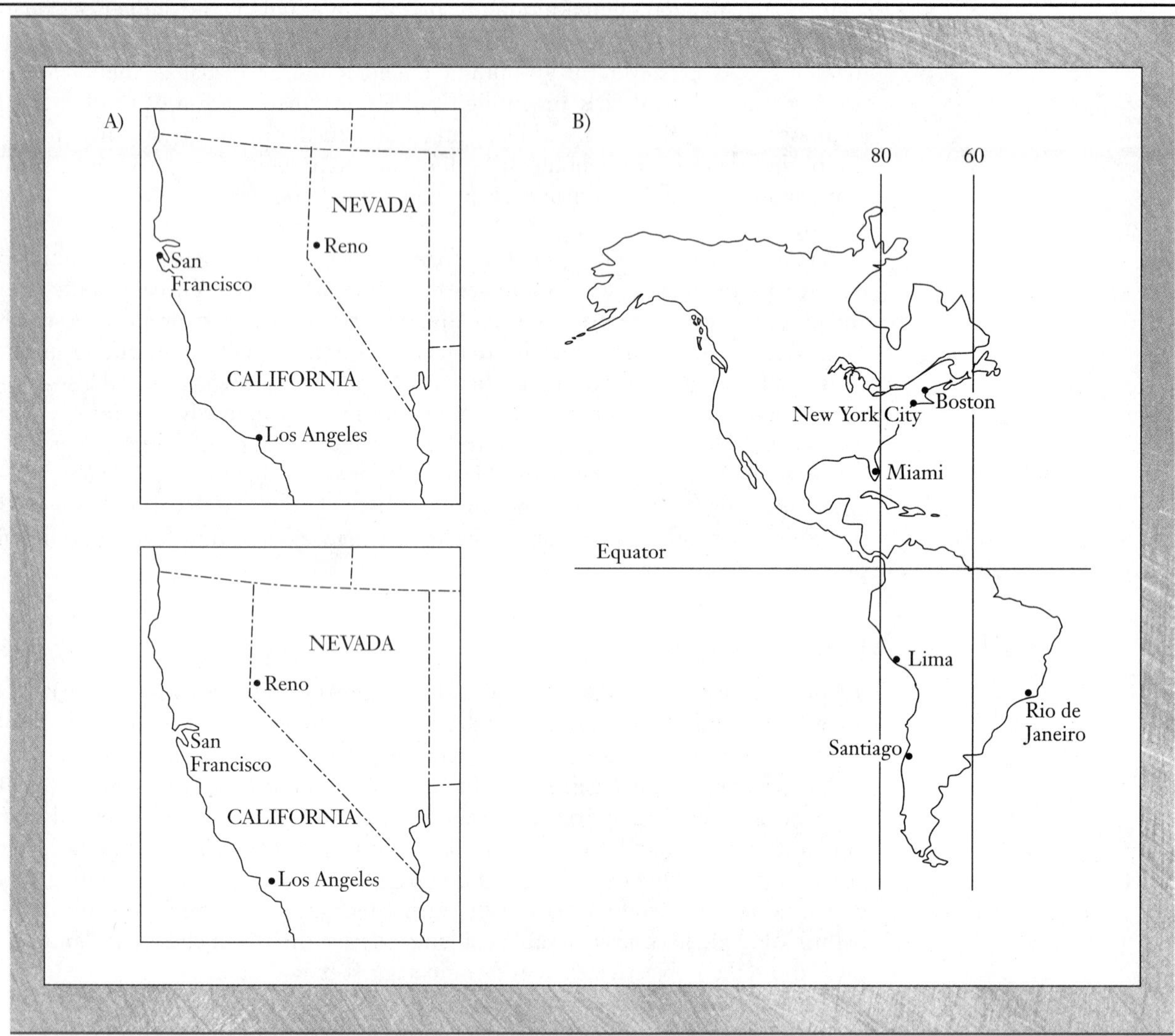

SOURCE: A. L. Glass and K. J. Holyoak, 1986. *Cognition.* 2nd ed. New York: Random House, pp. 141–143.

and one?" The boy responded, "A ball and a strike." This story vividly demonstrates how cultural or social contexts shape our beliefs and understandings.

Superstition can also be a source of bias and lead to poor decision making. Superstition is really nothing more than a false understanding of cause and effect, and superstitions often result from making incorrect inferences from past experiences. For example, the Vietnam disaster convinced many policymakers that the United States could not win a land war, and our country's experiences in Vietnam almost surely affected U.S. foreign policy for at least two decades and perhaps even now. Such a belief is superstitious because it ignores the many unique factors that made the U.S. position in Vietnam so intractable. Business managers can also be very superstitious. For example, a company may try a new strategy or tactic and it may fail. As a result, the company's managers may conclude that the strategy or tactic itself is unworkable even though it may have failed because of poor implementation.

Another bias very common in the business world is that most managers will pay more attention to those stimuli or aspects of the environment that confirm their mental models while ignoring or discounting evidence to the contrary. An accompanying Management Focus, "Good News, Bad News, and Attributions of Success and Failure," profiles Joseph Antonini, the former CEO of Kmart, and provides an excellent example of this bias. Kmart, with its performance lagging far behind the number one retailer, Wal-Mart, has been attempting to improve by updating its stores. Still, problems persist. Sales have lagged behind expectations and the company continues to suffer inventory problems. Yet, the Management Focus provides several illustrations of situations in which Mr. Antonini indicated he was tired of hearing "bad news" and wanted to hear more "good news."[20] Kmart's board eventually dealt with Mr. Antonini's bias for "good news" by firing him.

Because of rigidities, biases, and other limitations in managerial thinking, the chief executive officers and other top managers of declining companies must often be replaced before their strategies can be altered or their firms' performance levels improved. Unfortunately, as later chapters will emphasize, most boards of directors do not do an effective job of monitoring the financial performance of their companies or the performance of their firms' chief executive officers. Dismissal of a CEO is usually a final desperate measure taken by boards only after companies have experienced a severe decline in market standing, a severe downturn in financial performance, or—even worse—the risk of bankruptcy or failure.

Furthermore, a company's, or even an industry's, way of doing business may blind executives to new developments in the competitive environment.[21] The "we've always done it this way" mentality limits the ability of executives to accept new ideas or to challenge the conventional wisdom. For this reason, many companies turn to executives from other firms and even from firms in other industries when searching for new CEOs. The aim is to find executives whose thinking is not so tied to traditional beliefs or conventional ways of doing things. The Management Focus, "The Value of Outsiders as Chief Executives," examines a number of companies that have turned to outsiders for CEOs and considers both the advantages and the disadvantages associated with such a move.

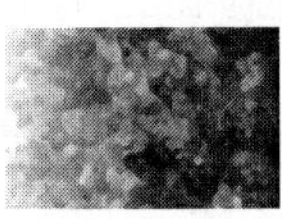

The Qualities of Effective Leaders and the Importance of Flexible Thinking

Mental models are prone to a number of limitations. They may fail to notice changes or other important stimuli in the larger environment. They do not change readily. Our thinking is subject to a number of inaccuracies, biases, superstitions, and social-psychological factors that prevent us from thinking effectively and rationally. In light of these limitations, let's now consider some of the qualities that may be helpful in being an effective manager and leader.

First, the managerial thinking approach to the study of strategic management that is the basis of this book suggests above all that *effective leaders are experts.* Managers must develop mental models that allow them to make good decisions, and one of the best ways to avoid making mistakes due to inaccurate thinking, biases, and other weaknesses is to become knowledgeable. Effective decision making and strategic

MANAGEMENT FOCUS

GOOD NEWS, BAD NEWS, AND ATTRIBUTIONS OF SUCCESS AND FAILURE

Joseph Antonini, Kmart's former chairman and chief executive officer, was like most of us — he didn't want to hear bad news. A *Wall Street Journal* article on Mr. Antonini noted that colleagues described him as "Teflon-coated":

> Complaints and unsolicited suggestions often slide right off. Positive feedback, Mr. Antonini maintains, is one reason he spends so much time visiting stores. "As CEO, you hear what's wrong all the time; you don't hear the good things," he says. "The best experience of my day is going to the stores." [1]

No doubt Kmart investors and Wall Street analysts wished that Mr. Antonini had been more sensitive to bad news. Under Mr. Antonini's leadership, Kmart's total sales surpassed Sears to become the largest retailer in 1990, but Kmart soon lost ground to fast-growing Wal-Mart. Wal-Mart's new stores and sophisticated inventory management system overwhelmed the dowdy image and "polyester palace" reputation of most Kmart stores and revealed some major weaknesses in Kmart's internal operations, especially its obsolete inventory systems.[2]

Almost everyone enjoys hearing "good news" and few people want to hear "bad news." We want to believe that our ideas are leading to good outcomes and we don't like to hear that our ideas are not working. Managers are no exception. They want to hear that their decisions are leading to effective strategies and higher performance levels, and they are loath to accept evidence that their strategies are proving ineffective. Yet, it's easy to see from the Kmart example that this tendency can have disastrous consequences for firms. If managers fail to accept the shortcomings of their strategies, then they may wait too long to take steps to change course. In Kmart's case, the company's board of directors finally lost its patience with Kmart's poor performance and Mr. Antonini's preference for good news and fired him.

Related to this phenomenon of paying more attention to good news or evidence that confirms our beliefs and less attention to evidence that might discredit our beliefs is the all-too-human tendency for individuals to take credit when something goes well, but to blame other individuals or circumstances for negative outcomes. These biases are referred to as *the self-serving bias*—the tendency to take personal credit for positive outcomes—and the *fundamental*

continued

management require competence and expertise. What does it mean to be an expert? Herbert Simon, the Nobel Prize-winning scholar, insists that an expert is an individual who knows 10,000 pieces of information about a particular phenomenon! Simon also argues that few individuals can develop such a body of knowledge in less than 10 years.

It's important to recognize, however, that it is not just the quantity of information or knowledge, but rather the quality, content, and timeliness of the knowledge possessed by the individual that will make him or her an effective leader. And, as an individual moves up through the ranks of a business organization, the content of the knowledge employed will have to change considerably. For example, an effective marketing manager will have to acquire totally new types of knowledge as he or she rises through the ranks and takes on general management responsibilities. The knowledge will have to be less specific to marketing and more focused on general management concerns and issues.

Moreover, research suggests that *effective leaders are able to link disparate strands of information and consider a broad array of scenarios and outcomes.* Effective general managers are able to see many different points of view and consider many different *attribution error*—the tendency to blame other individuals, circumstances, or exogenous factors when performance is below par.

In the business world, these biases are frequently seen in companies' letters to shareholders. It's quite common to read in letters to shareholders about chief executive officers taking credit for the strategies that have contributed to the bottom line or increased market share. Those same executives rarely take the blame for poor performance, however. Instead, they tend to blame exogenous factors, such as competitors, suppliers, customers, and, yes, even the weather for their companies' shortcomings.[3] A *Wall Street Journal* article, "A Chill Wind Blows Through the Pages of Earnings Reports," illustrates the extent to which managers will look for scapegoats for their firms' poor performance. The article noted that managers of all sorts of companies tend to blame harsh winter weather for poor performance, even when the winters are not unusually bad.[4]

In one sense, these common patterns of attribution represent good public relations. It's rarely wise in most business situations to highlight our weaknesses or our organizations' vulnerabilities, and, in most situations, we seek to cast ourselves and our firms in the best possible light. So it should be expected that managers would blame the weather for their firms' low performance levels rather than their own shortcomings. Such patterns of attribution can be dangerous, however, when they become something more than just good public relations and managers actually start to believe them. If managers refuse to listen to bad news and, even worse, refuse to believe that they might be responsible for their firms' shortcomings, then they will probably fail to respond effectively and their firms could seriously decline or even fail.

Next time you find yourself taking credit for something that goes right or blaming others or circumstances for something that goes wrong, ask yourself whether you're simply engaging in good public relations or whether you're falling victim to the self-serving bias and the fundamental attribution error. You're likely to learn a lot more from situations when you acknowledge your limitations and shortcomings and seek to grow from these experiences. ■

[1]Duff, C. 1993. Blue-light blues: Kmart's dowdy stores get a snazzy face-lift, but problems linger. *The Wall Street Journal*, November 5, A1.

[2]Ibid.

[3]Bowman, E. H. 1976. Strategy and the weather. *Sloan Management Review*, 17(2): 49–62; Noble, B. P. 1992. Paranoia in the ranks? No, realism. *New York Times*, August 23, F25.

[4]Ansberry, C. 1996. A chill wind blows through the pages of earnings reports. *The Wall Street Journal*, April 22, A1, A10.

possible outcomes. Moreover, effective managers not only can "see the forest for the trees," but good managers also "sweat the details." In other words, managers are not just "big picture" thinkers, but are also very much aware of the details.

In a number of interesting studies, researchers have compared grand masters to amateur chess players, and have found that both are equally well versed in understanding the rules, legal moves, and strategies of chess. What distinguishes the grand masters from amateur chess players is their ability to anticipate the consequences of a far greater number of possible moves when compared to amateurs. Similar to grand masters, expert managers are those who make more informed decisions by linking disparate strands of information and considering many different possible outcomes.

Finally, the text has already emphasized that managers' mental models must remain flexible and open to change if they are to keep pace with changes in business environments. Otherwise, managers risk having their firms pursue strategies that are no longer appropriate given changes in customer preferences, competitors' product and/or service offerings, and the development of new technologies.[22] It is essential, therefore, that *managers must be good learners*. To remain effective, managers must have their own personal programs of continuous learning that they can use to their advantage.

Management Focus

The Value of Outsiders as Chief Executives

What's more important: A thorough knowledge of a company and its industry, or broad general management skill and talent? During the 1990s, the boards of directors of many companies decided that a proven track record as a general manager was more important than specific company or industry experience, and many company and industry outsiders were hired as chief executive officers. In fact, a *Wall Street Journal* article reported that more than a third of the CEOs hired by major corporations in the 1990s were outsiders.[1]

Looking outside a company or its industry for top managers offers boards of directors a much larger and richer pool of talent, but the decision to hire a company or industry outsider is certainly a risky one. Outsiders will typically lack a detailed understanding of company and industry practices, an appreciation for the unique aspects of a company's culture, and the support of company veterans. And, newcomers, even fast learners, will need some time to come up to speed and be effective on the job.

Yet many of these qualities make outsiders very attractive to some boards of directors. They may conclude that a totally new perspective is needed and deliberately seek company or industry outsiders who will bring fresh ideas to their companies. They may also conclude that "the deck needs to be shuffled" and give new outsider chief executives the authority to remove company veterans and bring in new management talent. Two well-known consultants to many large companies have called such turnover in top management ranks, "gene replacement therapy."[2]

The record of outsiders as chief executive officers is somewhat mixed. Let's consider the results of two outsiders as CEOs in the computer industry. In 1983, Apple recruited John Sculley, who was then the president of PepsiCo, to be its new chief executive officer. While it is generally agreed that he transformed Apple into a more mature company with a broader product line, Apple's board eventually fired Mr. Sculley and it is now clear that he failed to provide Apple with a viable long-term strategy.

More recently, IBM hired industry outsider Louis Gerstner to be its chief executive. Mr. Gerstner had been a McKinsey consultant and, prior to accepting the position at IBM, he had been the CEO of RJR Nabisco. Assuming leadership of IBM at a time of crisis, Mr. Gerstner declared that "the last thing this company needs right now is a vision." Since he took over in 1993, Mr. Gerstner has been able to return IBM to profitability, but the company's growth has remained well below the computer industry average. A recent *Wall Street Journal* article described Mr. Gerstner's tenure at IBM as "impressive" but "incomplete," and suggested that the company may in fact need a vision for the future in order to achieve longer term success.[3] ■

[1]Helyar, J. and J. S. Lublin. 1998. The portable CEO: Do you need an expert on widgets to head a widget company? *The Wall Street Journal*, January 21, A1, A10.

[2]Hamel, G., and C. K. Prahalad. 1994. *Competing for the Future.* Boston: Harvard Business School Press.

[3]Ziegler, B. 1997. Gerstner's IBM revival: Impressive, incomplete. *The Wall Street Journal*, March 25, B1, B4.

Another way in which top managers can maintain flexibility and open-mindedness, while also avoiding the groupthink phenomenon, is to surround themselves with opinionated colleagues and to encourage them to offer dissenting opinions. Peter Drucker tells this anecdote about Alfred Sloan, GM's legendary chief executive:

> Sloan is reported to have said at a meeting of one of his top committees: "Gentlemen, I take it we are all in complete agreement on the decision here." Everyone around the table nodded assent. "Then," continued Mr. Sloan, "I propose we postpone further discussion of this matter until our next meeting to give ourselves time to develop disagreement and perhaps gain some understanding of what the decision is all about."

Drucker then makes this observation:

> Sloan . . . always emphasized the need to test opinions against facts and the need to make absolutely sure that one did not start out with the conclusion and then look for the facts that would support it. . . . *He knew that the right decision demands adequate disagreement.*[23]

Flexible thinking is also important for firms hoping to develop creative innovations, and the importance of creative innovations to the overall growth and well-being of our society cannot be underestimated. The spectacular success Apple Computer enjoyed in the early 1980s is but one example of the thousands of innovative firms that have had a profound impact on the growth of our economy. Apple's more recent slide from prominence is also an example of the danger firms can encounter when their managers remain inflexible or are unable to adapt to changes in the larger competitive environment.

Practical Usefulness of Understanding the Concept of Mental Models

The managerial thinking or mental models approach to the study of strategy has a number of practical implications:

- If you can "map" mental models and observe how they influence strategy, you can better understand firms' strategies and their competitors' likely reactions to those strategies. This understanding can help you (1) make better predictions about the future actions of competitors, and (2) recommend better strategies at the firms where you work. Success at predicting competitors' actions and recommending effective strategies can lead to greater influence and promotion to higher levels of responsibility.
- Furthermore, an understanding of mental models can improve your interpersonal skills. How many times have you said, "She just doesn't understand my point of view" or "He and I just don't see eye to eye"? Most interpersonal relations problems can be traced to individuals holding different mental models. In such cases, individuals who are trying to communicate with each other really *don't* understand each other's points of view. Understanding that disagreements and disputes often emerge because different individuals hold very different underlying assumptions, beliefs, and understandings about a particular phenomenon can, however, go a long way toward achieving consensus.

  Often, consensus requires making each individual's underlying assumptions or beliefs explicit. At this point, the various parties can evaluate the mental models held by the other parties and better appreciate why they hold the particular views they espouse. One additional advantage of making underlying assumptions and thinking explicit is to allow the various parties to learn from each other. Quite often it is not so much that one individual is "right" and that other individuals are "wrong," but rather that each individual is viewing the issue through a different lens. Such discussions about different underlying assumptions and thinking often lead to comments like, "Oh, I've never thought about it that way"—statements that suggest individuals are beginning to learn from one another.

- Finally, an understanding of mental models will help you better appreciate the need for updating your mental models on a timely basis. This chapter has already noted the tendency for mental models to be used over and over again, even when new information suggests that they should be updated. The chapter has described the risks associated with this reusing of old or dated models. By simply being aware of the inertia associated with your thinking and the risks associated with the use of dated or inappropriate models, you are much more likely to discipline yourself to pursue a program of continuous learning.

Conclusion

The overall aim of this chapter is to provide you with an understanding of mental models and how mental models influence decision making. The beliefs and understandings contained in managers' mental models determine what they notice, shape how they interpret the events, data, and environmental stimuli that they do notice, and influence the decisions that they make in response to their interpretations. Thus, mental models play a key role in strategic decision making and in the processes of strategy formulation and implementation.

The chapter also examined the sources of beliefs and understandings contained in mental models, including trial-and-error learning, imitation, and creativity. Powerful as they are in influencing decision making, mental models are also subject to a number of biases and limitations. The chapter reviewed these weaknesses and showed how they can lead to poor decision making and a failure of mental models to keep pace with changes in firms' competitive environments. Another section of the chapter reviewed some of the qualities of effective leaders and the importance of flexibility in managerial thinking. Finally, the chapter discussed the practical usefulness of understanding the concept of mental models.

As you continue reading and studying the material in this text, you might consider making your own thinking explicit. For example, what are your beliefs about industry environments? If you've had very little work experience, you are likely to have fairly basic or tentative beliefs and understandings about industry environments and competitive strategies. For example, you might distinguish between competitive and monopolistic markets, but have very little understanding of what makes these markets more or less competitive. Similarly, in terms of competitive strategy, you might also have some fairly simple yet strongly held beliefs about how business firms ought to compete based on your personal experience. You may have found after some either very good or very bad shopping experiences, for example, that you like to patronize businesses that offer good service. Thus, you may conclude that offering good service should be an important part of every company's competitive strategy. One important aim of any course in strategic management is to develop your knowledge of general management, so as this course progresses, you should see your own mental models of management becoming more complex and sophisticated.

The Appendix to this chapter offers two fairly straightforward methods for assessing and "mapping" mental models. You are encouraged to experiment with these two approaches, either to analyze the thinking of company managers or to assess your own beliefs and understandings of business phenomena. Regardless of your level of past work experience, the aim of this text is to encourage you to further develop your thinking so that you are prepared to take on management responsibilities in the future as well as to remain relevant and vital to the companies for which you choose to work.

Key Points

- The content of managers' mental models will influence the decisions they make and the strategic management of their firms.
- Mental models are developed through trial-and-error learning, by imitation, and through creativity.
- Mental models are incomplete representations of phenomena and are also subject to a variety of biases and social-psychological factors that can result in poor decision making.
- Mental models tend to be used over and over again even as the environment changes so that they become less and less accurate or appropriate. One key point of this chapter is that, just as business environments are changing all the time, so, too, must mental models change if managers hope to make appropriate and effective decisions.
- Some of the characteristics of effective managers and leaders include expertise, the ability to focus on the "big picture" as well as on the details, flexibility and a willingness to alter their beliefs and understandings, and an openness to new ideas and an appreciation of the value of alternative points of view.
- An understanding of the mental model concept can offer a number of practical advantages, including the ability to make better strategic recommendations, improved interpersonal relationships, and an acknowledgment of the need to change and update mental models on an ongoing basis.
- We can assess managers' mental models by analyzing what they say, write, and do. The two specific methods described and illustrated in the Appendix to this chapter are the word count technique and the analysis of cause-and-effect relationships.

Review and Discussion Questions

1. *Describe how mental models influence decision making and managerial behavior. Distinguish between categorical and causal beliefs and understandings and provide a few examples of each type of mental model.*
2. *What are the sources of mental models? Provide examples of your own beliefs or understandings that have been acquired from these different sources.*
3. *What are some of the problems associated with managerial thinking and mental models? How might these cognitive limitations and biases lead to poor decision making?*
4. *What does a managerial or cognitive approach to the study of strategic management suggest about the qualities of effective leaders?*
5. *Describe some of the practical benefits for you of understanding the concept of mental models.*

Suggestions for Further Reading

Donaldson, G., & Lorsch, J. W. 1983. *Decision Making at the Top.* New York: Basic Books.
Hamel, G., & Prahalad, C. K. 1994. *Competing for the Future.* Boston: Harvard Business School Press.
Senge, P.M. 1990. *The Fifth Discipline: The Art and Practice of Learning Organization.* New York: Doubleday/Currency.

Appendix to Chapter 2

Mapping Mental Models to Understand Strategic Decision Making

Mental models are unobservable—we have no direct process for obtaining an understanding of another individual's attitudes, beliefs, or understandings. Yet, we can construct "cognitive maps" of mental models by analyzing what we or others do, say, or write that can serve as powerful tools for industry and competitor analyses. Although a variety of methods have been developed for mapping mental models, we will consider only two relatively simple yet very effective methods for constructing cognitive maps. Our interest in exploring both of these mapping techniques is to illustrate and examine more closely the link between managers' mental models and the strategies of their firms. The various examples that follow should offer compelling evidence of the powerful influence of managerial thinking on strategic decision making.

The two cognitive mapping methodologies to be illustrated here involve content analysis of written documents or other materials. The written materials used in the examples are the letters to shareholders taken from firms' annual reports. Annual reports are a convenient data source for the analysis of managerial thinking because all publicly held companies provide such reports to their shareholders, so this data source is widely available and regularly updated. Content analysis of annual reports has been criticized because the annual reports are believed to be biased and written to frame issues in the best possible light for public relations purposes. Although annual reports are no doubt written in a way that portrays management as favorably as possible, content analysis of annual reports can still be useful because managers cannot intentionally mislead shareholders and because the material no doubt reflects the views of top managers. Furthermore, analysis of annual reports can be supplemented by content analysis of other company documents as well as the texts of speeches and interviews given by the chief executive officer.

The Word Count Technique

One mapping technique involves constructing simple maps by counting executives' use of key words. The goal of this content analysis technique is to identify key factors or issues emphasized in the thinking of top executives. The implicit hypothesis is that the thinking of executives—as revealed in their use (or lack of use) of key words—will be reflected in their firms' strategies. So, for example, if a particular firm's CEO mentions research and development over and over again in his or her letter to shareholders, then we can hypothesize that the firm emphasizes R&D activities or spends

MANAGEMENT FOCUS

ABRAHAM LINCOLN AND THE SECOND AMERICAN REVOLUTION

The word count technique has been used extensively in the study of history and political science to examine the relationship between the thinking of national leaders and their countries' policy decisions. In his collection of essays, *Drawn with the Sword: Reflections on the American Civil War*, James McPherson describes how the Civil War changed Abraham Lincoln's thinking about the identity of the country from a union or collection of states to a single, united nation:[1]

> Before 1861 the words *United States* were a plural noun . . . Since 1865, *United States* has been a singular noun. The North went to war to preserve the Union; it ended by creating a *nation.* This transformation can be traced in Lincoln's most important wartime addresses. The first inaugural address contained the word *Union* twenty times and the word *nation* not once. In Lincoln's first message to Congress, on July 4, 1861, he used *Union* forty-nine times and *nation* only three times. In his famous public letter to Horace Greeley of August 22, 1862, concerning slavery and the war, Lincoln spoke of the Union nine times and the nation not at all. But in the Gettysburg Address fifteen months later, he did not refer to the Union at all but used the word *nation* five times. And in the second inaugural address, looking back over the past four years, Lincoln spoke of one side's seeking to dissolve the Union in 1861 and the other side's accepting the challenge of war to preserve the nation.[1]

McPherson goes on to explain how this change in thinking about the identity of the United States was accompanied by a growth in the functions and role of the federal government (illustrating how beliefs influence action):

> The old decentralized republic, in which the post office was the only agency of national government that touched the average citizen, was transformed by the crucible of war into a centralized polity that taxed people directly and created an internal revenue bureau to collect the taxes, expanded the jurisdiction of federal courts, created a national currency and a federally chartered banking system, drafted men into the army, and created the Freedmen's Bureau as the first national agency for social welfare. Eleven of the first twelve amendments to the Constitution had limited the powers of the national government; six of the next seven, starting with the Thirteenth Amendment in 1865, radically expanded those powers at the expense of the states.[2]

So pivotal was this shift in thinking and its impact on national policy that Lincoln's presidency can truly be thought of as the "Second American Revolution." ■

[1]McPherson, J. M. 1996. *Drawn with the Sword: Reflections on the American Civil War.* New York: Oxford University Press, p. 64.

[2]Ibid, p. 64.

more on R&D than another firm in the same industry whose CEO does not mention R&D as frequently. Content analysis methodologies, such as the word count technique, have been used to examine the relationship between thinking and action in a number of fields. The accompanying Management Focus, "Abraham Lincoln and the Second American Revolution," illustrates use of the word count by a historian to study the relationship between presidential thinking and national policy.

ILLUSTRATION 1

Now, let's consider how the word count technique can be applied in a business setting to understand the influence of managerial thinking on a company's strategies. The example examines how the thinking of Vincent Sarni, recently retired chair-

EXHIBIT 2.4

An Illustration of the Word Count Technique Applied to Various Letters to the Shareholders of PPG Industries

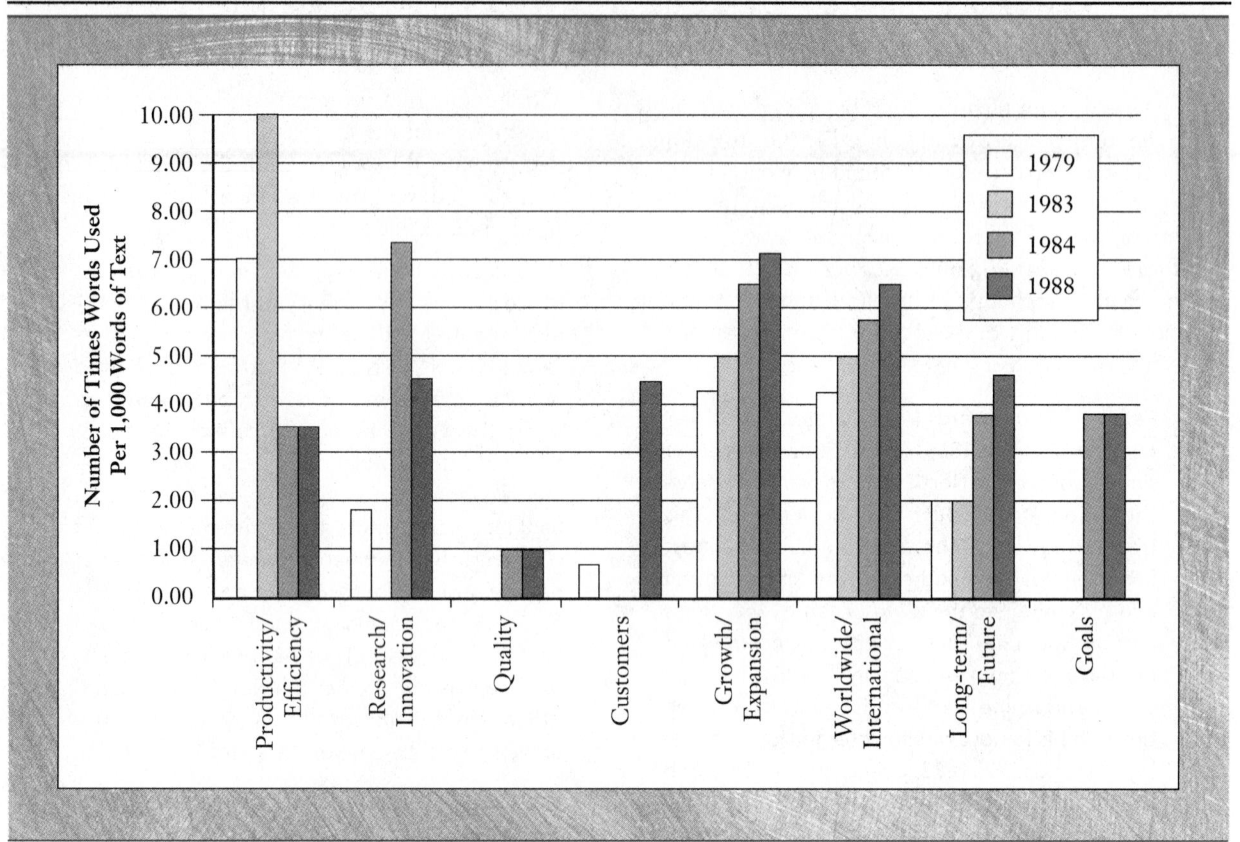

man and chief executive officer of PPG Industries, differed from that of his predecessor and how this difference in thinking led to different decisions and new strategies that improved PPG's performance. In this illustration, you'll see how the simple word count technique can be used to show that cognitive maps of Mr. Sarni's mental models are quite different from maps of his predecessor's mental models.

The success of the word count technique depends on the choice of words to be counted in the analysis. Words are not chosen randomly, but are instead carefully selected to capture managers' emphasis on key concepts in the hypothesized relationships. For this particular example, the hypothesis is that the many new products introduced by PPG and the strong growth the company experienced under Mr. Sarni's leadership can be traced to his beliefs, which were fundamentally different from his predecessor's beliefs. More specifically, this study hypothesizes that Mr. Sarni believed that PPG should pursue a strategy of new-product development through an emphasis on R&D, meeting customer needs, and domestic and international expansion, while his predecessor believed that PPG should pursue a strategy of producing low-cost commodity products.

To explore this working hypothesis, the words that were chosen for analysis included *productivity* or *efficiency*, *research* or *innovation*, *quality*, *customers*, *growth* or *expansion*, *worldwide* or *international*, *long-term* or *future*, and *goals*. Exhibit 2.4 shows the number of times each of these words was used in the 1979, 1983, 1984, and 1988 letters to shareholders. Comparing the number of times these words were used in the 1979 and 1983 letters to shareholders (before Mr. Sarni became CEO) with the number of times these words were used in the 1984 and 1988 letters to shareholders (after Mr. Sarni became CEO) shows that Mr. Sarni and his predecessor did indeed emphasize different concepts. The exhibit shows that Mr. Sarni emphasized the words *research*, *innovation*, *customers*, and *goals*, while his predecessor emphasized *productivity* and *efficiency*.

Further reading and research would lead to the conclusions that Mr. Sarni's mental models were different from his predecessor's and that Mr. Sarni's beliefs did have a strong influence on the strategies pursued by PPG Industries. Prior to Mr. Sarni becoming the company's chief executive officer, PPG participated in what were essentially commodity markets—paint and glass—primarily as a supplier to the automobile industry. Mr. Sarni's emphasis on research and innovation pushed the company to differentiate its products so that they would be less like commodities. During Mr. Sarni's tenure as CEO, the company did develop many new products, including Clear Coat paints (now widely used on new automobiles and trucks), new solar-efficient glass for use in homes and cars, and new environmentally safe inks and dyes. Furthermore, the share of PPG sales revenues coming from abroad also increased. These moves had a positive impact on the bottom line at PPG as well: PPG's return on equity in 1983, the year before Mr. Sarni became CEO, was 13 percent; by 1988, the company's return on equity had jumped to 22 percent.[24]

Illustration 2

Let's now consider another example in which the word count technique is helpful in illustrating the link between managerial thinking and strategic decision making. In 1984, two important regional bank holding companies, Mellon Bank and NCNB Corp. (now called NationsBank), both had approximately $20 billion in total assets. Over the next several years, however, the companies pursued very different strategies. Can this difference in strategies be attributed to differences in the mental models of the two companies' chief executives? Even a glance at the letters to shareholders of these two regional bank holding companies suggests striking differences between the two executives. Using the word count technique and analyzing these executives' use of just three words—*growth*, *expansion*, and *size*—revealed some striking differences between these two CEOs. While the CEO of Mellon Bank made only one reference to any of these words (or less than .5 percent of all words in the letter to shareholders), the CEO of NCNB made 37 references to these words (2 percent of all the words in the letter to shareholders)!

Did this difference in mental models have an impact on decision making at these two regional bank holding companies? They almost certainly did! As Exhibit 2.5 shows, by 1991, the total assets of NCNB had grown nearly five times to over $100 billion, while the total assets of Mellon Bank had actually fallen slightly.

Analysis of Cause-and-Effect Relationships

The second mapping technique requires more analysis than a simple count of words, but, as a consequence, the analysis of cause-and-effect relationships provides more detail about managerial thinking. As with the word count technique, the

EXHIBIT 2.5

The Change in Assets of Two Regional Bank Holding Companies

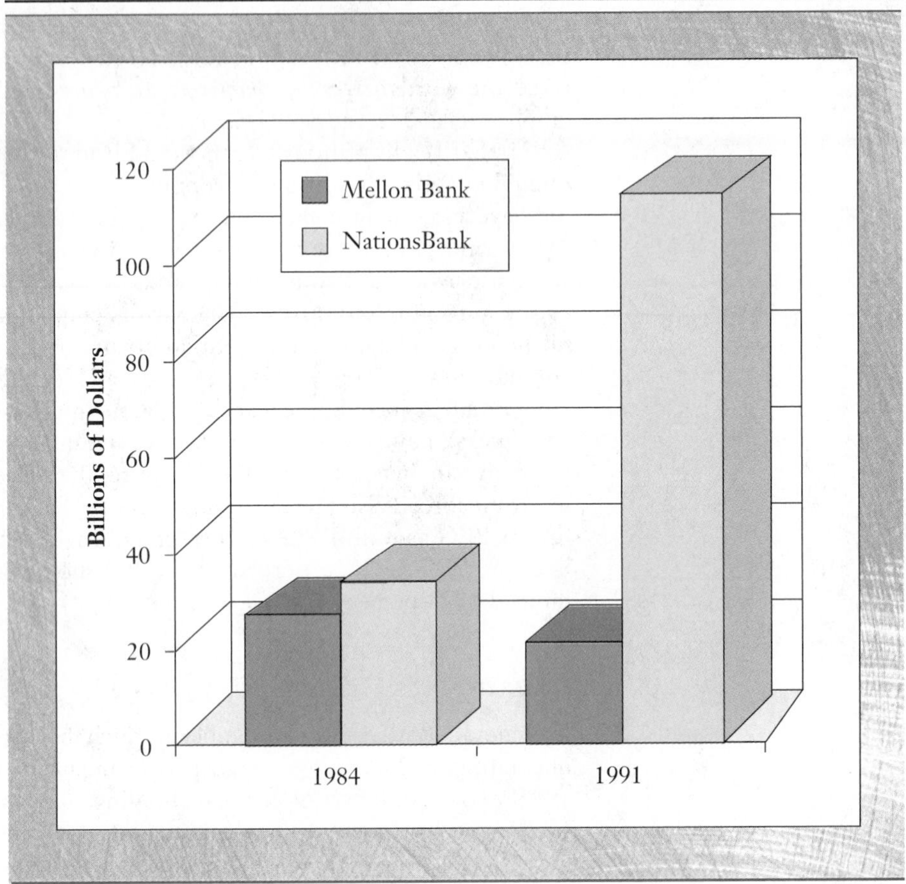

analysis of cause-and-effect relationships also involves content analysis of written documents, such as letters to shareholders. This time, however, the method analyzes not single words, but the cause-and-effect relationships embedded in the text. An analysis of cause-and-effect relationships requires researchers to first identify and document all the causal relationships contained in a body of text. For example, the hypothetical statement, "Sales revenues increased during the year due to a favorable economy and the introduction of several new products," contains two causal relationships: "A favorable economy" caused sales revenues to increase and "the introduction of several new products" also caused sales revenues to increase. These causal relationships would be coded by a researcher as shown in Exhibit 2.6.

As with the word count technique, the implicit hypothesis is that managers' understandings of cause and effect will be reflected in the strategies of their firms. So, for example, if a firm's top managers believe that advertising increases brand loyalty, which, in turn, increases sales, then we would expect to see that firm spend more on advertising than do other firms. If, on the other hand, a firm's top managers believe that customer service and product quality increase brand loyalty, then we would expect to see that firm place more emphasis on customer service and product quality.

EXHIBIT 2.6

Coding of the Cause-and-Effect Relationships Contained in a Simple Statement

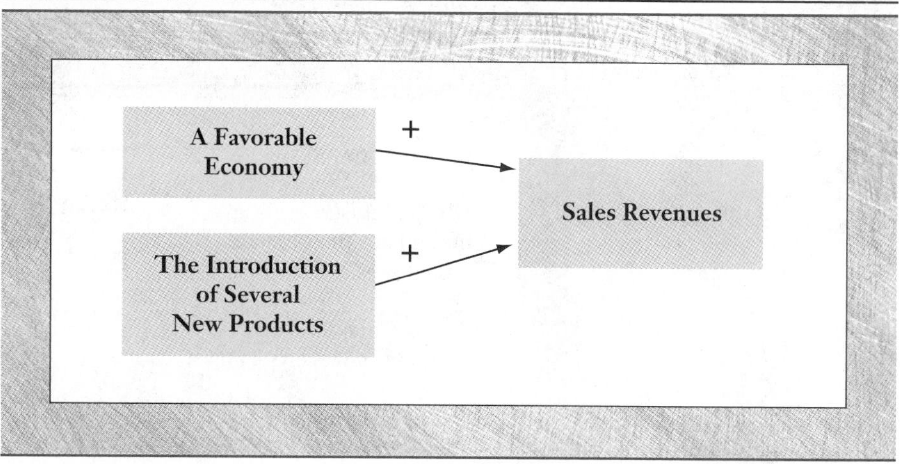

Earlier in the chapter, we mentioned the tendency for executives to take credit for their firms' successes while blaming other factors for the problems their firms experience. Researchers have, in fact, used the mapping of cause-and-effect relationships in letters to shareholders to document this tendency. Analyses of letters to shareholders have frequently found top managers attributing favorable outcomes to the strategies they have implemented while blaming low performance on poor general economic conditions or bad weather or natural disasters.[25]

Now, let's consider how the influence of managerial thinking on company strategies can be illustrated by mapping managers' cause-effect understandings. In this example, we'll consider two companies in the volatile retailing industry, Sears and Wal-Mart. During the 1980s, these two companies experienced very different fates. Sears, for years the largest retailing company in the world, saw its ranking among retailers slide from the number one position to number three behind Wal-Mart and Kmart. Wal-Mart, in contrast, emerged from obscurity as a local Arkansas retailer with stores primarily in small, rural towns to become the number one retailing company in the United States. Could the understandings of cause and effect held by the top managers of these firms explain these different outcomes?

To examine this possibility, the cause-and-effect relationships in the letters to shareholders in annual reports of both Sears and Wal-Mart were extracted and are summarized in Exhibits 2.7 and 2.8, respectively. A quick examination of Exhibit 2.7 reveals that Sears' top managers were preoccupied by the need to manage Sears' many businesses in retailing, insurance, financial services, and real estate. None of the causal relationships contained in the document deal specifically with the challenges of managing the company's troubled retail business. In fact, the last few cause-and-effect relationships contained in the letter to shareholders suggest that the CEO believed that Sears' retailing sales were not "caused" by anything Sears itself had done or could do, but were instead a function of a favorable macroeconomic environment, which includes an "increase in disposable income" and "no new taxes."

Contrast this map of cause-and-effect relationships with a map of the cause-and-effect understandings held by Wal-Mart's CEO, as illustrated in Exhibit 2.8. Every

EXHIBIT 2.7

Cause-and-Effect Relationships Contained in a Letter to Shareholders of Sears, Roebuck & Company

Cause		Effect
Everyday low pricing	+ →	Competitiveness
Divested Allstate's group life and health insurance businesses	+ →	Emphasis on consumer businesses
Selling Coldwell Banker commercial real estate unit	+ →	Emphasis on consumer businesses
Sale of Sears Tower	+ →	Relocation of offices to less costly facilities
Relocation of offices to less costly facilities	+ →	Reduce costs
Sale of Allstate's investment products through Dean Witter	+ →	Programs to link businesses
The Discover Card	+ →	Programs to link businesses
Growth of Dean Witter account executive force	+ →	Profits
Increase in disposable income, no new taxes	+ →	Allow consumers to increase spending on merchandise
Increase in disposable income, no new taxes	+ →	Stimulate investments in financial services
Increase in disposable income, no new taxes	+ →	Sales

causal relationship documented in the Wal-Mart letter to shareholders indicates the same desired end: customer satisfaction. No doubt this almost single-minded focus on customer satisfaction is reflected in Wal-Mart's superior retailing strategies.

CONCLUSION

As noted at the end of Chapter 2, one important practical application of knowledge about mental models is to understand and anticipate company and competitor strategies. If you can gain insight into managers' beliefs and understandings, then

EXHIBIT 2.8

Cause-and-Effect Relationships Contained in a Letter to Shareholders of Wal-Mart

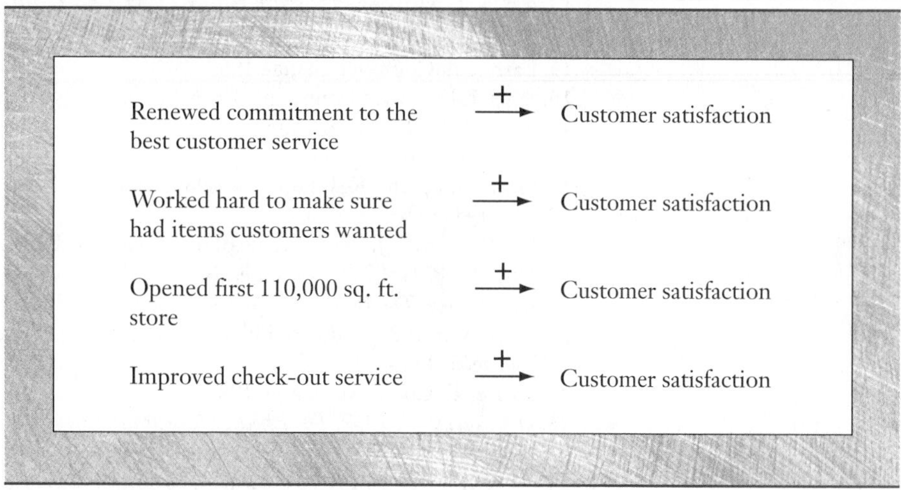

you are in an excellent position to predict what decisions they are likely to make and what strategies are likely to emerge. The mapping techniques that have been described and illustrated in this Appendix will allow you to make managers' (and your own) mental models more explicit.

Endnotes

1. Gibson, R. 1996. Quaker to cut its expenditures on Snapple unit. *The Wall Street Journal*, September 13, A5; Gibson, R. 1996. Quaker posts better-than-expected net, but disappoints with Snapple inaction. *The Wall Street Journal*, October 25, B2.
2. Hamermesh, R. G. 1977. Responding to divisional profit crises. *Harvard Business Review* 55(2):124–130.
3. Quoted in Mercer, D. 1987. *IBM: How the World's Most Successful Company Is Managed.* London: Kogan Page, p. 48.
4. Donaldson, G., and J. W. Lorsch. 1983. *Decision Making at the Top.* New York: Basic Books, p. 10.
5. See, for example, Carley, W. M. 1997. Charging ahead: To keep GE's profits rising, Welch pushes quality-control plan. *The Wall Street Journal*, January 13, A1, A6.
6. Frank, R., and J. S. Lublin. 1996. Dunlap's ax falls—6,000 times—at Sunbeam. *The Wall Street Journal*, November 13, B1, B9; Lublin, J. S., and M. Brannigan. 1996. Sunbeam names Albert Dunlap as chief, betting he can pull off a turnaround. *The Wall Street Journal*, July 19, B3.
7. Suris, O., and J. S. Lublin. 1997. Sunbeam's Dunlap sees evidence revamp is working. *The Wall Street Journal*, April 24, B4.
8. Carey, S. 1997. US Air's Stephen Wolf follows a familiar playbook. *The Wall Street Journal*, May 27, B4; Carey, S. 1997. US Airways' tentative pact with pilots moves carrier closer to Wolf's strategy. *The Wall Street Journal*, October 2, A4; Carey, S. 1997. US Air pilots approve contract in big victory for airline's chief. *The Wall Street Journal*, November 3, B4.
9. May, R. 1975. *The Courage to Create.* New York: Norton.
10. Ibid, p. 71.
11. Barr, P. S., J. L. Stimpert, and A. S. Huff. 1992. Cognitive change, strategic action, and organizational renewal. *Strategic Management Journal* 13 (special issue): 15–36.

12. Catton, B. 1955. *This Hallowed Ground.* New York: Washington Square Press, p. 471, emphasis added.
13. Hamilton, E. 1932. *The Roman Way.* New York: Norton, p. 209–211.
14. Senge, P. M. 1990. *The Fifth Discipline: The Art and Practice of the Learning Organization.* New York: Doubleday/Currency, p. 176.
15. Barr et al. Cognitive change 1982.
16. Janis, I. L. 1971. Groupthink. *Psychology Today*, November, 43–46.
17. Staw, B. 1981. The escalation of commitment to a course of action. *Academy of Management Review* 6: 577–588.
18. Glass, A. L., and K. J. Holyoak. 1986. *Cognition.* 2d ed. New York: Random House, pp. 141–143.
19. See Rosenthal, J. 1994. Frame of mind. *New York Times Magazine*, August 21, 16, 18.
20. Duff, C. 1993. Blue-light blues: Kmart's dowdy stores get a snazzy face-lift, but problems linger. *The Wall Street Journal*, November 5, A1, A6.
21. Huff, A. S. 1982. Industry influences on strategy reformulation. *Strategic Management Journal* 3: 119–131.
22. Barr et al. Cognitive change 1984.
23. Drucker, P. F. 1967. *The Effective Executive.* New York: Harper & Row, p. 148, emphasis added.
24. Norton, E. 1993. PPG's chairman, Sarni, will be a tough act to follow. *The Wall Street Journal*, January 22, B4.
25. Huff, A. S., and C. R. Schwenk. 1990. Bias and sensemaking in good times and bad. In *Mapping Strategic Thought*, edited by A. S. Huff. New York: Wiley.

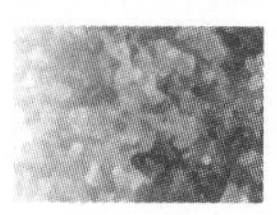

CHAPTER 3

AN INTRODUCTION TO COMPETITIVE ADVANTAGE

CHAPTER OBJECTIVES

The model of strategic management introduced in Chapter 1 and reprinted in Exhibit 3.1 suggests that general managers must make four crucial types of strategic decisions. They must:

- Define or position their firms in their competitive environments based on their understandings of industry structure and dynamics.
- Develop a business strategy based on their beliefs about how to compete in their firms' industries.
- Develop a corporate strategy based on their beliefs about the appropriate scale and scope for their firms, their understandings of how their firms' businesses are related, and their beliefs about how diversification should be managed.
- Create an organizational structure based on their beliefs about how to organize a business firm that will allow them to implement their firms' strategies.

Before beginning a detailed study of these topics, however, this chapter provides an introduction to the concept of competitive advantage. The specific objectives of this chapter are to:

- Provide a definition of and describe the characteristics associated with competitive advantage.
- Describe how organizations develop and maintain competitive advantage.
- Distinguish between content and process and emphasize the importance of organizational processes in developing and maintaining competitive advantage.
- Introduce the concept of the value chain and describe its usefulness as a tool for assessing organizational capabilities.
- Emphasize the importance of socially complex resources—such as trust, culture, and reputation, which are based on interpersonal relationships among managers, employees, customers, and suppliers.
- Emphasize that any source of competitive advantage can be rendered obsolete very quickly by changes in firms' competitive environments.

EXHIBIT 3.1

The Mental Models and Strategic Decisions Studied in This Text and Their Influence on Performance and Competitive Advantage

Managers' Mental Models
Their beliefs and understandings about
- Industry environments
- How to compete
- Appropriate size and diversity
- How to organize

Decisions about Business Definition

Decisions about Business Strategy

Decisions about Corporate Strategy and Diversification

Decisions about Organizational Structure

Market Position, Resources, and Capabilities

Performance and Competitive Advantage

Feedback
Reinforces or suggests changes in managers' mental models

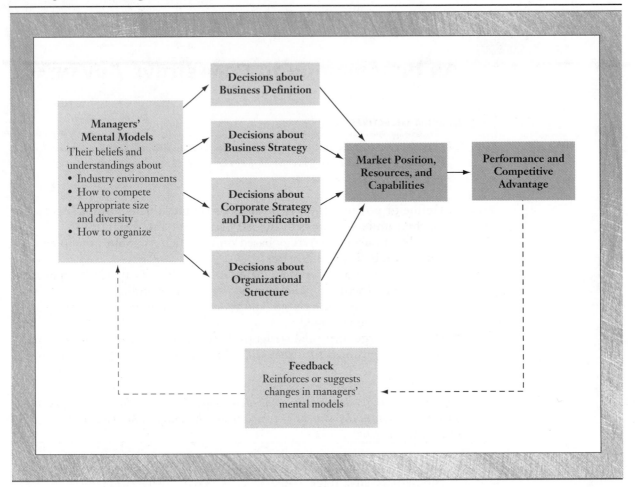

WHAT IS COMPETITIVE ADVANTAGE?

Let's begin with a definition: *Competitive advantage is the set of factors or capabilities that allows firms to consistently outperform their rivals.* Note that the objective of competitive advantage is to *outperform* rivals, not merely match the performance of other businesses. In other words, competitive advantage should allow businesses to enjoy high performance, and, though firms enjoying a competitive advantage do not necessarily have to be the highest-performing firms in their industries, they should be *among* the highest performers in their industries and do much better than the average. Moreover, another important aim of competitive advantage is for firms to enjoy *sustained* levels of high performance—in other words, a business should not enjoy just one or two or a few good years, but should *consistently* outperform rival firms and businesses. Many firms have shown that they have the ability to have a good year or two, but far fewer firms have shown the ability to enjoy *consistently* high levels of performance year after year.

How Is Firm Performance Assessed?

The term *performance* most commonly refers to financial performance, which can include net income, gross margin, or other absolute measures. Such measures can be helpful in assessing the growth of a particular firm or business over different time periods, but these absolute performance measures are not particularly helpful in comparing or contrasting firms of different size or firms that operate in different industries.

For example, two hypothetical firms might both have net income of $15 million, but one firm could be very large (say, $1 billion in total sales revenues) while the other firm might be much smaller (say, only $100 million in total sales revenues). Which of the firms is more profitable? If only net income is considered, the answer would be that the two firms are both equally profitable, but this answer is somewhat misleading given that one firm is so much larger than the other.

Thus, ratio measures are more useful for comparison purposes because they "standardize" absolute measures, such as net income, by dividing these measures by a common denominator. Some of the most common ratio measures are return on sales (net income/sales revenues), return on assets (net income/total assets), and return on equity (net income/total shareholders' equity), though many other ratio measures are also commonly used to assess the financial performance of business organizations. The return on sales for the first hypothetical firm mentioned earlier is only 1.5 percent, while the return on sales for the much smaller second firm is 15 percent. In other words, for every dollar of sales made by the first firm, it earns only 1.5 cents of net income, while the second firm earns 10 times as much net income for every dollar of sales. By controlling for firm size, the ratio measure—return on sales—suggests that the second, smaller firm is significantly more profitable than the larger firm. Because of the importance of financial statement analysis and the clues it can offer to analysts and strategists, the accompanying Management Focus on "Financial Statement Analysis" provides a summary of many of the most important and frequently used financial ratios.

Performance is, however, a multidimensional concept and, though financial performance measures are probably the most common, many other types of performance measures are also used to assess the performance and health of business firms. For example, stock market performance measures, such as one- and five-year market returns, which assess increases in the value of companies' stock prices over a particular time period, are commonly used. Earnings per share (EPS) is a ratio of a firm's net income divided by the total number of its common shares outstanding. Price/earnings (P/E) ratios are calculated by dividing the current market price of a company's common shares by its EPS. The resulting number is referred to as a company's "multiple." Historically, the average P/E ratio for stocks has been around 15; however, some stocks have very high P/E ratios. The P/E ratios of outstanding companies, such as Microsoft, Gillette, and Coca-Cola, are much higher than the historical average, often in the 40s, 50s, or even higher, reflecting investor confidence that these companies will continue to enjoy high earnings well into the future.

Market share is another important performance measure, especially in industries or markets in which important advantages can be derived from large size (i.e., economies of scale). On the other hand, firms that are deliberately pursuing very focused or niche strategies may find market share an irrelevant performance consideration. Many other performance measures are more industry specific. In retailing, for example, sales per square foot of retailing space is a common performance

MANAGEMENT FOCUS

FINANCIAL STATEMENT ANALYSIS

Financial statement analysis can be very useful in analyzing the financial health and prosperity of any business organization. Financial statement analysis can also offer important clues about the strategies firms are pursuing, so it can be an important tool for analyzing the strategies of competitors. In this Management Focus, we'll first consider four major types of financial ratios and then examine some additional ratios that are of special interest to strategists.

Financial performance ratios. Return on assets and return on equity are two of the most commonly used financial ratios and they both examine overall firm financial performance. They are calculated as:

Return on assets = Net income/Average total assets

Return on equity = Net income/Average total shareholders' equity

Operating performance and efficiency. A number of additional measures are helpful for examining more closely the performance and efficiency of firms' ongoing business operations. These ratios include profit margin, net profit margin, and the asset turnover ratio. They are calculated as:

Profit margin = Gross margin/Net sales

Net profit margin = Net income/Net sales

Asset turnover ratio = Net sales/Average total assets

Note that:

Net profit margin X Asset turnover ratio = Return on assets

This important relationship implies that managers can increase the overall profitability of their firms by (1) increasing the amount of profits earned from their companies' sales, and (2) increasing the volume of sales generated by their companies' assets. Some businesses are high volume—that is, they generate much of their profitability through a very high level of sales. For example, many retail establishments, especially grocery stores, tend to have fairly low net profit margins, but they aim to "make it up in volume" by generating a high level of sales and, therefore, have high asset turnover ratios. An "ideal" business will have both a high profit margin and a high sales volume or turnover ratio.

Liquidity ratios. Liquidity ratios assess the ability of firms to meet current financial obligations. The two best known measures of liquidity are the current ratio and the quick ratio (sometimes called the acid-test ratio). They are calculated as:

Current ratio = Current assets/Current liabilities

Quick ratio = (Current assets – Inventory – Prepaid expenses)/Current liabilities

continued

measure. In banking, net interest earned—the interest banks earn on their loans and other activities less the interest banks must pay to their depositors and other providers of funds—is an important measure of bank profitability.

More recently, "cycle time" and "time to market"—the time it takes to get new product ideas into production and available for consumer purchase—have become important performance measures, especially in high-tech industries or any markets in which new-product development efforts are critical to success.

While many performance measures are fairly straightforward and objective, other performance measures are more subjective. For example, customer perceptions of quality and business reputation are frequently measured, but they lack some of the objectivity of measures based on financial and stock market data. Just because some measures are more subjective than others does not mean, however, that they are unimportant or less relevant. Customer perceptions of product or service quality can make or break a company. In fact, when studying competitive advantage, it's important to

The quick ratio is obviously a much more stringent measure of a firm's ability to meet its current financial obligations because it includes only the most liquid current assets in the numerator.

Measures of debt and leverage. The most common measure of debt and leverage is the debt-to-equity ratio. It shows the extent to which companies' assets are financed by debt rather than equity, and it is calculated as:

Debt-to-equity ratio = Total liabilities/Total shareholders' equity

Another widely used measure of debt, which also measures an organization's solvency or its ability to meet its long-term financial obligations, is the times interest earned ratio. It is calculated as:

Times interest earned = Earnings before interest and taxes/Interest charges

In other words, the times interest earned ratio examines the extent to which a firm's current earnings are sufficient to meet its current interest payments.

Some financial ratios are of special interest to strategists. In addition to assessing firm performance, liquidity, and capital structure, financial ratios can offer important clues to understanding organizational strategies. Companies with high ratios of selling, general, and administrative expense to total sales or, more specifically, high levels of advertising and marketing expenditures to total sales, may be trying to build consumer awareness or customer loyalty through advertising and other marketing activities. Companies with high ratios of R&D expenditures to total sales may be working to develop new products or services or working to lower costs by developing more efficient production processes. Similarly, companies with high ratios of capital expenditures to total sales may be planning to increase production capacity.

Strengths and limitations of financial statement analysis. One major strength of financial statement analysis is the availability of data. Financial data for publicly held companies is widely available through company annual reports, documents filed with the Securities and Exchange Commission, and many popular databases. Many companies' financial statements are available on their Web sites and through EDGAR, an online service that provides access to records maintained by the Securities and Exchange Commission. Another advantage of financial statement analysis is that it relies on ratio measures so that companies can be readily compared with each other.

At the same time, financial statement analysis has a number of limitations. First, financial ratios and other measures are fairly meaningless in isolation. In other words, to be useful, financial ratios for a particular company must be compared against industry averages, other firms, or the firm's own past performance. Second, all financial data, no matter how recent, reflects what has happened rather than what will happen. Thus, financial ratios evaluate company performance by looking back rather than by looking ahead. This can be a problem, especially in high-velocity environments in which a firm's performance today says little about its ability to perform effectively tomorrow. ■

consider a variety of different types of performance measures. The best indication that a firm enjoys a competitive advantage would be high performance across a number of different performance dimensions over a number of years.

When using financial data to assess performance, users must be aware of the impact of extraordinary items and other accounting adjustments on net income. For example, an otherwise outstanding firm that enjoys a consistent record of excellent financial performance could have a major loss due to a fire at one of its facilities. This extraordinary item may, however, say little about whether the company enjoys a competitive advantage. At the same time, a firm reporting a series of restructuring charges over a period of several years should raise some skepticism: Why exactly is the firm undergoing so much restructuring? Why can't the company's managers get it on track? These points highlight the need to "look behind the numbers" when using financial data to assess competitive advantage. The documentation and "Notes to Accompany the Financial Statements" that are included in any company's annual report are often invaluable supplements to the financial statements. These observations also suggest the importance of consulting a wide variety of resources when evaluating companies, including newspaper and magazine reports, interviews with company executives, and even comments by the managers of competing firms.

In addition to annual reports, other useful sources of firm performance data include company 10Ks—documents that must be filed annually with the Securities and Exchange Commission by all publicly traded companies—Standard and Poors' *Industry Surveys*, Moody's *Manuals*, and industry and other trade publications. Many schools will have CD-ROM databases that can also be very helpful for conducting research on firms. For example, Standard and Poors' COMPUSTAT database contains current and historical accounting and market performance data on nearly 20,000 firms.

Competitive Advantage: The Importance of Firm-Specific Factors and Capabilities

The aim of strategic management is the development of sustainable competitive advantage. Given this book's definition of strategy as "a pattern in a stream of decisions,"[1] our focus is on the patterns of decisions that contribute to the development of competitive advantage and sustained high performance. The model of strategic management illustrated in Exhibit 3.1 shows that strategies do not directly affect firm performance, but that strategies affect performance through the development of firm-specific factors, capabilities, and competencies that are the sources of competitive advantage. This chapter considers how managerial thinking and decision making are associated with the development of firm-specific capabilities, including business definitions or market positions, strategies, and structures, that lead to sustained competitive advantage.

Only during the last decade has the strategic management field begun to appreciate the impact that firm-specific factors, capabilities, or competencies can have on firm performance levels.[2] In fact, only recently have firm-specific capabilities become the focus of academic research. One early study that demonstrated the importance of firm-specific factors found that firms in the *same* industry pursuing the *same* strategies had widely varying levels of performance.[3] This finding was important because it called into question traditional "structural" explanations for firm performance, which predict that firms in the same industry, especially firms pursuing similar strategies in the same industry, would enjoy roughly comparable performance outcomes.

A subsequent study also found significant performance differences among firms pursuing similar strategies.[4] These researchers reasoned that such performance differences must result from differences in organizational capabilities. In a follow-up study, these researchers did, in fact, find significant differences in the capabilities and resources of their sample firms, and they also found a significant relationship between firms' capabilities and their performance outcomes.

One way to explore the performance implications of firm-specific factors is through the "resource-based view of the firm."[5] This fairly new perspective is rooted in the important work of British scholar Edith Penrose,[6] who suggested that firms could be viewed as collections of productive resources. The central thesis of the resource-based perspective is that too little attention has been given to the importance of firm-specific factors and capabilities. Advocates of the resource-based perspective do not suggest that industry or market characteristics are unimportant, but they do argue that competitive advantage will be determined by the capabilities firms bring to their competitive arenas.

Criteria That Determine Whether Resources and Capabilities Can Provide Firms with Competitive Advantage

Although researchers have only begun to explore the implications of the resource-based perspective during the past decade, the central tenets of the theory suggest that firms will enjoy a sustained competitive advantage only if their capabilities are *valuable* and *rare*, *lack substitutes*, and are *difficult to imitate*.[7]

According to this logic, resources and capabilities that are not valuable obviously cannot be expected to generate any sort of competitive advantage. Similarly, if valuable capabilities are not rare, but are widely available to all firms in a particular market, the best that a firm can hope for is competitive parity with other firms. If resources and capabilities are both valuable and rare, and also difficult for rivals to imitate, then those resources can at least be a temporary source of competitive advantage. Finally, if resources and capabilities are valuable, rare, and difficult to imitate, and if those resources also lack viable substitutes, then those resources can be the source of sustained competitive advantage. This reasoning is summarized in Exhibit 3.2.

The Asymmetric Nature of Competitive Advantage

The four criteria that are common to the resources and capabilities that provide firms with a sustainable competitive advantage—valuable, rare, difficult to imitate, and without substitutes—imply that an essential characteristic of competitive advantage is *asymmetry*. In other words, uniqueness is an essential characteristic of any resource or capability that is to be the basis of competitive advantage. Thus, to enjoy a competitive advantage, a firm must do what its rivals cannot do, or, alternatively, if it does what its rivals can do, then it must do it better.

Exhibit 3.2

Estimating the Return-Generating Potential of Organizational Resources

Is a Resource ...				
Valuable	**Rare**	**Difficult to Imitate**	**Without Substitutes**	**Competitive Implications**
No	—	—	—	Competitive disadvantage
Yes	No	—	—	Competitive parity
Yes	Yes	No	—	Temporary competitive advantage
Yes	Yes	Yes	No	Competitive parity
Yes	Yes	Yes	Yes	Sustained competitive advantage

SOURCE: Adapted from J. B. Barney, 1991. Firm Resources and Sustained Competitive Advantage, *Journal of Management* 17: 99–120.

Although it is easy to identify a wide variety of tangible and intangible resources and capabilities that could be potential sources of competitive advantage, the resource-based view suggests that any resource or capability will only contribute to the development of competitive advantage if it is associated with "barriers" that prevent its acquisition or replication by competitors.[8] If a valuable resource or capability can be acquired or replicated by competitors, then any competitive advantage enjoyed by the firm will soon disappear.[9]

The Challenge of Defending Against Imitation

One of the most important challenges confronting any firm that seeks to enjoy a sustained competitive advantage is to defend against imitation. This challenge is made especially difficult in a market economy like ours where the managers of business firms not only have easy access to information, but also powerful incentives to learn about and acquire potentially valuable resources and capabilities.

Past research on the diffusion of innovations is particularly helpful in understanding the challenge of defending against imitation by rival firms. Studies have shown that ideas and innovations are diffused through the economy in a pattern that resembles a slanted "S-shaped curve" as illustrated in Exhibit 3.3. The curve suggests that for a relatively brief time—from t_0 to t_1—innovations may be proprietary to just one or only a very few firms, but that at some point—t_1 in the exhibit—the diffusion process begins. By t_2 in the exhibit, nearly all firms in the market or the entire economy have adopted the innovation. This pattern of adoption—in which only one person or firm or very few people or organizations employ a particular innovation, but very soon afterward nearly all people or firms have adopted the innovation—is seen across a wide variety of innovations, including everything from the use of new technologies in manufacturing to the spread of campus fashion trends among college students.

A resource or capability, like the value of an innovation, will contribute to competitive advantage only until the diffusion process begins. At the point t_1, any source of competitive advantage will begin to lose its rareness and, therefore, no longer guarantee sustained high performance. In fact, the resource-based view suggests that as a resource begins to be diffused through an industry or the entire economy, firms can expect the resource to offer only competitive parity with other firms.

Ways to Slow Down or Prevent Imitation

Managers can seek to prevent imitation by competitors in a number of ways. They can and often will seek to patent their firms' technologies or other resources that have the potential to provide a competitive advantage. A patent will provide firms with exclusive rights to a particular technology for 17 years. On the other hand, some managers are reluctant to patent their firms' technologies because they fear that the information contained in the patent might allow rivals to innovate or engineer "around the patent"—a process quite common in many high-technology industries.

Managers can also seek to have their firms own exclusive access to key resources or assets. Inco, for example, has long dominated the world nickel market largely because it owns such a vast majority of all known nickel deposits. Managers might also seek to exploit a resource as fully as possible before the diffusion process begins. For example, firms might take advantage of a particular technology by building

EXHIBIT 3.3

The Diffusion of Innovations

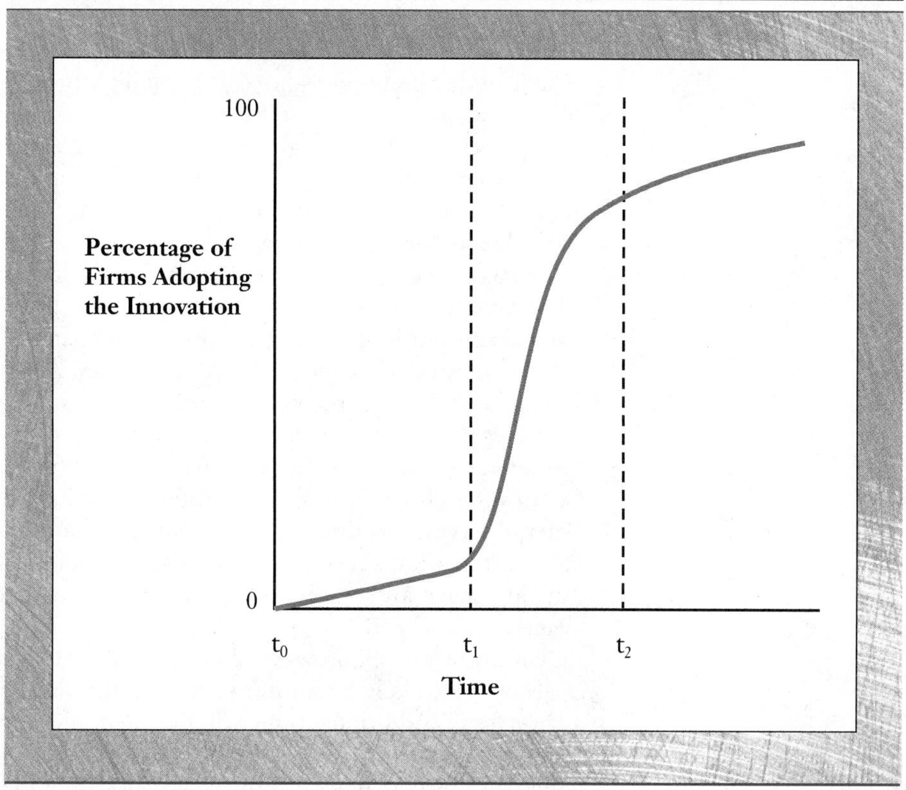

market share as fast as possible. This would not only build customer loyalty to the firms' products or services, but such a strategy could also allow the firm to enjoy economies of scale and develop an absolute cost advantage over potential rivals before they could adopt or exploit the new technology.

Finally, litigation is an atypical but frequently employed strategy that managers use to slow the diffusion process. Firms frequently sue their rivals in order to slow down the diffusion process. In fact, Intel has frequently and successfully used litigation as a competitive tactic in its efforts to slow competitors that are hoping to catch up with or "leap-frog" over Intel's technological advancements. Chapter 8 provides a closer look at litigation as a competitive tactic.

How Firms Develop Competitive Advantage: The Accumulation of Unique Capabilities

Competitive advantage is most likely to result from the development of unique capabilities that are built up through an ongoing process of resource accumulation.[10] Five factors contribute to this resource accumulation process, making capabilities more difficult to imitate and enhancing the potential of these capabilities to contribute to sustained competitive advantage. These five factors—time, building on past success, the interconnectedness of capabilities, investment, and causal ambiguity—are examined here.

TIME

The firm that builds a resource or capability through continuous investments over many years may enjoy a significant advantage over other firms that attempt to replicate this capability through larger investments made over a shorter time period. An analogy is the advantage a student who studies consistently throughout the semester enjoys over other students who attempt to cram an entire semester's worth of study into the week before the final exam.

As suggested by this analogy, the value of time is directly related to the extent of learning that occurs. A firm that uses time to learn or acquire unique capabilities can gain a significant advantage over its competitors. This experience or learning effect is illustrated by the advantage Southwest Airlines currently enjoys in the airline industry.[11] Over the years, Southwest has sought to improve the utilization of its planes through fast "turns" at airports so that passengers are unloaded, the planes are serviced, and passengers are quickly loaded for the next flight. So effective have Southwest's efforts been that it routinely turns its planes 10 or more times each day. After observing Southwest's success and attributing that success to effective equipment utilization, several other airlines, including United, Continental, and US Airways, have all sought to improve the number of turns they get from their planes.[12]

Unfortunately, Southwest's competitors have been unable to match Southwest's success, most likely because they need additional time to learn how to turn their planes faster. Additional time will give them not only more opportunities to learn from experience about how to improve their efficiency, but also time to modify union contracts that govern the work rules and practices of their flight personnel and ground crews.

BUILDING ON PAST SUCCESS

Most businesses find much truth in the statement, "Success breeds success." A history of accomplishments makes it easier to enjoy future success. Not only are winning firms likely to have more discretionary resources that can be reinvested to expand their businesses, but their reputations for success will also help them attract more assets and resources, helping to guarantee future successes and achievements. For example, leading business schools have no trouble recruiting outstanding students to their M.B.A. programs. Their students enjoy excellent placement prospects that further enhance the image and reputation of these leading schools, which, in turn, helps with their future recruiting efforts.

For the same reason, venture capital tends to flow to start-up firms that have executives or managers who have proven track records. Similarly, firms enjoying a reputation for success have no trouble recruiting outstanding employees. For example, many students majoring in finance are readily attracted to an outstanding investment bank like Goldman Sachs, just as many marketing students are attracted to companies like Procter & Gamble and biochemists are attracted to Merck because of their reputations as outstanding organizations.

Researchers have begun to study and recognize the importance of "path dependency"—the idea that decisions made at an earlier point in time will make some current options viable while foreclosing other options. Although not all decisions are path-dependent, many of the most important decisions made by managers tend to be highly dependent on past decisions and strategies. Firms on more successful paths or trajectories will almost always have a better array of options than will firms whose managers have made less optimal decisions or pursued less successful strategies in the past.

INTERCONNECTEDNESS OF CAPABILITIES

The ability to augment a particular resource or capability may be tied to or depend on the strength or value of other capabilities. For example, the extent to which a firm's technological capabilities are a source of competitive advantage may depend on its customer service capability, especially if the firm operates in an environment where customer requests and suggestions are an important source of information about future technological requirements.

One industry in which this interconnectedness among capabilities seems to be particularly important is pharmaceuticals. Merck's outstanding success suggests that high performance in the pharmaceutical industry is due to interconnectedness between a firm's R&D capabilities and its marketing skills. For Merck and other high-performing pharmaceutical companies, R&D capabilities provide a stream of new ethical drug products, but their marketing abilities allow them not only to "sell" these new products to the doctors who will be writing prescriptions for them, but also to gather information and other market intelligence that can then be relayed to their R&D departments, further enhancing the R&D process.

One important advantage Microsoft enjoys over Netscape and other Internet explorers in the market for Internet products and services is its near-monopoly in the market for personal computer operating systems. By "bundling" its Internet Explorer product with the Windows operating software it sells, Microsoft can place its explorer in every new personal computer that is sold. And, as users upgrade to new versions of Windows, Microsoft can quickly saturate the market with its Internet Explorer. Microsoft's rivals have argued that this interconnectedness gives Microsoft an unfair advantage and the Justice Department has pressed Microsoft to unbundle its products, and a major antitrust case now seems inevitable.

INVESTMENT

Investment is important to the development of unique and valuable capabilities for two reasons. First, the primary way in which firms develop capabilities is through investments that have been made in the past. Furthermore, because any resource or capability tends to deteriorate without sustained investment, resources and capabilities must be replenished if they are to continue to serve as sources of competitive advantage. "R&D know-how depreciates over time because of technological obsolescence, brand awareness erodes because the consumer population is not stationary (existing consumers leave the market, while new consumers enter) [and] consumers forget."[13] In fact, the value of all resources and capabilities will erode unless sustained by ongoing investment.

CAUSAL AMBIGUITY

The preceding four factors, either individually or in combination with other factors, can contribute to the development of competitive advantage. The likelihood of maintaining sustained competitive advantage is greatly enhanced, however, if resources or capabilities are shrouded in "causal ambiguity."[14] If competitors are unable to determine how or why another firm is enjoying a competitive advantage, their efforts to imitate the high-performing firm's success will obviously be greatly complicated.

It may be helpful to think about competitive advantage in terms of a conceptual flow chart like the one illustrated in Exhibit 3.4. To assess whether a particular firm enjoys a competitive advantage, the flow chart begins by asking whether the firm does what other firms cannot do, or whether the firm does what other firms can do but does it better. If the answer to either of these questions is yes, then the firm has met the first condition or requirement for enjoying a competitive advantage.

To determine whether the firm will enjoy a sustained competitive advantage from this asymmetry or potential source of competitive advantage, however, other conditions must be met. As already noted, this asymmetry must be valuable, rare, and difficult to imitate and must lack ready substitutes in order to provide the firm with a sustainable competitive advantage. If all these criteria are met, then the firm can expect to enjoy a sustained competitive advantage over its rivals.

To assess whether the potential source of competitive advantage is difficult to imitate, the flow chart also asks whether that source (1) was developed over time, (2) is based on past success, (3) incorporates an interconnected set of organizational resources, (4) is sustained by ongoing investment, and (5) is characterized by causal ambiguity. Again, if these criteria are also met, then the potential source of competitive

EXHIBIT 3.4

Competitive Advantage: A Conceptual Flow Chart

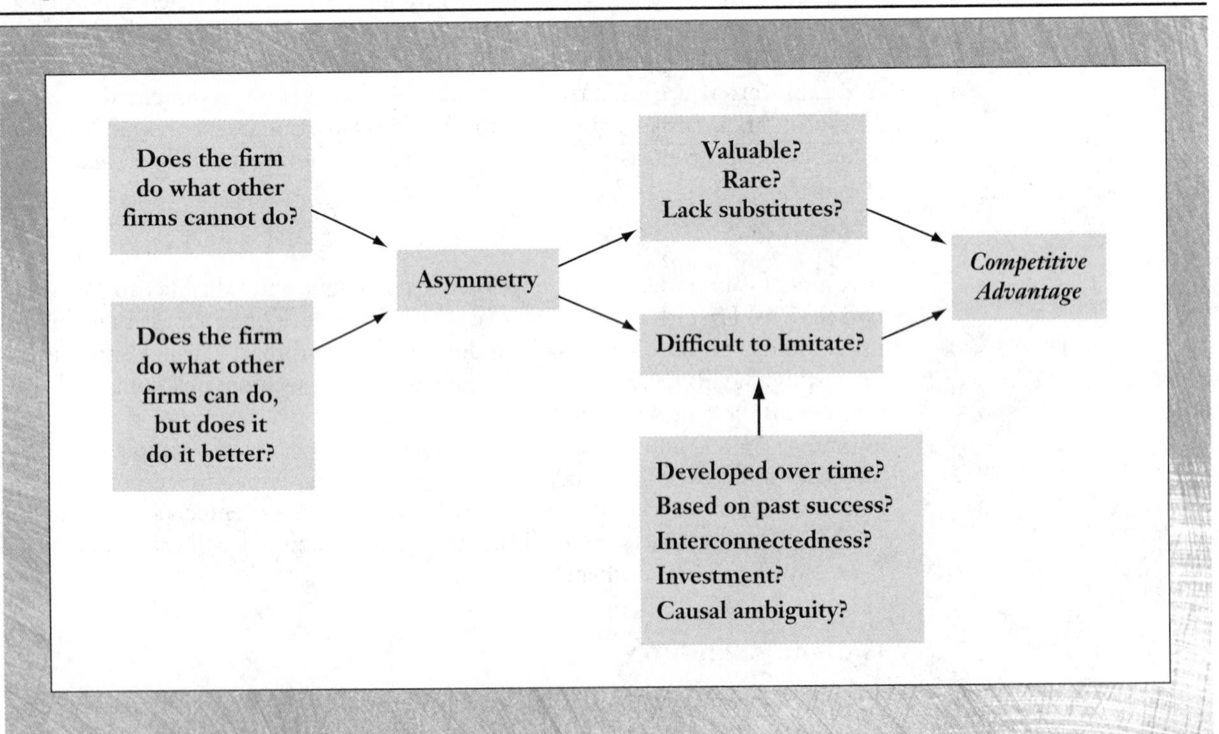

advantage is likely to be difficult to imitate, thereby increasing its value to firms seeking high performance.

The automobile industry offers an excellent illustration of how these factors work together to provide firms with a competitive advantage. The Management Focus, "The Value of Imitation in the Automobile Industry," describes how the Big Three U.S. automobile companies have widely copied or imitated many ideas, processes, and techniques from their Japanese competitors. Yet, the Big Three continue to lag behind Toyota and Honda. Although this chapter has already emphasized that imitation is unlikely to result in competitive advantage, the Management Focus examines why the Big Three have been unable to achieve even competitive parity with their Japanese counterparts.

How Firms Develop Competitive Advantage: Some Specific Routes Based on Our Model of Strategic Management

Competitive advantage will not just happen without a concerted effort or strategy, and several chapters in this book focus on specific ways managers can develop competitive advantage. Here, we provide an overview of these later chapters and a brief introduction to the various strategies that will be examined.

Business definition and positioning

Chapters 4 and 5 focus on industries and suggest a number of different frameworks or models managers can use to understand their firms' competitive environments. Chapter 6 then considers the importance of business definition or how managers position their firms in their industries. Business definition answers the who, what, and how questions, describing the customer wants or needs that a firm aims to meet (the who), the specific products or services it will be providing (the what), and the technologies it will employ to deliver those products or services (the how).

We will see that competitive advantage can be achieved through business definition if a firm's definition allows it to occupy (or be perceived as occupying) a unique position in its industry or competitive environment. Many firms have achieved a competitive advantage by developing distinctive business definitions. For example, over many years Harley-Davidson has developed a very distinctive business definition based on *The Wild One* image of its motorcycles. As an article on the company noted, "When you ride a Harley . . . you're doing something 'a little bit nasty.'"[15] "Harley bikers are known to wear T-shirts that say: 'I'd rather push a Harley than ride a Honda.'"[16]

Harley has done much to cultivate its image among the motorcycle-riding public. While Honda's early motorcycle advertisements in the United States had the theme "You meet the nicest people on a Honda," Harley has consistently targeted those riders who identified with the company's tough guy, nasty image. Furthermore, while most competitors offer a full line of motorcycle products, Harley has focused exclusively on building motorcycles for the "hog" segment of the motorcycle market— bikes with engines over 750 ccs. In fact, Harley has obtained a trademark for the term *hog* and is also seeking to trademark what it views as its distinctive "Harley sound."[17]

MANAGEMENT FOCUS

THE VALUE OF IMITATION IN THE AUTOMOBILE INDUSTRY

The automobile industry offers an excellent illustration of the return-generating potential of various organizational resources and capabilities. By the 1980s, Japanese automobile producers had developed a significant competitive advantage over their Big Three and European rivals. Tables 1, 2, and 3 compare and contrast Japanese automobile producers with the U.S. Big Three and European producers along a number of key performance dimensions at the end of the 1980s.

TABLE 1 *Summary of Assembly Plant Characteristics Volume Producers, 1989 (Averages for Plants in Each Region)*

	Japanese in Japan	Japanese in North America	American in North America	All Europe
Performance:				
Productivity (hours/veh.)	16.8	21.2	25.1	36.2
Quality (assembly defects/100 vehicles)	60.0	65.0	82.3	97.0
Layout:				
Space (sq. ft./vehicle/year)	5.7	9.1	7.8	7.8
Size of Repair Area (as % of assembly space)	4.1	4.9	12.9	14.4
Inventories (days for 8 sample parts)	.2	1.6	2.9	2.0
Workforce				
% of Workforce in Teams	69.3	71.3	17.3	.6
Job Rotation (0 = none, 4 = frequent)	3.0	2.7	.9	1.9
Suggestions/Employee	61.6	1.4	.4	.4
Number of Job Classes	11.9	8.7	67.1	14.8
Training of New Production Workers (hours)	380.3	370.0	46.4	173.3
Absenteeism	5.0	4.8	11.7	12.1
Automation:				
Welding (% of direct steps)	86.2	85.0	76.2	76.6
Painting (% of direct steps)	54.6	40.7	33.6	38.2
Assembly (% of direct steps)	1.7	1.1	1.2	3.1

SOURCE: IMVP *World Assembly Plant Survey*, 1989; and J. D. Power Initial Quality Survey, 1989.

TABLE 2 *Product Development Performance by Regional Auto Industries*

	Japanese Producers	American Producers	European Volume Producers	European Specialist Producers
Average Engineering Hours per New Car (millions)	1.7	3.1	2.9	3.1
Average Development Time per New Car (in months)	46.2	60.4	57.3	59.9
Number of Employees in Project Team	485	903	904	
Number of Body Types per New Car	2.3	1.7	2.7	1.3
Average Ratio of Shared Parts	18%	38%	28%	30%
Supplier Share of Engineering	51%	14%	37%	32%
Engineering Change Costs as Share of Total Die Cost	10–20%	30–50%	10–30%	
Ratio of Delayed Products	1 in 6	1 in 2	1 in 3	
Die Development Time (months)	13.8	25.0	28.0	
Prototype Lead Time (months)	6.2	12.4	10.9	
Time from Production Start to First Sale (months)	1	4	2	
Return to Normal Productivity after New Model (months)	4	5	12	
Return to Normal Quality after New Model (months)	1.4	11	12	

SOURCE: Kim B. Clark, Takahiro Fujimoto, and W. Bruce Chew. 1987. Product Development in the World Auto Industry, *Brookings Papers on Economic Activity*, No. 3; and Takahiro Fujimoto. 1989. Organizations for Effective Product Development: The Case of the Global Motor Industry, Ph. D. Thesis, Harvard Business School, Tables 7.1, 7.4, and 7.8.

continued

TABLE 3 *Cross-Regional Comparison of Suppliers*

Average for Each Region	Japanese Japan	Japanese America	American America	All Europe
Supplier Performance:[1]				
Die Change Times (minutes)	7.9	21.4	114.3	123.7
Lead Time for New Dies (weeks)	11.1	19.3	34.5	40.0
Job Classifications	2.9	3.4	9.5	5.1
Machines per Worker	7.4	4.1	2.5	2.7
Inventory Levels (days)	1.5	4.0	8.1	16.3
No. of Daily JIT Deliveries	7.9	1.6	1.6	0.7
Parts Defects (per car)[2]	.24	na	.33	.62
Supplier Involvement in Design:[3]				
Engineering Carried Out by Suppliers (% total hours)	51	na	14	35
Supplier Propriety Parts (%)	8	na	3	7
Black Box Parts (%)	62	na	16	39
Assembler Designed Parts (%)	30	na	81	54
Supplier/Assembler Relations[4]				
Number of Suppliers per Assembly Plant	170	238	509	442
Inventory Level (days, for 8 parts)	0.2	1.6	2.9	2.0
Proportion of Parts Delivered Just-in-Time (%)	45.0	35.4	14.8	7.9
Proportion of Parts Single Sourced (%)	12.1	98.0	69.3	32.9

NOTES AND SOURCES:

[1]From a matched sampled of 54 supplier plants in Japan (18), America (10 American-owned and 8 Japanese-owned), and Europe (18). T. Nishiguchi, *Strategic Dualism: An Alternative in Industrial Societies*, Ph. D. Thesis, Nuffield College, Oxford, 1989, Chapter 7, pp. 313–347.

[2]Calculated from the 1988 J.D. Power Initial Quality Survey.

[3]From the survey of 29 product development projects by Clark and Fujimoto. K. B. Clark, T. Fujimoto, and W. B. Chew, "Product Development in the World Auto Industry," *Brookings Papers on Economic Activity*, No. 3, 1987, page 741; T. Fujimoto, *Organizations for Effective Product Development: The Case of the Global Motor Industry*, Ph. D. Thesis, Harvard Business School, 1989, Table 7.1.

[4]From the IMVP *World Assembly Plant Survey*, 1990.

Confronted with this evidence and after several years of dismal performance, General Motors, Ford, and Chrysler all began an aggressive program of copying or imitating many Japanese manufacturing practices. All the Big Three companies adopted just-in-time inventory management methods, all sought to develop more cohesive work teams, and all adopted versions of lean production practices. General Motors even created Saturn as a new company within a company to employ Japanese manufacturing and work practices. This widespread imitation of Japanese practices has not, however, allowed any of the Big Three companies to enjoy a competitive advantage in the automobile industry. Studies show that it still costs the Big Three significantly more to produce each car, that each car produced by the Big Three requires more labor hours per vehicle, and that customer perceptions of quality still give the Japanese producers a significant edge over the Big Three.

Such an outcome could be expected by the framework described in this chapter: Imitation of other firms' resources or capabilities should only allow a firm to enjoy, at best, performance parity. Yet, why do the Big Three still lag so far behind their Japanese counterparts, and why have they been unable to achieve at least competitive parity with Toyota and Honda?

Again, the framework outlined in this chapter offers some important clues. First, Toyota and Honda enjoy the advantages of time. They have been developing and refining lean manufacturing techniques for so much longer than their Big Three rivals that they possess a significant lead in the accumulation of organizational knowledge and expertise. In addition, they have not stood still, waiting for the Big Three to catch up with them, but have continued to invest heavily to further improve their manufacturing and assembly skills.

The battle between the Japanese producers and the Big Three demonstrates an important truth about the nature of competitive advantage: Imitation of best practice in an industry will rarely lead to a competitive advantage. And, imitation may not even lead to competitive parity if industry leaders are determined to maintain their competitive edge. If managers at General Motors, Ford, and Chrysler are determined to catch up with and even surpass Toyota and Honda, they will most likely have to leap-frog over them by developing totally new capabilities that will be difficult to imitate. ■

The danger of relying on business definition alone as a basis for competitive advantage is that if customers lose this sense or perception of uniqueness, then the competitive advantage will also be lost. Coors illustrates just how fleeting a competitive advantage based on a distinctive image can be. So long as Coors remained a regional brewer with its beer available only in the West, the company enjoyed a unique and distinctive reputation. Beer drinkers from eastern and midwestern states would travel back from Colorado and other western states with trunk loads of Coors beer. As Coors achieved national distribution of its beer, however, the distinctiveness that it enjoyed due to its limited availability and Rocky Mountain image were lost.

Business Strategy

Though business definition is obviously important, most firms are not so fortunate to have the luxury of occupying, like Harley-Davidson, a unique position in the competitive space, or, if they do, they soon find competitors invading the same markets or niche segments. In addition, what starts out as a unique position in the marketplace can quickly lose its appeal if, as in the case of Coors, customers' perceptions change.

As a result, for most firms, competitive advantage depends not so much on having an effective business definition, but on being able to do what many other firms also do, but doing it better. Gap, one of the most successful specialty retailers, has a distinctive business definition, but many other specialty retailers serve similar customer groups, offering similar products, using the same retailing technologies—therefore, Gap's business definition is hardly unique. Gap, however, seems to have developed additional firm-specific capabilities that allow it to be more successful than many of its retailing competitors.

Chapters 7 and 8 take up the complex subject of business strategy. Again, based on our definition of strategy as a "pattern in a stream of decisions,"[18] we see business strategies resulting from a series of interconnected decisions. Chapters 7 and 8 seek answers to the question, "How should the business organization compete against its rivals in order to enjoy a competitive advantage?" Although it is convenient to separate decisions about business definition from decisions about business strategies, it should be fairly obvious that these concepts are tightly coupled. A firm's business definition will almost certainly influence how it decides to compete against its rivals. And, the capabilities that a firm develops as a result of its business strategies will also influence its definition or how it positions itself in the marketplace.

In Chapters 7 and 8, the text will not only provide a thorough introduction to the concept of business strategy, but it will also examine some of the interrelationships between managerial thinking, business definition, and business strategy. Chapter 7 describes "generic" strategies of cost leadership, differentiation, and focus. Chapter 8 examines the appropriateness of various business strategies in different industry contexts. It specifically examines the challenges of formulating and implementing business strategies in emerging and mature industry environments, as well as the unique challenges posed by firms operating in manufacturing and service industry environments. Chapter 8 also describes how some firms, like Nike, have been successful at developing a competitive advantage by totally reinventing their industries.

Corporate Strategy

Chapter 9 will consider how corporate strategy can be a source of competitive advantage. While business strategy addresses the question "How should the firm (or business) compete?" corporate strategy addresses several other important questions: What is the appropriate scale and scope of the enterprise? How are the businesses of the diversified firm related? How should the diversified firm be managed? In other words, the aim of corporate strategy, and the focus of Chapter 9, is to determine how large and how diversified organizations should be, how the businesses in diversified firms are related to each other, and how diversified firms should be managed to achieve high performance.

ORGANIZATIONAL STRUCTURE

Chapter 10 examines organizational structure. Structure has traditionally focused on how businesses and firms are hierarchically organized. In Chapter 10, however, we will consider many additional aspects or components of structure, including the importance of routines and standard operating procedures, information flows and systems, and organizational culture. We will also examine how these different components of structure can contribute to the development of competitive advantage. We will specifically consider how organizational structure can be used to improve the flow of information in an organization to facilitate coordination and organizational learning.

THE DISTINCTION BETWEEN CONTENT AND PROCESS

The distinction between *content* and *process* is particularly germane to this chapter's discussion of competitive advantage. Strategy content can be thought of as *what* a firm does, while process would be *how* a firm does or decides what it does. In terms of their ability to provide firms with sustained competitive advantage, organizational processes not only complement but also have distinct advantages over strategy content elements in managers' efforts to develop competitive advantage. First, because internal organizational processes are much less visible to outsiders, they are less amenable to imitation. Typically, the *content* of firms' strategies is not ambiguous. In fact, the content of firms' strategies, policies, and resource allocation patterns is usually quite apparent in publicly available information. And, competitors do seem to copy or imitate the content of their more successful rivals' strategies.

Consider, for example, the data portrayed in Exhibits 3.5 and 3.6. Exhibit 3.5 shows the profitability (as measured by net income[19]) of four leading firms in the pharmaceutical industry. The data show that Merck enjoys a significantly higher level of performance than its rivals in the pharmaceutical industry and that this performance advantage has persisted over time.

Merck's high performance is often said to result from the *content* of the company's strategy, namely its high level of R&D expenditures.[20] Yet, the data presented in Exhibit 3.6 reveal that although Merck invests considerable resources in R&D, it has never had the highest level of R&D spending (when adjusted for firm size) and its current level of R&D expenditures places the company at roughly the same level as its major competitors.[21] Furthermore, the data shown in Exhibit 3.6 suggest that, as predicted, many of Merck's rivals have imitated the content of Merck's R&D strategy by increasing their own levels of R&D expenditures over the last decade.

EXHIBIT 3.5

Net Income of Four Pharmaceutical Firms

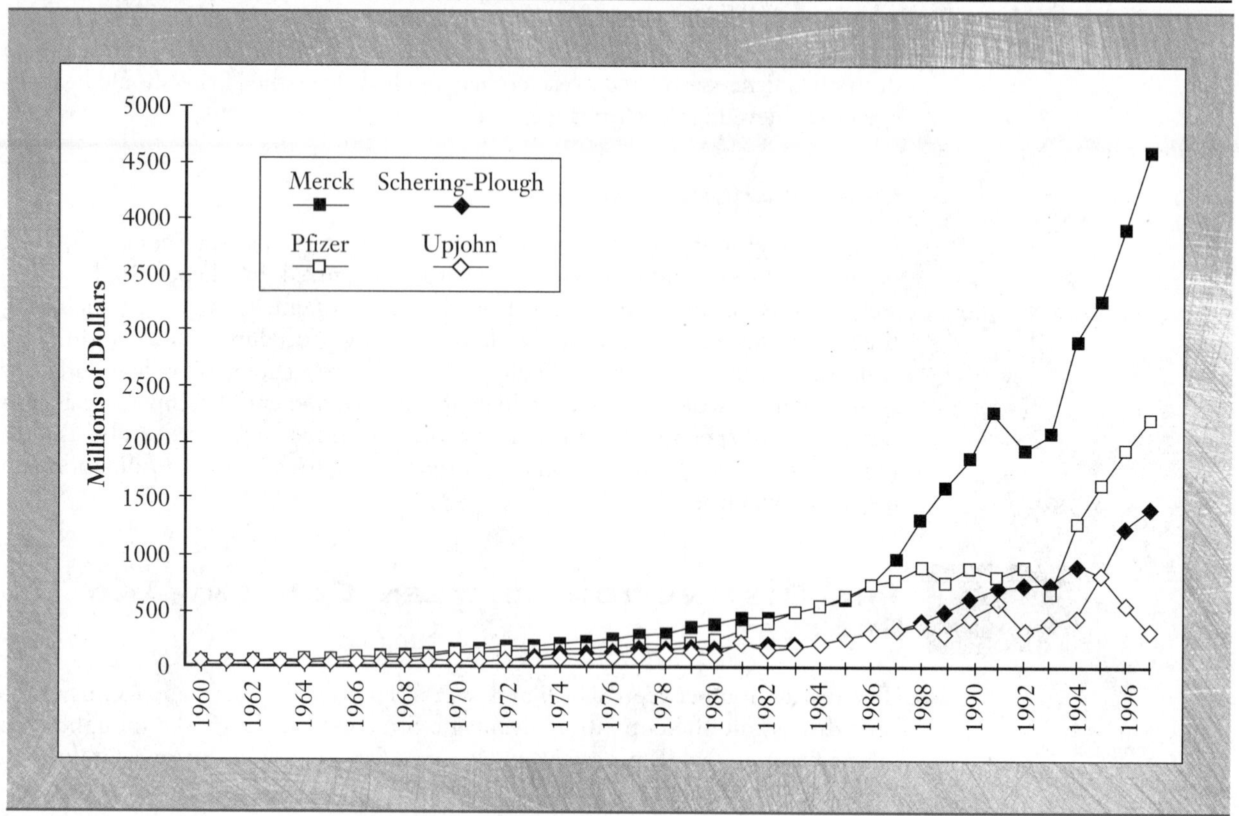

Exhibits 3.5 and 3.6 suggest that Merck's high performance is not due to the *content* of its R&D strategy. Instead, Merck's sustained high performance is more likely to be due to the *processes* the company uses to implement and manage its R&D program in order to yield so many new blockbuster drug products. And, the company continues to enjoy a sustained competitive advantage precisely because these organizational processes are difficult for its rivals to understand and imitate. Many industry observers are reaching this same conclusion. One article on the pharmaceutical industry noted, for example, that the problems associated with innovation and with the development of new products, services, and technologies lie "not with 'research' but with *how* research, or more precisely innovation, is managed."[22] The famous academics/consultants, Prahalad and Hamel, have emphasized that "cultivating core competence does *not* mean outspending rivals on research and development,"[23] and they document several examples in which highly successful firms have spent considerably less on R&D than their big-spending but less successful rivals.

A recent *Wall Street Journal* article on IBM described how the company has transformed its research and development program over the last few years. The company's managers now place much less emphasis on pure research activities, while giving priority to those projects and research initiatives that are most likely

EXHIBIT 3.6

R&D Spending as a Percent of Sales of Four Pharmaceutical Firms

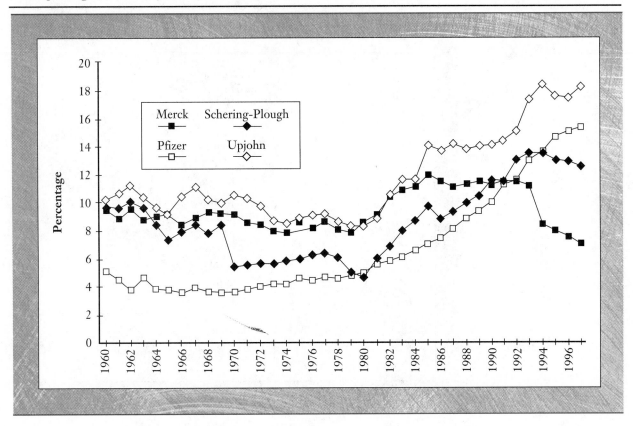

to yield commercial success. Though the company now spends $1 billion less on R&D than it did five years ago, IBM's research efforts have recently resulted in many more commercial applications.[24]

Managers seem to have an intuitive feel for both the importance of strategy process and the inability of strategy content variables to provide their firms with competitive advantage. Researchers have surveyed corporate managers to develop lists of resources that managers see as contributing to their firms' successes. Most of the items that the managers named were either intangible resources and capabilities, such as "culture" and "know-how," or subjective factors like "reputation for quality," "customer service/product support," and "name recognition," which are the products or results of their organizations' internal processes.[25]

Value Chain Analysis as a Way to Evaluate Organizational Processes

Value chain analysis can be a very helpful tool for evaluating the capabilities embedded in organizational processes. The value chain is simply a diagram illustrating the various value-adding processes that occur inside a firm or business. For example,

EXHIBIT 3.7

The Value Chain for a Hypothetical Manufacturing Firm

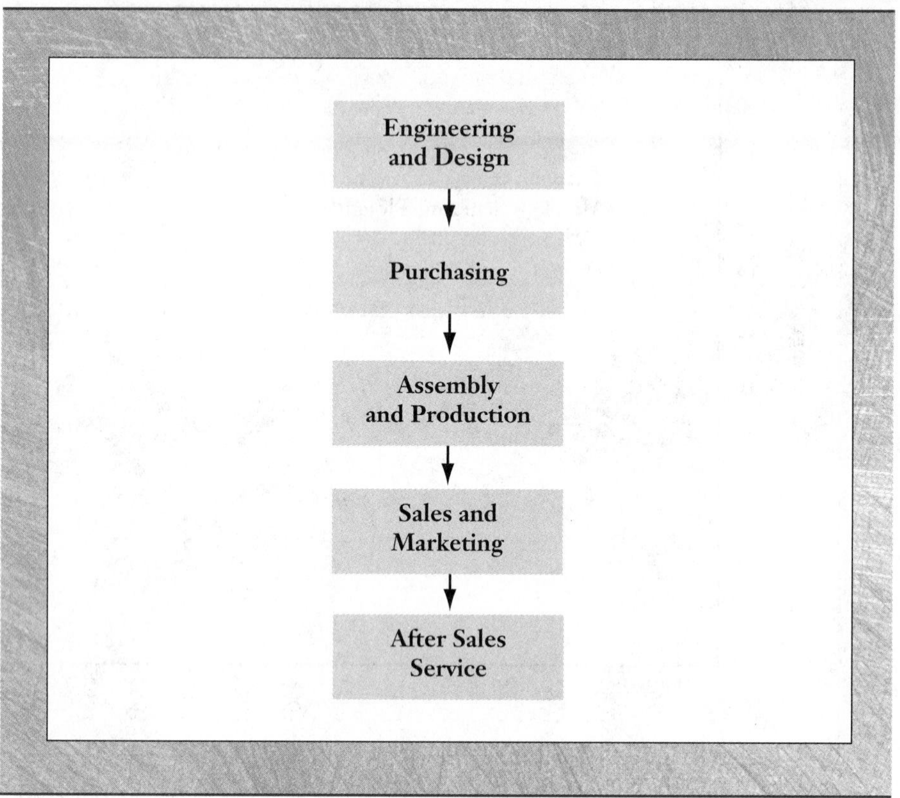

Exhibit 3.7 shows the value chain for a hypothetical manufacturing firm, showing the various value-adding processes from design, engineering, component and material procurement, manufacturing, marketing and sales, and after-sales service.

Analysis of the various links in the value chain can help managers evaluate the extent to which their organizations' processes contribute to competitive advantage. For example, in the case of the hypothetical manufacturing firm, analysis of the value chain might reveal that the company's marketing and sales capabilities are very weak and that they prevent the company from enjoying a competitive advantage relative to its rivals. Following this assessment of the value chain, the firm's managers could conclude that they should significantly augment the company's marketing and sales capabilities or, alternatively, they might conclude that they would be better off being a wholesaler and relying on other firms to market and sell their products. In later chapters, we will return to the value chain concept, illustrating a number of ways in which analyses of the value chain can provide managers with insights and assist in their quest for competitive advantage.

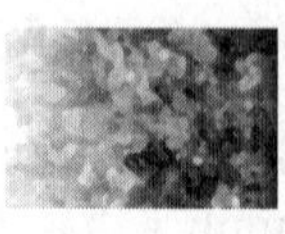

The Importance of Socially Complex Resources

The importance of strategy processes has led to a growing interest in socially complex resources. Socially complex resources have been defined as

> resources that enable an organization to conceive, choose, and implement strategies because of the values, beliefs, symbols, and interpersonal relationships possessed by individuals or groups in a firm. Some examples of these socially complex phenomena include organizational culture, trust and friendship among managers in an organization, the reputation of an organization among its customers, teamwork among managers and workers, and so forth.[26]

In other words, socially complex resources are the human equivalent of other, more tangible organizational capabilities and processes. Socially complex resources, such as organizational culture or reputation, can certainly be important potential sources of competitive advantage. The particular value of socially complex resources, and the reason they are described here, lies in the difficulty competitors will have in attempting to imitate them. For example, a reputation for high-quality products or outstanding service is not only a tremendous competitive asset but one that must be developed deliberately over time. It may be difficult for one firm to match or imitate another firm's reputation for excellent customer service unless it is willing to invest considerable resources over a long period of time.

Conclusion

This chapter has described the asymmetric nature of competitive advantage. Firms enjoy competitive advantage either by doing what other organizations cannot do or by doing what other organizations can do but doing it better. Thus, firms can gain a competitive advantage by occupying a unique niche or portion of their industries through a particularly effective business definition. Alternatively, firms can enjoy a sustainable competitive advantage by possessing capabilities that are *causally ambiguous* and *difficult to imitate.* If capabilities are not causally ambiguous and difficult to imitate, then rivals will quickly copy or match them, and this is why many of the resources and capabilities typically associated with high firm performance are not—and cannot be—the sources of sustained competitive advantage: An outstanding manager can be lured away by a more attractive compensation package. A new technology can be "reverse-engineered" and imitated. An organization's internal processes, on the other hand, are characterized by resources and capabilities that are much less amenable to replication. The factors that make a particular process advantageous may be quite invisible to outsiders. How, for example, can an outsider understand or begin to imitate the knowledge that has been accumulated by years of experience, learning, and trial-and-error by a team of outstanding scientists working in a research lab at Merck?

This chapter suggests, therefore, that an organization's internal processes are more likely than strategy content variables to be sources of sustained competitive advantage. Two firms can spend identical amounts of money on research and development (in other words, the strategy content of two firms can be identical on that particular dimension), *but, in the absence of luck, the firm with the better R&D process will enjoy higher performance.*

The chapter also reviewed the factors that contribute to the development of unique and valuable capabilities, such as an organization's internal R&D or manufacturing processes. These five factors—time, past success, interconnectedness, investment, and causal ambiguity—will make the capability more difficult to imitate and, therefore, increase the likelihood that the capability can be a source of sustained competitive advantage.

Although this chapter has suggested that a firm's internal processes are a critical resource that can be the source of sustained competitive advantage, it is important to remember that a particular internal process can quickly be rendered obsolete due to environmental shifts, such as changes in regulations or technologies. As a result, managerial attention needs to focus not only on the development of specific assets, but, more important, on the overall processes by which resources are accumulated and capabilities are developed. Managers will succeed in achieving sustained competitive advantage for their firm only if they acquire and develop resources that enhance their firm's current position while being mindful of the kinds of resources and capabilities that will be needed in the future. *This kind of creative thinking and foresight is perhaps the most valuable and least imitable of all organizational capabilities.*

Chapter 2 emphasized the tendency for managerial thinking to become dated—mental models appropriate at one time can become inappropriate as industry environments change. Similarly, any source of competitive advantage can become dated and useless as business conditions change. Furthermore, as any source of competitive advantage is likely to be tightly coupled with managerial thinking, they can mutually reinforce one another in ways that can be quite pathological for firms. Thus, managers must be particularly sensitive to changes in customers' needs and wants, the introduction of new product or service offerings, and the development of new technologies, any of which could jeopardize the effectiveness of any particular source of competitive advantage.

Key Points

- The chapter began by offering a definition for competitive advantage: *the set of factors or capabilities that allows firms to consistently outperform their rivals.*
- Firms that enjoy a sustained competitive advantage possess factors, capabilities, or competencies that are valuable, rare, difficult to imitate, and lack substitutes.
- As a result, a key characteristic of competitive advantage is asymmetry. Firms enjoy a competitive advantage by either doing what other firms cannot do, or, if they do what other firms can also do, by doing it better.
- Without resource "mobility barriers" to prevent the transfer of resources and skills across firms, capabilities and other sources of competitive advantage tend to be quickly diffused through an industry and the entire economy.
- Five factors that contribute to the development of sustained competitive advantage are: time, past success, interconnectedness of resources, investment, and causal ambiguity.
- Because they tend to be causally ambiguous and difficult to imitate, a firm's internal processes are more likely than the content of its strategies to be sources of sustained competitive advantage.
- Socially complex resources, such as reputation and organizational culture, can also be important sources of competitive advantage, again because they are so difficult to imitate.
- The value chain can be a very useful tool for analyzing organizational capabilities and processes and for assessing competitive advantage.
- Because a source of competitive advantage can become dated and useless over time, key management responsibilities are to be mindful of how vulnerable resources and capabilities are to imitation and obsolescence, and to anticipate the kinds of resources and capabilities that will be needed to compete effectively in the future.

Review and Discussion Questions

1. *What is competitive advantage? What does it imply if a firm is said to enjoy a competitive advantage? What are the criteria that determine whether resources or capabilities can provide firms with competitive advantage? Why is asymmetry or uniqueness so crucial to the development and maintenance of competitive advantage?*
2. *Describe how time, building on past success, interconnectedness of asset stocks, investment, and causal ambiguity are associated with the development and maintenance of competitive advantage.*
3. *The text's model of strategic management suggests that business definition, business strategy, corporate strategy, and organizational structure are various paths or routes that can lead to competitive advantage. Summarize how each is associated with the development and maintenance of competitive advantage.*
4. *Distinguish between strategy content and strategy process. Which is more likely to be a source of competitive advantage and why? Provide some specific examples of how strategy content and strategy process factors have contributed to firms' efforts to develop and maintain competitive advantage.*
5. *What is value chain analysis? How is it used to evaluate the effectiveness of organizational processes?*

Suggestions for Further Reading

Aaker, D. A. 1989. Managing assets and skills: The key to sustainable competitve advantage. *California Management Review, 31(2): 91–106.*

Barney, J. B. 1991. Firm resources and sustained competitive advantage. *Journal of Management*, 17: 99-120.

Dierickx, I., & Cook, K. 1989. Asset stock accumulation and sustainability of competitive advantage. *Management Science*, 35: 1504–1511.

Prahalad. C. K., & Hamel, G. 1990. The core competence of the corporation. *Harvard Business Review*, 68(3): 79–91.

Wernerfelt, B. 1984. A resource-based view of the firm. *Strategic Management Journal*, 5: 171–180.

Endnotes

1. Mintzberg, H. 1978. Patterns in strategy formation. *Management Science* 24:935–948.
2. Prahalad, C. K., and G. Hamel. 1990. The core competence of the corporation. *Harvard Business Review* 68(3):79–91.
3. Cool, K., and D. Schendel. 1988. Performance differences among strategic group members. *Strategic Management Journal* 9:207–223.
4. Lawless, M. W., D. D. Bergh, and W. D. Wilsted. 1989. Performance variations among strategic group members: An examination of individual firm capability. *Journal of Management* 15:649–661.
5. Barney, J. B. 1991. Firm resources and sustained competitive advantage. *Journal of Management* 17:99–120; Wernerfelt, B. 1984. A resource-based view of the firm. *Strategic Management Journal* 5:171–180.
6. Penrose, E. T. 1959. *The Theory of the Growth of the Firm.* New York: Wiley.
7. Barney, Firm resources, 1991.

8. Wernerfelt, Resource-based view.
9. Barney, J. B. 1986. Strategic factor markets: Expectations, luck, and business strategy. *Management Science* 42:1231–1241.
10. Dierickx, I., and K. Cool. 1989. Asset stock accumulation and sustainability of competitive advantage. *Management Science* 35:1504–1511.
11. See McCartney, S. 1996. Turbulence ahead: Competitors quake as Southwest Air is set to invade Northeast. *The Wall Street Journal*, October 23, A1, A6.
12. Quintanilla, C. 1994. New airline fad: Faster airport turnarounds. *The Wall Street Journal*, August 4, B1, B7.
13. Dierickx and Cool, Asset Stock, p. 1508.
14. Lippman, S. A., and R. P. Rumelt. 1982. Uncertain imitability: An analysis of interfirm differences in efficiency under competition. *Bell Journal of Economics* 13:418–438.
15. Quoted in Rose, R. L. 1990. Vrooming back: After nearly stalling, Harley-Davidson finds new crowd of riders. *The Wall Street Journal*, August 31, A1, A6.
16. Machan, D. 1997. Is the hog going soft? *Forbes*, March 10, 114, 117.
17. Rifkin, G. 1995. Type: Corporate chief. Passion: Riding Harleys. *New York Times*, January 14, F8.
18. Mintzberg, Patterns in strategy formation.
19. As noted earlier in the chapter, performance is a multidimensional concept, not adequately captured by a single, accounting-based measure, such as net income. Yet, by almost any performance measure, Merck enjoys significantly higher levels of performance than its rivals in the ethical pharmaceutical industry.
20. Weber, J. 1991. Merck needs more gold from the white coats. *Business Week*, March 18, 102–104.
21. Teitelman, R. , and A. Baldo. 1989. Grading R&D. *Financial World*, January 24, 22–24 also point to the discrepancy between Merck's relatively modest R&D expenditures and its strong financial performance.
22. Corcoran, E. 1992. Redesigning research. *Scientific American*, June, 102–110, p. 103, emphasis added.
23. Prahalad and Hamel, Core competence, p. 83.
24. Ziegler, B. 1997. Lab experiment: Gerstner slashed R&D by $1 billion; for IBM it may be a good thing. *The Wall Street Journal*, October 6, A1, A15.
25. Aaker, D. A. 1989. Managing assets and skills: The key to a sustainable competitive advantage. *California Management Review* 31(2):91–106; Hall, R. 1992. The strategic analysis of intangible resources. *Strategic Management Journal* 13:135–144.
26. Barney, J. B. 1992. Integrating organizational behavior and strategy formulation research: A resource-based analysis. *Advances in Strategic Management* 8:39–61; p. 44.

Chapter 4

Frameworks for the Analysis of Industry Environments

Chapter Objectives

In terms of the model of strategic management introduced in Chapter 1, Chapter 2 emphasized the importance of general managers in strategic decision making and Chapter 3 defined the concept of competitive advantage and described the ways in which competitive advantage can be developed and maintained. Chapters 4 and 5 begin our consideration of industry environments, the competitive arenas in which firms and businesses compete. As illustrated in Exhibit 4.1, managers' beliefs and understandings of their firms' business environments are important because they influence decisions about business definition and positioning and business strategy, topics covered in later chapters. Managers who develop insights about or novel understandings of their firms' industries may be able to uniquely define or position their firms or formulate particularly unique business strategies that can lead to the development of competitive advantage.

The specific aims of this chapter are to

- Develop your understanding of industries, the competitive environments in which firms offer products or services in an effort to compete for resources, customers, sales revenues, and profits.
- Introduce you to SWOT Analysis and the Five Forces Model, two frameworks that are commonly used by managers to analyze industries.
- Provide some specific illustrations of using the Five Forces Model for industry analysis.
- Assess the strengths and limitations of SWOT Analysis and the Five Forces Model as tools for analyzing industry environments.

Why Analyze an Industry's Environment?

When a roomful of executives is asked, "Is it fair to say that your industry is competitive?" a resounding "Yes!" is usually heard. This tends to happen regardless of industry or service sector, the size of the executives' organizations, whether the organizations

EXHIBIT 4.1

The Mental Models and Strategic Decisions Studied in This Text and Their Influence on Performance and Competitive Advantage

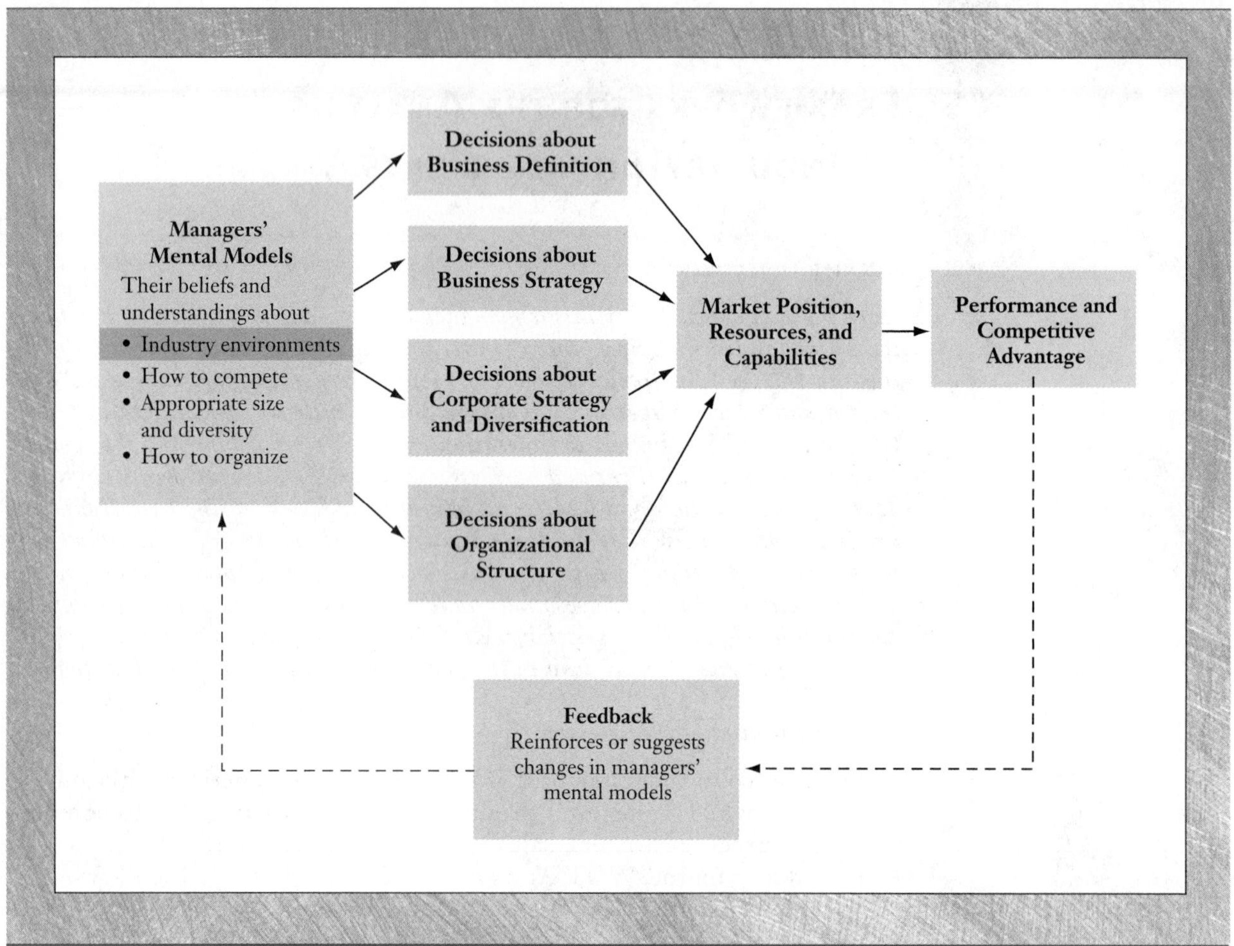

are domestic or global enterprises, or even whether they are businesses or not-for-profit organizations. Indeed, all organizations face competition — for resources, customers, sales revenues, and profits. All organizations also face uncertain and turbulent environments. Never has it been more important for managers to position their organizations strategically in order to compete successfully in the future. If only this could be done as easily as suggested by the Dilbert cartoon reprinted here!

Successful positioning, or what we call *business definition*, requires that managers thoroughly understand the dynamics of their industries, the trends in their firms' external environments, and the basic economics of their firms' markets — in short, managers must know how to analyze their industries. Once they have developed understandings — mental models — of their industry environments, they must then craft the strategies that will effectively position or define their firms in their industries and build unique competencies and capabilities that will provide them with competitive advantage.

Probably the most noteworthy characteristic of industry environments is the great extent to which they can vary. Some industries are highly competitive and

DILBERT

By Scott Adams

SOURCE: *Dilbert* reprinted by permission of United Feature Syndicate, Inc.

consequently not very profitable on average, while other industries are much less competitive and consequently enjoy much higher levels of average profitability. Some industries are mature, with growth coming primarily from replacement purchases or growth in the economy; other industries are only now emerging and beginning to experience rapid growth as large numbers of customers purchase the product or service for the first time.

Rapidly growing markets tend to be less competitive and often attract entry by new or existing firms. Emerging industries will provide managers and their firms with considerable discretion, opportunities to pursue a variety of different strategies, and even room for making mistakes. On the other hand, mature, concentrated industries provide competitors with very little breathing room; one firm's strategies or mistakes can have significant ramifications for the entire industry. For example, one firm's price reduction can set off an industrywide price war that reduces the margins of all companies in the industry.

How Much Does Industry Matter?[1]

When an industry with a reputation for bad economics meets a manager with a reputation for excellence, it's usually the industry that leaves with its reputation intact (quote attributed to Warren Buffett).

It should come as no surprise that firm performance levels depend a great deal on the attractiveness of the industries in which firms compete. Exhibit 4.2 shows the median return on assets of several different industries, illustrating the wide

EXHIBIT 4.2

Average Return on Assets in Different Industries

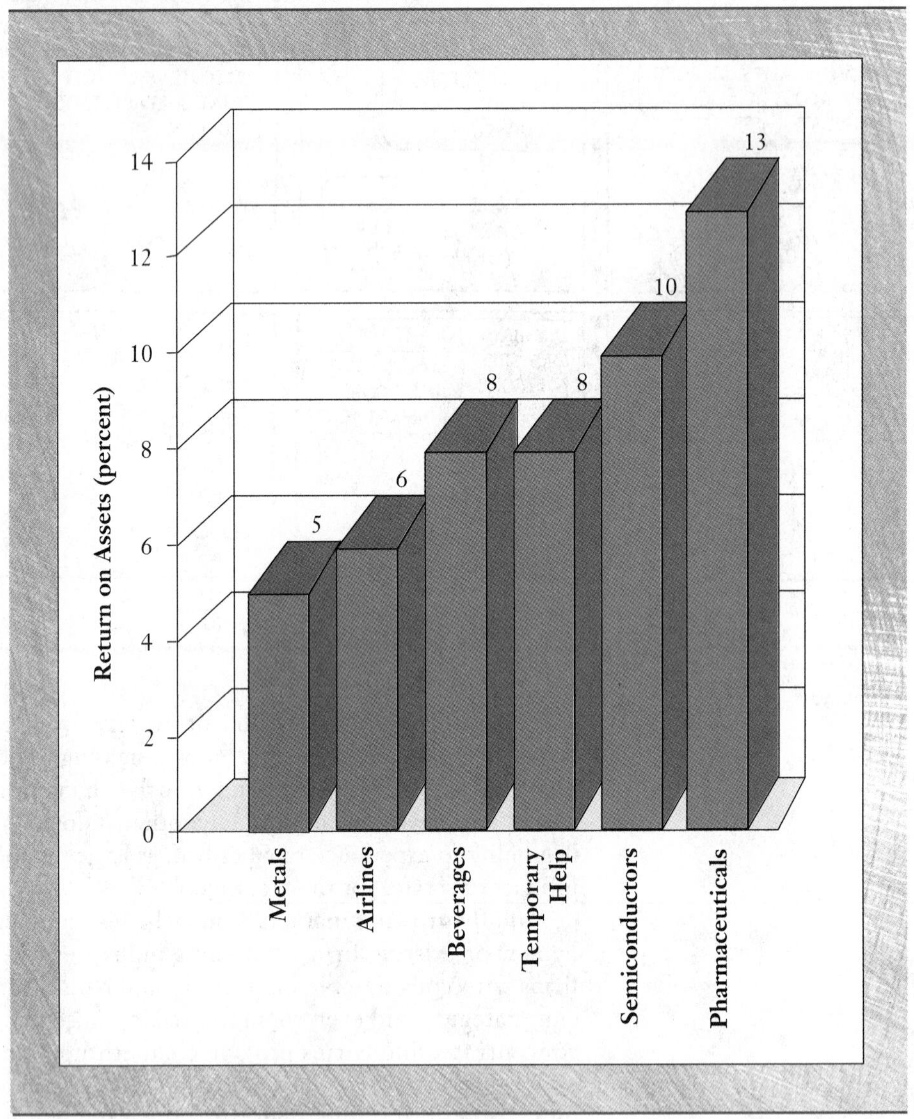

variation in average industry performance levels. For example, aside from a few start-up firms, nearly all companies in the highly profitable pharmaceutical industry enjoy high performance. In fact, the return on assets of even low-performing pharmaceutical firms would be the envy of many firms in some lower-performing industries.

Just how important is the influence of industry on firm performance? The evidence suggests that the influence of industry membership on firm performance is very strong. For almost any sample of firms, a regression equation using industry performance data (for example, average industry return on assets) to explain firm performance such as

$$ROA_{firm} = f\,(ROA_{industry})$$

will yield an r^2 of about .20. In other words, the variation in just this one variable — the average performance of all firms in an industry — will explain a great deal (approximately 20 percent) of the variation in the performance of any single firm in that industry. In fact, no other variable will consistently explain so much variation in firm performance.

Some economists seize on such findings to argue that industry is "all that matters,"[2] yet, as discussed in Chapter 1, such an industry "structuralist" argument is incomplete for several reasons.[3] First, industry returns can vary enormously from year to year. For example, Exhibit 4.3 illustrates the variation in return on assets over five years in the automobile industry. Note that the answer to the question of whether the automobile industry is a high-performing industry can depend a good deal on the year the question is asked. For example, firms in the U.S. automobile industry were, on average, modestly successful in 1993, 1994, and 1997. In 1995, however, the industry, on average, barely broke even and, in 1996, the industry lost money.

Furthermore, some industries are much more "cyclical" than others, meaning that average industry performance levels are heavily impacted by the macroeconomic business cycle. The U.S. auto industry is heavily influenced by macroeconomic conditions. General Motors, Ford, and Chrysler have enjoyed some very

EXHIBIT 4.3

Average Return on Assets in the U.S. Automobile Industry: 1993-1997

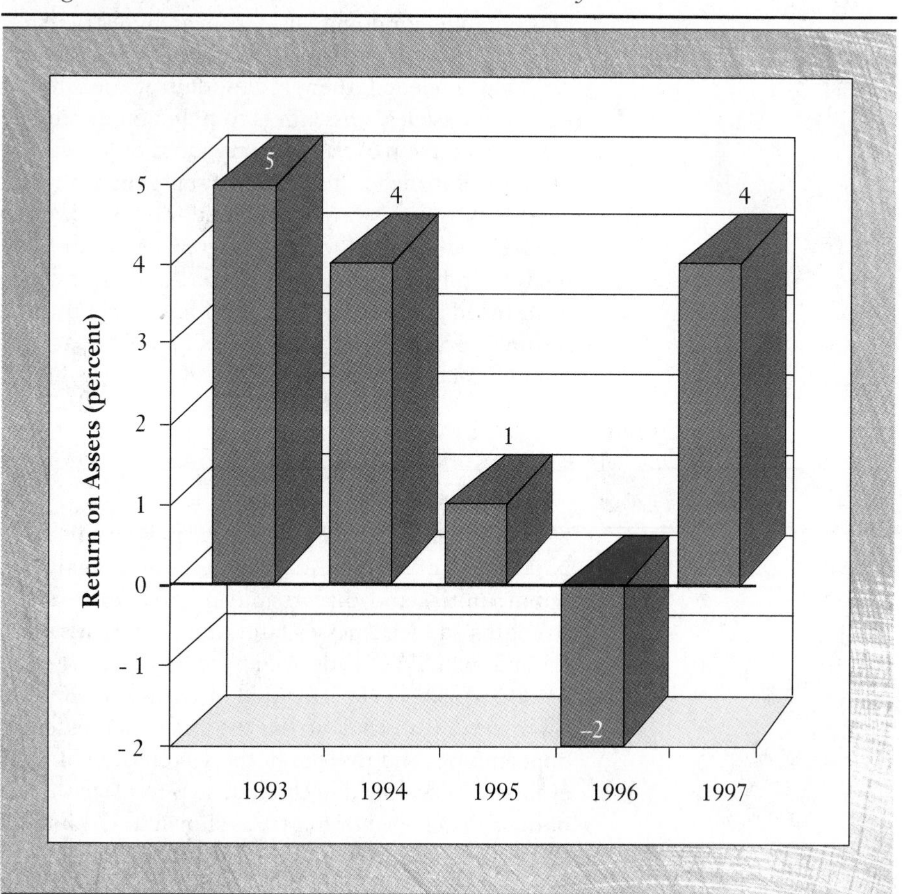

good years as the economy has remained strong and the dollar relatively weak. The future offers a much more uncertain outlook. Sales have been strong for several years now and many economists are questioning just how long automobile sales can stay so high. Furthermore, the strengthening dollar is making imported Japanese vehicles much less expensive relative to U.S.-built vehicles. A decline in automobile sales and more competition from Japanese producers could seriously erode the profits of the Big Three.

Industry averages also mask considerable variation in firm performance levels *within the same industry*. In fact, research evidence suggests that variations in average *intraindustry* profitability are approximately six times greater than the variations in average *interindustry* profitability.[4] In other words, the difference between the performance of the highest- and lowest-performing firms in any particular industry will be six times greater than the difference between the performance of the highest- and lowest-performing industries.

Exhibit 4.4 illustrates the wide differences in intraindustry profitability by profiling the high- and low-performing firms in two of the industries shown in Exhibit 4.2. Note, for example, that Nucor, one of the highest-performing firms in the steel industry (on average, a very low-performing industry), actually enjoys higher performance than many of the low-performing firms in the (generally high-performing) pharmaceutical industry.

In spite of these significant *intraindustry* differences in performance, Warren Buffett's comment at the beginning of this section still holds a great deal of truth, and given the choice of doing business in an industry that enjoys a consistently high level of profitability or doing business in an industry that suffers consistently low levels of profitability, most managers would opt to see their firms compete in the former.

What is needed, then, are models or tools for assessing the *relative* attractiveness of industries. Our aim is to help you develop an understanding of the factors that will tend to make an industry more or less attractive, while also describing some of the tools managers use to understand their firms' competitive environments. This chapter introduces two widely used frameworks or models for analyzing industries, *SWOT Analysis* and the *Five Forces Model*. Both frameworks are well known by academics and industry practitioners alike, and both frameworks have enjoyed widespread application in the business world. In fact, the managers of almost every business firm, whether large or small, have at one time or another conducted a SWOT Analysis or analyzed their industry using the Five Forces framework.

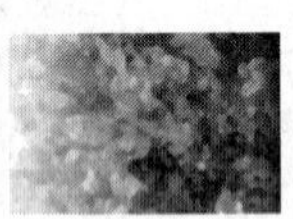

SWOT Analysis

SWOT Analysis has been used for many years to analyze industry environments. Not only can SWOT Analysis be used to analyze firms' external, environmental opportunities and threats, but it can also be used for analyzing firms' internal strengths and weaknesses (and therefore to assess competitive advantage). Hence, the acronym SWOT, derived from *Strengths*, *Weaknesses*, *Opportunities*, and *Threats*. SWOT Analysis is performed in two steps. First, managers thoroughly evaluate their *firm's* (internal) strengths and weaknesses and its *environmental* (external) opportunities and threats. In the second step of SWOT Analysis, managers use the evaluation developed in the first step to place the firm in one of the four quadrants of the SWOT grid or matrix as shown in Exhibit 4.5.

For example, if SWOT Analysis revealed that a firm enjoyed many internal strengths and few internal weaknesses, and many environmental opportunities and

EXHIBIT 4.4

High- and Low-Performing Firms in Two Industries

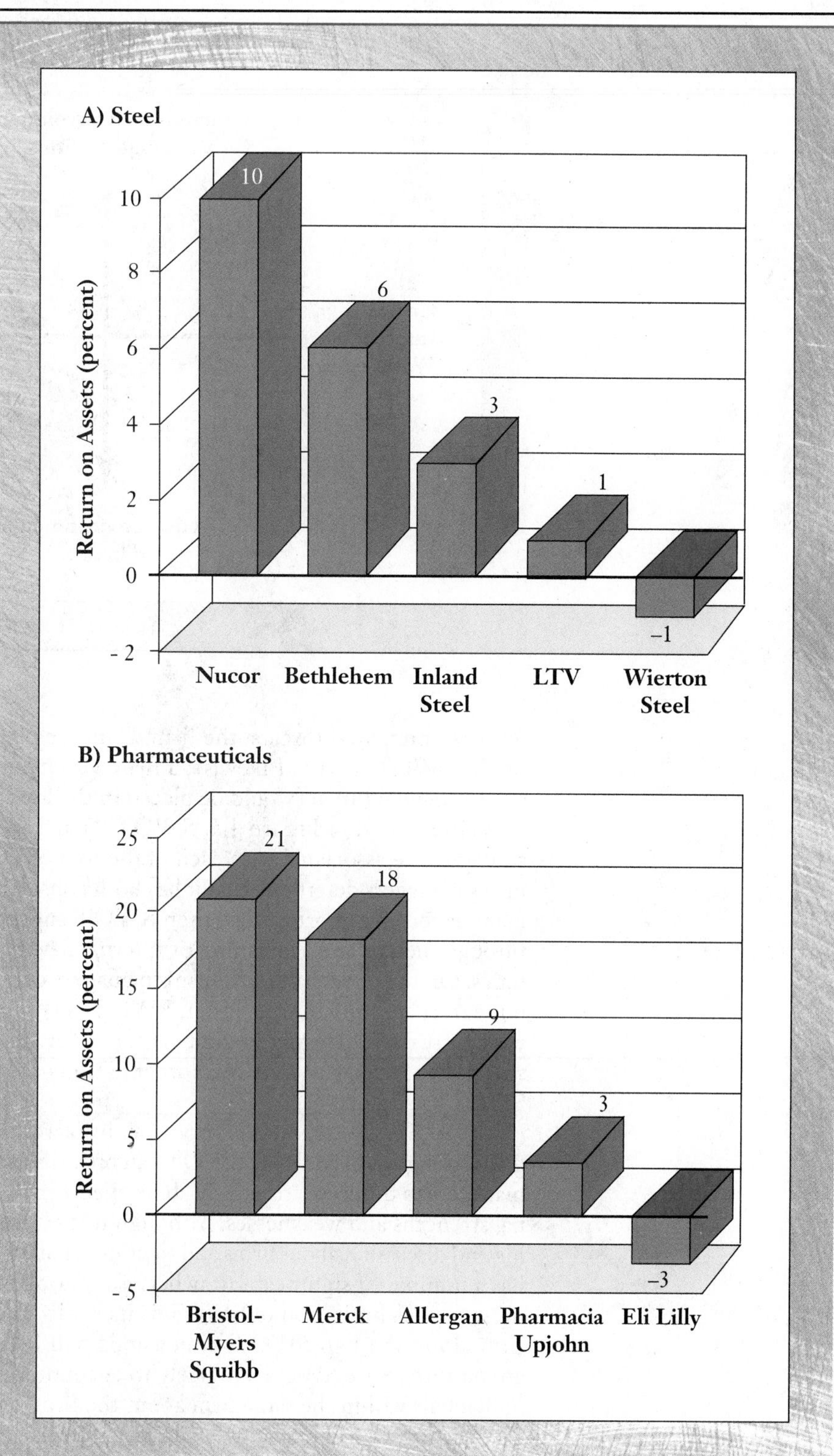

EXHIBIT 4.5

The Strengths, Weaknesses, Opportunities, and Threats Matrix

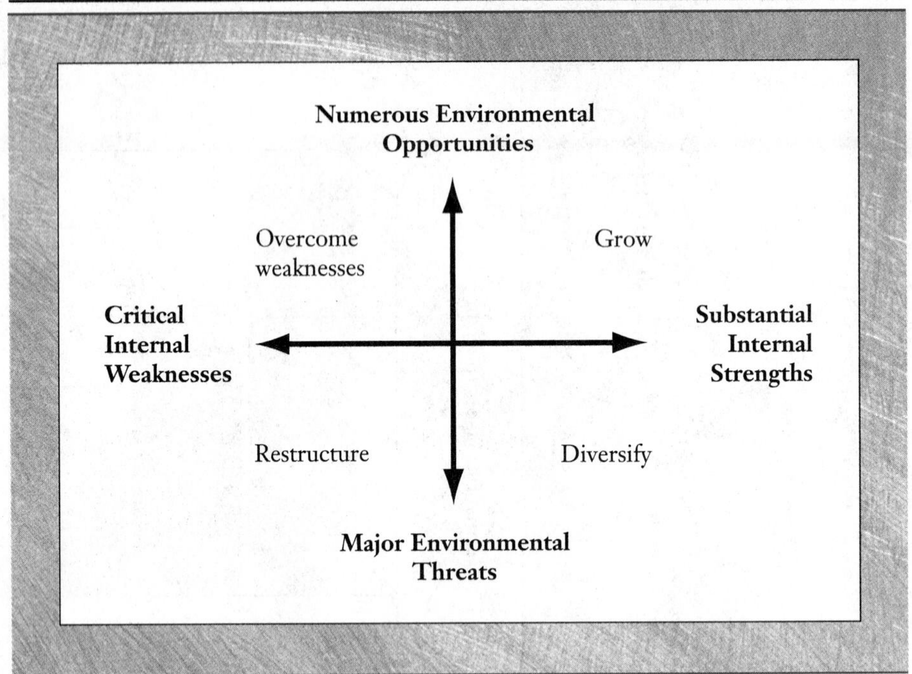

few environmental threats, the firm would be placed in the upper right quadrant on the SWOT matrix. Likewise, a firm with many internal weaknesses and many environmental threats would be placed in the lower left quadrant of the matrix.

As illustrated in Figure 4.5, SWOT Analysis is also prescriptive, and various strategies are associated with each of the four SWOT quadrants. For example, if a firm's managers determine that it has both considerable internal strengths as well as many external opportunities, then SWOT suggests that the firm should "grow" through merger and acquisition or internal development of new business opportunities. On the other hand, if a firm's managers determine it has internal weaknesses but external opportunities, then SWOT recommends that the firm "overcome weaknesses" by engaging in joint ventures, vertical integration, or unrelated diversification. Similar sets of recommendations are associated with the other two SWOT quadrants.

Use of SWOT Analysis is very straightforward, and this ease of use is one of its great strengths. In addition, SWOT can provide a very helpful framework for getting managers to think constructively about their firms' external environments and internal strengths and weaknesses. Although it is certainly helpful in stimulating thinking and discussion about firms and their external environments, SWOT Analysis also has a number of significant drawbacks as a tool for industry analysis. Perhaps the most serious limitation of SWOT is its subjectivity. Evaluating the position of a firm along the two SWOT dimensions will be quite subjective, and managers attempting to use SWOT are likely to encounter widespread disagreement among individuals within the same firm about the firm's position along these dimensions. Like the problem of one individual seeing "lemons" where another sees "lemonade," firms using SWOT Analysis will find managers disagreeing about whether a particular phenomenon in the firm's external environment is an opportunity or a threat. In fact, almost any event will offer a particular firm some opportunities while also posing some threats. A new technology, for example, can offer a firm the opportunity to develop a new product or it can represent a threat if the firm lacks the ability to develop or exploit that new technology.

Assessments of environmental opportunities and threats will also be biased by managers' perceptions of their firms' strengths and weaknesses. Managers of firms with many strengths are more likely to view environmental phenomena as opportunities, while the managers of firms with many internal weaknesses may view these same environmental phenomena as threats. Such interpretations will no doubt influence the strategies of these firms. If one firm's managers agree that their firm has a major opportunity while its competitors view this same phenomenon as a threat, the managers of the first firm are much more likely to pursue this opportunity while their competitors are more likely to take a defensive approach. For example, based on their organization's R&D strengths, managers might conclude that a rapid technological change offers their firm an important opportunity to develop new products, but the managers of a competing firm might see this same rapid rate of change as a threat. The first firm is much more likely to take an aggressive or proactive posture with respect to industry change.

Another drawback of SWOT Analysis is that its use is likely to yield few clear-cut recommendations. Very few firms are fortunate enough to have *only* external opportunities and internal strengths and very few firms are so unfortunate to have *only* external threats and internal weaknesses. In fact, almost all firms are going to face some combination of threats and opportunities in their external environments and they are also likely to possess some combination of internal strengths and weaknesses. Rather than finding themselves clearly or definitively in one of the four quadrants of the SWOT matrix, most firms will find themselves somewhere around the center of the matrix at the intersection of the two dimensions. So instead of providing managers with an obvious or clear-cut set of recommendations, SWOT is likely to suggest many contradictory strategies.

Thus, SWOT Analysis will almost always encourage some good thinking and dialogue about the firm and its industry, and managers using SWOT Analysis will almost always be able to list many strengths, weaknesses, opportunities, and threats. Many managers find, however, that SWOT's effectiveness or usefulness ends there and that it is not a particularly helpful tool for suggesting appropriate strategies for firms' unique circumstances.

The Five Forces Model

Because of its lack of prescriptive power, SWOT Analysis is a less than totally adequate tool for analyzing industries. In the late 1970s, Harvard Business School professor Michael Porter sought to fill this void first with a now-famous *Harvard Business Review* article[5] and then with his best-selling book, *Competitive Strategy*.[6] Porter's work offered a new framework for industry analysis that has enjoyed considerable popularity among business executives and has received a good deal of interest from the academic community as well. Porter's model examines five forces that influence or determine the structure of industries, and hence the average profitability or attractiveness of those industries. For each of the five forces, Porter identified sets of factors that would determine the presence and power of the force in a particular industry environment.

The Five Forces Model is based on the "structure-conduct-performance" framework of industrial organization economics. This framework suggests that the structure of an industry (e.g., the number and relative size of firms in the industry, barriers to entry, etc.) will have an impact on the conduct or competitive behavior of the firms in that industry (e.g., prices charged, rate of innovation, etc.). Industries characterized by a relatively small number of firms and industries that allow incumbent firms to keep new firms from entering the market will tend to be less competitive than industries that are populated by more firms. Firms in these more concentrated industries can charge higher prices than they would be able to in more competitive industries.

The second part of the structure-conduct-performance framework suggests that the conduct of firms will influence the average performance of firms in that industry. Obviously, if the structure of a particular industry allows firms in that industry to charge higher prices, then the firms in that industry will enjoy higher performance than would be the case if the industry was more competitive.

The implicit aim of industrial organization economics has been to understand the structural characteristics that allow industries to deviate from the perfectly competitive "ideal." Porter's model adopted the structure-conduct-performance framework, but Porter's work departed from the traditional industrial organization economics perspective in two significant ways. First, he recognized that if firms could either make their industries less competitive or shield themselves somehow from the competitive forces in their industries, then they could enjoy higher performance. Second, Porter's approach identified and described five specific "forces" that could be used to evaluate the structural characteristics of an industry.

The Five Forces Model is almost always depicted as shown in Exhibit 4.6. Exhibit 4.6 also provides a comprehensive list of factors for evaluating the intensity or power of each of the five forces. The logic behind the model is straightforward: *As the intensity of the forces increases, the industry environment becomes more hostile and overall industry profitability will decline.* In the following sections, the five forces and the sets of factors associated with each of the five forces are examined in more detail.

THE THREAT OF NEW ENTRY

If new rivals can enter an industry relatively easily, then the industry will probably be more competitive and it is less likely that the industry will enjoy high average profitability. Thus, it is desirable for incumbent firms — those already in an industry — to erect barriers to prevent other firms from entering the industry. What factors can serve as entry barriers, minimizing the threat of new firms entering an industry? In general, four types of factors can make entry less likely.

The first set of factors can be thought of as cost barriers. For example, if incumbent firms enjoy scale economies, the benefits of experience and learning effects, or privileged access to key raw materials or technologies, then potential entrants will necessarily enter the industry at a serious cost disadvantage. The concept of minimum efficient scale (MES) is closely related to the concept of economies of scale and refers to the level of production that is required in order to produce at the lowest level of average unit cost. Firms operating at MES are operating at a level of output that allows them to enjoy the lowest possible unit costs, as illustrated in Exhibit 4.7.

EXHIBIT 4.6
The Five Forces Model

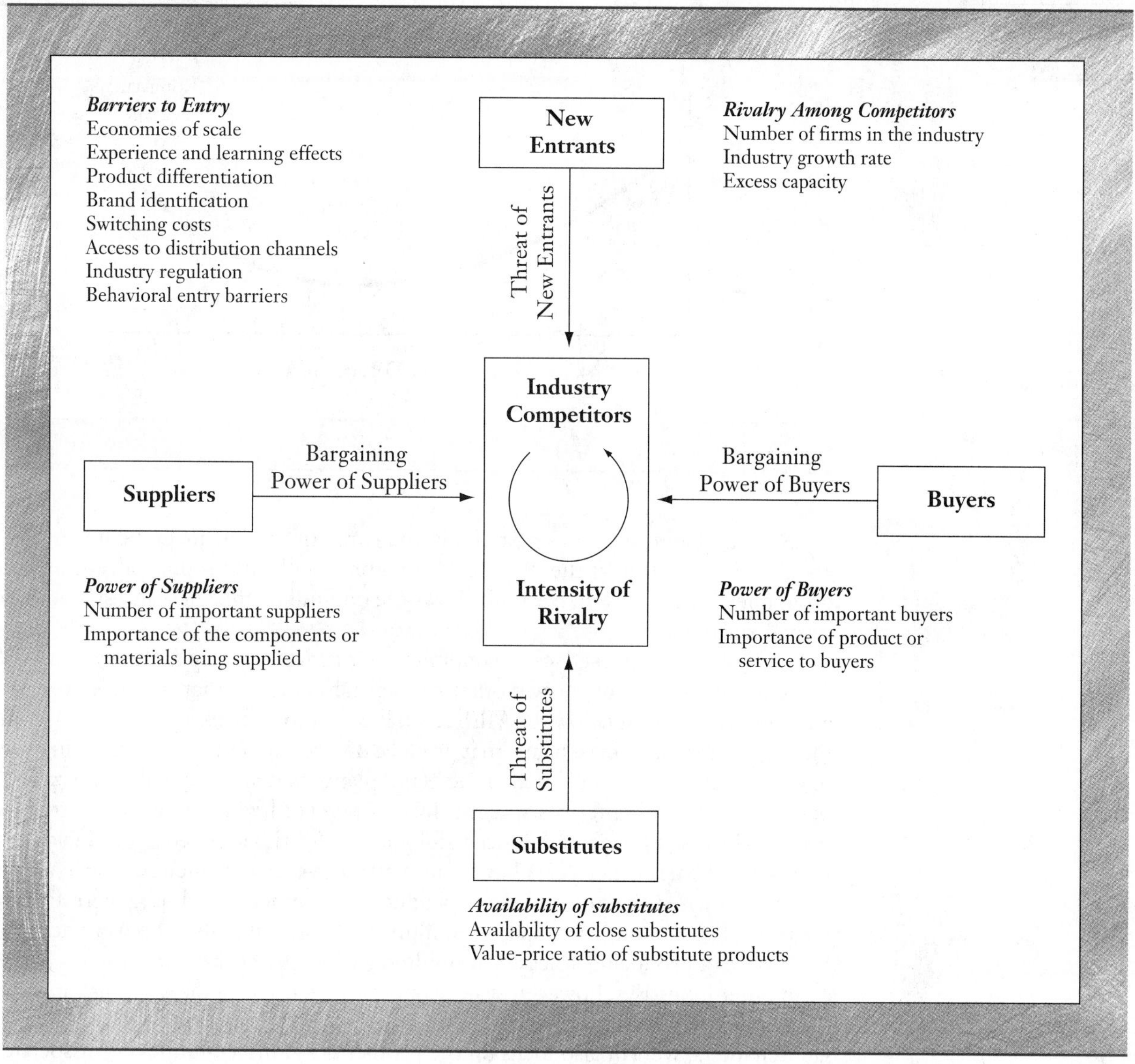

SOURCE: M. E. Porter. 1980. *Competitive Strategy*. New York: Free Press, p. 4.

The concepts of scale economies and MES are important because firms that do not produce at a volume of production to achieve minimum efficient scale necessarily incur a cost penalty relative to competitors with larger levels of output. Similarly, any firm that hopes to enter an industry must either enter at the level of

EXHIBIT 4.7

The Concepts of Scale Economies and Minimum Efficient Scale

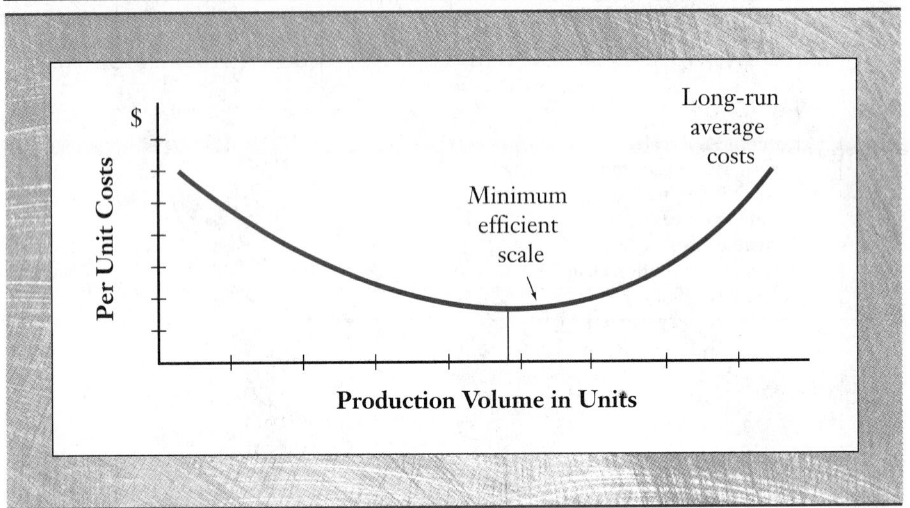

MES or risk facing a serious cost disadvantage relative to any incumbent firms that are already operating at the MES level. Exhibit 4.8 illustrates the concept of scale economies. The table in the exhibit shows the minimum efficient scale estimated for several key industries.

As Exhibit 4.8 suggests, scale economies offer firms operating at the level of MES a significant cost advantage over other firms or new entrants that are forced to operate at levels of output below the MES level. For example, firms manufacturing commercial aircraft must have plants that produce one-tenth of the total market in order to operate at minimum efficient scale. And, plants that are only half that size may have considerably higher costs, as much as 20 percent higher. The same is true for beer producers. Though many successful microbreweries (defined as producing less than 10,000 barrels per year) have found attractive market niches, nearly all the breweries owned by the major beer producers are much, much larger. In fact, to realize scale economies and operate at minimum efficient scale, a brewery needs to be capable of producing at least four million barrels per year.[7]

In other industries, however, scale economies are not a factor, so firms can enter these industries at a fairly small scale and not suffer a serious cost disadvantage. In later chapters, we will also focus on the problems — "diseconomies" — associated with large size. Firms in many industries encounter additional costs as their size increases. For example, in spite of the wave of consolidation that is sweeping through the banking industry, the evidence suggests that smaller banks (those with total assets between $50 million and $500 million) are more efficient and profitable than medium or large banks (those with total assets greater than $500 million).[8]

Another type of cost barrier is the cost advantages incumbent firms enjoy due to experience or learning. The concept of experience or learning effects suggests that as a firm's cumulative output doubles, unit costs of production will fall by some set percentage because the business is continually learning how to operate more efficiently and effectively. This experience effect, also called the "learning curve" effect, has been documented in a wide range of manufacturing and service activities in many different industries.

EXHIBIT 4.8

Minimum Efficient Scale in Several Key Industries

	Minimum Efficient Scale as Percentage of U.S. Output	Percentage Increases in Unit Cost at Half MES
Flour mills	0.7	3.0
Bread baking	0.3	7.5
Printing paper	4.4	9.0
Sulfuric acid	3.7	1.0
Synthetic fibers	11.1	7.0
Auto tires	3.8	5.0
Bricks	0.3	25.0
Detergents	2.4	2.5
Turbogenerators	23.0	n.a.
Diesel engines	21–30.0	4–28.0
Computers	15.0	8.0
Automobiles	11.0	6.0
Commercial aircraft	10.0	20.0

SOURCE: F. M. Scherer, *Industrial Market Structure and Economic Performance*, 2d ed. (Chicago: Rand McNally, 1980); U.S. Department of Commerce, Washington, D.C.

The concept of experience effects is illustrated in part A of Exhibit 4.9, which demonstrates the learning among workers using a punch press. Note that average output of inexperienced workers is less than 15 units per minute, but that output increases rapidly, eventually reaching 38 units per minute after 12,000 units have been produced. Part B of the exhibit shows how cost economies due to experience or learning effects documented during the production of the Model T allowed Ford to lower the car's price as cumulative production increased. When the car was first produced, it sold for more than $3,000, but learning economies allowed the price of the car to fall steadily until it sold for less than $1,000 in 1923.

Production of the Boeing 767 aircraft also offers some illustrations of learning or experience effects. The forward cabin on the first 767 required 6,000 hours and 47 days to construct. In addition, more than 12,000 production and design changes were made during the course of assembling the first 767. By the time Boeing had assembled the seventieth 767, however, far fewer hours were required and only 500 production changes needed to be made.[9]

Cost economies due to scale and learning are not guaranteed and do not occur without management effort. The accompanying Management Focus, "Problems in Realizing Scale and Learning Economies," describes some of the difficulties managers encounter as they attempt to capitalize on scale and learning effects.

A second set of factors that can minimize the threat of entry is associated with structural and marketing advantages enjoyed by incumbents. For example, if incumbent firms enjoy brand loyalty, then potential entrants will have to take satisfied customers away from products or services they are presently using and enjoying. Similarly, if incumbents enjoy access to

EXHIBIT 4.9

Experience or Learning Effects among Punch Press Operators and in the Production of Ford's Model T

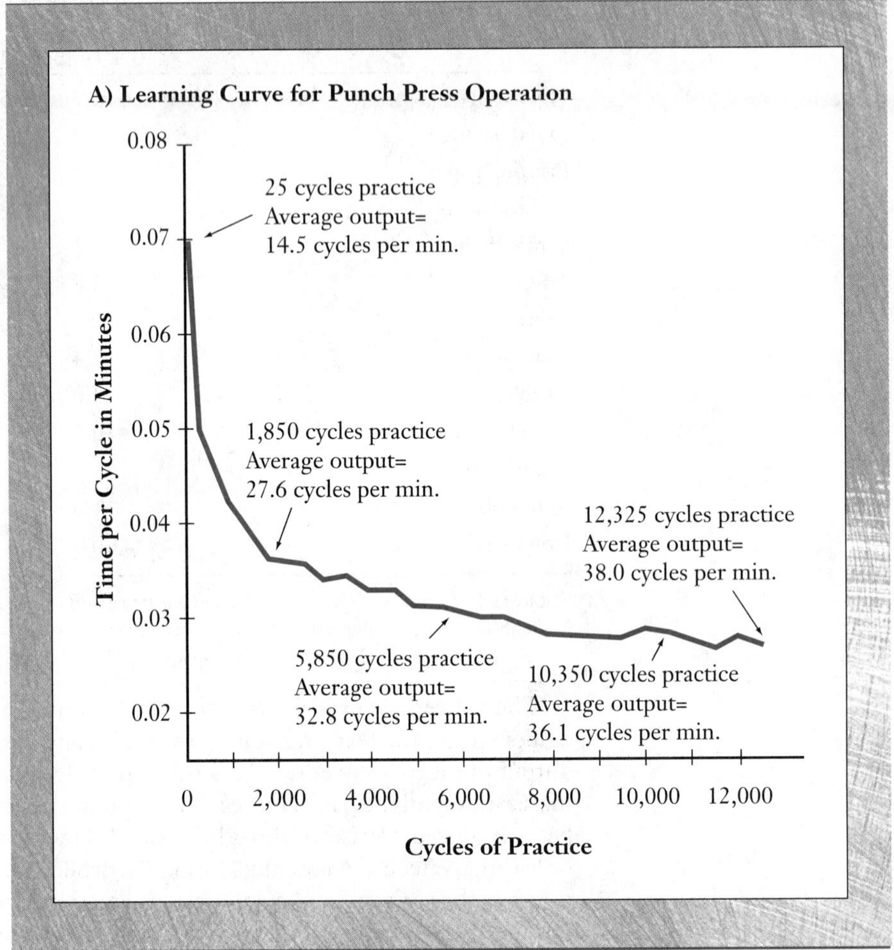

SOURCE: R. Barnes, *Motion and Time Study Design and Measurement of Work*, 7th ed. (New York: Wiley, 1980)

retail distribution channels, such as grocery store shelf space, then potential entrants will have to convince retailers to provide them with (often scarce) shelf space or similar opportunities to distribute their products.

The credit-card market offers a recent example of how companies can seek to prevent entry by limiting access to distribution. Visa and MasterCard have long required that member banks not issue American Express or Discover cards. As a result, American Express and Discover have had a great deal of difficulty getting banks to offer their cards since this would require banks to drop their Visa or MasterCard franchises. The Justice Department is now considering whether the requirements Visa and MasterCard impose on their member banks are a violation of U.S. antitrust laws.[10]

In addition, if customers of incumbent firms will incur "switching costs" by buying products or services from another firm, they will be more hesitant to shift their

EXHIBIT 4.9 CONTINUED

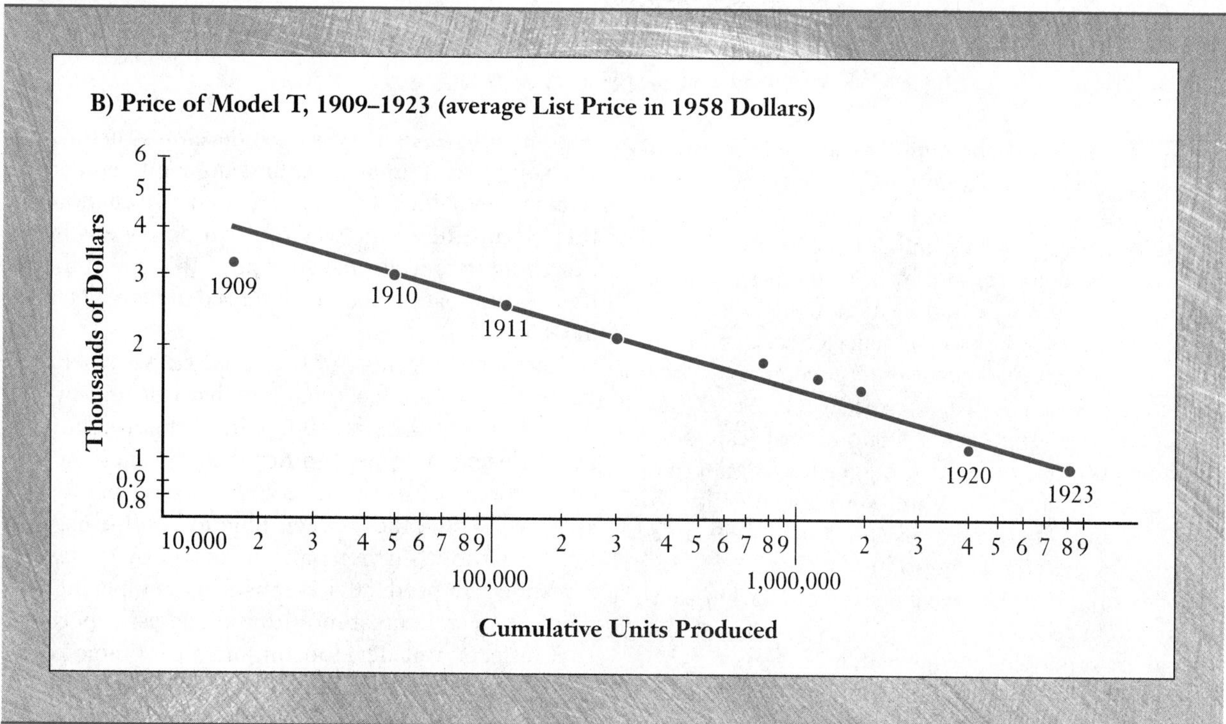

SOURCE: W. J. Abernathy and K. Wayne, "Limits of the Learning Curve," *Harvard Business Review* 52, no. 5 (1974): 109–119.

allegiance from an incumbent firm to a new entrant. A simple example of a switching cost is the cost that a company would incur by switching from Macintoshes to personal computers using the Microsoft operating system. Not only would the company incur the cost of acquiring the new computers and installing the new software, but the company would also have to provide training for its employees.

Government restrictions are yet another set of factors that can minimize entry. For example, when the airline, railroad, and trucking industries were still heavily regulated, potential entrants had to gain government authorization before they could begin service. Even deregulation may not increase the threat of competition, however. The airline industry has now been deregulated for more than a decade and a half, but many start-up airlines have been unable to reach potential passengers traveling to and from East Coast cities due to an important structural barrier—namely, the lack of access to boarding gates and takeoff and landing slots at eastern airports.[11] Similarly, all the major U.S. airlines have had difficulty expanding into Asian markets, as they are still heavily regulated by foreign governments that have denied entry to U.S. carriers.[12]

Finally, a fourth set of entry barriers referred to as "behavioral" entry barriers can be very effective in limiting entry. Incumbent firms might maintain low prices in order to discourage entry into what thus appears to be a low-profit industry. Or, incumbents might signal that they will lower prices

MANAGEMENT FOCUS

PROBLEMS IN REALIZING SCALE AND LEARNING ECONOMIES

The concepts of economies of scale and the experience curve are so intuitive and straightforward that students usually assume that they regularly occur and that few barriers or limitations exist that prevent them from being realized by firms and businesses. In fact, there's no guarantee that firms will enjoy economies of scale or experience effects, and managers must actively pursue these economies in order for them to be realized. As a recent *Wall Street Journal* article emphasized, "economies of scale don't come automatically from bigger market share or greater volume. Doughnuts are cheaper by the dozen only when bakers use the knowledge gained from increased production to shrink costs. Most firms squander executive energy on market share growth instead of exploiting the economies of scale that are supposed to come with it."[1]

The major challenge in realizing economies of scale is the significant amount of management attention and coordination that is required. Products and the delivery of services must be designed to capture economies of scale. Manufacturing and purchasing activities must be centralized and synchronized with logistical, marketing, and sales efforts in order to maximize throughput and minimize excessive inventories. Inevitably, as plant capacity levels are reached and as the costs of coordination increase, firms move beyond the lowest point on their long-run average cost curves and, without reengineering or changes to plant and equipment, firms will begin to experience increasing costs and diseconomies of scale.

Similarly, the benefits of experience or learning effects are only realized through management attention. The major challenge for managers is to capitalize on individual learning-by-doing to achieve overall improvements in productivity. Because inefficiencies in production processes can easily outweigh any benefits derived from experience or learning effects, managers must develop structures that minimize inefficiencies and augment and disseminate individual learning-by-doing throughout their companies. One way this can be done is by designing organizational structures that speed the flow of information (a topic discussed in more detail in Chapter 10).

Furthermore, most of the research on experience or learning effects suggests that learning-by-doing does not continue indefinitely. Studies show that firms enjoy some significant early experience effects for nearly all products and services, but after an initial period, these effects tend to become negligible without further mechanization or capital investment in productivity-enhancing equipment.[2] Thus, managers must monitor and assess experience effects and develop ongoing programs to maintain productivity improvement.

In addition, the management of human resources can have a major impact on the realization of experience effects. If a company recruits qualified employees, trains them, and begins to enjoy the benefits of their individual learning-by-doing, only to have them soon leave due to job dissatisfaction or other factors, then the company will fail to capitalize on this learning-by-doing and the potential for significant productivity gains from experience or learning effects will be lost. Human resources programs to retain qualified and trained employees are therefore very important in any work situation that is characterized by a significant degree of learning-by-doing. ■

[1] Miniter, R. 1998. The myth of market share. *The Wall Street Journal*, June 15: A28.

[2] W. J. Abernathy, "Limits of the Learning Curve," *Harvard Business Review* 52, no. 5 (1974): 109–119; and G. Hall and S. Howell, "The Experience Curve from the Economist's Perspective," *Strategic Managment Journal* 6 (1985): 197–212.

considerably if another firm enters the industry. Other types of "signaling" are also common. For example, firms often announce that they are planning to add additional capacity; this indicates to potential entrants that the industry might have excess capacity, which might in turn discourage entry. Or, companies could announce that they are about to unveil the next generation of a product, so that potential entrants would be concerned that they would be entering the industry with an obsolete product. Intel has used these tactics very effectively over the years as it has built its dominance in the market for microprocessors.

Signaling can often accomplish legally the same goals as collusive behavior that would violate antitrust laws. For example, the managers of one firm in an industry can announce that they intend to lower prices in an attempt to ward off entry by other firms. The managers of other firms can quickly follow the lead of the first firm's managers and also lower their prices. Such signaling behavior is perfectly legal and is quite common. On the other hand, if the managers of these same firms explicitly colluded by meeting in a hotel room or telephoning one another to discuss pricing patterns, then they would be engaging in illegal activities.

THE THREAT OF SUBSTITUTE PRODUCTS

The second of the five forces is the threat of substitute products. If substitute products or services are readily available, then firms in the industry are likely to suffer lower average profitability. A classic example of a substitute product is margarine for butter. More contemporary examples of substitute products are the personal computer for the typewriter, the use of aluminum versus the use of steel in manufacturing automobile engines, and home VCRs for movie theaters.

The extent to which products are substitutes for each other will depend on the value-price ratios of the two products. Two products or services might satisfy the same need or desire, but the extent to which they will be true substitutes for each other will also depend on the relative prices of the two products or services. For example, when VCRs were first introduced, their price was much higher than it is today. This meant that VCRs were essentially a luxury product that only a few consumers chose to buy. For most of the public, the high price of VCRs meant that the value-price ratio of going to a movie theater was much better than that of owning a VCR. As prices of VCRs began to fall, however, their value-price ratio became much more comparable to that of the movie theaters, and now it is safe to say that they are truly substitute products.

A recent *Wall Street Journal* article noted that one way the ready-to-eat cereal manufacturers are dealing with increasing competition from bagels and other substitute products is by cutting prices. Presumably, this move is aimed at improving the value-price ratio of cereal compared to that of bagels.[13] In addition to lowering prices, firms can also add capabilities and features to their products and services in an effort to make their value-price ratios more attractive. Steel manufacturers have begun providing a number of additional services, such as finishing and warehousing, in order to maintain steel's value-price ratio relative to aluminum.

THE POWER OF SUPPLIERS

The third force in the Five Forces Model is the power of suppliers. If the suppliers to an industry have enough power, they may be able to extract higher prices for critical components, thereby reducing average industry profitability. Though many factors influence the power of suppliers (see Exhibit 4.6), two factors are generally the most critical in determining supplier power. First, if only a few suppliers of a particular component exist relative to the number of buyers, then those suppliers will tend to have greater bargaining power. Second, if the component is a critical one or if it incorporates proprietary technology, then suppliers will generally have greater power.

The personal computer market offers some interesting examples of supplier power. The most critical component in any personal computer is the microprocessor. In the early history of personal computers, IBM was so powerful that it was able to demand that suppliers of critical components such as microprocessors agree to license their products and technology to other suppliers to guarantee a "second source." For example, IBM had selected Intel to make the microprocessors for its personal computers, but had also required Intel to license its technology to Advanced Micro Devices. With its significant technological capabilities and with the microprocessor so critical to the performance of personal computers, Intel's power grew considerably. By the time it had developed its 486 line of microprocessors, Intel declared that it would no longer license its proprietary technology to other semiconductor manufacturers. Given the enormous, almost monopoly-like power Intel enjoys, no personal computer manufacturer is really in a position to argue.

In 1990, Compaq announced that it was seeking another manufacturer as an alternative to Intel to provide it with microprocessors. Compaq even invested several million dollars in a small microprocessor manufacturing company in order to establish it as a suitable supplier. A Compaq executive was quoted as saying that the move was made "because strategically, we didn't like having Intel as a single source for such a vital part."[14] By early 1996, however, so powerful was Intel's grip on the market for critical microprocessors that Compaq was forced to admit that it was unable to secure an alternative source for the microprocessors used in its personal computers.[15]

On the other hand, many different companies produce other personal computer components, including disk drives, monitors, and keyboards — most of which incorporate less proprietary technologies. In these markets, producers enjoy very little supplier power, and personal computer makers can generally extract liberal price concessions from the producers of these components.

THE POWER OF BUYERS

Just as powerful suppliers can make an industry less attractive, so too can powerful buyers extract price concessions for products or services, also reducing industry profitability. As with the power of suppliers, two factors appear to be most critical in determining the power of buyers. First, if only a few buyers of a product or service exist relative to the number of firms in the industry, then those buyers will have greater bargaining power. Second, if the product or service is not particularly important to buyers or does not incorporate proprietary technologies, then buyers will have greater power. On the other hand, if the product or service is critical to the buyer or if the product or service is based on proprietary technology, then the power of buyers will be reduced.

One very good illustration of the power of buyers is in the automotive components industry. Literally thousands of small automotive components manufacturers exist around the world. Because there are so few buyers (i.e., automobile manufacturers) relative to the many component manufacturers, the buyers exercise a great deal of leverage over the firms in this industry, dictating product specifications, delivery schedules, and even the prices they will pay to these suppliers.

The power of buyers also helps to explain the fate of DeSoto, Inc., a paint manufacturer. For years, DeSoto was the sole supplier of paints to Sears, Roebuck and Company. At the time that Sears terminated its contract with DeSoto, DeSoto's sales to Sears represented over half of its total sales.[16] The impact on DeSoto from this loss of the Sears business was so devastating that the company was forced to sell its paint business to the Sherwin-Williams Company.

Rivalry

The fifth and final of the five forces is the extent of rivalry among existing firms in an industry. Greater rivalry usually reduces average industry profitability because rivalry will either drive down prices or increase the costs of doing business (as firms seek to add more features to their products and services without raising prices for those features). Many factors will tend to increase rivalry in an industry. Generally, the more firms in an industry, the greater will be the rivalry (e.g., the trucking industry), though highly concentrated industries with only a few major players can also be the scene of considerable rivalry and protracted price wars (e.g., the steel industry). As the number of firms in a particular industry increases, the industry will come closer to matching the conditions associated with perfect competition (i.e., many firms producing similar products, firms "taking" prices established by market competition, etc.). Mergers and acquisitions are often pursued in an effort to reduce rivalry and competition in an industry. For example, the Federal Trade Commission has argued against the acquisition of Office Depot by Staples and has charged that the acquisition is an effort by the managers of Staples to improve profit margins by reducing competition and rivalry in the market for office supplies.[17]

Also, the growth rate of an industry will affect rivalry; slower growth or declines in overall industry sales will tend to increase rivalry. Unable to meet their sales growth objectives from growing demand in the market, rivals in slow growth industries must compete to take market share from each other. The cigarette industry offers a recent example of how overall demand can affect the extent of rivalry in an industry. As seen in Exhibit 4.10, cigarette consumption fell steadily in the 1980s and early 1990s from nearly 650 billion cigarettes in 1981 to fewer than 500 billion in 1996. This decline in U.S. cigarette consumption was almost certainly a key factor behind the price wars that erupted among the leading cigarette manufacturers in 1995.

Excess capacity in an industry also tends to increase rivalry and usually results in lower prices, lower profit margins, and a less attractive industry. As firms in an industry with excess capacity seek to make full use of their own plant capacity, they collectively tend to create excess supply that in turn drives down price levels. Industries, such as airlines and steel, characterized by a high level of fixed costs seem particularly prone to this sort of behavior. A recent *Wall Street Journal* article suggested that the building of excess capacity and its downward pressure on prices in many different industries is one reason why inflationary pressures have remained so low in the United States over the last several years.[18] Two figures that accompanied the article illustrate this point well, and are reprinted in Exhibit 4.11. Part A of the exhibit shows the annual rate of growth in industrial capacity over the last several years, while part B shows the resulting beneficial impact this excess capacity has had on the rate of inflation.

An example of excess capacity that is visible to almost all consumers is the growth of retail shopping space. The increase in the square footage of retail shopping space is totally inconsistent with recent declining trends in shopping habits. Almost all industry analysts believe that the number of retail shopping outlets far exceeds the level of consumer demand, and this excess retailing capacity is almost certainly one of the major contributing factors behind the vigorous competition among retailers and resulting low levels of profits of firms in the retailing industry.[19]

EXHIBIT 4.10

Declining Cigarette Consumption: 1981-1996

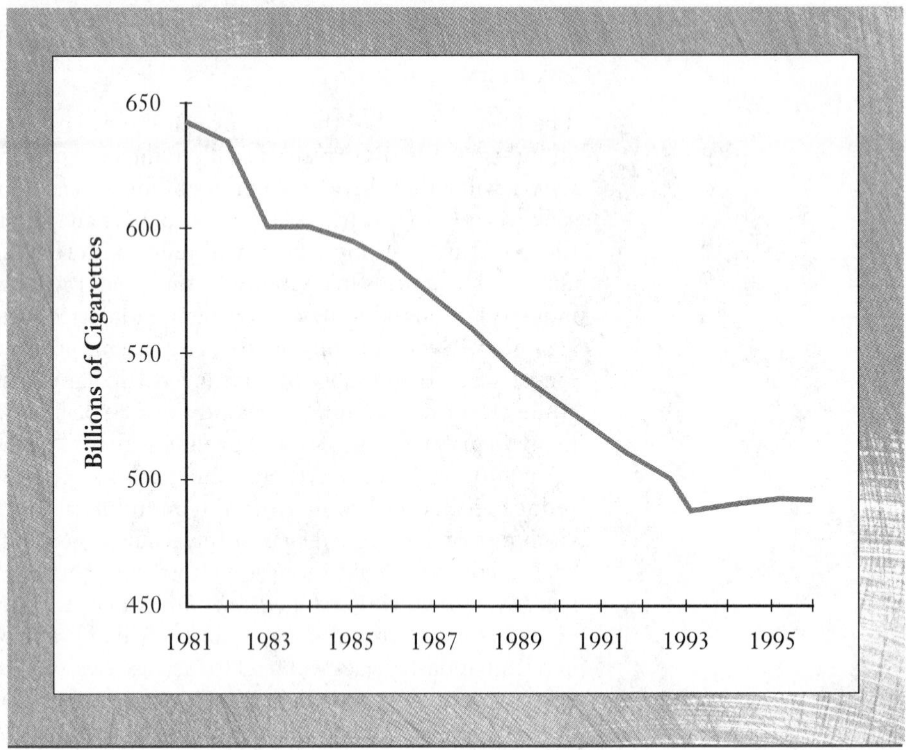

SOURCE: S. L. Hwang. 1997. Cigarette sales steady as young find habit hip. *The Wall Street Journal*, January 30; B10.

This section has focused on factors that tend to increase rivalry in an industry, but just as many factors tend to *increase* rivalry, so will several other factors *decrease* the level of rivalry in an industry. For example, in many emerging industries, firms must work together to gain consumer acceptance of new products and services, develop distribution channels, and establish industry standards. Similarly, any type of government regulation tends to decrease rivalry among firms in the regulated industry.

Nearly all the five forces are present at least to some extent in most industries, but it is the intensity of the various forces that will determine whether they have a significant impact on the profitability of a particular industry. The logic behind the Five Forces Model is straightforward: *As the intensity of the forces increases, the industry environment becomes more hostile and overall industry profitability will decline.* The next section describes how the Five Forces Model can be applied to analyze industry environments.

Application of the Five Forces Model

Perhaps the best way to illustrate the implications of the Five Forces Model is to use it to analyze some actual industries. This way you will be able to see how the

EXHIBIT 4.11

Industrial Capacity Grows, Keeping Prices Low

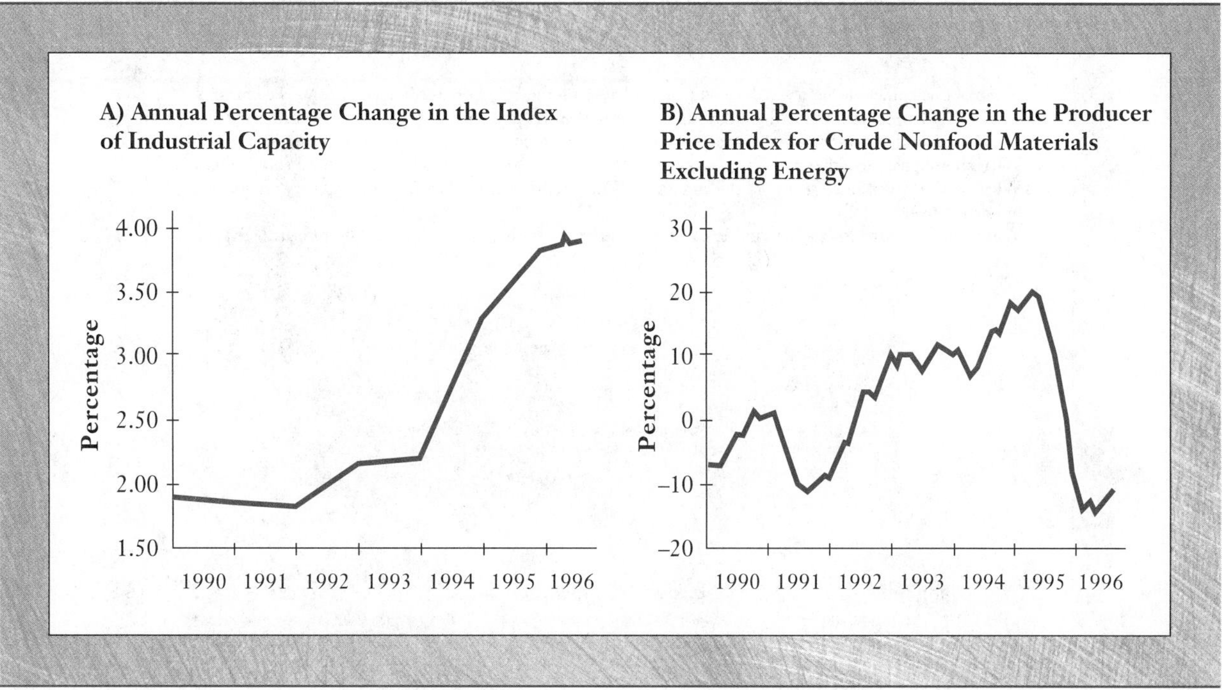

SOURCE: F. R. Bleakley. 1996. Capacity boosts take toll on many firms. *The Wall Street Journal*, October 21; A2.

structural characteristics of these industries influence the average profitability of firms in these industries. To get you started and to help you conduct your own industry analyses using the Five Forces Model, we've provided you with the guidelines summarized in Exhibit 4.12. These guidelines will help you to assess the intensity or strength of each of the five forces in Porter's framework.

To illustrate how you can use the Five Forces Model to analyze industries, we'll use the guidelines and criteria listed in Exhibit 4.12 to analyze two different industries. (The market for personal computers is also analyzed in the accompanying Management Focus, "Increasing Rivalry in the Market for Personal Computers.") You can then follow the approach we use as you analyze industries on your own. First, we analyze the steel industry, traditionally a low-performing industry. Then, we will analyze the pharmaceutical industry, traditionally a very high-performing industry.

STEEL: A FIVE FORCE CONSPIRACY

Firms in few industries have suffered through such a consistently low level of average industry performance as the integrated steel manufacturers. The Five Forces Model is particularly helpful in understanding why this is such a consistently low-performing industry. Recall that as the intensity of any of the five forces becomes higher, the industry becomes less attractive and industry performance tends to decline. In the steel industry, all but one of the five forces are quite intense. Supplier power is the only

EXHIBIT 4.12

Guide to Using the Five Forces Model for Industry Analysis

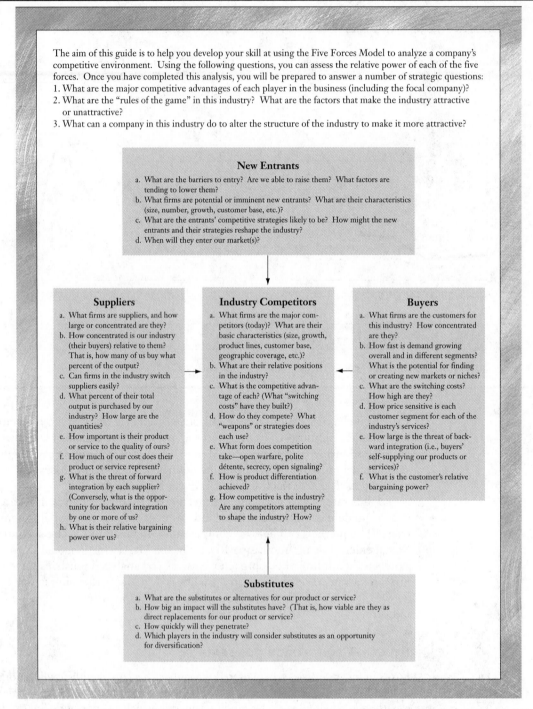

The aim of this guide is to help you develop your skill at using the Five Forces Model to analyze a company's competitive environment. Using the following questions, you can assess the relative power of each of the five forces. Once you have completed this analysis, you will be prepared to answer a number of strategic questions:

1. What are the major competitive advantages of each player in the business (including the focal company)?
2. What are the "rules of the game" in this industry? What are the factors that make the industry attractive or unattractive?
3. What can a company in this industry do to alter the structure of the industry to make it more attractive?

New Entrants

a. What are the barriers to entry? Are we able to raise them? What factors are tending to lower them?
b. What firms are potential or imminent new entrants? What are their characteristics (size, number, growth, customer base, etc.)?
c. What are the entrants' competitive strategies likely to be? How might the new entrants and their strategies reshape the industry?
d. When will they enter our market(s)?

Suppliers

a. What firms are suppliers, and how large or concentrated are they?
b. How concentrated is our industry (their buyers) relative to them? That is, how many of us buy what percent of the output?
c. Can firms in the industry switch suppliers easily?
d. What percent of their total output is purchased by our industry? How large are the quantities?
e. How important is their product or service to the quality of ours?
f. How much of our cost does their product or service represent?
g. What is the threat of forward integration by each supplier? (Conversely, what is the opportunity for backward integration by one or more of us?
h. What is their relative bargaining power over us?

Industry Competitors

a. What firms are the major competitors (today)? What are their basic characteristics (size, growth, product lines, customer base, geographic coverage, etc.)?
b. What are their relative positions in the industry?
c. What is the competitive advantage of each? (What "switching costs" have they built?)
d. How do they compete? What "weapons" or strategies does each use?
e. What form does competition take—open warfare, polite détente, secrecy, open signaling?
f. How is product differentiation achieved?
g. How competitive is the industry? Are any competitors attempting to shape the industry? How?

Buyers

a. What firms are the customers for this industry? How concentrated are they?
b. How fast is demand growing overall and in different segments? What is the potential for finding or creating new markets or niches?
c. What are the switching costs? How high are they?
d. How price sensitive is each customer segment for each of the industry's services?
e. How large is the threat of backward integration (i.e., buyers' self-supplying our products or services)?
f. What is the customer's relative bargaining power?

Substitutes

a. What are the substitutes or alternatives for our product or service?
b. How big an impact will the substitutes have? (That is, how viable are they as direct replacements for our product or service?
c. How quickly will they penetrate?
d. Which players in the industry will consider substitutes as an opportunity for diversification?

SOURCE: Adapted from Michael Porter, 1979 "How Competitive Forces Shape Strategy," *Harvard Business Review* 56(2): 137–145.

Management Focus

Increasing Rivalry in the Market for Personal Computers

The increasingly intense competition among personal computer manufacturers results from three of the five forces in Porter's model, while two of the forces play hardly any role in the industry at all. For example, few substitutes for the personal computer now exist. Although the typewriter can be a substitute for word processing and the adding machine or handheld calculator can be substitutes for some of the functions of spreadsheet programs, significant enhancements in personal computer technology, the growing popularity of personal computer applications, and falling PC prices have significantly improved the value-price ratio of personal computers relative to other products. In addition, aside from the power of large corporate buyers, the level of buyer power in the personal computer market remains fairly modest.

As indicated earlier in the chapter, personal computer makers do, however, face a good deal of supplier power from two key firms, Intel and Microsoft. These companies are in a very strong position relative to the computer manufacturers, basically dictating terms on two of the most important components in any personal computer, the microprocessor and the operating system. In addition, the personal computer market is faced with the threat of new entry and a good deal of rivalry, much of which can be explained by the way the industry has evolved.

In the early 1980s, when IBM was scrambling to introduce its own line of personal computers, the company's managers decided against developing a proprietary microprocessor and operating system. This decision allowed the company to bring its product to market very quickly. Yet, IBM's decision to rely on Intel and Microsoft to supply microprocessors and operating systems for its personal computers also had the unintended result of making entry into the personal computer market very easy for its rivals. Almost immediately, Compaq and a few other companies began manufacturing IBM "clones." Early on, these manufacturers enjoyed a friendly rivalry due to a very high demand for the new product and because many of the competitors had developed excellent reputations that allowed them some opportunities to differentiate their products.

By the early 1990s, however, the nature of competition in the personal computer market had changed dramatically. A flood of new "clone" manufacturers had begun operations, made possible by the independence of Intel and Microsoft and the widespread availability of manufacturers producing keyboards, monitors, disk drives, and other components. The computer makers also adopted mass marketing techniques, selling computers through electronics and appliance superstores like Best Buy and even through discount retailers such as Wal-Mart.

So dominant in the mainframe computer market, IBM never enjoyed the same reputation in the personal computer segment. Though IBM's reputation almost certainly encouraged the acceptance of personal computers among businesses, IBM did not and probably could not maintain a technological edge over its competitors, because all makers had access to Intel's microprocessors and Microsoft's operating systems. By the early 1990s, the personal computer had become a commodity product in which price was the most distinguishing feature among the various producers.[1]

With little leverage over Intel and Microsoft, with almost no barriers to entry, and with few distinguishing features other than price, the personal computer market will probably continue to be very competitive. Any decrease in PC sales, which have been growing at nearly 20 percent annually, would further intensify competition, and a serious decrease in demand could have severe consequences for industry players, even driving many weaker firms out of business. ■

[1] W. M. Bulkeley, Changed Industry: Computers Become a Kind of Commodity, to Dismay of Makers. *The Wall Street Journal*, September 5; 1991, A1, A4.

one of the five forces that is not really a factor in the steel industry because coal, oxygen, and iron ore are basic commodities and no raw material suppliers really exercise much market power over the major steel manufacturing companies.

The threat of new entry is, however, very real. The large investments required to open a steel mill would supposedly deter entry, but several minimill companies, which use scrap metal as a raw material, have successfully entered the steel industry since the mid-1970s. Many of these minimill companies, including Nucor and Oregon Steel, have grown to be major rivals to the traditional integrated steel manufacturers. In fact, Nucor, known for the efficiency of its minimills, is now the fourth largest steel manufacturer in the United States.

Threat of substitute products is also a major force in the steel industry. Aluminum manufacturers and other companies producing composite plastic materials are vying for many of steel's traditional markets. This is especially true in the automobile industry where, in an effort to reduce the weight of their cars and thereby improve fuel economy, automobile manufacturers have replaced much of the steel in cars with aluminum, plastic, and composite materials.[20]

The power of steel buyers is also significant. A relatively small number of companies account for a very large proportion of the steel used in manufacturing. In fact, firms in just two industry groups, automobile assembly and appliance manufacturing, account for a very large percentage of all steel purchases. As a result, these companies can exercise significant leverage over the various steel manufacturers. Often a threat from a buyer that it will take its business elsewhere is all that is necessary to get steel companies to roll back any planned price hikes. GM, the largest buyer of steel manufactured in the United States, has made some limited purchases of steel from Japanese steel manufacturers in order to extract price concessions from the U.S. steel producers. GM has also recently announced plans to broaden its base of steel suppliers in an effort to further reduce the prices it pays for steel.[21]

Finally, the steel industry is the scene of intense rivalry among manufacturers. The key reason for all the rivalry is the significant overcapacity that still exists despite the closing of many steel mills over the last two decades.[22] To spread their fixed costs over a large volume, all the major steel producers seek to keep their mills running at full capacity, but with more steelmaking capacity than steel demand, the excess production creates a glut on the market, which puts downward pressure on prices.[23] Further exacerbating domestic overcapacity is a major increase in imported foreign steel, particularly from Russia, Brazil, and Korea. In fact, U.S. steel imports reached an all-time high during 1996[24] in spite of overcapacity among the domestic producers.

Rivalry, resulting from a very crowded industry with excess capacity and growing pressure from foreign steel producers, is a key factor in understanding why the price of steel today is largely unchanged from the price of steel more than 20 years ago, in spite of inflation. The two graphs in Exhibit 4.13 illustrate how lingering overcapacity exerts considerable downward pressure on steel prices.

THE PHARMACEUTICAL INDUSTRY: THE BEST OF ALL POSSIBLE INDUSTRY WORLDS?

The pharmaceutical industry offers a marked contrast to the steel industry. Suppliers exercise little power over pharmaceutical companies because most of the raw material inputs are commodity chemical products that can be obtained from a large number of suppliers.

In addition, significant barriers to entry reduce the threat of new entrants. A company hoping to become a major player in the pharmaceutical industry must

EXHIBIT 4.13

Overcapacity in the Steel Industry and Its Downward Pressure on Steel Prices

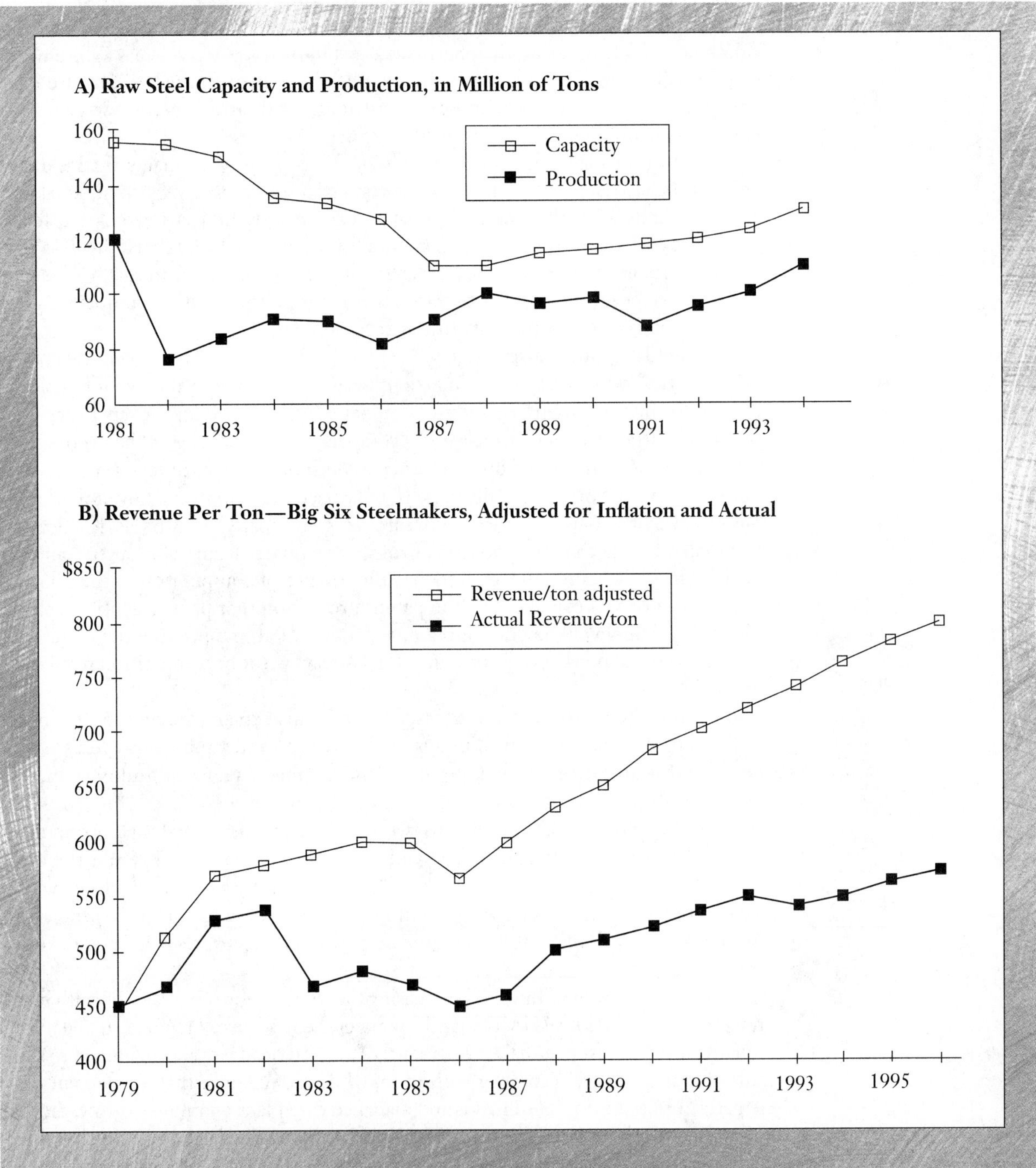

SOURCE: A) C. Ansberry and D. Milbank. 1992. Small, midsize steelmakers are ripe for a shakeout. *The Wall Street Journal*, March 4; B4; B) C. Ansberry. 1991. Men of steel see no end to leaden prices. *The Wall Street Journal*, March 19; A2.

be able to attract research and scientific talent, it must be able to obtain the financing that will allow it to operate for many years until new drug products are developed and approved by the Food and Drug Administration, and it must build a large professional sales force. For most companies, these requirements are significant obstacles to overcome. Even companies with vast financial resources have had considerable trouble entering the pharmaceutical industry. Several years ago, DuPont sought to become a major player in the pharmaceutical industry. In spite of its "deep pockets," DuPont found entry difficult, and, after only a few years, the company abandoned this diversification effort.

In addition to the barriers to entry that firms in the pharmaceutical industry enjoy, they also benefit because few true substitutes exist. A very small market of approximately $2 billion annually has emerged over the last few years offering organic, herbal, nontoxic, and other natural health products, but "healthy living" — possibly the greatest potential threat to the pharmaceutical industry — seems unlikely to emerge as a serious threat to the major pharmaceutical companies given the lifestyles of the vast majority of the U.S. population.

Also, until recently, buyers exercised very little control over pharmaceutical companies. A patient who was sick would take prescribed medications that would, typically, be paid for by the patient's insurance company. A sick patient is not in a very good position to argue with a pharmaceutical company about the price of the product, and when the tab is being picked up by a third party insurer, patients have few incentives or other reasons to worry about the price of pharmaceutical products. Given this lack of buyer power, it's no wonder that health care costs have soared over the last few decades!

Finally, unlike the steel industry, firms in the pharmaceutical industry enjoy an almost "friendly" competition. The friendly nature of competition in the pharmaceutical industry is explained by the patent protection that pharmaceutical companies enjoy whenever they develop a new product. Patents provide the companies with the right to market their products for 17 years without competition from other manufacturers.

The low intensity of each of the five forces helps explain the high performance of firms in the pharmaceutical industry. There are indications, however, that the comfortable situation enjoyed by firms in the pharmaceutical industry may be changing. In fact, the average performance of firms in the pharmaceutical industry could soon be much lower due to two important factors. First, patents on many important pharmaceutical products will be expiring soon.[25] As a result, the other major pharmaceutical companies as well as manufacturers of generic drugs will be able to introduce their own versions of many drugs that are currently proprietary products. This will inevitably increase competition and put pressure on companies' profit margins.

Second, the power of buyers is increasing due to the growing clout of health maintenance organizations (HMOs) and managed health care. HMOs are expanding rapidly; in 1993, just over half (52 percent) of all American workers belonged to some sort of managed care plan or organization, while today, more than 85 percent of all American workers do.[26] As HMOs and managed care plans continue to grow, they are becoming much more aggressive than insurance companies have been in bargaining with pharmaceutical companies. In some cases, HMOs have simply demanded that pharmaceutical companies lower their prices on various drug products. Several clashes between HMOs and drug firms have already been reported in the business press, and more can be expected. In most of the cases that have been reported to date, the HMOs have been very successful in obtaining price concessions or rollbacks.

Though they are often portrayed by the news media in a very negative light as ruthless organizations focused only on the bottom line, HMOs have done much to bring soaring health care costs under control. Already the impact of HMOs is being felt across the health care industry, and, as the chart in Exhibit 4.14 shows, the annual percentage increases in health care costs have been declining significantly since the late 1980s. Nearly all of this decline can be attributed to the growing buyer power of HMOs in the market for health care.

Limitations of the Five Forces Model

By offering a more concrete framework and by suggesting specific criteria or factors for evaluating the strength of each of the five forces, the Five Forces Model is more helpful than SWOT in conducting industry analysis and in understanding differences in average industry performance levels. Still, the model is not without its limitations. One key limitation is its inability to suggest strategies for managers. Porter concludes that managers have two options if they find their firms in unattractive industries. First, they can simply diversify their firms away from — or exit completely — the unattractive industry. Alternatively, they can attempt to minimize the impact of any of the five forces that are acting to make the industry unattractive.

The problem with the first recommendation is that few totally attractive industries exist. Almost every industry involves at least some unattractive characteristics, and the more attractive industries will generally be the most difficult to enter. In

EXHIBIT 4.14

The Impact of HMOs: Declining Rates of Increases in Health Care Costs

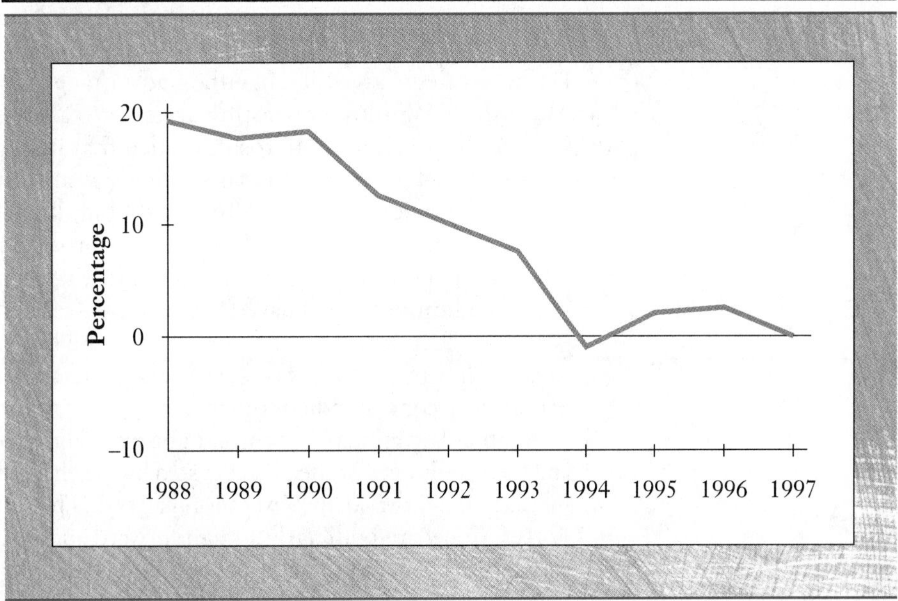

SOURCE: R. Winslow. 1997. Health-care costs may be heading up again. *The Wall Street Journal*, January 21; B1, B7; R. Winslow. 1998. Health-care inflation kept in check last year. *The Wall Street Journal*, January 20, B1, B4.

addition, firms often lack the resources necessary to diversify into other industries. Acquisitions of firms in other industries and the development of totally new products and services usually require a great deal of capital, and many firms lack either the necessary capital or access to capital from external sources. Moreover, diversification can be especially risky for firms that have no previous experience with diversification (an issue considered more fully in Chapter 9).

Managers can and frequently do pursue the second option, seeking to make their industries more attractive either by (1) reducing the power of the five forces, or (2) shielding or protecting their companies from the power of the five forces. For example, nearly all companies attempt to build brand loyalty through advertising or by offering good customer service. Companies also frequently seek to minimize the power of suppliers through backward integration in which they begin to manufacture their own components or merchandise.

It is important to emphasize, however, that many activities aimed at reducing competition in an industry are illegal. Firms must not be so eager to reduce competition in their industries that they unwittingly violate antitrust laws. For example, many activities aimed at preventing firms from entering an industry can be construed as restraint of trade. Collusion and price fixing are sometimes temptations for the executives of firms caught in intense rivalry and competitive pricing, but such collusive activities are also illegal.

An excellent illustration of collusion was provided by 21 private colleges and universities whose admissions and financial aid personnel would meet regularly to discuss the financial aid packages that they planned to award to admitted students.[27] Some people allege that the aim of these meetings was to minimize intercollegiate rivalry for promising college students by agreeing on the terms of the financial aid packages that would be offered to admitted students. The colleges and universities finally agreed to stop meeting collectively after the U.S. Justice Department announced that it planned a full-scale investigation of the collusive practice.

The current controversy between the Justice Department and Microsoft centers around Microsoft's "bundling" of its products[28] and whether Microsoft's marketing strategy gives it an unfair advantage over its competitors. Buyers of Microsoft's Windows operating system are also required to accept Microsoft's Internet browser, and Microsoft argued that its browser is just one of many features included in its Windows operating system. The Justice Department has disagreed, however, viewing Microsoft's bundling strategy as an effort to put companies producing competing Internet browsers at a significant disadvantage. This debate between Microsoft and the Justice Department is important because of the implications it will have for many high-tech companies. In the past, antitrust laws have been interpreted to discourage the bundling of products, but many of today's high-tech products — especially programs included in computer software packages — come bundled together.

Another key limitation of most industry analysis tools, including SWOT Analysis and the Five Forces Model, is suggested by the changes that are occurring in the pharmaceutical industry, which was just analyzed. Though SWOT Analysis and the Five Forces Model are both fairly straightforward and relatively easy to grasp and understand, many users of these industry analysis techniques often fail to appreciate the dynamic nature of the industries they are analyzing. Both frameworks provide their users with "snapshots" of industry environments, but many users then assume that the nature of competition in those industries will remain stable over time. In other words, many users of SWOT Analysis and the Five Forces Model apply these tools to study a particular industry at a point in time, but then fail to recognize how that industry is changing — for example, how HMOs are likely to change the nature of competition in the pharmaceutical industry. As two leading management authors have argued,

> Traditional competitor analysis is like a snapshot of a moving car. By itself, the photograph yields little information about the car's speed or direction — whether the driver is out for a quiet Sunday drive or warming up for the Grand Prix.[29]

As will be demonstrated in the next chapter, many — if not most — industry environments are very dynamic, and to use Hamel and Prahalad's analogy, it makes all the difference in the world whether competitors and would-be rivals are "out for a quiet Sunday drive or warming up for the Grand Prix." Developments in customer preferences, product and/or service offerings, and technologies can revolutionize industries overnight. Although SWOT Analysis and the Five Forces Model are widely used and can be very helpful in analyzing industries, these tools must be used with caution and a recognition that any conclusions may be quite fleeting as industry conditions change.

Perhaps one way to approach the task of industry analysis would be to begin by conducting analyses using SWOT Analysis and the Five Forces Model. These initial studies could be especially helpful in developing an understanding of a particular industry and identifying key competitive issues and factors. These same issues could then be further examined using a more dynamic model of industry structure and evolution, such as the one that is introduced in the next chapter.

Key Points

- Industry environments vary considerably. Some industries are relatively young, emerging industries while others are more mature; some industries are characterized by fierce competition while others are characterized by very little rivalry; and some industries are, on average, more profitable than others in any one year.
- SWOT Analysis can be used to analyze industry environments and organizational capabilities. It specifically examines organizational *Strengths* and *Weaknesses* and environmental *Opportunities* and *Threats*. The major limitation of SWOT Analysis is that it lacks objective dimensions, so any conclusions tend to reflect managers' subjective evaluations of their industry environments.
- The Five Forces Model analyzes five aspects of industry structure in order to assess the relative attractiveness of different industries.
- Use of the Five Forces Model is straightforward: *As the intensity of forces increases, the industry environment becomes more hostile and overall industry profitability will decline.*
- Both SWOT Analysis and the Five Forces Model are *static* frameworks. Users must recognize that most industry environments can be quite dynamic, and that any conclusions based on these models may not be appropriate in the future.

Review and Discussion Questions

1. *Describe the relationship between average industry performance and the performance of specific firms in an industry. How much does industry performance influence firm performance?*

2. *Describe how SWOT Analysis can be used as a tool for industry analysis. What are the limitations of SWOT Analysis?*
3. *What is the theoretical basis or foundation of the Five Forces Model?*
4. *Select an industry and analyze it using the Five Forces Model.*
5. *What are the limitations or shortcomings of the Five Forces Model as a tool for industry analysis?*

Suggestions for Further Reading

Hamel, G., and C. K. Prahalad. 1989. Strategic intent. *Harvard Business Review*, 67(3): 63–76.

McGahan, A. M., & Porter, M. E. 1997. How much does industry matter, really? *Strategic Management Journal*, 18 (special issue): 15–30.

Porter, M. E. 1978. How competitive forces shape strategy. *Harvard Business Review*, 56(2): 137–145.

Porter, M. E. 1980. *Competitive Strategy*. New York: Free Press.

Rumelt, R. P. 1991. How much does industry matter? *Strategic Management Journal*, 12: 167–185.

Schmalensee, R. 1985. Do markets differ much? *American Economic Review*, 75: 341–351.

Endnotes

1. This question has generated considerable empirical research among academics. Some key studies include R. Schmalensee, Do markets differ much? *American Economic Review* 75 (1985): 341–351; R. P. Rumelt, How much does industry matter? *Strategic Managemnt Journal* 12 (1991): 167–185; and A. M. McGahan and M. E. Porter, How much does industry matter, really?" *Strategic Management Journal* 18 (spec. issue, 1997): 15–30.
2. Schmalensee, R. 1985. Do markets differ much? *American Economic Review* 75: 341-351.
3. Rumelt, R. P. 1991. How much does industry matter? *Strategic Management Journal* 12: 167-185.
4. Ibid.
5. Porter, M. E. 1978. How competitive forces shape strategy. *Harvard Business Review* 56(2); 137-145.
6. Porter, M. E. 1980. *Competitive Strategy*. New York: Free Press.
7. Adams, W., and J. Brock, 1990. *The Structure of American Industry*. 9th ed. Englewood Cliffs, NJ.: Prentice-Hall.
8. Bollenbacher, G. M. 1992. America's banking dinosaurs. *The Wall Street Journal*, March 18; A14.
9. Garvin, D. A. 1992. *Operations Strategy*. Englewood Cliffs, NJ: Prentice-Hall.
10. Frank, S. E., and J. R. Wilke, 1997. Visa, MasterCard may face antitrust suit. *The Wall Street Journal*, February 7; A3, A4.
11. See for example, A. Q. Nomani, 1996. Eastern airports still out of reach to start-ups. *The Wall Street Journal*, April 25; B1; R. L. Rose, and J. Dahl, 1989. Aborted takeoffs: Skies are deregulated, but just try starting a sizable new airline. *The Wall Street Journal*, July 18; A1, A9.
12. McCartney, S., D. Brady, S. Carey, and A. Q. Nomani. 1996. Hot seats: U.S. airlines' prospects are grim on expanding access to Asian skies. *The Wall Street Journal*, September 25; A1, A13.
13. Miller, J. P. 1996. Cereal makers fight bagels with price cuts. *The Wall Street Journal*, June 20; B1.
14. *The Wall Street Journal*. 1990. Compaq said to seek alternative source for microprocessor. March 6; C9.

15. Templin, N. 1996. Compaq returns to "Intel Inside" fold after failing to find alternative chips. *The Wall Street Journal*, January 19: B3. 16.
16. *The Wall Street Journal*. 1990. DeSoto says Sears, its biggest customer, ended paint contract. February 1: A3.
17. Wilke, J. R. 1997. FTC says Staples' bid for Office Depot sought to remove most aggressive rival. *The Wall Street Journal*, May 20; A4.
18. Bleakley, F. R. 1996. Capacity boosts take toll on many firms. *The Wall Street Journal*, October 21; A2, A14.
19. Berner, R. 1996. Retailers keep expanding amid glut of stores. *The Wall Street Journal*, May 28; A21, A26.
20. Norton, E., and G. Stern, 1995. Heavy metal: Steel and aluminum vie over every ounce in a car's construction. *The Wall Street Journal*, May 9; A1, A8.
21. Adams, C. 1998. GM to broaden its steel suppliers world-wide. *The Wall Street Journal*, April 14; A4.
22. Ansberry, C. 1991. Men of steel see no end to leaden prices. *The Wall Street Journal*, March 19; A2; Norton, E. 1995. Price increase for steel isn't sticking, with inventory high, imports rising. *The Wall Street Journal*, February 2; A2.
23. Adams, C. 1997. Steel prices may decline due to excess in supply. *The Wall Street Journal*, June 12; A3, A11.
24. Adams, C. 1997. U.S. steelmakers face flood of imports. *The Wall Street Journal*, February 12; A2, A11.
25. Tanouye, E., and R. Langreth, 1997. Time's up: With patents expiring on big prescriptions, drug industry quakes. *The Wall Street Journal*, August 12: A1, A6.
26. Winslow, R. 1998. Health-care inflation kept in check last year. *The Wall Street Journal*, January 20; B1, B4.
27. Putka, G. 1991. Colleges cancel aid meetings under scrutiny. *The Wall Street Journal*, March 12; B1.
28. Bank, D. 1997. Why software and antitrust law make an uneasy mix. *The Wall Street Journal*, October 22; B1.
29. Hamel, G., and C. K. Prahalad, 1989. Strategic intent. *Harvard Business Review* 67(3): 64.

CHAPTER 5

A DYNAMIC MODEL OF INDUSTRY STRUCTURING[1]

CHAPTER OBJECTIVES

This chapter continues our focus on industry environments. Chapter 4 described two traditional frameworks for analyzing industries, SWOT Analysis and the Five Forces Model. The chapter concluded its discussion of these frameworks by observing that both SWOT Analysis and the Five Forces Model can provide "snapshots" of industries at a particular point in time, but managers who rely on these tools often fail to anticipate how industries will change over time or how firms and their rivals will respond to these industry changes.

Again, the objective of this second chapter on industries is to develop your understanding of business environments by focusing specifically on the dynamic nature of most industries. The specific aims of this chapter are to:

- Introduce a dynamic model of industry competition and evolution.
- Offer several specific observations about the evolution of industries based on this dynamic model, focusing specifically on the likely actions of new entrants to an industry and the responses of incumbent firms.
- Illustrate how this dynamic model can be used to analyze industries.
- Emphasize the managerial implications of this dynamic model of industry structuring.

INTRODUCTION

To illustrate the dynamic nature of industry environments, consider Tracy Kidder's description of the changes in the computer industry that led to the development of minicomputers in the 1970s:

> Scientists and engineers, it seems, were the first to express a desire for a relatively inexpensive computer that they could operate for themselves. The result was a machine called a minicomputer. In time, the demand for such a machine turned out to be enormous. Probably IBM could not have controlled this new market the way it did the one for large computers. As it happened, IBM ignored it, and so the field was left open for aspiring entrepreneurs.[2]

Near the end of the 1970s, history repeated itself when the computer industry was rocked by Apple's development and commercialization of the personal computer. Apple's phenomenal success is particularly noteworthy because, like DEC, Data General, and the other minicomputer entrepreneurs of the previous decade, Apple entered an industry occupied by major firms, including, of course, IBM. During the 1980s, history again repeated itself as "clone" manufacturers entered this industry to satisfy the enormous demand for personal computers. Like previous new entrants, many of these firms not only entered but profitably competed in an industry dominated by formidable rivals.

The ongoing evolution of the computer industry is inconsistent with the Five Forces Model and the structure-conduct-performance framework from industrial organization economics on which Porter's model is based. Recall that the Five Forces Model suggests that firms can erect a variety of entry barriers in order to prevent potential new rivals from entering an industry. Yet, in spite of entry barriers, new firms not only *do* enter industries but frequently enjoy remarkable success in competing against powerful incumbent firms. In fact, in many industries, the entry of new rivals is frequently associated with the subsequent decline of incumbent firms.[3] Thus, new frameworks and models are needed that will help to explain these patterns in the evolution of industries and provide managers with a better understanding of the dynamic nature of most industry environments.

As the pace of change has increased in many industries over the last several years, many more managers, consultants, and academics have become interested in understanding the processes of industry change and evolution. Several recent books, including Hamel and Prahalad's *Competing for the Future*[4] and D'Aveni's *Hypercompetition*[5] are aimed at helping managers not only understand and better anticipate the forces of industry change, but also fundamentally recreate their companies so that they can prosper in future competitive environments. As Hamel and Prahalad emphasize in their book:

> It is not enough for a company to get smaller and better and faster, as important as these tasks may be; a company must also be capable of fundamentally reconceiving itself, or regenerating its core strategies, and of reinventing its industry. In short, a company must also be capable of getting different.[6]

This chapter offers a model that explains how and why industries evolve. It focuses specifically on why newcomers tend to reshape industries in such fundamental ways, and why incumbent firms have such difficulties in responding to industry change. The chapter closes by suggesting ways in which managers can be more responsive to, anticipate, or even create changes in their industries. Future chapters elaborate on these suggestions, emphasizing not only how managers can develop competitive advantage, but also how they can maintain competitive advantage in the face of industry change. Note that the title of this chapter uses the word "structuring" rather than "structure." This choice is deliberate, emphasizing that industries are not static but that they are being continuously structured and restructured over time — an ongoing process of industry structuring.

The Building Blocks of a Dynamic Theory of Industry Structuring

The model introduced in this chapter suggests that industries are "structuring" over time, the result of an ongoing process that is tied to the cognitive understandings of managers. This model suggests that four factors — (1) changing industry dimensions, (2) shared norms held by the managers of firms in an industry, (3) managers' cognitive limitations, and (4) first-mover advantages — are helpful in explaining patterns in the evolution of most industries.

The model suggests that entrepreneurial activity plays a key role in the process of ongoing industry structuring because entrepreneurs see opportunities to (1) satisfy consumers' new wants and needs, (2) exploit new technological developments, and (3) offer new products and services. Entrepreneurs are also helped by the managers of incumbent firms who, because of cognitive inertia and limitations (discussed in Chapter 2), fail to see and exploit these same opportunities. This chapter will demonstrate how managerial thinking, over time, allows new entrants to become major players in their industries, shifting the locus of competition away from the incumbent firms, thereby undermining their dominant position.

Nor are the impacts of this entrepreneurial activity limited to intraindustry changes. Entrepreneurial activity in one industry can have profound effects on other industries; in some cases, changes can cause two or more industries to collide with each other, and totally new industries can emerge as a consequence. Chapter 1 described how traditional boundaries around industries are falling and new industries are emerging due to technological and other changes. For example, regulatory changes that initiated competition among banks, savings and loans, insurance companies, and investment banks have resulted in the emergence of a new financial services industry. Similarly, personal computers and the Internet have created a new means of distributing media content, and firms in industries as diverse as publishing, motion picture production, cable and network television, and computer software are now pursuing a variety of strategies in order to exploit these technological changes. These strategies and competitive interactions will result in a very different competitive landscape and possibly the emergence of a totally new industry.[7]

The Changing Dimensions of Industries

Our model of strategic management was portrayed in Chapter 1 (reprinted here as Exhibit 5.1) with managers at the center making a variety of decisions (based on their mental models), including decisions about their firms' business definitions, business and corporate strategies, and organizational structures. The model also places firms in industry or competitive environments consisting of customers, products and services, and technologies.

This illustration or characterization of firms operating in industries composed of customers, products and services, and technologies is based on the work of another strategy scholar who suggested that an industry can be thought of as an arena or a competitive "space" in which rivals compete along various dimensions. Abell suggested that industries are defined by firms that serve similar customers, meet similar customer needs, and employ similar technologies.[8] The model shown in Exhibit 5.1 can be expanded to portray industry as a three-dimensional "competitive space" delineated by customers (or "who" an industry serves), products and/or services (or "what" an industry offers), and technologies (or "how" those products or services are provided).

Traditional perspectives assume that changes in the dimensions of industries are relatively unimportant, that the size and shape of the competitive space are relatively stable over time, that industries remain in equilibrium, and that the locus of competition remains fixed on traditional patterns of interaction among participating firms.

EXHIBIT 5.1

Model of Strategic Management

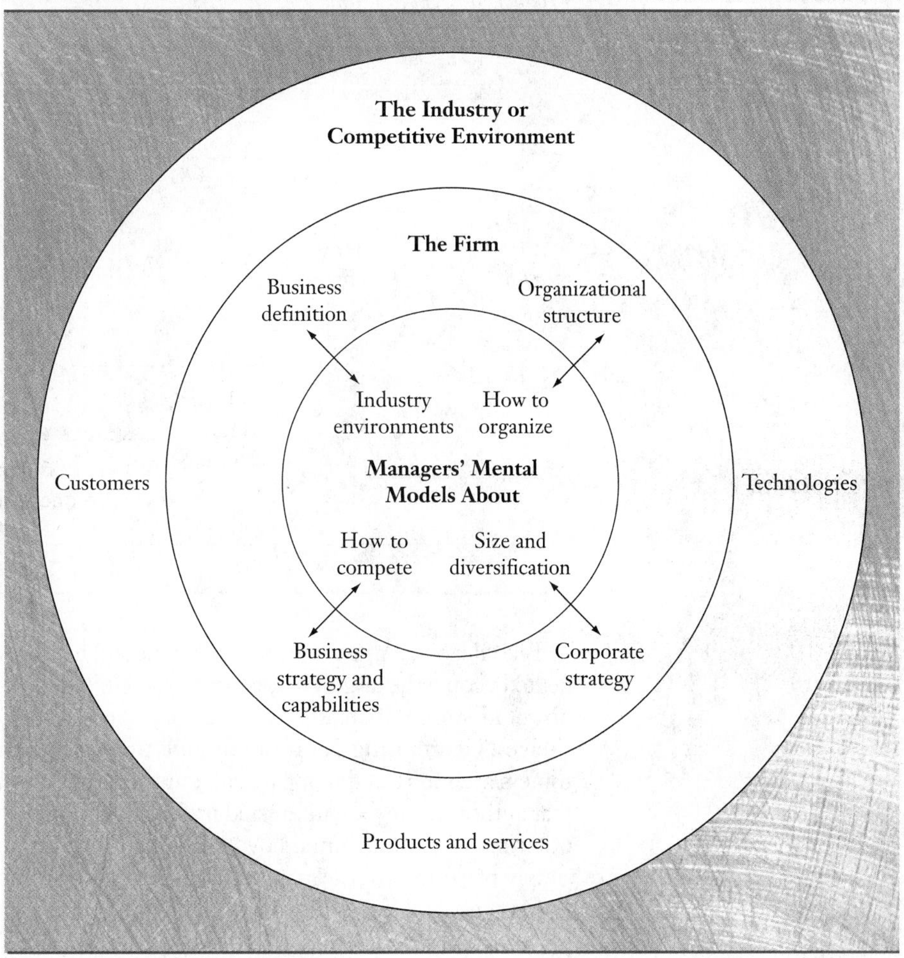

But, this is rarely the case. Consumer preferences and new product and process technologies are constantly evolving so that changes in industry dimensions are occurring all the time. As a result, an industry — or a competitive space — is very fluid. The arrows on each of the three dimensions of the figure in Exhibit 5.2 suggest this dynamic nature of industries.

Certainly the development of new technologies has a profound impact on industry environments. Entrepreneurial firms can exploit technological developments to create totally new products or services. For example, Peapod and Amazon (home pages of their Web sites are illustrated in Exhibit 5.3) are two new companies that owe their existence to the growing popularity of the Internet. Peapod (www.peapod.com) allows customers in major cities throughout the United States to order and purchase groceries using their personal computers and without ever leaving the comfort of their homes or apartments. Shoppers browse Peapod's extensive lists of items, select those items and the quantities they wish to purchase, and then indicate when Peapod should deliver those groceries to their home or apartment.

EXHIBIT 5.2

An Industry Environment Portrayed as a "Competitive Space" Defined by Customers, Products or Services, and Technologies

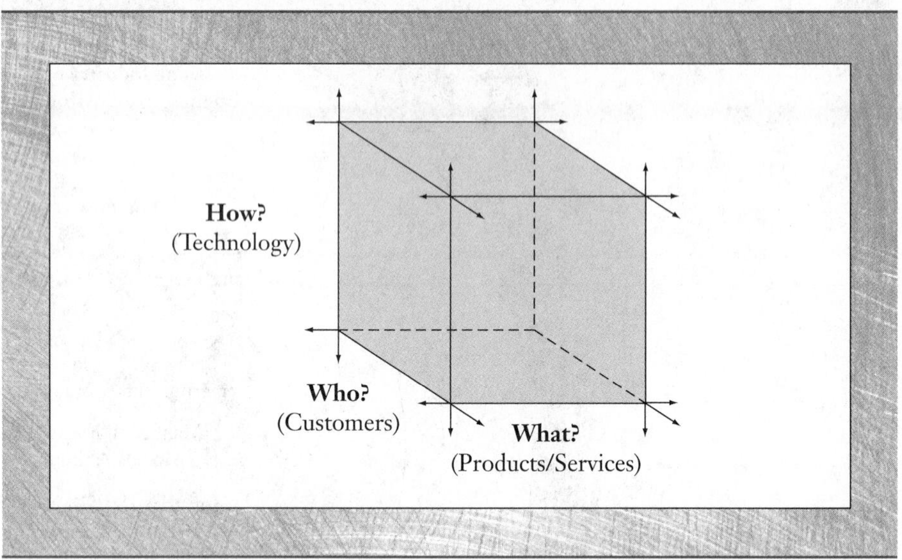

Like Peapod, Amazon (www.amazon.com) exploited growing interest in the Internet to become the largest bookstore in the United States, even though the company has no retail stores. Instead, customers can browse through Amazon's virtual "bookshelves," containing 2.5 million book titles, on their personal computers.[9] If customers are interested in a particular author, they can ask for a list of all the books by that author. If they are interested in a particular title, they can read reviews written by other readers and compiled by Amazon. Once customers make their selections, they simply place an order. Amazon then arranges for shipping. Other booksellers, such as Barnes and Noble and Borders, finally recognized the threat posed by Amazon and moved to offer their own sales sites on the Internet.[10] The accompanying Management Focus "Is Amazon's Lead Sustainable?" addresses the question of whether Amazon can maintain its position now that competitors have adopted the same technology.

In addition to the emergence of new technologies, demographic trends and shifts have an important impact on industry environments. The same desire for convenience that has encouraged many grocery customers to use the services provided by Peapod has given an important boost to companies like Boston Market. Boston Market thrives because it provides convenience. Far easier than the grocery shopping, cooking, and cleaning up that are required by home cooking, Boston Market provides its busy customers with quick, convenient meals that compare with home cooking. Similarly, as aging baby boomers begin to retire in the years ahead, they will create demand for many new services. New forms of health care and retirement living will inevitably emerge as entrepreneurs seek to meet the needs of this very large population.

As one or more of the dimensions in an industry changes, "holes" or new areas of opportunity are created. These holes create problems for industry incumbents for two reasons. First, firms operating in the industry may not perceive the emergence of these holes or opportunities, especially if they continue to enjoy satisfactory levels of performance. Second, new entrants that move into these holes (a focus of a later section of this chapter) may be so different — because they are serving different customers, providing

EXHIBIT 5.3

Home pages of Peapod (www.peapod.com) and Amazon (www.amazon.com)

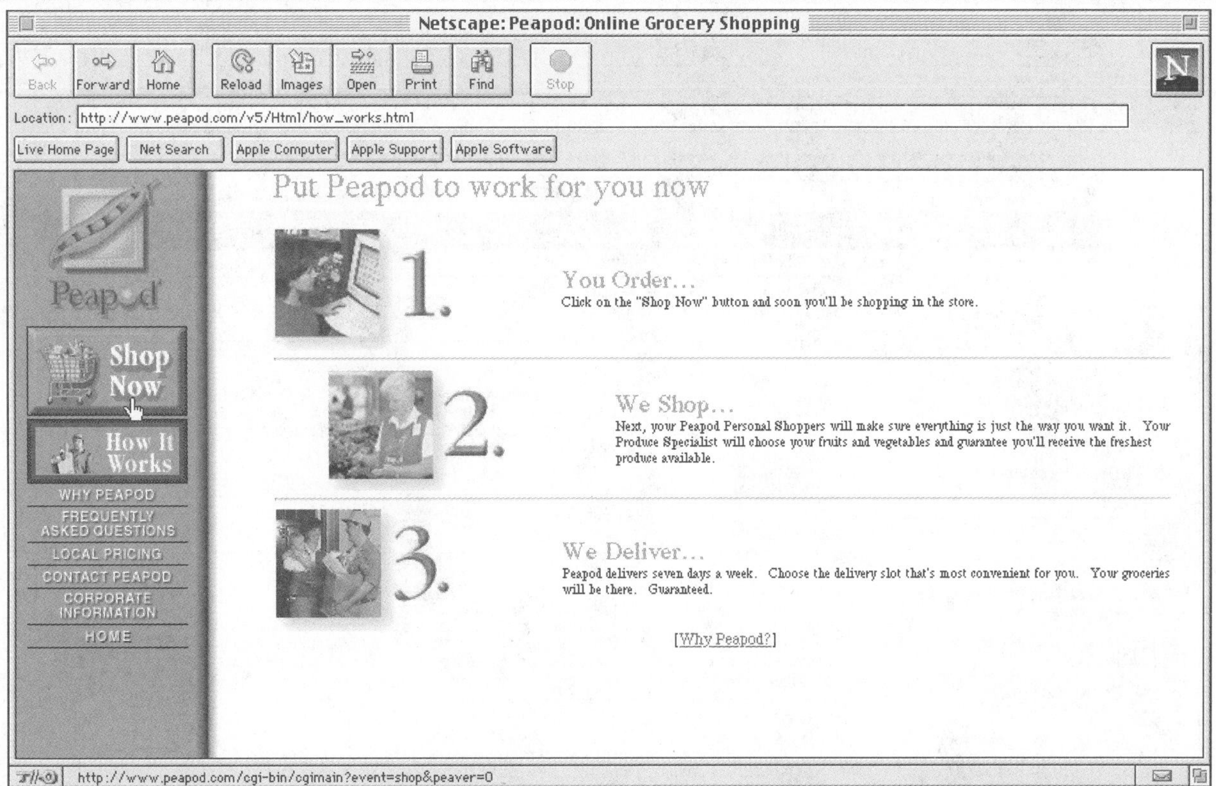

CONTINUED

different products or services, or using different technologies — that they are not recognized as serious threats by the managers of incumbent firms.

For example, steel minimill technology was developed by scientists in Nazi Germany toward the end of World War II when German steel plants could not obtain iron ore and other raw materials but did have ready access to scrap metal. The major integrated steel manufacturers failed to recognize the viability of minimill technology, and so this new technology remained dormant for more than 25 years until Nucor built its first minimill in the 1970s. As illustrated in Exhibit 5.4, Nucor entered the steel industry in the hole or opportunity created by the development of minimill technology. As suggested by the exhibit, Nucor's entry into the steel industry created no new products or services and developed no new customers; Nucor expanded the steel industry just by exploiting a previously unused technology.

INDUSTRY NORMS

Firms in the same industry typically share a common language and similar understandings about how to compete.[11] These shared industry norms result as managers of firms in the same industry move through the same educational programs, develop common professional networks, attend the same professional meetings, and read the same industry trade publications. These activities promote and reinforce conformity

EXHIBIT 5.3 *CONTINUED*

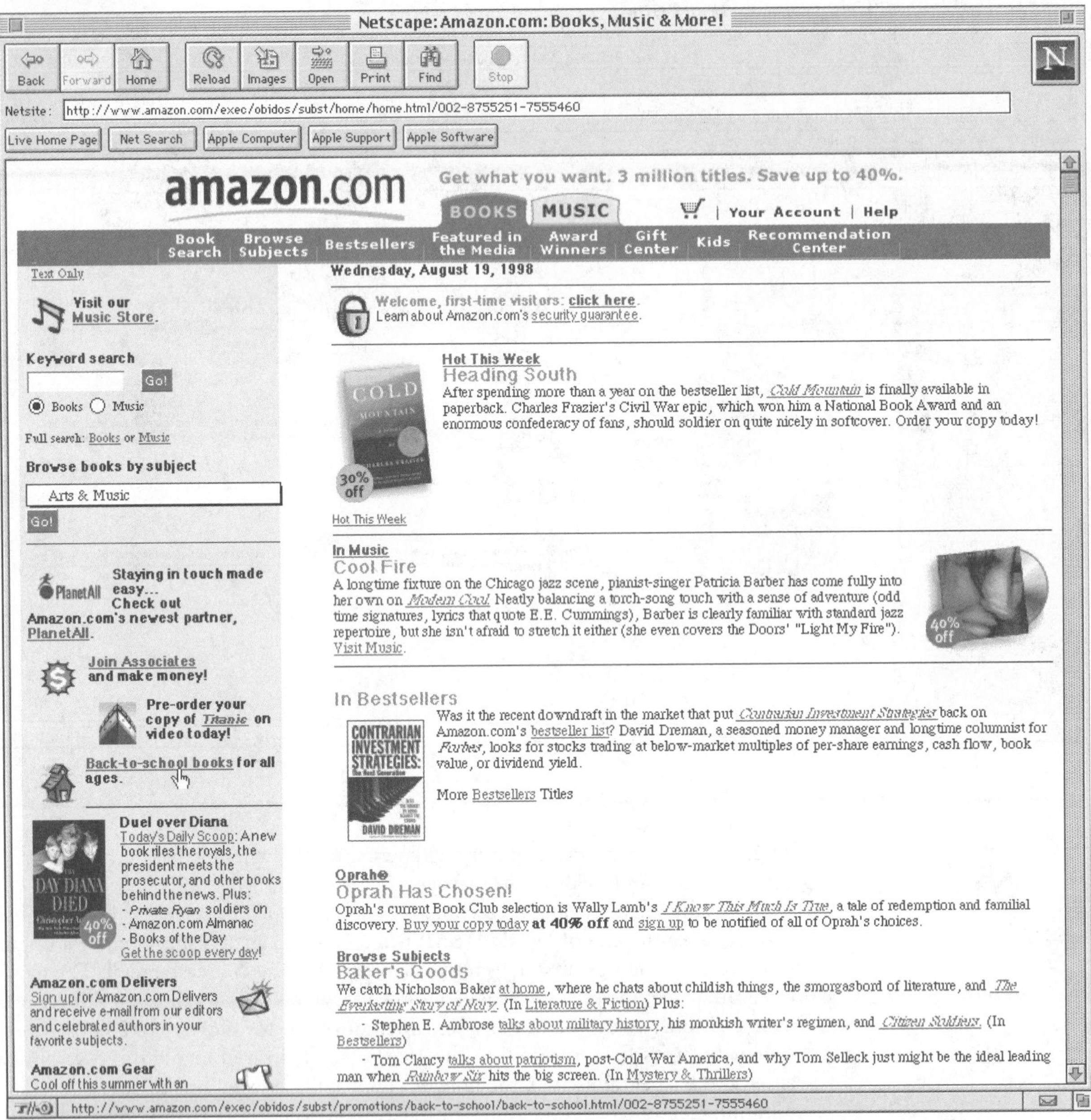

SOURCE: Amazon.com is a registered trademark or trademark of Amazon.com, Inc. in the U.S. and/or other countries.

to industry norms, and managers of firms in the same industries develop a "common body of knowledge."[12]

On the positive side, these shared norms help in providing industry standards, in encouraging consumer acceptance of products and services, and in facilitating incremental technological developments and improvements. On the other hand, these shared understandings remain relatively stable over time and can easily fail

MANAGEMENT FOCUS

IS AMAZON'S LEAD SUSTAINABLE?[1]

Amazon's success as an Internet business has been remarkable, but with both Barnes and Noble and Borders now selling books over the Internet, can Amazon sustain its competitive edge? After all, the competitive advantage framework introduced in Chapter 3 would suggest that once competitors imitate another firm's innovation, its lead or competitive advantage will quickly disappear, and the best the firm can hope for is competitive parity with its rivals. So, it's no wonder that after Barnes and Noble and Borders introduced their own online virtual bookstores, one pundit described the company as "Amazon-dot-toast" and a *Fortune* magazine headline read, "Why Barnes & Noble May Crush Amazon."

Still, Amazon may not only survive, it may well prosper and maintain its lead over its Internet competitors. Amazon benefits from time and investment — two factors that are key to developing the capabilities and resources associated with competitive advantage. By being the first to open its online bookstore, Amazon has a big lead over its new Internet competitors, considerably more experience, and many important advantages, including its reputation as a "first-mover." Amazon is already planning on offering books in German and Japanese in order to serve those important markets. The company has also been investing heavily in regional warehouses and distribution centers to better serve customers. To further improve distribution, Amazon has hired a logistics manager from Wal-Mart, a company widely regarded as having one of the best inventory and distribution systems of any retailer. In addition, Amazon has worked hard to build name recognition by making substantial marketing and advertising expenditures—over $100 million annually—and by placing advertisements in such publications as *The New Yorker* and *The New York Review of Books.*

Amazon has now served more than one million customers in 160 countries. The number of customers buying books from Amazon rose by more than 50 percent during the first three months after Barnes and Noble began selling books over its own Internet site! In fact, Amazon is by far the most important retail site on the Internet, and it receives more than four times as many hits as Barnes and Noble's Web site.

By having the advantage of being on the Web longer than any of its rivals, by seeking to develop a strong marketing presence and gain a large customer following while also developing a state-of-the-art inventory and distribution system, and by continuing to invest heavily in the business, Amazon is doing many of the things necessary to build a sustainable competitive advantage over its competitors. The company's experiences will offer many lessons for other entrepreneurial managers and their companies. ■

[1]Much of the information contained in this Management Focus appeared in A. Deutschman, "The Amazin' Amazon Man," *Gentlemen's Quarterly,* May 1998, 175–180, and G. Anders, "Amazon.com Sales More Than Quadruple," *The Wall Street Journal,* July 23, 1998, 85.

to keep pace with changes in the environment. As a result, the managers of incumbent firms might be vigilant in watching for new products and services, new customer groups, new technologies, and potential rivals, but they are likely to be watching for products and services, customers, technologies, and rivals that are consistent with or similar to current industry norms.

COGNITIVE LIMITATIONS

Even if shared industry norms blind managers to new rivals, shouldn't managers of incumbent firms at least notice major changes in industry dimensions, such as changes in consumer tastes and new technological developments? After all, many

EXHIBIT 5.4

The Development of Minimill Technology and Nucor's Entry Expanded the Steel Industry Along Only One Dimension: Technology

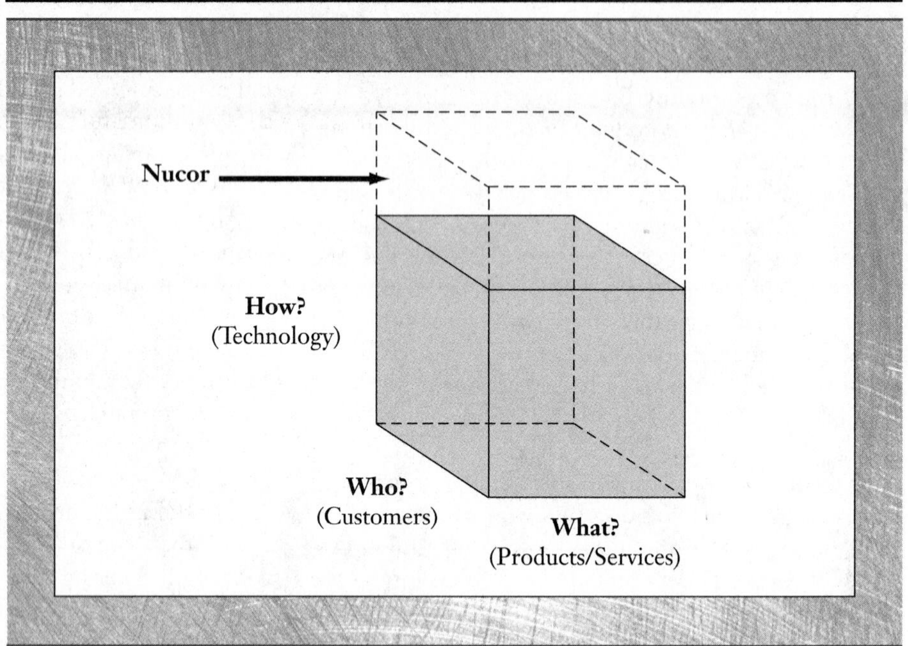

if not most firms employ sophisticated market research, forecasting, planning, and R&D departments that should alert top managers to important new developments in their industry environments. Evidence suggests, however, that even with all these resources, a number of factors may prevent managers from appreciating the importance of changing industry dimensions.

First, managers may simply fail to notice changes in their firms' environments. Most strategic issues "do not present themselves to the decision maker in convenient ways; problems and opportunities in particular must be identified in streams of ambiguous, largely verbal data."[13] Psychology researchers suggest that this problem is compounded because individuals make sense only of what they perceive to be key or important events. Individuals tend to recall the most obvious attributes of a particular situation. And, as noted in Chapter 2, individuals also seek confirmation for their beliefs[14] and will, therefore, pay greater attention to events that support their views—views that were formed by past experiences. "Managers operate on mental representations of the world and those representations are likely to be of historical environments rather than current ones."[15] "When faced with a totally new situation, we tend always to attach ourselves to the objects, to the flavor of the most recent past. *We look at the present through a rear-view mirror.*"[16]

Furthermore, managers often cannot make objective or rational evaluations of the data they collect, so a new rival offering a new and different product or service or employing a new and different technology might easily be ignored or rationalized away by incumbents. Traditional industry analysis tools assume that defining the nature of threats or rivals is not a problem. Yet, considerable evidence suggests that *defining the nature of a competitive threat is a problem* for the managers of incumbent firms. Changes in industry dimensions may not be perceived as important by the managers of incumbent firms, *especially if their firms continue to enjoy satisfactory levels of performance.*

Perhaps the most remarkable feature of organizational behavior is that the managers of complex organizations often develop and implement sophisticated strategies that are based on untested assumptions or understandings of the environment that may no longer be appropriate.[17] Moreover, many researchers have concluded that these understandings are so strongly held that they can be altered only by a crisis or calamity, such as a loss of profitability or even bankruptcy.

First-Mover Advantages

Traditional perspectives on industry structure suggest that following the entry of a new rival into an established industry, incumbent firms will move quickly to counter the initiatives of the new player. Yet, many factors may prevent the effective retaliation predicted by traditional models. First, as already suggested, managers of incumbent firms may simply fail to "see" the entrant. Given the effects of industry norms and managers' cognitive limitations, a new entrant could easily proceed to carve out a niche and establish a presence without being detected.

Second, even after a new entrant is detected, managers of incumbent firms will have to determine whether the new rival poses a serious threat, and, if so, how they should respond. The Five Forces Model emphasizes the importance of establishing "credible deterrence" to prevent other firms from entering the industry, but *the more relevant issue is whether incumbent firms identify the "credible threats" posed by new entrants.* New entrants are likely to be working in a previously unoccupied area of the industry or competitive space. The managers of incumbent firms could easily assume that the niches occupied by new entrants are neither viable nor large enough to be of concern.

This kind of myopic thinking, continuing over many years, may explain the decline of Western Union:

> Western Union's troubles grew out of a parochial mind-set that dates back 113 years. Then a high-tech giant sending messages by Morse code, the company turned down rights to the telephone, telling Alexander Graham Bell that sending voice over wire would never replace telegraph, particularly for business communication.[18]

A similar scenario helps to explain the emergence of natural cereals:

> After a rise in consumer interest in "health foods," all-natural cereals together had a market share of about 0.5 percent in early 1972. By early 1973 the naturals' share had climbed to about 4 percent, and in mid-1974 natural cereals accounted for about 10 percent of the market. Testimony and documentary evidence suggest that the shifts in consumer taste that led to this sharp increase in demand *were not well anticipated by most of the established firms.* As a result, a substantial new market segment was up for grabs.[19]

Additional research also suggests that when confronted by a threatening situation, managers seek more information in order to better understand the threat, but the information overload that results can create confusion. In this confusion, the true nature of the threat is obscured, and managers are more likely to shift their focus back to less strategic concerns. The paradox of information gathering is that, instead of leading to a better understanding, managers are likely to develop a "threat rigidity" so that they end up *actively ignoring* new rivals.[20]

Furthermore, even if the managers of incumbent firms do perceive the seriousness of the threat, new rivals will still enjoy a number of "first-mover" advantages. Once they recognize the threat posed by new entrants, the managers of incumbent firms will still have to determine how and when to retaliate. Some responses could emerge quickly. For example, incumbent firms could simply lower prices in order to improve the value-price ratio of their products. More elaborate responses, such as developing new products or services that are true substitutes for those offered by the entrant, may require large investments and considerably more time to implement, especially if the incumbent firms are large and bureaucratic.

Even fast responses may come too late, however. Research suggests that "first-movers" enjoy market share, pricing, and other advantages not enjoyed by "second-movers." Most studies conclude that first-mover advantages can continue for many years, so that even if incumbent firms respond quickly and are able to offer products that are close substitutes, a new entrant could still enjoy many advantages for many years.[21]

The Likely Outcome: The Strategic Retreat and Decline of Incumbent Firms

The evidence from many industries suggests that the likely outcome of the combination of the preceding four factors is not only that new firms enter established industries, but also that incumbent firms often retreat and enter periods of decline. Managers of incumbent firms typically describe their firms' retreats as a "rationalization" or a "downsizing," yet rarely do these strategic retreats result in a strengthened position. New rivals are rarely content to remain in smaller niches when they have opportunities to exploit their newly won customer loyalty, innovative products or services, and technologies to move into additional market segments. Drucker calls the advance of new rivals "entrepreneurial judo":

> Entrepreneurial judo aims first at securing a beachhead, and one which the established leaders either do not defend at all or defend only halfheartedly.... Once that beachhead has been secured, that is once the newcomers have an adequate market and an adequate revenue stream, they then move on to the rest of the "beach" and finally to the whole "island."[22]

Even when an incumbent's strategic retreat does provide it with a period of relief, the continuing advances of its rivals will sooner or later make the incumbent's situation untenable. The managers of incumbent firms may actually believe they are moving their companies to more defensible market segments; the paradox of strategic retreat is that competition usually intensifies along two fronts. First, competition increases because industry incumbents retreat to smaller segments of the industry, forcing them to compete more intensively for a smaller piece of the pie. Additional competition comes from the new rival or rivals that are seeking to expand from their "beachhead" into larger parts of the "island" or competitive arena.

The steel industry provides an excellent example of the dangers of strategic retreat and how retreat actually invites advances by new entrants. Nearly all the major integrated steel manufacturers have abandoned the market for steel rod and other structural products such as I-beams. This segment of the market has traditionally offered only low margins, and the major integrated mills have encountered intense competition not only from foreign steel producers but also from a growing number of domestic minimills, such as Nucor Steel. In retreating to what their managers believed to be the more defensible and higher-margin market for sheet steel, the major integrated mills have enjoyed very few benefits. Not only is the excess capacity of the major integrated producers now focused on a smaller segment of the total steel market, forcing downward pressure on sheet steel prices, but the minimills have not been content to remain in the structural steel segment of the market. Nucor, for example, has already constructed new mills that produce sheet steel, defying predictions that minimills would never be able to produce high-quality sheet steel.[23]

Traditional industry analysis tools assume that *incumbents and their rivals play the same game, battle on the same turf, and abide by the same rules*. From a strategic point of view, however, new entrants would be much more likely to think and act in new and totally different ways. Rather than invading an already crowded playing field, an entrant might seek to find or even create a new, more promising "game" to play — a game that has become possible due to changing industry dimensions, including new consumer demands and technological developments. And, because a new rival might choose to develop a totally new game rather than take on established firms in an old game, the rules of the game will also be different. The managers of incumbent firms may not even see this new game as a threat to their organizations, and the decisions they make may be totally inappropriate given changes in their industry environments. Research has shown that when confronted by new technologies, the managers of incumbent firms do not embrace the new technologies but instead seek to improve their own technologies even as these old technologies are quickly becoming obsolete.[24] For example, the most efficient steam locomotives and the most powerful vacuum tubes were developed *after* the introduction of diesel locomotives and transistors.[25]

Patterns in the Evolution of Industries

The model of industry structuring that we've just developed suggests that industries will evolve in common and fairly predictable ways. In this section, we describe some important characteristics of industry evolution and offer examples from many industries. We begin by examining the "attack" of new entrants and then consider how incumbent firms respond.

The "Attack" of New Entrants

The attack of new entrants is interesting for at least three reasons:

First, the managers of successful new rivals generally do not attack incumbent firms directly, but instead are more likely to enter an industry at the "holes" that are created by changes in industry dimensions, such as new consumer preferences and the adoption of new product and process technologies. The most dangerous new rivals are unlikely to attack the products or markets of incumbent firms directly. Potential rivals would be foolish to attack incumbent firms' positions when lucrative opportunities exist to create or meet new demands. New rivals are more likely to offer new or different types of products or services or to provide these products or services using new or different technologies.

Let's consider two examples from the automobile industry — first, we'll look at the classic story of how General Motors responded to Henry Ford's lock on the industry, and then we'll consider the Japanese invasion of the U.S. market in the 1970s and 1980s. In the early 1920s, General Motors faced the question of how to attack Ford, which at the time enjoyed a 60 percent share of the market for automobiles and trucks. At the same time, GM's Chevrolet unit had a mere 4 percent of the same market. Alfred Sloan, GM's visionary chief executive, summarized his company's situation this way:

> With Ford in almost complete possession of the low-priced field, *it would have been suicidal to compete with him head on*. No conceivable amount of capital short of the United States Treasury could have sustained the losses required to take volume away from him at his own game. The strategy we devised was to take a bite from the top of his position ... and in this way build up Chevrolet volume on a profitable basis.[26]

Note that Sloan recognized how foolhardy it would be for General Motors to take on the Ford Motor Company directly. Instead, GM's strategy was to offer cars that would be perceived as unique, aimed at buyers looking for vehicles that were more unusual than Ford's standardized cars. GM's strategy was phenomenally successful, and the company soon overtook Ford as the number one automobile manufacturer.

More recently, the successful entry of the Japanese automobile manufacturers into the U.S. market was possible because their small cars filled a new market demand for fuel-efficient vehicles that had not been well met by any of the Big Three producers. In fact, the Japanese invasion of the U.S. automobile market closely follows the dynamic model developed in this chapter. The Japanese manufacturers exploited changes in industry dimensions, namely the demand for more fuel-efficient cars and new production technologies. Because the U.S. Big Three producers possessed a quite different understanding of their environment, their managers failed to appreciate the seriousness of the threat posed by the Japanese producers. Brock Yates describes what he calls "the Detroit Mind," and he quotes a former U.S. automobile executive:

> If they [U.S. automobile executives] weren't isolated in Bloomfield Hills, driving their Cadillacs and Lincolns and Imperials, they'd understand why imported cars sell so well. Their automobiles are built to their life-styles, and they have no comprehension of why people in Los Angeles, San Francisco, Scarsdale, or Fairfield County, Connecticut, want Mercedeses, BMW's, and Hondas instead of Buicks and LeBarons.[27]

The Japanese producers further exploited the "blindness" of the Big Three producers by not attacking directly. Instead, the Japanese producers carved out and then dominated the small-car market, selling in what the Big Three producers regarded as an unattractive market segment due to the low margins of small cars. In describing the Japanese strategy, Yutaka Natayama, Nissan's representative in the United States, was quoted as having said, "What we should do is get better and creep up slowly, so we'll be good — and the customer will think we're good — before Detroit even knows about us."[28] Using the three-dimensional model of industries, the Japanese invasion of the U.S. automobile industry involved altering or expanding the industry along both the technological and product dimensions, as illustrated in Exhibit 5.5.

EXHIBIT **5.5**

The Japanese Invasion of the U.S. Automobile Industry: Expanding the Industry Along the Technological and Product Dimensions

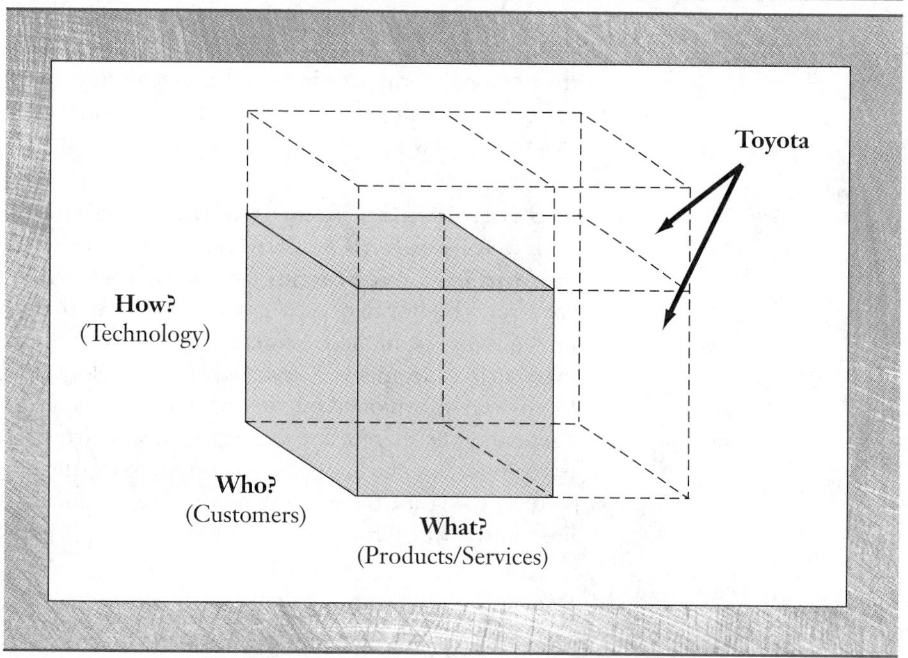

This pattern — of new entrants moving into "holes" in the competitive space or creating new competitive space rather than attacking incumbent firms directly — is observed in the experience of many industries. Apple Computer sought to tap the market for individual computing that had been ignored by virtually all other computer makers. Nucor did not attack the integrated steel manufacturers directly. In fact, Nucor began manufacturing structural steel products primarily for its own internal consumption.

The dynamic model also suggests that the managers of successful new entrants generally offer new products or services that capitalize on changes in more than one industry dimension. For example, a successful new entrant is likely to introduce a new product that not only responds to a change in consumer preferences but also incorporates a new technological development or a new production process. New rivals have many incentives to capitalize on changes in more than one industry dimension. By moving into a "hole" in the competitive space and by not only filling an unmet customer need but doing so in a novel way, a new entrant may be able to disguise itself even better from incumbent firms. Such a new rival might look sufficiently "different" to the managers of incumbent firms that they will have quite a difficult time recognizing the new entrant as a serious threat.

Again, the Japanese automobile manufacturers provide an example. Not only did they offer a new product — the small, fuel-efficient car—but they also exploited developments in manufacturing technology. Wal-Mart stores not only provided customers with a unique product mix, but the company also incorporated technological developments that allowed it to operate with a very low cost structure. Similarly, Apple not only sought to tap an unserved market for personal computing, but, to do so, the company took advantage of important advances in microprocessor technology. In fact, Apple offers a classic example of exploiting changes along more than one industry dimension. As illustrated in Exhibit 5.6, Apple's development of the personal computer involved the exploitation of a new technology (microprocessors) to develop a new product (the personal computer) that was then marketed to a totally new segment of computer users (individuals and households).

The model also suggests that the managers of successful new entrants seek to establish strong niches from which they then expand into ever larger areas in the competitive space. New entrants are rarely content to occupy niche positions in their industries. Although their initial presence may be modest, new entrants will have many incentives to move beyond their initial market segments. Consumers may develop a loyalty to the new entrant, and this loyalty can be exploited by offering a broader range of products or services. Similarly, the possibility of enjoying economies of scale from a broader application of the technology will also encourage a new entrant to expand beyond an initial niche position.

Over the years, the Japanese automobile manufacturers gradually expanded their car lines, introducing products that now fill the complete spectrum of the automobile market,

EXHIBIT 5.6

Apple's Entry into the Computer Industry Involved Expanding the Industry Along the Customer, Product, and Technology Dimensions

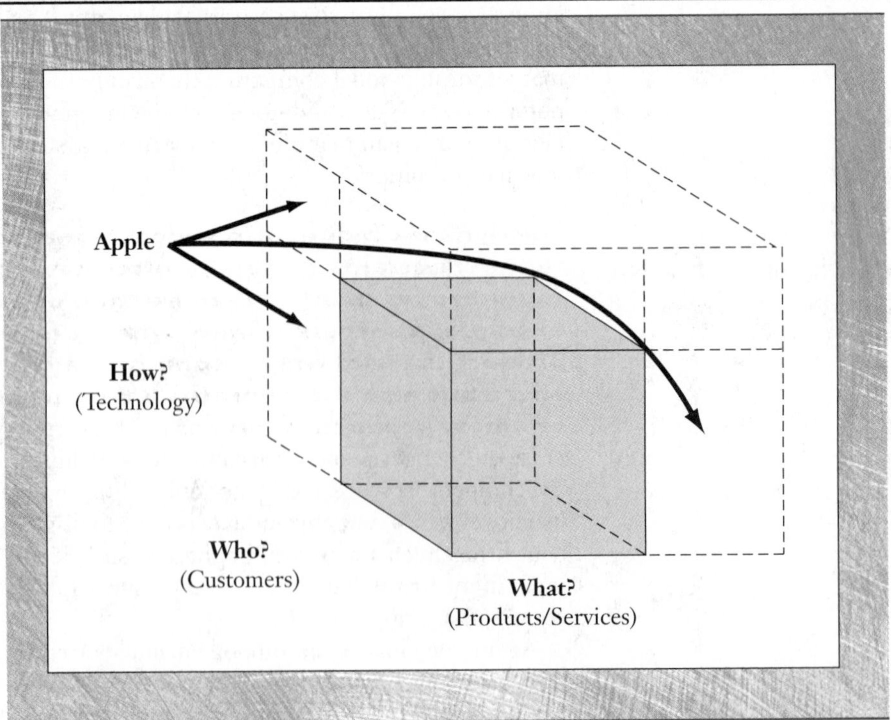

from small, fuel-efficient cars to sports cars, pickups, sport-utility vehicles, minivans, and luxury cars. In only a very short time, Wal-Mart grew from a small, regional company to surpass Sears as the nation's largest retailer. And, as already described, Nucor did not remain content producing structural steel products but is now seeking to apply its minimill technology to manufacture flat-rolled sheet steel, invading markets the large integrated steelmakers once thought were off limits to minimills.

Asleep at the Switch: Patterns in the Responses of Incumbent Firms' Managers

The preceding section focused on the characteristics of new firms entering established industries. This section focuses on three patterns that are common in the response of incumbent firms' managers to the entry of new rivals.

Managers of incumbent firms are rarely able to match new entrants' products, services, or technological capabilities. What do salsa, diesel locomotives, personal computers, mountain bikes, semiconductors, aluminum cans, varietal wines, and digital photography have in common? Each of these product categories was introduced by outsiders or new entrants to their respective industries. And, for most of these product categories, incumbent firms in the industry offered their own versions of these products only *after* the sales of these new products became fairly substantial. For example, before any of the major makers of condiments offered their own salsa products, salsa had already become the largest-selling condiment product.

In Chapter 2, we emphasized that managers' mental models are often locked in understandings of their competitive environments that do not allow them to recognize either changing industry dimensions or the presence of new rivals. In fact, managers may often fail to appreciate the challenges posed by new entrants until long after decline has already crippled their firms. In his company's 1982 annual report, David Roderick, the CEO of U.S. Steel, wrote that "we have been shocked out of our complacency and smugness. We now realize that American industry has no manifest destiny to be always first, always right, always best."[29] Roderick was shocked only because he and the managers of other integrated steel mills had been able to ignore for a very long time the existence of new competitors and the problems that were apparent and well documented by industry observers as early as the 1950s.

The result of this lack of awareness is that incumbent firms are rarely able to match the developments of new rivals. In those situations in which managers of incumbent firms are aware of the important developments in their industries, their companies will probably lack the necessary understandings (i.e., mental models), expertise, and technologies to respond effectively to the new entrants' initiatives. And, even in those cases in which incumbent firms can match a new rival's initiatives, the new rival may have already accrued significant first-mover advantages.

When confronted by new rivals, the managers of incumbent firms are likely to respond (1) by withdrawing to supposedly "safer" areas in the competitive space, (2) by diversifying, or (3) by improving current offerings of products and services. When confronted by a new entrant, incumbent firms might respond by vigorously challenging the new entrant's products or services or by acquiring, developing, or even improving on the new entrant's technology. The model offered in this chapter suggests, however, that such a vigorous response is unlikely. Asleep at the switch, the managers of incumbent firms are more likely to let considerable time pass before noticing the threat of a new entrant, and, then, they are likely to let even more time pass before taking action. By this time, the new entrant may have already secured a comfortable niche, may be enjoying a number of first-mover advantages, and may already be on its way toward challenging incumbent firms' positions of dominance. As a result, a counterattack by incumbent firms, if launched, will typically come too late to be effective.

At this point, incumbent firms will consider a number of other responses. For example, the managers of incumbent firms will often complain about unfair competition. This was certainly the case among managers of the automotive and steel industries who asked for quotas on imported automobiles and steel. Diversification into unrelated businesses is another strategy many industry executives have adopted in order to "escape" from markets that are becoming less attractive.

At the same time, managers are reluctant to abandon long-standing markets and to write off what had been productive investments.[30] A good deal of research evidence suggests that managers caught in such a situation may seek to "fight it out" by retreating to what they believe to be a more defensible niche. In fact, managers of incumbent firms often pursue improvements in existing products or services even though these products or services may have already been rendered obsolete by the products, services, or technologies introduced by a new entrant.[31] Whatever the initial response, the result is that incumbents tend to be more reactive than proactive. Incumbent managers are much more likely to retreat to what they believe will be more defensible positions than to launch effective counterattacks.

The managers of incumbent firms rarely enjoy any sort of long-run benefit from a strategic withdrawal from market segments invaded by new entrants. As already described, this retreat to supposedly more defensible positions is a paradox. Instead of finding a safe harbor, managers of incumbent firms are likely to find that competition has actually escalated. Competition among incumbent firms is likely to intensify as they begin serving a smaller segment of the industry. These incumbent firms will have excess capacity, and they will be fighting even more vigorously for shares of a smaller pie. Furthermore, competition from successful new entrants is likely to intensify as they proceed to move beyond their initial niche positions into additional areas in the competitive arena.

Often, successful new entrants totally restructure the industries they enter. For example, here's how two researchers analyzing the steel industry have assessed the impact of minimill producers like Nucor:

> Minimills have established more or less complete dominance in several product lines, and in these markets the integrated firms now exist on the forbearance of the minimills rather than the reverse. *The former fringe of the industry is now the principal locus of the restructuring forces that have been generated by overall secular decline. Far from being a dismissible appendage to the "real" steel industry, the nonintegrated sector has become its dynamic force.*[32]

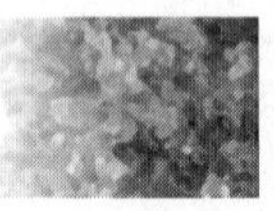

Using the Dynamic Model for Industry Analysis

Now that we have introduced a dynamic model of industry structuring and offered some specific propositions about the ways in which industries evolve, we want to describe how this dynamic model can be used to conduct analyses of specific industries. Although the dynamic model suggests that any industry can be analyzed along three dimensions — customers (the "who" dimension), products and services (the "what" dimension), and technologies (the "how" dimension) — use of the model requires that the analyst identify the relevant labels for the three dimensions.

For example, in analyzing the food industry, labeling groups based on chronological age might be relevant and provide useful labels for the customer (or "who") dimension. Babies have needs that are quite distinct from the wants of younger children. Similarly, working parents with school-age children have needs and wants different from those of senior citizens.

On the other hand, customer groups based on chronological age might not be particularly useful for analyzing the customer dimension of the automobile industry. For example, the automobile industry cannot really target buyers younger than 16 years old in most states. Furthermore, car-buying habits are much more likely to be influenced by such factors as disposable income and driving habits than by chronological age. Thus, for analyzing the customer dimension of the automobile industry, a far more useful set of labels might be "first-time car buyers" and "repeat buyers."

The major automobile companies develop much more detailed customer segmentation information through their market research efforts, but even this simple segmentation will be very helpful in understanding changes in the industry. For example, the Chrysler Neon, the redesigned Ford Escort, Saturn, and the new Chevrolet Cavalier were all introduced by the Big Three producers in the mid-1990s. They were key products for the Big Three because they were aimed at attracting first-time car buyers — an important customer segment in which the Big Three have lost ground to foreign automobile producers. First-time car buyers are important to automobile companies because many car buyers tend to buy the same brand of automobile if they have a positive experience. Unfortunately, none of the Big Three producers scored a "home run" among first-time car buyers with any of these models, suggesting that the weakness of these companies among this critically important customer group will continue for some time.

Similar types of analyses are required to develop labels for all three dimensions. The "what," or products and services, dimension poses some challenges. On the one hand, because any firm could hypothetically manufacture just about any product or provide any service, analysts might be tempted to define the products and services dimension too broadly. On the other hand, the products and services dimension must be broader than current conceptualizations of the industry or a single firm's own line of products or services so that the analysis can consider how the industry is likely to evolve. For example, Exhibit 5.7 offers one possible analysis of the products and services dimension of the computer industry.

Note that the analysis illustrated in Exhibit 5.7 includes not only personal computers, but also Internet service, software, high-technology components (such as microprocessors), other hardware components, workstations, minicomputers and mainframes, and information technology consultation services. By including such a broad range of products and services and by also labeling the various firms that produce and provide these products and services, the user can quickly get a feel for or an understanding of how the industry has evolved and which portions of the product dimension are more "crowded" than others. By doing some further research and attaching revenue and net income figures to the various products and services, the analyst can also get a feel for the relative size of these various product and service markets. Such an analysis would reveal, for example, that software,

EXHIBIT 5.7

An Analysis of the Products and Services Dimension of the Computer Industry

Internet Service	Software	High-Tech Components	Personal Computers	Workstations	Mini-Computers and Mainframes	Consulting Services
AOL, Yahoo!, Netscape, Microsoft	Microsoft	Intel, AMD	Compaq, H-P, IBM, Apple	H-P	IBM, Unisys	Andersen, EDS, IBM, Unisys

microprocessors, and consultation services generate the vast majority of the total net income generated by the computer industry.

Students often have difficulty in selecting appropriate labels for the technology or "how" dimension. In some cases, the analysis can be very straightforward. For example, in most manufacturing industries, the technology dimension is usually fairly clear. Exhibit 5.8 illustrates some possibilities for mapping the technology dimension of the automobile industry. Note in Exhibit 5.8 that the same firms have been placed on both diagrams, illustrating that there's no single "right" way to label these dimensions. Similarly, Exhibit 5.9 illustrates one way to map the technology dimension of the pharmaceutical industry. Note that although all the major pharmaceutical companies used to rely on random testing of chemical compounds to "discover" new drug products, they are now moving toward genetic research techniques to identify new treatment methods for diseases.

In analyzing any of the three dimensions, it is important to keep in mind the objectives of the analysis — to understand how the industry has changed and is likely to change, to identify areas of opportunity, and to rethink the structure of the industry. Thus, the choice of labels must help managers understand not only the nature of competition in the industry at the present time, but also how the various dimensions will be changing and how these changes will affect competition and the structure of the industry in the future.

Implications: Some Specific Recommendations for Managers

Given the dynamic model of industry structuring described in this chapter, how should managers formulate strategy? Before we suggest answers to this question, consider how one noted researcher has described the strategy formulation process:

> In general terms, strategy formation in most organizations can be thought of as revolving around the interplay of three basic forces: (a) an *environment* that changes continuously but irregularly, with frequent discontinuities and wide swings in its rate of change, (b) an organizational operating system, or *bureaucracy*, that above all seeks to stabilize its actions, despite the characteristics of the

EXHIBIT 5.8

Two Analyses of the Technology Dimension of the Automobile Industry

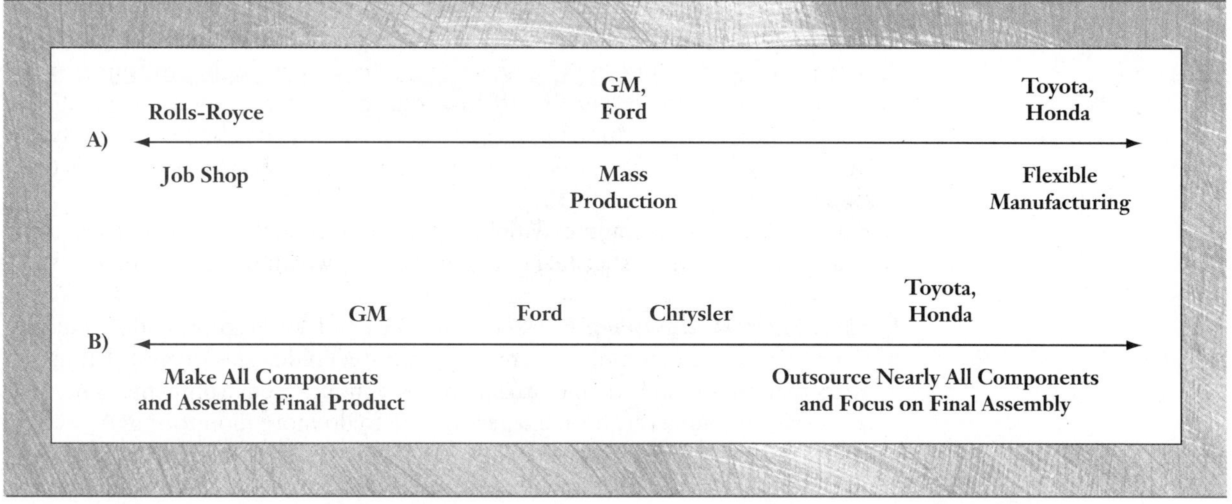

environment it serves, and (c) a *leadership* whose role is to mediate between these two forces, to maintain the stability of the organization's operating system while at the same time insuring its adaptation to environmental change.[33]

Note the similarities between the characterization of the strategy formulation process and the model of strategic management introduced in Chapter 1 of this text. Both include management, industry environment, and firm components. In addition, just as the environment is said to change "continuously but irregularly" in the preceding quotation, this chapter's model of industry structuring proposes that industries are not static, but continually evolving. Furthermore, as in the preceding paragraph, we have argued that the leadership or management component of the model often fails to maintain an alignment between firms and the environments in which they must compete.

EXHIBIT 5.9

An Analysis of the Technology Dimension of the Pharmaceutical Industry

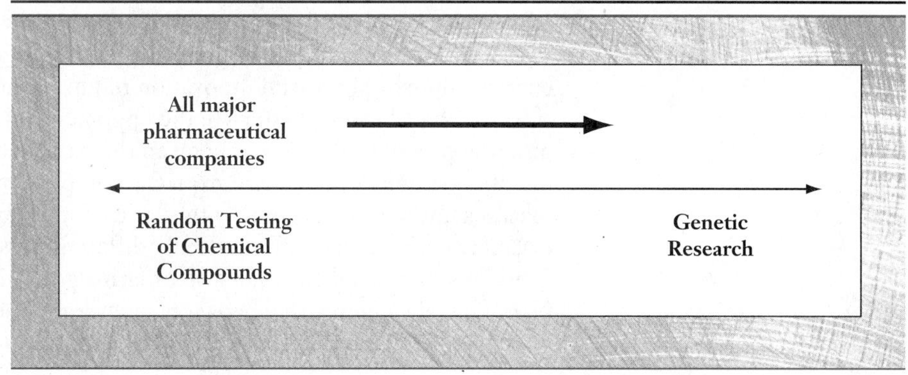

Our model of strategic management suggests that managers must not only understand the current relevant dimensions of their firms' industry environments, but they must also think about how these dimensions will change over time. They must also think creatively and imaginatively about where their firms should be in the evolving competitive environments. How, for example, can their firms be on the cutting edge, creating "new" competitive space by developing consumer interest in new products or services or by developing new technological capabilities? This kind of managerial thinking, insight, and creativity may be the most valuable resource organizations can possess, and it is certainly a key source of competitive advantage.

Beyond this broad recommendation, our dynamic model of industry structuring also suggests some more specific recommendations, which we outline here:

- *Managers must actively anticipate the future.* Many of the examples offered in this chapter from the automobile, computer, and steel industries suggest that managers tend to do too little monitoring of their industry environments. The answer is not, however, for managers simply to do more monitoring. As we've already suggested, monitoring is likely to be focused by past experience and industry norms. As a result, managers are likely to miss potentially important developments, and they are likely to look for potential new entrants that look like their own firms. In addition to monitoring, managers must more actively anticipate the future by exploring the unoccupied and newly emerging areas of opportunities both within *and outside* their industries.

  This means that more companies must adopt the strategies of companies like 3M and Rubbermaid. Both of these companies have explicit goals that a certain percentage of annual sales must come from products that did not exist in previous years.[34] Rubbermaid has described its emphasis on new products as one of its fundamental strengths: "Our goal is to have 30 percent of sales each year come from products which were not in the line five years earlier."[35]

  Some companies have gone even further. News articles about Sony have noted that the company schedules dates for the introduction of extensions to a new product and the date a replacement for a new product will be introduced *before the new product itself is introduced into the marketplace.*
- *Innovation is more important than imitation.* When the dimensions of industry environments are changing continuously, imitation should be less useful than innovation. In fact, as suggested in Chapter 3, competitive advantage is much more likely to result from innovation than from mere imitation. Firms that do copy other firms' innovations must focus more attention on adding knowledge and value to those innovations.
- *It's important to think like an industry outsider.* Innovations and strategic alternatives will not necessarily emerge from a better understanding of the industry's current context. Successful innovation requires that managers think like outsiders so that they can better see the opportunities that changes in industry dimensions will offer. This may mean that research and development staff members should be separated from the company bureaucracy. It might also mean paying more attention to the contrarian voices or iconoclasts within the organization who may offer radically different perspectives. New employees from outside the industry can also offer insightful ideas and suggestions. As Gary Hamel suggests, the managers of even the most successful industry incumbents must think like heretics and struggle against industry orthodoxy.[36]

- *Beware of success.* What causes or contributes to the failure of firms to keep pace with changes in their industry environments? It appears as though success in an earlier period is often responsible for decline in a subsequent period. In fact, although prosperity is the goal of the managers of every business enterprise, it appears that a certain adversity is associated with advantage. In most companies, success appears to lead to contentment and a self-satisfied sort of complacency among managers. Managers of these firms stop paying attention to changes in their industries, they do less monitoring of the competitive landscape, they tend to discount the activities of their competitors, they tend to assume that new technological developments will have no significant impact on their businesses. In short, these companies stop *learning*. Certainly an important challenge for managers of all firms is to unlock and stimulate the kinds of individual and organizational learning that will be associated with organizational renewal and vitality.

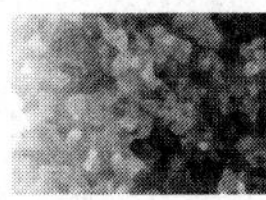

Conclusion

A key assumption of the model of industry structuring presented in this chapter is that industry environments are evolving over time as customer demographics change, as new products and services are introduced, and as new technologies emerge. Thus, an important insight is that managers must continuously reposition their firms over time in order to keep pace with changes in their firms' competitive environments. Entrepreneurial managers can anticipate changes in industry dimensions and literally create whole new markets. This is, of course, the genius of the founders of Apple Computer: They had the ability to see how changes in microprocessor technology would allow a great deal of computing power to be placed in a very small box, making possible a totally new product, the personal computer, that would appeal and be marketed to a totally new group of unsophisticated computer users.

The dynamic nature of industries is what makes business enterprise such an interesting field to join and study. Every day holds the promise of new developments and the opportunity to exploit changes in the competitive environment to create new products or services. Nothing can be assumed to remain stable or fixed for very long, as entrepreneurs rush to take advantage of changes in industry dimensions. Not only do these entrepreneurial efforts lead to the development of new products and services, but this activity is also a source of our society's wealth. A company like Apple, founded in a garage, becomes a *Fortune* 500 company within a decade, and along the way creates thousands of jobs, develops many new supporting industries, and generates millions of dollars of sales and profits. Columbia/HCA and other health maintenance organizations, which did not exist two decades ago, are now having a profound influence on how health care is administered in the United States.[37]

Although organizations are sometimes remarkably resilient, the record suggests that most companies have difficulty adapting to changes in their industries. Many companies fail to adjust to changes and find themselves blindsided by younger, more entrepreneurial competitors. Indeed, the paths of industry evolution are littered with the scarred remains of humbled or even bankrupt firms that once dominated their industries. Even Apple — a paragon of innovation — has become vulnerable to the fast pace of change in the personal computer market it helped to create.

MANAGEMENT FOCUS

APPLE'S FUTURE

Will Apple survive, and, if so, in what form? This seems to be one of the most frequently asked and debated questions in the computer industry these days. In spite of more than 22 million "fanatically loyal customers" who love their Macs, Apple is clearly at a crossroads. The personal computer market is now dominated by a "Wintel" coalition of personal computer makers assembling machines based on Windows software and Intel microprocessors. The commodity-like nature of the personal computer market has driven the prices of PCs — even Macintoshes — so low that Apple cannot simultaneously build its machines and afford R&D and the development of new software for Macs. Clearly, "business as usual" is not a viable option for Apple Computer, and its current market position is not viable in the long run.

The future for Apple Computer — a company that has been the source of so much innovation — is probably in more innovation, especially a groundbreaking innovation that would rival its development of the personal computer in the mid-1970s. At least one scenario sees Apple developing new ways for computer users to exploit the potential of the Internet. Apple already has considerable strengths in this market segment. "Macs are the most popular machines for Internet content creation, and Mac servers for World Wide Web sites rank No. 2 behind those of Sun."[1] According to this scenario, Apple will use sales of Macintoshes, and perhaps even fee revenue from licensing the Macintosh operating system to other computer makers, to fund the development of a new blockbuster computer product based on Internet technology.

Such a scenario raises some familiar questions. Would an Internet-based strategy be viable and could it lead to a sustainable competitive advantage? With so many fast-moving and powerful competitors in the computer industry and with the stakes so high for winners and losers, could Apple develop a product that would be truly proprietary, and, if so, for how long? Would the vast majority of personal computer users who use machines based on the Intel–Microsoft standard be required to sacrifice this technology in order to adopt Apple's new product, and, if so, how many of them would be willing to do so?

Like many of the companies described throughout this text, Apple Computer provides a fascinating real-time business case study. We can learn much by analyzing how Apple has reached its current juncture and by studying the company's current and future competitive moves. ■

[1]B. Schlender, Paradise Lost: Apple's Quest for Life After Death, *Fortune*, February 19, 1996, 64–74.

Key Points

- The fundamental assumption of this chapter is that industries are continuously structured and restructured over time.
- The model suggests that an industry can be thought of as a competitive arena or a "space" defined by firms sharing similarities along three dimensions — customers (the "who" dimension), products and services (the "what" dimension), and technologies (the "how" dimension).
- This model assumes that these three dimensions are continuously changing as customers develop new needs and wants, as new products and services are developed, and as new technologies emerge.
- These changes in industry dimensions create "holes" or opportunities in industry environments, and these holes invite invasion by entrepreneurial firms.
- At the same time, industry norms and cognitive limitations prevent the managers of incumbent firms from recognizing these same opportunities. They also prevent the managers of incumbent firms from recognizing the threat posed by entrepreneurial firms.

- The chapter offered six observations about the entry of new rivals into an industry and the response of incumbent firms to those new entrants:
  1. Successful new rivals generally do not attack incumbent firms directly, but instead are more likely to enter an industry at the "holes" that are created by changes in consumer preferences and the adoption of new product and process technologies.
  2. Successful new entrants generally offer new products or services that capitalize on changes in more than one industry dimension. For example, a successful new entrant is likely to introduce a new product that not only responds to a change in consumer preferences but also incorporates a new technological development or a new production process.
  3. The model also suggests that successful new entrants seek to establish strong niches from which they then expand into ever larger areas in the competitive space.
  4. Incumbent firms are rarely able to match new entrants' products, services, or technological capabilities.
  5. Incumbent firms confronted by new rivals are more likely to respond by withdrawing to supposedly "safer" areas in the competitive space, by diversifying, or by improving current offerings of products and services.
  6. Incumbent firms rarely enjoy any sort of long-run benefit from a strategic withdrawal from market segments invaded by new entrants.
- The chapter also suggested four implications for managers:
  1. Managers must actively anticipate the future.
  2. Innovation is more important than imitation.
  3. It's important to think like an industry outsider.
  4. Beware of success: Satisfaction or contentment can slow or prevent individual and organizational learning and renewal.

Review and Discussion Questions

1. *Why do managers need a dynamic model of industry structuring such as the one presented in this chapter? In what ways or along what dimensions are industries changing?*
2. *How do industry norms and managers' cognitive limitations prevent managers from anticipating or responding effectively to changes in their firms' environments?*
3. *What are the characteristics associated with the entry of new rivals into an established industry?*
4. *How are the managers of incumbent firms likely to respond to the entry of new rivals? What are some specific recommendations for managers suggested by the dynamic model introduced in this chapter?*
5. *Select an industry and analyze it using the dynamic model introduced in this chapter.*

Suggestions for Further Reading

Abell, D.F. 1980. *Defining the Business: Starting Point of Strategic Planning.* Englewood Cliffs, NJ: Prentice-Hall.

Cooper, A.C., & Schendel, D. 1976. Strategic responses to technological threats. *Business Horizons,* 19(1): 61–69.

D'Aveni, R. 1994. *Hypercompetition.* New York: Free Press.

Drucker, P.F. 1985. *Innovation and Entrepreneurship*. New York: Harper & Row.

Hamel, G., & Prahalad, C.K. 1994. *Competing for the Future*. Boston: Harvard Business School Press.

Kiesler, S., & Sproull, L. 1982. Managerial response to changing environments: Perspectives on problem sensing from social cognition. *Adminstrative Science Quarterly* 27: 548–570.

Urban, G.L., Carter, T., Gaskin, S., & Mucha, Z. 1986. Market share rewards to pioneering brands: An empirical analysis and strategic implications. *Management Science* 32: 645–659.

Yates, B. 1983. *The Decline and Fall of the American Automobile Industry*. New York: Empire Books.

ENDNOTES

1. Parts of this chapter are based on a paper entitled *The Cognitive Structuring of Industries*, written with Anne S. Huff, James O. Huff, and Jung-Taik Oh and presented at a conference on the Social Construction of Industries and Markets, sponsored by the University of Illinois in Chicago in April 1994.
2. Kidder, T. 1981. *The Soul of a New Machine*. New York: Avon Books, p. 12.
3. Cooper, A. C., and D. Schendel. 1976. Strategic responses to technological threats. *Business Horizons* 19(1): 61–69.
4. Hamel, G., and Prahalad, C. K. 1994. *Competing for the Future*. Boston: Harvard Business School Press.
5. D'Aveni, R. 1994. *Hypercompetition*. New York: Free Press.
6. Hamel and Prahalad, *Competing for the Future*, p. 16.
7. Bank, D. 1997. Why Microsoft wants to hook into cable TV. *The Wall Street Journal*, October 16, B1, B19; E. Shapiro, 1997. TCI may get investment by Microsoft. *The Wall Street Journal*, October 15, A3, A4.
8. Abell, D. F. 1980. *Defining the Business: Starting Point of Strategic Planning*. Englewood Cliffs, NJ: Prentice-Hall.
9. Deutschman, A. 1998. The amazin' Amazon man. *Gentlemen's Quarterly*, May, 175–180.
10. Reilly, P. M. 1997. Booksellers prepare to do battle in cyberspace. *The Wall Street Journal*, January 28, B1, B8.
11. Huff, A. S. 1982. Industry influences on strategy reformulation. *Strategic Management Journal* 3: 119–131; W.W. Powell and P.J. DiMaggio, Eds. 1991. *The New Institutionalism in Organizational Analysis*. Chicago: University of Chicago Press.
12. Hambrick, D.C. 1982. Environmental scanning and organizational strategy. *Strategic Management Journal* 3: 159–174.
13. Mintzberg, H., D. Raìsinghanì, and A. Théorêt. 1976. The structure of "unstructured" decision processes. *Administrative Science Quarterly* 21: 253.
14. Kiesler, S., and L. Sproull. 1982. Managerial response to changing environments: Perspectives on problem sensing from social cognition. *Administrative Science Quarterly* 27: 548–570.
15. Ibid, p. 557.
16. Marshall McLuhan, quoted in R.J. Barber. 1970. *The American Corporation: Its Power, Its Money, Its Politics*. New York: E. P. Dalton, p.3, emphasis added.
17. Hall, R. I. 1984. The natural logic of management policy making: Its implications for the survival of an organization. *Management Science* 30: 905–927.
18. Guyon, J. 1989. S.O.S.: Western Union, saved by a junk-bond deal, needs rescuing again. *The Wall Street Journal*, October 13, A1.
19. Schmalensee, R. 1978. Entry deterrence in the ready-to-eat breakfast cereal industry. *Bell Journal of Economics* 9: 318, emphasis added.
20. Staw, B. M., L.E. Sandelands, and J.E. Dutton. 1981. Threat-rigidity effects in organizational behavior: A multilevel analysis. *Administrative Science Quarterly* 26: 501–524.

21. Urban, G. L., T. Carter, S. Gaskin and Z. Mucha. 1986. Market share rewards to pioneering brands: An empirical analysis and strategic implications. *Management Science* 32: 645–659.
22. Drucker, P.F. 1985. *Innovation and Entrepreneurship*. New York: Harper & Row, p.230.
23. Adams, C. 1997. Nucor considers building a mill to roll steel plate. *The Wall Street Journal*, October 3, A5; C. Ansberry, & D. Milbank. 1992. Small, mid-size steelmakers are ripe for a shakeout. *The Wall Street Journal*, March 4, B4.
24. Cooper and Schendel, Strategic responses to technological threats.
25. Ibid.
26. Sloan, A.P. Jr. 1963. *My Years with General Motors*. New York: Doubleday/Currency. p.69, emphasis added.
27. Yates, B. 1983. *The Decline and Fall of the American Automobile Industry*. New York: Empire Books, pp. 80–81.
28. Shapiro, E. C. 1991. *How Corporate Truths Become Competitive Traps*. New York: Wiley, pp. 52–53.
29. Shapiro, *How Corporate Truths Become Competitive Traps*, pp. 3–4.
30. Porter, M. E. 1980. *Competitive Strategy*. New York: The Free Press.
31. Cooper and Schendel, Strategic responses to technological threats.
32. Barnett, D.F., and L. Schorsch. 1983. *Steel: Upheaval in a Basic Industry*. Cambridge, Mass: Ballinger, p.84, emphasis added.
33. Mintzberg, H. 1978. Patterns in strategy formation. *Management Science* 24: 941.
34. Mitchell, R. 1989. Masters of innovation: How 3M keeps its new products coming. *Business Week*, April 10, 58–63.
35. Rubbermaid, Inc. 1989. *Annual Report*.
36. Hamel, G. 1998. Will merger with DEC be Compaq's last hurrah? *The Wall Street Journal*, March 2, A18.
37. Krieger, L.M. 1997. Columbia/HCA's legacy isn't a fraud. *The Wall Street Journal*, October 27, A22; R. Winslow. 1998. Health-care inflation kept in check last year. *The Wall Street Journal*, January 20, B1, B4.

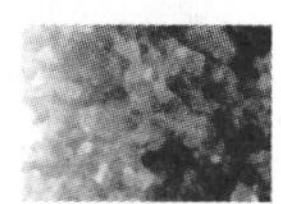

CHAPTER 6

BUSINESS DEFINITION

CHAPTER OBJECTIVES

As illustrated in Exhibit 6.1, this chapter describes how managers' mental models about their firms' industry environments influence their decisions about business definition and positioning—decisions that are certainly among the most important that any manager must make. The specific objectives of this chapter on business definition are to:

- Define the concept of business definition and emphasize both the importance and the creative nature of business definition.
- Describe the ways in which business definition can be a source or contribute to the development of sustained competitive advantage.
- Illustrate some effective business definitions.
- Emphasize the importance of redefinition, while also illustrating the challenges associated with redefinition.

WHAT IS BUSINESS DEFINITION?

The text has defined strategy as "a pattern in a stream of decisions," and certainly one of the most important decisions managers make is how they choose to define their firms and businesses. A firm's definition conveys what is most important about that company while also distinguishing the company from its competitors. Definitions give organizations identities that describe what is "central, distinctive, and enduring" about them.[1] Peter Drucker has emphasized that business definitions provide firms with a "theory of the business" that includes

> the assumptions that shape any organization's behavior, dictate its decisions about what to do and what not to do, and define what the organization considers meaningful results. These assumptions are about markets. They are about identifying customers and competitors, their values and behavior. They are about technology and its dynamics, about a company's strengths and weaknesses.[2]

Thus, definition allows a firm or a business to describe itself to employees, customers, and other constituencies while also distinguishing itself from other business organizations that may or may not be competitors. As Drucker suggests, definition

EXHIBIT 6.1

The Mental Models and Strategic Decisions Studied in This Text and Their Influence on Performance and Competitive Advantage

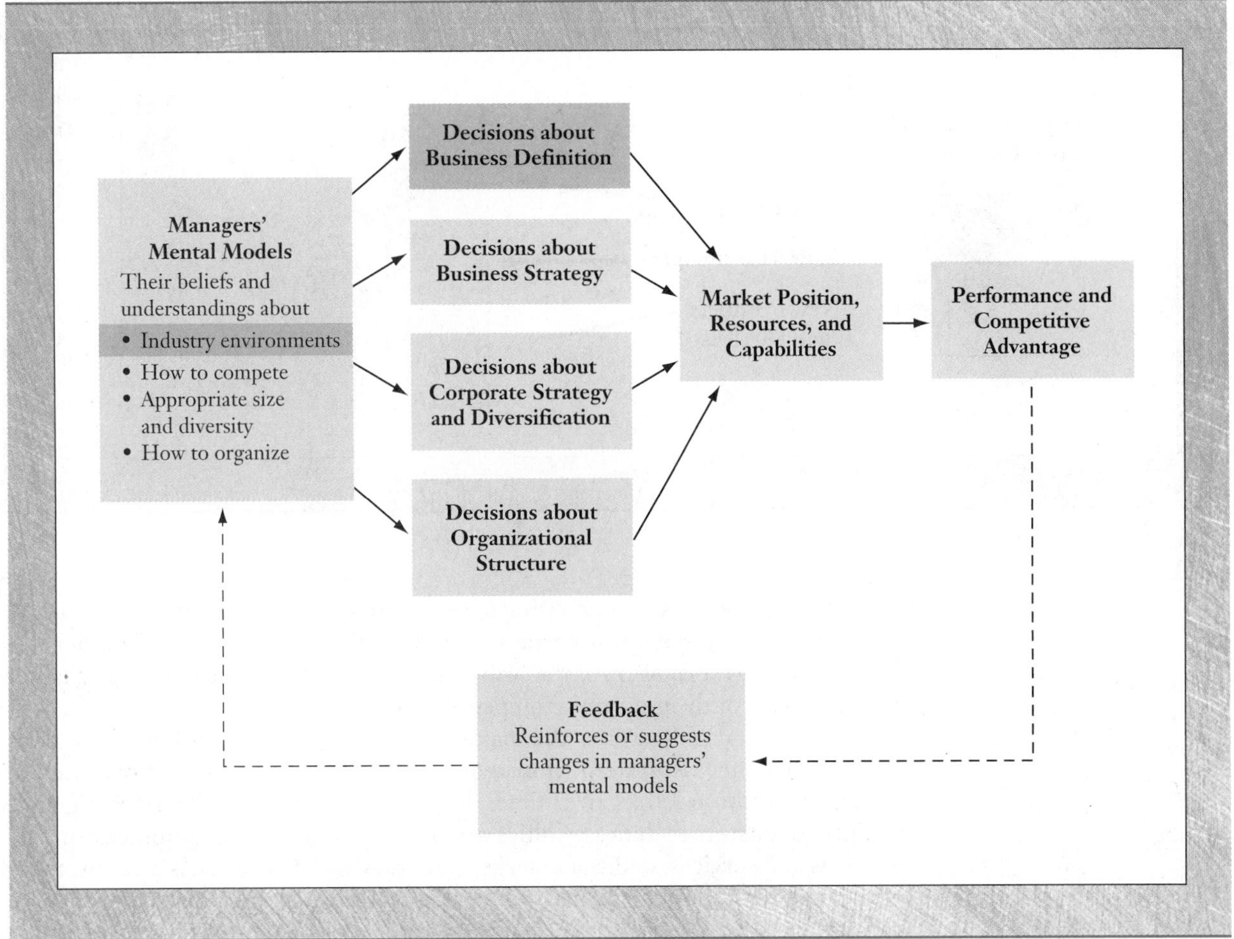

is related to a broader array of strategic issues because an organization's definition is tightly coupled with managers' understandings or beliefs about their firms' industries and rivals as well as their beliefs or understandings of their firms' competencies and strengths.

Business definition is both strategy content *and* strategy process. Business definition is strategy content in that, building on the dynamic model of industry analysis developed in Chapter 5, it describes *which customers the firm or business will serve, what products or services the firm or business will offer, and what technologies the firm or business will employ*. But business definition is also a strategy process—*the process by which firms and businesses select positions in their industry environments.*[3]

The process of business definition is illustrated in Exhibit 6.2. The exhibit depicts an industry as a locus of customers, products and services, and technologies—the three-dimensional competitive space introduced in Chapter 5. The left side of the exhibit illustrates the process of definition as the darker cube represents

EXHIBIT 6.2

The Processes of Business Definition and Redefinition

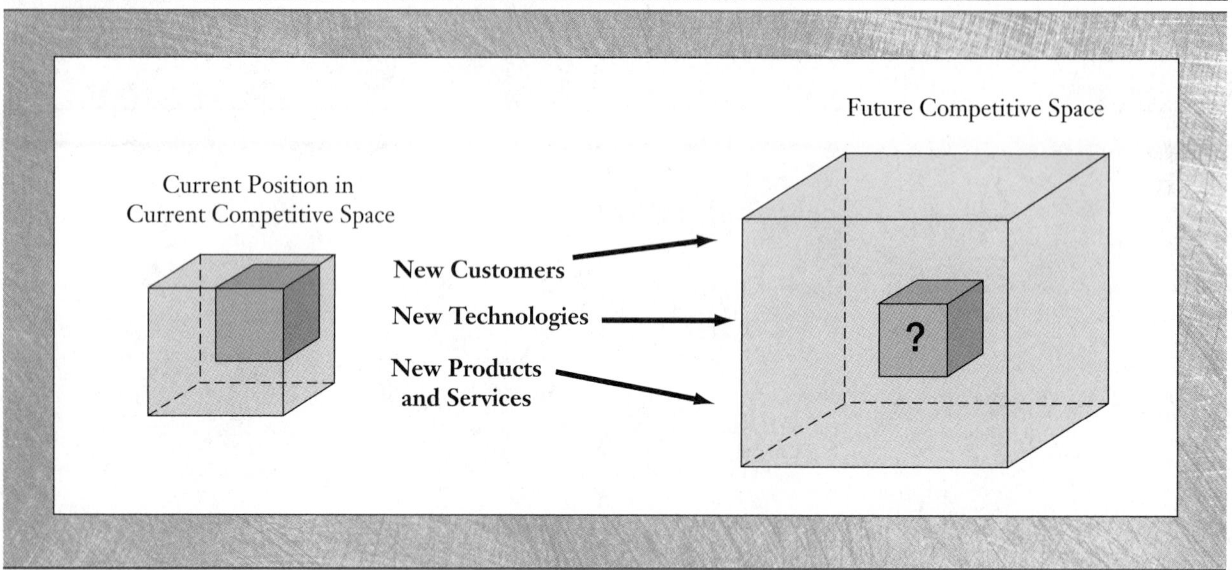

a particular firm or business choosing to serve certain customers, offer certain products or services, and employ certain technologies within the larger competitive arena. Obviously, managers of the firm or business could choose to occupy a larger or smaller part of the industry's competitive space.

The exhibit also illustrates the major challenge associated with business definition—that successful definition requires an ongoing process of *redefinition*. Notice in Exhibit 6.2 that, over time, the dimensions of the industry change due to shifts in customer demographics and preferences, the development of new products and services, and the emergence of new technologies. As a result, managers must redefine their firms and businesses in order to keep pace with these industry changes. Alternatively, managers can be proactive—pushing their firms to develop new products, services, and technologies and identifying new customer wants and needs—so that their firms are instrumental in reshaping industry boundaries.[4]

Notice that these descriptions of business definition refer to both firms *and* businesses. If a firm is a "single business firm," that is, if it engages in only a single business activity, then it will probably have a single business definition. On the other hand, diversified or multibusiness firms, which engage in many different lines of business, will need to have unique business definitions for each of their different businesses. In addition to developing unique definitions for each business, diversified firms will also need to develop some sort of overall definition for the firm—what Porter has called a "corporate theme"[5]—that describes the firm and suggests how (or whether) its various businesses are related to one another. Obviously, as the diversity of firms increases, the task of business definition becomes more complex and challenging. We focus more attention on the subject of business definition in diversified firms when we take up the challenges of managing corporate strategy and diversification in Chapter 9.

This chapter focuses on both the content *and* the process aspects of business definition. The following section describes the creative *process* by which business definitions are developed. This section is followed by a discussion of how the *content* of business definitions can be a source of or contribute to the development of competitive advantage. After focusing on some specific examples of effective business definitions *(content)*, the chapter then emphasizes the importance of *business redefinition* and describes many of the challenges surrounding the *process* of business redefinition.

Characteristics of the Business Definition Process

Several characteristics of the business definition process warrant comment.

First, business definition is fundamentally a creative process that can vitally influence the success of firms and businesses.[6] Most students are likely to think of business as a "science," much like engineering, because many business courses focus on "nuts and bolts" problems and provide students with models that often incorporate algebraic formulas. In a finance class, for example, you learn how to calculate the present value of future cash flows to assess requests for capital outlays. Students in marketing become familiar with the advanced statistical analysis techniques that are now so widely used in market research studies. One result of taking these courses is that some students get the idea that business is much like engineering, in which decisions can be guided by axiomatic or universal principles. In fact, many business students criticize organizational behavior, human resource management, and some strategy courses as lacking rigor because they don't require students to use their calculators or memorize mathematical formulas.

Though few business courses spend much time on the subject of creativity, many business activities require creative thinking. Why, then, are business school curricula populated by so many quantitative courses while at the same time offering so few courses that emphasize the creative aspects of business? At least two answers help to explain this imbalance. First, in many respects, accounting really is "the language of business," and however imprecisely accounting numbers value such resources as leadership, human capital, research and development, organizational knowledge, quality, customer satisfaction, and reputation, the business world nevertheless seeks to value all resource inputs, capabilities, and performance outcomes in quantitative terms. Another reason why business curricula often give little attention to the creative process is that it is not well understood. Lacking knowledge, tools, and textbooks with which to teach students about creativity, many faculty simply choose to ignore the subject.

Thus, we are all somewhat poorly prepared for considering the importance of creativity in the business world. Yet, no task is more fundamentally creative than business definition. Like the work of artists, the process of business definition brings something new into being—deciding that a business will provide a particular product or service, that it will serve a particular group of customers, that it will make use of a particular technology. And, given the dynamic, evolving industry environments in which business activity takes place, creativity becomes even more important. The famous psychologist, Rollo May, made these observations about the importance of creativity:

> Every profession can and does require creativity. In our day, technology and engineering, diplomacy, business, and certainly teaching, all of these professions and scores of others are in the midst of radical change and require courageous persons to appreciate and direct this change. *The need for creativity is in direct proportion to the degree of change the profession is undergoing.*[7]

Yet, May was also aware of the forces in our society that work against creativity; most specifically, May was concerned about a lack of will or passion:

> The fact that talent is plentiful but passion is lacking is a fundamental problem of creativity in many fields today, and our ways of evading the hard work of creativity have played directly into this trend. We worship technique and talent, so that we can evade the anxiety and struggle associated with creativity.[8]

Certainly it is good to remind ourselves that without the creative impulse as well as the entrepreneurial passion or will to transform ideas into reality, our economic landscape would be far less vibrant and our society would have far less economic growth and a lower standard of living than we presently enjoy.

A second characteristic of the business definition process is that effective business definitions rarely emerge without an extensive knowledge of the competitive landscape. In other words, *effective* business definitions are rarely the result of luck or whims, but are instead the outcome of expertise and hard work. May argued that creativity results from "encounter" or "engagement" with a particular issue or problem.[9] Furthermore, even though we tend to think of the *status quo* or the "conventional wisdom" as the opposite of creativity, May argued that an understanding of the structure of the problem or situation—what he called "form"—will actually increase the quality of the creative effort. May reasoned that an understanding of the problem or situation provides a context so that creative thinkers can know the full range of both the possibilities and the limitations associated with that particular problem or situation.

Certainly, the experiences of many important entrepreneurs confirm this characteristic of the creative process. John Deere's steel plow and Goodyear's development of vulcanized rubber followed years of experimentation and trial-and-error learning. Howard Head's metal skis were the result of his longstanding efforts to improve the quality of skis. Steve Wozniak and Steven Jobs did not "stumble" on the idea of personal computers, but, as electrical engineers, they were fully knowledgeable about the potential for microprocessors to place tremendous computing power in a very small box. These characteristics suggest another important feature of the business definition process.

An effective business definition not only will answer the Who, What, and How questions but also will be much more creative and unique than almost any corporate mission statement. Nearly all mission statements are long on lofty ideals and objectives, but they usually lack anything distinctive that would distinguish the organization from its competitors. Related to this point, effective business definitions are unlikely to emerge from a committee or task force set up to draft a mission statement. Often, the creative nature of an effective business definition dictates that it must be the inspiration of a key entrepreneurial thinker because a truly distinctive definition is unlikely to emerge from committee deliberations. In fact, one of the most important attributes a leader can give to his or her organization is an effective definition.

Another characteristic of the business definition process is that it implies that firms will necessarily engage in some activities and not engage in others. The word *decide*, like the word *scissors*, comes from the Latin *caedere*, which means "to cut," and it is important to remember that a decision to engage in one activity means that some other activity will not be done—it will be "cut" or eliminated. As students, you have decided to pursue business careers and, as a result, most of you have "cut off" the possibility of being doctors or scientists. Similarly, in selecting business definitions, managers are necessarily deciding that their firms will serve certain customers but not others, that their firms will provide certain products and services but not others, and that their firms will employ certain technologies but not others.

Sometimes, business definitions result from not deciding. In other words, business definition can be the product of proactive decision making, but business definition can also result from a passive acceptance of or being "boxed in" by market forces. Alfred Sloan, reflecting on his early years at General Motors, captured this tension between efforts to proactively create a business definition and falling victim to the forces of the marketplace:

> We did not know what we were trying to do except to sell cars. . . . Some kind of rational policy was called for. That is, it was necessary to know what one was trying to do, apart from . . . *what might be imposed upon one by the consumer, the competition, and a combination of technological and economic conditions.*[10]

The italicized portion of this quotation emphasizes the point that market and competitive forces can severely limit the freedom or flexibility a company's managers enjoy as they attempt to chart its course. Furthermore, if managers fail to explicitly define or redefine their firms, market forces and changes in the dynamics of the industries in which these firms operate can have a profound impact on the value of firms' business definitions.

Consider, for example, the case of Ziebart, for years a highly successful automotive rustproofing company. As the quality of automobiles improved and warranties were extended, the definitions of firms in the auto repair industry almost became superfluous. Recognizing that these trends could almost certainly drive the company out of business, Ziebart's managers decided that the company needed to diversify into additional automotive services including window tinting, sunroof installation, auto detailing, and security services.[11] Had Ziebart's managers not taken a proactive approach to business definition, the firm could easily have been overwhelmed by trends in its industry environment.

Not only must managers be cognizant of the need to redefine their firms over time in order to maintain alignment with the larger competitive environment, managers must also invest resources in their firms' definitions in order to build and maintain their strength. It is not enough to have a good concept or idea for a business definition; managers must invest continuously in order to establish their firms' definitions and then maintain the strength of those definitions in the marketplace. Chapter 3 emphasized that all assets—including an effective definition—will erode over time without a program of ongoing investment.

For example, Sears was for decades the largest retailer in the world, but by the 1970s, the company's focus had shifted to building a diversified retailing empire in insurance, financial services, and real estate. By the 1980s, Sears' retailing unit was in trouble. With its sales already surpassed by Wal-Mart and Kmart, Sears' retailing operations didn't seem to have either a focus or a niche in the retail marketplace. In spite of many well-known brand names, such as Kenmore, Craftsman, and Die-Hard, Sears' sales growth continued to lag behind that of its retail competitors. Only after a dramatic restructuring in which Sears shed nearly all its nonretailing operations and brought in a new CEO has the company been able to turn around its retailing operations.[12] Much of Sears' success has come from changing its definition so that it now places more emphasis on attracting female shoppers while still maintaining a focus on "tool guys."

A final characteristic of business definition that must be noted here is its fleeting nature. Though business definitions are typically built over long periods of time and with considerable investment, they can quickly become dated or irrelevant either by changes in the larger competitive environment or by the actions of managers. For example, the development of transistor technology doomed firms that had defined their businesses as vacuum tube manufacturers.[13] Similarly, Chapter 3 described how the decision to market Coors beer nationally rather than focusing solely on its Rocky Mountain base caused the beer to lose much of its mystique. The company's unique definition or position in the beer industry was apparently based almost solely on the product's scarcity. When the beer became widely available, the distinctiveness of the company's definition disappeared.

After reviewing many of the characteristics associated with the process of business definition, we now turn to an examination of the importance of business definition, focusing specifically on the ways business definition can contribute to competitive advantage. The chapter then explores the importance of business redefinition and the challenges associated with changing or altering business definitions.

Business Definition and Competitive Advantage

Both practicing managers and academic researchers have shown great interest in a number of related concepts, including "mission,"[14] "purpose," "vision,"[15] and "identity,"[16] all of which emphasize the importance of organizational "self-knowledge"—that the organization's definition and what distinguishes it from other organizations is somehow critical to its effectiveness. The underlying premise is that business definition can be an important source, or at least contribute to the development, of competitive advantage—the reason some firms enjoy higher performance than their rivals—not only because it determines how the organization sees itself and how others relate to the organization but also because it influences a wide range of other strategic decisions. Here, we suggest four ways in which business definition contributes to the development of competitive advantage. As suggested in Chapter 3, the key consideration in evaluating any source of competitive advantage is always the ease of imitation: Any source of competitive advantage that can be easily duplicated by rivals is unlikely to offer sustained levels of high performance.

Business Definition "Positions" a Firm or a Business in Its Competitive Space or Industry Environment

Business definition is the major way in which companies describe themselves to customers, employees, suppliers, and investors and also the primary way customers, employees, and other constituencies develop an image of companies.

MANAGEMENT FOCUS

TARGET'S DEFINITION HITS THE MARK

In the fast-changing world of retailing, many once formidable retailers have been sidelined. Montgomery Ward has filed for bankruptcy protection. Sears and J. C. Penney struggle to redefine themselves after years of being squeezed both by discount retailers, such as Wal-Mart, and by specialty retailers, such as the Gap, Limited, and Home Depot. So, given the competitive and crowded retail marketplace, what explains the tremendous success enjoyed by Target Stores, Dayton Hudson Corporation's largest retail division? It appears that much of Target's success is due to its business definition and unique position in the retailing marketplace.

Though classified by most industry analysts as a "discount retailer" like Kmart or Wal-Mart, Target is different. Target is a discount chain because of its emphasis on a high volume of sales and generally low profit margins. Yet, Target seeks to attract more upscale consumers by emphasizing fashion, carrying brand-name merchandise, and maintaining clean, attractive stores. And, the definition works: While the average shopper at a Wal-Mart store has household income of between $25,000 and $30,000, the average Target shopper has household income of $40,000.[1]

Part of Target's success in attracting such upscale consumers is its stock of high-quality merchandise. Noticeably absent is the "polyester palace" feel of many discount retail stores. Target's "clothing and housewares shelves offer attractive, inexpensive interpretations of specialty store merchandise, just a few aisles away from the less sexy but all-important items like milk, white T-shirts and potting soil. All this is wrapped in clever advertising that makes people feel that they are part of a big, hip national secret."[2]

In addition, every Target store's inventory is different and "targeted" to the particular community in which the store is located. Through a strategy of "micro-marketing," Target considers such factors as the demographics of the area, the climate of the region in which the store is located, popular leisure activities of the people living in the region, and special marketing opportunities in stocking each of its stores. For example, if two Target stores are located in the same city but one store is in a more affluent neighborhood, then that store will stock more upscale merchandise while the other store will stock more basic items. Stores located in midwestern states like Michigan will have snow shovels in the winter and gardening supplies in the spring, while stores in Florida will stock more beachwear. Target stores in Denver will stock Broncos jerseys while Target stores in the Chicago area will stock Bears jerseys. Likewise, Target stores in Ann Arbor will stock more University of Michigan clothing while Target stores in Lansing will stock more Michigan State merchandise.

Target also employs sophisticated inventory management tools to help in managing its micromarketing strategy and to minimize inventories while avoiding stock-outs. Computers automatically order snow shovels to arrive in Target's Michigan stores just before that first big snow in the winter, and the same inventory management programs automatically order garden supplies to begin arriving on store shelves just as spring begins. And, Target stores take customer convenience seriously by always trying to have enough cash registers operating so that customers do not have to stand in long lines. ■

[1]Steinhauer, J. The Store That Crosses Class Lines. *New York Times,* March 15, 1998, Section 3, pp. 1, 11.

[2]Ibid., p. 11.

Though definitions can be based on many different industry dimensions that will vary across companies and markets, this chapter builds on the framework introduced in Chapter 5 to describe how businesses come to be defined along three dimensions—customers, products and services, and technologies. For each of these three dimensions, business definition allows managers to describe or identify their companies while also helping customers, employees, and other constituencies to develop an image of their companies and how they differ from other business organizations.

Within almost any industry, one will find a number of different "strategic groups"—groups of firms pursuing similar strategies. For example, in the brewing industry, Busch, Miller, and Coors all pursue a national strategy in the United States. Microbreweries pursue a very different strategy, most serving only a local or small regional market. The objective of business definition is to somehow distinguish the firm from its competitors even though it might be pursuing strategies that are very similar to those of a number of other companies that are in the same strategic group.

The J. M. Smucker Company provides an excellent example of a company that has developed a very positive and effective business definition. A consistently high-performing company, J. M. Smucker has successfully defined itself as a manufacturer of the highest-quality jams, jellies, and other fruit products. The company's high-quality products have, in turn, attracted a loyal group of discerning customers who will pay a premium to use Smucker's fine products. Customers have so strongly accepted this definition that Smucker's products consistently receive more supermarket shelf space and sell for higher prices than their competitors' comparable products.

Like the J. M. Smucker Company, Gerber has also developed a very effective definition. Though two other companies produce baby food, Beech-Nut (owned by Nestlé) and Heinz, Gerber commands 70 percent of the U.S. baby food market, and parents prefer Gerber's products so much that most supermarkets will carry only two of the three baby food makers' products—Gerber and either Beech-Nut or Heinz. And, as with Smucker's jams and jellies, Gerber's products always command the vast majority of the shelf space devoted to baby food and tend to sell for a few more cents per jar than competitors' comparable products.

It is not that Smucker and Gerber do what other companies cannot do—in fact, both companies have well-established competitors. Rather, they have so carefully and effectively invested resources into crafting their definitions that they have come to be seen as so closely aligned with their product markets that consumers often do not consider other brands, even though choosing Gerber's baby food products or Smucker's jams means paying more per jar.

Furthermore, both companies have aggressively defended against attempts by other companies to copy or imitate them. For example, Smucker has sued Kraft to prevent it from adopting the distinctive "checkerboard" design that Smucker uses on its labels and jar lids. Gerber, which has long had the picture of a baby figure prominently on the jars of its baby foods, has also used litigation to prevent Beech-Nut from placing the picture of a baby on its jars. Are such simple factors as a checkerboard design on jar lids or the picture of a baby on a label really essential to these companies' definitions? We might think that they are trivial concerns, but it is instructive to see that the managers of these companies deem even these "minor details" as critical to their firms' success.

Business Definition Helps to Focus Management Attention on the Firm's Key Objectives, the Firm's Most Significant Strategic Issues, and the Firm's Most Important Rivals

There is an old saying that "the main thing is that the main thing must remain the main thing." Business definition can help to focus management attention on *the main thing*. Not only does business definition allow organizations to describe themselves to internal and external constituencies, but it also helps to focus management attention on key objectives, competitors, and other issues in the competitive landscape. In a classic article in the *Journal of Business Strategy*, Ram Charan, former Harvard professor and now management consulting guru, argued that before managers could effectively address other questions of strategy or competitive tactics, they needed to address key business definition questions,[17] including:

- Where are we now? Where are we taking the business?
- How are we going to position our business vis-à-vis the competition and the marketplace?

These are simple questions, yet they have profound implications for the success of any business organization. Business definition, by placing a firm in a particular portion of the industry or competitive arena, helps managers to focus their attention on a set of key strategic objectives and a much more limited set of relevant competitors, opportunities, and threats. It's not that managers can ignore more peripheral issues and competitors, but business definition allows managers to focus more of their attention on the most important objectives, direct competitors, and relevant issues.

BUSINESS DEFINITION INFLUENCES OTHER STRATEGIC DECISIONS

Business definition logically precedes most other strategic decisions.[18] Furthermore, once the business has been defined, managers will be able to quickly identify many other strategic questions that must be made. Consider the example of the Williams Companies. Before the mid-1980s, the primary business of the Williams Companies was to provide interstate gas transmission pipeline services. As natural gas prices began to fall in the 1980s, demand for Williams' gas transmission services also fell, lowering revenues and endangering the firm's profitability.

At this point, a young manager at Williams suggested the novel idea of entering the telecommunications business and running fiber optic cable through the firm's idle gas pipeline network. He reasoned that since breaks in fiber optic cable create major disruptions for companies that depend on communication networks, Williams could have a competitive advantage by touting that its fiber optic cables were protected by steel pipes.[19] Williams' telecommunications business, called WilTel, was a great success. In fact, most of Williams Companies' earnings over the last decade can be attributed to its WilTel telecommunications subsidiary.

What is noteworthy about Williams' decision to redefine itself and enter the fiber optic telecommunications industry is that this definition decision logically suggested other important strategic questions. For example, once the decision had been made to proceed with the telecommunications venture, Williams invested heavily in the business. During the late 1980s, nearly half of all the company's capital investment spending went toward this new subsidiary. Furthermore, recognizing that gas transmission pipeline employees knew nothing about the fiber optic telecommunications industry and that training would be time consuming and expensive, the company aggressively recruited new employees from competitors in the telecommunications industry.

By not only choosing to redefine itself, but also embracing its new definition and committing the necessary resources to implement its redefinition, Williams was able to establish itself as a unique (because of its ability to protect its fiber optic cable in steel pipes) and credible competitor in a totally new industry environment. As a result, the managers of the Williams Companies were able to do what few managers have been able to do without an incredible struggle—respond effectively and relatively painlessly to an unfavorable shift in their firm's industry environment by successfully redefining the company.

Business Definition Provides Meaning and Can Be Very Motivational

Finally, business definition has the ability to motivate managers and other employees. Many recent publications, including the best-selling book, *Built to Last*, by Collins and Porras, have emphasized the motivational aspects of such concepts as business definition, organizational identity, and vision. Firms that have strong business definitions provide managers and employees with a sense of meaning, purpose, and excitement that can arouse commitment and even passion.

Research suggests that effective business definitions can be much more tangible and motivational than financial objectives. Goals such as "increasing earnings per share" or "increasing shareholder value" are *not* examples of business definitions. Collins and Porras have this criticism of such goals:

> "Maximize shareholder wealth" does not inspire people at all levels of an organization, and it provides precious little guidance. *"Maximize shareholder wealth" is the standard "off-the-shelf" purpose for those organizations that have not yet identified their true core purpose.* It is a substitute ideology, and a weak substitute at that. Listen to people in great organizations talk about their achievements and you'll hear very little about earnings per share. Motorola people talk about impressive quality improvements and the effects of the products they create on the world. HP people talk with pride about the technical contributions their products have made to the marketplace. Nordstrom people talk about heroic customer service and remarkable individual performance by star sales people.[20]

Some Illustrations of Effective Business Definitions

To further demonstrate how business definition can contribute to competitive advantage, let's consider two examples that help to illustrate its influence on business success.

General Motors in 1921

As already suggested by the earlier quotation from Alfred Sloan's autobiography, *My Years with General Motors*, the problem for General Motors in the early 1920s was that the company had seven different car lines that lacked clear identities and vigorously competed with and took sales from each other. For example, Chevrolet, Oakland (later Pontiac), and Oldsmobile models all had similar specifications and sold at similar price points. As summarized by Sloan, this confusion had occurred because "we did not know what we were trying to do except to sell cars which, in a sense, took volume from each other."

To make sense of this chaos, Sloan argued that General Motors, like any other business, needed a definition, or what he called a "concept of the business:"

> After the two great expansions of 1908 to 1910 and 1918 to 1920—perhaps one should say because of them—General Motors was in need not only of a concept of management but equally of a concept of the automobile business. Every enterprise needs a concept of its industry. There is a logical way of doing business in accordance with the facts and circumstances of an industry, if you can figure it out. If there are different concepts among the enterprises involved, these concepts are likely to express competitive forces in their most vigorous and decisive form.[21]

Here, Sloan is making several points that have been emphasized throughout this textbook. First, he notes the importance of definition (e.g., "General Motors was in need . . . of a concept of the automobile business."). Second, he reinforces the fact that effective definitions are based on managers' understandings of their firms' industries (e.g., "Every enterprise needs a concept of its industry. There is a logical way of doing business in accordance with the facts and circumstances of an industry, if you can figure it out"). Finally, Sloan emphasizes that, by positioning firms in their industries, definitions determine how companies will compete for customers and sales (e.g., "If there are different concepts among the enterprises involved, these concepts are likely to express competitive forces in their most vigorous and decisive form.")

The definition or "concept" that Sloan imposed on the chaos of General Motors was the view that each of the different GM car lines should serve different but overlapping price points. The car lines and the actual price ranges assigned to each line in 1921 were:

Chevrolet	\$450 – \$600
Oakland (later Pontiac)	\$600 – \$900
Buick (four-cylinder)	\$900 – \$1,200
Buick (six-cylinder)	\$1,200 – \$1,700
Oldsmobile	\$1,700 – \$2,500
Cadillac	\$2,500 – \$3,500

Fundamental to Sloan's concept was the idea that the lowest-priced car line, Chevrolet, would offer automobiles that would not compete directly with Ford's Model T (which at the time sold for \$355 and enjoyed a market share of about 60 percent), but would be "so near the Ford price that demand would be drawn from the Ford grade and lifted to the slightly higher price."[22] Similarly, each of the other GM lines, Oakland, Buick, Oldsmobile, and Cadillac, respectively, would offer more features and slightly higher quality for which consumers might be willing to pay a premium.

So successful was Sloan's "concept" or definiton that General Motors quickly overtook Ford as the leader in overall market share, and this scheme of differentiated product lines selling at different price points also became a central component of GM's business definition. In addition to helping the struggling General Motors describe itself to customers, investors, and other external constituencies, Sloan's concept had several internal benefits that influenced strategic decision making at the company for many decades, helping GM's managers focus on a more finite set of competitive priorities, motivating managers to develop unique designs and styles, and improving manufacturing efficiency.

Sloan's "concept" of differentiated products selling at different price points was so powerful and so closely linked with the success of the company that when GM's troubles became widely evident in the late 1980s, many observers concluded that the company's problems resulted from violating Sloan's concept of the business. GM's detractors argued that all the company's models looked alike, regardless of their make, and that the highest-priced Chevrolet cost more to purchase than the lowest-priced Cadillac. Ronald Zarrella, recruited by General Motors from Bausch and Lomb to be its marketing chief in 1995, concluded that improving the focus and brand image of GM's overlapping divisions had to be his major objective.[23] Later in this chapter in a Management Focus, "General Motors at a Crossroads," we take a closer look at the challenges facing GM as it seeks to win back customers through redefinition.

THE COOPER TIRE AND RUBBER COMPANY

Another example of an effective business definition is provided by Cooper Tire and Rubber Company.[24] Although not nearly as well known as Goodyear or the other leading tire manufacturers, Cooper has enjoyed consistently high earnings in an industry that has seen considerable red ink during the last two decades. Why does Cooper perform so well in such an unattractive industry? Much of Cooper's success must be attributed to the company's business definition, which places it in a distinctive position in the industry: Cooper sells only replacement tires while most of its competitors serve the OEM tire market (i.e., automobile manufacturers) as well.

As a result of this distinctive position along the product dimension, Cooper does not compete in the cutthroat OEM tire market. Furthermore, because Cooper sells only replacement tires, it does not have to offer the technological advances that are required for competing in the OEM market, thereby minimizing its need for sizable R&D outlays. In addition, Cooper sells only through independent dealers and therefore avoids the overhead costs associated with retail distribution. Also, by not owning retail sales facilities, Cooper has developed considerable loyalty among independent retailers who must compete with the retail sales facilities of Goodyear and the other major tire manufacturers. Finally, Cooper has been able to cultivate a highly motivated workforce. Its employees stamp their names on the tires they manufacture, which provides them with a strong and very personal attachment to and identification with the company's products.

The success of Cooper's efforts to develop and maintain a distinctive business definition can be seen in the firm's outstanding financial performance. As shown in Exhibit 6.3, Cooper has consistently outperformed Goodyear, the leading tire manufacturer—a company many times its size.

CHARACTERISTICS OF EFFECTIVE BUSINESS DEFINITIONS

These two examples suggest three key characteristics of effective business definitions.

- *Distinctive.* The best business definitions give their companies distinct identities and place them in a unique position in the competitive space. In fact, if business definition is to be a source of sustained competitive advantage, then business definitions must not only be unique, but they must be difficult for other firms to imitate. Note in the General Motors example, Sloan did not seek to imitate Ford's standardized, mass-production definition of the automobile, but rather sought to have GM pursue a very different definition—one that allowed the

EXHIBIT 6.3

Cooper Consistently Outperforms Other Tire Manufacturers

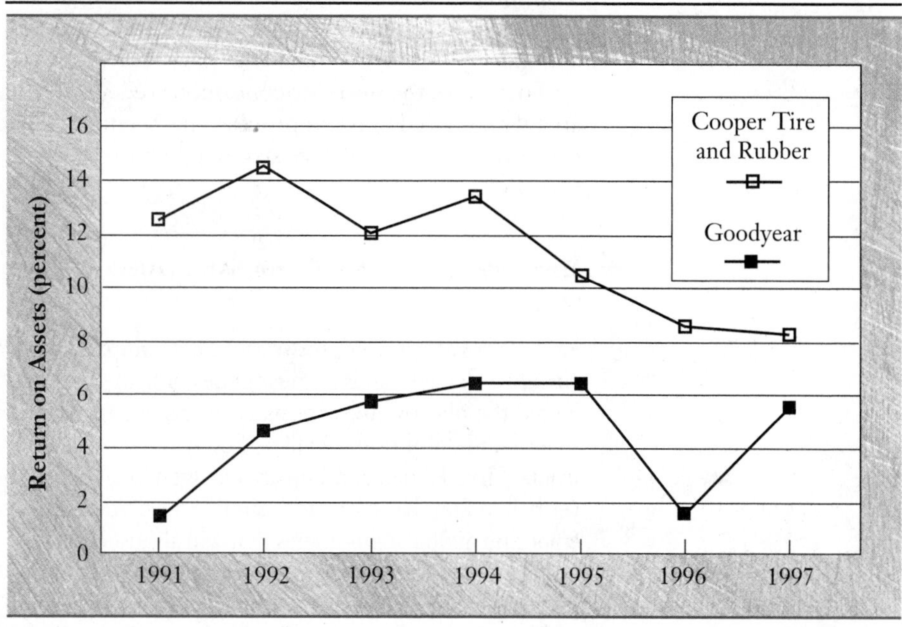

company to dominate the industry for a half century and, in the process, revolutionized the automobile industry by emphasizing car design and styling.

- *Timely and appropriate given the industry environment.* Second, a definition must be timely and appropriate given the industry. After reaching dominance, General Motors lost ground to other car manufacturers in the late 1970s and 1980s when its definition became "tired" and inappropriate given changes in customer demographics, demand for fuel-efficient cars, and new production technologies introduced by Japanese competitors.
- *Clear and readily understandable.* Not all business definitions can be unique and difficult to imitate, and, given the rapid rate of change in most industry environments, some business definitions will be less timely than others. Yet, all business definitions should be clear and readily understandable. The effectiveness of Smucker's definition is that simply by looking at the label, customers know that they are purchasing a high-quality product. All tire dealers know exactly what Cooper's business definition is and that it only sells replacement tires. Also, an effective business definition will be widely understood inside a company so that all its employees not only know the company's definition, but also support and "buy into" that definition.

The Need for Continuous Redefinition: Illustrations and Challenges

Although the following examples attest to the value of an effective business definition, the aim of this section is to emphasize that an outstanding business definition at one point in time is not sufficient. Industry environments can be incredibly dynamic, and the ongoing evolution of those environments requires that companies' definitions anticipate and respond to changes. Nike redefined the market for athletic shoes in the 1970s and 1980s, and a small, upstart company like Vans, Inc., appears to have done the same thing in the late 1990s.[25] Rivals must be on guard and quickly respond to such changes if they hope to remain viable.

To explore the need for continuous redefinition as well as the challenges associated with the redefinition process, this section includes several short case studies of companies that either have struggled or are currently struggling with the redefinition process.

EASTMAN KODAK COMPANY AND THE CHANGING PHOTOGRAPHY MARKET

Kodak provides a vivid illustration of a company caught in the midst of technological change—change that is requiring the company to rethink its definition. Kodak has dominated the photography industry ever since its founder, George Eastman, developed silver halide film in the 1880s. Today, Kodak is fighting battles along two important fronts. First, Kodak and Fuji are engaged in vigorous competition in the market for silver halide film. Kodak's more significant battle, however, is not with Fuji, but with the emerging digital technologies that will almost certainly render its silver halide film technology irrelevant. Already, Kodak must battle not only Fuji, but a new array of competitors, such as Canon, Sony, and Hewlett-Packard, in markets for digital products.

Digital photography is quickly becoming a quite viable substitute for traditional photographic film, but until very recently two factors have limited its widespread acceptance. First, digital photography has offered less clarity than traditional film photography. Until recently, digital photographs could not contain the same amount of "photographic information" as a typical 35 mm negative.[26] Second, the price of digital cameras—anywhere from several hundred to several thousand dollars each—has also slowed the acceptance of digital photography.

Digital competitors have moved rapidly to overcome these obstacles, however. The Olympus D-200L digital camera, priced at just $600, allows the user to record 80 low-resolution pictures or 20 high-resolution pictures at a time that can then be viewed on any personal computer with a Pentium microprocessor. Canon and Epson have already introduced new lines of computer printers that sell for less than $500 and are capable of producing high-quality, color photograph-like prints. Early in 1997, Hewlett-Packard introduced its "PhotoSmart" line of digital photography products. The product line includes a $399 digital camera and a $499 printer that can produce high-resolution photographs that have the same glossy look and feel of traditional photographs.[27] Many more new and affordable digital photography products are likely to be introduced in the near future by these competitors.

Kodak's managers have taken several steps to respond to its digital competitors. First, the company has shed businesses that were not central to its core imaging business. This effort began in 1993 when Kodak announced that it would spin off its giant Eastman Chemical Division. Then, in 1995, Kodak divested its Sterling Drug unit. Kodak had purchased Sterling Drug, best known as the maker of Bayer aspirin, in 1988 for $5.1 billion, yet the business failed to develop a single new ethical pharmaceutical product after being acquired by Kodak.

Second, Kodak's managers have begun pursuing ways of integrating digital technologies into its film photography business. The Photo CD product, introduced in 1992, was Kodak's first attempt to merge its silver halide film processes with digital technologies.

The Photo CD product was designed to allow users to take traditional silver halide photographs and transfer them to compact disks. Photographs could then be viewed on special photo-disk players. Sales of the Photo CD product have been poor, largely because consumers have refused to pay the high prices for the photo disks (approximately $20 for a 24-exposure film disk) and photo-disk players, which cost between $400 and $800.[28]

Finally, in perhaps the most important move to date, Kodak's board hired George Fisher, who was the CEO of Motorola, to be its new CEO.[29] Fisher has, in turn, recruited executives from other high-tech companies to help him engineer a turnaround at the insular Kodak, which has had a history of always promoting managers from within the company's ranks. Since arriving at Kodak, Fisher has consolidated all research and development of digital products in a single division.[30]

The outcome of this short case study on Kodak is still being written. For Kodak, the stakes are quite high. The company earns nearly all its revenues, net income, and cash flows from its film products. If Kodak successfully introduces digital photography products that "cannibalize" sales of its traditional film products, it could jeopardize its earnings and cash flow. At the same time, it would be even more foolish for Kodak to allow Sony, Canon, Hewlett-Packard, and other digital competitors to make any further inroads into the photography industry, for they will surely be formidable rivals.

Evidence suggests that Kodak has now reached a critical juncture. The company's sales did not grow in 1996,[31] and, with growing competition from Fuji in its traditional film business, earnings fell during 1997. To make matters worse, Kodak's digital product lines are very unprofitable. For the first nine months of 1997, Kodak lost $300 million on its digital products.[32] How Kodak's managers respond to the many challenges to its traditional business definition, and how they redefine the company in the midst of a technological revolution in its industry will provide an exciting "real-time" continuation of this case study. The next few years will bring further rapid advances in digital technology that will improve the quality and value of digital photography. As one reporter has observed, sophisticated digital technologies are currently "as out of place in Kodak's silver halide research labs as the first word processors would have been in a typewriter factory," and, depending on how well George Fisher steers Kodak into the digital age, the company "will emerge as either a smart example or a cautionary tale of what happens when a company stops fighting new technologies, and embraces them instead."[33] Redefinition would help Kodak's managers focus (no pun intended) their attention and energies on digital technologies and the company's most serious rivals—Canon, Sony, and Hewlett-Packard—*not Fuji.*

Seagram and Sons

Another interesting case of redefinition is offered by Seagram and Sons. Seagram has long been known best for its "brown liquors"—scotches, whiskies, and bourbons—but as the data in Exhibit 6.4 suggest, Seagram and other distilled spirits producers were confronted by a fairly dramatic decline in the consumption of alcoholic beverages that began in the early 1980s.

In response, Seagram pursued other initiatives. First, Seagram embarked on a strategy of unrelated diversification and sought to acquire Conoco. Conoco resisted Seagram's advances and found a "white knight" in DuPont, which subsequently acquired Conoco by issuing shares of its stock in exchange for Conoco's shares. Because Seagram had already acquired a large percentage of Conoco's outstanding shares at the time, DuPont's acquisition of Conoco meant that Seagram became

EXHIBIT 6.4

The Declining Market for Distilled Spirits, 1970-1995

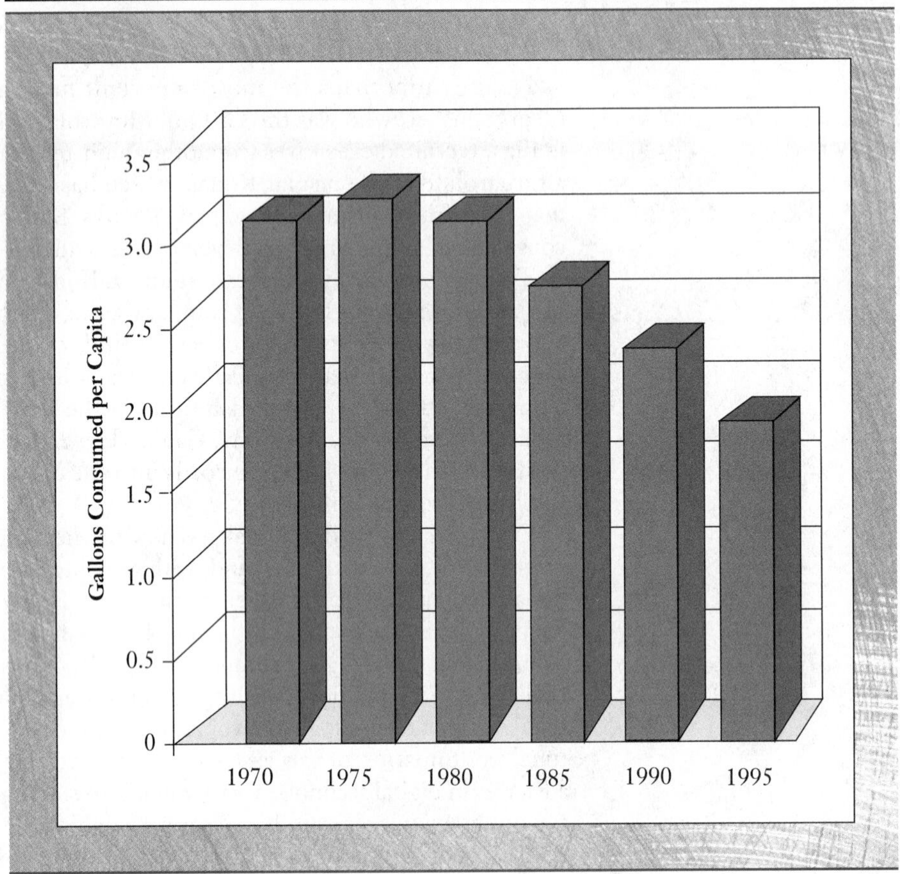

SOURCE: Statistical Abstract of the United States (Washington, D.C.: U.S. Superintendent of Documents, 1997), p. 150.

DuPont's largest shareholder, owning nearly 25 percent of DuPont's outstanding shares. In the years that followed, DuPont's dividend payments were Seagram's largest source of income and cash flow.

After failing to acquire Conoco, Seagram turned its attention to other companies in the beverage industry and acquired Tropicana, the largest maker of orange juice in the United States, in 1988. Later, Seagram acquired Soho, a maker of natural soda beverages. Seagram has also strengthened its position in distilled spirits by acquiring a number of strong brands from other manufacturers while shedding many of its weaker or less prestigious brands.

In 1995, Seagram sold its interest in DuPont to finance the acquisition of MCA, which owned Universal Studios. How this acquisition is related to Seagram's beverage businesses and how the company now defines itself are certainly interesting questions. The best explanation for Seagram's acquisition of MCA is that Edgar Bronfman, its chief executive, has had a long-standing interest in the motion picture industry and wanted to see the company acquire a motion picture studio. Most recently, Seagram has acquired PolyGram from Philips Electronics. PolyGram is

EXHIBIT 6.5

Seagram's Corporate History Since 1980

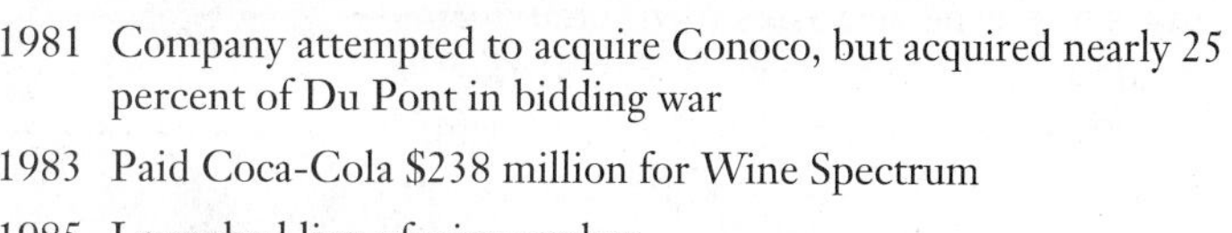

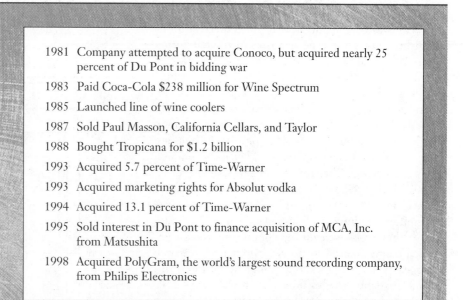

1981	Company attempted to acquire Conoco, but acquired nearly 25 percent of Du Pont in bidding war
1983	Paid Coca-Cola $238 million for Wine Spectrum
1985	Launched line of wine coolers
1987	Sold Paul Masson, California Cellars, and Taylor
1988	Bought Tropicana for $1.2 billion
1993	Acquired 5.7 percent of Time-Warner
1993	Acquired marketing rights for Absolut vodka
1994	Acquired 13.1 percent of Time-Warner
1995	Sold interest in Du Pont to finance acquisition of MCA, Inc. from Matsushita
1998	Acquired PolyGram, the world's largest sound recording company, from Philips Electronics

the world's largest sound recording company and owns some of the best-known record labels, including Motown, Decca, Mercury, and Deutsche Grammophon. Exhibit 6.5 provides a chronological summary of Seagram's shifting corporate terrain.

What can we make of Seagram's corporate history over the past decade? First of all, Seagram's business definition appears to be very unclear. Like Kodak, Seagram is not what it was before it began diversifying and yet it has not really become something new. After its acquisition of Tropicana in the mid-1980s, it was no longer just a "distilled spirits company," though it continued to make a number of acquisitions in distilled spirits. With its acquisitions of MCA and PolyGram, Seagram's revenues are now split between beverages and the entertainment business, so it is obviously no longer just a "beverage company." Thus, Seagram would appear to be an example of a company whose managers have not done an effective job of business definition. Why, then, is the Seagram example included here?

Though Seagram may lack a coherent business definition, it does illustrate the importance of responding proactively to a major decline in its core distilled spirits market. Not content to watch sales and earnings fall as the market for distilled spirits contracted, the company has aggressively sought new opportunities for growth. In fact, it's unfortunate that more companies aren't as proactive as Seagram. The challenge for Seagram's managers in the years ahead will be to prove that they can not only make acquisitions that help the company maintain revenue growth but that they can also develop a definition that helps them manage the company's business segments in a way that leads to competitive advantage and sustained high performance.

General Motors at a Crossroads

As illustrated in Figure 1, many of General Motors' car lines saw significant decreases in volume during the 1980s and early 1990s. For example, Oldsmobile sold more than 1.1 million cars in 1986. Oldsmobile cars were known for high-quality engineering and attractive styling. Since 1986, however, sales of Oldsmobile cars have fallen precipitously, reaching a low of 360,000 units in 1993. Similar declines are seen in GM's Chevrolet and Cadillac lines. Though the new Saturn division is a bright spot, Figure 2 shows that Saturn's sales—which have never exceeded 300,000 units—do not compensate for the significant volume declines in GM's other car lines.

What explains declining volume and the associated market share loss? GM's own market research suggests that its cars suffer from a definition problem. By failing to introduce new models and significant styling changes for several years, GM allowed many of its car lines to "age" in the minds of consumers. Oldsmobile offers perhaps the best example of this "aging" of its business definition. Focus group research found that consumers viewed Oldsmobile as "the car my father drives." A subsequent Oldsmobile advertising campaign sought to challenge and change this perception by claiming that Oldsmobile "is not the car your father drives." Nevertheless, Oldsmobile's definition has been badly tarnished. When Oldsmobile showed two versions of its Aurora model to focus groups—one version with the Oldsmobile logo and the other version without—reactions were surprising. Those focus groups viewing the Aurora without the Oldsmobile logo reported overwhelmingly positive reactions to the car, while those viewing the Aurora with the Oldsmobile logo reported far less positive reactions.

Cadillac also illustrates GM's definition problems. As recently as 1990, Cadillac held nearly one-fourth of the U.S. market for luxury cars. By 1996, however, Cadillac's share of the luxury segment had fallen to below 15 percent.[1] Cadillac's most serious problem is that the cars offered by Mercedes,

FIGURE 1

Unit Sales of Chevrolet, Oldsmobile, and Cadillac Cars

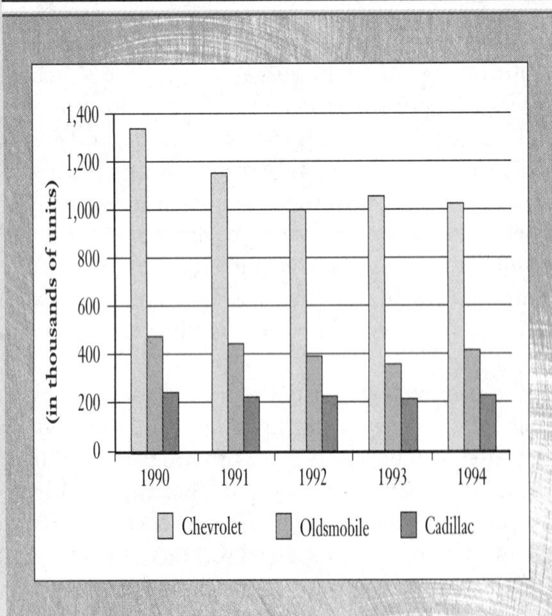

FIGURE 2

Unit Sales of Saturn Cars versus Unit Sales of Chevrolet, Oldsmobile, and Cadillac Cars

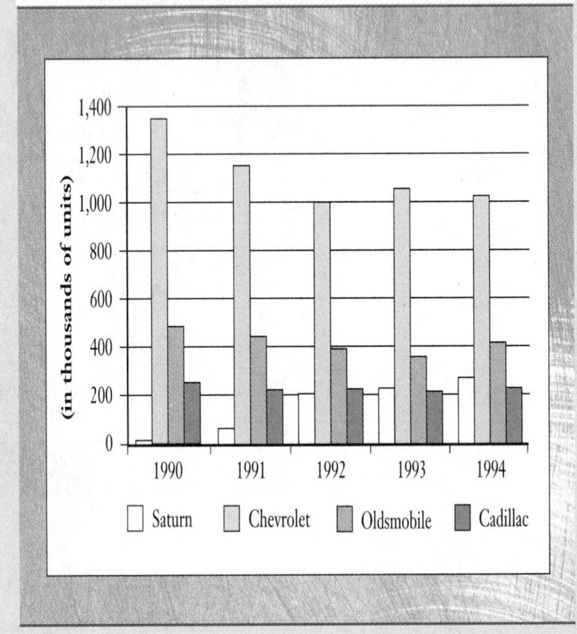

continued

BMW, Toyota's Lexus line, and other producers have come to be seen by consumers as more representative of what they expect luxury cars to look like than Cadillac's boxy, boat-like models. In response to this shift in consumer tastes, Cadillac is seeking to update its image by redesigning its Seville model and introducing a new model, the Catera, to give these cars a "new luxury look." Cadillac will also introduce its first sports utility vehicle in order to compete against other companies' luxury SUVs.

As noted earlier in the chapter, General Motors recruited an outsider, Ronald Zarrella from Bausch and Lomb, to improve the muddled image of its brands. Early on, Zarrella concluded that with 77 different car and truck lines, the company offered "too many models" and that the various GM divisions offered overlapping and poorly defined product lines.[2] As a first step, Zarrella sought to redefine the various GM divisions—something that had not really been done since Sloan's original concept of offering models at various price points. Figure 3 provides a description of Zarrella's definitions for each of GM's car and truck lines.

How well have Ronald Zarrella's marketing efforts worked over the past several years? At this point, it is probably still too early to pass judgment. A number of impressive reforms have been put in place. General Motors has adopted the practice of brand management, similar to the approach used by consumer product companies, in an effort to establish more distinct images for each of its many car lines. The company has also introduced 14 new models, many of which have won acclaim. Yet, during the last few years, General Motors' share of the U.S. automobile market has continued to slip from more than 50 percent in the early 1980s to 30.7 percent in 1997 and 28.6 percent in 1998.[3]

The General Motors example is interesting because it shows how aged or outdated business definitions can result in "negative brand equity." We typically think of brand names as adding equity or value to the products that carry them. Several of GM's brands, however, have lost a great deal of consumer appeal and may even detract from the company's efforts to sell its cars. General Motors has found, for example, that 35 percent of consumers

FIGURE 3

New Definitions for General Motors' Car and Truck Lines

GM marketing chief Ronald L. Zarrella's vision for GM's seven vehicle divisions:

Chevrolet: As GM's high-volume car and light-truck division, should offer affordability, dependability, reliability, and widest range of models.
Pontiac: GM's sportiest brand, standing for youthfulness and spiritedness, and featuring sleek, athletic, "in-your-face styling."
Saturn: A small-car division with a focus on "an overall shipping, buying, and ownership experience" targeting import-car buyers, and standing for "dependability, intelligence, friendliness."
Oldsmobile: "The logical place for Saturn owners to go" as they become affluent and want larger medium-priced cars; competitive against Audi, Acura, and entry-level Infiniti and Lexus.
Buick: GM's "premium American car," with products that are "substantial, distinctive, powerful, mature," targeting baby boomers in their 50s.
Cadillac: GM's luxury car division, with innovative, responsive, "sophisticated, highly perfected" cars that compete against Mercedes, BMW, Lexus "in all the markets of the world."
GMC: GM's "premium truck brand with differentiated products from Chevrolet."

SOURCE: G. Stern. 1995. GM's new marketing chief seeks clarity amid muddle of overlapping car lines. *The Wall Street Journal*, May 1, A3, A13.

continued

shopping for a new car won't even consider buying a GM vehicle! Certainly the future success of General Motors will depend on changing consumer perceptions; obviously this will not happen overnight.

Saturn, GM's biggest success at wooing back dissatisfied buyers in recent years, seems to have been limited by the company's decision to restrict Saturn's line to small cars rather than allowing it to include mid-size cars and sports utility vehicles. A recent *Business Week* article noted that "Buick, Olds, and Cadillac—fettered by stodgy images they've had trouble shaking—struggle to sell snazzy new vehicles such as the Regal, Intrigue, Silhouette minivan, Bravada SUV, and Catera. Many analysts believe similar models would fly out the doors at Saturn."[4] Saturn's lack of bigger models for its past customers to trade up to has almost certainly been responsible for its declining sales, which have fallen every year since 1994. ■

[1]R. L. Simison and R. Blumenstein, "Cadillac and Lincoln Try to Regain Their Cachet," *The Wall Street Journal,* July 3, 1997, B1, B7.

[2]G. Stern, "GM's New Marketing Chief Seeks Clarity Amid Muddle of Overlapping Car Lines," *The Wall Street Journal,* May 1, 1995, A3, A13.

[3]R. Blumenstein, "For GM's Marketing Chief, Some Bumps in the Road," *The Wall Street Journal,* August 8, 1997, B1, B2; A. B. Henderson, "U-Turn on Caddy Truck Detours GM Strategy," *The Wall Street Journal,* March 26, 1998, B1, B2.

[4]K. Kerwin, "Why Didn't GM Do More for Saturn?" *Business Week,* March 16, 1998, 62.

Redefinition at Steinway and Sons

Largely handcrafted, Steinway pianos have for years symbolized excellence and have long been the instruments preferred by concert pianists. Producing fewer than 5,000 pianos each year, the company fetches prices ranging from $10,000 for a basic upright to over $60,000 for a concert grand. Troubles began for Steinway in 1972, when the Steinway family sold the company to CBS. The small company became lost inside a giant conglomerate; management changes were frequent and many buyers became concerned about lower quality.

In 1985, ownership again changed hands when Steinway was acquired by John and Robert Birmingham in a leveraged buyout valued at $53.5 million. Nonmusicians, the brothers nevertheless set out immediately to implement modern manufacturing and management methods. They automated a number of processes and invested in new equipment, all with the aim of improving quality and raising productivity. The problem for the new owners, however, is that through automation of the company's manufacturing processes, the pianos have lost much of their uniqueness.[34] Buyers of these expensive instruments had come to expect that each piano would have its own unique tone, touch, and personality, so shopping for a Steinway involved selecting the piano that had a particular feel and sound. As the production of Steinway pianos has become more standardized, eliminating quality problems, the pianos have also lost their individual distinctiveness.

Ironically, as Steinway has lost much of its individuality and unique business definition, it has inadvertently imitated the strategy of one of its most established competitors, Yamaha, whose pianos have long been known for their consistently high-quality sound and feel. As emphasized in Chapter 3, imitation of another firm's successful strategy can sometimes provide a firm with competitive parity, yet it is unlikely to be a source of sustained competitive advantage.

Redefinition at Two Apparel Retailing Companies

"Oxxford Clothes has an image problem."[35] Long a maker of conservative business suits that sell for prices starting at $1,600, the company has come to be viewed as stodgy by many businessmen who prefer more fashionable suits sold by Armani and other Italian designers. In response, Oxxford Clothes has sought to update its image and has added a number of more fashionable suits to its collection, but it is finding that consumer perceptions are difficult to change.

Like Oxxford, Brooks Brothers, the well-known maker of conservative, if not stuffy, business attire, initiated a redefinition of its business soon after being acquired by the British retailer Marks and Spencer in 1988. Market research conducted by Brooks Brothers' new parent suggested that because of the shift toward more casual business attire, the company was failing to serve a large and growing segment of the business clothing market.

Altering its inventory mix, Brooks Brothers stores soon began carrying more casual clothing, including more blazers and casual slacks. Sales of the new, more casual clothing lagged behind expectations, however, so Marks and Spencer conducted additional research, the findings from which were quite surprising. The company found, for example, that customers liked the new, more casual clothing lines. The merchandise wasn't selling well, however, because Brooks Brothers' sales personnel were not selling the new lines. When asked why they were not more aggressively pushing the casual clothing lines, sales personnel stated, "It isn't what we do."

The Brooks Brothers example suggests that it is not enough for top managers to adopt a new business definition, but that the entire organization must "buy into" any new definition in order for it to be effective. Brooks Brothers has subsequently retrained many of its employees, and sales as well as profits have shown growth during the past few years.[36]

GALLO'S EFFORTS TO RECAST ITSELF IN THE VARIETAL WINE SEGMENT

For much of its life, the E. & J. Gallo Winery successfully defined itself as a producer of low-cost table wine, typically selling wine for less than \$5 to \$6 per bottle. Over the last several years, however, Gallo has sought to enter the higher-priced varietal wine segment in which wine sells at various price points ranging from \$6 to \$16 per bottle. To the dismay of Gallo's managers, the company enjoyed little success in redefining itself as a producer of varietal wines. In spite of major advertising campaigns aimed at improving the image of the company's products, consumers seem reluctant to pay more than \$5 to \$6 per bottle for Gallo wines. Apparently, the image that customers hold of Gallo as the producer of low-cost table wines simply prevents the company from breaking the price threshold that separates the low-cost table wine and varietal wine categories.

For many years, consultants and industry observers suggested that Gallo could enter the higher-priced varietal wine market, but that it would have to use a different name in order to overcome the image consumers have of Gallo as the maker of low-cost table wines.[37] Such a tactic has been employed successfully by many other wine makers; for example, Glen Ellen, a varietal wine maker whose wines generally sell in the range of \$5 to \$7 per bottle, offers a higher-priced line of wines carrying the Benziger name. Gallo's managers long resisted the suggestion that it offer a wine under any other name, but the company recently introduced wines using the Turning Leaf brand name. Noticeably absent from bottles of Turning Leaf wines: the Gallo name!

The Gallo example suggests just how important business definition can be. Although Gallo has never enjoyed much success at breaking into the varietal wine segment because of its low-cost jug wine image, its Turning Leaf chardonnay rose from obscurity to become the second-best-selling chardonnay in less than one year. Gallo's success with its Turning Leaf brand has even prompted a lawsuit from Kendall-Jackson, maker of the number-one selling chardonnay. Kendall-Jackson argues that Gallo copied its "colored leaf" logo and the "gradual, tapered neck" of its bottles.[38]

Kendall-Jackson may well be concerned about trademark infringement, but it is probably just as likely that Kendall-Jackson is hoping the publicity surrounding the lawsuit will make wine drinkers aware of Gallo's parentage of Turning Leaf wines.[39]

MONSANTO

Unlike Kodak, General Motors, and some of the other companies profiled here, Monsanto has been very proactive in changing its business definition. And, unlike Seagram, Monsanto's managers have been quite certain about how they wanted to change the company's definition. Thus, Monsanto offers an excellent example of redefinition because of the success it has enjoyed in transforming itself.

Though Monsanto had long been a major player in the commodity chemicals industry and a maker of agricultural herbicides and pesticides, Monsanto's managers became convinced of the promise of biotechnology for agricultural applications by 1980. In the years since, Monsanto's managers have aggressively invested in its agricultural biotechnology business, and Monsanto's shift in focus was completed in 1996 when the company's managers announced that it would split into two parts: Monsanto would focus on biotechnology, and a newly formed company, Solutia, would operate Monsanto's former commodity chemicals businesses. Exhibit 6.6 offers a brief history of Monsanto's acquisitions and investments in biotechnology.

THE CHALLENGES ASSOCIATED WITH REDEFINITION

The preceding case studies suggest a number of observations about the process of redefinition. First, these case studies underscore a point made at the outset of this

EXHIBIT 6.6

Monsanto's Acquisitions and Investments in Biotechnology

June 1995	Acquired 49.9 percent of Calgene, a biotechnology company
November 1995	Paid $25 million for rights to Ecogen's plant gene technology
February 1996	Acquired large stake in DeKalb Genetics, a corn seed producer
April 1996	Paid $150 million for Agracetus, a company that pioneered use of "gene gun" technology
September 1996	Acquired Asgrow Seed, a major producer of soybean seeds
December 1996	Announced that it will spin-off chemicals business
May 1998	Agreed to acquire DeKalb Genetics and Delta Pine & Land (a cotton seed producer)
June 1998	Agreed to merger with American Home Products

chapter: Business definition and redefinition are creative and ongoing processes. Business definition and redefinition are rarely, if ever, "typical business decisions" in the sense that they are based on financial or quantitative criteria and data. For example, if Kodak used present value or rate of return criteria to evaluate whether it should move more aggressively toward a digital future, it would surely reject such an option. It is highly unlikely that investments in digital products and technologies would show higher rates of return than additional investments in Kodak's silver halide film business. Decisions about business definition and redefinition almost certainly have to be made using different criteria and decision processes.

At the same time, decisions about business definition and redefinition cannot be made blindly. In fact, it is probably fair to argue that managers must know a good deal about the direction they want to take their firms; they cannot simply come to work one day and decide to redefine their firms to serve new customer groups by making products that their companies have never made before, using totally different technologies. Kodak is probably able to make the decision to move toward a more digital future *because* it has already invested sizable sums in researching and developing digital technologies. Monsanto's transformation from commodity chemical company to biotechnology company came after a number of successful initiatives helped to convince its managers that the company had a viable future in biotechnology.

Though Seagram's definition seems quite vague, with few if any obvious linkages or relationships among the company's distilled spirits, and motion picture businesses, the Seagram case study does highlight another key point about the redefinition process: *Sooner is probably better than later*. As noted earlier, Seagram moved quickly to diversify as the market for distilled spirits began to decline. Though Seagram can be faulted for the decisions it has made since, it must still be applauded for being so proactive. General Motors would certainly have benefited from being more proactive in updating the image of its car lines!

Finally, all these case studies illustrate that business definition and redefinition require a "leap" as well as considerable investment. Hamel and Prahalad have coined the phrase "strategic intent" to describe the significance of these redefinition efforts.[40] Hamel and Prahalad define strategic intent as an ideal "destiny" or competitive position that firms hope to achieve over the next several years or even decades of effort and investment. Monsanto is realizing so much success from its redefinition effort because its managers have been willing both to take calculated risks and to make large investments in transforming the company. It's probably fair to argue that the success of Kodak's efforts to redefine itself as a digital company will depend on the level of investment it makes in digital technologies. When General Motors spent billions of dollars to acquire EDS and Hughes, it chose not to invest those same dollars in its automotive business. That additional investment could have helped to maintain GM's position in the all-important family sedan and luxury car markets.

Even as we emphasize the importance of timely redefinition, these short case studies suggest that redefinition is rarely easy. Many firms have encountered a variety of problems and met considerable resistance as they have sought to change or alter their definitions. The Gallo case study illustrates that firms can develop such strong definitions that the loyalty of customers, employees, and other constituencies to those definitions can limit the ability of firms to redefine themselves with anything short of Herculean efforts.

The evidence suggests a management paradox: It appears that the companies that have the greatest difficulty in changing their definitions are those that have been most effective in forging distinctive definitions in the past. In fact, it is probably safe to argue that *the degree of difficulty associated with business redefinition will be directly related to the level of recognition and distinctiveness that a firm's definition has enjoyed in the past.*

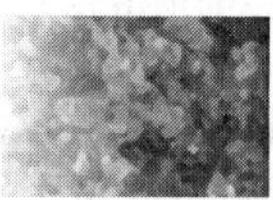

Managers and Their Role in Business Definition

One rather obvious conclusion that emerges from this discussion is that top managers should place a great deal of emphasis on business definition and redefinition. Business definition is the creative task of selecting a mission or vision for the firm, and it includes fundamental decisions about customers to be served, products or services to be offered, and technologies to be employed. As suggested by many of the examples offered in this chapter, once managers have made fundamental business definition decisions, other important strategic questions are likely to become more apparent and straightforward.

It is also important to emphasize that business definition is *not* strategic planning. Good definitions provide firms with *visions* rather than *plans*. Unlike formal planning processes that develop strategies based on analyses of companies' existing competitive environments, the processes of business definition and redefinition should allow firms to shape proactively their own destinies and create totally new competitive environments, transcending the barriers posed by existing industry structures. In other words, through business definition, firms play offense rather than defense.

Furthermore, as managers work to develop their firms' visions or missions and seek to develop unique business definitions, they can then focus their attention on a smaller portion of the competitive environment. While this narrowing of a company's range of vision does pose some increased danger of being "blind-sided," it greatly reduces what is perhaps the biggest obstacle confronting most firms: the analysis of too many different business opportunities. Managers who are more certain about their firms' definitions will have less trouble deciding which opportunities are worth pursuing and which would be unrelated to the visions of their firms.

Related to this last point, another important advantage of effective definition and timely redefinition is that it should shorten considerably not only the time required to formulate strategy but also the time required to implement strategy. A widely held vision or understanding of a firm's purpose should facilitate decision making by providing managers with a blueprint that provides direction for the future of their businesses and firms. Research has revealed that it is not uncommon in most large business firms for 80 percent of middle-level managers to be uncertain about their firms' strategies. Obviously this is going to greatly complicate the strategy implementation process. By defining the business—clearly articulating a mission or vision for the organization—firms could do much to create greater constancy and consistency of purpose (to paraphrase Dr. Deming).

Finally, this chapter has emphasized that continuous redefinition is essential if firms are to stay relevant and avoid decline. Organizations that undergo periodic redefinition will not only be more innovative, but they will also be more responsive to day-to-day challenges and changes in their competitive environments.

Key Points

- Business definition is a fundamental, perhaps the most fundamental, business decision that managers must make.
- Good business definitions reflect creative exploitation of developments in firms' competitive environments.
- Effective business definitions share the following characteristics:
  1. They are distinctive and set companies apart from competitors.
  2. They are timely and appropriate given the industry environments in which companies are competing.
  3. They are clear and readily understandable by customers as well as employees, suppliers, and other constituencies.
- Business definition can contribute to the development of competitive advantage in at least four ways:
  1. An effective business definition can uniquely position a firm in its industry.
  2. An effective business definition can help to focus management attention on a firm's key objectives, its most significant strategic issues, and its most important rivals.
  3. An effective business definition does not answer other strategic questions, but it does make those questions more obvious and should improve strategic decision making and the implementation of strategies.
  4. An effective business definition provides managers and employees with a sense of meaning and purpose that can be very motivational.
- Firms that are defined and then continuously redefined are much more likely to keep pace with changes in their competitive environments, and they are also much more likely to have clearer understandings of how resources should be allocated.
- Redefinition poses many challenges. Firms must frequently make significant investments in new markets and technologies without clear evidence that those investments will pay off. Furthermore, redefinition often requires companies to radically alter the perceptions and beliefs of customers and employees.

Review and Discussion Questions

1. *What is business definition? In what ways is business definition a creative process?*
2. *How can business definition contribute to the development and maintenance of competitive advantage?*
3. *What are the characteristics of effective business definitions?*
4. *Why must managers be concerned about the process of business redefinition? What makes business redefinition so difficult for the managers of many firms?*
5. *How is business definition related to managerial thinking and mental models?*

Suggestions for Further Reading

Abell, D.F. 1980. *Defining the Business: Starting Point of Strategic Planning.* Englewood Cliffs, N.J.: Prentice-Hall.

Collins, J.C., & Porras, J.I. 1994. *Built to Last: Successful Habits of Visionary Companies.* New York: HarperBusiness.
Drucker, P.F. 1994. The theory of the business. *Harvard Business Review,* 72(5): 95–104.
Hamel, G., & Prahalad, C.K. 1989. Strategic intent. *Harvard Business Review,* 67(3): 63–76.
Sloan, Jr., A.P. 1963. *My Years with General Motors.* New York: Doubleday/Currency.

ENDNOTES

1. Albert, S., and D. Whetten, 1985. Organizational identity. In L. L. Cummings and B. M. Staw, eds. *Research in Organizational Behavior,* 7:263–295. Greenwich, Conn: JAI Press.
2. Drucker, P. F. 1994. The theory of the business. *Harvard Business Review* 72(5):95.
3. Abell, D. F. 1980. *Defining the Business: Starting Point of Strategic Planning.* Englewood Cliffs, N.J.: Prentice-Hall.
4. Exhibit 6.2 illustrates an industry that expands over time, suggesting that new customers are being served, new products or services are being introduced, and new technologies are being incorporated. It's important to emphasize that all industries do not expand over time as illustrated in the exhibit. The newspaper market, for example, has contracted considerably since the end of World War II. At that time, many households subscribed to two major daily newspapers and, to meet this demand, many cities had at least two daily newspapers. For example, in Washington, D.C., the *Washington Post* was the "morning" newspaper while the *Evening Star* was published in the afternoon to summarize the day's news. The advent of television has had a major impact on newspaper readership, and today, less than half of all American households subscribe to a daily newspaper. Thus, the newspaper market has contracted considerably over the past several decades.
5. Porter, M. E. 1987. From competitive advantage to corporate strategy. *Harvard Business Review* 65(3):43–59.
6. Abell, *Defining the Business.*
7. May, R. 1975. *The Courage to Create.* New York: Norton, pp. 21–22.
8. Ibid., p. 88.
9. Ibid.
10. Sloan, A. P., Jr., 1963. *My Years with General Motors.* New York: Doubleday/Currency, p. 60.
11. Miller, K. 1990. Repair industry struggles to survive cars' high quality. *The Wall Street Journal,* January 5, B2.
12. Dobrzynski, J. H. 1996. Yes, he's revived Sears. But can he reinvent it? *New York Times,* January 7, F1, F8; Mundt, K. 1997. Why Sears survived—and Ward and Woolworth's didn't. *The Wall Street Journal,* June 28, A18.
13. Cooper, A. C., and D. Schendel, 1976. Strategic responses to technological threats. *Business Horizons* 19(1):61–69.
14. Selznick, A. 1957. *Leadership in Administration: A Sociological Interpretation.* New York: Harper & Row.
15. Collins, J. C., and J. I. Porras, 1994. *Built to Last: Successful Habits of Visionary Companies.* New York: HarperBusiness; L. Larwood, C. M. Falbe, M. P. Kriger, and P. Miesing, 1995. Structure and meaning of organizational vision. *Academy of Management Journal* 38:740–769.
16. Albert and Whetten, Organizational identity.
17. Charan, R. 1982. How to strengthen your strategy review process. *Journal of Business Strategy* 2(3):53.
18. Abell, *Defining the Business.*
19. The story of Williams Companies' redefinition is told in an article by Solomon, C. 1989. Bright idea: How Williams Companies turned oil pipelines to conduits of data. *The Wall Street Journal,* July 11, A1, A5.
20. Collins and Porras, *Built to Last,* p. 227.

21. Sloan, *My Years with General Motors*, p. 58.
22. Ibid, p. 68.
23. Stern, G. 1995. GM's new marketing chief seeks clarity amid muddle of overlapping car lines. *The Wall Street Journal*, May 1, A3, A13.
24. Hymowitz, C., and T. F. O'Boyle, 1991. Two disparate firms find keys to success in troubled industries. *The Wall Street Journal*, May 29, A1, A9.
25. Pereira, J. 1998. Going to extremes: Board-riding youths take sneaker maker on a fast ride uphill. *The Wall Street Journal*, April 16, A1, A8.
26. Holusha, J. 1992. American snapshot, the next generation. *New York Times*, June 7, F1, F6.
27. Gomes, L. 1997. H-P to unveil digital camera and peripherals. *The Wall Street Journal*, February 25, B7.
28. Deutsch, C. H. 1996. Picture it: More paths to profits. *New York Times*, December 2, C1, C10.
29. Bounds, W. 1995. George Fisher pushes Kodak into digital era. *The Wall Street Journal*, June 9, B1, B4.
30. Deutsch, Picture it.
31. Nelson, E. 1997. Kodak says sales are "essentially flat," and stock price gets pummeled 10.5 percent. *The Wall Street Journal*, March 24, A4.
32. Johannes, L. 1997. Kodak profit fell 43 percent in third quarter on losses in digital-imaging products. *The Wall Street Journal*, October 15, B2; E. Nelson, 1997. Kodak posts 16 percent decline in earnings; stock price drops 11 percent to 52-week low. *The Wall Street Journal*, July 17. A3.
33. Deutsch, Picture it, p. C10.
34. Valente, J. 1991. Sour notes: In clash between art and efficiency, did Steinway pianos lose? *The Wall Street Journal*, March 27, A1, A10.
35. Berner, R. 1997. An old clothier learns some new tricks. *The Wall Street Journal*, July 24, B1, B5.
36. Parker-Pope, T. 1996. Brooks Brothers gets a boost from new look. *The Wall Street Journal*, May 22, B1, B4.
37. Fisher, L. M. 1992. The Gallos go for the gold, and away from the jugs. *New York Times*, November 22, F5.
38. King, R. T., Jr. 1996. Grapes of wrath: Kendall-Jackson sues Gallo Winery in a battle over a bottle. *The Wall Street Journal*, April 5, B1, B2.
39. Rigdon, J. I. 1997. Wine-bottle design suit could have a spillover effect on other products. *The Wall Street Journal* March 31, B9D.
40. Hamel, G., and C. K. Prahalad, 1989. Strategic intent. *Harvard Business Review* 67(3),63–76.

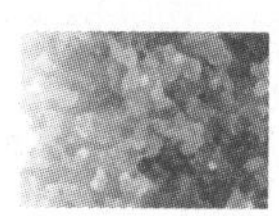

CHAPTER 7

BUSINESS STRATEGY AND COMPETITIVE ADVANTAGE

CHAPTER OBJECTIVES

Chapter 7 is the first of two chapters on business strategy. This chapter introduces the concept of "generic" business strategies, describing the objectives, characteristics, and limitations of the various generic strategies. Chapter 8 continues the study of business strategy by examining the challenges of formulating and implementing business strategies in emerging and mature industry contexts. Chapter 8 also considers the unique challenges associated with developing a competitive advantage in both manufacturing and service industries.

The specific objectives of Chapter 7 are to:

- Introduce the concept of generic business strategies and describe the generic business strategies of cost leadership, differentiation, and focus.
- Describe the organizational resources and capabilities associated with these generic business strategies, and suggest how managers can identify opportunities for reducing costs and differentiating their businesses.
- Identify and discuss a number of the implications of generic business strategies, focusing specifically on the special challenges of commodity markets (e.g., the tendency to compete on price alone) and the factors that limit the effectiveness of differentiation strategies (e.g., private-label competition, discounting, and commoditization—the tendency for differentiated products to lose their distinctiveness).

BACKGROUND

This chapter and the one that follows focus on business strategy. As suggested by the text's model of strategic management (reprinted in Exhibit 7.1), the overall aim of these two chapters is to stimulate your thinking about how managers formulate business strategies aimed at developing and sustaining competitive advantage. While the previous chapter emphasized the importance of business definition, or the task of positioning firms in their competitive arenas, these two chapters examine how firms should compete in their industries. As suggested by the model,

EXHIBIT 7.1

The Mental Models and Strategic Decisions Studied in This Text and Their Influence on Performance and Competitive Advantage

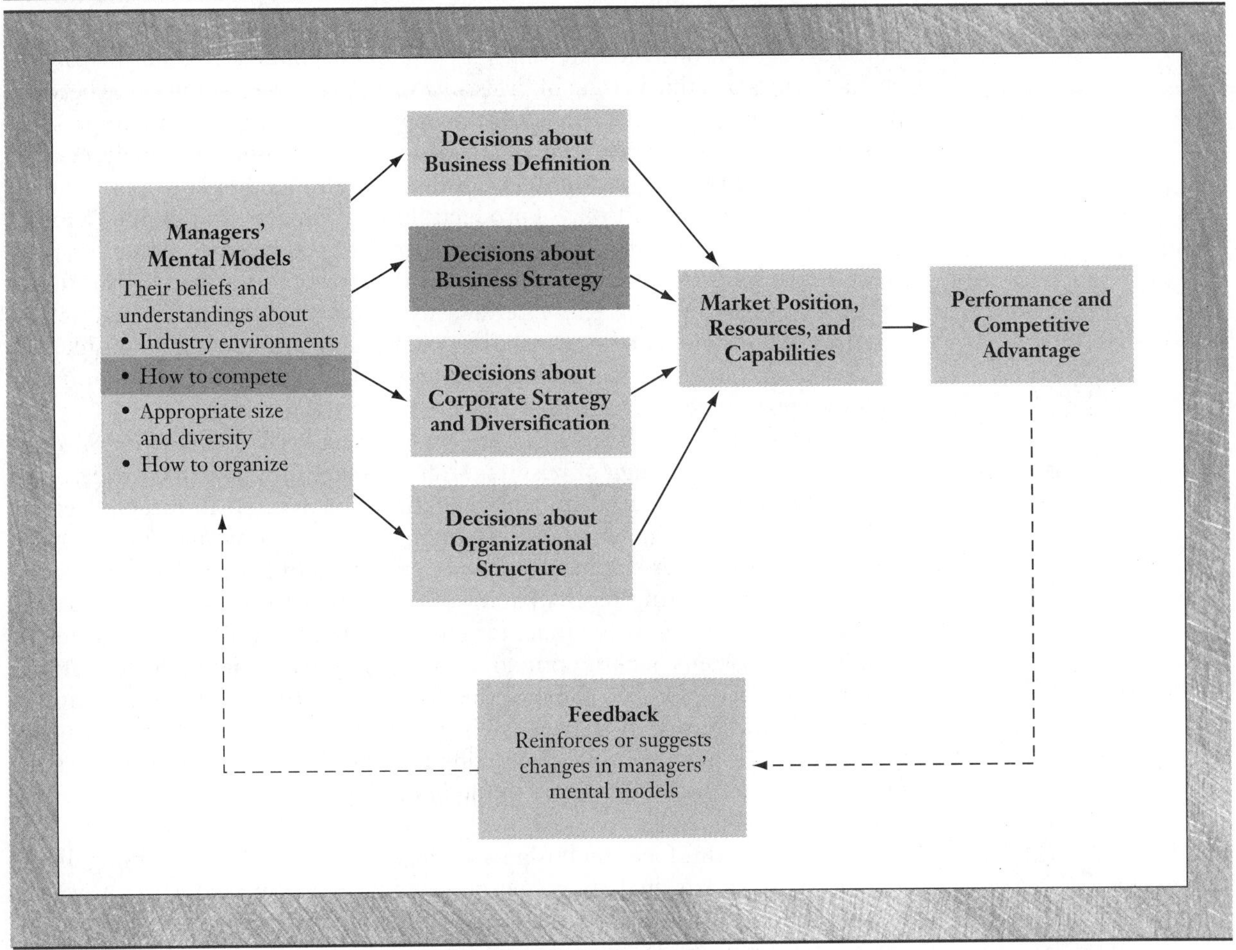

managers' decisions about business strategy are influenced by their beliefs and understandings about how their firms should compete.

Though the text and the model explicitly distinguish between the concepts of business definition and business strategy, it should be fairly obvious that managerial thinking and decisions about business definition and business strategy are very much interrelated or "tightly coupled" in that they are mutually dependent and can become mutually reinforcing. For example, the managers of companies like Saks Fifth Avenue and Neiman Marcus, which have defined their firms as exclusive, high-end retailers, necessarily pursue different business strategies than Wal-Mart and Kmart — stores that dominate the discount segment of the retailing industry. No doubt the definitions these companies have adopted have influenced their choice of business strategies. In addition, over time, the various strategies that companies pursue further enhance or reinforce their business definitions.

Over the years, researchers have sought to develop typologies of business strategies, based on the assumption that there are observable patterns or regularities in the way firms compete. One early typology suggested that firms tend to pursue one of four different types of business strategies.[1] According to this typology, firms could be *prospectors*, pursuing entrepreneurial exploration of their competitive environments with the aim of developing new product and market opportunities. Firms could also be *defenders*, seeking stability by maintaining current market positions and defending against encroachment by other firms. The characteristics of a third group of firms, *analyzers*, place them somewhere between prospectors and defenders, balancing the opportunity-seeking nature of prospectors against the risk aversion of defenders. Thus, like prospectors, analyzers seek to exploit new market opportunities, but they will also tend to draw most of their revenue from a stable portfolio of products. Finally, the typology defined a fourth group of firms as *reactors*. While the strategies of prospectors, defenders, and analyzers were all to some extent proactive, the strategies pursued by this fourth group of firms would be characterized by inconsistencies and a reactionary response to environmental change. Thus, the reactor strategy is not considered a viable one, and firms pursuing such a strategy would either have to adopt one of the other three types of strategy or face eventual decline.

The publication of Michael Porter's widely read book, *Competitive Strategy*, introduced a new typology of business strategies that quickly gained widespread popularity among both academics and practicing managers.[2] In this chapter, we will examine Porter's generic business strategies of *cost leadership*, *differentiation*, and *focus*. This chapter emphasizes Porter's typology of generic business strategies because his writing has had an important impact on the business world, and, as with his Five Forces Model for industry analysis, nearly all managers are familiar with Porter's generic strategies. In addition to explaining Porter's strategies, the chapter examines some of the problems associated with operating in commodity markets or industries. This discussion will suggest the many benefits companies can enjoy by differentiating their products or services. At the same time, the chapter highlights some of the limitations of differentiation as a viable business strategy.

In Chapter 8, this focus on business strategies is extended by examining different industry contexts, including emerging and more mature industries as well as manufacturing and service industries. We will see that new challenges and insights emerge by examining the relationship between business strategy and competitive advantage through the lenses of these various industry contexts.

Generic Business Strategies

To begin, let's review the three generic strategies described by Michael Porter in his book, *Competitive Strategy*. Porter's three generic strategies emerge from a two-by-two matrix defined along one axis by market breadth and along the other axis by the source of strategic advantage. Porter argued that any particular company's market breadth can be either broad, aimed at serving an entire industry or a very broad segment of an industry, or narrow, focusing on a particular industry niche. Similarly, Porter suggested that companies can seek to gain a strategic advantage in one of two ways — either by achieving lower costs than their competitors or by offering products and services that are perceived as unique in some way. Porter's matrix and its resulting generic strategies are illustrated in Exhibit 7.2. The matrix offers a useful way of thinking — or mental model — about business strategy.

EXHIBIT 7.2

A Matrix Describing Porter's Three Generic Strategies

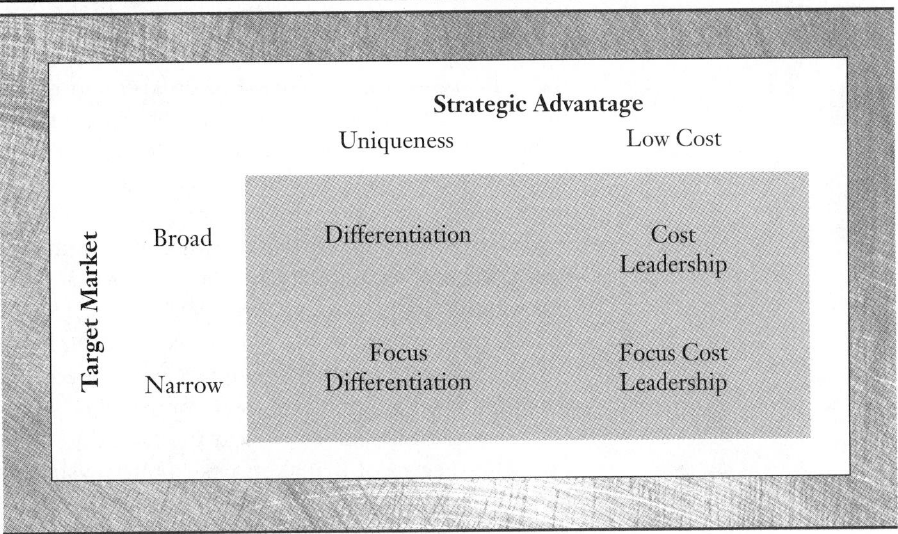

SOURCE: M.E. Porter. 1980. *Competitive Strategy.* New York: Free Press.

COST LEADERSHIP

As seen in the matrix illustrated in Exhibit 7.2, the generic business strategy of cost leadership is aimed at a broad market segment and is based on the strategic advantage of low cost. The idea behind the generic strategy of cost leadership is straightforward: Firms with costs lower than those of their competitors are likely to enjoy a competitive advantage in the marketplace if they can maintain this cost advantage over time. Furthermore, by serving a broad market segment, firms pursuing the generic strategy of cost leadership will seek to exploit economies of scale and experience or learning effects by maximizing sales volume.

A few points about the strategy of cost leadership are worth emphasizing. First, a strategy of cost leadership is probably most effective in those industries or markets in which the material or physical characteristics or reputation of a particular product or service are less important than its price. For example, the business strategy of cost leadership is particularly well suited for firms competing in commodity markets in which one company's products are indistinguishable from other companies' products. On the other hand, a strategy of cost leadership is likely to be ineffective for firms competing in markets in which products or services are readily differentiated along tangible or intangible characteristics. For example, a strategy of cost leadership would probably be less effective in the market for legal services because most individuals seeking legal assistance would be more interested in the reputation and past success of a particular law firm and less concerned about its fees.

Second, a successful "cost leader" develops a competitive advantage, not by selling cheap merchandise or products and services that are perceived as inferior or of poor quality, but by offering products and services of comparable industry quality standards at lower prices than most industry competitors. Especially in the past few years, quality has become a sort of *sine qua non* for companies in nearly all industries. Packard

Bell, the manufacturer of low-priced personal computers, illustrates how quality problems can damage the reputation of a company in spite of its low prices. Packard Bell certainly offers customers low prices, but its recent problems with product quality have made many customers wary of buying the company's personal computers.[3]

Furthermore, a successful cost leader need not always offer the lowest prices in the industry. As our discussion of differentiation will emphasize, customer perceptions are often just as important, if not more important, than reality. Thus, what is important to the success of a cost leadership strategy is that the prices of a particular company's products or services are *perceived* by customers to be lower than the prices of other firms in the industry. For example, Kmart and Wal-Mart compete vigorously with each other in the discount segment of the retailing industry. What is important or significant to the success of Wal-Mart's strategy of cost leadership is not whether its prices are lower than Kmart's for every item in its stores, but that customers *perceive* that Wal-Mart's stores offer better value than Kmart's stores.

Still, firms are unlikely to enjoy a cost leadership position for long if their prices consistently exceed those of their competitors, so the prices of successful cost leaders must routinely match or beat the prices of other industry competitors. Therefore, the success of firms' efforts to pursue successful cost leadership strategies depends a great deal on their ability to achieve an overall low cost position.

To achieve an overall low cost position in their industries, firms will typically seek to maximize market share. Greater sales volume allows these firms to exploit economies of scale as well as experience or learning effects (as discussed in Chapter 4), helping these firms to lower their per unit manufacturing or production costs. In addition to exploiting economies of scale and learning effects, successful cost leadership strategies are often characterized by:

- capital-intensive manufacturing or production processes that reduce labor costs,
- process (rather than product) engineering skills that are aimed at lowering manufacturing and production costs, and
- products that are designed to be manufactured easily and products that are designed to share many common components,

These characteristics help firms minimize production costs and exploit economies of scale. In addition, many successful cost leaders have developed

- sophisticated materials procurement and inventory management systems, and
- low-cost distribution systems,

which can offer significant cost savings.[4] For example, Wal-Mart's state-of-the-art inventory and distribution management systems are almost certainly important factors that contribute to the company's significant cost advantage in the retailing industry. Finally, a management or company culture that emphasizes

- close supervision of labor,
- tight cost control, and
- incentives based on cost and quantitative targets

can be particularly helpful to firms pursuing cost leadership strategies.

The value chain concept can be a very useful tool for managers who are pursuing a cost leadership strategy. Exhibit 7.3 illustrates the value chain for a hypothetical manufacturing firm first introduced in Chapter 3. Recall that the value chain depicts the various value-adding processes inside a business organization. Analysis of the various links in a company's value chain can be particularly helpful in assessing the ability of the organization to pursue a successful cost leadership strategy. For example, analysis of the value chain depicted in Exhibit 7.3 would lead managers to raise a number of questions: Are the company's products engineered and designed for ease of manufacture? Do the company's purchasing practices provide it with the lowest possible raw material costs? Could the company save money by purchasing materials from fewer suppliers? Is the production process as efficient as possible? Could the company lower its costs by increasing the level of mechanization? Does the company have any opportunities to cut the costs of its sales and marketing activities? Could the company save money by having other firms distribute its products, allowing the company to focus on engineering and manufacturing?

DIFFERENTIATION

As seen in Exhibit 7.2, firms pursue differentiation strategies when they aim to serve a broad segment of their market by offering products or services that are

EXHIBIT 7.3

Using the Value Chain for a Hypothetical Manufacturing Firm to Assess Its Ability to Pursue a Strategy of Cost Leadership

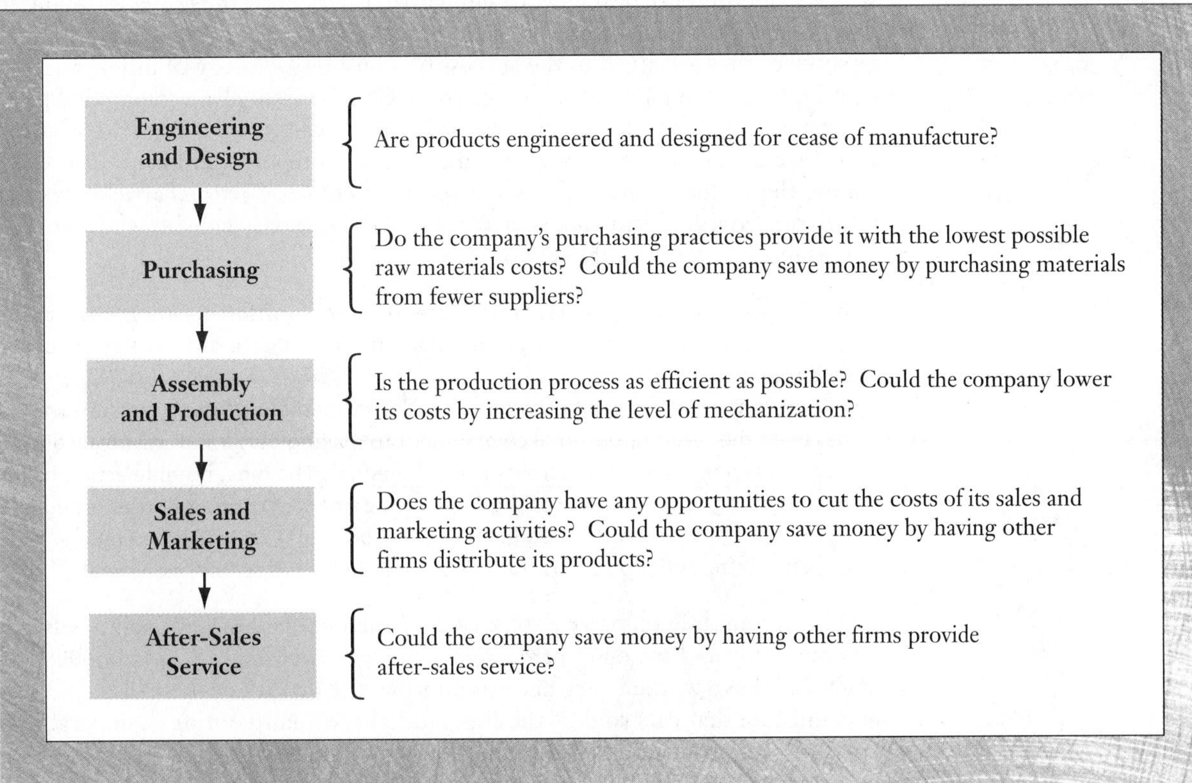
Engineering and Design
Are products engineered and designed for cease of manufacture?
Purchasing
Do the company's purchasing practices provide it with the lowest possible raw materials costs? Could the company save money by purchasing materials from fewer suppliers?
Assembly and Production
Is the production process as efficient as possible? Could the company lower its costs by increasing the level of mechanization?
Sales and Marketing
Does the company have any opportunities to cut the costs of its sales and marketing activities? Could the company save money by having other firms distribute its products?
After-Sales Service
Could the company save money by having other firms provide after-sales service?

perceived as unique. This suggests that the strategy of differentiation is likely to work best in those markets with products and services that lend themselves well to differentiation. The experience of firms in many industries suggests, however, that nearly all products and services — even many commodity products and services, such as colas and hair care — can be effectively differentiated. Perhaps no company has been as effective as Morton International at differentiating a product — in Morton's case, salt — that is one of the most basic of all commodities. The distinctive blue label showing the company's "When it rains it pours" slogan and the picture of a girl, with an umbrella, spilling salt is one of the business world's best-known icons.[5] Morton's differentiation strategy has helped the company dominate the various markets for its salt products, enjoying higher prices than its competitors for commodity products that are virtually indistinguishable from those offered by its rivals.

Intel represents another remarkable example of a firm that has been able to differentiate a commodity product.[6] Intel's well-known "Intel Inside" advertising campaign has been a great success. Developed in 1991 as a way to distinguish its microprocessors from those of Advanced Micro Devices and other semiconductor manufacturers, the advertising campaign has not only improved the company's name recognition, but also helped to give Intel's microprocessors a premium or higher-quality image in the minds of personal computer buyers. Many anecdotes exist about the success of Intel's efforts to differentiate its microprocessors; one story describes an older, grandmotherly woman who went to buy a personal computer. Admitting that she knew nothing about personal computers, she did insist that whatever machine she bought had to have an "Intel Inside."

As with the strategy of cost leadership, a few points about the generic business strategy of differentiation must be emphasized. First, it is the *perception* of differences and not the actual material or physical characteristics of competing products or services that is critical to the success of a business strategy of differentiation. Consider, for example, the market for colas: Cola is essentially a commodity product, yet the billions of dollars spent each year by Coca-Cola and PepsiCo on advertising are aimed at convincing consumers that there are significant differences among the various brands of colas. A recent *Wall Street Journal* article included this quote from Roberto Goizueta, Coca-Cola's legendary chief executive, on the importance of product differentiation:

> If the three keys to selling real estate are location, location, location, then the three keys of selling consumer products are differentiation, differentiation, differentiation.
>
> In recent years, we can honestly say that every marketing victory we have won has been the result of our total commitment to making our brands clearly distinctive from every other item on the grocery shelf .... The most notable action has been our ongoing expansion of the famous trademarked contour bottle throughout the entire world-wide packaging line for Coca-Cola, arguably the single most effective differentiation effort the soft-drink industry has seen in many years.[7]

The automobile industry also illustrates the important relationship between differentiation and customer perceptions. For several years, U.S. automobile manufacturers have worked very hard to improve the quality of their cars, and data now indicate that cars sold by the Big Three have quality ratings comparable to those of cars produced by the Japanese automobile companies. Still, customers believe that the quality of U.S.-built cars lags behind that of Japanese cars, and it is this perception that counts in the marketplace. Several years will probably be required before consumer perceptions of quality catch up with or match reality in the automobile industry.

Moreover, because they are often built as much on customer perceptions as they are on actual or tangible differences in the material or physical characteristics of products and services, successful strategies of differentiation can be "fragile" or short-lived, especially in industries or markets where fads or fashion swings occur frequently. In many markets, the introduction of new products or services can also wreak havoc on companies' differentiation strategies, especially if those new products or services possess real or perceived features that are quickly accepted or come to be demanded by consumers.

Porter suggested that because a successful strategy of differentiation depends on real or perceived uniqueness, firms pursuing differentiation strategies must develop

- strong marketing capabilities, and
- a reputation for quality or uniqueness.[8]

In addition, product (as opposed to process) innovation is important for firms pursuing differentiation strategies because they must develop totally new products or extensions of existing products that will be viewed as unique. Thus, firms pursuing differentiation strategies must also seek to enhance their

- creativity and research capabilities,
- coordination among R&D, marketing, and manufacturing, and
- ability to attract highly skilled labor, scientists, or creative people.

As with the strategy of cost leadership, analysis of the various links in a company's value chain can also be helpful in assessing the ability of the organization to pursue a successful differentiation strategy. Analysis of the links in the value chain of the hypothetical manufacturing firm depicted in Exhibit 7.4 would suggest a number of opportunities to differentiate the company's products: Are products engineered and designed to provide superior quality or other unique features for which customers are likely to pay a premium price? Have the company's purchasing managers identified the very best raw materials suppliers? Have the company's suppliers offered ideas or suggestions for how they could assist the company in differentiating its products? Will the production process ensure that only the highest-quality products are made? Do the company's sales and marketing activities lead to superior customer satisfaction?

Focus

As suggested by Exhibit 7.2, when strategies of differentiation or cost leadership are not aimed at broad market segments, but instead are targeted at a narrow industry niche or market segment, they are called focus strategies. Firms pursuing focus strategies seek the same strategic advantage — overall lower cost or perceived uniqueness — as firms pursuing cost leadership or differentiation strategies, but they target or "focus" that strategic advantage on a particular market segment or niche. Thus, there are really two possible focus strategies — a *focus differentiation* strategy of offering products or services that are perceived as unique to a narrow

EXHIBIT 7.4

Using the Value Chain for a Hypothetical Manufacturing Firm to Assess Its Ability to Pursue a Strategy of Differentiation

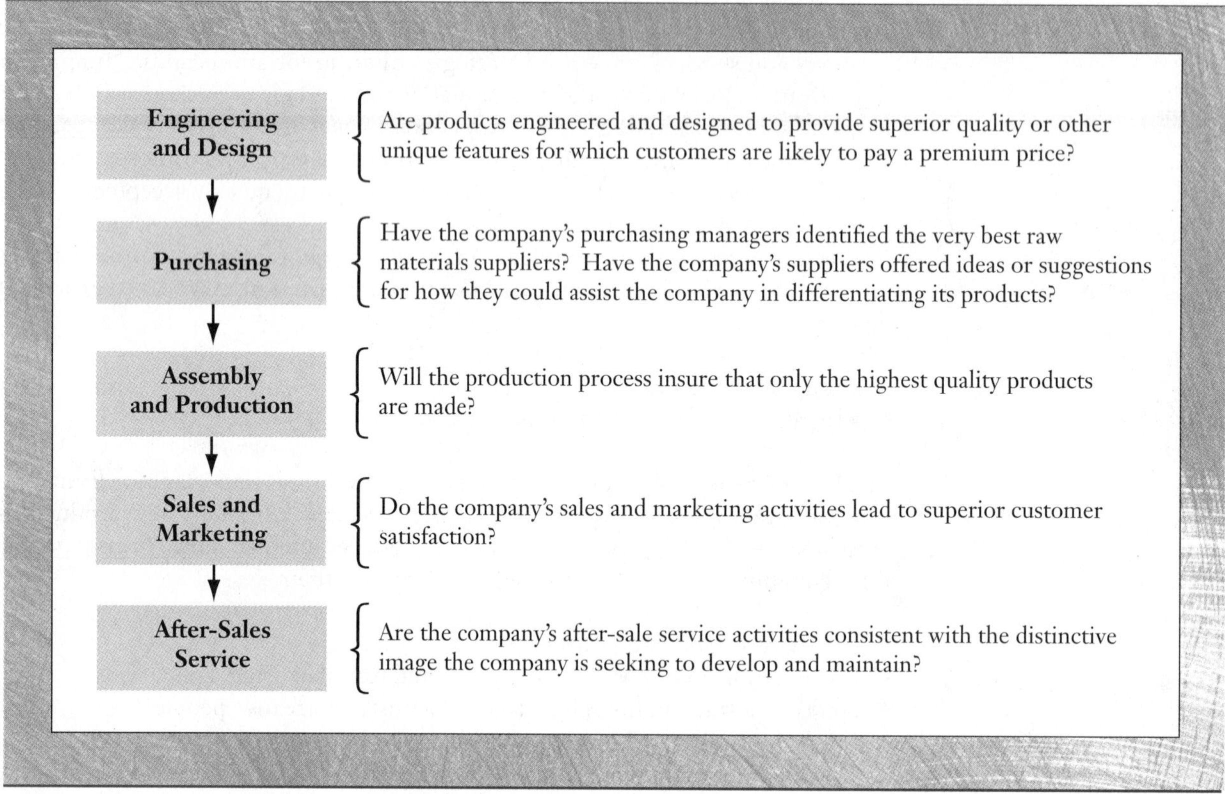

market niche, as well as a *focus cost leadership* strategy of offering low-cost products or services to a narrow market niche.

The automobile business of Rolls-Royce represents one of the best examples of a focus differentiation strategy. Rolls-Royce is obviously not seeking to sell its automobiles to a broad segment of the market; in fact, Rolls-Royce is not even seeking to sell its cars to buyers in the luxury segment of the market. Instead, the company focuses only on those buyers in what might be characterized as the ultra-luxury segment of the market — those consumers who are willing to pay between $178,000 and $376,000 for an automobile.[9] A focus strategy requires managers to be particularly attentive to defining the company's target market. Changes in customer demographics, competing products, and new technologies could quickly wipe out a narrow target market. In fact, some evidence suggests that Rolls-Royce's market niche may be shrinking because fewer and fewer buyers remain in this ultra-luxury segment of the automobile market. Recent losses in Rolls-Royce's automobile division are causing the company's corporate parent, Vickers PLC, to consider the sale of the business to another automobile manufacturer.

Langlitz Leathers, a small company manufacturing leather clothing, has been called the "Rolls-Royce of Leather Jackets," and offers an excellent illustration of a company successfully pursuing a focus differentiation strategy.[10] Although many other manufacturers produce high-end leather jackets and pants, Langlitz

MANAGEMENT FOCUS

FOCUS STRATEGIES

So many firms enjoy high performance by pursuing focus strategies that it's clear that market share is not a prerequisite to high performance. In fact, a recent study involving more than 3,000 companies found that firms with the largest market shares rarely enjoy the highest rates of return.[1] Yet focus or low market share strategies can also have their pitfalls and require significant management effort and talent. Recall that a focus strategy assumes that a cost leadership or differentiation strategy will be targeted or focused on a narrow market niche. As a result, managers of firms pursuing focus strategies must develop the capabilities and resources necessary to be a successful cost leader or a successful differentiator.

Furthermore, because managers of firms that are pursuing focus strategies are seeking to serve very narrow niches, business definition becomes especially crucial. Managers and employees of companies that are pursuing focus strategies must know and understand exactly what niches they are seeking to serve. And the market size of the niche can be very important. Too narrow a niche will leave a company with too few customers, and sales revenues will be too low to maintain viability. On the other hand, a company that seeks to serve too wide a niche may confuse its customers. Consider the dilemma faced by companies selling designer jeans. They could probably serve a larger group of customers and even increase their sales revenues by lowering their prices. Yet, by lowering their prices, they could alienate their former customers if they interpreted the lower prices and larger market as diminishing the exclusivity of the product. One company that has successfully pursued a focus strategy for many years is Rolex. The company aims to serve only the highest end of the wristwatch market. Its prices reflect this exclusivity, and, to reinforce this image among its customers and potential customers, the company advertises in publications and magazines that cater to its upscale clientele.

In addition to focusing much attention on business definition, managers of companies pursuing focus strategies must be particularly sensitive to changes in the dimensions of their industries. Because their companies are serving such narrow niches, even fairly modest changes in their industries could wipe out the markets for their highly focused products or services. For example, New York City once had a number of African-American community newspapers. Though their circulation numbers were never large relative to other New York newspapers, these newspapers played an important civic and cultural role in their respective communities. As reading habits changed and fewer and fewer households subscribed to newspapers, all newspapers suffered declines in circulation, but many of these very focused newspapers were forced to cease publication.

On the other hand, niche markets can sometimes grow and become large industries in their own right, and managers must be prepared to take advantage of these opportunities. For example, in its early years, Federal Express served a niche market for a relatively small number of all postal and freight customers — those who had to have their letters and packages delivered overnight. As Federal Express developed this market niche, however, the number of customers who "absolutely, positively" had to have their packages delivered overnight grew substantially, and the overnight mail business has now become an industry in its own right with a very large base of customers and many competitors. ■

[1]R. Minter, "The Myth of Market Share," *The Wall Street Journal*, June 15, 1998, A28.

is distinguished by the fact that it makes only six garments a day — just 1,600 items per year. Furthermore, just as scarcity once contributed to the perceived distinctiveness of Coors, the long wait created by Langlitz's limited production capacity actually adds to the allure or perceived uniqueness of the company's leather goods.

"Stuck in the Middle"

Porter also argued that some firms do not pursue a viable business strategy, and he labels these firms *stuck in the middle*. According to Porter, firms become stuck in the middle for one of two reasons. First, they might fail to pursue successfully any of the generic business strategies. For example, a firm might pursue a strategy of differentiation, but, failing to become a successful differentiator, the firm becomes "stuck": It has failed to differentiate itself from its competitors, but, by trying to pursue a strategy of differentiation, the firm has also failed to develop the capabilities or resources that would make it a successful cost leader.

Porter suggested a second way firms might become stuck in the middle: Firms that attempt to pursue more than one generic strategy will most likely become stuck in the middle. He argued:

> Successfully executing each generic strategy involves different resources, strengths, organizational arrangements, and managerial style .... Rarely is a firm suited for all three.
>
> The firm stuck in the middle must make a fundamental strategic decision. Either it must take the steps necessary to achieve cost leadership or at least cost parity, which usually involve aggressive investments to modernize and perhaps the necessity to buy market share, or it must orient itself to a particular target (focus) or achieve some uniqueness (differentiation). The latter two options may well involve shrinking in market share and even in absolute sales.[11]

Porter's assertion that firms simultaneously pursuing more than one generic strategy will wind up stuck in the middle is challenged later in this chapter, and several firms are identified that successfully pursue both cost leadership and differentiation strategies.

Some Illustrations of Generic Business Strategies

The end of this section identifies some specific firms in various industries and describes their strategies in terms of Porter's typology, but first, consider Exhibit 7.5, which provides stylized illustrations of successful cost leadership and differentiation strategies. Exhibit 7.5 shows three sets of bar graphs, depicting hypothetical per unit sales prices, costs of goods sold, and gross margins for the products or services of three different firms — an "average industry competitor," a "successful cost leader," and a "successful differentiator." Notice that although the successful cost leader's product or service is priced just below the industry average, its unit costs are much lower than those of the average industry competitors. Because of this significant per unit cost advantage, the successful cost leader enjoys margins that are much higher than those of the average industry competitors.

The successful differentiator, on the other hand, offers a product or service that is perceived as unique. The successful differentiator, therefore, is able to charge prices that are significantly higher than the industry average. The higher prices the successful differentiator enjoys come at a cost, however: Differentiation requires additional costs either for tangible features, such as more expensive raw materials, or to pay for research and development of unique physical characteristics or for advertising to inform or persuade consumers that the product warrants its higher

EXHIBIT 7.5

A Hypothetical Illustration of Successful Cost Leadership and Differentiation Strategies

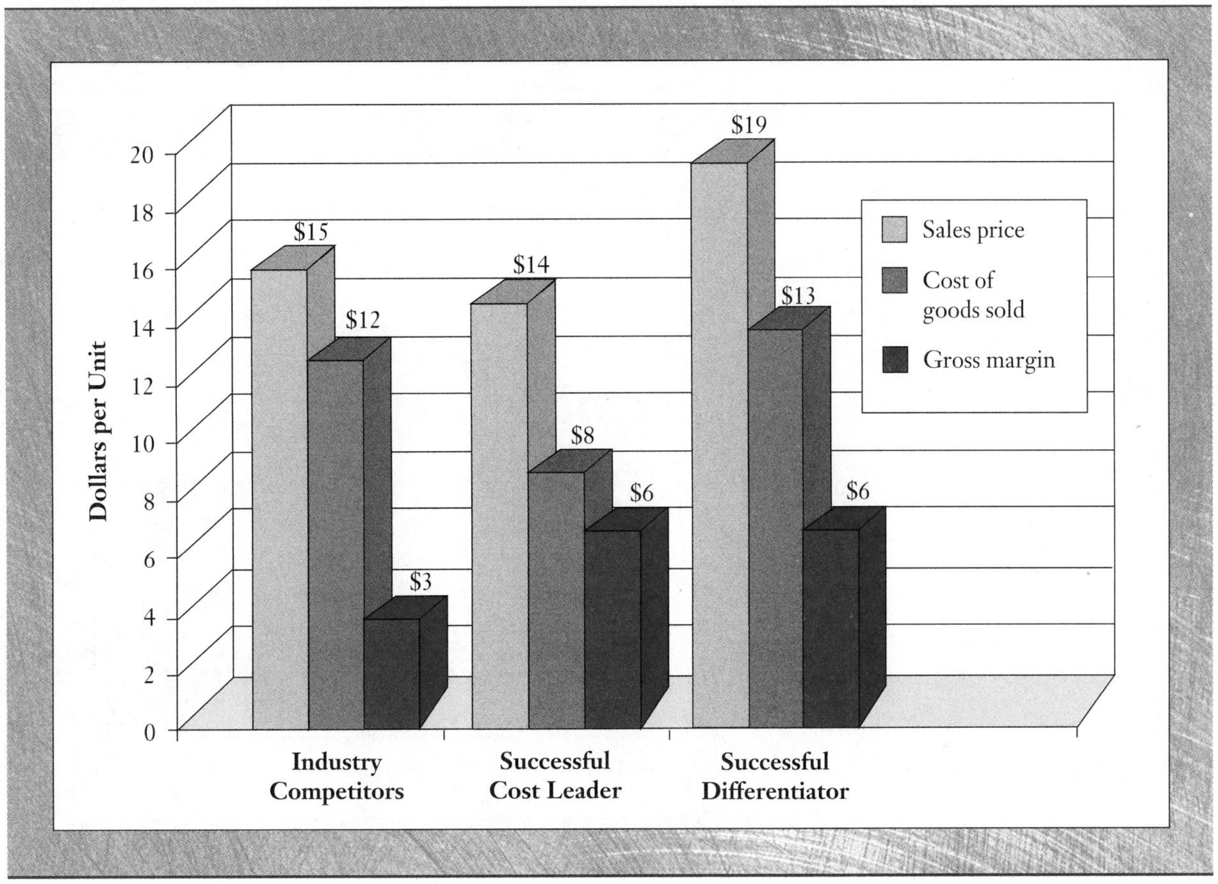

price. Notice in Exhibit 7.5 that the differentiator's costs are higher than the industry average. Still, the successful differentiator's higher prices provide it with a very satisfactory margin compared to that of competitors.

Exhibit 7.6 goes a step further by applying the same analysis illustrated in Exhibit 7.5 to three firms in the retailing industry—Wal-Mart, May Department Stores, and Sears. As you can see from Exhibit 7.6, Wal-Mart offers a prototypical example of a successful cost leader. The company's zeal for low costs is reflected in its low level of selling, general, and administrative (SGA) expenses compared to total sales revenues. In 1996, SGA expenses represented only 16 percent of Wal-Mart's total sales revenues.

On the other hand, May Department Stores provides a very good illustration of a successful differentiator. May's department store chains include Lord & Taylor, Foley's, Filene's, and Famous-Barr, all of which seek to provide customers with unique shopping experiences. This uniqueness, as Porter suggested, has a cost, which is reflected in higher selling, general, and administrative expenses. May's SGA expenses represent 19 percent of the company's sales revenues. Still, the company's ability to charge higher prices due to the unique shopping experience May's stores offer their customers allows the company to earn a satisfactory return on

EXHIBIT 7.6

Wal-Mart, May Department Stores, and Sears as Examples of Porter's Generic Strategies: Selling, General, and Administrative Expenses as a Percentage of Sales Revenues

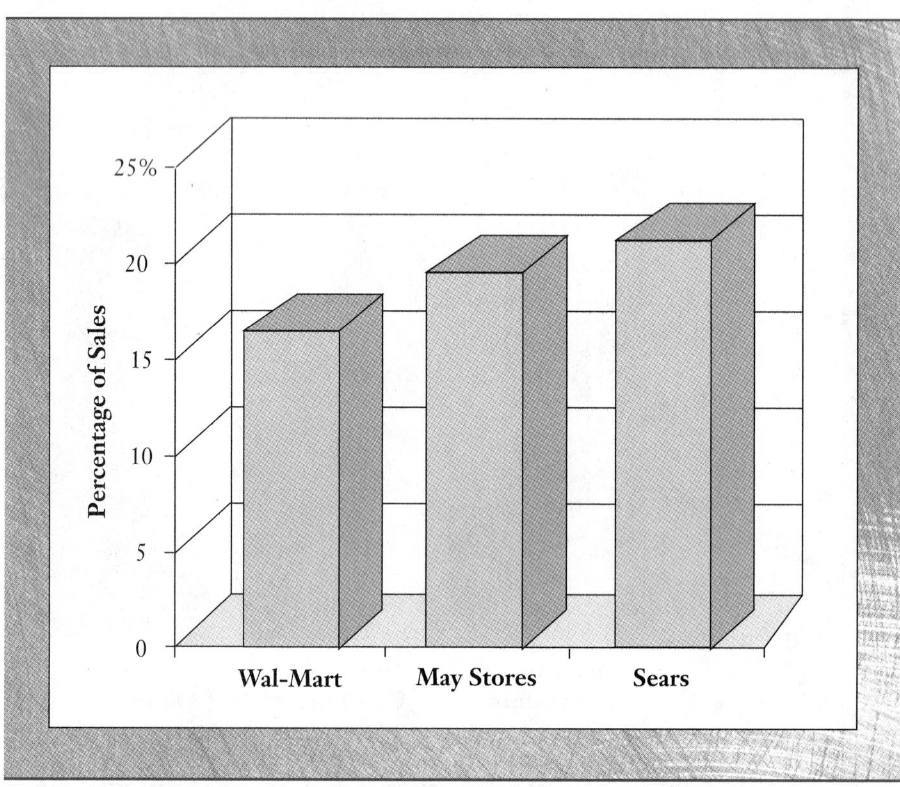

sales. May's 6 percent return on sales makes it one of the most profitable retailing companies.

Sears has made great strides in improving its performance over the past few years, yet Sears still seems "stuck in the middle." As illustrated in Exhibit 7.6, its SGA expenses as a percentage of total revenues are higher than those of both Wal-Mart and May, but Sears is certainly not a successful differentiator — its return on sales is only half the return on sales enjoyed by May. And, with such high costs, Sears is obviously not a successful cost leader.

To further illustrate the concept of generic strategies, we've included in Exhibit 7.7 some specific companies classified according to the generic strategy each is pursuing.

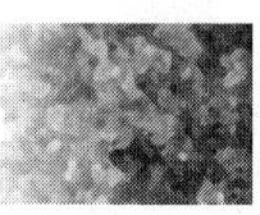

The Efficiency and Effectiveness of Generic Strategies

Now that the concept of generic business strategies has been introduced and illustrations of successful cost leadership and differentiation strategies have been provided, this section and the next several sections take up several additional issues

EXHIBIT 7.7

The Generic Strategies of Companies in Various Industries

Industry	*Cost Leadership*	*Differentiation*	*Focus*
Airline	Southwest	American	Kiwi
Automobile	Kia	General Motors	Rolls-Royce
Retailing	Wal-Mart	May Stores	Starbucks
Wristwatch	Timex	Seiko	Rolex

that will help to make this introduction of business strategies more complete. This section considers the efficiency and effectiveness of generic strategies, emphasizing two important points:

- First, none of Porter's generic strategies is, by definition, optimal; the appropriate generic strategy for any particular firm will depend on its managers' beliefs, its industry context, its business definition, and its capabilities.
- Second, both cost leadership and differentiation strategies can be *efficient* and *effective*.

The first point is fairly straightforward. Porter has made no claim that any one of his generic strategies is better than the others. The choice of generic strategy will necessarily be a function of a variety of factors, including the beliefs and understandings of a firm's managers, the nature of its industry, its business definition, its internal capabilities, and the nature of competition in its industry. In the next few sections and in Chapter 8, the text examines in more detail how industry context can influence the choice of generic strategies.

The second point may seem somewhat counterintuitive. Because we tend to equate the concepts of efficiency and effectiveness with low costs, it is easy to see how a strategy of cost leadership can be described as "efficient" or "effective;" it is less obvious to see how a strategy of differentiation can be called either "efficient" or "effective" because successful differentiators will almost certainly have higher costs than successful cost leaders.

Efficiency and effectiveness mean more than "low costs," however. A more accurate definition of *efficiency* is "the ratio of outputs to inputs." Similarly, a more complete definition of *effectiveness* is "firm performance relative to average industry performance." Using these definitions, it is much easier to see that both cost leadership and differentiation strategies can be efficient and effective. The first strategy increases profit margins by lowering costs, while the latter strategy increases profit margins by allowing firms to charge higher prices for products that are perceived as unique. In either case, the generic strategy can be efficient if it increases the ratio of outputs (i.e., sales price) to inputs (i.e., per unit costs). Note, for example, in the hypothetical examples illustrated in Exhibit 7.5, that both the successful cost leader and the successful differentiator enjoy comparable profit margins that are much higher than the average industry competitor's profit margin.

Successful cost leadership strategies and successful differentiation strategies are *efficient* because the resulting ratio of outputs (i.e., gross margin) to inputs (i.e., cost of goods sold) is greater than that enjoyed by the average industry competitor. Moreover, successful cost leadership and differentiation strategies are more *effective* because they allow firms to enjoy higher performance relative to the average industry competitor. The breakfast cereal industry illustrates this point. Kellogg, General Mills, and the other name-brand cereal makers are pursuing differentiation strategies. Because of advertising and promotion, their costs are almost certainly higher than those of store-brand cereals. Yet their differentiation strategies can still be *efficient* if they enjoy higher ratios of margin to cost of goods sold than their store-brand competitors. Their strategies can also be effective if they enjoy higher levels of performance than their store-brand competitors.

The Unattractive Characteristics of Commodity Markets, and the Challenges of Price Competition and "Commoditization"

Firms can be successful and enjoy high levels of profitability in commodity markets, but these markets tend to be less attractive and more challenging than markets that provide greater opportunities for differentiation. Although many firms do well in spite of selling commodity products or services, participation in commodity markets can be particularly challenging for a number of reasons. First, and most important, competition in commodity markets is almost always vigorous, and is primarily focused on price because commodity products or services have few other distinguishing features. Thus, in order to enjoy competitive advantage in commodity markets, firms must (1) become successful cost leaders, or (2) find some way, as Coca-Cola and PepsiCo have done with their colas or as Morton has done with its salt products, to differentiate what are essentially commodity products.

Furthermore, the profitability levels of firms in commodity markets tend to be heavily impacted by business cycles. In many commodity markets, firms will have invested heavily in fixed plant and equipment. In these industries, firms are always seeking to spread fixed costs over as large a volume of production as possible in order to reduce overall per unit costs. As a result, firms will attempt to maintain high levels of production even during recessionary periods. The oversupply that typically results almost always depresses price levels in an industry.

Finally, with few features other than price to distinguish among competitors, customers rarely develop a strong loyalty to a particular firm or its products and services and will frequently switch to a different supplier based on only very small differences in price. This lack of customer loyalty can invite entry by additional competitors — remember from Chapter 4 that customer loyalty was identified as an important barrier to entry — and such entry can further intensify competition, increase supply, and depress prices in the industry.

For all these reasons, commodity markets tend to be less attractive than markets in which firms have more opportunities to differentiate themselves. Unfortunately, over the past several years, firms in several industries have seen their markets become more commodity-like. This "commoditization" has affected a diverse set of industries, including the markets for air travel, photographic film, personal computers, and disposable diapers, and has required firms in these markets to alter their business strategies accordingly.

EXHIBIT 7.8

Book and Actual Prices for Large Turbine Generators, 1948-1962

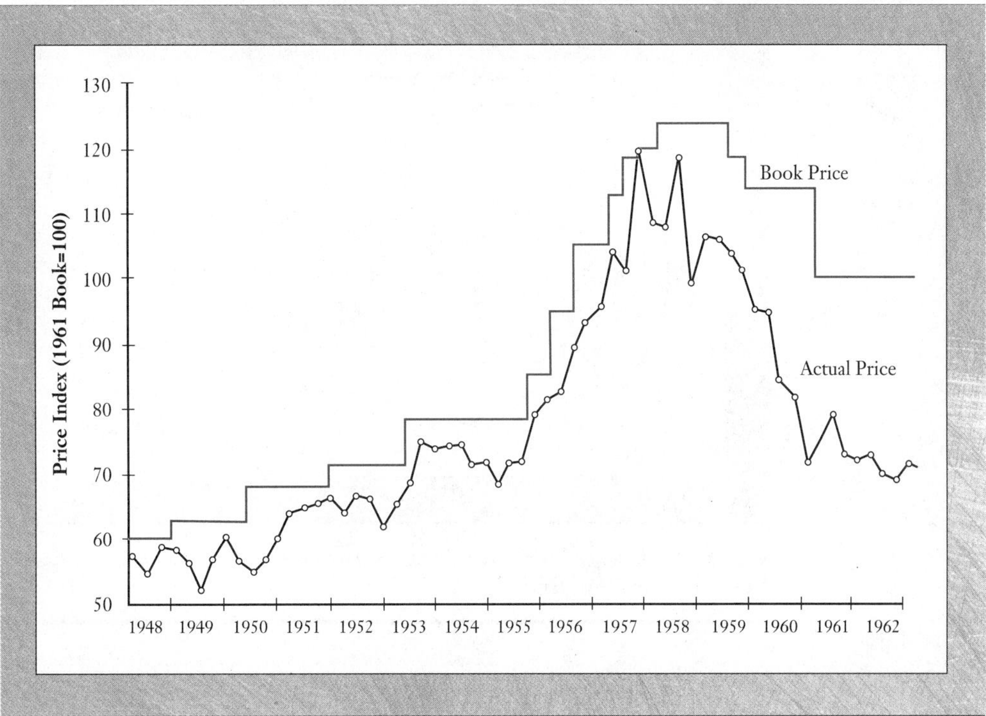

SOURCE: M. E. Porter and P. Ghemawat. 1980. *General Electric vs. Westinghouse in Large Turbine Generators.* Boston: HBS Case Services, Harvard Business School.

SOME OBSERVATIONS ON PRICE COMPETITION

As just noted, competition in commodity markets often centers on price because the products offered by competitors in these markets tend to be similar with few distinguishing characteristics. It's not uncommon for price competition to deteriorate into all-out price wars in which firms slash prices to a point where no firms — even those firms with the lowest costs — break even. Many industries, including the airline, railroad, steel, and photographic film industries, have been the scene of price wars. During the economic recession of the early 1990s, for example, *vicious price competition among the major airlines caused firms in the industry to lose all the money the industry had ever made!*[12]

In another famous price war between the General Electric Company and Westinghouse Electric Corporation in the market for large turbine generators, prices for generators fell by as much as 40 percent over a four-year period during the late 1950s and early 1960s as illustrated in Exhibit 7.8.[13] The pricing battle eventually prompted GE and Westinghouse to adopt common book prices and discounting formulas as a way to end their price war. Though these pricing practices helped to end the companies' price war, the Department of Justice concluded by the early 1970s that such practices represented a form of collusion. It forced GE and Westinghouse to sign a consent decree agreeing that they would end their practices of openly publishing book prices and discounting formulas.

EXHIBIT 7.9

Peter Senge's Systems Archetype of Escalation

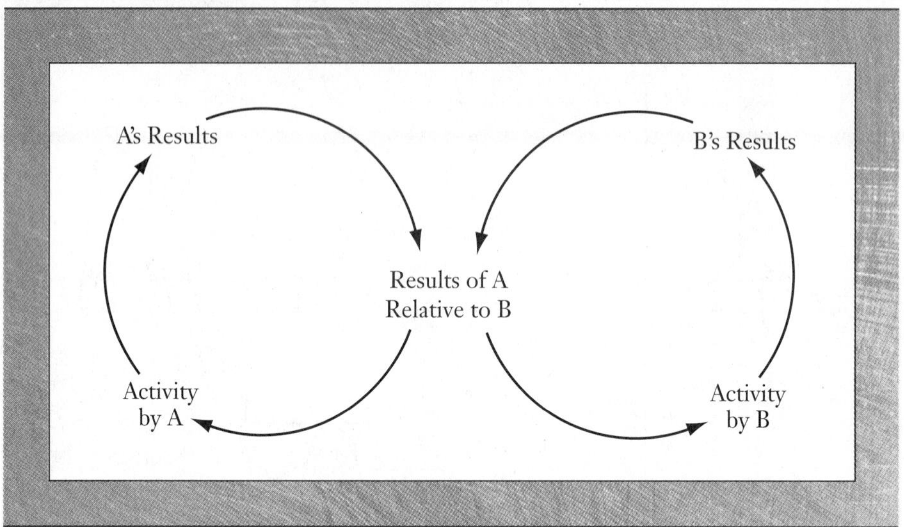

SOURCE: P. M. Senge. 1990. *The Fifth Discipline: The Art and Practice of the Learning Organization.* New York: Doubleday Currency.

Though the business world and the study of management offer very few clear-cut rules or axioms, one almost certain rule is that *price wars are never a good idea!* The important lesson to learn from these examples of vicious price competition in the airline and electric turbine generator industries is that a price war can hurt all competitors. It is said among businesspeople that a price war is like getting into a fight with a skunk: You might win the battle, but you'll still wind up stinking pretty bad. Consumers would appear to be the big winners in any price war. They relish the low prices, and, at least in the short run, price wars do offer consumers significant savings. Yet, over the long run, price wars are not good for consumers, either. Lower prices will lead companies to reduce spending on R&D and innovations that would improve product features or service.

Though structural factors, such as excess capacity, are often blamed for price wars, there is also a managerial component that is at least as important as structural phenomena in explaining vigorous price competition. In fact, structural and managerial phenomena are often tied together in mutually reinforcing ways. For example, high levels of fixed investment, underutilized capacity levels, and undifferentiated products or services are all important structural explanations for price competition, but so, too, are such managerial phenomena as the tendency for actions to escalate or for managers to intervene to "fix" situations. In his widely read book on management, *The Fifth Discipline*, Peter Senge suggests that many of these managerial phenomena often fail to correct and may even worsen many situations because they attack the more obvious symptoms of a problem rather than dealing with the underlying or root causes.[14]

Senge suggests that much managerial behavior conforms to what he calls "systems archetypes" — patterns of actions that produce fairly predictable outcomes. Exhibits 7.9 and 7.10 illustrate two of Senge's archetypes—"escalation" and "fixes that fail." Exhibit 7.9 illustrates the phenomenon of escalation that was introduced in Chapter 2. The exhibit shows how actions can easily escalate beyond the players' original intent, and it suggests why price competition can so often lead to an uncontrolled price war. For

EXHIBIT 7.10

Peter Senge's Systems Archetype of Fixes That Fail

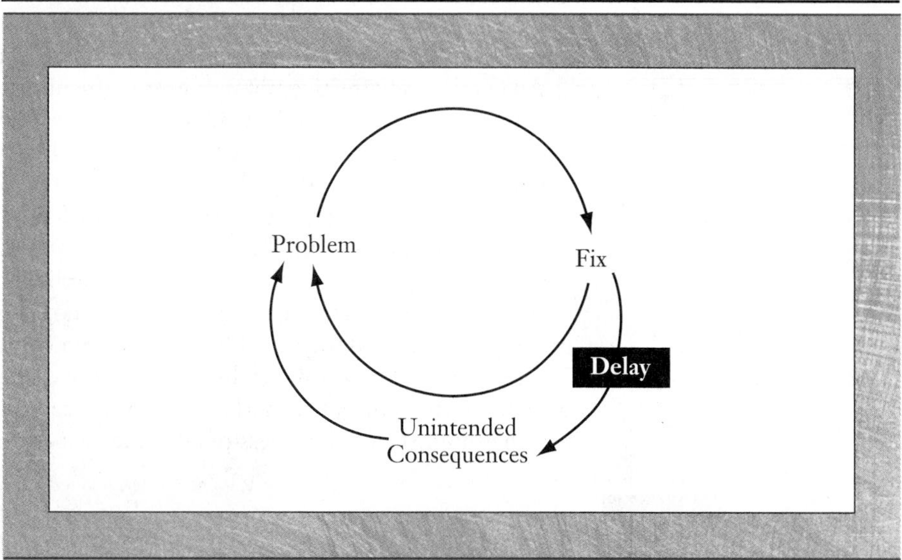

SOURCE: P. M. Senge. 1990. *The Fifth Discipline: The Art and Practice of the Learning Organizaiton.* New York: Doubleday Currency.

example, confronted by overcapacity, the managers of firm A might lower their company's prices. This price reduction might succeed in increasing A's sales volume and market share. The managers of firm B, comparing their company's results with those of firm A, might conclude that they have no other choice but to lower their company's prices to match or even beat A's prices in order to maintain sales volume and win back market share. It is easy to see that such a process could quickly get out of hand as each competitor seeks to maintain or increase its market share.

Likewise, Exhibit 7.10 illustrates how vigorous price competition can become a "fix that fails." For example, confronted by a structural problem, such as overcapacity, the managers of both firm A and firm B adopt a "fix" — in this example, price competition — that produces unintended consequences — frequently, prices that are below cost — that do nothing to address the underlying structural problem (i.e., overcapacity) but further aggravate the companies' situation.

So, if the axiom is to avoid getting involved in price wars, what *should* managers do if they are confronted by an aggressive competitor that seems all too eager to initiate a price war? This is a difficult question with no easy or clear-cut answers. Matching the competitor's prices could almost certainly result in just the sort of escalation phenomenon that could lead to an all-out price war in which all participating companies could sustain serious losses. On the other hand, if managers fail to match the lower prices of an aggressive competitor, then their firm will surely lose sales and market share.

Perhaps the best advice is for managers to be proactive. Rather than allowing industry conditions to deteriorate to a point where a price war becomes inevitable, managers are well advised to take steps to avert such a crisis. As in many other situations, the best defense is often a good offense. First, managers can work with key customers to negotiate long-term contracts. Such contracts may require managers to offer some price concessions initially, but they would help to maintain price levels during periods of weak demand. Second, managers can signal to their firm's competitors that they are well prepared or positioned to weather a protracted price war as a way of discouraging competitors from lowering their prices. For example, managers could announce that they were working to substantially lower (or had succeeded in lowering) their firm's break-even point.

An even more effective, though more difficult, strategy is for managers to work to differentiate their firm's products or services so that customers will come to perceive the firm's products or services as qualitatively better. This is, of course, much more difficult to do if the firm participates in commodity markets. Even in these markets, however, there are ways to differentiate what are essentially commodity products. Offering higher quality, greater sensitivity to customers' needs, and more convenient shipping and delivery services, as well as providing such additional services as warehousing, finishing, or component assembly that are valued by customers, are all ways to differentiate even commodity-like products. Though differentiation can be one of the most effective strategies for managers who find their firms in commodity markets, the next section will describe some of the factors that limit the effectiveness of even the best differentiation strategies.

THE LIMITS OF DIFFERENTIATION

Given the discussion in the preceding two sections about the unattractive characteristics of commodity markets and the vigorous price competition that is often present in such industries, differentiation would appear to be an attractive strategic alternative. The success of the generic strategy of differentiation depends, however, on two critical factors.

First, consumers must value the product or service characteristics on which managers have based their differentiation strategies. A company can come to dominate a market by differentiating its product or service in a particular way, but if customer tastes change, then the differentiating characteristics or features that have given the firm its dominant position in the market can become irrelevant.

This point may seem fairly obvious, but, as suggested in Chapter 2, company managers can become so caught up in their own worlds that they lose sight of what customers value. One example is provided by the competition between Motorola and the Finnish company, Ericsson, for portable telephones. Motorola, which has long been obsessed with product quality, has claimed recently that its portable telephones are so well built that they will last 1,000 years. Many customers — most of whom will live far less than 1,000 years — seem less than impressed by Motorola's claim, and growing numbers of consumers have been buying Ericsson's portable phones because of their unique designs and colors.[15] The differentiating characteristics that customers appear to value in the market for portable telephones would seem to be design and color rather than quality and product durability.

Alternatively, a company can come to dominate its industry by offering a differentiated product or service, but if customer preferences change and the product or service is no longer desired by customers, then the effectiveness of the company's differentiation strategy becomes irrelevant and the company must search for new products or services that are more congruent with customer needs and wants. For example, the rapid proliferation of Chinese restaurants has caused sales of Chun King and La Choy, well-known brands of canned Chinese food, to stagnate.[16]

Similarly, data suggest that sales of minivans have begun to soften after reaching a peak of over 1.2 million units in 1992 as customers are increasingly choosing to buy four-wheel drive sports utility vehicles instead.[17] Although it is too early to conclude that the popularity of minivans is truly waning, Chrysler's dominance of this segment of the automobile industry will become irrelevant if a large percentage of consumers decide they prefer sports utility vehicles over minivans. It doesn't matter if you have the world's best minivan if consumers decide they want sports utility vehicles instead. Cadillac seems to have already suffered this fate. Mercedes, BMW, and Lexus have managed to redefine the luxury car market so that Cadillac's boxy, boat-like models, while certainly differentiated, are inconsistent with luxury buyers' preferences; as a consequence, Cadillac has seen its market share lead in the luxury car market disappear.

The second factor that is key to the success of any differentiation strategy is the ability of firms to maintain the perception of uniqueness in their products or services. One of the biggest threats to the strategy of differentiation appears to be the proliferation of private-label and store-brand products. Some product categories have seen considerable private-label competition. Store brands of butter now account for nearly half of all sales of this product. Private labels have even won over 20 percent of the market for peanut butter, putting considerable pressure on Jif, Peter Pan, and other name brands. On the other hand, some companies seem to be remarkably immune to the threat of private-label products, and some product categories have seen almost no private-label competition. For example, Exhibit 7.11 shows nine companies that have been market share leaders in their product categories since 1923, and Exhibit 7.12 shows six product categories that have had almost no private-label invasion.

During the past few years, private-label manufacturers have made two advances that threaten the ability of consumer products companies to maintain the perception of uniqueness that their products have enjoyed, thereby undermining their strategies of differentiation. First, it appears that the quality of private label and store brands has improved while their prices continue to be much lower than those of

EXHIBIT **7.11**

Companies That Have Maintained Market Share Leadership Since the 1920s

Shelf Life

Here are some of the most durable brand names, with their market rank in 1923 and today:

Category	*Leading Brand in 1923*	*Current Rank*
Cameras	**Kodak**	No. 1
Canned fruit	**Del Monte**	No. 1
Chewing gum	**Wrigley's**	No. 1
Crackers	**Nabisco**	No. 1
Razors	**Gillette**	No. 1
Soft drinks	**Coca-Cola**	No. 1
Soap	**Ivory**	No. 1
Soup	**Campbell**	No. 1
Toothpaste	**Colgate**	No. 2

SOURCE: M. Lander, 1991. "What's In a Name? Less and Less," *Business Week*, July 8, 66–67.

EXHIBIT 7.12

Product Categories That Have Been Immune to Private-Label Invasion

Category	*Private Label Share*
Baby food	*0.0%*
Beer	*0.1%*
Shaving cream	*0.6%*
Bar soap	*0.8%*
Deodorant	*1.3%*
Toothpaste	*2.0%*

SOURCE: E. Shapiro, "Price Lure of Many Private-Label Products Fails to Hook Many Buyers of Baby Food, Beer," *The Wall Street Journal,* May 13, 1993, B1, B8.

name-brand products. As consumers try private label and store brands and find comparable quality at far lower prices, their perception of the value-price relationship will change, and they may become reluctant to pay premium prices for name-brand products. As a result, the private-label invasion has the potential to seriously erode the loyalty that consumers have traditionally placed in name-brand products.

Furthermore, as in most economic downturns, the most recent economic downturn in the early 1990s saw many consumers switching to lower-priced private-label and store-brands. What made this recession unique, however, was that a far higher percentage of formerly loyal consumers switched from name brand to private label or store brands and that more consumers did not return to the name brand products after the recession ended.

These two factors—value to consumers and perception of uniqueness—are critical to the success of any strategy of differentiation. Yet, differentiation strategies can be threatened by three factors: (1) private label and store brand competition, (2) discounting and (3) commoditization.

Private-label and store-brand competition. Private-label and store-brand competition poses a serious threat to any strategy of differentiiation because of its potential to change consumers' perceptions of the value-price ratio of name-brand products. Differentiation implies that consumers will pay higher prices for products and services, but that additional value will be derived from such purchases. If consumers purchase lower priced private-label products and find that they enjoy the same level of value as they do from much higher priced name-brand products, then they will seriously question future purchases of name-brand products and services.

Many major manufacturers of name-brand products have already had to wrestle with challenges from private labels and store brands. For example, Procter & Gamble has encountered considerable private-label and store-brand competition in many of its product categories. In many cases, this competition has forced the company to lower its prices in order to maintain competitive value-price ratios with private-label products. Exhibit 7.13 illustrates the extent to which Procter & Gamble was forced by market conditions during the last economic downturn to lower prices on several major name-brand products.

The Kellogg Company offers another example of a famous consumer products company that has seen its strategy of differentiation threatened by many of the factors described here. For years, Kellogg's has dominated the ready-to-eat breakfast cereal industry. Today, however, the company's dominance is threatened — first, by sluggish demand as consumers appear to be choosing bagels and other more convenient items over cereal for breakfast. Furthermore, not only is Kellogg's waging a battle with other name-brand cereal manufacturers, such as General Mills, but the market for ready-to-eat breakfast cereals is also the scene of vigorous competition from private-label and store-brand cereals. Sales of private-label and store-brand cereals have grown from approximately $150 million in 1988 to approximately $550 million in 1995 — an increase of more than 40 percent annually — as the private-label and store-brand manufacturers have improved the quality of their cereals while also charging prices that are often $1 or more per box less than the leading name-brand cereals.[18]

Discounting. Some companies and whole industries have diminished their ability to maintain their differentiation strategies by engaging in discounting. Discounting "cheapens" or weakens the effectiveness of differentiation strategies by giving

EXHIBIT 7.13

Procter & Gamble Company: List Price Reductions on Major Products, 1992–1994

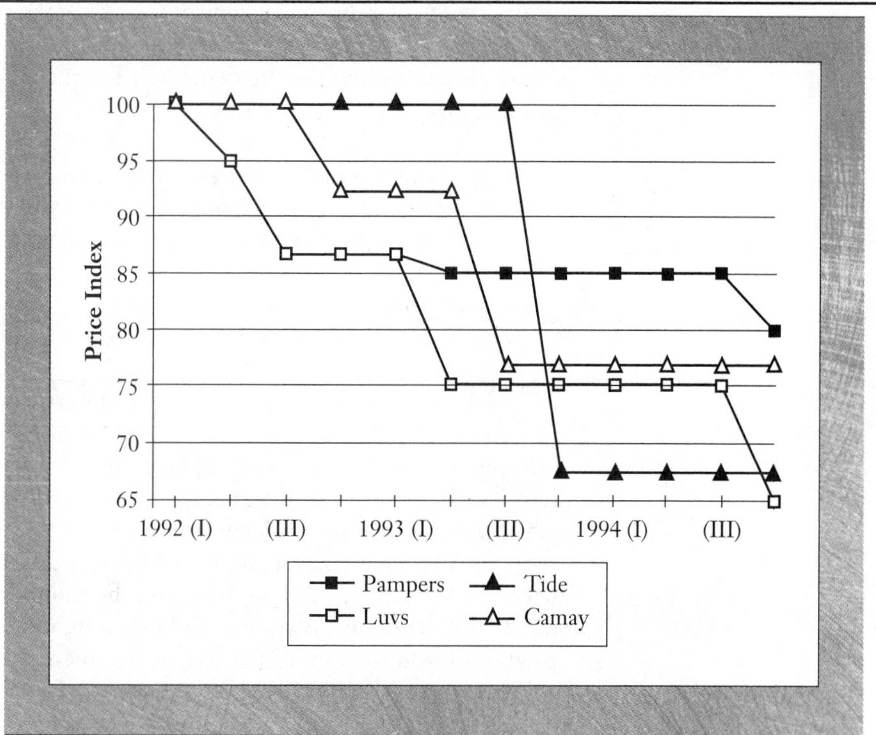

consumers the idea that they do not necessarily need to pay more for products or services that should be perceived as unique and therefore worth higher prices. Nowhere are the problems of discounting more obvious than among department stores, whose customers have become almost addicted to sales and other promotions.[19] As department stores have come to realize the harm that frequent sales have done to profit margins, they have made an effort to scale back their reliance on sales as a promotion technique. For example, Dayton Hudson sought to reduce the number of sales at its Dayton's, Hudson's, and Marshall Field's stores from over 140 in 1995 — about one sale every other day — to less than half that number in 1996.[20]

Commoditization. Finally, several factors can lead to a gradual loss of distinctiveness, or what we call commoditization. In some cases, famous consumer product brands have suffered from a benign neglect in which companies have failed to invest in maintaining the brand image of these products. Referring to Chapter 3 where investment was described as a key factor associated with the development and maintenance of competitive advantage, it appears that at least some of the problems the major consumer products companies have had with their name-brand products have resulted from their own inaction. Ajax, Brylcreem, Aqua Velva, Lifebuoy, Duncan Hines, Aunt Jemima, Mrs. Paul's frozen seafood, and Log Cabin syrup are all examples of once-famous name-brands that have lost their cachet as well as market share largely because companies failed to sustain adequate levels of advertising and marketing.[21]

In other cases, companies have "crowded out" their own products by introducing new products. For example, Coke's introduction of Diet Coke marginalized the role of its Tab product. Similarly, Procter & Gamble has tried in vain to maintain the market position of its Camay soap, but a good deal of Camay's troubles are due to growing competition from Procter & Gamble's own successful introduction of a similar competing product, Oil of Olay bar soap.[22]

Procter & Gamble has begun to recognize that its own marketing and product proliferation efforts have been a source of confusion for consumers. A recent *Wall Street Journal* article on the company noted that customers' buying habits have changed significantly in recent years:

> Today's average consumer, more often than not a woman, takes just 21 minutes to do her shopping — from the moment she slams her car door in a supermarket parking lot to the moment she climbs back in with her purchases. In that time, she buys an average of 18 items, out of 30,000 to 40,000 choices. She takes less time to browse; it is down 25 percent from five years ago. She isn't even bothering to check prices. She wants the same product, at the same price, in the same row, week after week.[23]

The article also noted that in spite of these changes in consumer buying habits, Procter & Gamble was routinely "making 55 price changes a day across 110 brands, offering 440 promotions a year, [and] tinkering with package size, color and contents" with the result that the company offered as many as 35 varieties of its Bounce fabric softener just in its North American markets.[24] In response to this consumer research, P&G has taken a number of steps, including drastically reducing the number of variations on each product, and the number of product promotions it conducts, and the company is also working more closely with retailers to improve the promotion and in-store displays of its products.[25] P&G's new approach will probably have several positive benefits. First, greater consistency in pricing and product promotion will help P&G reinforce customers' perceptions of its products. In

Management Focus

Commoditization

Over the past several years, many once-differentiated products and services have become much more commodity-like, and competition in these markets now focuses largely on price. Airline seats, disposable diapers, and photography film are all products or services that have become commodities. For most vacation travelers, one airline seat is pretty much just as comfortable (or rather, uncomfortable) as any other airline seat, so they buy tickets primarily on the basis of which airline is offering the lowest fare. Similarly, with Fuji's entry into the film market, Kodak has been forced to compete on the basis of price because differences between the two companies' film products are not apparent to many consumers.

Another example of commoditization is the shift that has occurred in the market for personal computers. As personal computers began to be sold through mass market outlets such as Best Buy, and as consumers became less willing to pay higher prices for PCs that they perceived to be similar to or difficult to distinguish from competing products, manufacturers of personal computers were forced to rethink their strategies of differentiation.

In fact, this trend toward commoditization in the personal computer market has had a profound effect on the strategies of several PC manufacturers. Perhaps most interesting is the case of Compaq. For many years, Compaq aggressively pursued a strategy of differentiation, emphasizing the quality of the materials and workmanship of its PCs. Compaq's prices — typically far higher than those of competitors—reflected this strategy of differentiation. When confronted by the trend toward commoditization that threatened the company's strategy of differentiation, Compaq's chairman, Ben Rosen, actually commissioned several Compaq workers to go "under cover" and explore the possibilities for lowering Compaq's costs of production so that it might offer its own machines at far lower prices.[1] What these covert employees found was surprising. In many cases, when they contacted suppliers and vendors of component parts, they were able to obtain lower prices than these same manufacturers were charging Compaq!

Their covert investigation laid the groundwork for a dramatic change in Compaq's strategy. Almost overnight, Compaq shifted from pursuing a differentiation strategy, adopted a cost leadership strategy, and slashed prices. By moving quickly and by successfully adapting to this changed industry environment, Compaq is now a successful cost leader and holds the number one position in the personal computer market. ■

[1] Allen, M. 1992. Bottom fishing: Developing new line of low-priced PCs shakes up Compaq. *The Wall Street Journal*, June 15, A1, A6.

addition, by reducing the number of variations of its products, P&G can realize significant cost economies in manufacturing, distribution, and advertising.

Do Some Companies Successfully Pursue Both Differentiation and Cost Leadership Strategies?

Porter argued that because of the resources, capabilities, and skills required, managers will find it very difficult for their companies to successfully pursue more than one generic strategy simultaneously, and he argued that companies pursuing more than one generic strategy are likely to find themselves "stuck in the middle." Still, it's worth noting that more than a few high-performing companies seem to be both successful cost leaders and successful differentiators. Certainly, in many industries, it appears that firms must have strength along one of these dimensions with at least parity with their competitors along the other dimension.

Consider, for example, Anheuser Busch. The company owns the most modern breweries in the industry and enjoys a significant cost advantage over its rivals. At the same time, Busch has always been very successful at differentiating its products through its marketing and advertising campaigns. As noted earlier in the chapter, Morton International, the famous salt producer and also an important manufacturer of specialty chemicals, has pursued a very successful differentiation strategy even though salt is one of the most basic of all commodity products. Over the years, however, Morton International's managers have also won a reputation as successful cost cutters, and they have aggressive goals for improving profit margins over the next several years by further reducing the company's operating costs.[26]

The success of a number of Japanese companies also seems to be built on their simultaneous pursuit of both cost leadership and differentiation strategies. Canon's success in the market for photocopiers was built largely on differentiating its products from those of Xerox while also pursuing economies of scale and other cost efficiencies.[27] Similarly, Toyota appears to have successfully pursued cost leadership and differentiation strategies. For many years, Toyota has been one of the lowest-cost producers of automobiles in the world, and, over the past decade, Toyota's innovative automobile designs have redefined several key segments in the automobile market, especially the high-volume family sedan segment, where its Camry model has been a best-seller, and the luxury car segment, where its Lexus models have been very well received.

Porter is right to be concerned that the simultaneous pursuit of both cost leadership and differentiation strategies will require large commitments of organizational resources (as well as managerial talent). Still, the nature of competition in many industries today dictates that firms must frequently compete along both cost and differentiation dimensions. Some recent research studies have also found that the managers of most firms emphasize capabilities associated with more than one generic strategy, further indicating that the strategies are not mutually exclusive.

Moreover, a growing body of evidence suggests that many management efforts contribute to both lower costs and greater differentiation. For example, quality improvements enhance customers' perceptions of the value of products and services and can be an excellent way to differentiate a company's products and services. Yet many quality improvement efforts also contribute to lower costs by improving manufacturing processes, reducing scrap and waste, and lowering inspection costs.

New developments in many industries are suggesting new competitive dimensions that go beyond cost and differentiation. In some high-velocity manufacturing industries, for example, it can be very important to bring new products to market quickly. Firms in these industries must emphasize design and engineering so that new products move quickly from the concept or idea stage to production. Costs and differentiation may be important in these industries, but fast response or "fast cycle time" may be much more important to firm success.

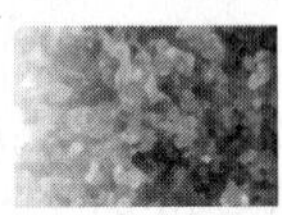

Conclusion: Generic Strategies, General Managers, and the Development of Sustained Competitive Advantage

One question that is certainly appropriate at this point goes back to the discussion of competitive advantage found in Chapter 3: If competitive advantage is based on asymmetry, then how can "generic" strategies, such as cost leadership, differentiation, or focus, be sources of competitive advantage? In other words, how can "generic" strategies, which any firm can pursue, possibly give rise to the asymmetry that is the essential characteristic of competitive advantage?

Content or Process as Sources of Competitive Advantage

This is a challenging question for the field of strategy. The answer, as we suggested in Chapter 3, is that the ability of any of these strategies to provide a firm with a competitive advantage typically comes not from the *content* of the strategy but from the way the firm chooses to formulate and implement the strategy and the unique capabilities the firm develops. It is not enough for managers to decide that their firm should adopt a strategy of cost leadership because many firms — even many firms in the same industry — will be pursuing a strategy of cost leadership. For a firm to achieve a competitive advantage by pursuing a cost leadership strategy, it will have to pursue that strategy in a distinctive way and develop unique capabilities. Thus, the decision to select a particular strategy is only a preliminary step. The array of associated decisions that must follow this first decision about strategy content will prove to be much more influential in determining whether that strategy leads to a competitive advantage.

The Role of General Managers

Of course, managers play a critical role in developing and sustaining competitive advantage. One possible way, but certainly not the only way, to think about the role of managers in developing competitive advantage is depicted in Exhibit 7.14. As illustrated in this exhibit, a company's top managers might begin by defining the business in a particular way. As indicated at the beginning of this chapter, the choice of business definition should suggest an appropriate business strategy, such as cost leadership or differentiation. The choice of business strategy would be followed by a resource accumulation *process* that would focus on the acquisition of key resources and the development of the capabilities needed to execute the business strategy in a singularly or uniquely effective way. Time, success, interconnectedness, and continued investment would be expected, over time, to provide firms with resources and capabilities that are rare, valuable, nonsubstitutable, and inimitable — unique resources and capabilities that can be sources of competitive advantage. As noted earlier in this chapter, many of these decisions are very much interrelated or "tightly coupled" so that the process is not likely to be as rational or as neat as suggested in Exhibit 7.14. For example, a particularly strong resource or capability might influence managers to define their firm in such a way as to take advantage of that capability. The dotted arrows in Exhibit 7.14 suggest some of the many possible relationships.

Two points seem particularly significant: First, as this description suggests, it is *not* the choice of generic strategy that leads to competitive advantage, but the resource accumulation *process* that gives rise to unique and valuable capabilities and resources that are sources of competitive advantage. Second, whether these resource accumulation processes occur in the order illustrated in Exhibit 7.14 or in some other fashion, it is important to recognize that the processes are not random or haphazard but that they are guided by managers' beliefs and understandings. In fact, the role of "architect" that managers play in guiding their firms through the decisions

EXHIBIT 7.14

A "Mental Model" of Competitive Advantage

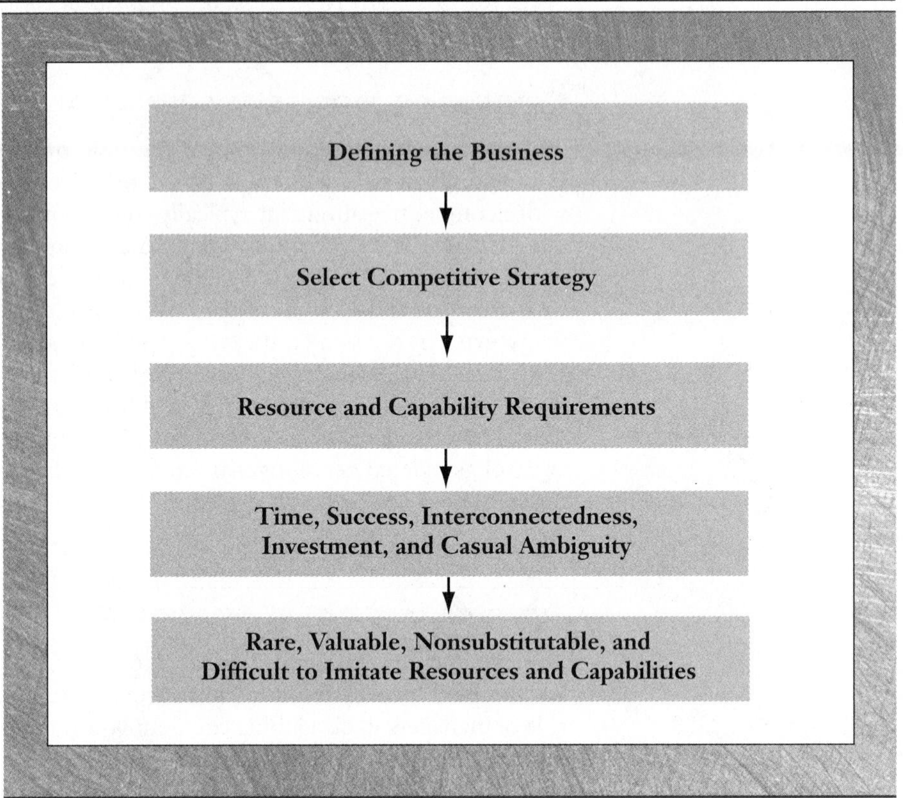

illustrated in Exhibit 7.14 is crucial or fundamental to the success of business organizations. In the next chapter, we see how these processes play out in a variety of different industry contexts.

Key Points

- *Cost leadership*, *differentiation*, and *focus* represent three alternative generic business strategies.
- Each of the generic strategies has its own set of required organizational resources and capabilities.
- Commodity markets, in which products or services of competing companies are perceived to have few differences, have a number of unattractive characteristics — most significant, perhaps, is that firms tend to compete on the basis of price. As a result, managers will often seek to differentiate their firms' products and services.
- Successful differentiation strategies require (1) that consumers value the product or service characteristics on which managers have based their firms' differentiation strategies, and (2) that firms can maintain the perception of uniqueness that is vital to the success of any differentiation strategy.
- At the same time, a number of factors limit the ability of firms to differentiate their products and services, including

1. Competition from private-label and store-brand products
2. Discounting, which tends to erode customers' perception of product or service uniqueness and value
3. Commoditization, or the tendency for once-differentiated products to become more commodity-like over time

- Competitive advantage is best derived by developing and possessing unique and difficult-to-imitate resources and capabilities.

Review and Discussion Questions

1. *Distinguish among the generic strategies of cost leadership, differentiation, and focus. What are the organizational resources and capabilities associated with each?*
2. *What factors make commodity markets attractive? How can firms be most successful in commodity markets?*
3. *Why should price wars be avoided if at all possible? What can managers do to avoid having their firms compete solely on the basis of price?*
4. *What factors tend to limit the ability of managers to pursue differentiation strategies?*
5. *How can generic business strategies provide firms with the asymmetry or uniqueness associated with competitive advantage?*

Suggestions for Further Reading

Miles, R. E. & Snow, C. C. 1978. *Organizational Strategy, Structure, and Process.* New York: McGraw-Hill.

Porter, M. E. 1980. *Competitive Strategy.* New York: Free Press.

Endnotes

1. Miles, R. E., and C. C. Snow, 1978. *Organizational Strategy, Structure, and Process.* New York: McGraw-Hill.
2. Porter, M. E. 1980. *Competitive Strategy.* New York: Free Press.
3. Carlton, J. 1996. Tight squeeze: Packard Bell is beset by new competition, customer complaints. *The Wall Street Journal*, March 26, A1, A10.
4. Porter, *Competitive Strategy.*
5. Brush, M. 1997. At Morton, much more than a dash of cash. *New York Times*, June 1, Section III, 5.
6. Mitchell, R. 1991. Intel isn't taking this lying down. *Business Week*, September 30, 32–33.
7. *The Wall Street Journal.* 1997. Roberto Goizueta in his own words. October 20, B1.
8. Porter, *Competitive Strategy.*
9. Rose, M. 1997. Is independence a luxury Rolls-Royce can't afford? *The Wall Street Journal*, June 9, B5.
10. Berner, R. 1996. The Rolls-Royce of leather jackets is hard to come by. *The Wall Street Journal*, November 22, A1, A10.
11. Porter, *Competitive Strategy*, p. 42.
12. Dempsey, P. S. 1993. The bitter fruits of airline deregulation. *The Wall Street Journal*, April 8, A15.
13. Porter, M. E., and P. Ghemawat, 1980. *General Electric vs. Westinghouse in Large Turbine Generators.* Boston: HBS Case Services, Harvard Business School.

14. Senge, P. M. 1990. *The Fifth Discipline: The Art and Practice of the Learning Organization.* New York: Doubleday/Currency.
15. Meeks, F. 1994. Watch out, Motorola: Newcomer to cellular phone equipment making inroads. *Forbes*, September 12, 192–198.
16. Elliott, S. 1993. The famous brands on death row. *New York Times*, November 7, F1, F6.
17. Blumenstein, R. 1997. Chrysler's October car sales fell 8 percent stung by 10 percent decline in minivan sales. *The Wall Street Journal*, November 4; A4; K. Bradsher, 1997. Start expanding that garage for Detroit's next generation. *New York Times*, June 17, A1, C6; *New York Times*. 1997. Driving habits: From cliché to cliché. May 18, Section 3, 2.
18. Burns, G. 1995. A Froot Loop by any other name...: Ralcorp's private-label cereals are gobbling market share. *Business Week*, June 26, 72, 76.
19. Bird, L. 1996. Back to full price: Apparel stores seek to cure shoppers addicted to discounts. *The Wall Street Journal*, May 29, A1, A10.
20. Ibid.
21. Balu, R. 1998. "Orphan" brands grow with new parent. *The Wall Street Journal*, April 2, B1, B14; Elliott, The famous brands on death row.
22. Elliott, The famous brands on death row.
23. Narisetti, R. 1997. Too many choices: P&G, seeing shoppers were being confused, overhauls marketing. *The Wall Street Journal*, January 15, A1.
24. Ibid.
25. Ibid.
26. Brush, At Morton, much more than a dash of cash.
27. Ishikura, Y. 1983. *Canon, Inc.: Worldwide Copier Strategy*. Boston: HBS Case Services, Harvard Business School.

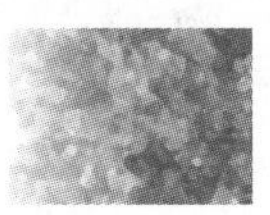

Chapter 8

Business Strategy and Competitive Advantage in Different Industry Contexts

Chapter Objectives

The previous chapter introduced the concept of business strategy by describing Porter's typology of generic business strategies—cost leadership, differentiation, and focus. [1] *Chapter 7 also suggested some of the unattractive characteristics of commodity markets and the dangers of price competition while noting the advantages as well as the limitations of the business strategy of differentiation. This chapter continues the focus on business strategies introduced in Chapter 7 by considering the special challenges facing firms in different industry contexts.*

The overall objective of this chapter is to develop your thinking—your mental models—about business strategy and competitive advantage in different industry contexts. Because of the many differences across industry environments, developing and maintaining a competitive advantage is much more challenging than merely selecting an appropriate generic strategy! In fact, managers must consider many more competitive dimensions than product or service cost, uniqueness, and market breadth—the dimensions that are the basis of generic strategies. The aim of this chapter is to explore many of the other factors managers must consider in formulating and implementing business strategies.

Life cycle models suggest that products and services pass through successive periods of emergence, rapid growth, maturity, and eventual decline as illustrated in Exhibit 8.1. Life cycle models have been extended beyond products and services to describe the emergence, growth, maturity, and eventual decline of companies and industries as well. The first two sections of this chapter focus specifically on the emerging and mature phases of the industry life cycle (the shaded portions of the life cycle illustrated in Exhibit 8.1). Although the growth and decline phases are also important, the emerging and mature phases present very difficult challenges that often prove critical to the long-run success of firms. During the growth phase, market demand is growing rapidly so any one firm's growth does not necessarily come at the expense of other firms in the industry. Furthermore, the growth phase can be very forgiving: Strategic mistakes made during the growth phase can usually be overcome because industry demand is growing so quickly; mistakes made during the emerging or mature phases of the industry life cycle, however, can have devastating consequences.

The first two sections of this chapter take a close look at emerging and mature industry contexts and consider some of the challenges managers face when their firms operate in these industry environments. (Chapter 12 deals

EXHIBIT 8.1

The Industry Life Cycle

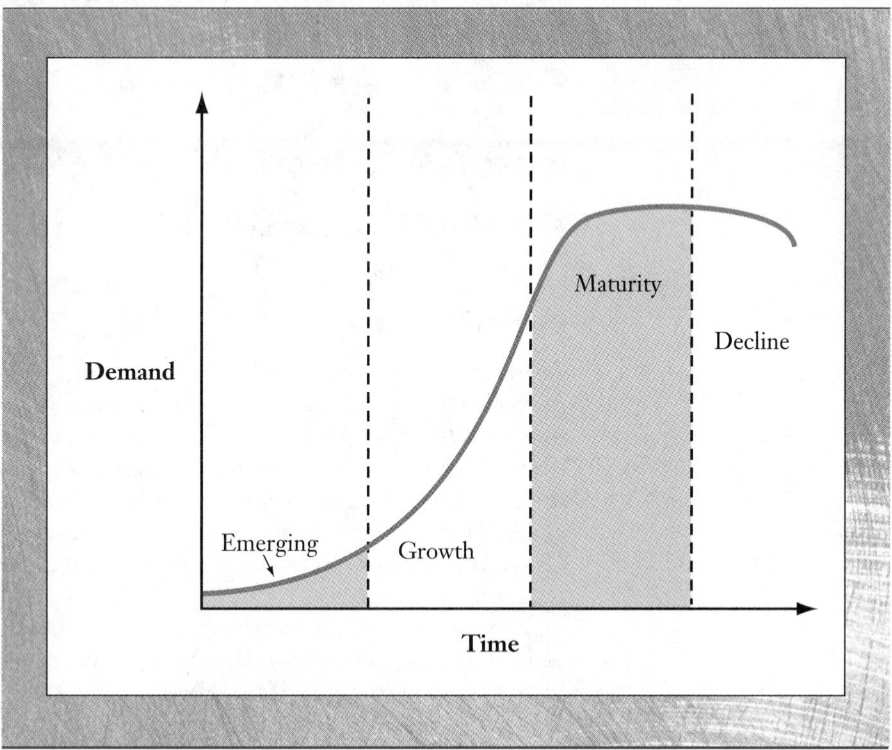

with the problem of decline, or, more specifically, how managers can avoid seeing their firms enter periods of decline.) In the last section, this chapter will compare and contrast manufacturing and service industries, and it will describe how the pursuit of competitive advantage differs across manufacturing and service industry environments. The specific objectives of this chapter are to:

- Describe the characteristics of emerging industry environments and the special challenges they pose for firms seeking to develop a competitive advantage in those industries.
- Describe the advantages and disadvantages associated with first- and second-mover strategies, and identify some of the factors that are essential to success in emerging industry environments.
- Examine the challenges associated with achieving and maintaining competitive advantage in mature industry contexts, and describe some specific ways to improve competitiveness in mature industries.
- Compare and contrast the characteristics of manufacturing and service businesses, and describe the challenges of achieving and maintaining competitive advantage in both manufacturing and service industries.

Competition in Emerging Industries and the Value of First-Mover and Second-Mover Strategies

As emphasized in Chapter 5, industry environments are constantly in flux. Some industry environments have proven particularly dynamic over the last decade as new customer preferences have emerged, new products and services have been developed, and new technologies have been exploited. As suggested by the book's model of strategic management (shown in Exhibit 8.2), the managers of firms operating in these dynamic industry contexts will develop mental models about their industry environments as well as mental models about how they should compete. These beliefs and understandings will influence how they position their firms in these emerging competitive environments and will also influence managers' decisions about whether their firm should be a first-mover, that is, whether their firm should be the first to seize and exploit new market opportunities, or whether their firm should wait until another, pioneering firm has entered the market.

Exhibit 8.2

The Mental Models and Strategic Decisions Studied in This Text and Their Influence on Performance and Competitive Advantage and Performance

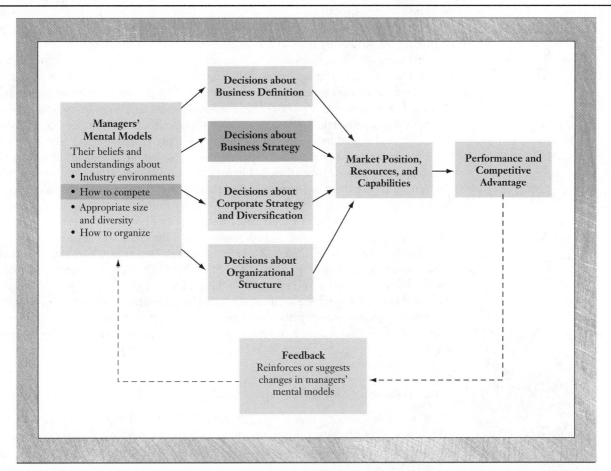

In many cases, managers do not have a choice. Because successful entry into and development of new markets entails a certain degree of luck, firms cannot always be first-movers. In fact, there are advantages as well as disadvantages associated with both first-mover and second-mover strategies. For example, it is not always desirable or advantageous to be a first-mover, and even when it might be, a first-mover strategy will not guarantee a competitive advantage. The next few paragraphs examine the advantages and disadvantages of first- and second-mover strategies, suggesting some of the factors managers must consider in making important decisions about entering emerging industry environments.

Empirical research suggests that first-movers often enjoy a number of advantages that persist over time.[2] In many respects, first-mover strategies have many of the same qualities and objectives as the generic strategy of differentiation. Perhaps the most important advantage is a positive reputational effect. A firm that successfully pursues a first-mover strategy can come to be so closely associated with the new product or service in the minds of customers that subsequent entrants will have a difficult time overcoming that loyalty. If a first-mover fills a new portion of a market's competitive space and if that first-mover can achieve a high level of customer satisfaction, then subsequent entrants will have a difficult time displacing the first-mover from its status as market leader.

In addition, first-movers can come to be recognized as particularly innovative firms, which can positively influence customers' perceptions of the other products or services these firms offer. Finally, by aggressively entering an emerging market segment before other firms, first-movers have an opportunity to move down the experience or learning curve so that they have the potential to enjoy a significant absolute cost advantage over any firms that enter the segment later.

On the other hand, first-movers sometimes stumble badly, and their strategies can fail to win customer acceptance. Sometimes in the rush to bring new products or services to market quickly, first-movers will offer products or services that are poorly designed or even defective. First-movers might also launch new products or services with inadequate marketing or promotional efforts. Sometimes first-movers are so overwhelmed by customer acceptance of a product or service that they are simply not prepared to meet customer demand. As a result, orders go unfilled and customers can become dissatisfied. These errors provide opportunities for second-movers, allowing them to learn from and then exploit first-movers' mistakes.

Furthermore, when second-movers can quickly imitate the products or services of first-movers, it is often in their best interest to let first-movers pay for research and development, marketing and advertising, and the costs associated with opening distribution channels. Second-movers can then "piggyback" on the efforts of first-movers, while avoiding many of the costs that the first-movers have incurred.

So, both first-mover and second-mover strategies have advantages and disadvantages and, as we will see, neither strategy always guarantees success.[3] The risks for firms considering either first- or second-mover strategies are heightened by two factors that characterize the dynamic emerging industry contexts in which these decisions must often be made: (1) ambiguity, and (2) short product life cycles.

The Ambiguity of Emerging Markets

First, the managers of firms in these dynamic industry contexts face a great deal of ambiguity and uncertainty about the attractiveness of emerging market opportunities. For example, uncertainty exists with respect to all of the following:

- *Demand*. Will a new product or service be accepted by consumers? Will it appeal to broad market segments or will it remain a novelty? Will the new product or service be a fad, selling very well for a short time with demand then falling off sharply?
- *Industry infrastructure*. Most emerging industry environments lack an infrastructure of established markets, buyers, suppliers, distribution channels, and a common language and set of norms. As a result, the preconditions and requirements for industry success are often unknown by the players in the industries. Furthermore, managers of firms participating in these emerging industries must cooperate and even collaborate to develop the needed infrastructure. The Internet offers many interesting illustrations of the challenges that firms face in moving into emerging markets in which the infrastructure is largely undefined. Companies—like Netscape—that offer key products or services that address this lack of infrastructure can have an enormous impact, rapidly propelling an emerging industry forward.
- *Industry standards*. Additional ambiguity exists until an emerging industry settles on a uniform set of product or service standards. Will the firm's product or service set the standards or will a competing product with different standards come to be preferred by consumers? In the latter case, how quickly can other firms adopt the new industry standard? What costs will be incurred by switching to the new industry standard?
- *The nature of competition*. Perhaps most uncertain of all is the nature of the competitive environment. What other firms will choose to compete in this market? Will those firms seek to dominate the market or will they be willing to accept more modest shares of the emerging market? What strengths and weaknesses will these competitors bring?

Product Life Cycles in Emerging Markets Can Be Very Short

In addition to ambiguity, another troubling characteristic of many emerging market opportunities is that product life cycles may be very short. Though emerging market opportunities are often characterized by an almost explosive growth in demand, many of these opportunities now have very short life cycles. For example, in the market for CT scanners, less than two years elapsed between the first sale and market saturation; EMI sold its first CT scanner in 1974 and by 1976, the industry had the capacity to manufacture 900 units even though only 500 units were sold that year.[4] An even more startling example is offered by the market for personal computers: Product life cycles can be as short as four months from a product's introduction until demand for that product will start to decline!

As a result, firms that choose to compete in emerging markets—regardless of whether they choose to pursue first- or second-mover strategies—not only face the challenge of introducing their new product or service offerings, but because product life cycles can be so short, they must also quickly establish competitive advantage. If neither first- or second-mover strategies guarantee success in emerging markets, what, then, does determine success?

Successful First- and Second-Movers: The Importance of Three Factors

Exhibit 8.3 shows successful and unsuccessful first- and second-movers. Some first-movers have enjoyed considerable success. For example, consider Chrysler's success

EXHIBIT 8.3

Successful and Unsuccessful First- and Second-Movers in Various Industries

	First-Mover	Follower
Win	Chrysler (minivan) Searle (NutraSweet) Du Pont (Teflon)	IBM (personal computer) Matsushita (VHS video recorders) Seiko (quartz watch)
Lose	RC Cola (diet cola) Bowmar (calculator) DeHavilland (Comet)	Kodak (instant photography) Northrop (F20) DEC (personal computer)

SOURCE: D. J. Teece, Profiting from Technological Innovation: Implications for Integrating, Collaboration, Licensing, and Public Policy; *The Competitive Challenge: Strategies for Industrial Innovation and Renewal*, ed. D. J. Teece. Cambridge, Mass: Ballinger, 1978, pp. 185–221.

with the minivan. After Chrysler's successful introduction of its minivan in the early 1980s, virtually all automobile companies introduced their own minivan designs. In spite of this competition, Chrysler continues to enjoy a wide market share lead over other manufacturers. On the other hand, some first-movers have seen dramatic failure. EMI, the British recording company that brought the world the Beatles, introduced the CT scanner in 1974. By 1976, sales had peaked and major competitors had entered the market. Competitive conditions in this emerging industry created a financial crisis for EMI that was resolved only when it was acquired by Thorn Electronics.

What distinguishes the winners from the losers in Exhibit 8.3? Research by David Teece, a professor at the University of California, suggests that three factors may be significant influences on whether first- and second-mover strategies are successful:[5]

- *Dominant design.* It appears that much of the success of either first- or second-movers depends on their developing what becomes the dominant design for the new product or service. Arguably, Chrysler was saved from bankruptcy by its introduction of the minivan in 1982. Today, more than 15 years after the introduction of its first minivans, Chrysler continues to dominate this market segment in spite of competition from nearly every other automobile manufacturer in the world. Much of Chrysler's success with its minivan product can be traced to the fact that, in spite of considerable imitation, no other manufacturer has "gotten it right" the way Chrysler did in its original design and its more recent model updates.

  Anecdotal evidence suggests, however, that being a first-mover offers no guarantee that a company's product or service will become the dominant design. The experience of DeHavilland, maker of the Comet, the aviation industry's first commercial jet aircraft, illustrates how a first-mover can be a "loser." DeHavilland's early customers complained of design flaws in the Comet. The company was slow to respond to these concerns, and, as a result, the DeHavilland design was rejected shortly after its introduction as customers flocked to what was to become the dominant design for jet aircraft, second-mover Boeing's 707.

Similarly, technically superior designs do not necessarily become dominant designs. The QWERTY typewriter (and now personal computer) keyboard is often cited as an example of a product that became the dominant design in spite of being technically inferior. Sony's first-mover product, the BETA VCR technology, though widely regarded as the technologically superior design, failed to become the dominant design as the market converged instead on the VHS technology.

- *Inimitability*. If an innovative product or service is easy for competitors to imitate, then it matters little whether a firm is a first- or second-mover. RC Cola has long been one of the most innovative soft-drink manufacturers. It was, for example, the first company to offer soft drinks in cans, and its Diet-Rite cola was the first diet cola to be introduced. Yet none of these innovations has provided the company with any long-term competitive advantage because of the ease with which RC's competitors could imitate them.

  Even innovations that are patented are subject to imitation. Many companies have successfully innovated or engineered around patents. Canon's successful entry into the market for photocopiers came after its researchers had developed a "new process" that avoided infringement of Xerox's many patents.[6] Still, companies must be careful when attempting to innovate around another company's patents. After Polaroid's success at creating instant photography, Kodak sought to be a successful second-mover in the fast-growing market for instant photography products. After Kodak entered the market with its own instant photography products, Polaroid successfully sued Kodak charging patent infringement. In its judgment against Kodak, the court awarded Polaroid over $900 million in damages.
- *Interconnectedness*. Finally, Teece suggests that interconnected resource capabilities and requirements can also be an important factor distinguishing between successful and less successful first- and second-movers. Similar to the logic presented in Chapter 3, if the successful introduction of a new product or service requires an interconnected set of resources or capabilities, then both first- and second-movers will face greater costs to bring new products or services to market. Potential second-movers may find it both time consuming and expensive to duplicate the success of a first-mover if that success is based on an interconnected set of resources and capabilities. Similarly, first-movers will have a difficult time maintaining their lead if second-movers have a better endowment of the interconnected resources.

  EMI's inability to enjoy any sort of long-term advantage from its development of the scanner—a technology so important that the EMI research team that developed the scanner won the Nobel Prize in medicine in 1977—was probably due to its lack of related, interconnected resources and capabilities.[7] For example, EMI had no previous medical technology sales experience and it had no U.S. sales force, even though the United States was likely to be the largest market for the CT scanner technology. On the other hand, EMI's major competitor in the market for CT scanners, General Electric, had long been a major player in X-ray and other advanced medical technologies. And, General Electric had an established sales and marketing organization to support its advanced medical technology products.

IBM, though a second-mover in the market for personal computers, initially enjoyed great success in this business because of its reputation for product quality and service. In many respects, IBM's reputation allowed it to do what Apple and other PC manufacturers could not do—namely, to persuade businesses to buy personal computers in large quantities.

NutraSweet: A Case Study of a Very Successful First-Mover Strategy

NutraSweet, the artificial sweetener developed by Searle, offers a case study of a very successful first-mover strategy. When health concerns were raised about cyclamates, a new market for alternative artificial sweeteners emerged. Searle's development of aspartame proved to be very much the "right product at the right time." After developing aspartame, Searle patented the new product, but several years passed before Searle won approval from the Food and Drug Administration to market its new product. At this point, Searle's managers sought, and successfully won, the right to extend the life of aspartame patents so that the company would continue to have exclusive rights to market aspartame for several additional years after winning FDA approval for sale of the product.

Searle's patents on aspartame expired in 1992, but the company has maintained its dominance of the artificial sweetener market, suggesting that the company's success is based on more than patent protection. In fact, much of Searle's success with aspartame can be attributed to steps the company's managers took to make its success difficult to imitate and to the interconnected set of capabilities the company developed to support its product. For example, early on, Searle entered into an agreement with a Japanese company, Ajinomoto, the low-cost maker of a key aspartame ingredient, phenylalanine. In this pact, Ajinomoto agreed to supply phenylalanine exclusively to Searle; furthermore, Ajinomoto agreed to provide Searle with the technology to manufacture phenylalanine so that Searle could also become a low-cost producer of this key ingredient.

In addition, Searle adopted the NutraSweet brand name for aspartame and even developed a logo that it required all buyers of NutraSweet to place on their packaging.[8] Such marketing efforts were aimed at bolstering NutraSweet's brand recognition and developing a following for the product among consumers. These steps not only gave the company a significant cost advantage over any would-be rivals, but they also led to the development of an interconnected set of manufacturing and marketing capabilities that have strengthened the company's position in the artificial sweetener market.

The Challenges of Mature Industry Environments

The first part of this chapter examined the factors that make emerging industry environments so challenging. It focused specifically on the ambiguity that characterizes these industry environments and also noted the tendency for product life cycles in these emerging industry environments to be increasingly short. Just as challenging for managers, if not more so, are mature industry environments.

Unattractive Characteristics of Mature Industry Environments

As noted at the beginning of this chapter, all phases of an industry life cycle present their own challenges, but managers of firms operating in mature industry contexts face especially formidable challenges, several of which are described here:

MANAGEMENT FOCUS

Some Thoughts on Litigation for Competitive Purposes

A topic very much related to first- and second-mover strategies is the frequent use of lawsuits by first-movers against their second-mover rivals. The use of lawsuits is probably not thought of as a typical business strategy or tactic, and few if any strategy texts discuss the use of litigation for competitive purposes, yet so many companies have successfully used litigation in their competitive interactions with rivals that the subject warrants some discussion here. As noted earlier in the chapter, Polaroid's successful suit against Kodak not only drove Kodak from the instant photography market, but also brought Polaroid $900 million in damages. Litigation can be used by firms to defend against the imitation or infringement of patents, but when it is used as a competitive weapon, firms can derive several additional advantages.

First, litigation can be expensive for smaller or weaker rivals that might lack the resources and "deep pockets" of industry leaders, and a lawsuit can force a smaller or weaker rival to divert resources from more important R&D or marketing efforts in order to pay attorneys' fees and other legal costs. As a result, the smaller or weaker firm may simply decide that it cannot afford to compete against the stronger rival. Or, if it remains in the market, the smaller or weaker firm may lack the resources to compete effectively.

Litigation can also be used to slow down or even stymie competitors or would-be rivals. In the late 1960s and early 1970s, for example, Procter & Gamble successfully used litigation or the threat of legal action to slow the expansion of its rivals, Johnson & Johnson and Weyerhaeuser, in the emerging disposable diaper market.[1] These lawsuits and threats of legal action bought time for Procter & Gamble, allowing it to establish a dominant position in the emerging market for disposable diapers.

Another example of a firm using litigation to slow the advance of a rival is the lawsuit brought by Digital Equipment Corporation against Intel. In its lawsuit, Digital claimed that Intel's Pentium series of microprocessors violated a number of patents associated with the technology incorporated in Digital's own microprocessors. A *New York Times* story suggested, however, that Digital's lawsuit was not really aimed at Intel's Pentium line of microprocessors.[2] Instead, the story suggested that Digital's real objective was to slow Intel's introduction of its next generation of chips, which carries the code name Merced, because the Merced, Intel's first 64-bit microprocessor, would compete directly with Digital's own 64-bit Alpha microprocessor.

In settling the suit only a short time later, Digital agreed to sell its Alpha technology and manufacturing facility to Intel for $700 million and an additional $800 million in product discounts over many years.[3] Analysts have interpreted this chain of events favorably. Intel takes over the development and production of a super-fast chip that Digital had never been able to turn into a commercial success, and the sale provides Digital with a huge infusion of cash, giving the company time to develop a growth strategy.

Finally, over time, firms can develop a reputation as being particularly litigious. Such a reputation has the same effect as raising the barriers to entry of an industry or market because the managers of potential rivals would have to anticipate that the entry of their firms into these markets will result in potentially costly litigation. Ironically, Intel—the firm that Digital sued—has proven itself to be one of the most aggressive litigators in any industry. Intel has aggressively used litigation to defend its microprocessors from imitation and to slow down product launches by "clone" manufacturers, such as Advanced Micro Devices.[4] As a recent *Forbes* article noted, "Companies sue each other all the time. It is part of life in present-day America. But when you get sued by Intel you know you've been sued."[5] In fact, it is

continued

probably fair to say that litigation is one of the most distinguishing characteristics of the competitive rivalry among Intel, Advanced Micro Devices, and other firms in the semiconductor market. ■

[1]Porter, M. E. 1980. *The Disposable Diaper Industry in 1974.* Boston: HBS Case Services, Harvard Business School.

[2]Zuckerman, L. 1997. For Digital's chief, a last grab for glory. *New York Times,* May 25, section 3, 1, 6.

[3]Auerbach, J. G. 1997. Alpha male: Digital's Palmer faces an unsettled future after Intel settlement. *The Wall Street Journal,* October 30, A1, A10.

[4]Hill, C. W. L. 1997. Establishing a standard: Competitive strategy and technological standards in winner-take-all industries. *Academy of Management Executive* 11(2):19.

[5]McHugh, J. 1998. Don't mess with me. *Forbes,* March 23, 42.

- *Stagnant demand and excess capacity.* In most mature markets, growth in demand will have either slowed or become stagnant, but because firms in the industry have become used to increasing demand, they are likely to be adding capacity in anticipation of continued growth. And, because capacity tends to be added in "lumpy" increments, there is a tendency for capacity expansion to grow faster than demand as the industry begins to mature. This tendency is illustrated by the figure in Exhibit 8.4 in which demand is depicted as a solid line while capacity is shown as a dotted line.

  The strategic challenge this poses for managers is that if capacity exceeds demand over fairly long periods, it tends to invite price competition. If each firm in the industry maintains high levels of output in order to make full use of plant capacity, then the excess supply that results must inevitably put downward pressure on prices as the market seeks to clear the surplus. As suggested in Chapters 4 and 7, excess capacity is a major reason for downward pressure on prices in many industries.

  In spite of a worldwide glut of automobile production capacity, the major automobile companies and even some companies that have had no prior experience in the automobile industry continue to open new production facilities.[9] The giant South Korean conglomerate, Samsung, which has never been a player in the automobile industry before, is now planning to open a plant that will produce 80,000 cars annually. And, nearly all the Japanese transplants have plans to increase production capacity in the United States. Clearly, excess capacity does not always discourage new entry. Current worldwide automobile production capacity is now estimated at more than 70 million vehicles, even though demand for automobiles is more than 30 percent below this capacity! This excess capacity will almost surely put downward pressure on automobile prices at some point in the future.
- *Exit barriers.* Exit barriers complicate the problem of excess capacity. As discussed in Chapter 4, exit barriers are often associated with idiosyncratic assets that have no "second-best use," such as jet aircraft, steel mills, refineries, and automobile production plants. Managers are reluctant to take these idiosyncratic assets out of production as their firms would most likely incur sizable restructuring charges or write-offs. As a result, exit barriers hinder what might otherwise be a more orderly shake-out of weak competitors that would alleviate the excess capacity problem.
- *A lack of innovation.* As the growth in demand for products or services slows, managers of incumbent firms may stop investing in product or process innovations. Because of stagnant growth, proposals that might improve products or services and lead to higher demand often fail to meet rate of return and other investment

EXHIBIT 8.4

The Tendency for Capacity Expansion to Grow Faster Than Demand in Mature Industry Environments

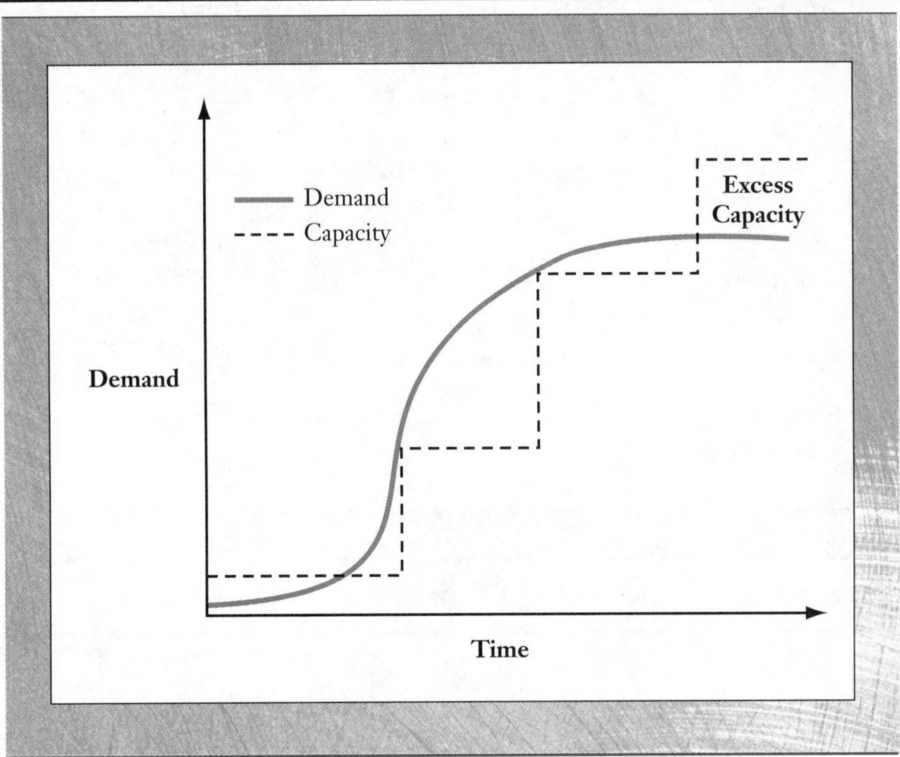

hurdles. As a consequence, the rate of innovation in the industry begins to lag. The ensuing lack of innovation has several unfortunate consequences.

First, a lack of innovation will further customers' perceptions that the industry offers nothing new that would warrant a replacement purchase, further reducing demand. For example, the market for personal computers has maintained a strong sales growth rate even though analysts have long predicted that the market would soon mature. The rapid rate of innovation in this market is almost certainly responsible for the continuing growth in demand for personal computers. Newer, faster microprocessors allow personal computers to perform more complex tasks, which encourages other firms to write more sophisticated software applications, which, in turn, further stimulates consumer demand for personal computers. If the pace of innovation in this industry were to slow, demand would most certainly fall as consumers would find fewer reasons for buying new personal computer models.

Second, as firms in an industry engage in less innovation activity, their products and services may come to appear more and more like commodities. Without discernible differences across products or services, firms will be pressured by consumers to compete on the basis of price, which can escalate into all-out price wars.

- *Pressure from new entrants.* Furthermore, by failing to innovate, incumbent firms in a mature industry actually invite entry because more entrepreneurial managers will see opportunities to appeal to customers by offering new products or

EXHIBIT **8.5**

Benchmarking, Organizational Learning, and Firm Performance Over Time

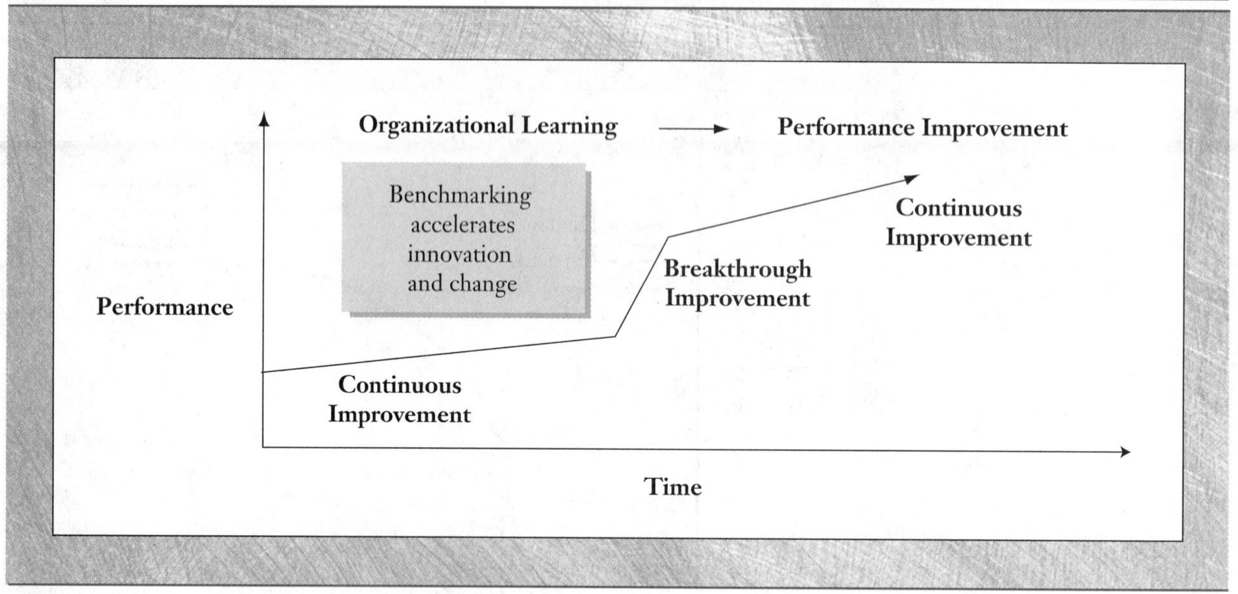

SOURCE: E. Pappacena (Arthur Andersen & Co.), *Benchmarking for Success* (presentation).

services or by employing new technologies. If new entrants do invade, they will further intensify competition in what has already become an unattractive industry. Again, the steel industry offers an excellent example of how minimills saw an opportunity to employ an alternative technology—the electric arc furnace—in order to enter the steel industry profitably.

Thus, high-performing firms face the challenge of maintaining their competitive advantage as their industry environments become increasingly unattractive. Alternatively, firms that have never enjoyed a competitive advantage in an industry might see opportunities for developing one as the industry shifts to a more mature context.

WAYS TO IMPROVE THE ATTRACTIVENESS OF AND ACHIEVE COMPETITIVE ADVANTAGE IN MATURE INDUSTRY ENVIRONMENTS

This section considers a number of methods or tools that managers have employed in order to thrive in more mature industry environments. We first introduce, describe, and evaluate the effectiveness of benchmarking. We will then examine how firms have gained competitive advantage by totally rethinking their value chains. Finally, we will describe the importance of aggressive product and process innovation.

Benchmarking and its usefulness in developing and maintaining competitive advantage. A technique for developing competitive advantage that many firms have adopted over the last several years is benchmarking. Benchmarking can be defined as *comparing and measuring a firm's business processes against the best practice of those processes by any organization in any industry in the entire* *world*. As suggested by Exhibit 8.5, the objective of benchmarking is to foster organizational learning to achieve improvements in firm performance. Note that the illustration in Exhibit 8.5 assumes that ongoing organizational learning and improvement will be taking place. The objective of benchmarking is to accelerate that organizational learning and improvement so that performance "breakthroughs" can be achieved.

When a firm decides to undertake a benchmarking effort, it must first break down its own operations into discrete value-adding activities or processes. One way this can be done is by examining the firm's "value chain." Chapter 3 introduced the value chain concept, and Exhibit 8.6 illustrates the value chain for a hypothetical manufacturing firm, showing the various value-adding processes from design and engineering, to component and materials procurement, and manufacturing, to marketing and sales, and after-sales service.

After identifying discrete value-adding activities or processes, the next step in benchmarking is to measure those processes and compare the firm's performance against the best practice of any firm in the world. Best practice of a particular process might be done by a competitor in the firm's own industry. For example, Ford Motor Company has long benchmarked hundreds of its own internal processes against Toyota's performance of those same processes. One central idea of benchmarking, however, is that firms should not limit their search for best practice to their own industries. Some of the most famous examples of best practice bench-

EXHIBIT 8.6

The Value Chain for a Hypothetical Manufacturing Firm

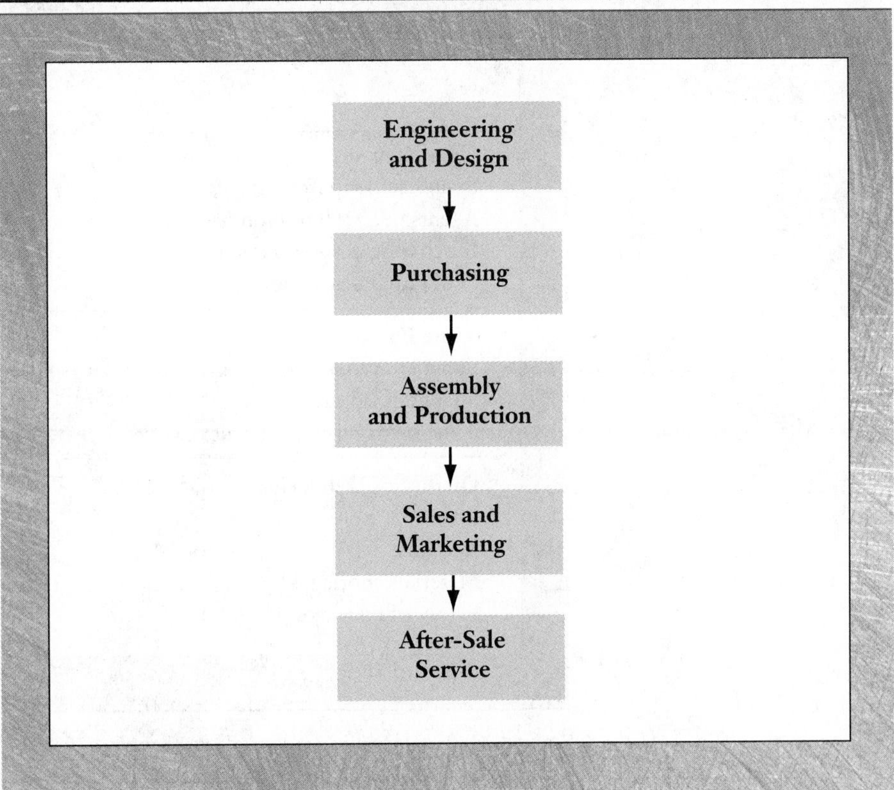

marking involve situations in which firms look at very different industries. For example, to better improve its customer service processes, Xerox benchmarked itself against L. L. Bean, a firm that is widely regarded as one of the very best customer service providers in the world.

A company should achieve two objectives from any benchmarking effort. First, the company should get a set of metrics that contrast its performance of a particular process with best practice. Exhibit 8.7 shows the outcome of a "typical company's" comparison of its procurement activities against best practice.

More important than these numbers, however, a firm engaging in a benchmarking study should gain some tangible ideas about how it can dramatically improve its own performance. These ideas, in turn, should stimulate a good deal more organizational learning so that dramatic improvements in overall firm performance are realized. During a benchmarking analysis of best practice, some ideas will be quite obvious and can be quickly copied or imitated. Other, more complex ideas will require considerably more "learning by doing" or study in order for the benchmarking firm to match and exceed the level of best practice.

The results of a successful benchmarking effort can be impressive. Exhibit 8.8 illustrates the improvements General Electric was able to achieve in its dishwasher business after a benchmarking study. Note the dramatic improvements in

EXHIBIT 8.7

A Benchmarking Study Comparing a Firm's Procurement Activities with Best Practice

	Typical Company	*World-Class Company*
Cost Factors		
Suppliers per purchasing agent	34	5
Agents per $100 million of purchases	5.4	2.2
Purchasing costs as a percentage of purchases made	3.3%	0.8%
Time Factors		
Supplier evaluations (weeks)	3	0.4
Supplier lead times (weeks)	150	8
Time spent placing an order (weeks)	6	0.001
Quality of Deliveries		
Late	33%	2%
Rejected	1.5%	0.00001%
Materials shortages (no. of instances per year)	400	4

SOURCE: O. Port, "Quality," *Business Week*, November 30, 1992, 66–72.

EXHIBIT 8.8

Results of Benchmarking at General Electric's Dishwasher Business

	1980–1981 (actual)	*1983 (actual)*	*1984 (actual)*
Service call rate (index)	100	70	55
Unit cost reduction (index)	100	90	88
Number of times handled (tub/door)	27/27	1/3	1/3
Inventory turns	13	17	28
Reject rates (mechanical/electrical test)	10%	3%	2.5%
Productivity (labor/unit index)	100	133	142
Other: 70 percent fewer part numbers, 20 pounds lighter, worker attitudes (positive 2X, negative 0.5X)			

SOURCE: R. H. Hayes and S. C. Wheelwright, *Restoring Our Competitive Edge: Competing Through Manufacturing* (New York: Wiley, 1984).

rejection rates, inventory turns, and labor productivity that are documented in the exhibit.

After the emphasis Chapter 3 gave to the asymmetric nature of competitive advantage, a good question is how benchmarking—with its emphasis on comparing firms' processes and capabilities with best practice—can result in competitive advantage? If the essence of benchmarking is the emulation of best practice, then it seems reasonable that benchmarking will be unable to provide firms with the asymmetry that is essential to achieving competitive advantage. According to the logic introduced in Chapter 3, wouldn't it seem that benchmarking, at best, could only result in competitive parity? The answer to this question is that the aim of benchmarking is not merely to copy or imitate successful firms, but rather to motivate organizational learning and improvements so that firms engaging in benchmarking studies develop their own unique competencies. Furthermore, as emphasized in Chapter 3, effective organizational processes will prove very difficult for other firms to imitate. Instead, managers can use benchmarking to spur their own thinking and creativity so that their firms develop their own unique and effective processes. As Steven Walleck, a consultant for McKinsey & Company, has argued:

> Managerial innovation will be required to adapt the important characteristics of successful approaches in ways that best fit a company's own situation. *The purpose of benchmarking is to expose managers to new ways of doing things in order to spark creativity, not to create efficient copy cats*.[10]

In fact, it's safe to say that *the greater the differences or disparity between the focal firm and the firm being benchmarked, then the greater the need for learning and innovation on the part of the focal firm.*

Rethinking the value chain. Another way managers can lead their firms to competitive advantage when operating in mature industry environments is to rethink their firms' value chains. Very much related to benchmarking, rethinking the value chain involves careful analysis of each of the various links in firms' value chains. The analysis includes reconsidering which of the various links add or could potentially add value and which of the links are unlikely to contribute to the development of competitive advantage.

Early on, we asked how a company like Nike could come to dominate so completely the athletic shoe industry when it owns no shoe manufacturing facilities. The answer to this provocative question is that the managers of many companies, including Nike, have rethought their industries' value chains. In the case of Nike, the company's managers realized that with the widespread availability of low-cost shoe manufacturing facilities in the Far East, it did not need to have its own manufacturing facilities. Furthermore, the company's managers realized that the best way to add value was to develop and exploit marketing, promotion, and new-product development capabilities that would allow Nike to differentiate its products from those of its rivals. Thus, it is fair to say that Nike is really more of a *marketing company* than an *athletic shoe company*. Nike's marketing and promotion capabilities have helped the company to push aggressively into just about every sporting activity. A

DOONESBURY

by Garry Trudeau

SOURCE: *Doonesbury* © 1997 G. B. Trudeau. Reprinted with permission of Universal Press Syndicate. All rights reserved.

couple of Doonesbury cartoons illustrate just how ubiquitous the Nike "swoosh" has become.

Though less dramatic than Nike, the managers of many other companies have also come to realize that by rethinking their value chains they can find and exploit new ways to increase profitability. Nowhere are these new tactics more visible than in the ever-changing retail industries. While many retailers sought to perfect a "one-size-fits-all" strategy in which uniform or standardized products and services are delivered through common distribution channels and aimed at serving the broadest possible target markets, many newer retailers have realized that a large number of consumers are willing to sacrifice service in order to enjoy lower prices. As a result, firms like Dell Computer, Costco, and Charles Schwab have emerged as major players in their respective retail markets.[11] These firms have realized that many consumers who "know what they want" do not benefit from some product attributes or service activities and would gladly give up some product features or customary levels of service if they could obtain lower prices as a result.

Gibson Greetings and Sara Lee have recently announced programs that will in many ways make them look much more like Nike. Gibson Greetings plans to outsource the manufacturing and printing of all its greeting cards.[12] Sara Lee's plan calls for it to eliminate nearly all its own manufacturing operations and contract out for all its production needs.[13] By eliminating its manufacturing facilities, the company will be able to focus more of its management attention on marketing and new-product development

EXHIBIT 8.9

Productivity (Sales per Employee) at Nike and Sara Lee

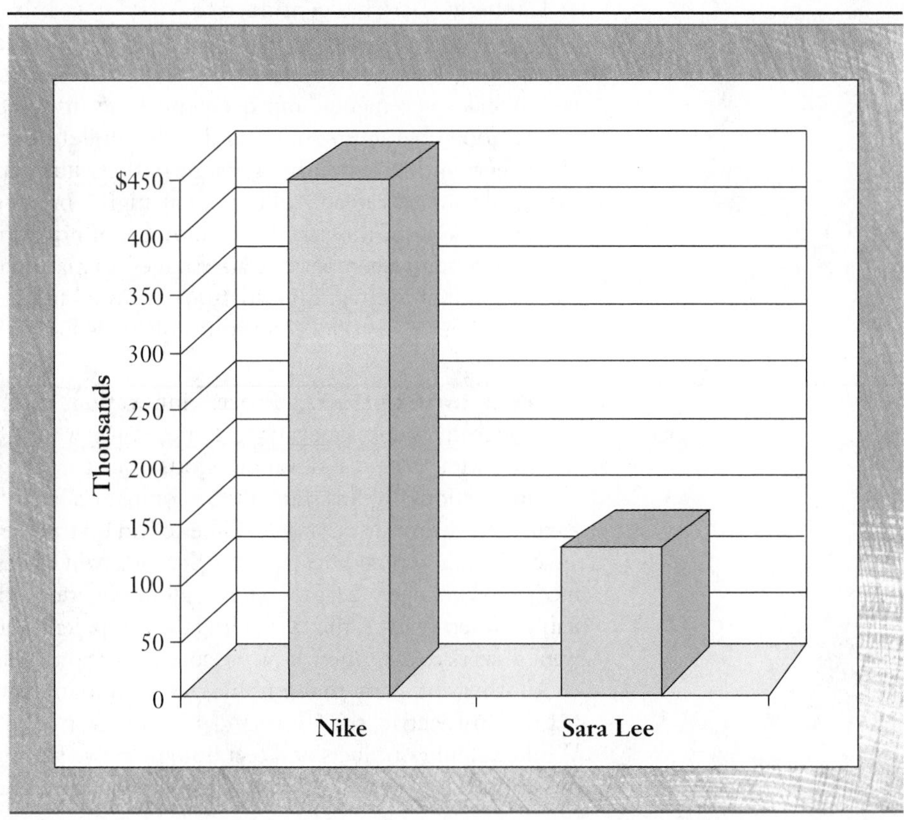

activities. Furthermore, the move will almost certainly improve the productivity of the company. Exhibit 8.9 compares the sales per employee of Nike with the current level of sales per employee at Sara Lee. Sara Lee is almost certainly hoping to see its level of sales per employee increase to the level enjoyed by Nike and other companies that have eliminated those links in their value chains that do not contribute value.

Product innovation. Innovation can occur along two fronts, both of which will change the value-price relationship associated with a given product or service. Product innovations provide new or improved features or attributes that deliver more value. Process innovations typically allow firms to make or deliver better products or services or to make or deliver those products or services at a lower cost and price.

Product innovations have a remarkable record of revitalizing mature markets. Product innovation worked well in the automobile industry for many decades. The Big Three would routinely alter their cars by adding features (e.g., power steering, power brakes, air conditioning, the automatic transmission) or by making superficial changes in car body design (tail fins, a little more or a little less chrome, changes in the arrangement of the headlights). Only after the successful invasion of the U.S. market by Japanese manufacturers in the 1970s and 1980s did the U.S. manufacturers emphasize the importance of manufacturing *process* innovations that would improve quality.

Consider also the impact the mountain bike has had on the bicycle industry. The developer of the mountain bike supposedly tried to sell the idea to Schwinn, whose managers rejected the offer, believing that riders would object to the bike's fat tires. Of course, all that remains of the shortsighted Schwinn company today is its name, which was acquired by another bike manufacturer; the company has gone out of business and been liquidated.

Kimberly-Clark has continued to enjoy remarkable success in the disposable diaper market even as number one Procter & Gamble has been forced to lower prices on its Pampers and Luvs lines. Why? Probably because Kimberly-Clark has continued to make incremental improvements to its disposable diapers (e.g., velcro fasteners, cartoon characters, boys' and girls' models, better absorbency, a little more elastic here and there). Although none of these innovations has been particularly dramatic, consumers remain willing to pay higher prices to receive the added benefits.

Perhaps one of the very best examples of how product innovation can allow a firm to maintain a competitive advantage in a mature industry is offered by Gillette, whose product innovation efforts are profiled in the accompanying Management Focus, "Gillette's Product Innovation Efforts Fuel a Blockbuster Product."

Process innovation. Process innovations can be just as valuable if not more valuable than product innovations. For example, while Gillette's managers are obviously obsessed with product innovation efforts, they appear to be equally obsessed with process innovations, as illustrated in the company's manufacturing processes. To manufacture the Sensor, for example, Gillette had no trouble finding equipment that would attach the tiny springs to each of the Sensor's twin blades. The problem was, the equipment wouldn't operate fast enough to allow Gillette to make the Sensor cartridges profitably. Nevertheless, Gillette acquired the equipment, and the company's engineers then went to work to determine how the speed of the production process could be increased.

Another company that emphasizes such manufacturing process improvements is Lincoln Electric, the Cleveland-based maker of electric arc welding equipment. While welding products and technologies have seen few changes over the past several decades, Lincoln focuses on process innovations that lower manufacturing

MANAGEMENT FOCUS

GILLETTE'S PRODUCT INNOVATION EFFORTS FUEL A BLOCKBUSTER PRODUCT

When Bic, the French maker of ballpoint pens, introduced the disposable razor in 1974, Gillette's managers thought that disposables might win a mere 10 percent of the wet-shave market, but by the late 1980s, 60 percent of all the razors sold were disposables. Though Gillette was able to maintain a market share lead over other razor manufacturers by introducing its own disposable razors, the lower profit margins of disposables were hurting Gillette's overall profitability. The challenge for Gillette was to regain a competitive advantage by developing a razor that would win back customers yet be very difficult for competitors to imitate. The result was the Sensor razor.

The Sensor is a twin-blade razor that offers a very close shave because each of the twin blades is mounted on springs that allow the blades to follow the contours of the shaver's skin. The Sensor has been a runaway hit for Gillette, allowing the company to earn high profits and increase its stock price dramatically. An innovation effort that borders on obsession supported Gillette's development of the Sensor. Consider these passages from a *Wall Street Journal* article on Gillette:

> Nowhere is the obsession more evident than at the South Boston manufacturing and research plant. Here, some 200 volunteers from various departments come to work unshaven each day. They troop to the second floor and enter small booths with a sink and mirror, where they take instructions from technicians on the other side of a small window: try this blade or that shaving cream or this aftershave, then answer questionnaires. Besides men's faces, the research includes the legs of women volunteers...
>
> For a close look at the mechanics of shaving, Gillette uses a boroscope—a video camera attached to a blade cartridge using fiber optics. Magnifying the film hundreds of times, researchers can precisely determine how twin blades catch the whiskers, pull them out of the follicles and cut them. Sometimes they collect debris after test shaves and measure the angle of the cut whiskers; the flatter the angle, the less force it took to cut the hair.
>
> "We test the blade edge, the blade guard, the angle of the blades, the balance of the razor, the length, the heft, the width," explains Donald Chaulk, vice president of the shaving technology laboratory. "What happens to the chemistry of the skin? What happens to the follicle? We own the face. We know more about shaving than anybody. I don't think obsession is too strong a word." He pauses. "I've got to be careful. I don't want to sound crazy."[1]

But it is precisely this obsession that has helped Gillette to maintain its dominant position in the shaving industry, and it is this same research effort that was behind Gillette's recent introduction of the MACH3, the first three-blade razor.[2] ■

[1]Ingrassia, L. 1992. The cutting edge: Using advanced technology, Gillette has managed an unusual feat. *The Wall Street Journal*, April 6, A6.

[2]Maremont, M. 1998. How Gillette brought its MACH3 to market. *The Wall Street Journal*, April 15, B1, B4.

costs. Lincoln routinely buys new capital equipment and then the company's own engineers modify that equipment to increase its productivity on the assembly line.

Over the past two decades, the vast majority of U.S. manufacturing companies have adopted some form of just-in-time production practices. The impact has been profound. In 1983, the ratio of inventory to gross domestic product was 24 percent; by 1996, this ratio had fallen to just 17 percent. In the early 1980s, nearly 20 percent of the gross domestic product was accounted for by expenditures on logistics

EXHIBIT 8.10

GE Dishwashers: Several Models, All Based on a Common Platform

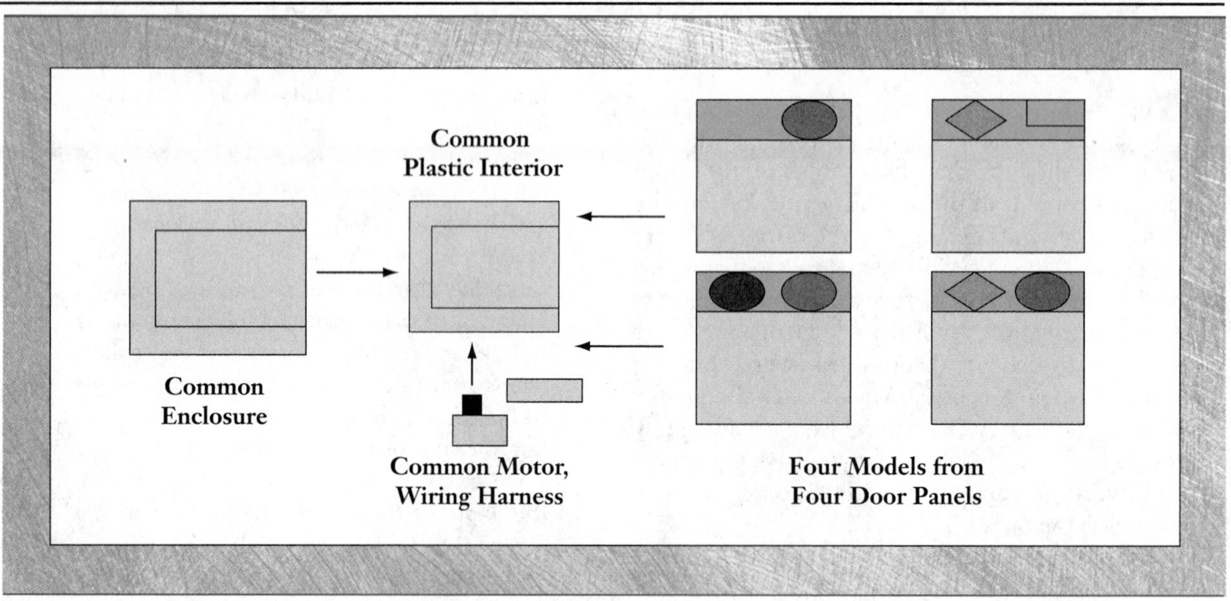

SOURCE: R. Sanchez and D. Sudharshan, "Real-Time Market Research," *Marketing Intelligence and Planning* 11, 7 (1993): 29–38.

and transportation. By 1996, logistics and transportation costs represented just 11 percent of the gross domestic product.

Another important process innovation tool is modular design. The idea behind modular design is to build a number of different product models or variations, all based on a common product "platform." One company that has benefited from modular design is General Electric. Several years ago, the company considered closing its dishwashing manufacturing operations due to low market share and poor profitability. Given one last opportunity to turn the situation around, the managers of GE's dishwasher business took some fairly dramatic steps. In addition to automating many of the plant's operations, GE's dishwasher business also adopted modular design. As illustrated in Exhibit 8.10, all of GE's dishwashers incorporate many common "modules," such as the same enclosure, the same interior, and the same motor and wiring harness. Any differences in GE's dishwasher models, such as different wash cycles and other options, are incorporated in the door panel. Thus, the company enjoys the benefits of offering several different models, all based on a common platform. Such an approach to manufacturing allows companies to produce a number of different products or models while also enjoying considerable economies of scale in the production and assembly of common components.

Competition in Manufacturing and Service Industries

This final section compares and contrasts the characteristics of manufacturing and service firms and describes some of the competitive challenges that are unique to firms in each of these two sectors.

The Revolution in Manufacturing

After several years, in the late 1970s and early 1980s, during which many observers concluded that manufacturing was "dead," we've now witnessed a revolution in manufacturing in the United States as well as in other industrialized nations. After two decades of declining manufacturing efficiency and competitiveness, many U.S. manufacturing industries are enjoying a renaissance, and a growing number of manufacturing companies are establishing or reestablishing a competitive advantage in both domestic and international markets. Richard Schonberger, a consultant to many manufacturers, has pointed out that many American companies grew complacent during the 1960s and early 1970s.[14] Schonberger uses a simple metric, inventory turnover, to illustrate not only the decline in U.S. manufacturing competitiveness but also how, after about the mid-1970s, many of these companies began to improve the efficiency of their operations. Exhibit 8.11 (A) shows the decline of manufacturing efficiency before the mid- to late 1970s while part B shows the subsequent improvements in manufacturing efficiency after 1980.

What factors have been responsible for the dramatic improvement in manufacturing sector profitability, and why have so many manufacturing companies been successful at establishing a competitive advantage? At least five interconnected factors have spurred many firms to improve their manufacturing operations:

- *Increased competition*. Increased competition from both foreign and domestic rivals alerted many firms to the need for improving the efficiency and productivity of their manufacturing operations. The impact of competition from Japanese automobile producers on the U.S. automobile industry is perhaps the most obvious example, but the impact on the chemical, electronics, and consumer products industries also illustrates how growing competitive pressures have forced manufacturers to improve their operations. Technology has also played a role in increasing the level of competition present in many industries. As more entrepreneurial firms have used technology to improve product offerings or generate manufacturing process improvements, more established firms have come under increasing pressure to maintain market share and increase profit margins.
- *Productivity improvement*. In response to mounting competitive pressures, manufacturing firms have pursued a broad range of efforts to improve the efficiency of their operations. As the data presented in Exhibit 8.12 suggest, the results of these efforts have provided many firms with spectacular gains in productivity.
- *Benchmarking and value chain analysis*. Benchmarking was discussed earlier and is mentioned again here only because of its importance in contributing to improvements in manufacturing efficiency and productivity. Nearly all manufacturing operations have conducted some sort of benchmarking or value chain analysis exercises over the last several years, and these studies have proved helpful in identifying those activities or operations that add or contribute value and those that don't.
- *Reengineering and outsourcing*. Many firms have gone beyond benchmarking studies and value chain analyses and have sought to "reengineer" activities throughout their firms. Popularized by Michael Hammer and James Champy in their best-selling book, *Reengineering the Corporation*, the concept of reengineering encouraged managers not just to improve their companies' activities, but to fundamentally rethink their business operations.[15] The impact of Hammer and Champy's book has been nothing short of phenomenal as companies and consulting practices have rushed to adopt the reengineering dogma. Reengineering studies at thousands of companies led to reductions in the number of management layers, staffing cuts, the reorganization of work activities, and the merger or consolidation of various departments.

EXHIBIT 8.11

The Decline and Improvement in Manufacturing Efficiency: Inventory Turnover Ratios of Selected U.S. Manufacturing Companies

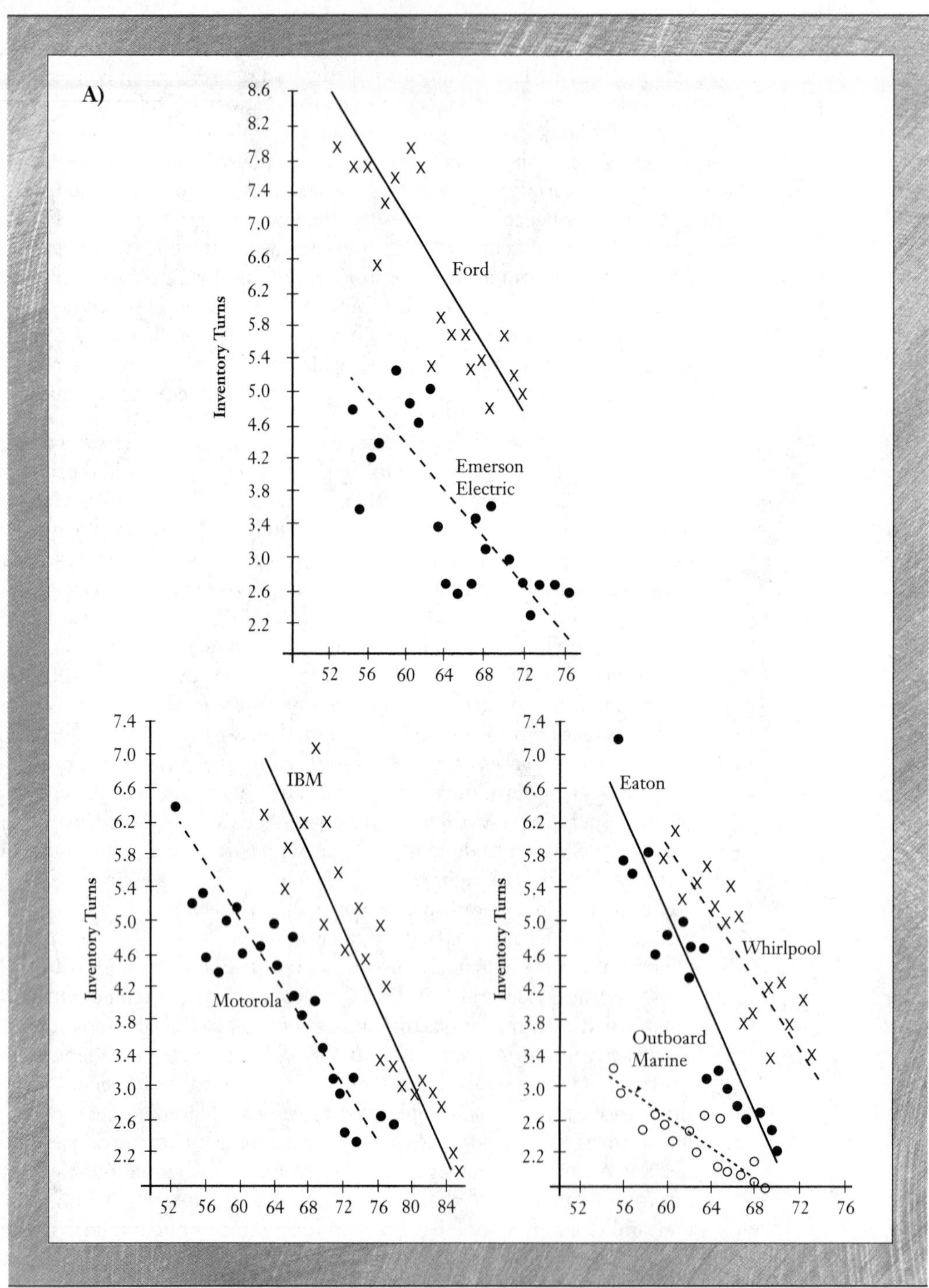

CONTINUED

EXHIBIT 8.11 CONTINUED

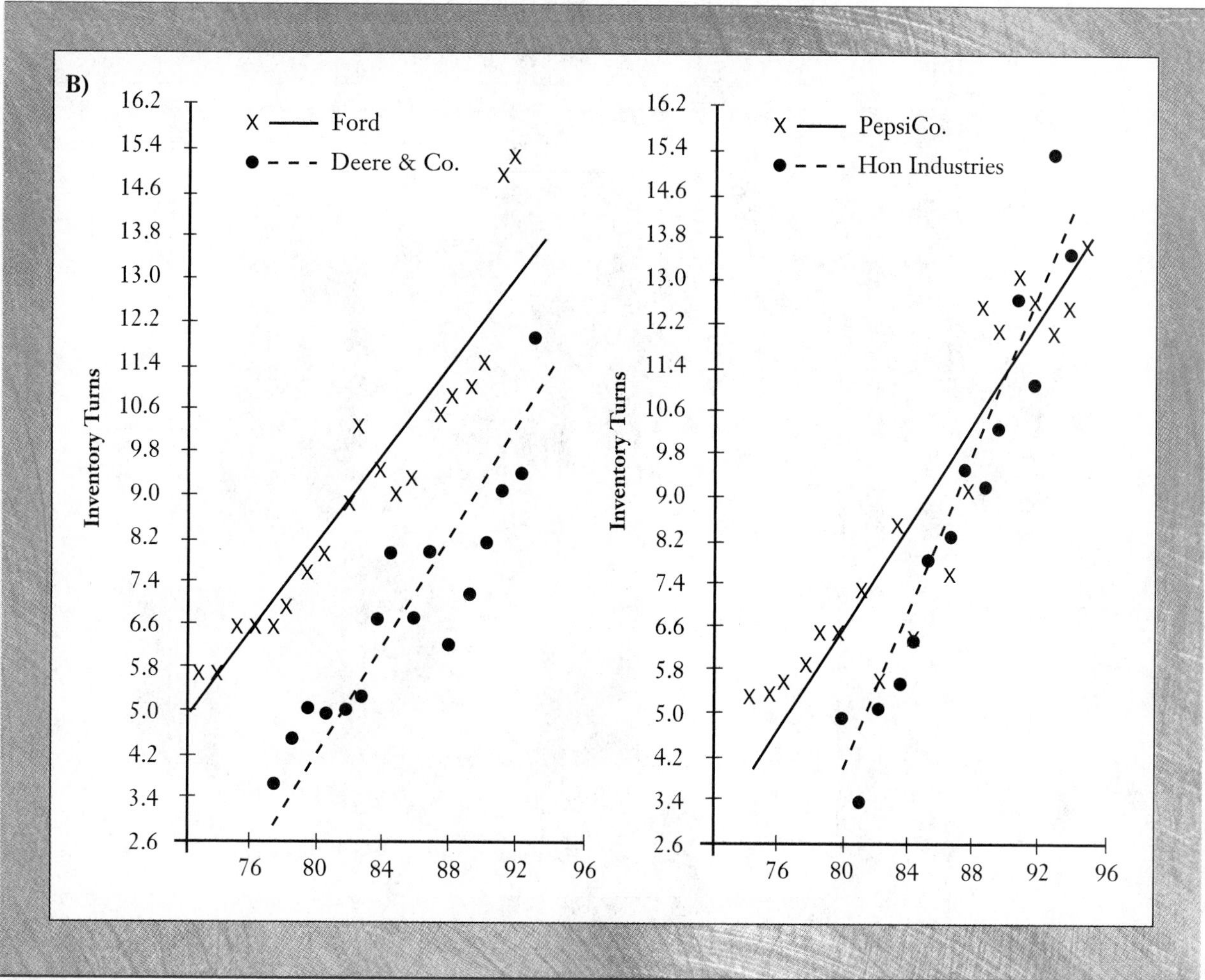

SOURCE: R. J. Schonberger, *World Class Manufacturing: The Next Decade* (New York: Free Press, 1996).

Even more significant, reengineering also encouraged firms to begin outsourcing more and more activities. Though the outsourcing of components has long been a common practice among manufacturing firms, the reengineering movement proved to be a major catalyst for firms to begin outsourcing many more activities that were either not critical to the success of their operations or unlikely to be sources of competitive advantage. Firms found that they could outsource everything from janitorial and secretarial services to data processing, payroll administration, and even, in the case of the Southern Pacific Railway, train dispatching.[16]

Recently, however, many managers have begun to question the zeal with which their firms have pursued reengineering activities. The major concern among managers is that although reengineering efforts can be effective at cutting costs, they do little to increase revenue or market penetration.[17] In other words, reengineering is a defensive strategy that offers managers little guidance about how to grow their businesses. As a result, companies are likely to continue

EXHIBIT 8.12

Improvements in Manufacturing Productivity

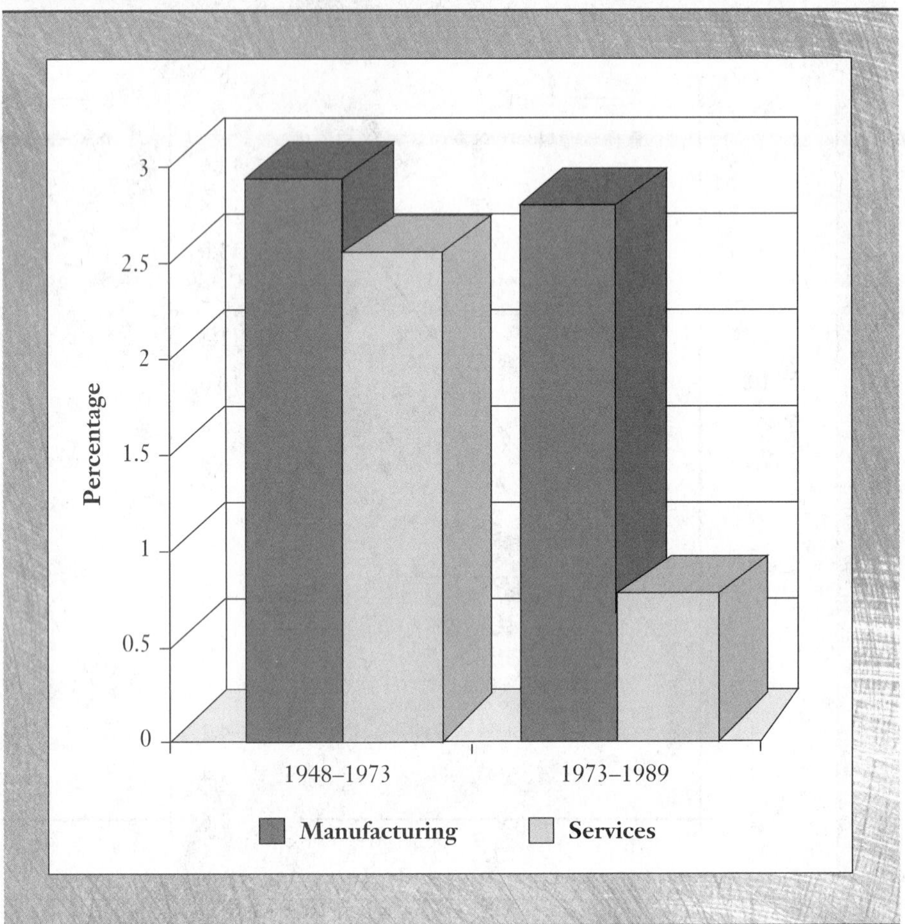

SOURCE: J. B. Quinn and M. N. Baily, "Information Technology: Increasing Productivity in Services," *Academy of Management Executive* 8(3): 1994, 28–48.

pursuing reengineering efforts in the future, but those efforts will be accompanied by additional emphasis on strategies aimed at sales revenue growth.

- *Quality*. Over the past decade, the importance of quality has become axiomatic among nearly all firms. Although quality improvement had formerly been viewed as a zero-sum game (i.e., improvements in quality would increase costs and come at the expense of lower profit margins), the last several years have shown that improvements in quality that are accompanied by improvements in manufacturing processes can actually result in lower costs and higher profit margins.

The remarkable improvements in manufacturing efficiency have not, however, been mirrored by similar improvements in service sector efficiency. In fact, the growth rate of service sector productivity lags far behind the rate of productivity improvement in manufacturing. The next few sections focus on the service sector and the challenges managers face in attempting to improve productivity in service business contexts.

EXHIBIT 8.13

Value Added by the Agricultural, Manufacturing, and Service Sectors

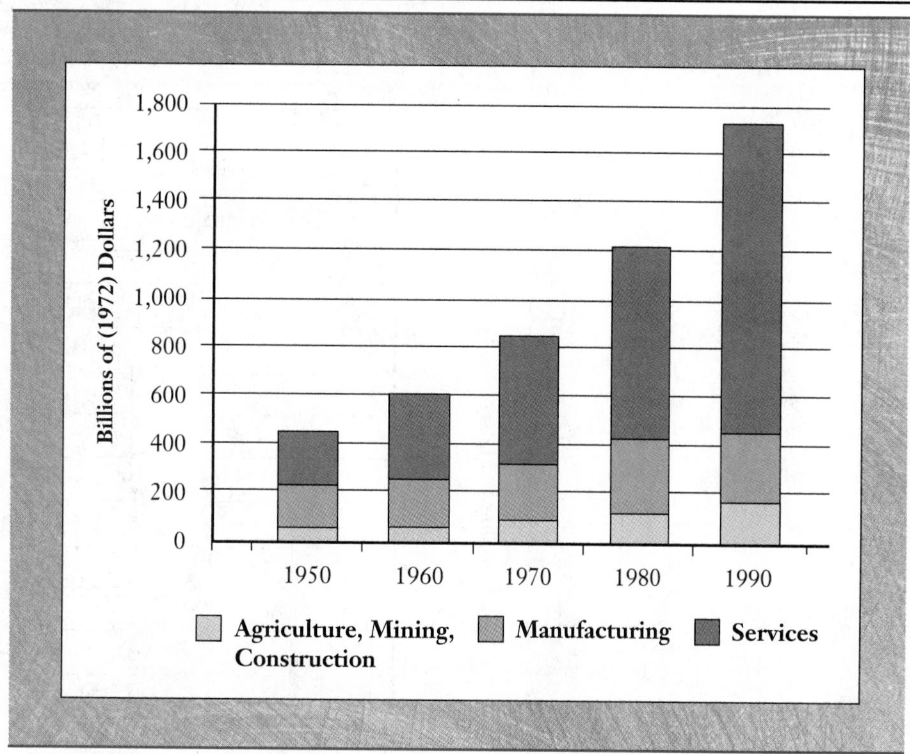

SOURCE: J. B. Quinn, *Intelligent Enterprise* (New York: Free Press, 1992).

THE GROWING SERVICE SECTOR, THE NATURE OF SERVICE WORK, AND THE PROBLEM OF SERVICE PRODUCTIVITY

The growth of the service sector is probably one of the most taken-for-granted features of the economic landscape, but a few illustrations of the importance of services are worth noting here. Exhibit 8.13 shows the value added by the agricultural, manufacturing, and service sectors, and vividly illustrates the growing importance of services to the overall economy. Exhibit 8.14 offers additional evidence of this profound shift and shows how employment patterns have changed in the United States since 1950. Note that during the 1980s, service sector employment grew by nearly 30 percent while manufacturing employment actually fell by nearly 2 percent.

In addition to the absolute and relative growth of the service sector, another interesting development is the entry of many traditional "manufacturing companies" into service businesses. For example, in 1995, $20 billion of IBM's $70 billion in total revenues came from services. Even General Electric has seen the sales of its service activities increase over the last several years; by 1995, services accounted for 10 percent of GE's revenues. Such trends are likely to continue as more firms pursue new opportunities for growth—most of which will be in the service sector.[18]

Firms in service industries face many of the same challenges confronting manufacturing companies. Both types of firms must attract and keep customers, offer

EXHIBIT 8.14

Changing Employment Patterns from 1950 to 1990

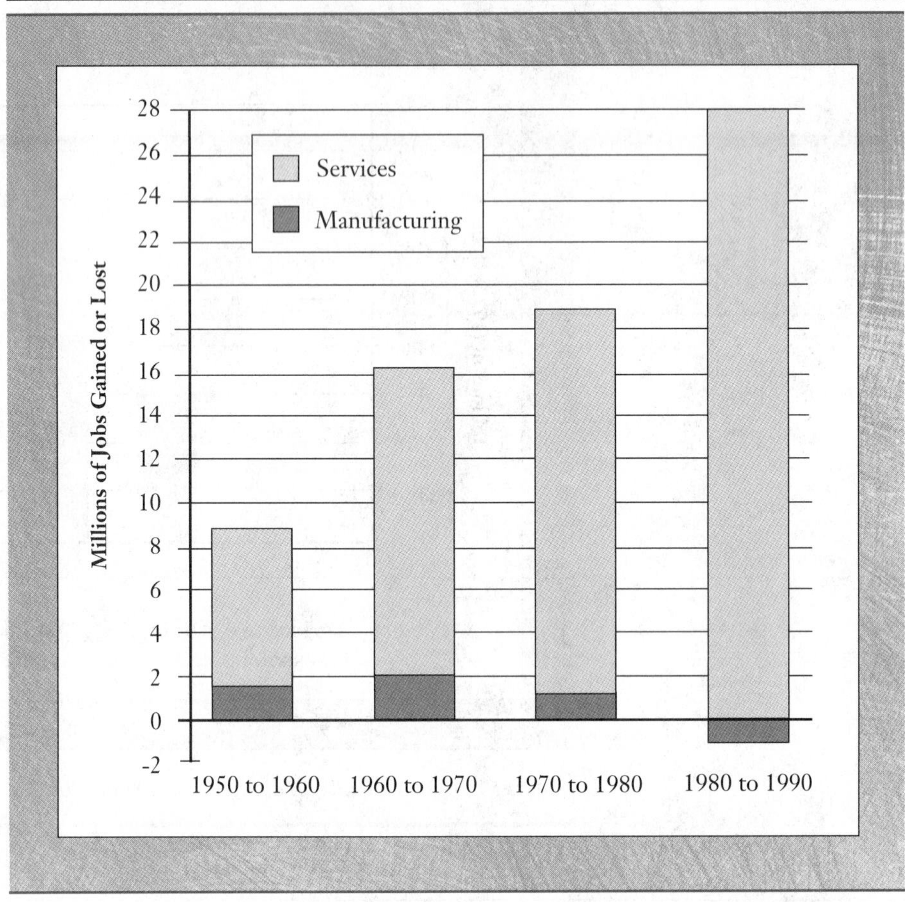

SOURCE: J. B. Quinn, *Intelligent Enterprise* (New York: Free Press, 1992).

quality products or services, and develop the capabilities that will allow them to compete effectively in their industry environments. At the same time, service industries have several unique characteristics that pose special challenges for managers:

Services cannot be inventoried. First, unlike most manufacturing firms, service firms cannot maintain an inventory of services. In other words, most service firms cannot manufacture or make their services "ahead of time" and hold them in inventory for resale at a later date or time. Instead, services—including everything from a haircut to travel on an airplane—are typically provided in "real time" while the customer waits. If a manufacturing company produces a defective product, it may be detected during the manufacturing process and either reworked or scrapped before reaching—and disappointing—a customer. In nearly all service businesses, however, a faulty or substandard level of service will be immediately apparent to the customer. Although this distinction between manufacturing and service businesses may seem obvious, it is vitally important to the success of service firms. Managers of service firms must attempt to ensure that every encounter with a customer meets a high level or standard of quality.

The service "encounter" is personal. Second, while the relationship between the manufacturers of most products and the customers buying those products tends to be impersonal and somewhat objective, the relationship between most service providers and their customers tends to be more personal and based much more on perceptions and other less objective or tangible factors. The personal nature of the relationship between customers and service providers in most service industries suggests that these firms have considerable opportunities to differentiate themselves, and many businesses work very hard to be perceived as offering excellent service.

Consider, for example, the market for hair care. While some consumers view haircuts and other hair care services as commodity-like services and will seek out the lowest-cost providers, a large percentage of consumers will develop personal and loyal relationships with their hair care professional. Indeed, such loyal relationships between customers and service providers are a hallmark of many service industries, including the markets for doctors, lawyers, and other professionals, and retailing industries of all types. Often, these relationships are based not only on the quality of the services these professionals provide but also on less objective factors. When asked why they use a particular doctor, for example, people are as likely to say "Because she listens to me" or "Because he is always available to meet with me" as they are to comment on the quality of the doctor's medical advice or recommendations.

The personal and less objective nature of the relationship most service providers have with their customers has a number of drawbacks, however. Because of the personal nature of most service businesses, a great deal of organizational knowledge or expertise resides not in the management of the firm but with the actual service provider. Consider again the example of hair care: Customers are likely to be more loyal to their particular barber or stylist than they are to the hair care establishment because of the personal relationship they have established. If their barber or stylist decides to leave one firm and move to another, customers are likely to follow the barber or stylist to the new firm. As a result, service firms must emphasize human resource policies and programs that help them retain the best employees.

Automating or improving the efficiency of services can be challenging. Third, because of the personal and "real-time" nature of most service industries, service firms cannot use the same techniques as manufacturing firms to improve productivity. For example, many services do not lend themselves well to automation. Although the banking industry has made great strides in automating many of its services through the installation of automatic teller machines and telephone banking systems, it is doubtful that other services, such as hair care, legal assistance, and medical care, will ever be fully automated.

Also, the productivity of service businesses can rarely be improved by simply reducing employee headcount. Although an executive like Albert J. ("Chainsaw Al") Dunlap can lay off 6,000 of the 12,000 employees of a manufacturing company like Sunbeam, executives of service firms do not have the same discretion. Layoffs of employees may reduce payroll expense, but many service firms have found that layoffs adversely affect service quality and lead to the loss of customers. For example, when the Carlson Travel Network decided to improve productivity by laying off travel agents, customer service suffered severely—not because the company's remaining travel agents couldn't handle customers' requests for travel arrangements, but because those agents did not have the expertise—in this case, the relationship knowledge—to know that when a particular customer called to request an airline ticket to Los Angeles, that customer would also expect the travel agent to reserve a particular type of rental car and a room at a preferred hotel. As a consequence, the travel agency suffered considerable embarrassment and ill will when customers would arrive at their destinations without rental car and hotel reservations.[19]

Delta Air Lines offers another vivid example of how cost-cutting approaches that have long been common among manufacturing firms can backfire when used in a service industry context.[20] To trim its costs, Delta reduced its headcount from nearly 70,000 to less than 60,000 employees in less than two years. Although the cuts were helpful in improving Delta's profits, service levels definitely suffered. The carrier fell to last place in on-time performance among the major airlines, and at an airline that once prided itself for its excellent service, customers now often wait in long lines to check bags and purchase tickets.

Improving the Productivity of Service Work

Because of the unique characteristics of service work and because many of the practices that have been used to improve efficiency and productivity in the manufacturing sector are often counterproductive when applied in service businesses, firms in the service sector have had to develop new, more appropriate methods or techniques for increasing productivity. Some techniques that firms have adopted include bundling or cross-selling services, increasing or improving the rate of organizational learning, and restructuring work practices:

- *Bundling or cross-selling* involves exposing customers to a broader array of a company's service offerings. For example, a customer might come into a bank to make a deposit. The teller, while processing the transaction, would also ask the customer whether he or she might need a loan or whether the customer could use any of the bank's investment services. Such bundling or cross-selling typically requires that employees have additional training so that they are knowledgeable about their firms' service offerings and how they might identify those customers who would be most likely to make use of the firms' other services.
- Managers of service firms are also achieving productivity gains through the *more effective use of organizational knowledge and learning*. Retailing offers an excellent example of how service firms are realizing significant productivity gains by better using information and organizational knowledge. For example, bar coding and computer technology have allowed retailing firms to monitor their customers' buying habits, identify popular items and detect fashion trends, and realize significant improvements in the management of their inventories.
- Managers of many service firms have also *reorganized their firms' structures to eliminate inefficiencies and bottlenecks*. In many cases, service firms have given "frontline" employees more authority to satisfy customers. Rather than having unhappy customers wait for a manager to show up to rectify unsatisfactory situations, many companies now give employees the authority they need to satisfy these customers.

All these steps reinforce many of the observations made by the authors of a recent *Harvard Business Review* article, "Managing Our Way to Higher Service Sector Productivity."[21] The authors argued that the most important factor in improving service sector productivity is *management*, and they cited numerous

EXHIBIT 8.15

Differences in Productivity Across Three Insurance Companies

General Expenses ÷ Premiums (in cents per dollar)			
Year	*Connecticut Mutual*	*Phoenix Mutual*	*Northwestern Mutual*
1988	20.9	16.7	6.8
1989	19.8	15.7	6.9
1990	20.2	14.9	7.4
1991	20.9	15.6	6.3

SOURCE: M. Van Biema and B. Greenwald, "Managing Our Way to Higher Service Sector Productivity," *Harvard Business Review* 75, 4 (1997): 87–95.

examples to show how service firms operating in the same industry with the same technologies using people with the same skill levels can nonetheless achieve remarkably different levels of productivity from their workers. One such example compares the productivity of various companies in the insurance industry and is included here in Exhibit 8.15. Van Biema and Greenwald propose a "management-driven revival in service productivity" that is based on (1) sustained management attention, (2) application of "productivity-enhancing strategies," (3) appropriate and effective use of labor-saving technologies, and (4) the "implementation of carefully conceived, parallel human-resources and workforce-management strategies."[22]

CHAINS, FRANCHISING, AND COMPETITIVE ADVANTAGE IN SERVICE INDUSTRIES

One final topic that deserves some discussion in this chapter is the growth of franchising and retailing chains in many service industries. Perhaps the growth of chains and franchising is best illustrated by some statistics from the restaurant industry. Today, in the United States, there are nearly 10,000 McDonald's restaurants, over 11,000 Subways, more than 8,000 Burger Kings, 4,200 Domino's Pizzas, and 3,400 Little Caesars restaurants, and then there are the countless Taco Bells and KFCs, and the thousands of upscale dining franchises, such as the Olive Garden, Red Lobster, Macaroni Grill, and the Outback Steakhouse. A drive through any city or a walk through any shopping center will reveal the extent to which retailing chains and franchises have become a dominant feature of the economic landscape.

Much of the literature that has examined the growing presence of retailing chain stores and franchising in our urban areas is very critical. Chains and franchising are blamed for the "homogenization" of our cities. This homogenization is so pervasive today in the United States that an individual walking through a shopping mall in suburban Maryland would see almost all the same stores that another individual walking through a shopping mall in suburban Atlanta, Chicago, Denver, Miami, or Los Angeles would see. James Howard Kunstler's book, *The Geography of Nowhere: The Rise and Decline of America's Manmade Landscape*, takes these arguments even further and suggests that the growth of shopping malls and the associated proliferation of retailing chains and franchising has led to the destruction of our communities and especially our cities' downtown areas.[23] Kunstler further argues that the growth of shopping malls on the periphery of cities has required nearly everyone to own a car in order to enjoy "first-class citizenship" in the modern city.

Other articles and books have also argued that chain stores and franchising are responsible for the loss of many small, unique, and locally owned businesses, and that the strategies of Wal-Mart, Barnes and Noble, and many other chains have driven many smaller, independent retailers out of business. Some communities have reacted by adopting zoning laws that seek to prevent retailers—specifically, Wal-Mart—from entering their borders. A book published by the National Trust for Historic Preservation, *How Superstore Sprawl Can Harm Communities and What Citizens Can Do About It*, seeks to assist these efforts.[24]

Although much of the literature takes a very dim view of the growth of chain stores and franchising, a few more positive observations are also warranted. First, the chain store and franchising phenomena are likely to be an important part of the economic landscape for many years to come. Most retail chains have ambitious expansion plans, and nearly any retailing concept can be franchised. As a result, it's likely that the role of chain stores and franchising will grow rather than diminish.

Second, it is also important to recognize that chain stores and franchising have a number of important economic and strategic advantages over other forms of business. For example, chains and franchise organizations typically enjoy economies of scale in purchasing, distribution, and marketing and advertising that give them an important edge over smaller, independently owned businesses.

Furthermore, chains and franchise organizations are almost ideally designed to promote organizational learning. Both chains and franchise organizations can develop and perfect a particular concept and then expand by opening other establishments based on this concept or by selling franchises to independent entrepreneurs. Unlike most entrepreneurial activity, however, the chain or franchise is pursuing a concept that has already proven itself at another location. In addition, over time, the chain develops a tremendous amount of information and learning about customer preferences, marketing, sourcing, and logistics. With effective structures, this organizational learning and knowledge can be widely shared across all chain or franchise outlets. And, as the chain or franchise continues to expand, its knowledge base continues to grow.

Conclusion: The Importance of Managerial Thinking and Organizational Learning in Developing Effective Business Strategies

While Chapter 7 introduced the concept of business strategy and described generic strategies of cost leadership, differentiation, and focus, this chapter has emphasized some of the complexities associated with the formulation and implementation of business strategies in different industry contexts, including emerging and mature industries as well as manufacturing and service industries. It's not that generic strategies are inappropriate in any of these industry contexts, but the development of competitive advantage requires managers to do more than select an appropriate generic strategy. Although the choice of generic strategy can be helpful in developing the unique and difficult-to-imitate resources and capabilities that are essential to the development of competitive advantage, every firm must pursue specific strategies that are tailored to its industry or market.

Thus, one important, but largely implicit, theme throughout this entire chapter is the importance of managerial and organizational learning. All the industry contexts that have been described in this chapter present their own unique challenges. It is the responsibility of the managers of firms operating in these different industries to acquire the knowledge necessary to guide their firms so that appropriate business strategies are formulated and implemented.

As noted at the beginning of this chapter, the product life cycle concept has been applied to industries, suggesting that industries and markets move through a predictable cycle of emergence, rapid growth, maturity, and eventual decline. The text has emphasized that many entrepreneurs have ideas that can radically alter their firms' industries or create totally new industries. As markets emerge and rapid growth begins, however, many entrepreneurial firms lack the managerial talent and skill to maintain a competitive advantage. Most entrepreneurs are very knowledgeable about their products or services, but they often lack the managerial know-how to deal with the challenges of emerging industry environments. As a consequence, many start-up firms go through "growing pains" and many even go out of business because their owners do not acquire the necessary managerial know-how or turn their firms over to professional managers.

Similarly, many successful established firms operating in mature industry environments stop innovating and, as a consequence, their sales begin to stagnate. Instead of pursuing innovations that might invigorate their firms, managers remain content with existing products and services. In both these examples—entrepreneurs operating in the emerging market and the managers of established companies operating in mature markets—firms encounter difficulties because their managers fail to acquire the knowledge necessary to develop and maintain competitive advantage.

Similarly, managers of firms in manufacturing and service industries need to develop specialized knowledge and expertise. The chapter has suggested that the remarkable renaissance among U.S. manufacturing companies is almost certainly due to the application of new knowledge and organizational learning that have been translated into strategies that have dramatically improved productivity. If service sector productivity also improves, it will most likely occur because managers and their firms have developed new insights and knowledge that suggest new strategies.

Key Points

- Managers of firms operating in emerging industries face a number of challenges, including a great deal of ambiguity and uncertainty, as well as industry and product life cycles that can be very short.
- Neither first- nor second-mover strategies are necessarily optimal for firms operating in emerging industries—both have advantages and disadvantages, and firms pursuing both first- and second-mover strategies have been successful and unsuccessful in developing sustainable competitive advantage.
- Producing products and services that become the dominant design in an industry, producing products and services or developing processes and capabilities

that are difficult for competitors to imitate, and possessing important and valuable interconnected assets are all ways to improve competitiveness in emerging industry environments.

- Managers of firms operating in mature industry environments face a number of difficult challenges, including stagnant demand and excess capacity, exit barriers, a lack of innovation that makes products and services less attractive to customers, and competition from new entrants.
- Managers of firms in mature industry environments can take steps to develop and maintain competitive advantage, including benchmarking, rethinking the value chain, and product and process innovation.
- The manufacturing sector of the economy has enjoyed remarkable improvements in efficiency and productivity. The much larger service sector has not shared in these efficiency gains.
- Managers of firms in service industries face many challenges that are quite different from those faced by the managers of firms operating in manufacturing industries.
- Close management attention, appropriate use of technology, and the development of organizational routines and standard operating procedures can lead to major improvements in service sector efficiency and productivity.
- One of the most important reasons why chains and franchises have enjoyed great success is their ability to accumulate, store, and apply organizational learning to enhance efficiency and productivity.

Review and Discussion Questions

1. *Describe the concept of industry life cycle and what it implies about the sales of firms in industries at various points in the industry life cycle.*
2. *What are the special challenges of emerging markets?*
3. *Describe the three factors that are helpful in distinguishing between successful and unsuccessful first- and second-movers.*
4. *What are the unattractive characterisitcs of mature industry environments? What can managers of firms in mature industries do to develop or maintain competitive advantage?*
5. *What factors have contributed to a renaissance in many manufacturing industries? Why have these same factors not led to significant improvements in service industry productivity? What can be done to improve service sector productivity?*

Suggestions for Further Reading

Hammer, M., & Champy, J. 1994. *Reengineering the Corporation: A Manifesto for Business Revolution.* New York: HarperBusiness.

Schnaars, S. P. 1986. When entering growth markets, are pioneers better than poachers? *Business Horizons*, 29(2): 27–36.

Teece, D. J. (Ed.) 1987. *The Competitive Challenge: Strategies for Industrial Innovation and Renewal.* Cambridge, MA: Ballinger.

Urban, G. L., Carter, T., Gaskin, S., & Mucha, Z. 1986. Market share rewards to pioneering brands: An empirical analysis and strategic implications. *Management Science*, 32: 645–659.

Van Biema, M., & Greenwald, B. 1997. Managing our way to higher service-sector productivity. *Harvard Business Review*, 75(4): 87–95.

ENDNOTES

1. Porter, M. E. 1980. *Competitive Strategy*. New York: Free Press.
2. Urban, G. L., T. Carter, S. Gaskin, and Z. Mucha, 1986. Market share rewards to pioneering brands: An empirical analysis and strategic implications. *Management Science* 32:645–659.
3. Schnaars, S. P. 1986. When entering growth markets, are pioneers better than poachers? *Business Horizons* 29(2):27–36.
4. Bartlett, C. A. 1983. *EMI and the CT Scanner*. Boston: HBS Case Services, Harvard Business School.
5. Teece, D. J. 1987. Profiting from technological innovation: Implications for integration, collaboration, licensing, and public policy. In *The Competitive Challenge: Strategies for Industrial Innovation and Renewal*, edited by D. J. Teece. Cambridge, Mass: Ballinger.
6. Ishikura, Y. 1983. *Canon, Inc.: Worldwide Copier Strategy*. Boston: HBS Case Services, Harvard Business School.
7. Bartlett, EMI and the CT Scanner.
8. Shapiro, E. 1989. NutraSweet's bitter fight: A bid to defend its sole product as patents fall. *New York Times*, November 19, section 3, 4.
9. Reitman, V. 1997. Detroit challenge: Japanese car makers plan major expansion of American capacity. *The Wall Street Journal*, September 24, A1, A12; M. Schuman and V. Reitman, 1997. Full speed ahead: A worldwide glut doesn't sway Samsung from auto business. *The Wall Street Journal*, August 25, A1, A10.
10. Walleck, A. S. 1991. A backstage view of world-class performers. *The Wall Street Journal*, August 26, A10.
11. Morrison, D. J. 1996. Retail's shrinking middle. *The Wall Street Journal*, October 21, A20.
12. Coleman, C. Y. 1998. Gibson Greetings will outsource manufacturing of all of its cards. *The Wall Street Journal*, April 1, B6.
13. Rose, R. L., and C. Quintanilla, 1997. Sara Lee's plan to contract out work underscores trend among U.S. firms. *The Wall Street Journal*, September 17, A3, A6.
14. Schonberger, R. J. 1996. *World Class Manufacturing: The Next Decade*. New York: Free Press.
15. Hammer, M., and J. Champy, 1994. *Reegineering the Corporation: A Manifesto for Business Revolution*. New York: HarperBusiness.
16. Lee, L. 1995. Rent-a-techs: Hiring outside firms to run computers isn't always a bargain. *The Wall Street Journal*, May 18, A1, A9.
17. White, J. B. 1996. Next big thing: Reengineering gurus take steps to remodel their stalling vehicles. *The Wall Street Journal*, November 26, A1, A10.
18. Deutsch, C. H. 1997. Services becoming the goods in industry. *New York Times*, January 7, C1, C4.
19. Harper, L. 1992. Hazardous cuts: Travel agency learns service firms' perils in slimming down. *The Wall Street Journal*, March 20, A1, A9.
20. Brannigan, M., and E. de Lisser, 1996. Ground control: Cost cutting at Delta raises the stock price but lowers the service. *The Wall Street Journal*, June 20, A1, A8.
21. Van Biema, M., and B. Greenwald, 1997. Managing our way to higher service sector productivity. *Harvard Business Review* 75(4):87–95.
22. Ibid, p. 95.
23. Kunstler, J. H. 1993. *The Geography of Nowhere: The Rise and Decline of America's Manmade Landscape*. New York: Simon & Schuster.
24. Beaumont, C. E. 1994. *How Superstore Sprawl Can Harm Communities and What Citizens Can Do About It.* Washington: National Trust for Historic Preservation.

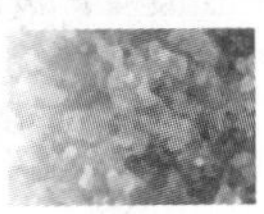

CHAPTER 9

CORPORATE STRATEGY AND DIVERSIFICATION

CHAPTER OBJECTIVES

We now turn our attention to corporate strategy and diversification. In terms of our model of strategic management, illustrated in Exhibit 9.1, decisions about corporate strategy and diversification are influenced by managers' beliefs about the appropriate size and diversity of their firms, their beliefs about how their firms' businesses are related to each other, and their beliefs about how diversification should be managed.

Corporate strategy and diversification are, however, multifaceted topics, and our exploration of these topics will build on many of the issues that have been discussed in previous chapters. We will see, for example, that successful corporate strategy requires the effective management of business definition or positioning at both the business and corporate levels, the development of unique organizational capabilities for the management of diversification, and the use of complex organizational structures. Above all, this chapter will emphasize the importance of managerial thinking, knowledge, and learning in guiding these management activities. In fact, the chapter will argue that successful diversification and the effective formulation and implementation of corporate strategies require a great deal of managerial and organizational learning.[1]

The specific objectives of this chapter are to:

- Define corporate strategy, describe some of the reasons firms diversify, identify and describe different types of corporate diversification, and assess the advantages and disadvantages associated with each.
- Identify sources of synergy in diversified firms and explain why synergies are so difficult to achieve.
- Explore the complex relationship between corporate diversification and firm performance.
- In particular, explore the influence of managers and managerial thinking on the relationship between diversification and performance.

EXHIBIT 9.1

The Mental Models and Strategic Decisions Studied in This Text and Their Influence on Performance and Competitive Advantage

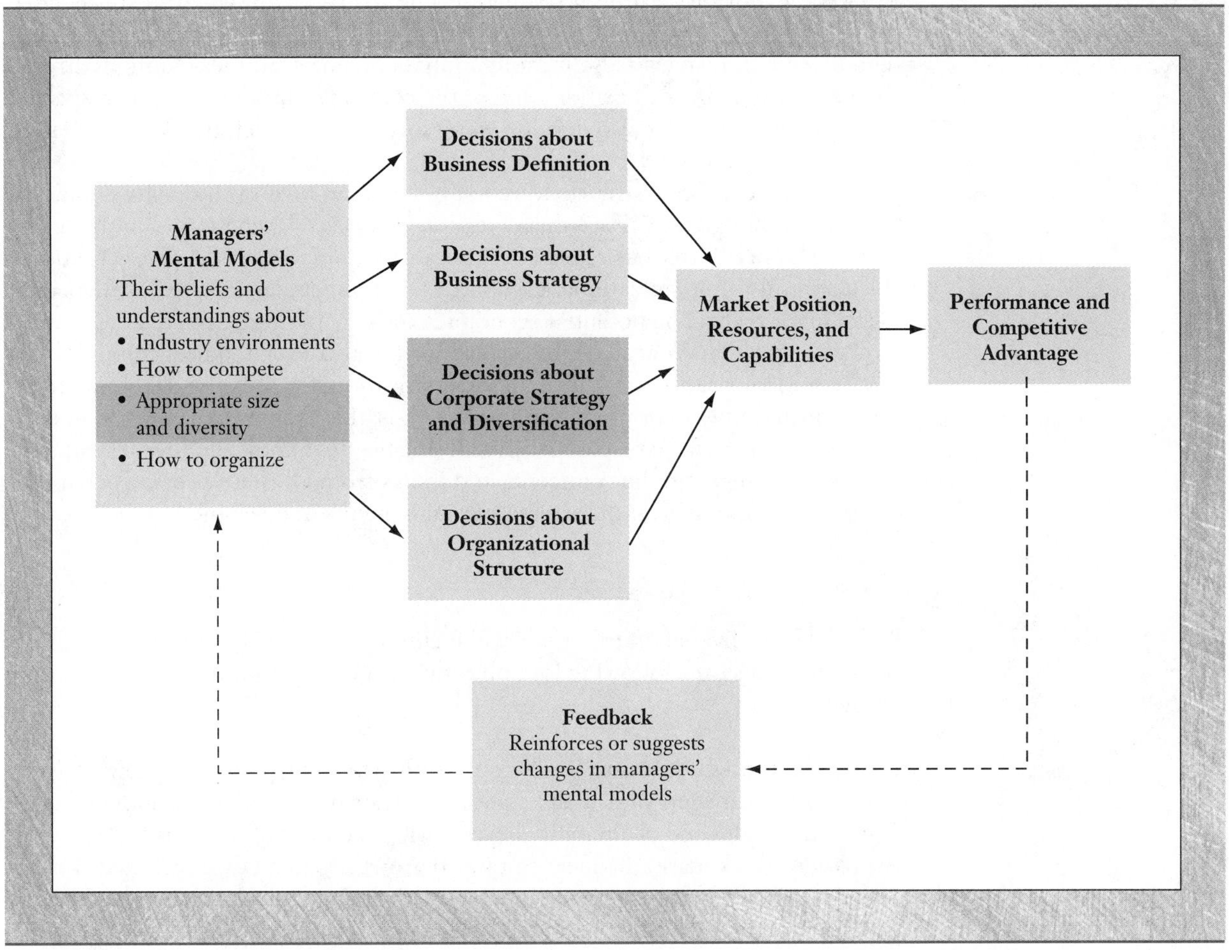

A Definition of Corporate Strategy, Why Firms Diversify, and Different Types of Diversification

As indicated in Chapters 1, 3, and 7, business strategy addresses the question How should the firm or business compete in a given competitive environment? Corporate strategy, on the other hand, addresses the question What is the appropriate scale or scope of the enterprise? Corporate strategy therefore influences how large and how diversified firms will be. Thus, in many respects, this chapter on corporate strategy and diversification is related to the chapter on business definition because diversification decisions are really decisions about the definition of the firm. A firm can be a "single business firm" operating in a single industry environment with a fairly apparent definition. On the other hand, a large and widely diversified firm with many different businesses, each operating in a different industry, faces the challenges of defining each of its various businesses as well as developing an overall corporate or firm definition. Steinway, the manufacturer of fine pianos, operates in a fairly small portion of the musical instruments industry, offering a limited line of products to a select group of customers who are willing to pay from $30,000 to $70,000 or more for a fine instrument. The firm's business definition is fairly straightforward. In contrast, the managers of General Electric, with businesses in such diverse industries as household appliances, entertainment, and jet aircraft engines, must define or position each of the company's businesses in its respective industry, but they must also develop some sort of unified definition for the enterprise as a whole.

Successful corporate strategies are not only the product of successful definition, however. Although we will see that diversified firms need some sort of unifying definition, or what Porter has called a "corporate theme,"[2] successful diversification is also the result of organizational capabilities or competencies that allow managers to exploit or realize the potential economies and other synergies that large size and diversity can offer. We will see that diversification also often requires complex organizational structures, and, above all, diversification requires the development of unique management knowledge and skills. Thus, this chapter logically follows earlier chapters on managers, competitive advantage, definition, and business strategy because it brings together concepts and issues from all these previous chapters. Chapter 10 elaborates on the structural requirements of diversified firms.

WHY DO FIRMS DIVERSIFY?

Why do firms diversify rather than stay focused on a single business? Though not an exhaustive list, the following four objectives appear to motivate most decisions to diversify:

1. *To grow.* Growth seems to be an implicit objective in nearly all organizations, and many managers pursue diversification strategies in order to maintain growth in sales and profitability beyond what their firms' core businesses can provide. Stock markets appear to reward growth companies, which may further encourage many managers to pursue growth through diversification. Other research studies have documented a strong correlation between firm size and executive compensation, suggesting that managers who pursue aggressive growth strategies are engaging in self-serving behavior. Still other researchers have suggested that managerial "hubris" — pride or status that comes from managing a large business enterprise — may also explain decisions to diversify. Whatever the source, it appears that the desire to grow motivates much diversification activity.
2. *To more fully utilize existing resources and capabilities.* Managers may also pursue diversification strategies because they believe their firms possess underutilized resources or capabilities that can be further exploited by diversifying into other markets or industries. Obvious examples of underutilized resources include factories or distribution channels operating below capacity, but underutilized capabilities might also include skills at sales and marketing as well as general management skill and knowledge.
3. *To escape from undesirable or unattractive industry environments.* The desire to escape from unattractive industry environments is also a powerful motivation for managers to pursue diversification strategies.[3] Managers of firms engaged in

a declining industry often face the choice of seeing their firms fail or pursuing diversification into a more promising industry. It is currently uncertain how federal and state governments will move to further restrict tobacco use, but all the major tobacco companies have prepared for further restrictions by diversifying into other industries.

4. *To make use of surplus cash flows.* Firms will often generate surplus cash flows or cash flows above and beyond their own investment needs. Managers are understandably reluctant to simply give these surplus cash flows to shareholders in the form of higher dividends. Yet large cash balances often attract corporate raiders or unsolicited takeover offers because raiders or other firms can use these cash balances to pay for the acquisition. As a result, managers often pursue diversification strategies as a way to make use of cash balances and avoid a hostile takeover.

TYPES OF DIVERSIFICATION

Although all corporate strategies are somewhat unique, we will describe four broad categories or types of diversification strategies: vertical integration, horizontal or related diversification, conglomerate or unrelated diversification, and global diversification. We will also focus on the advantages and disadvantages associated with each type.

Vertical integration. Vertical integration refers to a strategy of acquiring control over additional links in the value chain of producing and delivering products or services. *Backward integration* refers to a strategy of moving closer to the sources of raw materials by acquiring resource suppliers or by manufacturing the components needed for the production of a final product. *Forward integration* is just the opposite and refers to a strategy of moving closer to the end user. It may include acquiring or establishing retail outlets for the distribution, sale, or after-sale service of the company's products or services.

Firms in some industries, such as the petroleum industry, tend to be more vertically integrated than firms in other industries, but the extent of vertical integration among firms within the same industry can also vary considerably. For example, various divisions of General Motors manufacture nearly 70 percent of the components needed in the assembly of GM automobiles, while Chrysler and most Japanese manufacturers produce less than 30 percent of the components needed in the assembly of their automobiles. Exhibit 9.2 illustrates the concept of vertical integration and distinguishes between forward and backward integration.

The advantages of vertical integration include greater control over the costs and supply of components. Furthermore, vertical integration avoids the transactions costs associated with dealing with vendors or retailers. Although many transactions are straightforward, firms can encounter a variety of problems in dealing with vendors, and, when lawyers get involved in disputes, the time and expense in resolving disagreements can become quite costly. Vertical integration eliminates this type of problem. Two additional advantages of vertical integration include the ability to protect proprietary technology and to protect a company's reputation. If a firm believes it has a technology that gives it a significant advantage over its competitors, it may not wish to share that information with any outside vendors that might also do business with the firm's direct competitors. Similarly, a company may wish to maintain or cultivate a reputation for outstanding quality

EXHIBIT 9.2

Vertical Integration and an Illustration of Forward and Backward Integration

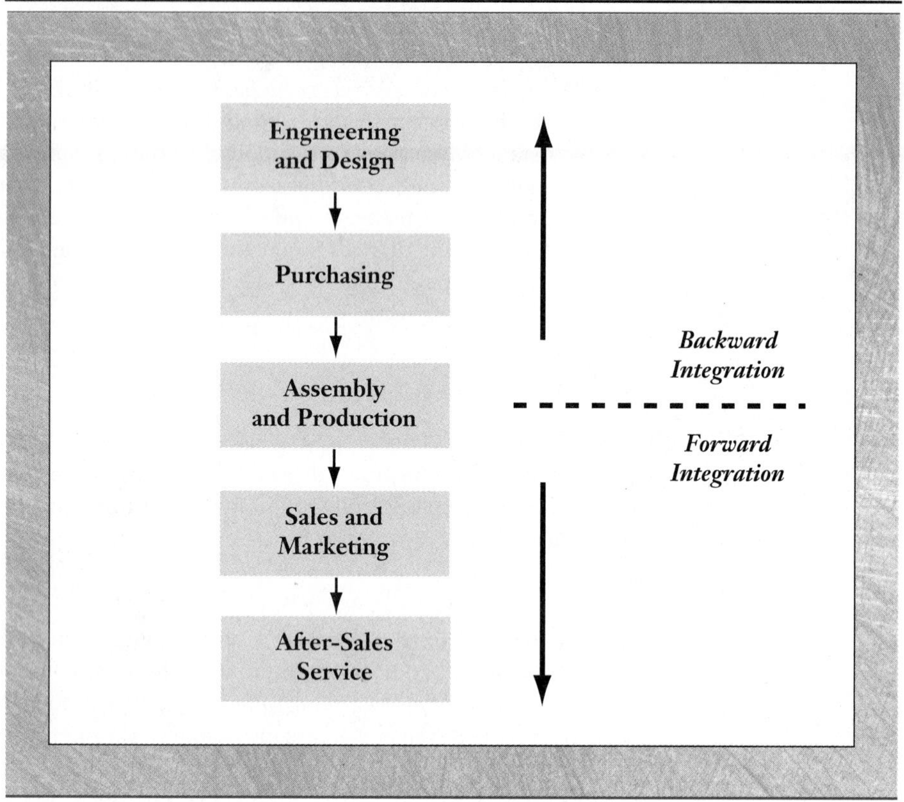

or service. In this case, it may choose to open its own retail outlets or after-sale service centers to ensure that its customers will obtain the high level of service it wants them to receive.

Vertical integration can also have a number of disadvantages, however. First, the vertically integrated firm will almost necessarily have higher fixed overhead costs than a less integrated competitor. Only if lower direct costs can compensate for these higher fixed overhead costs will the firm enjoy higher profits than its less integrated competitors. This is the struggle now facing General Motors. The company has higher overhead costs than other automobile companies due to its more extensive vertical integration. In addition, GM pays the employees making its components union wages, whereas many of the suppliers to Chrysler or the Japanese producers pay far lower wages to their nonunion employees. Thus, not only does GM have higher fixed overhead costs, but it also fails to enjoy any lower direct product costs as a result of its vertical integration. Furthermore, although vertical integration can eliminate the costs of haggling with outside vendors or retailers, integrated firms must still deal with the transfer pricing dilemma — the price one division pays another division for components or services — which can create serious morale and other internal problems, potentially as serious as legal disputes with outside vendors.

Furthermore, demand uncertainty can also create problems for the vertically integrated firm. If demand for a company's products exceeds the capacity of the

EXHIBIT 9.3

The Advantages and Disadvantages of Vertical Integration

Advantages	***Disadvantages***
• Greater control over costs and supply of components • Avoidance of transactions costs • Ability to protect proprietary technology • Ability to maintain or cultivate a reputation for outstanding quality or service	• Higher overhead costs • Transfer pricing dilemmas • Low demand can lead to underutilization of plant capacity and high demand can result in a dependence on outside suppliers • Technological change can leave vertically integrated firms stuck with older technology

company's component assembly operations, then the company will have to turn to outside vendors that may not be enthusiastic about dealing with a customer that only buys when demand is high and when the vendors are already operating at full capacity to meet the needs of their more reliable buyers. On the other hand, if demand is far below factory capacity, the vertically integrated firm is left with unused capacity and uncovered fixed costs.

Finally, if a company operates in an industry in which technology is changing rapidly, then vertical integration can be a very poor strategy for that firm. Less integrated firms can switch quickly to vendors offering the latest components or using newer, lower cost, or more sophisticated processes to produce components, leaving the more integrated firm "stuck" with older components manufactured by less efficient, more costly processes.

This discussion of the advantages and disadvantages of vertical integration is summarized in Exhibit 9.3.

Horizontal or related diversification. Horizontal or related diversification refers to a strategy of adding related or similar product or service lines to the existing core business, either through the acquisition of competitors or through the internal development of new products or services. Horizontal or related diversification strategies can vary considerably. For example, many banks have acquired or merged with other banks over the past decade as a wave of consolidation has swept over the banking industry. In most of these mergers or acquisitions, few totally new products or services are offered as a result. Thus, it appears that the major objective of these mergers and acquisitions is to realize economies of scale.

Although many bank mergers (such as the merger between Chemical Bank and Chase Manhattan) appear to be motivated by opportunities to achieve greater economies of scale, other banks have acquired or merged with brokerage and insurance firms in order to expand the range of products offered to their customers. The merger between Citicorp and the Travelers Group brings together a global banking powerhouse, brokerage and investment banking services, and a major insurance company.

Thus, related diversification strategies can allow firms to expand their product or service offerings as well as move into new geographical areas. For example, a few years ago, International Paper acquired Hammermill. International Paper's goal was to broaden its product line, and the acquisition of Hammermill allowed the company to improve its competitive position in the printing paper segment. International Paper was then able to apply its existing general management and marketing talent over a broader product line. For International Paper, the goal was not simply to achieve economies of scale, but also to grow and to more fully use existing management, production, and marketing resources.

The benefit of related or horizontal diversification is the opportunity to exploit economies of scale, especially in the case of mergers between firms producing the same product or service. Yet, as noted in Chapter 4, economies of scale do not simply or automatically emerge as firm size increases. Significant management attention and coordination may be required in order to realize economies of scale, and this management effort is not costless. Obviously, any benefits of economies of scale should exceed the management coordination costs incurred to realize those economies.

Furthermore, as suggested in Chapter 4, merging firms may already be operating at minimum efficient scale, in which case a merger with a company that participates in a related industry could cause the combined firm to operate at a level of output that places it on the upward-sloping portion of the long-run average total cost curve. Certainly economies of scale can be enjoyed in many industries by increasing output, but, as we saw in Chapter 4, the minimum efficient scale in many industries occurs at fairly low levels of output. Once firms expand output beyond the minimum efficient scale, bigness for the sake of bigness is likely to yield few additional economies and is likely to create additional administrative and coordination challenges and problems.

While related diversification offers the promise of economies and other advantages, the problems encountered by many firms pursuing related diversification are the management of complexity and the difficulties of coordinating different but related businesses. In many cases, related diversification means that firms will acquire companies or product lines that they hope will complement existing businesses or product lines, and the hope is that these businesses, once combined, can share resources and capabilities. Yet, as noted earlier, the coordination required to achieve these economies is not without cost. A few years ago, Philip Morris, which already owned General Foods, acquired Kraft. Given the many corporate restructurings and top management changes that have occurred since this acquisition, it is probably safe to conclude that Philip Morris did not have an easy time integrating the General Foods and Kraft business lines.

Brunswick provides another example of the difficulties of managing related business lines. Over the years, Brunswick has acquired a number of different companies in the bowling and boating industries that were formerly competing companies. For example, in its boating business segment, Brunswick now owns many different boating lines serving the pleasure, sport, and fishing boat markets, including Bayliner, Laguna, Maxxum, Arriva, Cobra, Sea Ray, and Ski Ray. The challenge for Brunswick's top management is to coordinate the activities of these various boating lines and foster a "healthy competition" between them that benefits the company as a whole while also avoiding conflicts and disputes between the different boating lines that would be detrimental to the company. It is not an easy task to walk the fine line between managing a healthy internal competition among different product lines and an unhealthy situation in which distinct businesses cannibalize each other's sales! A senior corporate development officer at Brunswick described this challenge:

> It's actually easier to manage diversification in unrelated markets. The complexity for Brunswick comes from the management of these diversified marine businesses. The very nature of having a common industry is what creates all of our problems. Why would you buy related companies that compete with each other? In bowling and marine we have companies that compete with each other. It is this aspect of diversification that creates problems for us. Diversification is not the problem. If you had total diversification, it would be a lot easier to manage.[4]

Clearly, the management of related businesses poses a major challenge for the managers of diversified firms.

Conglomerate or unrelated diversification. Conglomerate or unrelated diversification is, however, no panacea. Firms pursue unrelated diversification strategies for a variety of reasons. One primary reason is to continue to grow after a core business has matured or is threatened. This, of course, explains the unrelated diversification of the giant tobacco companies Philip Morris and R. J. Reynolds, which have both aggressively diversified into food and consumer products businesses.

Firms will also diversify into unrelated businesses in order to reduce cyclical fluctuations in revenues and cash flows. A small company in Michigan that sells both bikes and hockey equipment illustrates this benefit of unrelated diversification. During the spring and summer, the company enjoys a good business selling bikes and biking equipment. Then, in the fall, just as the biking business enters a seasonal downturn, sales of hockey equipment begin to increase. In this way, the company is able to better balance its sales revenues and cash flows throughout the year.

The major problem or disadvantage associated with unrelated or conglomerate diversification is that firms often acquire businesses that top managers do not understand. As a result, they may rely on strict financial controls and objectives in order to manage or gauge the success of these businesses. This can result in an emphasis on short-term performance at the expense of long-run strategic objectives.

And, when problems develop in the businesses of a conglomerate firm, top managers will probably have no technical knowledge of the businesses, their manufacturing processes, their major customers, or their investment needs, and thus, they will probably have few insights into how they should intervene to correct the problems. As a result, many conglomerate firms have explicit policies stating that low-performing businesses that cannot be quickly turned around will be divested.

Exhibit 9.4 summarizes the advantages and disadvantages of both related and unrelated diversification strategies.

Global diversification. Although some companies, such as Boeing, Caterpillar, and Kellogg, have been in global markets for decades, many U.S. firms have only recently "discovered" global diversification. The trend toward expansion into global markets is usually motivated by the desire to grow or by pressures from global competition. Many U.S. firms have ventured abroad only because the rate of sales growth has begun to slow in their domestic markets. For example, although Kellogg has been active in global markets since the early 1930s, its major U.S. competitor, General Mills, has remained focused on the domestic market. Only recently, as the U.S. cereal market has matured, has General Mills formed a venture

EXHIBIT 9.4

The Advantages and Disadvantages of Related and Unrelated Diversification

A. Related Diversification

Advantages	*Disadvantages*
• Opportunities to achieve economies of scale and scope • Opportunities to expand product or service offerings or to move into new geographical areas	• Complexity and difficulty of coordinating different but related businesses

B. Unrelated Diversification

Advantages	*Disadvantages*
• To continue to grow after a core business has matured or started to decline • To reduce cyclical fluctuations in sales revenues and cash flows	• Managers often lack technical expertise or detailed knowledge about their firm's many businesses

with Nestlé to market its breakfast cereals in foreign markets. Similarly, the merger between Daimler and Chrysler comes in response to the increasing globalization of the automobile industry.

Firms can take many different routes as they seek to serve global markets. The simplest route is exporting. Other options include licensing or franchising with foreign firms. Or, like General Mills, companies can establish joint ventures or strategic alliances overseas. The most complex route, also involving the greatest risks, is to establish wholly owned foreign subsidiaries.

Regardless of the mode firms use to enter foreign markets, all global diversification efforts entail significant challenges. Probably the most difficult challenge for many managers of U.S. firms is to appreciate the unique cultures and customs of foreign markets, and the need for products and technologies to be modified to accommodate these markets. A few examples will illustrate the problems that managers have created for their companies when they have failed to learn about their foreign markets. GM tried to export the Chevy Nova to Mexico, unaware of the fact that the literal Spanish translation of "no va" is "no go." Similarly, criticisms of the "closed" Japanese market for U.S. automobiles might be more credible if the Big Three manufacturers were exporting vehicles that had steering wheels on the right-hand side to accommodate Japanese driving custom. Even the Japanese can make mistakes, however. When

Honda first began exporting its motorcycles to the United States, the engines were not designed to meet the demands of the wide open spaces of the U.S. countryside, and would often fail.

McDonald's has now entered the Indian market and has carefully tailored its menu to avoid offending the largely Hindu population.[5] The Big Mac with its "two all-beef patties" was replaced with the "Maharaja Mac," which features "two all-mutton patties." McDonald's has also enjoyed a great deal of success in Japan recently with a series of ads that emphasize a very un-Japanese theme (yet one that has resonated well with Japanese consumers) — close relationships between fathers and their children — that is part of a worldwide emphasis on family members and relationships.[6] This ability to tailor business practices to local tastes while also developing global advertising and marketing themes illustrates the great skill that many multinational companies have to develop in order to be successful worldwide.

This discussion about different types of diversification strategies may suggest that it is relatively easy to categorize multibusiness firms into one of the four diversification strategies just described. In fact, this is not the case at all. For example, consider IBM's takeover of Lotus Development Corporation. It could be argued that this represents an example of vertical integration. By acquiring Lotus, IBM is simply expanding its reach into additional software market segments, thereby broadening its presence in an important link in the computer market value chain. On the other hand, most of the public announcements that accompanied the takeover suggested that IBM was pursuing a strategy of related diversification, seeking to offer its customers a broader and complementary product line that includes a full range of hardware and software products. A skeptic might argue, however, that the acquisition of Lotus was really an unrelated diversification, claiming that hardware and software products are so totally different as to represent two distinct industries. Certainly, the cultures of the two companies put them worlds apart.

The message here is that the "relatedness" of firms' diversification strategies is largely a product of top managers' own understandings and sensemaking activities — their mental models. Sara Lee, selling its famous Sara Lee food products, Hillshire Farm and Jimmy Dean brands of meat products, Hanes and Champion brands of knitwear, Kiwi shoe polishes, Isotoner gloves, and Coach leather products (to name just a few of its major product lines), is widely viewed as a conglomerate firm. But, Sara Lee's top managers have a very different view, seeing all of their company's products as related along a number of dimensions:

> In the late '70s and early '80s, we got out of a lot of commodity businesses, non-food businesses, non-consumer products businesses. We like to think of ourselves as a consumer packaged-goods products company, offering products that are high repeat purchase, basic items in people's diets or wardrobes, products that are not subject to big fashion swings, product categories that are marketing sensitive that allow us to differentiate ourselves. *Those commonalities you can point to in all of our businesses.*[7]

Later in the chapter, we will see that how firms' managers understand the relationships among their various businesses as well as their beliefs about how diversification should be managed will determine to a large extent whether their firms' corporate strategies are successful.

The Aim of Corporate Strategy: Synergy

While all the corporate strategies just reviewed offer a number of potential advantages, the many disadvantages associated with each strategy can easily overwhelm the benefits of diversification. The important point is this: *The aim of diversification should be to create value or wealth in excess of what firms would enjoy without diversification.*

In discussing the performance implications of diversification, strategists and company managers frequently use the term *synergy* to describe the gains in value that should be derived from a particular diversification strategy. Often synergy is expressed in the mathematical "shorthand" of 2 + 2 = 5, the point being that the whole should be greater than the sum of its parts. In the case of one firm acquiring another, for example, synergy implies that the value of the combined firm after the acquisition should be greater than the value of the two firms prior to the acquisition. Synergy is obtained in three ways: (1) by exploiting economies of scale, (2) by exploiting economies of scope, and (3) through the efficient allocation of capital. Each of these three sources of synergy, and several examples of each, will be discussed here.

Economies of Scale

Of the three sources of synergy, the concept of economies of scale is probably the easiest to understand. Economies of scale exist when unit costs decline with increases in production. For example, say a company can manufacture 100,000 units at $1.00 each. It will enjoy economies of scale if it can produce 150,000 units at $.90 each. A practical definition or way to think about the concept is that economies of scale occur when firms "use the same resource to do more of the same" and thereby realize lower per unit costs. Building on the example just cited, a company with a factory manufacturing 100,000 units might acquire a competitor and consolidate manufacturing operations so that after the acquisition the same factory might manufacture 150,000 units at a lower per unit cost. As noted earlier, many bank mergers appear to be motivated by a desire to achieve greater economies of scale. By centralizing "back office" activities, such as check clearing and loan processing, many banks have been able to realize significant economies of scale. For example, analysts estimate that economies of scale resulting from the merger of Chase Manhattan and Chemical Bank will result in an annual reduction in costs of more than $1.5 billion.[8]

Yet, as noted in Chapter 4 as well as earlier in this chapter, economies of scale are not free and may require considerable management effort and coordination. The important point to remember about economies of scale is that diversification or any other corporate strategy pursued primarily for the sake of expansion or firm growth will not necessarily enhance shareholder value.

Economies of Scope

The concept of economies of scope is related to yet different from economies of scale. Whereas economies of scale refers to using the same resource to do more of the same things, economies of scope refers to "using the same resource to do different things" and achieve lower unit costs. For example, one reason the decision to manufacture disposable diapers was a natural diversification move for both Procter & Gamble and Kimberly-Clark was that both companies had extensive experience in manufacturing and marketing brand-name sanitary paper products. Both companies could apply this know-how or expertise to the manufacture and marketing of a completely new brand-name paper product, disposable diapers.

The Efficient Allocation of Capital

Even though the efficient markets hypothesis proposed by finance researchers holds that stock markets take into consideration all available information in assessing the value of firms, many top executives of diversified firms believe they have the ability to find undervalued companies or other attractive investment opportunities. They then seek to acquire these undervalued companies or exploit these opportunities and, through their investments, improve their operations and add value to these businesses. The following statement by a top strategic planning executive at a *Fortune* 500 firm illustrates the logic of deriving synergies through the allocation of capital:

> When [a business] is part of a larger corporation there's a larger pool of investment, and when there is recognition of a major growth opportunity in one of your companies, you can pour more money into it than a banker would or maybe the equity market would be willing to do.... When a market is growing at a double-digit rate, we're pouring a lot of money into it. I don't think [businesses] could get that kind of investment on their own.[9]

Here's another statement by a top strategic planning executive at a different *Fortune* 500 firm describing his company's strategic use of capital:

> The ability to shift resources from one business to another — today we have a defense business which five years ago was our largest group, and based on where we are in the world today, the prospects for that business are not very good. We hope to be able to take assets out of that business and redeploy them in other businesses that are going to turn around and do well. That's really a form of capital market. It may be saying that we are better capital allocators than Wall Street. We certainly have better information than they do.[10]

Whether firms have information better than that of Wall Street investment bankers is a controversial question, likely to generate a good deal of discussion if posed to groups of academics, top managers, and Wall Street investment bankers. It's certainly possible that corporate executives may have access to inside information that assists them in their investment decision making. The accompanying Management Focus, "Portfolio Management Techniques and the Efficient Allocation of Capital Inside Diversified Firms," explores how the concept of portfolio management has been used by managers to create synergies through the allocation of capital within diversified firms.

This introduction to the ways in which companies can achieve synergies through diversification does not reflect the challenges and problems associated with actually achieving these synergies. It is one thing to believe that a particular diversification move might yield significant synergies or that a particular management technique might make the process of formulating corporate strategy easy. As we will see in the next section, however, it is a very difficult challenge to achieve those synergies once a business has been acquired or a new product line has been introduced.

MANAGEMENT FOCUS

Portfolio Management Techniques and the Efficient Allocation of Capital Inside Diversified Firms

Following the wave of diversification activity that occurred during the 1960s and early 1970s, portfolio management techniques emerged as a very popular tool for managers to think about and develop corporate strategies. Developed initially by the Boston Consulting Group (BCG) and then significantly augmented by the contributions of other consulting organizations and the managers of diversified corporations, nearly all portfolio management techniques involve analyzing a diversified firm's businesses along two dimensions — the business's market attractiveness and its competitive position. Though many different portfolio management techniques have been developed, we focus here on only one, the Boston Consulting Group's "Growth-Share Matrix" — probably one of the best-known portfolio models.

Use of the BCG Growth-Share Matrix (illustrated in Figure 1) begins by analyzing and placing the diversified firm's businesses along these two dimensions. In BCG's Growth-Share Matrix, market attractiveness is assessed by the industry growth rate, while competitive position is assessed by examining each business's relative market share. As the diversified firm's businesses are analyzed along these two dimensions, they are then placed on the matrix, with each circle representing one business. The circles are scaled according to the size of the business, so that larger circles represent larger businesses.

FIGURE 1

The Boston Consulting Group's Growth-Share Matrix

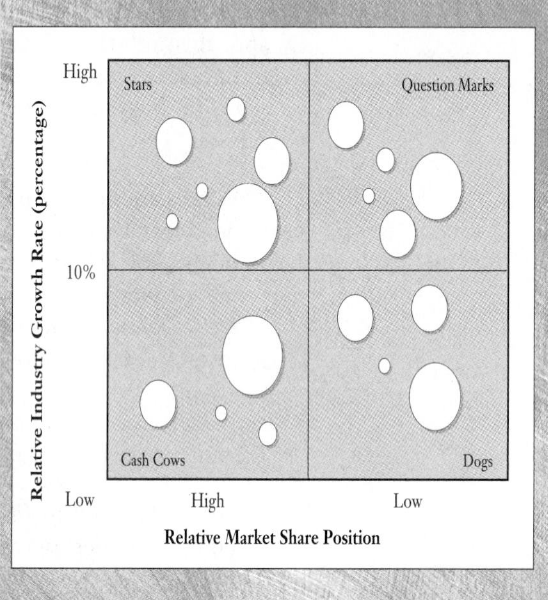

Nearly all portfolio management techniques are based on three sets of concepts. First is the concept of product or industry life cycle, introduced in Chapter 8. Life cycle models suggest that all products or services have a natural pattern of emergence, rapid growth, maturity, and eventual decline. Portfolio models build on the life cycle concept to argue that the portfolio of businesses owned by a diversified firm should include a variety of businesses at all stages of the product life cycle; firms with no mature businesses may lack stability and steady cash flows, while firms relying only on slow-growing mature businesses risk eventual decline.

Most portfolio models also build on the concepts of experience or learning curve effects and scale economies. The greater the cumulative output of a particular business the lower its per unit costs should be, and higher levels of output are likely to be associated with economies of scale. A business's competitive position — market share in the BCG Growth-Share Matrix — thus becomes a proxy for experience curve effects and scale economies. The greater a particular business's market share the more likely that it is rapidly moving down the experience curve and enjoying economies of scale.

The final concept on which all portfolio models rest is the efficient allocation of capital. Portfolio management techniques view firms as "internal capital markets." Central to all portfolio models is the idea that the businesses of diversified firms are not allowed to operate independently but that corporate

continued

managers will actively intervene to transfer capital from some businesses to others. In fact, portfolio models assume that the major task of corporate managers is to balance cash flows between cash-generating and cash-requiring businesses.

Using Portfolio Models to Formulate Corporate Strategy

The four quadrants in the Growth-Share Matrix illustrated in Figure 1 are labeled based on their cash flow characteristics. Businesses in the "Cash Cows" quadrant are, because of their high relative market shares but relatively low rates of growth, most likely to be very successful mature businesses. These businesses are assumed to be generating large amounts of surplus cash. This cash can be transferred to "Question Marks," emerging businesses that have the potential to become "Stars" but need additional capital to fund expansion and marketing activities. "Dogs" are businesses that, because of their low relative market shares and low growth, are deemed to contribute little value to the corporate portfolio; most portfolio models suggest that these businesses should be divested.

The ideal portfolio will vary considerably depending on the unique characteristics and circumstances of different diversified firms, but one central objective of portfolio management is balance across the quadrants. No managers would want their firms to have only "Dogs." Similarly, a company with a vast majority of its businesses in the "Cash Cows" quadrant might be generating a great deal of cash flow, but it may have few opportunities for future growth. Thus, portfolio management techniques, such as the BCG Growth-Share Matrix, can be very helpful tools for generating thought and discussion among managers about the various businesses of their diversified firms.

More elaborate portfolio models may offer additional insights, but they can also be much more complex and time consuming to use. Furthermore, all portfolio models must be used with caution because a number of factors (discussed below) limit their effectiveness as analytical frameworks. Nevertheless, portfolio models can be very useful in stimulating thought and discussion among managers, and they may be particularly effective at getting managers to vocalize their beliefs and understandings — their mental models — about their firms' diversification strategies.

Limitations of Portfolio Management Techniques

Though widely taught and used, portfolio management models have a number of limitations, and fewer managers of large diversified companies appear to be relying only on portfolio management models to guide the formulation of their corporate strategies. One concern or limitation is whether portfolio models, such as the BCG Growth-Share Matrix, are really very useful for most companies. Because competitive position in the BCG Matrix is determined by relative market share, by definition, only one business in an industry will be on the left side of the matrix's *relative* market share dimension. Many companies enjoy great success without their businesses having large market shares (in other words, their businesses are either "Dogs" or "Question Marks"). In addition, the emphasis of portfolio models on cash flow management ignores the challenge of building linkages across businesses in order to achieve economies of scale and scope.

Furthermore, many of the basic assumptions underlying portfolio models do not hold upon closer examination. For example, research has shown that "Dogs" can be a "manager's best friend" and that these low-growth, low-share businesses do not necessarily have the unattractive profitability and cash flow characteristics that most portfolio models assume.[1]

Perhaps the biggest factor limiting the use of portfolio management techniques is the pressure firms receive from investors when they reallocate cash internally. Pressure from corporate raiders and institutional investors during the past decade has made it unlikely that firms can transfer large amounts of cash from profitable business units to "Question Mark" businesses with high risks. Instead, institutional investors will pressure firms to divest these "Question Mark" businesses in order to "increase shareholder value." ■

[1] D. C. Hambrick and I. C. MacMillan, 1982. The product portfolio and man's best friend. *California Management Review* 25(1): 84–95.

Problems in Exploiting Potential Synergies

In this section, we explore some of the many reasons why firms fail to realize hoped-for synergies from their diversification activities.[11]

Poor Understanding of How Diversification Activities Will "Fit" or Be Coordinated with Existing Businesses

First, it appears that many diversification efforts fail because managers have not given adequate thought to how a new business will be related to their firms' existing businesses. As a consequence, many new businesses offer few if any potential economies or opportunities to generate synergies. It is even conceivable, as humorously suggested by the accompanying *Far Side* cartoon, that new businesses could result in *negative* synergies.

Without an understanding of how newly acquired or internally developed businesses are related to existing businesses, firms' managers will have few clues as to how these businesses will share activities, skills, and other organizational resources.

Far Side

by Gary Larson

Source: *The Far Side* © 1980 Farworks, Inc. Used with permission. All rights reserved.

And, without a plan for realizing these economies, it is unlikely that synergies will be generated or shareholder value enhanced. Porter has suggested that diversified firms need to develop "corporate themes" that explicitly suggest how businesses will be related and how synergies will be derived from firms' portfolios of businesses.[12] And, he argued that these corporate themes must do more than simply sound plausible, that they must clearly demonstrate linkages and potential synergies among businesses and suggest how those synergies will be derived. In elaborating on this concept of a corporate theme, Porter concluded:

> It is all too easy to create a shallow corporate theme. CBS wanted to be an "entertainment company," for example, and it built a group of businesses related to leisure time. It entered such industries as toys, crafts, musical instruments, sports teams, and hi-fi retailing. While this corporate theme sounded good ... none of these businesses had any significant opportunity to share activities or transfer skills among themselves or with CBS's traditional broadcasting and record businesses.... Saddled with the worst acquisition record in my study, CBS has eroded the shareholder value created through its strong performance in broadcasting and records.[13]

Apparently, other media companies learned little from the dismal experiences of CBS. A recent *Wall Street Journal* article reviewed the performance of several media companies after they had made large acquisitions.[14] Graphs contained in the article showed that nearly all the companies have failed to generate synergies that would impress shareholders. (Exhibit 9.5 reprints these graphs.) The article raised the question of whether these companies have really thought through the potential for synergies among their various businesses:

> ...the rationale driving their megamergers — control over every aspect of their businesses — has fundamental flaws. Their operations are diffuse, stretched from R-rated movies and retail video stores to trade magazines, animated cartoons and elementary-school textbooks.[15]

The article specifically questioned whether potential synergies really exist between businesses that *provide* media content and those that *deliver* media content:

> ...the notion that the marriage of content and distribution is always desirable has turned out to be questionable. Mergers such as Disney/ABC and Time Warner/Turner and Viacom's purchase of Paramount Communications and Blockbuster were based on the theory that studios had to be linked with networks, TV stations, cable systems and retailers to give their product a direct pipeline to viewers and to avoid being shut out by rivals.[16]

Yet, the record of most of these media companies suggests that few synergies really exist between media content and distribution. Companies producing very good media content should, in fact, want the widest possible distribution, just as companies distributing media content should want to buy the best content from any media producer.[17]

Risks Associated with the Acquisition Process

The risky characteristics of the acquisition process are also responsible for many acquisitions not living up to their expected synergies. One of the most serious

EXHIBIT 9.5

Stockholder Reactions to the Megamergers of Several Large Diversified Media Companies

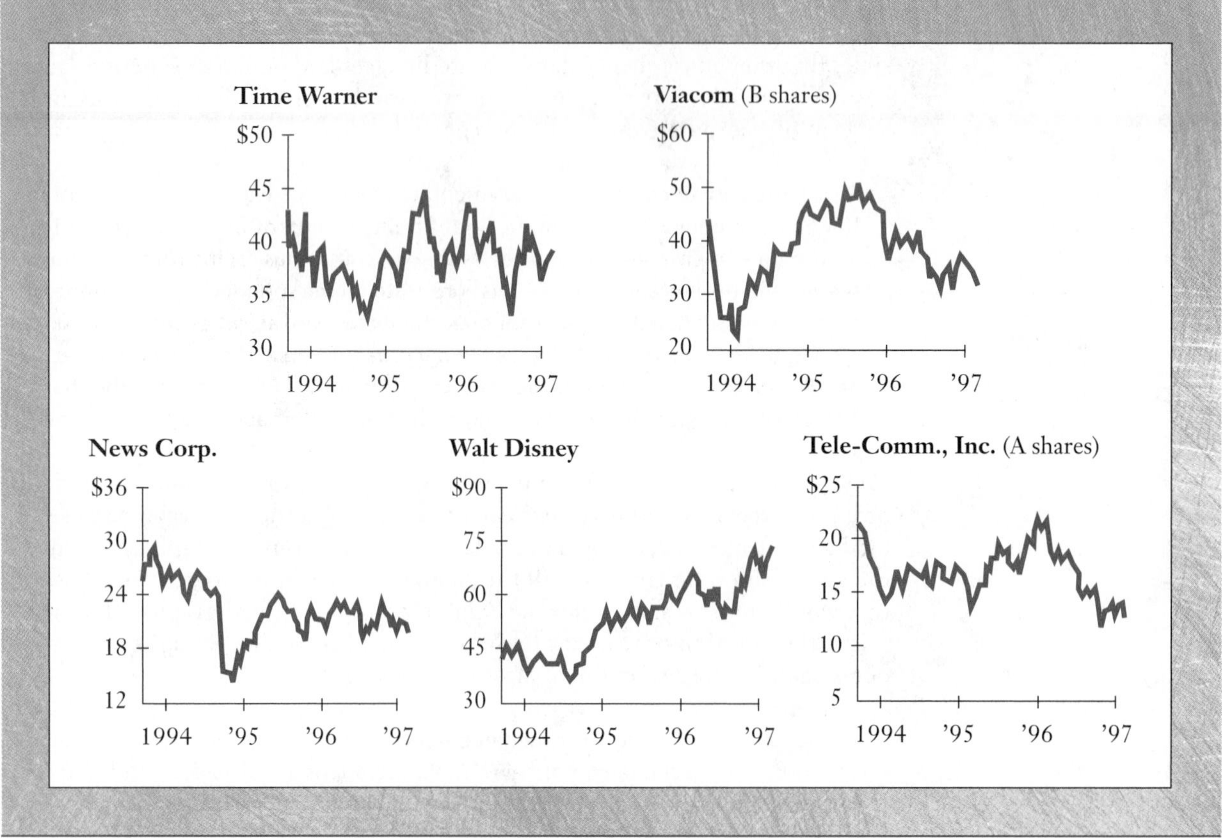

NOTE: Charts show weekly closing stock prices.
SOURCE: L. Landro, "Back to Reality: Entertainment Giants Face Pressure to Cut Costs, Get Into Focus," *The Wall Street Journal*, February 11, 1997, A1, A10.

mistakes managers can make is to fail to conduct an adequate strategic analysis of the acquisition candidate. This can be due to several factors. For example, managers will often try to complete an acquisition deal quickly before other potential buyers have an opportunity to become interested in the acquisition target and possibly begin a "bidding war" that would raise the price of the acquisition. Bidding wars can result in the price of an acquisition rising way above the true economic value of the target company.

The data summarized in Exhibit 9.6 show how the stock price of Conoco increased as Seagram and DuPont engaged in a bidding war for the company. As seen in the exhibit, the per share price of Conoco hovered around $60 during the first five months of 1981, falling during May to about $50. As the summer progressed and both Seagram and DuPont entered into a bidding war, however, the value of Conoco's shares skyrocketed, and DuPont eventually paid almost $100 per share to acquire Conoco. The final acquisition price of Conoco was so much higher than the company's prevailing stock price before the bidding war that we have to conclude that DuPont paid almost twice as much as Conoco was really worth.

EXHIBIT 9.6

Impact of Bidding War Between Seagram and DuPont on Stock Price of Conoco, 1981

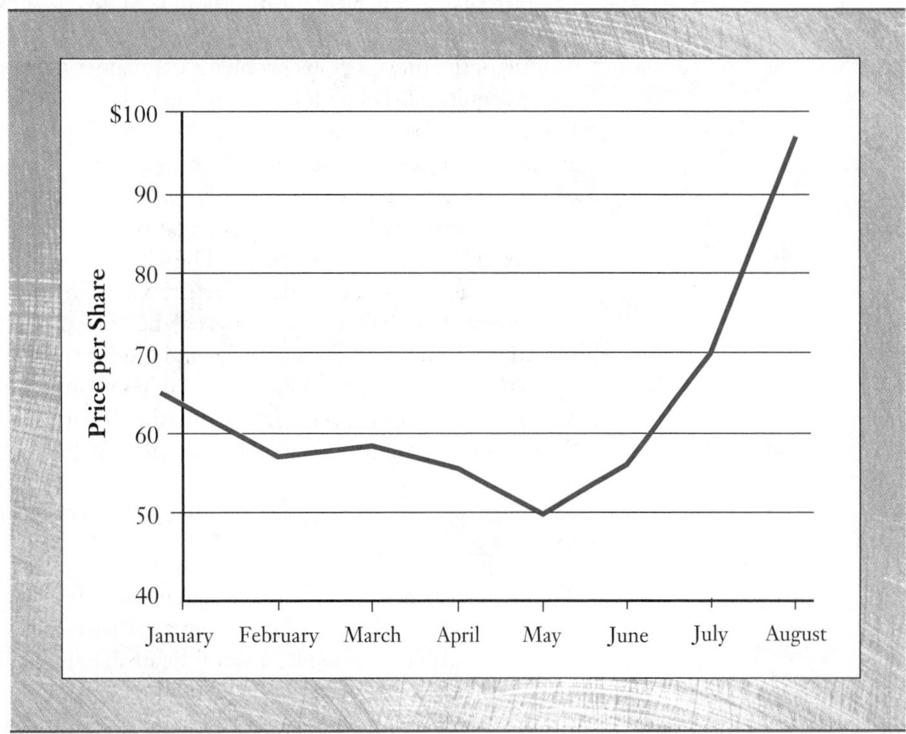

Bidding wars are an excellent example of the escalation of commitment problem described in Chapter 2. There, we discussed how managers will continue to pursue a particular course of action — in this case a bidding war — even after it becomes clear that the strategy is inappropriate or that the company will pay too much for the acquisition.

Companies do not have to enter into bidding wars to pay too much for an acquisition, however. Companies will sometimes make very high offers in order to scare off other potential bidders. This appears to have been IBM's strategy in its acquisition of Lotus Development Corporation. Yet, even as IBM avoided a bidding war, its acquisition of Lotus for $64 per share was so much higher than Lotus's book value that IBM will be taking special accounting charges of $900 million over several years to write down the value of its acquisition.

Furthermore, because of biases in their thinking, managers will often focus on the attractive features of an acquisition candidate, while giving less attention or weight to the candidate's negative features. This is complicated by opportunism on the part of the managers of the acquisition candidate — once they agree to the acquisition of their company, they are motivated to get the best possible price for their shareholders. As a result, they will not be forthcoming about any problems or weaknesses that would cause the acquiring company to lower its offer.

After making an acquisition, managers must integrate the new business into their company's existing portfolio of businesses. The integration of a new business with existing operations poses a new set of challenges, especially for the managers of firms that make only occasional acquisitions and therefore lack experience at managing the integration process. Should a new business be allowed to operate on a stand-alone basis, or should the new business be incorporated into the operations of the existing core business? Should IBM, for example, attempt to integrate its own software programming activities with those of Lotus? How much freedom should GM give its new Saturn division, which, until recently, has enjoyed brisk sales, but has remained unprofitable?

One of the most serious problems companies encounter in their efforts to integrate newly acquired firms with their existing businesses is differences in organizational cultures. This is certainly one of the major fears of analysts who have commented on IBM's acquisition of Lotus — that the cultures of the two companies are so different that many of Lotus's most talented employees will feel stifled by the IBM culture and take jobs elsewhere. Problems of melding disparate cultures can be particularly difficult for firms making international acquisitions. The acquisition of the pharmaceutical firm Upjohn, based in Kalamazoo, Michigan, by the Swedish company Pharmacia illustrates just how severe these cultural problems can be. The combined companies have clashed on everything from management styles and the appropriate length of vacations to whether cigarettes and wine would be allowed in company dining rooms.[18] An accompanying Management Focus, "The Culture Clashes That Often Follow Mergers and Acquisitions," examines in more detail this problem of combining diverse cultures.

Problems Associated with the Internal Development of New Businesses

The difficulties associated with realizing synergies are not limited to firms that choose to diversify through acquisition. Managers who start new businesses internally often encounter problems as well. Most of the problems associated with internally developed diversification activities are caused by the considerable time and investment that are required to launch new businesses. Furthermore, managers usually face a great deal of difficulty assessing the risks associated with a new investment opportunity. In addition, the available capital budgeting tools offer little assistance in helping managers weigh or assess these risks. It's not surprising then that, although some new product introductions are overnight successes, research suggests that, *on average*, most new product lines require 10 years before generating positive cash flows and net income.[19] As anyone who has had even an elementary finance class knows, an investment project that doesn't return a positive cash flow during the first 10 years of its life is likely to have a very low net present value no matter how large the positive cash flows are after year 10!

As a consequence, many companies are simply unwilling to fund such speculative investment proposals. Of course, low estimates of cash flow are often caused by the difficulties of adequately forecasting the future. Unwillingness to take risks may also explain why U.S. companies are often the first to develop the new products that are made commercial successes by other companies, especially Japanese companies. For example, the fax machine and the telephone answering machine were developed by U.S. companies, but when forecasts of demand for the products were low, their U.S. inventors allowed foreign manufacturers to introduce and enjoy success from the products that they had developed.

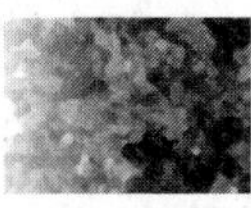

Diversification and Performance: The Score

Given the potential for corporate strategy to generate synergies as well as the very real problems of actually achieving those synergies, what is the relationship between diversification and firm performance? In other words, can corporate strategy and

Management Focus

The Culture Clashes that Often Follow Mergers and Acquisitions

After the merger of the Pennsylvania Railroad and the New York Central — one of the most famous yet least successful mergers in business history — the clash between the two companies' cultures was so severe that former employees organized themselves into red and green "teams" reflecting the respective corporate colors of the two predecessor companies. So it's not surprising that a recent study suggested that clashing cultures are the leading cause of failure in unsuccessful mergers.[1] Some acquiring companies have found the difficulties associated with integrating disparate cultures so challenging that they deliberately maintain acquired businesses as stand-alone entities and make no attempt to integrate their operations with the core business of the company. Even more serious clashes are likely as companies increasingly merge with foreign firms which have unique national cultures.

Managers of acquiring companies can, however, take some initiatives to minimize clashes between cultures. Here are some suggestions:[2]

- First, clearly divide power among top managers. Attempts to split authority among top managers by having co-CEOs or by sharing managerial responsibilities in other ways almost always fail, so acquiring companies should clearly define roles among all top executives.
- Second, managers of acquiring companies can formulate integration "teams" composed of representatives from both the acquired and the acquiring companies to relieve tension among employees; to highlight and combine the best capabilities, characteristics, and resources of both the acquiring and acquired companies; and to help in blending cultures.
- Third, managers of acquiring companies can effectively communicate with employees. Employees hold fast to their companies' cultures because they provide meaning at a time of great anxiety. Rather than contributing to employees' fears by allowing rumors to run rampant, the managers of acquiring companies should communicate clearly and frequently with their employees. Communication methods that managers of acquiring companies have used include frequent newsletters, video conferences, retreats, focus groups and surveys, and Internet Web sites.
- Finally, top managers can design and implement compensation plans that reward cooperation and teamwork. Compensation plans can send an important message that employees who "get on board" and emphasize teamwork and the overall organization will be rewarded. ■

[1] J. S. Lublin and B. O'Brian, 1997. Merged firms often face culture clash. *The Wall Street Journal*, February 14, B7.

[2] Ibid.

diversification be sources of sustained competitive advantage? Unfortunately, answers to these questions are not at all obvious or straightforward. Generally, academics, consultants, and the financial community have taken a dim view of diversification. In their well-known book, *In Search of Excellence*, Peters and Waterman exhorted managers to "stick to the knitting" and avoid extensive diversification beyond their firms' core businesses.[20]

Many research studies support Peters and Waterman, suggesting that diversification beyond a core business leads to lower performance. For example, in a classic *Harvard Business Review* article, Michael Porter studied the diversification activities of 33 large companies between 1950 and 1986 and found that, on average, each of these 33 firms made 80 diversification moves, of which 70 percent were acquisitions of other businesses, 20 percent were by start-up, while 10 percent were joint ventures with other firms. Porter concluded that the results of this diversification activity were largely disastrous: More than 60 percent of all the acquired businesses were subsequently divested. Of those acquisitions that involved moving into unrelated markets, more than 74 percent of the acquired businesses were divested.[21]

A number of other studies have sought to "decompose" the sources of business unit performance. In other words, these studies have sought to determine how much various factors, including industry attractiveness, business strategy, and corporate strategy, contribute to the performance of business units. Exhibit 9.7 summarizes the findings of one of these studies, and, as the exhibit suggests, industry attractiveness (i.e., average industry performance) and business strategy together explain more than 99 percent of the variation in business unit performance. Corporate parentage, on the other hand, explains less than 1 percent of the variation in business unit performance. In short, corporate strategy has no apparent effect on business unit performance!

Additional studies have reinforced the conclusion that corporate strategy rarely makes a significant contribution to shareholder value. One study reported that firms that had "de-diversified" saw improvements in stock market performance while those that had diversified actually saw their stock market value decline.[22] A *Wall Street Journal* article reported the findings of another research study that found greater levels of diversification were associated with lower levels of productivity.[23] Thus, many research studies mount a strong case against corporate diversification, and, during the past decade, many business leaders and investors have concluded that Peters and Waterman were right — firms should stick to their knitting. Many widely diversified firms have de-diversified in order to focus on a narrower range of industries or markets.

The situation is not so simple, however, and the view that diversification is necessarily associated with lower performance overlooks much evidence of successful

EXHIBIT 9.7

The Influence of Industry Attractiveness, Business Strategy, and Corporate Strategy on Business Unit Performance

Percent of variation in performance due to:	
Industry membership	16.1 %
Corporate strategy	0.8
Business strategy	83.0
Total	99.9%

SOURCE: R. P. Rumelt, "How Much Does Industry Matter?" *Strategic Management Journal* 12:167–185.

diversification. In fact, researchers have failed to find a consistent empirical relationship between diversification and performance, in spite of extensive research over more than 20 years. While many studies have concluded that firms pursuing single business or related diversification strategies enjoy higher performance than firms pursuing unrelated strategies, other research studies have reached the opposite conclusion.[24] Furthermore, one scholar has noted that "high-performing diversified firms exist in sufficient numbers ... to throw doubt on the proposition that diversification is not a workable strategy."[25]

Part of the confusion about the relationship between diversification and performance may result from differences in the questions researchers study or the methods they employ. For example, one study cited earlier examined the relationship between *changes* in diversification and *changes* in stock market performance. It did not examine the relationship between *overall* levels of diversification and firm performance. During the period studied, the stock market may well have rewarded companies that increased their focus — indeed, those firms that de-diversified during this time may have made very poor diversification decisions in the past — but this does not warrant the conclusion that the market necessarily penalizes all diversified companies. Similarly, the study that examined the contributions of industry attractiveness, business strategy, and corporate strategy to overall business unit performance levels did not distinguish between what we might call "successful" and "unsuccessful" diversifiers.

A more recent study that did distinguish between successful and unsuccessful diversified firms may offer some helpful insights on the relationship between diversification strategy and firm performance.[26] That study classified over 180 *Fortune* 500 firms into groups based on their diversification and performance characteristics. The resulting diversification–performance groups, which are illustrated in Exhibit 9.8, offered a number of surprising findings:

First, the categorization of firms into the four diversification–performance groups is remarkably balanced. In other words, high-performing firms are just as

EXHIBIT 9.8

Distribution of a Sample of Fortune *500 Firms Among Diversification-Performance Groups*

	Low-Performing Firms	High-Performing Firms
Less Diversified	47	46
More Diversified	46	47

likely to be more diversified as they are to be less diversified, and low-performing firms are just as likely to be less diversified as they are to be more diversified. Furthermore, the study found no significant performance differences between the high-performing more- and less-diversified groups of firms. In short, *higher levels of diversification are not incompatible with high performance, and higher levels of diversification do not necessarily imply that firms will suffer lower performance levels.*

This same study also sought to identify how high- and low-performing diversified firms might differ along a number of strategic dimensions (including the attractiveness of the industries in which they operate, their growth rates, and their levels of capital expenditures, R&D, and leverage). Surprisingly, these analyses also revealed few significant differences.

So what do the findings of many, many research studies suggest about the relationship between diversification and firm performance? Here are some observations that seem warranted:

- First, though diversification has been disastrous for many firms, diversified firms can also be very successful.
- Second, studies have found no obvious differences between high- and low-performing diversified firms along several important strategic dimensions. In other words, high- and low-performing diversified firms do not differ along tangible characteristics.

Thus, as suggested in Chapter 3, successful strategies result from more intangible factors or characteristics. In the next section, we argue that the specific intangible factors that are associated with effective corporate strategies are managers' beliefs about how their diversified firms' businesses are related and their understandings about how diversification should be managed.

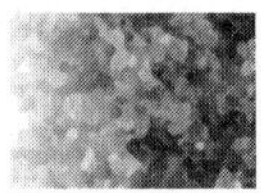

The Crucial Role of Managers

This last point — that successful diversification strategies result from the ability of managers to develop skill and competency at managing diversification — fits well with the themes we have emphasized throughout this book. We have consistently argued that competitive advantage is unlikely to emerge from factors that are obvious or resources that can be easily acquired. Managerial beliefs, knowledge, skills, and understandings as well as supporting management processes, routines, and standard operating procedures, all of which have been developed over time, can be valuable resources that are difficult for rival firms to imitate. And, we believe that such socially complex resources are likely to be the deciding factor in predicting the success of firms' corporate strategies. Most practicing managers and most researchers in the strategic management field would agree that managers occupy a central role in the strategy formulation and implementation processes. One noted researcher has, in fact, argued that management skill is "the critical resource" of successful diversified firms.[27]

In terms of our model of strategic management, managers must develop two very important types of mental models in order to achieve successful diversification. As illustrated in Exhibit 9.9, managers must have well-developed understandings of their firms' diversity and the relatedness that defines their companies and suggests how their businesses are related to each other. Managers must also have well-developed beliefs

EXHIBIT 9.9

How Managers' Beliefs and Understandings Influence the Relationship between Diversification and Performance

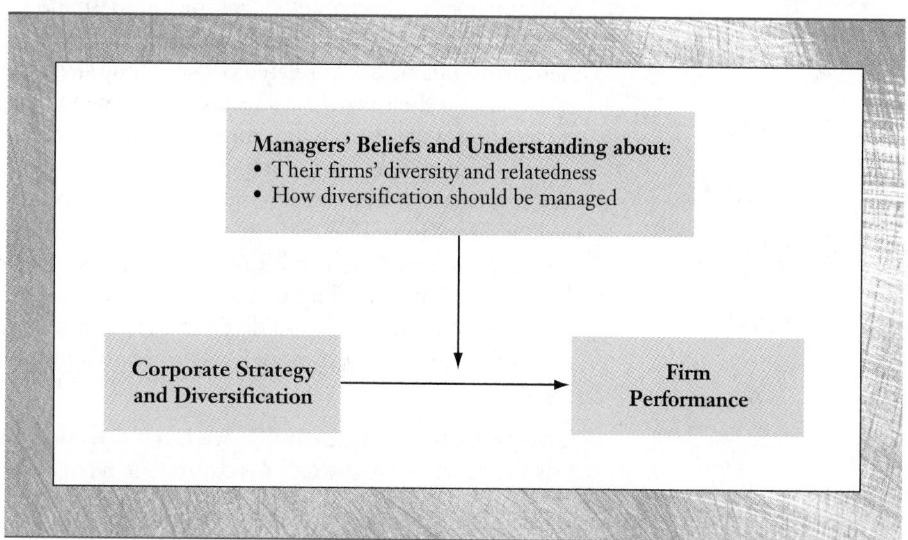

about how diversification should be managed in order to achieve synergies. In the next two sections, we focus on these two different sets of beliefs and understandings.

MANAGERS' UNDERSTANDINGS OF THEIR FIRMS' DIVERSITY AND RELATEDNESS

Managers' understandings of how their firms' businesses are related are important for at least two reasons. First, understandings of diversity and relatedness will influence how managers describe their organizations to important stakeholders.[28] Such understandings of diversity and relatedness can provide diversified firms with "corporate themes" that help "unite the efforts of business units and reinforce the ways they interrelate."[29] The ability to articulate a coherent identity may be especially important in the case of widely diversified firms that have business units operating in many different product markets that have no obvious linkages with one another. The task of articulating a coherent identity or understanding of how business units are related becomes not only more important but also more difficult as diversity increases because individual business units may have their own strong identities tied to strong brand names or cultures.[30]

Second, managers' understandings of diversity and relatedness will also describe or suggest how their firms' businesses are related to each other. Traditionally, we have assumed that the businesses in a diversified firm's portfolio were related if they shared product-market characteristics, such as a common production technology or similar customers or distribution channels. Research has now demonstrated that the managers of diversified firms develop unique understandings of how their firms' businesses are related to each other that may include but also go well beyond similarities in product-market characteristics.[31]

For example, studies have shown that while some managers consider their firms' businesses to be related because their products share common physical characteristics, common manufacturing processes, or common customers, other managers tend to see their firms' businesses as related because they share a wide variety of common marketing and product differentiation characteristics. As noted earlier in the chapter, Sara Lee's businesses sell a diverse array of products, but nearly all those products share common marketing characteristics, including brand names, strong market share positions, and a reliance on advertising. Research has also shown that other managers see their firms' businesses as related because they share common financial characteristics so that even if their firms' businesses participate in many different product markets, all the businesses are expected to meet common financial objectives.

These idiosyncratic understandings of relatedness and diversity are potentially very important to the development of a competitive advantage in the management of diversification. The managers of nearly all diversified firms are likely to have understandings of such traditional concepts as economies of scale and scope, and they are probably seeking to exploit these concepts. It is the more unique understandings of relatedness and diversity that top management teams have developed over time that are much more likely to contribute to competitive advantage.[32]

Managers' Beliefs About How Diversification and Corporate Strategy Should Be Managed

A second set of understandings includes managers' beliefs about how diversification and corporate strategy should be managed. Because the management of diversification is a complex activity, managers must develop a set of beliefs about how they should manage their diversified firms. In other words, top managers of diversified firms must learn about the management of diversification "as a distinct process and skill."[33] Managers' understandings of how corporate strategy should be managed and their ability to leverage their firms' competencies will not only influence day-to-day decision making and the longer-run direction of firms' diversification strategies, but these understandings will also have the potential to be an important source of competitive advantage.

The distinct process and skill of managing diversification may include (but is not limited to) understandings and knowledge about:

- how to coordinate the activities of businesses in order to achieve synergies,
- how to allocate resources to the various businesses in a diversified firm,
- whether various functional activities, such as engineering, finance and accounting, marketing and sales, production, and research and development, should be centralized at the corporate headquarters or be decentralized and operated by business unit managers, and
- how to compensate and reward business unit managers so that their goals and objectives are best aligned with the overall goals and objectives of the organization.

The "Learning Hypothesis"

As organizations diversify beyond a core business, they inevitably learn through trial and error.[34] Learning occurs as managers' understandings of cause and effect are shaped and influenced by their evaluations of the success of past strategic decisions.[35] Unlike management beliefs borrowed or copied from competing firms or acquired by hiring executives from other firms, the beliefs acquired through trial-and-error learning may contain unique insights that can become embedded in an organization's routine operating procedures. These insights may also be embedded in interconnected organizational processes that are difficult for other firms to imitate.[36]

Consider, for example, the daunting complexity associated with an acquisition, just one of many important corporate strategy activities pursued by diversified firms. One researcher has concluded that

> more than 2,000 major steps and more than 10,000 non-routine decisions are required to completely integrate an acquisition of any size into a large corporation. In addition, the sequence of many of these steps is critical..., which adds greatly to the complexity of the problem.[37]

Given the complexity of acquisitions, managers who have had little experience in making acquisitions will almost certainly make mistakes, often serious mistakes. By engaging in a number of acquisitions over time, however, managers can develop an expertise about how the acquisition process should be managed. Thus, the "learning hypothesis" suggests that *those firms with management teams that have more experience at managing diversification will enjoy higher performance than those firms with management teams that are less experienced at managing diversification*.

Much evidence supports the learning hypothesis. A *Business Week* article reported the results of a study that examined the performance of 248 acquiring firms.[38] The study found that only 54 percent of the less-experienced acquirers (i.e., those firms that had made five or fewer acquisitions) had returns above their industries' average returns, while 72 percent of the "active acquirers" (i.e., those firms that had made six or more acquisitions) enjoyed above-average returns.

A *Wall Street Journal* article on the banking industry made the same observation. In many cases, active acquirers have outperformed other regional bank holding companies. The article described Wells Fargo, First Bank System, Norwest, and Banc One as having management teams with "an excellent record of adding value through acquisition,"[39] and, as Exhibit 9.10 shows, several acquisitive banks have enjoyed outstanding performance in the stock market.

These empirical findings lend support to the observations of a McKinsey consultant, who has argued that "the people who are good at diversifying do it all the time. They have mechanisms in place, they've been through the process a number of times. They know what kinds of businesses they can and can't manage."[40]

The learning hypothesis is also supported by the experience of companies that have diversified globally. Kellogg provides an excellent example of the relationship between learning and performance. At Kellogg, company executives believe that two types of learning are critical. First, when Kellogg enters a new country, the company must learn how to sell cereal to the people in that particular country. In addition, however, the people in that country must learn — largely from Kellogg's teaching — to like cereal. For example, when Kellogg entered the Japanese market (where the traditional breakfast consists of warm fish and rice), it found that consumers viewed cereal as junk food — that because of their shape, cornflakes reminded consumers of potato chips. As a result, Kellogg learned that it needed to market the nutritional value of its cereal products to Japanese consumers. Kellogg very much believes that cereal consumption in a particular market is a function of how long the company has been in the country, and, therefore, how much the company has learned about selling cereal in that market.

EXHIBIT 9.10

Stock Market Performance of Five Bank Holding Companies That Are Active Acquirers

Stock	*Five-Year Performance**
Wells Fargo	+234%
First Bank System	+195
Norwest	+142
NationsBank	+118
Banc One	+44

*Stock price change August 31, 1991–September 10, 1996

SOURCE: S. E. Frank, "In Bank Deals, Consider This: Buy the Buyer," *The Wall Street Journal*, September 11, 1996, C1, C2.

THE FUTURE OF CORPORATE DIVERSIFICATION: SOME OBSERVATIONS ON DIVESTMENT ACTIVITY, CORPORATE RESTRUCTURING EFFORTS, AND OUTSOURCING

Over the past several years, we have seen many widely diversified firms shed business units in order to "focus" on a core business or a set of core businesses. In this section, we examine this restructuring activity and assess the future of diversification while also offering some observations about possible future trends in corporate strategy.

Based on anecdotal evidence and stories from the business press, it is easy to conclude that diversification is on the wane and that the large, widely diversified firm is becoming obsolete. Nothing could be further from the truth. Evidence supplied by Cynthia Montgomery of the Harvard Business School shows that the level of diversification among the 500 largest public companies in the United States actually increased in recent years.[41]

Furthermore, there are many good reasons to believe that diversification will continue to be an important feature of the economic landscape. Extensions of existing product lines, exploitation of economies of scale and scope, and expansion into new geographical areas remain compelling reasons for firms to move into new markets or to pursue new business opportunities. Firms will also continue to diversify into new businesses to reduce their reliance on declining business lines or industries. Given the dynamic nature of the economy, we can expect that firms will seize opportunities resulting from demographic shifts, the development of new products and services, and the emergence of new technologies, to diversify into new arenas.

Much of the de-diversification and restructuring activity that has occurred over the last several years can be explained by the failure of these firms to develop effective understandings of how their businesses were related or fit together.

Sears' grand strategy for developing a consumer retailing powerhouse based on its merchandising, insurance, real estate, and financial services businesses failed because the company was never able to realize the anticipated synergies. Furthermore, Sears' diversification activities had a devastating impact on the company's merchandising operations as managers lost sight of the need for Sears' stores to maintain a strong business definition in the ever-changing retail marketplace.[42]

In addition, as noted in Chapter 8, many companies are restructuring their operations to emphasize those value-chain activities that contribute to their competitive advantage while outsourcing other, less critical activities. We can expect to see more of this activity in the future. It is also likely that we will see fewer vertically integrated firms as many firms that are currently vertically integrated rethink this strategy. Just as the managers of Nike and Sara Lee have radically rethought their firms' value chains, many vertically integrated firms are likely to focus more attention on those links in their value chains that are or can be sources of competitive advantage while contracting with other companies for those products or services provided by less important links in their value chains.

Given that so many corporate restructurings have occurred over the past few years, it is worth asking, "What has been the impact of all this restructuring activity on bottom line performance?" Some evidence certainly suggests that restructurings have improved the performance of diversified firms. The chapter referred earlier to a research study that found the stock market rewarded firms that increased their focus on a core business or set of core businesses.[43] Other evidence also indicates that the performance levels of many businesses improve after they are divested by corporate parents, suggesting that they may have been suffering some sort of "negative synergy" when a part of a larger diversified organization. On the other hand, we have already pointed out that these studies examined the relationship between *changes* in diversity and *changes* in stock price; they say nothing about the relationship between *absolute* levels of diversification and firm performance. It's logical to conclude that the firms most likely to de-diversify may be those that are having the most trouble managing diversification. Therefore, it is not surprising that the stock market rewards those firms when they shed the units they are having difficulty managing!

Furthermore, much evidence suggests that "corporate breakups are no panacea."[44] A recent *Wall Street Journal* article noted that, although the stock market often has a favorable initial reaction to announcements of spinoffs or restructuring plans, these restructuring efforts rarely correct companies' more fundamental problems.[45] For example, AT&T's decision to divest its ill-fated acquisition of NCR was warmly received by the stock market, yet it is now apparent that fundamental problems remain at AT&T that have not been "solved" by spinning off NCR. A new CEO, Michael Armstrong, is now struggling with these problems. His first major move, AT&T's acquisition of TCI, has, however, been greeted with skepticism in the stock market.

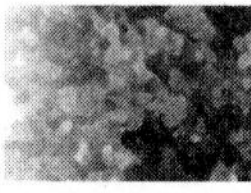

Conclusion

Corporate strategy is concerned with the appropriate scale and scope of business firms. While this chapter has sought to introduce a number of important corporate strategy topics, to review the relevant literature and research findings, and to suggest appropriate conclusions, we have necessarily been selective in our coverage of this material. Whole books have been devoted to the subject of diversification, there are journals totally focused on mergers and acquisitions, and a large percentage of all articles in the business press focus on corporate strategy topics. As a result, this single chapter on corporate strategy is necessarily incomplete. With this caveat, however, let us now offer a few summary observations to bring some closure to this chapter:

- First, size alone does not guarantee firms an advantage. Firms can achieve economies of scale through bigness, but, as we saw in Chapter 4, minimum efficient scale in many industries occurs at fairly low volume levels. The chapter has also emphasized that the coordination required to exploit economies of scale and scope is not costless. We will further emphasize in Chapter 10 that size creates additional challenges and difficulties, including problems of communication and coordination.
- At the same time, the challenges of managing diversification should not suggest that diversification is somehow a wrong or failed strategy. The evidence we have offered in this chapter indicates that high-performing firms are just as likely to be more diversified as they are to be less diversified, and low-performing firms are just as likely to be less diversified as they are to be more diversified. Furthermore, statistical tests comparing and contrasting the mean levels of performance across the high-performing more- and less-diversified groups and across the low-performing more- and less-diversified groups are not significantly different. In short, *higher levels of diversification are not incompatible with high performance, and higher levels of diversification do not necessarily imply that firms will suffer lower performance levels.*
- We have argued that the critical factor in determining success is the level of management expertise in formulating and implementing corporate strategy. Few tasks are as difficult as managing a diversified firm, and even the most talented management teams are likely to encounter constraints on the amount of diversity they can manage. The evidence presented in this chapter suggests that the management teams of large, diversified firms possess a variety of well-developed mental models that provide them with powerful understandings of how to manage their firms. Experienced managers possess (1) well-developed understandings that allow them to articulate clearly the purpose or definition of their firm to both external constituencies and their own employees, and (2) a highly developed set of cause-effect understandings of those factors that contribute to high performance. These cause-effect understandings play a key role in the selection of strategies and the development of management processes. Many diversification studies have failed to find a strong relationship between diversification and performance because they have lacked measures to assess the quality of managerial understandings.

These conclusions suggest that managers and the skills they bring to their firms are key or fundamental organizational resources that will determine whether those firms enjoy sustained competitive advantage. The quality of the mental models that managers develop is especially vital in determining the success of their firms' diversification strategies.

Key Points

- Corporate strategy is concerned with determining the appropriate scale (size) and scope (extent of diversification) of business firms. Firms can be small or large and they can focus on a single line of business or they can participate in many diverse industries.
- Firms diversify for a variety of reasons, including the desire to grow, to more fully utilize existing resources and capabilities, to escape from undesirable or unattractive industry environments, and to make use of surplus cash flows.
- Vertical integration, horizontal or related diversification, conglomerate or unrelated diversification, and global diversification are four major types of diversification. Each has a number of advantages and disadvantages associated with it and each entails a number of unique management challenges.
- The aim of all corporate strategies should be to achieve synergies. The divisions, segments, and businesses of a firm should create more value together than they would on their own as independent businesses.
- Three ways for firms to achieve synergies are to (1) exploit economies of scale, (2) exploit economies of scope, or (3) "beat the market" in the efficient allocation of capital.
- Several factors complicate firms' efforts to achieve synergies, including:
  1. A poor understanding of how diversification activities will "fit" or be coordinated with existing businesses.
  2. Dangers or risks associated with the acquisition of businesses.
  3. Problems associated with the internal development of new businesses.
- As a result, the relationship between diversification and performance is complex. The conventional wisdom suggests that higher levels of diversification lead to lower levels of performance; however, this conventional wisdom has received very little empirical support. Moreover, many successful, highly diversified firms exist.
- Managers' beliefs and understandings play a key role in influencing the relationship between diversification and firm performance. Two specific beliefs or understandings that are key to the successful management of diversification are:
  1. Managers' understandings of how their firms' businesses are related.
  2. Managers' beliefs about how diversification and corporate strategy should be managed.
- Learning from experience is key to developing skills at managing diversification, and the chapter specifically hypothesizes that *those firms with management teams that have more experience at managing diversification will enjoy higher performance than those firms with management teams that are less experienced at managing diversification.*

Review and Discussion Questions

1. *How does corporate strategy differ from business strategy? What is the primary focus of each type of strategy?*
2. *Why do managers pursue diversification strategies? What are the various types of corporate or diversification strategies, and the advantages and disadvantages of each?*
3. *How can managers achieve synergies through corporate or diversification strategies? What are the factors that often prevent managers from achieving or realizing synergies from their firms' diversification strategies?*

4. *What does research say about the relationship between diversification strategy and firm performance?*
5. *The chapter suggests that managers and managerial thinking play a crucial role in the success of diversification strategies. Describe how managers and managerial thinking can influence the success of firms' diversification strategies.*

Suggestions for Further Readins

Biggadike, E. R. 1979. The risky business of diversification. *Harvard Business Review*, 57(3): 103–111.

Montgomery, C. A. 1994. Corporate diversification. *Journal of Economic Perspectives*, 8: 163–178.

Porter, M. E. 1987. From competitive advantage to corporate strategy. *Harvard Business Review*, 65(3): 43–59.

Prahalad, C. K. & Bettis, R. A. 1986. The dominant logic: A new linkage between diversity and performance. *Strategic Management Journal*, 7: 485–502.

Ramanujam, V., & Varadarajan, P. 1989. Research on corporate diversification: A synthesis. *Strategic Management Journal*, 10: 523–551.

Rumelt, R. P. 1974. *Strategy, Structure and Economic Performance*. Cambridge, MA: Harvard University Press.

Thackray, J. 1991. Diversification: What it takes to make it work. *Across the Board*, November, 17–23.

Endnotes

1. Senge, P. M. 1990. *The Fifth Discipline: The Art and Practice of the Learning Organization*. New York: Doubleday/Currency.
2. Porter, M. E. 1987. From competitive advantage to corporate strategy. *Harvard Business Review* 65(3):43–59.
3. Rumelt, R. P. 1974. *Strategy, Structure and Economic Performance*. Cambridge, Mass: Harvard University Press.
4. Stimpert, J. L. 1992. *Managerial Thinking and Large Diversified Firms*. Unpublished doctoral dissertation, University of Illinois at Urbana-Champaign.
5. Biers, D., and M. Jordan, 1996. McDonald's in India decides the Big Mac is not a sacred cow. *The Wall Street Journal*, October 14, A13.
6. Ono, Y. 1997. Japan warms to McDonald's doting dad ads. *The Wall Street Journal*, May 8, B1, B12.
7. Stimpert, *Managerial Thinking and Large Diversified Firms*.
8. *Economist*. 1996. The bankers marched in two by two. April 6, 75–76.
9. Stimpert, *Managerial Thinking and Large Diversified Firms*.
10. Ibid.
11. See also P. L. Zweig, 1995. The case against mergers. *Business Week*, October 30, 122, 124–6. 128, 130.
12. Porter, From competitive advantage to corporate strategy.
13. Ibid., p. 59.
14. Landro, L. 1997. Back to reality: Entertainment giants face pressure to cut costs, get into focus. *The Wall Street Journal*, February 11, A1, A10.
15. Ibid., p. A1.
16. Ibid., p. A10.
17. Orwall, B., and K. Pope, 1997. Relativity: Disney, ABC promised "synergy" in merger; so, what happened? *The Wall Street Journal*, May 16, A1, A9.
18. Frank, R., and Burton, T. M. 1997. Side effects: Cross-border merger results in headaches for a drug company. *The Wall Street Journal*, February 4, A1, A12.
19. Biggadike, E. R. 1979. The risky business of diversification. *Harvard Business Review* 57(3):103–111.

20. Peters, T. J., and R. H. Waterman, 1982. *In Search of Excellence: Lessons from America's Best Run Companies*. New York: Harper & Row.
21. Porter, From competitive advantage to corporate strategy, p. 45.
22. Jarrell, G. A. 1991. For a higher share price, focus your business. *The Wall Street Journal*, May 13, A14.
23. Lichtenberg, F. R. 1990. Want more productivity? Kill that conglomerate. *The Wall Street Journal*, January 16, A22.
24. Ramanujam, V., and P. Varadarajan, 1989. Research on corporate diversification: A synthesis. *Strategic Management Journal* 10:523–551.
25. Milton Leontiades, quoted in J. Thackray, 1991. Diversification: What it takes to make it work. *Across the Board*, November, 17–23.
26. Stimpert, J. L., and I. M. Duhaime, 1996. *Theoretical Perspectives on Diversification: An Empirical Examination*. Paper presented at the Academy of Management, Cincinnati, August.
27. Rumelt, *Strategy, Structure and Economic Performance*, p. 156.
28. Halloran, K. D. 1985. The impact of M&A programs on company identity. *Mergers and Acquisitions*, 20(1):60–66.
29. Porter, From competitive advatage to corporate strategy, p. 59.
30. Hall, G. E. 1987. Reflections on running a diversified company. *Harvard Business Review* 65(1):84–92.
31. Stimpert, J. L., and I. M. Duhaime, 1997. In the eyes of the beholder: Conceptualizations of relatedness held by the managers of large diversified firms. *Strategic Management Journal* 18:111–125.
32. Barney, J. B. 1992. Integrating organizational behavior and strategy formulation research: A resource-based analysis. *Advances in Strategic Management* 8:39–61.
33. Prahalad, C. K., and R. A. Bettis, 1986. The dominant logic: A new linkage between diversity and performance. *Strategic Management Journal* 7:488.
34. Kazanjian, R. K., and R. Drazin, 1987. Implementing internal diversification: Contingency factors for organization design choices. *Academy of Management Review* 12: 342–354.
35. Porac, J. F., H. Thomas, and C. Baden-Fuller, 1989. Competitive groups as cognitive communities: The case of Scottish knitwear manufacturers. *Journal of Management Studies* 26:397–416; G. R. Salancik and J. F. Porac, 1986. Distilled ideologies. In *The Thinking Organization*, edited by H. Sims and D. Gioia. San Francisco: Jossey-Bass.
36. Barney, Integrating organizational behavior and strategy formulation research; I. Dierickx and K. Cool, 1989. Asset stock accumulation and sustainability of competitive advantage: Reply. *Management Science* 35: 1504–1511.
37. Wallace, F. D. 1969. Some principles of acquisition. In *The Corporate Merger*, edited by W. W. Alberts and J. E. Segall. Chicago: The University of Chicago Press, p. 173.
38. Zweig, The case against mergers.
39. Frank, S. E. 1996. In bank deals, consider this: Buy the buyer. *The Wall Street Journal*, September 11, C1.
40. Thackray, Diversification, p. 18.
41. Montgomery, C. A. 1994. Corporate diversification. *Journal of Economic Perspectives* 8:163–178.
42. Patterson, G. A., and F. Schwadel, 1992. Back in time: Sears suddenly undoes years of diversifying beyond retailing field. *The Wall Street Journal*, September 30, A1, A16.
43. Comment, R., and G. A. Jarrell, 1995. Corporate focus and stock returns. *Journal of Financial Economics* 37:67–87; Jarrell, For a higher share price, focus your business.
44. Guyon, J. 1996. Hanson spinoff plans haven't raised shareholder value. *The Wall Street Journal*, September 26, B4; R. Lowenstein, 1997. Corporate breakups are no panacea. *The Wall Street Journal*, June 5, C1.
45. Lowenstein, Corporate breakups are no panacea.

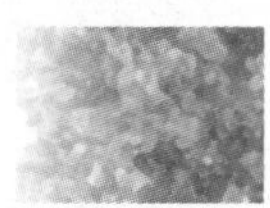

CHAPTER 10

ORGANIZATIONAL STRUCTURE AND THE IMPLEMENTATION OF STRATEGY

CHAPTER OBJECTIVES

Largely unaddressed so far in this book is the relationship between organizational structure and the implementation of strategy. Although the text has emphasized that firms differ greatly in their ability to implement strategies effectively, it has not really focused on organizational structure as a potential source of competitive advantage. The overall aims of any organizational structure are to implement the strategic initiatives that managers have formulated and to make organizations responsive to their managers, their shareholders or owners, and developments in their larger competitive environments. By developing especially effective structures, managers can give their organizations a significant competitive advantage.

The specific objectives of this chapter are to:

- Define structure and describe its role in the implementation of strategy.
- Identify and describe the different components of organizational structure.
- Identify some of the problems associated with organizing and describe how the various components of organizational structure can be used to overcome these organizational problems that are common to nearly all firms and businesses.
- Discuss some of the emerging issues that are likely to have an impact on organizing and organizational structures in the future.

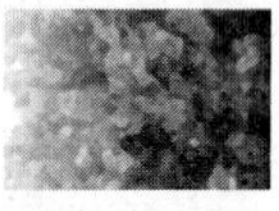

HISTORICAL OVERVIEW AND THE CHARACTERISTICS OF BUSINESS ORGANIZATIONS

In spite of their prominence in our society, it is worth noting that large, complex business organizations are a relatively new phenomenon, less than 150 years old. As Harvard professor Alfred Chandler has noted:

> Before 1850 very few American businesses needed the services of a full-time administrator or required a clearly defined administrative structure. Industrial enterprises were very small, in comparison with those of today. And they were usually family

> affairs. The two or three men responsible for the destiny of a single enterprise handled all its basic activities — economic and administrative, operational and entrepreneurial .[1]

The emergence of the railroads and other large industrial enterprises in the mid-1800s, however, drastically changed the nature of business administration. The construction of railroads linking eastern cities with the American heartland required large organizations. One of the first major railroads, the New York and Erie, had over 4,000 employees by the early 1850s, and the Pennsylvania Railroad had nearly 50,000 employees by the late 1880s.[2] The new challenges of managing and coordinating such large organizations forced managers to focus on developing sophisticated structures.

Chandler makes clear, however, that it was not only the size but also the complexity of the tasks to be performed by these organizations that required new administrative and organizational structures:

> No existing business required so many, so varied, and so intricate short-term operating decisions, and none called for such difficult long-term decisions as to pricing and allocation of resources. Thus, even before financiers and speculators grasped the possibilities of the corporation as an engine for exploitation and manipulation, railroad managers were devising ways to transform it into the basic institution for the management of modern large-scale business enterprise.[3]

Thus, the growing size and complexity of the railroads and other early industrial firms did much to develop the contemporary concepts of business administration and organization. Over the last 150 years, business enterprises have evolved considerably and nearly all modern organizations have the following characteristics:[4]

- *Division of labor*. Employees in most companies generally do not perform a wide variety of duties; instead, work is organized so that employees specialize in a particular task or set of related tasks. Organizations recruit or train specialists to perform these tasks, and such a division of labor allows these specialists to become increasingly adept at performing their job duties. For example, it would be very uncommon for a company to hire an individual to make some sales calls in the morning, do some manufacturing work in the early afternoon, and then perform some bookkeeping activities before leaving work at the end of the day. Instead, organizations hire marketing, manufacturing, and accounting specialists who then work within their respective areas of functional expertise.
- *Hierarchy*. Hierarchy is another characteristic of nearly all business organizations. Hierarchy is the "organization chart," or the arrangement of managers and employees into superior-subordinate relationships. The concept of *hierarchical levels* refers to the levels of managerial decision-making activity. A "tall" structure would have many (perhaps as many as eight) hierarchical levels from the CEO down to the lowest level of subordinates, while a "flat" structure would have fewer (perhaps only three) hierarchical levels. Closely related to the concept of hierarchical levels is the concept of *span of control*. Span of control refers to the number of subordinates reporting to a manager. The greater a manager's span of control, the more subordinates that manager would have reporting to him or her.
- *Decisions are based on rules, policies, and standard operating procedures that seek to promote efficiency*. In most organizations, employees are not free to do whatever

they want in any way they wish. Instead, their actions are guided by uniform rules, policies, and standard operating procedures that aim to promote efficiency and standardization. In most organizations, such policies and standard operating procedures are a very important component of structure, and, as we shall discuss later, such rules and standard operating procedures can have significant positive benefits and, at times, some negative consequences for organizational performance.

- *Tendency to become inflexible and resist change.* As noted at the end of Chapter 5, one key characteristic of most organizations is their stability. Most organizations rigidly adhere to their rules, policies, and standard operating procedures even when circumstances might suggest that exceptions or changes in policies might be warranted. Once set in motion, organizations can become quite resistant to change, preferring to "do things the way they've always been done." As a result, most organizations are hostile to innovation and tend to resist leadership that would initiate change.

The remainder of this chapter is organized as follows: First, we define structure and take a closer look at the various components of organizational structure. We then consider some of the central issues and problems that are common to nearly all organizations and discuss how structures can be altered or modified to alleviate some of these problems. Finally, we describe several emerging issues that are likely to have an impact on how organizations structure their operations in the future.

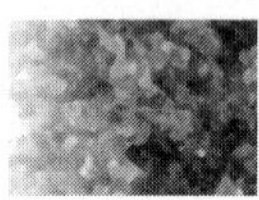

A Definition of Organizational Structure

Although hierarchy is the most obvious or visible component of structure, organizational structure includes much more than hierarchy or organization charts. Another important component of organizational structure is the written and unwritten rules, standard operating procedures, and systems that constitute organizations' marketing, production, personnel, and compensation policies as well as their accounting, financial control, and information systems. In addition, the lifeblood of any organization is the information and knowledge that resides in and is passed among organizational members and their departments. Finally, we have come to realize that an organization's culture or "informal structure" can be just as important as if not more important than its formal structure of hierarchy, policies and systems, and flows of information.

Thus, we will define structure broadly to include any *mechanisms that facilitate the formulation and implementation of strategy and the overall coordination of the business enterprise*. These mechanisms include:

- hierarchical reporting relationships,
- policies, standard operating procedures, and control systems,
- information systems and flows of information moving through organizations, and
- culture.

The challenge confronting general managers is to combine these components into unique organizational structures that (1) effectively implement chosen strategies, and (2) make their firms responsive to the leadership of owners and managers as well as to changes in the larger competitive environments in which firms operate.

EXHIBIT 10.1

The Mental Models and Strategic Decisions Studied in This Text and Their Influence on Performance and Competitive Advantage

Managers' Mental Models
Their beliefs and understandings about
- Industry environments
- How to compete
- Appropriate size and diversity
- How to organize

Decisions about Business Definition

Decisions about Business Strategy

Decisions about Corporate Strategy and Diversification

Decisions about Organizational Structure

Market Position, Resources, and Capabilities

Performance and Competitive Advantage

Feedback
Reinforces or suggests changes in managers' mental models

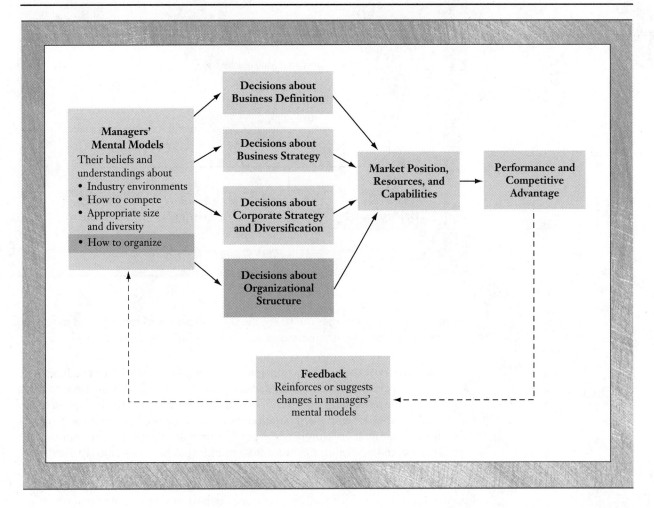

As suggested by our model of strategic management, illustrated in Exhibit 10.1, decisions about organizational structure will be influenced by managers' beliefs about how to organize and implement strategy. As suggested in Chapter 2, managers' beliefs and understandings are likely to be developed by their own trial-and-error learning, imitation of other firms' effective structures, and their own creativity and ingenuity.

THE COMPONENTS OF ORGANIZATIONAL STRUCTURE

HIERARCHY

Hierarchy is both the most visible and the most widely studied aspect of structure. This section focuses on three types of hierarchical structures — functional, multidivisional,

EXHIBIT 10.2

An Illustration of Functional Structure

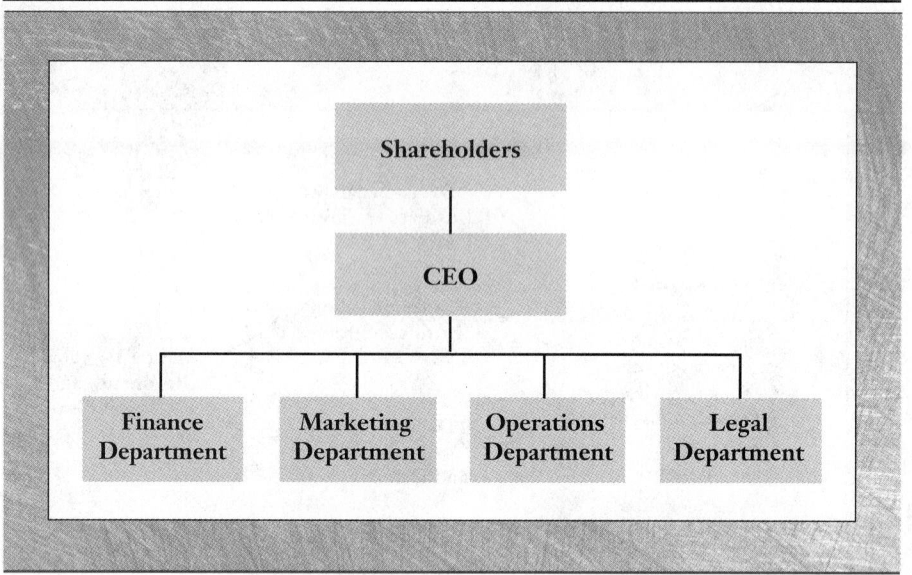

and matrix — and examines the strengths and limitations of each type of structure. Later in the chapter, we examine some new types of hierarchical structures.

Functional structure. Functional structures organize activities around functional activities or departments, such as manufacturing, marketing, research and development, and sales, as illustrated in Figure 10.2. The principal advantage of the functional structure is that its division of the organization into departments allows employees to specialize and become increasingly adept at what they do. Because of its emphasis on specialization and efficiency, the functional structure has been described as the natural way for most firms, even fairly large firms, to organize their operations.[5]

Yet many problems are associated with functional structures. First, communication and motivational difficulties can be particularly vexing in functional organizations. The various departments of a firm organized along functional lines must communicate with each other, but because of the structure's design, most information must flow up through functional "chimneys" before it can flow across to another functional department.

Though it might seem logical that an employee in the manufacturing or production department who has a marketing question could simply telephone or e-mail a colleague in the marketing department, this is rarely done in practice. Rather than simply telephoning a colleague in the marketing department, the manufacturing employee with a question would instead write a memorandum to his or her manager who might then relay the request to the vice president of manufacturing who would then forward the request to the vice president of marketing who would forward the memo to a marketing manager who would then deliver the memo to the employee he or she deems most qualified to answer the query.

Why this cumbersome process? Primarily because it keeps employees' supervisors informed and allows them to provide their input to policy questions. Furthermore, the process leaves what is referred to as a "paper trail," allowing employees to show that they have kept supervisors informed. At the same time, however, the process increases the amount of time required to transmit data, slows decision making, and increases the likelihood that both the request for data as well as the reply will be distorted or altered as they move through the organization's hierarchy.

Also, in most functional organizations, some departments are designated *profit centers* — seen as responsible for generating the company's revenues, while other departments are designated *cost centers* — seen perhaps as important, but not responsible for generating revenues. Without responsibility for generating revenue, employees in cost centers can develop morale and motivation problems.

Finally, functional structures tend to overload top managers.[6] Because most information goes up before it goes across departments in functional organizations, much management time is spent just relaying information. Furthermore, disputes that inevitably arise between functional departments must be refereed by top managers.

If these motivational and informational limitations become so severe that they prevent managers from noticing or responding to changes in their competitive environments, or if these problems limit the ability of their firms to effectively implement strategies, then changes in the hierarchy may be needed. Most managers have found that as organizations grow and become increasingly diversified, they must make major changes to their firms' hierarchies. One early organizational innovation developed in response to these challenges was the adoption of multidivisional structures.

Multidivisional (product, geographical) structure. As just suggested, the growth and increasing diversity of some early corporate giants during the first decades of the twentieth century resulted in a variety of organizational problems, including inefficiencies in information flows and top management overload. Through a process of trial-and-error learning, managers of several large firms began to develop multidivisional structures.[7] Multidivisional structures are based on the reality that many firms consist of several distinct operating segments or businesses. Instead of operating and trying to coordinate the activities of these different businesses as if they were a single firm, the multidivisional structure explicitly divides these businesses into autonomous units or "divisions." As illustrated in Exhibit 10.3, these divisions can be made along business or product lines as illustrated in part A of the exhibit, or along geographical lines as illustrated in part B.

A few firms adopted multidivisional structures early in the twentieth century, but, as Exhibit 10.4 shows, most large, diversified organizations quickly adopted multidivisional structures in the post-World War II years.[8] In fact, the adoption of the multidivisional structure by nearly all *Fortune* 500 firms in the years after World War II is an excellent example of how imitation by managers leads to the diffusion of innovations throughout the economy.

The divisionalization of business activities that characterizes the multidivisional structure has a number of advantages for large, diversified firms. First, the multidivisional structure decentralizes decision making, freeing firms' top managers from day-to-day decision making so they can focus on more strategic issues. In the multidivisional organization, most tactical and strategic decisions affecting each division are made by the managers in those divisions. Thus, corporate-level managers can focus on the allocation of capital to the various divisions, the overall direction of the firm, and decisions to buy or sell businesses.

EXHIBIT 10.3
Illustrations of Multidivisional Structures

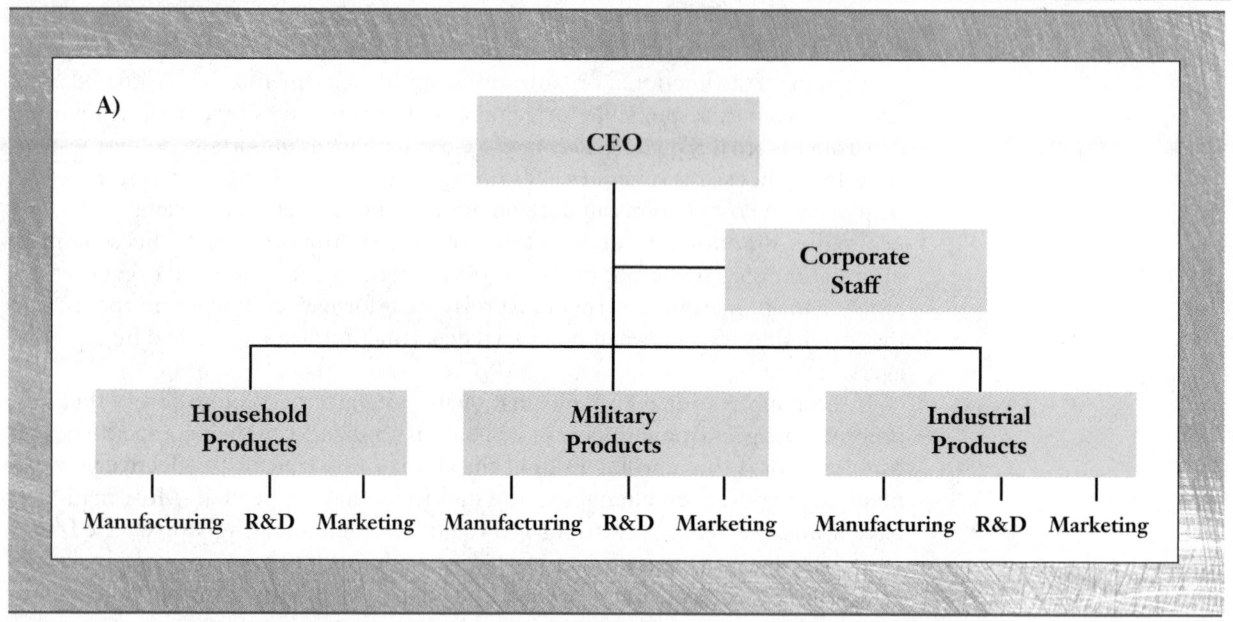

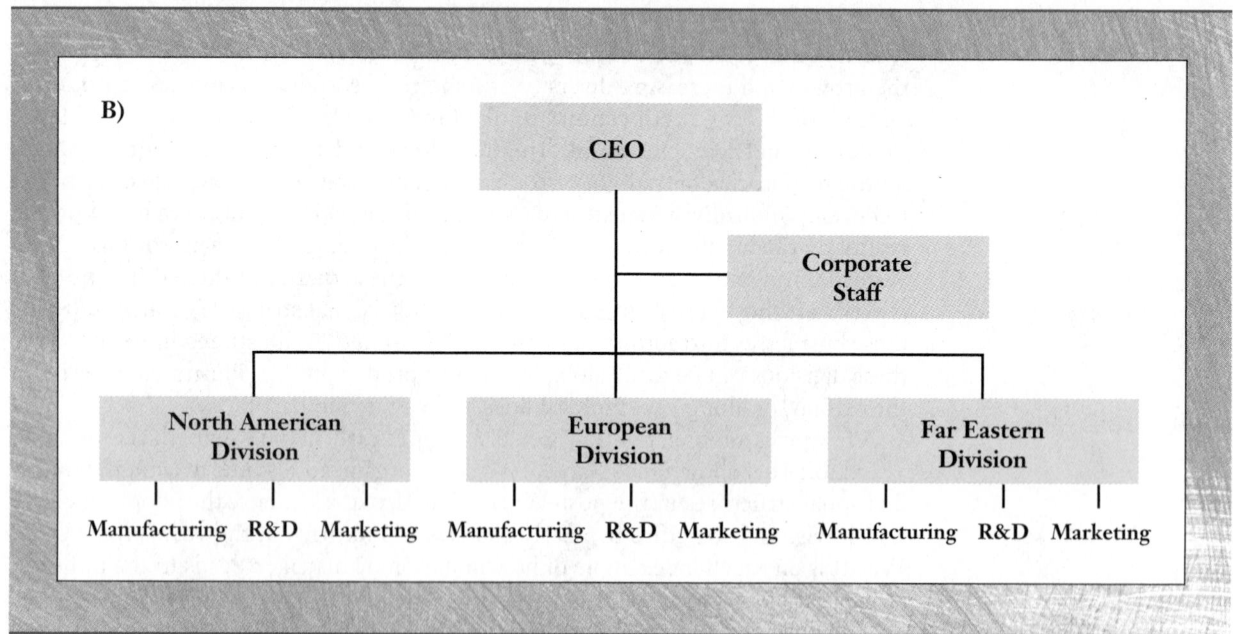

Furthermore, the multidivisional structure improves accountability. A key component of any multidivisional structure is the "corporate staff" (illustrated in Exhibit 10.3), which serves both advisory and audit functions. The corporate staff holds division managers responsible for decisions made in their units by measuring and monitoring the performance of each division. Thus, the corporate staff "keeps score," summarizing for corporate managers how each of their firms' various divisions are performing.

EXHIBIT 10.4

Adoption of the Multidivisional Structure by Fortune 500 Firms After World War II

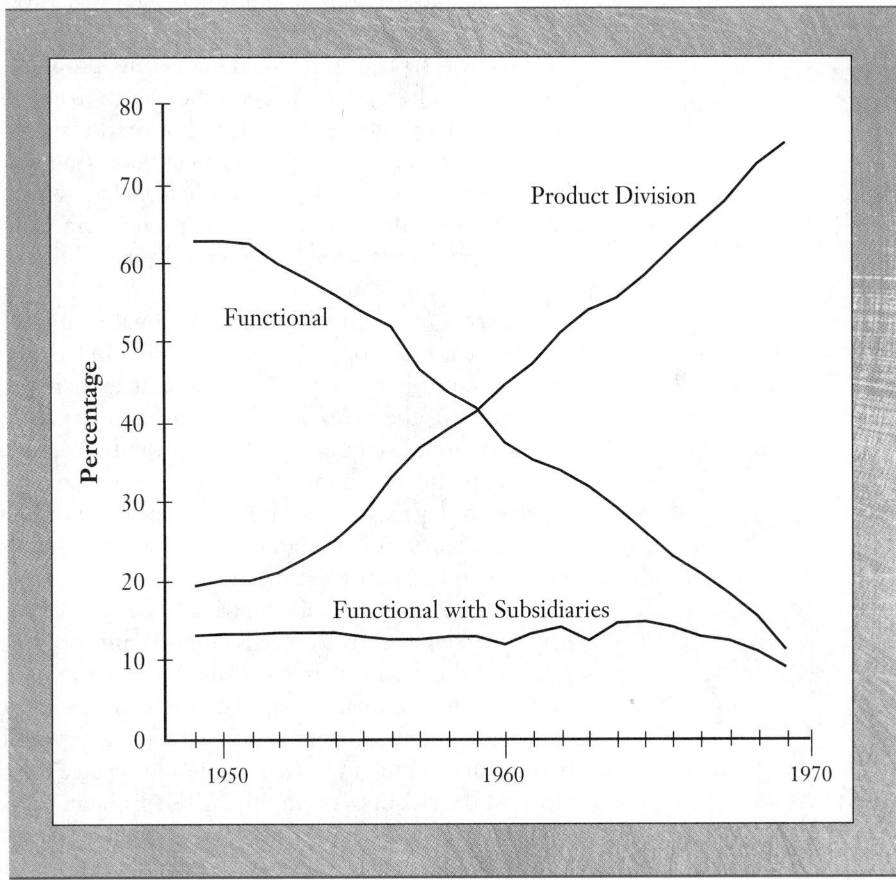

SOURCE: R. P. Rumelt, *Strategy, Strucutre and Economic Performance* (Cambridge, Mass.: Harvard University Press, 1974).

In addition, the multidivisional structure can improve the allocation of resources by requiring all divisions to submit investment proposals to the corporate staff, which then applies common criteria (i.e., return on capital or hurdle rate requirements) to evaluate and fund these investment proposals. In many respects, this internal competition for capital is the most distinctive feature of the multidivisional enterprise. Cash flows in the multidivisional firm are always sent to the corporate treasury and

> are not automatically returned to their sources but instead are exposed to an internal competition. Investment proposals from the several divisions are solicited and evaluated by the general management.... *this assignment of cash flows to high yield uses is the most fundamental attribute of the [multidivisional] enterprise.*[9]

In other words, one division may generate considerable cash flow, but if it has fewer profitable opportunities for reinvesting those cash flows, the cash can be reallocated to other divisions in the organization that have more profitable investment opportunities.

In spite of their many advantages over functional structures when firms become very large and diversified, multidivisional structures also suffer from a number of limitations and disadvantages. First, each division in a multidivisional firm will have its own array of functional marketing, production, and service departments as illustrated in Exhibit 10.3. Instead of centralizing all manufacturing or marketing activities in a single manufacturing or marketing department, the multidivisional firm will typically have as many manufacturing and marketing departments as it has divisions. As a result, many functional activities will necessarily be duplicated once or many times in the multidivisional firm. This duplication is costly and can prevent firms organized along multidivisional lines from realizing many potential economies of scale and scope.

A second problem with multidivisional firms is that top managers can become very far removed from divisional activities. In fact, it is not uncommon for top managers of multidivisional firms to have little if any expertise about the activities or operations of the various divisions of their firms. Though a key advantage of the multidivisional structure is that it provides top managers with time to focus on "the big picture" and more strategic issues, managers may, as a consequence, lack the day-to-day experience or familiarity with divisional operations that can be crucial when reviewing investment proposals or when dealing with strategic issues or a crisis within a particular business.

The transfer pricing dilemma is another problem common to any multidivisional firm in which one division sells components, products, or services to another division in the same firm. In spite of a long history of working with transfer pricing problems, few companies have been able to develop solutions that leave both selling and buying divisions totally pleased. The key problem is determining the appropriate prices supplying divisions should receive for the transferred goods and services. At the risk of oversimplifying the problem, it is easy to see that if prices are set equal to market prices (or higher), supplying divisions are likely to be pleased but buying divisions may feel that they should receive some sort of price break or that they are not enjoying the same sort of flexibility that they would have if dealing with external suppliers. On the other hand, if prices are set lower than market prices, buying divisions may be pleased but supplying divisions are likely to feel cheated. In either case, morale problems in one of the divisions may ensue.

Finally, multidivisional structures can result in a short-term focus and an undesirable level of competition for resources among divisions. Because investment dollars tend to be allocated to those divisions showing the most promise and because firms tend to promote those managers who show the best results, division managers may feel tremendous pressure to report strong performance in the short run. By emphasizing short-run performance goals, however, division managers may pursue activities that will actually harm their business units over the longer run. For example, expenditures for marketing and R&D efforts may be needed to maximize long-term market share and profitability, yet these expenditures will reduce a division's quarterly net income. A division executive hoping to "look good" or aiming to improve the division's results might decide to forgo these expenditures, thereby improving the next quarter's results at the expense of longer-term performance.

Matrix structure. Matrix structures represent a hybrid hierarchy in which a functional structure is overlaid or placed on top of a multidivisional (or geographical or product) structure. Exhibit 10.5 shows the matrix structure adopted several years ago by Chrysler Corporation. The matrix structure illustrated in Exhibit 10.5 shows that Chrysler is organized along both product lines (e.g., small-car platform team, large-car platform team, minivan platform team) as well as functional lines (e.g., engineering, production, marketing, finance). Employees retain functional specialties, such as engineering, marketing, or production, but the company has placed employees in "cross-functional" product teams. As a result, engineers, marketing, and production people all work together on the small-car platform team or the minivan platform team. Other types of matrix structures are obviously possible; a firm pursuing a global strategy, for example, might be organized along both product and geographical lines.

Matrix structures are especially useful in a situation like Chrysler's when traditional functional or multidivisional structures inadequately distribute information throughout the organization. In the past, the "chimney" problem (described earlier in the section on functional structure) has been particularly acute at U.S. automobile companies. Engineers often designed cars that were difficult to build and/or that consumers didn't want. Ensuing discussions to correct problems and communicate across engineering, production, and marketing departments would take months or even years. Already the advantage of cross-functional product teams is seen in much shorter product development lead times and significantly lower product development costs at the major automobile companies.[10]

Some pharmaceutical companies are now making use of "drug discovery teams" to speed the development of new products. Like cross-functional teams, these drug

EXHIBIT 10.5

The Matrix Structure Used at Chrysler Corporation

	Engineering	Sales and Marketing	Production
Small-Car Operations			
Large-Car Operations			
Minivan Operations			
Jeep/Truck Operations			

discovery teams consist of researchers with different types of expertise but focusing on a common problem. Working closely together, these discovery teams develop a common body of knowledge or team mental model that facilitates research.[11]

Although the major advantage of the matrix structure is its ability to improve information flows, the matrix structure also has a number of limitations. One problem is often referred to as the "two-boss problem." Employees working in a firm organized as a matrix will find that they often report to two bosses. In the Chrysler example described earlier, an engineer working on the minivan platform team is responsible to the head of the engineering department as well as to the head of the minivan platform team. Thus, if goals are not congruent throughout the firm or if the organization lacks an effective mechanism for settling conflicts and disagreements, the matrix structure can become unworkable. In fact, matrix structures have often produced either power struggles or outright anarchy as product managers struggle with functional managers.

Another problem that is sometimes encountered in matrix organizations has been referred to as "groupitis," or the tendency for cross-functional team members to believe that every decision needs to be made as a group.[12] Although group decision making offers many benefits, it can also slow progress if the group becomes bogged down in deciding too many details.

Another limitation of the matrix form that Chrysler and some high-technology companies have encountered is that specialists who are working on a product team often become so involved in working on the product that they lose touch with their specialty area. For example, some automobile companies have found a trade-off between the benefits of better information flow from having their engineers involved in product teams and the cost of having those engineers unaware of new developments in engineering technologies. Some companies have dealt with this challenge by having employees rotate into and out of product teams on fairly strict schedules.

We've already described how different hierarchies are more and less effective at moving information. For example, we noted that the automobile industry has embraced matrix structures and cross-functional teams as ways of better sharing information and overcoming the limitations of moving information through or between functional silos or chimneys. Whenever the context demands the dissemination and application of information, we can expect more and more companies in different industries to adopt matrix structures and cross-functional teams as ways to improve decision making. Later in this chapter, we examine the *virtual* or *modular* structures and other new structural forms that many companies are adopting in order to more effectively manage information flows.

Many global companies have adopted matrix structures as a way to manage their international business activities. The accompanying Management Focus, "Structures for Managing the Global Organization," describes matrix, hybrid, and other types of structures that many large firms have adopted in their efforts to improve coordination and information flows.

Policies, Standard Operating Procedures, and Control Systems

Though organizational charts or hierarchies of supervisor-subordinate relationships are the most visible aspect of structures, much of the actual work of organizations and the implementation of strategies is accomplished through their policies, standard operating procedures, and control systems. Most organizational behavior is

STRUCTURES FOR MANAGING THE GLOBAL ORGANIZATION

Global companies have special requirements that create significant organizational challenges. The structures that the managers of global companies adopt must assist them in their efforts to exploit opportunities to achieve economies of scale by centralizing their marketing and production activities whenever possible. At the same time, the structures of international companies must also accommodate differences in national cultures and variations in business practices. And, as in any organization, the structures of international companies must serve to coordinate business activities and to move information quickly and accurately across borders and around the world.

Global companies have dealt with these organizational challenges in many ways, but they have almost always involved the adoption of more complex hierarchical structures. Many global companies have adopted multidivisional structures, organizing different product lines or different regions of the globe into semi-autonomous divisions. For example, Figure 1 shows a hypothetical global company with its headquarters in New York City, but with North American, European, and Far Eastern divisions.

Such a multidivisional structure has a number of advantages for the global business organization. It decentralizes decision making, giving much authority to geographical division managers so that their divisions can be especially responsive to the unique needs of local markets and cultures. Such decentralization and delegation also frees top corporate managers from much day-to-day decision making, allowing them to focus on more strategic issues and problems. Still, in spite of their many advantages, all multidivisional structures have a number of disadvantages. They often duplicate many functional activities, including marketing and production, reducing opportunities to achieve economies of scale. Furthermore, multidivisional structures often fail to ensure coordination and are

FIGURE 1

A Multidivisional Structure for a Hypothetical Global Company

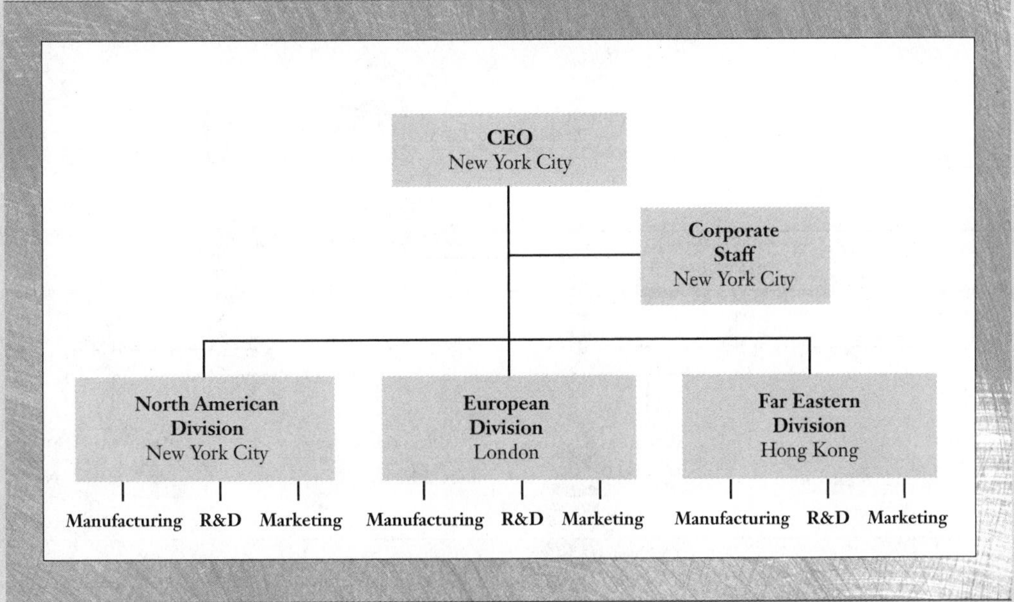

continued

FIGURE 2

The Matrix Structure Adopted by One Global Company

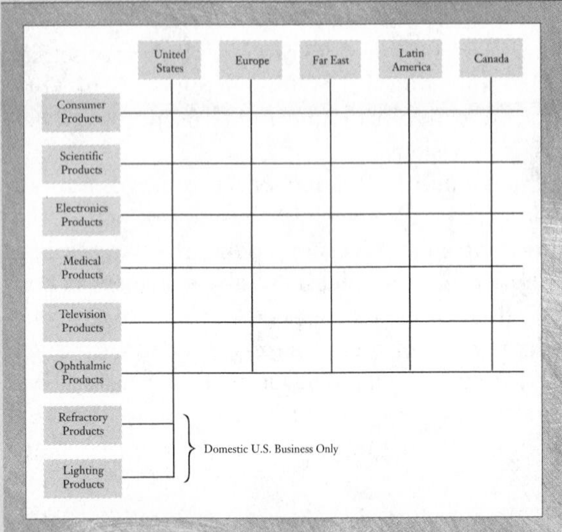

SOURCE: C. A. Bartlett and M. Y. Yoshino, *Corning Glass Works International* (B-1). Boston: HBS Case Series.

often ineffective at distributing information to and between operating divisions.

To improve coordination and information flow, many global companies have adopted matrix structures. For example, Figure 2 illustrates the matrix structure adopted many years ago by one large global company. This company had eight major business lines and operated in the United States Canada, Latin America, Europe, and the Far East. Its matrix structure created product-market teams to focus on each of the company's businesses in each of its international markets.

Other managers have been reluctant to adopt matrix structures for many of the disadvantages and shortcomings described in the text, but they have also found that multidivisional structures do not adequately distribute information or provide enough coordination of business activities. As a result, managers of many companies have developed new, hybrid types of organizational structures. For example, as illustrated in Figure 3, the Kellogg Company is organized as a multidivisional

FIGURE 3

Kellogg's Multidivisional Structure with Liaison Roles

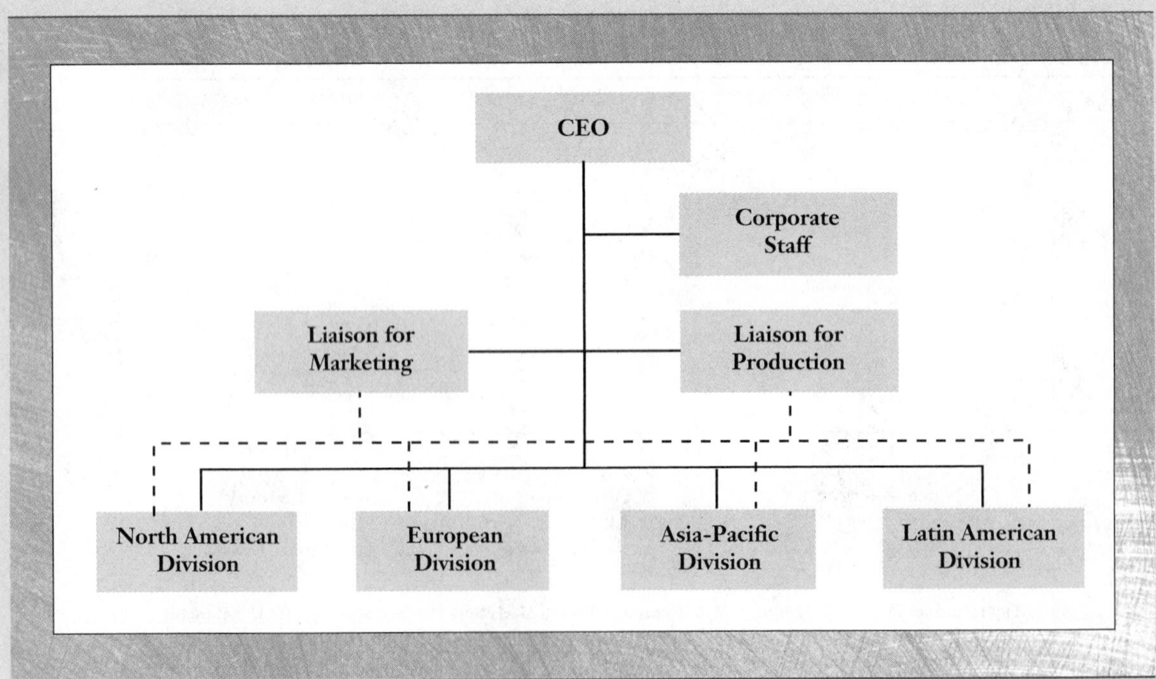

continued

with various geographical areas organized into different divisions, but the company has also created "liaison roles" in order to better distribute information about functional activities across its geographical divisions.

The job of the marketing and production liaison personnel is to coordinate functional activities across the geographical divisions and improve communication between the company's headquarters in Battle Creek, Michigan, and the various geographical divisions. In addition, these liaisons share ideas developed in one division with the managers of all the other divisions. Though the managers holding these liaison roles have no line authority, they report directly to the CEO of the company, thus ensuring that they have sufficient prestige and visibility to obtain the cooperation of division managers.

With more and more companies pursuing global diversification strategies, we can expect a growing number of firms to experience problems of strategy implementation, organizational control and coordination, and information flow. This will almost surely prompt companies to experiment with new hierarchies and other structural innovations. The global companies that develop especially effective structures can come to enjoy significant advantages. ■

highly routinized; rather than "reinventing the wheel" every time a unit of work must be performed, organizations standardize many activities and functions in order to increase efficiency and reduce variability.

Thus, most organizations have thick policy manuals describing routines and standard operating procedures for accomplishing an array of tasks, including everything from market research, engineering, and personnel recruitment to manufacturing, marketing, sales, and after-sales service activities. Furthermore, even strategic tasks, such as performance monitoring and the review of investment proposals, are routinized. As a result, accounting data from one period are comparable with data from other periods, and investment proposals are not considered uniquely but in light of uniform financial criteria.

The importance of this component of organizational structure should not be underestimated; indeed, it is probably fair to state that organizations' policies, standard operating procedures, and control systems play a critical role in influencing their successes as well as their failures. On the positive side, high performance is almost always associated with an effective set of policies, procedures, or systems. A low-cost, high-quality manufacturing operation is based on a set of policies and procedures that reflect a tremendous amount of learning and experience. As suggested in the preceding chapter, firms make a series of successful acquisitions not because of luck or the intuition of their top managers, but because they have developed a set of procedures that helped them identify attractive acquisition candidates, execute the purchases, and successfully integrate the new units. Managers of many organizations believe that their firms' financial control systems are important sources of competitive advantage.

At the same time, organizations' procedures and systems can be pathological. Highly routinized policies and procedures can limit organizational flexibility and adaptability, and can make organizations very unresponsive to changes in their competitive environments. Recall from Chapter 6 that we suggested that managers' understandings of their firms' definitions tend to become tightly coupled with their firms' strategies, policies, and procedures. Because of this tight coupling and because firms' policies and procedures tend to be so highly routinized, managers can come to use their organizations' policies, procedures, and systems over and over again in an automatic, almost unthinking way. Although this automatic or reflexive use of policies, procedures, and systems minimizes ambiguity and promotes rapid decision making, it can become a serious liability if environmental conditions or competitive circumstances change.

Organizational policies and procedures can also unwittingly reward the wrong types of behaviors and, therefore, produce undesirable results. One example of how a company's systems can have an adverse effect on strategy and performance is provided by the Harvard Business School case study of the Dexter Corporation.[13] In this case, one of Dexter's businesses manufactures a key component for firms in the rapidly growing semiconductor industry. One Dexter executive summarizes the company's problem this way:

> We were doing very well but we were underinvesting in what turned out to be a very high-growth industry. We weren't putting in the marketing dollars and we weren't putting in the R&D dollars. We were growing . . . at close to 20 percent, however, the semiconductor market was growing at 30 percent. So we were losing market share and didn't know it.[14]

And what role did Dexter's structure play in fostering this problem? First, until the time of the case, Dexter lacked some sort of monitoring system for gauging company performance against the competitive environment. The case also suggests a second factor, however. The casewriter again quotes the same Dexter executive:

> I would say going back one, two, or three years ago, that due to the constraints of the profit-sharing and the incentive program for the divisions, we probably underinvested in our two growth businesses.[15]

In other words, the company's own compensation system—which rewarded division executives on the basis of their division's bottom line return on investment — discouraged division executives from spending what was needed for marketing and R&D efforts in order to maximize the company's long-run performance outcomes.

INFORMATION SYSTEMS AND INFORMATION FLOWS

Although a traditional aim of structure has been the organization of work — especially physical work or tasks — to implement or achieve strategic objectives, it now appears that the implementation of strategy is becoming increasingly dependent on the acquisition, storage, distribution, and application of information. Many companies have found that information and systems for managing the flow of information can be important sources of competitive advantage. The text has already noted how Wal-Mart has successfully exploited information and information technology to provide it with one of the most sophisticated logistics and inventory management systems of any retailing firm. Nearly all large retailing firms have come to realize that their ability to manage information about their costs, inventories, and customer preferences and shopping patterns can have a profound impact on their success.

One important factor behind the revolution in manufacturing is the incorporation of information technology to handle the flow of materials and labor through the manufacturing process. Computerized information systems allow companies to process vast amounts of marketing, production, and human resources data. Highly sophisticated information systems, such as MRP (materials requirement planning) and SAP, not only schedule production processes but they also automatically order raw materials, control inventories, and maintain general ledgers and other accounting records.

Following deregulation, airline companies responded to the challenge of strategically managing information by developing elaborate computerized reservation systems. The objective of these computerized reservation systems is yield management, or maximizing revenue per flight by determining the optimal number of seats to be sold at higher business class fares and at lower leisure class fares. The reservation systems use computer technology to process and analyze data on thousands of variables so that the carriers can "predict with almost pinpoint accuracy how many business customers would want seats on a particular flight."[16] Here's the impact of this sophisticated information technology on just a single American Airlines flight:

> Take Flight 2015, American's popular 5:30 p.m. departure from Chicago to Phoenix. Its 125 coach seats are divided among seven fare "buckets," with round-trip tickets ranging from $238 to $1,404. In the weeks before each Chicago-Phoenix flight, American's yield-management computers constantly adjust the number of seats available in each bucket, taking into account tickets sold, historical ridership patterns and connecting passengers likely to use the route as one leg of a longer trip.
>
> If advance bookings are slim, American adds seats to low-fare buckets. If business customers buy unrestricted fares earlier than expected, the yield-management computer takes seats out of the discount buckets and preserves them for last-minute bookings that the database predicts will still show up.
>
> With 69 of 125 coach seats already sold four weeks before one recent departure of Flight 2015, American's computer began to limit the number of seats in lower-priced buckets. A week later, it totally shut off sales for the bottom three buckets, priced $300 or less.
>
> One day before departure, with 130 passengers booked for the 125-seat flight, American still offered five seats at full fare because its computer database indicated ten passengers were likely not to show up or take other flights. Flight 2015 departed full and no one was bumped.[17]

Obviously, it is not enough to simply collect and manipulate information. The proliferation of computers and other information technology has vastly increased the ability of companies to collect, store, and distribute information. How that information is used and whether it is used in a way that offers companies a competitive advantage—as in the American Airlines example— has quickly become the central question for the managers of firms in many industries. This increasing demand for and importance of information and coordination continues to tax traditional organizational structures, and firms have responded in a variety of ways. The accompanying Management Focus, "The Strategic Use of Information," describes how several companies have both successfully used and failed to use information technology to develop competitive advantage in their industries.

ORGANIZATIONAL CULTURE

If we think of organizations' hierarchical reporting relationships and their policies, procedures, and systems as more formal aspects of structure, then their cultures are a more informal but no less important aspect of structure. Anyone who has been involved for any length of time in businesses, schools, clubs, or religious institutions

Management Focus

The Strategic Use of Information

Several years ago, Frito-Lay gave each of its 10,000 route salespeople handheld computers.[1] In the process, the company transformed these workers from "laborers" to "knowledge workers." Instead of simply ordering merchandise and restocking shelves, these employees now play central roles in collecting and analyzing marketing data. Information that these employees enter into their handheld computers is sent daily to Frito-Lay's Dallas headquarters. There, the information is compiled so that the company's top managers can have access to the latest sales and market share information on every outlet selling Frito-Lay products. In addition to having accurate and up-to-date information on the sales of its products, the company benefits because its managers are able to make decisions faster. Here's how Frito-Lay's president described this advantage:

> Recently, I noticed red numbers (indicating reduced market share) for tortilla chips in our central business region. I punched up another screen display and located the problem: Texas. I kept punching up new screens and tracked the red numbers to a specific sales division, and, finally, the chain of stores. The numbers pinpointed the problem area and, after additional research, revealed the culprit: the introduction of a generic store-branded product. We quickly formulated a counter-strategy and sales climbed again. Time invested: a couple of weeks. Before ... finding such a problem and correcting it took the better part of three months.[2]

What makes Frito-Lay's strategic use of information so remarkable is how few companies have adopted similar practices. Many companies have employees on the front lines working every day with customers, and — like Frito-Lay's route salespeople who have valuable market knowledge that they could pass on to top decision makers — these employees could be much more valuable as "knowledge workers," providing top managers with accurate and timely data to improve decision making. Yet, few companies exploit this knowledge source.

For example, railroad train employees pass by many plants and warehouses every day as they deliver and pick up freight. They know whether their companies serve a particular location, they know what other railroads or trucking companies serve a particular location, and they know how current traffic levels compare with past traffic levels. Unfortunately for their companies, these employees are never asked to supply marketing or sales personnel with information. Similarly, overnight express delivery employees visit many if not most of the same customer locations every day. They know whether their competitors also serve these locations, they know how their company stands relative to the others, and they know how current volumes of business differ from past volumes. Unfortunately, again, their companies do not ask them to share this important marketing knowledge.

As information and knowledge become even more important keys to building and sustaining competitive advantage, companies — like Frito-Lay — that have developed structures and information systems to effectively capture and exploit knowledge will become tough to beat in the battle for market position and high performance. ■

[1]Beeby, R. H. 1990. How to crunch a bunch of figures. *The Wall Street Journal*, June 11, A14.

[2]Ibid.

knows that nearly all organizations have cultures — widely shared norms and values — that have a powerful influence on their activities and operations. And, culture can have significant positive and negative impacts on performance. In fact, an organization's culture can be both an important source of sustained competitive advantage[18] as well as a serious drag on its effectiveness.

In many cases, an organization's culture reflects the myths and realities surrounding a founder or a key leader of the company. For example, following World War II, W. D. Brosnan became the president of the Southern Railway Company at a time when the company was facing a serious financial crisis. Brosnan's charismatic leadership saved the company from its financial problems and made the company one of the most efficient railroads in the United States. In the process, Brosnan so firmly implanted his attitude and outlook on the company that years after his retirement, nearly every employee still had a favorite "Brosnan story" and many employees had a sign on their desks reading "IT CAN'T BE DONE" with a big red X through the " 'T," reflecting Brosnan's "can do" attitude.

An organization's culture can also be derived from or associated with its definition or identity so that those characteristics that make the organization distinctive in the eyes of customers or other external constituencies are also internalized as norms or values by the organization's employees. For example, Old Kent Financial Corporation, a bank holding company headquartered in Grand Rapids, Michigan, has enjoyed nearly 30 years of continually rising earnings. The norm or value that the company's employees have internalized from this exemplary record of financial performance is that they are "winners" and that they work for a "winning" organization.

These examples also suggest how culture gets transmitted to employees. Quite often, new employees are socialized into an organization's culture as veteran employees pass along stories and myths. Stories about a dynamic leader, an employee's extraordinary efforts, a remarkable turnaround that saved the company from bankruptcy, or any other epic offer new employees a powerful model for their behavior. Visible symbols, such as the Southern Railway "IT CAN'T BE DONE" signs, also play an important role in socializing new employees.

The development and communication of effective cultures can be an important source of competitive advantage because they can provide employees with a sense of meaning and purposefulness. In his remarkable little book, *Leadership Is an Art*, former Herman Miller CEO, Max DePree, writes,

> Every family, every college, every corporation, every institution needs tribal storytellers. The penalty for failing to listen is to lose one's history, one's historical context, one's binding values....
>
> As a culture or a corporation grows older and more complex, the communications naturally and inevitably become more sophisticated and crucial. An increasingly large part that communication plays in expanding cultures is to pass along values to new members and reaffirm those values to old hands.
>
> A corporation's values are its life's blood. Without effective communication, actively practiced, without the art of scrutiny, those values will disappear in a sea of trivial memos and impertinent reports.
>
> There may be no single thing more important in our efforts to achieve meaningful work and fulfilling relationships than to learn and practice the art of communication.[19]

Effective cultures also motivate the types of behaviors that are important to organizational success. For example, if culture helps to foster certain norms and behaviors that are desired by the organization or consistent with its goals and objectives, then culture can take the place of much supervisory activity.[20] In other words, organizations can establish formal supervisory and other structural controls to ensure employee compliance, and/or they can develop informal structural mechanisms, such as a strong culture, that can socialize employees into the organization's norms, goals, and objectives and encourage appropriate employee behaviors—a less expensive and usually far more effective alternative.

On the other hand, culture can also slow or retard organizational adaptation to change. If employees become so entrenched in their organization's way of doing things that they cannot objectively evaluate new developments in their firm's environment, then culture can have devastating consequences. Donald Katz, in his analysis of the decline Sears, Roebuck experienced in retailing, found that the company's strong culture had prevented its managers from understanding the changes that were occurring in retailing:

> None of the consultants [hired by Sears] had ever encountered such awesome cultural and political impediments to altering an economic organization. They all sensed the richness and religiosity of the contrived family of Sears, and though they believed it continued to be the best of America in so many ways, they believed also that the Sears system was inimical to the survival of a great enterprise.[21]

Thus, culture can be a double-edged sword, providing meaning, helping to socialize new employees, and motivating desired behaviors, but culture can also be dangerous if it prevents managers and employees from being open to new ideas and new developments in their firms' competitive environments.

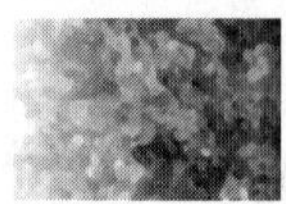

Central Issues and Problems in Organizing

When an individual sits down to play a video game, his or her commands are executed immediately and precisely. General managers, in spite of impressive job titles, high-paying salaries, and willing subordinates, face a much different situation, however. In spite of their power and prestige, even the chief executive officers of the world's largest corporations find that the most carefully designed strategies often fail to get implemented because of a variety of organizational issues and problems. Here we will review some of these issues and describe how managers can use the various components of organizational structure to resolve these problems.

Centralization versus Decentralization

One important issue that all managers confront is the appropriate degree of centralization and decentralization. The more managers centralize decision making, the more control they can exercise over their firms. Centralized decision making can facilitate rapid implementation of strategies. It can also improve coordination, and a high degree of centralization may be required in vertically integrated organizations when different business units depend on each other for raw materials, components, and services. Effective management of related diversification strategies may also require a good deal of centralization in order to ensure that economies of scale and scope are realized by the related business units.

At the same time, decentralization can have a number of advantages. Decentralization gives lower-level employees and managers more opportunities to participate in organizational decision making. Decentralized decision making can enhance their esteem and morale by making them feel as though they play important roles in their firms. Furthermore, because lower-level managers and employees are more likely to be aware of unique or special circumstances surrounding various issues, decentralization of decision making is likely to lead to better decisions. And, because lower-level employees and managers are probably the first to become aware of changes or the potential for changes in the competitive environment, decentralized decision making can improve organizational flexibility and responsiveness to environmental change.

Centralization and decentralization thus have both advantages and disadvantages, and the appropriate degree of centralization or decentralization will be determined by firms' unique missions and needs. The various hierarchical structures that have been described here vary significantly in terms of their centralization and decentralization with functional structures being the most centralized and the cross-functional teams found in most matrix structures quite decentralized from top management. The degree of centralization can vary considerably inside any type of structure, however. For example, even in relatively decentralized multidivisional structures in which division managers are given a good deal of responsibility and control over their units' activities, accounting, finance, and treasury operations and decision making are almost always centralized in the corporation's headquarters.

Communication and Language Problems

It is interesting to consider that an organization with eight hierarchical levels and a span of control of eight individuals per manager — not unreasonable assumptions — would have the theoretical capacity to employ 16,777,216 individuals! Yet, even the largest corporations rarely have more than a few hundred thousand employees. And, though it is certainly conceivable that organizations could have very tall hierarchies with a dozen or more levels of superior-subordinate reporting relationships, it is rare for even the largest business organizations to have more than eight hierarchical levels. What explains the difference between "theoretical capacity" and the actual size of today's largest corporations, and why do organizations rarely have more than eight hierarchical levels?

Although several factors limit the size of organizations, the most important limiting factor is communication. All modern organizations suffer language and other communication problems; research suggests that these problems intensify as organizational size and diversity increase. An excellent illustration of these organizational communication problems is provided by the children's game of "telephone" in which one child in one corner of a room relays a message to the next child who relays the message to the next child and so on until a much-distorted message reaches the last child in the far corner of the room. In the children's game of telephone, the distortion of the original message will vary directly with the number of participants in the game. The same distortion occurs in organizations as information flows across hierarchical levels or from one department to another.

Researchers have long been aware of such communication problems. One organizational scholar writing in the late 1960s noted that

> a [manager] faces a world of vast scope, and therefore he must rely primarily on a formal information system to filter out "noise" and less important data and to provide an abstraction of the real world that preserves essential information about significant events.[22]

But he also acknowledged that data flowing through the organization can become so distorted that the resulting information "cannot convey what is going on in the world." As a result, managers work "in an analogue, abstract world."[23] Other researchers have made the same observation, noting that "almost all organizational structures tend to produce false images in the decision maker, and the larger . . . the organization, the better the chance that its top decision-makers will be operating in purely imaginary worlds."[24]

Nor has information technology enabled firms to overcome these limitations. According to Martin S. Davis, former chairman and chief executive officer of Paramount,

> complexity has narrowed the capacity of managers. There are limits to the information they can absorb and the operating details they can monitor. Managers can be spread so thin that they overlook areas of true opportunity. *The information age has not necessarily been accompanied by an ability to interpret and use the greater fund of information advantageously.*[25]

In most organizations, however, the problem is even more complicated than is suggested by these concerns about information distortion and data overload because business firms are political organizations. Self-interested managers will often find it expedient to alter or otherwise intentionally distort a particular communication. Harvard professor Richard Hamermesh has argued that information, and especially "bad news," moves very slowly through organizations.[26] Managers who have unfavorable information to pass along have strong incentives either to alter or to slow down this information before passing it along. The result is a loss of management control, and strategy implementation inevitably suffers.

It is probably impossible to totally alleviate organizational communication problems. Certainly no hierarchical structure is free of communication problems. In fact, the various hierarchical structures that have been described in this chapter were all developed, at least in part, to alleviate communication problems and improve organizational responsiveness. The multidivisional structure aimed to reduce the problem of top management overload that often develops in functionally organized firms, yet it has failed to completely eliminate communication problems. As a consequence, many firms have adopted matrix structures to improve communication, coordination, and information flows. Future evolutions in organizational structure will almost certainly continue to address the communication problems that are inherent in all organizations.

Conflict

Because organizational life is political, conflict is an inevitable part of all organizations. Some conflict is almost unavoidable as many business situations invite disagreements and animosities among individuals and departments. Some of these situations have already been alluded to. For example, the transfer pricing problem, found in any company in which one division produces a component or raw material or provides a service for another department, invites conflict. Functional rivalries are also often a source of conflict. Manufacturing managers often claim that engineers design products that are difficult to build or assemble, while engineers often feel as though manufacturing managers lack appreciation for the "elegance" of their product designs. Sales and marketing personnel will often conclude that accounting or finance departments prevent them from selling products or services by keeping prices high, while accounting and finance personnel often claim that sales and marketing departments are trying to "give away" their companies' products or services.

Considerable evidence suggests that an emphasis on "superordinate goals" (i.e., goals that are more important to all organizational members than their individual or group goals) can do much to reduce conflict among employees, departments, and business units. Superordinate goals can have powerful motivational impacts on employees.[27] Compensation systems can also be designed to motivate employees and managers to work to achieve overall organizational objectives rather than their own parochial interests.

At the same time, it's important to emphasize that conflict is not entirely negative. If conflict brings out different opinions and leads to a greater exploration of strategic options, it can be very beneficial for organizations. In fact, organizations without any conflict or disagreements are likely to be particularly vulnerable to the forces of environmental change because they may lack ideas for how change should be addressed.

SUBORDINATION OF OWNERS' AND MANAGERS' INTERESTS AND PROBLEMS OF MOTIVATION

A related problem is referred to as the "agency problem" — the tendency for the interests of principals (owners) and their agents (managers) to diverge.[28] The same agency problems exist within organizations between top managers and their subordinates, and no organizational structure, however carefully designed, can completely alleviate these agency and motivation problems.

In fact, problems of agency afflict all organizations at multiple levels: At the senior management level, for example, the objective of maximizing shareholder wealth will often take a back seat to other objectives that may be more aligned with the interests of managers and employees. At lower levels, many employees are extremely conscientious and often willing to do the work of several of their more average performing colleagues, but other employees are shirkers who will gladly let their more ambitious colleagues take up the slack. Furthermore, employees will naturally work harder on those initiatives to which they are more committed and on those that they see as serving their own best interests.

One way to think about agency and motivation problems is to contrast the behaviors of renters and homeowners. As students or young professionals, many of you have had the experience of renting apartments. As renters, you are essentially "agents" renting from a "principal" — it is not *your* apartment, you simply live there, and you have few incentives to take extra care of the apartment or engage in preventive maintenance. Many renters care for an apartment only enough to be able to get back their security deposits. Once you become a homeowner, however, you become a "principal." The home or apartment that you have bought is now your own property, you have a vested interested in its condition and maintenance, and you will probably be much more motivated to care for it and to engage in remodeling and preventive maintenance activities.

Obviously, one way for organizations to wrestle with the motivation problem is to develop in their employees a sense of ownership. This can be done in many ways. For example, Chapter 6 suggested that effective business definitions can have powerful motivational impacts on employees if they "buy in" or become committed to their organizations' definitions. As with conflict, motivational problems can also be addressed by designing compensation systems that reward the achievement of superordinate organizational goals. Nearly all companies now have compensation plans that award bonuses to top managers for meeting organizational goals and objectives. A few progressive firms even have companywide bonus plans so that all employees reap rewards when the firm meets key objectives. A strong organizational culture can also foster a high level of employee motivation and morale.

As already noted, these issues and problems are an inevitable part of organizational life. We've already suggested some ways in which the various components of structure can be used to deal with these issues and problems. Multidivisional structures are necessarily more decentralized than functional structures, and we've already noted that one of the key advantages of the multidivisional structure is its ability to improve decision making in large and diversified companies. Matrix structures can further decentralize decision making to product teams. Matrix structures also provide excellent forums for conflicting points of view to be heard and addressed in an effective manner. Personnel and compensation policies can do much to align employee interests with the superordinate goals and objectives of their firms. Similarly, effective organizational cultures can be highly motivational and can often minimize the need for more elaborate hierarchical structures.

Top managers' mental models — their beliefs and understandings about how to organize and implement strategy — determine how they combine the various structural components of hierarchy, standard operating procedures and policies, information systems, and culture into effective organizational structures. Unfortunately, many managers fail to give adequate attention to structural issues and questions, preferring instead to focus their attention and energy on the formulation of strategy. As a consequence, many very good strategies never live up to their potential but become "unrealized strategies" because of ineffective implementation.

Emerging Issues and New Types of Organizational Structure

This final section considers how the changing nature of work, demands for information, and emerging human resource management issues are encouraging the development of new organizational structures.

The Changing Nature of Work

The rapid rate of technological change, especially the rapid pace of developments in information technology, is having a profound impact on the nature of work in most industries. As noted in the introductory chapter, products and services are becoming increasingly knowledge intensive. This shift toward more knowledge-intensive products and services has placed important new demands on workers. As the study *Workforce 2000*, prepared by the Hudson Institute, suggests, these transformations in the economy will require a more educated and knowledgeable workforce. The study estimates that by the year 2000, "a majority of all new jobs will require post-secondary education."[29]

Even more profound than these changing educational requirements, however, are the changes that are occurring in the nature of work itself. Few workers are important today for their physical labor or physical skills. Instead, workers are becoming important for the knowledge and expertise they possess. Here's how one participant at a conference sponsored by the late Commerce Secretary Ron Brown and former Labor Secretary Robert Reich described this transformation in the nature of work:

> [W]e began to realize that when we looked at the social and technical changes that needed to take place in the work force and the workplace ... that the real technology was in people's heads.
>
> The real cutting edge competitive piece to this was not the hardware that sat in front of them [i.e., employees] or necessarily the social systems that were around them. It was the knowledge in workers' heads. That is the competitive edge.[30]

As noted earlier in the chapter, the traditional aim of structure has been to organize work — physical work — in order to implement strategies effectively. Employees were organized into functional departments so they could specialize and become increasingly proficient at their tasks. Today, however, few tasks allow employees the luxury of working in isolation, unaware of what other employees in other parts of the organization are doing. Organizational structure takes on added importance because of this changing nature of work. Even in manufacturing companies, employees are becoming less and less important for their physical labor. As in the service sector, nearly all manufacturing employees are now "knowledge workers," important not for their physical labor but for their expertise and know-how. These shifts imply that we will see major changes in human resource management and new types of organizational structures in the years ahead.

Human resource management issues

As a consequence of the changing nature of work, companies need to focus more effort and energy on how jobs are designed, how work is organized, and how knowledge will be accumulated, stored, and shared with other employees as well as with customers and suppliers. In other words, companies will need to place a new emphasis on human resource management issues and policies, which often get short shrift.

The management of knowledge workers requires a radical rethinking of traditional organizational structures. At present, we know very little about the management of knowledge workers in any industry. The traditional, functional division of labor approach may enhance efficiency, but an unintended consequence of this approach is the "dumbing down" of work so that it becomes a repetitious, thoughtless, and mind-numbing exercise. One industry observer has argued that the problem with many traditional assembly line jobs is not the time lost as workers pass parts from one workstation to the next or the high incidence of costly repetitive stress injuries; instead, the problem is that employees "doing the same task repeatedly twenty-five hundred times a day cannot think, record data, study, teach, learn, maintain, improve, and otherwise perform as a world-class work force."[31]

A better approach is to organize work in such a way that employees become managers of their own processes, that they take responsibility for developing their knowledge and skills, and that they have opportunities for sharing their knowledge and skills with other employees, customers, and suppliers.[32] And, it is important that we retain knowledge workers because they "become about three times more productive after ten years with the same employer than when they started work," and their "knowledge is key to keeping customers — whose longevity is the source of repeat sales and referrals."[33]

New types of structures

We are also likely to see the emergence of new types of organizational structures that meet the information needs of the new work. Certainly we can expect that the trend toward the use of more cross-functional teams and matrix structures will continue. As discussed in the preceding two chapters, the managers of many firms have evaluated their value chains and concluded that many activities that their firms have traditionally performed have not contributed to competitive advantage, and they have now begun to contract with suppliers for these activities. It is conceivable, in fact, that many organizations could be radically restructured so that nearly all the activities they now perform could be supplied by outside vendors.

The resulting *virtual* or *modular* organizations focus on the one or few activities that are critical to their success while outsourcing nearly all other functional activities. Companies like Nike and Liz Claiborne operate in this way. As discussed in Chapter 8, Nike designs and markets footwear, but outsources all its production needs, leaving the company free to focus on those activities — marketing and product design — that provide it with its competitive advantage. Similarly, Liz Claiborne designs clothing lines, but, like Nike, Liz Claiborne contracts with other companies to produce its apparel products. Retail department and specialty stores sell the merchandise of both companies.

While Nike and Liz Claiborne are perhaps extreme examples, we see many organizations contracting out for services that have traditionally been handled in-house by functional departments. For example, Xerox has recently contracted with EDS to manage all its data-processing operations. Chapter 8 described how both Sara Lee and Gibson Greetings are now contracting for the manufacture of all their products. Future changes in technology and business practices will only continue to push organizations toward greater outsourcing. Organizational boundaries will become more fluid as firms rethink which activities and functions must be performed "inside the organization" and which activities can be outsourced to other firms.

Many observers have criticized organizations that have outsourced manufacturing and other activities, arguing that these firms are "hollowing" themselves and that they risk losing control of critical functions. Others have argued just the opposite, however. Dartmouth professor James Brian Quinn is one of the leading advocates of restructuring efforts that allow firms to focus attention on critical activities while outsourcing many less critical activities. In his defense of outsourcing, Quinn argues that:

- Intellectual and service activities now occupy the critical spots in most companies' value chains — regardless of whether the company is in the service or manufacturing sector—and if companies are not "best in world" at these critical intellectual and service activities, then they are sacrificing competitive advantage by performing those activities internally or with their existing levels of expertise.
- Each company should focus its strategic investments and management attention on those capabilities and processes — usually intellectual or service activities — where it can achieve and maintain "best in world" status.
- The specialized capabilities and efficiency of outside service suppliers have so changed industry boundaries and supplier capabilities that they have substantially diminished the desirability of much vertical integration, and, strategically approached, outsourcing does not "hollow out" a corporation, but it can decrease internal bureaucracies, flatten organizations, and give companies a heightened strategic focus, vastly improving their competitive responsiveness.[34]

In other words, companies must focus on those value-chain activities that are critical to their success, while the efficiency and quality of outside vendors allows companies to outsource their less central activities.

Peter Drucker has concluded that the virtual corporation may well become the dominant form of organizational structure in the years ahead.[35] Drucker argues that it is not just because virtual organizations contract out less critical activities, allowing them to focus their attention and resources on those activities that are sources of competitive advantage. Drucker's more important observation is that contracting out these more peripheral activities may be a way to actually gain an additional advantage over competitors who keep these activities inside the organizational hierarchy. Drucker reasons that when employees are involved in an activity that is not central to the success of an organization (such as sorting the mail, janitorial work, manufacturing of components), they have only limited promotion opportunities and will therefore suffer from low morale and low job performance. By contracting out these peripheral activities, however, employees working for those contract organizations will have greater opportunities for advancement and will therefore have higher morale and be more effective in performing the duties and responsibilities of their jobs.

These radical changes in the nature of work, new human resource practices, and the introduction of new organizational forms cannot help but have a major impact on the careers of individuals now entering the workforce. An entry level job as a computer programmer for a major firm might appear to offer a secure future, but what if that company contracts with Andersen Consulting, EDS, IBM, or Unisys to manage these operations? When evaluating a firm's offer of employment, it will become increasingly important to consider the extent to which that position and department contributes to the overall competitive advantage of the firm.

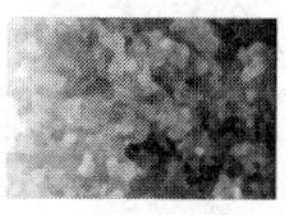

Conclusions

The optimal organizational structure for any firm involves balancing many different components of structure and dealing with a number of complex topics and issues, such as conflict, employee motivation, the appropriate degree of centralization and decentralization, and communication and language problems. In making important decisions about organizational structure, managers must weigh many considerations, but well-designed structures are essential if strategies are to be effectively implemented and if organizations are to be responsive to changes in the competitive environment.

Organizing and organizations will continue because they provide the necessary context and continuity that knowledge workers require in order to function effectively. In short, organizational structures convert the creativity and expertise of knowledge workers into desired firm outcomes.[36] Yet, we know very little about how firms foster individual and organizational learning or what can be done to improve their ability to exploit this learning. One of the Big Three automobile companies recently undertook a study of its product development efforts and found that it had learned very little from its past mistakes and successes; every new vehicle development effort was essentially starting at zero, and the same mistakes were being committed over and over again with each new vehicle. On the other hand, a small coffee shop in Colorado Springs asks every employee, before punching out, to write comments in a running log about what went right or wrong; likewise, before they can begin working, arriving employees must read all comments that have been added since their last shift. These two examples are anecdotal, but the extremes they illustrate suggest the pressing need for thinking and research on organizational learning.

As the intellectual or knowledge component of work continues to increase, managers will place ever greater pressure on their firms' structures to acquire and disseminate information and knowledge and to facilitate individual and organizational learning.[37] In addition, firms will continue to rethink their value chains as discussed in Chapter 8. This will almost surely lead to more and more companies focusing on key value-adding activities that can be sources of competitive advantage, while contracting with other firms to perform less critical functions. Finally, because yesterday's source of competitive advantage — whether it be an effective business definition, a low-cost manufacturing capability, or a strong organizational culture — can quickly become tomorrow's competitive *disadvantage*, managers and their firms must become even more responsive to changes in their competitive environments.

Key Points

- Organizational structure includes *the mechanisms that facilitate the formulation and implementation of strategy and the overall coordination of the business enterprise.*
- The objectives of structure are to implement strategies and to make organizations responsive to their owners (shareholders), managers, and the competitive environment.
- Structure includes hierarchical reporting relationships, formal organizational control systems, flows of information, and organizational culture.
- Three traditional types of hierarchical structure are the functional, multidivisional, and matrix forms, each having some advantages as well as disadvantages and limitations.
- Though less visible than hierarchical structures, organizational control systems, flows of information, and organizational culture are other important components of organizational structure.
- Any structure will face a number of issues and problems, including communication and motivational problems, control loss, and the danger that owners' interests will be subordinated to managers' interests. Effective organizational structures can mitigate, but not completely eliminate, these problems.
- The competitive environment and the changing nature of work will lead companies to adopt new human resource management practices and to develop new structures, including virtual forms of organization.

Review and Discussion Questions

1. *What are the primary purposes of organizational structures? What are the various components of organizational structure?*
2. *Distinguish between functional, multidivisional, and matrix hierarchical structures, and describe the advantages and limitations associated with each.*
3. *Assess the importance of standard operating procedures and information systems in the successful implementation of strategies.*

4. *Identify some of the central issues and problems managers face in organizing. What implications do these issues and problems suggest about the appropriate characteristics or features of firms' structures?*
5. *What are some emerging factors or issues that are affecting organizational structures and leading to new types of structures? In the future, how will organizational structures differ from those found in most organizations today?*

Suggestions for Further Reading

Barney, J. B. 1986. Organizational culture: Can it be a source of sustained competitive advantage? *Academy of Management Review,* 11: 656–665.

Chandler, A. D., Jr., 1962. *Strategy and Structure: Chapters in the History of the Industrial Enterprise.* Cambridge, MA: MIT Press.

Quinn, J. B. 1992. *Intelligent Enterprise: A Knowledge and Service Based Paradigm for Industry.* New York: Free Press.

Williamson, O. E. 1975. *Markets and Hierarchies: Analysis and Antitrust Implications.* New York: Free Press.

Endnotes

1. Chandler, A. D., Jr., 1962. *Strategy and Structure: Chapters in the History of the Industrial Enterprise.* Cambridge, Mass: MIT Press, p. 19.
2. Chandler, A. D., Jr.,1965. *The Railroads: The Nation's First Big Business.* New York: Harcourt, Brace.
3. Ibid., p. 97.
4. Weber, M. 1947. *The Theory of Social and Economic Organization.* New York: Free Press.
5. Williamson, O. E. 1975. *Markets and Hierarchies: Analysis and Antitrust Implications.* New York: Free Press.
6. Ibid.
7. Chandler, *Strategy and Structure.*
8. Chandler, *Strategy and Structure;* R. P. Rumelt, 1974. *Strategy, Structure and Economic Performance.* Cambridge, Mass: Harvard University Press.
9. Williamson, *Markets and Hierarchies,* pp. 147, 148, emphasis in original.
10. Blumenstein, R. 1997. Tough driving: Struggle to remake the Malibu says a lot about remaking GM. *The Wall Street Journal,* March 27, A1, A8.
11. Wasserman, M. E. 1998. *Examining the Relationship between Research and Development Resource Flows and Knowledge-Based Capabilities: Integrating Resource-Based and Organizational Learning Theory.* Unpublished doctoral dissertation, Michigan State University.
12. Davis, S. M., and P. R. Lawrence, 1978. Problems of matrix organizations. *Harvard Business Review* 56(3):131–142.
13. White, R. 1979. *The Dexter Corporation.* Boston: HBS Case Services, Harvard Business School.
14. Ibid., p. 11.
15. Ibid., p. 12.
16. McCartney, S. 1997. Ticket shock: Business fares increase even as leisure travel keeps getting cheaper. *The Wall Street Journal,* November 3, A1, A10.
17. Ibid., p. A10.
18. Barney, J. B. 1986. Organizational culture: Can it be a source of sustained competitive advantage? *Academy of Management Review* 11: 656–665.
19. DePree, M. 1989. *Leadership Is an Art.* New York: Dell Publishing, pp. 82, 108.
20. Etzioni, A. 1965. Organizational control structure. In *Handbook of Organizations,* edited by J. G. March. Chicago: Rand McNally.
21. Katz, D. R. 1987. *The Big Store: Inside the Crisis and Revolution at Sears.* New York: Viking, p. 41.

22. Emery, J. C. 1969. *Organizational Planning and Control Systems: Theory and Technology*. New York: Macmillan.
23. Ibid., p. 114.
24. Boulding, K. R. 1966. The economics of knowledge and the knowledge of economics. *American Economic Review* 56(2): 8.
25. Davis, M. S. 1985. Two plus two doesn't equal five. *Fortune* 112(13):177, 179 emphasis added.
26. Hamermesh, R. G. 1977. Responding to divisional profit crises. *Harvard Business Review* 55(2):124–130.
27. Kramer, R. M. 1991. Intergroup relations and organizational dilemmas: The role of categorization processes. In *Research in Organizational Behavior*, edited by B. Staw and L. Cummings 13:191–228. Greenwich, Conn: JAI Press.
28. Berle, A. A., and G. C. Means, 1932. *The Modern Corporation and Private Property*. New York: Macmillan.
29. *Workforce 2000: Work and Workers for the Twenty-first Century*. 1987. Indianapolis: Hudson Institute. p. xxvii.
30. Kevin P. Boyle, quoted in U.S. Department of Commerce, and U.S. Department of Labor. 1993. *The Work Place of the Future*. Washington, D.C.: U.S. Government Printing Office.
31. Schonberger, R. J. 1996. *World Class Manufacturing: The Next Decade*. New York: Free Press.
32. Senge, P. M. 1990. *The Fifth Discipline: The Art and Practice of the Learning Organization*. New York: Doubleday/Currency.
33. Ibid., p. 213.
34. Quinn, J. B. 1992. *Intelligent Enterprise: A Knowledge and Service-Based Paradigm for Industry*. New York: Free Press, pp. 32–33.
35. Drucker, P. F. 1989. Sell the mailroom. *The Wall Street Journal*, July 25, A16.
36. Drucker, P. F. 1994. The age of social transformation. *Atlantic Monthly*, November, 53–80.
37. Senge, *The Fifth Discipline.*

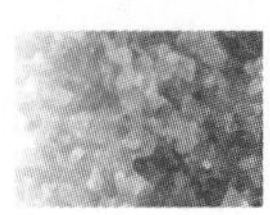

CHAPTER 11

ORGANIZATIONAL RESPONSIVENESS: THE ROLE OF BOARD GOVERNANCE AND STRATEGIC PLANNING

CHAPTER OBJECTIVES

Chapter 10 emphasized that one important function of organizational structure is to make the organization responsive to changes in its larger environment. Throughout, the text has emphasized the dynamic nature of business environments and argued that firms must anticipate or quickly respond to changes in their industries if they are to remain viable. The last two chapters of this text focus specifically on the challenges of organizational responsiveness and the management of strategic change. This chapter begins this study by considering the role of boards of directors and the effectiveness of strategic planning processes, while Chapter 12 focuses on the difficult process of managing strategic change.

This chapter has several objectives. Its specific goals are to:

- Describe the composition, purposes, and limitations of boards of directors.
- Analyze and assess the board of directors as a strategic management mechanism.
- Describe strategic planning processes.
- Evaluate the strengths, limitations, and overall effectiveness of strategic planning processes.
- Describe some alternatives to traditional strategic planning processes.
- Briefly describe the corporate governance and strategic planning practices employed by European and Japanese firms.

INTRODUCTION

This chapter considers two important strategic management "mechanisms": boards of directors and strategic planning processes. Boards of directors are an essential component of all corporations. State laws that govern the issue of corporate charters require corporations to elect boards of directors. Furthermore, all business organizations, even small business organizations, should engage in some type of planning processes if for no other reason than to ensure that sufficient cash will always be on hand to pay employees and suppliers.

To begin our study of boards of directors and strategic planning processes, consider the following questions:

- With so many experienced executives, often CEOs of major companies, sitting on boards of directors, why do some firms still become misaligned with their competitive environments and experience poor performance and even failure?
- Even though nearly all companies employ some sort of strategic planning process, many companies are surprised by changes in their industry environments. Why aren't strategic planning processes more effective at making organizations responsive to their competitive environments?

This chapter seeks to answer these questions by assessing the merits as well as the limitations of boards of directors and strategic planning processes. This chapter argues that boards of directors and strategic planning processes are quite often less than effective, and are certainly no substitute for the leadership provided by general managers. The chapter examines many of the limitations of boards of directors and strategic planning processes and also considers some ways in which the effectiveness of both mechanisms might be improved. The chapter begins with a discussion of boards of directors. Strategic planning processes are taken up in the second half of the chapter.

Boards of Directors

All publicly held corporations are required by state laws to have boards of directors in order to represent their shareholder owners. Yet boards tend to meet fairly infrequently, perhaps only once each quarter. Even then, much of the work of boards of directors is carried out in standing committees. Typically, most boards of directors have an executive committee that works closely with their companies' top managers, an audit committee responsible for fiduciary oversight of the company, a compensation committee responsible for establishing compensation plans aimed at promoting the maximum performance from top managers, and a nominating committee responsible for selecting candidates to serve on the board of directors. Companies' board members, their affiliations, and board committee assignments are almost always identified in the last few pages of their annual reports as well as in official documents, such as companies' 10K reports, that they are required to file with the Securities and Exchange Commission. For example, Exhibit 11.1 lists the members of the boards of directors of Gap, Inc., and Nike, showing their affiliations and their committee assignments, taken from the most recent annual report available on each company's Web site (www.gap.com and www.nike.com).

Insiders, Outsiders, and the Current Interest in Board Governance

During the past several years, researchers and major institutional investors (such as insurance companies, mutual funds, and pension funds) have begun to focus more attention on the composition of boards of directors. Of particular interest to academic

EXHIBIT 11.1

The Boards of Directors of Gap and Nike

company
gap
gapkids
store locator
advertising
GAP
financial information
company home
our community
community relations
environmental principles
employment
careers in our stores
careers at our headquarters
university recruiting
company benefits
financial information
annual report
current stock price
SEC filings
quarterly earnings reports
monthly sales report
investor faq
frequently asked questions
about this site
about the company in general
about the stores
about the clothes
about sourcing
about advertising
investor information
The Gap, Inc. 1996 Annual Report
Directors
Adrian D. P. Bellamy (b,c)
Chairman of the Gucci Group N.V.; Director of The Body Shop International PLC; and Paragon Trade Brands, Inc. Director since 1995.
John G. Bowes (b,c)
Former Chairman of Kransco Group Companies. Director since 1974.
Millard S. Drexler
President and Chief Executive Officer of the Company; and Director of Williams-Sonoma, Inc. Director since 1983.
Donald G. Fisher (c)
Chairman and founder of the Company; Director of The Charles Schwab Corporation; and AirTouch Communications. Director since 1969.
Doris F. Fisher
Merchandising consultant and founder of the Company. Director since 1969.
Robert J. Fisher
Chief Operating Officer of the Company; and Director of Sun Microsystems, Inc. Director since 1990.
Lucie J. Fjeldstad (b,c)
President of Video and Networking, Tektronix, Inc.; Formerly President of Fjeldstad International; Vice President and General Manager of Multimedia, IBM; Director of Keycorp, Entergy; and Bolt Beranek & Newman. Director since 1995.
William A. Hasler (a,c) Dean, Haas Graduate School of Business, University of California, Berkeley; Formerly Vice Chairman of KPMG Peat Marwick; Director of Tenera Inc.; Aphton, Inc.; Walker Interactive Systems Inc.; and TCSI. Director since 1991.
John M. Lillie (b,c)
Former Chairman and Chief Executive Officer of American President Companies, Ltd.; Director of Vons Companies; Consolidated Freightways, Inc.; The Harper Group, Inc.; and Walker Interactive Systems Inc. Director since 1992.
Charles R. Schwab (a,c)
Chairman and Chief Executive Officer of The Charles Schwab Corporation; Director of Transamerica Corporation; AirTouch Communications; and Siebel Systems, Inc. Director since 1986.
Brooks Walker, Jr. (a,c)
General Partner of Walker Investors; Director of Pope & Talbot, Inc.; and AT&T Capital Corporation. Director since 1972.
(a) Audit and Finance Committee
(b) Compensation and Stock Option Committee
(c) Corporate Governance Committee
previous
index
next

CONTINUED

EXHIBIT 11.1 *CONTINUED*

William J. Bowerman
Deputy Chairman of the Board of Directors
Eugene, Oregon

Thomas E. Clarke (1)
President and Chief Operating Officer, NIKE, Inc.
Beaverton, Oregon

Jill K. Conway (4) (5)
Visiting Scholar
Massachusetts Institute of Technology
Boston, Massachusetts

Ralph D. DeNunzio (3) (4)
President, Harbor Point Associates, Inc., private investment and consulting firm
New York, New York

Richard K. Donahue
Vice Chairman of the Board
Lowell, Massachusetts

Delbert J. Hayes (2) (3)
Newberg, Oregon

Douglas G. Houser (2)
Assistant Secretary, NIKE, Inc.
Partner—Bullivant, Houser, Bailey, Pendergrass & Hoffman, Attorneys
Portland, Oregon

John E. Jaqua (4)
Secretary, NIKE, Inc.
Partner—Jaqua & Wheatley, P.C., Attorneys
Eugene, Oregon

Philip H. Knight (1)
Chairman of the Board and Chief Executive Officer, NIKE, Inc.
Beaverton, Oregon

Kenichi Ohmae
Former Chairman of the Board
McKinsey & Company
Tokyo, Japan

Charles W. Robinson (3)
President, Robinson & Associates venture capital
Santa Fe, New Mexico

A. Michael Spence (2)
Dean, Graduate School of Business
Stanford University
Palo Alto, California
Lowell, Massachusetts

John R. Thompson, Jr. (4)
Head Basketball Coach
Georgetown University
Washington, D.C.

(1) Member — Executive Committee (2) Member — Audit Committee
(3) Member — Finance Committee (4) Member — Personnel Committee
(5) Member — Compensation Plan Subcommittee

SOURCE: Data on board membership and commettee assignments provided by Web sites for Gap and Nike.

researchers and institutional investors alike is the ratio of *insiders* to *outsiders* serving on boards of directors. Outsiders are defined as directors who are not current or former members of the top management team, their associates, or family members, and are not employees of the firm or its subsidiaries. As can be seen by a review of the affiliations of the directors of Gap and Nike, the outside members of the boards of large organizations are most often chief executive officers or other top officers of other corporations, but directors are also often lawyers or representatives of not-for-profit or other public interest organizations. Insiders, on the other hand, are defined as directors who are current or former managers, their associates, or employees of the firm. Chief executive officers are almost always members of their companies' boards of directors, and CEOs also frequently serve as chair of the board.

For the last several decades, conventional wisdom has held that boards should be controlled by outside directors. Since the 1930s, academic scholars have argued that the interests of owners (shareholders) and the interests of managers are likely to diverge.[1] According to these arguments, shareholders are primarily interested in maximizing their returns from their investment in the stocks of particular firms, while managers are more interested in maintaining employment and maximizing their compensation. It is easy to see that the aims of shareholder owners (so-called "principals") might come into conflict with the aims of managers (who serve as the "agents" of the shareholder owners). Thus, this potential divergence in interests is called the *agency problem*, and agency theory — a body of academic literature that focuses on agency issues and questions — suggests that boards of directors with a majority of outsiders will do a better job of representing and protecting the interests of shareholder owners than will a board controlled by a majority of company insiders.

Chapter 1 highlighted the growing importance of institutional investors, which now account for over half of all equity ownership in the United States. They have used their growing clout and influence to pressure companies to maintain high levels of performance, but also to alter the composition of their boards of directors. Nearly all institutional investors and other shareholder groups have subscribed to the view that companies' boards should be dominated by a majority of outsiders, and a few institutional investors — including TIAA-CREF, one of the largest pension funds in the country — have even gone on record insisting that a company must have a majority of outside directors before they will invest in the company's shares.

The California Public Employees' Retirement System (Calpers), the largest public employees' pension fund in the United States with $113 billion in assets, has recently issued a set of guidelines for an "ideal" board of directors.[2] Included in these guidelines are recommendations that (1) boards should be composed of a majority of outside directors, (2) the chairman of the board should be an outside director, (3) former CEOs should not serve as members of their companies' boards of directors, and (4) directors should receive only cash or stock as compensation for their services and should not receive other benefits, such as retirement plans. Many investor groups have also suggested that boards should have directors who are women and racial minorities in order to encourage diversity and to better represent the larger society.

Though the agency perspective is widely embraced, research studies examining board composition and firm performance have failed to document a consistent relationship between composition (usually defined as ratios of inside or outside directors to the total number of directors) and firm performance. Although some studies seem to support the conventional wisdom, finding a positive relationship between firm performance and the percentage of *outside directors* on boards of directors, other studies find positive relationships between firm performance and the percentage of *inside directors!* Many other empirical studies have found no significant correlation between board composition, however defined, and firm performance.

Two factors may be responsible for this lack of consistency in empirical research studies examining the relationship between board composition and firm performance. One explanation is that the agency perspective is too simplistic and not complex enough to deal adequately with a subject as complicated as the relationship between boards of directors and firm performance. The second explanation is that all boards, regardless of their composition, face certain limitations or hurdles that hinder effective decision making. The next two sections consider both of these explanations.

Limitations of the Agency Perspective

In spite of some well-publicized abuses in which managers have clearly put their own interests ahead of their firms' shareholder owners,[3] agency arguments are undermined by at least two limitations. First, agency theory assumes that all managers aim to advance their own interests at the expense of those of shareholders. Yet, it is clearly possible that many top executives are actually motivated to be diligent and effective stewards of their shareholders' interests. Agency theory arguments simply do not consider the possibility that managerial self-interest seeking might vary considerably across any sample of managers.[4]

Furthermore, among large corporations, the vast majority of corporate boards has been dominated by outsiders since the 1930s. The chart shown in Exhibit 11.2 clearly shows that the overwhelming majority of corporate directors are outsiders and that the proportion of outsiders on boards continues to increase. Thus, the emphasis that institutional investors have placed on board composition is focused on a very small number of companies that still have a majority of insiders.

Exhibit 11.2

The Historical Dominance of Outside Directors on the Boards of Directors of Large Corporations

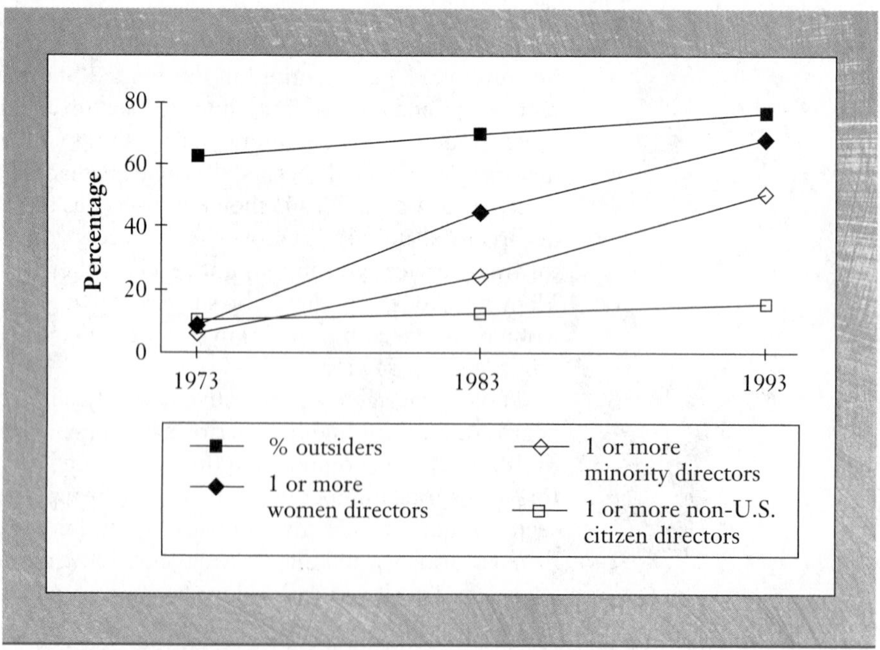

Note: Figures for non-U.S. directors are for 1972 and 1989.

Source: Michael Useem, *Investor Capitalism: How Money Managers Are Changing the Face of Corporate America* (New York: Basic Books, 1996).

Finally, agency theory arguments also fail to consider the possibility that inside directors might bring important or even critical expertise to board deliberations. For example, in evaluating risky investment projects or considering long-term strategy, outside directors may have few insights that are helpful in assessing different options, while the knowledge and expertise of insiders might be particularly valuable. Some empirical research suggests that this argument has merit. For example, one study used agency theory arguments to hypothesize that companies with boards composed of a higher percentage of outside directors would spend more on research and development because their boards would be more inclined to support speculative projects that might increase returns to shareholders. In fact, the study found just the opposite — that boards with a higher proportion of inside directors were associated with higher levels of R&D spending.[5]

Limitations of Boards of Directors

Another reason for the lack of consistent findings across studies that have examined the relationship between board composition and firm performance is that, regardless of their composition, boards face a number of structural constraints and other drawbacks that limit their ability to formulate and implement strategy effectively. These limitations of boards of directors include:

- *Board meetings that do not provide a forum for effective strategic management.* The boards of directors of most major corporations meet only rarely. Even the most active boards tend to hold fewer than eight meetings a year. Those meetings that are held are unlikely to promote substantive discussions about companies' affairs. Martin Lipton, a leading corporate attorney, and Jay Lorsch, a professor at the Harvard Business School, make these observations about the nature of board meetings:

  > Even with committee meetings and informal gatherings before or after the formal board meeting, directors rarely spend as much as a working day together in and around each meeting. Further, in many boardrooms too much of this limited time is occupied with reports from management and various formalities. In essence, the limited time outside directors have together is not used in a meaningful exchange of ideas among themselves or with management/inside directors.[6]

  Thus, it appears that the aim of most board meetings is to keep directors informed of company activities rather than to engage them in meaningful discussions of competitive environments or to involve them in any serious way in the strategy formulation and implementation processes.
- *Furthermore, most board members have too many competing responsibilities to have the time necessary for any meaningful leadership role.* As already noted, many board members are important executives — typically CEOs — of other companies, and their other, usually primary, duties simply prevent them from devoting much time to their board member responsibilities.
- *Moreover, even if they had the time, most outside board members lack expertise about their companies or the industries in which their companies compete.* Directors who do not have business experience are especially handicapped by their lack of intimate knowledge or expertise about their companies and their companies' industries and competitors. In addition, directors typically must rely on their

companies' chief executive officers to provide them with data and other information.

- *Finally, research suggests that board members are typically chosen for "who they are" and not for "what they know."* Individuals tend to be nominated to serve on boards of directors because they are friends or acquaintances of company executives or other directors, and not because the company needs some particular expertise or set of skills.

These limitations suggest that boards may have difficulty doing anything more than simply following the lead of their companies' CEOs. In fact, most research studies support such a "rubber stamp" perspective: In a survey of banking industry CEOs, one researcher found that only 2 percent of the CEOs considered their boards of directors "critical" to the success of their firms. Another researcher conducted extensive interviews with directors and concluded that they are little more than "ornaments on a corporate Christmas tree" — that they are not extensively involved in strategy formulation, that they do not typically ask important or discerning questions of management, and that they are seldom extensively involved in recruiting top managers.[8] Furthermore, this researcher concluded that boards have only a very limited array of strategic options. One of these is the drastic step of firing or removing the chief executive officer, but the study noted that this step is rarely done proactively, and tends to occur only "when results deteriorate to an almost fatal point."[9]

A number of well-publicized business failures also point to directors who were "blind" to serious business problems that preceded bankruptcy or firm failure.[10] In their analysis of and attempt to understand the causes behind the failure of the Penn Central (at the time, the largest bankruptcy ever), Daughen and Binzel concluded that the company's directors had

> sat around the big polished table as representatives of the railroad's stockholders, whose interests they were supposed to protect. But in most cases all they did was sit. With few exceptions, they appeared to be blind to the onrushing events that sent the Penn Central hurtling off the tracks.[11]

More recent anecdotal evidence also supports the view that boards rarely intervene to manage strategy in an overt way except in crisis situations.[12] Even then, as one study concluded, board involvement seems limited to replacing the chief executive officer.[13] Over the last several years, the boards of many well-known companies, including American Express, Kodak, IBM, Apple, and General Motors, have all fired their CEOs. In each case, the board took this drastic action only after the company had suffered a severe decline in financial or operating performance and institutional investors had demanded changes.

THE ROLE OF BOARDS OF DIRECTORS IN STRATEGY FORMULATION AND IMPLEMENTATION

Given the lack of strong research evidence about a direct link between board composition and firm performance and the apparent support for a "rubber stamp" perspective, is there no role for the board of directors in the strategic management of business firms? To address this question, consider four short case studies that provide illustrations of boards of directors in action.

Sears, Roebuck and Co. By the late 1980s and early 1990s, Sears was in trouble. Its corporate strategy of creating a one-stop retailing powerhouse offering everything from financial, insurance, and real estate services to power tools and clothing was not working. The profitability of the company's merchandise retail unit had declined dramatically and Sears lost market share to both Kmart and Wal-Mart. The company's board of directors finally took action to address these problems but it took a major event with potentially very serious financial consequences — Moody's decision to review and possibly downgrade its ratings on Sears' debt — for the board to recognize that it needed to become more involved in strategy formulation.[14] Even then, it took the board many months to reach its decision to de-diversify or break up Sears' retail and financial services businesses.

Though it did take Moody's decision to review Sears' debt to force the company's board to act, this case does illustrate some positive aspects of the board's role in strategy formulation and implementation. First, the board *did* act. Though it may not have been particularly proactive, the board did act before the company's problems reached crisis proportions. Furthermore, the diversification strategy that Sears had been pursuing had been developed over many years; any moves to undo such a long-standing strategy *should* probably require a good deal of careful deliberation.

General Motors. In his classic autobiography, *My Years with General Motors*, Alfred Sloan offers his thoughts on the functions of a company's board of directors. One paragraph in Sloan's book describes both the information that is provided to GM directors as well as how the company's directors could use this information to assist them in their strategic management role:

> [T]he General Motors board receives a comprehensive picture of the enterprise and its operations. Reports from its Executive and Finance committees are presented monthly, and those from other standing committees periodically, covering their actions. A visual presentation on a screen sets forth for examination every material aspect of the corporation's position, financial, statistical, and competitive, and a forecast of the immediate future. This is supported by explanatory comments and also by a summary of the general business outlook. In addition, operating officers make oral reports on the corporation's business in various areas. Also, formal presentations are made to the board regularly by various staff vice presidents and top operating executives covering developments in their fields of responsibility. Board members then ask questions and seek explanations. This audit function, as the General Motors board exercises it, is of the highest value to the enterprise and its shareholders. *I cannot conceive of any board of directors being better informed and thus able to act intelligently on all the changing facts and circumstances than is the board of General Motors.*[15]

Yet, as Exhibit 11.3 shows, General Motors' market share declined precipitously during most of the 1980s, and, during this entire decade, the board was apparently content to do nothing to stem GM's diminishing position in the automobile industry. Only when the company appeared on the verge of a financial calamity did General Motors' board finally take action.[16] In fact, the behavior of GM's board during the 1980s differs markedly from Sloan's description. The crisis situation that finally forced the board to act resulted in a decision to fire the company's chief executive officer, Robert Stempel, a fairly drastic step and one that is rarely, if ever, taken proactively.

Archer-Daniels-Midland. Finally, consider the case of Archer-Daniels-Midland, the giant grain processing company based in Decatur, Illinois. When Michael

EXHIBIT 11.3

A Decade of Decline at General Motors

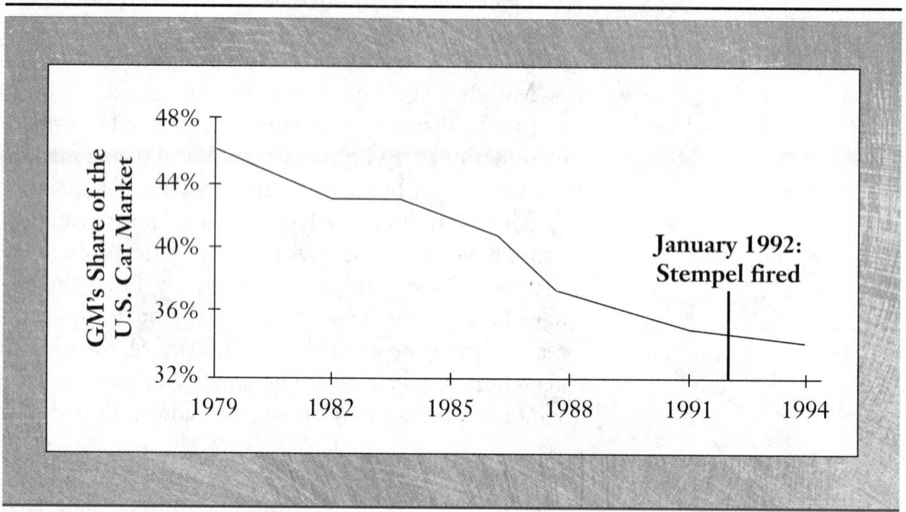

Andreas, son of the company's chairman and chief executive officer Dwayne Andreas, was alleged to have been involved in a scheme to fix prices on a number of the company's products, shareholder attention became focused on the composition of ADM's board of directors. The attention brought to light that ADM's 17-member board was loaded with inside directors. As shown in Exhibit 11.4, of the 17 members on the board, 9 were current or retired ADM executives or relatives of current ADM executives.

EXHIBIT 11.4

Members of the Board of Directors of the Archer-Daniels-Midland Company (January 1996)

Insiders	*Outsiders*
Dwayne Andreas	Gaylor Coan
Ralph Bruce	John Vanier
John Daniels	Brian Mulroney
Lowell Andreas	"Happy" Rockefeller
Martin Andreas	Glenn Webb
Michael Andreas	Ross Johnson
H. D. Hale	Ray Goldberg
James Randall	Robert Strauss
Shreve Archer	

MANAGEMENT FOCUS

Cypress Semiconductor's T. J. Rodgers Airs His Views on Corporate Governance

A seemingly innocuous letter sent by Sister Doris Gormley to T. J. Rodgers, CEO of Cypress Semiconductor, touched a raw nerve.[1] Sister Gormley, representing the Sisters of St. Francis, wrote to Mr. Rodgers, asking that he and his board consider adding women or representatives of racial minorities to Cypress's board of directors. Mr. Rodgers responded to Sister Gormley's request with a six-page letter that makes a case for choosing directors on the basis of background qualifications, knowledge, and expertise, rather than gender or racial characteristics. Sister Gormley's letter and excerpts of Mr. Rodgers's letter are reprinted here in Figure 1. ■

[1]See E. J. Pollock, "Angry Mail: CEO Takes on a Nun in a Crusade Against 'Political Correctness,'" *The Wall Street Journal,* July 15, 1996, A1, A7.

FIGURE 1

Excerpts of Letters Written by Sister Doris Gormley and T. J. Rodgers

The Wall Street Journal Interactive Edition — July 15, 1996

This is the full text of Sister Doris Gormley's letter:

The Sisters of St. Francis of Philadelphia
Our Lady of Angels Convent -- Glen Riddle
Aston, Pennsylvania 19014
(610) 558-1421

Dear Mr. Rogers:

The Sisters of St. Francis of Philadelphia, a religious congregation of approximately 1000 women, is the beneficial owner of 7000 shares of stock in Cypress Semiconductor Corporation.

We believe that a company is best represented by a Board of qualified Directors reflecting the equality of the sexes, races and ethnic groups. As women and minorities continue to move into upper level management positions of economic, educational and cultural institutions, the number of qualified Board candidates also increases. Therefore our policy is to withhold authority to vote for nominees of a Board of Directors that does not include women and minorities.

It appears from the proxy statement which does not include pictures that Cypress Semiconductor has no women or minority Directors. We have voted our proxy accordingly, and we urge you to enrich the Board by seeking qualified women and members of racial minorities as nominees.

Sincerely,

Doris Gormley, OSF
Director, Corporate Social Responsibility

continued

FIGURE 2

Excerpts of Letters Written by Sister Doris Gormley and T. J. Rodgers

Cypress

May 23, 1996

Doris Gormley, OSF
Director, Corporate Social Responsibility
The Sisters of St. Francis of Philadelphia
Our Lady of Angels Convent -- Glen Riddle
Aston, PA 19014

Dear Sister Gormley:

Thank you for your letter criticizing the lack of racial and gender diversity of Cypress Board of Directors. I received the same letter from you last year. I will reiterate the management arguments opposing your position. Then I will provide the philosophical basis behind our rejection of the operating principles espoused in your letter, which we believe to be not only unsound, but even immoral, by a definition of that term I will present.

The semiconductor business is a tough one with significant competition from the Japanese, Taiwanese, and Koreans. There have been more corporate casualties than survivors. For that reason, our Board of Directors is not a ceremonial watchdog, but a critical management function. The essential criteria for Cypress board membership are as follows:

- Experience as a CEO of an important technology company
- Direct expertise in the semiconductor business based on education and management experience
- Direct experience in the management of a company that buys from the semiconductor industry.

A search based on these criteria usually yields a male who is 50-plus years old, has a Masters degree in an engineering science, and has moved up the managerial ladder to the top spot in one or more corporations. Unfortunately, there are currently few minorities and almost no women who chose to be engineering graduate students 30 years ago. (That picture will be dramatically different in 10 years, due to the greater diversification of graduate students in the '80s.) Bluntly stated, "a woman's view" on how to run a semiconductor company does not help us, unless that woman has an advanced technological degree and expererience as a CEO. I do realize there are other industries in which the last statement does not hold true. We would quickly embrace the opportunity to include any woman or minority person who could help us as a director, because we pursue talent—and we don't care in what package that talent comes.

I believe that placing arbitrary racial or gender quotas on corporate boards is fundamentally wrong. Therefore, not only does Cypress not meet your requirements for boardroom diversification, but we are unlikely to, because it is very difficult to find qualified directors, let alone directors that also meet investors' racial and gender preferences. ...

Finally, you ought to get down from your moral high horse. Your form letter signed with a stamped signature does not allow for the possibility that a CEO could run a company morally and disagree with your position. You have voted against me and the other directors of the company, which is your right as a shareholder. But here is a synopsis of what you voted against:

- Employee ownership. Every employee of Cypress is a shareholder and every employee of Cypress—including the lowest-paid—receives new Cypress stock options every year, a policy that sets us apart even from other Silicon Valley companies.

continued

FIGURE 2 CONTINUED

- Excelllent pay. Our employees in San Jose averaged $78,744 in salary and benefits in 1995. (That figure excludes my salary and that of Cypress's vice presidents; it's what "the workers" really get.)
- A significant boost to our economy. In 1995, our company paid out $150 million to its employees. That money did a lot of good: it bought a lot of houses, cars, movie tickets, eyeglasses, and college educations.
- A flexible health-care program. A Cypress-paid health-care budget is granted to all employees to secure the health-care options they want, including medical, dental, and eye-care, as well as different life insurance policies.
- Personal computers. Cypress pays for half of home computers (up to $1,200) for all employees.
- Employee education. We pay for our employees to go back to school, and we offer dozens of internal courses.
- Paid time off. In addition to vacation and holidays, each Cypress employee can schedule paid time off for personal reasons.
- Profit sharing. Cypress shares its profits with its employees. In 1995, profit sharing added up to $5,000 per employee, given in equal shares, regardless of rank or salary. That was a 22% bonus for an employee earning $22,932 per year, the taxable salary of our lowest-paid San Jose employee.
- Charitable work. Cypress supports Silicon Valley. We support the Second Harvest Food Bank (food for the poor), the largest food bank in the United States. I was chairman of the 1993 food drive, and Cypress has won the food-giving title three years running. (Last year, we were credited with 354,131 pounds of food, or 454 pounds per employee, a record.) We also give to the Valley Medical Center, our Santa Clara-based public hospital, which accepts all patients without a "VISA check."

Those are some of the policies of the Board of Directors you voted against. I believe you should support management teams that hold our values and have the courage to put them into practice. So, that's my reply. Choosing a Board of Directors based on race and gender is a lousy way to run a company. Cypress will never do it. Furthermore, we will never be pressured into it, because bowing to well-meaning, special-interest groups is an immoral way to run a company, given all the people it would hurt. We simply cannot allow arbitrary rules to be forced on us by organizations that lack business expertise. I would rather be labeled as a person who is unkind to religious groups than as a coward who harms his employees and investors by mindlessly following high-sounding, but false, standards of right and wrong. ...

In conclusion, please consider these two points: First, Cypress is run under a set of carefully considered moral principles, which rightly include making a profit as a primary objective. Second, there is a fundamental difference between your organization's right to vote its conscience and the use of coercion by the federal government to force arbitrary "corporate responsibilities" on America's businesses and shareholders.

Cypress stands for personal and economic freedom, for free minds and free markets, a position irrevocably in opposition to the immoral attempt by coercive utopians to mandate even more government control over America's economy. With regard to our shareholders who exercise their right to vote according to a social agenda, we suggest that they reconsider whether or not their strategy will do net good—after all the real costs are considered.

Sincerely,

T. J. Rodgers
President and CEO

SOURCE: Text for both letters obtained from *The Wall Street Journal* Interactive Edition.

In response to criticisms about the composition of the ADM board, a committee composed of ADM outside directors recommended a number of reform measures that would change significantly the composition and nature of the ADM board of directors in an effort to make the board more independent of top management. Among the most significant recommendations made by the committee — all of which were aimed at giving outside directors greater control and influence over the board — were the following:

- The board should be made up of a majority of outsiders.
- The number of management (i.e., insider) directors, including the chief executive officer, should be limited to no more than three members.
- The number of board members should be reduced from 17 to between 9 and 15.
- New nonmanagement directors should be less than 70 years old.

After the release of these recommendations, eight of ADM's directors — most of whom were ADM insiders — announced that they would not stand for reelection to the board, thus greatly limiting the role of insiders on the board.[17]

What can we conclude or learn from these short case studies? Did Sears and GM suffer from low performance because of something their boards of directors did or didn't do? Certainly the boards of directors at both companies could have been more proactive in assessing their companies' performance levels, questioning their managers' plans, and monitoring the implementation of those plans. Yet in both cases, many of the problems these companies encountered can be traced to a failure on the part of their managers to understand the pace of change in their industries. Having been so successful for so long, managers at both companies found it inconceivable that their firms could be displaced from their dominant positions in their respective industries.

A similar question can be posed about the board of directors at Archer-Daniels-Midland — could the company's directors have done more to prevent the alleged price-fixing activities? This case illustrates the problems board members face in gaining access to information and their detachment from the day-to-day operating activities of the firm. Certainly, ADM's board members would not have condoned price-fixing or other illegal activities, but the board, which was heavily influenced by the company's forceful chief executive, Dwayne Andreas, and weighted down with company insiders, was unlikely to question or engage in a proactive review of the company's internal business practices.

Will the changes in board composition that have been recommended be able to prevent future illegal activities at ADM? This is a more difficult question to answer. Certainly, the attention and the current legal investigation surrounding ADM executives who have been indicted in the price-fixing case will do much to discipline other ADM managers. It's unlikely, however, that the current or any future board of directors will monitor extensively the day-to-day operating activities of ADM. The limitations of boards that have been described earlier in this chapter suggest that such extensive intervention is unlikely.

Finally, the debate between Sister Doris Gormley and Cypress Semiconductor's CEO, T. J. Rodgers, suggests another view of boards of directors — a view that calls into question much of the past research that has documented a "rubber stamp" role for boards of directors. Mr. Rodgers's response to Sister Gormley indicates that he believes that directors have a very important role to play in strategy formulation and implementation, so much so that directors *must* be selected on the basis of expertise rather than to achieve demographic heterogeneity.

These short case studies offer no consistent assessment of the role of boards of directors in the strategy formulation and implementation processes. As already noted, empirical studies that have examined the relationship between board composition and firm performance levels offer no definitive evidence to support control by insiders or outsiders. Moreover, recommendations for board reform, like those suggested by the committee of ADM's outside directors, seem quite reasonable, but given the many structural limitations that board members face (i.e., many competing duties and responsibilities, board meetings that do not provide a forum for strategy formulation and implementation, lack of expertise, etc.), it is difficult to believe that these recommendations will either improve company performance or prevent illegal activities.

A recent study by professors John Core, Robert Holthausen, and David Larcker of the Wharton School at the University of Pennsylvania found six characteristics of boards of directors that are associated with lower levels of firm performance.[18] According to the study, companies had poorer stock market performance if:

- the chairman of the board and the chief executive officer are the same person,
- the board of directors is large,
- the chief executive officer appoints or nominates outside directors,
- outside directors have business dealings with the company,
- outside directors are age 70 or older, and
- outside directors serve on many other boards.

Again, though, one must question whether altering any of these characteristics would really improve the internal functioning of boards of directors by involving directors more seriously in the formulation and implementation of strategies or by making them more proactive in questioning the strategies and performance outcomes of their companies.

Perhaps the one safe conclusion that can be drawn from these short case studies and this chapter's discussion of boards of directors is that board governance is an issue or a problem *because internal governance by top managers appears to be a problem.*[19] Perhaps Cypress Semiconductor's T. J. Rodgers is aware of how difficult it is for his top management team to forecast the future of their company's fast-changing industry. This may explain why he is so adamant about having a board composed of experts who can help his management team understand future trends and proactively formulate strategies. The case studies also suggest that boards have had to intervene in such an overt way precisely because company managers often fail to maintain high levels of performance or prevent other top managers from engaging in illegal activities. *These case studies suggest that if top managers could be more proactive in anticipating and responding to environmental change or company shortcomings, then their boards of directors would have less cause for intervention.*

These case studies also suggest that few boards of directors are prepared to challenge the bureaucratic management cultures that seem to dominate many companies. Improving responsiveness to environmental change and opportunities appears to be one of the most important challenges confronting companies operating in today's fast-changing competitive environments, yet companies approach these challenges with bureaucratic cultures and planning processes. The following quote has been attributed to Ross Perot, founder of Electronic Data Systems (acquired and then later divested by General Motors) and a former GM board member:

> We taught EDS employees that when they see a snake, they should shoot it. GM employees are taught that when they see a snake, they should form a committee to study the snake.

One product of a bureaucratic management culture is a belief in the usefulness of strategic planning processes. Implicit in such a view is that important events can be anticipated, that plans can be developed to meet almost any circumstance, and that these plans can be implemented fairly easily. The remainder of this chapter focuses on the strengths and limitations of these planning processes.

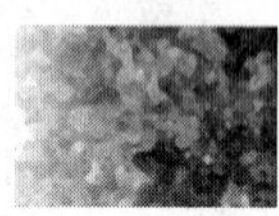

Strategic Planning Processes

We now turn to strategic planning processes. All organizations of any size must plan, and planning tends to be done on many levels, from the development of overarching five- and ten-year strategic plans for the entire firm to the handling of daily cash receipts and disbursements, which is necessary to ensure that sufficient cash is always available to meet a firm's current liabilities and other obligations. The focus of this section is on strategic planning processes. The section first considers the value of strategic planning. It then considers some of the factors that explain why planning efforts often fall short of expectations. Finally, some new approaches that show promise in improving the effectiveness of planning efforts are reviewed.

Advantages of Strategic Planning

First, consider the advantages that strategic planning should provide: Strategic planning should allow firms to determine what needs to be done *now* to maximize *future* performance. In the planning process, today's management problems and today's business performance should be irrelevant. The aim of planning should be to stop putting out today's fires (at least for a while) and focus on what the firm should be doing to maximize its performance in the future. Strategic planning should also provide opportunities for managers to question the basic assumptions underlying their firms' strategies. Take, for example, the case of Sears: Strategic planning should have forced the company's top managers to recognize some of the fundamental changes that had been occurring in the retailing industry over the last two decades *before* the company's merchandising operations began experiencing serious performance problems.

Limitations or Problems Associated with Strategic Planning

Yet, in spite of these advantages and the need for all organizations to engage in some sort of planning and coordination activities, the effectiveness of strategic planning processes tends to be limited by a number of factors. These include the following limitations:

- *Planning often fails to acknowledge the emerging nature of much strategic activity.*[20] As described in Chapter 1, the strategy formulation and implementation processes do not occur in isolation, but must contend with emerging events in firms' external industry environments. Unfortunately, nearly all traditional planning processes tend to assume away the possibility of unanticipated events

EXHIBIT 11.5

Forecasting Procedures Used in the Planning Processes of Many Companies

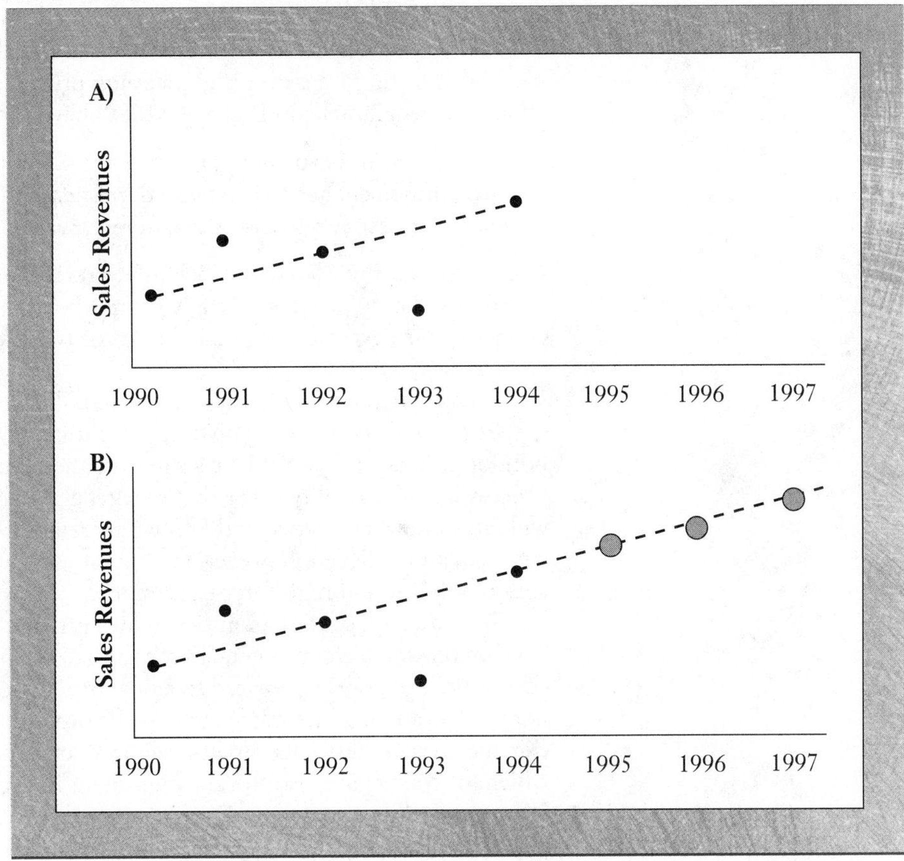

emerging in firms' external environments, such as the development of new technologies, the introduction of new products or services, and the emergence of new competitors. As a result, most planning processes leave firms poorly prepared to cope with emerging events.

- *Too often planning relies on regression-based forecasting procedures that merely extend present trends into the future*. As a consequence, plans get "locked in" and actually reduce the flexibility of strategic thinking; instead of questioning basic assumptions, planning actually reinforces current thinking.

To show how such forecasting procedures actually lock in current strategies, Exhibit 11.5 offers a simplified illustration of the kind of forecasting procedures employed by many companies. Let's assume that a company wants to forecast future sales revenues for a particular product line for the next three years. As shown in part A of the exhibit, typical forecasting procedures use regression to explain *past* sales revenue levels. As suggested in part B of the exhibit, the next step in forecasting future sales revenue levels is to extend this regression line into the future. Unfortunately, such procedures typically ignore or assume away the possibility of any changes in the external industry environment that might impact on company revenues.

This illustration of forecasting procedures helps to explain how companies like GM and Sears, which have long employed sophisticated planning processes, can enter periods of decline. Instead of recognizing how drastically their respective business environments had changed and taking new courses of action, their managers' outdated views were actually reinforced by their companies' reliance on forecasting and planning processes that "locked in" outmoded strategies. As Hamel and Prahalad (1989) have noted:

> Although strategic planning is billed as a way of becoming more future oriented, most managers, when pressed, will admit that their strategic plans reveal more about today's problems than tomorrow's opportunities.[21]

Because of their tendency to "lock in" or reinforce outdated strategies, traditional forecasting processes simply cannot be used for planning purposes when companies are experiencing major shifts or turbulence in their industry environments.

- *The strategic planning process typically produces "point estimates" rather than a range of possible outcomes.* More sophisticated forecasting procedures typically produce both optimistic and pessimistic scenarios, and all participants in any planning process would probably agree that the "true" forecast of future business activity will fall somewhere between these two extremes. What gets printed, distributed, and believed, however, are "point estimates" — often simply the averages of the low and high forecast numbers.

  The drawback of these point estimates is that all too often firms fail to develop reasonable contingencies for the low or high forecasts. As a result, companies are poorly prepared to adjust production, marketing, and even financial strategies when demand exceeds or falls short of expectations. (Finance researchers have already begun to criticize the use of point estimates, which, of course, are also the key ingredient in capital budgeting analyses.)
- *Plans often suffer from a phenomenon that Senge calls "eroding goals."* Ambitious plans should motivate companies and their employees to "work harder" to achieve challenging goals. But all too often, companies find it convenient or expedient to lower their goals when they find their plans too ambitious or challenging. Thus, organizational goals and objectives, much like personal goals and objectives, can slowly erode over time so that what was considered unacceptable performance at an earlier point can slowly become seen as satisfactory.[22]

  Exhibit 11.6 illustrates this tendency toward "goal erosion." Part A of the exhibit illustrates how gaps between goals and current performance levels should increase pressure and encourage efforts to achieve goals. All too often, however, the disparity between goals and current performance levels actually results in pressures to lower or scale back ambitious goals, as illustrated in part B of the exhibit. Thus, it is not enough to set ambitious goals; companies must also pursue those goals with unwavering vigilance.

  IBM has long had a stated goal or objective of achieving a return on equity of 20 percent; over the last decade, however, its investors have often had to be content if the company merely returned a profit. Wal-Mart's investors became quite addicted to the company's ability to generate double-digit increases in same-store sales revenues year after year. When, during the last couple of years, Wal-Mart's sales growth slipped into single-digit (though still impressive) rates of growth, the company's stock price languished; and investors have been unimpressed as the company's top managers have explained that it was unrealistic for investors to expect

FIGURE 11.6

Goal Attainment versus Eroding Goals

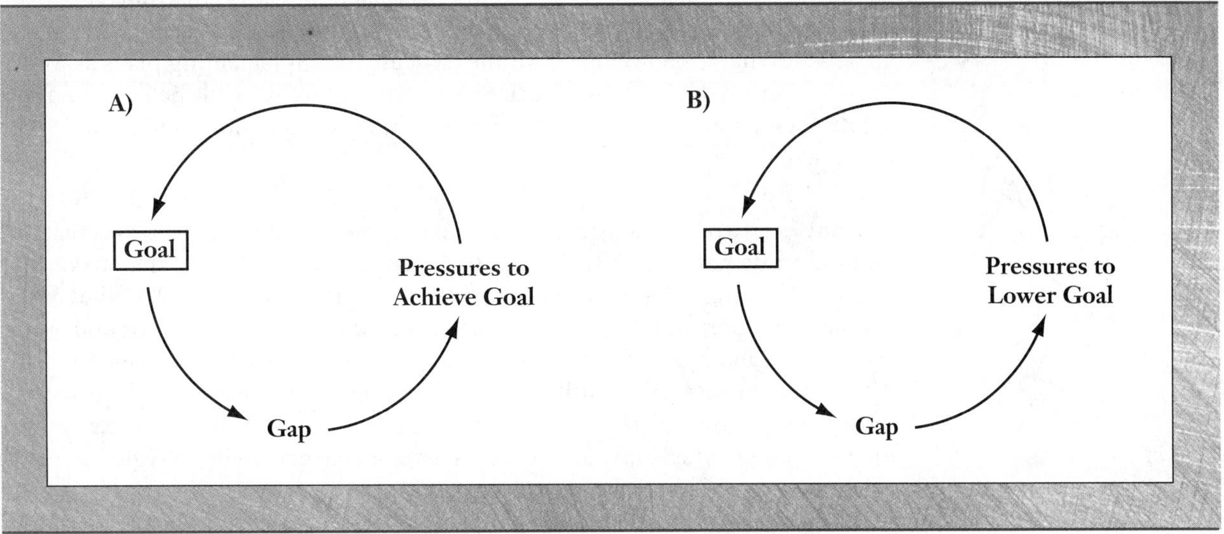

that double-digit sales growth would continue indefinitely.[23] Both of these company examples illustrate that to be effective, goals and objectives must be rigidly adhered to and not allowed to erode.

- *Planning data are often used — incorrectly — for evaluating the performance of management personnel.* Incentive bonuses are often awarded to executives for "meeting the plan." This creates serious disincentives for incorporating challenging goals or objectives in the planning process. If an executive is going to be evaluated on meeting the plan, he or she is much more likely to offer modest, "sure bet" estimates of likely future performance rather than suggesting challenging, "stretch" goals. Such built-in structural disincentives only reinforce other factors that contribute to the conservative, risk-averse character of most large business organizations.
- Finally, *for all the time and other resources required by formal planning processes, it is unclear that planning has any impact on firm performance.* Strategic planning processes in most firms tend to be very bureaucratic, and few of the executives who participate in annual strategic planning processes find them a useful or even relevant exercise. As a result, critics have charged that:

> Most corporate planning is like a ritual rain dance: it has no effect on the weather that follows, but it makes those who engage in it feel that they are in control. Most discussions of ... planning are directed at improving the dancing, not the weather.[24]

More recently, a larger number of business executives and scholars have concluded that traditional strategic planning doesn't work. William Starbuck, a management professor at New York University, has observed that "companies are no longer doing strategic planning. This is the inevitable consequence of engaging in an activity which has no consequences." And, in a 1990 *Fortune* magazine article, traditional strategic planning processes were characterized as "overly bureaucratic, absurdly quantitative, and largely irrelevant."[25]

NEW APPROACHES TO PLANNING

Recognizing that nearly all organizations of any size must plan but also acknowledging that traditional approaches to strategic planning are less than effective, managers have shifted their attention to alternative approaches to strategic planning—approaches that acknowledge both the difficulty of implementing plans as well as the emergent nature of much strategic activity. Here we will focus on two new approaches that have generated much recent interest, scenario planning, and vision or "strategic intent."

Scenario planning. Unlike traditional strategic planning processes that rely on forecasting procedures that extend past trends into the future, the objective of scenario planning is for managers to develop several different but plausible scenarios for their companies.[26] Each scenario is based on a different set of underlying assumptions about the future, and each suggests a different set of strategies or plans. Although managers might still "bet" on the particular scenario they believe to be most plausible, scenario planning encourages managers to "hedge their bets" in order to preserve flexibility and to be prepared to change their strategies quickly if events deem another scenario more appropriate.

The advantages of scenario planning are obvious. Instead of putting an unwarranted faith in the "point estimates" that emerge from traditional strategic planning processes, executives participating in a process of formulating possible future scenarios are forced to acknowledge the likelihood of many possible outcomes. Furthermore, because the development of different scenarios also requires managers to formulate different sets of plans and strategies, managers are forced to consider a much broader array of strategic alternatives. Thus, managers are much less likely to develop a strong psychological commitment to a single course of action.

Vision or strategic intent. Another newer approach to planning has been proposed not only as an addition to traditional strategic planning processes, but also as a reaction to the reengineering dogma of the last decade. This approach emphasizes the importance of commitment to a company vision or set of enduring core values.[27] Management consultants Hamel and Prahalad have coined the term "strategic intent" to refer to goals or destinies that represent significant leaps for organizations, achievable only after five or ten years or even longer.[28] Advocates of an emphasis on vision or strategic intent claim that a clearly articulated and widely held vision or destiny can be very motivational for company employees who are likely to find traditional strategic plans too abstract or meaningless.

Vision or strategic intent represents something far more tangible than the hyperbole contained in most organizations' mission statements. Hamel and Prahalad tell this story, which illustrates the meaninglessness of most corporate mission statements:

> Recently one of us made a presentation to the top 15 officers of a large multinational company. We showed them their company's mission statement. No one demurred; yes, that looked like their mission statement. Only what was there on the screen was actually the mission statement of their major competitor!
>
> What value is a mission statement, we asked, if it is totally undifferentiated? What chance does it offer to stake out a unique and defensible position in an already overcrowded market?

Hamel and Prahalad answer their own questions, noting that "it's not surprising that when a company's mission is largely undifferentiated from that of its competitors, employees may be less than inspired."[29] Collins and Porras also argue that more concrete and tangible company visions give employees meaning and are much more motivational than a set of financial goals or an undifferentiated mission statement.[30]

Furthermore, advocates suggest that a vision, far from limiting a company or slowing its responsiveness to changing industry environments, can actually help companies deal more effectively with rapid industry change. According to this argument, by focusing company efforts on the pursuit of an enduring set of core values, the managers of firms with strategic intent or powerful visions of their firms' futures will have a much better idea of how to deal with emergent issues. It's not that a powerful vision reduces the amount of emergent activity or the number of emergent issues confronting managers. Rather, a powerful vision will help company managers know how to deal with or respond to emergent activity or which emergent activity to "select into."

Here is a comment from a chief executive of a major U.S. automotive components company that relies on a strong and widely held company vision to guide its decision making and strategic activities. This passage illustrates how a widely held vision can be of significant help to companies as they deal with a variety of strategic issues:

> I just spent five hours in here this morning with ... the guy who runs the ride control [business] in the U.S. We're talking about his opportunities.... When I have significant discussions, say three or four times a year for five hours, this guy knows exactly what's in my head, I know exactly what's in his head, we don't have to have anything written down, we don't have to have any criteria, we don't have to have any policy manuals. He knows which rainbows to chase, which rainbows not to spend any time on, and it's not because I have given him an edict. It's because he's told me all the opportunities, we've discussed them, we've begun to sort them out, and he knows how fast I want to grow, how much capital is available, whether he ought to use the cash flow from this business to put in another business.
>
> This is the way you run a business and I think the management schools would say, "We don't want guys running a business by the seat of their pants." We're not running a business by the seat of our pants, but we know it so well and we've talked about it so thoroughly that when an opportunity pops up, it's yes or no. It's quick, it's easy. [The business schools would] say, "Oh that's seat of the pants; you're shooting from the hip." That's the farthest thing from the truth.[31]

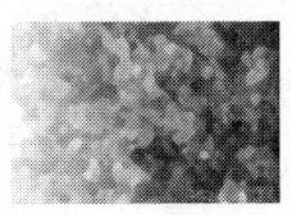

Conclusion

This chapter concludes by reviewing the questions posed at the beginning of the chapter:

- With so many experienced executives, often CEOs of major companies, sitting on boards of directors, why do some firms still experience such poor performance?
- Even though nearly all companies employ some sort of strategic planning process, many companies are surprised by changes in their industry environments. Why aren't strategic planning processes more effective, and what is so difficult about formulating and implementing strategic plans?

MANAGEMENT FOCUS

Corporate Governance and Strategic Planning in European and Japanese Companies

It is instructive to consider some of the corporate governance and strategic planning practices of companies operating in international contexts. An interest in board governance in England has mirrored recent shareholder activism in the United States. As in the United States, much of this interest has focused on the composition of boards of directors. A report of the so-called Cadbury Committee, published in 1992, detailed a "Code of Best Practice," which suggested several recommendations, including the need for boards to meet regularly, for boards to be composed of a majority of independent (outside) directors, for all directors to be appointed for specified and limited terms and for directors to have free access to company information.[1]

Firms in Germany have long been governed under a system of shared governance — "*Mitbestimmung*" or *codetermination* — in which a company's managers and its workers elect an equal number of directors. Although such an arrangement has worked well for German companies for many decades, it now appears that this approach has limited the ability of German companies to respond to growing competitive pressures from foreign companies. In particular, German companies have been unable to lay off workers or otherwise improve the efficiency of their operations.[2] As a result, investment in Germany, even investment by German companies, has lagged and economic growth has slowed. This slow growth and its accompanying high levels of unemployment have now become important economic and social issues in Germany (as well as in many countries throughout the European continent), which may create pressures for changing existing corporate governance practices.

Japanese corporate governance and strategic planning practices also provide a number of contrasts. It is frequently noted that banks, as both creditors and shareholders, play a much larger role in the capitalization or financing of most Japanese corporations. Some researchers have hypothesized that this makes Japanese corporations less susceptible to pressures for short-term financial performance than their U.S. competitors, and it is widely believed that Japanese corporations are freer to pursue longer-run strategies of market penetration and market share growth and have more discretion in allocating resources to research and development and to expansion projects.

In addition, Japanese corporations not only tend to "promote from within" but also appear to emphasize functional experience and expertise in operations or production as promotion criteria. This emphasis on operating, production, and technical experience may have its roots in a long-standing Japanese fear of "capitalistic industry." Summarized many years ago by Japanese industrialist Okochi Masatoshi, the primary defect of Western "capitalistic industry" is that it

> controls industrial management and authority. Not only does science come under this control as well, but managers do not recognize its value nor do they succeed in understanding it because they lack the knowledge. Most engineers ... combine science with jobs in industry, so one would expect them to have constant contact with the latest scientific developments. Yet they are no more than employees, and, however often they suggest innovations, managers who do not understand them cannot judge the merits of these proposals. Or, even if managers more or less understand a proposal, their first concern is how much money it will cost. Then they usually try to postpone a decision until they have accumulated more profits. The primary defect of capitalistic industry is that businessmen lack this understanding but still control managerial authority in industry.[3]

It also appears that, although Japanese corporations make use of traditional strategic planning processes, Japanese executives are more reluctant than managers in the United States to accept "point estimates." The flatter, more horizontal organizational

continued

structures that characterize most Japanese corporations may promote greater communication and discussion about possible future scenarios and more consideration of alternative strategies. In his comparison of Japanese and U.S. capital budgeting practices, James Hodder found that

> Japanese firms generally appear to be much less "numbers driven"... Japanese firms have done a better job of focusing attention on critical input assumptions including possible scenarios and management responses. They seem to place enormous emphasis on involving all managers even remotely connected with a project in the proposal generation and evaluation process. This tends to head off problems resulting from different parts of the firm operating with differing sets of expectations. It may also be that verbal discussions of complex issues (such as estimating future demand or production costs) are superior to written memos and formal projections.[4] ■

[1]The full text of the report of the Cadbury Committee appears in *International Corporate Governance* by Robert Tricker (New York: Prentice Hall, 1994).

[2]See, for example, G. Steinmetz, "German Firms Falter in Struggle to Regain Competitive Edge," *The Wall Street Journal*, June 12, 1997, A14.

[3]M. A. Cusumano, 1990. "Scientific industry": Strategy, technology, and entrepreneurship in prewar Japan. In W. D. Wray, ed., *Managing Industrial Enterprise: Cases from Japan's Prewar Experience*, Cambridge, Mass: The Council on East Asian Studies, Harvard University.

[4]J. E. Hodder, 1986. Evaluation of manufacturing investments: A comparison of U.S. and Japanese practices. *Financial Management* 15(1):22.

This chapter has suggested a number of answers to these questions. The chapter reviewed two corporate governance mechanisms — boards of directors and strategic planning processes. Although the merits of boards of directors that are composed of experienced and talented outside directors would seem to recommend the board as an important vehicle for strategy formulation and implementation, we have also seen that boards of directors are often hampered by several constraints that can limit their effectiveness. In fact, considerable evidence suggests that boards rarely intervene in strategy formulation and implementation in a proactive way. Instead, financial crises will prompt boards to act, but even then their involvement appears to be limited to removal and replacement of the chief executive officer. Though a number of proposals for board reform have been offered — all aimed at giving outside directors more authority and control over corporate governance — we conclude that board governance is primarily an issue *because of the failures or shortcomings of internal governance*. In other words, board governance tends to be problematical because top managers fail to anticipate or respond effectively to changes in their companies' external business environments. The importance of top managers and their role in strategic management is the topic we examine in the next chapter.

Similarly, we have reviewed the merits and limitations of traditional strategic planning processes. Again, the aims of strategic planning are certainly constructive. Yet, in application, traditional strategic planning processes rarely live up to expectations, and the chapter has detailed many of the reasons for their disappointing results. Not the least among the reasons for disappointment with strategic planning is the very nature of business environments. Because business environments are constantly in a state of flux, few of the most important new developments can be adequately anticipated by traditional strategic planning processes that incorporate forecasting procedures that rely so heavily on past results to anticipate future trends. Recent innovations in strategic planning focus on improving the ability of managers to anticipate future events through scenario planning. The concepts of strategic intent and vision are also being widely embraced by managers as ways to focus attention on future business environments and objectives.

Key Points

- Boards of directors and strategic planning processes are two important strategic management mechanisms.
- All public companies are required to have boards of directors. Most boards are organized into committees, including executive, audit, compensation, and nominating committees. Boards are composed of insider and outsider directors. Recent attention has focused on the composition of boards of directors, and the prevailing wisdom suggests that boards should be controlled by a majority of outside directors.
- Research finds no consistent correlation between board composition and firm performance. This may be explained by the limitations of boards of directors, which include outside directors who have little time, many competing responsibilities, and little knowledge or expertise about the companies at which they serve as directors.
- Boards of directors tend to take decisive action only when their firms are confronted by financial distress; even then, their actions are usually limited to replacing the chief executive officer.
- Board governance is problematic to a large extent because top managers *fail to respond to or anticipate* changes in their firms' competitive environments.
- Strategic planning should allow firms to question basic assumptions and select strategies to maximize future performance. In practice, however, most strategic planning processes are likely to reinforce existing assumptions and often contribute to eroding goals and expectations.
- Dissatisfaction with traditional strategic planning processes has encouraged interest in new approaches to planning, including *scenario planning* and the concepts of *strategic intent* and *vision*.

Review and Discussion Quesitons

1. *What is the primary purpose of a board of directors?*
2. *Much interest focuses on board composition, i.e., the number of outsiders relative to the number of insiders on company boards. Define board insiders and outsiders. What are the supposed advantages of having a majority of outsiders on company boards? What does research suggest about the relationship between board composition and company performance?*
3. *What are some of the limitations of boards of directors? Assess the effectiveness of boards of directors in the formulation and implementation of strategy.*
4. *What are the advantages of strategic planning? What are the limitations of strategic planning processes?*
5. *What are some of the new approaches to strategic planning being adopted by the managers of many firms? What advantages do these new approaches have over more traditional strategic planning processes?*

Suggestions for Further Reading

Berle, A. A., & Means, B. D. 1932. *The Modern Corporation and Private Property*. New York: Macmillan.

Byrne, J. A. 1996. Strategic planning: It's back! *Business Week*, August 26: 46–52.

Collins, J. C. & Porras, J. I. 1994. *Built to Last: Successful Habits of Visionary Companies*. New York: HarperBusiness.

Hamel, G., & Prahalad, C. K. 1989. Strategic intent. *Harvard Business Review*, 67(3):63–76.

Endnotes

1. Berle, A. A., and B. D. Means, 1932. *The Modern Corporation and Private Property*. New York: Macmillan.
2. Bryant, A. 1997. Calpers draws a blueprint for its concept of an ideal board. *New York Times*, June 17, C1, C9.
3. For example, *Barbarians at the Gate* by B. Burrough and J. Helyar (New York: Harper & Row, 1990), the best selling book documenting the leveraged buyout of RJR-Nabisco, describes some of the management excesses at the company; among them, so many corporate jets that the company's pilots referred to themselves as the RJR Air Force.
4. Perrow, C. 1986. *Complex Organizations*. 3rd ed. New York: Random House.
5. Baysinger, B. D., R. H. Kosnik, and T. A. Turk, 1991. Effects of board and ownership structure on corporate R&D strategy. *Academy of Management Journal* 34:205–214.
6. Lipton, M. and J. W. Lorsch, 1992. A modest proposal for improved corporate governance. *The Business Lawyer* 48(1):64.
7. Bavly, D. 1986. What is the board of directors good for? *Long Range Planning* 19:20–26.
8. Mace, M. L. 1971. *Directors: Myth and Reality*. Cambridge, Mass: Harvard University Graduate School of Business Administration.
9. Ibid., p. 41.
10. Daughen, J. R. and P. Binzel, 1971. *The Wreck of the Penn Central*. Boston: Little, Brown; P. M. Sweezy, 1972. The resurgence of financial control: Fact or fancy? In *The Dynamics of U.S. Capitalism*, edited by P. M. Sweezy and H. Magdoff. New York: Monthly Review Press.
11. Daughen and Binzel, *The Wreck of the Penn Central*, p. 17.
12. Ingrassia, P. and J. B. White, 1992. Major overhaul: Determined to change, General Motors is said to pick new chairman. *The Wall Street Journal*, October 23, A1, A6; Patterson, G. A. and F. Schwadel, 1992. Sears's decision on breakup took months to make. *The Wall Street Journal*, October 2, A3, A6.
13. Boeker, W. 1992. Power and managerial dismissal: Scapegoating at the top. *Administrative Science Quarterly* 37:400–421; W. Boeker and J. Goodstein, 1993. Performance and successor choice: The moderating effects of governance and ownership. *Academy of Management Journal* 36:172–186.
14. Patterson and Schwadel, Sears' decision on breakup took months to make.
15. Sloan, A. P., Jr., 1963. *My Years with General Motors*. New York: Doubleday/Currency, p. 188, emphasis added.
16. Ingrassia and White, Major overhaul.
17. Kilman, S. and T. M. Burton, 1996. Two more ADM directors are stepping down. *The Wall Street Journal*, September 17, B4.
18. Browning, E. S. 1997. Wharton study connects strengths and flaws of directors to companies' financial returns. *The Wall Street Journal*, April 25, C2.
19. Prahalad, C. K. 1996. *Managing Discontinuities*. Talk presented at the annual meeting of the Strategic Management Society. Phoenix.
20. Mintzberg, H. 1978. Patterns in strategy formation. *Management Science* 24:934–948.
21. Hamel, G. and C. K. Prahalad, 1989. Strategic intent. *Harvard Business Review* 67(3): 66.
22. Senge, P. M. 1990. *The Fifth Discipline: The Art and Practice of the Learning Organization*. New York: Doubleday/Currency.

23. Helliker, K. and B. Ortega, 1996. Falling profit marks end of era at Wal-Mart. *The Wall Street Journal*, January 18, B1, B11.
24. Ackoff, R. L. 1981. On the use of models in corporate planning. *Strategic Management Journal* 2:359.
25. Henkoff, R. 1990. How to plan for 1995. *Fortune*, December 31, 70.
26. Wood, W. 1997. So where do we go from here? *Across the Board*, March, 44–49.
27. Collins, J. D. and J. I. Porras, 1994. *Built to Last: Successful Habits of Visionary Companies.* New York: HarperBusiness.
28. Byrne, J. A. 1996. Strategic planning: It's back! *Business Week*, August 26, 46-52; Hamel and Prahalad, Strategic intent; G. Hamel, and C. K. Prahalad, 1994. *Competing for the Future*. Boston: Harvard Business School Press.
29. Hamel and Prahalad, *Competing for the Future*, p. 145.
30. Collins and Porras, *Built to Last.*
31. Quoted in J. L. Stimpert, 1992. *Managerial Thinking and Large Diversified Firms.* Unpublished dissertation, University of Illinois at Urbana-Champaign.

CHAPTER 12

THE MANAGEMENT OF STRATEGIC CHANGE

CHAPTER OBJECTIVES

The importance of managers anticipating and responding effectively to ever-changing business environments has been consistently emphasized throughout this text. Chapter 12 returns to this theme and examines in some detail the factors that limit the ability of managers to anticipate and respond to changes in their firms' industries. The chapter also suggests some ways in which managers and organizations might be more responsive to and even proactive in dealing with environmental changes. All these suggestions are related in some way to managerial and organizational learning, so the chapter also describes different types of organizational learning and their relationship to strategy formulation and implementation.

The specific objectives of this chapter are to:

- Review and further explore the factors that inhibit managerial responsiveness to changes in industry environments.
- Describe different types of organizational learning and their relationship to strategy formulation and implementation.
- Identify factors that influence the rate and extent of organizational learning.
- Offer some recommendations for managers and their organizations that aim to make firms more responsive, innovative, and adaptive.

INTRODUCTION

A key premise of this text is that nearly all business environments are in a state of ongoing change or disequilibrium. For example, the main point of Chapter 5 was that the various dimensions of industries are continually shifting as customer needs and wants change, as new technologies emerge, and as new products and services are introduced into the marketplace by entrepreneurial firms. Firms must either (1) stay aligned with changes in their competitive environments by responding quickly to these changes, or (2) actively anticipate changes in customer demographics, future technologies, and potential new products and services and thereby recreate their industries. One way to think about the relationship between firms and their competitive environments is illustrated in Exhibit 12.1. Recall that this exhibit was introduced in Chapter 1 as an alternative way

EXHIBIT 12.1
Model of Strategic Management

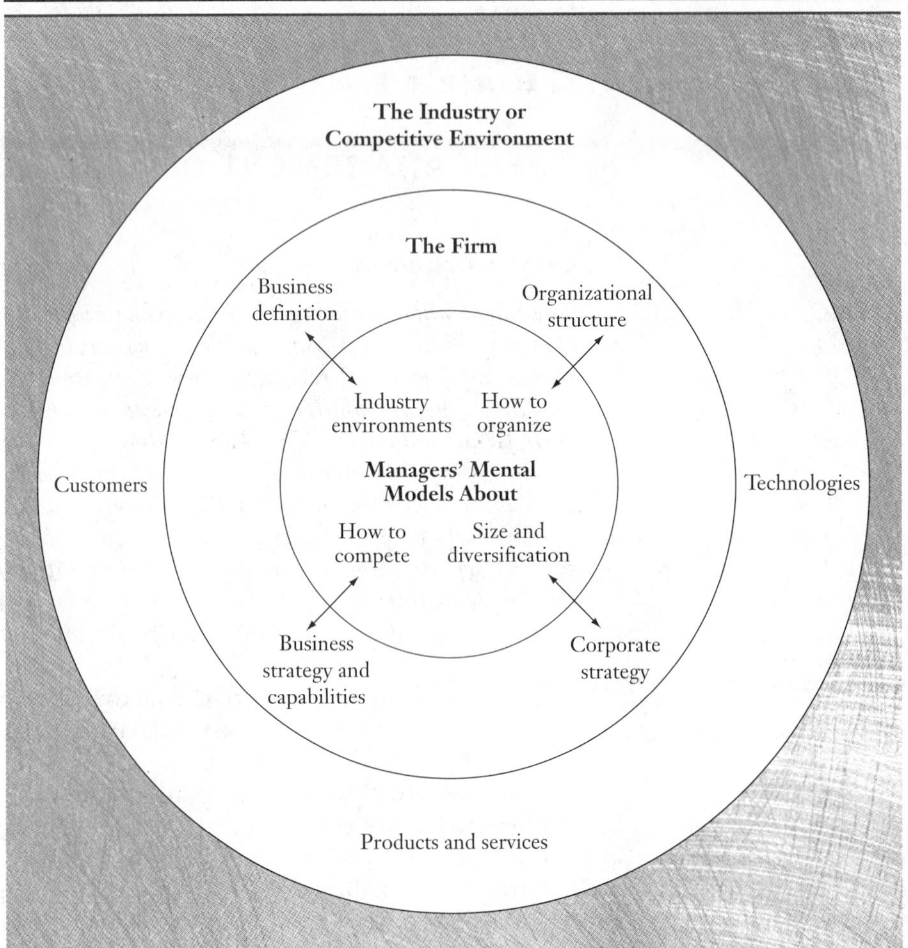

to conceptualize the model of strategic management that provides the foundation for this text. The exhibit highlights the importance of firms maintaining an alignment with their industries. Note that the arrows indicate that industry changes should elicit a response from firms *and* that firms— especially entrepreneurial firms — have opportunities to change and shape their industries as well.

The interactions between firms and their environments that are portrayed in Exhibit 12.1 do not occur frictionlessly, however. As illustrated in Exhibit 12.1, managers play a key role in this relationship between industry and firm change. Because managers' mental models influence strategic decision making, managerial thinking must anticipate or respond quickly to environmental change if their firms are to stay aligned with their industries. Yet, the text has emphasized the difficulty managers have in anticipating and recognizing changes in their business environments. Chapters 1, 2, and 5 noted that managers' mental models do not always keep pace with changes in the larger environment. As a consequence, managers of business firms are often unable to see industry changes or to appreciate fully the consequences these industry changes might have for their firms.

The price for failing to keep pace with industry changes can be devastating. In the early 1990s, IBM eliminated 180,000 jobs, chopped $1 billion from its research budget, wrote off $28 billion in restructuring charges, and watched the per share value of its stock fall from a high of over $125 in the late 1980s to less than $50 in late 1993.[1] Between 1989 and 1992, General Motors' cumulative losses exceeded $13 billion, and the company announced plans to lay off more than 100,000 employees. In addition to direct impacts on employees and shareholders, the write-offs and reductions in investment and R&D that accompany corporate restructuring efforts have far-reaching negative consequences.

The danger of falling out of step with industry changes will almost certainly increase in the future as international competition intensifies, as existing and new technologies continue to be exploited, and as shifts in consumer demographics lead to new customer needs and wants. Organizational change will, therefore, be essential to firm survival. In fact, so important is the management of change to organizational success, that the field of strategic management might more appropriately be called "strategic change management."

This chapter is divided into two main sections. The first section reviews and explores further the factors that slow managerial responsiveness to environmental change. The second section offers recommendations for how managers can overcome these factors and become more responsive to or proactive in dealing with environmental change.

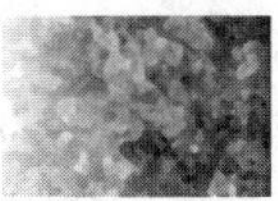

Cognitive, Organizational, and Industry Factors That Contribute to a Lack of Responsiveness

Many factors slow or limit the responsiveness of managers. This section begins by examining some of the cognitive factors that limit the ability of managers to notice, interpret, and act on environmental stimuli. It then turns to some of the organizational and industry factors that also limit the responsiveness of managers and their firms to environmental change.

Managerial Thinking and Environmental Change

The academic research literature has shown that managers can fail to anticipate or adequately respond to change for a number of reasons. First, managers can simply fail to *notice* change in their business environments. As a result, they are "blindsided" by changes that were totally unanticipated. Second, research has also shown that managers can be aware of changes in their industries, but they may fail to *interpret* these changes correctly. They may then underestimate the importance of these environmental changes, they may wait too long to respond, or they may not respond at all. Finally, research evidence has also shown that managers may correctly see or notice changes, that they may even correctly interpret the likely impact of these industry changes, but that they might still fail to adopt an appropriate course of *action*. In the next few sections, we examine in more detail each of these limitations or weaknesses associated with managerial thinking.

The problem of noticing. Two researchers, Sara Kiesler and Lee Sproull, have written about the problems of responding to environmental change and have suggested that

> [a] crucial component of managerial behavior in rapidly changing environments is problem sensing, the cognitive process of noticing and constructing meaning about environmental change so that organizations can take action.[2]

Note the implications of this statement: Noticing is crucial because if environmental changes are not noticed, action will not be taken. In many ways, the problem of noticing is similar to the "boiled frog experiment."[3] In the experiment, a frog is first placed in a pot of boiling water. As soon as the frog lands in the water, it jumps out. The frog is then placed in a pot of lukewarm water and the heat is turned on. The frog fails to notice the warming temperature, however, and ends up being boiled.

Considerable anecdotal and empirical evidence suggests that managers are like the frog — they swim along comfortably in their firms' current environments and fail to notice how their industries are changing. How is it possible that experienced and competent managers can simply fail to notice important changes in their organizations' environments? Recall from Chapter 2 that one of the key roles played by managers' mental models is to focus their attention on those aspects of the environment that are deemed important. Indeed, without this focusing characteristic of mental models, we would be overwhelmed by the incredible array of environmental stimuli that are constantly bombarding us. In fact, without this focusing function of our mental models, few if any of us would be able to live effectively in this complex world. The downside of this focusing function is that we miss much of the activity in our environments.

As a result, managers are almost certainly scanning their environments, but their mental models are likely to be focusing attention on those aspects of their firms' business environments that are deemed most salient or most important by their current mental models. Because managers are more committed to their firms' ongoing strategies than they are to noticing unrelated data and other environmental stimuli, they will "actively ignore" data that are inconsistent with those strategies.[4] Thus, changes may be occurring in their industries, but managers may simply fail to detect these changes because their attention is focused on their firms' strategies and other related aspects or features of their firms' business environments.

The problem of noticing industry changes is also compounded because these changes are unlikely to stand out or be overtly obvious to managers. Chapter 5 noted that "most strategic decisions do not present themselves to the decision maker in convenient ways; problems and opportunities in particular must be identified in streams of ambiguous, largely verbal data."[5] Other researchers have concluded that many potentially important changes go unnoticed by managers for long periods simply because they have failed to track them.[6]

Thus, most research suggests that changes must often be dramatic or have major consequences for firms before their managers will take notice of them. Noticing changes depends on those changes being seen as "breakpoints."[7] Stated another way, the changes that tend to be noticed are those changes that are significant, sudden, or catastrophic. Unfortunately, when managers and their firms are eventually blindsided by significant, sudden, or catastrophic changes in their industries, it is often too late for them to respond effectively. As a result, many of these blindsided firms go into decline and some never fully recover.

Interpretation of data. Even when managers notice changes in their industries, they may still fail to interpret correctly or appreciate fully the potential

EXHIBIT 12.2

Survivors versus Bankrupts: Return on Assets in Years Prior to Bankruptcy

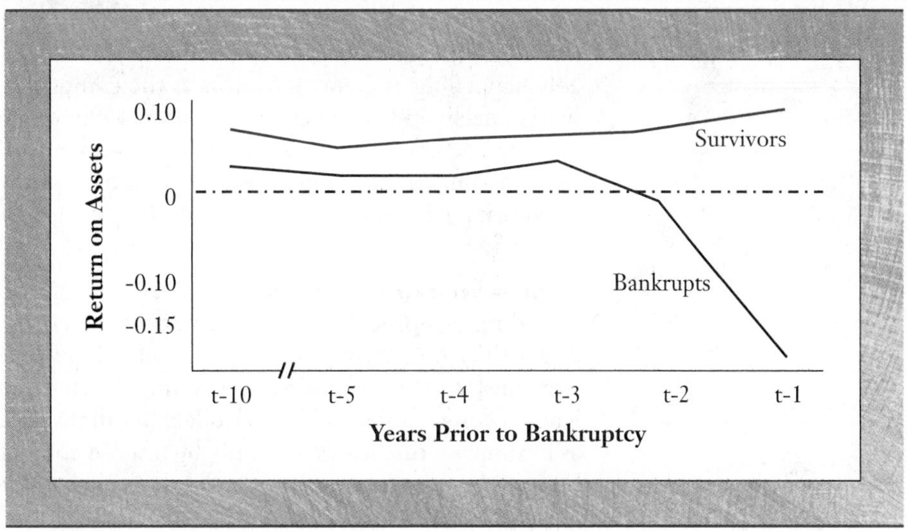

SOURCE: D. C. Hambrick and R. A. D'Aveni, "Large Corporate Failures as Downward Spirals," *Adminstrative Science Quarterly* 33:1–23.

consequences of these changes for their firms. A number of studies suggest that "seeing is not always believing." For example, a study that examined companies in the declining railroad industry during the 1950s and 1960s found that railroad managers noticed or were aware of the significant competitive threat posed by trucks and an improved national highway system by the early 1950s, yet those same managers continued to believe that government regulation, the railroad labor unions, and even the weather were more serious problems than competition from trucks.[8]

Another study compared the financial performance of matched pairs of sample firms from a variety of industries.[9] In each pair, one firm went bankrupt while the other firm survived. As illustrated in Exhibit 12.2, one of the most interesting findings of this study is that *significant performance differences between the bankrupt and survivor firms appeared as early as 10 years before the failing firms declared bankruptcy!*

Certainly the managers of the low-performing firms noticed that their firms were underperforming industry competitors, so why, given such a long lead time, were the managers of the low-performing firms unable to formulate and implement strategies that would have changed the course of their histories and avoided eventual bankruptcy? And, in the case of the railroads, why, given managers' awareness of the threats posed by trucks, did they continue to focus their attention on other factors, such as government regulation and the weather? One possible explanation for this problem of interpretation is that managers' mental models will allow them to rationalize away unfavorable stimuli. Chapter 2 emphasized the tendency for managers to give more weight to data that confirm their beliefs while discounting data that would require them to alter their mental models.

The managers of declining firms might therefore be able to overlook poor performance on one dimension (say, return on assets) if they can focus instead on some more positive dimension of performance (such as an increase in sales). In the case of the railroads, for example, decline in the railroad industry was *relative* rather than *absolute*, so railroad managers could ignore market share losses and take consolation in the fact that they were continuing to handle increasing volumes of freight in spite of increasing competition from trucks. Something similar was probably happening at General Motors as the company's share of the U.S. automobile market declined from over 50 percent in 1980 to only about one-third of the market a decade later. During most of the 1980s, General Motors enjoyed record profits, so as long as the company was earning high profits, its managers had the luxury of ignoring the consequences of its declining market share.

Limits on organizational action. Finally, even when managers are aware of and fully appreciate the seriousness of the changes that are occurring in their competitive environments, they may still fail to formulate appropriate responses or strategies to meet these threats. A company that offers a good example of this problem of taking effective action is Kodak. Recall that in Chapter 6 we described Kodak as a company threatened not only by intense competition in its photographic film business but also by important technological changes that are making digital imaging a viable alternative to traditional silver halide film technology. The available evidence suggests that Kodak's leadership is fully aware of the potential consequences of this profound technological change. Kodak's board of directors almost certainly recruited the company's current chief executive, George Fisher, from Motorola — a company at the forefront of digital technologies — because the directors knew and understood that the company needed a leader who would be familiar with digital technologies. Furthermore, since arriving at Kodak, Fisher has made it clear that Kodak's future must be in exploiting digital technologies.

Yet, Kodak has yet to score any significant "wins." Its Photo-CD and Advantix digital camera have been major product flops, and the company has failed to become recognized as a major player in the market for digital photography products. In July 1997, Kodak announced that its digital businesses, which have annual sales of $1.5 billion, had already lost more than $100 million during the first six months of the year.[10]

The managers of the Big Three automobile companies probably deserve a similar criticism for their lack of action. Since coming to a full appreciation of the threat posed by Japanese automobile manufacturers as recently as the early 1990s, all of the U.S. Big Three have adopted new strategies to improve their manufacturing processes and the quality of their product offerings. But, as noted in Chapter 3, most of the strategies they have adopted are attempts to imitate the practices of their Japanese competitors,[11] and few if any of their strategies are really new or particularly novel. As a result, though the Big Three have achieved remarkable improvements in manufacturing efficiency and product quality, they have also failed to leapfrog ahead of Toyota, Nissan, and Honda, and they are unlikely to do so at any time in the near future and certainly not until they have devised truly original strategies.[12]

IBM also illustrates the problems associated with taking action. After becoming IBM's first outsider CEO, Louis Gerstner's first objective was to simply return the company to profitability, and his strategies focused primarily on cost cutting. Only more recently, as the company has become profitable again, has attention turned to more aggressive strategies to increase sales revenues. Yet, organizational factors have slowed many of IBM's initiatives. The story of IBM's revival is still being written as this book goes to publication. How IBM's story unfolds will prove to be an interesting "real-time" case study in strategic management.

Two different types of organizational learning and the tendency for organizations to emphasize low-level learning

In addition to cognitive factors, failures in organizational learning also limit organizational adaptation and change. This book has emphasized the importance of managerial and organizational learning, but has avoided until now a detailed discussion of learning. Here, we examine one of the most important organizational learning issues, the distinction between lower-level learning and higher-level learning. Lower-level learning is characterized by improvements in or refinements of existing beliefs, understandings, and organizational processes. In contrast, higher-level learning involves developing totally new beliefs, understandings, and organizational processes.

One leading organizational scholar has distinguished between these two types of learning by describing lower-level learning as the "exploitation of the known" and higher-level learning as "exploration of the new."[13] Both types of learning are absolutely critical to organizational effectiveness. Without lower-level learning to refine and improve existing organizational processes, firms will be less likely to develop or maintain competitive advantage. Without higher-level learning and the "exploration of the new," firms can develop *competency traps* in which they become increasingly adept at routines and processes that are no longer appropriate because of changes in their environments. These organizations are vulnerable to being blindsided by new rivals, newly developed technologies, and the introduction of new products and services. Thus, both types of organizational learning are absolutely essential to maintain organizational effectiveness over the long run. Firms must get better and better at what they already do while also exploring new opportunities.

One of the best ways to depict the importance of lower-level learning is to refer to experience or learning curve effects that were introduced in Chapter 4. As illustrated in Exhibit 12.3, lower-level learning leads to refinements of existing organizational knowledge and processes that allow firms to reduce unit costs as cumulative output increases. Lower-level learning through experience effects offers companies important dividends. Problems arise, however, when companies' managers emphasize lower-level learning at the expense of higher-level learning — their firms get better and better at what they already know how to do, but run the risk of failing to develop new capabilities or being blindsided by new rivals, new products and services, and new technologies.

The railroads offer an excellent illustration of lower-level learning and the tendency for firms to fall into competency traps. During the 1950s, railroad managers realized that by increasing capital intensity (i.e., by replacing steam locomotives with more powerful diesel locomotives and by acquiring larger freight cars) they could reduce the number of employees needed to move the same quantity of freight. Their investments in capital equipment had the intended effect. Dieselization and larger freight cars allowed railroad companies to operate longer trains carrying far more freight than in the past. Because fewer trains were needed, the railroads were able to reduce the number of train crew employees. In fact, railroad employment fell from 1.2 million employees in 1950 to 780,000 employees in 1960! The railroads enjoyed great success at reducing employment levels, but fewer trains meant slower freight service at exactly the same time trucks were beginning to offer faster and more reliable service. The railroads got more efficient at doing what they had always done, but their managers missed the most important development in transportation in the twentieth century.

EXHIBIT 12.3

An Illustration of Experience Effects

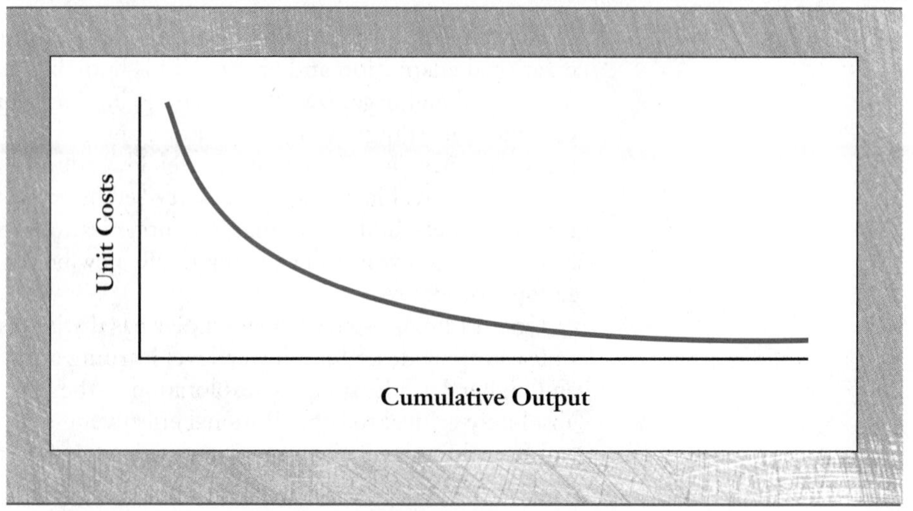

Unfortunately, most firms tend to allocate more resources to lower-level learning (the "exploitation of the known"), while failing to engage in enough higher-level learning (the "exploration of the new"). Such an allocation of resources is clearly detrimental to long-run effectiveness, but it is not surprising that managers make this trade-off. In fact, managers have good reasons to emphasize lower-level learning over higher-level learning. Lower-level learning is likely to have fairly immediate, predictable, and positive impacts on firm performance, while higher-level learning is much more speculative and much less likely to have an immediate or a positive impact on bottom-line financial performance. Furthermore, lower-level learning allows managers and their firms to continue doing more or less what they have been doing, while higher-level learning may suggest pursuing totally new and different markets and strategies. In fact, as the Kodak example suggests, the exploration of the new — in Kodak's case, attempts to incorporate digital technologies to develop new photography products — typically requires considerable investment and often results in many years of financial losses before firms see any significant benefits.

In spite of its costs and speculative nature, higher-level learning is essential to the survival of firms. What seems to be lacking is a clear understanding of the factors that contribute to or foster higher-level learning. Research evidence suggests that at least two factors influence the extent of higher-level learning:

- First, higher-level learning is most likely to result from *problemistic search*; in other words, when routine policies or procedures fail to deal effectively with organizational problems or crises, managers initiate search activity that leads to higher-level learning in order to solve these organizational problems.[14] Managers' aspirations—or their desired levels of performance—are also an important influence on the rate of organizational learning. When organizational performance fails to match high aspiration levels, managers will be more likely to engage in problemistic search activity. On the other hand, if aspiration levels are low, even low performance may not initiate problemistic search.[15] Thus, an important prerequisite of higher-level learning is for managers to have high aspiration levels and to notice problems and shortcomings in performance early on. Furthermore, managers must interpret these problems and performance shortcomings correctly so that, rather than rationalizing them away, they initiate problemistic search, which leads to higher-level learning.

The bottom-line message from research on these issues is more than a little counterintuitive: *Too much success breeds complacency and a failure to engage in higher-level learning*. One organizational researcher has summarized his findings by noting that "organizations are often poisoned by their own success" because they are "unable to unlearn obsolete knowledge in spite of strong disconfirmations." He concluded that *"shortages are useful to prevent organizations from dying from wealth."*[16]

The losses experienced by the major airlines during the early 1990s prompted many industry leaders and observers to call for a return to regulation of the industry. They viewed deregulation as a "disease" that had led to fare wars and financial losses. Yet, the disease afflicting the airline industry had less to do with deregulation, and a great deal more to do with the loss of high-paying business travelers due to massive layoffs and the introduction of information technology that supplanted the need for much business travel.[17] In fact, between the mid-1980s and the early 1990s, businesses permanently eliminated more than two million middle- and upper-level manager positions. The airline industry needed to learn how to be profitable without so many high-fare business flyers.

Although the fare wars that followed were a textbook example of the market dealing with the excess capacity in the industry, the losses that resulted gave managers tremendous incentives to learn how to scale back capacity and how to compete in this changed industry environment. Though it has taken many years, nearly all the major carriers have now learned how to be successful in this new market, and airline margins are as high as they have ever been. No managers want to see their companies lose money, but losses do provide tremendous incentives for those managers to engage in organizational learning.

- Another factor that is important to the success of higher-level learning efforts is *absorptive capacity*,[18] which has been defined as the ability of firms to "recognize the value of new information, assimilate it, and apply it to commercial ends."[19] Firms with higher levels of absorptive capacity are better able to scan their external environments, recognize the importance of significant developments, such as an emerging technology, and then assimilate that knowledge into the organization. What determines a firm's absorptive capacity? It appears as though a firm's absorptive capacity is a function of its existing knowledge base. In other words, like the old saying "it takes money to make money," the ability of an organization to recognize new developments and assimilate new knowledge is a function of its current stock of knowledge.

  Here again, we see the importance of time, which was also emphasized in Chapter 3 when examining the factors that are associated with the development of competitive advantage. The organization that spends considerable time studying a particular technology is much more likely to understand and to assess the value of new developments in that technology than a firm that has only recently become interested in that technology.

EXHIBIT 12.4

The Attraction-Selection-Attrition (A-S-A) Cycle

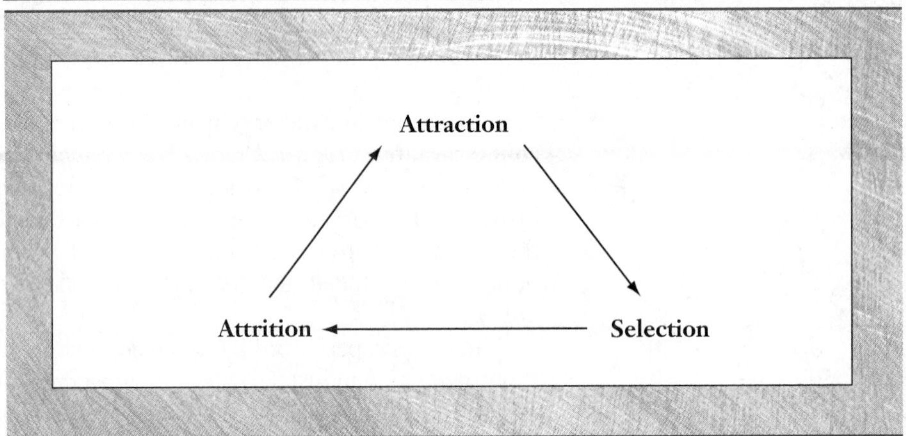

SOURCE: B. Schneider, "The People Make the Place," *Personnel Psychology* 40:437–453.

HOMOGENEITY IN MANAGERIAL THINKING

Another important organizational factor that limits managerial responsiveness to environmental change is homogeneity in managerial thinking. Many large organizations are caught in an "Attraction-Selection-Attrition" cycle (illustrated in Exhibit 12.4) that tends to promote homogeneity in managerial thinking.[20] According to this model, only certain people are attracted to particular firms. Of those attracted, companies will select, primarily on the basis of "fit," an even more limited group of individuals to join. Over time, those employees who find that they do not "fit" well with these companies will be more likely to leave. The A-S-A cycle therefore predicts that the thinking of employees within their respective companies will become more and more homogeneous over time. As a result, those managers who are promoted to top management positions are likely to think very much alike.

Although this "thinking alike" can certainly facilitate rapid decision making, it can also have very serious negative consequences for firms operating in fast-changing environments. A management team composed of like-thinking individuals is much more likely to notice important environmental changes too late or to misinterpret the nature of those changes. Organizations can overcome the dangers of like-minded thinking in at least two ways. One would be to give greater attention to "contrarian voices." Within nearly all organizations are managers and employees whose ideas are at odds with the prevailing wisdom. Often shunted aside, these individuals and their ideas tend to be ignored. Furthermore, they are the managers who Schneider would argue are most likely to "attrit," or leave their organizations. Yet, it is precisely these contrarian members who are most likely to see aspects of changing industry environments that are ignored by top managers, and they are also most likely to be able to suggest new ideas and strategies for coping with these industry changes.

A second way organizations can overcome the dangers of like-minded thinking would be to encourage greater turnover among top management ranks. Most research on turnover has focused on the negative organizational consequences (such as the loss of skilled employees and added recruiting and training costs) of turnover among lower-level employees. Far fewer studies have focused on either the positive or functional aspects of turnover among top managers. Some research evidence does suggest, however, that a lack of turnover among top managers can have a negative impact on organizations. Studies have shown that executives become more and more committed to the *status quo* as they remain in the same position, continue in employment with the same company, or stay in the same industry.[21] As a result, companies with long-tenured executives run the risk of getting "locked in" to the *status quo* and pursuing strategies that are inappropriate given changes in their industry environments.

Danny Miller, a researcher who has shown a great deal of interest in top management issues, found that firms were much more likely to be appropriately aligned with their industry environments when their CEOs had served for less than 10 years. Firms with CEOs who had served for more than 10 years tended to exhibit greater misalignment with their industry environments, and this misalignment was associated with lower levels of firm performance. Based on his findings, Miller concluded that long-serving chief executives become "stale in the saddle."[22]

Research studying the impact of employee turnover and workforce heterogeneity on organizational learning has concluded that both contribute to greater knowledge generation.[23] One important study found, for example, that the absence of turnover and workforce heterogeneity can lead to situations in which all of an organization's members become well-versed in its routines and procedures. At some point, an information equilibrium is reached, and, without new personnel, ideas for changing or improving organizational routines and procedures are not forthcoming and very little new knowledge accumulates. Failure to introduce new thinking into a closed system leads to stagnation, and an organization's capacity for change can fall below the rate of change in its environment.[24]

The value of introducing new individuals into an organization comes not from their superior knowledge; in fact, this same study asserted that organizational veterans almost always have more knowledge about their firms. Instead, the value of new individuals is the new knowledge they contribute. Newcomers may be less knowledgeable than veterans, but what they know is less redundant, is often insightful, and offers more opportunities for improving existing routines or suggesting new procedures.[25]

The decline of the railroad industry was probably due in large part to a lack of heterogeneity and turnover among top railroad managers. From 1885 through 1913, nearly 20 percent of all senior managers in railroad companies had come from other industries. By 1940, however, only about 5 percent of all senior managers had come to railroad companies from other industries.[26] One railroad industry observer has suggested that because of the tendency to promote from within,

> [o]utside inputs were often ignored or suppressed. Rather than being change seekers, the railroads attempted to accommodate the changing environment by retarding the change or accommodating the new situation with minimum change to the way business was conducted.[27]

The tendency to promote from within had also

> contributed to an attitude of suspicion of any value or idea that is generated outside the system, and, as in many closed social systems, the belief that insiders are more worthy and trustworthy than outsiders and *behavior that rejects anything "not invented here."* . . .

> This system of self-selected men of patience turned away or discouraged those whose impatient questioning and aggressiveness might have introduced a challenge to their seniors and conventional wisdom. The railroads might have profited more from men with ... *willingness to be aggressive and less patient.*[28]

THE POWER OF INDUSTRY INFLUENCES

Institutionalized industry practices can also limit organizational change. In Chapter 5, we emphasized that competition among firms in the same industry results in a good deal of imitation and industry-wide institutionalization of common business practices.[29] Firms in the same industry also develop a common language and similar understandings about how to compete. Managers of these firms develop a "common body of knowledge"[30] that is reinforced by reading the same publications, participating in professional networks and trade associations, and moving across firms.

Chapter 5 noted that these industry influences play an important, positive role in facilitating the emergence of industry standards that, in turn, encourage customer acceptance of products and services. On the other hand, Chapter 5 also described how these industry norms can "blind" managers to new opportunities and technologies, alternative bases of competition, and potential competitors. Thus, these institutional contexts in which firms compete will reinforce existing patterns of competition, and firms seeking to adopt new strategies will have to contest industry norms and influences. Firms that deviate from these industry standards — by introducing totally new products and services or by incorporating totally new technologies — face considerable upside, but also significant downside, risks. As a result, many firms choose the safer route of incremental changes in product or service offerings.

Furthermore, selecting a totally new course is rarely an obvious or a straightforward process for most established firms. Accounts of organizations struggling to formulate totally new strategies suggest that the process is a painful and highly uncertain one, characterized by periods in which organizations are "groping" or "in flux," without a clear definition or focus.[31] Again, many firms choose to remain content pursuing strategies that are consistent with industry norms rather than face the ambiguity and uncertainty associated with formulating and implementing totally new strategies.

The result, as suggested in Chapter 5, is that incumbent firms in established industries are often quite vulnerable to the "attack" of new entrants that fill unmet customer needs or wants, offer new products or services, or exploit emerging technologies. Apple's development of the personal computer, the Japanese invasion of the U.S. automobile industry, Nucor's development of minimill technology in the steel industry, and the eclipse of the railroads by trucks are just a few of the examples cited throughout this text that illustrate how vulnerable incumbent firms can be to new entrants that are motivated by ideas that lie outside industry norms and traditional patterns of competition.

This section has described four major factors that can slow the responsiveness of managers and limit their ability to anticipate environmental change. These factors include: (1) cognitive limitations and problems associated with noticing, interpreting, and responding to environmental change, (2) the tendency for managers to emphasize low-level learning over high-level learning, (3) the tendency for organizational hiring and promotion practices to foster homogeneity in managerial thinking, and (4) the power of institutionalized industry practices to focus managerial attention on the *status quo*. McDonald's illustrates well how these factors can conspire to limit responsiveness. The accompanying Managerial Focus, "McDonald's in Need of a Revival," describes how many of these factors have slowed the company's response to changes in the fast-food industry.

McDonald's in Need of a Revival[1]

As one of the largest restaurant chains in the world, McDonald's has some tremendous business strengths:

- Its 42 percent share of the burger segment of the fast-food market puts it way ahead of its major competitors, Burger King and Wendy's. In the United States alone, McDonald's serves more than 20 million people every day. In other words, nearly one in ten people in the United States eats at McDonald's daily.[2]
- In just the last 10 years, the company has opened 50 percent more stores in the United States.
- Kids love its Happy Meals.
- At the same time, McDonald's is truly an international company with one of the best-known brand names in the world, and with half of its sales and 60 percent of its profits coming from overseas restaurants.

But in spite of all these strengths, McDonald's is plagued by some significant and chronic weaknesses:

- McDonald's share of the overall fast-food market is declining due to competition from both Burger King and Wendy's as well as from non-burger fast-food chains.
- Even as the company has increased the number of its restaurants by 50 percent over the last 10 years in the United States, domestic sales have increased by only 18 percent and operating profits have grown only 2 percent during the same period. Thus, when McDonald's opens new restaurants in the United States it does not experience a net increase in business but rather takes business away from its preexisting restaurants.
- Over the last two years, as the average stock market performance of the S&P 500 grew by 63 percent, McDonald's stock price grew by a mere 3 percent. Investors buying McDonald's stock have earned less than if they had put their money in a bank savings account.
- McDonald's industry is changing. While consumers of fast food have traditionally emphasized convenience over quality and taste, recent surveys have found a major shift in consumer preferences. In one recent poll, "more than 90 percent of consumers listed both taste and quality as 'very important' factors in their choice of a restaurant, while location and speed were selected by barely half."[3]
- Quite simply, McDonald's has lost momentum, and it risks losing its dominant position in the restaurant industry.

What has gone wrong at McDonald's? In many respects, McDonald's offers an excellent illustration of many of the topics and issues described in this chapter:

First, the company's top managers have not noticed or not understood the extent of change in their industry, and they have not responded effectively to it. Major demographic changes, the proliferation of fast-food chains serving everything from burgers to vegetarian entrees, and changes in consumer tastes and preferences have all had a dramatic impact on the restaurant industry and especially its fast-food segment. Such changes in a firm's industry environment should prompt its managers to evaluate the changes and consider appropriate responses, including the formulation and implementation of totally new strategies.

Yet, in a recent *Business Week* article, McDonald's chairman was quoted as saying, "Do we have to change? No, we don't have to change. We have the most successful brand in the world."[4]

> As the company's performance has deteriorated, top execs have tended to blame others. They have publicly blasted dissident franchisees, whom they dismiss as a small faction. Negative news accounts are chalked up to misperceptions by reporters. And one persistently critical Wall Street analyst ... was barred from the company's latest biennial briefing.[5]

continued

In short, McDonald's managers appear to be actively ignoring bad news rather than dealing proactively with industry change.

McDonald's is dominated by homogeneous thinking at the top. McDonald's executive ranks are dominated by an old guard of top executives, most of whom began working at the company when Richard Nixon was president.[6] McDonald's has long promoted from within, rarely considering outsiders for top management positions. And, although executive recruiters once looked to McDonald's management ranks for candidates for other companies' management positions, the current view among most recruiting firms is that McDonald's Oak Brook headquarters offers few new or exciting ideas. McDonald's board of directors is also dominated by insiders. Of the 15 members on McDonald's board, only four can be classified as independent outsiders who have no business dealings with McDonald's. As a result, board members — most of whom benefit from the *status quo* — are unlikely to recommend significant changes.

Finally, McDonald's has "exploited the known" but failed to "explore the new." While Wendy's has introduced everything from stuffed pitas to spicy chicken sandwiches to fuel continuous sales gains, McDonald's new-product introductions have been erratic and, for the most part, failures. Over the years, McDonald's has experimented with everything from pizza to fried chicken, fajitas to pasta, and — its most recent new-product flop — the McLean Deluxe, but few of these items remain on its menus. Furthermore, most of these menu items have involved variations on what McDonald's already does rather than anything truly new or particularly innovative.

> McDonald's seems to have fallen into the hell that traps many of the best companies at some point in their lives. Having established a dominant position under a previous generation, it is bedeviled by a reverence for the old formulas, while its leadership takes weak steps and then denies all problems.[7]

Changes may be on the way for McDonald's, however. In mid-1998, the company's board promoted Jack M. Greenberg to serve as its president and CEO. What makes Greenberg's appointment significant is that he is the first McDonald's CEO to have had significant management experience outside the company. Mr. Greenberg came to McDonald's from Pizza Hut in 1982 to serve as the company's chief financial officer. In another sign that signals change, Mr. Greenberg has appointed Alan Feldman, another Pizza Hut management veteran and a newcomer to McDonald's, to run the company's troubled U.S. operations. Mr. Greenberg has also signaled that he expects McDonald's to pursue a more innovative course in the future by stating that "innovaiton will occupy a good deal of my effort. Innovation has always driven our growth, and I want an environment that fosters and rewards it."[8] ■

[1]This Management Focus is based largely on a *Business Week* article by David Leonhardt (1998), "McDonald's: Can It Regain Its Golden Touch?" March 9, 70–77.

[2]D. Upton and J. Margolis, J. 1992. *McDonald's Corporation 1992 Operations, Flexibility and the Environment*. Boston: HBS Case Services, Harvard Business School.

[3]Leonhardt, "McDonald's" p. 74

[4]Quinlan, quoted in Leonhardt, "McDonald's," p. 71.

[5]Leonhardt, "McDonald's" p. 72.

[6]Ibid.

[7]H. W. Jenkins, Jr., 1998. How to save McDonald's. *The Wall Street Journal*, March 18; A23.

[8]R. Gibson, "McDonald's Makes Changes in Top Management," *The Wall Street Journal*, May 1, 1998, A3.

Implications and Recommendations

The previous section implies that, without intervention, managers will be less responsive than they should be to changes in their firms' industry environments. This section offers three recommendations aimed at improving the responsiveness of managers and their firms. Our first two recommendations assume that managers need to think like outsiders, and we offer some specific proposals for how this "outsider" thinking can be encouraged. Our final recommendation focuses on the importance of higher-level learning, and we offer some ideas for how this higher-level learning can be institutionalized in business organizations.

Advantage comes from thinking (and acting) like an outsider

As already suggested in Chapter 5, one clear implication of the various factors just reviewed is that advantage comes not only from thinking like an outsider, but also by taking risks that would be considered unconventional given industry norms and standards. The factors reviewed in the previous section also suggest that one important way in which firms can think and act like outsiders is for top managers to give greater credibility to contrarian voices or outliers within their own organizations.

Rather than see these contrarian individuals or "renegades" become alienated and eventually leave as the A-S-A cycle suggests they will, organizations would benefit by giving greater attention and credence to their maverick views. As suggested earlier, these contrarian individuals are much more likely to see and anticipate industry changes, and they are much more likely to understand how their firms could proactively respond to these changes. Gary Hamel has described the process of strategic change as "a fight with orthodoxy" and suggested that it is fueled by new voices, new conversations or connections among new voices, new perspectives, and experimentation. He concludes that *"heretics — and not profits — create company futures!"*[32]

This recommendation has important implications for companies' human resource management practices. If most organizations select new employees on the basis of "fit," then these hiring practices are responsible for much of the "thinking alike" that can be so detrimental and stultifying for business organizations. The challenge for the future will be for firms to develop new recruitment and selection practices that ensure greater diversity in thinking among employees. It will not be enough, however, to simply alter recruitment and selection patterns in an effort to increase cognitive diversity. Employees who hold maverick views must be supported within the organization or they will leave.

Research by Robert Burgelman of Stanford University suggests that middle-level and senior-level managers play important roles in accommodating and supporting new points of view.[33] According to Burgelman, middle-level managers play an important role as "champions" of new ideas, while senior-level managers must alter the "strategic context" of their firms in order to accommodate these new ideas. The ideas of new employees are unlikely to have any beneficial impact without managers who are willing to "champion" these ideas or an organizational "context" that welcomes them.

Demographic diversity versus "genetic diversity"

Over the last decade, a major and long overdue emphasis on diversity has pushed business organizations to improve their records at both hiring and promoting minorities and women into top management positions. Although many firms are to be applauded for their efforts to improve diversity in their ranks, it should be remembered that the *economic* value of demographic diversity is the possibility that it will also lead to greater cognitive diversity — or what Hamel and Prahalad have called "genetic diversity" — by introducing more divergent and contrarian points of view into organizations. Hamel and Prahalad argue that:

> [i]t is important to distinguish between genetic diversity and cultural diversity. Many laggards are international companies. Many possess enormous cultural diversity in their ranks. Many celebrate diversity as a source of strength and innovation. Yet much of the potential for creativity offered by cultural diversity is often surrendered to an allegiance to very undiverse views about the industry and how to compete in it.
>
> Enlarging managerial frames [i.e., managers' mental models] depends, more than anything else, on curiosity and humility. It is these traits that make a senior manager willing to tolerate first-level employees who think the boss is a neanderthal, and to exercise the patience required to span the hierarchical divides that form a barrier to "upward learning."[34]

Thus, employees who bring new and diverse points of view to an organization expand or enlarge companies' "gene pools," and Hamel and Prahalad argue that more than a few companies are in need of "gene replacement therapy." Managers who fail to promote demographic diversity in their firms may be missing a major opportunity to realize economic benefits by recruiting employees with new viewpoints and understandings. Equally at fault are the managers who promote demographic diversity but then fail to tap divergent points of view within their ranks.

Organizational Learning and Strategic Change

The factors noted earlier in the chapter also suggest that organizational learning is essential if organizations are going to formulate and implement strategic change successfully. The ability to balance the allocation of resources between "the exploitation of the known" *and* "the exploration of the new" is essential if firms are to develop their capabilities and competencies while also avoiding the possibility of being blindsided by changes in their industries. As business environments change, managers and firms must not only develop and deploy new knowledge, but they must also "selectively forget" knowledge that has become dated or obsolete.[35]

Just as we have described two different levels or types of organizational learning, so too can we distinguish between two different types of organizational change. First-order — or evolutionary — change can be thought of as refinements to existing products or services or technologies. Product line extensions, software upgrades, and new models are all examples of first-order changes. Second-order — or revolutionary — change involves introducing totally new product lines or totally new services, reaching totally new groups of customers, or adopting new technologies. First- and second-order changes have also been called competence-enhancing and competence-destroying changes, respectively, because first-order change involves enhancing or extending existing knowledge and capabilities while second-order change usually means that existing knowledge and capabilities are made irrelevant.

Just as all organizations need to engage in both lower- and higher-level learning, organizations must also engage in both first- and second-order change. Yet, acknowledging the importance of both types of organizational change is much easier than actually implementing change. Improvements Kodak makes to its silver halide film technologies (i.e., a first-order change) do very little to stop the photography industry's rush toward digital technologies (i.e., a second-order change). As noted in Chapter 6, however, Kodak cannot simply abandon its silver halide film business because it is the source of nearly all the company's sales revenues, profits, and cash flow. Thus, the rate of change and the appropriate amount of first- and second-order change are key questions for general managers.

The points that have been made earlier in this chapter suggest that it's unlikely that managers and their firms will simply "embrace" or welcome change. Thus, managers must seek to institutionalize change. One way in which some firms have been successful at institutionalizing change is through product development. Traditional product planning efforts typically begin to design new products only *after* demand for old products begins to fall. At this point, the firm will have already missed important opportunities for influencing customer buying habits, and may even lose considerable ground to new products developed by more proactive rivals.

To overcome these limitations, many companies are adopting product planning strategies that attempt to *institutionalize innovation* in their product development efforts. Chapter 5 described the efforts of companies like 3M and Rubbermaid that now require a certain percentage of each year's sales to come from products that did not exist previously. Sony has gone a step further. When it introduces a new product, Sony also specifies the date when the next generation of that product will be introduced. One research study has suggested that an ongoing series of first-order changes creates an experimental atmosphere within organizations that facilitates timely second-order changes.[36] According to this study, ongoing change prevents managers from concluding that they've ever "learned enough" or that they can become complacent. Furthermore, experimentation and first-order change can lead to the discovery of important new areas of opportunity that result in major second-order changes.

Conclusion

In his recent book, *Competitive Advantage Through People*, Jeffrey Pfeffer asks readers to go back to 1972 and predict which companies would generate the highest returns for their stockholders over the next 20 years. He goes on to note that the conventional, structuralist wisdom would suggest selecting firms in industries

> with barriers to entry, low supplier and buyer bargaining power, few ready substitutes, and a limited threat of new entrants to compete away economic returns. Within such industries, other conventional analyses would urge you to select firms with the largest market share, which can realize the cost benefits of economies of scale. In short, you would probably look to industries in which patent protection of important product or service technology could be achieved and select the dominant firms in those industries.[37]

But, Pfeffer goes on to note that you would have much better luck selecting the highest performing firms if you had taken "this conventional wisdom and turned it on its head." The highest performing firms during this 20-year time frame (ranked by stock market performance) were Southwest Airlines with a stock appreciation of 21,775 percent, Wal-Mart with an increase in stock value of 19,807 percent, and Tyson Foods, a poultry processor, whose stock increased by 18,118 percent. Pfeffer notes that

> during this period, these industries ... were characterized by massive competition and horrendous losses, widespread bankruptcy, virtually no barriers to entry [after airline deregulation in 1978], little unique or proprietary technology, and many substitute products or services. And, in 1972, none of these firms was ... the market share leader, enjoying economies of scale from moving down the learning curve.[38]

In Chapter 1 of this text, we argued that the field of strategic management has long been dominated by a structuralist point of view — that firm performance is largely a function of external forces, primarily industry structure, and that high performance and competitive advantage result from an ability to "strategically manage" these structural forces. Pfeffer's observations should help to emphasize a point we made in Chapter 4 about the structuralist perspective: Although industry structure is almost certainly an influence on firm performance, it is not the only influence, and within both high- and low-performing industries, we find both high- and low-performing firms. Although industry structure is part of the firm performance "story," it is only one, fairly small part of the story.

Recapitulation: The Key Roles of General Managers

The perspective that has guided the writing of this book suggests that general managers, and *not* industry forces, are a much more important influence on organizational success. Managerial thinking, rather than industry structure, influences the choice of strategies that allow high-performing firms either to occupy unique positions in their competitive arenas or to possess unique competencies that cannot be easily duplicated by their rivals. The success of Southwest Airlines comes not from competing in an attractive industry — recall that during the most recent industry downturn in the early 1990s, the airline industry lost more than twice the total accumulated profits earned by all carriers since the 1920s![39] Instead, Southwest's high performance results from managerial thinking that viewed the airline industry in nontraditional ways, placed the company in a unique position in the airline industry, and led the company to develop unique and difficult-to-imitate capabilities and competencies that give it the lowest cost structure of any of the major airlines.

The study of business administration has tended to focus on evaluating, financing, and accounting for investments in physical assets. A key lesson of this book is that *investments in physical assets are less important than the managerial thinking that guides these investment decisions*. In other words, managers' understandings of their firms' competitive environments and their beliefs about how their firms should compete are far more critical to their firms' success than is any set of physical assets. And, the relative importance of managerial thinking, organizational learning, and other intangible organizational assets will almost certainly continue to increase in the years ahead.

Throughout this chapter, we have argued that managers must pursue two types of learning and initiate two types of organizational change. They must pursue what they already know — in other words, they must seek to apply and refine existing knowledge in order to develop the capabilities and competencies that will provide their firms with a competitive advantage. At the same time, they must focus on "exploring the new" in order to proactively redefine their businesses and develop the capabilities and competencies that will be needed to enjoy a competitive advantage in the future. Unfortunately, a good deal of the evidence offered in this book suggests that managers show a preference for the known over the more speculative unknown.

In the early 1960s, Peter Drucker published *Managing for Results*. That book made many of the same points that have been emphasized throughout this book, suggesting that these points may be timeless truths. For example, Drucker worried that most managers show a tendency to fight today's fires rather than pursue tomorrow's opportunities, noting that "all one can hope to get by solving a problem is to restore normality. All one can hope, at best, is to eliminate a restriction on the capacity of the business to obtain results. The results themselves must come from the exploitation of opportunities."[40]

Drucker also emphasized the importance of firms occupying unique positions in their competitive arenas. He suggested that managers ask themselves, "What do we do ... that no one else does well?"[41] Drucker also understood the dynamic nature of markets and industries that was emphasized in Chapter 5 of this text. Early in his book, Drucker noted that "what exists is getting old" — that no product or service is likely to remain relevant forever — and that "any leadership position is transitory and likely to be short-lived."[42] Finally, Drucker emphasized repeatedly the importance of managerial decision making in determining organizational success:

> The key decisions on the idea of the business [i.e., business definition], its excellence and its priorities can be made systematically or haphazardly. They can be made in awareness of their impact or as an afterthought to some urgent triviality. They can be made by top management or by someone way down the line who, in disposing of a technical detail, actually determines company character and direction.
>
> But somehow, some place, these decisions are always made in a business. Without them no action whatever could really be taken.
>
> There is no formula to yield the "right" answers for these key decisions. But if given haphazardly and without awareness of their importance they will inevitably be the wrong answers. To have even a chance of being right, the key decisions have to be made systematically. This is one responsibility top management can neither delegate nor leave to others.[43]

Great "Dramas" in Business

Throughout this text, we have offered many examples of contemporary business issues and described the strategic dilemmas currently faced by many companies: The attempts of the Big Three U.S. automobile companies to regain leadership in the (now) worldwide automobile industry, the ascendency of digital companies like Intel, Microsoft, and Yahoo!, IBM's spectacular yet incomplete turnaround, Apple's struggles to reinvent itself, the ongoing development of new medical technologies for fighting disease, the emergence of health maintenance organizations and their impact on the delivery of health care, Kodak's efforts to remake itself in a digital future — these are great dramas in the business world that are currently being acted out on a global stage. We can learn much from these companies by seeking to understand the complex relationships among the thinking of their top managers, the dynamic nature of their industry environments, their struggles to redefine themselves in a new competitive landscape, and their strategies to maintain or regain competitive advantage. This is certainly a most exciting time to be entering the world of business, and we await your contributions.

Key Points

- A lack of responsiveness to and the inability to anticipate environmental change is a major organizational problem, probably far greater than most other business problems.
- A lack of responsiveness appears to be related to four factors: (1) problems of managerial cognition, including problems of noticing and interpreting environmental stimuli and problems of taking action; (2) a preference for and an emphasis on lower-level learning over higher-level learning; (3) homogeneity in managerial thinking; and (4) the limiting influence of industry norms and standards.

- By thinking (and acting) like industry outsiders, by emphasizing higher-level organizational learning, and by institutionalizing change, managers can become more responsive to environmental change.
- Finally, the chapter closed by describing again the important roles played by general managers and by reiterating the fundamental importance of managerial decision making. Many current examples of firms working to remake themselves offer real-time "dramas" that can teach us much about the management of strategic change.

Review and Discussion Questions

1. *Describe how managers' cognitive limitations and biases contribute to a lack of responsiveness to environmental change.*
2. *Which seems to be more difficult for managers — noticing strategic change or correctly interpreting and responding to strategic change?*
3. *Distinguish between low-level and high-level learning and describe the importance of each. Why is high-level learning so important to the management of strategic change? What can managers do to encourage more high-level learning?*
4. *How does homogeneity in managerial thinking contribute to a lack of responsiveness to environmental change? Why do organizations tend to develop homogeneity in managerial thinking? What can top managers do to encourage more diversity in managerial thinking?*
5. *What can managers do to improve their ability to anticipate and respond effectively to strategic change? Select a firm that has suffered a major decline and identify and describe the factors that were responsible for the firm's downturn.*

Suggestions for Further Reading

Barr, P. S., Stimpert, J. L., and Huff, A. S. 1992. Cognitive change, strategic action, and organizational renewal. *Strategic Management Journal*, 13(special edition): 15–36.

Hambrick, D. C., and D'Aveni, R. A., 1988. Large corporate failures as downward spirals. *Administrative Science Quarterly*, 33: 1–23.

Hamel, G., and Prahalad, C. K. 1994. *Competing for the Future*. Boston: Harvard Business School Press.

Hedberg, B. 1981. How organizations learn and unlearn. In P. C. Nystrom and W. H. Starbuck (Eds.), *Handbook of Organizational Design*, 1: 3–27. New York: Oxford University Press.

Kiesler, S., and Sproull, L. 1982. Managerial response to changing environments: Perspectives on problem sensing from social cognition. *Administrative Science Quarterly*, 27: 548–570.

March, J. G. 1991. Exploration and exploitation in organizational learning. *Organization Science*, 2: 71–87.

Schneider, B. 1987. The people make the place. *Personnel Psychology*, 40: 437–453.

Endnotes

1. Miller, M. W. 1993. As IBM losses mount, so do the complaints about company perks. *The Wall Street Journal*, October 27, A1.

2. Kiesler, S., and L. Sproull, 1982. Managerial response to changing environments: Perspectives on problem sensing from social cognition. *Administrative Science Quarterly* 27:548.
3. Senge, P. M. 1990. *The Fifth Discipline: The Art and Practice of the Learning Organization.* New York: Doubleday/Currency.
4. Kiesler and Sproull, Managerial response to changing environments.
5. Mintzberg, H., D. Raìsinghanì, and A. Théorêt, 1976. The structure of "unstructured" decision processes. *Administrative Science Quarterly* 21:253.
6. Starbuck, W. A., and F. J. Milliken, 1988. Executives' perceptual filters: What they notice and how they make sense. In *The Executive Effect: Concepts and Methods for Studying Top Managers,* edited by D. C. Hambrick. Greenwich, Conn: JAI Press.
7. Kiesler and Sproull, Managerial response to changing environments.
8. Barr, P. S., J. L. Stimpert, and A. S. Huff, 1992. Cognitive change, strategic action, and organizational renewal. *Strategic Management Journal* 13(special issue):15–36.
9. Hambrick, D. C., and R. A. D'Aveni, 1988. Large corporate failures as downward spirals. *Administrative Science Quarterly* 33:1–23.
10. Nelson, E., and J. B. While, 1997. Blurred image: Kodak moment came early for CEO Fisher, who takes a stumble. *The Wall Street Journal,* July 25, A1, A6.
11. Stertz, B. A. 1992. Importing solutions: Detroit's new strategy to beat back Japanese is to copy their ideas. *The Wall Street Journal,* October 1, A1, A12; J. B. White, 1992. For Saturn, copying Japan yields hot sales but no profits. *The Wall Street Journal,* October 1, A10.
12. Womack, J. P., D. T. Jones, and D. Roos, 1990. *The Machine That Changed the World.* New York: Rawson Associates.
13. March, J. G. 1991. Exploration and exploitation in organizational learning. *Organization Science* 2:71–87.
14. Cyert, R. M., and J. G. March, 1963. *A Behavioral Theory of the Firm.* Englewood Cliffs, N.J.: Prentice Hall.
15. Cohen, W. M., and D. A. Levinthal, 1989. Innovation and learning: The two faces of R&D. *Economic Journal* 99: 569–596; W. M. Cohen, and D. A. Levinthal, 1990. Absorptive capacity: A new perspective on learning and innovation. *Administrative Science Quarterly* 35:128–152; T. K. Lant, and D. B. Montgomery, 1987. Learning from strategic success and failure. *Journal of Business Research* 15:503–517.
16. Hedberg, B. 1981. How organizations learn and unlearn. In *Handbook of Organizational Design,* edited by P. C. Nystrom and W. H. Starbuck. New York: Oxford University Press, emphasis added.
17. Banks, H. 1994. A sixties industry in a nineties economy. *Forbes,* May 9, 107–112.
18. Cohen and Levinthal, Innovation and learning; Cohen and Levinthal, Absorptive capacity.
19. Cohen and Levinthal, Absorptive capacity, p. 128.
20. Schneider, B. 1987. The people make the place. *Personnel Psychology* 40: 437–453.
21. Finkelstein, S., and D. C. Hambrick, 1996. *Strategic Leadership: Top Executives and Their Effects on Organizations.* St. Paul: West Publishing.
22. Miller, D. 1991. Stale in the saddle: CEO tenure and the match between organization and environment. *Management Science* 37:34–52.
23. March, Exploration and exploitation in organizational learning.
24. Ibid., p. 80.
25. Ibid., p. 79.
26. Wyckoff, D. D. 1976. *Railroad Management.* Lexington, Mass: Lexington Books.
27. Ibid., p. 87.
28. Ibid., p. 99, emphasis added.
29. DiMaggio, P. J., and W. W. Powell, 1983. The iron cage revisited: Institutional isomorphism and collective rationality in organizational fields. *American Sociological Review* 38:147–160; A. S. Huff, 1982. Industry influences on strategy reformulation. *Strategic Management Journal* 3:119–131.

30. Hambrick, D. C. 1982. Environmental scanning and organizational strategy. *Strategic Management Journal* 3:159–174.
31. Mintzberg, H. 1978. Patterns in strategy formation. *Management Science* 24:934–948.
32. Hamel, G. 1996. *Strategy in the New Economy: Issues and Opportunities.* Talk presented at the annual meeting of the Strategic Management Society. Phoenix.
33. Burgelman, R. A. 1983. A process model of internal corporate venturing in the diversified major firm. *Administrative Science Quarterly* 28: 223–244.
34. Hamel, G., and C. K. Prahalad, 1994. *Competing for the Future*. Boston: Harvard Business School Press, p. 63.
35. Hamel, *Strategy in the New Economy.*
36. Barr, et al., Cognitive change, strategic action, and organizational renewal.
37. Pfeffer, J. 1994. *Competitive Advantage Through People*. Boston: Harvard Business School Press, p. 4.
38. Ibid.
39. Dempsey, P. S. 1993. The bitter fruits of airline deregulation. *The Wall Street Journal*, April 8, A15.
40. Drucker, P. F. 1964. *Managing for Results: Economic Tasks and Risk-Taking Decisions.* New York: Harper & Row, pp. 5–6.
41. Ibid., p. 116.
42. Ibid., p. 7–8.
43. Ibid., p. 202.

PART 2

CASES

CASE 1

THE ALASKAN GOLD MINE: PART I

You have taken a three-month option on a possible gold mine in Alaska. It took you two months of dangerous journey to get there. After two weeks of exploration (and recuperation), you have got your health back except for your injured left hand, which sometimes can suddenly become quite weak. In the last 24 hours, you have finally discovered gold in what appears to be good quantity. You have exactly two weeks to get to the claims office. If you arrive late and attempt to secure the property with the owners knowing you have visited it, they will probably hold an auction, at which you, given your limited resources, could easily be outbid. Here are your alternatives:

1. Wait three to four weeks until the weather warms up and enjoy a safe trip home.
2. Go over the mountains. This is dangerous. It is sometimes impassable. It is quick, however (7 to 10 days), if you can make it without harm. If you encounter storms or are injured before you reach the top, you will probably have to turn back. In either case, you may perish, because the longest part of the journey is on the way over the top.
3. Go through the valley passes. This is less dangerous and is usually passable. It is slow and tiring, however. You can probably make it in two to three weeks.

The weather is only moderately favorable; a mountain storm may be brewing. You will know within 48 hours if the storm is coming and will know whether the mountain is passable (if the storm comes) about one day later.

4. Wait two to four days, take #2 if the weather permits; if not, take #3. (There is no advantage to waiting if you prefer #3 anyway, and waiting to take #1 = #1.)

What do you do? (Circle your answer.) #1 #2 #3 #4

Authored by Jeffrey Barach, Graduate School of Business, Tulane University, New Orleans, Louisiana, 1977. Reprinted by permission. Revisions by Professor L. J. Bourgeois made with permission.

CASE 2

THE ALASKAN GOLD MINE: PART II

Assume you chose the valley passes (Alternative 3). Five days later you are halfway there. You have pushed too hard and sprained your ankle. Pat, an old friend on a trapping expedition, comes along and takes you to a cabin. Pat could get to the claims office in town and offers to take you. If you were well, you could do it easily in 7 days, but you cannot make it alone without a few days of rest and then 10 days to two weeks of travel. Traveling together, you might take 10 to 14 more days to get there. If you tell Pat about the gold and make a deal, Pat alone could get there in 8 to 10 days.

You are not sure whether Pat can exercise the option and file the claim correctly, because Pat is not bright, tends to drink in excess, and is not the single-minded hustler that you are. Pat is a simple, decent person who likes trapping but would, you suspect, both need and desire financial independence. You think you could trust Pat if you offer to split 50-50, because Pat would need your expertise and help to capitalize on the discovery.

What is your decision?

Go it alone ______

Go with Pat ______

Send Pat ______

Explain in detail your best strategy for success and how you plan to carry it out:

____

____

____

____

____

____

____

CASE 3

ASTRAL RECORDS, LTD., NORTH AMERICA

The date was August 24, 1993, and Sarah Conner felt overwhelmed and more than a little disoriented. Only two days ago, she had rushed from her office at Bendini, Lambert & Locke (BLL), a well-known venture-capital firm, to board the company jet for Knoxville, Tennessee, where she would assume operating control of Astral Records, Ltd., North America (Astral N.A.). One week earlier, Astral N.A.'s president and chief executive officer, Sir Maxwell S. Hammer, had been killed in a tragic hunting accident. As the owner of 60 percent of the company, BLL had felt an immediate need to protect its investment. Accordingly, BLL's managing director, T.J. Lambert, had asked Conner to run the company while the firm planned its next moves. He had assured her that she would be in Pigeon Forge, Tennessee, for at least a year.

Conner was the obvious choice. After graduating from Wellesley College in 1982 with a degree in classical music, she had gone to work for Galaxy Records, first in marketing and later in production. In 1987 she was admitted to the Darden Graduate School of Business Administration, where she was president of the Entrepreneurs Club, a Shermet scholar, and, upon graduation, a recipient of the Faculty Award for academic excellence. Hoping to combine her love of music with her business acumen, she joined BLL as assistant manager of the entertainment portfolio. That BLL was acquiring new music-industry companies made it the perfect and first choice among her several job offers.

Conner had progressed quickly during her four years at BLL. Nevertheless, she was rather surprised at how quickly she had been asked to assume operating control of one of the fastest growing compact-disc (CD) manufacturers in the world. In two weeks she was scheduled to meet with BLL's principals. They wanted a status report, a set of recommendations, and an action plan for the next year. She knew that a number of important issues were likely to need attention in the wake of Sir Maxwell's death.

THE CD INDUSTRY

In principle, CD technology was an evolutionary refinement of records and tapes. Under the old technology, music and voice were converted into electronic impulses that were then embedded in a medium such as vinyl or magnetic tape. These impulses were then decoded and amplified to reproduce the original music. CDs, however, represented a huge technological leap forward. Sound was converted into digital code that could then be decoded by a laser to reproduce exactly the original digital information.

This case was prepared by Lynn A. Isabella, Associate Professor of Business Administration, and Ted Forbes. Revised August 1994.

CDs were produced in two steps. First, a "master" was made. An extremely flat, glass master disc received an adhesive and a thin (0.12 micron) layer of light-sensitive photoresist on one side. The photoresist was then exposed to a 100-milliwatt laser beam that applied the sequence of coded digits in real time to the photoresist. After an alkaline bath removed unwanted resist, a pattern of micropits was left. A nickel impression, known as the "father," was made from the glass master. The positive "mothers" that were produced from the negative father were used to make the stampers of the polycarbonate substrate.

Because the photoresist was damaged when it was developed, the exposed glass master could normally be put to use only once. Four or five nickel mothers were usually made from a single father. Another four or five stampers could be sputtered in metal from each mother, for a total of up to 25 stampers from the single master disc. The master could thus become the source of up to 10,000 discs per stamper, or 250,000 CDs.

In the second step, a mold received polycarbonate resin that was stamped to make the hard, transparent CD wafer. A vaporized metal layer, usually aluminum, was applied in a vacuum chamber as the surface that reflected the laser beam for player reading. Then came another hard, protective resin layer, the printed label, automatic inspection, and packaging.

CDs were first mass-produced in 1980. Since then, CD technology had seen mostly refinements rather than breakthroughs. For example, in 1989 CD-production cycle times were 13 seconds; now those times were less than 7 seconds, and leading-edge technology produced CDs in less than 5 seconds. The machinery was more efficient and less expensive than the old equipment, with the cost of a new small plant in the range of \$8–\$10 million.

Although industry dynamics had stabilized in recent years, predicting volume and designing appropriate capacity were as much art as science. "Correct capacity, either annually or monthly, is like an Indiana spring. It's only two or three days a year. You're either over or under capacity. If we weren't talking about being over capacity, we'd be talking about a shortage; it's never correct very long," stated Robert McGee, executive director of ComDisc, a trade association.

Quality had improved dramatically over the past 10 years. In most plants, quality control was completely automated. The implementation of statistical process controls had a tremendous impact. In 1986 industry reject rates were approximately 12 percent. By 1993 rates were as low as 1.5 percent. "The discs coming off the machines today are simply better quality. Because of our knowledge and machine consistency, inspection is made easy," said Billie Holliday, director of quality for Celestial Records.

As the technology matured, producers discovered that cover art was increasingly important in selling CDs. Many CD replicators now had 5-color capacity. Most CD producers used silk-screen printing, and the large operations used offset printing. Over the years, packaging was standardized around the "jewel box," a hard, plastic case used to hold both the CD and accompanying liner notes. Efforts to move toward "environmentally friendly" packaging had not succeeded.

Wholesale prices for finished product averaged \$1.30. Packaging costs were approximately 23 cents per disc and the finished disc itself cost approximately 90 cents. Industry analysts asserted that price competition among disc replicators had come down to pennies and half pennies, as opposed to differences of 15–25 cents in the late 1980s. "When the business is soft and you establish a price, it's very difficult to establish a higher price once business picks up. The gross margins on CDs have eroded tremendously over the past five years. I don't see any more maneuvering left on the price," said Eleanor Rigby, record-industry analyst with Sergeant and Pepper Investments.

Record labels contracted with manufacturing facilities to produce the finished product. The labels then sold, either directly or through a distributor, to the retail outlets. Sales from label/distributor to retail outlets were on a consignment basis. Continued Rigby,

> Although quantity discounts are available, most labels are placing smaller orders and then reordering on a more frequent basis to keep inventory at manageable levels. There are only so many returns a label can take and still turn a profit, so we're seeing labels be a bit more cautious about their opening orders and then coming back for more in a shorter turnaround period than before.

Recent advances in laser technology had opened up the market in both the computer and video arenas. Because the technologies were essentially the same, audio CD manufacturers could easily produce CD-ROM discs for computers or laser discs for video. Sam Cooke, vice president of marketing and sales, Galaxy Records, asserted,

> Quality of the CD in the industry is fairly standard now. A disc we stamp is the same quality as any of the other major houses. What might set a company apart, though, is what we do in terms of fulfillment services, packaging and design, and drop shipping. Customer service has definitely become the buzzword among replicators for the '90s.

Company History

Astral Records was founded by Count Francisco Smirnov, a Franco-Russian nobleman, in 1967 in Wollaston-on-Heath, England. Smirnov was a professional musician who had a vision of building a new kind of record company. Appalled by the quality of records at that time, Smirnov set out to construct a studio whose sole purpose would be to produce classical-music record masters of a quality greater than that of any other company in the world. The count had been disappointed to learn that the long-playing records made from his masters were little better in sound quality than most others on the market. Undaunted, he decided to move into manufacturing.

Smirnov's vision was of a utopian musical village, where classical musicians and company directors would reside in luxury and elegance. The count wanted nothing to impede the creative process: "Beautiful music can only happen in beautiful surroundings. If society continues to ignore the high arts, then society will be led into a barbarian condition."

In 1975 Astral purchased a 50-room Georgian mansion on 187 acres near the top of the Cynwyr valley not far from Wales. Each step in the production process would be carried out onsite. The ballroom was turned into one of the most elegant recording studios in the industry. The count and five of the seven managing directors continued to live the vision, residing in the exquisitely furnished headquarters and taking all their meals together. Key business decisions were often made casually over lunch and dinner. Recording musicians were invited to live on the grounds for as long as they needed to complete their projects.

Astral Records might well have continued to operate in this idyllic setting, but for a major technological breakthrough. The count was captivated by the emerging compact-disc technology. He immediately saw the medium's potential for producing virtually flawless recordings. The combination of pure digital sound and laser technology became the count's obsession, even though he would be going up against the industry giants.

Instead of simply licensing CD technology from the giants, the count and his researchers decided to develop their own process. In eight months they developed production capabilities that not only saved them millions in royalty fees, but also won them a Queen's Award for technological achievement. Astral Records was the first company in the United Kingdom to produce CDs, two years ahead of its major competitors. By the mid-1980s, more than 50 record labels were using Astral's facilities to record, produce, and manufacture CDs. Astral's own labels constituted a mere 10 percent of the company's sales.

Astral's bold, yet whimsical, business decisions had been wildly successful. In 1980 Astral Records, Ltd., U.K., employed 27 people and grossed 600,000 pounds. By 1992 the company had 500 employees and turned a pre-tax profit of £2.7 million on sales of £20 million.

Astral Records, Ltd., North America

In 1986 the count entered into negotiations with Bendini, Lambert & Locke to secure capital for a planned expansion into the U.S. market. The market for CDs was booming and the plant in England was struggling to keep pace with demand. One night Smirnov had a vision of the new facility: It would be nestled among mountains and streams surrounded by lush pastures. In 1987, in exchange for 60 percent ownership of the U.S. operation, BLL financed the construction of a $14 million plant on 265 acres in Pigeon Forge, Tennessee. The count chose Sir Maxwell S. Hammer, an English aristocrat and hunting partner, to run the U.S. operation. "I shall endeavor to carry the mission of Astral Records to the States," Sir Maxwell stated.

Astral Records, Ltd., N.A., was predominately a manufacturing facility, capable of pressing 100,000 CDs per day. Ninety percent of its business was producing CDs for a variety of other record labels. Diverging from the Astral, U.K., core business and classical tradition, Sir Maxwell had begun to explore recording and producing CDs beyond Astral's classical catalog, which contained 300 titles. Sir Maxwell's wide-ranging interests ran from classical to blues to rock and roll to new age to rap. Having seen the phenomenal sales of many of the artists whose CDs Astral manufactured under contract, Sir Maxwell entered into negotiations with a variety of country, world-music, and new-age artists to bring them under Astral's own labels.

Under Sir Maxwell's leadership, Astral Records quickly became known as the premier CD manufacturer in the United States. Astral's stringent quality-control standards were far higher than those set by its competitors. Within the industry, an Astral CD was widely believed to be playable without error on any CD player. "It's quality. I think if we lost that, then the company would be truly adrift. Music and all the arts are extremely fragile creations and it's quite simple to lose that very thing after which you are chasing," said Mr. Kite, Astral's celebrated music director.

Sir Maxwell built a reputation as an innovator in the industry. Astral invented multisonic recording, a method of capturing reverberated sounds from the rear of the orchestra. Astral also pioneered the use of new packaging systems that used recycled paper. The company's current research focused on creating the ability to compress feature-length motion pictures onto a standard 5-inch disc. In his last interview before his death, Sir Maxwell stated, "People no longer want to just hear music; they want to see it. Video is the future."

He had also embarked on a path of expansion in order to increase capacity in a growing market. In 1991 the company completed a $3-million capital project that increased capacity by 40 percent. Production lines were expanded from five to eight, and two new mastering systems were added. Astral represented the latest in CD-manufacturing systems.

Sir Maxwell ran the U.S. operation as though it were his own colonial outpost. "Sir Max," as his employees called him, affectionately referred to his top managers as "toppers." He quickly established a reputation as a demanding taskmaster, and he insisted on being involved in every aspect of the business. He oversaw every major decision. Not surprisingly, the managers and employees at Astral were feeling adrift in the wake of Sir Maxwell's death.

Sarah Conner Takes Charge

At 8:00 A.M., Sarah Conner sat in the walnut-paneled conference room overlooking the Great Smokey Mountains. Sir Maxwell's office was elegant, but Conner did not feel comfortable in it yet. In front of her was an assortment of memos, phone messages, faxes, and other correspondence that had accumulated, mostly over the past week (see the exhibits that follow). Conner believed she needed to deal with all of these papers and also begin preparing the report for the upcoming meeting with the partners from BLL. The next couple of weeks promised to be interesting.

ASTRAL RECORDS, Ltd. *North America* *Pigeon Forge, TN* **Tel. (615) 356-9889**

TO: All Astral Toppers

FROM: Sir Maxwell S. Hammer

DATE: August 18, 1993

SUBJECT: Staff Meeting

Please join me for high tea in the boardroom on August 24th at 3:00 P.M.

ASTRAL RECORDS, Ltd. *North America* *Pigeon Forge, TN* Tel. (615) 356-9889

August 24, 1993

Sarah—

Welcome to Astral. We are all glad to have you with us.

I've gone ahead and told our toppers that you would want to meet them at 3p.m. as was scheduled. It was so shocking about Sir Max!

I'm sure you'd appreciate some advice from an "old pro." (I've been Sir Max's right-hand man since the beginning.) Sir Max commanded respect and you should do the same. Make quick decisions. The E.P.A. can wait, for example, but that conflict in production needs your attention. I won't put too much stock in O'Reilly or Sandy either. I'll stop by around 2 p.m. to brief you on what Sir Max would have wanted.

Wallace Alexander

Wallace Alexander
Assistant to the President

To Ms. Conner

Date 8/23 Time 10:03 ☒ AM ☐ PM

WHILE YOU WERE OUT

M Prof. Calhoun

of Univ. of Tennessee

Phone (____) ________________

Area Code Number Extension

TELEPHONED	✓	PLEASE CALL	✓
CALLED TO SEE YOU		WILL CALL AGAIN	
WANTS TO SEE YOU		URGENT	

RETURNED YOUR CALL ☐

Message Confirming student visits tomorrow @ 10am. Final count—50 MBA students for tour & mgmt. briefings. Look forward to continuing relationship with Astral.

Operator

ASTRAL RECORDS, Ltd. *Wollaston-on-Heath* *England* Tel. 098-765-54

August 22

Dearest Sarah,

Alas, I wish the circumstances surrounding your arrival were more joyous. Sir Max was a dear friend and a valued associate.

The directors and I would like to formally welcome you into the company. We will hold a Fox Hunt here at the compound on September 7. The Hunt will be in your honor. Please plan to arrive on the fifth, and stay through the tenth.

We eagerly anticipate your arrival!

Count Francisco Smirnov
P.O.R., R.E.G., R.D.G.

ASTRAL RECORDS, Ltd. *North America* *Pigeon Forge, TN* Tel. (615) 356-9889

August 20, 1993

TO:	Bart O'Reilly Vice President, Operations Astral NA	FROM:	Roberta Prospect District Sales Manager
CC:	Sir Maxwell S. Hammer		
FAX:	804-555-1234	FAX:	804-458-0000

URGENT ACTION REQUEST!!!!!!!

Purchasing personnel from Republic Music Distributors, Inc., are on their way to see us once again, and we need your help. Can you meet with me on Wednesday, August 25, to help us figure a way out of the current order backlog—particularly since Republic is my largest customer? Currently, we have a production run that is out-of-spec on color and electrical properties, but Republic is still willing to take it. Our plant manager is balking at shipping anything out-of-spec.

The new equipment still has problems. The plant manager and the staff have been working around the clock, it seems, to get the utilization promised by the equipment manufacturers. They have made great progress in stabilizing the production processes, particularly in view of the new technology in the NCC-1701A equipment, but there are still problems.

My issue at the moment is the plant's unwillingness to be a bit flexible in what it ships out to Republic. Here is the latest incident. This afternoon, I called our shipping department to verify that the Republic order would be

(continued on next page)

2

picked up by Smith's Transfer. We had promised a ship date of Tuesday of this week, and I have been reassuring Republic's purchasing agent all week that this shipment would be made by the week's end.

When I found out the products were being scrapped, I really hit the ceiling. I felt like this action would be the last straw with Republic. We will lose all credibility if we don't get product to them by next Thursday. There is no way to meet their needs if we start a new production run. I was able to get the current run placed on hold by the Q.A. manager. The plant manager promises a new run from NCC-1701A by next Friday afternoon. Even if this run goes perfect, and we airship, the product will arrive too late for Republic to meet its customer ship date.

I proposed to the plant manager and quality assurance manager that the plant work overtime on Monday and Tuesday, sorting the products on electrical properties conformance. The purchasing people at Republic said they would be willing to accept "sorted-product." Moreover for this *one order*, they would allow off-specification occurrences for the color schemes on the various outside graphics. (We will have to process all of the 8,000 units through the certifier to sort "good/bad" on electrical properties. There are nine critical electrical performance attributes that must meet specifications.) Then the color consistency must be checked visually by our people. This visual check is a manual process and will take a lot of labor, particularly since the visual check requires a tricky disassembly step to remove the protective shield covering the minted surface.

So, I can get the purchasing people at Republic off my back with this one-time stop gap sort, and yet the plant manager refuses to schedule the overtime. He says that my proposal and the plant's TQM initiative don't go hand-in-hand. Their TQM activities have been underway for eight months, so I don't see how the actions would impact his TQM implementation. We need to be more customer focused at Astral.

Please call me later today and give me some help on this one. Thanks.

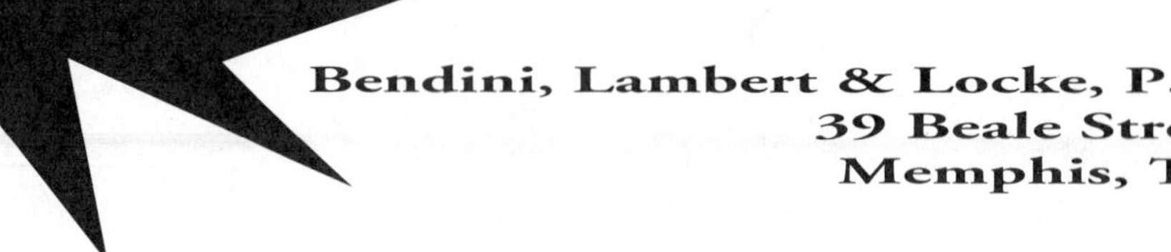

Bendini, Lambert & Locke, P.A.
39 Beale Street
Memphis, TN

FACSIMILE TRANSMISSION

TO: Sarah Conner
Astral Records, NA

FROM: T.J. Lambert
Partner, BLL

DATE: August 24, 1993

MESSAGE:

Sarah.... Welcome to Astral. Hope your flight on the Lear was enjoyable. Just wanted to once again let you know that we are expecting great things from you. This Astral Records affair has cost us a great deal more money than we had anticipated. Arthur and I know that you will work your magic on Astral in short order. Let's get this company straightened out.

As we set up before you left, Arthur, Helen and I will be coming to Astral on September 7th to meet with you. Please arrange appropriate accommodations for us. You know what we like.

By the way, we have been unable to locate the financial model you built for the TechnoWiz deal. As I recall, this was an extremely complex spreadsheet. Celia, your former secretary, left unexpectedly last Friday and no one can find her files. Can you build it for us again by the end of this week as we hope to complete this deal immediately?

Look forward to seeing you in two weeks. Best of luck.

"WE COVER THE WORLD WITH CHEMICALS"

POLYCARBONATE SUBSTRATE INC.
R.D. #3
BOX 4788
KENNER, LOUISIANA

TO: Sir Maxwell S. Hammer

FROM: J. Cash
Manager, Accounts Receivable

DATE: August 9, 1993

SUBJECT: Overdue Account

This is to notify you that Astral Records, North America, is more than 90 days overdue in its payment to us. You currently owe us $27,914.22.

If payment is not received by August 26, 1993, we will not deliver the next shipment of resins. Thank you for your prompt attention to this matter.

To Ms. Conner

Date 8/23 Time 1:43 ☐ AM ☒ PM

WHILE YOU WERE OUT

M Bea Walters

of Billboard Magazine

Phone (____)____________________

Area Code Number Extension

TELEPHONED		PLEASE CALL	✓
CALLED TO SEE YOU		WILL CALL AGAIN	
WANTS TO SEE YOU		URGENT	

RETURNED YOUR CALL	

Message

Would like interview ASAP regarding management transition.

Operator

ASTRAL RECORDS, Ltd. *North America* *Pigeon Forge, TN* Tel. (615) 356-9889

TO: Sir Max

CC: Bart O'Reilly
Vice President, Manufacturing

CC: Safety Committee

FROM: Mr. and Mrs. Richard Clark
Shipping Department

DATE: August 16, 1993

As you may know, the September 1993 Safety Day plans are almost finished. We had a chance to see the last working document that was prepared by the Plant Safety Committee. We are really upset and want to see you ASAP. Can we schedule ourselves into one of your "open doors" later this week?

For the fourth year in a row, there will be a Safety Day exhibition on Home Safety. We applaud Home Safety as one of the key themes. However, this year's focus on "Construction of a Deer Stand: Safety and Safe Hunting" is offensive to many of us. First, it is a fact that 38% of our plant employees are female, and they have no interest in hunting, particularly shooting deer from a stand placed off the ground in trees somewhere on the company's property. Certainly, you understand this point personally. Second, we think it is time to step up to the environmental issues and get our employees involved with recycling (newspapers, aluminum cans, plastic bottles, glass). Can't you order the Safety Committee to drop the "Deer Stand Construction" exhibition? After all, we think productivity/absenteeism and quality suffer at the opening of deer season every year. It is time, we think, to de-emphasize hunting and get people to stay focused on what they are paid to do.

ASTRAL RECORDS, Ltd. *North America* *Pigeon Forge, TN* Tel. (615) 356-9889

TO: Sir Max

CC: G. Scott Herron
Vice President, Marketing and Sales

FROM: Larry Taylor
Account Manager

DATE: August 13, 1993

SUBJECT: Unauthorized Return of Merchandise

Harris' Sound Machine, the largest chain of retail music stores in New York City, has informed me they intend to return 1,252 CDs with the title, "Buddy Holly's Greatest Hits," and are asking for a full refund. They claim the CDs arrived damaged. The one they sent me looks like it was cut with a knife used to open the shipping cartons. Since this is a slow seller, I am somewhat doubtful about how the CDs were damaged. Please let me know what to do.

YURBANK

"SERVING PIGEON FORGE'S FAMILIES AND BUSINESSES SINCE 1929"
2300 MAIN STREET
PIGEON FORGE, TN

TO: Sir Maxwell S. Hammer

FROM: C. Hewitt Farmington
Senior Relationship Manager
YurBank

DATE: July 1, 1993

SUBJECT: Renewal of Revolving Credit Agreement

Sir Max, this is to remind you that your revolver with the bank is due for review and renewal at the end of this month. As it currently stands, the bank is committed to lend you up to $500,000 at LIBOR + 1% with a 0.5% fee on the unused portion of the commitment. In light of the growth of last year's sales and your expectation of future growth, I recommend that we increase the commitment to $600,000. I do not expect the pricing structure to change before the end of this month.

Our understanding is that the line is used for seasonal working capital needs and as such your company will be out of the bank loan for at least 45 days during the next 12 months. Part of the purpose of the review is to see if the financial condition of the company has changed substantially since last year. Historically, your peak loan needs have occurred from September through December. My back-of-the-envelope calculations show that increasing the revolver will not violate the debt-to-equity covenant of the term loan unless equity is unexpectedly low prior to or during your peak seasonal need.

Is the early part of next week too early for your people to get the financials prepared so we can discuss things? I'll check back with you in a day or so to confirm.

To Astral Records

Date 8/23 Time 8:00 ☒ AM ☐ PM

WHILE YOU WERE OUT

M Tony Witherspoon

of Environmental Protection Agency

Phone (____) ________ Area Code Number Extension

TELEPHONED	✓	PLEASE CALL	
CALLED TO SEE YOU		WILL CALL AGAIN	
WANTS TO SEE YOU	✓	URGENT	✓
RETURNED YOUR CALL			

Message

Fish kill in local river downstream of plant. E.P.A. requests full site inspection Wed a.m., Aug. 25.

Operator

ASTRAL RECORDS, Ltd. *North America* *Pigeon Forge, TN* Tel. (615) 356-9889

TO: Sir Max

CC: G. Scott Herron
Vice President, Marketing and Sales

FROM: John Henry
Account Manager
Mississippi See Dee

DATE: August 10, 1993

SUBJECT: Contract Negotiation 1994/1995

Mississippi See Dee's has a fast-growing collection of Delta Blues. (They own the rights to much of John Lee Hooker's, Jimmy Reed's, and Lightnin' Hopkins' titles.)

Larry Johnson, their purchasing agent, says he is willing to increase our share of their business from 15% to 20% if we can guarantee two-week delivery of titles and reduce prices by 5%. I think this is a great opportunity to increase sales.

ASTRAL RECORDS, Ltd. *North America* *Pigeon Forge, TN* Tel. (615) 356-9889

TO: Richard & Emma Clark

CC: Sir Max
Bart O'Reilly, Vice President, Manufacturing

FROM: Maggie May

DATE: August 17, 1993

Will you two get off it! Who do you think you are suggesting that women don't enjoy hunting? I'll have you know I've been hunting since I was six when my daddy let me load his gun. I won't miss deer season and, believe me, these safety reminders are important. Not all women want to join your sewing circle, Emma. So stop writing memos to the VP and accusing us of not doing our work. If you are writing memos, how can you two be doing your own jobs!

To Astral

Date 8/24 Time 10:06 ☒ AM ☐ PM

WHILE YOU WERE OUT

M Tony Witherspoon

of E. P. A.

Phone (____)

Area Code Number Extension

TELEPHONED	✓	PLEASE CALL	
CALLED TO SEE YOU		WILL CALL AGAIN	
WANTS TO SEE YOU		URGENT	

RETURNED YOUR CALL	

Message

Suggests Astral legal counsel be present during tomorrow's inspection.

Operator

ASTRAL RECORDS, Ltd. *North America* *Pigeon Forge, TN* Tel. (615) 356-9889

TO: Sir Max

CC: Bart O'Reilly, Vice President, Manufacturing
G. Scott Herron, Vice President, Marketing and Sales

FROM: Phil Kreutzman
Purchasing

DATE: August 11, 1993

SUBJECT: Proposal for New Plastic Packaging Material

As you know, our packaging costs are substantial. I have a new plastic supplier who can cut our total COGS by 20%. Eventually, costs might be even lower.

The advantage of this company's new formula is that it is *completely* biodegradable in 10 years. The disadvantage is that the package will no longer be serviceable after 3–5 years of normal usage. Should we pursue this project?

ASTRAL RECORDS, Ltd. *North America* *Pigeon Forge, TN* **Tel. (615) 356-9889**

TO: Sir Maxwell S. Hammer

FROM: Richard Cory
Treasurer

DATE: July 3, 1993

SUBJECT: Approval of New Packaging Equipment

Below is a summary of the analysis we have been conducting on some new packaging equipment. Based on a discounted cash flow analysis, we estimate that the $1MM investment will increase firm value by $200,000. If we order by the end of this month, we should have the equipment installed and running in time for the increase in production that always occurs around October. The supplier will accept installment payments of $400,000, $300,000, and $300,000 over the next three months as payment. Since we are currently out of the bank, we could use the revolver line to make the $400,000 initial payment.

I hope the numbers on the attached sheet help show the merits of the new system. Frankly, Sir Max, it is rare that such a good opportunity comes around. The sooner we start using it, the better.

(continued on next page)

2

Cash Flow Analysis
New Packaging Equipment

Initial investment:	$1.0MM
Projected annual savings:[a]	$160M
Corporate tax rate:	34%
Economic/depreciable life:	7 years

Cash flow summary ($000):

Year →	0	1	2	3	4	5	6	7
Investment	(1000)							
After-tax savings		106	106	106	106	106	106	106
+ Depreciation		143	143	143	143	143	143	143
Total after-tax cash flows	(1000)	248	248	248	248	248	248	248

Net present value = $209,000
Internal rate of return = 16.1%
Payback = 4 years

[a]After depreciation, before taxes.

YURBANK

"SERVING PIGEON FORGE'S FAMILIES AND BUSINESSES SINCE 1929"
2300 MAIN STREET
PIGEON FORGE, TN

TO: Sir Maxwell S. Hammer

FROM: C. Hewitt Farmington
Senior Relationship Manager
YurBank

DATE: August 10, 1993

SUBJECT: Renewal of Revolving Credit Agreement

Things have changed. The credit review committee has put your company on its credit watch list because of our increasing exposure and the growth-induced strain on your balance sheet. They do not want to renew the revolver unless you can give us some sort of indication of how you are going to manage the growth of the firm going forward. Frankly, there is a general concern that your company is growing beyond its financial capabilities and that we might find ourselves with a bad term loan and very little usable collateral.

I spent the better part of an hour arguing with the credit committee, and I can tell you that these people are serious. This is all part of the tightened credit standards that were instituted following the S&L crisis. The only way I can see us doing business in the future is for you to strengthen the balance sheet with an equity infusion. The investment banking folks here would be very interested in helping you take the company public. I think you should consider it. The equity markets are very strong these days, and you may not be able to get a better price in the near future if this bull market turns bearish.

Sorry to catch you with this news with such little notice, but there was nothing I could do. I will meet anytime you are available. Obviously, time is of the essence.

ASTRAL RECORDS, Ltd. *North America* *Pigeon Forge, TN* Tel. (615) 356-9889

TO: Sir Maxwell S. Hammer

FROM: Abby McDeere
Chief Legal Counsel

DATE: July 17, 1993

SUBJECT: Lawsuit against Astral

Please be advised that MasterVision Associates of Burbank, California, has filed suit in the Los Angeles Superior Court against us. They are a worldwide optical disc licensor. They charge that some of our CD manufacturing equipment infringes on their patents. They are seeking unspecified "substantial damages" and note that there is still litigation pending from 1988 when they accused us of two other optical disc patent violations.

The resolution of these charges is uncertain. I will keep you advised.

ASTRAL RECORDS, Ltd. *North America* *Pigeon Forge, TN* Tel. (615) 356-9889

TO: Sir Max

FROM: Sandy Bien-Fait
Human Resource Manager

DATE: August 16, 1993

SUBJECT: Hiring

Sir Max —

We can't afford to lose any more time addressing the issue of hiring. The increase in production has strained the existing shift personnel. And, as I mentioned last week at our weekly tea, the surrounding area just doesn't have the numbers of workers we need. Either we have to pay more or get them from somewhere else. I need authorization to hire 20 shift workers immediately.

Also, Sir Max, I think it is time to eliminate playing a musical instrument as a hiring criterion. We have simply run out of musicians in the community.

ASTRAL RECORDS, Ltd. *North America* *Pigeon Forge, TN* Tel. (615) 356-9889

TO: Sir Max

FROM: Margaret Lee
Public Relations

CC: Bart O'Reilly
Vice President, Operations

DATE: March 7, 1993

SUBJECT: CD Rot

There have been an increasing number of articles in the trade press describing a phenomenon known as "CD rot." If the CD rot stories are true, certain CDs may begin to self-destruct within 8–10 years because the ink used for labeling begins to eat into the protective lacquer coating. This in turn can oxidize the aluminum layer resulting in an unplayable CD.

Although we have not yet had any inquiries or returns due to "CD rot," we should nevertheless be prepared to respond to this possible crisis.

ASTRAL RECORDS, Ltd. *North America* *Pigeon Forge, TN* Tel. (615) 356-9889

TO: Sir Max

FROM: Carl Christie, Ph.D.
Research and Development

DATE: August 16, 1993

SUBJECT: Project FutureVision

We are at the breakthrough stage on Project FutureVision. Compression technologies are progressing at an acceptable rate, and we anticipate being able to place full-length motion pictures with Dolby Surround Sound tracks on a 5-inch disc within the next 6 months.

I don't need to tell you about the commercial possibilities. However, the lab is feeling the pinch financially right now. My people have estimated that we need another $3.5 million within the next month in order to complete our work. Since you have been so generous in the past, I know that we all can count on your continued support.

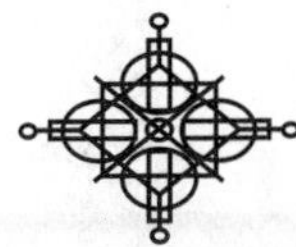

ASTRAL RECORDS, Ltd. *North America* *Pigeon Forge, TN* Tel. (615) 356-9889

TO: Sir Maxwell S. Hammer

FROM: Abby McDeere
Chief Legal Counsel

DATE: August 10, 1993

SUBJECT: Lawsuit against Astral

On August 7th, I met with Richard Milhous, Chief Legal Counsel for Master-Vision. After protracted discussion and negotiation, they have offered a settlement for all litigation pending against us.

They have offered to settle for either a one-time cash payment of $5 million or a 4-cent-per-disc royalty over the next 10 years of production.

We must respond by the 24th of August. Please advise me of your decision.

ASTRAL RECORDS, Ltd. *North America* *Pigeon Forge, TN* Tel. (615) 356-9889

TO: Sir Max

FROM: Bruce Park-Asbury
Shift Supervisor

CC: Sandy Bien-Fait
Human Resource Manager

DATE: August 17, 1993

SUBJECT: Employee Reprimand

This is the third time that I have had to reprimand Sonny Barger for being insubordinate. I am at my wits end with him and don't know what to do.

On February 7, Barger refused to clean up his work area, and I gave him a formal reprimand. On March 23, Barger was found taking an unauthorized cigarette break and was again reprimanded. On August 16, Barger left his station 15 minutes before quitting time to run to his car to turn on the air conditioning. I suppose so it would be cool when he got out. I wrote him up for this incident. He told me to watch out, he was going to get me and "the whole damn company."

I honestly believe that Barger is trying to undermine my authority as shift supervisor. If something doesn't change, I may have to leave Astral.

CROSBY, SELLS, CASH AND YOUNG

CERTIFIED PUBLIC ACCOUNTANTS KNOXVILLE, TN

TO: Sarah Conner

FROM: Janet Young

SUBJECT: Audit Planning Meeting

DATE: August 23, 1993

I wanted to make sure that you were aware of the planning meeting to discuss our audit of Astral's financial statements for the fiscal year ended December 31, 1993, that is scheduled for 10:00 A.M. on Friday, September 10th. We hope to begin our preliminary audit work on Monday, September 27th.

Please be advised that we intend to continue our discussion about Astral's contingent environmental liabilities. We told Sir Max last year that the 1993 financial statements would likely contain at least footnote disclosure of environmental issues and, perhaps, even reflect actual environmental liabilities. Please be prepared to bring us up to date on all environmental matters.

Also, we just heard about the "CD rot" problem. This could have a material effect on Astral's financial statements. We are anxious to learn more about it from your production personnel. Finally, we will need current information about actual and pending litigation. What is happening regarding the MasterVision case?

I look forward to meeting you. If you need to reschedule our meeting, that's OK, but we don't have a lot of flexibility. Please let me know ASAP.

ASTRAL RECORDS, Ltd. *North America* *Pigeon Forge, TN* Tel. (615) 356-9889

TO: Sir Max

FROM: Ed Heath
Foreman, Waste Disposal Unit

SUBJECT: Equipment Maintenance

DATE: August 13, 1993

The PCB filtration actuators are breaking down regularly these days. We really need to replace these units. I know replacements are very expensive, but this stuff is really toxic and these units are almost to the end of their serviceable life. It won't take much to cause a major problem. In fact, just yesterday, one of our technicians knocked the master valve loose and it took us almost three hours to clean up the spill.

I've talked with the finance people a number of times about getting replacements, but I can't seem to get an answer. We need to move on this soon.

August 17, 1993

Sir Maxwell S. Hammer
President and CEO
Astral Records, N.A.
Pigeon Forge, TN

Sir Max:

DECEMBER is thrilled that Astral Records is interested in placing them under contract. Plans are well underway for the signing party and free concert in Pigeon Forge on the 26th.

I know this will be the beginning of a successful relationship. Attached is our sketch for the cover art of our first CD.

Regards,

Matthew D. Booth

Matthew D. Booth
Business Manager, DECEMBER

Attachments: 1

DECEMBER

For the World is Hollow and I Have Touched the Sky

DECEMBER is
Kevin Albers—Keyboards
Matt Booth—Bass Guitar
Michael King—Vocals
Bryce Smith—Drums

Lighting Techs:
George Ackert, Steven Harper

Road Crew:
Kevin Asherfeld, Dave Erickson

Recorded at: SRS Austin TX

Engineered by: Ben Blank

Send all correspondence to:

DECEMBER
P.O. Box 49188
Austin, TX 78765
(512) 472-8943

Thanks to:
Steven, George, Kevin, Dave, Jim, Sharron, Tim, Matt, Jeanette W., Mark P., and Liberty Lunch. Grace Wall, Derek "Matt kicked me out of the band" Brownlee. Jan Long, Mark A., Dave H., and especially Jill Isreal, and Lisa McBride.

Back-up vocals on
Darkest Cave by:
Jill Isreal

Lyrics to *A Letter to Vernon Lee*
Inspired by the play *Madame X*
by Anne Ciccolella

ASTRAL RECORDS, Ltd. *North America* *Pigeon Forge, TN* Tel. (615) 356-9889

Sir Max,

You should know that Roberta Prospect was seen leaving Arnold Smither's house yesterday morning at 6 a.m.! Smither is the purchasing manager at Republic Records. Aren't they one of our biggest customers? I think this is just scandalous.

Your faithful employee

(Sorry, but I can't sign my name.)

ASTRAL RECORDS, Ltd. *North America* *Pigeon Forge, TN* Tel. (615) 356-9889

TO: Sarah Conner

FROM: Richard Cory
Treasurer

DATE: August 24, 1993

SUBJECT: Capital Structure Summary

In response to your request, I am summarizing Astral's current financial structure below. Note that the line of credit and 5-year term loan are with YurBank and that the 15-year subordinated debt is a loan obtained at a favorable rate from BLL in 1987. As you can see, we have just about reached our debt limit. We probably should discuss this at your convenience. However, the sooner the better.

CAPITAL STRUCTURE ($ MILLIONS)	
Line of credit	0.5
Term loan	3.0
Subordinated debt	10.0
Equity	6.5
Total	20.0

CASE 4

INTERNATIONAL COLOUR ENVELOPE ADVISORS A/S

Never prostitute yourself for the sake of business.
Never do something if you do not believe in it.

Gorm Kristiansen, 1992

Gorm Kristiansen sat at his desk looking out of the window at the summer rain. He was contemplating the future of the company he had worked so hard to build. The financial situation of International Colour Envelope Advisors A/S (ICEA) was tight: ICEA was growing too quickly; he was unable to buy the machinery necessary to fill all of the orders that ICEA could possibly generate; and getting loans in Denmark was very difficult because the economy was not healthy and many small businesses had failed. If Kristiansen could not get the working capital he needed, he might have to consider making a public offering of ICEA stock—an option he would rather not have to think about right now. Kristiansen preferred to retain his 100-percent control of ICEA.

Coupled with the financial dilemma was the problem that growth had caused in the company's culture. The culture that was appropriate for a small living-room-based enterprise might not be appropriate for the growth opportunities ICEA now faced. The business had started out with 3 people but had grown to 72. What sorts of changes would have to be made for ICEA to remain successful? Could the informality of the ICEA workplace be maintained?

COMPANY HISTORY

Kristiansen had started out as a partner in a small company in Pandrup, Denmark, that sold printed business forms. In the course of day-to-day business, he had met several individuals who were involved in the photo-processing industry. Kristiansen had learned that this industry was particularly lucrative and had decided to look for ways to enter into it. He and his partners had decided to buy photo wallets and film mailers from an Austrian company, then sell them to photo processors. By 1979, the photo side of Kristiansen's business accounted for 60 percent of the company's turnover and 80 percent of its profits. Kristiansen was the only one of the partners taking care of the photo business, so he wanted to split the company up and take on the photo business himself. Nevertheless, he owned only 12½ percent of the company's shares. He stated that "my partners ended up kicking me out of the business entirely."

Kristiansen had to start all over again and build a business from scratch. In 1980, Kristiansen decided to start his own company to target the photo-wallet and

This case was prepared by Maria Holcomb, Darden MBA 1993, under the supervision of L. J. Bourgeois.

film-mailer market. He named it International Colour Envelope Advisors (ICEA). Kristiansen worked out of his home as an agent once again, buying mailers and photo wallets from the same Austrian company he had dealt with before. He had two persons working with him: one worked in the living room, another in the children's room; meetings were held in the kitchen. Soon no space was left unclaimed in the house.

ICEA began by selling to Scandinavian photo processors. At the time, it competed with six to eight suppliers, including Kristiansen's old partners. Two years into his business, Kristiansen had become successful enough to dominate the Scandinavian wallet-and-mailer market, which caused his former partners to exit the business, along with many smaller suppliers of these products. Kristiansen credited his highly targeted strategy for this success. Photo mailers and wallets were not the other companies' essential business, so they had not felt overly threatened by Kristiansen's presence there and had been willing to let him dominate this small segment of the market. Kristiansen's success, however, did lead to a backlash from his Austrian supplier, Paka. Paka not only sold supplies to agents like Kristiansen but also had direct customers within the photo-processing business. Suddenly, Paka found itself in a predicament: Kristiansen was able to buy product from Paka and sell it to his customers at a much higher price than Paka was selling to its direct customers. (Kristiansen attributed his ability to command higher prices to the excellent relationships he built with his customers.) Kristiansen was earning so much money that Paka raised its prices to him. This increase put pressure on Kristiansen's margins, which meant that Kristiansen had to create an alternative to keep Paka from increasing its prices further. In 1982, Kristiansen decided to begin producing the mailers and wallets himself.

"I just wanted to have a small amount of production to keep them [Paka] quiet. This was a strategic move on my part," recalled Kristiansen. "I got a partner who would take care of the production management, and I handled the sales. I brought in another person as the company's accountant to handle all of the financial details."

Kristiansen applied for a government loan to pay for his first machinery. The loan was granted and production began. Once production began, however, Kristiansen discovered that, in order to make a profit, he would have to run high-scale production, which meant that he no longer needed to buy from Paka at all. Paka retaliated by beginning to push its products heavily in the Scandinavian market. In response, ICEA attacked Paka's other European markets. ICEA would soon become a dominant force in the marketplace.

The Photo Market in Europe

The European photo market was characterized by the demand created by consumers' need for developed film, which led to laboratories' and dealers' need for processing products, including photo mailers and envelopes. Photo mailers were the special envelopes used to send exposed rolls of film from the photo dealer to the processing lab. Photo envelopes were the colorful envelopes used to return the processed photographs to the consumer. In this business, prosperity depended a great deal on consumers' desire to take pictures.

In Europe, the principal markets for photo supplies were experiencing a rise in demand for pictures, measured in terms of exposed film, of 2 percent to 5 percent a year. Because the proliferation of dealers and labs in Europe offered consumers more choice, consumers were beginning to demand better service and quality from photographic suppliers. Dealers and processors had to find ways to differentiate themselves so they could stay in business, and they put emphasis on the quality of the finished product, price, quick development, safe delivery, and personal service.

The advent of new technologies, such as CDs, videos, and computers, was not expected to impact the market for paper prints to any great extent. Because of this expectation, large photo producers such as Kodak were spending millions of dollars to build factories that produced regular films for exposure. Suppliers to the photo market, however, needed to be aware that new technologies existed that might come into play in the future.

Within the photo-processing industry, an increasing number of mergers and acquisitions of photo labs were taking place, resulting in large chains of photo laboratories across Europe. Many of the acquisitions were done by multinational photo producers (e.g., Kodak and Fuji) that wanted to control the total photo experience. These companies wanted to have a hand in everything from the production of film to the processing of exposed film.

In order to grow their businesses, labs and dealers were concentrating to a greater degree than before on customer segmentation, offering services based on the individual needs of different customer groups. For example, households that used a great deal of film would be given one set of coupons or promotions to reinforce usage, while individuals who took very few pictures would be given a different set of coupons to encourage them to try the product. These activities led to an increased need for database technologies within labs and dealerships to help keep up with sales activities and distribution. Photo labs were also entering the direct-mail market so they could bypass photo dealers altogether.

At the same time, the photo-lab suppliers were developing in two different directions. They were either concentrating on price competition or developing products and services of high quality or distinction that would help labs improve their service and quality images.

Photo-Wallet and Mailer Suppliers

The three main suppliers of photo envelopes and mailers in Europe at this time were ICEA, Kieser, and Paka-Seetal (see Exhibit 1 for the competitors' European market shares). Kieser was a German company that was able to run its production

Exhibit 1

European Market Shares for Print-Wallet, Workbag, and Mailer Markets, 1991

	Print Wallets	Workbags	Mailers
Paka-Seetal	45%	20%	25%
Kieser	0	44	35
ICEA	21	1	25
Others	34%	35%	15%

operations efficiently, so it was able to sell at very low prices. The quality of Kieser's products, while good, was not considered to be as high as that of either ICEA or Paka-Seetal. Kieser sold its products through a direct sales force, as well as through agents who represented many suppliers of photo products.

Paka-Seetal, an Austrian company, was a high-quality, low-cost producer. Although it was considered to be a good service provider to its customers, the company was not able to help customers design new or different products. If the specific product that a customer needed was not available in the current catalog, the customer had to compromise. Paka-Seetal sold by means of a direct sales force, as well as through agents. Paka-Seetal, like Kieser, sold other products to other industries; the company did not specialize in the photographic industry.

The third competitor was ICEA, a small Danish company that focused on the photo market. ICEA produced photo mailers and wallets and helped dealers and labs develop databases for keeping up with their customers. ICEA had also entered into the photo mail-order market. ICEA was known for its high-quality products and its customer service. If a photo lab or dealer wanted a particular product, ICEA salespeople would do whatever was necessary to get that product produced. ICEA priced its products at a slight premium, but customers believed the price was justified by the specialization and the service. ICEA sold exclusively through a direct sales force.

Originally, suppliers had had to use different sales approaches with photo labs and dealers in each of the European countries. Even if a lab was part of a chain, its needs were distinct because of the variations in language and marketing among European countries. The situation had begun to change, however. As companies like Kodak began to create large networks of labs throughout Europe, and with the advent of the European Common Market, large multicountry contracts were beginning to come into play. It was very important for suppliers to have the service, price, quality, and capacity necessary to fulfill these contracts. This trend also meant that suppliers were beginning to depend on fewer customers for their sales. The loss of a single large customer could be devastating.

ICEA

ICEA was involved in the design and production of photo wallets and mailers. ICEA also helped customers develop databases that enabled labs and dealers to keep track of who their customers were and when and how customers were being served. The data could then be used to formulate marketing plans. In addition, ICEA had entered into the photo-developing mail-order arena by helping mail-order companies handle their customers. ICEA had a computerized system that inserted information and mail-order forms into envelopes, labeled the envelopes, and sent out the mailings for mail-order houses. If a mail-order processor had 300,000 customers on file, ICEA would do the total mailing for the mail-order house. ICEA could also personalize each packet for each customer and insert different information into different customers' mailings.

ICEA stressed quality and service in all that it did. The salespeople worked closely with each customer to help develop the product best fitted to the customer's needs. ICEA handled everything from the design to the production of the wallets and mailers. Kristiansen's basic principle for his company was to sell an idea first, then sell the product. For this reason, ICEA organized its five-person sales force by customer rather than by country. In this way, no overlap occurred, because one salesperson could see to all of a customer's needs. The travel expenses within this system were very high because a customer might have locations in several different countries, but ICEA believed that handling sales this way gave better service and increased quality.

All salespeople had assistants, called order administrators, for planning orders and making quotations. Order administrators planned all production in and out of house, planned deliveries, and drew up contracts. These assistants went out into the field with the salespeople twice a year so the customers could get to know them. ICEA always wanted its customers to be able to reach a familiar person.

The hiring of new office staff could be a problem, because ICEA dealt with a very specialized industry; it took one to two years for ICEA to train a fully functional employee. ICEA tried to hire either product specialists or language specialists. Hiring a person who was both was difficult. A language specialist was better than a product specialist because ICEA dealt with customers in many different countries. Training consisted of six months of education in production to learn about the products. Then, six months were spent in the sales department with a salesperson. Finally, after assisting another order administrator for six months, the trainee was ready to be on his or her own.

Company Culture

Although ICEA had grown from a small entrepreneurial company that employed 2 people to one that employed 72, its underlying culture had not changed a great deal. Indeed, maintaining the entrepreneurial feel of the company had been of prime importance to all involved. One of ICEA's employees summarized the atmosphere in this way: "This is a very laid-back place. You have your job. You have to do it. You know that. And it is informal. In many companies, the management is up on a pedestal and everyone else is somewhere below. It is not like that at ICEA. Everyone is very accessible." Unfortunately, the lack of an evolving culture was beginning to present problems to the management and the staff of the company. (See Exhibit 2 for ICEA's organization chart.)

Exhibit 2

International Colour Envelope Advisors Organizational Chart

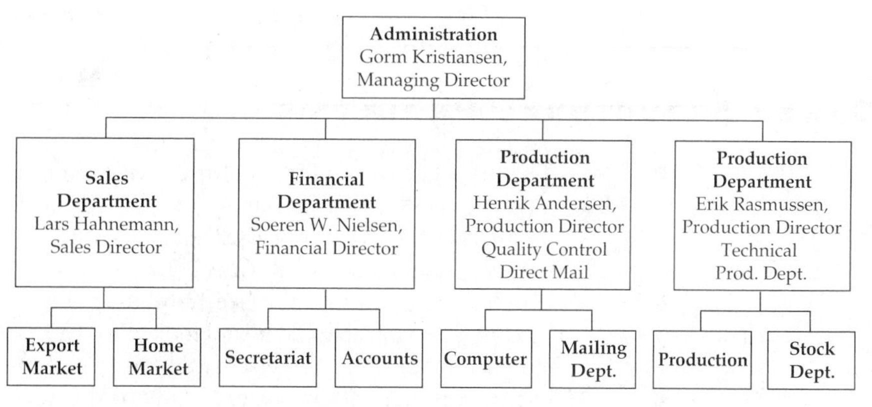

ICEA was considered by its sales and administrative people to be a very dynamic place to work. When employees were asked to describe the atmosphere at ICEA, the two words they used most frequently were "flexibility" and "engagement." The nature of the business and ICEA's desire to accommodate its customers meant that the employees had to be flexible in their day-to-day activities. Adaptability was very important because one never knew what might occur on a given day; the staff had to be ready for changes in customers' needs right up to the moment that printing occurred. People at ICEA had to be willing to work with these changes to get things done on time. Consequently, people were very involved with their work. Everyone still believed that the work they did had a major impact on the success of the company.

The workforce of ICEA was divided into two very different and separate groups: administration and production.

The front-office staff (administration and sales) were willing to do whatever it took to make the company succeed. They were amenable to coming in early and staying late—anything to make sure that their tasks were accomplished. These jobs were definitely not 9 to 5. Everyone in the sales and marketing departments felt as if ICEA were one big family.

The employees in production, however, did not necessarily feel the same way. Although the employees of the production department were very loyal to the company, they sometimes felt forgotten by management in the front office. Because three shifts were always running, management was not always aware of the great job that someone on the third shift might have done. Because production ran 24 hours a day, the technical staff were not together all the time. In addition, because two-thirds of the staff were not around during normal working hours, they were not necessarily aware of what was happening in the front office. Thus, the production staff did not feel like a family in the same way that the administrative staff did.

It was very hard for people to describe, but a separation seemed to exist between the sales department and the production department. As one sales employee stated, "The people in production think differently than do the people in sales, and this difference has sometimes led to friction."

Furthermore, the production employees had gone on strike six months earlier. At first, it had simply been a work slowdown, but a three-day strike eventually occurred. The entire process of negotiations had taken about two months. Although the strike was mostly about monetary issues, the nonmonetary issues still lingered. After the strike, people had to get over a lot of bad feelings. A loss of trust had occurred between management and the production staff.

Other Structural Problems

The informality of ICEA's culture was leading to problems as the company grew. There was no formal written policy that outlined company structure, responsibilities, decision-making processes, and so forth. In 1990, the employees had together written a document called *ICEA Thoughts*, which was intended to outline the company's strategy until 1995 (see Exhibit 3). This document talked about the past, laid out a mission statement, and looked to the future. Unfortunately, after this document was typed up and circulated, it seemed to fade from sight. It was put away in a file cabinet and forgotten. Many of the newer employees who had started at the company after 1990 did not even know of its existence. Some of the older employees had only vague memories of what the document actually said.

EXHIBIT 3

Excerpts from *ICEA Thoughts*

TOWARD YEAR 1995

ICEA has now lived through, and—strange as it may sound—survived its first hard years after a "difficult delivery." But, we made it, thanks to an unconquerable will, an incredible performance, and a good solidarity, and lately we have glimpsed improved results in our accounts.

We are now in midstream. Shall we lean back in our chairs and enjoy that we did succeed after all, or shall we try to create an even healthier and more competitive company that is able to deal with the challenges of the future?

In ICEA, we have decided to do the latter. The future has a lot of challenges to offer ICEA, and already now, we have to prepare ourselves to take up these challenges. The competition is hard and will be even harder. And winning is what we like best.

If ICEA is to obtain results on a long view in terms of increased income and competitive improvements, it is important that we "set out" properly. Therefore, we present the targets and the lines for our work until the year 1995. The year 1995 is close enough to be realistic, and yet so far away that we can adapt ourselves to it.

The most important element is our customers, and it must not be forgotten that ICEA's most important task is not to "sell," but to fulfill the customers' needs for products and services. This is a long view, the only way to make an income and to grow. In most cases, the customers can choose between several suppliers. We are, on the contrary, in our capacity as a supplier, dependent on our customers.

ICEA's future depends on the contribution made by each of us—also you—in common to fulfill customers' needs. The customer orientation must be intensified, and both the sales staff and the production staff are to cooperate on making the product-and-service package as attractive as possible to the customer. We also have to improve our internal efficiency considerably through a more formalized control and through information about the activities in ICEA.

It is time to start now!

WE HAVE A MISSION

ICEA will, on its own and in cooperation with partners, develop, produce, and sell solutions to fulfill the photo laboratories' needs in connection with their servicing of the final photo user.

ICEA's product concept is built up with the photo laboratory in the center strongly attached to its three basic needs:

- Marketing
- Production control
- Distribution

(continued)

ICEA's product-and-service package is directed to fulfillment of the individual customer's special needs for "tailor-made" solutions—partial as well as total solutions.

In this way, ICEA will contribute to the biggest possible dividend on the activities of the company to the shareholders and to good jobs for the employees, with development and career possibilities for each individual employee.

Good for Good People . . . This Is ICEA

In ICEA, the employees are the most important resource, because ICEA is completely dependent on human beings and human relations.

The quality of ICEA's employees in production as well as sales and administration is of vital importance to the success of the company.

Our contact to our customers is of the utmost importance . . . as *all our activities start here*. In ICEA all employees are—at any time—representing the company.

We believe that success is made through a positive and active performance by each individual employee, no matter what his position in the organization. The employees have a joint responsibility.

We like to be busy—and we like to set high targets and to reach them.

And It Is Still Our Customers Who Are Paying Our Salaries

A good employee is trying to solve problems and is not only focusing on questions of guilt or pointing out problems.

We like employees who are prepared and capable of working in an environment requiring the key factors of professional competence, efficiency, cooperation, joint responsibility, and flexibility.

We will improve the qualifications of employees through training and increased information, which will make their jobs meaningful and make them understand ICEA's growth and direction of development.

ICEA will offer good employees permanent and lasting working conditions with salaries according to the work performed and modern welfare arrangements.

Good Quality . . . This Is ICEA

Good quality = more satisfied customers = higher profitability. Therefore, ICEA's main task is to create products and services with which the customers will be satisfied. In the long run, this is the only way to make income and to grow.

There is only one reason for charging a good price for a product or a service: the quality is good according to the customers' judgments.

(continued)

Excerpts from *ICEA Thoughts*

We believe that the employees whose work is of good quality can be proud of their company and satisfied with their work.

If ICEA is to function as a single unit qualitywise, it is necessary that all employees show a positive attitude toward quality.

A good quality of products and services, which will meet the requirements of our customers, is not made by the production staff alone. There are many conditions and activities in ICEA which influence the quality of products and services.

It is important for ICEA that all conditions that influence the quality—both the construction quality of products and processes and the production quality and the marketing quality of sales and services—are systematized.

The way we do our jobs, and the cooperation which can be established across the various functions to make sure that the customers get the right production and service quality, are all factors which influence quality and quality control.

One of the most essential messages we will bear in mind in our efforts to make good quality in all functions is

Do it right each time!

This message clearly expresses the basics—it is better and more inexpensive to do things right the first time.

ICEA's Image

We want to establish at any time by means of our first-class products and customer service that

ICEA is an active, creative company oriented toward the photo laboratories—that we are the only company which is professionally fulfilling the photo laboratories' requirements for marketing, production control, and distribution.

ICEA is the only right choice for the good photo-lab customer and for good employees.

There is no reason to hide that we are on the right road, that we are very good at our work and have success. This attracts good customers and creates new successes.

What about the Culture?

The ICEA spirit is, however, not only a question of strategy, good sales, income, and cost control.

The inner value—which is so difficult to measure—the way we behave toward each other every day is also of vital importance.

We have a good place of work which is to be made even better. What active part do you want to play in this process?

One difficulty arose because of all the extra work people were asked to do; employees stated that they sometimes felt as though they were not appreciated for all their hard work.

Henrik Andersen, production director, acknowledged this problem:

> I think that we sometimes forget to take care of people's time. A major project comes up and you think that a certain individual would be best to handle that project. Then it is given over to that person regardless of how busy he or she may be. Even if a person is very busy, he will not say no. This leads to some frustration on the part of the employees.

Another problem was the lack of a formalized communication system. Although ICEA did have an open-door policy that encouraged people to discuss their ideas, if someone was not in the office at the time a particular subject was discussed, he or she might never be informed about the outcome of that discussion. The problem of information exchange among sales, administration, and production was becoming especially acute. For many years, ICEA had not been particularly effective in telling its production employees what was going on in the sales department: Memos were posted, but they were not always read. Production staff became frustrated because they never really understood why the salespeople were constantly making changes. Production believed that it would make more sense to do large runs of standardized products rather than small quantities of many different products. There also seemed to be a lack of communication between sales and production people regarding the degree of quality necessary for shippable products.

Some believed that management needed to do a better job of instilling in the technical staff a true understanding of how necessary quality was and what ICEA's quality standards were. Because ICEA promoted its products' quality, it was very important for everyone in the company to realize that attention to detail was critical. This lack of communication about quality was demonstrated in an incident where one million envelopes came out spotted. Production had let these envelopes run through the printers even though the envelopes would not be acceptable to a customer. It was a huge waste, and nothing was done about it until it was too late. When asked about the incident, Kristiansen said, "I do not know if the production employees could not fix the problem so they let the envelopes continue through the system, or if they simply did not care that the problem existed."

Some efforts were being made to address the communication problems between management and production. More meetings were held with production employees to keep them informed, work groups had been formed, and time and money were being spent on training. Newsletters were placed in each employee's pay envelope. Several sales managers indicated that they believed it would be a good idea to take production employees out on sales calls or to trade shows so they could get firsthand knowledge of how ICEA tried to meet its customers' demands.

Even though the employees recognized that some changes in the company's culture and structure were necessary for the continued strength of the business, most were resistant to change. They seemed to fear that the introduction of more structure into ICEA would ruin the company. Everyone wanted to maintain the flexibility that the flat organizational structure permitted. Most people equated more structure and enhanced communication systems with extra paperwork and an impersonal workplace.

Decision-Making Process at ICEA

Some employees believed that teamwork was an important aspect of decision making within the company. Others pointed out that, even though decisions might be discussed, Kristiansen ultimately made most of the decisions for the company. Lars Hahnemann, sales director, stated, "Apart from price setting and sales contracts with customers, Gorm is making almost all the decisions, big and small." Klaus Pinsker, sales manager, elaborated further:

> If we could get into an organization where we would be free of frustrating, impulsive decisions from Gorm, things would run more smoothly. He has ideas on many levels that do not belong to his kind of job. For example, at the beginning of this week he decided that everyone should have a clean desk, and he wanted everyone to straighten his desk. But there is only a limited area of space, and I have a reason for having certain things on my desk. These are ideas outside of Gorm's level of dealing, things which should not belong to his job function.

Another sales manager related another example of Kristiansen's involvement in all decisions of the company:

> Last spring, a fuss developed in the company canteen's kitchen about how to organize the dishes. Gorm involved himself 100 percent in deciding how the dirty plates should be stacked. It was completely crazy . . . the staff in the kitchen was completely furious. This kind of discussion should not involve the general manager of the company. It should have been resolved by the canteen manager. If general management is involved in this type of problem, the employees start to wonder why he has so much time for this. Doesn't he have more important things that he should be attending to?

No one was saying that Kristiansen should not be making decisions for his company. The consensus, however, was that he needed to place limits on his involvement with some of the more mundane decisions—decisions that could be handled quite competently by others in the organization.

In the early years, when ICEA was small, it was possible and necessary for Kristiansen to have a hand in all aspects of running the business. He knew all of the customers. He knew what was needed to make his company perform well. As the company grew, however, Kristiansen had been unable to let go of some of his decision-making power. Several members of the executive board believed that Kristiansen realized he could no longer make every decision for every aspect of day-to-day life within ICEA. Unfortunately, Kristiansen had not been able to relinquish this authority.

Flemming Larson, a salesperson, summed up the situation this way:

> Gorm does have to learn something. He has to learn how to go from the role he was in before, where he oversaw all aspects of the company. He has to become the general manager of the company and not the manager of the kitchen, etc. But before he can step out of the old role, the general directors of the company must be ready. If Gorm is always there to pick them up whenever they fall down, then they will never learn to keep themselves from falling. This is not just a requirement for Gorm. Everyone in this organization has to do things differently. We will

> have to go through turbulence. First-line management needs more responsibility, and Gorm needs to back off somewhat. He should take a chance not to get himself involved. If something goes wrong, he should leave it be and let others learn how to pick up after themselves.

Gorm Kristiansen

Gorm Kristiansen was a dynamic man. While attending The Executive Program (TEP) at the Darden Graduate School of Business Administration during the summer of 1992, he was described by one program manager as looking exactly like a Viking should look. She said, "He is tall and broad shouldered with blond hair and a scruff of a beard." Several people in the ICEA organization said that he had more ideas than was humanly possible to act on.

During his summer at TEP, one story that circulated about Kristiansen involved his relationship with his local airport. Apparently, Kristiansen was always running late and in danger of missing his plane. To avert disaster, he would simply call the airport to let them know he would not be on time. The people at the airport knew him well and would hold the plane for him. This story typifies the self-confidence that Kristiansen was able to project. (He was usually the last one in at TEP classes as well. Upon his late arrival, his fellow TEPers would greet him in unison with a hearty "Gorm!")

Kristiansen began ICEA from the ground up. He saw the possibility of creating a market niche in the photo-wallet-and-mailer market, and he decided to take advantage of that niche. Kristiansen was not averse to taking risks. Rather, the only thing that frustrated him was seeing an opportunity and being unable to seize it.

The employees of his company all admired him because of his abilities. They liked the fact that Kristiansen was accessible to them. They enjoyed being able to see and interact with him on a daily basis. According to Larson, "Gorm is really the picture of the entrepreneurial personality. His personality comes straight out of the book. He is the theoretical picture of the great innovator. He has a lot of ideas and energy. That is why we are one of the major companies in this business. We are of importance to the market."

When asked why the company had no formal policy or marketing plan, Kristiansen stated that he did not make a big plan because he was afraid that, if he came in with a big plan and was unable to fulfill it, he would jeopardize his position with his employees. He said, "I have no end goal for this company. I want things to be done better every day." Kristiansen characterized ICEA as a rolling ball. He had a feeling about where the company was going, but things moved so quickly in the industry that, if he locked the company into a definite strategy or investment plan for a certain number of years, he believed that he could lose out on something else that would be more important. He added:

> It is not a question of changing the strategy of the company. It is a question of constantly working with it. We must constantly evaluate it, constantly modify it. This does not mean that you change everything. We must modify our plans as necessary. We must be determined. We must make decisions whenever they need to be made. We must not allow things to change by coincidence.

When employees were asked what would happen when Kristiansen retired or left the company, most responded that he would be irreplaceable. The company would lose some of its dynamics. Henrik Andersen, production director, summed it up best: "Gorm knows every machine and wants to be a part of everything. If we hired a professional general manager, it would mean more paperwork and less flexibility."

Financial Difficulties

One of the major problems facing ICEA was a lack of capital. The company had simply grown too fast to meet its monetary needs. The problem weighed heavily on the minds of everyone there.

ICEA was able to generate more orders than it could possibly fill. In addition, large customers like Kodak were demanding higher quality than ever before. New printing machines were needed to make enough high-quality products to meet demand. Hahnemann stated that extra capacity was desperately needed. ICEA was fighting hard to maintain deliveries on time. Normally, ICEA was able to deliver on time, but during peak seasons timely delivery was quite difficult. Nevertheless, because ICEA's sales were based on service, timely delivery was extremely important. ICEA's financial director, Soeren Nielsen, believed that a new printing line could add 12 percent to 40 percent more to the company's bottom line because it would give ICEA the capacity to increase its sales.

Securing financing for expansion, however, was a very large problem. ICEA was currently carrying 37 million Danish kroner (DKK) in short-term debt. The building and machinery were financed through long-term bank loans, while everything else was financed through short-term credit. The amount of interest ICEA had to pay on this debt was dragging the company down. Short-term interest rates were at 15 percent; long-term rates were 9 percent. ICEA wanted, at the very least, to consolidate DKK 10 million of the short-term debt into a long-term loan. Nielsen believed that converting the short-term debt into a long-term loan would give the company more flexibility; ICEA would be able to budget better for the future, and it would feel more secure.

ICEA had several strikes against it whenever it presented its case to the banks. One problem was that the economy in Denmark had been in recession, and many small businesses had failed. Danish banks had lost so much money that they were becoming extremely careful about lending to small businesses.

A second difficulty was that the company had very specialized machinery that the banks did not want to accept as collateral. The buildings that housed ICEA were located in an area of the country that decreased their worth. Had the buildings been nearer to Copenhagen, they probably would have been worth an additional DKK 2 million.

A third problem was the company's financial condition (see Exhibits 4, 5, and 6 for financial statements). ICEA's total equity capital to assets was very low when compared with the amount of debt it was carrying. In addition, ICEA had suffered a loss in 1990 owing to difficulties with a new machine, renovation of old machines, and the loss of a subsupplier at the last moment for the production of print wallets for a major customer. In order not to lose this large customer, ICEA had produced the wallets itself, causing unplanned, heavy extra charges. This loss severely weakened ICEA's financial position, leading most banks to think twice before considering a loan.

If a loan was unavailable, the only way ICEA could get the money it needed for new machinery was to generate it internally. Nielsen stated, however, that internal funds generation would be very difficult because the printers were already running

EXHIBIT 4

International Colour Envelope Advisors Income Statement and Balance Sheet 1989–1992 (in thousands of Danish kroner; DKK 5 = US$1)

	1989	1990	1991	1992
INCOME STATEMENT				
Net turnover	73,206	76,669	75,897	86,752
Variable costs	−46,457	−50,876	−46,283	−51,452
Contribution margin	26,749	25,793	29,614	35,300
Overhead costs	18,099	20,762	20,280	18,325
Return before interest and depreciation	8,650	5,031	9,334	16,975
Depreciation	3,313	4,023	4,273	5,504
Return before interest	5,337	1,008	5,061	11,471
Interest expenses	2,854	3,700	2,975	2,340
Return before extraordinary items	2,483	−2,692	2,086	9,131
Extraordinary items	0	+99	+116	−4,349
Pretax return	2,483	−2,593	2,202	4,782
BALANCE SHEET	1989	1990	1991	1992
Equity capital	4,007	2,031	3,563	15,388
Equity capital including responsible loan capital	8,455	6,407	8,021	15,388
Total balance-sheet amount	46,666	54,193	57,434	44,983
Rate of return	11.4%	1.9%	8.8%	25.0%
Profit ratio	7.3%	1.3%	6.8%	13.2%
Contribution margin ratio	36.5%	33.6%	39.0%	40.7%
Capacity ratio	1.48	1.24	1.46	1.93
Index turnover	100	105	104	119
Index overhead costs	100	115	112	101

NOTE: The key figures have been calculated on the basis of the return before extraordinary items.

at 120 percent capacity, working 24 hours a day, seven days a week. Because the machines had to be run overtime, ICEA incurred overtime costs. Overtime at ICEA, as stipulated in the union contract, was 2.5 times regular pay. A printing technician at ICEA made the equivalent of US$30/hour on regular time and US$75/hour overtime. Nielsen stated, "If we got money for new machinery, we could save all of that overtime pay, and we could have enough money to pay all of the interest on the new loan."

Nielsen believed that ICEA had a 50-50 chance to get the bank loan it needed. Thus, Kristiansen saw himself as being in a deadlocked situation:

EXHIBIT 5

International Colour Envelope Advisors Profit-and-Loss Account
January 1, 1992, to June 30, 1992 (in thousands of Danish kroner)

	REALIZED 1/1/92 TO 6/30/92	BUDGET 1/1/92 TO 6/30/92	REALIZED 1/1/91 TO 6/30/91
Turnover	41,482	39,503	40,373
Variable costs			
Wages	4,950	3,792	4,392
COGS	20,611	20,537	21,074
Total	25,561	24,329	25,466
Contribution margin	15,921	15,174	14,907
Overhead costs			
Sales	2,134	2,277	2,153
Production	4,720	4,410	5,445
Administration	3,241	2,724	3,019
Other (income)	(270)	(248)	(344)
Total overhead	9,285	9,163	10,273
Return before depreciation	6,096	6,011	4,634
Depreciation	2,201	2,590	2,211
Return before interest	3,895	3,421	2,423
Interest	1,390	1,419	1,458
Bad debts	00	100	0
Return before extraordinary items	2,505	1,902	965
Extraordinary income	1,520	00	79
Pretax return	4,025	1,902	1,044

I could attack the market heavily right now because there is high demand for our products, but I cannot do so with our current presses. I want to keep the majority of my company's shares. If I were to sell 50 percent of ICEA's shares, then I could solve the money problem. But, if I sold 50 percent, the buyer could demand first rights over the other 50 percent of the shares, which I would still hold. I would give up a bit of control. It would be a sacrificial move to do this.

CONCLUSION

ICEA was at a turning point. The confusion over where the company's culture should go, in combination with financial difficulties, put pressure on Kristiansen and his managers. Decisions would have to be made as to the best course for the company to follow so it could continue its success.

EXHIBIT 6

International Colour Envelope Advisors Balance Sheet as of June 30, 1992 (in thousands of Danish kroner; DKK 5 = US$1)

	REALIZED 6/30/92	REALIZED 1/1/92
ASSETS		
Intangible fixed assets		
Goodwill	200	400
Deposit—rent	143	143
Depreciation	(100)	(100)
Total intangible fixed assets	243	443
Tangible fixed assets		
Building	7,402	7,385
Technical plants	17,822	15,617
Machines, fixtures, fittings	2,369	1,782
Computer equipment	1,043	816
Automobiles	288	584
Prepayments	1,832	2,517
Depreciation	2,101	0
Total tangible fixed assets	28,655	28,701
Financial fixed assets		
Sparekassen Nordjylland, account held as collateral	4,970	6,900
Shares—FRS + Sparekassen	22	22
Total financial fixed assets	4,992	6,992
Total fixed assets	33,890	35,966
Goods in stock		
Raw materials	3,756	3,090
Finished articles + merchandise	2,441	2,381
WIP	445	880
Total stocks	6,632	6,351
Credits		
Trade debtors	17,901	11,083
Provision for loss	(80)	(146)
Sundry loans	101	18
Accruals	2,204	146

(continued)

SOURCE: ICEA, July 15, 1992. All numbers are as presented in the original report.

EXHIBIT 6 (CONTINUED)

International Colour Envelope Advisors Balance Sheet as of June 30, 1992 (in thousands of Danish kroner; DKK 5 = US$1)

	REALIZED 6/30/92	REALIZED 1/1/92
Loan MK	243	247
Total credits	20,369	11,348
Liquid reserves	221	856
Total net current assets	27,222	18,555
Total Assets	61,112	54,521
LIABILITIES		
Equity capital		
Share capital	3,000	3,000
Reserves	00	00
Carried forward to next year	563	563
Return of the period	4,025	00
Total equity capital	7,588	3,563
Contingent taxation		
Set-aside for contingent taxation	669	669
Liable loan capital		
Long-term debt		
RRF Danmark (credit assoc.)	2,244	2,264
Industriend Realkr. Pond (credit assoc.)	1,433	1,449
Finansiaeringsinst. (credit assoc.)	2,728	3,288
Rongerieget DR Hypotekb. (credit assoc.)	3,450	3,450
Advance payment (regional development grant)	1,520	3,450
Installment payments (1992)	(466)	00
Total long-term debt	10,909	13,901
Short-term debt		
Short-term share of long-term debt	466	0
Bank debt	16,259	18,111
Trade creditors and costs due	13,571	12,176
Current accounts with ICEA Ruvertering I/S	127	148
Other short-term debt	3,302	1,590
V.A.T., etc., due	3,763	(95)
Total short-term debt	37,488	31,930
Total debt	48,397	45,831
Total Debt Plus Equity	61,112	54,521

CASE 5

JIFFY LUBE INTERNATIONAL, INC.

In November 1988, Jiffy Lube's chief executive officer, Jim Hindman, was pondering the future of his company from his offices at the company's Baltimore, Maryland, world headquarters. Less than 10 years before, he had purchased this tiny franchise chain of retail fast-oil-change centers and turned it into the internationally recognized industry leader. In fact, the industry had literally grown simultaneously with his company. Jiffy Lube International (JLI) now boasted about 1,000, mostly franchised, centers and reported more than $250 million in systemwide revenues (including those of its franchisees) during the fiscal year ended March 31, 1988.

Despite its phenomenal growth and the fact that JLI now had about three times as many centers as its closest competitor, the company was under considerable pressure from the financial community and the press. The price of JLI's common stock was at its lowest point ever, and the business press had been increasingly negative in its assessment of JLI's financial condition. Moreover, a Washington-area TV station (located next door to JLI's headquarters) had recently broadcast a damaging news segment that suggested that consumers were taking considerable risks by having their cars serviced at local Jiffy Lube centers; and a Philadelphia TV station was planning a five-part segment there soon.

During the last several months, Hindman and his senior management team had formulated a new strategy to take Jiffy Lube through its next phase of development. The emphasis was to shift from growth to consolidation. Because the elements of this new strategy had not yet been widely communicated outside the company, Hindman thought now would be a useful time to consider where the company was going in light of where it had been.

THE JIFFY LUBE SERVICE CONCEPT

Jiffy Lube emphasized preventive automotive maintenance rather than repair. At its drive-up centers, it offered a complete fluid-maintenance service for all types of automobiles, vans, and light-duty trucks. Customers needed no appointment, and most centers were open between 8 A.M. and 7 P.M., Monday through Saturday. The standard 14-point service was advertised to take only 10 minutes. For an all-inclusive price averaging about $22, the "J-Team" would:

- change the oil (with a well-known brand, usually Pennzoil)
- replace the oil filter
- lubricate the chassis

This case was prepared by Kathi Breen, Darden MBA 1988, under the supervision of John L. Colley Jr., Almand R. Coleman Professor of Business Administration, and L. J. Bourgeois III, associate professor of business administration.

- check and top off all other fluids:
  - —transmission fluid
  - —brake fluid
  - —power steering fluid
  - —differential fluid
  - —windshield washer fluid
  - —battery fluid
- inflate the tires to proper pressure
- examine the air filter (for excessive dirt)
- vacuum the interior of the vehicle
- examine the windshield wiper blades
- clean the windows (or wash the car, where available)

For an extra charge, Jiffy Lube provided ancillary services and products, including flushing and filling the radiator, gear-box service, recharging air-conditioner freon, changing automatic transmission fluid and filter, and installing new air filters, breather elements, windshield wiper blades, and radiator coolant. These add-on services increased the average ticket by about $6.

The typical Jiffy Lube center looked distinctly different from a gas station. It was clean (with no grease spots or dirty tools lying about) and efficiently designed, and it had a comfortable waiting room for customers. Exhibit 1 shows the layout of a Jiffy Lube center with two service bays, each capable of accommodating two cars simultaneously (some centers had three bays and/or a car-wash facility). Cars were driven into one of the bays, entering from the back and exiting to the front. This drive-through design significantly increased the center's capacity as compared with a traditional service station's drive-in/back-out design. Also, JLI centers had a bi-level layout: The floor had an open pit through to the basement over which the car was positioned for servicing. This setup allowed one "lube tech" working below the car to drain the oil and check the chassis and transmission lubrication while two others worked simultaneously at floor level replacing the oil filter, adding new oil (from pull-down hoses), vacuuming the interior, etc.

While the car was being serviced, customers could relax in the waiting room with free coffee and an assortment of magazines or watch the lube techs work through the window. When servicing was complete, the lead technician gave the customer a personal explanation of the exact services performed, at which time the technician could point out any problems and offer ancillary services that could be done on the spot. To encourage repeat business, Jiffy Lube either left a card in the car (noting the mileage at which the next service should be done) and/or mailed a reminder to the customer's home at the appropriate time.

Jiffy Lube's service objectives were modeled after those used by McDonald's: quality, service, cleanliness, and value. To those four, Hindman added another for JLI: convenience. As he often said, "We're selling convenience, not oil." JLI attempted to provide consistent quality across its nationwide system, but visits by this case writer to two centers suggested that service quality varied considerably and that the standard service sometimes took longer than 10 minutes.

The Quick-Lube Industry

The quick-lube (also known as fast-oil-change) industry was one segment of the automotive aftermarket, which included muffler shops (e.g., Midas), Aamco

EXHIBIT 1

Design of a Typical Jiffy Lube Center

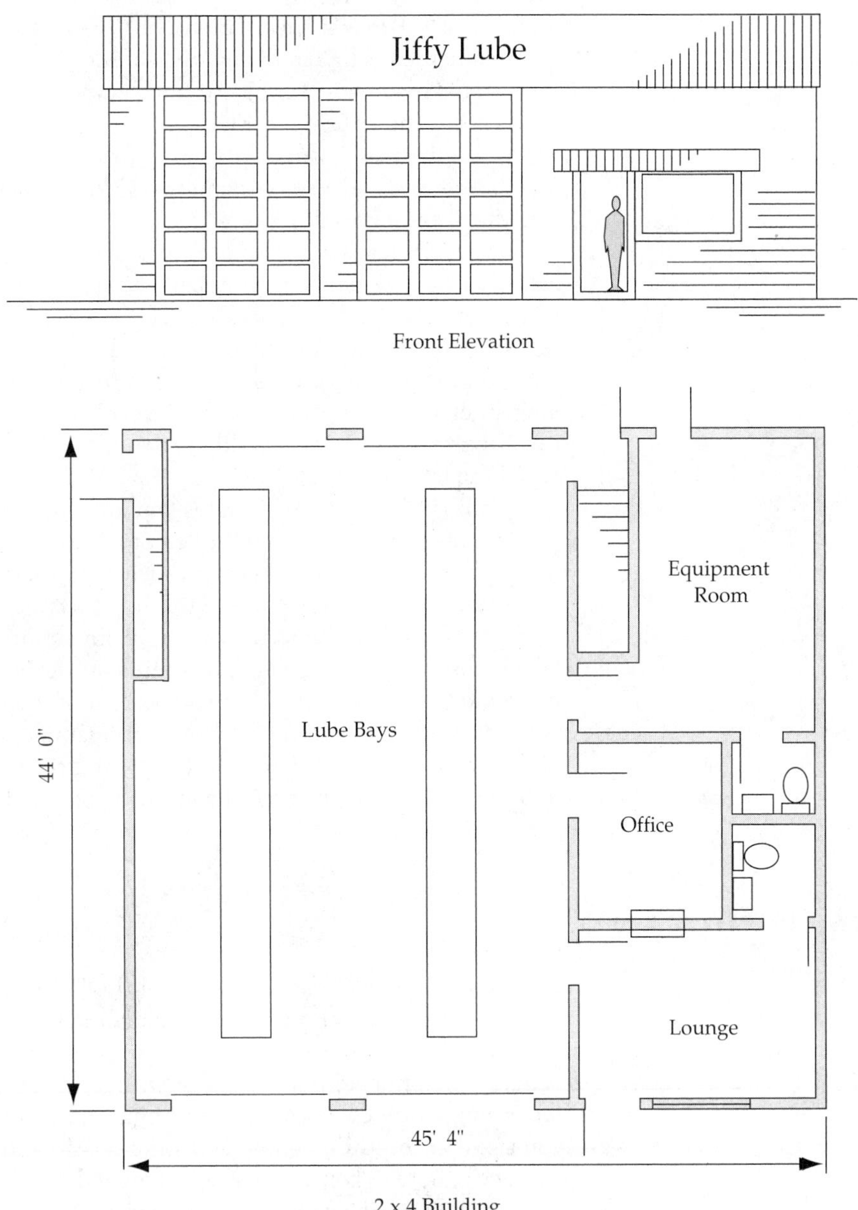

SOURCE: JLI drawing.

transmission specialists, and Goodyear tire/brake centers. Like them, quick-lube centers specialized in one service to focus their message to consumers and achieve operational efficiencies.

The growth of automotive specialty repair/maintenance firms had resulted largely from a steep decline in the number of full-service gas stations over the last

15 years. The oil price shocks of the 1970s drove many gas stations out of business, and most of the remainder dropped repair services to become gas-only outlets. According to information obtained by JLI, there were 226,000 service stations in the United States in 1972, 90 percent of them full-service outlets. By 1986, there were about 110,000 service stations, less than 30 percent full-service.

Despite the decline in the number of service stations, there were more automobiles on the road than ever before, and people were keeping them longer. The number of autos and light-duty trucks grew from 102 million in 1972 to 160 million by 1986, and their average age increased from 5.7 to 7.2 years. The increase in two-income families had also led people to spend money to save time and hassle in getting their cars serviced.

Car owners had several options for obtaining regular fluid-maintenance service. Auto dealers and independent repair shops were available but required that the car be left for a day while this minor work was squeezed in between larger jobs. A local full-service gas station normally charged a lower price than Jiffy Lube for a basic oil change (averaging \$12–\$15), but the service required an appointment and took longer (about 45 minutes), because the car had to be raised and lowered twice on the lift. Finally, a car owner could change his or her own oil, which was messy and took time from other activities.

In late 1988, the United States contained over 3,500 quick-lube centers. The exact number of operators was difficult to determine, because quick-lube service was being provided not only in centers such as JLI's, but sometimes in dedicated bays at gas stations and other auto service shops. About 5 percent of all oil changes were performed by quick-lube centers, up from about 2 percent in 1982. The quick-lube industry was expected to grow rapidly over the next several years, with potential market share as high as 35 to 40 percent of the U.S. oil-change market. Longer new-car warranties offered by U.S. auto manufacturers, which required evidence of regular service, might also contribute to growth. Moreover, there was thought to be a large unfilled market of consumers who did not change their oil as often as they should.

Jim Hindman

Hindman was the prime motivator in the JLI organization. Jiffy Lube's culture had been shaped by his personal code of ethics, which he communicated often and consistently. In "Ain't It Great!" a bound collection of his personal philosophy as delivered in letters to franchisees and in speeches to training classes, he said, "With the wrong attitude you can do everything right and fail, but with the right attitude you can do everything wrong and still succeed." For Hindman, the right attitude was "we're here to help... do what's right and reasonable, even when no one is looking... fairness to the customer... and always work harder than the next guy."

Hindman's background illustrates his self-reliance and drive to achieve. He described himself in a Jiffy Lube public relations release as having been "a strong-willed kid and a street fighter. You'd have to kill me to whip me." He spent part of his childhood in a boys' home, caring for himself and two younger brothers. He put himself through college and graduate school, spent nine years as a hospital administrator, later formed a partnership that built and operated 32 nursing homes, and bought several other businesses. By 1970, at age 35, he was a millionaire.

As he became successful in business, Hindman began to devote time to his college sport, football. In 1977, he became head football coach at Western Maryland

College, working without salary and helping to finance the team by buying equipment and funding scholarships. During his four years as head coach, Hindman turned a losing team into a winning one with an overall record of 21-7-8. He said in a JLI publication:

> I believe firmly in the importance of the old-fashioned American work ethic and the team spirit. This was the philosophy that helped our football team achieve success, and the disciplines that it takes to be a success in football are the same ones it takes to be successful in business.

The Birth of JLI

When a Western Maryland College student complained about the lack of opportunities for young people to make a million dollars today, Hindman was so incensed that he bet the student he (Hindman) could do it again. He later explained that JLI "was born as a personal challenge to the negativism that runs rampant through much of our society. And the growth, success, and health of the chain proves that opportunity is alive and well today."

In mid-1979, Hindman's partnership purchased the trademark, logo, and franchise agreements of a nine-outlet fast-oil-change company in Salt Lake City named Jiffy Lube. He renamed it Jiffy Lube International, Inc., envisioning that JLI would expand to national and even international prominence.

Initially, Hindman both developed company-owned centers and sold franchises, many to his friends and associates. In 1982, however, he decided JLI didn't have the resources to be in both types of business, because a large network of company centers required a large corporate staff to manage it. That year, JLI sold all its stores to franchisees and focused on selling individual new franchises. When Hindman purchased JLI in 1979, his major objective was to reach 100 centers, considered a critical "level of respectability" for a franchisor. It took Jiffy Lube five years to reach that goal.

Growth Strategies

After reaching 100 stores in fiscal 1984, Hindman set a new goal of 1,000 centers by the end of fiscal (March 31) 1989. His strategy was to preempt significant competition before it could get started, and achieve a wide enough scale to support a national advertising effort. (National advertising was considered critical to maximizing daily car counts and establishing Jiffy Lube as the industry leader.) So, the 1,000-store goal became JLI's overriding strategic objective, and it affected almost every action the company took through the end of fiscal 1988.

To accelerate growth, in 1984, JLI began selling area-development rights, which granted an investor the exclusive right to develop and operate Jiffy Lube centers within a particular Area of Dominant Influence (ADI), an advertising term of the Arbitron Rating Service that referred to population centers. The area developer paid a negotiated, nonrefundable fee up front that varied by the potential number of centers to be built, the demographics of the area, and the difficulty of development there. The area developer's continuing right to exclusivity depended on opening a specified number of centers within each year of its five-year contract; in practice, JLI usually granted extensions. The rights to virtually all of the top 30 ADIs had been sold by the end of fiscal 1987.

The area-development program spurred fast growth in the number of franchised Jiffy Lube centers, and area-development fees became an important source of revenue for JLI. JLI discovered that area developers were investors rather than operators, however, who relished "doing deals" over managing their stores and ensuring proper customer service. Hindman believed that this characteristic was a prime reason for the lack of franchisee profitability in some areas, and this problem was to be explicitly addressed in his new strategy.

JLI had also grown by acquiring smaller chains and converting independents to the Jiffy Lube system. In its acquisitions, price had been less a concern than store location and competitive position, because Hindman believed that quick-lube shops would only become more valuable as the industry grew. Most stores JLI acquired were later sold to franchisees, and some acquisitions were made directly by franchisees but financed by JLI. The company also added centers by convincing independent quick-lube operators to become JLI franchisees. Jiffy Lube converted 26 such independents during fiscal 1986, 75 in fiscal 1987, and 83 in fiscal 1988. To encourage these conversions, JLI had sometimes waived initial franchise fees, offered reduced royalty rates for a year or two, and/or provided funds to enable the physical conversion of the centers. JLI rarely built new company-owned centers.

Jiffy Lube's strategy for organizing this growth was to concentrate its centers in the largest (metropolitan) ADIs in order to reach national advertising scale quickly. Furthermore, JLI built "clusters" of centers within each ADI, rather than individual stores in outlying areas, to enhance consumer awareness of both the quick-lube concept and of Jiffy Lube. JLI wanted its name to be the first thing that came to mind when consumers thought about getting an oil change. Clustering was also thought to preempt local competition, and it clearly offered economies of scale in local advertising, distribution of product to the centers, and store management. The distribution of Jiffy Lube centers across the country in June 1988 appears in Exhibit 2.

EXHIBIT 2

Distribution by State of Centers Open at June 30, 1988

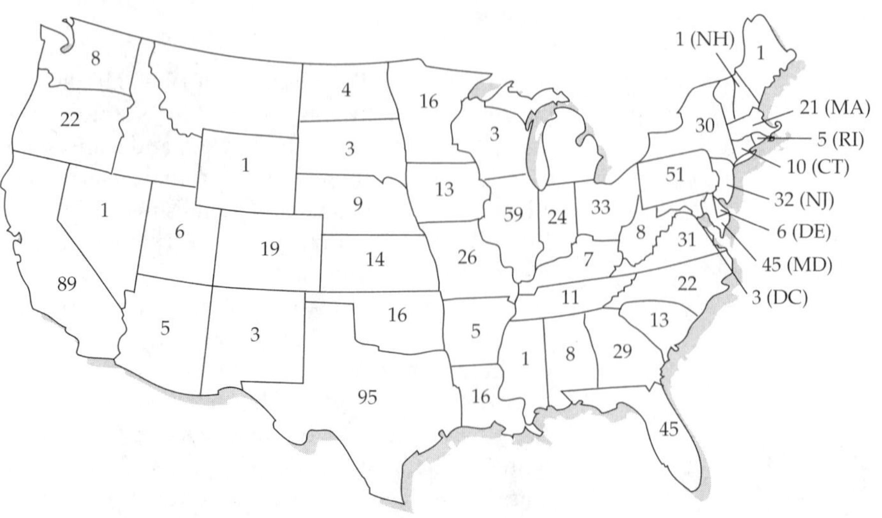

SOURCE: JLI map.

During this high-growth period from 1984 through early 1988, JLI had pursued several goals simultaneously: expanding to 1,000 centers as quickly as possible, increasing daily car counts across the system, and improving the quality of Jiffy Lube service to the consumer. As the summary operating data in Exhibit 3 show, the results were impressive. By November 1988, JLI had more than 1,000 stores, systemwide revenues increased from $28 million in 1984 to $252 million in 1988, and the average daily car count rose from 35.9 in fiscal 1984 to 43.1 in fiscal 1988. The break-even car count (systemwide) was about 35 cars per day, but some centers regularly serviced over 100 a day.

From the beginning, Hindman had dreamed of expanding overseas, which he did in 1988. By March 31, JLI had opened 9 stores in Canada, 5 in Europe, and 1 in

EXHIBIT 3

Jiffy Lube International, Inc. Summary Operating Data

	FISCAL YEAR ENDING MARCH 31				
	1988	1987	1986	1985	1984
NUMBER CENTERS OPEN					
Co-owned	71	29	14	21	1
Franchised	737	532	334	187	119
International	15	—	—	—	—
Total	823	561	348	208	120
NUMBER STATES WITH JL CENTERS	44	39	33	28	23
System sales	$252,082	$151,590	$91,201	$48,750	$27,762
Average ticket price/ vehicle served	$27.63	$27.78	$27.01	$26.24	$24.86
Average no. of vehicles/day	43.1	42.2	41.8	44.0	35.9
Effective royalty rate	5.2%	5.3%	4.6%	4.6%	4.8%

	APRIL 30		
	1988	1987	1986
JLI CORP. EMPLOYEES			
Senior management	16	15	14
Management and professional	77	69	24
Field operations	55	40	25
Clerical	128	81	51
Company-owned centers	855	351	146
Total	1,131	556	260

SOURCE: JLI stock offering prospecti (1986 and 1987) and March 31, 1988, 10-K report to the Securities and Exchange Commission (SEC).

Australia and had another 33 under development abroad. JLI's international strategy was to find local companies to assume a master license, which entitled them to receive initial franchise fees and a share of the royalties of operating centers. In effect, the master licenser was a subfranchisor, investing its own time and money to develop the area. JLI provided support in training, standards, and operating methods and received lower royalties than in the United States because of its reduced role. Elf France, a division of Elf Aquitaine (France's largest oil company), had obtained a direct license for most of Western Europe, and JLI had established an office in Paris to manage its international expansion effort.

Managing Growth

The Role of JLI Corporate Headquarters

As a franchisor, JLI's most significant responsibilities were assisting its franchisees in developing and operating their centers, maintaining systemwide operating standards, and managing the national marketing effort.

Jiffy Lube provided *development assistance* by helping franchisees select sites, manage construction of the centers, and locate financing. All sites had to be approved by JLI, which generally used the criteria listed in Exhibit 4. The company also supplied franchisees with standard center designs and operating procedures and trained new franchisees and store managers.

To provide *operating assistance*, JLI maintained a field force of district managers (DMs). There were 20 DMs in the field to service 753 franchised centers in fiscal 1988; by the end of fiscal 1989, JLI projected it would have 34 DMs to service 970 franchisees. The functions of the field force included training and supervising new center managers and lube techs, communicating JLI's operating standards and merchandising techniques, and troubleshooting operational problems. Apart from the field force, JLI headquarters staff provided training for center personnel, as well as help in organizing regional advertising co-ops and fleet-maintenance programs.

In 1983, JLI acquired Heritage Merchandising to achieve economies of scale through centralized purchasing of nonoil products. As a wholly owned subsidiary, Heritage supplied both franchisees and company-owned centers with 90 percent of their oil filters and air filters as well as other operating supplies and equipment. From its national network of eight public warehouses, Heritage could reach almost all centers within 48 hours. Heritage also distributed various products to outside customers.

If a franchisee had financial or operational problems, JLI might elect to assist in several ways: arranging additional financing, facilitating a transfer of the license agreement to a new franchisee, extending payment terms on accounts and notes due to JLI, or, as a last resort, repurchasing the franchise rights. In such circumstances, JLI had repurchased franchise rights to 16 centers in fiscal 1987 and 41 centers in fiscal 1988. Historically, JLI had been quite successful in buying back financially distressed centers, turning them around, remarketing them to new franchisees, and recovering at least its acquisition cost.

Maintaining Standards. The relationship between JLI and its franchisees was like a partnership, because the company did not enjoy direct authority over

EXHIBIT 4

Preferred Site Parameters for Center Locations

The following preferred site parameters are used in the selection of free-standing sites and shopping center pad locations.

LOCATION

- Corner: most desirable
- Inside: preferably with left-hand turn
- Near shopping center and major food stores
- Near other successful services and fast-food restaurants
- Good visibility from both directions

PROPERTY SIZE

- Range: 10,000–15,000 square feet
- A smaller size may be acceptable, depending upon other characteristics of the site
- With common ingress and egress, as little as 4,000 square feet can be utilized

STANDARD BUILDING SIZE

Building	Size	Square feet
2 × 4	46' × 48'	2,208
1 × 3	34' × 61'	2,074
3 × 6	46' × 61'	2,806

ZONING

- Local zoning that will allow a fast-lube center or that can be rezoned

TRAFFIC

- 20,000 plus cars per day
- Two-way, undivided traffic
- Traffic speed of 35 mph or less

AREA

- Population of 60,000 within a 3-mile ring
- Median income of $21,000

TERMS

- Lease
- Purchase
- Build-to-suit

PRICE

- The prevailing price per square foot or front foot in the market area

SOURCE: JLI pamphlet for prospective landlords.

franchises. Under its franchise agreements, JLI could, however, inspect franchise centers at any time to ensure that employees were using approved products and following Jiffy Lube procedures. The company used both field personnel and "mystery shoppers" (who posed as customers and reported back to headquarters) to monitor franchise operations. If a franchisee failed to operate a center according to JLI's standards, the company had the right to revoke the franchise rights and obtain control of the center. This step had been taken for the first time only recently; in its quest for growth, JLI had not always enforced strict adherence to its operating policies.

In mid-1986, JLI made a substantial effort to encourage improved service quality throughout the system. To focus its efforts, the company introduced the "Zero Defects Program" around which to rally franchisees and store managers through working toward the stated goal of 100 percent defect-free performance for every customer. To convey this new attitude to customers, a plaque containing the Jiffy Lube Pledge of Quality was displayed prominently in every store; it encouraged customers to contact JLI headquarters directly if dissatisfied with their service. JLI also developed a computerized tracking system to follow and analyze defects when they did occur.

To help support this renewed focus on quality, JLI significantly expanded its training programs. Previously, the company had offered only a two-week program for franchisees and store managers at headquarters; at this time, it introduced standard training consisting of videotapes and workbooks to "certify" lube techs at the individual center sites.

JLI also expanded its field force, recruiting people who were particularly suited to lead franchisees in the quality-improvement effort. The field force, which in fiscal 1987 consisted of only nine DMs covering 545 franchised centers, was given responsibility for performing the newly introduced operational audits; under this system, DMs formally measured centers on 150 attributes of service. Finally, JLI established a customer service department to follow up on every complaint received at headquarters. During 1988, the number of complaints averaged about 100 a month; the most common was that the customer didn't get the full 14 points of service.

Marketing. Jiffy Lube was the only quick-lube chain with a national advertising effort. Each center contributed 3 percent of gross revenues to a National Ad Fund, which was used to produce commercials, buy media time, and create signs and other materials for systemwide promotions. The fund's expenditures had grown dramatically, from $510,000 in fiscal 1985 to $8.1 million in fiscal 1988. The fund's emphasis had been on TV commercials featuring well-known TV personalities (Dick Van Patten and family, Sally Struthers, Sherman Helmsley) with the theme: "We treat you like family." Over and above its contribution to the National Ad Fund, each franchisee was required to spend 5 percent of gross sales on local and regional advertising, often through co-ops arranged by JLI.

JLI's Senior Management

Several times over the years, Hindman had hired an outside executive to add skills to the organization and manage JLI's operations; in each instance, however, he was unable to feel comfortable relinquishing control. The most recent such executive was J. Richard Breen, hired in April 1986 as president and chief operating officer. Before coming to JLI, Breen had been president of Tenneco Automotive International (which owned Speedy Muffler King and several other automotive aftermarket businesses); also, he was a former executive vice president of Fram International (which manufactured and sold oil filters). Breen's largest contribution had been developing and spearheading the corporate effort to improve franchise service quality. He resigned on September 1, 1987, to become a franchisee. (In fact, several former executives had become franchisees.)

JLI's present senior management consisted of

- **W. James Hindman,** age 53, chairman, president, and CEO. He owned about 22 percent of JLI's outstanding common stock and was said to control another 8 percent through relatives and associates.
- **Edward F. Kelley, III,** age 35, executive vice president and chief financial officer. Kelley had been an assistant coach to Hindman at Western Maryland College and was one of JLI's six founding stockholders. He was responsible for finance, accounting, headquarters administration, and the Heritage Merchandising subsidiary. He also coordinated the remarketing of company-owned stores. His prior positions included vice president of operations and senior vice president of the Eastern Region.
- **Nicholas A. Greville,** age 44, executive vice president. He had joined JLI in 1985 and was responsible for operations (including both franchise and company-owned stores) and marketing. His offices were located at the JLI Western Region headquarters in California. Greville had formerly been with Midas Mufflers for 11 years in various sales and management positions.
- **Neal F. O'Shea,** age 58, senior vice president. O'Shea was responsible for all international operations and development. An officer of JLI since 1980, he was formerly vice president of franchise development.
- **Eleanor C. Harding,** age 38, vice president and treasurer. She had joined JLI in 1986 after three years as a manager of corporate finance at Black & Decker. Before that, she had been a vice president of Loyola Federal Savings & Loan.

Financing Growth

Development of Centers

In 1988, developing a new Jiffy Lube center from the ground up cost about a half million dollars, as shown in Exhibit 5. Franchisees had always been responsible for financing the development of their own stores, but to spur growth of the system, JLI assisted wherever possible. Sometimes the company helped franchisees negotiate "build-to-suit" leases, especially in the early years. It also helped franchisees find construction loans (sometimes providing them itself) and helped arrange permanent financing of real estate and construction expenditures from mortgage lenders with which it had developed relationships. With respect to real estate, JLI had come to prefer owning or leasing center sites and buildings itself and subleasing them to franchisees, which was thought to provide better control over the use of these properties. It also allowed JLI to profit on the spread between its mortgage/lease cost and rental revenue. A significant proportion of franchise sites were now subleased

EXHIBIT 5

Costs to Develop a New Jiffy Lube Center in 1988

	Estimated Range	
	Low	High
TYPE OF EXPENDITURE		
Purchase real estate	$100,000	$350,000
Site improvements/construction	225,000	250,000
Start-up operating costs:		
License fee	15,000	35,000
Equipment/fixtures	38,000	78,000[a]
Initial inventory	17,500	17,500
Working capital/prepaid expense	35,900	43,400
First month's rent	4,000	5,000
Total start-up cost	110,400	178,900
Total to develop center	$435,400	$778,900

[a]Includes $40,000 for car wash facility.

SOURCE: JLI March 31, 1988, 10-K report to the SEC.

from the company, as shown in Exhibit 6. Another way JLI helped its franchisees develop centers was by providing acquisition financing for the purchase of competing stores in their territories. Finally, JLI had often provided loan and lease guarantees of franchisee debt to third parties.

JLI Corporate Financing History

JLI's need for capital was driven by its decision to help finance the growth in centers, which it considered vital. During the early years, JLI had literally lived from hand to mouth, stretching payments and patching together loans from unlikely sources. In 1981, Pennzoil had provided a crucial $1 million when it bought preferred stock with warrants (which Hindman later repurchased) for 30 percent of JLI. In 1985, its major source of mortgage loans (Old Court Savings & Loan) was closed by federal regulators, which precipitated a crisis in funding completion of several centers then under construction. Until as late as 1986, Hindman himself often lent the company large sums of money, and he sometimes waived his salary.

In December 1985, JLI privately placed a $10.5 million loan (with warrants) with Bridge Capital Investors, a well-known New York investment company. This mezzanine financing introduced Jiffy Lube to Wall Street and lent the company an aura of legitimacy to help prepare it for going public. Seven months later, in July 1986, JLI had its initial public offering of common stock on the NASDAQ, which netted the company $28 million and introduced both the quick-lube concept and Jiffy Lube to the investing public. The offering price was $15 per share, but investor interest pushed the price to $21 later that day; it later settled in at about $17.[1] In

EXHIBIT 6

Ownership of Center Locations during Fiscal Years 1986–1988

FYE 3/31/86

	Operated by		
	Company	Franchisee	Total
SITES			
Owned by company	3	33	36
Leased by company[a]	11	54	65
Owned/leased by franchisees	0	247	247
	14	334	348

FYE 3/31/87

	Operated by		
	Company	Franchisee	Total
SITES			
Owned by company	8	49	57
Leased by company[a]	21	113	134
Owned/leased by franchisees	0	370	370
	29	532	561

FYE 3/31/88

	Operated by		
	Company	Franchisee	Total
SITES			
Owned by company	14	84	98
Leased by company[a]	57	220	277
Owned/leased by franchisees	0	448	448
	71	752	823

[a]Includes sites where company owns buildings and improvements.

SOURCE: JLI stock offering prospecti (1986 and 1987) and March 31, 1988, 10-K report to the Securities and Exchange Commission (SEC).

March of 1987, the stock price peaked at $49, when it was split 2-for-1. During the next quarter, the stock hit an all-time high of $25¼ (adjusted for the split) but had dropped by the time JLI completed its second offering in June 1987. At an offering price of about $15 per share (adjusted), the company raised $34 million. Since that offering, the stock had declined steadily, and it currently traded around $6–$7 per share.

JLI Operating Performance

As shown in the financial statements in Exhibit 7, JLI's corporate revenues were derived from four general areas. Revenues from *operations* represented sales of the company-owned centers. *Franchising* revenues included area-development and

Exhibit 7

JLI Financial Statements for Fiscal 1986–1988 and Interim September 30, 1988

INCOME STATEMENT	6 mos. 9/30/88	1988	1987	1986
REVENUES				
Sales—company stores	$12,556	$18,974	$ 8,079	$ 7,825
Initial franchise fees	1,631	4,706	3,327	2,490
Area development fees	46	5,719	4,481	2,150
Franchise royalties	8,518	12,133	7,551	3,847
Heritage Merchandising	14,657	21,490	13,505	8,792
Rental income	10,216	14,048	6,495	4,288
Other operating revenue	639	1,132	732	59
Total revenue	$48,263	$78,202	$44,170	$29,451
EXPENSES				
Company stores	$15,168	$18,739	$ 7,331	$ 6,548
CGS—products	11,727	16,993	11,217	7,492
Rental properties	7,534	10,397	5,259	4,065
S, G, & A	13,574	21,447	13,029	9,281
Prov. bad debt	1,260	1,391	681	271
Total expenses	$49,263	$68,967	$37,517	$27,657
OPERATING INCOME	(1,000)	9,235	6,653	1,794
OTHER INCOME/(EXPENSES)				
Other income	$ 2,741	$ 4,947	$ 1,940	$ 824
Interest expense	(2,604)	(2,138)	(1,362)	(1,197)
Minor int. in loss	0	(132)	(213)	41
Total other	137	2,677	365	(332)
Income before tax	(863)	11,912	7,018	1,462
Income tax expense	(448)	5,003	3,333	720
Income before extra items	(415)	6,909	3,685	742
Extraordinary items				
NOL carryforwards				470
Debt extinguished			(219)	
Total after-tax	0	0	(219)	470
Net income	(415)	6,909	3,466	1,212

(continued)

master license fees, initial franchise fees, and royalties. Initial franchise fees were earned when a new center was opened and varied according to each franchise agreement. JLI's average initial franchise fee had been rising; it was $20,900 during the two-year period including fiscal 1987 and 1988, up from $17,300 during fiscal 1985–1986. Royalties, earned monthly, were usually 5 percent of each

EXHIBIT 7 (CONTINUED)

JLI Financial Statements for Fiscal 1986–1988 and Interim September 30, 1988

BALANCE SHEET

	Interim 9/30/88	1988	1987	1986
ASSETS				
Cash and S-T investment	2,146	3,497	1,277	2,474
Accounts and fees receivable	23,919	19,753	7,584	6,771
Notes receivable	13,318	11,844	4,682	1,811
less allowance	(2,551)	(2,054)	(935)	(299)
Net receivables	34,686	29,543	11,331	8,283
Inventory	4,973	4,932	1,217	752
RE held for resale	0	0	0	2,719
Other current assets	3,339	1,742	1,130	258
Total current assets	45,144	39,714	14,955	14,486
Accounts and fees receivable	1,135	1,185	933	783
Stores held for resale	11,376	4,644	2,663	0
Notes receivable	25,715	22,668	9,616	3,181
Inv./Adv.—affiliates	3,875	2,138	2,217	237
FA leased to franchisees				
Construction advances	5,460	15,860	8,592	0
Land	22,066	16,654	8,966	3,613
Buildings and equipment—gross	17,338	9,840	9,807	9,299
Financing leases	77,136	61,624	26,658	7,694
Construction-in-progress	14,171	14,617	4,298	0
Gross	136,171	118,595	58,321	20,606
Less accumulated depreciation	N/A	(1,222)	(938)	(885)
Net	136,171	117,373	57,383	19,721
Net property and equipment	21,246	15,329	1,885	4,271
Intangible assets (net)	13,032	14,783	9,104	6,227
Other assets	7,281	7,929	3,687	1,787
Total assets	264,975	225,763	102,443	50,693

(continued)

EXHIBIT 7 (CONTINUED)

JLI Financial Statements for Fiscal 1986–1988 and Interim September 30, 1988

	9/30/88	1988	1987	1986
LIABILITIES				
Accounts payable/accruals	11,755	10,045	6,926	3,905
Income tax payable	0	125	2,241	0
Notes payable	0	0	1,981	2,403
Construction advance—real estate held for resale	0	0	0	2,331
CMLTD	10,589	17,561	1,047	1,355
Total current liabilities	22,344	27,731	12,195	9,994
Long-term debt	91,927	74,911	21,797	9,971
Substantial debentures	19,309	4,299	4,887	9,736
Capital leases	48,456	36,130	18,969	9,586
Def. tax/other liabilities	1,126	1,805	1,054	504
Def. franchise fees	1,306	1,500	872	4,131
Total long-term liabilities	162,124	118,645	47,579	33,928
Total liabilities	184,468	146,376	59,774	43,922
Minority interest	0	0	3,173	10
Common stock	381	380	294	180
PIC-Paid-in-Capital	77,513	75,979	39,479	10,222
Retained earnings	6,217	6,632	(277)	(3,467)
Less due for common stock	0	0	0	(175)
Less treasury stock	(3,604)	(3,604)	0	0
Total equity	80,507	79,387	39,496	6,760
Total liabilities + equity	264,975	225,763	102,443	50,692

SOURCE: JLI Annual Reports and September 30, 1988, 10-Q report to the SEC.

franchise's gross revenues during a store's first year of operation and 6 percent thereafter. Revenues from *distribution* represented sales of supplies and equipment by Heritage Merchandising to franchisees and outside customers. *Real estate* revenue was rental income JLI earned by subleasing properties to franchisees. Over the years, JLI had recorded significant revenue from *other sources*, including gains on the sale of real estate and company-owned centers and interest on short-term investments and notes receivable from franchisees.

During the past several years, nonrecurring revenues (such as area-development fees, initial franchise fees, and gains on the sale of real property) had contributed a significant portion of total revenues. However, these revenues were expected to decline in relative importance as growth slowed. Rental income would become more significant, because JLI had bought many properties during the past two to three years; lease rates on new centers were typically low in the early years and rose as the centers matured. Also, area-development revenues had been dramatically reduced by a recent order of the Securities and Exchange Commission requiring JLI (and all franchisors) to recognize area-development fees over the term of a contract rather than in current income, as previously done.

The largest drain on JLI earnings was from company-owned centers held for resale. Exhibit 8 shows data on the growth and operations of company-owned centers over the last few years. JLI intended to keep some stores in order to remain knowledgeable about center operations and to test new methods. Over the last two years, however, it had purchased a substantial number of distressed centers to turn around and remarket. At the end of fiscal 1988, JLI classified 34 of its 71 centers as held for resale. During fiscal 1988, operating losses on such centers totaled $950,000.

EXHIBIT 8

Jiffy Lube International Data on Company-Owned Centers

	INTERIM 9/30/88	3/31/88	3/31/87	3/31/86
# COMPANY-OWNED CENTERS AT END OF PERIOD				
To keep	25	37	8	14
Held for resale	81[a]	34	21	0[b]
Total	106	71	29	14
CHANGES IN # CENTERS DURING THE PERIOD				
Acquisitions	34	88	61	1
# Centers built by company	21	9	0	0
# Centers sold/leased	(20)	(55)	(45)	(8)
# Centers closed	0	0	(1)	0
Net change in centers	35	42	15	(7)
CENTERS HELD FOR RESALE ($000)				
Assets (year end)	$11,376	$4,644	$2,663	N/A
Results of openings				
Sales	6,783	6,664	2,951	N/A
Operating expenses	9,650	7,614	3,282	N/A
Operating loss	(2,867)	(950)	(331)	N/A
Gain—sale of centers	($17)	$1,242	$1,000	$317

[a]Twenty-eight of these centers were located in Houston, Texas.

[b]Before fiscal year 1987, JLI did not classify centers as held for resale.

SOURCE: JLI stock offering prospecti (1986 and 1987), March 31, 1988, 10-K and September 30, 1988, 10-Q reports to the SEC.

During the second quarter of fiscal 1989, losses from centers held for resale caused Jiffy Lube to post its first quarterly net loss since going public. For the six months, JLI reported a loss of $415,000 on revenues of $48.3 million. During the same period a year earlier, revenues had been 39 percent lower, but net income was $3.3 million. Systemwide sales for the first six months of fiscal 1989 were $172.8 million, up 50 percent over the previous year. During those months, JLI had acquired 70 centers intended for resale.

JLI Financial Condition

JLI's assets consisted primarily of accounts and notes receivable from franchisees, and real property (most of which was leased/subleased to franchisees). Accounts receivable encompassed all amounts currently due from franchisees, including initial franchise fees on a quarterly payment plan, royalties, rents, and Heritage receivables. A small portion was area-development fees. Accounts receivable were usually personally guaranteed by franchisees. Notes receivable represented amounts due from franchisees under long-term arrangements with scheduled payments. Of the total, 50 percent represented financing of franchisees' acquisitions; 30 percent, working-capital financing for stores in the early stages of growth; 10 percent, term payments of area-development fees; and 10 percent, miscellaneous. Notes receivable were always personally guaranteed and were usually collateralized by a pledge of center assets.

Fixed assets consisted mostly of land and buildings, except for the equipment in company-owned centers (center equipment had historically been financed for individual franchisees by Pennzoil). Fixed assets leased to franchisees at fiscal year end 1988 were about $117 million, of which $85 million represented land and buildings owned by JLI; the remainder was mostly leased property that was subleased to franchisees. Separately, assets of centers held for resale totaled about $4.7 million.

Jiffy Lube had assumed considerable debt in its acquisition of real estate and operating centers. At the end of fiscal 1988, total long-term debt and capital leases of $129 million balanced equity of $79 million. To reduce the impact of future real estate acquisitions on its balance sheet, JLI had formed the Jiffy Lube Insured Income Limited Partnership (JLIILP), which raised $40 million in a public sale of units in early 1988. This vehicle would not only allow JLI to keep future assets and liabilities off its balance sheet, it would also generate property-management income for the company. In an innovative twist, the rents payable by franchisees were 80 percent insured (for the first seven years) by United Guaranty Commercial Insurance Company of Iowa.

Another significant off-balance-sheet issue was the high level of JLI's contingent liabilities. During its growth period, the company had often guaranteed loans and leases for franchisees who acquired or leased center sites and related equipment. The properties were pledged as collateral for these guarantees. Such guarantees totaled $58.2 million in fiscal 1988, up from $24.7 million in 1987 and $1.5 million in 1986.

The Pennzoil Strategic Alliance

In March 1988, JLI signed a 20-year Strategic Alliance Agreement with Pennzoil Products Company, which, with 21 percent of U.S. motor oil sales, was the leading motor oil company in the United States. The agreement continued the close relationship the two companies had developed over the years. Pennzoil promised to discontinue financing new independent quick-lube operators and to assist JLI in converting as many of its 750 qualifying independents as possible to the Jiffy Lube system. Pennzoil also committed to make equipment loans to all new franchisees approved by JLI, which formalized the financing of individual franchise equipment it had provided for years. Moreover, Pennzoil agreed to contribute $.20 for each gallon of motor oil purchased by the Jiffy Lube system to JLI's National Ad Fund; this contribution would equal about $4 million in fiscal 1989. Finally, Pennzoil agreed to pay JLI an "administrative fee" of $.05 per gallon sold through the JLI system and to release individual franchisees from any obligations to purchase Pennzoil oil and air filters under existing motor oil supply arrangements.

For its part under the Strategic Alliance, JLI agreed to pay Pennzoil 25 percent of the royalties it would collect from Pennzoil independents who converted. (These independents would pay no initial franchise fee.) JLI also committed to designate Pennzoil as the Jiffy Lube system's "oil of choice," use its best efforts to persuade all JLI franchisees to use it (over 80 percent of the system already did), and feature Pennzoil in its national ads. Finally, JLI promised to place the Pennzoil logo on its own private brand of oil filters and pay Pennzoil $.04 per filter sold.

The conversion of Pennzoil independents was progressing slower than planned. JLI had hoped to convert 350 operators during fiscal 1989 but had converted only 100 by November 1988. The company changed the projection to about 100 a year for the next two to three years. JLI believed, however, that Pennzoil's contribution to its National Ad Fund was more important than the conversion of independents.

Quick-Lube Competition

Jiffy Lube was the market leader in both sales and number of centers, as the list of major competitors in Exhibit 9 shows. Like Jiffy Lube, most of the large national chains were affiliated with one of the top motor oil marketers. Minit Lube, the second largest chain (about 300 stores), was owned by Quaker State, which had about 17 percent motor oil market share. Minit Lube was the only major chain with a strategy of growing through company-owned stores instead of franchises. The third largest chain was Instant Oil, at about 178 stores; it was owned by Ashland Oil, whose Valvoline motor oil had about 13 percent market share. Instant Oil had been attempting to grow through acquisition of smaller chains and construction of company-owned stores. It recently announced an intention to concentrate on franchising, however, with a goal of 1,500 franchised centers by 1995.[2] The fourth-largest quick-lube chain, Grease Monkey, had about 120 stores and was independent of any oil company. Its stores were virtually all franchised and were located mostly in the western states in a shotgun pattern, often near Jiffy Lube centers.

Smaller, local and regional quick-lube chains abounded, some with fewer than 10 stores. New independents seemed to be springing up all the time. These competitors often attempted to steal Jiffy Lube's customers by advertising 15-, 16-, or up to 21-point services, claiming to take nine minutes instead of Jiffy Lube's ten, and circulating discount coupons.

EXHIBIT 9

Information on Quick-Lube Industry

The industry's only aftermarket weekly...48 Mondays...$85/year

AUTOMOTIVE WEEK

Automotive Week Publishing Co.
P.O. Box 3495
Wayne, NJ 07470-3495
210/694-7792 FAX 201/694-2817
Circulation/Subscriptions: 201/694-6078
CHUCK LAVERTY, *Editor and Publisher*

Car Care Mall News
Car Care Mall Seminars
Car Care Mall Directory
Toll-Free and FAX Directory
Autoparts and Service Market Data
Mailing Lists/Direct Mail/Surveys

ISSN 0889-3948

APRIL 4, 1988 VOLUME XIV, NUMBER 13

Good morning, here's the week's news:

A telephone survey by Automotive Week (on March 30th) shows that **the Top Twelve quick lube chains in North America will boost their facility count by an impressive 67% by the end of 1989, and a further 54% by the end of 1990**...See table below...A major new entry into the U.S. market by 1989 will be the **Mr. Lube** unit of **Exxon,** which recently acquired control the the Edmonton/Canada-based firm (now 50 centers) through its Imperial Oil affiliate...The firm projects about **500 U.S. quick lubes** by the Mid-Nineties, and 140 in the Canadian market...Similar rapid-growth patterns are projected for the smaller independents like Speedee Oil Change (Metarie, LA), which currently has 32 operating, but expects more than 10-fold growth to 365 in the next 21 months...

...The independents are also reaching out to many new markets from their historic base of operations, e.g., **Econo Lube 'N Tune** (Newport Beach, CA) will this year open in **Seattle, Georgia,** the **Mid-Atlantic States** and **Massachusetts, Texas, New Mexico,** and **Colorado**...

	Company/Base	Current 3/1988	Projected 12/1989	Projected 12/1990
1.	Jiffy Lube Int'l/Baltimore, MD	779	1250	1550
2.	Quaker State-Minit Lube/Salt Lake City, UT	290	490	735
3.	Rapid Oil-Valvoline/Minneapolis, MN	127	275	400
4.	Grease Monkey/Denver, CO	116	240	330
5.	Econo Lube N Tune/Newport Beach, CA	101	200	250
6.	Autospa/Great Neck, NY	88	N/A	N/A
7.	McQuik's Oil/Muncie, IN	64	100	130
8.	60 Minute Tune (+Lube)/Seattle, WA	51	N/A	N/A
9.	Mr Lube-Exxon/Houston, TX	50	134	640
10.	Laser Lube/Mount Laurel, NJ	39	189	400
11.	Oil Express/Hinsdale, IL	34	74	115
12.	Speedee Oil Change-Tune Up/Metarie, LA	32	365	597
	TOTALS:	1771	2952	4550
	PERCENT GAIN:		+66.7	+54.0%

Source: Automotive Week, from company-supplied data. (C) Automotive Week, 1988.

...**Speedee Oil** is extending into many Eastern markets, including **New England,** and the Atlanta Region...**60 Minute Tune,** which also performs fast-lube service, disclosed earlier that it is entering **Southern California,** Texas, and other markets East of the Rockies from its Bellevue, WA, base of operations...

...The fast-lube market—which accounts for **less than 15% of the total oil and lube business**—is highly fragmented...In addition to our chart, we believe there are as many as 100 chains with five to 25 centers, and another 1,500 performing dedicated quick-lube operations (i.e., offering general lube services without appointment and within 30–45 minutes...Some major oil chains have erected "quick lube" signage at their gas pumps, but most often the claim isn't delivered: "Next-day" or "Drop Off Your Car" schedules are commonplace.) **More on this market inside.**

FINGERHUT SUED BY INDEPENDENT SALES REP AGENCIES...SEE TOP OF PAGE FOUR.

SOURCE: *Automotive Week*, reprinted by telephone permission.

Recent Negative Publicity

Service Quality

In the recent Washington TV broadcast, a two-part news report on quality problems at local Jiffy Lube centers, the reporter elicited on-camera horror stories from consumers. In one, Jiffy Lube had drained a car's old oil but hadn't replaced it with new oil. Later, the engine seized and had to be replaced at a cost of $3,500. JLI responded to these allegations by explaining that, out of the thousands of cars serviced daily, very few had such problems; furthermore, the company had promptly paid for those that did occur. The reporter conceded that area consumer protection agencies had received few complaints against Jiffy Lube but pointed out that the centers hired unskilled labor, training them with a series of videotapes and workbooks. "After all, Jiffy Lube says, lube technicians don't have to be mechanics."[3]

The company had been recently notified of the Philadelphia TV station's planned five-part news segment on Jiffy Lube on "The Consumer's Friend" portion of its show. In early 1987, the former area developer there had agreed to discontinue what the Pennsylvania attorney general charged were deceitful sales practices.[4] Employees had been selling unnecessary transmission and differential fluid changes by showing customers a sample of their cars' "dirty" fluid compared with one of new, "clean" fluid; in fact, automobile performance was not affected by the color of these fluids. Since then, JLI had instructed all its centers to stop showing such "comparisons" to customers and had repurchased this area from the developer.

Financial Condition

In August 1988, *The Wall Street Journal* titled its "Heard on the Street" column "Jiffy Lube Raises Some Eyebrows with Loans to Its Franchisees for Their Up-Front Expenses." The article reported that the stock, then trading at about 9½, had "plummeted nearly 50 percent from its 52-week high of 18¼," and that the outstanding short position was 2.4 million shares (about 16 percent of all outstanding stock). The writer asserted that investor concern over financial interdependence between JLI and its franchisees had caused the decline. He cited one case of a troubled franchisee, Lone Star Lubrication, which owned 67 centers in Texas and Oklahoma. Lone Star had lost $4.2 million during fiscal 1988 and owed a total of $9.5 million in long-term debt (two-thirds of it to JLI). Lone Star had projected it would turn profitable in fiscal 1990, however, assuming growth to 85 centers and an increase in its average car counts from 27 to 49 per day.

JLI responded in the article by noting that most of its loans and leases to franchisees were secured by real estate in prime locations and explained that it had financed the franchisees in order to build its 1,000-store nationwide network quickly to win market share before competitors did.[5]

Jiffy Lube's New Strategy

The planned shift in strategic emphasis from growth to consolidation focused on improving the quality of service at Jiffy Lube centers and increasing individual franchisee profitability. Financially, JLI would step back from direct financing of franchisees and attempt to facilitate third-party financing. JLI planned also to cut

$3 million in annual sales and general and administrative expenses to help offset current losses.

To increase franchisees' profitability, Hindman set a goal of 65 cars per day systemwide. The company had analyzed historical center data, which showed that systemwide car counts increased with the age of a center, but the Jiffy Lube system was still young: in May 1988, 72 percent of centers were under three years old, 58 percent were less than two years old, and 32 percent were less than a year old. Exhibit 10 shows a graph of the trend in Jiffy Lube center car counts over the past four years. Exhibit 11 shows that, during fiscal 1988, every age category experienced higher daily car counts than during fiscal 1987. JLI's growth was built on the premise that car counts would continue to increase over time.

Resizing Program

In analyzing franchisee performance, JLI found that small operators (those with fewer than 10 stores) clearly outperformed those who controlled larger areas. The cost advantages of clustering were outweighed by the dilution of management attention. JLI's new strategy was to carve up the ownership of large areas and encourage more individual owner/operators. Under its new Expansion Qualification Policy, the company would no longer approve new sites under area-development agreements if a franchisee's existing sites were not performing well, or if the developer lacked sufficient start-up capital. The company also planned to encourage

Exhibit 10

Jiffy Lube International, Inc. Trend in Daily Car Counts over Time

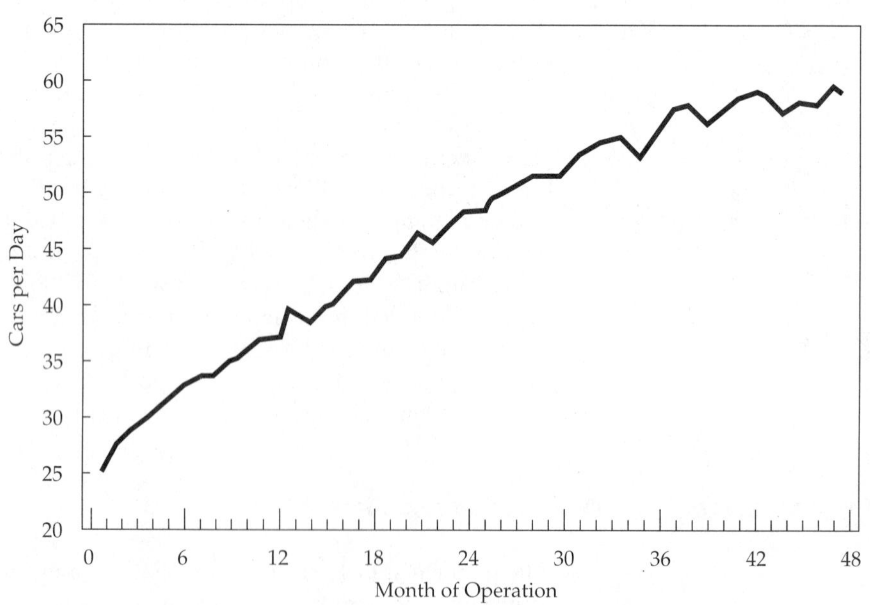

Source: JLI internal analysis.

EXHIBIT 11

Jiffy Lube International, Inc. Comparison of Daily Car Counts by Age Category Fiscal Year 1987 versus 1988

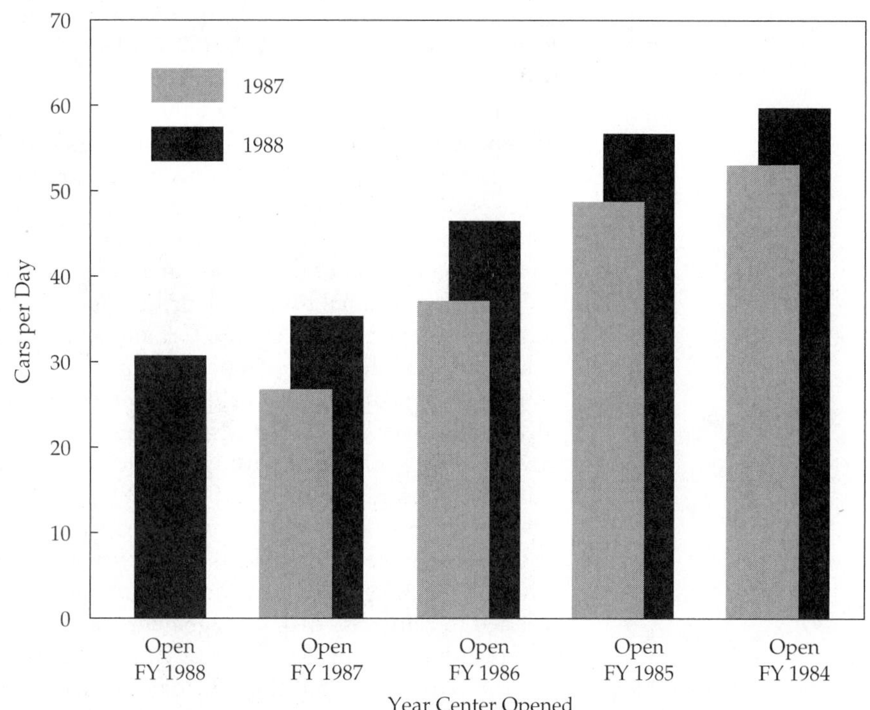

On average, centers in every age category experienced car count increases over the previous year.

SOURCE: JLI internal analysis.

large operators to reduce their debt to JLI by selling assets (i.e., stores). Since the company had to approve any new franchisee, it would participate in the remarketing effort. In fact, to facilitate the resizing program, JLI would probably be forced to repurchase the rights to some stores in the interim before selling them to new franchisees.

OTHER OPERATIONAL PLANS

JLI planned to make a major effort to recertify all lube techs at Jiffy Lube centers. With the relatively high employee turnover typical of a mostly teenaged workforce, the company had found it difficult to maintain its earlier certification program. Jiffy Lube also intended to commission a time-and-motion study to reexamine car-servicing procedures (unchanged since the early days of the chain) and to test the 10-minute claim. JLI would continue to expand its field force and reduce the number of centers per DM in an effort to enforce its operating standards more diligently than in the past.

Financial Restructuring Program

JLI had recently announced a seven-step program to reduce its financial leverage. Parts of the plan were already underway. The first element involved restructuring JLI's existing liabilities, replacing some short-term debt with long-term debt. JLI had recently placed $15 million of convertible subordinated debentures with Pennzoil and, separately, $54 million of senior notes maturing over 3 to 10 years with a group of insurance companies.

The second element of the financial restructuring was selling assets. The company planned to sell and lease back its new $10-million headquarters building, purchased in April 1988. JLI also hoped to sell $15 million to $20 million of other real estate (store sites to franchisees) and some of the $30 million of notes receivable. The company had recently received a commitment from Sanwa Business Credit to purchase $5 million of these notes at a minimal discount.

Third, JLI planned to control further increases in debt by initiating an aggressive accounts-receivable collection effort and restricting financing of franchisees. Such loans would be limited to 50 percent financing to facilitate the purchase of company-owned centers and working-capital financing for new centers through its SBIC subsidiary. (SBIC loans were consolidated on JLI's balance sheet but were government guaranteed without recourse to the company; $2.7 million of such loans had been made so far in fiscal 1989.) JLI believed it could attract about 100 new franchisees a year without providing significant start-up financing.

The fourth element of the program was to limit loan and lease guarantees and initiate a tracking system to control outstanding contingent liabilities. Fifth, JLI planned to centralize cash management and capital budgeting to improve expenditure planning. Sixth, JLI would rely more heavily on off-balance-sheet financing, like the JLIILP created the previous spring, to fund the purchase of new center sites. Finally, the company would seek to become more effective at helping franchisees find independent sources of financing. JLI had recently hired a manager who had experience in this area with another franchisor.

Questions to Consider

Hindman wondered whether the new strategy had addressed the most important issues facing his company and whether the plan would satisfy the concerns of the financial community. How would he manage the franchisees differently now? What was the impact of the large number of company-owned centers?

Would the new plans help JLI maintain its market position? Hindman was convinced that the JLI service concept, if properly implemented, worked in all parts of the country. Thus, he believed that both his earlier growth strategy and the national advertising effort were justified. Jiffy Lube was by far the largest chain in the quick-lube industry; could the company sustain competitive advantage and improve profitability for both itself and the franchisees?

Endnotes

[1]"Striking It Rich," *Warfield's Magazine*, Baltimore, October 1986.

[2]"Ashland's Valvoline Plans to Franchise Quick-Lube Outlets, Stepping Up Rivalry," *The Wall Street Journal*, October 24, 1988.

[3]"Jiffy Lube Auto Shops Accused of Inefficient Services," Eyewitness News, WUSA Television, Washington, D.C., October 17–18, 1988 (from a transcript provided by Radio-TV Monitoring Service, Inc.).

[4]"Quick-Grease Artists: Fast-Lube Shops Slip into Area Market," *Washington Post,* April 27, 1987.

[5]*The Wall Street Journal,* August 29, 1988.

CASE 6

CROWN CORK AND SEAL COMPANY, INC.

In 1977, Crown Cork and Seal Company was the fourth-largest producer of metal cans and crowns in the United States.[1] Under John Connelly, chairman and CEO, Crown had raised itself up from near bankruptcy in 1957. After 20 years of consistent growth, the company had emerged as a major force in both the domestic and international metal container markets (see Exhibit 1).

During those 20 years, Crown Cork and Seal had concentrated its manufacturing efforts on tin-plated cans for holding beer, soft drinks, and aerosol products. By 1977, however, the ozone controversy and the trend toward legislative regulation of nonreturnable containers was threatening Crown's domestic business. Was it time for a change in Crown's formula for success or merely time for a reaffirmation of Connelly's basic strategic choices?

To explore these questions, this case looks at the metal container industry, Crown's strategy and position within that industry, and the nature of the problems facing the company during mid-1977.

THE METAL CONTAINER INDUSTRY IN 1977

The metal container industry included 100 firms and a vast number of product lines. This section describes the product segments in which Crown competed, examines the industry's competitive structure, and looks at three industrywide trends: (1) increasing self-manufacture, (2) new material introductions, and (3) the effect of the "packaging revolution" on the competitive atmosphere.

THE PRODUCTS

Metal containers made up almost a third of all packaging products used in the United States in 1976. Metal containers included traditional steel and aluminum cans, foil containers, and metal drums and pails of all shapes and sizes. Of these, metal cans were the largest segment, reaching a value of $7.1 billion in 1976. Cans were being used in more than three-fourths of all metal-container shipments.

Cans were composed of two basic raw materials: aluminum and tin-plated steel. Originally, they were formed by rolling a sheet of metal, soldering it, cutting it to the right size, and attaching two ends, thereby forming a three-piece, seamed can. In the late 1960s, a new process introduced by the aluminum industry made possible a two-piece can. The new can was formed by pushing a flat blank of metal into a deep cup, which eliminated the need for a separate bottom. The product makers adopted the term "drawn and ironed" from the molding procedure.

 This case was prepared by Karen D. Gordon, John P. Reed, and Richard Hammermesh as the basis for class discussion rather than to illustrate either effective or ineffective handling of an administrative situation.

EXHIBIT 1

Crown Cork and Seal Company, Inc. Financial Statement, 1956–1976 ($ thousands except where indicated otherwise)

	1976	1975	1974	1973	1972	1971	1966	1961	1956
Net sales	$909,937	$825,007	$766,158	$571,762	$488,880	$448,446	$279,830	$176,992	$115,098
Cost of products sold									
(excluding depreciation)	757,866	683,691	628,865	459,183	387,768	350,867	217,236	139,071	95,803
Selling and administrative expense	31,910	30,102	28,649	23,409	20,883	21,090	18,355	15,311	13,506
% of net sales	3.5%	3.6%	3.7%	4.1%	4.3%	4.7%	6.6%	8.7%	11.7%
Interest expense	3,885	7,374	6,973	4,407	4,222	5,121	4,551	1,252	1,150
Depreciation expense	26,486	25,402	25,525	20,930	18,654	16,981	9,381	4,627	2,577
Taxes on income	43,500	34,925	33,298	26,725	24,900	24,560	12,680	7,625	105
Net income	$ 46,183	$ 41,611	$ 39,663	$ 34,288	$ 31,193	$ 28,474	$ 16,749	$ 6,653	$ 277
% of net sales	5.1%	5.0%	5.2%	6.0%	6.4%	6.3%	6.0%	3.8%	.2%
Earnings per common share	$ 2.84	$ 2.43	$ 2.20	$ 1.81	$ 1.58	$ 1.41	$ .80	$ .28	$ (.01)
Plant and equipment									
Expenditures	$ 21,568	$ 47,047	$ 52,517	$ 40,392	$ 28,261	$ 33,099	$ 32,729	$ 11,819	$ 1,931
Accumulated investment	398,377	401,657	371,297	335,047	316,266	313,214	223,153	107,258	65,196
Accumulated depreciation	149,306	143,406	129,924	116,191	105,377	101,314	68,359	45,004	31,167
Current asset/liability ratio	1.8	1.6	1.4	1.6	1.7	1.6	1.5	2.7	3.2
Long-term debt	$ 25,886	$ 29,679	$ 34,413	$ 37,922	$ 31,234	$ 41,680	$ 57,890	$ 17,654	$ 21,400
Short-term debt	2,984	30,419	45,043	28,504	17,221	31,381	44,784	5,190	6,500
Shareholders' investment	316,684	292,681	262,650	243,916	230,366	211,847	110,841	77,540	50,299
Number of									
Preferred shares	0	0	0	0	0	0	79,370	139,540	275,000
Common shares, average	16,235,040	17,137,030	18,000,792	18,894,105	19,726,799	20,211,810	20,606,835	21,594,720	24,155,800

SOURCE: Crown Cork and Seal Company, Inc., 1976 Annual Report, pp. 4–5.

The aluminum companies that developed the process, Alcoa and Reynolds, had done so with the intention of turning the process over to can manufacturers and subsequently increasing raw-material sales. However, when the manufacturers were reluctant to incur the large costs involved in line changeovers, the two aluminum companies began building their own two-piece lines and competing directly in the end market.

The new can had advantages in weight, labor, and materials costs and was recommended by the Food and Drug Administration, which was worried about lead from soldered three-piece cans migrating into the can's contents. Tin-plated can producers soon acknowledged the new process as the wave of the future. They quickly began to explore the possibilities for drawing and ironing steel sheets. By 1972 the technique was perfected, and investment dollars had begun to pour into line changeovers and new equipment purchases. Exhibit 2 illustrates the rapid switch to the two-piece can in the beverage industry. In the beer segment alone, almost half of the total cans used in 1974 were made by the new process.

Growth

Between 1967 and 1976 the number of metal cans shipped from the manufacturers grew at an average of 3.4 percent annually. As shown in Exhibit 3, the greatest gains were in the beverage segment, while shipments of motor oil, paints, and other general packaging cans actually declined. A 6 percent decline in total shipments in 1975 turned around as the economy picked up in all areas except basic food cans. For the future, soft drink and beer cans were expected to continue to be the growth leaders.

Exhibit 2

Beverage Can Shipments (billion cans)

	1972	1973	Change 1972–1973	1974	Change 1973–1974
SOFT DRINK CANS					
Total	15,596	17,552	+12.5%	17,980	+2.4%
Three-piece	14,217	15,779	+11.0%	15,589	−1.2%
% of total	91.2	89.9		86.7	
Two-piece	1,379	1,773	+28.6%	2,391	+34.9%
% of total	8.8	10.1		13.3	
BEER CANS					
Total	21,801	24,131	+10.7%	26,077	+8.1%
Three-piece	14,746	14,363	−2.6%	13,237	−7.8%
% of total	67.6	59.5		50.8	
Two-piece	7,055	9,768	+38.5%	12,840	+31.4%
% of total	32.4	40.5		49.2	

Source: *Metal Can Shipments Report 1974*, Can Manufacturers Institute, p. 6.

EXHIBIT 3

Metal Can Shipments 1967–1976 (000 base boxes)

	1967	1972	1973	1974	1975	1976
TOTAL METAL CANS	133,980	168,868	180,482	188,383	177,063	179,449
BY PRODUCT						
Food cans	67,283	64,773	68,770	73,104	68,127	64,984
Beverage cans	42,117	75,916	84,617	89,435	85,877	90,084
Soft drinks	14,580	31,660	35,631	36,499	33,284	39,488
Beer	27,537	44,256	48,986	52,936	52,593	50,596
Pet foods	5,797	6,694	7,121	7,083	6,057	6,121
General packaging cans	18,783	21,485	19,974	18,761	17,002	18,391
Motor oil	n/a	3,095	2,756	2,533	n/a	n/a
Paints	n/a	6,086	5,562	5,202	n/a	n/a
Aerosols	n/a	5,877	6,103	5,765	4,808	5,097
All other	n/a	6,427	5,553	5,261	n/a	n/a

NOTE: A base box contains 31,360 square inches.

SOURCE: Standard and Poor's Industry Survey, *Containers, Basic Analysis,* March 24, 1977, p. C123; *Metal Can Shipments Report 1974,* p. 6.

INDUSTRY STRUCTURE

In 1977 the U.S. metal can industry was dominated by four major manufacturers. Two giants, American Can and the Continental Can Division of the Continental Group, together made up 35 percent of all domestic production. National Can and Crown Cork and Seal were also major forces with market shares of 8.7 percent and 8.3 percent, respectively (see Exhibit 4).

Equipment. A typical three-piece can line cost $750,000 to $1 million. In addition, expensive seaming, end-making, and finishing equipment were required. Since each finishing line could handle the output of three or four can-forming lines, the minimum efficient plant required at least $3.5 million in basic equipment. Most plants had twelve to fifteen lines for the increased flexibility of handling more than one type of can at once. However, any more than fifteen lines became unwieldy because of the need for duplication of setup crews, maintenance, and supervision.

The new two-piece can lines were even more expensive. Equipment for the line itself cost approximately $8.5 million, and the investment in peripheral equipment raised the per-line cost to $10 million to $15 million. Unlike three-piece lines, minimum efficient plant size was one line, and installations ranged from one line to five lines.

Conversion to these two-piece lines virtually eliminated the market for new three-piece lines. No firms were installing new three-piece lines, and the major manufacturers were selling complete, fully operational three-piece lines "as is" for $175,000 to $200,000. Many firms were shipping their old lines overseas to their

EXHIBIT 4

Comparison of 1976 Performance of Major Metal Can Manufacturers ($ millions)

	Continental Group	American Can	National Can	Crown Cork and Seal
TOTAL COMPANY PERFORMANCE				
Sales	$3,458	$3,143	$917	$910
Net income	$118.3	$100.9	$20.7	$46.2
Sales growth, 1967–1976	147%	107%	317%	202%
Profit growth, 1967–1976	51%	33%	160%	145%
Return on equity, five-year average	10.3%	7.1%	11.9%	15.8%
Debt ratio	34%	35%	46%	23%
METAL CAN SEGMENTS (DOMESTIC)				
Sales	$1,307.8	$1,177.6	$616.0	$575.0
Pretax income	$73.0	$64.9	$36.4	$49.0
as a % of sales	5.6%	5.4%	5.0%	8.5%
Market share	18.4%	16.6%	8.7%	8.3%
Number of can plants	70	48	41	26
INTERNATIONAL (SALES OF ALL PRODUCTS)				
Sales	$1,147.2	$475.1	n/a	$343.0
Net income (before taxes)	$63.4	$41.5	small loss	$39.4

SOURCE: *Wall Street Transcript*, November 3, 1975, pp. 41, 864, and company 10-K reports.

foreign operations where growth potential was great. There were few entrenched firms, and canning technology was not well known or understood.

Pricing. The can industry was very competitive. The need for high capacity utilization and the desire to avoid costly line changeovers made long runs of standard items the most desirable business. As a result, most companies offered volume discounts to encourage large orders. From 1968 to 1975, industrywide profit margins declined 44 percent, reflecting sluggish sales and increased price competition. This trend hurt the small company, which was less able to spread its fixed costs. Raising prices above industry-set norms, however, was dangerous. Continental tried this in the fall of 1963 with the announcement of a 2 percent price hike. Other manufacturers refused to follow its lead, and by mid-1964 Continental was back to industry price levels with a considerably reduced market share.

Distribution. Because of the product's bulk and weight, transportation was a major factor in a can maker's cost structure. (One estimate put transportation at

7.6 percent of the price of a metal can, with raw materials playing the largest part at 64 percent and labor following at 14.4 percent.) A manufacturer's choice of lighter raw materials and plant location could have a large impact on total costs. Most estimates put the radius of economical distribution for a plant at between 150 and 300 miles.

Suppliers and Customers

At one time the big U.S. steel companies were the sole suppliers of metallic raw material used by the metal container industry. Can companies, in turn, were the fourth-largest consumers of steel products. During the 1960s and 1970s, aluminum—and to a lesser extent, fiber-foil and plastic—suppliers increasingly entered traditional tinplate markets.

On the customer side, over 80 percent of the metal can output was purchased by the major food and beer companies. Since the can constituted about 45 percent of the total costs of beverage companies, most had at least two sources of supply. Poor service and uncompetitive prices could be punished by cuts in order size. Because can plants were often set up to supply a particular customer, the loss of a large order from that customer could greatly cut into manufacturing efficiency and company profits. As one can executive caught in the margin squeeze commented, "Sometimes I think the only way out of this is to sell out to U.S. Steel or to buy General Foods."[2]

Industry Trends

Three major trends had plagued the metal container manufacturers since the early 1960s: (1) the continuing threat of self-manufacture; (2) the increasing acceptance of other materials such as aluminum, fiber-foil, or plastic for standard tinplate packaging needs; and (3) the "packaging revolution" leading to new uses and thus new characteristics for containers.

Self-Manufacture

In the years 1971 to 1977, there had been a growing trend toward self-manufacture by large can customers, particularly of the low-technology standard items. As shown in Exhibit 5, the proportion of "captive" production increased from 18.2 percent to

Exhibit 5

Metal Can Production by Market (%)

	1970	1971	1972	1973	1974	1975	1976
For sale	81.8	80.9	80.8	78.2	76.7	73.7	74.2
For own use	18.2	19.1	19.2	21.8	23.3	26.3	25.8

25.8 percent between 1970 and 1976. These increases seemed to come from companies gradually adding their own lines at specific canning locations rather than from full-scale changeovers. However, the temptation for major can users such as food and beer producers to begin making their own cans was high. As a result of such backward integration, Campbell Soup Company had actually become one of the largest producers of cans in the United States. The introduction of the two-piece can was expected to dampen the trend toward self-manufacture, since the end users did not possess the technical skills to develop their own two-piece lines.

New Packaging Materials

Aluminum. The greatest threat to the traditional, tin-plated can was the growing popularity of the new, lighter-weight aluminum can. The major producers of this can were the large aluminum companies, led by Reynolds Metals and Aluminum Company of America (Alcoa). Some traditional tin-plated can producers, such as Continental and American, also produced a small proportion of aluminum cans.

From 1970 to 1976 aluminum usage for cans increased, moving up from 11.6 percent to 27.5 percent of the total metal can market. It was expected to reach a 29 percent share in 1977 (see Exhibit 6). In absolute numbers, steel use remained fairly level while aluminum use tripled in those years (see Exhibit 7). Most of the inroads were made in the beer and soft-drink markets, where aluminum held 65-percent and 31-percent shares respectively in 1976. Additional gains were expected, as aluminum was known to reduce the problems of flavoring, a major concern of both the brewing and soft-drink industries.

Aluminum had several other important advantages over tinplate. First, its lighter weight could help reduce transportation costs. In addition, aluminum was easier to lithograph, producing a better reproduction at a lower cost. Finally, aluminum was favored over steel as a recycling material, because the lighter aluminum could be transported to recycling sites more easily, and recycled aluminum was far more valuable.

Aluminum's major disadvantage was its initial cost. In 1976 the stock to manufacture 1,000 12-ounce beverage cans cost $17.13 using steel and $20.81 using aluminum. Moreover, "in early 1977, steel producers raised the price of tinplate by only 4.8 percent, in contrast to an increase for aluminum can stock of about 9.7 percent. [They did this] in an effort to enhance the competitiveness of steel vis-à-vis aluminum."[3] Some industry observers also expected the gap to widen as the auto

Exhibit 6

Metal Can Production by Material (%)

	1970	1971	1972	1973	1974	1975	1976
Steel	88.4	86.9	82.6	81.4	79.0	74.7	72.5
Aluminum	11.6	13.1	17.4	18.6	21.0	25.3	27.5

EXHIBIT 7

Metal Can Shipments (million base boxes)

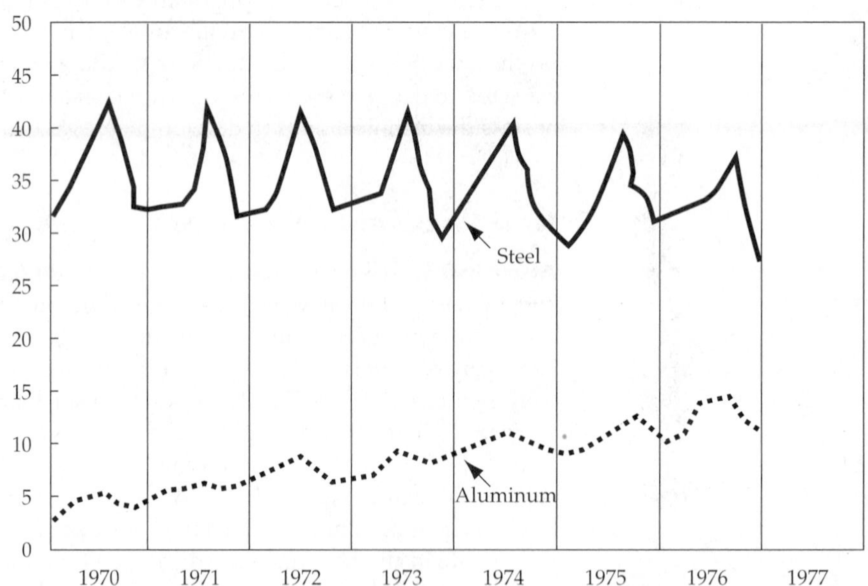

SOURCE: Standard and Poor's Industry Survey, *Containers, Basic Analysis,* March 24, 1977, p. C123.

companies increased their usage of aluminum and thus drove up aluminum prices. The two-piece tin-plated cans were also considerably stronger than their aluminum counterparts.

Other Materials. Two other raw materials threatened tinplate as the primary product in making containers: the new paper-and-metal composite called fiber-foil and the growing varieties of plastics. Fiber-foil cans were jointly developed by the R. C. Can Company and Anaconda Aluminum in 1962 for the motor oil market. They caught on immediately, and by 1977 this composite material was the primary factor in the frozen-juice-concentrate container market as well. Plastics represented the fastest growing sector of the packaging industry and the principal force in packaging change. The plastic bottle offered an enticing variety of advantages over glass bottles, including weight savings, resistance to breakage, design versatility, and thus lower shelf-space requirements. While can makers felt little initial effects from the introduction of plastics, they too could suffer if plastic bottles began to replace the cans being used as packaging for carbonated soft drinks.

The Packaging Revolution

Not only was the traditional package being reshaped and its materials reformulated, but by the 1970s containers also served a new purpose. Starting in the late 1950s the package itself became increasingly important in the marketing of the product it contained. The container was an advertising vehicle, and its features were expected to contribute to total product sales. This had serious implications for the metal can industry. Although the tin can was functional, aluminum was easier to lithograph, and plastic enabled more versatile shapes and designs. Pressure for continuing innovation to enhance marketing meant that companies had to make greater R&D expenditures in order to explore new materials, different shapes, more convenient tops, and other imaginative ideas with potential consumer appeal.

Increasingly, metal can companies would have to contend with the research and marketing strengths of such giant integrated companies as Du Pont, Dow Chemical, Weyerhaeuser, Reynolds, and Alcoa. In response to the integration of packaging by these major material suppliers, some metal can manufacturers began to invest in their own basic research. In 1963, American announced the start of construction on a research center where investigations in such areas as solid-state physics and electrochemistry might reveal potential sources of new products.[4]

The Competition

By the late 1960s all three of Crown Cork and Seal's major competitors had diversified into areas outside the metal container industry. However, in 1977 all three still remained major producers of metal cans (see Exhibit 4).

Continental Group

Because of the extent of its diversification, Continental changed its name in 1976, making Continental Can only one division of the large conglomerate. Although only 38 percent of the total company's sales were in cans, it still held the dominant market share (18.4 percent) of the U.S. metal can market. The remainder of Continental's domestic sales were in forest products (20 percent) and other plastic and paper packaging materials (9 percent).

In 1969 Continental began focusing its investment spending on foreign and diversified operations. In 1972, the company took a $120-million after-tax extraordinary loss to cover the closing, realignment, and modernization of its domestic can-making facilities over a three-year period. Of the $120-million loss, close to 70 percent resulted from fixed-asset disposals, pension fund obligations, and severance pay. By 1976 almost one-third of the company's revenues came from its overseas operations, which covered 133 foreign countries. Domestic investment went primarily to paper products and the plastic bottle lines. Very little was allocated for the changeover to new two-piece cans.

American Can

American also reduced its dependence on domestic can manufacture and, even more than Continental, emphasized unrelated product diversification. American competed in the entire packaging area—metal and composite containers, paper, plastic, and laminated products. In 1972, American "decided to shut down, consolidate, or sell operations that had either become obsolete or marginal [which] resulted in an after-tax extraordinary loss of $106 million."[5]

By 1976, 20 percent of the company's sales came from consumer products such as household tissues, Dixie paper cups, and Butterick dress patterns. American's large chemical subsidiary brought in 15 percent of sales and another 15 percent came from international sales. Return on sales for the domestic container segment of American's business had remained stable at about 5 percent for the last five years. For this period American's average return on equity (7.1 percent) was the lowest of the four major can manufacturers, a result of relatively poor performance in its diversified areas (see Exhibit 4).

National Can

National's attempt to join the trend toward diversification achieved somewhat mixed results. Until 1967 National was almost solely a can producer. After that, through acquisitions the company moved into glass containers, food canning, pet foods, bottle closures, and plastic containers. However, instead of generating future growth opportunities, the expansion into food products proved a drag on company earnings. Pet foods and vegetable canning fared poorly in the 1974–1975 recession years, and the grocery division as a whole suffered a loss in 1976. As a result, National began a stronger overseas program to boost its earnings and investment.

Crown Cork and Seal

While its three major competitors turned to diversification, Crown Cork and Seal continued to manufacture primarily metal cans and closures. In 1976 the company derived almost 65 percent of its sales from tin-plated cans; crowns accounted for 29 percent of total sales and 35 percent of profits. The remaining sales were in bottling and canning machinery. In fact, Crown was one of the largest manufacturers of filling equipment in the world. Foreign sales—of crowns primarily—accounted for an increasingly large percentage of total sales (Exhibit 8). In 1976, Crown's return on sales was almost twice that of its three larger competitors. Over the previous ten years Crown's sales growth was second only to National Can, and Crown was first in profit growth. The following sections describe Crown's history and strategy.

Crown Cork and Seal Company

Company History

In August 1891 a foreman in a Baltimore machine shop hit upon an idea for a better bottle cap—a round piece of tin-coated steel with a flanged edge and an insert of natural cork. This crown-cork top became the main product of a highly successful small venture, the Crown Cork and Seal Company. When the patents ran out, however, competition became severe. The faltering Crown Cork was bought out in 1927 by a competitor, Charles McManus, who then shook the company back to life, bursting upon the "starchy" firm, as one old timer recalled, "like a heathen in the temple." *Fortune*, in 1962, described the turnaround:

> Under the hunch-playing, paternalistic McManus touch, Crown prospered in the thirties, selling better than half the U.S. and world supply of bottle caps. Even in bleak 1935 the company earned better than 13% on sales of $14 million.
>
> Then overconfidence led to McManus' first big mistake. He extended Crown's realm into canmaking. Reasoning soundly that the beer can would catch on, he bought a small Philadelphia can company. But reasoning poorly, he plunged into

EXHIBIT 8

Estimated Breakdown of Crown Cork and Seal's Sales and Pretax Income

	($ MILLIONS)			(PERCENTAGES)		
	1974	1975	1976[a]	1974	1975	1976[a]
A. SALES						
Domestic						
Cans						
Beer	180	209	232	23.5	24.7	24.6
Soft drinks	120	128	140	15.7	15.2	14.8
Food	55	65	70	7.2	7.7	7.4
Other (mainly aerosols)	100	91	101	13.0	10.7	10.7
Total cans	455	493	543	59.4	58.3	57.5
Crowns	25	29	32	3.3	3.4	3.4
Machinery	20	24	27	2.6	2.8	2.8
Total domestic	500	546	602	65.3	64.5	63.7
International						
Cans	46	57	73	6.0	6.7	7.7
Crowns	200	220	242	26.1	30.0	25.6
Machinery	20	24	28	2.6	2.8	3.0
Total international	266	301	343	34.7	35.5	36.3
Total, domestic and international	766	847	945	100.0	100.0	100.0
B. PRETAX INCOME						
Domestic						
Cans	41.0	43.0	46.0	53.9	52.2	50.9
Crowns	2.0	2.0	3.0	2.6	2.4	3.3
Machinery	1.5	2.0	2.0	2.0	2.4	2.2
Total domestic	44.5	47.0	51.0	58.5	57.0	56.4
International						
Cans	4.0	6.0	8.0	5.3	7.3	8.9
Crowns	25.6	26.4	28.4	33.6	32.1	31.4
Machinery	2.0	3.0	3.0	2.6	3.6	3.3
Total international	31.6	35.4	39.4	41.5	43.0	43.6
Total, domestic and international	76.1	82.4	90.4	100.0	100.0	100.0
C. PRETAX MARGINS						
Domestic						
Cans				9.0	8.7	8.5
Crowns				8.0	6.9	9.4
Machinery				7.5	8.3	7.4
Total domestic				8.9	8.6	8.5
International						
Cans				8.6	12.5	11.0
Crowns				13.0	12.3	11.6
Machinery				10.0	12.5	10.7
Total international				11.9	11.8	11.5
Total, domestic and international				9.9	9.7	9.6

[a] 1976 figures are estimated and thus do not match actual numbers on other exhibits.

SOURCE: *Wall Street Transcript*, November 3, 1975, pp. 41, 865.

> building one of the world's largest can plants on Philadelphia's Erie Avenue. It grew to a million square feet and ran as many as fifty-two lines simultaneously. A nightmare of inefficiency, the plant suffered deepened losses because of the McManus mania for volume. He lured customers by assuming their debts to suppliers and sometimes even cutting prices below costs. The Philadelphia blunder was to haunt Crown for many years.[6]

With all his projects and passion for leadership, McManus had no time or concern for building an organization that could run without him.

> Neither of his two sons, Charles Jr. and Walter, was suited to command a one-man company, although both had been installed in vice presidents' offices. Crown's board was composed of company officers, some of whom were relatives of the boss. The combination of benevolent despotism and nepotism had prevented the rise of promising men in the middle ranks. When McManus died in 1946, the chairmanship and presidency passed to his private secretary, a lawyer named John J. Nagle.
>
> In a fashion peculiar to Baltimore's family-dominated commerce, the inbred company acquired the settled air of a bank, only too willing to forget it lived by banging out bottle caps. In the muted, elegant offices on Eastern Avenue, relatives and hangers-on assumed that the remote machines would perpetually grind out handsome profits and dividends. In the postwar rush of business, the assumption seemed valid. The family left well enough alone, except to improve upon the late paternalist's largess. As a starter, Nagle's salary was raised from $35,000 to $100,000.
>
> Officers arrived and departed in a fleet of chauffeured limousines. Some found novel ways to fill their days. A brother-in-law of the late McManus fell into the habit of making a day-long tour of the junior executives' offices, appearing at each doorway, whistling softly, and wordlessly moving on. After hours, the corporate good life continued. More than 400 dining and country club memberships were spread through the upper echelons. A would-be visitor to the St. Louis plant recalls being met at the airport, whisked to a country club for drinks, lunch, cocktails, and dinner, and then being returned to the airport with apologies and promises of a look at the plant "next time."[7]

Up to the early 1950s, Crown ran on a combination of McManus momentum and the last vestiges of pride of increasingly demoralized middle managers, who were both powerless to decide and unable to force decisions from above.

> Dividends were maintained at the expense of investment in new plant; what investment there was, was mostly uninspired. From a lordly 50% in 1940, Crown's share of U.S. bottle cap sales [in the early 1950s] slipped to under 33%. In 1952 the chaotic can division had such substantial losses that the company was finally moved to act. The board omitted a quarterly dividend. That brought the widow McManus, alarmed, to the president's office. President Nagle counseled her to be patient and leave matters to him.[8]

Matters soon grew worse. A disastrous attempt at expansion into plastics followed a ludicrous diversification into metal bird cages. Then in 1954 a reorganization, billed to solve all problems, was begun. The plan was modeled after Continental's decentralized line and staff. The additional personnel and expense were staggering, and Crown's margins continued to dip. One observer noted, "The new suit of clothes, cut for a giant, hung on Crown like an outsized shroud." The end seemed near.

John Connelly Arrives

John Connelly was the son of a Philadelphia blacksmith who, after working his way up as a container salesman, formed his own company to produce paper boxes. His interest in Crown began when he was rebuffed by the post-McManus management, which "refused to take a chance" on a small supplier like Connelly. *Fortune* described Connelly's takeover:

> By 1955, when Crown's distress had become evident to Connelly, he asked a Wall Street friend, Robert Drummond, what he thought could be done with the company. "I wrote him a three-page letter," Drummond recalls, "and John telephoned to say he'd thrown it into the wastebasket, which I doubted. He said, 'If you can't put it into one sentence you don't understand the situation.'" Drummond tried again and boiled it down to this formula: "If you can get sales to $150 million and earn 4% net after taxes and all charges, meanwhile reducing the common to one million shares, you'll earn $6 a share and the stock will be worth $90."[9]

That was good enough for Connelly. He began buying stock and in November 1956 was asked to be an outside director—a desperate move for the ailing company.

> The stranger found the parlor stuffy. "Those first few meetings," says Connelly, "were like something out of *Executive Suite.* I'd ask a question. There would be dead silence. I'd make a motion to discuss something. Nobody would second it, and the motion would die." It dawned on Connelly that the insiders knew even less about Crown than he did.
>
> He toured the plants—something no major executive had done in years. At one plant a foreman was his guide. His rich bass graced the company glee club, and he insisted on singing as they walked. Connelly finally told him to shut up and sit down. The warning system silenced, Connelly went on alone and found workers playing cards and sleeping. Some were building a bar for an executive.
>
> At another plant he sat in on a meeting of a dozen managers and executives, ostensibly called to discuss the problem posed by customers' complaints about poor quality and delivery. The fault, it seemed, lay with the customers themselves—how unreasonable they were to dispute Crown's traditional tolerance of a "fair" number of defective crowns in every shipment; how carping they were to complain about delays arising from production foul-ups, union troubles, flat tires, and other acts of God. Connelly kept silent until a pause signaled the consensus, then he confessed himself utterly amazed. He hadn't quite known what to make of Crown, he said, but now he knew it was something truly unique in his business life—a company where the customer was always wrong. "This attitude," he told the startled executives, "is the worst thing I've ever seen. No one here seems to realize this company is in business to make money."[10]

The Crisis

In April 1957, Crown Cork and Seal was on the verge of bankruptcy. The 1956 loss was $241,000 after preferred dividends, and 1957's promised to be worse.

Bankers Trust Company had called from New York to announce the withdrawal of their $2.5 million line of credit. It seemed that all that was left was to write the company's obituary when John Connelly took over the presidency. His rescue plan was simple—as he called it, "just common sense."

Connelly's first move was to pare down the organization. Paternalism ended in a blizzard of pink slips. The headquarters staff was cut from 160 to 80. Included in the departures were 11 vice presidents. The company returned to a simple functional organization, and in 20 months Crown had eliminated 1,647 jobs or 24 percent of the payroll. As part of the company's reorganization, Connelly discarded divisional accounting practices; at the same time he eliminated the divisional line and staff concept. Except for one accountant maintained at each plant location, all accounting and cost control was performed at the corporate level; the corporate accounting staff occupied one-half the space used by the headquarters group. In addition, the central research and development facility was disbanded.

The second step was to make each plant manager totally responsible for plant profitability, including any allocated costs. (All company overhead, estimated at 5 percent of sales, was allocated to the plant level.) Previously, plant managers had been responsible only for controllable expenses at the plant level. Under the new system, the plant manager was responsible even for the profits on each product manufactured in the plant. Although the plant manager's compensation was not tied directly to profit performance, one senior executive pointed out that the manager was "certainly rewarded on the basis of that figure."

The next step was to slow production to a halt and liquidate $7 million in inventory. By mid-July Crown paid off the banks. Planning for the future, Connelly developed control systems. He introduced sales forecasting, dovetailed with new production and inventory controls. This move took control away from the plant managers, who were no longer able to avoid layoffs by dumping excess products into inventory.

By the end of 1957 Crown had, in one observer's words, "climbed out of the coffin and was sprinting." Between 1956 and 1961 sales increased from $115 million to $176 million, and profits soared. After 1961 the company showed a 15.45 percent increase in sales and 14 percent in profits on the average every year. However, Connelly was not satisfied simply with short-term reorganizations of the existing company. By 1960, Crown Cork and Seal had adopted a strategy that it would follow for at least the next 15 years.

Crown's Strategy

Products and Markets

Recognizing Crown's position as a smaller producer in an industry dominated by giants, Connelly sought to develop a product line built around Crown's traditional strengths in metal forming and fabrication.[11] He chose to return to the area he knew best—tin-plated cans and crowns—and to concentrate on specialized uses and international markets.

A dramatic illustration of Connelly's commitment to this strategy occurred in the early 1960s. In 1960 Crown held over 50 percent of the market for motor oil cans. In 1962 R. C. Can and Anaconda Aluminum jointly developed fiber-foil cans for motor oil, which were approximately 20 percent lighter and 15 percent cheaper than the metal cans then in use. Crown's management decided not to continue to compete in this market and soon lost its entire market share.

In the early 1960s Connelly singled out two specific applications in the domestic market: beverage cans and the growing aerosol market. These applications were called "hard to hold," because the cans required special characteristics either to contain the product under pressure or to avoid affecting taste. The cans had to be filled in high-speed lines. In the mid-1960s, growth in demand for soft-drink and beer cans was more than triple that for traditional food cans.

Crown had an early advantage in aerosols. In 1938 McManus had tooled up for a strong-walled, seamless beer can, which was rejected by brewers as too expensive. In 1946 it was dusted off and equipped with a valve to make the industry's first aerosol container. However, little emphasis was put on the line until Connelly spotted high growth potential in the mid-1960s.

In addition to the specialized product line, Connelly's strategy was based on two geographic thrusts: expand to national distribution in the United States and invest heavily abroad. The domestic expansion was linked to Crown's manufacturing reorganization; plants were spread out across the country to reduce transportation costs and to be nearer customers. Crown was unusual in that it set up no plants to service a single customer. Instead, Crown concentrated on providing products for a number of customers near their plants. Also, Crown developed its lines totally for the production of tin-plated cans, not for aluminum. In international markets Crown invested heavily in undeveloped nations, first with crowns and then with cans as packaged foods became more widely accepted.

MANUFACTURING

When Connelly took over in 1957, Crown had perhaps the most outmoded and inefficient production facilities in the industry. In the post-McManus regime, dividends had taken precedence over new investment, and old machinery combined with the cumbersome Philadelphia plant had given Crown very high production and transportation costs. Soon after he gained control, Connelly took drastic action, closing down the Philadelphia facility and investing heavily in new and geographically dispersed plants. From 1958 to 1963, the company spent almost $82 million on relocation and new facilities. By 1976, Crown had 26 domestic plant locations versus 9 in 1955. The plants were small (usually under 10 lines versus 50 in the old Philadelphia complex) and were located close to the customer rather than the raw material source.

Crown emphasized flexibility and quick response to customer needs. One officer claimed that the key to the can industry was "the fact that nobody stores cans" and when customers need them, "they want them in a hurry and on time. . . . Fast answers get customers."[12] To deal with rush orders and special requests, Crown made a heavy investment in additional lines, which were maintained in set-up condition.

MARKETING/SERVICE

Crown's sales force, although smaller than American's or Continental's, kept close ties with customers and emphasized Crown's ability to provide technical assistance and specific problem solving at the customer's plant. This was backed by quick manufacturing responses and Connelly's policy that, from the top down, the customer was always right. As *Fortune* described it:

> At Crown, all customers' gripes go to John Connelly, who is still the company's best salesman. A visitor recalls being in his office when a complaint came through from the manager of a Florida citrus-packing plant. Connelly assured him the problem would be taken care of immediately, then casually remarked that he planned to be in Florida the next day. Would the plant manager join him for dinner? He would indeed. As Crown's president put the telephone down, his visitor said that he hadn't realized Connelly was planning to go to Florida. "Neither did I," confessed Connelly, "until I began talking."[13]

Research and Development

Crown's R&D focused on enhancing the existing product line. According to Connelly, "We are not truly pioneers. Our philosophy is not to spend a great deal of money for basic research. However, we do have tremendous skills in die forming and metal fabrication, and we can move to adapt to the customer's needs faster than anyone else in the industry."[14] Research teams worked closely with the sales force, often on specific customer requests. For example, a study of the most efficient plant layout for a food packer or the redesign of a dust cap for the aerosol packager were not unusual projects.

Crown tried to stay away from basic research and "all the frills of an R&D section of high-class, ivory-towered scientists." Explained John Luviano, the company's new president:

> There is a tremendous asset inherent in being second, especially in the face of the ever-changing state of flux you find in this industry. You try to let others take the risks and make the mistakes as the big discoveries often flop initially due to something unforeseen in the original analysis. But somebody else, learning from the innovator's heartaches, prospers by the refinement.[15]

This sequence was precisely what happened with the two-piece drawn and ironed can. The original concept was developed in the aluminum industry by Reynolds and Alcoa in the late 1960s. Realizing the can's potential, Crown, in connection with a major steel producer, refined the concept for use with tinplate. Because of Crown's small-plant manufacturing structure and Connelly's willingness to move fast, Crown was able to beat its competitors into two-piece can production. Almost $120 million in new equipment was invested from 1972 through 1975, and by 1976 Crown had 22 two-piece lines in production—far more than any competitor.[16]

Crown was also credited with some important innovations. The company initiated the use of plastic as a substitute for cork as a crown liner, and in 1962 it introduced the first beverage-filling machine that could handle both bottles and cans.

Financing the Company

After Connelly took over, he used the first receipts from the inventory liquidation to get out from under the short-term bank obligations. He then steadily reduced the debt-equity ratio, from 42 percent in 1956 to 18.2 percent in 1976. In 1970 the last of the preferred stock was bought back, eliminating preferred dividends as a cash drain. From 1970 on, the emphasis was on repurchasing the common stock (see Exhibit 1). Each year Connelly set ambitious earnings goals, and most years he achieved them, reaching $2.84 per share in 1976. That year marked a critical time for Connelly's financial ambitions. As he said in the 1976 annual report:

> A long time ago we made a prediction that some day our sales would exceed $1 billion and profits of $60.00 per share. Since then the stock has been split 20-for-1 so this means $3.00 per share. These two goals are still our ambition and will remain until both have been accomplished. I am sure that one, and I hope both, will be attained this year [1977].

International Expansion

Another aspect of Crown's efforts was its continuing emphasis on international growth, particularly in developing nations (Exhibit 9). With sales of $343 million and 60 foreign plant locations, Crown was, by 1977, the largest producer of metal cans and crowns overseas. In the early 1960s, when Crown began to expand internationally, the strategy was unique. In many cases the company received ten-year tax shelters as initial investment incentives. At that time Connelly commented:

> Right now we are premature but this has been necessary in order for Crown to become established in these areas. . . . If we can get 20% to 40% of all new geographic

Exhibit 9

Crown Cork & Seal's Facilities

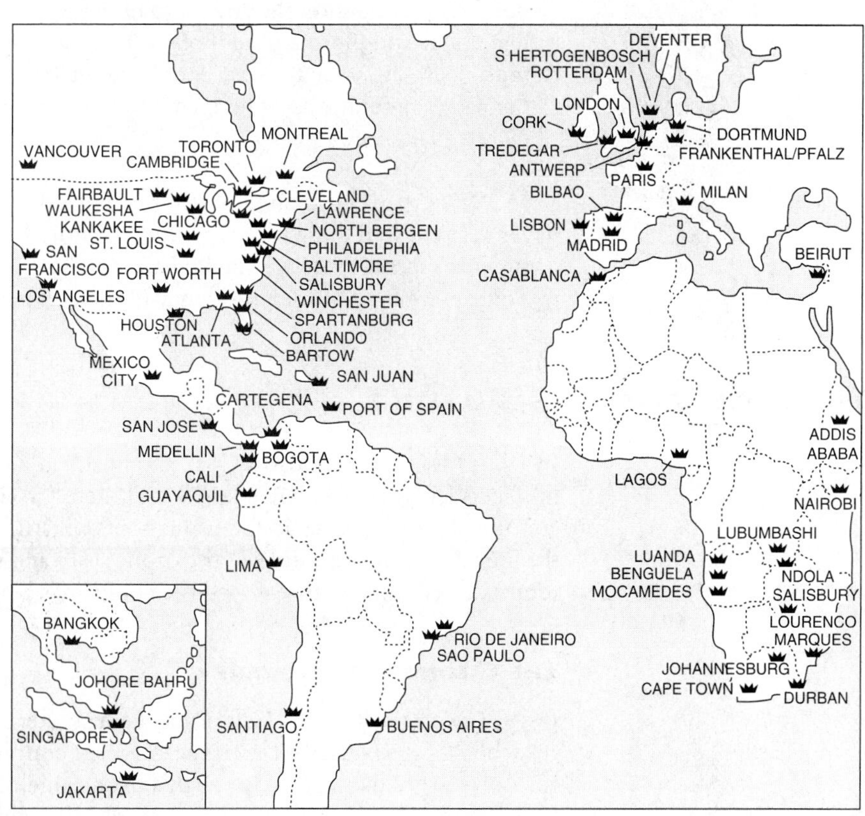

Source: Crown Cork and Seal Company, Inc., 1972 Annual Report.

> areas we enter, we have a great growth potential in contrast to American and Continental.... In 20 years I hope whoever is running this company will look back and comment on the vision of an early decision to introduce canmaking in underdeveloped countries.[17]

John Connelly's Contribution to Success

Many claimed that John Connelly himself was the driving force behind Crown's dramatic turnaround and that it was his ambition and determination that kept the company on the road to success. Connelly has been described as a strong-willed individual whose energetic leadership convinced and inspired his organization to meet his goals.

Yet Connelly was no easy man to please. He demanded from his employees the same dedication and energy that he himself threw into his work. As one observer wrote in 1962:

> At fifty-seven Connelly is a trim, dark-haired doer. The seven-day, eighty-hour weeks of the frenetic early days are only slightly reduced now. The Saturday morning meeting is standard operating procedure. Crown's executives travel and confer only at night and on weekends. William D. Wallace, vice president for operations, travels 100,000 miles a year, often in the company plane. But Connelly sets the pace. An associate recalls driving to his home in the predawn blackness to pick him up for a flight to a distant plant. The Connelly house was dark, but he spotted a figure sitting on the curb under a street light, engrossed in a loose-leaf book. Connelly's greeting, as he jumped into the car: "I want to talk to you about last month's variances."[18]

In 1977, at age 72, Connelly still firmly held the reins of his company.[19] "He'll never retire. He'll die with his boots on," noted one company official.[20] Despite comments such as these, Connelly had raised John Luviano—age 54 and a 25-year veteran at Crown—to the presidency of the company.

Outlook for the Future

In 1977, observers of Crown Cork and Seal had a favorite question: How long can this spectacular performance last? Until then, Crown's sales and profit growth had continued despite recession, devaluation, and stiff competition from the giants of the industry. However, in 1977 the ozone scare and the potential legislation on nonreturnable containers threatened the company's beverage and aerosol business.

The Ozone Controversy

In 1973 two University of California chemists advanced the initial theory that fluorocarbons—gases used in refrigerators, air conditioners, and as a propellant in aerosols—were damaging the earth's ozone shield. (Ozone forms an atmospheric layer that prevents much of the sun's ultraviolet radiation from reaching the earth's surface.) Their theory was that the fluorocarbons floated up into the stratosphere where they broke up, releasing chlorine atoms. These atoms then reacted with the ozone molecules, causing their destruction. The problem was compounded because after the reaction the chlorine atom was free to attack other ozone molecules, causing accelerated breakup of the ozone layer. Proponents of the theory asserted that "fluorocarbons have already depleted ozone by 1 percent and will eventually deplete it by 7 percent to 13 percent, perhaps within 50 to 80 years, if the use of fluorocarbons continues at recent levels."[21]

Proponents of the theory argued that there was real danger in allowing the destruction of the ozone shield. As this shield was depleted and more radiation passed through, they predicted, the number of cases of skin cancer would rise alarmingly. Dr. Sherwood Rowland, one of the original proponents of the theory, explained:

> If aerosol use were to grow at 10% annually (half the growth rate of the 1960s), stratospheric ozone content would fall by 10% by 1994. Scientists figure this would mean a 20% increase in ultraviolet radiation reaching the earth and cause by itself at least 60,000 new cases of skin cancer annually in the United States, roughly a 20% increase.[22]

They also cited the possibility of crop damage, genetic mutation, and climatic change.

Although many studies were in progress, by the end of 1976 the theory had not yet been conclusively proven. There were still some major questions about the types and amounts of reactions that would take place in the stratosphere. Nonetheless, most tests supported the basic thesis that fluorocarbons were in some way damaging the ozone layer.

After the ozone theory was publicized, the reaction against aerosols was severe. Aerosols provided about 60 percent of the fluorocarbons released into the air annually. In 1974 aerosol production declined almost 7 percent in reaction to the recession and the fluorocarbon problem. Only 2.6 billion aerosol containers were used, down from 2.9 billion in 1973. Action began immediately—on the scientific front to test the ozone theory and on the legislative front to restrict the use of fluorocarbons.

Soon a bitter battle broke out between industry spokespeople and those advocating an immediate ban. One industry spokesperson, who requested anonymity, said, "All the scientific theories against fluorocarbons are just that—theories, not facts. What we need is more research before there are any more bans or badmouthing. We don't want another false scare."[23] A member of the Natural Resource Defense Council looked harshly upon the aerosol industry's position. "It's like Watergate," he said. "They want to see a smoking gun. We'll have to wait 25 years for that, and by then irreparable damage will have been done."[24]

Despite industry protests and with the support of some additional studies, state legislators began to introduce antifluorocarbon bills. Georgia led the way in June 1975 by passing a bill banning fluorocarbon aerosols effective March 1, 1977. Successful industry lobbying kept other actions to a minimum until May 1977, when federal agencies proposed a nationwide ban. Calling fluorocarbons an "unacceptable risk to individual health and to the earth's atmosphere," the commissioner of the Food and Drug Administration outlined a three-step phaseout of fluorocarbon manufacture and use.[25] The first step in the ban would be a halt to all manufacture of chlorofluorocarbon propellants for nonessential uses. This ban would take effect October 15, 1978. In the second step, on December 15, 1978, all companies would have to stop using existing supplies of the chemicals in making nonessential aerosol products. The third step would be a halt to all interstate shipment of nonessential products containing the propellant gases. This part of the ban would go into effect April 15, 1979.[26]

The Future for Aerosols. Opinions differed widely as to the extent of the problems the ozone issue would cause the industry. By 1977, the latest estimates were that the fluorocarbon ban would cost container manufacturers more than $132 million in lost sales from 1977 to 1980. This was much less than most of the original estimates due to the success of efforts in the previous two years in finding fluorocarbon substitutes. Most of the solutions involved finding substitute propellants or changing the aerosol valve.

A propellant is the pressurized gas used to hold the suspended molecules of aerosol products as they are sprayed out. Until the early 1970s the most common propellant material was fluorocarbon, which was used in about half of the aerosol cans sold. By 1977 the possibility of substituting hydrocarbons was being explored for many applications. However, although they were less expensive, hydrocarbons were known to be more flammable and thus more dangerous to mix with the many personal-care products that include alcohol as an ingredient. Other proposed alternatives included using carbon dioxide or special pressurized cans that did not release propellants at all.

In May 1977 the new Aquasol valve looked to be one of the most promising ways of eliminating fluorocarbons. Developed by Robert Abplanalp, the inventor of the original aerosol valve, the Aquasol used a dual-duct system (rather than the traditional one-duct) that kept the product separate from the propellant. Abplanalp claimed that fillers could get twice as much product into a can with the new valve because the product did not have to be mixed with the propellant. Also, hydrocarbons could be used more safely for many applications.

Industry Recovery. By 1977 recovery in the aerosol market had already begun, with shipments for 1976 up 6 percent. It seemed likely that this trend would continue because of the strong appeal aerosols had for the consumer. In a 1974 study over 59 percent of the population had heard of the ozone problem, yet about 25 percent said they would be "very disturbed to do without" aerosol products. Industry optimism was moderated, however, by the growing popularity of pump sprays and other nonaerosol products, and by the tendency of the consumer not to differentiate between fluorocarbons and aerosols using other propellants.

Regulating Nonreturnable Containers

Crown's future was also threatened by moves to legislate restrictions on the use of nonreturnable containers. By 1976 Oregon, Vermont, and South Dakota already regulated the use of disposable containers. Laws requiring mandatory deposits for most beverage containers were approved in November 1976 by voter referendums in Maine and Michigan, while they were turned down by narrow margins in Massachusetts and Colorado. The existing laws required a 5-cent deposit on all bottles and cans, refundable when the empties were brought back for recycling or reuse. Nationally, the Environmental Protection Agency banned throwaways from federal property—parks, federal buildings, and military posts—starting in October 1977.

The main problem was litter. Although it was estimated that only 1 percent of the American population were litterers, the extent of the damage was staggering. Unfortunately, disposable cans contributed significantly to the problem. While containers made up only 8 percent of the solid waste in the United States, they made up 54 percent to 70 percent of highway litter by volume. A second issue was the potential savings of raw materials and energy that could be obtained from reusing containers.

Economic Impact. Part of the controversy involved the potential economic impact of legislative bans on nonreturnables. Industry sources agreed that the laws would bring an increase in beer and soft drink prices and eliminate thousands of jobs. The environmentalists countered that consumers paid 30 percent to 40 percent more for beverages in throwaway containers. "Any increased cost due to retooling would be offset by savings in the use of returnable bottles or recycled cans," claimed a spokesperson for the Michigan United Conservation Clubs. He added that "any jobs lost in the canning or bottling industries would be offset by additional jobs in transportation and handling."[27]

Prospects for the Future. Despite a powerful industry lobby, the fight against nonreturnables gained momentum. In July 1977 legislation was being considered by the Congressional Committee on Energy and Natural Resources to require deposits on throwaways nationwide. Although the Senate had once rejected a ban on pull tops, some states, including Massachusetts, had passed such bills effective in 1978. Returnable bottles, which could be used by more than one manufacturer, were being encouraged under the new laws, but it seemed unlikely that cans would be totally banned. Instead, various schemes for deposits and recycling were emphasized. Proposals were made that metal cans be collected, crushed, melted, and reused to make new cans. Under the new system it was uncertain who would pay the extra transportation costs and whether lower raw material prices to the can maker would result. Unfortunately for tinplate users like Crown, the new system favored aluminum cans because of the higher value of the reclaimed metal and the recycling network that already existed for aluminum products.

Crown's Future Growth

Crown's usual optimistic forecasts continued into 1977. The 1976 Annual Report all but ignored the aerosol and bottle bill issues. The strategy stayed the same: no major basic R&D efforts, but quick attention to meeting customer needs and leadership in new applications that involved the traditional metal can. Thus, despite current problems in its markets, some industry observers saw no reason why the company's good record wouldn't continue:

> Even with Connelly's eventual retirement, his Number 2 man seems certain to keep Crown on its upward profits growth trend. While others—like National Can—have ventured into uncharted and at times unprofitable waters, Crown has prospered by doing what it knows best. Under that strategy, prosperity is likely to continue reigning for Crown.[28]

ENDNOTES

[1]Crowns are flanged bottle caps, originally made with an insert of natural cork—hence the name Crown Cork and Seal.

[2]"Crown Cork and Seal Company and the Metal Container Industry," HBS Case Services No. 6-373-077, Harvard Business School.

[3]Standard and Poor's Industry Survey, *Containers, Basic Analysis,* March 24, 1977, p. C123.

[4]"Crown Cork and Seal Company and the Metal Container Industry," HBS Case Services No. 9-373-477, p. 14. Harvard Business School.

[5]Crown Cork and Seal Company Annual Report, 1972, p. 3.

[6]"The Unoriginal Ideas That Rebuilt Crown Cork," Fortune, October 1962, pp. 118–64.

[7]Ibid.

[8]Ibid.

[9]Ibid.

[10]Ibid.

[11]In 1956 Crown's sales were $115 million compared with $772 million for American and $l billion for Continental.

[12]"Crown Cork and Seal Company and the Metal Container Industry," HBS Case Services No. S373477, p. 28. Harvard Business School.

[13]"The Unoriginal Ideas," p. 164.

[14]"Crown Cork and Seal Company and the Metal Container Industry," HBS Case Services No. S373477, p. 30. Harvard Business School.

[15]Ibid., p. 29. Luviano became president in 1976, while Connelly remained chairman and chief operating officer.

[16]In 1976, there were 47 two-piece tinplate and 130 two-piece aluminum lines in the United States.

[17]"Crown Cork and Seal Company and the Metal Container Industry," HBS Case Services No. S373477, p. 33. Harvard Business School.

[18]"The Unoriginal Ideas," p. 163.

[19]Connelly reportedly owned or controlled about 18 percent of Crown's outstanding common stock.

[20]*Financial World,* November 26, 1975, p. 12.

[21]*The Wall Street Journal,* December 3, 1975, p. 27.

[22]Ibid.

[23]*New York Times,* June 22, 1975, p. F3.

[24]Ibid.

[25]*New York Times,* May 12, 1977, p. 1.

[26]Ibid.

[27]*New York Times,* October 30, 1976, p. F1.

[28]*Financial World,* November 26, 1975, p. 12.

Case 7

Georgia Digital Reproduction, Inc.

On Wednesday, August 10, 1988, Richard Taylor, GDR's third president, heard that the Bank of Maryland would not extend a working-capital loan to his company, Georgia Digital Reproduction, Inc. (GDR). That was bad news. During June, GDR had taken down the last $100,000 of a shareholders' $250,000 note. GDR's only remaining funds were $46,512 in cash and a $130,000 bank line of credit backed by shareholder letters of credit. Clearly GDR could not qualify for more bank financing. Taylor was well aware of GDR's financial position (summarized in Exhibit 1) and that he needed to decide on a new strategy for his Norcross, Georgia, company. Was conserving cash while searching for more equity financing what GDR needed, or was that just part of a major overhaul?

GDR Background

Georgia Digital Reproduction was an electronic design and marketing company with 13 employees that subcontracted all its manufacturing. In pursuit of its corporate mission and company objectives (see Exhibit 2), GDR had developed two electronic product lines: (1) a group of digital recorders, electronic devices that recorded and stored audio messages in chip memory for repeated playback, and (2) a series of Travelers' Information Stations (TIS), short-range AM transmitters that broadcast messages repeated by an accompanying digital recorder.

Digital recorders were configured as units to feed recorded announcements to loudspeakers in tour and airport shuttle buses (suggested list price, $5,000–$18,000), as bugle systems for playing bugle calls over the public address systems at military bases ($6,500–$20,150), and as message dispensers in amusement/theme parks, museums, and public parks ($270–$410 for single-channel record and playback units and $2,500–$16,050 for multichannel record and playback units). Each stored message required its own channel; so, for example, a bugle system for storing and playing "Taps," "Reveille," "To the Colors," and "Mess Call" required four channels and had a higher selling price than a two-channel system with only "Taps" and "Reveille" capability. Prices varied also with the mechanical enclosure.

The most common application for TIS units was transmitting weather, parking, or other information on AM 530 or 1610 to motorists' radios along highways, in state and national parks, entering airports, and around university campuses.

This case was prepared by Ambrose S. Kalmbach, Darden 1989, under the supervision of Associate Professor L. J. Bourgeois III and Assistant Professor Andrea Larson.

EXHIBIT 1

Georgia Digital Reproduction, Inc. Financial Statements

	1984	1985	1986	1987	1988							1988
					Jan	Feb	March	April	May	June	July	YTD
REVENUES												
Trade products	147,465	149,002	43,598	347,765	24,822	37,245	100,086	81,787	6,721	122,124	32,568	405,335
Other services	0	0	0	0	0	300	421	9,652	0	250	500	11,123
Total revenue	147,465	149,002	43,598	347,765	24,822	37,545	100,507	91,439	6,721	122,374	33,068	416,458
Cost of Sales												
Trade products	91,687	94,858	39,968	167,710	11,424	18,254	58,922	52,745	3,921	33,125	16,102	194,493
Other services	0	0	0	0	0	200	1,621	4,585	250	473	198	7,327
Total cost of sales	91,687	94,858	39,968	167,710	11,424	18,454	60,543	57,330	4,171	33,598	16,300	201,820
Gross Margin	55,778	54,143	3,630	180,055	13,398	19,091	39,964	34,109	2,550	88,776	16,768	214,638
OPERATING EXPENSES				Note 1								
Staff, staff related	0	0	166,296	347,762	61,094	44,373	47,209	46,244	49,079	50,156	50,818	348,905
General & admin.	60,187	89,759	47,172	186,810	42,776	58,232	13,367	8,361	17,400	18,679	21,678	169,035
Sales & marketing	19,451	93,062	76,956	101,647	1,701	5,103	14,421	6,195	8,267	2,940	2,201	40,965
Total oper. exp.	79,637	182,821	290,424	636,219	105,571	107,708	74,997	60,800	74,746	71,775	74,697	558,905
Other Inc./(Exp.)	(8,255)	52,998	(1,860)	(41,473)	1,829	1,431	(5,243)	(6,237)	(5,629)	(8,924)	(8,812)	(42,533)
Pretax Income/(Loss)	(32,114)	(75,680)	(288,654)	(497,637)	(90,344)	(87,186)	(40,276)	(32,928)	(77,825)	8,077	(66,741)	(386,800)
	Note 2		Audited		Unaudited							

(continued)

Note 1: Composition of 1987 Operating Expenses is estimated; however, the total is audited.

Note 2: Unaudited estimates derived from CPA reviewed data (not GAAP certified) for GDR and its predecessor company. Predecessor's data has been shifted from a July 31 fiscal year to GDR's December 31 fiscal year via calendar proration.

EXHIBIT 1 (CONTINUED)

Georgia Digital Reproduction, Inc. Financial Statements

	1984	1985	1986	1987	1988						
					Jan	Feb	March	April	May	June	July
ASSETS											
Current Assets											
Cash & equivalents	577	15,088	1,914	267,468	149,761	24,445	2,249	7,825	11,451	8,226	6,512
Accounts receivable											
Trade	22,883	7,907	6,345	29,670	35,639	52,987	148,515	195,002	133,238	234,342	168,293
Shareholder	(44,138)	48,629	0	0	253,000	253,000	203,000	150,000	100,000	0	0
Inventory	68,379	39,986	6,865	63,730	45,504	44,697	32,432	23,212	39,389	47,836	119,370
Prepaid expenses	0	0	2,663	5,692	4,218	4,218	4,218	4,639	16,389	4,859	13,445
Total cur. assets	47,701	111,610	17,787	366,560	488,122	379,347	390,414	380,678	300,467	295,263	307,620
Equip., furn., fixts.	4,730	8,441	19,134	20,583	20,483	20,815	22,573	21,573	21,573	28,643	34,496
Less accum. depr.	(718)	(2,160)	(1,151)	(5,126)	(1,941)	(1,971)	(1,977)	(2,007)	(2,287)	(2,287)	(2,587)
	4,012	6,281	17,983	15,457	18,542	18,844	20,596	19,566	19,286	26,356	31,909
Other Assets											
Org. cost net amort.	341	250	11,907	9,944	54,413	53,266	52,119	50,972	49,822	45,222	40,622
Patents	0	0	9,489	10,464	9,489	9,489	9,489	9,489	9,893	9,893	9,894
Total assets	52,054	118,141	57,166	402,425	570,566	490,946	472,618	460,705	379,468	376,734	390,045
	Note 3		Audited		Unaudited						

(continued)

Note 3: Unaudited estimates derived from CPA reviewed data (not GAAP certified) for GDR and its predecessor company. Predecessor's data has been shifted from a July 31 fiscal year to GDR's December 31 fiscal year via calendar proration.

EXHIBIT 1 (CONTINUED)

Georgia Digital Reproduction, Inc. Financial Statements

	1984	1985	1986	1987	1988						
					Jan	Feb	March	April	May	June	July
LIABS. & CAPITAL DEFICIENCY											
Current Liabilities											
AP & accr. exp.	56,116	100,087	162,449	241,789	197,721	174,584	193,392	196,813	206,342	198,478	250,152
Notes payable—cur.	36,875	24,367	26,250	176,374	90,000	90,000	90,000	90,000	87,500	85,000	84,028
Cur. capital leases	0	0	4,352	5,420	5,874	5,874	5,874	5,874	5,875	5,875	5,875
Outstg. line of credit	0	0	0	0	0	0	35,000	50,000	40,000	40,000	70,000
Deferred revenue	0	0	0	999	999	1,700	0	0	0	0	0
Total cur. liabs.	92,991	124,454	193,051	424,582	294,594	272,158	324,266	342,687	339,717	329,353	410,055
Long-term bank debt	0	0	70,000	438,386	0	0	0	0	0	0	0
Capital leases	0	0	11,005	5,608	5,412	5,412	4,984	4,548	4,107	3,659	3,010
Total liabilities	92,991	124,454	274,056	868,576	300,006	277,570	329,250	347,235	343,824	333,012	413,065
STOCKHOLDERS' EQUITY											
Series A Convert., Voting PS	0	0	4,091	8,426	8,158	8,158	8,427	8,427	8,427	8,427	8,427
Addit. PIC PS	0	0	325,909	475,963	474,474	474,474	474,474	474,474	474,474	474,474	474,474
Addit. PIC PS optns.	0	0	0	93,987	0	0	0	0	0	0	0
CS $.10 par	800	100	5,000	5,000	5,000	5,000	5,000	5,928	5,928	5,928	5,928
Addit. PIC CS	0	0	5,490	5,490	5,490	5,490	5,490	7,593	7,593	7,593	7,593
Subordinated debt	0	0	0	0	850,000	850,000	850,000	850,000	850,000	850,000	850,000
Deficit accumulated	(41,737)	(5,009)	(557,380)	(1,055,017)	(1,072,560)	(1,159,746)	(1,200,022)	(1,232,950)	(1,310,775)	(1,302,698)	(1,369,439)
Total equity	(40,937)	(4,909)	(216,890)	(466,151)	270,562	183,376	143,369	113,472	35,647	43,724	(23,017)
Total liabs. & equity	52,054	119,545	57,166	402,425	570,568	460,946	472,619	460,707	379,471	376,736	390,048
	Note 4		Audited		Unaudited						

Note 4: Unaudited estimates derived from CPA reviewed data (not GAAP certified) for GDR and its predecessor company. Predecessor's data has been shifted from a July 31 fiscal year to GDR's December 31 fiscal year via calendar proration.

EXHIBIT 2

Georgia Digital Reproduction, Inc. Corporate Mission Statement

Georgia Digital Reproduction, Inc., designs and markets record/playback digital equipment and related services for communications applications using innovative technologies resulting in flexible, cost-effective, energy-efficient products.

COMPANY OBJECTIVES

1. Build a long-term profitable company.
2. Work in a positive, growth-oriented environment.
3. Manage for and expect superior performance by everyone.
4. Exploit and maintain leadership in record/playback digital equipment technology applications.
5. Attain a reputation for commitment to quality of product and all business affairs.
6. Remain diversified in customers and vendors.
7. Sell products requiring installation and service through dealers/distributors except government agencies and corporate accounts.
8. Price products and services at standard (suggested retail) lists with standard discounts recognizing value in use and not commodity.

SOURCE: GDR company records.

Roadside signs informed motorists of the radio-based service. These units had suggested list prices between $8,300 and $12,050 (see Exhibit 3).

Most of GDR's sales were direct from the home office; a growing volume, however, was coming through George Sherman, the Western Region sales manager in GDR's California office. Additionally, Stephen Naegle, GDR's director of national sales, was dedicated to building a dealer and distributor network. GDR had set minimum stocking and purchasing requirements for its distributors and dealers to maintain. Just recently it had received orders from two possible candidates—EBI of Florida, a trade-show booth and exhibit distributor, and Lyons Communications of California—and it had made a promising contact with American Communications, Inc. (ACI).

THE FAMILY BUSINESS

GDR's predecessor company had been founded in 1982 by Arthur Butler, now GDR's vice president of research and development. Arthur had been involved in audio electronics for more than 40 years and was experienced in radar, black-and-white and color TV, AM and FM broadcasting, computer peripherals, and telephone equipment. He anticipated a demand for TIS units in 1982 shortly after the Federal Communications Commission (FCC) authorized two AM radio channels to

EXHIBIT 3

TIS Sales Brochure

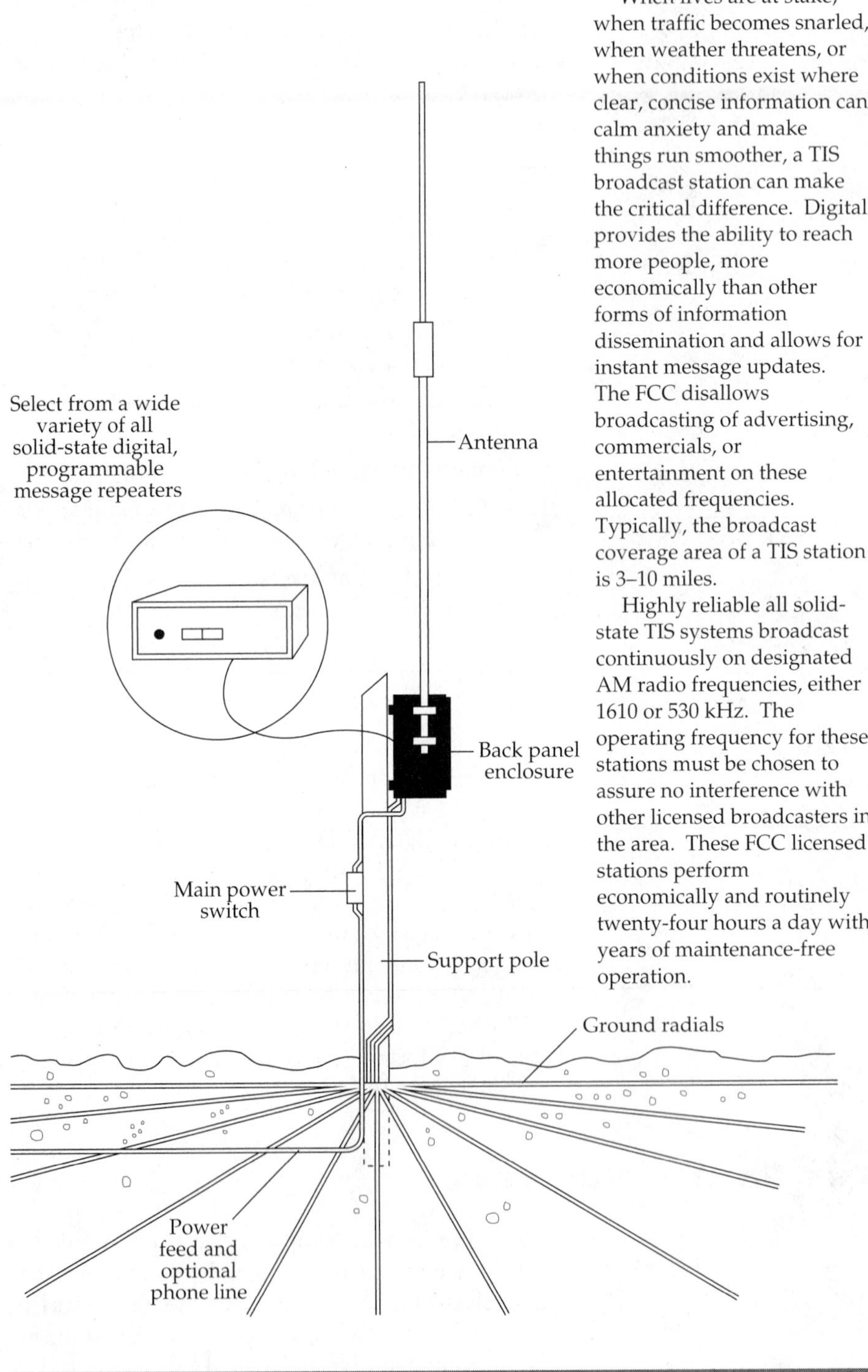

When lives are at stake, when traffic becomes snarled, when weather threatens, or when conditions exist where clear, concise information can calm anxiety and make things run smoother, a TIS broadcast station can make the critical difference. Digital provides the ability to reach more people, more economically than other forms of information dissemination and allows for instant message updates. The FCC disallows broadcasting of advertising, commercials, or entertainment on these allocated frequencies. Typically, the broadcast coverage area of a TIS station is 3–10 miles.

Highly reliable all solid-state TIS systems broadcast continuously on designated AM radio frequencies, either 1610 or 530 kHz. The operating frequency for these stations must be chosen to assure no interference with other licensed broadcasters in the area. These FCC licensed stations perform economically and routinely twenty-four hours a day with years of maintenance-free operation.

be used as TIS channels for transmission of voice information, but not music, to travelers in a three-to-five-mile radius. These channels could be licensed only to government agencies. Butler designed the TIS units for this emerging market.

This new company, consisting of Butler, his daughter Barbara Gibson, and her husband, Phillip, designed the first 10-watt AM TIS unit and started selling it. Butler did the design and engineering work, Barbara handled marketing and sales activities, and Phillip flew all over the country installing the units.

In most early applications, TIS transmitters got their signals from continuous-play cassette players manufactured by other companies. The nonstop wear caused frequent cassette failures and necessitated expensive maintenance and repair trips. Many units were in remote locations. In late 1982, Butler responded by designing a digital recorder/player using 64K dynamic RAM (random access memory) chips. GDR was incorporated as a sister company in early 1983 to handle the redesigned digital recorder/player product line. It also was operated by Butler and his team. A digital recorder sales brochure is shown in Exhibit 4.

Butler spent most of 1983 designing a console for the National Oceanic & Atmospheric Administration (NOAA). This unit could play weather reports to eight incoming phone calls simultaneously. NOAA had promised to buy four but took delivery of only one console. No other applications of this product were developed.

Late in 1984, GDR greatly improved the digital recorders by incorporating 64K static RAMS (SRAMs). With the addition of a small lithium battery, SRAMs retained the recorded messages through power outages. Various SRAM-based products were sold to national and state parks, the U.S. Department of Transportation, the U.S. Army Corps of Engineers, and several national and international airports. Most products had unique features to meet individual customers' needs. Although revenues doubled every year—1983, $42,000; 1984, $94,000; and 1985, $178,500 (fiscal year ending on July 31)—the company continued to run a deficit.

The First Administration

Venture Capital

Realizing that they lacked the resources for a major marketing effort, Butler and Phillip and Barbara Gibson decided to find outside capital. Barbara Gibson spent the last few months of 1985 writing a business plan for presentation at the 1985 Georgia Venture Fair. Their talking Kellogg's Corn Flakes box was the major attraction, and they initiated discussions with Southeast Venture Partners, a prominent venture-capital firm in Atlanta. In early 1986, Southeast agreed to invest $330,000 in June 1986, followed by $100,000 at the beginning of 1987, for partial ownership of GDR, provided that Butler consolidate all operations into GDR, assume the vice presidency of R&D, and recruit a new president.

GDR Staffs Up

During 1986, GDR hired five key employees. Sean Knox accepted the presidency after 14 years in the furniture industry. He had successfully started one company and turned around four others. Stephen Naegle was hired as vice president of sales and marketing. He had 10 years in the banking industry and 4 years marketing and

EXHIBIT 4

Digital Recorder Sales Brochure

DR410 and DR420 W2 Models Are Complete Solid-State Recorder/Players in Compact Aluminum Housings

Change messages yourself. Here is compact flexibility that puts audio where you need it. Featuring a rugged, all-aluminum housing and simple controls, the W2 fits almost anywhere and can be ordered with memory of a few seconds to over ten minutes.

The DR-W2 features:

- Multiple message stacking
- User programming without specialized equipment
- Adjustable sampling frequency from 2.5 kHz to 10 kHz
- High-quality sound reproduction
- Memory protection for power outages and storage
- Economical design with attractive pricing
- Unsurpassed power efficiencies at 12 VDC

The DR-W2 comes complete with an 8-ohm stand-alone speaker and a UL listed 110 VDC power converter. Functions include a start switch, audio-in plug, record/play mode switch, power jack, and wiring position bus for speaker and remote start. An ultrasonic sensing kit is available as an option to automatically activate the unit by detecting motion in the sensor range.

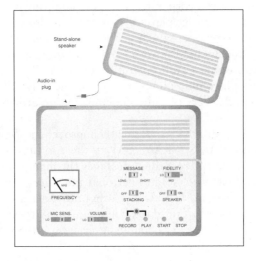

DR410 and DR420 OEM Products Easily Conform to New or Retrofit Environments

Assembled board-level products are available on all DR410 and DR420 components to incorporate with or add on to existing products.

All board-level products have been tested and carefully packaged for easy handling and safe storage. Board-to-board connectors and simple cabeling are included to make a complete player/recorder.

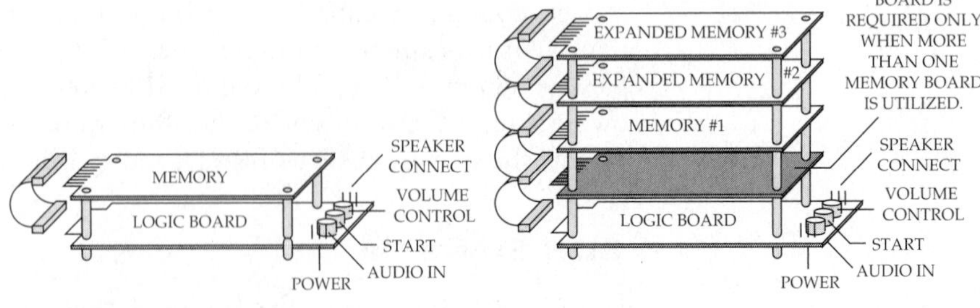

selling corporate communication programs. The vice president of manufacturing position was filled by Vernon Simms, a long-time friend of Butler's who had 20

EXHIBIT 5

Georgia Digital Reproduction, Inc. Organization Chart as of September 15, 1987

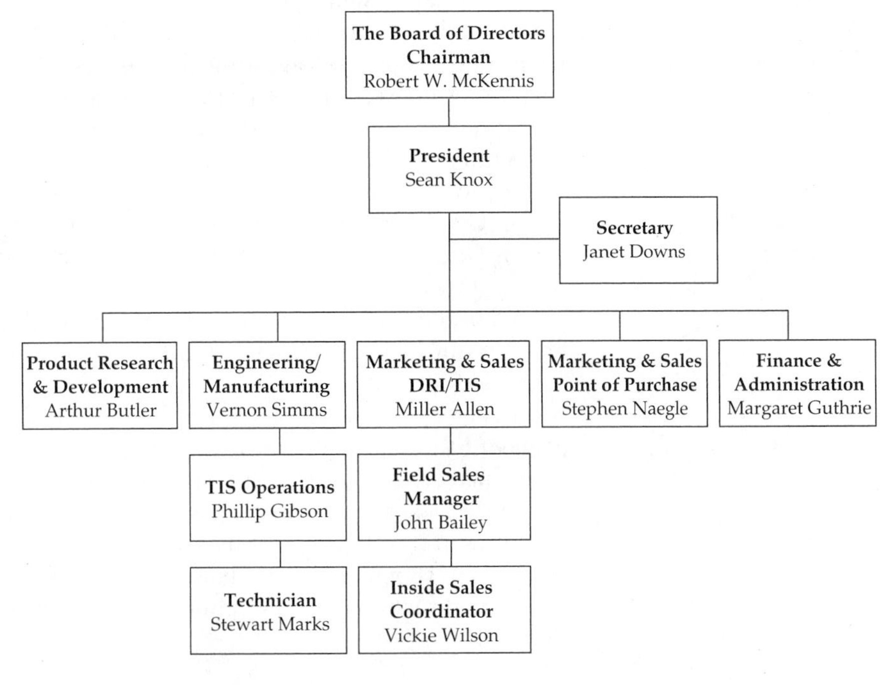

years' experience with ITT Telecom, CTI Data, NCR, and Control Data. Margaret Guthrie came on board as controller and chief financial officer. She was a CPA with 5 years in public accounting, 2 years as general accounting supervisor for a CAD/CAM workstation manufacturer, and 2 years as corporate accounting manager for a musical instrument manufacturer. Finally, John Bailey became TIS national sales manager.

Because of the restructuring, GDR finished fiscal 1986 with revenues of $80,000 ($23,000 for the last five months of calendar 1986 as the company shifted its fiscal year to the calendar year). GDR's resulting organization is shown in Exhibit 5.

The Big Account Targets

Under Sean Knox's leadership, GDR targeted high-potential accounts. Knox and Stephen Naegle made cold calls themselves; however, these efforts required considerable travel, which depleted much of GDR's cash. As these excursions continued, Sean Knox's management style was increasingly seen by many as autocratic. He held few meetings to discuss plans or results.

As part of this effort, GDR first pursued the point-of-purchase (POP) advertising boom. POP advertising was already a $9 billion market, of which $25 million was electronic, and experts expected the electronic segment to expand to $200 million by 1990. The POP revolution was accelerating; consumers were apparently making more of their buying decisions in stores.

GDR approached several large consumer-goods companies to demonstrate its digital recording and playback technology as an enhancement to retail displays. GDR's appeal was that audio inducements similar to the talking Kellogg's Corn Flakes box could spur sales. After much effort, GDR presented the idea to Coca-Cola's southeast regional sales manager, whose only response was a letter to the district sales managers suggesting that they share the idea with their advertising agencies. Anheuser-Busch had a similar reaction. No sales resulted.

Fortunately, other marketing efforts expanded the company's base of sales, and during the first half of 1987, GDR sold digital recorders to many new customers. These included Anchorage National Park, The Tennessee Valley Authority, Fort Bragg (U.S. Army), King's Dominion, Sea World of Florida, The Raleigh-Durham Airport, and a number of state transportation departments. Although sales grew rapidly, expenses ballooned.

To bolster its marketing effort, GDR split the marketing and sales department in mid-1987 by making Stephen Naegle vice president of POP and hiring Miller Allen to be vice president of GDR/TIS. Allen had nine years of experience with three advertising and marketing companies in New York City and eight years as an independent communications and marketing consultant. Vickie Wilson was also hired as the marketing manager. She was responsible for proposal and quotation coordination, customer order entry and expediting, distribution of general sales and product literature, product price lists, and discount schedules. The increased salary expense was supported by an additional $100,000 from Southeast and by a $200,000 line of credit with Georgia Republic Bank backed by letters of credit from GDR's shareholders.

A New Business Plan

The third quarter of 1987 introduced a shift in GDR's marketing strategy. Instead of approaching the POP market directly, GDR opted to develop alliances with other firms active in the field. In July GDR signed a contract with Intermark, a leader in state-of-the-art POP marketing systems, selling all rights to GDR's technology for both domestic and international marketing to Intermark for $60,000. Sean Knox (president) negotiated the entire contract, and neither of the sales vice presidents, Miller Allen and Stephen Naegle, were consulted about the contract, nor had either of them seen the agreement. The Intermark alliance affected only one of the six market segments that GDR had described in its revised business plan dated October 1, 1987.

The second segment cited in the business plan was Short Range Broadcasting (SRB). If a TIS unit transmitted at .1W instead of 10W, it could cover about a ¼-mile radius; thus, it would not need licensing from the FCC and could use voice, music, or commercials. One application would be a "talking house" for the real-estate market. An independent source had estimated the market to be 190,000 realty offices with 20 active listings, on average, yielding a $760-million market.

The third segment was the elevator and fire alarm industry. Although little market data were available, the applications were numerous. Several recently built hotels had talking elevators. Busch Gardens in Tampa, Florida, had already bought several digital recorders for fire alarms and voice evacuation directions.

The fourth segment was the transportation industry. This segment included 16,319 airports worldwide, bus stations, train stations, shuttle buses, tramways, and other mass transit. For example, in an airport, TIS transmitters could direct automobiles as they entered parking lots, and digital recorders could announce public information on the shuttle buses. These airport applications could easily reach $15 million. GDR saw great promise in this market segment, because through one of its major customers, the New York/New Jersey Port Authority, the company had made direct contact with Hudson General Management Corp., one of the largest firms in the United States managing transportation facilities.

The fifth market segment, government entities, was the prime target for TIS units. The Army Corps of Engineers operated 600 lakes and dams and hundreds of waterway projects, each a possible TIS installation. Additionally, the 197 domestic military bases were prime candidates for new multichannel digital recorders to replace the old cassette bugle systems. There were also more than 1,000 national and state parks that could need TIS units, and each of the 380 U.S. Weather Service offices could use $9 million to $11 million in consoles like the one sold in 1984. Also considered in this segment were the 105 nuclear power plants in the United States, the 220 foreign operating plants, and the 176 plants under construction worldwide, in which digital recorders could be installed to expedite evacuations.

The final market segment was replacement of the installed base of cassette players manufactured by other companies. The national parks had at least 10,000 of these older units, but GDR had not explored this segment extensively.

Progress and Disappointment

By the end of 1987, sales had expanded to $347,765 through shipments to customers like the University of North Carolina for the U.S. Olympic Festival. This festival introduced Richard Taylor to GDR. He had spent 14 years coordinating the safety and transportation aspects of special events such as the 1987 Olympic Festival. When the festival ended in September 1987, Taylor began work for GDR.

The sales growth in 1987 enabled the company to assume $750,000 in debt toward the end of the year, but new problems arose. Personality clashes caused the resignation of Sean Knox, Vernon Simms (vice president, manufacturing), John Bailey (national sales manager), and Barbara Gibson (founder Arthur Butler's daughter) in November and December of 1987. After conducting a search for a new president, GDR's board of directors promoted Richard Taylor to the position.

The business plan Taylor inherited had been designed for $1 million in equity, but in reality was funded with $750,000 of debt. Not only did Taylor face $250,000 less in capital than planned and accrued liabilities from Knox's excursions, but GDR was also saddled with the interest expense and the cash drain of the debt.

The Second Administration

Product-Line Expansion

Taylor's attention turned toward expanding GDR's product line. Early in 1988 Arthur Butler and Carol Campbell, a young electrical engineer, designed, prototyped, and built 19 multichannel digital recording units. Products in this new DR460 family used 256K SRAM memory chips and could store and play up to 16 different 45-second messages. All 19 units were shipped to the New York/New Jersey Port Authority for installation in buses. Although Campbell was pleased with the successful effort, she was troubled because time had not allowed adequate lab testing of the new design. Exhibit 6 shows a brochure for this product.

EXHIBIT 6

Multichannel Sales Brochure

Multi-Channel Message Dispatch System

MODEL DR-464

The efficient way to solve transportation information problems

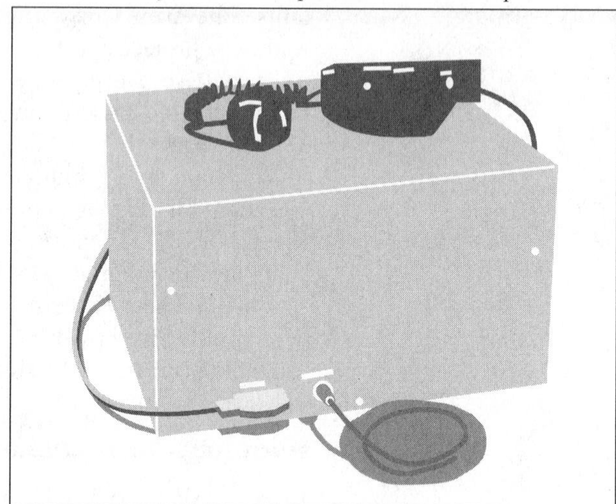

Features:

- All solid-state.
- No tapes to break, replace, or clean.
- Fool-proof operator console.
- Multiple language capability.
- User reprogrammable.
- No anticipated maintenance or service, ever!
- One-year warranty on parts and labor.
- Battery supported memory.
- Crisp, clear sound reproduction.
- No rewinding.
- Compact size.

For use on

- Buses
- Trains/subway cars
- Trams
- Excursion boats/ferries
- People movers
- Monorails

This truly outstanding messaging system is the only all solid-state recorder/player specifically designed for on-vehicle use. Buses, trains, trams, and people movers now have a compact energy efficient way to communicate with passengers thanks to our digital audio technology.

Permanent messages or on-site reprogramming allows the user flexibility never before available for mass transit vehicles. Messages may be loaded by microphone, cassette player, or through our optional, special high-speed digital loader.

The Model DR-464 may be ordered with any number of channels, to a maximum of 16, and has the capacity to store up to 11 minutes per channel of accumulated message time. Each channel is selectable by dialing the channel number on the remote driver console and the message is activated with a simple push of the start button.

All solid-state technology is your assurance of high performance, reliability, and years of maintenance free operation. The Model DR-464 has been carefully designed to withstand shock and vibration and all electronic components are housed in an all-aluminum and weather-resistant case. Nothing on the market today can compare in size, audio quality, and overall performance.

(continued)

Next, Arthur Butler interfaced an electronic timer to a DR460 unit and created a replacement for worn-out cassette bugle systems at military bases. He also designed a dial-up interface for the TIS transmitters. Now, instead of being delivered physically to the TIS location, new messages could be phoned to the TIS unit. This enhancement gave GDR the broad line of products shown in Exhibit 7.

EXHIBIT 6 (CONTINUED)

Multichannel Sales Brochure

Multi-Channel Message Dispatch System

MODEL DR-462

TECHNICAL SPECIFICATIONS

Audio:
  Input: In record, –5 dbm @ 600 Ohm unbalanced
  Output: low impedance for speakers, 10-watt audio power
Operation environment: –30°C to 75°C
Power requirements: 1.5 watts plus audio power to 10 watts 12 VDC nominal
Dimensions: Electronic cabinet: 17 9/16" × 10 9/16" × 16"
  Console: 6.5" × 1.9" × 6.5"
Memory: Type: 256K Static RAM (CMOS)
  Capacity per board: 8 memory chips per board
  Number of boards (memory): max. of 16 bds. per channel and 16 channels per system
  Battery to support memory: 3VDC Lithium Battery
Board size: Logic Board: 13 5/8" × 2 1/16"
  Memory Board: 13" × 3" × 1/2"

EXHIBIT 7

Georgia Digital Reproduction, Inc. 1988 Product Line

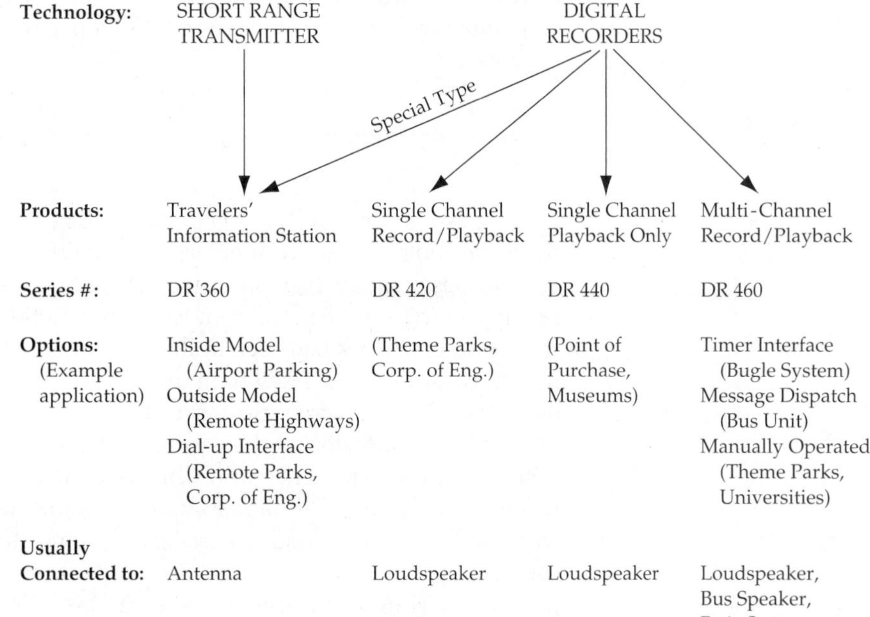

The Competitive Situation

The electronic basis of GDR's products gave them several inherent advantages over mechanical cassette systems. The digital recorders were more power efficient, more reliable, and virtually maintenance free with no degradation of sound quality, because no parts or tapes wore out. Users of digital recorders did not have to store, duplicate, or replace tapes; moreover, the wait for cassette tapes to rewind was eliminated, because GDR's electronic products instantaneously reset to the message's beginning for replay.

The company's products were built from commercially available components, but GDR was the only company combining these particular technologies. The 12-volt power requirement allowed installation of GDR products in transportation vehicles; a small battery let the SRAMs retain their data when the ignition was off.

Few cost-competitive products existed in either GDR's TIS or digital recorder markets, but several companies sold substitute products that met the various customer needs GDR was attempting to meet. Three companies—Vari-Tech, McKenzie Laboratories, and 360 Systems—offered alternatives to cassette players. Thirteen other companies manufactured products for related applications and could be drawn into GDR's market if the potential continued to materialize.

GDR faced stiff competition in one arena: TIS sales to government agencies such as national parks. Government sales were almost always by sealed bids and were awarded on price after a three- to six-month wait. ISS, a one-man distributorship in Michigan, competed strictly on price, 30 percent of GDR's price. A recent GDR study concluded that only $24,000 worth of the $300,000 of product put out to bid in 1988 was actually awarded. Although ISS got all of the bids, the dollar value was relatively low.

To address ISS's aggressive approach, Richard Taylor had sent a letter suggesting that ISS become a GDR distributor. Taylor was disappointed by ISS's reply, which cited poor ethics by GDR prior to Taylor's arrival, when GDR had distributed ISS literature copied on GDR letterhead. Sean Knox had halted the counterfeited literature distribution only after ISS's legal counsel sent a letter. Taylor responded with a letter explaining GDR's personnel changes, but he received no response.

Events during the Summer of 1988

As he contemplated GDR's strategic needs in August 1988, Taylor thought back to the past summer. GDR's cumulative loss for the year through July 31 was $386,800 and growing because sales were significantly below forecast. The October 1, 1987, business plan had forecasted $461,000 year-to-date sales with Intermark. In reality, Intermark sales had been less than $5,000. Taylor's summer communications with Intermark had been futile, so he did not know why Intermark had placed no significant orders. Excluding expected Intermark revenues, GDR sales were down only 3 percent from the forecast.

One bright spot during the summer was the hiring of Diane Conner, with more than ten years' experience in inventory control, as director of engineering and manufacturing. (See Exhibit 8 for latest organization chart.) Within three months with GDR, she had devised a part-numbering system, organized all GDR's inventory, started qualified-vendors lists, and was working toward incorporating the part-numbering scheme into engineering. (GDR had some bills of material, but they weren't integrated into the inventory system, nor were part numbers on any

EXHIBIT 8

Georgia Digital Reproduction, Inc. Current Organization Chart

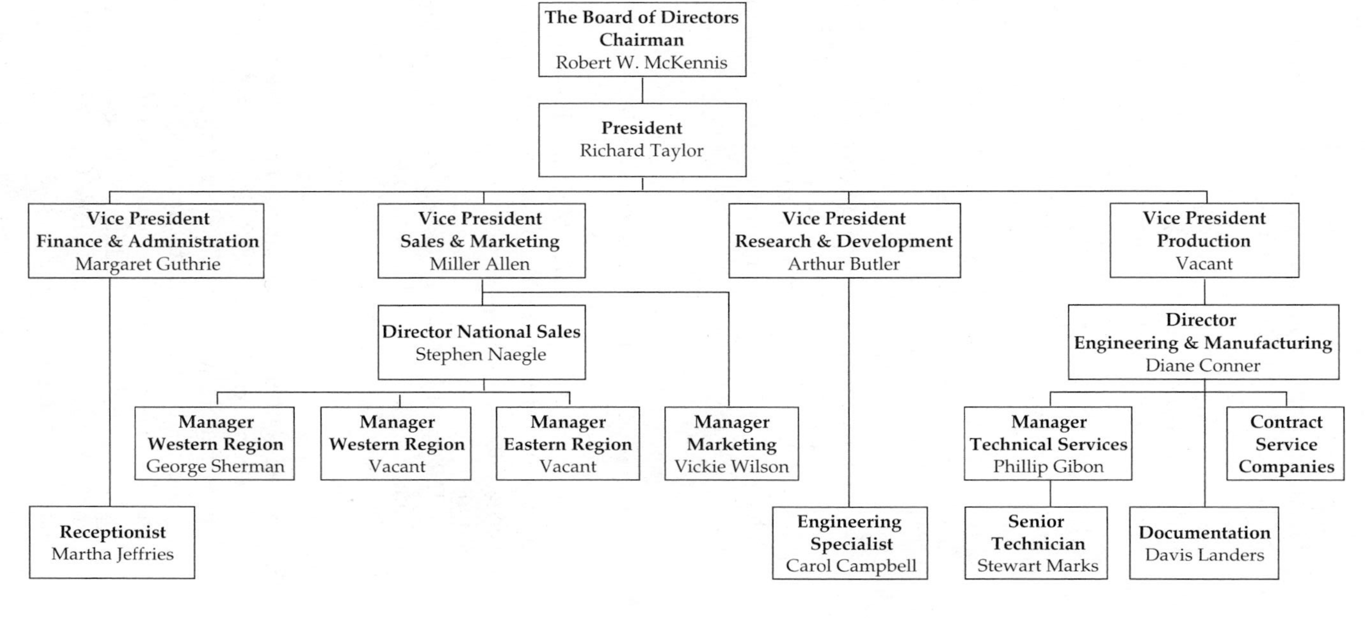

schematics.) She was also responsible for planning and coordinating GDR's production subcontractor, Electronic Circuits, Inc. (ECI). This responsibility required visits to ECI and the writing and distribution of a weekly report.

During the summer, GDR had sent letters similar to Exhibit 9 to the commanders of 25 U.S. Army bases. Four responded with orders for bugle systems, DR460s. When the purchasing officer at one fort requested that the unit include battery backup, GDR's sales representative saw nothing unusual and shipped the order with the standard battery backup that enabled the message memory to be maintained through power outages. In reality, the fort wanted the clock/calendar chip battery backed up to maintain time and date through power failures also. That request required a top-priority design change by Butler.

There were other sales-order problems. Once Stephen Naegle quoted a DR460 based on 64K SRAMs, but GDR had upgraded to 256K SRAMs six months previously. Another problem occurred when an order of DR460s was taken on July 12 for Anaheim, California. The city wanted the units with dial-up control; GDR promised shipment by July 30, but the dial-up control circuitry had not yet been designed for the DR460. This caused another panic design effort by Butler.

To Carol Campbell, Butler's engineering specialist, every unit being sold seemed to be a "custom sales job." Even when the salespeople talked to Butler in advance about a possible order, the problems persisted. Campbell explained the situation as "Arthur says yes to whatever sales says, but sales doesn't ask or say what they should, because they don't know what to ask or say." In a separate conversation, Miller Allen said, "Maybe we just need a better list of questions to ask our customers." Campbell saw it differently: "Sales thinks they know the product; all they really know is what it used to be."

In another incident, a TIS order for the U.S. Army Corps of Engineers had been quoted, and the Corps was very pleased with the price. As Phillip Gibson (manager of technical services) assembled the order, however, he realized the quote included only the enclosure, the transmitter, and a filter board. The power supply, the audio processor board, and the back panel had all been omitted. In the rush to correct the order by the January 1 shipping date, the wrong frequency option was shipped.

GDR's problems were not restricted to booking and shipping orders. GDR had sold four bugle systems, but difficulties with three of them required Campbell's help at the army bases. No major technical issues had to be resolved; the army personnel simply could not program the timer that triggered the bugle calls because GDR had shipped the bugle systems with no documentation. The expense of Campbell's trips had not been included in the prices quoted.

The technical side of GDR also had problems. Butler had incorporated several design changes without considering the cost and scheduling impact. Since most communication with ECI, the manufacturing subcontractor, was verbal, GDR had little documentation of these changes or of overall product design. As the situation worsened, Taylor requested that ECI be paid only for those items on official GDR purchase orders issued by Diane Conner, which improved her control over the manufacturing process.

GDR's Current Situation

After reviewing the development of Georgia Digital, Taylor began to think through the company's current operations and strategy.

EXHIBIT 9

Example of Direct-Mail Letter to Army Base

Georgia Digital Reproduction, Inc.
2110-15 Technology Dr.
Norcross, GA 30092

August 18, 1987

Captain David Jenkins
Base Commander
Northside Army Ammunition Plant
P. O. Box 3258
Northside, CA 95637

Reference: Solid State Bugle Calls

Dear Captain Jenkins:

I'd like to introduce you to a concept that is revolutionizing the way the U.S. Army wakes up each morning. Georgia Digital Reproduction, Inc., Model 460 Multi-Channel Digital Recorder/Player automatically plays bugle calls at predetermined times, day after day, year after year—it even calculates for leap year!

All solid-state technology means no maintenance and no repair. Standard audio connections make our player directly suitable to match with existing public address or amplifier systems. Low power requirements allow for convenient auxiliary battery backup during any power outages.

You may select only the bugle calls you use most or an entire set of all the official U.S. Army calls.

For more information on how you can get your base up on time, please call (404) 834-1733.

Regards,

Vickie Wilson

Vickie Wilson
Inside Sales Coordinator

MA/vw

PRODUCT DESIGN AND MANUFACTURING

Arthur Butler did the initial design and breadboarding (a quick method of physically verifying a paper design). The verified design was then given to Dixie Circuits in Marietta, Georgia, for circuit-board layout and prototype building. After Butler tested and approved the prototypes, the design was given to ECI for manufacture.

ECI operated in a storefront in Roswell, Georgia, and all product was built by hand. Most of the company's employees were experienced electronics assemblers and worked at ECI as a second job in the evenings. ECI had been in business for three years and had six customers; GDR and General Electric made up most of the company's business. ECI bought most of the parts used to assemble GDR products.

Marketing

In July 1988, GDR had hired a recent college graduate to test-market a .1W FM transmitter/tape player manufactured by a third party for "talking house" applications. The long-term goal would be to penetrate the real estate market and then upgrade the customers to digital recorders. If the effort was successful, GDR would act as a distributor. The unit would sell for about $350.

For TIS sales, Taylor thought from his experience with universities, a direct mailing to large universities would be an effective addition to government sales. By the end of this month, August 1988, Marketing Manager Vickie Wilson would send out letters to 50 universities in California and Texas. September's mailing would promote bugle systems to Air Force bases, and October's would target more universities.

Other efforts to develop distribution of GDR products were not progressing. The opportunity with ACI of Detroit to coordinate alarm and safety equipment had bogged down this week. The national sales manager of ACI had visited GDR and informed the company that ACI was still interested but needed more time. The information was disappointing, because Naegle and Allen had just spent a week in Chicago at a kickoff meeting for ACI dealers. Fortunately, ACI had given GDR approval to work directly with ACI's six largest dealers.

A new market opportunity had recently arisen in discussions with one of the nation's largest aircraft manufacturers. The Federal Aviation Administration's recent announcement requiring installation of cockpit voice recorders (CVRs) in all existing and newly manufactured commuter aircraft had prompted this company to approach GDR. Both companies thought a viable digital solid-state CVR (DSS-CVR) could be developed, and the aircraft company had sent GDR a letter of understanding describing possible DSSCVR products and initial specifications. The letter stated, "Physical size is an important consideration." Taylor thought that GDR could have a prototype by the end of January 1989.

Stephen Naegle, the national sales director, estimated that the commuter aircraft market for DSSCVRs could be 10,000 units worth $20 million and that the commercial aircraft market was four times larger. The pilots' preflight checklist and the flight attendants' well-known monologues could also be done by a digital recorder.

Naegle had also contacted the Naval Air Command concerning DSSCVRs and was progressing on a proposal. According to the usual schedule for such projects, GDR would deliver the first prototypes to the Navy in mid-1991. Naegle's thoughts on the project were, "You can never have it too small. . . . I can't see any down side . . . and technologically I think we're pretty much there."

Employees

Taylor's thoughts shifted from GDR's marketing efforts to the strengths and weaknesses of the staff (see Exhibit 8 for current organization). Recently he had discussed with Marketing Manager Vickie Wilson the need to stay focused on the tasks delegated to her. She had been letting several priorities slide and had been repeatedly making small but important errors. Some of the difficulty with Wilson was attributable to her boss Miller Allen's management style.

Although Allen delegated well, he often failed to check on progress. His previous experience as a consultant helped him develop good sales literature and nurture relationships with customers, but it had not required extensive supervisory effort. He was also able to set up deals, but he could not consistently close them.

Both Allen and Stephen Naegle would often close customers' sales by offering discounts. Not only could this upset current and future dealers and distributors, it also lowered GDR's margins. Taylor wanted to price GDR's products by value to the customer, not cost multiples and discounts.

Naegle had slightly different characteristics from Allen. He managed his subordinates better and was also adept at "managing" superiors. He was a good, responsive team player. He built customer relationships well and could close almost any sale to an interested buyer, but he lacked experience in closing tough sales and in negotiating. Unfortunately, he also aggravated the technical staff by making design suggestions.

GDR had a very talented R&D engineer in Arthur Butler, but because GDR had no manager of production, Butler was overly involved in manufacturing coordination. Administration was not Butler's forte, and he candidly didn't want that responsibility. Moreover, Butler was not concerned with career development; he wanted to work with what he loved—product design and development. Instead, he had to coordinate manufacturing situations, which did not fit his background. He preferred that Carol Campbell attend the recently instituted weekly staff meetings as the R&D/engineering representative. Taylor viewed this situation not as a shortcoming in Butler's abilities but as a problem in company staffing.

Campbell's attendance at staff meetings had two disadvantages. She often needed to discuss technical situations with Butler before replying to questions, and she became defensive in discussions concerning product design problems. Although Campbell was an eager contributor, she was fairly new to the company and did not have the technical base that would substitute for Butler's.

Phillip Gibson, the manager of technical services, was a contrast to Campbell. As one of the original three founders, Gibson had grown with GDR. He was an excellent broadcast engineer and was critical to the support of the TIS product line, which he knew better than anyone else.

Recently much of the administrative work had been handled by Diane Conner in engineering and manufacturing. Although Conner had done a superb job organizing GDR's inventory and establishing a part-numbering system, Taylor had been disappointed with her supervisory capabilities. She was a superb doer but was overwhelmed by the management of three subordinates and GDR's contract relationships.

When Taylor had succeeded Sean Knox as president of Georgia Digital, he realized that everyone was doing everyone else's job. Taylor's priority was to focus each employee on his or her own talents, skills, job, and responsibilities.

FUTURE COURSE

Taylor knew that the cash crunch at Georgia Digital was very real. Margaret Guthrie had done almost everything possible to ease it. She had negotiated with ECI to stretch the $80,000 due ECI on August 31 to $10,000 due every two weeks.

She was discussing factoring GDR's receivables, which would provide an additional rolling line of credit for 90 percent of everything under 90 days, capped at $200,000. Despite Guthrie's efforts, however, both she and Taylor were concerned that, unless GDR's cash position improved, the company might have difficulty making future payrolls. Taylor knew that any major changes would need approval of GDR's board of directors.

GDR under Richard Taylor had a very open atmosphere, and people freely expressed their opinions. He decided to seek clues to a strategy for GDR in some of the points his staff had made.

- Diane Conner (engineering and manufacturing) was surprised at the lack of manufacturing experience in the company.
- Margaret Guthrie (finance) felt that the toughest thing to handle was changing priorities coming from several people.
- Phillip Gibson (technical services) stated, "Marketing doesn't know enough to sell the products or even write up an order. None of them have electronic backgrounds."
- Carol Campbell (electrical engineering) noted, "At one point in time, sales was selling stuffed printed circuit boards, and all of a sudden we had a system."
- Conner's summation was, "The circuitry's all done. Our packaging needs to be improved. Documentation needs to be done. Basically the back end is unfinished."
- Stephen Naegle (director of national sales) seemed unsure: "I really haven't had a problem with missed orders. . . . It's helter skelter back there."
- Campbell said, "Marketing is constantly asking us to make up this and that. I don't know what they are doing with all those sample units. Maybe they are leaving them with customers."
- Guthrie felt GDR needed to be poised for a big manufacturing hit.
- Naegle explained the custom-order tendency: "We always did it that way; any sale is seductive."
- Campbell warned, "We need to be aware of sending prototypes to customers. Boards with jumpers [wires added to correct design errors] are not reliable."
- Naegle also expressed a word of warning: "We know some needs; needs are not markets."
- Guthrie thought, "We need to build to inventory, but we can't take the inventory-obsolescence risk unless the market and application solidifies."
- Naegle acknowledged that "developing a distributor/dealer network is labor intensive and tough."
- Campbell showed her foresight: "What's going to happen when Arthur Butler leaves?"
- Naegle expressed his slant: "I'm on the road trying to book that one big piece of business."
- Miller Allen (vice president of sales and marketing) stated the challenge as "selling new products to new environs for new customers."

CASE 8

IRAN OFFICE AUTOMATION COMPANY

It was early January 1995 as Kayvan Noori sat in his office looking out at the snow-covered mountain ranges north of Iran's capital city, Tehran, contemplating his future. Kayvan was a second-year MBA student at the University of Virginia and had returned to Tehran to spend the winter vacation with his family. During that period, he and his father, Mahmoud Noori, often discussed the future of the family company, Iran Office Automation Company, Ltd., the strategic choices it faced, and Kayvan's career options upon receiving his MBA in May.

IRAN OFFICE AUTOMATION COMPANY, LTD.

Iran Office Automation Company, Ltd. (IOAC) was established in 1964 by Mahmoud Noori. By 1994, IOAC was the oldest and largest office machines company in Iran. The company remained privately held by Mahmoud Noori and his brother, both of whom were actively involved with its management. IOAC exclusively represented the following international manufacturers and their products in Iran:

Sharp Corporation, Osaka, Japan: Since 1964

- Photocopy machines and supplies
- Calculators
- Cash registers
- Facsimile machines
- Bank-teller machines (government orders only)
- Notebook computers
- Computer monitors

Glory Co., Ltd., Osaka, Japan: Since 1986

- Banking and cash-handling equipment (government orders only)

Seiko Epson Corporation, Tokyo, Japan: Since 1991

- Epson brand of computer printers

Olivetti S.P.A., Ivrea, Italy: Since 1991

- Personal computers
- Notebook computers
- Banking systems
- Electronic typewriters

This case was prepared by Amir Massoud Amiri, Darden 1995, under the supervision of Jeanne M. Liedtka, Associate Professor of Business Administration.

IOAC imported, marketed, sold, and serviced the office equipment of the companies it represented. Nationwide sales were made through a network of approximately 750 dealers, and a direct sales force sold to the government and large private customers. The company provided after-sales service through 120 service dealers and its own team of 125 technicians. (Exhibit 1 provides the list of IOAC's installed machine population and service coverage channels.) In all, the company employed 280 personnel, and revenues from local operations reached a record $45.4 million in 1992.

In Kayvan's opinion, IOAC had both survived the Iranian revolution of 1978 and maintained its leadership in Iran's turbulent environment by being innovative and flexible. For example, throughout the eight-year Iran/Iraq war, when the importation of nonessential products was restricted, IOAC maintained its own critical flow of supplies and spare parts (especially for photocopiers) by using airline passengers as carriers from Dubai (The United Arab Emirates). Since the process was costly, margins were low, and the risk was high, most competitors opted to cease operations altogether, and a few limited their transactions to sporadic government orders only. As a result of its persistence, IOAC's Sharp brand copiers were the main operational copiers in Iran for eight years. Although IOAC made no substantial profits during this period, it seized a leading market share in key products. By the time restrictions for imports were lifted in April of 1989, IOAC had firmly established its 750-strong dealer network, and continued to maintain a leading market share for nearly all its products. In 1993, IOAC held an 85 percent share of the Iranian copier market.

At the end of 1994, IOAC was more than triple the size of its closest competitor and was the only company that covered the complete range of office machines in Iran. IOAC distributed approximately 600 different products through 750 dealers nationwide. The copier department alone ordered and distributed more than 15,000 items monthly.[1] At such volumes, territory management, price control, and

EXHIBIT 1

IOAC's Installed Machine Population and Service Coverage Channels

PRODUCT	INSTALLATION 1985–1993	IOAC SERVICED	DEALER SERVICED
Copiers	50,000+	40%	60%
Facsimiles	11,600	60	40
Printing calculators	210,000	35	65
Other calculators	2,400,000	30	70
Cash registers	3,000	70	30
Electronic typewriters	1,700	0	100
Bank-teller terminals	8,300	100	0
Bank note counters	5,800	100	0
Personal computers	17,000	90	10
Notebook computers	1,900	90	10
Printers	29,000	95	5

SOURCE: IOAC Company Profile 1993.

account management became very complicated, especially in developing countries such as Iran. The slightest shortage in supplies resulted in dealer-initiated arbitrage and high price fluctuations. Customers became frustrated and the brand image suffered. Excess inventory and good dealer management were fundamental for nationwide product availability and price stability.

Nationwide after-sale service was another one of IOAC's critical operations. In the office machine industry, a brand's reputation and popularity depended on the quality of service provided for it. IOAC provided the best after-sale service in the industry. It was the only company that guaranteed service in under 20 hours for any location outside Tehran. This was particularly difficult in Iran, where transport infrastructures were limited and inefficient. IOAC maintained its superior after-sale service through careful coordination of service affiliates, a large and continuously replenished inventory of spare parts, and ongoing training of dealers and technicians.[2] IOAC's service operation was hard to replicate since it would have required substantial investment of capital, human resources, and training. According to Mahmoud Noori: "Today all of IOAC's managers understand after-sales service and customer satisfaction. It's the backbone of the company, an integral part of our culture."

Localized marketing was another strength. IOAC had its own advertising and publication department, which translated all product and technical manuals into Farsi (Iranian) and coordinated the company's advertising with numerous outside agencies. All advertising catered to local tastes and needs. In the late 1980s, IOAC initiated the use of city walls and buses as advertising vehicles. In 1994, it introduced direct mail. Furthermore, IOAC had been the largest advertiser in Iran in 1989, 1990, and 1991. Actual advertising had been reduced in recent years, but the advertising and publication department had been expanded to provide greater support for IOAC's products.

IOAC also enjoyed greater flexibility over its local competitors by owning a shipping and financing subsidiary in Dubai, the United Arab Emirates. The subsidiary, Gulf Mercantile & Investment Co., financed and coordinated most of IOAC's imports. This added speed to IOAC's operations, as Dubai's economic infrastructure was better suited for international trade than Iran's. The smaller operation of competitors prevented them from maintaining similar subsidiaries in Dubai.

To date, IOAC had survived a revolution and maintained a vigorous operation under a variety of conditions, including war, hyperinflation, depression, volatile exchange rates, adverse government regulations, and constant uncertainty. Resourceful managers, agility, and speed were central to its success. According to Mahmoud Noori:

> One of our main strengths is management's understanding of how to operate in very haphazard environments such as the Middle East. Our managers make fast decisions and move quickly to adapt to new situations. The whole operation, the whole culture of the company, is based on this fast management of change.

A comprehensive information system further enhanced management's effectiveness. Both offices in Tehran and Dubai were fully computerized in order to keep up-to-date accounting books, inventory, and shipping data. In addition, a current database on all sales transactions was maintained. This provided management with instant financial, dealer, and product data. Instantaneous access to information had been instrumental in management's speed and agility.

Ultimately, customers remained loyal to IOAC due to its ability to provide products, supplies, service, and spare parts, regardless of economic conditions.

Despite IOAC's solid positioning within the Iranian office machines market, its future prosperity was threatened by grave macroeconomic issues which plagued its home territory. IOAC's revenue grew 81 percent between 1989 and 1990. It grew another 77 percent in 1991, but growth dropped to 8 percent in 1992. During 1993, IOAC's revenue declined by 9 percent and by 1994 the decline reached 55 percent. Forecasted decline for 1995 was expected to be greater than 50 percent again.

The substantial fluctuation in revenues was directly related to Iran's weakening economy. Iran had entered a recession in 1992, and the economy had continually deteriorated ever since.

Iran

Iran's population of 64 million was growing at 3.5 percent annually. Its GNP equivalent of $90 billion, growing at 7 percent, had not absorbed a 30 percent unemployment rate, and inflation had risen from 23.7 percent in 1992[3] to 60 percent in 1994.[4] With oil prices likely to remain low for years,[5] Iran's annual hard currency revenues from petroleum could fall to $12 billion, a drastic drop from the $18 billion revenue it had generated in 1992.[6] With nonpetroleum exports generating another $4 billion, its total hard currency revenue of $16 billion would not cover its $21 billion of imports.[7] Consequently, Iran's $30 billion debt to foreign countries was likely to rise. In addition, Iran was unlikely to receive any further credit from abroad after it defaulted on $8.7 billion of overdue foreign debt in 1993. A further $8 billion of debt was thought to be due and it was unclear if Iran had the resources to pay.[8] Finally, Iran could not increase its oil production from 3.6 million barrels a day, since an investment of $10 billion was required to increase production capacity by 1 million barrels.[9]

In order to preserve its scarce reserve of hard currency, in May 1994 the Iranian government began to restrict imports, raise custom duties, and establish a number of regulations that practically blocked the import of nonessential goods and the repatriation of hard currencies. These actions had halved imports, deepened the recession, produced an acute shortage of foreign goods, and intensified inflation. The exchange rate had been destabilized and could fluctuate up to 15 percent in a single day.[10] It seemed unlikely that the Iranian economy would rebound any time soon.

Options

Iran's weakening economy had become a major concern for IOAC, prompting management to consider alternative growth options. Kayvan's father and uncle had identified a number of unique and promising business opportunities in the Middle East. However, the windows of opportunity were limited, and management constraints within the company only allowed for the pursuit of a single option. All of IOAC's executives were fully engaged in managing its ongoing operations, and none could be reassigned to start a new venture. In addition, finding experienced managers or MBA graduates from top business schools was very difficult in Iran. This left Kayvan as the only immediate candidate for starting a new venture. Although Kayvan was excited about the prospect of working with the family company to help expand its operations in the region, he was concerned about choosing the right option.

Kayvan reflected on the four most promising options before the firm. Within Iran, there was a manufacturing opportunity (Exhibit 2) and a telecommunications option (Exhibit 3). Outside of Iran, there was the booming market of the United Arab Emirates (Exhibit 4) and the highly promising markets of the Commonwealth of Independent States (Exhibit 5), which had recently separated from the former Soviet Union. Kayvan glanced at the notes he had compiled on each of the options. He wondered how to go about choosing the best alternative. He thought about two recent comments his father had made:

> We have to expand beyond office machines and computers to communications and local manufacturing. Communications is where the world is heading and we need manufacturing in order to maintain our operation in case the government restricts imports even further. We have to evolve into a conglomerate.
>
> Iran is one of the few countries in the world that has 15 neighbors, and it is very rich in natural and human resources. We have to expand our operations into neighboring countries. The CIS are particularly interesting because they are far, far behind in the industries we specialize in. Dubai, on the other hand, it is like Hong Kong being re-created—can we afford to miss such an opportunity?

The snow-covered mountains had turned orange in the sunset. Looking at them, Kayvan wondered what kind of data could help him in his decision. He felt he was running out of time, and yet he was not quite sure what to do next.

Endnotes

[1]The copier department carried 190 different products. Of these, there were eight current copier models and their accessories. For each copier model there were unique supplies such as toner, developer, and drums that had to be replenished or changed on a regular basis. In addition, IOAC had to maintain supplies for many operational but discontinued models that dated as far back as 1974. The average inventory held by the copier department was 40,000 items.

[2]IOAC's service department maintained an inventory of 3 million spare parts, representing 180,000 different items.

[3]Central Intelligence Agency, "Iran," *The World Factbook 1993*, 185–187.

[4]"Iran: Tied Economy, Tied President," *The Economist*, 16 July 1994, 37–38.

[5]James Tanner, "Oil Prices Seem Likely to Stay Low for Years," *The Wall Street Journal*, 21 March 1994.

[6]"Iran: Tied Economy."

[7]Central Intelligence Agency, "Iran," 185–187.

[8]"Iran: Tied Economy."

[9]Hossein Askari, "It's Time to Make Peace with Iran," *Harvard Business Review* (January/February 1994), pp. 50–63.

[10]"Iran: Tied Economy."

EXHIBIT 2

Iran Office Automation Company: Manufacturing Option

IOAC had recently purchased the complete knock down (CKD)[1] electronics manufacturing facilities of a start-up company that had failed. The US$800,000[2] factory consisted of a 300-square-meter building and dedicated machinery for mounting electronic components onto prefabricated circuit boards and the assembling of parts into final electronic products. An additional capital investment of US$200,000 in machinery and equipment was needed to make the factory fully operational. The factory was designed to assemble a large variety of electronic products, ranging from consumer electronics, computers, printers, and monitors, to mobile phones and digital telephone switches.

IOAC structured the factory as a wholly owned autonomous subsidiary under the name of Iran Office Automation Manufacturing Co. Ltd. (IOAM) and retained four of the factory's previous staff: the factory manager, a production engineer, a quality controller, and an accountant. IOAC had no previous experience in manufacturing. IOAM itself had no existing contracts with any original manufacturers and was not producing anything.

According to Mahmoud Noori, the purchase of the factory was a strategic move designed to provide IOAC with the option of local production in case the government tightened its restriction on imports. Also, Mahmoud considered the purchase a bargain since it would have taken two years to build a comparable factory and secure the multitude of permits needed for production. Feasibility studies were under way to evaluate the options of producing computers, printers, or monitors in case the import of these products was restricted. However, there were no immediate plans for production.

Kayvan looked at some figures his father had scribbled on a piece of paper:

Hungary: 124 personal computers per 1,000 people.
Population 10.3 million, growing 0 percent annually.
GDP per person = $4,010.

Iran: 4.5 personal computers per 1,000 people.
Population 64 million, growing at 3.5 percent annually.
GDP per person = $440.

In the past there were 65 printers and 90 monitors per 100 personal computers sold in Iran (10 percent of computers are imported with monitors). Existing personal computer installation in Iran was approximately 40,000 units.

Kayvan wondered if he should initiate some sort of operation rather than leaving the factory as a strategic option. If so, what should he produce and what sort of data would he need to help him with this decision?

[1] A complete knock down operation is a common manufacturing setup in developing countries where base components and parts of predesigned products are imported and assembled locally. Although the process is less efficient than importing complete products, cheaper local labor or favorable government import tariffs for local manufacturers, or both, make them economically attractive options.

[2] Financial figures are provided in U.S. dollars equivalent to local currencies. In the case of the Iranian rial, which experienced significant exchange rate fluctuations during the period of the case, the spot rate at the date of each transaction has been used.

EXHIBIT 3

Iran Office Automation Company: Telecommunications Option

IOAC had recently approached Telefonaktiebolaget LM Ericsson of Sweden to discuss the possibility of a joint venture in order to take advantage of Iran's newly emerging mobile phone market.

In 1994, the government-owned Telecommunication Company of Iran (TCI) provided only 3.5 million digital phone switchlines to service Iran's 11 million households and thousands of businesses. In order to obtain a regular phone line, customers had to deposit 500,000 rials (U.S $182, at U.S $1= 2,750 rials), which was over a month's average salary, and wait one to two years before being provided with a telephone service. The going rate for the purchase of an immediate phone line from existing holders was between 2.5 million and 3.0 million rials, depending on the area.

In 1991 TCI awarded Nokia of Finland the contract for an initial 10,000-line mobile phone scheme for the Tehran area.[1] In May of 1994, 5,000 mobile phone lines were offered to the public for the first time. The subscription, which included the telephone number, cost 5 million rials, while the cellular phone unit cost 3.5 million rials. This translated into $3,090 for a single mobile phone system. Despite the high price, all lines were sold within the first month. The going rate to buy a subscription for a line from existing holders was 9 million rials. Mobile phone air-time was approximately 200 rials per minute, versus the 30 rials per minute for the regular telephone rate.

Since the government had growing problems in funding the mobile phone projects, new bids for the six largest cities included provisions for private-sector involvement.[2] Part of the provisions required local partnership, transfer of technology, and local assembly of handsets and switchboards. Investment estimates for a 10,000-line capacity GSM Relay Station and citywide antennas was approximately $15 million.[3] This did not include the start-up cost for the support organization needed to market and administer the system.

Due to the declining demand in IOAC's traditional office machines market and the incredible opportunities arising in the emerging mobile phone market, IOAC was considering whether to enter the telecommunications industry. Having no prior experience in that industry, IOAC sought a joint venture partner that could assist them in this new market. Their first choice was Ericsson of Sweden.

Ericsson was the world leader in mobile telephone systems, serving 13.2 million subscribers in 64 countries. In 1994, Ericsson commanded 40 percent of the world analog systems and more than 50 percent of the global

[1]"Phone bids reinvited; Iran," *MEED Middle East Business Weekly*, 21 January 1994, 15.

[2]Ibid.

[3]A mobile telephone system consisted of radio-based stations linked by telephone exchanges. Each base station covered a geographical area or "cell." When a subscriber moved within the area covered by a cellular mobile telephone system, the telephone call was transferred automatically from cell to cell. GSM (Global system for mobile telecommunications) was the pan-European standard for digital cellular mobile telephone systems that had been accepted in many parts of the world.

(continued)

EXHIBIT 3 (CONTINUED)

Iran Office Automation Company: Telecommunications Option

digital systems.[4] They were the seventh-largest producers of general telecommunications equipment[5] with 1993 net sales of 62.9 billion krona[6] ($8.08 billion).[7] Ericsson's product portfolio covered all types of telecommunications equipment, including:

AXE:	*Digital telephone switches for wired and mobile networks.*
ETNA:	*Transport networks.*
TMOS:	*Management and operations support system.*

Radio-Based Stations *for analog and digital mobile telephone systems.*

Mobile telephones

Mobitex:	*Systems and equipment for mobile data communications.*
MD110:	*Digital systems for business communications with 50 to 20,000 connections or more.*
Business Phone	*Small digital telephone systems.*
Freeset:	*Systems and telephones for cordless business communications.*
Eripax:	*Data network products.*
Eripower:	*Power systems for telecommunications equipment, computers, etc.*
Mini-Link:	*Microwave links.*[8]

Ericsson also supplied a range of products within the electronic-defense system.

Ericsson had built a dominant presence in the Middle East since the 1950s. The firm estimated that almost 50 percent of installed telephone capacity in the region involved its technology.[9] As the Swedish krona had lost over 40 percent of its value against the deutsche mark since 1991,[10] lower comparative prices had prompted Ericsson to target some of the remaining German-dominated communication markets in the Middle East. Iran was a case in point where Siemens and Alcatel had dominated its telecommunications market for decades.[11] Ericsson, in contrast, opened its first branch office in Iran only in 1991. Using Sweden's exchange-rate advantage, Ericsson was determined to capture a piece of Iran's extensive telecom expansions.

Kayvan wondered if IOAC should enter a completely new market such as telecommunications. If so, would IOAC's alliance with Ericsson be feasible?

[4]Ericsson Annual Report 1993.
[5]"Wireless Outstrips Main Lines," *Communication Daily*, 25 October 1994, 2.
[6]Ericsson Annual Report 1993.
[7]"Exports Roar Ahead After the Recession, Special Report: Scandinavia," *MEED Middle East Business Weekly*, 28 October 1994, 12.
[8]Ericsson Annual Report 1993.
[9]"Ericsson in the Middle East: No Lowball Bids or Free Extras," *Crossborder Monitor*, 29 June 1994.
[10]*MEED*, 28 October 1994.
[11]"Ericsson in the Middle East."

EXHIBIT 4

Iran Office Automation Company: United Arab Emirates and Dubai Option

The United Arab Emirates (UAE) was located in the southeast corner of the Persian Gulf below Iran (see map).[1] The UAE consisted of seven emirates, the largest of which was Abu Dhabi (the capital) and the second largest, Dubai. The UAE had an open economy and one of the world's highest incomes per capita outside of the OECD ($13,800 for 1992). It was a modern state with a high standard of living for its population of 2.7 million. Their gross domestic product stood at $35 billion, with exports of $21 billion (66 percent of which was crude oil) and imports of $14 billion (1991 f.o.b. est.). At existing levels of production their crude oil could last for over 100 years. Unemployment was negligible and inflation stood at 1 percent.[2] UAE's exchange rate was fixed against the dollar and extremely stable.

Approximately 70 percent of UAE's trade was done through Dubai. Dubai's non-oil trade had been growing at an annual rate of more than 20 percent in the past five years. Total economic growth for Dubai was 37 percent in 1992 and 48 percent in 1993. Dubai imported from 124 countries and re-exported to 120 countries; Dubai was considered one of the top 15 international shipping centers, with one of its three main ports being the largest man-made container harbor in the world. Re-export of goods was tax free, and turnaround time was a rapid 24 hours. In 1992, re-exports stood at $2.45 billion.[3] Goods sold within Dubai had a mere 4 percent tariff.

Consequently, Dubai had evolved into one of the mercantile capitals of the world. Merchants from all over the Middle East, Russia, the Commonwealth of Independent States, and the Far East went there to either purchase or sell goods. Sanyo, Sony, Panasonic, Toshiba, and Yashica were a few of the many Japanese companies that had established a distribution center in Dubai within the past three years.

Gulf Mercantile & Investment Co. was IOAC's shipping and financing subsidiary in Dubai, established in 1980. Kayvan wondered if IOAC should expand its operations in Dubai given Iran's worsening economic condition, lack of hard currency, and mounting import restrictions. If so, what kind of operations should be established there?

[1]Central Intelligence Agency, "Middle East Map," *The World Factbook 1993.*
[2]Central Intelligence Agency, "United Arab Emirates," *The World Factbook 1993,* 399–401.
[3]Robin Allen, "Survey of Dubai," *Financial Times,* 3 November 1993, 2.

(continued)

EXHIBIT 4 (CONTINUED)

Iran Office Automation Company: United Arab Emirates and Dubai Option

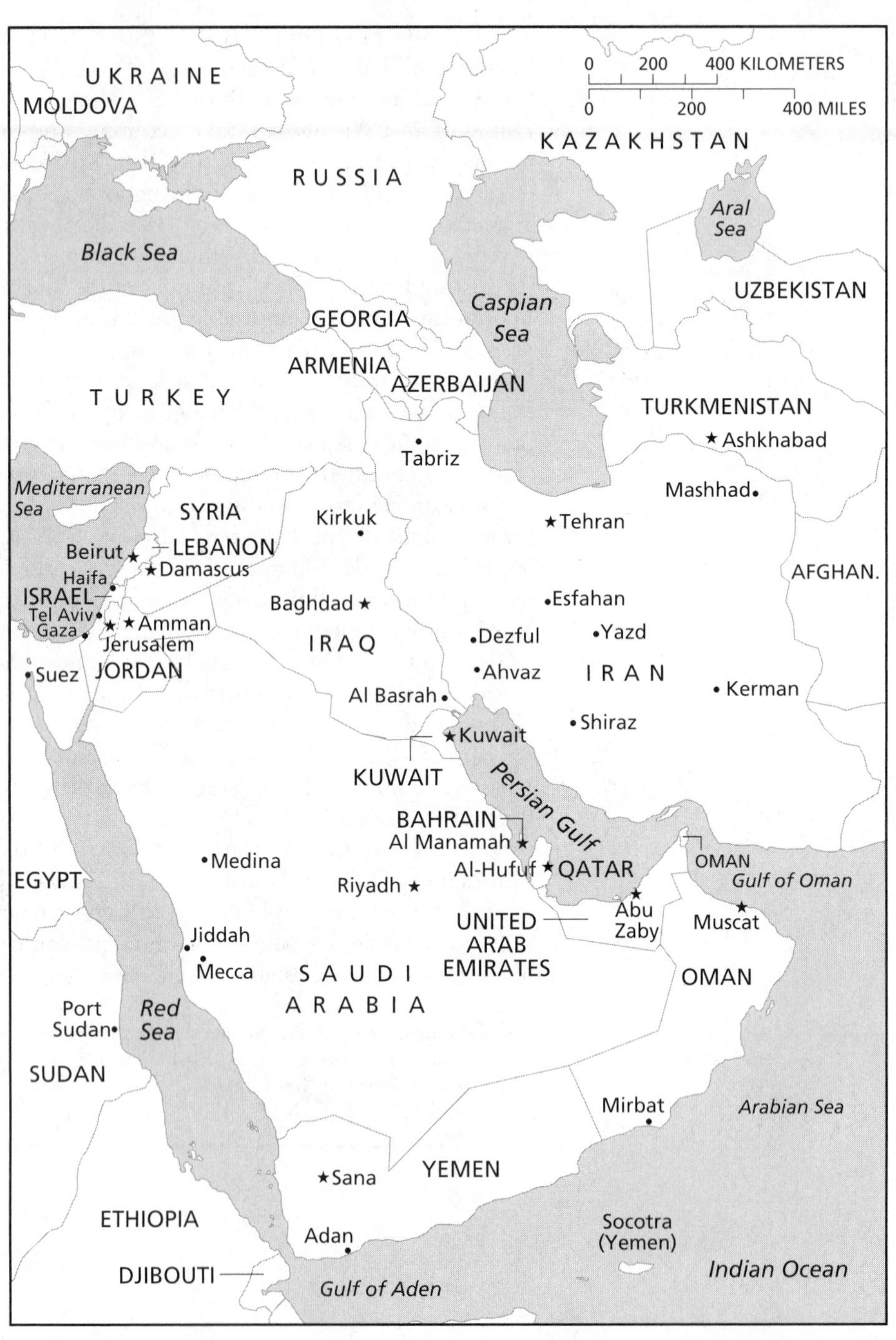

EXHIBIT 5

Iran Office Automation Company: The Commonwealth of Independent States Option

Kayvan thought that some of the independent republics of the former Soviet Union, especially the ones north of Iran, would provide a unique growth opportunity for IOAC. In particular, Kazakhstan, Uzbekistan, and Turkmenistan seemed promising (see map).[1]

Most of the republics of the Commonwealth of Independent States (CIS) had gained their independence from the former Soviet Union in 1991. New governments, constitutions, and legal systems were introduced shortly thereafter. Their transition from a centralized to a free-market economy had been impeded by many problems, ranging from ethnic disputes and political instability to lack of market pricing, hyperinflation, and the demand for property rights. The republics also faced an acute shortage of goods and services, since their markets and distribution channels were in infancy.

Nonetheless, some republics had achieved political stability and controlled substantial resources, which could fuel their economic growth and accelerate their move toward a free-market economy. For example, Kazakhstan had vast oil, coal, and agricultural resources, combined with a 100 percent literate labor force of 7.6 million.[2] Uzbekistan was ranked as the fourth-largest global producer of cotton and had vast natural reserves of gold, uranium, and silver. Uzbekistan also commanded a 100 percent literate labor force of 7.94 million.[3] Turkmenistan boasted one of the largest natural gas reserves and also had oil, coal, and sulphur.[4]

Kayvan wasn't quite sure how to approach the CIS option. Should he choose the CIS over Dubai? If so, what kind of operations could he start there?

[1]Central Intelligence Agency, "Commonwealth of Independent States Map," *The World Factbook 1993.*

[2]Ibid., "Kazakhstan," 205–207.

[3]Ibid., "Uzbekistan," 407–409.

[4]Ibid., "Turkmenistan," 391–393.

(continued)

EXHIBIT 5 (CONTINUED)

Iran Office Automation Company: The Commonwealth of Independent States—Central Asian States

Case 9

Southwest Airlines

It was March 1992, and Herb Kelleher, Southwest Airlines' chief executive officer, was laughingly describing the way in which he was about to settle a dispute with Stevens Aviation over the right to use the ad slogan "Just Plain Smart," which Stevens maintained it had developed first. Kurt Herwald, chairman of Stevens Aviation, and Kelleher had decided they would settle things the "old-fashioned way" in a best-of-three arm-wrestling match in the Dallas Sportatorium.

This unusual method of negotiation was entirely in keeping with Herb Kelleher's "disarming" style, which, for some observers, was the principal reason for Southwest's 19 straight profitable years. Many in the industry, however, pointed to a variety of other factors that ensured the Dallas-based airline would continue to maintain its top record of achievement. The bottom line for Southwest Airlines was that it provided high value for low cost and consistently delivered what it promised.

History

Southwest Airlines was founded in 1967 by Rollin King, a former investment counselor who had been operating a small air-taxi service in Texas. The impetus behind King's organization of Southwest Airlines was his perception of a growing unmet need for improved intercity air service within Texas.

In the late 1960s, Houston, Dallas, San Antonio, and Fort Worth were among the fastest growing cities in the United States. Although each had its own airport, a huge new airport, the Dallas/Fort Worth Regional Airport, was then under construction that would serve both Dallas and Fort Worth. These four cities were primarily served by two Texas-based carriers, Braniff International Airways and Texas International Airlines (TI). For the most part, service to these cities by Braniff and TI consisted of "legs" of interstate flights; in other words, a Braniff flight might stop at Dallas on its way from New York to San Antonio.

In his talks with consumers prior to embarking on the Southwest venture, King was struck by the amount of dissatisfaction with the current service and discovered that the market was bigger than many realized. Together with his lawyer Herb Kelleher, King was able to raise enough capital to incorporate the airline. On February 20, 1968, Kelleher obtained the Certificate of Public Convenience and Necessity from the Texas Aeronautics Commission, which granted Southwest Airlines the right to provide intrastate air service between Dallas/Fort Worth, Houston, and San Antonio. Southwest's competitors reacted immediately by asking the Texas courts to enjoin issuance of the certificate, maintaining that service was already provided on the proposed routes and that the market was not large enough to support another carrier. The ensuing litigation kept the company's lawyers occupied for several years.

This case was prepared by Charlotte Thompson under the supervision of Professor Elliot N. Weiss.

In 1970, King brought Lamar Muse aboard as president, director, and treasurer. An independent financial consultant and former president of Universal Airlines, Muse had become attracted to Southwest after reading about its legal battles and realizing that the market for this kind of carrier was growing: "There was so much interline traffic that most of the seats were occupied by those people. While Braniff had hourly service, there really weren't many seats available for local passengers." Muse also commented that both Braniff and TI, in part because their local service was merely a leg of interstate flights, were rarely on time, and people thus tended to fly only when they absolutely had to.

On June 18, 1971, amid a heavy advertising campaign to promote the new airline and restraining orders issued by judges after complaints by its competitors, Southwest launched 6 round-trip flights between Dallas's Love Field and San Antonio and 12 round-trip flights between Dallas and Houston. The takeoff proved to be less than auspicious. In its first 11 months of operation, Southwest lost $3.7 million. Some days saw the airline carrying a total of only 150 passengers on its 18 round-trip flights. Nevertheless, Muse persevered with his ideas by offering unbelievable prices, gimmicks, and creative advertising.

In Texas, 1972 became the year of the fare war. To compete with Southwest, competitors slashed fares and began offering more in terms of service, for example, free beer, hot and cold towels, one-dollar drinks on routes Southwest flew, and more frequent service. When Braniff decided to offer a half-price fare, Muse countered with a giveaway: free bottles of premium liquor to passengers who paid full fare; passengers who did not want the liquor would pay half fare. Because corporations were used to paying full fare, business travelers became the happy recipients of premium liquor. During the promotion, Southwest became not only the largest distributor in Texas of Chivas, Crown Royal, and Smirnoff, but also the winner in the fare war. After 1972, Southwest consistently made a profit (see Exhibit 1).

HERB KELLEHER

In March 1977, Lamar Muse resigned as president and chief executive officer of Southwest Airlines, and Herb Kelleher was named to replace him. Kelleher, a student of philosophy and literature who later graduated at the top of his law-school class at New York University, was wedded to the Southwest cause from the very beginning. Kelleher did not merely believe in Southwest's mission; in some ways, the initial legal battles with Southwest's competitors enraged him to the point where he knew he had to win. Kelleher likened Southwest's struggles with its competitors to the trench warfare of World War II, and he was determined that Southwest would eventually be able to engage the enemy on its terms, not theirs.

Early on, Kelleher established a reputation for doing the unusual. At company functions he would appear as Elvis Presley or Roy Orbison and perform "Jailhouse Rock" or "Pretty Woman." One Halloween night he showed up at Southwest's hangar in drag, as Corporal Klinger from *M*A*S*H*, to thank mechanics for working overtime. Although Kelleher's behavior was somewhat unconventional for a chief executive officer, his efforts paid off. His colleagues credited much of Southwest's "magic" to him. "Herb has a nice, light perspective on life," stated Jim Wimberly, head of Southwest's ground operations. "We both like Wild Turkey, and we smoke a little too much."

Known for his extreme tenacity and limitless energy, Kelleher slept only four hours a night, read two or three books a week, and chain-smoked. Gary Barron, Southwest's chief operations officer, called Kelleher "the smartest, quickest

EXHIBIT 1

Southwest Airlines Profits, Revenues, and Number of Passengers

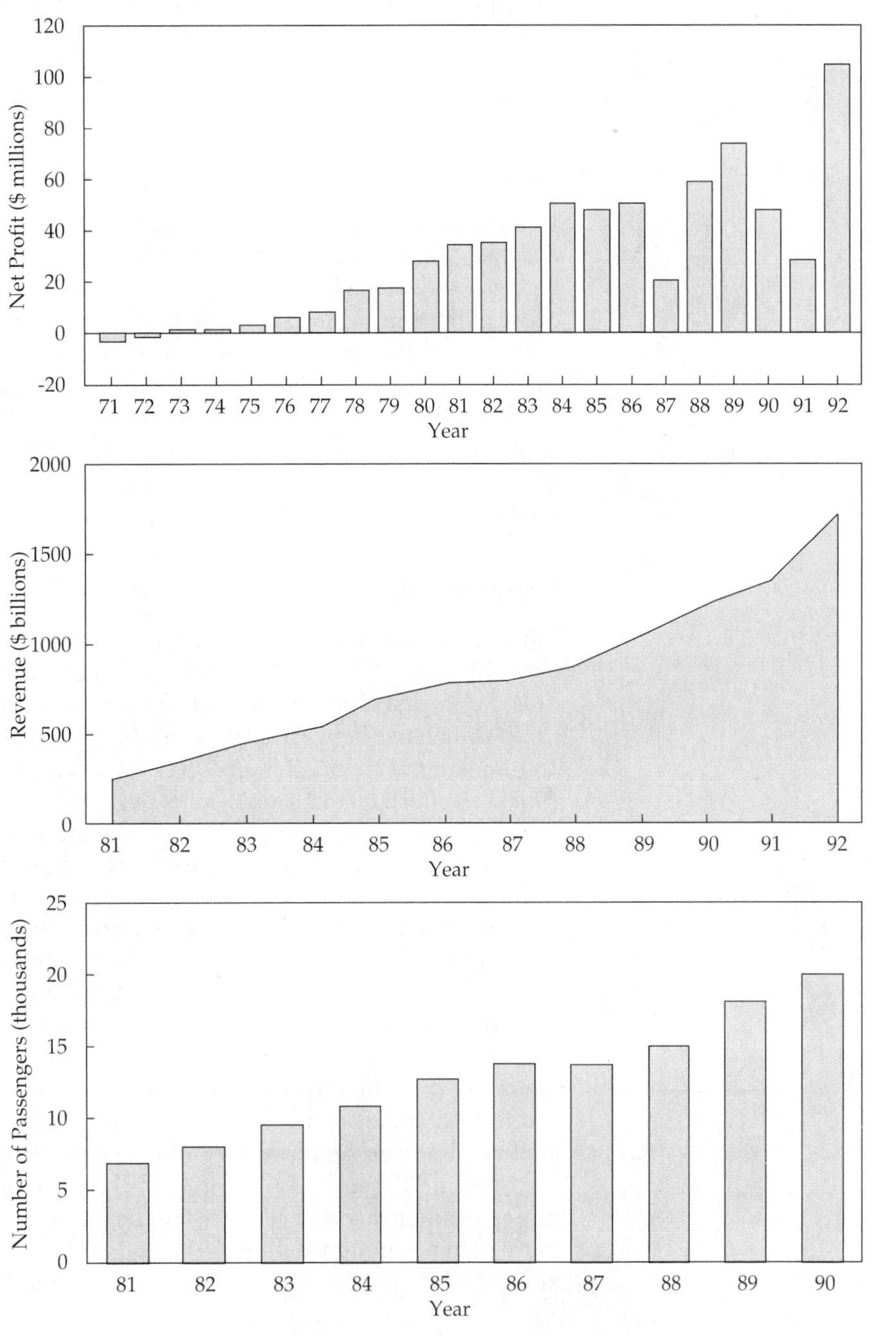

lawyer—not to mention the best judge of people" he had ever seen.[1] Kelleher was widely credited with much of the airline's success for promoting and maintaining both a culture that favored people and a coherent business strategy that was consistently successful yet deceptively simple. "People always want high-quality service at a lower price, provided by people who enjoy what they do," he maintained.[2] The results of Kelleher's efforts: Southwest's overall costs were the lowest of any major carrier, yet its workers were among the best paid.

Operations

Start-Up

Initial operations for Southwest Airlines began under extreme pressure and tight deadlines. Additional capital for start-up expenses had to be raised, personnel had to be hired and trained, and a multitude of marketing problems had to be resolved. Most important, Muse and King had to make key decisions on the number and type of aircraft to be used. Many weeks of high-pressure negotiations with representatives of several airplane manufacturers resulted in the purchase of three Boeing 737-200 aircraft. This decision proved to be a crucial one for Southwest, not only because the airline would continue to use the same type of aircraft for many years, but also because the planes required fewer crew members than the aircraft used by Southwest's competitors.

Scheduling

Initial decisions regarding scheduling were constrained by the fact that Southwest only had three airplanes. After studying flight times and on-the-ground (turnaround) times, Muse and King concluded that they could offer flights at 75-minute intervals using two planes between Dallas and Houston (the most important route) and at 150-minute intervals (2.5 hours) between Dallas and San Antonio using one plane, which amounted to 12 round-trips per day between Dallas and Houston and 6 round-trips per day between Dallas and San Antonio. Because of low weekend demand, Muse and King decided to fly less frequently on Saturdays and Sundays.

In spite of all their well-laid plans, however, scheduling proved to be a problem. In the first two weeks, the airline reported an average of 13.1 passengers per flight on the Dallas–Houston route and 12.9 passengers on the Dallas–San Antonio route. Because of the lack of planes, management concluded that Southwest was unable to compete effectively and thus set about improving its schedule frequencies. The delivery of the fourth plane in late September helped immensely; but perhaps more important than the arrival of the fourth plane was the company's ability to deliver a turnaround time of ten minutes. Proving its ability to turn a constraint into a competitive advantage, Southwest was able to initiate hourly service between Dallas and Houston and flights every two hours between Dallas and San Antonio by orchestrating maintenance and servicing to the point that no plane stayed on the ground more than ten minutes. This development proved to be a real innovation in the industry; the company became known for its "quick turns."

Strategy and Service

From the beginning, Southwest management's idea was to offer no-frills, low-cost flights to and from secondary airports, and the airline clung tenaciously to this initial strategy. Management's focus was the "short-haul, point-to-point" strategy, which advocated short flights (average flight time of 55 minutes) to uncrowded airports for quick turnarounds. This adherence to a short-haul strategy enabled Southwest to distinguish itself from its competitors, many of whom failed. Several airlines started out in the short-haul business, only to become tempted by the more glamorous routes. "Suddenly they were competing with big people who knew what they were doing," stated Gary Barron. "They got their brains beat out. Southwest will take Lubbock to Little Rock any old time." As Salomon Brothers analyst Julius Maldutis pointed out, "They stay out of the major vegetable patches with big elephants."[3]

Most of Southwest's competitors used a "hub-and-spoke" system in which big planes fly to major airports (hubs) and then link up with smaller airports (spokes). Southwest developed no recognizable hub, preferring instead to maintain a "spiderweb" system in which one strand at a time is spun.[4] Kelleher's reason for implementing this strategy was that a hub-and-spoke network tied up too many valuable assets at too few pressure points, whereas a spiderweb system would allow maximum flexibility to disperse assets and reduce stress in the system.

Southwest's "no-frills" policy included no baggage transfers, no meals, no assigned seats, and reusable boarding cards. When a passenger decided to fly Southwest, he or she would show up at the airport at the designated time, get a ticket at the counter printed out by a machine (at the time, the competition was issuing handwritten tickets), take a reusable boarding card, and board the plane to sit wherever he or she preferred. On board, the passenger could enjoy a drink or two and some peanuts, but nothing more. The reason behind the no-frills policy was that there were other things to offer customers that gave better value: frequent, reliable, on-time flights and very low prices. For Southwest, quality was not a filet mignon dinner with a fine wine; it was on-time flights and no lost baggage.

Southwest's management also made a decision not to subscribe to expensive computerized reservation systems that would link them with travel agencies, opting instead to market the airline through other means. Although initially the airline hired a small sales force that promoted Southwest among travel agents and corporate accounts (companies whose personnel flew Southwest on a regular basis), Southwest used travel agents relatively infrequently because of the small margins it made on ticket sales.

One way the airline was able to keep its costs down was through contracting for such things as major maintenance, data processing, and legal services. Southwest also contracted for about two-thirds of its monthly jet-fuel supply and purchased the rest on the spot market.

Southwest's policy with regard to costs and service paid off: its average number of flights per plane per day was 10.5, whereas the industry average was 4.5; its planes were in the air 11 hours a day (industry average, 8 hours a day), which was an especially significant statistic in that its flights were the shortest of any airline. Given that short flights made for higher fuel costs and a greater number of landing fees than did long flights, Southwest could be especially proud of its cost of 6.5 cents per available seat-mile, the lowest in the industry. Southwest's secret was that it made extremely good use of its most expensive asset: its planes (see Exhibit 2).

New Markets

Part of Southwest's strategy was to investigate potential markets carefully. As flamboyant as Kelleher often portrayed himself, he admitted to being a very cautious businessman. In 1991, 34 cities formally requested that Southwest operate from

EXHIBIT 2

Southwest Airlines Number of Workers and Airplanes

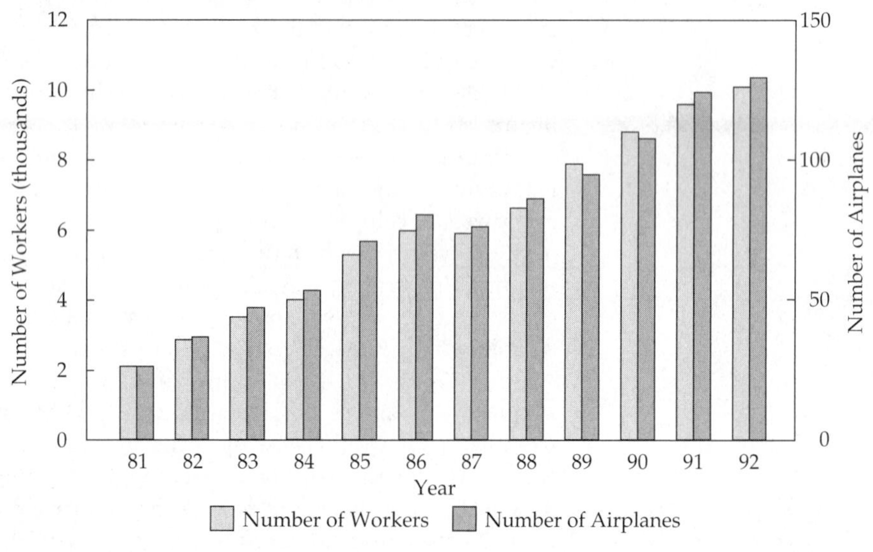

their airports. Southwest chose only one, Sacramento, and it did so only after USAir left. As Gary Barron put it, "We search out markets that are overpriced and underserved."[5] Small cities and small airports meant that Southwest could get its planes in and out quickly.

Once Southwest decided to enter a market, however, it did so with full force. The airline offered so many flights that customers merely had to show up at the airport and take the next cheap flight out. This part of the strategy not only enabled the airline to spread its fixed costs over many seats, but also served a marketing function in that Southwest could really "make a statement" in a new airport.

After years of patient watchfulness and careful consideration, Southwest decided to enter the California market. In 1983, it began offering flights on the San Diego–San Francisco route but did not expand service until 1989. The California intrastate market was ideal for Southwest: it combined short-haul, high-frequency routes with good weather and a populace appreciative of Southwest's "unconventional behavior." The airline employed a relatively simple strategy of offering service in the mainly suburban areas outside Los Angeles and San Francisco at prices as low as $19 and no higher than $64 for a one-way flight.

Not surprisingly, Southwest's expansion into California led to a series of fare wars as the major airlines tried to keep Southwest from stealing customers. The intensely competitive market in California saw some losers: USAir and American were forced out of the California intrastate market almost entirely. As airline analyst Harold Shenton noted, "Most of the big airlines are trying to protect long-haul revenue, so they're not dependent on local traffic and they're weakening in the markets outside Los Angeles and San Francisco."[6]

Southwest undercut its California competitors and emerged victorious in the fare battles. The airline continued to use such tactics as offering free tickets in a "Fly

One Way, Get One Way Free" campaign and a $59 unrestricted one-way fare for all intrastate California flights as part of the airline's "California State Fare" promotion. Southwest's California campaign was so successful that Southwest saved its California fliers more than $40 million in 1991.

Marketing

Positioning

Southwest decided from the beginning that it would differentiate itself from its competitors by creating a "fun" image. In contrast to Texas International, which was perceived as dull, and Braniff, which was seen as conservative, Southwest's personality and theme were focused on the concept of "love"; flight attendants wore brightly colored hot pants, and inflight drinks and peanuts were known as "Love Potions" and "Love Bites."

As Southwest began working with the Bloom Agency, a large regional advertising agency, to create its public image, it concurrently came up with a model for the type of person it wanted to hire: the "entire personality description model," which was used as a guide in the recruiting process. Adjectives such as "young and vital," "exciting," and "dynamic" were sprinkled throughout the personality-model statement.

Herb Kelleher's fun-loving personality served to reinforce Southwest's lively image among its employees and encouraged them to pass it on to passengers. Employees took to donning holiday costumes such as rabbit garb for Easter, and every holiday became an excuse for inflight parties with balloons and cake.

In 1986, the airline introduced the concept of "Fun Fares," which ranged in price from $19 to $85 for a one-way ticket. A new summer uniform for flight attendants was used to promote the fares: surfer shorts, knit shirts, and tennis shoes.

Under an agreement signed with Sea World of Texas in 1988, Southwest launched "Shamu One," its flying killer whale in the form of a 737-300 airplane. The painted plane became so popular throughout Texas that Southwest painted two more to resemble Sea World's most popular attraction.

Pricing

Pricing decisions were a particularly important part of Southwest's overall strategy. Muse and King spent a great deal of time discussing the pricing issue with executives of Pacific Southwest Airlines, which had revolutionized commuter air travel in California through a combined strategy of low fares and aggressive promotion. At the time, Braniff and TI fares from Dallas to Houston were $27 and from Dallas to San Antonio, $28. Muse and King looked carefully at preoperating expenditures, operating costs, and market potential and finally decided on an initial fare of $20 for both routes. To operate at a break-even capacity, Southwest would require an average of 39 passengers per trip, a number the two executives considered reasonable given that the airline would have an initial price advantage over its competition. Before the break-even figure of 39 passengers per flight could be reached, however, they expected an initial period of deficit operations, a development they were willing to accept to get the airline off the ground. Clearly, the marketing campaign would be crucial to their future decisions on pricing.

Southwest was only five months old when Muse decided to try something revolutionary in the airline industry. Because the crew had been flying an empty plane from Houston to Dallas at the end of each week for weekend servicing, Muse came up with the idea of offering a fare of $10 for this last flight of the week. Within a period of two weeks, the plane was flying from Houston to Dallas with a full passenger load.

The success of the two-tier pricing system did not escape Muse, who soon decided to cut fares on the last flight of *each day* in all directions, which meant that any passenger flying Southwest after 7:00 P.M. on any day of the week would need a mere $10 to climb aboard. A few months later he was able to raise both prices (regular and "night"), but he continued the two-tier pricing system because of its ability to attract passengers.

Pricing was a key part of Southwest's strategy, and the company was leery of fare increases. From 1972 to 1978, Southwest did not have a single fare increase. "We base our pricing on profit rather than market share," contended Southwest Vice President for Finance Gary C. Kelly.[7]

Southwest's rock-bottom prices won both admiration and scorn from competitors, many of whom immediately dropped their prices when Southwest entered their markets. Many were also resentful: One American Airlines executive commented, "Value isn't quality; it's getting what you pay for."[8] Some competitors accused Southwest of "airline-seat dumping," although the airline made money on its routes from day one.

Promotion

Southwest defined its target market not as the passengers flying with other airlines, but as the people who were using other modes of transportation. As Southwest's director of sales and marketing stated, "We're not competing with other carriers. We want to pull people out of backyards and automobiles, and get them off the bus."

Southwest's promotions were aimed primarily at regular business commuters, who constituted 89 percent of Southwest's traffic. Accordingly, the airline used a heavy advertising campaign and a small sales force targeted specifically at the business traveler. Initially, the airline was striving for name recognition, but its marketing efforts quickly expanded to create an image via mass communications. With a first-year advertising budget of $700,000, this strategy was implemented in a number of ways, including teaser ads announcing incredibly low fares and a follow-up phone number, and the Sweetheart Club, in which secretaries received one "sweetheart stamp" for each Southwest reservation they made for their bosses. For every 15 stamps, the secretary would receive one free ride on Southwest.

Building a Reputation

Although at first many observers believed Southwest's "fun" image and no-frills flights would be the last choice for business travelers and cause the airline to take an immediate nosedive into bankruptcy, the skeptics soon stopped laughing. Initially unprofitable, Southwest ended 1973 in the black and celebrated its millionth passenger early in 1974. As the airline continued to expand its routes to cities such as Corpus Christi, Austin, El Paso, Oklahoma City, New Orleans, and Albuquerque, its management continued to maintain its reputation as the feisty underdog that was consistently able to offer low prices and superior, reliable service. (See Exhibit 3 for a comparison of 1991 revenues, profits, and passenger-miles for the major U.S. airlines.)

In 1988, the U.S. Department of Transportation rated Southwest as having the best on-time performance, the lowest number of lost-baggage complaints, and the lowest number of customer complaints among all domestic airlines (see Exhibit 4).

EXHIBIT 3

Airline Revenues, Profits, and Passenger-Miles for 1991

AIRLINE	REVENUE ($ MILLIONS)	PROFIT ($ MILLIONS)	PASSENGER-MILES (BILLIONS)
Alaska Air Group	1,116	10.3	5.4
America West	1,420	−222.0	3.0
American	12,993	−240.0	82.3
Continental	5,551	−305.7	41.4
Delta[a]	9,171	−324.4	62.1
Northwest	7,534	−3.1	53.2
Southwest	1,324	26.9	11.3
Trans World	3,688	34.6	28.0
UAL	11,748	−331.9	82.3
U.S. Air Group	6,533	−305.3	34.1

[a]Fiscal year ended June 30, 1991.

SOURCE: "Unfriendly Skies," *Fortune*, November 2, 1992, p. 92.

EXHIBIT 4

Performance of Major U.S. Air Carriers for 1992

AIRLINE	ON-TIME PERFORMANCE[a] (RANK)	BAGGAGE PROBLEMS[b] (RANK)	CONSUMER COMPLAINTS[c] (RANK)
Alaska Air Group	84.6 (4)	6.04 (7)	0.48 (2)
America West	88.9 (2)	4.42 (2)	1.50 (9)
American	82.1 (6)	4.73 (3)	1.40 (8)
Continental	79.0 (10)	6.13 (10)	1.17 (7)
Delta	79.1 (9)	5.71 (6)	0.58 (3)
Northwest	86.1 (3)	5.49 (5)	0.74 (4)
Southwest	92.1 (1)	3.72 (1)	0.24 (1)
Trans World	82.1 (5)	6.06 (8)	2.82 (10)
UAL	81.3 (7)	5.30 (4)	1.05 (6)
U.S. Air Group	79.6 (8)	6.10 (9)	0.85 (5)
Average	**82.3**	**5.36**	**1.03**

[a]Percentage of flights operating within 15 minutes of their scheduled times.

[b]Reported baggage problems per 1,000 passengers.

[c]Complaints per 100,000 passengers.

SOURCE: U.S. Department of Transportation's *Air Travel Consumer Reports*.

Southwest was particularly proud that it was the first airline to "win" all three categories since the department began tracking airline performance. Southwest then proceeded to win the "Triple Crown" the following four years.

Personnel

The company's philosophy toward recruitment and its employees remained consistent throughout its history: Southwest looked for people who were energetic and who wanted to work hard and have fun at the same time. Kelleher maintained that the most important step was choosing the right people, because "if the employees aren't satisfied, they won't provide the product we need."[9]

This philosophy proved effective. Although Southwest's workforce was more than 90 percent unionized, the employees owned 11 percent of the company. The average employee age was 34 years, one of the industry's lowest, yet the annual average employee pay ($42,000) was among the industry's highest. Although the airline industry was notorious for contentious labor-management relations, Southwest's employees enjoyed sunny relations with management. One reason for the smooth sailing was that employees had a stake in the company's success. Another reason was that Southwest managed to make employees feel as if they were part of an extended family, even if it was a $1.2-billion family.

Southwest management did not try to hide the fact that the main reason for the airline's success was the commitment of its employees. The quick turnaround time was a perfect example. As Gary Barron stated:

> Our employees bust their butts out there. Ground crews of six (12 is the industry average) perform 40 or 50 tasks during the 15 minutes that the plane is on the ground. [Jim] Wimberly [head of ground operations] likens those 15 minutes to a ballet, in which everything must be perfectly executed, and if it isn't, the employees have to be flexible enough to adjust. Because of employee commitment, Southwest has consistently kept to its 15-minute "turn" (planes of major airlines spend usually an hour at the gate) and is consequently on time.

Another example of employee loyalty was the automatic ticket machines at Southwest counters that took credit cards and dispensed tickets in just 20 seconds. These efficient machines were built by Southwest employees in their off-hours. Stated Andy Donelson, station manager at Dallas's Love Field, "The machine was thought up by a bunch of guys in a bar one night in Denver."[10]

Annual turnover was 7 percent, the industry's lowest. In 1990, 62,000 people applied for jobs at Southwest. Only 1,400 were hired.

Corporate Culture

Southwest's culture was perhaps best experienced by strolling down the hallway of the company's Dallas headquarters, where 20 years of Southwest Airlines history could be witnessed through mannequins attired in the various uniforms of Southwest personnel and hundreds of photos of employees. Each year the company hosted a banquet at which outstanding employees were recognized, much in the manner of the Emmy Awards. Kelleher could be seen at these functions mingling with employees from all levels of the company, calling them by name, laughing uproariously with them, and hugging and kissing them.

Even customers were brought into the family circle. Each month Southwest invited its frequent fliers to company headquarters to interview prospective employees, the logic being that the company wanted to hire people who matched customers in personality. The 5,000 letters a month Southwest received from its customers were all answered by the staff; Kelleher himself usually read around 200 letters a week.

Kelleher's role in the formation of Southwest's familial culture was crucial. Jim Wimberly stated that Kelleher had "a knack of really being with you, even if you're one person in a crowd of 1,000."[11] Kelleher firmly believed that employees who were committed to a mission would be more productive than uncommitted employees, and he spent a lot of his time fostering this attitude: "Southwest has its customers, the passengers; and I have my customers, the airline's employees. If the passengers aren't satisfied, they won't fly with us. If the employees aren't satisfied, they won't provide the product we need."

Once a quarter, Kelleher would join his employees to load baggage, serve drinks at 30,000 feet, or hand out boarding passes. Every Friday he wore brightly colored shirts and shorts, regardless of the business to be conducted that day.

Kelleher seemed to have found a formula that worked. During 1990, rising fuel costs caused Southwest to suffer a fourth-quarter loss of $4,581,000. Employees voluntarily created a "Fuel from the Heart" program in which they incurred payroll deductions to purchase fuel for the airplanes. Kelleher was so moved that he dedicated his opening letter to them in the company's 1990 annual report.

As bright as Southwest's history had been, there had also been a few dark clouds. Perhaps the darkest cloud was Southwest's purchase of Muse Air in June 1985. Kelleher changed the airline's name to TranStar, and it operated profitably for two years, until the larger Continental Airlines began an "impossible fare war" by moving into Houston's Hobby Airport. TranStar, with only 18 operating planes, proved to be no match for Continental with its fleet of 618 planes and considerable financial resources. In 1987, Kelleher was forced to liquidate TranStar's assets and report a loss in the first quarter of that year.

Although many observers were quick to praise the airline, some analysts were not as enthusiastic about Southwest's future. The industry itself has always been a risky one, and the prospects of endless competition, unpredictable fuel prices, and fickle customers gave financial analysts reason to advise caution when investing in Southwest. The TranStar case was a good example of how quickly success could turn sour in such a high-risk industry, and how even bright, savvy managers could make disastrous mistakes. Analysts also pointed out that large airlines had the deep pockets necessary to subsidize some of the more important routes if they deemed them important, whereas Southwest did not have much of a cushion.

Conclusion

The Southwest success story served as a model for others in the airline business, but none were able to match the airline's stellar record. Southwest's strategy of high value and low cost had worked for 20 years; what would the future hold? Kelleher's goal for the airline was simple: Increase the number of seats by 15 percent each year and keep costs down. He feared the complacency suffered by many airlines when things appear to be going well. "Our job is to never lose focus on keeping our costs low and to never suffer an excess of hubris so we take on too much debt," he commented. "When you think you've got it all figured out, then you're probably already heading downhill."[12]

Endnotes

[1]*Inc.*, January 1992, p. 67.
[2]Ibid., p. 66.
[3]*Financial World*, May 28, 1991, p. 19.
[4]*Inc.*, January 1992, p. 66
[5]Ibid., p. 68.
[6]Ibid., p. 70.
[7]*AW*, March 5, 1990, p. 36.
[8]*Time*, March 2, 1992, p. 15.
[9]*AW*, March 5, 1990, p. 36.
[10]*Inc.*, January 1992, p. 70.
[11]Ibid., p. 67.
[12]Ibid., p. 72.

CASE 10

THE BACOVA GUILD, LTD.

INTRODUCTION

Ben Johns, president of The Bacova Guild, Ltd., picked up the phone to get an update from his partner Pat Haynes, who was attending the August 1991 National Hardware Show in Chicago, Illinois.

"Well, Rubbermaid went ahead with it," Haynes said. "Their poly mailbox is being highlighted in the New Product Exposition. It looks like a one-piece mold, but it is really unattractive. What's more is they're asking two times the going rate, listing at an average of $14.99!"

"The problem," Johns reflected, "is that with a name like Rubbermaid you might be able to get away with it."

"I don't know," Haynes responded. "Rubbermaid has a lot of overhead, and it is accustomed to very high margins. And word with retailers is that they're being extremely heavy handed, saying 'You *will* buy our boxes or else.' Retailers are upset."

Johns pointed out, "Like it or not, Rubbermaid has quite a bit of leverage with those retailers. It also has a great reputation among consumers.

"The good news is Rubbermaid's entry could be a big plus for the industry. It will bring some credence to the market while putting an upward pressure on prices," Johns continued.

"Regardless, this development really puts some pressure on us for speeding up our strategic planning process. We'll wrap up here late Thursday night. Let's sit down first thing Friday morning," Haynes suggested.

As he hung up, Johns couldn't help but wonder what this latest development meant for this small manufacturer located near Hot Springs, Virginia. Since peaking in 1987, Bacova's sales had declined steadily. (See Exhibits 1 and 2.) While the numbers for the first half of 1991 looked promising, Bacova was having an increasingly difficult time handling competition from larger and more powerful companies. Management's response at this crucial turning point would determine if Bacova would reach the partners' goal of having a $25 million to $30 million business by 1997.

THE EARLY YEARS

Malcolm Hirsh, an industrialist from Peapack, New Jersey, purchased the entire "company town" of Bacova, Virginia, in 1965. The name came from BAth COunty, VirginiA. After purchasing the town, Hirsh founded The Bacova Guild, Ltd. He

This case was prepared by Eileen Filliben, Darden MBA/J.D. 1994, under the supervision of John L. Colley Jr., Almand R. Coleman Professor of Business Administration.

EXHIBIT 1

The Bacova Guild, Ltd. Audited Financial Data ($1,000s)

	1981	1982	1983	1984	1985	1986	1987	1988	1989	1990
Sales	776.3	1,116.1	1,681.2	2,420.7	3,808.2	9,559.8	19,090.4	15,766.7	14,380.5	13,371.1
Cost of goods sold	506.7	711.8	983.6	1,403.9	2,097.4	5,660.6	11,946.6	10,525.9	10,239.8	9,537.7
Gross margin	269.6	404.3	697.6	1,016.8	1,710.8	3,939.2	7,143.8	5,240.8	4,140.7	3,833.4
SG&A	259.4	308.5	520.6	774.5	1,242.8	2,229.7	3,649.8	3,623.1	4,228.0	3,486.3
Interest expense	32.8	34.6	32.1	30.4	89.1	129.4	224.7	287.3	304.1	338.6
Finance charges	0.0	0.0	(2.5)	(5.8)	(8.3)	(3.5)	(17.1)	9.5	(16.7)	(13.6)
Other income and expenses	(11.7)	(15.3)	(4.7)	(21.8)	(35.8)	(7.0)	(23.7)	(76.4)	(72.8)	(17.5)
Net pretax earnings	(10.9)	76.5	152.1	239.5	423.0	1,590.6	3,310.1	1,397.3	(301.9)	39.6
Taxes	0.0	11.9	54.1	89.3	180.5	782.8	1,489.0	531.0	0.0	0.0
Net earnings	(10.9)	64.6	98.0	150.2	242.5	807.8	1,821.1	866.3	(301.9)	39.6
COGS/Sales	65.3%	63.8%	58.5%	58.0%	55.1%	59.0%	62.6%	66.8%	71.2%	71.3%
Gross margin	34.7%	36.2%	41.5%	42.0%	44.9%	41.0%	37.4%	32.2%	28.8%	28.7%
SG&A/Sales	33.4%	27.6%	31.0%	32.0%	32.6%	23.2%	19.1%	23.0%	29.4%	26.1%
Net margin	−1.4%	5.8%	5.8%	6.2%	6.4%	8.4%	9.5%	5.5%	−2.1%	0.3%

EXHIBIT 2

The Bacova Guild, Ltd. Annual Dollar Sales

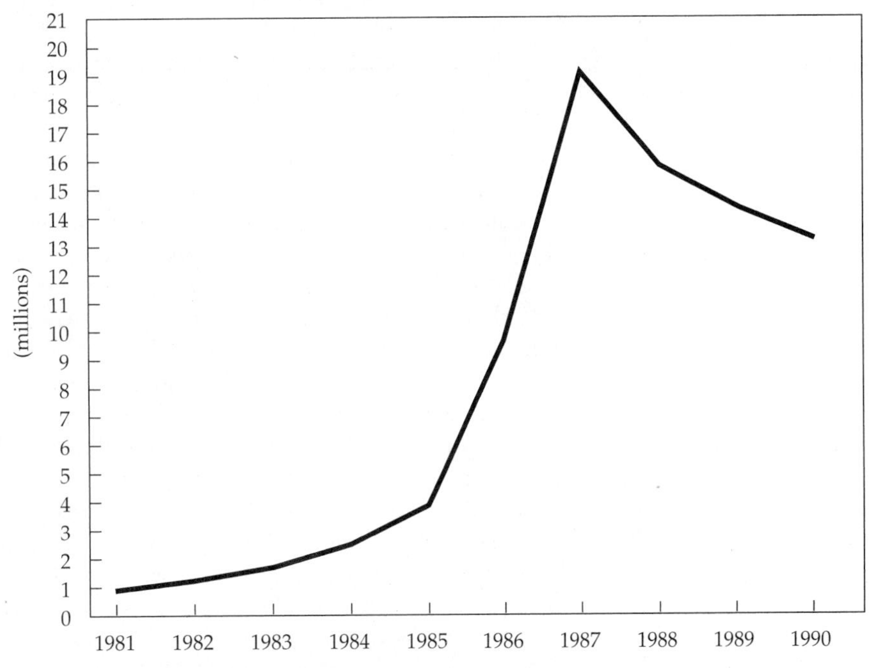

joined forces with Grace Gilmore, a commercially successful artist who had a love for painting birds and wildlife. Several years earlier, while living in New Bern, North Carolina, Grace and her husband William perfected the process of silk screening on transparent paper and laminating it in fiberglass. This new technology allowed Grace Gilmore's beautiful wildlife paintings to be preserved and even shaped to be used as inlays for various product applications. The company began producing a variety of laminated fiberglass gift items with Gilmore's designs, including outdoor thermometers, place mats, outdoor cast iron furniture with decorative table tops, and the original Bacova mailbox, which remains the classic Bacova Guild item.

To maintain Bacova's elite appeal, Hirsh kept distribution limited. The company sold its products, primarily the mailboxes (which could be personalized with the name and address of the purchaser), to specialty gift shops and direct mail companies, such as Abercrombie & Fitch, Orvis, and L.L. Bean (roughly 600 accounts).

New Owners, New Products, New Markets

In 1981, Hirsh sold the business to two young entrepreneurs. Patrick R. Haynes Jr., a tennis pro at the nearby Homestead Resort, and Benjamin I. Johns Jr., a former tennis pro at the Homestead, teamed up and bought Bacova, which had 25 employees, one small building, and 600 customers. In 1980, the business lost $40,000 on sales of $550,000.

The new owners believed the business had to grow to become profitable. Its product line consisted of three rural mailboxes, an ice bucket, an outdoor thermometer, two porch boxes, a picnic basket called the Kool Basket, and a wood tray. The new owners began an aggressive program of expansion with regard to products they sold and markets they served. They took the wildlife designs, the screen printing, and the fiberglass lamination process that had worked with the mailboxes and began to market a wider variety of products, such as ice buckets, window thermometers, card tables, television trays, and bird feeders. All of these products, along with the mailboxes, were purchased from outside manufacturers and then decorated with a laminated Bacova design. The company tried to expand its customer list by aggressively participating in more gift trade shows and producing a full-color wholesale catalog. These efforts quickly showed results as the firm was profitable in 1982.

In 1983, Bacova created a new line of products by printing its traditional designs on indoor/outdoor mats, thus beginning Bacova's diversification into the textile industry. These doormats could be personalized in the same manner as the mailboxes, and they were very successful with gift shops and mail order companies. These mats, 20" by 30", wholesaled for $11.25 ($13.75 if personalized) and retailed for $22.50. In addition to earning $98,016 on sales of $1.7 million in 1983, the company also realized an important lesson: Its real strength was in its screen printing expertise and capacity.

The doormats that Bacova developed appealed to mass merchandisers in addition to the specialty gift shops. One large discount chain approached the manufacturer and requested a similar mat at a lower price point. In 1985, a turning point for the company, a smaller (18" by 27"), less expensive version of the Bacova doormat was introduced to the discount chain for $6.25 wholesale, $13.50 retail, and sales soared. Then came a request for a mat to meet a $9.99 price point. Johns and Haynes hesitated at first because they had built the business to nearly $4 million in sales and were afraid to tamper with success. The company was able to market a rug that would retail at $9.99 with a switch from acrylic to nylon and a change in the printing process to one where the image went to a sheet of paper and then from the paper to the carpet.

Initially some retailers complained about the new rugs' tacky, "velvet Elvis" look. Fortunately, innovations in dryer technology allowed a switch to polypropylene material, which gave the rugs the sophisticated silk-screen look that was Bacova's trademark. In 1986, the revolutionary AccentMat was introduced, wholesaling at $3.80 and easily meeting the $9.99 price point. AccentMats soon became the leading seller among Bacova products.

This success inspired a similar strategy with the mailboxes. By 1986, Bacova had developed a process for silk screening its traditional images on the reverse side of a flexible piece of polycarbonate that could be fitted over a standard rural mailbox. The new mailbox was called AccentBox, and it sold for about half the price of the Classic Bacova Mailbox because the cover was riveted on, not hand-laminated. This less expensive version of the mailbox was very popular with the retailers. The company's sales leapt to $9.6 million in 1986 and $19 million in 1987. The success of these two product lines demonstrated to Bacova management the potential of marketing to mass merchandisers.

The 1987 Peak

During the mid-1980s, Bacova constantly expanded its workforce and facilities. It built an addition onto the original facility, added a new manufacturing/screen-printing facility, and leased a building in an industrial park in the next town. It also made arrangements with a carpet manufacturer in Georgia. Bacova would typically source the manufactured product from the outside, create a series of designs, screen print the designs, and market the product through its growing network of manufacturers' representatives. Bacova could introduce a new product in this manner at such a low cost that it generally did not bother to do any preliminary market testing.

By the end of 1987, sales had grown to $19 million and profits were $1.8 million. The company was selling hardware products, including mailboxes, covers, and accessories, and textile products, including a wide variety of mats and rugs. Textiles had a record year in 1987, particularly the AccentMats, which accounted for approximately $8 million in sales. Each product line included some higher-priced items that were sold to the specialty gift shops and mail-order companies. Sales and profits declined each year after 1987 as the economy worsened and Bacova continued to face price competition from other manufacturers. In 1990, Bacova earned only $39,539 on sales of $13.4 million. (Exhibits 1 and 2 present financial data for the years 1981–1990.)

COMPETITION

Mailbox sales were divided into the following categories: steel (70 percent), plastic (20 percent), and wood (10 percent). Bacova was sourcing its standard metal mailboxes from the Solar Group in Taylorsville, Michigan. Another primary manufacturer sold nearly 90 percent of all plain steel mailboxes directly to the same mass merchandisers that Bacova was targeting. Bacova's success in creating the decorative mailbox market had attracted the attention of its mailbox supplier. By the end of 1987, the top competitors became aware of the market Bacova had created, and retailers began to ask these competitors why they did not provide a decorative box.

Sales of mailboxes declined rapidly as competition increased. When Steel City entered the market in 1988 with its answer to the AccentBoxes, Bacova was forced to cut its wholesale price from $13.50 to between $7.00 and $7.50. The growing textile division was partially offsetting the lost mailbox sales, but the outlook for Bacova was not optimistic. Management knew that unless it found a way to differentiate itself and compete by creating and filling a profitable niche, the AccentBox was destined to be priced out of the market.

The Solar Group, Bacova's supplier, approached Johns and Haynes to see if it could buy Bacova panels. Johns and Haynes knew their panels were the highest quality and most appealing on the market and thought that by selling them to the Solar Group they would forfeit their advantage in the marketplace. This option did not appear to have any long-term potential. After the Solar Group had improved its own processes for making panels, it would no longer need Bacova. As a result of this conflict of interests, Bacova began to source its mailboxes from Fulton, which served hardware distributorships and which therefore was not a competitor in Bacova's distribution channels.

MARKETING AND SALES

Bacova had a vice president of sales and three regional sales managers who oversaw the activities of approximately 25 independent manufacturers' representative organizations, including about 130 reps. These salespeople sold Bacova's products through a variety of retail outlets. Retailers were moving to eliminate as many vendors as possible; being able to offer one-stop shopping was a real advantage.

The problem with working with mass merchandisers, reported Tim Lindhjem, regional sales manager, was that they can "kill a category within two years because of the downward pressure on prices." He believed hardware stores held the key to Bacova's success.

THE POSTMASTER SYSTEM

In 1988, Bacova decided to try to differentiate itself by creating a total mailbox system, designed to take the mailbox product a step further, to incorporate plastics to create a wider range of products and prices, and to satisfy consumer demand for easier installation. The process of buying a mailbox and a post, setting the post in the ground, and figuring out a way to attach the box to the post usually became an all-day affair. The total system proposed by Bacova was called PostMaster and included a molded polypropylene mailbox (the Poly-Box), a PVC cross-mount or top-mount post kit that could be installed with no digging or concrete, a universal mounting plate that would hold any standard rural mailbox, a newspaper tube, and a Bacova design on a sheet of polycarbonate that snapped in place over the mailbox. These products would be sold separately, and the covers could be personalized and snapped on or off the Poly-Box so they could be changed for different holidays or special occasions. Bacova sold a variety of interchangeable covers, including collegiate and National Football League designs. The PostMaster system could also be used with a standard metal mailbox, such as the AccentBox or the Classic Bacova Mailbox.

After deciding to go with this PostMaster System, Bacova made arrangements to have the Poly-Box molds manufactured in Taiwan from its own designs. This was Bacova's first experience with trying to design something and having someone else manufacture it. The molds turned out to be poorly designed and low in quality. The company scrapped everything that had been done in Taiwan and hired a product-development consulting firm to help design the box and the packaging and engineer the system more efficiently. Those costs are broken down in Exhibit 3. The development of the PostMaster System represented nearly an $800,000 investment.

Bacova introduced the plastic PostMaster boxes, the post kits, and the other accessories in the beginning of 1990. These boxes were well received by the marketplace, although they cannibalized sales of the AccentBoxes (see Exhibits 4 and 5). Plastic boxes were definitely thought to be the wave of the future. They had none of the denting, rusting, or rotting characteristics of the metal boxes, cost less to make, and wholesaled for more.

EXHIBIT 3

Bacova Guild PostMaster Development Costs

Original mailbox mold (Taiwan)	$133,158
Second mailbox mold (U.S.)	244,430
Post system mold	127,000
Design consultant	276,252
Total	$780,840

EXHIBIT 4

Bacova Guild Historical Mailbox Sales

	1987	1988	1989	1990	1991 Est.
ACCENTBOXES					
Total sales	$2,612,686	$3,615,756	$2,751,523	$631,007	$455,600
Quantity sold	193,195	278,813	247,076	59,159	38,512
Average price	$13.52	$12.97	$11.14	$10.67	$11.83
POSTMASTER BOXES					
Total sales	0	0	$675,601	$1,397,576	$1,880,200
Quantity sold	0	0	92,229	178,832	338,775
Average price	0	0	$7.33	$7.82	$5.55

EXHIBIT 5

Cannibalization by PostMaster

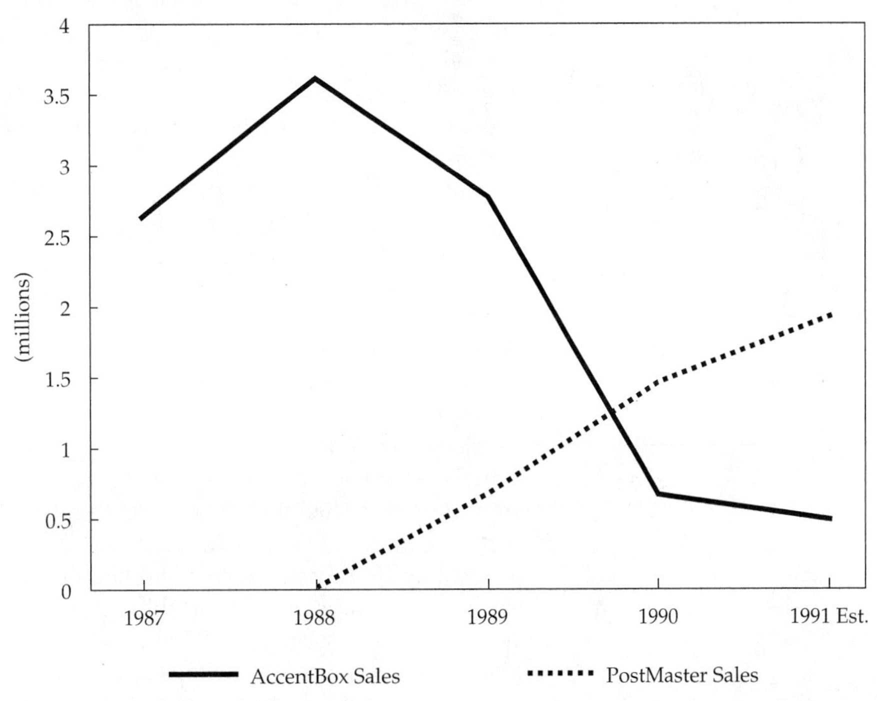

It had been a major decision for Johns and his partner to undertake the investment in the PostMaster System. They had created a successful product, but it appeared that they had not been able to distance themselves adequately from their larger competitors. Johns wondered if the PostMaster System had been a worthwhile venture. The company evaluated projects using a 15 percent hurdle rate. The U.S. molds could be depreciated straight line over ten years. Had this been a sound decision on a net present value basis? What other qualitative benefits did the PostMaster System provide?

Looking Forward

Both Johns and Haynes believed their company to be at a turning point. Within the next five years, they would like to see Bacova reach $25 million to $30 million in sales with 30 percent gross margins. They knew that things would have to change, though, in order for them to meet their goal.

In assessing which way to go, Johns turned to several trusted industry allies for suggestions. Feedback from the market showed that Bacova was highly respected and known to have superior creativity and design. Its quality, service, and delivery were regarded as above average.

Still, several suggestions were made:

1. Focus on high-quality, crafted products.
2. Go after mom-and-pop retailers who are very loyal and who are willing to pay more for innovation and service.
3. Reduce the amount of paperwork manufacturers' reps need to do.
4. Provide better supporting material for new-product introductions.
5. Either support or withdraw products like the veggie markers, driveway markers, and single numbers, which are always shown at shows but which have no supporting materials.
6. Redesign the conference booth to be more inviting. Make it larger. Highlight new products.
7. Expand the mailbox line so that Bacova can walk into a retailer and offer to supply the entire mailbox department.
8. Add a larger box size in black.
9. Develop more case-cut packaging that goes from truck to floor with little effort.

While these suggestions were all worthwhile, Johns knew the company needed a "big picture" adjustment, one that would have to come from senior management. How the company reacted to the "accelerated rate of change in the marketplace" would dictate its future.

Johns reflected on the lessons he had gleaned from Michael Porter's *Competitive Strategy*, a book he had just read. In this analysis, Porter discussed the two main strategies a company may take in order to gain a competitive advantage in the marketplace. The first involved cost and keeping it as low as possible. The second focused on differentiation, or the ability to add features that separated a product from the rest of the pack.

The key to success for any company was to recognize which single or combination strategy it intended, or was best-suited to employ, and then to make sure that all elements of its marketing, pricing, and distribution were consistent with this strategy.

Clearly, Bacova started out as a specialty gift supplier, charging premium prices. Then, when Johns and Haynes took over and wanted to expand the business, they used upgrades in technology to introduce products such as AccentMats and AccentBoxes that were differentiated and yet low cost. They expanded into mass distribution to keep up with demand and initially earned handsome returns. Unfortunately, given the economics of the business, competitors soon copied Bacova's designs. The company was forced to compete on price and was suffering the low profits of a commodity business. Was Bacova best suited to compete in this arena? If not, where should it compete and how?

Still there were problems with Bacova's current structure as Charlie Bower, vice president of sales and marketing, pointed out:

> Bacova is a niche business. It has to be more. Right now the textile and hardware businesses are so diverse that it has been very difficult to focus strategically. . . . If we do focus, textiles would be the way to go. They are higher margin and more closely tied to Bacova's strength in printing designs.

One manufacturers' rep felt it would be a mistake to divest its mailbox business: "There are synergies between the two, and Bacova would lose some significance to retailers if it were just a textiles firm."

Cedar Works Acquisition

A second option came with Bacova's opportunity to purchase Cedar Works, a small manufacturer of top-of-the-line cedar mailboxes. Charles Bower commented on the prospect:

> Strategically, it would be good to go wood. It broadens the product line and typically commands higher margins. Steel City and Solar have both gotten into the cedar business and have hurt Cedar Works considerably. In fact, Cedar Works lost its Home Depot, Lowes, and Hechinger accounts to these larger competitors. It still retains Wal-Mart, though, which would be a great customer to have.
>
> Cedar Works has the best wood boxes in the business but needs lower costs. Bacova might be able to help. The problem is we can't afford to pay a lot. Even if we could, it comes down to buying a client list. And the main noteworthy client with Cedar Works is Wal-Mart.

Johns had very little financial information on Cedar Works since they were only in preliminary discussions. He knew sales for fiscal year ending June 30, 1990, were about $4 million, with net profit of $190,000. (See Exhibit 6 for a 1990 income statement.) Johns expected 6 percent growth per year. Word in the industry was that Cedar Works might go for as high as $4 million. After ten years, industry experts thought the business might be worth as much as $5.88 million. Would this acquisition make sense for Bacova? How much could Johns and Haynes offer to pay for Cedar Works?

A third option was for the company to focus on its competitive advantage and get back to being a supplier of premium products. Bacova was the undisputed design leader and the favored supplier among gift accounts and upscale hardware stores. Should the company rethink its marketing and distribution to get back to premium craftsmanship at a higher price?

EXHIBIT 6

Cedar Works, Inc. 1990 Income Statement

Sales	$3,968,693
COGS	2,935,894
Gross margin	1,032,799
Expenses	651,675
Operating income	381,124
Other expenses	88,920
Net income before taxes	292,204
Taxes	101,774
Net income	$ 190,430

Johns knew his management team would be returning from the Chicago Hardware Show on Friday. He wanted to have thought through the options by then and be prepared to present them with his plan.

CASE 11

WOMEN'S WORLD BANKING: THE EARLY YEARS

It was January 1990. Michaela Walsh had to make a major decision, whether to end her tenure as president of Women's World Banking (WWB) or to stay on for a few more years. She had repeatedly talked with members of the board of directors about leaving in the fall of 1990, but no one seemed to believe her. On the one hand, she had accomplished her goal—to establish an internationally respected and innovative financial institution. In many ways, Walsh's vision for WWB had been realized: The organization had grown to 44 affiliates in 35 countries through which $11.6 million had flowed to entrepreneurs in less economically developed areas around the world who otherwise might never have started or built their own businesses. On the other hand, was WWB on sufficiently stable foundations? Who should the successor be? Walsh knew the organization's future depended on its capacity to strengthen and expand its management and services. Walsh's thoughts shifted to plans for her next innovative project, the creation of a venture-capital fund. The excitement of this new challenge was as compelling as the demands of WWB in its early years had once been. She knew she had to make a decision because discussion of a successor would need to take place at the upcoming board meeting in April.

BEGINNINGS

The seeds for WWB were planted in 1975 at the United Nations International Women's Year Conference in Mexico City. The conference, which launched the United Nations Decade for Women, stressed the high cost of traditional cultural practices and legal and financial requirements that undermined women's active participation in the economic mainstream. Walsh attended the conference as an observer at the request of her employer at the time, the Rockefeller Brothers Fund. A group of fifteen delegates—women from diverse cultures—met to discuss obstacles to women's participation in business and agreed that access to credit and business training were major hurdles all over the world. This group resolved to create a vehicle to support women who had entrepreneurial qualities but who lacked the capital and management skills to build viable businesses. These delegates became the nucleus for Women's World Banking.

This case was prepared by Andrea Larson, assistant professor of Business Administration, with the help of Jeanne Mockard, research assistant. Revised 1/97.

START-UP

By 1977, the founding fifteen women had become the Committee to Organize Women's World Banking.[1] In addition to her responsibilities at Rockefeller Brothers Fund, Walsh spent the next two years working with the group, researching questions such as how to build a development bank and how these financial institutions worked. She was convinced of the need for an independent organization supported by the United Nations but not under its direction. The Committee to Organize WWB used a United Nations' grant to hold meetings in five locations around the world to explore the idea and to cover the costs of lawyers to set up the legal structure. The need to establish an international structure flexible enough to accommodate the diversity of activities and participants was recognized at the outset. The Netherlands offered the opportunity to set up a global financial institution that could be independently registered in other countries. Dutch incorporation also served to confirm the international identity of the organization.

Walsh believed strongly that the organization should retain a legal status under Dutch law that allowed it to fall between profit and nonprofit. She asserted that

> you are less than whole when you are dropped into the nonprofit category. So we don't want the institution locked into a nonprofit status without flexibility for alternative sources of revenue.

Accordingly, in the face of those who would have formed a United Nations-backed development bank modeled on existing institutions, she argued in favor of building a new institution with a capitalization that would throw off income, support operations, and provide funds to guarantee credit to local businesswomen. The *Stichting* (a Dutch term for "corporation") to promote Women's World Banking was organized in 1979 under Dutch law "to advance and promote the full participation of women and their families in local and global economies."

In the late 1970s and early 1980s, through a difficult process involving many cold calls and rejections, Walsh raised funds that WWB used to guarantee loans. By 1983, WWB had received funds totaling approximately $900,000 to finance planning and initial operations. The money came primarily in the form of gift donations from government organizations concerned with economic development issues and entrepreneurship. Norway was first to participate, followed by Holland and Sweden. Canada and the United States also contributed.

At first Walsh had difficulty defending her vision of the new institution. The government sponsors had their own ideas about the new organization. All the contributors recommended that the new financial entity manage projects in less developed countries and invest directly in the poor. Walsh knew, however, that projects typical of development-oriented organizations usually died out at the end of three years. Despite pressures to conform to the more accepted way of investing development monies, she envisioned WWB building a stable worldwide organization, and she charged her detractors with being interested in reporting money spent, not in seeing actual returns on money invested. Her perspective, based on investment-management experience, emphasized long-range financial returns and careful cash-flow management. In what was then considered an innovative step, Michaela Walsh placed the initial donations in a permanent capital fund.

WWB encompassed WWB/New York (the New York City communication hub and service center), the WWB regional coordinators, the board of trustees, and the WWB Capital Fund. According to its charter, WWB was founded

> to advance and promote the direct participation of women and their families in the full use of the economy [by operating] as an independent financial institution to provide loan guarantees or other securities to banks and other financial institutions, and to provide technical and other advice and assistance to direct and indirect beneficiaries of guarantees.

WWB's philosophy discouraged subsidizing loan interest rates to women, because the organization's objective was to teach women to compete in the marketplace. In order to accomplish this goal, WWB worked with local entrepreneurs and local financial institutions through a global network of affiliates, a group of associated yet independent local organizations that, by 1985, formed the core of the WWB organization.

The Affiliates

The real work of WWB was accomplished through the web of worldwide affiliates. These local groups provided the link between WWB/New York City, participating local banks, and entrepreneurs. Under the program, local banks extended credit to individuals because loans were guaranteed jointly by the affiliate and the WWB organization.

The first step in WWB's work was the incorporation of an established local organization as an affiliate of the WWB network. Typically these local organizations were composed of a small number of women who had successfully started businesses or who had tried to start a business and were frustrated by the lack of training and access to capital for women in their locales. Banks were generally reluctant to fund small businesses because banks saw them as risky. Like all entrepreneurs, women had to overcome this obstacle, then fight additional battles, primarily a lack of collateral. In many societies, tradition dictated that most property and resources be registered legally in the husband's name. Some countries' laws prevented women from holding collateral in their own names. The alternatives were few. For individuals without assets and without access to capital through formal avenues, the only source was moneylenders, who charged rates of up to 10 percent per day.

WWB required affiliate applicants to meet certain requirements prior to incorporation. First, and most important, a fund had to be raised from local sources. Capital was generated from individual contributions and fundraising events. Once a certain level of funds was raised, WWB and the new affiliate signed an agreement stipulating the requirements for affiliation:

1. Local incorporation
2. Adherence to the objectives of WWB
3. Capital funds of US$20,000 (within 5 years)
4. Board of directors to include at least one banker and one lawyer
5. Annual self-assessment report
6. Schedule of membership and service fees

No other controls were imposed. As long as these requirements were met, each affiliate established the organization and strategy that worked best in its local situation. Every affiliate was responsible for its own financial viability and internal administration. This structure kept decision making at the local level and enabled the WWB network to meet the different business and cultural needs of the female entrepreneurs it reached all over the world.

The direct lending programs of affiliates proved to be a profitable business for some. Portfolios included small loans to individuals and groups of self-employed women, loans to microenterprise groups, and lines of credit for working capital. Direct assistance was also provided to businesswomen who sought access to banks.

EXHIBIT 1

Women's World Banking: Revenue Breakdown

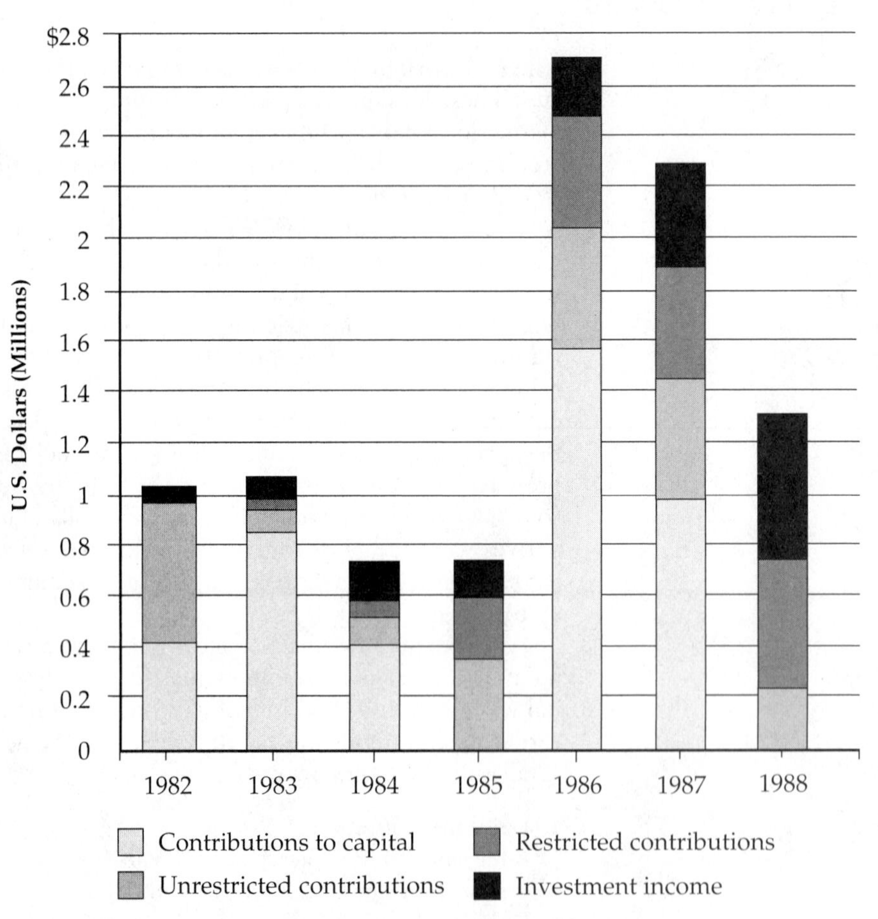

SOURCE: Company records.

EXHIBIT 2

Women's World Banking: Consolidated Fund Balances

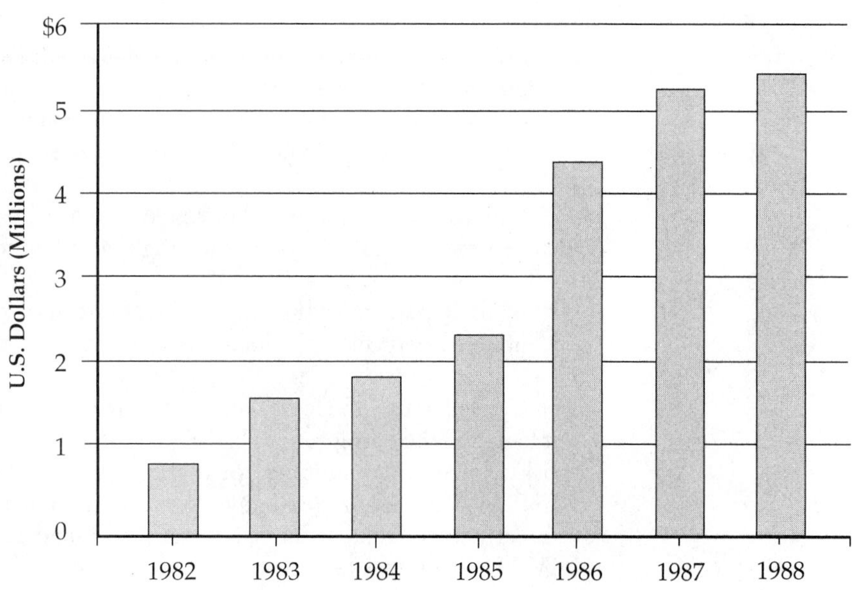

SOURCE: Company records.

Affiliates structured their local programs according to unique local needs and linked up with WWB through the Management Institute Program, the Affiliate Exchange Program, or other international meetings. Although a loan-guarantee program was often part of an affiliate's partnership with WWB, loan guarantees were not a necessary component; when offered, guarantees were usually combined with a variety of local program offerings. As of March 1990, WWB affiliates had participated in over 56,000 loans totaling $11.6 million, including 5,800 covered under WWB's loan-guarantee programs. (See Exhibits 1 and 2 for 1982–88 revenues and fund balances.)

THE LOCAL PARTNERSHIP

Once an affiliate was approved, a set of relationships had to be built and managed at the local level to move the financial resources from banks into the hands of the entrepreneurs. In order to receive a loan guarantee from WWB, a prospective borrower had to meet certain standards. She had to have a viable business plan and she had to be willing to participate with the affiliate to learn any management skills required to run the business.

The affiliate then played the role of intermediary, presenting the entrepreneur's case to the bank as an acceptable investment opportunity. The affiliate handled most of the bank's paperwork requirements and often negotiated the terms of credit on behalf of the loan applicant. This role was essential because it linked capital to individuals who otherwise had no other economic opportunities. Mary Okelo, the founder of the Kenya affiliate and former vice president of the African Development Bank, explained:

> An illiterate peasant woman in the village with a practical and viable business proposal cannot walk into those marble buildings and state her own case. She needs someone to take her to the bank manager and say, "I can vouch for this person," and to say to her, "Don't worry, we are behind you."

Once the bank loan was approved, the local bank would lend money in local currency at commercial rates knowing that it had the following guarantees:

- up to 50 percent of the loan was guaranteed by the WWB Capital Fund
- up to 25 percent of the loan was guaranteed by the local affiliate's fund

Consequently, the local bank normally only risked 25 percent of the capital that it lent, and the entrepreneur had a guarantee for 75 percent of the loan. This shared risk assured the commitment of all participants to the success of the enterprise. Over time WWB encouraged banks to increase their portion of the risk, do business directly with female owners, and accept women as regular clients, which freed the WWB guarantees for new borrowers.

Since the inception of its Loan-Guarantee Program, WWB had backed 5,800 loans totaling $2,662,068. The ratio of losses to loans disbursed was low: $73,720, or approximately 2.75 percent over ten years. The low default rates were explained by local political conditions rather than by business failure. The first loan losses, reported in 1988, raised concerns that time and budgetary constraints had led to deficiencies in loan-approval and monitoring procedures in certain affiliates. Inexperienced younger affiliates also reported that significant resources were required for effective monitoring of the borrowers. In some cases, however, losses were unavoidable. Walsh stated the case for losses in 1989:

> When soldiers raze markets and inventory is destroyed, as it was in Haiti, the money is not recoverable.

THE CLIENT

WWB's clients were women in less developed economies who owned and operated small and microbusinesses or who wished to do so. Most of these women lived in urban or rural poverty, and the vast majority had never had access to the services of established financial institutions. (The mix, however, of microbusiness activity and sophisticated entrepreneurs in any given affiliate's portfolio could vary.) Entrepreneurs operated in all sectors of local economies, ranging from agriculture to marketing of goods and services to small-scale manufacturing (see Exhibit 3). Regardless of their business experience, women received from affiliates the training and services that assured entrepreneurs access to the mainstream economy and that brought them, often for the first time, into sustained relationships with financial institutions. This strategy had the dual impact of providing female entrepreneurs access to credit at market interest rates and recognizing them as full

EXHIBIT 3

Examples of Funded WWB Affiliate Projects, 1989

GHANA

1. Poultry
2. Garment industry
3. Bakery/catering industry

UGANDA

1. Nursery school
2. Poultry farm
3. Vegetable and fruits farm
4. Handicrafts center
5. Carpentry shop and school
6. Home weaving operation
7. Dairy-cow raising
8. Chick hatchery
9. Vegetable farm
10. Vegetable farm cooperative
11. Tomato grower
12. Restaurant
13. Potato grower
14. Piggery
15. Piggery

KENYA

1. Market stall—fruit
2. Market stall—fruit and vegetable
3. Dentist
4. Dress shop/realty company
5. Dress shop
6. Market stall—fruit and vegetable
7. Beauty salon

MALAYSIA

1. Swim instructor
2. Restaurant

RWANDA

1. Slaughterhouse/butchershop—cooperative
2. General store
3. Market stall—roof tiles
4. Small shop—palm oil
5. Handicrafts center

partners in the local business community. Consequently, the women were better able to provide for themselves and their families, create jobs in the community, and influence local economic development strategies.

Growth in Affiliates and Services

The first affiliate began in Cali, Colombia, in May 1981. The second affiliate was established in western India. Others followed quickly in Brazil, Ghana, the Philippines, Thailand, the United States, Egypt, Kenya, Nigeria, Uruguay, Bangladesh, and Indonesia. By 1984, WWB had 21 affiliates and 19 in formation (see Exhibit 4). The WWB Loan-Guarantee Program, which formed the heart of this growing affiliate network, was unique for the time: It differentiated the affiliates and WWB from organizations with similar objectives.

The need to provide more systematic contact with affiliates resulted in the creation of regional coordinators. In 1985, WWB established a regional coordinator's office in Nairobi, Kenya. In 1986, a regional office for the Latin American and Caribbean region was established. Part-time regional coordinators for North America (based in Charleston, West Virginia) and for the Asia/Pacific region (based in Kuala Lumpur, Malaysia) were also set up. The regional offices needed to be upgraded to provide sufficient technical support to affiliates at various stages of development. Several models for regional coordination were under discussion. An experienced banker who had been active in establishing the WWB Bolivia affiliate provided one prototype: She became the Latin American/Caribbean coordinator in 1989, dividing her time evenly between New York and the affiliates.

With a regional organization level coalescing, Walsh recognized the need to set up systems and standardize procedures as much as possible yet maintain the flexibility to adapt them as necessary. By 1986, the WWB executive committee and representatives of twenty-seven potential affiliates had agreed on the formal requirements for affiliation, drafting a model affiliation agreement in three languages. Though later amended, this document served in 1990 as the standard document of compliance for the organization (see Appendix). A loan-guarantee agreement for affiliate programs was written and formalized to stipulate the obligations among the two guarantor parties (WWB and the local affiliate) and the local bank. Accounting systems had to be established and an operations manual written to explain the WWB Loan-Guarantee Program, although by 1988, this project was not yet completed. In 1987, WWB instituted its Start-Up Loan Program, which permitted affiliates to borrow up to $15,000 to cover operating expenditures over the first few years, repayable to WWB after three years.

When WWB was founded, its goal was to establish twelve affiliates within five years. That goal was surpassed and, in fact, the number of affiliates had reached thirty-seven by 1987. As of September 1990, WWB's global organization incorporated forty-eight legally established affiliates in thirty-seven countries, and an additional fifty groups had expressed interest in WWB affiliation. While the organization spanned six continents, the majority of affiliates were in Latin America, the Caribbean, Africa, and Asia. Despite the expansion, one board member commented, "WWB has not been growth oriented. We do not want rapid growth; we want stable, strengthened small businesses run by women." Whether desired or not, the demand for WWB's programs was not slowing, and growth had its challenges: Regions and affiliates sometimes became fractionalized due to competition

EXHIBIT 4

Development of WWB Affiliate Network

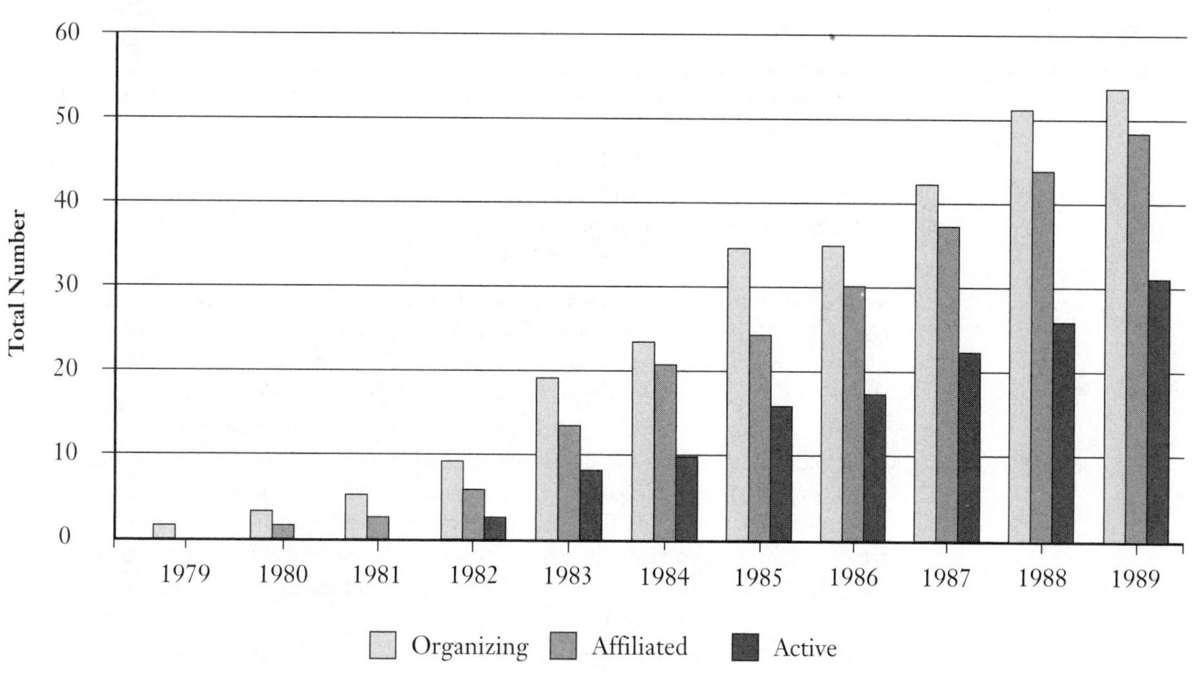

SOURCE: Company records.

for resources. Each time global meetings were held and affiliate representatives gathered, however, commonalities were reinforced and the network grew stronger.

WWB Programs for Strengthening Affiliates

WWB developed and began to implement a number of programs for regional and international meetings in response to the expressed needs of affiliates who were at different stages of development. The WWB Affiliate Exchange Program, the publication of newsletters, and the regular international and regional affiliate meetings all contributed directly to the exchange of acquired knowledge and experience within the global WWB network. The WWB Management Institute, the WWB Start-Up Loan Program, the WWB Loan-Guarantee Program, and fund-raising assistance were designed to provide the tools for affiliates to operate as effective intermediaries for financial, managerial, and technical services for small and microenterprises.

The WWB Affiliate Exchange Program. WWB established its Affiliate Exchange Program in 1987. It was designed to enable affiliates to share ideas, information, expertise, and experience. Under this program, members of new affiliates would visit experienced, successful affiliates to learn how to develop business plans, design and manage programs, develop credit and training systems, and raise funds locally. Established affiliates could also initiate exchanges among themselves to learn methods for moving closer to financial self-sufficiency, improving management of credit systems, expanding portfolios, and providing better technical and management services. An exchange visit could be for one to two weeks, and expenses consisted of travel and a consulting fee paid to the affiliate providing technical assistance. Half of all expenses were paid by the affiliate receiving assistance, and the remaining half were covered by WWB. This program was not used extensively but showed great promise.

WWB Management Institute. The WWB Management Institute (MI) was established in 1989 as a vehicle for WWB affiliates to strengthen their business planning, management capabilities, and structures. MI was set up in response to the growing complexity of management challenges facing affiliates as they progressed through stages of institutional and program development. Some of the topics addressed by MI included financial and strategic planning, credit delivery systems, savings mobilization, client relations, marketing of services, and personnel management. The WWB Affiliate Management Program (AMP) involved three weeks of intensive training, field consultations, and an evaluation week. The methodology focused heavily on affiliate case studies, practical exchange of experience, and preparation of business plans. AMP was expected to be instrumental in building shared values, strong know-how, and sound business plans among WWB affiliates.

The pilot AMP took place from July 1989 to February 1990 for fifteen participants from nine WWB affiliates. The second AMP series was to be launched in July 1990. The pilot AMP was a major success: Its courses had a tremendous impact on the participants, as witnessed by the affiliates themselves throughout the evaluation session and as observed by the trainers. The impact was assessed on two levels: (1) participants instituted many improvements in their day-to-day operations, ranging from redesigning their loan procedures to developing more effective ways to work with staff; (2) the experience reinforced the increased self-confidence of the participants, the sense of ownership of WWB as their network, and the integrity and philosophy of Women's World Banking.

WWB Publications. Over the years, WWB produced a number of basic business publications to help strengthen affiliate operations. These included manuals such as: *How to Start an Affiliate*, *How to Set Up a Loan-Guarantee Program*, *How to Set Up a Loan-Reporting System*, and *How to Develop Fund-Raising Proposals*. WWB and its affiliates also published training tools for WWB clients. In addition, WWB produced materials to provide information about Women's World Banking and to promote the WWB image, such as the Annual Report, a trilingual brochure, the WWB Global Self-Assessment, WWB regional newsletters, and the WWB Global Trade Atlas.

Evaluation of Results. For the past six years, WWB had organized annual affiliate self-assessments. These self-assessments served as planning and evaluation tools for affiliate managers. They also provided WWB with a means to gauge the progress of affiliates at various stages of development, the coverage and impact of affiliate programs, the status of affiliate finances and organization, plans for the future, and service needs from WWB/NYC and the WWB network.

This evaluation also pointed out, however, the organizational stresses of a geographically far-flung and philosophically decentralized network. Walsh was seen as "a strong and visionary president continually attracting a talented and dedicated group" to work at all levels of the organization. Nevertheless, the report pointed to the need for a comprehensive, detailed impact analysis of affiliate programs and a more systematic development of the range of affiliate counseling and loan activities. Of thirteen affiliates visited by the evaluation team, four were found to be "experiencing serious problems in either internal management and systems or in program delivery and monitoring or both." Although this was seen as a relatively good performance for a network of local institutions that often worked with volunteers and limited budgets, the report recommended greater involvement at the senior levels of WWB in the creation and delivery of local programs.

The WWB Self-Assessment Form proved to be a necessary information vehicle for the organization. It received criticism, however, for being cumbersome and not completely useful for assessing overall program results.

WWB/NYC

The New York City hub office had remained small because Walsh had wanted to keep overhead expenditures low. WWB/NYC reduced overhead costs by relying for backup on the board's operating committees and on outside consultants who received guidance from either the president or the executive committees. On average, six permanent employees staffed the New York City office. This strategy made sense during the early growth period, when a top-heavy administrative structure was unnecessary and would have drained scarce resources. Consultants brought in to evaluate WWB in 1989, however, concluded that the small staff and the president's central role had led Walsh to assume a high concentration of day-to-day responsibilities. That burden made it hard for her to focus on strategic issues and staff development. Limited staffing also made it difficult for WWB/NYC to respond in a timely way to the ever-increasing needs of the culturally diverse affiliate network.

Board of Trustees

WWB was governed by a board of trustees that met annually. In 1990, the board was composed of twenty experienced finance, legal, and development specialists of many nationalities. Affiliate leaders from Colombia, Costa Rica, the Dominican Republic, Ghana, Thailand, India, and the Netherlands were members of the board; many were illustrious business leaders and stateswomen. Esther Ocloo was a leading businesswoman and development expert from Ghana. Beatrice Harretche was a leading development and commercial banker from Latin America. WWB's present chair, Ela Bhatt, was the founder of SEWA, a model financial institution providing lending, savings, and organizing services for self-employed women in India; Bhatt had been a member of Parliament and, in 1990, was a member of India's Planning Commission. The large board of committed professionals of international stature enhanced WWB's identity.

In addition to its fiscal responsibility to the Stichting, the board of trustees was responsible for approving the affiliate organizations, which were the raison d'etre of the group, and for setting operating policies of the institutions. The board established operating committees and assigned at least two trustees to each. Only the board could grant authority to the committees, but they reported to and were coordinated by an executive director. The committees met quarterly or as duties required. A strong executive committee provided leadership through quarterly meetings; the large and diverse board provided a range of expertise and acted as a general policy advisory group for the executive committee. A finance committee, a nominating committee, and an operations committee also met together quarterly (see Exhibit 5).

The board was active and wanted to be kept informed about all aspects of WWB. The quarterly meetings of the executive and finance committees required a great deal of preparation and follow-up paperwork by the WWB/NYC staff.

EXHIBIT 5

Women's World Banking: January 1990 Organization Chart

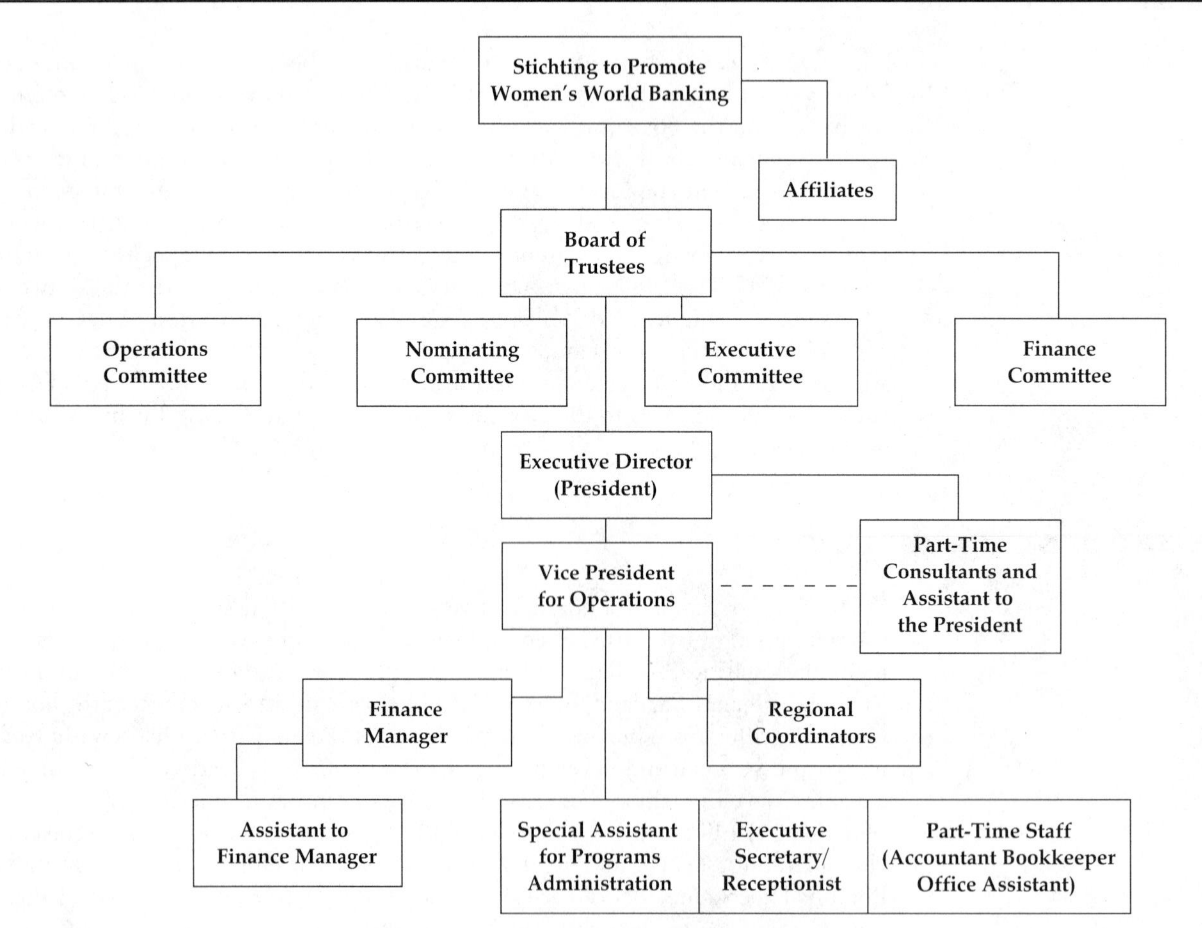

The WWB Capital Fund

The WWB Capital Fund totaled US$80,000 in 1979. By 1990, it had grown to US$6.5 million. The fund was divided into three approximately equal parts. A third of the fund was invested through Clemente Capital in a diversified portfolio of international equity markets. Clemente Capital was an international investment firm managing over US$7 billion in assets. Its founder, Lilia Clemente, a Filipino, started her company in the building that housed WWB/NYC, shared a copying machine with WWB, and had grown alongside WWB. Another third of the fund was placed with the investment firm C&S and invested in diversified domestic equities. The last third was managed by WWB's finance manager and was invested in easily accessible, short-term instruments for immediate cash needs.

The funds were invested conservatively according to the finance committee's criteria. Investment income averaged 5.5 percent of fund balances during the 1980s. This income provided funding for WWB/NYC's operating budget. The finance committee limited withdrawals from the fund in any given year to 5 percent of total capital to avoid depleting the real value of the fund.

The ten-year assessment by outside consultants completed in 1989 concluded that, although WWB had created an innovative organization based on the strength of the capital-fund idea, the narrow base of the fund and changing patterns of donors represented a challenge to the medium-term viability of the system. Donor support was declining as priorities changed and development monies moved toward country-specific and project-based funding. Walsh was concerned about a fall in donor income between 1986 and 1990.

Michaela Walsh

Michaela Walsh made the transition to WWB from Wall Street. She began her Wall Street career as an office manager with Merrill Lynch, first in Kansas City and then in New York City in the late 1950s and 1960s. When she discovered Merrill Lynch's internal training programs were not open to women, she attended night school on her own and soon became a registered stock-and-bond trader. She joined the new international department and became Merrill Lynch's liaison for its representatives, opening branch offices around the world. It was an exciting time: Fifteen offices were established within two years, giving Michaela a taste of opening service businesses in global environments. When the opportunity arose she left the New York office for five years to help start and operate the Middle Eastern office in Beirut, Lebanon. Another opportunity soon presented itself: When international brokerage firms were allowed to trade foreign securities out of London for the first time, she moved to the London office to set up new operations. With the business established two years later, she needed a new challenge and went back to New York City to go back into sales. When she found sales jobs were not available for women, she left Merrill Lynch for another, smaller regional investment banking firm, Boettcher and Co.

Despite achieving partner status at Boettcher and Co. and setting up the company's New York City offices, she increasingly questioned her commitment to her career path. She was making a good income, but was not satisfied with that alone. In 1972, she left investment banking to work for the Rockefeller Brothers Fund. After one year with the Fund's portfolio management group, Walsh headed a research project that analyzed and predicted the effects on the economy of cultural changes and new ideas that emerged from the turbulent 1960s. Based on her research, she recommended innovative ventures and activities for Rockefeller family investments. During this period she was involved with a group of people financing the 1975 United Nations Women's Year Conference, and her employer requested that she attend the event.

The path that led Walsh from the Women's Year Conference to establishing and serving as president of WWB had been an exhilarating and fulfilling one. She had used her financial background to build an innovative financial institution that, by 1990, was respected around the world. The WWB network had raised awareness of the need for an emphasis on the role of women in the economy. For example, as a result of active efforts by WWB affiliates in several African countries, government units working on behalf of women and the family (in some cases at the ministerial level) had significantly increased. In France, due to a concerted effort by the WWB affiliates, the government had announced plans to set aside specific loan funds for women in business.

In addition to raising awareness, WWB had reached an estimated 56,000 women and men directly and through loan programs and had indirectly reached a substantially larger number of their families and communities. For example, one small loan of US$300 to a group of 12 women in Uganda for an agricultural cooperative ultimately benefited more than 100 women, men, and children in the village due to increased production and income.

By 1990, WWB was recognized in the development sector as a reputable organization. Its affiliate structure, its focus on microenterprise, and its Loan-Guarantee Program had been imitated, and, reflecting the impact of the WWB philosophy, these models had become widely accepted over time as an integral part of development assistance programs. WWB was continuing to grow in scope and scale. On the other hand, because its pioneering approach of loan guarantees and direct affiliate loans was no longer unique, it had to compete more aggressively for funds to finance its continued expansion.

Was this the time for Walsh to step down? She was considering a small number of people who could ably serve as her successor. Did she want to separate completely from WWB or remain involved? If she stayed active, in what capacity should she serve? Walsh knew her organization well and knew it had weaknesses that needed to be addressed. How should they be prioritized and who was the best person to address them?

ENDNOTE

[1]The fifteen were Martha Bulengo, Patricia Cloherty, Gasbia El Hamamsy, Annie Jiagge, Lucille Mair, Bertha Beatriz Martinez-Garza, Esther Ocloo, Caroline Pezzullo, Virginia Saurwein, Leslie Sederlund, Leticia Ramos Shahani, Margaret Snyder, Martha Stuart, Zohren Tabatabai, and Michaela Walsh.

APPENDIX

Model Affiliation Agreement between Stichting to Promote Women's World Banking and (Affiliate)

Whereas, Stichting to Promote Women's World Banking ("WWB") has been organized to advance and promote the direct participation of women and their families in the full use of the economy, particularly those women who have not generally had access to the services of established financial institutions;

Whereas, WWB has decided that it would be desirable to establish a formal relationship with and grant the status of "Affiliate of WWB" to organizations which have been established with the specific purpose to further the goals of WWB in whole or in part;

Whereas, the granting of such status will help promote the formation, growth, and cooperation of institutions around the world mutually devoted to each other in support of such objectives;

Whereas, for such purposes and as more fully set forth below [Affiliate] proposes to enter into such a relationship with WWB;

Now therefore, WWB and [Affiliate] hereby agree as follows:

1. [Affiliate] represents and agrees as follows:
   (a) It has been duly established in [city and country] as a legal entity (describe status, e.g., corporation, association, foundation, cooperation society) and will maintain such status.
   (b) The objective of [Affiliate] is to advance and promote the direct participation of women and their families in the full use of the economy and it will use its best efforts to carry out such objectives in accordance with the philosophy, policy, and practices of WWB in cooperation, whenever feasible, with other Affiliates.
   (c) Capital Funds of not less than the equivalent of US$20,000 (such equivalent to be determined at the time of contribution) have been contributed to the Affiliate for use in its operations, provided that at least 50% has been obtained from local, independent sources. [Affiliate] will use its best efforts to obtain such additional funds from such sources that may be necessary to maintain its Capital Funds at that level.

      It is the goal that at least 50% of any additional Capital Funds will be obtained from local independent sources.

<u>(Alternative paragraph for affiliates starting with US$5,000).</u>

   (c) Capital Funds shall be provided on the following basis:
      (i) Not less than the equivalent of US$5,000 (such contribution to be determined as of the time of contribution) has been contributed to [Affiliate] for use in its operations.

SOURCE: From company records.

(continued)

APPENDIX (CONTINUED)

Model Affiliation Agreement between Stichting to Promote Women's World Banking and (Affiliate)

(ii) An additional contribution will be made to [Affiliate] of not less than US$5,000 within three years from the date when this agreement is effective.

(iii) An additional contribution will be made to [Affiliate] of not less than US$10,000 within five years from the date when this agreement is effective, provided that by the end of the three-year period and the end of the five-year period at least 50% (fifty percent) of the total required for that period has been obtained from local, independent sources. [Affiliate] will use its best efforts to obtain such further additional funds from such sources that may be necessary to maintain its Capital Funds at the levels provided above.

It is the goal that at least 50% of any additional Capital Funds will be obtained from local, independent sources.

(d) The Board of Directors of [Affiliate] has and will continue to have at least one member with substantial banking experience and one member who is a lawyer with banking or business experience.

(e) [Affiliate] will furnish to WWB, on a date to be agreed with WWB, the following reports and information:

(i) Reports of activities under its loan guarantee programs.

(ii) Self-Assessment Reports.

(iii) Reports of affiliate activities; financial statements; annual reports; information regarding its membership, management, and staff; information regarding its attendance at conferences and seminars; and such other reports and information as shall be agreed with WWB.

(f) [Affiliate] will establish and maintain a minimum schedule for membership fees, fees for services, meetings, furnishing of information, and other relevant services.

2. (a) Before [Affiliate] shall present a written request to accept funds or borrow from sources originating, or from entities whose principal office is located outside the Affiliate's home country, or from an international organization, it shall notify WWB and shall advise WWB of the details of such proposed acceptance or borrowing of such funds.

(b) If the President, upon receipt of such information, believes that the proposed acceptance or borrowing of such funds raises an issue of policy for WWB or may be inconsistent with the fund-raising activities of WWB or another Affiliate, the President shall

(i) So notify [Affiliate] and

(ii) Consult with [Affiliate] to try to resolve any difficulties

(continued)

APPENDIX (CONTINUED)

Model Affiliation Agreement between Stichting to Promote Women's World Banking and (Affiliate)

regarding the proposal. Failing such agreement, either the President or [Affiliate] can bring the matter to the Board of Trustees.

(c) The Board of Trustees or the Executive Committee acting for the Board shall then examine the matter and as soon as practicable, but no later than within three (3) months of the receipt of information under paragraph (2) above, decide whether to consent to the proposed acceptance or borrowing of funds. If, after due consideration, the consent is not given, [Affiliate] will not accept or borrow such funds.

3. WWB grants the status of "Affiliate of WWB" to [Affiliate]. This status entitles [Affiliate]
   (a) To present itself as such.
   (b) To use the name "Women's World Banking" in its title.
   (c) To avail itself of the support of WWB in the advancement of [Affiliate]'s objectives. The rights stated in the prior sentence shall cease if this agreement is terminated under paragraph (7).

4. WWB shall provide to [Affiliate] the following:
   (a) Assistance in setting up its loan and guarantee operations.
   (b) Information and assistance in evaluating loan applications and monitoring loans.
   (c) Assistance in developing fundraising strategies.
   (d) Opportunities for exchanging information regarding the operations of WWB and the other affiliates and other matters of common interest.
   (e) Information and assistance regarding the expansion of loan portfolios.
   (f) Assistance in protecting its name.

5. Neither WWB nor [Affiliate] shall be responsible for the debts or obligations of the other.

6. This agreement shall become effective when the following shall have occurred:
   (a) It shall have been signed by authorized representatives of each party.
   (b) [Affiliate] shall have furnished to WWB evidence satisfactory to it of the accuracy of the representations made by it in paragraph 1 above.

(continued)

APPENDIX (CONTINUED)

Model Affiliation Agreement between Stichting to Promote Women's World Banking and (Affiliate)

(c) WWB, acting upon the instructions of the Board of Trustees or the Executive Committee, as the case may be, shall have notified [Affiliate] in writing or by cable that it is satisfied with such evidence and this agreement is thereupon effective.

7. Either party can terminate this Agreement at any time by notice in writing or by cable to the other party. Thirty days (30) after such notice is sent, the Agreement and all rights and obligations thereunder will be terminated.

______________________	______________________
[Affiliate]	Women's World Banking
[Title]	President
Date:	Date:

CASE 12

COPELAND CORPORATION/BAIN & COMPANY: THE SCROLL INVESTMENT DECISION[1]

In late January 1989, Joanna Engelke and David Bechhofer of Bain & Company were preparing for the initial meeting of the Copeland engagement team. Engelke and Bechhofer had circulated a memo outlining their thoughts (Exhibit 1), together with excerpts from an investment research paper on Emerson Electric, Copeland's parent company (Exhibit 2) and overheads used during a Copeland management presentation to Emerson's board of directors in May 1988 (Exhibit 3). Timing was critical because the Bain team hoped to have recommendations for Copeland's management by May 1, 1989, concerning a capital appropriations request for a major addition to Scroll's compressor capacity.

Interviews with Ed Purvis, Copeland's senior marketing manager for the air conditioning department, and Howard Lance, Copeland's president of sales and marketing, were scheduled for the following week.

This case was prepared by Jeanne M. Liedtka, Associate Professor of Business Administration, and John W. Rosenblum, Tayloe Murphy Professor of Business Administration.

[1]This case is to be used in conjunction with the Darden Video Module "Copeland/Bain."

EXHIBIT 1

To: Mike D'Amato
Vern Altman
From: David Bechhofer
Joanna Engelke
Date: January 23, 1989
Subject: Overview of Copeland Corporation

The following is a summary of the information that we have learned about Copeland. I hope that it will be valuable as background for the discussions this Thursday in Sidney, Ohio.

HISTORY

Copeland Refrigeration Corporation was founded in Michigan in 1933. The name was changed to Copeland Corporation in 1972 and incorporated in Delaware. The name change signified the growing importance of the air conditioning market in the company's sales mix. In 1981, the company was taken private by Henry Hillman for $215mm. Hillman had been the lead shareholder with 36 percent of the stock prior to the leveraged buyout. He combined the company with Pameco (Pam eee' co), a refrigeration and air-conditioning parts distributor, and formed Cop-Pam Holdings.

In 1986, Emerson purchased the company for $541mm. The logic to the acquisition was that it gave Emerson a full line in the refrigeration and air-conditioning parts business and fit well with the electric-motor division. Before the acquisition was complete, Copeland signed an exclusive distribution agreement with Pameco for aftermarket parts.

While all the annual data is not available, Copeland has grown from $200mm in sales ($12mm profit) in 1976 to $575mm in sales ($31mm profit) in 1986.

TECHNOLOGY

(With apologies to the mechanical engineers in the room)

Copeland's sales are dominated by the compressor business, with more than 90 percent of revenue coming from sales of new compressors, rebuilt compressors, and compressor parts. Historically, the two main technologies have been hermetic and semihermetic compressors. Hermetic (.25–22 hp) compressors are completely sealed and difficult-to-repair units that are oriented toward the residential air-conditioning market. Semihermetic (.25–80 hp) compressors are repairable and rebuildable, larger, more expensive, and oriented toward the refrigeration and commercial air-conditioning markets.

The company has also developed and built condensing units that combine a compressor and an electric motor in one package.

(continued)

EXHIBIT 1 (CONTINUED)

The current "hot" product is the compliant Scroll compressor. While most compressors use a plunging action to compress the relevant gases, the Scroll compressor uses a spiral squeezing action. The value gained is that it is smaller, more efficient, and has fewer moving parts (lower cost) than older technologies. It is currently being targeted for the residential air-conditioning OEM (Original Equipment Manufacturer) market.

The buzzword in the business these days is "variable speed." The ability to combine compressors with variable-speed motors creates a system that is inherently more efficient. Consequently, those companies that can integrate these products should have an advantage. Although Emerson has both motor and compressor divisions, we believe that some competitors may be farther along in this technology.

MARKETS (CUSTOMERS)

The compressors are sold in three definably different markets (or market segments): refrigeration, commercial air conditioning, and residential air conditioning. The refrigeration market includes products such as supermarket display cases and walk-in refrigerators and freezers. Copeland has built a strong position in both the OEM business and the aftermarket. There is a large market for rebuilt compressors and for compressor service. (When the display cabinet dies, prompt service turnaround is critical.)

The other end of the spectrum for Copeland is the residential air-conditioning market, where cost and efficiency are critical. Copeland seems to be competitive in the market as well, particularly with its new products.

Overall, the refrigeration and air-conditioning markets appear to be flat for the next five plus years, driven at least partially by the cyclicality of the housing market.

Less than 10 percent of Copeland's sales come from outside the United States, which is both a competitive risk and a marketing opportunity. We would hypothesize that there are no clear technological barriers to penetrating the world markets.

MANUFACTURING (COST)

All of the Copeland product lines are produced in focused manufacturing facilities. The decision was made in the late 1970s and early 1980s to focus those facilities by product and end market rather than technology or process. It appears that Copeland is a relative model of manufacturing efficiency, and at least part of its competitive advantage comes from its cost position.

The company is backward integrated into stampings (Shelby Manufacturing Company in Sidney) as well as some other key parts. In 1986, Copeland had more than 20 plants, and it is unclear how many acquisitions, divestitures, and closings the company has undergone since then.

(continued)

EXHIBIT 1 (CONTINUED)

COMPETITORS

If one defined the relevant marketplace as those domestic companies that only manufactured compressors, then the top competitor would be Tecumseh, with slightly lower market share than Copeland. Bristol would be a distant third. Tecumseh appears to be more mass-market oriented, aiming for high-volume, lower-price business. (Tecumseh followed this same strategy very successfully against Briggs and Stratton in the small-engine market, capturing customers such as Sears in the lawn-mower market.) In air conditioning there are at least some manufacturers (Carrier and Trane) that have backward integrated into compressors. It is unclear what the relative economics are in this case.

There are also clearly some overseas manufacturers, including a number of Japanese companies. One article described Whirlpool's shifting $50mm of Emerson hermetic motor sales to a foreign supplier who could provide both motors and compressors in 1985.

Our hypothesis would be that there are some major risks from both offshore and vertically integrating companies that may begin to have an impact on the compressor market with the decline in end-market growth.

EXHIBIT 2

Excerpts from Goldman Sachs Investment Research Paper on Emerson Electric Company (March 26, 1987)

Despite more than $11 million in amortization per year resulting from its acquisition, Copeland's operating income should be relatively flat in fiscal 1987 and increase more than 10 percent in fiscal 1988. However, with 2 percent to 3 percent projected gains in residential air-conditioning shipments and a slowdown in commercial construction, two important Copeland end markets, revenues should be stable. Still, we view the acquisition of Copeland, the leading manufacturer of air-conditioning and refrigeration compressors, as an excellent move.

Copeland has rather consistently maintained 10 percent operating margins, which compare quite favorably with competitors such as Tecumseh. From 1980 to 1985, sales compounded at 8 percent; in calendar 1986, they rose 12 percent to $578. Approximately 23 percent of its sales are outside the United States. Copeland's three main markets are residential air conditioning, commercial air conditioning, and commercial refrigeration. The residential air-conditioning and commercial-refrigeration sectors are extremely attractive given the large replacement markets. Copeland is the dominant company in these two markets.

In refrigeration, a malfunctioning compressor can result in substantial losses at a supermarket from spoilage. The implicit cost of a new compressor becomes almost immaterial. What is required is an efficient service/wholesaling network, and Copeland has the largest. According to industry sources, approximately 40 percent to 50 percent of the air-conditioning and refrigeration-compressor market is tied to replacements. *In sum, Copeland's strengths are its quality products, strong market shares, service franchise, and an orientation away from commodity-oriented import markets.* However, it was also the company's technology that ultimately attracted Emerson.

Copeland plans to introduce a new compressor in fiscal 1987 called the Scroll. Compared with existing technologies characterized by reciprocating and rotary compressors, the Scroll has several advantages. It is more efficient as it is almost constantly "pushing out" small amounts of coolant compared with larger and less-frequent discharges by the others.

The Scroll also has fewer moving parts, which makes it smaller and easier to produce at a lower cost. The technology behind the Scroll dates back to 1903; however, computerized design and manufacturing have finally allowed it to be produced economically and perform as expected. Hitachi is the other major producer of Scroll compressors, but Copeland's weighs less and takes up less space. Scroll technology fits in extremely well with Emerson's work on variable-speed motors. The combined technologies offer significant energy savings as the Scroll is highly efficient at various speeds. The Scroll compressor will initially be targeted at the residential air-conditioning market.

EXHIBIT 3A

Excerpts from Emerson Board Meeting, May 1988

Copeland Focused on High-Volume, Value-Oriented Markets

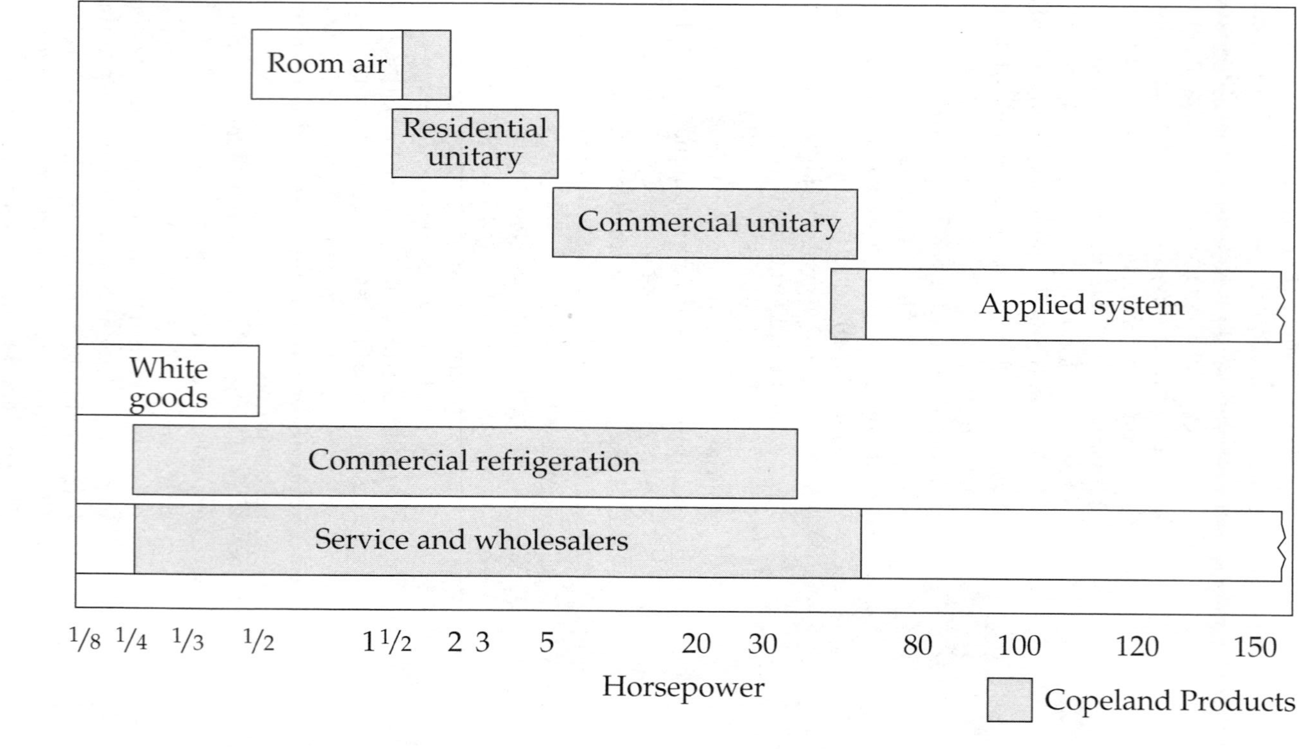

EXHIBIT 3B

Excerpts from Emerson Board Meeting, May 1988

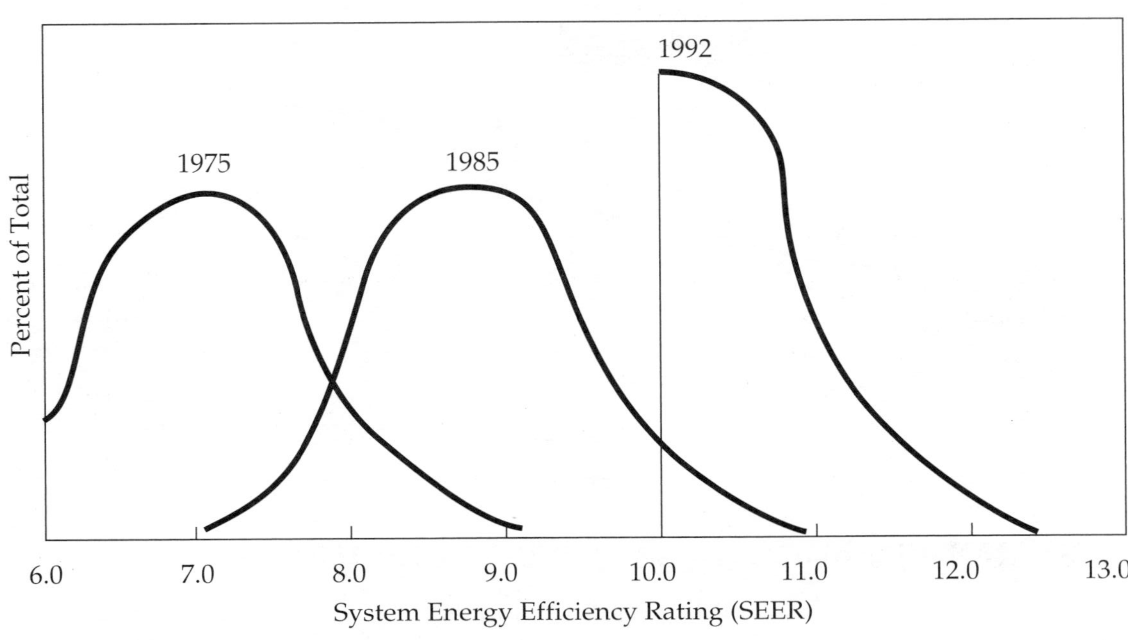

EXHIBIT 3C

Excerpts from Emerson Board Meeting, May 1988

U.S. Residential Air-Conditioning Market

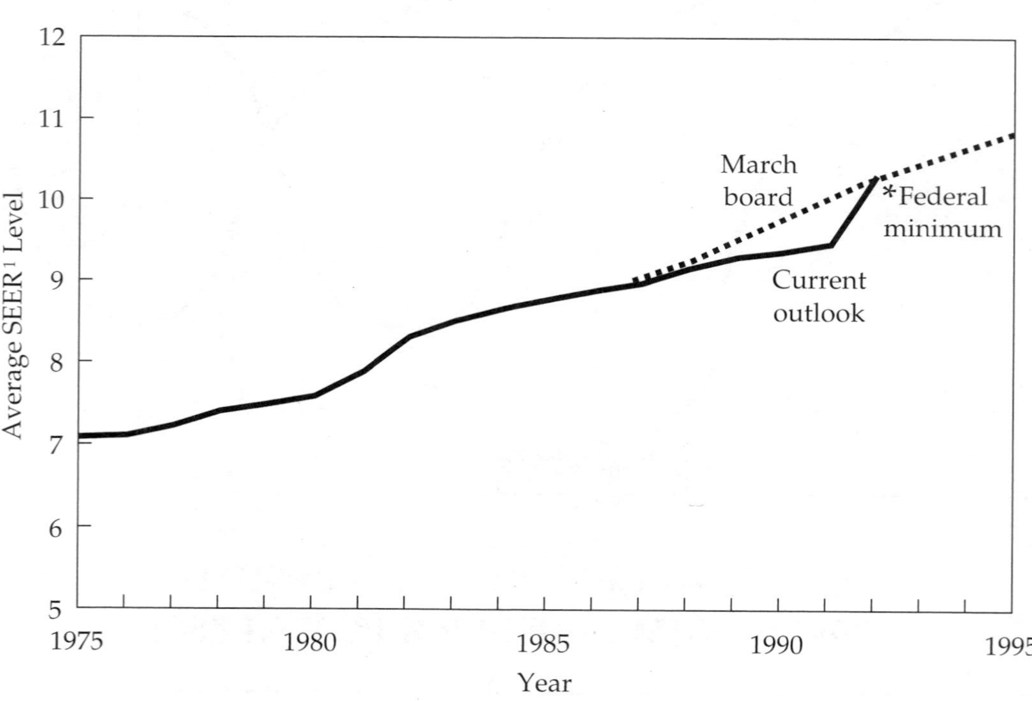

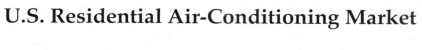

[1]System Energy Efficiency Rating.

EXHIBIT 3 D

Excerpts from Emerson Board Meeting, May 1988

Unitary A/C Scroll Demand, 1½- to 5-Ton

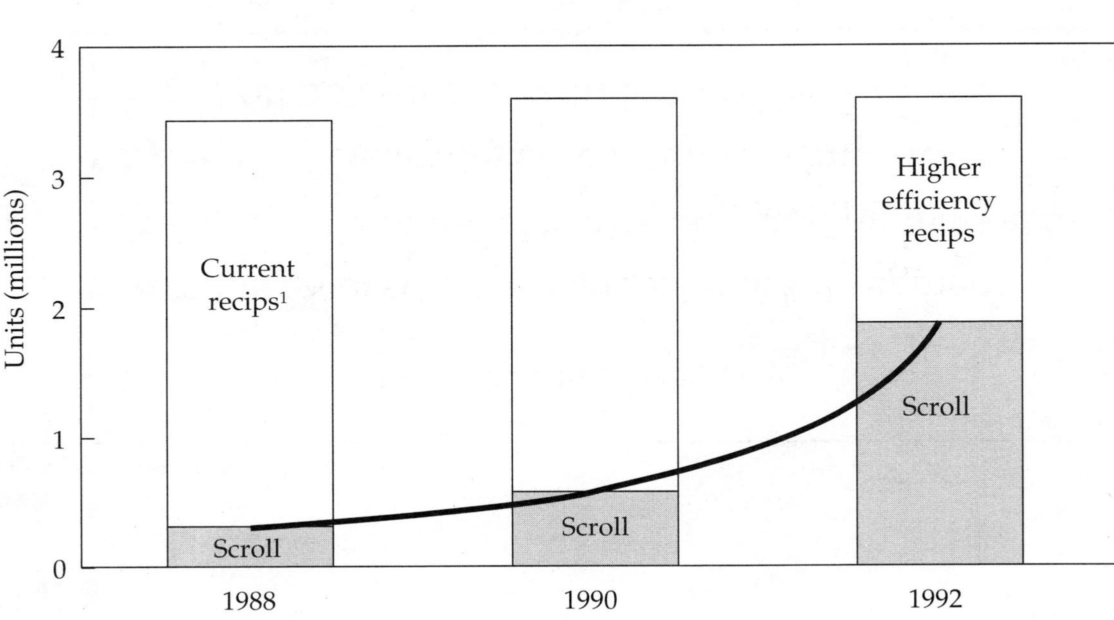

[1]Reciprocating compressor.

EXHIBIT 3E

Excerpts from Emerson Board Meeting, May 1988

Scroll Market Summary

- Scroll is focused on the largest market segment.
- It serves 80% of the U.S. air-conditioning market.
- System efficiency levels continue to improve.
- Scroll offers best cost solution to OEMs.

EXHIBIT 3F

Excerpts from Emerson Board Meeting, May 1988

Eight Major Manufacturers Control 87% of the Residential Market

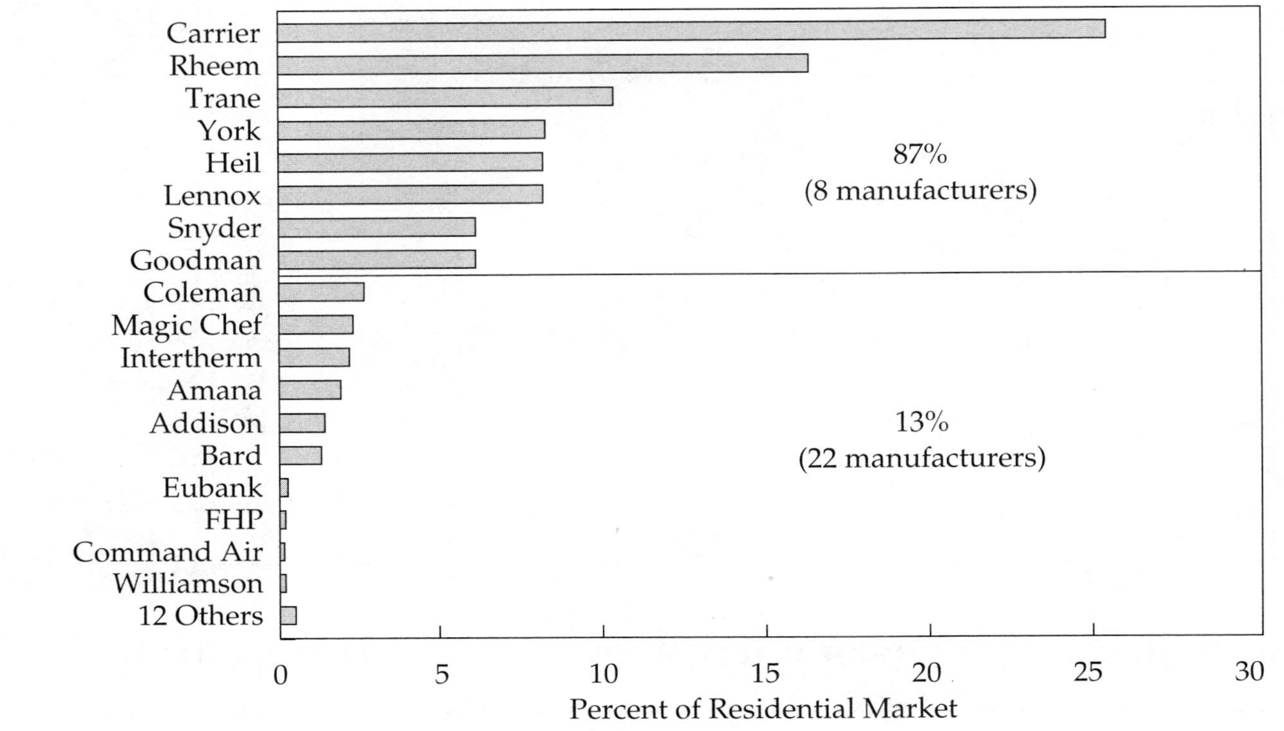

EXHIBIT 3G

Excerpts from Emerson Board Meeting, May 1988

Share Shift Occurring among Major Residential Manufacturers

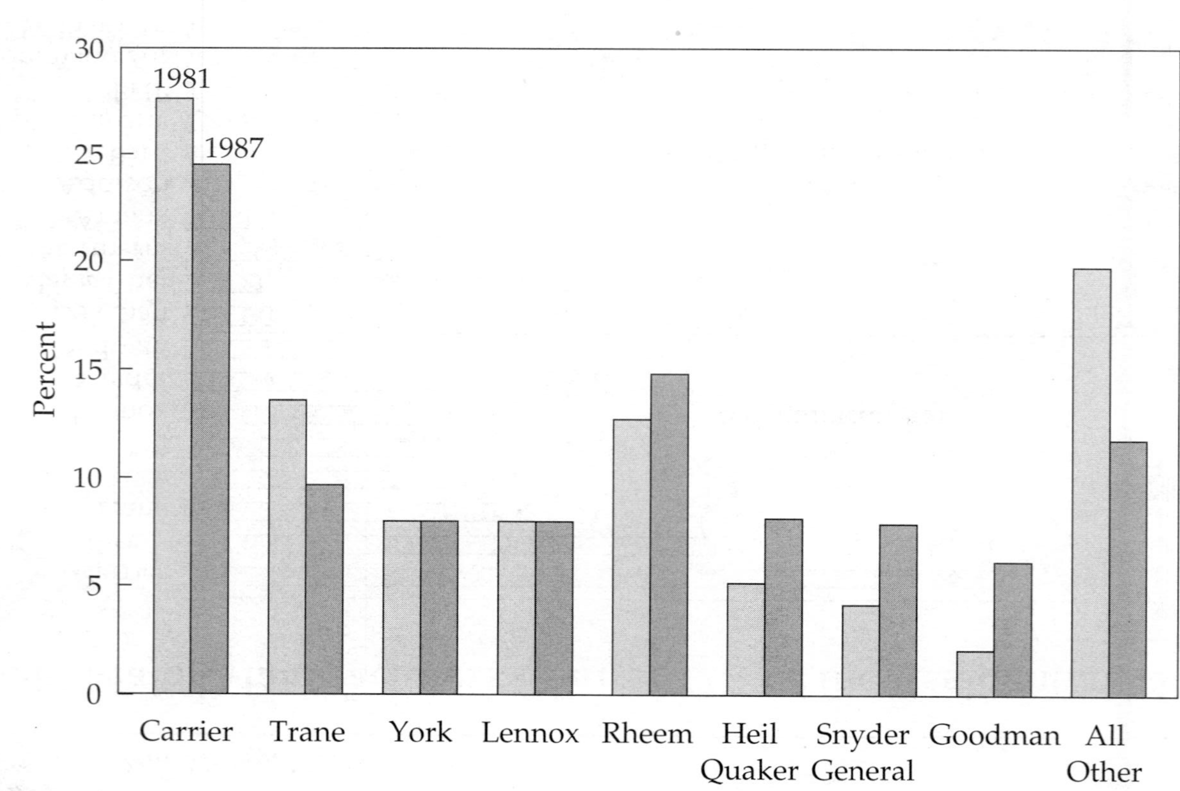

EXHIBIT 3H

Excerpts from Emerson Board Meeting, May 1988

Scroll Reduces Cost for OEMs
System Design Options
Heat Pump

With Scroll

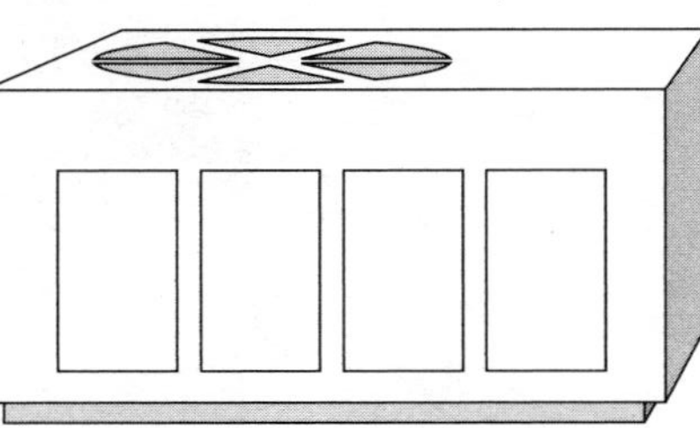

With Recip

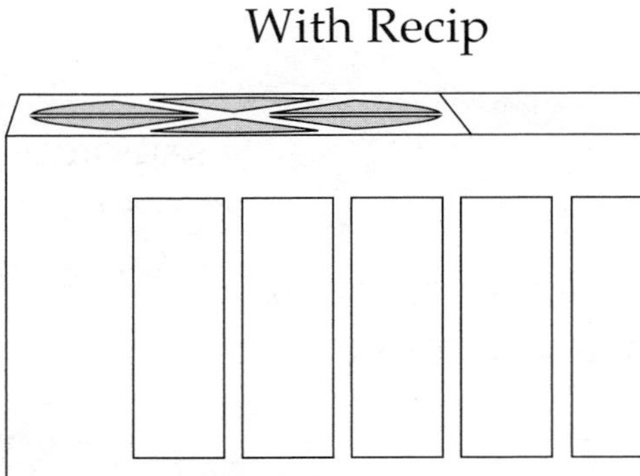

Cost Savings:
- Coil
- Cabinet
- Components

EXHIBIT 31

Excerpts from Emerson Board Meeting, May 1988

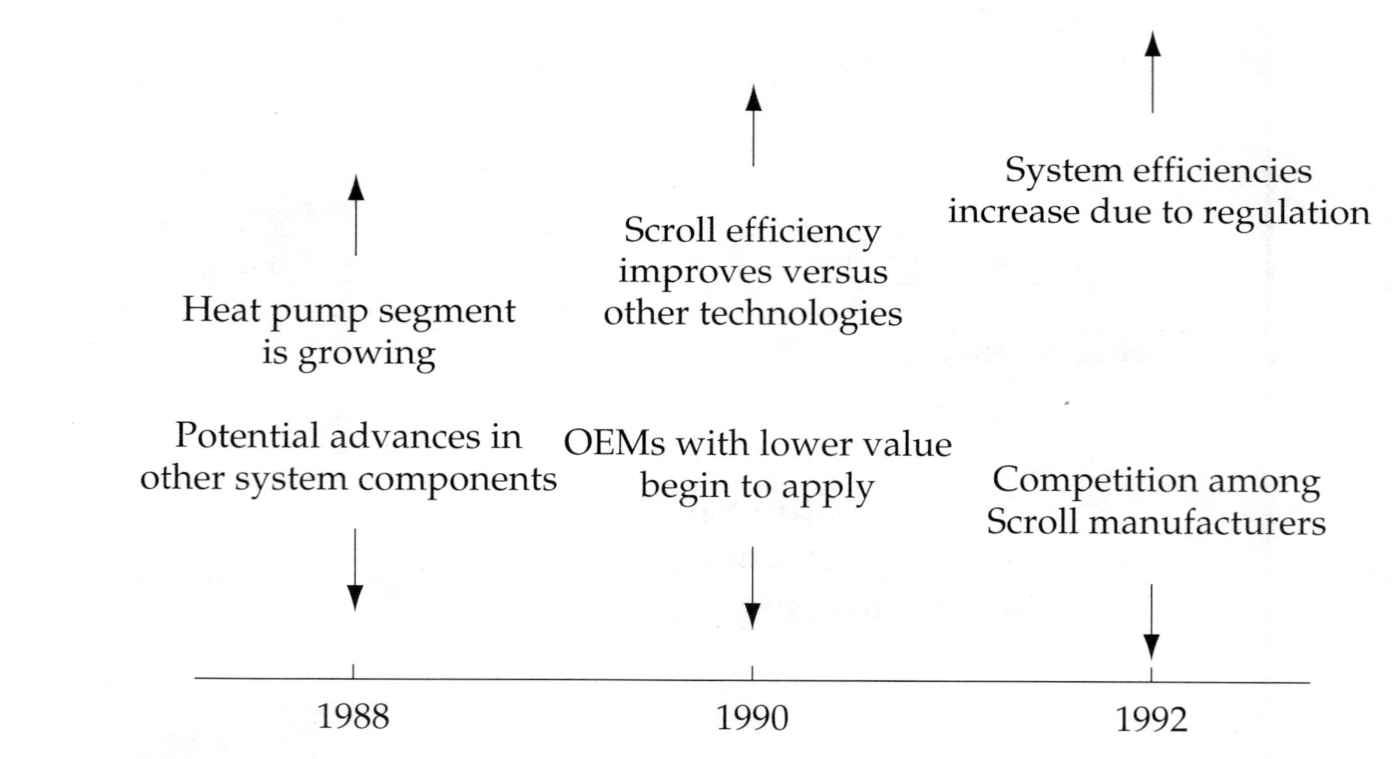

EXHIBIT 3 J

Excerpts from Emerson Board Meeting, May 1988

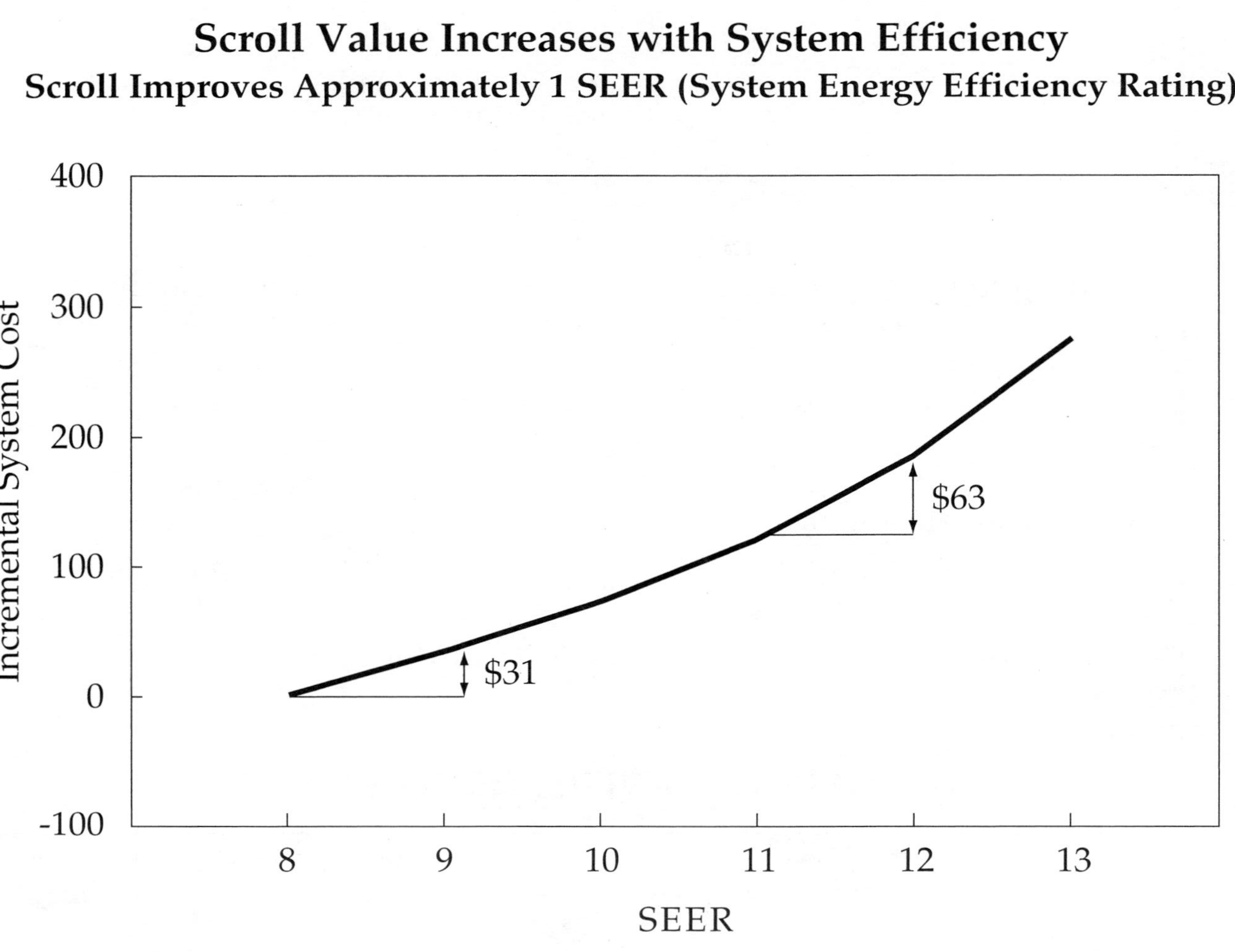

EXHIBIT 3 K

Excerpts from Emerson Board Meeting, May 1988

Scroll Value Is Higher in Heat Pumps

Heat Pump

- Larger coils
- Handle more refrigerant
  - -suction accumulators
  - -start kits
  - -crankcase heaters
- Scroll simplifies design task

Air Conditioning

- Smaller coils
- Less refrigerant
  - -crankcase heater only

Scroll Value	Heat Pump	Air Conditioner
Coil	$18	$11
Cabinet	7	4
Components:		
suction accumulator	10	—
crankcase heater	3	3
	$38	$18

EXHIBIT 3L

Excerpts from Emerson Board Meeting, May 1988

Japan Produces More Compressors Than Any Other Nation

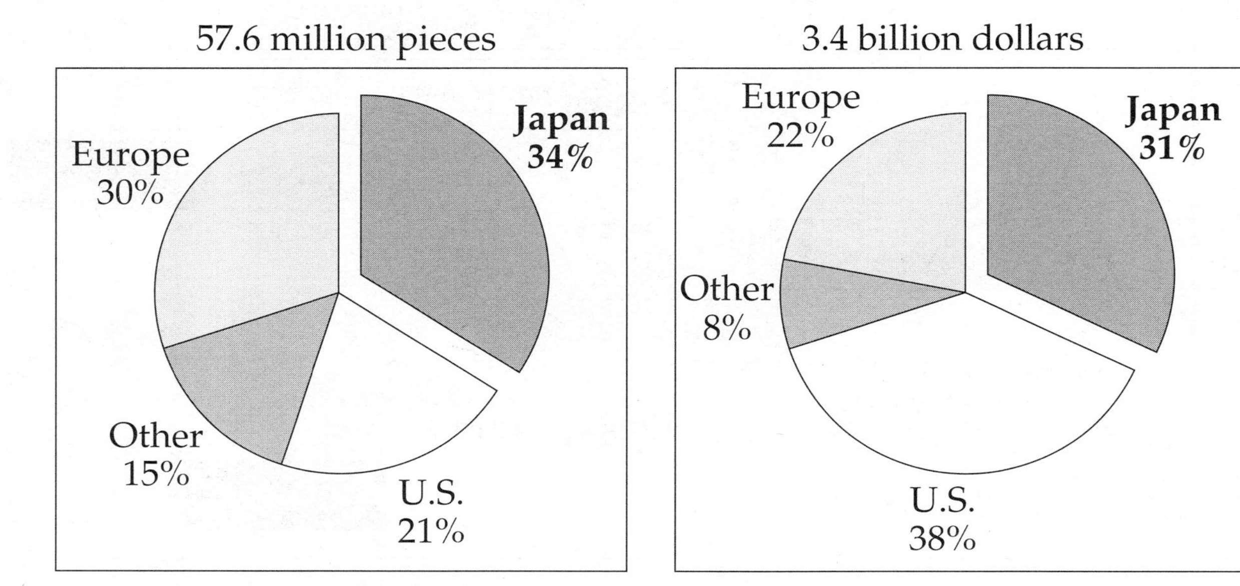

EXHIBIT 3M

Excerpts from Emerson Board Meeting, May 1988

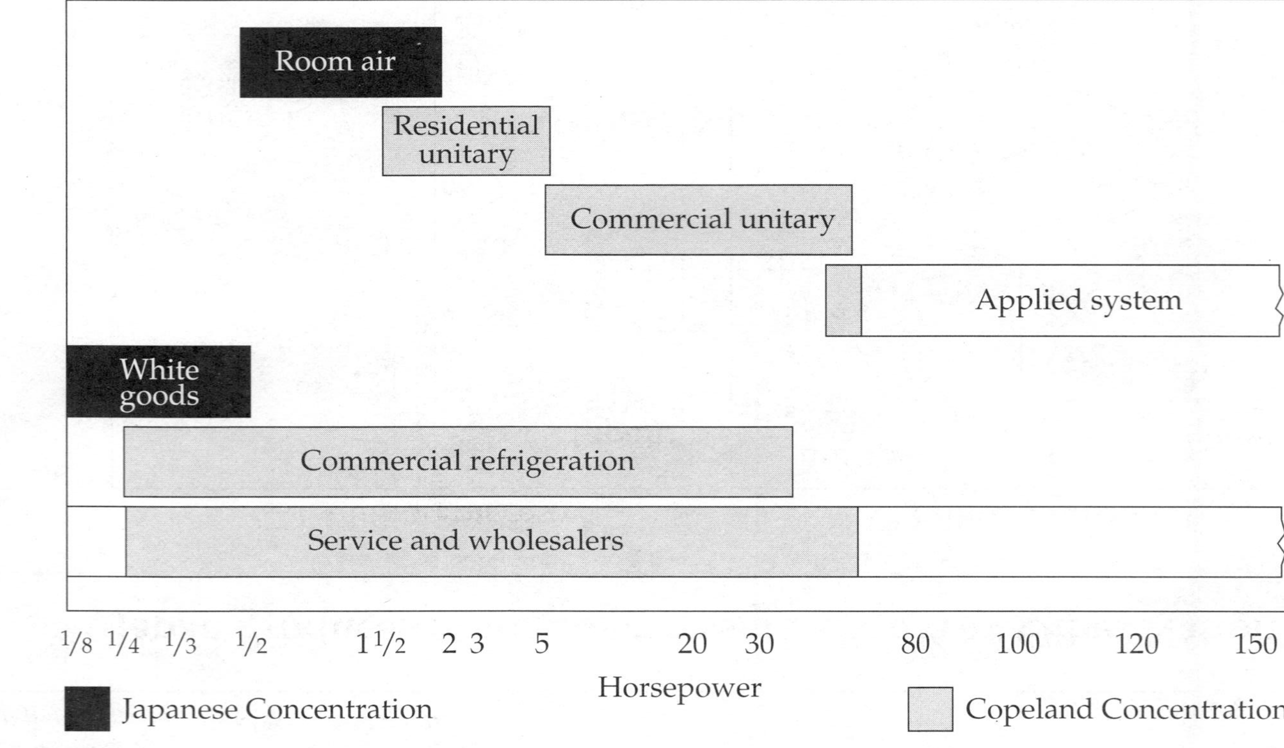

EXHIBIT 3N

Excerpts from Emerson Board Meeting, May 1988

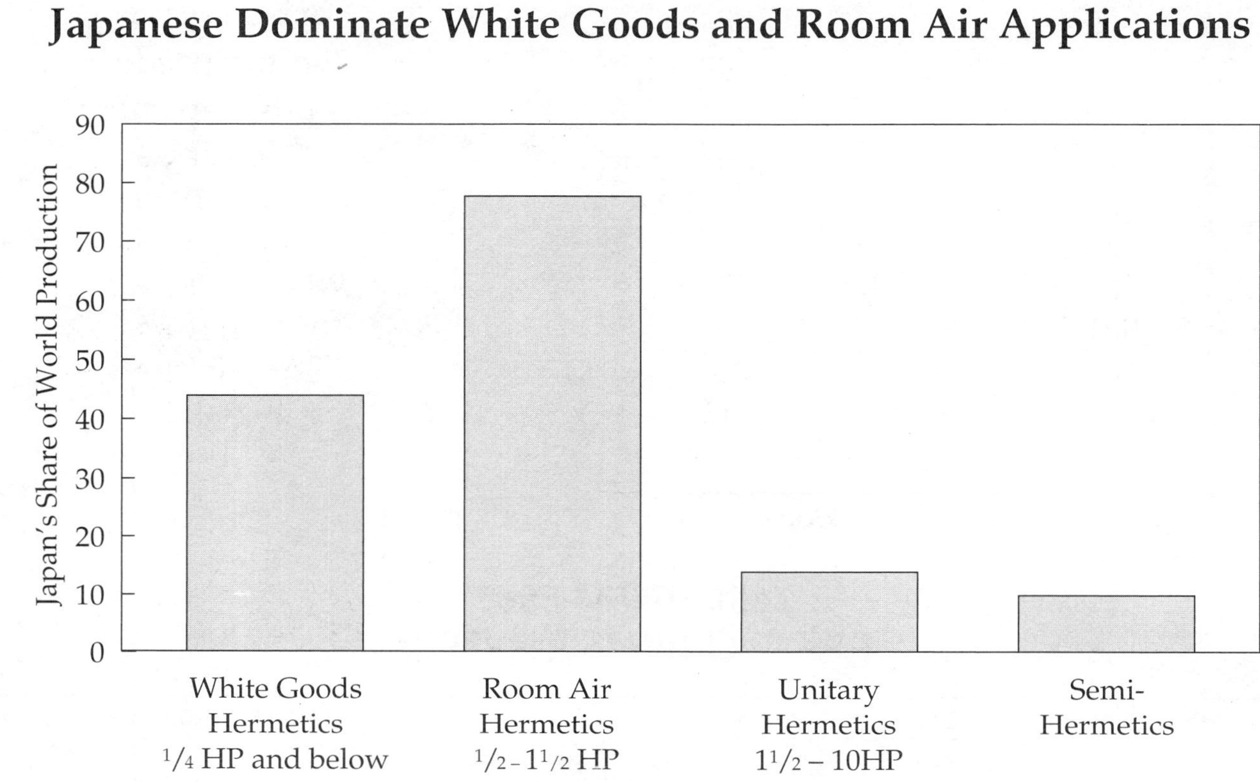

EXHIBIT 30

Excerpts from Emerson Board Meeting, May 1988

Japanese Scroll Demand
1988 versus 1992

	Actual 1988	Forecast 1992
Demand		
• Hitachi	110	140
• Melco	20	220
• MHI	20	130
• Matsushita	20	100
• Daikin	—	230
• Toshiba	—	120
• Sanyo	—	60
Total demand	**170**	**1,000**
Capacity (total)	250	1,500
Excess capacity	80	500
Exports	10	300–400

EXHIBIT 3P

Excerpts from Emerson Board Meeting, May 1988

Summary

- The Japanese are major competitors in the world compressor industry.
- Japan has succeeded in markets not targeted by Copeland.
- In the future, the Japanese will place more emphasis on compressors greater than 2 horsepower.
- Several Japanese A/C OEMs will develop Scroll production capabilities.
- By 1992, the Japanese could have 400,000 units available for export.
- Technology and cost advantages protect Copeland from Japanese competition in the short term.
- In the long run, Copeland must prepare to be a significant player in Japan.

EXHIBIT 3 Q

Excerpts from Emerson Board Meeting, May 1988

Copeland Competitive Position Forecast for 1992

	Copeland Scroll	Best Japanese Scroll
E.E.R. (CHEER)*	19.5	18.0
Cumulative Production volume	3.0M	1.0–1.5M
Production capacity	5x M	x M

*CHEER is the rating standard used by the company to rate compressor performance. Higher compressor efficiency at CHEER equates to lower system operating cost.

EXHIBIT 3R

Excerpts from Emerson Board Meeting, May 1988

Scroll Marketing Strategy Summary

- Target Scroll to highest value segments
- Target recips to lowest value segments
- Minimize penetration of Scroll competitors
- Increase total market share
- Opportunity for strategic alliance with Carrier or Trane to further increase share
- Flexibility is augmented with CR6* capacity

*Higher efficiency reciprocating compressor

EXHIBIT 3S

Excerpts from Emerson Board Meeting, May 1988

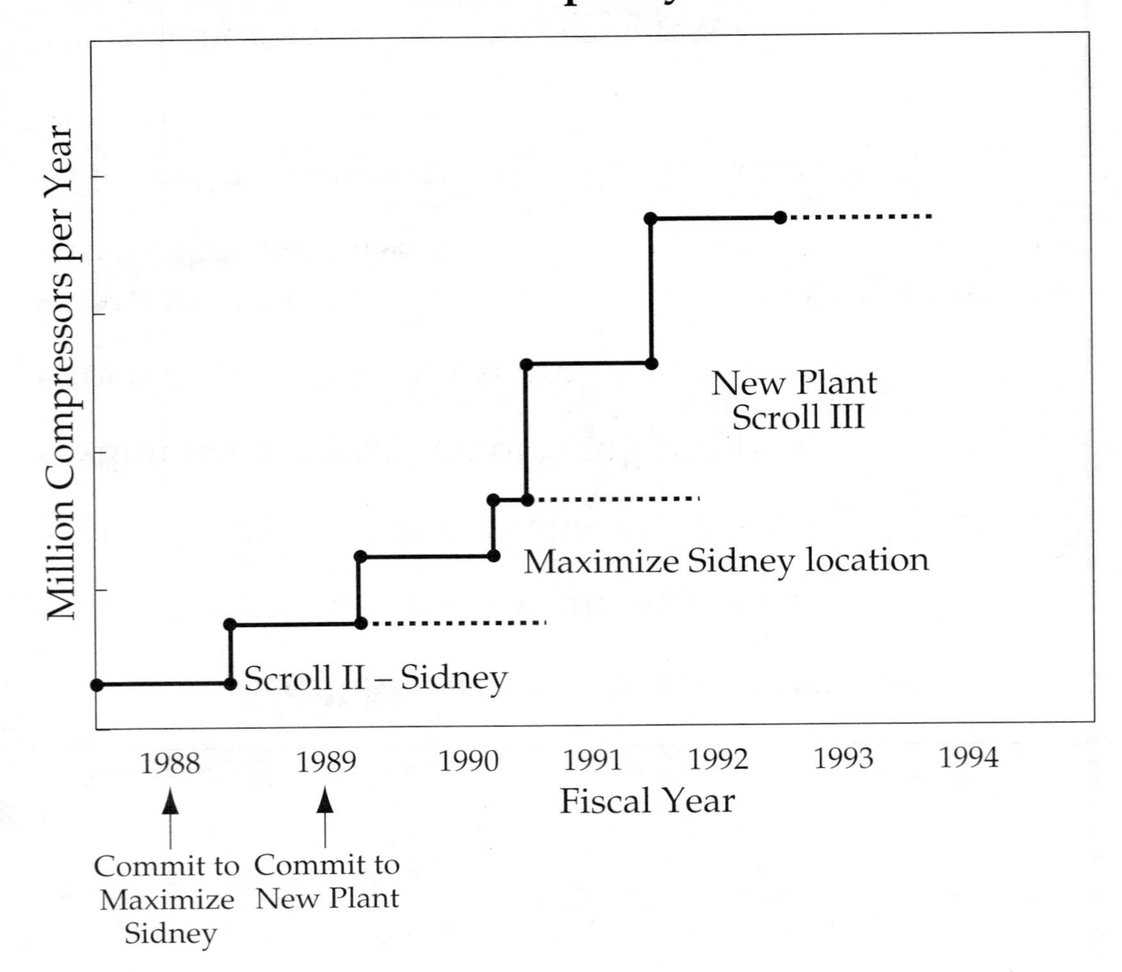

CASE 13

FALLS RIVER CENTER, INC.

Betsy Dalgliesh watched her new Macintosh as the screen saver sent a spray of rainbow-hued fireworks across the screen. As she looked at her computer, she wondered if this would be just what she and Rick Haupt, cofounder of Falls River, needed to get organized. Until now a jumbled mess of paperwork thrown in old shoe boxes represented the filing system for Falls River.

Somehow Dalgliesh wasn't convinced that this new computer, the Quicken software package, and a few sessions with their accountant would be enough to carry their growing experiential learning company to the next stage. Just being "people people and not businesspeople" had been enough to turn Haupt and Dalgliesh's belief in experiential learning into a profitable business; but the strains and pains of growth were all too evident. Falls River was at a turning point. If they wanted to expand in a growing market, Dalgliesh knew it would take more than just a computer. But then again, it wasn't clear that fast growth was what they wanted.

INDUSTRY BACKGROUND

The first outdoor education program was developed during World War II by Kurt Hahn, an expatriate German educator, to train young British sailors in marine and survival skills. He called this program "outward bound" because this was the expression sailors used when they were going out to sea.[1]

Outward Bound USA was chartered in 1961 and ran the first U.S. wilderness program in Colorado in 1962. By 1993, Outward Bound conducted more than 600 courses a year for such diverse groups as inner-city children and cancer patients.

Few of these programs were designed for the corporate world. To fill this need, many new programs sprung up, and corporate adventure training expanded rapidly so that by 1992 more than 100 training organizations provided corporate adventure or experiential learning.[2] These programs ranged in size from a one-person operation to big programs like Pecos River, which required several hundred employees to run a 1,000-person program in a day. People involved in experiential learning program organizations formed a grassroots association, the Association for Experiential Education, based in Boulder, Colorado, to provide a psychological as well as physical meeting place for practitioners. The association sponsored annual conferences and addressed issues associated with very diverse areas of hands-on learning, including, for example, apprenticeship.

Adventure or experiential learning programs focused on building leadership and teamwork skills, and generally fell into two main categories: wilderness and "outdoor-centered" programs. The programs could last from a few hours to several weeks, as

This case was written by Christine Lotze, Darden 1992, and Jamie Berger, Darden 1992, under the supervision of Professor L. J. Bourgeois.

in the case of some wilderness programs. The wilderness programs involved outdoor living and vigorous activities such as mountain climbing or white-water rafting. Outdoor-centered programs consisted of "high ropes" activities, which took place at elevations high above the ground, and "low ropes," which involved either team problem solving or individual initiative. Wilderness programs and high ropes were more expensive, with wilderness programs averaging $2,800 per participant. Low ropes averaged $300 per participant.[3] Another estimate of the cost of low ropes per participant was from $100 to $300 per day with $600 to $1,200 being the range for high ropes.[4]

One study found the proportion of wilderness and outdoor-centered programs to be 23 percent and 77 percent, respectively. Of outdoor-centered program participants, 70 percent were top executives or middle-level managers, 20 percent were sales representatives or supervisors, and 10 percent were other nonmanagers. The wilderness training programs focused on developing leadership and decision-making skills, while the outdoor-centered programs focused on team building, self-esteem, leadership, problem solving, decision making, and a sense of corporate ownership.[5] One study estimated that 13.8 percent of companies used outdoor education training. Pecos River, the largest of the outdoor education training centers with 400 full-time employees, had a gross income of approximately $20 million in 1991.[6]

Despite debate over the programs' effectiveness with regard to the transfer of the course learning to actual business situations, the experiential learning programs were expected to continue to grow in number. Bob Carr, president of the Association for Experienced Based Training, estimated that, in 1990, more than $227 million, or one-half of 1 percent of the total spending of corporate America on training, was spent on experiential-based training. He predicted "that figure will increase significantly in the next five years."[7]

History of Falls River

Betsy Dalgliesh and Rick Haupt came to Falls River with a wide range of experiences relating to experiential learning. Dalgliesh received an undergraduate degree in education and pursued graduate work in social psychology, educational foundations, and counseling and experiential education. Her initial contact with experiential learning, during her early 20s, was with a wilderness program that worked with schools in northern Georgia. Later, with Outward Bound in their professional development programs, she gained much grounding in the field. Dalgliesh also at one point joined the Santa Fe Mountain Center in New Mexico—a wilderness program for adjudicated youth. Here she became interested in building a business and developed a fund-raising program that continues to be successful for this organization. In 1984 Dalgliesh became involved in professional development with a consulting group in New Hampshire. Dalgliesh had also found that her work with children in summer camp for the previous 21 years complemented these experiences. (See Exhibit 1 for a biographical sketch.)

Since his experience as a Peace Corps Volunteer in South America, Rick Haupt had been a licensed professional counselor. He became interested in experiential learning after doing Outward Bound work in the Peace Corps, and in 1986 he continued his work with Outward Bound as an instructor. Haupt and Dalgliesh met at Outward Bound and were later reconnected through mutual friends in Charlottesville, Virginia, in 1987. Dalgliesh was doing experiential learning work, and

EXHIBIT **1**

Betsy Dalgliesh Biographical Sketch

Betsy Dalgliesh has been committed to creating positive learning experiences for a variety of populations for almost 20 years. After receiving a B.A. from Hollins College, she trained at Dartmouth College's Outward Bound Leadership Program and with Wolfcreek Wilderness School in Georgia. She worked as an environmental educator, outdoor instructor, and camp director, emphasizing the connections between personal growth and the natural environment.

Subsequent work with North Carolina Outward Bound's Professional Development Program established her belief that business and community groups can greatly benefit from opportunities to experience challenge, self- and team reliance, and adventure. As president and co-owner of Falls River Center in Charlottesville, she designs and conducts action-learning programs that utilize outdoor activities to stimulate leadership and develop effective interpersonal skills. She is the 1994 recipient of the Association for Experiential Education's Practitioner of the Year Award.

One particular interest is in program development. She has designed outdoor programs for youth leaders, families in crisis, teachers, and managers. At Santa Fe Mountain Center, she developed a fund-raising program to support wilderness experiences as adjunct therapy for at-risk youth. She also participated on the coordinating team that initiated a national leadership conference for minority youth.

As an affiliate consultant with Action Learning Associates and Peak Performance of Colorado Springs, Colorado; Hollander, Kerrick Cappy and Associates of Peterborough, New Hampshire; Blue Ridge Consultants of Sugar Grove, North Carolina; TeamCraft of Austin, Texas; and North Carolina Outward Bound School, she has worked in leadership and team development programs for Federal Express, Frito-Lay, Hoescht-Celanese, GE, Anheuser-Busch, Trammel Crow, Dana Corporation, Ciba-Geigy, Dial Page, and Carolina Power & Light.

Dalgliesh lives in Albemarle County near the Blue Ridge Mountains of Virginia, where she enjoys hiking, mountain biking, canoeing, and cross-country skiing with her husband and their dog. Another passion is adventure travel. She speaks Italian and has a working knowledge of French and Spanish.

Haupt thought she might be interested in his idea of building a ropes course on his land. They met every week for a year, and Dalgliesh, who was traveling a great deal for a Harcourt Brace Jovanovich leadership program in Florida, realized she could do the same work in Charlottesville. They decided ropes training had real potential in the area, and building the course would be a great way for Haupt to utilize his 80-acre wooded land in Afton, Virginia, and to spend more time outdoors. (Exhibit 2 contains a biographical sketch on Haupt.)

EXHIBIT 2

Rick Haupt Biographical Sketch

Vice president and co-owner of Falls River Center, Inc., Rick Haupt draws much of his experience from his time spent as an Outward Bound instructor and at Project Adventure corporate training programs where experiential learning was combined with ropes course activities. Since 1988 he has been intensely involved with Falls River in its leadership, team development, and corporate training programs.

Haupt attended Ohio State University for undergraduate studies where he also played halfback under football coach Woody Hayes and was on the 1961 national championship team. He did his graduate studies in psychiatry at The Johns Hopkins School of Medicine and graduated in 1977.

In 1964 Haupt served for two years as a Peace Corps Volunteer in the Central American Republic of Panama. He has traveled extensively in Central and South America, Puerto Rico, and the Caribbean, and throughout Europe. He is fluent in Spanish.

Since 1980 Haupt has been in private practice as a psychotherapist doing individual, family, and couples counseling. More and more he has combined the issues of trust, communication styles, and teamwork on the ropes course as a therapeutic tool for families and couples.

Born in a small farming community in the Midwest, Haupt has lived on the East Coast since 1970. He currently lives in rural Virginia with his wife and three daughters.

His hobbies include jogging, biking, tennis, rock climbing, white-water canoeing, scuba diving, canyon hiking, and family wilderness outings.

While neither were particularly interested in running their own business—experiential or otherwise—they agreed that doing so could be fun and creative, and meet their common individual goals. Dalgliesh, in talking with teachers and administrators in the surrounding school system, thought that there was a demand for a program that encouraged and developed teamwork.

In 1988, each provided one-half of the $20,000 initial investment to found the Falls River Center, Inc. Their vision for the business was to stay flexible and to customize their programs to meet individual needs. They felt that Falls River should be a place away from the workplace where people were encouraged to grow both professionally and spiritually. "We believe that when people participate in their own learning it can be very powerful," explained Dalgliesh. "Falls River's method is to develop a process where the group can analyze its own problems and challenges and then learn how to overcome them."

The company's overriding goal was quite simple—to have fun. The founders planned on actively running the programs and working directly with the groups, as well as customizing and planning the programs, and taking care of the more arcane side of the business.

The course was designed for one-day, task-oriented sessions, rather than the long programs offered by Outward Bound and others. (See Exhibit 3 for the Falls River mission statement.) Outward Bound was brought in to build the course and to train Haupt and Dalgliesh and eight new facilitators on course techniques and safety procedures. The facilitators were part-time employees with varying degrees of knowledge in experiential training, but most had a background in counseling and group dynamics. By the spring of 1988 the Falls River complex was opened with an initial rush of business from public schools and hospitals in the area.

Two of the facilitators, Peggy Amacker and Scott Ziemer, had been part of Falls River from the start. Amacker, a native of Charlottesville, studied communications and business at North Carolina State University and subsequently worked in administration for two years in an outdoor education program in New Hampshire/Peterborough at Boston University's 860-acre Sergeant Camp. She then joined an international program in Seattle that involved dialog training for children living in conflict areas. Amacker specialized in the Middle East and trained Palestinian and Jewish children in dialog training to run programs for their peers in their home countries. Amacker found out about Falls River through an ad in a local paper that called for people with ropes course experience to come and "test" a new course. After signing on, Amacker served as both a trainer and an administrator, providing bookkeeping and logistical support.

Ziemer, an armed forces dependent, moved frequently during his childhood. After receiving a B.A. in social science from Hiram college in Hiram, Ohio, he

EXHIBIT 3

Falls River Center Mission Statement

Our mission is to provide the highest quality action-oriented training programs to intact work teams and the community at large with a goal of professional and personal revitalization.

We accomplish this by developing a safe physical and emotional environment for our participants and providing the highest level of safety and ethical standards in the experiential education field. We respect individual differences, encourage sound environment practices, and value our role of service to the community.

Falls River Center is open to all people regardless of race, gender, age, sexual orientation, or physical abilities.

Statement of Ethical Practices

Falls River Center is committed to providing the highest level of quality in programming, staff, and business operations. Our staff agrees to demonstrate and develop the concepts of compromise, cooperation, empathy, acceptance, and compassion, both in facilitation of programs and in the operation of the corporation. We demonstrate respect for others' rights, styles, and standards. We will, to the best of our ability, maintain the highest level of emotional and physical safety.

worked as a carpenter and eventually co-owned a construction business. Later, he directed the ropes course and counseling services at a drug and alcohol treatment center for children. After hearing about Falls River from an acquaintance of Haupt and Dalgliesh, in 1989 Ziemer came to Charlottesville working part-time in carpentry; as a tree surgeon; as a builder, designer, and maintainer of equipment and grounds; and as a facilitator at Falls River.

MARKETING

Initially, there were no marketing efforts at Falls River because Dalgliesh knew the Charlottesville schools were interested in participating in experiential learning programs and Haupt had several therapeutic groups that were interested. They recognized a growing demand for the type of programs they planned to offer and were encouraged by local hospitals and schools to open Falls River.

Haupt and Dalgliesh were encouraged by friends to pursue target marketing immediately, but they planned to "get really good" before they expanded their marketing endeavors. This objective, combined with having enough clients (30 program-days per year) to keep them in business for quite a while, allowed Haupt and Dalgliesh to avoid marketing aggressively. In their second year of operation, the Albermarle County school system was their biggest client; however, with the recession and budget cuts in late 1990, business was much harder to generate.

It was informal word of mouth, or personal marketing, that brought the contract that marked a turning point for Falls River. At a Charlottesville Christmas party in December of 1989, Dalgliesh talked about Falls River and its objectives with a man who had expressed considerable interest in the programs. "Would you be able to run 240 people through your program?" he asked. The person at the cocktail party, John Rosenblum, dean of the Darden Graduate School of Business at the University of Virginia, was very interested in incorporating the Falls River program into the second-year MBA leadership course, which would push the course along the "new wave" in management education.

While they had never dealt with groups that large, Dalgliesh realized that becoming associated with a business school with a national reputation could be tremendous for the long-term growth of Falls River, not to mention the revenue involved. Afterward, several Darden faculty members came to tour Falls River. In the spring of 1989, it was agreed that in October the 240 second-year MBAs would come to Falls River in groups of 60 per day, over four days. This initial contract resulted in several annual contracts with the Darden School: three years of the second-year MBA program, three years of Darden's flagship senior executive program ("TEP"), and six to eight clients from TEP-participant mailings, as well as an additional annual Darden executive program with the Bacardi Corporation. The contacts from the TEP and executive programs opened new avenues for business.

With the Darden contracts in place, Haupt and Dalgliesh began formal marketing efforts. Marketing decisions were difficult since Haupt, Dalgliesh, Ziemer, and Amacker had no formal marketing experience. This lack of knowledge coupled with their lack of a defined target group made their marketing efforts even more perplexing. All four knew they must bring in other business to be able to drop their less profitable groups. Knowing that corporate groups tended to be less price sensitive than other groups, they wanted to pursue these groups so they might also be able to provide their services to other nonprofit groups that could not afford to pay the full rate.

While word of mouth was their most successful form of advertising to date, they also ran a series of ads in the two local papers, *The Daily Progress* and *The Observer*, and in a local business journal. They sent out an extensive mailing to local business leaders, school systems, many groups at the University of Virginia, and others who had expressed interest. (See Exhibit 4 for Falls River brochure.) Unfortunately, they were not able to gauge the success of the ads. Haupt and Dalgliesh thought the mailing had a 0 percent return, while Amacker felt that the budget cuts announced at UVA (University of Virginia) the week of the mailing thwarted the effort.

Amacker found that in eliminating groups that were not cost-effective, Falls River began to get a reputation for being "expensive and not giving breaks." This, she said, was rather unfortunate since "many groups that might not even consider us would have found our rate within their price range."

Prices at Falls River were determined on a case-by-case basis. As of 1990 they had defined three price categories:

- Students up to high-school level
- Professional and community groups
- Organizational rate/corporate

Falls River did not make any profits on the student rates; it only hoped to cover its costs. Profit came from corporate programs with rates ranging from $125 to $250 per person, which was still below the average charge of $300 per person for similar programs. For a group of 100 to 300 persons, $150 per person was considered a good rate in the industry. Falls River had bid on jobs and had been selected even though it was the high bidder. Dalgliesh believed this was a result of the personal attention Falls River afforded its clients. Students were offered a one-half day rate averaging $30 to $40 per person and $50 to $60 for elementary or middle-school students. Other companies, such as Pecos River, charged far more than Falls River's $125–$250 range for a day. Pecos River might charge $1,000 per participant for a similar program and pay its facilitators less than half of what Falls River did. The cost of a Falls River program could also include a consulting fee, depending on the work done for a company. For example, if considerable work was required prior to the program, an additional consulting fee ranging from $100 to $1,500 per day might be charged. Dalgliesh felt very strongly about telling corporations that their fee rates allowed Falls River to offer programs to deserving groups not able to afford the standard pricing.

Dalgliesh and Haupt also wanted to educate potential consumers about Falls River's unique services. Falls River offered client group programs and "open" programs. Client groups usually involved intact work groups or companies in transition and required a needs assessment. For a needs assessment, Falls River would gather information from a contact person and/or as many people in the company as it could and ascertain the client's current state, desired state, and how the program could facilitate transition to the desired state.

Open programs allowed couples or individuals to engage in the Falls River experience. Dalgliesh found these "messier to run" since participants had vastly different agendas and goals for the program, and these were usually determined at the program rather than being carefully planned in advance. The number of client-days of open programs was low compared to client group program days; with approximately

EXHIBIT 4

Falls River Center Promotional Brochure

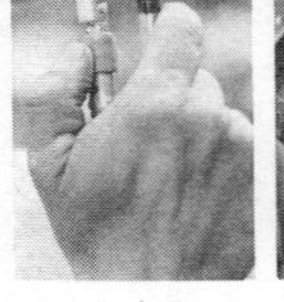

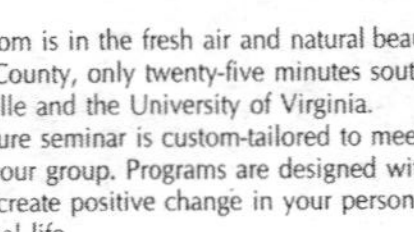

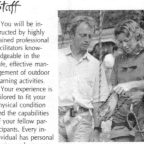

Falls River Center

Falls River is an adventure-based training center that offers dynamic opportunities for personal growth through safe, challenging activities.

Programs offered by Falls River can be used to achieve the following outcomes:

- **Improve individual and group planning, decision-making, and problem-solving processes.**
- **Enhance self-esteem and self confidence.**
- **Learn to manage stress and to function effectively in difficult situations.**
- **Develop team cohesion and team effectiveness.**

Your classroom is in the fresh air and natural beauty of Albemarle County, only twenty-five minutes south of Charlottesville and the University of Virginia.

Each adventure seminar is custom-tailored to meet the needs of your group. Programs are designed with your input to create positive change in your personal and professional life.

"Not a day goes by that I don't associate back to the Ropes Course and use the strength I gained to get through tough times. By showing me how I can face fear (the Course) has allowed me to take new risks. If I can do the Ropes Course, then I can do anything!"
Elaine Connors, Owner
Charlottesville restaurant

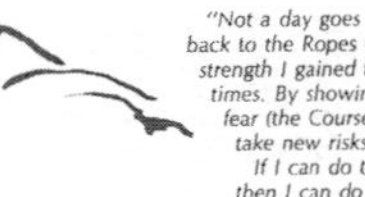

Many Falls River programs take place at the Low Ropes Challenge Course, which consists of courses built of ropes and cable no higher than five feet from the ground. Here you will embark on a carefully crafted series of interactive tasks designed to build trust and increase your ability to be an effective member of a problem-solving team. Each event presents a different challenge in which you must discover the resources within your team and work cooperatively to achieve your goal.

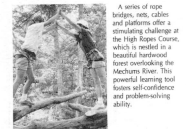

A series of rope bridges, nets, cables and platforms offer a stimulating challenge at the High Ropes Course, which is nestled in a beautiful hardwood forest overlooking the Mechums River. This powerful learning tool fosters self-confidence and problem-solving ability.

"The challenges offered at Falls River give educators, who often work in isolation, the opportunity to see how their cooperative efforts can exceed individual efforts in reaching goals."
Pamela Moran,
Staff Development Coordinator,
Albemarle County Public Schools

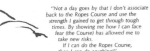

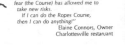

Following each exercise, time is reserved to debrief and explore how your group chose to work together, and how well your actions worked. You are encouraged to support each other with feedback and to share your observations. This often creates a forum for drawing analogies to the work environment.

The program demonstrates how a group of individuals can increase its resources and meet significant challenges when its members choose to work cooperatively as a team.

Underlying all is the sense of camaraderie gained by working together and enjoying each other in a beautiful outdoor setting.

"The ride on the "Zip Line" is a real experience in letting go of control and trusting something outside yourself...the course is very good for building group cohesion and cooperative spirit. Going through this course is a wonderful life experience."
Peter Sheras, Director of Clinical Psychology,
University of Virginia

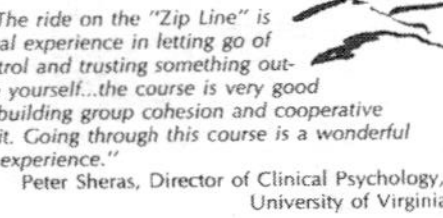

Managers of large and small corporations, administrators of schools and hospitals, educators from all levels, and helping professionals from social agencies participate in programs offered by Falls River. Students from area schools and churches have benefited from their experiences as well.

Falls River Center, Inc. is an Institutional Member of The Association for Experiential Education and The Virginia Association for Outdoor Adventure Education.

Photos by Phillip Beaurline. Cover photo and photo of Low Ropes Course by Cynthia DeCanio.

Staff

You will be instructed by highly trained professional facilitators knowledgeable in the safe, effective management of outdoor learning activities.

Your experience is tailored to fit your physical condition and the capabilities of your fellow participants. Every individual has personal choice and you are encouraged to determine your personal limits.

Falls River Center, Inc. was founded in 1989 and is owned and operated by Rick Haupt and Betsy Caldwell Dalgliesh.

Rick is a licensed professional counselor in private practice for the past twelve years. In 1986 he became an Outward Bound instructor. He has a passion for creating a place in the wilderness in which people can grow and work together. He was a Peace Corps volunteer in South America and has travelled extensively in South America and in Europe. He is associated with Project Adventure in their Adventure Based Counseling Program.

Betsy is an experiential education consultant with twenty years of experience in leadership and team development programs. She instructs for North Carolina Outward Bound's Professional Development Program, The Santa Fe Mountain Center, and Action Learning Associates, as well as a number of other highly esteemed training programs. She has served on the Boards of the Virginia Council for Outdoor Adventure Education and the Association for Experiential Education.

For further information,
Please call
(804) 971-8599

600 client-days per year, about 50 client-days were open programs. At the 600 client-days per year level (equivalent to 30–35 actual days per year), Falls River could be considered a small operation. Most of the other experiential learning companies had more than 1,000 client-days per year.

Falls River differed radically from other experiential learning firms in that, because of Falls River's relatively small size, it had the flexibility to offer its clients personalized programs. As mentioned above, a Falls River staff person would perform a needs assessment—discussing in detail with the client the areas of concern and getting a feel for the company culture and the context in which the participants worked. The Falls River staff would incorporate this information into the program development and then after completing the program the staff would follow up with the company and the participants. (See Exhibit 5 for a sample custom program.)

Falls River's unique customized service required each facilitator to be able to take a group through a range of learning experiences (e.g., "the spider web," "the wall," or "Jacob's Ladder"), follow its development, and constantly make adjustments as the group's journey progressed. Comparable firms offered "off the shelf" programs, such as the ones offered by Pecos River, with instructors who were very narrowly specialized and tended to perform only one type of activity (e.g., "the wall") with every group. In these types of programs, a client group might be facilitated by a separate specialist in each of the activities.

Human Resources

The Falls River Center had no full-time employees. The first eight facilitators were trained during the first year of operations for programs with schoolteachers, administrators, students, and therapeutic groups. Haupt and Dalgliesh required each of these facilitators to have a counseling background since the skills necessary to be a competent facilitator—particularly in touchy situations—had a lengthy development process. Of these facilitators, only Ziemer and Amacker worked on more than a per-program contract basis. They became intimately involved in the course improvement, administrative tasks, and marketing of Falls River.

In the first year Haupt and Dalgliesh found themselves doing most of the work themselves. Amacker developed a self-managing system for the paperwork submitted by the facilitators and wrote a safety manual for the course. Neither Haupt nor Dalgliesh had any business or finance background, but Haupt kept the books until 1991 when he turned the finances over to Dalgliesh.

Haupt and Dalgliesh complemented each other well as the leaders of the organization. Dalgliesh was constantly focused on the emotional needs of her employees, tried to keep the energy level high, and provided an organizational framework while Haupt always had time to listen, provided stability, and paid attention to the small details that created a special touch. Haupt's calm consistency balanced Dalgliesh's high-gear state just before programs were about to take off. Dalgliesh's good organizational skills helped keep Haupt's "laid-back" nonlinear style from digressing into chaos.

Their differences were well illustrated in their descriptions of an awful day. Haupt's idea of an awful day was one where he would have to "shoot from the hip" and was not grounded. This was not an issue for Dalgliesh because she always spent considerable time planning ahead. For Dalgliesh an awful day was "having to manage the office and be 15 different people" to meet everyone's needs. However, they

EXHIBIT 5

Falls River Center Action Learning Session for CAE Electronics
Tentative Program Design (10/28/92)

GOALS

Identify strategies and behaviors that help the team to "win." Develop ways to take these winning strategies back to the workplace. Have fun with each other in an outdoor setting away from work.

PRECEDING AFTERNOON

Meet with participants for introductory briefing. Framing the day, goals articulated, what to wear/bring. Medical release forms.

PROGRAM DAY

9:00 A.M. All group opening.
Warmups.
Communication barriers.

9:30 Divide into six teams for Action Learning sequence.

Group Juggle—Team members toss "products" to their customers, focusing on pleasing the customer (good passes) and zero defects (no dropped balls), while remaining in touch with the Big Picture (what the rest of the team is doing).

Issues: *What is a mistake?*
Who owns the mistakes?
How was customer satisfaction created?
Importance of keeping the big picture in mind.
How is this activity like the workplace?

Speedball—Task is changed; time focus is added.

Issues: *What were the breakthroughs in solving this problem?*
Were everyone's ideas heard?
What does it take for an idea to get put into action?

Mission Possible—Group is paired: one is area supervisor, the other is frontline worker; supervisors are given the task that blindfolded workers are to perform. Supervisors can communicate, give vision, guide worker, but only workers may handle the tools to complete the task (delivering a product—represented by a bucket—into a new marketplace given time and other constraints).

Issues: *Importance of clearly articulating a vision.*
Communicating a task to someone who cannot see what the problem is.
Teaming to get jobs done.
What learnings can we take with us from this?

Traffic Jam—Half the group changes places with the other half with certain constraints around their movement patterns.

(continued)

EXHIBIT 5 (CONTINUED)

Falls River Center Action Learning Session for CAE Electronics
Tentative Program Design (10/28/92)

Issues: *How does our "social architecture" affect our ability to resolve problems?*
What causes frustration level to rise?
How can we resolve this as effectively as possible?

Quality Web—Group must plan and execute the passing of each individual through a "web," where each opening may only be used once. Group determines the standards to which it wants to adhere.

Issues: *Planning versus execution.*
Who assumed leadership?
Did leadership change, and why?
What are the operating norms?
Which of these do you like, and which would you like to change?

Blindfold Squares—While all are blindfolded, group is given the challenge of creating a certain pattern with lengths of rope, within a time constraint.

Issues: *How do we approach a challenge that none of us can see?*
What were examples of effective leadership?
What got in the way?
What are our learnings?

Corporate Islands—Entire group stands on small island, which represents "current reality." Island ten feet away represents its "desired state." The group has "resources," human, financial, and technical (represented by three boards). The challenge is for the group to reach its desired state, using its resources, without touching the ground.

Issues: *Was everyone able to see the problem?*
Was the vision clear?
What are other challenges in our current reality?

The Wall—Entire group attempts to get over a 14-foot wall, utilizing only each other as resources. (May or may not use this.)

The above are suggested activities. (Each team will do a subset.) Options remain flexible as we further refine needs and objectives and depending on how the day itself progresses.

12:00–12:45 P.M.	Catered lunch at Big Top in Meadow.
11:15–4:00	Choice of two: Jacob's Ladder, Zip Line, Leap of Faith, along with other initiatives if they choose.
3:15–3:45	Small group debriefs (some may have to happen during your assigned flex time).
4:00	All groups meet at Zig Zag clearing for final wrap-up.
4:15	Participants leave, staff debrief.

did share a commitment to delivering "high-quality, totally safe, and the best possible programs in the field."

As the business grew, several strains appeared. Dalgliesh's and Haupt's philosophy was always that "most important is having fun." As administrative tasks began to take them away from the programs, both felt that they could not take on more than their current workload. Haupt found himself "overwhelmed" and faced a low point as the tensions of balancing a healthy family life, his therapeutic practice, and Falls River seemed to be pulling him in too many directions. They both found themselves strapped, particularly with large programs such as the 240-person program for Darden. Furthermore, these large programs required that they bring in additional facilitators beyond the original group, usually from outside of Charlottesville. At first, they found it difficult to find enough qualified persons. After the first few programs, however, word of mouth gave Falls River a reputation for being a great place to work. The special attention and expense they put into preparing the facilitators and making their stay comfortable paid off; soon they began receiving requests from people who wanted to work in the next program.

In addition to the increased staff, the program methodology was changed, particularly with regard to the large corporate groups. Having more than 60 participants required a new level of planning, as did groups approaching 60 on high-ropes courses, because the staff had to be at least doubled. New ropes stations had to be built. They now had enough sites to accommodate 120 comfortably on low ropes. For corporate groups the large staff required more sophisticated management techniques and formal training on Falls River's rules and safety procedures. Tying the exercises and the learning to the participants' workplace was essential and required additional training for the facilitators.

Finances

Haupt and Dalgliesh started the company as 50/50 shareholders. They each invested $10,000 to create this subchapter S business. When asked if the business was profitable, Dalgliesh replied: "No, not yet. We haven't made back our initial investment, although we did each receive $7,000 last year."

With their lack of formal business skills, they found "learning the language of business difficult." As the business grew, they began to realize that their simplified accounting procedure was no longer adequate. They had been keeping all of their receipts and contracts in paper boxes and logging transactions in a book. Haupt and Dalgliesh found the language of the "business world" very perplexing. Terms such as "equity" and "fair market value" were difficult to comprehend. Trying to make sense of tax laws and legal terms was even worse.

One of Dalgliesh's learning challenges was doing a payroll. She had "never done a payroll before," much less one for 28 employees. The increase in employees reclassified Falls River and generated new concerns with insurance and taxes. She also found herself learning rudimentary accounting (see Exhibit 6 for sample book page and accountant's review) to keep track of the cash flow. She found "doing the books" very complicated and time-consuming and ran into the typical cash-flow problems of a growing small business. In June of 1991 she found herself facing a rather unexpectedly large insurance and tax bill without the money to pay for it. She realized how important it was to plan ahead and to build in cushions when large increases in the payroll required larger amounts of cash.

EXHIBIT 6

Falls River Center Ratio Analyses and Financials, December 31, 1991

Introduction

The following graphic ratio analyses are calculated from the accounting data provided. They are meant to serve only as an aid to understanding your business. They are useful in charting the progress of a business over time, as well as comparing the business to industry averages. (The different ratios will differ greatly across industries.) As such, ratios are important and useful tools. However, they must be interpreted with care and discretion.

Only some of the ratios are discussed below. Others, such as "Net sales" or "Gross profit margin on sales," should be obvious. If you are uncertain what these other ratios mean, please feel free to ask.

Ratio

This popular ratio measures the ability to pay current liabilities (due within one year) from cash and other assets that can be quickly converted to cash ("current assets"). A current ratio of 2.0 (2:1) is generally accepted as a healthy relationship between current assets and current liabilities. It is calculated by dividing current assets by current liabilities.

Debt-to-Equity Ratio

This ratio compares the firm's debt financing with the amount of owner/stockholder financing. It is commonly used by banks and other long-term creditors, who prefer a low debt-to-equity ratio because it implies less risk for the creditors. It is calculated by dividing total liabilities by total equity.

Employee Costs to Sales

This valuable ratio compares the cost of employees to the dollar amount of sales generated. It is useful to look at it over time and determine the trends. It is calculated by dividing the total of salaries, payroll taxes, and employee benefits by net sales.

(continued)

Although Dalgliesh kept the books, they decided to turn the books over to the accountant every quarter. Yet, even with the accountant, Haupt and Dalgliesh were barely able to distinguish a balance sheet from an income statement, referring to them as "those things we get from the accountant."

As a result of their lack of business expertise, they faced a surprising disappointment after the excitement of the success of their first 240-person Darden program. While the business school had been their largest revenue program, they realized

EXHIBIT 6 (CONTINUED)

Falls River Center Ratio Analyses and Financials, December 31, 1991

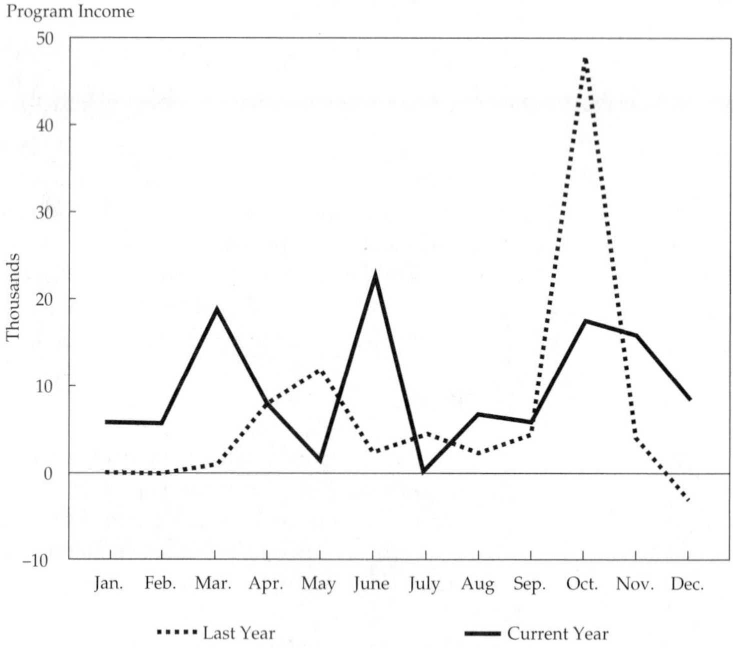

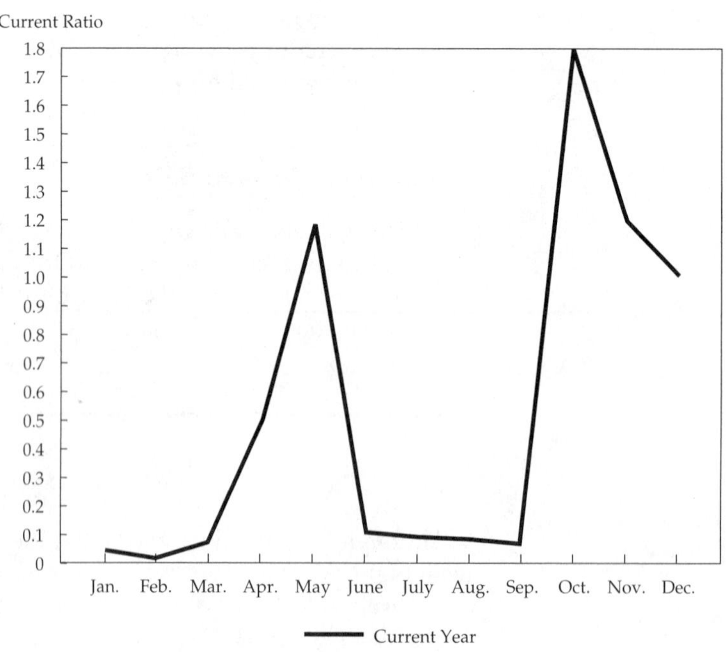

(continued)

EXHIBIT 6 (CONTINUED)

Falls River Center Ratio Analyses and Financials, December 31, 1991

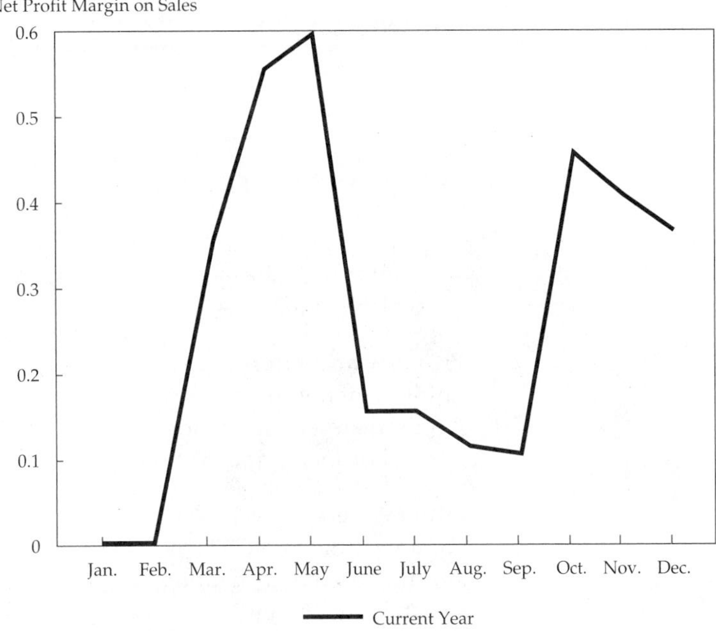

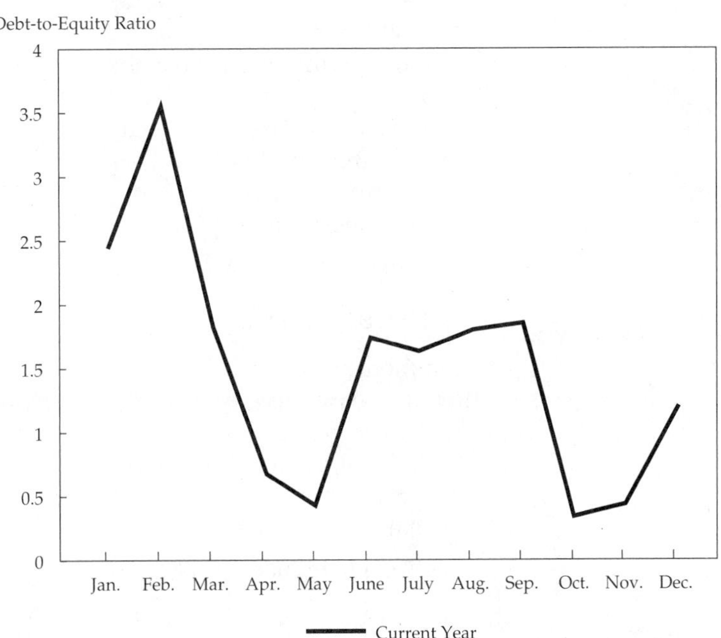

EXHIBIT 6 (CONTINUED)

Falls River Center Ratio Analyses and Financials, December 31, 1991

BALANCE SHEET

	1991	1992
ASSETS		
Current Assets		
Cash in bank	$12,689.37	$14,451.32
Money market account	.00	5,168.11
Accounts receivable—return checks	.00	273.00
Total current assets	12,689.37	$19,892.43
Property and Equipment		
Equipment and furniture	21,995.00	27,123.90
Accumulated depreciation	(11,038.07)	(14,930.90)
Total property and equipment	10,956.93	12,193.00
Other Assets		
Organization costs	1,655.00	1,655.00
Accumulated amortization	(801.00)	(1,131.98)
Total other assets	854.00	523.02
Total assets	$24,500.30	$32,608.45
LIABILITIES		
Current Liabilities		
Employee withholdings payable	$ 1,469.99	$ 204.83
Payroll taxes payable	1,223.75	292.43
Loan payable shareholder—current	11,238.00	.00
Total current liabilities	$13,931.74	$ 497.26
Long-term liabilities	.00	.00
Total long-term liabilities	.00	.00
Total liabilities	$13,931.74	$ 497.26
OWNER'S EQUITY		
Common stock	$ 1,000.00	$ 1,000.00
Retained earnings	3,578.00	31,122.66
AAA distributions— Betsy Dalgliesh	(10,777.05)	(24,658.05)
AAA distributions—Rick Haupt	(10,777.05)	(24,658.05)
Net profit/loss	$27,544.66	$49,304.63
Total owner's equity	$10,568.56	$32,111.19
Total liabilities and equity	$24,500.30	$32,608.45

(continued)

EXHIBIT 6 (CONTINUED)

Falls River Center Ratio Analyses and Financials, December 31, 1991

INCOME STATEMENT

	1991	Ratio	1992	Ratio
REVENUE				
Program income	$84,488.25	100.00	$117,792.40	100.00
Interest income	.00	.00	168.11	.14
Total revenue	$84,488.25	100.00	$117,960.51	100.00
OPERATING EXPENSES				
Advertising	$ 1,908.53	2.26	$ 1,467.38	1.24
Amortization	331.00	.39	330.98	.28
Bank charges	.00	.00	21.31	.02
Contract labor	1,100.50	1.30	320.00	.27
Depreciation	3,853.07	4.56	3,892.83	3.30
Donations	25.00	.03	.00	.00
Dues and subscriptions	170.00	.20	203.97	.17
Entertainment/meals—programs	1,163.64	1.38	506.06	.43
Entertainment/meals—other	606.60	.72	672.77	.57
Equipment rental	1,641.20	1.94	1,178.68	1.00
Insurance	2,731.00	3.23	3,081.00	2.61
Legal and accounting	825.00	.98	1,675.00	1.42
Licenses and permits	168.65	.20	277.96	.24
Miscellaneous expenses	208.03	.25	200.00	.17
Office supplies and expense	1,457.90	1.73	1,862.99	1.58
Penalties	140.50	.17	199.32	.17
Postage and delivery	.00	.00	208.70	.18
Program expenses	.00	.00	1,110.66	.94
Reference materials	50.00	.06	40.70	.03
Rent	4,000.00	4.73	3,250.00	2.76
Repairs and maintenance	1,275.03	1.51	727.55	.62
Subcontractor fees	1,750.00	2.07	14,700.00	12.46
Supplies	914.80	1.08	2,421.99	2.05
Taxes—payroll	2,990.56	3.54	2,739.67	2.32
Taxes—other	212.85	.25	140.61	.12
Telephone	53.89	.06	3.56	.00
Training and development	2,168.26	2.57	273.00	.23
Travel	1,202.06	1.42	1,877.69	1.59
Wages	24,195.52	28.64	13,284.50	11.26
Wages—officers	1,800.00	2.13	11,987.00	10.16
Total operating expenses	$56,943.59	67.40	68,655.88	58.20
Net income/loss	$27,544.66	32.60	$ 49,304.63	32.60

(continued)

EXHIBIT 6 (CONTINUED)

Falls River Center Ratio Analyses and Financials, December 31, 1991

STATEMENT OF RETAINED EARNINGS

	1991	1992
Retained earnings	$3,578.00	$ 9,568.56
Net income	27,544.66	49,304.63
Dividends declared	.00	.00
Adjustments to retained earnings		
AAA distribution—Betsy Dalgliesh	(10,777.05)	(13,881.00)
AAA distribution—Rick Haupt	(10,777.05)	(13,881.00)
Total adjustments	(21,554.10)	(27,762.00)
Total retained earnings	$9,568.56	$31,111.19

STATEMENT OF CASH FLOWS

	1991	1992
Cash Flow from Operating Activities		
Net income/loss	$27,544.66	$27,648.70
Depreciation	3,853.07	1,921.19
Net receivables	.00	(203.00)
Inventory	.00	.00
Prepaid expenses	.00	.00
Accounts payable	.00	.00
Notes payable	.00	(11,238.00)
Taxes payable		
Federal withholding	506.00	(376.59)
FICA withholding	835.99	(309.92)
Virginia withholding	128.00	(148.94)
Payroll taxes payable	1,223.75	(441.96)
Interest payable	.00	.00
Leases payable	.00	.00
Other current liabilities	.00	.00
Total cash flow from operating activities	$34,091.47	$16,851.48

(continued)

EXHIBIT 6 (CONTINUED)

Falls River Center Ratio Analyses and Financials, December 31, 1991

	1991	1992
Cash Flow from Investing Activities		
Property, plant, and equipment		
Equipment and furniture	(800.00)	473.00
Intangible assets		
Accumulated amortization	331.00	165.50
Other assets	.00	.00
Total cash flow from investing activities	(469.00)	638.50
Cash Flow from Financing Activities		
Long-term debt	.00	.00
Common stock	.00	.00
Additional paid-in capital—common	.00	.00
Retained earnings		
AAA distribution—Betsy Dagliesh	(10,777.05)	(3,881.00)
AAA distribution—Rick Haupt	(10,777.05)	(3,881.00)
Total cash flow from financing activities	(21,554.10)	(7,762.00)
Net increase/decrease in cash	$12,068.37	$ 9,727.98
Beginning cash balance	621.00	9,891.45
Net increase/decrease in cash	12,068.37	9,727.98
Ending cash balance	$12,689.37	$19,619.43

(continued)

that Falls River had barely broken even after expenses. Haupt and Dalgliesh understood that they would have to develop a better understanding of the company's cost structure before they quoted a price to the school again.

When it came to new equipment, Amacker asserted that Falls River was the best place she had ever worked. In most places Amacker found it "a battle to get new equipment." Haupt and Dalgliesh "were very willing to put more money into equipment despite a tight money supply." When an instructor mentioned a new helmet that would be a great safety improvement for the high ropes, he found ten of them out at the course the next week.

If money were not so tight, Amacker was certain they could do better marketing by improving their brochure and video. While Haupt and Dalgliesh were more than willing to spend money on equipment, they were apprehensive about buying office equipment such as a computer. However, Amacker convinced them that a "computer was as worthwhile as new equipment for the course," and in late 1991 Falls River purchased a Macintosh LC, which now held a prominent position in the office.

The Future

The work with Darden had become an excellent source of business for Falls River. Darden had run its second-year leadership class through the course for the second year in a row, and the continued positive feedback boded well for a third year. In addition, the school's executive education programs' participants were being introduced to Falls River programs, generating excellent word-of-mouth publicity in the business world, which resulted in their latest and largest program, the Bacardi Annual Sales Convention.

The program would be the first not run at the Falls River facility but at the convention site in Scottsdale, Arizona. At the convention 156 people would be run through a "series of moderately physical and cognitive 'challenges,'" designed to focus on the "values" that Bacardi wanted its sales and marketing organization to internalize (e.g., quality, productivity, long-term vision).

Since Falls River's work was with only one of the five companies under the Bacardi corporate umbrella, a successful program could translate into invaluable word of mouth within this corporation as well as the business community at large.

Falls River's payroll had jumped from 8 to more than 30; and Dalgliesh and Haupt, who had averaged 8–10 hours per week, now estimated that the company took up 20–24 hours per week. Clearly, it would require an even greater time commitment if it were to grow any further. Overall, the growth potential and business outlook was very good for the partners of a company whose founding goal was to "have fun."

As Dalgliesh considered how much time and effort growing the business would require, she wondered what she and Haupt—who was already having trouble balancing Falls River, his private practice, and time with his family—should do. Dalgliesh was very sensitive to the fact that programs being at Falls River had an impact on the Haupt family; there were possibly other sites, but Falls River was such a beautiful location. Besides, Dalgliesh's passion was not in building ropes courses; it was not her energy that would build another course. Her passion was in the process that happened there and that could happen anywhere. Dalgliesh knew that they "could do really well if they had ten more programs a year," yet it was not her goal to double the business. The idea of doubling the profits, however, did have a certain appeal. She knew it would be to their advantage to increase their business and understood that Haupt had larger financial ambitions than she did. They both wanted to see the company "run easier and better."

If they grew, would she spend even more time on administrative tasks instead of the part she loved: working with and creating the programs? Could they keep people like Amacker and Ziemer, who had become integral to their business, without the security of a full-time position? Dalgliesh knew Ziemer really wanted to work full time, and Amacker was ready and willing also. She began to think about what it would take to bring in the extra ten programs needed to do really well. They had flopped at marketing before, but how else could they bring in new business? What would the ten programs allow them to do? Perhaps Amacker could take over the office work as a full-time employee. Perhaps, she mused, they should just concentrate on continually improving their existing quality programs and forget about growth.

Endnotes

[1]Richard Wagner et al., "Outdoor Training: Revolution or Fad?" *Training and Development Journal*, March 1991.
[2]Richard Broderick, "Learning the Ropes," *Training*, October 1988.
[3]Wagner, "Outdoor Training."
[4]Brad Lee Thompson, "Training in the Great Outdoors," *Training*, May 1991.
[5]Wagner, "Outdoor Training."
[6]Thompson, "Training in the Great Outdoors."
[7]Ibid.

Case 14

National Guitar Summer Workshop, Inc.

Eyes closed, biting his lower lip, Tom Dempsey improvised several bars of "All of Me" on his jazz guitar. Seated around him in a semicircle were the members of Tom's morning Jazz Workshop with their guitars on their knees, anxiously awaiting their turn to echo what they had just heard. The six students in the room at the Canterbury School in New Milford, Connecticut, were an odd assembly of boys and men ranging from Frank, the 55-year-old physician from New Jersey, to Mike, the 16-year-old student at Scarsdale High School.

Although it was August and the Canterbury School was not in session, the campus was abuzz with people, the types of which the founders would definitely not have approved—the school had been rented out for the summer. Next to the main entrance, tee-shirted teenagers with long hair smoked cigarettes around a large makeshift ashtray. Middle-aged men with varying degrees of facial hair strolled across the campus with instrument cases slung casually over their shoulders. The clues to this unusual activity led to an office to the right of the main building's entrance. Through the door in the outer office, surrounded by a small crowd of people, sat the charismatic bundle of energy responsible for the summer activity at the Canterbury School. David Smolover, the 44-year-old son of a Scarsdale cantor, was the founder and managing director of the National Guitar Summer Workshop (NGSW), the largest guitar camp currently operating in the United States, and, for the past eight years, the Canterbury School's regular summer tenant.

Every summer since 1984, Smolover had assembled a faculty of guitar teachers and professional musicians to offer an intensive series of one-, two-, and three-week instructional sessions to teenage Generation Xers with dreams of being the next Kurt Cobain, aging baby boomers trying to recapture something they lost at Woodstock, and hobbyists with the leisure time and capital to devote to improving their jazz and classical-guitar skills. Over the past 12 years, core members of the faculty, staff, and returning campers had formed a summer family, with Smolover as a crisis-solving father figure. This close-knit familial structure worked quite well, enabling the NGSW to increase annual tuition income from $64,004 in 1984 to $854,000 in 1995 (see Exhibits 1, 2, and 3). This increase was accomplished through expanded enrollment at New Milford and the creation of four satellite campuses: California in 1989, Toronto in 1993, Nashville in 1995, and Freiburg, Germany, in 1996. In addition, Smolover increased NGSW's visibility by creating the music-publishing subsidiary Workshop Arts, Inc., producing a guitar newsletter, sponsoring a Guitar Expo, and establishing an affiliation with a small music-store chain, Daddy's Junky Music Stores, Inc.

In the fall of 1996, NGSW stood at a crossroads. Despite steady growth in attendance from 1984 to 1993, between 1993 and 1996 attendance leveled off (see

This case was prepared by Orson Watson, research associate, under the supervision of L. J. Bourgeois, professor of Business Administration. Research funding was provided by the Batten Center for Entrepreneurial Leadership.

EXHIBIT 1

National Guitar Summer Workshop, Inc.: Statement of Income and Expenses

	1993		1994		1995	
	Actual	Percentage	Actual	Percentage	Actual	Percentage
INCOME						
Fees	$806,691.86	99.6%	$727,505.62	101.0%	$872,188.53	99.2%
Refund of fees	(9,224.95)	(1.1)	(10,238.26)	(1.4)	(17,435.00)	(2.0)
NMW reimbursements	—	—	1,590.41	0.2	4,452.00	0.5
Company sponsorship	—	—	1,900.00	0.3	2,500.00	0.3
Workshop Arts reimbursements	—	—	—	—	19,020.50	2.2
Miscellaneous fees	—	—	—	—	(952.31)	(0.1)
Refund of photo	(196.00)	(0.0)	—	—	—	—
Fees for expo	28,942.60	3.6	—	—	—	—
Bad-customer checks	(14,186.64)	(1.8)	(325.00)	(0.0)	(400.00)	(0.0)
Foreign collection	(1,905.00)	(0.2)	—	—	—	—
Total income	$810,121.87	100.0%	$720,432.77	100.0%	$879,373.72	100.00%
EXPENSES						
Transfer to NMEW account	$10,000.00	1.2%	—	—	—	—
NMEW expenses	1,244.86	0.2	$41,569.00	5.8%	—	—
NMW expenses	274.69	0.0	2,167.80	0.3	—	—
Workshop Arts	—	—	—	—	$2,319.59	0.3%
Guitar-repair supplies	2,070.61	0.3	1,512.84	0.2	1,907.92	0.2
Salaries, part-time employees	141,985.70	17.5	134,981.23	18.7	116,350.98	13.2
Salaries, subcontractors	29,649.38	3.7	38,099.50	5.3	53,373.67	6.1
Salaries, full-time employees	18,560.00	2.3	20,288.00	2.8	24,080.00	2.7
Salaries, royalties	2,117.60	0.3	1,517.70	0.2	1,796.00	0.2
Salaries, newsletter	—	—	—	—	1,500.00	0.2
Salaries, bonuses	24,900.00	3.1	3,800.00	0.5	2,775.00	0.3
Salaries, officers	57,000.00	7.0	60,000.00	8.3	60,000.00	6.8
Salaries, officers' bonuses	1,787.00	0.2	—	—	1,000.00	0.1
Master-artist fees	28,550.00	3.5	31,614.93	4.4	40,621.05	4.6
Advertising, magazine	30,391.03	3.8	35,435.99	4.9	34,257.42	3.9
Advertising, production	317.69	0.0	294.83	0.0	561.43	0.1
Advertising, other	340.17	0.0	5,044.32	0.7	1,067.62	0.1
Accounting	2,568.00	0.3	3,355.70	0.5	2,510.00	0.3
Newsletter	—	—	—	—	8,419.30	1.0
Printing, brochure	21,119.82	2.6	15,063.14	2.1	22,289.48	2.5
Printing, textbooks	4,045.40	0.5	2,752.08	0.4	2,814.46	0.3
Printing, offset	3,320.92	0.4	4,435.76	0.6	6,066.02	0.7
Alfred textbooks	—	—	4,000.00	0.6	10,000.00	1.1
Textbooks (other publishers)	—	—	870.90	0.1	328.32	0.0

(continued)

EXHIBIT 1 (CONTINUED)

National Guitar Summer Workshop, Inc.: Statement of Income and Expenses

	1993		1994		1995	
	Actual	Percentage	Actual	Percentage	Actual	Percentage
Auto expense	$2,487.63	0.3%	$1,922.97	0.3%	$2,393.69	0.3%
Auto lease	5,482.38	0.7	3,932.58	0.5	4,219.53	0.5
Auto rental	356.18	0.0	1,175.52	0.2	2,863.60	0.3
Bank-service charges	1,552.27	0.2	394.64	0.1	968.18	0.1
Credit-card discounts	6,625.38	0.8	5,305.21	0.7	7,478.22	0.9
Bank-debt memo	—	—	460.00	0.1	—	—
Contributions	50.00	0.0	150.00	0.0	500.00	0.1
Dues and subscriptions	665.95	0.1	421.70	0.1	235.00	0.0
Store	13,116.97	1.6	11,818.67	1.6	22,425.69	2.6
Equipment rental	3,107.89	0.4	2,443.64	0.3	1,530.47	0.2
Freight	2,664.74	0.3	2,013.84	0.3	3,880.24	0.4
Insurance—workers' comp.	1,469.00	0.2	1,232.00	0.2	4,425.00	0.5
Insurance—automobile	1,036.48	0.1	2,879.86	0.4	2,725.62	0.3
Insurance—liability	4,063.00	0.5	2,444.00	0.3	2,385.00	0.3
Insurance—equipment	371.95	0.0	—	—	—	—
Insurance—officers' life	228.54	0.0	228.54	0.0	228.54	0.0
Insurance—officers' health	3,213.51	0.4	3,378.47	0.5	4,075.00	0.5
Legal	1,348.72	0.2	1,699.00	0.2	1,116.84	0.1
Laundry	1,082.95	0.1	807.83	0.1	1,064.00	0.1
Miscellaneous expenses	4,487.16	0.6	5,072.40	0.7	2,121.06	0.2
Musical equipment	5,138.07	0.6	350.24	0.0	914.93	0.1
Office supplies	3,290.88	0.4	3,203.88	0.4	4,383.78	0.5
Computer expenses	2,103.03	0.3	3,272.43	0.5	2,132.61	0.2
Computer lease	2,186.94	0.3	1,925.36	0.3	517.96	0.1
Copier expenses	246.65	0.0	471.26	0.1	800.00	0.1
Outside services	291.50	0.0	—	—	—	—
Postage expenses	17,962.31	2.2	15,522.07	2.2	19,138.99	2.2
Postage, Federal Express	939.75	0.1	1,069.25	0.1	1,740.94	0.2
Postage, meter lease	—	—	—	—	948.70	0.1
Bulk-mailing expenses	—	—	879.15	0.1	1,858.67	0.2
Mailing lists	880.95	0.1	107.57	0.0	609.92	0.1
Water	—	—	—	—	42.73	0.0
Rent, Connecticut facility	233,210.00	28.8	220,112.50	30.6	244,504.50	27.8
Rent, California facility	39,462.76	4.9	37,994.50	5.3	24,549.54	2.8
Rent, Canada facility	11,183.73	1.4	1,100.00	0.2	21,606.31	2.5
Rent, office	—	—	—	—	2,410.00	0.3
Rent, Tennessee campus	—	—	—	—	7,612.22	0.9
Supplies expenses	652.48	0.1	—	—	—	—
Taxes, personal property	38.63	0.0	—	—	—	—
Taxes, Ct. unemployment (UC2)	606.20	0.1	907.77	0.1	7,663.09	0.9
Taxes—other	—	—	168.00	0.0	—	—
Telephone Network Plus	—	—	1,577.87	0.2	—	—

(continued)

EXHIBIT 1 (CONTINUED)

National Guitar Summer Workshop, Inc.: Statement of Income and Expenses

	1993		1994		1995	
	Actual	Percentage	Actual	Percentage	Actual	Percentage
Taxes, federal unemployment (940)	—	—	—	—	$1,273.63	0.1%
Taxes, California unemployment	—	—	—	—	2,545.14	0.3
Telephone, ATT	$1,974.48	0.2%	$458.28	0.1%	305.76	0.0
Telephone, SNET	4,416.08	0.5	4,276.75	0.6	7,321.05	0.8
Telephone, MCI	6,870.11	0.8	5,261.62	0.7	40.60	0.0
Telephone, Sprint	1,233.34	0.2	777.64	0.1	—	
Telephone, LAS	1,263.92	0.2	1,686.22	0.2	1,461.25	0.2
ITS Phone	—	—	497.62	0.1	6,459.87	0.7
Telephone equipment	225.00	0.0	—	—	—	—
Entertainment	3,354.05	0.4	1,240.32	0.2	2,414.50	0.3
Travel (master artists)	—	—	—	—	15,494.48	1.8
Lodging (travel)	766.32	0.1	145.00	0.0	—	—
Lodging, master artists	1,147.91	0.1	1,511.43	0.2	3,190.49	0.4
Travel	14,066.35	1.7	21,105.56	2.9	11,021.22	1.3
Training and seminars	138.88	0.0	89.70	0.0	117.00	0.0
Recruitment fees	—	—	—	—	687.30	0.1
Studio	2,983.73	0.4	3,018.48	0.4	5,269.37	0.6
Total expenses	790,287.62	97.6	783,315.17	108.7	857,710.49	97.5
Net operating income (loss)	$19,834.25	2.4%	$(62,882.40)	(8.7)%	$21,663.23	2.5%
OTHER INCOME AND EXPENSES						
State license	—	—	$650.00	0.1%	$650.00	0.1%
Newsletter	—	—	—	—	119.85	0.0
Fines and penalties	$25.00	0.0%	—	—	—	—
Temporary distribution	271.75	0.0	—	—	—	—
Total, other income and expenses	296.75	0.0	650.00	0.1	769.85	0.1
Net income (loss) before taxes	19,537.50	2.4	(63,532.40)	(8.8)	20,893.38	2.4
INCOME TAXES						
Awards and prizes	—	—	—	—	$2,000.00	0.2%
Total income taxes	—	—	—	—	2,000.00	0.2
Net income (loss)	$19,537.50	2.4%	$(63,532.40)	(8.8)%	$18,893.38	2.1%

Exhibit 3). While the New Milford "mother campus" continued to be NGSW's cash cow, of the four other satellite campuses only the Nashville campus turned a profit. In addition, several of the NGSW's diversified ventures had either collapsed or were producing disappointing returns.

EXHIBIT 2

National Guitar Summer Workshop, Inc.: Balance Sheet (December 31)

	1993	1994	1995
ASSETS			
Current assets:			
Bank of Boston	$ 3,646.23	$ 1,622.16	$ 871.87
New Milford Bank & Trust	99,835.22	44,411.76	29,993.69
Bank of America	1,113.68	120.73	1,550.03
Petty cash	800.00	800.00	1,000.00
Cash transfers	12,750.50	15,265.50	15,265.50
Loans and exchanges	7,249.50	7,249.50	7,249.50
Loan to P. L. Castleman	1,000.00	1,000.00	1,000.00
Loan receivables—Workshop Arts	(6,742.50)	(47,338.66)	(48,559.16)
Loan receivables—NGSW	16,541.75	16,541.75	16,541.75
Loan receivables—NMW	2,000.00	2,000.00	2,000.00
Total current assets	$138,194.52	$41,672.74	$26,913.18
Property and equipment:			
Equipment	$ 56,291.56	$56,291.56	$56,291.56
Accumulative depreciation—equipment	(53,105.60)	(53,105.60)	(53,105.60)
Total property and equipment	$ 3,185.96	$ 3,185.96	$ 3,185.96
Other assets:			
Organizational costs	$ 166.00	$ 166.00	$ 166.00
Accumulative amortization—organizational costs	(166.00)	(166.00)	(166.00)
Total assets	$141,380.48	$44,858.70	$30,399.14
LIABILITIES AND EQUITY			
Current liabilities:			
Notes payable—short term			$ 60,000.00
Sales taxes payable	$ 191.19	$ 401.19	4,865.45
Payroll taxes payable	(17,631.21)	(39,194.20)	(66,822.77)
Current portion, long-term debt	75,000.00	75,000.00	75,000.00
Notes payable	557.86	(11,075.11)	(76,245.34)
Accrued taxes	16,051.00	16,051.00	16,051.00
Total current liabilities	$74,168.84	$ 41,182.88	$12,848.34
Equity:			
NGSW retirement trust	$ (5,000.00)	$ (5,000.00)	$ (5,000.00)
Common stock	1,000.00	1,000.00	1,000.00
Retained earnings	51,794.30	71,328.38	2,477.58
Net income (loss)	19,537.50	(63,532.40)	18,893.38
Total equity	67,331.80	3,795.98	17,370.96
Total liabilities and equity	$141,500.64	$44,978.86	$30,219.30

EXHIBIT 3

National Guitar Summer Workshop, Inc.: Tuition Income History, 1984–1995

Year	Tuition as of June 1	Total Tuition for Year
1984	$ 44,725	$ 64,004
1985	120,070	152,370
1986	134,702	208,372
1987	233,830	304,125
1988	323,494	447,974
1989	363,446	517,141
1990	355,785	527,062
1991	494,272	682,540
1992	536,705	714,270
1993	523,972	735,213
1994	520,067	679,384
1995	660,749	854,000

Meanwhile, the core NGSW family began to experience growing pains. Several of the core staff members stated that in the beginning they were treated respectfully as professional members of an educational institution. Classes were small and instruction was tailored to meet the individual needs of a fairly serious student body. In 1996, however, they complained that in recent years the bottom line had taken precedence. Instructor wage rates remained static. One instructor complained that he felt like an underpaid babysitter for maladjusted upper-middle-class youth. As one of the camp's longtime assistant directors observed:

> It's as if you build a sturdy one-room log cabin with a stove in the middle to house your nuclear family. As you have more children, you hastily add more rooms. Before you know it, you have this great big ten-room house. Unfortunately, the heat does not get to all of the rooms.

To put NGSW's strategic options in context, this case will examine the guitar business, shifting demographic trends, and affiliated service industries to identify the nature of the problems facing NGSW during the second half of the 1990s.

Industry Trends

The success and growth of the NGSW in the second half of the 1980s correlated directly to the resurgence of an American guitar industry that faced near extinction in the early 1980s, and to shifting demographic trends that created a market for guitar instruction in two distinct age groups.

Guitar Industry: Early 1980s

In the early 1980s, tight credit and high interest rates placed musical-instrument retailers—with traditionally slow turnover and chronic dependence on borrowed capital—in crisis. Between 1980 and 1989, more than 1,200 instrument dealers in the United States went out of business. A shift in popular musical tastes away from the guitar-based bands of the 1960s and early 1970s directly contributed to a drop in the demand for guitars. The popularity of digital synthesized music and guitar-less bands, such as Spandau Ballet and Devo, featured on the new music-video venues, led to industrywide speculation that the guitar could go the way of the accordion. In addition to historically high interest rates and cutbacks in consumer spending, the music industry faced several other critical problems. As the baby boom went bust in 1981, the industry faced a shrunken potential market with the smallest group of children between the ages of 5 and 18 since 1957.[1]

The 1982 meeting of the Guitar Music Marketing Association marked an industry low point. Several guitar manufacturers described the industry's future as "bleak." Dave Sutton, of Gibson Guitar, Inc., the second-largest guitar manufacturer in the United States, stated: "This business is in a state of crisis. Unless we can devise a new means of effectively marketing guitars to a larger segment of the population, I'm not sure we'll all be here next year."[2] It was during this time that the NGSW was founded.

Mid-1980s Industry Rebound

Poor sales in the early 1980s led to inventory surpluses and falling instrument prices, especially for electric guitars. For most of the 1970s, electric-guitar manufacturing was dominated by two American companies, Fender Musical Instruments, Inc., and Gibson Guitar Corporation. The average retail price for a professional quality instrument stood at $700, with depressed annual sales of 375,000 in 1980. In 1980, Peavey Electronics, Inc., introduced a successful professional quality instrument with a retail price of $399. The quality and successful sale of the Peavey instruments paved the way for a flood of lower-priced imported electric guitars from Korea and Japan. By 1983, the average price of professional quality Fender and Gibson electric guitars had dropped to under $600. This improvement in the retail price, along with the guitar-based heavy-metal and new-age music trends of the late 1980s, pushed annual sales of electric guitars to a record 625,000 units in 1989.[3]

The rebound in acoustic guitars took a more demographic route. During the mid-1980s, baby boomers entering their late thirties developed acute yearnings for the acoustic sounds of their youth. A late 1980s revival reintroduced acoustic-guitar music in car commercials, TV series themes, and revival-rock concerts. An early 1990s country-music (traditionally acoustic based) revival fed the trend. Acoustic-guitar sales rose from a low of 500,000 units in 1983 to 800,000 units in 1989.[4]

1990s Guitar-Industry Boom

Many of the near-bankrupt U.S. guitar manufacturers were sold in the late 1980s and early 1990s to Asian investors and a new generation of entrepreneurs. Demographics, easier credit, and popular-music trends created a steady growth trend in the guitar market in the 1990s. The number of guitar players between the ages of 12 and 24 increased steadily.

Combined worldwide sales of guitars and amplifiers were $1.3 billion in 1994 with guitar sales totaling $665.8 million and sound amplification totaling $609.2 million, a 23 percent increase over 1994. Total annual U.S. guitar sales in 1995 were approximately $300 million. Fender Musical Instruments accounted for 50 percent of U.S. guitar sales, nearly twice the volume of its closest rival, Gibson Guitar Corporation of Nashville. In the same year, acoustic-guitar sales remained virtually unchanged at 558,000 units, while electric guitars increased 38 percent over 1994 to 547,261 units. With over 100 percent markups, guitars and related products represented one of the highest-margin products at retail in 1995.[5]

In addition to strong sales in 1995 and 1996, there was unprecedented coverage of guitar-related stories in the general media. During 1995, *Time*, *Newsweek*, *USA Today*, the *New York Times*, and the major television networks devoted significant space to guitar-related stories. The boom in instrument sales bolstered sales in related product categories, most notably guitar-related publishing, guitar collectibles, advertising, sponsorship, and music education.[6]

Demographic Trends

General Trends

Following the 1980s recession, Americans had more money to spend on music, and lower credit-card interest rates encouraged them to do so. During the 1990s, population trends also played a big role, as the number of school-aged children in their prime music-learning years climbed to levels not seen since 1970. These forces, along with breakthroughs in education research and computer technology, pushed increasing numbers of Americans toward musical instruments.

According to the Gallup Organization, in 1994 the United States had more than 62 million amateur instrumentalists over the age of 5. Six in ten American households included someone who had experience playing a musical instrument. In nearly half of households that had a musical instrument, one or more people played that instrument. While 60 percent of people who used to play an instrument said they would try again, the other 40 percent said that nothing could coax them back. One-third of the potentially reclaimed instrumentalists cited lack of time as the crucial issue. Others said they would play if they owned an instrument, if the hobby was more affordable, if they could take lessons, or if they had others to play with. Only 1 percent of the former players blamed their disinterest on a lack of talent.[7]

Musicians were almost equally split between the sexes. The amateur-musicians category consisted of 52 percent female and 48 percent male. Despite the aging of baby boomers, the median age of instrumentalists between 1985 and 1994 remained at 28. The share of players aged 50 and older remained constant, but the share aged 5 to 17 and 35 to 49 increased with the baby boomers and their kids, while the share aged 18 to 34 decreased with the baby bust. The 17 percent share held by adults aged 50 and older was predicted to grow as the baby boomers moved into this age group.[8] (See Exhibit 4 for U.S. demographics.)

People with more money were more likely to own instruments. Of households with annual incomes over $55,000, 56 percent owned instruments, compared with 31 percent of those earning $25,000 and under. The most popular instruments were piano, owned by 34 percent of households, and guitars, owned by 22 percent. Guitarists were overwhelmingly male. As a percentage of current and former musicians aged 5 and older who preferred particular instruments, 36 percent of males and 8 percent of females selected guitars as their favorite instruments.[9]

The guitar was the quintessential trendy instrument. While many young people started guitar lessons, few continued long-term. The common cliché among guitar instructors was that "it is the easiest instrument to learn, yet the most difficult to master."

EXHIBIT 4

U.S. Resident Population, by Age and Sex: 1970–1994 (in thousands)

Year	Total all years	Under 5 years	5–9 years	10–14 years	15–19 years	20–24 years	25–29 years	30–34 years	35–39 years	40–44 years	45–49 years	50–54 years	55–59 years	60–64 years	65–74 years	75–84 years	85 years & over	5–13 years	14-17 years	18-24 years	Median age (yr.)
1970 Total	203,235	17,163	19,969	20,804	19,084	16,383	13,486	11,437	11,113	11,988	12,124	11,111	9,979	8,623	12,443	6,122	1,408	36,675	15,851	23,714	28.0
Male	98,926	8,750	10,175	10,598	9,641	7,925	6,626	5,599	5,416	5,823	5,855	5,351	4,769	4,030	5,440	2,437	489	18,687	8,069	11,583	26.8
Female	104,309	8,413	9,794	10,206	9,443	8,458	6,859	5,838	5,697	6,166	6,269	5,759	5,210	4,593	7,002	3,684	919	17,987	7,782	12,131	29.3
1980 Total	226,546	16,348	16,700	18,242	21,168	21,319	19,521	17,561	13,965	11,669	11,090	11,710	11,615	10,088	15,581	7,729	2,240	31,159	16,247	30.022	30.0
Male	110,053	8,362	8,539	9,316	10,755	10,663	9,705	8,677	6,862	5,708	5,388	5,621	5,482	4,670	6,757	2,867	682	15,923	8,298	15,054	28.8
Female	116,493	7,986	8,161	8,926	10,413	10,655	9,816	8,884	7,104	5,961	5,702	6,089	6,133	5,418	8,824	4,862	1,559	15,237	7,950	14,696	31.3
1985 Total	237,924	17,842	16,665	17,027	18,727	21,265	21,671	20,025	17,604	14,087	11,606	10,854	11,229	10,906	16,858	8,890	2,667	29,893	14,888	28,902	31.4
1990 Total	248,718	18,757	18,035	17,060	17,886	19,135	21,328	21,833	19,846	17,589	13,744	11,313	10,487	10,625	18,046	10,012	3,022	31,826	13,340	26,950	32.8
Male	121,244	9,599	9,232	8,739	9,175	9,744	10,703	10,862	9,834	8,677	6,739	5,493	5,008	4,947	7,907	3,745	841	16,295	6,857	13,738	31.6
Female	127,474	9,158	8,803	8,322	8,711	9,391	10,625	10,971	10,012	8,912	7,004	5,820	5,479	5,679	10,139	6,267	2,180	15,532	6,482	13,212	34.0
1994 Total	260,341	19,727	18,859	18,753	17,616	18,326	19,177	22,177	21,961	19,699	16,679	13,191	10,936	10,082	18,712	10,925	3,522	33,863	14,428	25,263	34.0
Male	127,076	10,094	9,657	9,602	9,036	9,311	9,619	11,058	10,920	9,728	8,181	6,410	5,244	4,740	8,290	4,206	980	17,339	7,412	12,856	32.9
Female	133,265	9,633	9,201	9,150	8,580	9,015	9,558	11,119	11,040	9,970	8,498	6,781	5,692	5,342	10,422	6,719	2,542	16,524	7,016	12,407	35.2
Percent:																					
1970	100.0	8.4	9.8	10.2	9.4	8.1	6.6	5.6	5.5	5.9	6.0	5.5	4.9	4.2	6.1	3.0	0.7	18.0	7.8	11.7	
1980	100.0	7.2	7.4	8.1	9.3	9.4	8.6	7.8	6.2	5.2	4.9	5.2	5.1	4.5	6.9	3.4	1.0	13.8	7.2	13.3	
1990	100.0	7.5	7.3	6.9	7.2	7.7	8.6	8.8	8.0	7.1	5.5	4.5	4.2	4.3	7.3	4.0	1.2	12.8	5.4	10.8	
1994	100.0	7.6	7.2	7.2	6.8	7.0	7.4	8.5	8.4	7.6	6.4	5.1	4.2	3.9	7.2	4.2	1.4	13.0	5.5	9.7	
Male	100.0	7.9	7.6	7.6	7.1	7.3	7.6	8.7	8.6	7.7	6.4	5.0	4.1	3.7	6.5	3.3	0.8	13.6	5.8	10.1	
Female	100.0	7.2	6.9	6.9	6.4	6.8	7.2	8.3	8.3	7.5	6.4	5.1	4.3	4.0	7.8	5.0	1.9	12.4	5.3	9.3	

SOURCE: *Statistical Abstract of the United States*, 1995, U.S. Department of Commerce, Economic and Statistics Administration, Bureau of Census.

Of current and former players, 85 percent began playing between the ages of 5 and 14. School programs played a pivotal role in the music market. Of teen musicians in 1994, 63 percent learned at school, 27 percent took private lessons, and the rest were self-taught.[10]

Guitar Trends

More than with most classical instruments, there was a direct correlation between guitar sales and popular-music trends. The aging baby boomers who made up most of the born-again guitar hobbyists were the product of the popularity of guitar-based bands of the 1950s and 1960s, and in their youth the boomers drove guitar sales in the 1960s and 1970s. Likewise, the popularity of synthesized music and guitarless bands in the 1970s and early 1980s directly contributed to the guitar-industry slump of the early 1980s, and the emergence of heavy-metal music bands featuring virtuoso electric guitar in the mid-1980s contributed to the 1990s guitar boom. By 1994, however, the heavy-metal craze had ended, and the trend in popular music began again to shift away from virtuoso guitar-based bands toward song-driven guitar music that did not require a high level of musical expertise. In short, the popular guitar music of the 1990s was easier to play.

Music Education

The mid-1990s reawakening of the guitar industry and positive demographics led to a renaissance of music-education programs. Traditional school-based music programs, which had been hurt by the recessionary school budgets of the early 1980s, began to reemerge in the 1990s. Advances in computer technology created a world of new guitar-related options. In addition, an educated American middle class created a growth market in educational travel, including a number of music camps, such as guitar programs.

School-Based Programs

In the 1990s, school-based music programs benefited from improved demographics and the official reacknowledgment of the link between the study of music and improved academic performance. Both 1995 and 1996 were growth years for school-based music-education programs. Bill Schultz of Fender stated:

> The most encouraging fact driving the growth in the guitar business is the fact that young kids have a strong desire to play the guitar. School guitar programs have been tried before, but we feel that we are finally homing in on an approach that will work and will get thousands more kids involved in music.[11]

In 1995, Fender instituted programs with the Boys and Girls Clubs of America, with curricula developed by the NGSW, as a means of building future markets for its products. Industry-sponsored outreach programs took advantage of the low-cost imported guitars and enabled them to offer quality entry-level instruments to first-time buyers. At the other end of the spectrum, middle-aged baby boomers who grew up on rock-and-roll developed a taste for high-end (over $3,000) and collectible guitars in record numbers.

The guitar industry, in partnership with the Music Educators National Conference, embarked on a long-range program to introduce guitars into those school music programs traditionally dominated by band instruments. In 1987, the industry introduced and sponsored International Guitar Month as a means of providing in-school demonstrations and celebrity workshops to attract future players. They also created initiatives to expand their female, senior, and ethnic markets.

Music Software

Computers and music software had the potential to revolutionize the process of learning to play an instrument. Although the computer-assisted music market was still in its infancy in 1995, according to a Louis & Harris Associates survey of 402 home-computer users who made or recorded music on their home machines, 94 percent of computer musicians were men. Most music-software users were also college graduates under age 40. Of the computer musicians, 93 percent also played a "regular" musical instrument. Nearly one-third of this group expressed an interest in making music with their computers, and 15 percent planned to purchase music-related computer equipment within the next year. The dramatic growth in home-computer usage, coupled with the fact that there were approximately 62 million amateur musicians in the United States in 1995, meant that the nontraditional segment of the music-products industry was poised for growth.[12]

In the 1990s, the fastest-growing music product in the United States was music software for personal computers. According to a 1990 Gallup survey for the American Music Conference, 11 percent of American households contained at least one person who had used a personal computer to make music. Music software improved rapidly. A home computer with $10,000 of add-on memory and processing kits was capable of doing everything that a $200,000 synthesizer used by pop groups and recording studios could do in 1991. Sales of electronic musical instruments (including guitars) accounted for over half of all instrument sales in the United States in 1995.

Despite favorable projections, in 1996 instructional-music software was still in its embryonic stage as CD-ROM computer video had not yet been perfected. As a result, instructional-music software still had to overcome the major obstacle of interactivity. No matter how sophisticated the computer equipment, music lessons were, by nature, interactive. Numerous guitar-related Web pages, including one for NGSW, sprang to life in 1995 and 1996. In 1996, an Internet user could purchase new and collectible guitars, download guitar music, read guitar magazines, and connect to hundreds of guitar-related sites from the "Guitar Page" Web site without leaving home.

This connection between guitar players and the Internet correlated directly with the shared demographics between Internet users and guitar players. A December 1995 Nielsen Media Research study on the demographics of Web users found that 65 percent of all Web users were male; 55 percent had college degrees and 26 percent had graduate degrees; 56 percent were between the ages of 25 and 44; 37 percent worked in a professional field, 12 percent in a technical field, and 14 percent in managerial positions; and 55 percent of Web users had annual incomes of greater than $55,000.[13]

Educational Travel

The educational-travel market became a growth industry in America in the 1990s. U.S. vacationers developed a taste for special-interest and educational travel (including adult and family learning camps), a category that accounted for roughly 10 percent of U.S. vacation itineraries in 1995. This demand for tangible vacation experiences was largely a function of shrinking leisure time. It was not entirely clear whether the growing popularity of adult learning camps resulted from developments in the education or leisure industries. Karen Cure, editor of *Fodor's Great American Learning Vacations*, observed this growth trend for over 20 years: "When I started travel writing in the early seventies, these camps were like little jewels you found that nobody knew about. . . . Today all the special-interest magazines are jampacked with listings."[14] Books like *Fodor's Great American Learning Vacations* described hundreds of vacation possibilities, from foreign-language programs to painting and guitar workshops. Kay Kohl, head of the National University Continuing Education Association in Washington, D.C., described the increased interest in learning vacations as natural to a U.S. population that was better educated than ever before: "We have more college graduates than we had years ago. . . . When they think how they will spend their leisure time and disposable income, education is very appealing."[15]

Recognizing this trend, the Disney Corporation created the Disney Institute at Disney World in 1996, where they offered nine courses ranging from cooking to guitar at a cost in excess of $200 a day. The growth of guitar programs (dubbed "camps" by the families and spouses of attendees) was the result of shifting demographics and parallel growth trends in the guitar-manufacturing industry, the computer-software industry, and the educational-travel market.

Puget Sound Guitar Workshop

The oldest of all guitar summer camps was the Puget Sound Guitar Workshop, which had been around for 22 summers prior to 1996. A much more rustic affair than NGSW, it was located in a wooded setting about one-and-a-half hours from Seattle, Washington, where campers stayed in cabins and tents. The workshop enrolled an average of 115 students each week and had a staff of 18 instructors. Over 30 classes were offered each session during the three daily class periods. These ranged from level 1 (complete beginners) to level 4 (accomplished amateurs and professional musicians). The focus was on acoustic-guitar styles (finger picking, flat picking, blues, bluegrass, swing, and jazz). Unlike NGSW, Puget Sound's campers were evenly divided between men and women. Puget Sound's priority was to make an effort to bring in female teachers, which they reported as key to making women feel welcome. Tuition for the Puget Sound Guitar Workshop was $450 a week.

Sound Acoustic Music Camp

This camp was sponsored by the Puget Sound Guitar Workshop, but focused on letting intermediate and advanced students work on ensemble playing. A much smaller undertaking than Puget Sound (10 students per class, approximately 100 total attendees, for only one week), it concentrated on bluegrass, "old-time" music, and jazz. Like the Puget Sound camp, the Sound Acoustic Music Camp was also held in a rustic, woodsy setting. Tuition for the Sound Acoustic Music Camp was also $450 a week.

Augustana Heritage Center

The Augustana Heritage Center was located at Davis and Elkins College in Elkins, West Virginia. This camp was an all-around "folk-life center," of which guitar was one of many components. Other components included dance, folklore, and crafts. Augustana strove for a "family-friendly" environment, in which entire families could attend the camp with activities designed for each age group.

University of Wisconsin–Green Bay's Guitar/Bass-Guitar Camp

This program covered all musical styles and was specifically designed for teens. During its guitar week, the Green Bay camp offered a combination of rock and academic musicianship. In addition to guitar week, the Green Bay camp offered weeklong instruction in piano, jazz, school band, orchestra, and chorus.

California Coast Music Camp

The California Coast Music Camp, a nonprofit corporation, was founded in 1991 to educate the public in music and related art forms. "Inspired" by the Puget Sound Guitar Workshop, the California Coast Music Camp sponsored a weeklong summer adult music camp, which offered over 30 classes taught by nationally recognized artists. Guitar, bass, voice, fiddle, banjo, mandolin, percussion, and songwriting classes were among the offerings, which covered numerous styles—jazz, folk, blues, swing, and Brazilian. Instructors were professional musicians, composers, artists, and music teachers. The camp provided round-the-clock musical opportunities, such as jam sessions, song circles, open microphones, special-interest workshops, and dances. Concerts were given by the instructors to expose campers to the various styles and musicianship of their teachers. During the year, the California Coast Music Camp sponsored an ongoing concert series. Some concerts were accompanied by daytime workshops led by the same performers. As a nonprofit corporation, the camp used these events as fund-raising opportunities. Tuition for the week-long adult music camp was $400.

National Guitar Summer Workshop

David and Barbara Smolover

David Smolover, a product of the 1960s, was a member of the very generation that elevated rock groups and their lead guitarists to the status of cultural icons. A self-described ex-hippie, David had spent his childhood in a musical household. His father was a professionally trained opera singer who made his living as a cantor in Scarsdale, an exclusive suburb of New York City. Smolover began taking guitar lessons at age 13.

Like many of his peers, Smolover spent the late 1960s and early 1970s at a number of campuses in pursuit of a degree. During those years, he earned a living playing gigs as a professional guitarist and giving guitar lessons on the side. He finally settled in Seattle, where he graduated in 1975 from his fourth college, the University of Washington, with a degree in education.

Smolover continued to teach and play guitar professionally in Seattle. He eventually met his wife, Barbara, a graphic designer, and returned to the East Coast to settle down close to his parents. In 1982, the Smolovers purchased a house in Lakeside, Connecticut, a rural community in the northwestern part of the state.

Lakeside was an ideal location for a guitar teacher. First, northwestern Connecticut was a "boarding-school capital." Second, Lakeside was within striking distance of Fairfield County, Connecticut, and Westchester County, New York (where Smolover's parents lived), counties with the fifth- and eighth-highest per capita income in the United States, respectively. Here, too, were a steady supply of teenage guitarists with financially supportive parents. Finally, Lakeside's proximity to New York City provided Smolover with professional musical opportunities as well as an extensive community and network of professional musicians.

Smolover's services were in high demand in the early 1980s; so much so that he began to spread himself too thin: "I had access to all the students I could handle, but seeing them all was becoming too much for me. I was spending four hours a day commuting between Connecticut and Westchester."

Despite the time and hard work, Smolover quickly discovered that teaching students individually maximized his per-student earnings potential. This became a major consideration when Barbara became pregnant with their only child.

Beginning of the National Guitar Summer Workshop

Smolover realized that a majority of his Scarsdale students spent their summers at one of the numerous summer camps scattered throughout upstate New York and New England. He asked some of his students if they would be interested in attending a week of intensive all-day group guitar lessons. In the summer of 1983, Smolover conducted the first weeklong intensive guitar workshop with five students in the garage of his father's Scarsdale home. He immediately realized that he had tapped into a niche market. He began to investigate the possibility of expanding the program out of his father's garage into a facility that would provide not only practice space, but also room and board.

Fortunately, in addition to being the boarding-school capital, northwestern Connecticut was also one of the summer-camp capitals of the Northeast. Smolover consulted with various summer-camp managers who, not viewing a prospective guitar summer camp as a competitor, taught him the ropes of camp management: small margins and a constant struggle to squeeze profits out of camp tuition. Smolover's current system of calculating camp expenses and revenues based on "bed spaces" was learned under their tutelage.

Realizing that his dream of a summer guitar workshop was in reach, Smolover went in search of a facility. For the right price, Connecticut offered numerous boarding schools with ready-made dining, sleeping, recreation, and practice facilities that were empty during the months of July and August. His rounds of the various boarding schools led him to the South Kent School, where the business manager (an amateur guitarist) offered him not only a fair price for the summer rental of the school's facilities, but also help in securing a bank loan of $20,000. In the summer of 1984, with a $20,000 investment and a second mortgage on the Smolover's Lakeside home, the first session of the National Guitar Summer Workshop was held at the South Kent School in South Kent, Connecticut.

The NGSW's first session was advertised in national guitar magazines and by direct mail to local high schools and music schools on the East Coast. To attract the widest possible variety of students, the NGSW offered intensive classes in a variety of traditional styles—classical, jazz, acoustic, and rock. To staff the camp, Smolover drew from a pool of professional musicians and music teachers from the New York area who were either out of work or between gigs during the summer.

While Smolover and his wife were the only full-time administrators of the camp, many of the early instructors also doubled as camp managers, assisting in the day-to-day problems of feeding, housing, and controlling teenagers for one summer week. With 1984 tuition income of $64,004, the first summer of the NGSW was a success.

GROWTH AND PROCESS DEVELOPMENT IN THE LATE 1980s

In 1985, total tuition income more than doubled, to $152,370 (see Exhibit 3). The increase in enrollment was so dramatic between 1984 and 1987 that the NGSW had to seek larger quarters twice, moving to the Darrow School in New Lebanon, New York, in 1987, and then again in 1988 to its present location at the Canterbury School. Smolover installed a computer system in 1987 and began to keep detailed data on camp attendance, demographics, and effective advertising in 1991, going back to 1984.

In the early years, word-of-mouth established the NGSW's reputation as a serious summer-music program. Approximately 28 percent of NGSW alumni returned to the camp for subsequent sessions. Learning from the other camp managers in the area, Smolover developed a student/faculty hierarchy common to most summer camps, where returning workshop participants became CITs (Counselors in Training), enabling them to work their way up from paying student to low-paid junior staff. Several of the better former students returned in later years as full NGSW instructors.

A set salary scale was established for instructors. Instructors were classified as independent contractors, with wage increases dependent upon their tenure at the camp (see Table A). Roughly 80 to 90 percent of the faculty were "returnees." The top salary of $525 a week reflected the plentiful supply of guitar musicians and instructors in the New York area. Guest artists such as Chet Atkins, Pat Martino, and Joe Satriani taught special workshops for a one-time fee ranging from $700 to $3,500, depending on their level of celebrity.

Table A
NGSW Instructor Salary Scale

Category	Per Week
CITs	$150
First Year	375
Second Year	450
Third Year	525

As NGSW grew, Smolover formalized the management structure. He and Barbara were the sole owners and, in the beginning, the NGSW's only full-time employees. A layer of four directors and four associate directors was created to take on the added administrative and management tasks associated with the NGSW's growth. Directors' tasks, however, were never strictly delineated. Duties included everything from room assignments, employee relations, dorm monitoring, coordinating guest-artist visits, and generally acting as a buffer between Smolover and the day-to-day running of the camp. According to Paula Dutton, a longtime NGSW employee and director, "Everyone is expected to be able to do everyone else's job." Director salaries ranged from $600 to $825 a week, plus a bonus in good years (see Table B).

Table B

NGSW Director Salary Scale

Year	Per Week
First Year	$600
Second Year	650
Campus Director	825

Because there was no set method for teaching guitar, NGSW standardized its teaching methods and printed its own instructional guitar books. A minimum-qualification standard was established for faculty hiring, and new instructors were required to undergo two days of training prior to the beginning of the summer session.

Growth and Stagnation in the 1990s

NGSW was not the only guitar camp to emerge in the United States in the guitar boom years, nor was it the first. However, it was by far the most comprehensive program focused exclusively on the guitar.

Between 1984 and 1990, the NGSW experienced rapid growth. Thanks to the popularity of heavy-metal music among American youth, growth remained healthy until 1993. To improve NGSW's position within the summer-guitar-program market, Smolover expanded beyond the Connecticut campus with satellite campuses in other locations, broadened his advertising base, and diversified into complementary businesses.

Satellite Campuses

In 1989, Smolover opened the NGSW's first satellite campus at Dominican College in San Rafael, California, moving to Scripps College in Claremont, California, in 1991. This campus allowed NGSW to take advantage of the West Coast market by reducing the cost of attending the workshop for West Coast residents. In 1993, NGSW added a second satellite campus, at Humber College in Toronto, Canada, and in the summer of 1995 NGSW opened a third campus, in Nashville at Middle State University, to take advantage of the growing popularity of country and western music—one of the few popular-music mediums that had nearly always featured guitar playing. The fourth satellite campus was opened in Freiburg, Germany, in 1996 to capitalize on the longtime popularity of American guitar music in Europe. The satellite campuses were all based on the Connecticut campus model. Unlike the Connecticut program, however, which ran for six weeks, the satellite campuses only offered one one-week session each. Each NGSW satellite campus was managed autonomously by one of the NGSW directors, with all finances flowing through Connecticut. The Connecticut campus absorbed all the administrative costs, while each satellite was considered profitable if it covered its direct operating costs (e.g., facilities and salaries). Despite this expansion, the Connecticut campus remained the largest and most profitable (Exhibit 5).

EXHIBIT 5

National Guitar Summer Workshop Satellite Campuses, Attendance and Profitability, 1991–1996

Campus	Average Number of Students per Week	Break-Even Point
Connecticut	190	155
Toronto	40–60	60
Nashville	57–65	60
California	65–100	60

NGSW Weekly Attendance at Campus Locations
(in "bed spaces")

	Ses 1	Ses 2	Ses 3	Ses 4	Ses 5	Ses 6	Ses 7	Calif	Can	Tenn	Total
1996	80	166	182	193	197	154	180	65	34	56	1,307
1995	102	161	196	194	211	166	179	93	56	63	1,421
1994	73	145	195	164	197	175	155	71	62	67	1,304
1993	48	170	223	192	224	188	169	76	81	58	1,429

NOTE: Ses = session or week at the Connecticut campus.

CURRICULUM

Students selected a major area of study from the following NGSW major specializations: Rock, Jazz, Electric Blues, Finger Style, Guitar Skills, Bass, and Classical Guitar. Major courses were offered by style and level according to student preference and ability. On a typical day, students would attend two hours of classes in their major in the morning and one hour in the afternoon. Students also selected two minor subjects, which were one hour long and met once a day. In the evening, students worked on an ensemble piece that they would perform together at the end of the week in concert. Students could also opt to take a special seminar, which consisted of five-day classes taken in place of the major/minor curriculum, with fewer performance opportunities. These seminars usually featured major artists and ran five hours a day.

COSTS

In 1996, tuition at the Connecticut campus was $575 a week. The Canterbury School's weekly room and board costs averaged $177.50 per student (Exhibit 6). The combined NGSW break-even point was 1,320 bed spaces per summer across all campuses. Between 1992 and 1996, total room and board costs averaged $238,000.

MARKETING AND ADVERTISING

NGSW's marketing consisted mainly of direct mail and print advertising. In 1995, NGSW spent $20,000 on printing costs and $8,000 on postage, sending 10,000

EXHIBIT 6

Tuition and Direct Cost per Week at the National Guitar Summer Workshop

Year	Tuition	Cost
1984	$345	$80
1985	360	90
1986	375	100
1987	395	125
1988	395	135
1989	415	137
1990	435	139
1991	455	140
1992	475	145
1993	495	150
1994	510	167
1995	560	172
1996	575	177.50
1997	—[1]	140[2]

[1]Not established yet.
[2]Decrease in cost due to a guaranteed flat fee.

NGSW packages to music stores, 1,000 to guitar teachers and college music departments, 8,500 to high schools, and an undetermined number to NGSW alumni and others who had requested information on the workshop in previous years. NGSW also mailed to names on the Guitar Foundation of America mailing list for an additional $10,000 in postage. With the exception of 1994, when the U.S. Postal Service failed to deliver the NGSW bulk mailing, NGSW was successful with its mass-mailing campaigns. (The postal error resulted in a drop in brochure requests, attendance, and revenues for 1994.)

In addition, NGSW took out five months' worth of ⅓-page black-and-white ads in guitar trade magazines and the *New York Times*. NGSW also utilized magazine postcard inserts, which had a higher response rate than the print ads (see Table C). NGSW's magazine-advertising costs ranged between $30,391 in 1993 and $35,000 in 1995.

In 1996, NGSW introduced its Internet Web site. Despite increased advertising budgets, NGSW's visibility in a growing number of guitar trade publications, and mass mailings, NGSW hit a ceiling of 5,500 total inquiries and requests for information received in a given year (see Table D). Breaking the 5,500 barrier became an obsession with Smolover. In 1997, he planned to purchase the subscription list of various guitar magazines (totaling 80,000 names) at a cost of $30,000. With a 1 percent return on direct mail, this was expected to net 800 responses.

Table C

Where 1995 Attendees Learned about NGSW

Source	Number of Students
Referrals	292
Alumni	156
Guitar Player (magazine)	136
Posters	73
Guitar (magazine)	55
Acoustic Guitar (magazine)	53
New York Times	44
Guitar World (magazine)	42
Performing Songwriter	23
Guitar schools	22
Internet	15
Finger Style Guitar (magazine)	14
Guitar Solo (magazine)	5
Bass Player (magazine)	3
Downbeat (magazine)	3
Camp referral service	3
Jazz Times	1
Miscellaneous	14

Table D

NGSW Brochures Requested, 1993–1996

	1993	1994	1995	1996
Brochures requested	5,439	4,444	5,481	5,461

Camp Attendance

With the exception of 1994, camp attendance had been fairly constant (see Table E). The average length of stay by NGSW students, 88 percent of whom were male, was 1.4 weeks in 1992, declining to 1.3 weeks in 1996. To an extent, the decrease in enrollment after 1993 was anticipated by Smolover (1993 was the last year of the heavy-metal boom). The absence of a new lead-guitar pop-music trend signaled that the decline could continue until the end of the decade. In addition, middle-aged, born-again guitarists—the second traditional NGSW demographic group—were also projected to drop off (see Exhibit 7). People entering middle age in the second half of the 1990s were the disco-era population; their relative lack of interest in the guitar contributed to the guitar-industry collapse in the late 1970s. In other words, the next wave of middle-aged guitar players would be the teenagers who were taking heavy-metal guitar lessons in the early 1990s. Despite the leveling off, Smolover managed to maintain decent profits by cutting costs and increasing tuition and fees.

Among the annual returning baby boomers were a Washington, D.C., judge, a business-school professor, and Dr. Frank Forte, a 57-year-old oncologist and medical-school professor. When asked about the spartan quarters at the school—bare rooms, no air-conditioning, baths and phone down the hall—Dr. Forte commented: "I wouldn't have it any other way. There is no phone, newspaper, patients. It's not competitive (like college)—it's laid back."

Table E

NGSW Attendance and Attendance Deposits, 1991–1996

(in number of bed spaces; 1 bed space = 1 session attendance)

	1991	1992	1993	1994	1995	1996
March	281	301	124	137	171	162
April	368	365	379	327	407	306
May	484	424	589	494	476	465
June	295	349	320	264	297	347
July	81	82	95	73	134	53
August	21	19	19	2	10	
Accepted	1,530	1,540	1,526	1,297	1,495	1,333
Refunds	–80	–104	–97		–73	–56
Actual	1,450	1,436	1,429	1,297	1,422	1,277

Human Resources

Including Smolover, the NGSW had four year-round employees: Michael Allain was employed full-time at the NGSW's main Lakeside, Connecticut, office and was responsible for booking artists and lining up instructors for the summer; Nathaniel Gunod was the director of Workshop Arts, the NGSW's publishing arm; and Paula Dutton, an associate director and former NGSW main office manager, was generally acknowledged to "run the place," capable of performing numerous administrative tasks while maintaining sanity in a sea of creative personalities.

Musicians as managers was a recurring problem at NGSW. Of the eight NGSW directors and associate directors, seven were professional musicians. One NGSW administrator observed that the energy of the musician-managers was not always focused on NGSW management because they would rather be playing the guitar.

EXHIBIT 7

Age Breakdown of NGSW Attendees (Actual), 1991–1996

Age	1991	1992	1993	1994	1995	1996
12	5	4	6	7	15	15
13	20	25	34	19	43	48
14	69	94	108	85	94	91
15	139	128	132	134	136	126
16	162	160	159	123	112	116
17	118	115	105	77	87	81
18	56	60	51	58	42	40
19	33	27	29	32	23	24
20	30	34	30	13	14	25
21	35	22	26	19	26	12
22	12	19	14	22	10	15
23	25	8	16	10	15	7
24	15	17	15	11	13	12
25	9	15	19	10	21	10
26	25	9	20	11	10	18
27	13	20	9	9	11	6
28	19	10	15	10	13	6
29	16	12	14	14	15	11
30–34	72	75	77	63	93	56
35–39	62	60	70	52	95	58
40–44	42	39	64	76	95	86
45–49	16	22	27	24	43	56
50–54	7	9	7	13	15	27
55–59	0	5	5	4	7	5
60–64	2	1	1	2	6	2
65–70	1	1	2	4	4	1
unknown	35	36	14	23	32	23
Total	1,038	1,027	1,069	925	1,090	977

While Smolover was well liked among the faculty and staff, in 1996 some of the NGSW instructors were disgruntled. Although Smolover had established a graded salary scale in the late 1980s, the scale remained unchanged in 1995. In addition, the 1993 tax code required Smolover to withhold 12.5 percent of instructors' salaries. One longtime NGSW instructor who began attending the camp as a teenager and worked his way up to the top instructor salary grade explained:

> I came here every summer between age 15 and 18. Dave and the other instructors were like a family to me. Even in my early years as an instructor, it felt like we were all working together to make this place work. Now I feel like a temporary employee. Dave no longer remembers all the campers by name, and there are all these "directors" and "assistant directors."

Another camper-turned-instructor complained that the camp had gotten too big.

> When I was a teenager, I worked and saved money so that I could spend a week here in the summer. The instructors were well trained and the other students in my classes were pretty serious. The two-day instructors' seminar exists in name only. I feel like a babysitter. I have more teenagers and fewer adults in my class. Many of these teenagers are not serious. Their parents just want to get rid of them for the summer. I have one kid in my group whose parents sent him here for six weeks. It's gotten so bad that the camp now has a rule that students on Ritalin will not be allowed to attend class unless they have taken their medication.

Yet another instructor complained: "Dave's heart used to be into this place. Now he's got all of these other things on the side that I think he's just in the camp for the money."

But not all instructors were disgruntled. NGSW had maintained a 90 percent faculty-retention rate over its 13 years, and some of the newer instructors were delighted to be invited to participate. Jack Grassel, 40-year-old music-department chairman at Milwaukee Area Technical College, had applied for 10 years to be on the NGSW faculty. A former child prodigy who had performed in everything from small jazz clubs to Broadway musicals, Grassel was delighted when finally invited to teach at the Connecticut campus in 1995. "I was so excited. The experience here is wonderful. The [jazz] students are here because they want to be, and are dedicating 24 hours a day for a week at a time to their music. Teaching them is a real shot in the arm—it recharges my batteries before the fall semester starts again."

NGSW Diversification

A joke circulated among the NGSW staff in 1996: When David Smolover finds an empty closet, he starts a new business, preferably with someone else's money. This joke was not very far from the truth. Between 1989 and 1996, Smolover and the NGSW started several guitar-related ventures. Smolover was an energetic idea man, and he was constantly dreaming up proposals for guitar-related businesses that would popularize the NGSW name and keep it afloat. Many of his ideas did not always take flight, however, and as one NGSW staff member put it: "He gets an idea in his head and works on it day and night. Then if something goes wrong, or it gets too complicated, he completely loses interest." Smolover had dreams of expansion, but his staff members saw an NGSW that was in a constant state of crisis. Even the NGSW's longtime office manager and Smolover devotee stated: "If this place gets any bigger it will be over my dead body." The following is a sampling of some of Smolover's NGSW-related ventures.

Workshop Arts

In 1989, Smolover established Workshop Arts, a publishing and recording arm of the NGSW. Workshop Arts was directly responsible for developing programs and curricula for the NGSW, publishing more than 40 texts each summer. Between 1990 and 1995, Workshop Arts published/recorded 30 books with accompanying audiotapes (copublished with Alfred Publishing), produced two instructional videos, and recorded one instructional CD. Workshop Arts materials were distributed worldwide through Alfred Publishing. This venture became increasingly profitable, reporting pretax net-income growth from $11,218 in 1994 to $40,572 in 1995 (see Exhibit 8).

EXHIBIT 8

Workshop Arts Statement of Income and Expenses

	1993		1994		1995	
	Actual	Percentage	Actual	Percentage	Actual	Percentage
REVENUES						
Sales—Products	$11,729.60	10.4%	$4,017.82	3.9%	5,888.80	3.7%
Alfred royalties	12,702.16	11.3	27,999.27	27.3	45,294.84	28.2
Editorial fees	87,960.00	78.3	70,570.92	68.8	109,474.50	68.1
Total revenues	112,391.76	100.0	102,588.01	100.0	160,658.14	100.0
Factory overhead	313.16	0.3	—	—	—	—
Total cost of sales	313.16	0.3	—	—	—	—
Gross profit	$112,078.60	99.7%	$102,588.01	100.0%	$160,658.14	100.0%
SELLING EXPENSES						
Salaries—sales	$ 7,500.00	6.7%	$ 12,000.00	11.7%	$15,500.00	9.6%
Reimbursement to NGSW	—	—	—	—	1,020.50	0.6
Royalties	18,743.42	16.7	12,645.32	12.3	24,317.34	15.1
Author buyout fees	4,000.00	3.6	14,500.00	14.1	17,643.75	11.0
Studio fees	5,984.80	5.3	2,846.50	2.8	9,065.50	5.6
Photography	—	—	2,402.30	2.3	932.00	0.6
Advertising	574.90	0.5	1,215.53	1.2	1,338.69	0.8
Typesetting	21,288.80	18.9	17,795.25	17.3	21,610.00	13.5
Proofreading	2,633.73	2.3	2,165.90	2.1	2,543.90	1.6
Lino output	4,777.32	4.3	2,119.30	2.1	1,608.29	1.0
Printing	1,115.99	1.0	76.55	0.1	0.00	0.0
Duplication	2,321.20	2.1	903.25	0.9	1,391.83	0.9
Nabanco fee	15.84	0.0	—	—	—	—
Miscellaneous expense—sales	—	—	23.93	0.0	—	—
Book orders	—	—	—	—	200.00	0.1
Travel	896.43	0.8	5,739.42	5.6	5,724.44	3.6
Total selling expenses	$69,852.43	62.2%	$74,433.25	72.6%	$102,896.24	64.0%
GENERAL AND ADMINISTRATIVE						
Salaries and wages	$500.00	0.4%	$1,000.00	1.0%	—	—
Auto expense	188.34	0.2	—	—	—	—
Auto rental	235.06	0.2	—	—	$388.69	0.2%
Bank-service charges	194.50	0.2	54.55	0.1	257.29	0.2
Dues and subscriptions	80.00	0.1	0.00	0.0	36.00	0.0
Refund	49.90	0.0	—	—	—	—
Computer/printer lease	9,369.21	8.3	4,507.68	4.4	958.38	0.6

(continued)

EXHIBIT 8 (CONTINUED)

Workshop Arts Statement of Income and Expenses

	1993		1994		1995	
	Actual	Percentage	Actual	Percentage	Actual	Percentage
Computer	—	—	$3,029.68	3.0%	$1,422.61	0.9%
Legal and accounting	$1,118.00	1.0%	350.00	0.3	817.00	0.5
Miscellaneous expenses	1,404.14	1.2	—	—	114.82	0.1
Office expenses	3,071.45	2.7	1,623.17	1.6	2,050.89	1.3
Outside services	366.08	0.3	—	—	—	—
Postage expenses	4,059.62	3.6	2,207.82	2.2	3,647.76	2.3
Packaging	79.18	0.1	—	—	42.95	0.0
Supplies expenses	675.78	0.6	—	—	—	—
Repairs and maintenance	—	—	509.08	0.5	—	—
Rent expenses	—	—	—	—	600.00	0.4
Telephone	3,761.35	3.3	3,266.51	3.2	4,644.44	2.9
Travel and entertainment	421.14	0.4	9.50	0.0	117.15	0.1
Lodging	—	—	318.66	0.3	2,091.53	1.3
Food	92.43	0.1	60.00	0.1	0.00	0.00
Total general and administrative	25,666.18	22.8	16,936.65	16.5	17,189.51	10.7
Net operating income (loss)	16,559.99	14.7	11,218.11	10.9	40,572.39	25.3
Net income (loss) before tax	$16,559.00	14.7%	$11,218.11	10.9%	$40,572.39	25.3%
INCOME TAXES						
Federal income tax	—	—	—	—	$6,501.00	4.0%
State income tax	—	—	—	—	1,715.00	1.1
Total income taxes	—	—	—	—	8,216.00	5.1
Net income (loss)	$16,559.99	14.7%	$11,218.11	10.9%	$32,356.39	20.0%

(continued)

Smolover had plans to expand this venture into interactive video on the Internet as soon as the technology became cost effective (see Exhibit 9).

NATIONAL MUSIC WORKSHOP (NMW)

Smolover established the National Music Workshop in 1993 in partnership with Daddy's Junky Music Stores, a northeastern regional music-store chain with nine locations. In an effort to broaden the base of the NGSW, the NMW was a music-education program that offered NGSW-modeled instruction to locals serviced by Daddy's Junky Music Stores. Through the stores, potential guitar students had access to private lessons, group classes, and NGSW seminars. At the end of 1995, the NMW reported a net loss of $4,642 (see Exhibit 10).

EXHIBIT 8 (CONTINUED)

Workshop Arts Balance Sheet (December 31)

	1993	1994	1995
ASSETS			
Current assets:			
Bank of Boston	$ 869.49	$ 869.49	$ 869.49
New Milford Bank & Trust	12,295.52	152.33	15,210.22
Cash transfers	—	5,765.00	4,765.00
Loans and exchanges	(500.00)	(500.00)	(500.00)
Total current assets	12,655.01	6,286.82	20,344.71
Total assets	12,665.01	6,286.82	20,344.71
LIABILITIES AND EQUITY			
Current liabilities:			
Notes payable—short term	(10,669.41)	(28,265.71)	(47,265.71)
Current portion, long-term debt	(20,371.38)	(20,371.38)	(20,371.38)
Total current liabilities	(31,040.79)	(48,637.09)	(67,637.09)
Equity:			
Retained earnings	24,169.72	40,729.71	51,947.82
Initial cash-balance offset	2,937.65	2,937.65	3,639.15
Net income (loss)	16,559.99	11,218.11	32,356.39
Total equity	43,667.36	54,885.47	87,943.36
Total liabilities and equity	$12,626.57	$ 6,248.38	$20,306.27

COMPLETE GUITARIST NEWSLETTER

Noticing the absence of an education-centered guitar magazine, in 1994 Smolover founded the *Complete Guitarist Newsletter*. This bimonthly publication featured articles on the practical aspects of becoming a professional musician, the legalities of copyrighting, and guitar-playing lessons, written by heavy-hitters in the professional guitar world. The subscription cost was $15 a year, and the first two issues were distributed free of charge to NGSW alumni and guitar teachers. Unfortunately, the newsletter never generated a profit, and publication was discontinued at the end of 1995.

GUITAR EXPO

In 1994, the NGSW cosponsored three Guitar Expos with *Guitar Player* magazine in New York, San Francisco, and Boston. The Guitar Expos were weekend events consisting of exposition space managed and rented out by *Guitar Player* to guitar-related merchandisers. During the expo, the NGSW conducted a series of workshops, demonstrations, and seminars based on their standardized curriculum. The NGSW's involvement in the expo resulted in a $30,000 loss for the NGSW, which withdrew its sponsorship in 1995.

EXHIBIT 9

Workshop Arts Information Sheet

Established in Connecticut in 1989 by the National Guitar Summer Workshop.

Description: Publishing (Workshop Arts) and recording division (Workshop Sounds). Developing programs and curricula for the National Guitar Summer Workshop provided us with a unique perspective in regard to instructional materials. The NGSW publishes over 40 texts each summer. Over the past five years we have published/recorded 30 books with accompanying audiotapes (Workshop Arts copublishes these materials with Alfred Publishing), produced two videos, and recorded one CD.

Products: Educational books, tapes, and videos.

Videos:
The Essentials of Classical Guitar
A Musician's Guide to Publicity and Promotion
Reference:
Mode Encyclopedia
The Stand-Alone Series:
Blues (with cassette or CD)
Fusion (with cassette or CD)
Contemporary Rock (with cassette or CD)
Jazz (with cassette or CD)
Rockabilly (with cassette or CD)
Heavy Metal (with cassette or CD)
Classic Rock (with cassette or CD)
Funk (with cassette or CD)
Blues and Beyond (with cassette or CD)
Classical Repertoire:
Towns & Cities
Workshop Sounds:
1993 Sampler

Methods:
Beginning Rock Guitar
Intermediate Rock Guitar
Mastering Contemporary Rock
Beginning Blues Guitar
Intermediate Blues Guitar
Advanced Blues Guitar
The Technique Series:
Bending (with cassette)
Speed (with cassette)
Metal Techniques (with cassette)
Slide (with cassette)
Tapping (with cassette)
Finger Style (with cassette)
Scales and Modes:
Pentatonics (with cassette)
Mixolydian (with cassette)
Dorian (with cassette)
Alternate Tuning
Jazz for the Rock Guitarist

Market: The national distribution network of Alfred Publishing sells these books worldwide.

NATIONAL SCHOOL OF MUSIC (NSM)

In 1995, Smolover proposed the creation of the National School of Music as a year-round expansion of the NGSW summer program. The plan called for purchasing a campus in Connecticut to create two programs: an accredited music conservatory that would offer a two-year degree in contemporary music, and a college-preparatory program for teenagers. At the NSM, students could major in guitar playing, recording technology, or guitar building. For an application pool, the NSM collegiate program would draw on the 5,000 or so NGSW alumni who would be entering the 18-to-25 college-age group.

EXHIBIT 10

National Music Workshop Statement of Income and Expenses

	1995	
	Actual	Percentage
INCOME		
Fees	$52,055.06	99.8%
Fees from courses	106.00	0.2
Total income	$52,161.06	100.0%
EXPENSES		
Miscellaneous expenses	$ 50.00	0.1%
Refunds	119.00	0.2
Tax deposits paid to NGSW	5,481.81	10.5
Loan repayment—NGSW	500.00	1.0
Salaries and wages	20,342.60	39.1
Salaries, bonuses	250.00	0.5
Awards	300.00	0.6
Salaries, subcontractors	275.00	0.5
Advertising	1,694.45	3.2
Printing	411.30	0.8
Bank-service charges	183.00	0.4
Computer	2,200.00	4.2
Miscellaneous expenses	130.00	0.2
Office expenses	772.59	1.5
Postage expenses	424.29	0.8
Rent, Daddy's Junky Music	18,875.00	36.2
Telephone	1,552.95	3.0
Telephone—SNET	1,718.23	3.3
Travel and entertainment	1,361.45	2.6
Lodging	162.15	0.3
Total expenses	56,803.82	108.9
Net operating income (loss)	(4,642.76)	(8.9)
Net income (loss) before taxes	(4,642.76)	(8.9)
Net income (loss)	$ (4,642.76)	(8.9)%

(continued)

Several colleges and music institutes offered degrees in contemporary music. The NSM's primary competition included the Berklee School of Music in Boston and Musicians Institute in Hollywood, California. The Berklee School of Music offered a four-year bachelor of arts degree and had 2,500 full-time students, 1,250 of whom majored in guitar. In 1996, tuition was approximately $12,000 a year. Room and board for freshmen was an additional $6,000 a year. The graduation rate for freshmen at Berklee was well under 50 percent. Musicians Institute, which was purchased in 1995 by ESP Guitars (a Japanese guitar manufacturer) for $10 million,

EXHIBIT 10 (CONTINUED)

National Music Workshop Balance Sheet (December 31, 1995)

ASSETS	
Current assets:	
Bank of Boston	$ 1,224.05
Total current assets	1,224.05
Total assets	$ 1,224.05
LIABILITIES AND EQUITY	
Current liabilities:	
Credit card—VISA	$ (152.00)
Sales taxes payable	1,122.00
Payroll taxes payable	5,724.45
Total current liabilities	$6,694.45
Equity:	
Retained earnings	$ (827.64)
Net income (loss)	(4,642.76)
Total equity	$(5,470.40)
Total liabilities and equity	$ 1,224.05

offered a one-year certificate program. Until 1996, students did not receive college credit for their year of study. In 1996, enrollment was approximately 1,000 students, 750 of whom were guitarists. The tuition was $9,500 a year, with no housing provided.

NGSW's community-music program would draw its applicants from Connecticut-area public and private schools. The program would provide students 12 to 18 years of age with a college-preparatory curriculum in the arts—music, dance, fine arts, and creative writing. The second program would consist of private and group instruction in the NSM arts areas. Smolover expected the NSM to have advantages over its competitors in terms of curriculum, location, and price. As of 1996, Smolover had not found financial backing for this project.

Borders Books and Barnes & Noble

In 1996, the NGSW contracted with Barnes & Noble and Borders Books to provide weekly in-store arts events (for the nominal fee of $150 per event), including musical demonstrations, art demonstrations, and readings for children. NGSW's rationale for stepping out of its traditional guitar-related role was to increase its exposure in central Connecticut as a precursor to the proposed NSM community-arts program. The NGSW planned to expand its exposure as an arts "provider" by compiling a database of its artists and arts services and marketing them to local school boards and municipalities.

As he placed the remaining rented Peavey amplifiers on the UPS truck, shut down the computer, and closed the administrative offices of the Canterbury School for the last time in 1996, Smolover wondered what strategy or strategies he needed to pursue to ensure the survival and prosperity of NGSW.

ENDNOTES

[1]"1980–1989: Tumultuous Times in the New Global Market; Musical Instrument Industry," *Music Trades* 139 (January 1991):186.
[2]Ibid.
[3]Ibid.
[4]Ibid.
[5]"The Music Products Industry Census: Overview," *Music Trades* 144 (April 1996):84.
[6]Ibid.
[7]Tibbett L. Speer, "Marketing to Musicians," *American Demographics* (March 1996):30.
[8]Ibid.
[9]Ibid.
[10]Ibid., 30–31.
[11]"Going Out on a Limb: Top Suppliers Try Their Hand at Predicting Future—Industry Overview," *Music Trades* 143 (January 1996):125.
[12]Speer, "Marketing to Musicians," 32.
[13]Kim Cleland, "Study: Typical Web User Is College-Educated Male," *Business Marketing* (December 1995):22.
[14]Richard O'Mara, "Adults Happy Campers, Too; Learning Camps Serve Wide Interests," *Baltimore Sun*, September 3, 1995, 4G.
[15]Ibid.

CASE 15

MARRIOTT CORPORATION

Bill Marriott Jr., president and CEO of the ninth largest hotel chain and the third largest server of food in the United States, was concerned. Although he had led the company through an impressive 12 years of growth, with sales increasing almost nine times, earnings seven times, and return on equity more than doubling, the annual compounded growth rate was only 17.3 percent, which was below the company's 20 percent goal and compared poorly with the 20.5 percent for the previous 15 years. Furthermore, the company's major source of growth, hotels, appeared to be facing a decline in growth rate. According to Fred Malek, executive vice president for Marriott's Hotel Group, "We can't maintain our rate of room growth at 20 percent. We see a compound growth rate of 16 to 17 percent for the next three years, but beyond 1986 the markets will be fully supplied and our growth rate could decline to 10 to 12 percent."

Bill Marriott was "getting heat" from Tom Curren, his senior vice president for planning, to branch out of full-service hotels for the first time. It was clear to Marriott that some change was needed:

> I have seen chains that have adopted a no-growth approach in the hotel business, and I have seen them go out of business. The reason is that a good person, after he's been in the same job for five years ... starts looking around for something else. And then the whole ball of twine starts to unravel. You lose your senior people ... then your properties start deteriorating, service starts going, and you start losing money.

Don Washburn, the vice president of hotel planning and the newest member of the Marriott management team, also was concerned. As the "product champion" for a new chain of Marriott budget hotels, he had been assigned by Bill Marriott the task of developing a detailed implementation plan that could generate substantial future growth for the company. It was clear to Washburn that although Bill Marriott was open minded about such a chain, he was still skeptical about execution of the concept and wanted to see the project move faster. Other managers were not just skeptical; they were opposed to the new concept.

COMPANY BACKGROUND

In 1927 John Willard (Bill) Marriott opened a small root beer stand in Washington, D.C. A decade later, after opening his eighth stand, now called Hot Shoppes, he expanded into in-flight catering of the airlines. In the early 1950s he built his first hotel and took his company public. (For more information on J. W. Marriott and the early days of his company, see Exhibit 1.)

This case was prepared by Jim Kennedy, Research Associate, under the supervision of Professor William E. Fulmer.

EXHIBIT 1

The Founding of Marriott: Bill Marriott Sr.

John Willard (Bill) Marriott was born in the Marriott Settlement near Ogden, Utah, on September 17, 1900. The son of a sheep farmer, he was a third-generation Mormon, whose grandfather moved to Utah in 1854 with the second wave of Mormons.

At the age of 19, J. W. Marriott, as encouraged by his church, set out to preach the gospel of Mormonism for two years. His father sold the family car and his mother her gold watch and chain to finance his mission to New England. While there, he received a rude awakening one night when an angry mob chased him and his partner out of town by torchlight and with gunfire. After completing his mission in another state, he returned home by way of Washington, D.C. It was September, and J. W. took special note of how the soda pop vendors were selling cart after cart of soda pop and ice cream in the sweltering heat.

At home he discovered that the postwar depression in livestock prices had forced his father to borrow nearly $50,000 from the Ogden State Bank. J. W. quickly concluded that his life was somewhere else and that his ticket out was education. The fact that he had never finished high school did not deter him; he convinced an administrator at recently established Weber State Junior College in Ogden to enroll him and allow him to make up high school credits and arrange odd jobs to pay tuition. In 1923 J. W. was a member of the first graduating class. The next fall he enrolled at the University of Utah, where he met Alice ("Allie") Sheets. They were engaged in 1926, just before J. W.'s graduation.

After graduation J. W. returned to Weber College to teach English and theology and to help with fund-raising. He became intrigued, however, with a new drink being sold from stands in Salt Lake City—A&W Root Beer. After learning that franchises were available and that some vendors made enough in the summer months to take the rest of the year off, he borrowed $1,500 and invested $1,000 of savings in franchises for Baltimore, Richmond, and Washington, D.C.

In 1927, just prior to Allie's graduation and their wedding, J. W. returned to Washington to open a small root beer stand on 14th Street, N.W. The A&W franchise agreement forbade the sale of any product other than A&W Root Beer, but, realizing that in winter people would lose interest in cold drinks, J. W. successfully sought a change in his franchise agreement so that he could sell food. Drawing on her western background, Allie cooked tamales, chili, hot barbecue sandwiches, and hot dogs in their apartment, and J. W. served customers in a nine-stool unit. At the suggestion of a customer, the stand was named the Hot Shoppe—a name "so bad it's good," Allie said.

After the success of the original Hot Shoppe, J. W. opened another on Ninth Street, N.W. Then for the third Hot Shoppe, he looked for a location that would allow plenty of parking for curb service because he had decided

(continued)

EXHIBIT 1 (CONTINUED)

The Founding of Marriott: Bill Marriott Sr.

to use a new invention—a tray that affixed to an open car window—to introduce the first drive-in restaurant east of the Mississippi River. With an expanded menu that included salads and ham sandwiches flavored with Allie's own sauce, the third Hot Shoppe, opened in 1929, served as a model for others to come. The new sandwiches sold for 15 cents, the tamales and hot dogs for 10 cents, and the drinks for a nickel. By the time the stock market crashed, the Marriotts were selling $1,400 of food and drink each day from the three units.

As the chain grew throughout the 1930s, J. W. and Allie continued to visit every restaurant every day—ordering meals, talking to customers, and even checking the garbage cans. After the fifth unit, J. W. began using central mass production and procurement systems.

In 1937 Hot Shoppe number eight was built near Washington's old Hoover Airport. Not only did people stop, eat in their cars, and watch the planes take off and land, but the manager noticed that travelers on their way to the airport would stop in, buy food to go, and take it on the plane with them (in-flight service at the time was primitive at best). So Hot Shoppes began selling box lunches for airline travelers, along with large thermos bottles of milk and coffee. Soon J. W. convinced Eastern Air Lines to buy Marriott bag lunches for its passengers. As Hot Shoppes expanded geographically, so did the in-flight catering, and soon the company was serving the Newark and Chicago airports.

J. W. opened his first contract cafeteria in 1942 and soon had the Navy as a customer.

Hot Shoppe number eight was located between two heavily traveled highways and about a half mile from National Airport. After successfully resisting pressure from two government agencies to sell the land for an approach to the 14th Street bridge, in 1950 J. W. purchased the adjoining eight acres for $60,000 per acre. The site provided the perfect location for his latest project: a $7 million motor hotel that, in J. W.'s words, would be "the logical extension of Hot Shoppes' traditional concern for the American family on wheels."

Considered upscale at the time, the 370-room unit was the largest motor hotel in the world and featured such amenities as soundproofing, drive-in registration, a Hot Shoppe overlooking the swimming pool, an observation deck to view the Washington skyline, TV sets in every room, king-size beds, wall-to-wall carpeting, and baby-sitters on call. Allie picked the red-and-gold room decor, the family hung pictures on the walls, and Bill Jr., just out of the Navy, supervised the final months of construction and the grand opening with daughter Debbie cutting the yellow ribbon.

In the early 1950s, J. W., seeing the growth of other area companies that had gone public, sold 229,880 shares of Hot Shoppes, Inc., to the public (for $10.25 a share) and 18,000 shares to employees (at $7.54 a share). The family retained control of about two-thirds of the company's 704,800 shares.

The success of the first hotel led J. W. Marriott to construct additional properties, and by 1958 the hotel division had been established, with J. Willard Marriott Jr. (Bill Jr.), as vice president. According to J. W., "I think we're opportunists in a way. I never had any great dreams about what I was going to do. But what I was doing I wanted to make successful. When I made that successful, I wanted to go on to something else."

In 1960, to the dismay of many traditional Mormons, the Philadelphia Marriott opened with the company's first cocktail lounge. As J. W. explained to the church elders, "If I want to stay in the hotel business, I've got to sell liquor."

By 1964 J. W. Marriott was worried, however. Although he operated 45 Hot Shoppes, four hotels, and the airline catering service, he was experiencing some health problems and the company appeared to be a "runaway horse." For example, in 1964, 17 new eating establishments were opened (three cafeterias, three restaurants, six parkway and turnpike establishments, and five institutional cafeterias); Bill Jr. was building hotel number five (a 500-unit in Atlanta), was about to start construction on another one in New Jersey, was breaking ground in Boston, and had three more on the design boards. In J. W.'s opinion, the company was plunging into debt like a "ne'er-do-well crap shooter" and it was Bill Jr.'s hotels that were responsible.

According to J. W. Marriott, "I told my sons that this is a tough business and that you'd better be a stockbroker or something." Despite his reservations, in late 1964, he decided that the time for change had come. At an announcement ceremony in November, he named Bill Jr. president of the company. Earlier that year, as he had wrestled with the decision, he had written Bill Jr. an outline of his management philosophy (Exhibit 2).

J. Willard Marriott Jr.

According to a 1985 *Management Review* article:

> When Bill Marriott talks, his attitude is open and warm, his voice young and lively—almost preppy. His vocabulary is speckled with "gosh," "gotta," and "sure betcha." He believes in God, country, and family, and thinks good character is a "must" in a manager. In a one-hour interview he uses the word "fun" six times—and each time the word is used in relation to running his business.[1]

As a kid, Bill, along with his younger brother, Dick, frequently accompanied his father on business trips and began working with the company part-time as soon as he was old enough to get a permit. During college Bill started most mornings at 4:00 A.M. at the Salt Lake Hot Shoppe with the breakfast chef. He worked the grill, the fountain, the deep fryer, and the salad block.

In college Bill had all of the advantages of an oldest son of a multimillionaire. Nevertheless, the former Eagle Scout dressed plainly, made consistently high grades, and graduated from the University of Utah with top honors from the business school and the Navy ROTC. His only indulgence was the flame-red Jaguar that he sported around campus. According to Bill, "When you are raised in a religious family, you have to be a person of character and good standards to be accepted."

EXHIBIT 2

Letter from J. W. Marriott Sr., to J. W. Marriott Jr.

January 20, 1964

Dear Bill:

I am mighty proud of you. Years of preparation, work, and study have shown results.

A leader should have character, be an example in all things. This is his greatest influence. In this you are admirable. You have not taken advantage of your position as my son. You remain humble.

You have proved you can manage people and get them to work for you. You have made a profit—your thinker works. You are developing more patience and understanding with people, more maturity.

It is not often that a father has a son who can step into his shoes and wear them on the basis of his own accomplishments and ability. Being the operating manager of a business on which probably 30,000 people depend for a livelihood is a frightening responsibility, but I have the greatest confidence you will build a team that will insure the continued success of a business that has been born through years of toil and devotion by many wonderful people. I have written down a few guideposts—all born out of my experience and ones I wish I could have followed more closely.

Love and best wishes.
Sincerely,
(signed) Dad

Bill's 15 "guideposts":

1. Keep physically fit, mentally and spiritually strong.
2. Guard your habits—bad ones will destroy you.
3. Pray about every difficult problem.
4. Study and follow professional management principles. Apply them logically and practically to your organization.
5. People are No. 1—their development, loyalty, interest, team spirit. Develop managers in every area. This is your prime responsibility.
6. Decisions: Men grow making decisions and assuming responsibility for them.
   a. Make crystal clear what decisions each manager is responsible for and what decisions you reserve for yourself.
   b. Have all the facts and counsel necessary—then decide and stick to it.
7. Criticism: Don't criticize people but make a fair appraisal of their qualifications with their supervisor only (or someone assigned to do this). Remember, anything you say about someone may (and usually does) get back to them. There are few secrets.

(continued)

EXHIBIT 2 (CONTINUED)

Letter from J. W. Marriott, Sr., to J. W. Marriott, Jr.

8. See the good in people and try to develop those qualities.
9. Inefficiency: If it cannot be overcome and an employee is obviously incapable of the job, find a job he can do or terminate *now*. Don't wait.
10. Manage your time.
    a. Short conversations—to the point.
    b. Make every minute on the job count.
    c. Work fewer hours—some of us waste half our time.
11. Delegate and hold accountable for results.
12. Details:
    a. Let your staff take care of them.
    b. Save your energy for planning, thinking, working with department heads, promoting new ideas.
    c. Don't do anything someone else can do for you.
13. Ideas and competition:
    a. Ideas keep the business alive.
    b. Know what your competitors are doing and planning.
    c. Encourage all management to think about better ways and give suggestions on anything that will improve business.
    d. Spend time and money on research and development.
14. Don't try to do an employee's job for him—counsel and suggest.
15. Think objectively and keep a sense of humor. Make the business fun for you and others.

After a stint in the navy, Bill Jr. married his college sweetheart, and he joined the Marriott Corporation in 1956. He spent his first six months in the restaurant division but was soon transferred to public relations. Later that year he began coordinating the final stages of construction of the company's first hotel—The Twin Bridges. By 1958 Bill was running the newly formed hotel division, and one year later he was also named president of Hot Shoppes.

Although the growth was not as fast as he would have liked, within a year Bill had opened three more hotels: "I felt that the company had to grow and that to grow we had to have more hotel units. Hotels are a greater challenge than restaurants. They generate higher profits." Bill financed the growth by debt. "As my father was always saying, he owed $2,000 when he first came to Washington in 1927 as a young man; now he owes $20 million, and that, he says, is progress!"

In 1964, at the age of 34, Bill was named executive vice president of the company and later that year was elected president. In 1967 the company's name was changed to Marriott Corporation and one year later was listed on the New York Stock Exchange. In 1972 Bill was officially designated chief executive officer (CEO).

After assuming control of the company, Bill realized that the rapid growth it had been experiencing required management expertise that the company did not have. "I had to terminate between 20 and 30 people. My dad could never have done what I did." Some of those let go were relatives and longtime family friends of his father. He compensated most of them handsomely and allowed many to retire.

Friends say that the ordeal made him physically sick. He quickly moved to bring in outside professional management.

In 1975, when earnings per share dipped slightly after years of growth, Bill decided that there were too many unproductive assets and a lack of marketing and finance professionals in the company. He hired new managers who could begin to dispose of unproductive businesses and concentrate on expanding hotels at a faster rate. When the recession of 1979–1980 helped to depress the stock price below $25, management spent $259 million to buy back a third of its stock.

Under Bill Marriott Jr., the company grew through expansion of the hotel operations and acquisition of restaurant and travel-related businesses:

1965–1970: *Big Boy and Roy Rogers franchises and a travel agency (since sold).*

1970–1975: *Sun-Line cruise ships, Great America theme parks (since sold), and Farrell's ice cream parlors (since sold).*

1975–1984: *Host International airport restaurants and Gino's fast-food restaurants for conversion to Roy Rogers units.*

By 1984 Bill Jr. was president and CEO of the largest private employer in the Washington area (20,000 employees) and one of the largest in the United States. His 1.1 million shares of Marriott stock made him a very rich man, but according to Bill it was not the money that satisfied him: "You get to a point where it's not really that any more. Then most businesspeople, they're in it for the pride of accomplishment and the success in what they do. It's fun to do things and get things done. The key is to keep that going." He also adds, "If you don't generate excitement, you don't generate much."

According to *Business Week*, Bill was a "self-confessed, Type-A, workaholic" who regularly spent 70 to 80 hours a week on the job, about half of it on the road. It is estimated that he traveled 200,000 miles a year on company business, visiting 100 hotels and 25 flight kitchens and eating at company restaurants as often as five times a week. In 1982 he spent 180 days on the road. Bill said he practiced "management by moving around" (Exhibit 3):

> That's not original, but it's what I do. You can check up and appraise how things are really going if you get down on the line. You can get a feel if the people are up or down, if they're being motivated and care. You can see if a place is getting worn. You don't see that if you're sitting behind your desk.
>
> I have a nice office. It would be a lot more fun to sit in the easy chair in the office and read reports and talk on the telephone every now and then and think up great strategic ideas rather than fly 200,000 miles every year to visit another hotel, or a flight kitchen, or a customer.
>
> I found that the successful managers in our hotels stay out of their offices. They are out inspecting rooms, checking restaurant food and service, pouring coffee at breakfast in the dining room, welcoming our guests when they check in, and bidding them goodbye when they check out. They are walking the property, listening to the guests and the employees, looking for problems to solve and solving them.

According to *The Washingtonian*, when traveling,

> Bill asks guests at a hotel what they think, what they like and don't like. He joins a stranger at breakfast to check the service. He asks a flight attendant about the

EXHIBIT 3

"KEEPING IN TOUCH," FEBRUARY 27, 1985, *THE WALL STREET JOURNAL*

WASHINGTON— J. Willard Marriott Jr., the Chief Executive Officer of Marriott Corp., is wandering around the basement of his flagship hotel here. Randomly yanking a dinner plate out of a storage cabinet, he spots a splotch of dried food. "You really ought to soak some of these dishes," he reminds the hotel manager.

. . . .

Often he checks out his hotels at odd hours: midnight in the kitchen, for instance, or 5 A.M. in the laundry room. "When you start trying to anticipate what he'll find, you get better as a manager," says John Dixon, the general manager of the new JW Marriott hotel here.

On a recent visit, Mr. Marriott found plenty. Seconds after entering the atrium-style lobby, his eyes darted left to a pink marble pillar. On a visit to the hotel a few weeks before, Mr. Marriott had noticed an unwaxed strip about half-an-inch wide circling the pillar's base. "I see you cleared up that problem. Looks good," he said approvingly, shaking Mr. Dixon's hand.

A few minutes later, Mr. Marriott was in the kitchen. Looking like a man running for office, he greeted about a dozen employees with firm pumps of the hand, a broad smile and a "Hi, how ya doin'?" He addressed a few of the old-timers by their first names and embraced one.

Then he grimaced as he discovered a batch of hash browns left over from breakfast two hours earlier, a violation of one of the strict written rules that dictate food portions and preparations. "This is a penny business," says Wes Merhige, the general manager of the Santa Clara, California Marriott, "and Bill knows how to keep track of the pennies."

Before his two-hour tour ended, Mr. Marriott peeked in on the front desk, the laundry ("good, no wrinkles"), the loading dock, the exercise spa, storage lockers ("what's hidden in here?") and about half-a-dozen rooms and suites. At the employee cafeteria, he swept through the room, shaking hands with at least 50 startled workers.

In fact, Mr. Marriott is so involved in every detail of his business that he selects the color of the carpeting for hotel lobbies.... Mr. Marriott believes his involvement has given the company an advantage. "The edge in this business is people," he says. "I'm trying to communicate that I care and that the role they play in the organization is an extremely vital one."

---

food that's being served—and gets an opinion from the passenger next to him as well.

He's quick to suggest changes. On a visit to the Boston Long Wharf Marriott, he thought the carpet in the lobby looked dirty, and ordered it replaced with a darker color. The Newport Beach Hotel had bought 50 clay pots and filled them with flowers; Bill thought they looked so good he ordered similar planters for all the California Marriotts.[2]

Although he admitted that travel was a strain, he saw it as "part of the culture of doing business today." He rejected the idea of a corporate plane, however, choosing to fly commercial coach most of the time: "Too expensive. It would drive me crazy knowing two guys were sitting around out there with their meters ticking, waiting for me to fly off." He told an anecdote about his father's thriftiness:

> I have a lot of great people working for the company, among them a half dozen so-called superstars who report to me, who think we should have a corporate jet. And I remind them that, although we are a $3 billion company and probably the only one in the country that does not have a $3 million jet, we do have 17 beautiful used Rambler automobiles that belong to my father. Anytime they want to use one of those, they are privileged to ask his permission (he probably won't let them do it). You see, he served on the board of American Motors many years ago and was on long enough to get a new car every year at cost. When he went to turn in his current car for a new model, they would never give him the cost back on the car, so we now have 17 used Ramblers in our family.

In general Bill believed "Work is good and necessary. That was the attitude around me when I was growing up. My father worked hard. My mother worked hard. I was *expected* to get all *A*s when I was in school or I sure was asked why." (For more information on some of Bill Marriott's other interests, see Exhibit 4.)

Another characteristic of Bill Marriott's management style was described by one of his managers:

> He's got to be one of the world's greatest listeners. He conveys to you that you have his full attention. He can handle great diversity. He tolerates spirited diversity of opinion in meetings; he doesn't squelch it. Consequently, most decisions are reached by talking them through. Once there were two schools of thought about an issue. After 30 minutes of debate, no one had changed their opinion and someone remarked, "That's why we have a chief executive."
>
> Bill said, "Oh hell" and made the decision. But that's not the typical way a decision is reached at Marriott. Bill prefers to have a consensus develop from the dialogue.

Another executive commented on his leadership:

> He doesn't run a financial holding company. His leadership can attract strong people to him. He can create a climate where there is healthy disagreement. In the Finance Committee, he says, sometimes he doesn't get a word in edgewise. He's secure enough in his leadership that you don't have people jockeying to be president next year. He provides a stable climate that allows people to use their strengths. He utilizes his counselors very well.

One of his counselors was his father. Although Bill was quick to give his father credit for "getting the company started," "making it work," and "establishing the culture," he once remarked,

> Working for your father is very difficult. You say things to your father that you would never say to your boss, and he says things to you he'd never say to a subordinate.
>
> Whenever there was a major decision, he [his father] would tell me all the things he saw wrong with it—and, believe me, there were plenty. But if I insisted on going ahead he never stopped me, because the decision was mine and I knew I had better make it work. I also knew that if I was going to make it work I had better anticipate the problems before they hit me head on. I had to be sure, as much

Exhibit 4

Other Interests of Bill Marriott Jr.

Bill devoted time to the Boy Scouts, Chamber of Commerce, and Business-Industry Political Action Committee and gave about 15 to 20 hours a week (evenings, Saturdays, and Sundays) as well as 10 percent of his gross income to his church. Not only was his family instrumental in building the Washington Mormon temple, but Bill, a former bishop, was currently president of the Washington "stake," the equivalent of a diocese, and oversaw the spiritual well-being of 35,000 Mormons:

> I don't know how much you know about our church, but it is basically a lay church. We have no paid ministry, and so they put us all to work. They installed me as a bishop about 12 years ago. I was really the parish priest. I had 750 members in my ward: I had a lot of singles, I had Spanish, and I had American families. I had all kinds of diverse people to take care of.
>
> I spent 30 hours a week listening to marital problems, youth problems, father problems, mother problems, parenting problems. And I think it did more to develop me as an executive than any experience I have ever had, because I was put into a position of having to deal with people's lives, people's aspirations and hopes and sorrows and fears.
>
> I preached funerals; I performed marriage ceremonies. I did everything that the parish priest or the parish minister does in other churches. And so I learned firsthand again the... importance of being empathetic toward people, taking care of people, learning to listen to people, and learning to help them solve problems. It was a great reinforcement for me in the business world and probably one of the great experiences in my life.
>
> In many of my counseling sessions, I saw that if I listened they solved their own problems. I have definitely learned to listen better and to be more compassionate. When you listen to a woman with kids who is divorcing, you become exposed to people and their problems in their own context, not just how you saw them before. I've learned to deal with people whose lives have not been as fortunate as mine. I've learned to deal with compassion. It's given me understanding.
>
> I think my people feel I am a pretty good listener. I'll listen to what they say, and I'll try to get their input. But I'm still willing to make the decisions.

The *Washingtonian* article tied together Bill Jr.'s Mormon heritage with his life and philosophy:

> He believes the Mormon doctrine—God lives on a planet and has a wife—and he follows the church's puritanical scriptures: no liquor, tobacco, or caffeine. His verities are God, country, hard work, self-denial, and strength of character....
>
> Bill Jr. says that the Mormon emphasis on family has made him a better executive. In many ways, the Marriott Corporation is an extension of the Marriott family. Bill Jr. says that the Mormon ethic of hard work has become the company's ethic. "We try to instill the Mormon ethic in the employees," explains his brother Dick. "But we don't preach the Mormon doctrine here. We just have a good Christian work ethic."

(continued)

EXHIBIT 4 (CONTINUED)

Other Interests of Bill Marriott Jr.

> He's a family man. He tries to get to his youngest son's soccer games every Saturday. He spends his free time with his wife and kids; he never misses Sunday dinner, and the whole Marriott clan gets together for Mother's Day, Father's Day, Christmas, and Easter. He has simple tastes. He lives in a small two-story colonial house in Chevy Chase. He buys his suits off the rack at Joseph Bank. His one passion is speed: During college he drove a Jaguar; later, he zipped around in a Lamborghini; he is now the proud owner of a new Jaguar sedan. He also likes to race powerboats.

During the summer of 1983, although the plan had been discouraged by the Marriott board, Bill raced up the Mississippi River in an effort to set a new record for the 673-mile race:

> It was like being in a black closet with sort of a pale light in front of you from the buoys. So at night for about two hours there was a risk. You don't know if you're going to hit a boat; you don't know if you're going to run aground; you don't know if you're going to hit a big log.

Yet, he described it as

> more fun than anything I've done in years. I thought as I was driving that boat, "Not only am I doing something I like to do, but I am also trying to achieve something. I'm moving toward a goal. I'm not out for a joy ride in a boat riding around in a circle. I'm headed from Point A to Point B in an attempt to get there faster than anyone else has ever done it before."

> as possible, that the light at the end of the tunnel was that ray of hope that we all look for when we make decisions, and not the Santa Fe Super Chief.
>
> If I have had any success in business, I think it is because I have had a teacher who was willing to let me make mistakes and then to know that I had to fix them. . . . I guess that is why I try hard not to veto the recommendations of those who work for me.

In 1984, at the age of 83, as chairman of the board, J. W. Marriott still took an active role in the business, talking to his son almost every day and studying memos and cost reports. He and his wife, also on the board, owned 862,412 and 939,431 shares of Marriott stock, respectively. He once observed, "People say 'Weren't you ever satisfied?' I've never been satisfied. I see things now that haven't been right all along."

Management Practices

Although Bill Jr. considered his father "one of the pioneers of the chain restaurant systems," he would rather "perfect than pioneer." In reflecting on his approach, he commented, "To make the right decisions, you have to have a thorough understanding of your people, your business, and your products. Lacking that, you make bad decisions." A key to Marriott's success, he believed, was its employees (Exhibit 5)—motivating, teaching, helping, and caring about them. Bill Sr. explained:

> If your managers can treat your people right and be sincerely interested in them, then you'll be successful. We must be interested in people, all people. I believe that the success of our company from the very beginning was simply because we have been interested in our people. When we had only a few restaurants, the people who worked for us were just like members of our own family. If they got sick, we went to see them. If they had trouble, we tried to get them out of trouble, and they, in turn, developed a warmth and a loyalty to us that money couldn't buy. . . . Those who work for us must like us. If they like you and have respect for you, then they will do almost anything for you. They will look after your customers properly, and a spirit of friendliness will pervade your whole organization. And what a wonderful thing that sort of harmony is.

The company was decentralized when it came to recruiting, training, and staffing, with each division, hotel, or restaurant hiring its own employees. College recruiting was coordinated centrally (with Bill Jr. occasionally joining in), but each division recruited for itself at approximately 40 colleges and at seven MBA programs. In this recruiting effort, Bill Jr. wanted recruiters to look for certain qualities—people skills ("Some of the brightest often don't have people skills"), high motivation, and willingness to sacrifice:

> I have been concerned that our business schools around the country are not graduating businessmen. I would go to business colleges and universities and try to talk to and recruit graduates. The ones that I talked to seemed to be anxious to become administrative assistants, strategic planners, financial analysts, treasurers. I asked them, "Do you want to learn to cook? Do you want to work in a kitchen? Do you want to carry suitcases, to check in people at the front desk? Would you like to learn the business?"
>
> And the answer was almost always, "No, why would I do that when I can work on corporate strategy or make big financial transactions?" And I told them that by not wanting to learn the basics of the business, they were not developing a foundation of knowledge and skill that would equip them to move into a senior manager's position, which is what they all wanted to do anyway. They did not realize that, to be truly effective future managers, they had to learn to manage in their own particular sphere in business.
>
> I was also not able to convince them that the truly effective manager succeeded because he had the knowledge and the skill [that] gave him the self-confidence to operate comfortably as the boss. They had thought the operations people would respect and perform for them even if they didn't understand the business.

He also believed effective managers let their people try new things and yet held them accountable:

> It is not really the mistake that concerns and upsets me nearly as much as the refusal by someone to try and make it work. For I believe we must try and try and never give up until success is achieved. We must be willing to take some risks. The guy that shot the hole-in-one had to get on the golf course in the first place.

EXHIBIT 5

Dave Roberts, John Dixon, and Donna Moore: Three People Who Show Why Marriott Is a Winner

Dave Roberts started working for Marriott Corporation nine years ago as a grill man at a local Hot Shoppes Jr. He worked part-time at a Roy Rogers while he studied at the University of Maryland. Then he decided to become a restaurant manager, so he took a three-week course at Marriott headquarters on how to run a Roy Rogers. He worked as a management assistant for a couple of months, then was named a unit manager. He took charge of a Roy Rogers in Waldorf, Maryland; then he supervised the openings of some of the newly converted Gino's; now he's managing Roy Rogers number D55 on upper Connecticut Avenue. And he's looking up: In three years, he hopes to be a district manager.

He is blond, blue-eyed, and 26. He wears wire-rimmed glasses. He gets to the restaurant at six every morning to supervise the opening. The tables have to be sparkling clean; the salad bar has to be prepped; the beef roasts have to go into the oven at eight o'clock. He stays "till death do us part," sometimes as late as ten at night. He usually works the night shift on Fridays.

On the job, Roberts wanders from station to station making sure that the cooking is up to standard, that the person at the cash register is working efficiently, that the tables are cleaned after each diner leaves. He handles all customer complaints. He's in charge of ordering supplies for the unit and counting the receipts every night. He watches who comes in. There's a regular clientele: elderly residents of the Van Ness community down the street, UDC students, IBM employees from the offices upstairs. And Roberts supervises the three management trainees who are at his store for three weeks to learn how a real Roy Rogers works.

His favorite job is spotting management potential. If Roberts thinks that one of his hourly workers could handle a supervisory job, he suggests that the employee apply for a training course. The employee goes to headquarters for two months to learn some management basics, then comes back to Roberts's shop to learn how to run each of the hourly stations. Next, a management internship, assisting a manager like Roberts. In the past year, Roberts has spotted seven trainees. One left the company when her husband moved out of the area; another couldn't handle the pressure of a management job; five now manage Roy Rogers units.

The long hours don't give Roberts much time to spend with his wife, Maya, an advertising executive at Sentinel Publications. When he can, he works at fixing up the couple's new house in Crofton, Maryland. He also plays tennis and rides his bike. Roberts loves his job, and he was tickled a couple of months ago when he met cowpuncher Roy Rogers in person at the opening of a new unit. "He was a lot smaller than I'd imagined," says Roberts. "I thought he was a tough, tall cowboy. He's small and delicate." Roberts wasn't disillusioned, however, and he's never given a thought to leaving the company. "There's never a day the same as the next," he says. "There is always something out of the ordinary. I like that."

John Dixon was no novice when he joined Marriott Corporation three years ago: For eight years, he'd been a

(continued)

EXHIBIT 5 (CONTINUED)

general manager at the Hyatt Hotel on Union Square in San Francisco. But Dixon still had to go through the Marriott management training program. He started with a weeklong course called "Introduction to Management," which taught him how Marriott Corporation deals with people. Then he went to food school for a week to learn to cook from the company's recipe cards. After that, Dixon spent three months training at the Tysons Corner hotel. The first day he worked on the loading dock, unpacking boxes from delivery trucks. The next day he was in the kitchen, first as a banquet cook, then as a line cook. He worked at the front desk making reservations, checking in guests. He was a housekeeper for a day, learning how to make up a room. The manager at Tysons Corner gave Dixon written tests on what he was learning. Dixon passed with flying colors.

Finally Dixon was named a "resident" at the Crystal City Marriott. That meant he was responsible for hotel operating areas like housekeeping and the front desk. A year after he joined the company, Dixon was made a general manager at Tysons Corner. He worked there for a year. Then he was tapped to be manager of the new JW Marriott at National Place.

He's a big man with a jaunty mustache. He wears a three-piece suit and a gold pocket watch. He's a bachelor. Mostly, however, he's in the office: eight in the morning till eight at night. And he couldn't be prouder of his job. The new hotel will be a showcase that Bill Marriott says will "represent what the new Marriott hotels stand for."

"It will be a very special hotel," says Dixon. There will be two concierge floors, a floor of luxurious suites overlooking Pennsylvania Avenue, and a presidential floor offering full butler service. Rates start at a steep $98 a night; the largest suites will go for $750.

For the past two years, Dixon has supervised a sales team and has put together a 700-person hotel staff. Once the hotel opens, he'll be the head troubleshooter, and he expects guests to come to his mezzanine office and tell him if the hotel is doing something wrong. He loves his work. He recently took a course in advanced management techniques, and he hopes to move up the management ladder, perhaps opening another larger hotel in the next few years. "What I like best about this company is the pace," he says. "It's exciting. It's challenging. This is not a company that has found its place under the sun."

Donna Moore has been running the Marriott hotel gift shops for nine years. When she took the job, the shops weren't managed as a unit. Each one had its own image and did its own purchasing; the quality varied considerably from hotel to hotel—and Bill Marriott wasn't happy about that. Moore's assignment was to make the shops more uniform and more profitable. And she has. The gift shops are now geared to the Marriott business guest—they sell everything from ashtrays to Hathaway shirts to designer stockings to Kachina dolls. Goods are bought at headquarters; quality and service are tightly controlled. The bottom line: Marriott gift shops are about twice as profitable as the top New York department stores.

The secret, says Moore, is hard work. Moore supervises everything: floor plans, hiring, training, merchandising. She spends half her time on the road visiting gift shops, talking to regional managers, examining merchandise. She is always looking for new items, and her friends never stop making suggestions. Often those aren't helpful, but a few work out. A friend in California showed Moore a handmade doll last year; Moore ordered some samples from the maker in North Carolina

(continued)

EXHIBIT 5 (CONTINUED)

and liked them so much she asked the woman for 1,200 dolls—three times what the woman can deliver this year. Sometimes, Moore develops her own product ideas. When the JW Marriott opens next month, the gift shop will boast a Gund bear with a custom sweater reading, "JW Bear," a Moore innovation. J. Willard Marriott Sr. got a sample for Christmas. "He's a teddy bear," says Moore.

She is a small woman with red hair and brown eyes. She lives in Annapolis with her husband, a boat maker. Moore has a daughter and a fourteen-month-old granddaughter. She spends her free time sailing: Mexico, the Caribbean. For years she worked at Joseph Magnin, a women's retailer based in San Francisco. She left when Cyril Magnin retired and the company stopped being a family enterprise.

Her next goal at Marriott is to spin off the gift shops as a separate division, run as a retail outfit instead of a hotel unit. She thinks that would be more profitable. "Working for Marriott is fantastically exciting," she says. "This is still a family business. If Mr. Marriott sees something he likes or doesn't like in the shops, I hear about it. There is lots of contact with the people at the top. It is important to have people talk to you on a first-name basis. It's thrilling for me."

Bill Jr. also believed that it was important to know what prospective employees had "done with their lives" and what their relationships with their spouses and families had been like. He believed, "We are living in a much more righteous and puritanical society than just a few years ago. Much of what has happened in the way of business scandals that have almost ruined companies is making businesspeople much more cognizant of honesty and good character in managers." He also believed that another advantage to the business of good character was honesty in giving opinions: "I don't want a bunch of yes men. Your people are your best resource. If they aren't helpful, why have them? You want people to challenge you. You've got to have good advice."

Another quality Marriott was seeking in recruiting was the ability to get along with all types of people; the company wanted corporate people who were not "too entrepreneurial." As Bill Jr. explained, "We are in the people business, and from waiters to maids to truck drivers, our employees must be able to get along pleasantly with others all day long."

As *The Washingtonian* described Marriott,

> It's an egalitarian company, with few perks for executives: no company plane, no limos, no executive dining hall. Top executives lunch at the employee cafeteria; the fancy health club at headquarters is open to all employees for $1 a month—and even Bill Jr.'s brother Richard, vice president in charge of restaurants, has to reserve his racquetball court in advance.

Bill Jr. also insisted on giving people "a fair shake." Consequently, every employee received a formal performance evaluation at least once a year that identified both strengths and areas that needed improvement, including suggested ways for improving. Each division was required to follow certain guidelines in matters of discipline. In particular, except for a few very serious offenses, no one could be fired unless warned in writing three times. Bill Jr. maintained,

> It seems like common sense to me. When you abdicate in fairness or responsibilities, the union takes over by default.... In a lot of companies there is a very hostile attitude. Let's admit it. There are people who like to fire people. Some managers may not know it, but they have created a fear-oriented attitude. They may call it "productivity-oriented," but if their people are afraid of them and tattle on each other, it's no good.

Although compensation standards were established for the corporation as a whole, with a 28-grade salary structure, each division was able to adjust its compensation levels to remain competitive in its respective markets. Ninety percent of Marriott employees were paid on an hourly basis, and except for 10 percent who had come with acquisitions, none were union members.

Part of the fair shake was a companywide profit-sharing plan, under which the company donated an average of $1.55 for every dollar paid in by an employee. Recently a retired dishwasher had received $104,000 after 17 years with the company, a secretary $149,000 after 20 years, and a top executive $477,000 after 21 years.

Partially as a result of some "bad experiences" in hiring people from outside into line positions, Marriott emphasized internal promotion and training. For example, 30 percent of Marriott's managers were estimated to have started as hourly employees. Furthermore, the company spent $20 million annually on training. The *Washingtonian* article noted:

> Perhaps the most important part of the training program is attitude. It's hard to teach an employee to be nice, but Marriott tries with twelve rules, printed in each job manual: (1) Listen to guest complaints. (2) Filter through to the real problem. (3) Develop alternative solutions. (4) Act immediately and visibly. (5) Never promise what you cannot deliver. (6) Defer that which is beyond your authority to control. (7) Look for something (however unimportant) in the guest's remarks with which you can agree. (8) Give the guest your individual attention. (9) Smile and be pleasant. (10) Initiate the conversation. (11) Give your name. (12) Follow up on any guest complaints to insure satisfaction.

New managers and executives at Marriott spent as much as eight months working in the field. Bill Jr. explained that they needed exposure to actual operations:

> What happens with MBAs is they come in here and like strategy; they become junior CEOs. That's OK, but they've had a steady dose [of that] for two years. Involvement in the details gives you the basis for planning. If you know your business, you understand what's going on out there, and you can't be led along by strategists or theorists who don't know the real world you operate your business in.

He added,

> Today many people say the image of a Marriott manager is a person who is leaning over to pick up the piece of paper off the lobby floor. Well, I've caught myself picking up pieces of paper off the floor at the Sheraton, the Hyatt, the Hilton, even in airports—and I end up putting them back down where they belong.

Operations at Marriott were strictly controlled. For example, each hotel maid had a list of 66 things to do in cleaning a room: Step number 7—dust the tops of pictures; Step number 37—make sure the Bible and telephone books are in good condition. Bill Jr. asserted, "The more the system works like the army, the better." After all, he said, "We make our profit in small increments, not home runs." In the restaurants, each portion, plate, and presentation was standardized; the cooks, regardless of their authority or training, were forbidden to deviate from the 6,000 carefully tested and approved (in central kitchens) Marriott recipe cards: "Deviation from the standard written specification may not be made without prior approval and written consent of the vice president of food and beverages." In 1981 at an American Bar Association luncheon, the system resulted in 600 burned chickens. Nevertheless, the ABA was trying to book another Marriott hotel for 1986.

Each month top managers received, via computer terminals in every office, the equivalent of a 50-page report on how the company was doing. It included such information as profit margins, revenues, customer counts, and occupancy rates. It was management's goal to develop computerized information networks that linked each restaurant, hotel, and flight kitchen to its respective regional office and divisional center in Washington.

Bill Jr. met frequently with senior executives and kept a loose-leaf notebook that listed everything he had asked anyone to do. He also read letters from 20 random Marriott guests each week. As he said in one of his magazine ads: "I have to make sure we do things right. After all, it's my name over the door."

Divisional Structure

In the words of one executive, Marriott was "a loose confederation of businesses" that emphasized "high-quality growth" (Exhibits 6–8). It was divided into three strategic business units: restaurants, contract food services, and lodging. Each was led by an executive vice president.

The restaurant group, headed by Dick Marriott, a Harvard MBA who owned 1.3 million shares of Marriott stock and served on the board, basically consisted of Roy Rogers and Big Boy restaurants. With a menu that included chicken, burgers, roast beef sandwiches, and hot-topped potatoes, Roy Rogers sought to provide high-quality fast food to adults in the Mid-Atlantic and Northeastern states from 388 company-operated and 131 franchised units. Big Boy was a full-service coffeehouse restaurant that featured breakfast bars and a greenhouse effect. Marriott held franchise rights for 26 states, where it operated 209 units and was responsible for the franchises of another 636 units.

Contract Food Services, headed by Bob Schultz, the former president and CEO of Barwick Corporation and an executive with both Colt Industries and General Housewares, supplied food for more than 350 airlines, businesses, health care facilities, and educational institutions. This group was divided into four divisions: airline catering, airport operations, food service management, and highway restaurants. Airline catering, or in-flight services, served 150 airlines from 90 flight kitchens worldwide. Airport operations included terminal vending machines and restaurants. The acquisition of the Host chain in 1982 for $148 million aimed at giving Marriott a greater presence in this area. Marriott estimated that 60 percent of all people who flew in the United States passed through a Marriott/Host terminal facility. Food Service Management included institutional feeding, especially company cafeterias.

EXHIBIT 6 (CONTINUED ON NEXT PAGE)

Marriott Corporation Financial History, 1975–1985

	Years							
	1984	1983	1982	1981	1980 (53 weeks)	1975	5-Year Compound Growth Rate	10-Year Compound Growth Rate
SUMMARY OF OPERATIONS[1]								
Sales	3,524,937	2,950,527	2,458,900	1,905,659	1,633,892	775,866	19.8%	17.7%
Earnings before interest and taxes	284,794	240,331	200,345	173,339	150,278	63,160	16.4%	16.5%
Interest cost, net	48,691	55,270	66,666	52,024	46,820	23,017		
Income before income taxes	236,103	185,061	133,679	121,315	103,458	40,143	17.5%	18.9%
United States and foreign income taxes	100,848	76,647	50,224	45,176	40,567	15,995		
Income from continuing operations	135,255	108,414	83,455	76,139	62,891	24,148	16.9%	18.8%
Net income	139,765	115,245	94,342	86,136	72,030	24,148	14.5%	19.2%
Funds provided from continuing operations[2]	322,485	272,655	203,556	160,770	125,790	75,486	22.4%	16.8%
Capital expenditures and acquisitions net of hotel sales	286,289	499,439	483,498	247,999	168,289	132,500	13.2%	6.2%
CAPITALIZATION AND RETURNS								
Total assets	2,904,669	2,501,428	2,062,648	1,454,876	1,214,264	830,975		
Total capital[3]	2,330,683	2,007,507	1,634,504	1,167,458	977,690	739,311		
Shareholders' equity	675,560	628,204	516,005	421,729	311,505	263,730		
Debt and capital lease obligations	1,115,287	1,071,611	889,325	607,743	536,607	405,658		
Percent to total capital	47.9%	53.4%	54.4%	52.1%	54.9%	54.9%		
Return on average shareholders'equity	22.1%	20.0%	20.0%	23.4%	23.8%	9.5%		
Return on average total capital (before interest and taxes)	14.1%	14.4%	14.8%	17.6%	18.0%	9.1%		

	YEARS							
	1984	1983	1982	1981	1980 (53 weeks)	1975	5-Year Compound Growth Rate	10-Year Compound Growth Rate
PER SHARE AND OTHER DATA								
Fully diluted earnings per share:								
Continuing operations	5.01	3.90	3.04	2.83	2.27	.69	24.1%	21.8%
Net income	5.18	4.15	3.44	3.20	2.60	.69	21.6%	22.2%
Cash dividends	.465	.38	.315	.255	.21	—	22.3%	
Shareholders' equity	26.22	23.37	19.43	16.12	12.43	7.68		
Quoted market price at year-end	73.50	71.25	58.50	35.88	31.75	15.46	33.4%	27.4%
Shares outstanding	25,760,968	26,876,344	26,554,692	26,158,762	25,061,265	34,358,503		
Hotel rooms:								
Total	60,873	54,986	49,432	40,419	30,169	16,072	18.3%	15.7%
Company-operated	50,930	45,909	41,126	33,088	23,704	12,987	19.4%	16.1%
Employees	120,100	109,400	109,200	81,800	67,300	47,600	12.8%	10.5%

[1]Operating results have been restated for theme park operations discontinued in 1984.

[2]Funds provided from continuing operations consist of income from continuing operations plus depreciation, deferred taxes, and other items not currently affecting working capital.

[3]Total capital represents total assets less current liabilities.

SOURCE: Annual Report, 1984.

EXHIBIT 7

Marriott Corporation Income Statement, 1982–1984
(dollars in thousands, except per share amounts)

SALES	1984	1983	1982
Lodging	1,640,782	1,320,535	$1,091,673
Contract food services	1,111,300	950,617	819,824
Restaurants	772,855	679,375	547,403
Total sales	$3,524,937	$2,950,527	$2,458,900
OPERATING INCOME			
Lodging	$161,245	$139,706	$132,648
Contract food services	90,250	73,300	51,006
Restaurants	76,220	61,634	48,492
Total operating income	327,715	274,640	232,146
Interest expense	(61,638)	(62,786)	(71,760)
Interest income	12,947	7,516	5,094
Corporate expenses	(42,921)	(34,309)	(31,801)
Income before income taxes	135,255	108,414	83,455
Income from discontinued operations	4,510	6,831	10,887
Net income[1]	$139,765	$115,245	$ 94,342
PRIMARY AND FULLY DILUTED EARNINGS PER SHARE			
Continuing operations	$5.01	$3.90	$3.04
Net income	$5.18	$4.15	$3.44

[1]Discretionary cash flow for 1984 = $278 million; 1983 = $246 million; 1982 = $192 million.

SOURCE: Annual Report, 1984.

Highway restaurants operated Marriott Restaurants on some major turnpikes and thoroughfares.

The Lodging Industry and the Hotel Group

The daily average number of hotel/motel rooms in the United States had experienced constant growth in recent years. One industry source estimated the numbers to be 2.2 million in 1978, 2.3 million in 1980, and 2.4 million in 1982. During the same period, average room rates increased from the low $30s to approximately $50 in 1982.

Marriott research identified 2,150,000 competitive rooms in the lodging industry, broken down into 80,000 luxury, 620,000 quality, 750,000 moderate, and 700,000 budget rooms. Other analysts identified only the three large segments, while some segmented by price band or price/value, an attempt to measure the amenities provided against the price.

EXHIBIT 8

Marriott Corporation Balance Sheet, 1983–1984 (dollars in thousands)

ASSETS	1984	1983
Current assets:		
Cash and temporary cash investments	$ 22,656	$ 92,279
Accounts receivable	195,874	151,975
Due from affiliates	46,467	17,655
Inventories, at lower of average cost or market	111,722	95,806
Prepaid expenses	53,330	43,655
Total current assets	430,099	401,370
Property and equipment, at cost:		
Land	141,714	171,984
Buildings and improvements	245,367	373,593
Leasehold improvements	658,815	716,461
Furniture and equipment	415,634	475,003
Property under capital leases	77,566	86,539
Construction in progress	668,845	388,025
	2,207,941	2,211,605
Depreciation and amortization	(375,108)	(419,823)
	1,832,833	1,791,782
Other assets:		
Investments in and advances to affiliates	268,177	68,412
Assets held for sale	230,760	81,312
Cost in excess of net assets of business acquired	26,742	26,380
Other	116,058	132,172
	641,737	308,276
Total assets	$2,904,669	$2,501,428

(continued)

Revenues for most U.S. hotels came from room rentals (60 percent), food sales (24 percent), beverage sales (10 percent), and miscellaneous services (6 percent). The gross profit on a room was often as high as 70 percent, which did not reflect depreciation or debt-service costs. For food the gross profit was 15 percent to 20 percent.

Hotel properties were managed in a variety of ways, but the two most common were management contract and franchise. Under management contract, chains agreed to sell their properties, in whole or in part, and contracted to operate them for the owners. Usually the fee was a percentage of the gross revenues or gross profit. This method had grown increasingly popular in recent years. Hilton Hotels, for example, managed 35 properties under contract in 1983 and received $20.5 million in contract fees; they collected only $23 million in franchise fees from 194 franchised properties.

With franchise arrangements, hotels were neither owned nor operated by the hotel company. Instead, the company received a percentage of revenues in exchange

EXHIBIT 8 (CONTINUED)

Marriott Corporation Balance Sheet, 1983–1984 (dollars in thousands)

LIABILITIES AND SHAREHOLDERS' EQUITY	1984	1983
Current liabilities:		
Short-term loans	$ 7,486	$ 8,895
Accounts payable	252,806	194,499
Accrued wages and benefits	129,452	111,420
Other payables and accrued liabilities	152,654	149,308
Current portion of debt and capital lease obligations	31,588	29,799
Total current liabilities	573,986	493,921
Debt:		
Mortgage notes payable	632,923	491,999
Unsecured notes payable	420,860	509,144
Total debt	1,053,783	1,001,143
Capital lease obligations	61,504	70,468
Other long-term liabilities	99,323	55,175
Deferred income	160,371	4,834
Deferred income taxes	280,142	247,683
Shareholders' equity:		
Common stock, 25.8 and 26.9[1] million shares outstanding, respectively	29,419	29,422
Capital surplus	145,756	140,882
Deferred stock compensation and other	3,141	4,160
Retained earnings	622,283	494,585
Treasury stock, at cost	(125,039)	(40,845)
Total shareholders' equity	$ 675,560	$ 628,204
Total liabilities and shareholders' equity	$2,904,699	$2,501,428

[1]Marriott family holdings are approximately 22%.

SOURCE: Annual Report, 1984.

for the use of the company name, advertising support, and reservation system. Most large chains were heavily franchised. For example, in 1983, 1,489 of Holiday Inn's (HI) 1,707 properties and 255,213 of its 310,337 rooms were franchised. Most of those properties were 10 to 20 years old, and approximately 50 percent of HI's 600-plus franchise holders owned 2 or fewer properties. The typical HI franchise agreement required an initial payment of $300 per room plus 4 percent of revenues.

The customer base for domestic hotels could be divided into three groups: pleasure, business, and personal markets. Approximately 180 million Americans took at least one pleasure trip of greater than 100 miles from home each year. They accounted for about 40 percent of all hotel nights sold. Approximately 18 million people took business trips each year and accounted for 45 percent of the hotel rooms sold. In contrast to business travel, which was generally paid by employers, personal travel, such as job hunting, funeral attendance, and so forth, was usually at the traveler's expense; it accounted for the remainder.

In recent years hotel construction had been concentrated at the upper end of the market, primarily because of rapidly escalating construction costs. Two industry rules-of-thumb held that room rates should equal $1 for every $1,000 of construction cost applicable to a given room, and that breakeven was an occupancy rate of 55 to 60 percent. In many markets, owners of commercial-class hotels, which cost about $95,000 a room to build, could not charge sufficiently, while operators of luxury hotels, which cost about $125,000/room, could. Some firms, such as HI's Crowne Plazas and Ramada's Renaissance Hotels, were aggressively pursuing the higher segments with traditional rooms, while other firms, such as Quality Inns and Brock Hotels, had announced plans to enter the all-suite market. Other hotels were diversifying into gaming (gambling casinos). In 1983, Ramada Inns derived 55 percent of revenues and 45 percent of operating profits from gaming operations; HI earned 37 percent and 40 percent, respectively.

There had also been growth in the budget end of the market (Exhibit 9). The companies ranged from the economy segment (Motel 6, Super 8, Econo Lodge, Red Roof, and Scottish Inns) that could be built for $15,000 to $20,000 a room and charged $18 to $29; to "luxury budget" (Days Inns, La Quinta, and Comfort Inns) at $30,000 to $37,000 to build and $25 to $39 in room rates.

The Marriott Hotel Group, headed by Fred Malek, former Green Beret and Harvard MBA, operated 142 hotels and resorts in almost all of the top U.S. markets plus Mexico, Central America, the Caribbean, Europe, and the Middle East. From 1975 to 1984, the number of Marriott rooms increased from 14,000 to more than 60,000 and by 1990 was expected to reach more than 100,000—a rate faster than any of the other major hotel chains:

	Number of Rooms	
Chain	1975	1982
Holiday Inn	240,500	265,585
Best Western	82,841	150,188
Ramada Inns	87,251	86,503
Sheraton	74,500	79,803
Hilton Hotels	59,931	80,473
Friendship Inns	59,000	84,000
Howard Johnson's	57,800	59,360
Days Inns of America	36,992	43,549
Trusthouse Forte (TraveLodge)	29,404	29,000
Quality Inns International	31,975	48,350
Best Value Inns/Superior Motels	14,400	21,300
Motel 6	21,788	33,166
Hyatt Hotels	19,500	36,300
Marriott Hotels	14,953	42,182
Rodeway Inns International	18,855	17,860
Westin Hotels	13,213	14,012
La Quinta Motor Inns	5,762	14,705

By 1985, 80 percent of Marriott's rooms would have been built during the previous decade, 90 percent built or renovated in the previous five years, and 26 percent would be less than two years old. Marriott estimated that 60 percent of its rooms were in the quality group and 20 percent in each of the luxury and moderate groups.

EXHIBIT 9

Top 50 U.S. Economy/Limited-Service Lodging Chains

Chain Name	Ownership Structure	Number of Properties	Number of Rooms	Average Property Size	Geographic Concentrations[a]	Published Room Rate Ranges: Single
1. Days Inns	Company owned/ Franchised	291	45,410	156	MA, USA, ENC, WSC, UM, LM, P	$23.88–$56.00 X-Person $5
2. Motel 6	Company owned	394	43,881	111	National	$16.95 X-Person $4
3. La Quinta Motor Inns	Company owned/ Franchised	157	19,545	124	SA, ENC, ESC, WNC, WSC, UM LM, P	$29.00–$49.00 X-Person $5
4. Econo Lodges	Franchised	233	17,561	75	National	$21.95–$39.95 X-Person $4
5. Super 8 Motels	Company owned/ Franchised	234	14,967	64	National and Canada	$21.88–$42.88 X-Person $5
6. Hospitality International (Master Host/ Red Carpet/ Scottish Inns)	Franchised	161	13,265	82	MA, USA, SA, ENC, ESC, WSC	$22.00–$34.00 X-Person $5
7. Red Roof Inns	Company owned	123	13,161	107	NE, MA, USA, SA, ENC, ESC, WNC, WSC	$21.95–$26.95 X- Person $5
8. Comfort Inns (a division of Quality Inns)	Franchised	130	11,599	89	NE, USA, SA, ENC, ESC, WNC, WSC, UM, LM, P, CANADA	$21.00–$52.00 X- Person $5
9. Knights Inn	Company owned	60	6,594	110	USA, ENC, SA, MA	$24.00–$32.00 X-Person $5

[a]Geographic Concentrations Legend

Region	States	Region	States
New England (NE)	ME, NH, VT, MA, CT, RI	West North Central (WNC)	IA, KS, MN, MO, NE, ND, SD
Mid Atlantic (MA)	NY, NJ, PA	West South Central (WSC)	AR, LA, OK, TX
Upper South Atlantic (USA)	MD, DE, WV, VA	Upper Mountain (UM)	CO, ID, MT, UT, WY
South Atlantic (SA)	FL, GA, NC, SC	Lower Mountain (LM)	AZ, NV, NM
East North Central (ENC)	IL, IN, OH, MI, WI	Pacific (P)	CA, OR, WA
East South Central (ESC)	AL, KY, MS, TN		

(continued)

SOURCE: *Hotel & Management*, April 1985.

The "mix of property types" included downtown locations (32 percent), airports (24 percent), suburban sites (28 percent), and resort areas (16 percent).

Marriott targeted four groups for its hotels: high-income business travelers (40 percent), conventioneers (30 percent), well-to-do pleasure travelers (15 percent),

EXHIBIT 9 (CONTINUED)

Top 50 U.S. Economy/Limited-Service Lodging Chains

Chain Name	Ownership Structure	Number of Properties	Number of Rooms	Average Property Size	Geographic Concentrations	Published Room Rate Ranges: Single
10. Affordable Inns (Regal 8)	Company owned	50	5,604	112	ENC, ESC, WNC, WSC, UM, IM	$19.88–$23.88 X-Person $5
11. Western 6 Motels	Company owned	54	5,346	99	WSC, UM, LM, P	$24.95–$29.95 X-Person $5
12. Vagabond Inns	Company owned	47	3,841	82	WSC, LM, P	$21.95–$38.95 X-Person $5
13. Imperial 400	Company owned/ Joint venture	67	3,674	55	MA, USA, SA, ENC, WNC, WSC, UM, LM, P	$23.95–$33.95 X-Person $5
14. Drury Inns	Company owned	29	3,456	119	ENC, ESC, WNC, WSC, UM	$28.00–$44.00 X-Person $6
15. Chalet Suisse Int'l	Company owned	30	3,025	101	NE, MA, SA, ENC	$23.70–$26.70 X-Person $4
16. L-K Motels/ Penny Pincher Inns	Company owned	54	2,849	53	SA, ENC, ESC	$20.00–$29.00 X-Person $4
17. Sixpence Inns	Company owned	24	2,653	111	NE, ENC, LM, P	$21.00–$24.00 X-Person $5
18. Thrifty Scott Motels	Company owned/ Joint venture	32	2,627	82	WNC, UM	$20.90–$29.90 X-Person $4
19. Exel Inns	Company owned	20	2,345	117	ENC, WNC, WSC	$18.95–$33.95 X-Person $5
20. Shoney's Inns	Company owned/Franchised	19	2,299	121	SA, ESC, WSC	$23.00–$45.00 X- Person $5
21. Budgetel Inns	Company owned/ Joint venture	21	2,184	104	NE, SA, ENC, ESC, WNC, WSC	$21.95–$28.95 X-Person $5
22. Lexington Hotel Suites	Company owned	15	2,173	145	WSC, LM, P	$32.00–$52.00 X-Person $6
23. Family Inns	Franchised	26	2,171	84	SA, ENC, WSC	$21.95–$27.95 X-Person $5
24. Ha'Penny Inns	Company owned	18	2,106	117	P	Not available
25. Turnpike Properties (Cricket Inns)	Company owned	14	1,717	123	SA, MA, ESC, WNC	$24.95–$34.95 X-Person $5

(continued)

and contract rooms for flight crews (15 percent). Company research showed that those planning meetings used Marriott more often than any other chain.

The average Marriott hotel stressed service over architecture. Each offered a full line of services (restaurants, gift shops, automatic checkout, bellhops, convention and

EXHIBIT 9 (CONTINUED)

Top 50 U.S. Economy/Limited-Service Lodging Chains

Chain Name	Ownership Structure	Number of Properties	Number of Rooms	Average Property Size	Geographic Concentrations	Published Room Rate Ranges: Single
26. Passport Inns	Franchised	22	1,630	74	SA, ENC, ESC, WNC, WSC	$24.00–$50.00 X-Person $5
27. Luxury Budget Inns	Company owned	18	1,459	81	MA, USA	$19.95–$29.95 X-Person $4
28. Texian Inns	Company owned	12	1,380	115	WSC	$38.00–$45.00 X-Person $5
29. E-Z 8 Motels	Company owned/ Franchised	17	1,342	79	LM, P	Not available
30. Shilo Inns	Company owned	15	1,315	88	UM, P	Not available
31. Dillon Inns	Company owned	11	1,263	115	ENC, WNC, WSC	$25.95–$39.95 X-Person $5
32. America's Best Inns	Company owned/ Franchised	9	1,104	123	ENC, WNC, ESC	$21.95–$29.95 X-Person $4
33. Skylight Inns	Company owned	9	1,004	112	SA, ENC	$34.95–$39.95 X-Person $5
34. Koala Inns	Company owned	10	973	97	NE, MA	$29.95–$48.00 X-Person $5
35. Mid Continent Inns	Company owned/ Franchised	15	961	64	SA, ENC, ESC, WNC, WSC	Not available
36. Travel Host Motor Inns	Franchised	18	847	47	WNC, UM	$18.95–$22.90 X-Person $5
37. McIntosh Motor Inns	Company owned	7	813	116	MA	$23.95–$29.95 X-Person $5
38. Bargaintel Inns	Company owned	8	812	102	ENC	$24.95–$27.95 X-Person $5
39. Budgeteer Inns	Company owned	6	778	130	ENC	$21.95–$33.95 X-Person $5
40. Stratford House Inns	Company owned/ Franchised	11	770	70	WNC, WSC	$31.00–$42.00 X-Person $5
41. Roadstar Inns	Company owned	9	709	79	ENC, WNC	$23.95–$29.95 X-Person $5
42. Econ-O-Inn	Company owned	8	688	86	WNC	$21.95–$26.95 X-Person $4

(continued)

ballroom space, pool and recreation areas) and such features as French milled soap and all-cotton towels. A full-scale hotel usually required one employee for every room and one manager for every ten employees. The average room rate for Marriott's full-scale hotels was $80 to $100 a night, compared to a 1983 lodging industry average of $51.90.

EXHIBIT 9 (CONTINUED)

Top 50 U.S. Economy/Limited-Service Lodging Chains

Chain Name	Ownership Structure	Number of Properties	Number of Rooms	Average Property Size	Geographic Concentrations	Published Room Rate Ranges: Single
43. Prime Rate Motels	Company owned	8	677	85	WNC, UM	$21.00–$28.00 X-Person $5
44. Signature Inns	Company owned	6	670	112	ENC	$34.00–$38.00 X-Person $5
45. Pony Soldier Motor Inns	Company owned	8	669	84	UM, P	Not available
46. Interstate Inns	Company owned/ Franchised	17	600	35	WNC, WSC, UM	$20.00–$25.00 X-Person $4
47. Hampton Inn Hotels (a division of Holiday Inns)	Company owned/ Franchised	4	488	122	SA, ESC, WNC, WSC	$29.95–$36.95 X-Person $5
48. Tapadera Motor Inns	Company owned	7	481	69	UM, P	Not available
49. Tourway Inns	Company owned	5	476	95	SA	Not available
50. Wynfield Inns	Company owned	3	408	136	SA, UM	$32.00–$38.00 X-Person $5

Marriott's hotel occupancy rate usually averaged at least 10 points higher than the industry, which in recent years had ranged from the low 60s to low 70s. In 1981 Marriott's occupancy rate, at 79 percent, was 16 percentage points above the industry average. To assure such high rates, Marriott was constantly changing. Recently the company had developed an automatic check-out system in which the bill was slipped under the door at night, and it was working on an automatic check-in system. Management monitored the complimentary items left in the room to see what was used. When they discovered that bath crystals were not being used, those were replaced with cable television at no additional cost. Some hotels boasted a "concierge floor," where for an extra $10 guests got bigger rooms, complimentary breakfast and bar, and a concierge. In 1982 the company set up 28 model rooms and questioned 1,000 people for two hours each about the layout, color, and furnishings.

When taken as a whole, food and beverage contributed 35 percent of industry sales and 37 percent of Marriott sales. Whereas the industry reported 15 percent of gross income from food, Marriott achieved 50 percent to 60 percent higher profit margins on food services by consolidating purchases from all of its kitchens and putting the giant contracts out to bid once a year.

Since 1980 the company had financed the construction of more than $3 billion of lodging facilities. To combat high interest rates, the company began to sell the hotels as soon as construction was completed, either as equity interest partnerships (usually to large institutions such as Equitable Life Assurance Society) or as limited partnerships. Potomac Hotel Limited Partnership put up $18 million and borrowed $365 million from banks to buy 11 hotels in 1983, and Marriott expected to raise $1 billion from them in 1984. Chesapeake Hotel Limited Partnership owned 9 Marriott hotels. Marriott was the general partner, and all partnerships agreed to hire Marriott under management contract to operate the hotels. The contracts usually were for 75 years and paid Marriott a fee of 3 percent to 8 percent of operating revenues, plus an incentive fee of 20 percent to 30 percent of cumulative operating profits, making the contracts among the most generous in the industry. According to Marriott's chief financial officer, "We don't just broker a deal. We take a position and sell it off." In 1985 Marriott either owned or managed 80 percent of its rooms, making it the largest operator of hotel rooms in the United States.

Marriott's rapid growth had been managed without any apparent loss of ability to build and operate quality hotel facilities. The company's guest ratings increased significantly in 1984 in the areas of check-in and checkout, efficient reservations, meeting facilities, and friendliness of employees. In fact, Marriott led all chains in the latter category and was one of America's two most preferred business hotels. According to Bill Jr., "We receive over a thousand customer comment forms and letters every day..., and the most complimentary...are those written by guests who are impressed by our people and by some small thing that one of our staff went out of his or her way to do for them." The rooms were also rated particularly high. The company had received more four- and five-star awards than any other U.S. hotel chain.

Bill Jr. took a special interest in the hotels: "It's fun to build hotels; it's fun to make money. Being a playboy or a semi-playboy, that's really not fun. I like the pace. There's something different all the time. It's challenging." He added, "It's dirty work but the opportunities for people with brains are incredible in this industry."

Planning the Future at Marriott

In 1977 Bill Jr. had hired Tom Curren away from McKinsey & Co. to become the first full-time staff member to focus primarily on strategic issues. After earning his MBA from the Wharton School in 1967, Curren had served a stint in the Navy Supply Corps and later worked with Compton Advertising and McKinsey. Until 1980 Curren's work was primarily project-oriented planning with a heavy financial emphasis—for example, stock valuations, debt policy, and determining hurdle rates.

In 1980 Curren began working to increase the number of people doing strategic thinking in the organization and began systematically examining new business opportunities for Marriott. According to Bill Jr., "We decided that by 1990 we would have saturated the upscale market that had been our area—we would have a Marriott everywhere that it was important for us to have one. If we wanted to grow, we would have to find another area."

As stage one of early business development, Curren worked with a small task force and a developmental budget and, under a steering committee of two senior executives, began "idea generation" about alternative new businesses. The task force was expected to help answer such questions as, What are our most attractive market segments? On what basis could Marriott build a meaningful competitive advantage? Is there a way to enter the business profitably? Curren wanted the alternatives to meet three objectives: (1) build or maximize shareholder wealth, (2) maintain the values of the company, and (3) allow for Marriott to control its own destiny.

Among the alternatives being considered were the following:

- ***All Suites.*** Although several companies had launched all-suite hotels, it was not clear if these were a fad or a serious alternative to traditional hotels.
- ***Upscale Hotels.*** Bill Jr. was known to be interested in architect John Portman's plan to build a 1,877-room, 48-story hotel, with a 1,507-seat theater and some 1,400 lounge and restaurant seats in New York's Times Square—an area one developer called a "cesspool." Bill Jr. had once remarked, "I had a chance to buy... [Portman's Hyatt Regency in Atlanta] and if I had, there would be no Hyatt chain today. But I didn't understand the importance of architecture then." Portman wanted to combine the $400 million Times Square project to a $250 million, 1,674 room unit in Atlanta.
- ***Time-Sharing Condominiums.*** Time-sharing facilities that allowed owners to purchase a condo for certain specified weeks of the year might allow a number of carryovers from Marriott's lodging business that would permit efficiencies in operations.
- ***Retirement Communities.*** Units for approximately 400 people that offered residential, recreational, and health care facilities might be a good fit with the company's food and lodging strengths.
- ***Casinos.*** The company had recently purchased the Seaview Resort and Country Club near Atlantic City, New Jersey, that could easily be outfitted for gambling.
- ***Funeral Homes.*** Not only were there Marriott skills that could be successfully brought to the funeral industry, but the company could provide a useful service and enter a very profitable industry.
- ***Downscale Hotels.*** The company had had no experience running a limited-service facility, but the move was a possibility. Bill Jr. had at one time expressed an interest in purchasing La Quinta Motor Inns but rejected the idea because of the asking price.

The Clubcourt Project

After considering the options, Curren decided to recommend undertaking an "initial business analysis" of a downscale hotel, code-named Clubcourt. Bill Jr., "whose knowledge of the business is the best in the building," according to Curren, agreed that the idea was worth further exploration.

Curren hired Don Washburn from Booz, Allen & Hamilton to be vice president of hotel planning. Washburn, a Northwestern MBA, had started his career with Inland Steel in 1963 but later joined Quaker Oats in brand management. When the Justice Department sued the large cereal companies for monopolistic behavior, Washburn found himself on the team preparing the analysis for Quaker's defense. Since it appeared that the proceedings would stretch for years, Washburn decided to attend law school in the mornings and work afternoons and nights. Ultimately, he ended up as an attorney on the case. When the government dropped Quaker from the case in 1978, Washburn moved to Booz, Allen & Hamilton and one year later to Marriott.

In describing his decision to join Marriott, Washburn observed,

> The job seemed to fit me. The first part of my work combined the skills of a consultant and a brand manager: Where were the markets? Then I needed to be creative and find a way to fill it; then ramrod the process of creating and introducing the product.
>
> I found the place very cooperative. There was a lot of conventional wisdom built around full-service hotels and some resistance to thinking about new ideas. The company, however, is filled with some of the best people I've known—honest, hard-working, dedicated to quality. I was impressed. With their participation, I was able to make headway.
>
> Because of our high growth, you find very little petty conversation. Everyone is focused on growth. When you have growth goals you have to focus on things that create value. In our meetings we are very candid. You don't have time for maneuvering. The world will move past you. We all like each other. We have a lot of respect for each other. It's very nice.
>
> We like the business and the people we work with. I think we look forward to getting to work. Times like these don't last forever. It's a challenge for a CEO to keep them going. Bill Marriott has kept them going for many years.

Curren and Washburn, as part of their "category assessment," began a thorough research effort, using various analytical models of the lodging market, to determine where a real need existed. They had concluded that there were at least four segments (classified by room rates) below Marriott's current hotels: under $30s, low to mid-$30s, high $30s to low $40s, and mid-$40s to low $50s. They also began breaking down the lodging experience into its smallest parts to determine what constituted "value" for the guest. Through an extensive motivational segmentation research effort that in the first year cost $400,000, they tried to determine a variety of price/value trade-offs and develop a better understanding of industry trends.

As the concept of Clubcourt became better known within the company, the initial response outside the team, especially from the Hotel Group, was less than enthusiastic. When Don tried to recruit people to work on the project, most people had little interest and saw it as high risk. Many wanted to stay with the glamour of the larger hotels. Some managers feared the possibility of cannibalization and, as a result, worried about its prospects. Others argued that a lower-line product was not consistent with Marriott's values. In addition, there were questions of how quality-sensitive the market was and how Holiday Inn would react to a move into its niche. It was estimated that, if Clubcourt cost around $50,000 a room to build and rooms were priced at $50, break-even occupancy might be as high as 75 percent.

Curren and Washburn therefore hit the road, with Washburn personally staying in or inspecting more than 200 moderate-priced hotels to evaluate how the competition did business and determine if there were any geographical differences that should be considered. The road time exposed them to a number of interesting ideas. For example, in Dallas they liked the size and feel of one hotel. In San Diego, they noted several hotels that had a centralized computer system. Washburn described what they discovered:

> First, we analyzed our competition at all levels of the lodging industry. Then we studied the consumer at these levels. By comparing the results of these two studies, we determined which segments were most vulnerable. We found more

customers in the mid-price segment dissatisfied with existing supply than any other segment.

They concluded that, although the markets were changing rapidly, the largest group of travelers placed most value on five characteristics: (1) an attractive, comfortable, functional room; (2) a relaxing, secure environment; (3) a simple restaurant with good food; (4) friendly, helpful employees; and (5) all at a good price. In general, Washburn believed that a Marriott mid-price hotel should give people "an 'Ahaaaa!' experience": "When you've done a good job of creating an experience people wanted but didn't expect—people say 'Ahaaa! That is what I've been looking for!'"

When Curren and Washburn presented the five-point proposal at a meeting with Bill Marriott Jr., the Hotel Group head, and the executive vice president of finance, Marriott was positive about the concept but skeptical about the execution of the idea. What would the physical facilities look like? How would it be managed and staffed? What level of service could be provided? He also expressed a desire to see the project move faster. Before it could be presented to the finance committee, which he chaired, and ultimately to the eight-member board of directors, it was necessary that a "full business concept" be developed.[3] Only if the finance committee approved could the venture start-up phase begin where, under the sponsorship of one of the four executive vice presidents, the idea would be test-marketed and, if successful, followed by a national roll-out.

In Curren's opinion, the decision whether to go with Clubcourt would be "80 percent based on superior execution." It was up to Don Washburn to take the lead in developing a detailed implementation plan that would win Bill Marriott's and the board's approval.

Endnotes

[1]S. M. Sullivan, "Money, Talent, and the Devil by the Tail: J. Willard Marriott," *Management Review*, January 1985, p. 19.

[2]Hope Lampert, "How Did This Quiet, Nice, Religious Man Become One of the Most Successful Businessmen in the Country?" *The Washingtonian*, January 1984, p. 151.

[3]The board members were J. W. Marriott, Alice Marriott, Bill Marriott, Dick Marriott, Thomas Piper (Harvard Business School professor), Harry Vincent Jr. (vice chairman of Booz, Allen & Hamilton), Frederick Deane Jr. (chair and CEO of Bank of Virginia), and Don Mitchell (director of other corporations).

CASE 16

HEWLETT-PACKARD (CONDENSED)

For John Young, the 53-year-old president of Hewlett-Packard (HP), 1986 was shaping up as the worst year in recent history. Not only were profits declining, but with the electronics industry slumping and with HP now using fewer internally manufactured components in its products, HP was overstaffed by 1,500 to 2,000 people. Furthermore, HP had "bet the store" on a radical technology to stay in the computer business. By mid-1986 it was clear that what some were calling the "biggest gamble" in the company's 47-year history had encountered new delays. Dave Packard, age 73, and Bill Hewlett, age 72, controlled 30 percent of the company's stock but would soon be playing a much smaller role in the company than in the past. The future course for HP was largely in Young's hands.

COMPANY BACKGROUND

In 1939 Bill Hewlett and Dave Packard, both Stanford graduates, set up shop in a one-car garage. Their first product was a new type of audio oscillator used to test sound equipment; Walt Disney Studios ordered eight of them to improve the sound in the movie *Fantasia*. HP's products for the first 20 years were primarily electronic test and measurement instruments for engineers and scientists. Since then HP had added computers, peripherals, calculators, medical electronic equipment, instrumentation for chemical analysis, and solid-state components.

THE HP WAY

During the company's early years, the founders developed a number of management concepts that evolved into a set of corporate objectives and a business style known as "the HP Way." First put into writing in 1957, these objectives remained the fundamental, active guiding forces at HP. The HP Way was reflected directly in a statement of company objectives distributed throughout the organization (see Exhibit 1). According to Dave Packard,

> Early in the history of the company, while thinking about how a company like this should be managed, I kept getting back to one concept: If we could simply get everybody to agree on what our objectives were and to understand what we were trying to do, then we could turn everybody loose and they would move along in a common direction.

This case, a condensation of UVA-BP-268, was prepared by Professor L. J. Bourgeois III. The original case was prepared by Professor William E. Fulmer. Revised January 1994.

EXHIBIT 1

Excerpts from HP's Statement of Corporate Objectives

The achievements of an organization are the result of the combined efforts of each individual in the organization working toward common objectives. These objectives should be clearly understood by everyone in the organization and should reflect the organization's basic character and personality.

OBJECTIVES

1. PROFIT: To achieve sufficient profit to finance our company growth and to provide the resources we need to achieve our other corporate objectives.

   . . . It is the one absolutely essential measure of our corporate performance over the long term. . . .

   . . . Our long-standing policy has been to reinvest most of our profits and to depend on this . . . to finance our growth. This can be achieved if our return on net worth is roughly equal to our sales growth rate.

   . . . Profits vary from year to year . . . our needs for capital also vary, and we depend on short-term bank loans to meet those needs. . . . However, loans are costly and must be repaid; thus, our objective is to rely on reinvested profits as our main source of capital.

   Meeting our profit objective requires that . . . every product . . . is considered a good value . . . , yet is priced to include an adequate profit.
2. CUSTOMERS: To provide products and services of the greatest possible value to our customers, thereby gaining and holding their respect and loyalty.

   . . . products that fill real needs and provide lasting value. . . .
3. FIELDS OF INTEREST: To enter new fields only when the ideas we have, together with our technical, manufacturing, and marketing skills, assure that we can make a needed and profitable contribution to the field.

   . . . The key to HP's prospective involvement in new fields is *contribution.* This means providing customers with something new and needed, not just another brand of something they can already buy.
4. GROWTH: To let our growth be limited only by our profits and our ability to develop and produce technical products that satisfy real customer needs.
5. OUR PEOPLE: To help HP people share in the company's success, which they make possible; to provide job security based on their performance; to recognize their individual achievements; and to help them gain a sense of satisfaction and accomplishment from their work.

   . . . Relationships within the company depend upon a spirit of cooperation among individuals and groups, and an attitude of trust and understanding on the part of managers toward their people. These relationships will be good only if employees have faith in the motives and integrity of their peers, supervisors, and the company itself.

(continued)

EXHIBIT 1 (CONTINUED)

Excerpts from HP's Statement of Corporate Objectives

...Job security is an important HP objective...the company has achieved a steady growth in employment by consistently developing good new products, and by avoiding the type of contract business that requires hiring many people, then terminating them when the contract expires. . . .

6. MANAGEMENT: To foster initiative and creativity by allowing the individual great freedom of action in attaining well-defined objectives.

   . . . insofar as possible, each individual at each level in the organization should make his or her own plans to achieve company objectives and goals. After receiving supervisory approval, each individual should be given a wide degree of freedom to work within the limitations imposed by these plans, and by our general corporate policies. . . .

7. CITIZENSHIP: To honor our obligations to society by being an economic, intellectual, and social asset to each nation and each community in which we operate.

   ...to make sure that each of these communities is better for our presence.

SOURCE: "Human Resources at Hewlett-Packard," pp. 28–29.

In addressing a training class for company managers, Packard had observed,

> I think we've done a really remarkably good job to maintain this so-called "HP Spirit" as the company has grown larger. . . . Let's work on that because it is just one of the real strengths. It's the key to productivity and to leadership and continuing progress and success in our company.

One HP manager noted that the subtlety of the system made it difficult to describe:

> It is basically a faith in people to use their discretion and to be sure along the way to make some mistakes as well as to make some contributions in a way that, over time, generally will continue to take the company in the direction it wants to go—consistent with its basic underlying set of objectives. These objectives continue to drive us, they really do.

According to a vice president,

> There is something useful in not being too precise—a value to fuzziness. No one can really define the HP Way. If it weren't fuzzy, it would be a rule! This way leaves room for judgment. Without that, there wouldn't be room for the constant micro-reconciliations needed in a changing world. This is designed as an adaptive company.

Another vice president said,

> There's not a lot of flexibility in the way you use the process. The process has got a very good track record, and people don't like you to mess with it. Also, if individuals start to mess with the process, then I think the company breaks down pretty quickly.

New employees were not always enthusiastic. According to a relatively new MBA, "It can also feel intrusive. It can feel presumptuous, and it's much, much more demanding than any other company that I've ever been affiliated with.... You just have to do the right thing." Another relatively new employee described his adjustment to it:

> We hear about the "HP Way" almost ad nauseam. It's sort of "truth, justice, and the HP Way." I went through a real struggle with the concept. Initially exposed to it, I thought: Boy! There's an awful lot that makes sense. But I guess I came to the point where I said this is over-indoctrination...some of it must be baloney. I've come not quite full circle, but part way back to the realization that, gee, there is an awful lot that is distinctive, an awful lot that is good in the HP Way, an awful lot that as an employee I feel grateful for.

Telling company stories was part of the HP Way: Naming Bills and Dave's first instrument the "200A" so that people would not know that they were just starting out; Dave's smashing of an instrument in a lab because it was poorly designed and unreliable; and the avoidance of layoffs in 1970 by having all employees take a 10 percent pay cut and work nine out of ten days (the "nine-day fortnight," in HP lore).

As the organization grew and word-of-mouth storytelling became more difficult, executive seminars and courses for supervisors were increased. Materials were presented to all HP employees, approximately 30 employees at a time, as a four half-day course called "Working at HP." The first part dealt with the history of HP and the HP Way, and the remaining sessions provided comprehensive coverage of personnel policies, performance evaluations, salary administration, and personal development. The program was considered most effective if attended after about six months of employment at HP.

Hiring Policies

HP tended to hire people straight out of college and steep them in the corporate tradition. According to a division manager,

> There are a lot of different types of people who have been successful in the company. There is no prescription for background. There probably *is* a prescription for style. If you look at the makeup of the Executive Committee or the Operations Council, there are very definitely some different personalities and different styles. But the similarities are probably greater than the differences when it comes to style. Each one of these people has strong belief in individual freedom. We can accept widely different backgrounds but don't accept divergent style.

Turnover (5 to 10 percent in 1983) was low by industry standards, and, even after leaving, many employees remained loyal. HP also had shown a willingness to rehire people who had left to try other fields or to start their own companies.

People were rarely hired directly as managers. As Packard explained,

> Now there are some who say that a person is a good manager who has mastered managerial technique; he can manage anything. Well, maybe he can. But I hold very strongly that he can manage it a hell of a lot better if he really knows the territory.

Structural Devices and Work Systems

At HP a division was an integrated, self-sustaining organization with a lot of independence. The objective was to create a working atmosphere that encouraged solving problems as close as possible to the level where they occurred.

HP worked to keep the product divisions relatively small (about 1,000 people) and well defined. In 1980 HP had 40 divisions and 10 groups, by 1982 more than 45 divisions and 12 groups (Exhibit 2). According to a general manager in 1982,

> New divisions tend to emerge when a particular product line becomes large enough to support its continued growth out of the profit it generates. Also, new divisions tend to emerge when a single division gets so large that the people involved start to lose their identification with the product line.

The product divisions were considered HP's tactical business units, each responsible for its own R&D, manufacturing, marketing, finance, and personnel management. All sales organizations reported to the group level (e.g., the Computer Group), however, and were separate from the product divisions. Divisions were kept small to allow considerable individual freedom while maintaining a focused business purpose.

Each of the six major product groups in 1982 had developed a selling strategy that was highly individualized for its particular market, yet according to the vice president of marketing,

> Many of our customers, especially the major accounts, need products and service from two, three, or more product lines. So there has to be a lot of interaction [among] the salespeople in servicing these customers. They have to work together as a team, using common sense as to who should lead the team.

Each division was measured along two dimensions: (1) financial results of the actual manufacturing of products in the division and (2) the total worldwide activity in the division's product lines, wherever they were manufactured. (Divisions could produce other divisions' products to improve service and reduce transportation costs around the world.) Reporting of worldwide results was accomplished by adjustments to the divisional profit-and-loss statement. Intracompany sales discounts (structured to minimize customs and tariffs) were reversed so the selling division would consider domestic and international customers evenly. Because of the many "incestuous" products, which divisions bought from each other, incorporated into more complex assemblies, and then sold as combined products, each division was allowed credit for only the value it added (which was negotiated among the divisions). In addition, a "license fee" was paid by divisions manufacturing products designed by other divisions. A division could thus be both receiving fees for products it had designed that were made by other divisions and also paying fees to

EXHIBIT 2

Hewlett-Packard Corporate Organization, November 1982

Board of Directors Dave Packard, Chariman of the Board
Bill Hewlett, Chairman, Executive Committee

Chief Executive Officer John Young, President

Administration
Bob Boniface, Executive Vice President

Operations
Paul Ely, Executive Vice President
Bill Terry, Executive Vice President
Dean Morton, Executive Vice President

Corporate Staff

Corporate Controller
Jerry Carlson
Controller

Corporate Services
Bruce Wholey
Vice President

General Counsel
and Secretary
Jack Brigham
Vice President

International
Bill Doolittle
Senior Vice President

Government
Affairs
Bob Kirkwood
Director

Patents and Licenses
Jean Chognard
Vice President

Personnel
Bill Craven
Director

Public Relations
Dave Kirby
Director

Marketing
Al Oliverio
Senior Vice President

Treasurer
Ed van Bronkhorst
Senior Vice President

EUROPE
Franco Mariotti
Vice President

Field Sales Regions
- France
- Germany
- Northern Europe
- South/East Europe
- United Kingdom

Manufacturing
- France
- Germany
- United Kingdom

INTERCONTINENTAL
Alan Bickell
Managing Director
Field Sales Regions
- Australasia
- Far East
- Japan
- Latin America
- South Africa

Manufacturing
- Brazil
- Japan
- Malaysia
- Mexico
- Puerto Rico
- Singapore

U.S./CANADA
SALES
Field Sales Regions
- Eastern
- Midwest
- Neely (Western)
- Southern
- Canada

Corporate
Marketing
Operations
- •Parts Center

Computers

TECHNICAL
COMPUTER GROUP
Doug Chance
Vice President

- •Data Systems
- •Roseville
- •Desktop Computer
- •Engineering Systems
- •Boblingen Desktop
- •YHP Computer
- •Computer I.C.
  - •Cupertino I.C.
  - •Systems Technology

BUSINESS
COMPUTER GROUP
Ed McCracken
General Manager

- •Computer Systems
  - •Roseville
- •Info Networks
  - •Office Systems Pinewood
  - •Office Systems Cupertino
  - •Grenoble Datacomm
- •Mfg. Productivity
  - •Financial Systems
- •Boblingen General Systems
- •Info. Resources
- •Guadalajara Computer

COMPUTER
PERIPHERALS
GROUP
Dick Hackborn
General Manager

- •Boise
- •Disc Memory
- •Greeley
  - •Singapore
- •Vancouver
- •Bristol

COMPUTER
TERMINALS
GROUP
Cyril Yansouni
General Manager

- •Personal Office Computer
- •Roseville Terminals
- •Grenoble
- •Puerto Rico

COMPUTER MARKETING GROUP
Jim Arthur, Vice President

- •Computer Support
- •Application Marketing
- •Personal Computer Marketing
- •Systems Re-marketing
- •Computer Supplies

Instruments

MICROWAVE AND
COMMUNICATIONS
INSTRUMENTS
GROUP
Hal Edmondson
General Manager

- •Colorado Telecom
- •Queensferry Telecom
- •Stanford Park
- •Spokane
- •Signal Analysis
- •Network Measurements
- •Santa Rosa Technology Center

ELECTRONIC
MEASUREMENTS
GROUP
Bill Parzybok
General Manager

- •Boblingen Instrument
- •San Diego
- •Colorado Springs
- •Logic Systems
- •YHP Instrument
- •Loveland Instrument
- •Lake Stevens Instrument
- •New Jersey
- •Santa Clara
- •Integrated Circuits
  - •Santa Clara
  - •Loveland
  - •Colorado Springs

INSTRUMENT MARKETING GROUP
Bob Brunner, General Manager

- •Instrument Support

COMPONENTS
GROUP
John Blokker
General Manager

- •Microwave Semiconductor
- •Optoelectronics
  - •Visible Products
  - •Interface Products
  - •Singapore
  - •Malaysia

Components
Sales/Service

ANALYTICAL
GROUP
Lew Platt
General Manager

- •Avondale
- •Scientific Instruments
- •Waldbronn

Analytical
Sales/Service

MEDICAL
GROUP
Dick Alberding
Vice President

- •Andover
- •Boblingen Medical
- •McMinnville
- •Waltham
- •Medical Supplies

Medical
Sales/Service

PERSONAL
COMPUTATION
GROUP
Dick Moore
General Manager

- •Corvallis
- •Personal Computer
- •Corvallis Components
- •Brazil
- •Singapore

(Computer
Marketing Group)

HP LABORATORIES
Research and
Development

John Doyle
Vice President

RESEARCH
CENTERS
Computer
Research

Physical Research

Technology
Research

Corporate
Development
Dave Sanders
Director

Internal Audit
George Abbott
Manager

Corporate
Manufacturing
Services
Ray Deméré
Vice President

other divisions for products of others it was making. These fees were percentages of sales revenues negotiated among the divisions.

The adjusted worldwide profit-and-loss statement was the basis for allocation of each division's R&D funds (usually 9 percent of sales). This policy rewarded the innovative divisions with additional funds for further innovation and acted as an indirect form of asset allocation. Plants started purely as desirable manufacturing activities could attain full divisional status only by somehow creating a new product. Then it would be allocated R&D funds—the key to growth.

Balance sheets were produced only at the group level. HP felt that below that level the large allocations necessary for such items as corporate overhead, the sales force, and marketing assets created too much distortion to make the statements useful.

Capital allocations were negotiated during the yearly budgeting process. Although divisions were expected to be self-financing over any period of time, for start-ups or major expansions in any one year, a division might be allowed to spend more capital than it could provide for itself. Most capital-rationing negotiations were resolved within the group.

A corollary to the division and group focus was the moderate size and influence of the corporate staff. The special "cross-boundary" types of projects that were often undertaken by corporate staffs in other companies were at HP given to *ad hoc* task forces drawn from many parts of the company. According to Bill Hewlett,

> Our strength lies in the fact that our divisions have real freedom of choice in their operations, yet we have learned to talk across these divisional and group boundaries. This has enabled us to share our problems and strengths, thereby building a much stronger company.

HP used a large number of task forces and committees. Task forces were temporary assignments with a specified deadline. The task force would typically consist of five to ten people, often from different functions and levels within HP and including the people most affected by the particular project. Committees, or councils, were ongoing teams concerned with issues affecting either a single part of the company or the whole organization.

Packard described the cooperation as follows:

> One of the things that we have tried to achieve and I think we have achieved is this concept of teamwork. That's one of the reasons we don't have special awards for a division for something that it does particularly well. The only way this company is going to run successfully is if we can insure that there is a maximum flow of information and cooperation between all the elements of it.
>
> . . . I've often expressed this in terms that everyone in the company is equally important. It's just as important that the person who is responsible for sweeping the floor does a good job as it is if Bill and I do a good job.

Communications

Most places throughout HP had no doors to individual offices. Top executives, including the president, had offices within large administrative areas that were divided by freestanding, low partitions. An open-door policy was stressed. According to an HP group vice president,

> Employees have every bit as much access to John Young as I do. They don't see him as frequently, because they don't have as many reasons to talk to him. But the door is as open to them as it is to me.

Common coffee breaks had become practically a ritual at HP, with the company providing coffee and croissants to all employees every morning and afternoon. There were periodic "beer busts" and picnics for the whole plant, often at recreational facilities owned by the company. Management meetings and retirement and division parties often included spoofs written by employees, and managers normally cooked and helped serve other employees at division picnics. Frequent plant meetings were held to discuss the latest company and plant news. A loudspeaker system allowed the announcement of company operating results and discussions of topics of general interest.

Managers at all levels were encouraged to spend a part of each day wandering through the organization, often without specific purpose other than to see what was going on and to build new channels of communication. This practice was called "management by wandering around" (MBWA). According to the HP employee magazine,

> There had to be a way of describing the extra step that HP managers needed to take in order to make the HP open-door policy truly effective. It was not enough to sit and wait for people to come through the door with their problems and ideas—they probably wouldn't in many cases. The managers had better get off their chairs and go out and get in touch with people. In that way people would know the managers were accessible whenever they had something important to communicate.
>
> Straightforward as it sounds, there are quite a few subtleties and requirements that go with MBWA. For one thing, it is not always easy for managers to do—so some of them do it reluctantly or infrequently. And its purpose is not always apparent to people—especially new HP people—at the receiving end of visits, so they may view it suspiciously and respond uneasily.

Promotion and Reward Systems

People at HP referred to the "career maze" to describe the cross-functional, cross-divisional, and lateral moves that often occurred. According to one employee, "If you're doing an excellent job within the HP context, that means you're affecting and involved with a lot of other people in a lot of functional areas. And as openings come up, there are going to be people aware of your skills." A manager noted, "In my first eight years, I guess I had about seven or eight different jobs and four different functions. A couple of them were lateral moves." According to a group manager, another advantage of HP's frequent use of task forces was that "it also gives a lot of visibility to people."

All employees were salaried, and all aspects of salary administration were open. Each employee saw his or her wage curve and the one on the level above. Performance appraisal and salary administration made use of wage curves, where various levels were set to be competitive with relevant labor markets. Individual pay was set by a combination of relevant experience and "sustained performance," with the emphasis on performance. Within each wage curve, normal distribution was expected to result in 10 percent exceptional performers, 40 percent very good, 40 percent good, and 10 percent acceptable or new in the range. Unacceptable performance resulted in counseling, repositioning, or firing. Because sustained performance was emphasized, dramatic changes in performance were rare. Those whose performance declined were given small or no increases.

A bonus plan was initiated in 1940, and all employees were included in it, as well as being eligible for stock options. When an HP employee married, he or she was recognized by the gift of a silver bowl, and the birth of an employee's first child was recognized with a blanket.

In 1973 flexible hours were introduced for all HP employees. According to an HP group vice president, "People making PC boards here don't punch time clocks, and they haven't for over the 15 years I've been here. They do have flexible hours. They got them as soon as I did."

The HP Way of Doing Business

Just as the internal management of HP was dictated by the HP Way, an "HP Way of Doing Business" provided guidelines for running the company. First, HP maintained a pay-as-you-go attitude. The absence of long-term borrowing helped maintain a stable financial environment during depressed business periods. Packard noted the importance of this policy:

> In some industries, particularly those [that] require large capital investments, the pay-as-you-go approach is not feasible. There is also a school of thought in management that capital needs should be attained by leveraging equity financing with large amounts of debt. This school of thought says you can make your profits go further if you do this. Whatever the arguments, it is not Hewlett-Packard Company policy to lever our profits with long-term debt. We want every manager to know this and to act accordingly. . . . I see no possible circumstance that would justify a change.

According to a vice president,

> Our feeling is there is enough risk in the technology—we have all we can handle there. This philosophy provides great discipline all the way down. If you want to innovate, you must bootstrap. It is one of the most powerful, least understood influences that pervade the company.

A second major element of the HP Way of Doing Business was that any market expansion or leadership was based on new products. A dominant emphasis at HP had been for R&D to create products that would compete by new technical contributions rather than through marketing or other competitive devices. HP products were thoroughly designed, tested, and specified before being brought to market. HP's approach traditionally was to design its products first and worry about how much they were going to cost later. HP management had always placed great emphasis on product development programs, which they considered a fundamental strength of the company. An indication of the importance of this effort was the fact that more than half of 1982 orders came from products introduced during the prior three years.

HP avoided doing contract work and instead designed general-purpose devices suitable for a broad range of customers. All commercial customers bought from one catalog that listed almost all the products HP made. Only exterior modifications such as special colors or extra protection for environmental extremes were made. The basic designs or purposes of the instruments were not modified. These rules were the same for government purchases.

A focus on technical contributions and profit rather than volume had led HP to conclude that trying to gain market share with a low introductory price was not appropriate for the company. Dave Packard believed that "market share is not an objective, but a reward." He noted,

> It is just as easy to make a profit today as it will be tomorrow. There are, of course, occasions when actions should be taken [that] will jeopardize the short-term profit. These need to be considered very, very carefully because, more often than not, they tend to be rationalizations [that] simply put off what you should be doing today. . . .
>
> If a new product is really as good as we think it is going to be, we'll be able to sell more than we can make in the initial period anyway, and so you are jeopardizing the whole situation with really nothing to gain. . . . You can reduce the price later on, if, in fact, you are able to achieve your lower production costs and keep your costs down.

Another significant element of the HP Way of Doing Business was to stress honesty and integrity in all matters as a guiding principle for HP employees. For example, there was no tolerance for dishonest dealings with vendors or customers, and open and honest communication with employees and stockholders alike was stressed.

John Young[1]

In May 1978, one day before his 65th birthday, Bill Hewlett resigned from his position as chief executive officer of HP. He was appointed chair of the executive committee and joined David Packard, chairman of the board, in semiretirement, although he remained very active in HP affairs. John Young, who had succeeded Bill Hewlett as president and chief operating officer in November 1977, was named CEO.

Young, an athletic-looking 46-year-old who had capped his electrical engineering degree from Oregon State with an MBA from Stanford University, joined HP in 1958. Ten years before Young was named CEO, some of his peers had already pegged him as the heir apparent. *Fortune* later noted, "The praise strains belief. 'John Young is ideal for Hewlett-Packard, a gift from heaven,' exclaims a retired board member." A close observer said, "I've worked with thousands of leading businessmen, and he's absolutely at the top of the heap." *Fortune* continued with these observations:

> He has been described as a cool, confident, television surgeon. "When I first met him," says a company veteran, "he seemed so smooth and polished that I wanted to take his pulse to see if he was alive." Ernest C. Arbuckle, a former dean of Stanford Business School and a retired Hewlett-Packard director who lives next door to Young, puts it more sympathetically: "It's not easy to get under his skin. He's extremely self-controlled. I've never seen him get angry. But that's also the Hewlett-Packard way. You want to get the best out of people, so you control yourself."

Fortune also asked Young to contrast his management style with those of Hewlett and Packard:

> Young tends as always to be modest. "Bill is a brilliant engineer and Dave is a great businessman," he says. "I stress organization, planning, and the process." Young builds consensus decisions by asking penetrating questions and listening closely to the answers. Robert Minge Brown, a corporate lawyer and former director, describes Young as far and away the best-organized manager who ever made a presentation to the board. Young's memory for details is prodigious: though he crowds more events into his schedule than most people can believe, he keeps the schedule in his head, not in an appointment book.

Fortune used terms like "fierce determination" and "a powerful drive to master new skills" to describe Young:

> He is an accomplished pilot and fly-fisherman. "For him, even relaxation is highly focused," observes Tom McCabe, the tennis pro Young retains to be on the other side of the net whenever Young wants him there. "After he gets through with a lesson, there are puddles of good, honest effort all over the court."
>
> Young uses his superb organizational skills to make plenty of time for his wife, Rosemary (they met in first grade), and their three grown children. "He is getting way up there to being a pretty important guy," says his father. "But he doesn't get excited about it. Everything gets kept track of. He has time for his family, no matter what." Young calls his parents once a week. Several times a year he gathers the clan at his rustic 40-acre spread not far from Klamath Falls (Oregon). The highlight of these trips: fishing for trout along the six miles of Five Mile Creek.

According to one insider, "His style is to lead people where he wants them to go rather than tell them what to do."[2] One of the areas where Young had led HP was into computers.

HP and Computers

HP backed into the computer business in 1966 by introducing a minicomputer intended for controlling HP instruments; in fact, it was called an instrumentation computer. After a weak start with its initial entrance into business computers (1971), HP reintroduced the HP3000 in 1973. According to *Fortune*,

> In early 1973, David Packard threw a fit about the company's fledgling minicomputer business, which in 1972 had made only $100,000 on $100 million in revenues. He dispatched Paul Ely, then general manager of the microwave division, to straighten things out.[3]

By 1975 the HP3000 had firmly established HP as a leading computer manufacturer. In fact, the small, time-sharing HP3000 minicomputer was a primary contributor to the development of "distributed data processing," which expanded computing power beyond the data processing department.

In 1980 John Young launched a recruiting campaign to beef up R&D in the computer area. Longtime R&D head Bernard Oliver had focused HP Labs on physical-science problems instead of the software and design issues crucial to developing new computers. Of 200 HP Labs professionals, only 50 had been working in the computer field. When Oliver retired in 1981, Young appointed Doyle, the company's personnel director, to the post. Doyle recruited a team of 220 computer-oriented professionals and started forming HP's first research partnerships with universities. Young then raised R&D spending from 8.8 percent to more than 10 percent of sales.[4]

Young's prize catch in 1981 was Joel Birnbaum, who for five years had been the head of computer sciences at IBM's Thomas Watson Research Center. He had been at IBM when the pioneering work was done on RISC (reduced instruction-set computing) computers in the 1970s. RISC represented a shift from building more functions into computers to increasing speed by leaving out complex functions. The technology had been the subject of experimentation for ten years when Birnbaum and several former IBM researchers brought the concepts to HP. Young soon vetoed at least four competing approaches to building high-powered computers. He agreed with Birnbaum that HP should be making simple computers.

In 1981 Young championed a much publicized effort to launch a 32-bit desktop workstation for engineers. The basic computer was ready to go in time, but parts of the system that were being developed in other divisions, such as software, held up the launch for nearly a year. Nevertheless, by 1982 HP had succeeded in penetrating the explosive market for small-to-medium-sized (less than $250,000 system price) computers.

By 1982, computer products sales for HP reached $2.2 billion (out of total HP sales of $4.25 billion from a line of more than 5,000 products). Total sales had grown at a compound annual rate of 24.3 percent over the previous ten years, while earnings had increased tenfold. About half of the company's sales were to the United States, with the rest to other parts of the world. There were 40 manufacturing locations spread across the United States and 10 others around the world. In addition, there were more than 240 sales and service locations. More than half the 68,000 worldwide workforce had been with HP for less than three years. Also by 1982, 22 of the divisions were directly related to computers, and the portion of total revenues attributable to computer products had increased from 16.8 percent in 1971 to 51 percent in 1982.

This dramatic shift had been especially challenging to HP because of the differences between the instrument and computer businesses. Instruments were essentially stand-alone products, whereas computers required a systems integration. In instruments, HP could rely on its technological superiority to sell customers premium-priced products. Furthermore, instrument customers could be left with the job of tailoring the equipment to their own particular needs because they were usually technical people. Those market segments were well defined, and HP held the leadership position in most product categories. Information processing markets, in contrast, were not clearly defined and were marked by fierce competition. Computer customers demanded increasingly better performing products at lower prices. They often wanted ready-to-use products designed for specific applications.

The systems approach required for designing and selling computers presented a problem for the HP way of doing business. According to Young, his biggest challenge in 1982 was "to orchestrate the divisions and provide a strategic glue and direction for the computer effort, while keeping the work units small." He added, "Having small divisions is not the only way to organize a company, but having organizations that people can run like a small business is highly motivational, especially for professionals. Keeping that spirit of entrepreneurship alive is very important to us."[5]

Based on 1981 revenues, HP was ranked the seventh largest computer manufacturer in the world. Only HP and DEC (Digital Equipment Corporation) had grown at more than 30 percent a year between 1978 and 1981. A study by an independent market research firm in 1981 indicated that only four computer firms would exceed $5 billion in sales by 1985 and suggested that HP would maintain the fastest growth rate, nearly 30 percent a year, between 1980 and 1985. Having been the pioneer system in the market for interactive business systems for online processing, in mid-1983 the HP3000 remained the leader, with 12,000 systems installed worldwide. A 1982 survey of minicomputer users, conducted by Datapro Research Corporation, attested to HP's ability to satisfy its customers. When asked if they would recommend the HP3000, 95 percent of HP3000 users said yes.

HP's ability to manage such rapid growth while maintaining a healthy working environment was acknowledged in a 1982 *Fortune* survey, in which HP was ranked the second most admired U.S. corporation, following IBM. It was recognized as being among the top three companies in each of five areas: ability to attract, develop, and keep talented people (number one ranking); innovativeness; quality of product; management reputation; and investment value.

An example of the innovation that had allowed the continued development of technically outstanding products was the HP9000, introduced in 1982, which had the power of a mainframe in a desktop unit. Some considered it the ultimate personal computer for scientists and engineers. The HP9000 incorporated HP's new integrated-circuit technology, which allowed up to 600,000 transistors to be put onto a single silicon chip.

By the mid-1980s the number of divisions at HP was 50, producing 9,000 products. Autonomy in proliferating divisions had resulted in some overlapping products. Customers complained about products developed in one HP division not being compatible with products from other divisions. The company's position in one of the most critical markets, personal computers, was threatened by a lack of cohesive effort between three geographically separated divisions. Each was individually engaged in the design, manufacture, and marketing of personal computers. According to a division marketing manager,

> With three independent divisions working on personal computers, there was no well-defined strategy. Products overlapped, and distribution channels were not standardized. This internal competition, while providing benefits up to a point, resulted in an inefficient use of the company's resources.

In an effort to coordinate its more than 20 information processing divisions, HP used a computer strategy council composed of that business's top management. The computer strategy council, set up by Young and headed by Executive Vice President Paul Ely Jr., addressed issues ranging from product introductions to data communications standards.

In addition, HP used an experimental program-management style to provide unified direction on cross-divisional projects, and it improved planning through a number of task forces and committees. Despite some positive outcomes from these efforts, however, some observers were concerned that these coordinating activities might be damaging HP's entrepreneurial spirit.

In 1982 employee turnover and concern for the health of HP's entrepreneurial spirit led Young to commission a survey of 12,000 employees to pinpoint problems. In addition, HP improved its benefit program and launched new efforts to communicate with employees, especially when divisions were split up or moved. He noted, "We're constantly dealing with the trade-offs. We work hard at creating an exciting environment, but in the computer area interdependence is also very important."[6] He also commissioned McKinsey and Company to begin studying HP's marketing abilities.

The 1983 Reorganization

In early 1983 HP announced the most significant restructuring of its computer operation since the company entered the information processing business (Exhibit 3).[7] The organization had two major purposes, as outlined in a letter from Ely to the company's top 150 customers:

1. Unify our development and manufacturing activities in three strategic centers: system processors, personal computers, and networks. This will . . . provide a more cohesive product offering for customers.
2. Combine the marketing of all HP computers into a single organization to improve our effectiveness in interacting with our customers.

The 1983 reorganization began in January with the consolidation of the Personal Computation Group and the Computer Terminals Group. The new group, the Personal Computer Group, would be responsible for developing and manufacturing personal computers, terminals, personal computer peripherals, and other personal computation products, such as calculators. This change provided for the first time a cohesive overall strategy for HP's personal computer efforts. Decisions about marketing and R&D could now be made at the group level by a single manager. Before the reorganization, the only common manager for the separated divisions had been the company president. According to Young, "Creating the personal computer group was an extremely good way of getting a focus on marketing. It was a way of communicating to everyone that this [i.e., marketing] was okay, that it's okay to eat quiche."

The most undefined of HP's five reorganized computer groups was the Business Development Group (BDG), which was responsible for the strategic marketing and business-development activities for all HP computer products. BDG would generate three-year plans to position HP in three key markets: computer-integrated manufacturing, office automation/personal computers, and commercial data processing. These plans would be developed in conjunction with the divisions involved in the particular market.

Another significant change was the creation of two sales centers, in California and in Germany, under BDG. The sales centers would consolidate into single locations all the sales development activities previously conducted in each individual division. The primary role of sales development was to support and help motivate the sales force. Sales development provided the interface between the product divisions and the sales force. In the past, when sales representatives or HP customers wanted information, they were often forced to deal with several sales groups. With the change, the sales centers would serve as the sole source of information. HP termed it "one-stop shopping."

Opinions as to the benefits of the 1983 reorganization and the need for it were generally favorable. According to a group vice president,

EXHIBIT 3

Hewlett-Packard Corporate Organization, June 1983

Board of Directors Dave Packard, Chariman Bill Hewlett, Vice Chairman

Chief Executive Officer John Young, President*

Administration
Bob Boniface, Executive Vice President

Corporate Staff

Corporate Controller
Jerry Carlson
Controller

Corporate Services
Bruce Wholey
Vice President

General Counsel
and Secretary
Jack Brigham
Vice President

International
Dick Alberding
Senior Vice President

Government
Affairs
Bob Kirkwood
Director

Public Relations
Dave Kirby
Director

Patents and Licenses
Jean Chognard
Vice President

Personnel
Bill Craven
Director

Marketing
Al Oliverio
Senior Vice President

Treasurer
Ed van Bronkhorst
Senior Vice President

EUROPE
Franco Mariotti
Vice President

Field Sales Regions
France
Germany
Northern Europe
South/Eastern Europe
United Kingdom
Manufacturing
France
Germany
United Kingdom

INTERCONTINENTAL
Alan Bickell
Managing Director
Field Sales Regions
Australasia
Far East
Japan
Latin America
South Africa
Manufacturing
Brazil
Canada
Japan
Malaysia
Mexico
Puerto Rico
Singapore

U.S./CANADA
SALES
Field Sales Regions
Eastern
Midwest
Neely (Western)
Southern
Canada
Corporate
Marketing
Operations
•Parts Center

Operations

Bill Terry, Executive Vice President

Instruments

ELECTRONIC MEASUREMENTS
GROUP
Bill Parzybok, General Manager
•Boblingen Instrument
•San Diego
•Colorado Springs
•Logic Systems
•Santa Clara
•YHP Instrument
•Loveland Instrument
•Lake Stevens Instrument
•New Jersey
•Integrated Circuits
•Santa Clara
•Loveland
•Colorado Springs

MICROWAVE AND
COMMUNICATIONS INSTRUMENTS
GROUP
Dick Anderson, General Manager
•Colorado Telecom
•Queensferry Telecom
•Stanford Park
•Spokane
•Signal Analysis
•Network Measurements
•Santa Rosa Technology Center

INSTRUMENT MARKETING GROUP
Bob Brunner, General Manager
Sales: N. America/Europe/Intercon.
•Instrument Support

Paul Ely, Executive Vice President

Computers

COMPUTER
PRODUCTS GROUP
Doug Chance
Vice President
•Data Systems
•Computer Systems
•CSY/Roseville
•Ft. Collins Systems
•Engineering
Productivity
•YHP Computer
•Computer I.C.
•Cupertino I.C.
•Systems
Technology
•Corvallis
Components
•Boblingen
Computer Products

PERSONAL
COMPUTER GROUP
Cyril Yansouni
General Manager
•Roseville Terminals
•Portable Computer
•Grenoble Personal
Computer
•Personal Office
Computer
•Vancouver
•Personal Software
•Puerto Rico
•Singapore
•Brazil

INFORMATION
PRODUCTS
GROUP
Dick Hackborn
Vice President
•Boise
•Disc Memory
•Greeley
•Computer
Peripherals
Bristol
•Roseville
Networks
•Information
Networks
•Colorado
Networks
•Grenoble
Networks

BUSINESS
DEVELOPMENT
GROUP
Ed McCracken
General Manager
•Systems Marketing
Center
•Business
Development Center
•Business
Development Europe
•Information
Resources
•Systems
Re-Marketing
•Guadalajara Computer
•Manufacturing
Productivity
•Application Marketing
•Office Productivity

COMPUTER MARKETING GROUP
Jim Arthur, Vice President
Sales: N. America/Europe/Intercon.
•Computer Support
•Application Marketing
•Computer Supplies

Dean Morton, Executive Vice President**

Medical

MEDICAL GROUP
Ben Holmes, General Manager
•Andover
•Boblingen Medical
•McMinnville
•Waltham
•Bedside Terminals
•Medical Systems
•Medical Supplies

Analytical

ANALYTICAL GROUP
Lew Platt, Vice President
•Avondale
•Scientific Instruments
•Waldbronn

Components

COMPONENTS GROUP
John Blokker, General Manager
•Microwave Semiconductor
•Optoelectronics
•Visible Products
•Interface Products
•Singapore
•Malaysia

CORPORATE
MANUFACTURING
Hal Edmondson
Vice President

HP LABORATORIES
John Doyle
Vice President
Research and
Development

RESEARCH
CENTERS

Computer
Research

Physical Research

Technology
Research

CORPORATE
DEVELOPMENT
Dave Sanders
Director

INTERNAL AUDIT
George Abbott
Manager

Corporate & Support Functions
Business Segments
Division
Operation
* Chairman, Executive Committee
** Chairman, Management Council

> The top managers of the computer groups [computer strategy council] have been discussing a reorganization of this magnitude for some time. I proposed a structure similar to this one about two years ago to John Young and Paul Ely. Although John and Paul agreed such a change was needed, they felt the organization (i.e., the people) were not ready for such a change.
>
> We could have forced the restructuring earlier. Instead we chose to allow the organization to go through its own osmosis in coming to accept that such changes were needed. We may have waited a couple years, but I believe it would have taken just as long for people to absorb something forced on them, if ever. People are more committed when they come to the conclusion on their own. This osmosis process is much like Japanese consensus management.

A marketing manager commented,

> Until now HP has tried to manage its computer business much like it has run the instruments business—with decentralized divisions selling stand-alone products based on technological superiority. The computer marketing managers, division managers, and group managers all knew HP had to become more marketing-oriented, but the organization structure didn't allow for it.

Another group vice president reflected,

> A single entrepreneur has only a few people to communicate his vision to. A large organization must establish and communicate boundaries, set objectives, and let people loose.
>
> There is a big difference between being independent and being entrepreneurial. Independence implies there may not be a cohesive overall fit among the pieces of an organization. Entrepreneurial units, on the other hand, can be managed to fit together if direction is provided. HP's divisions have always had innovation, pride, and openness. The reorganization will get them operating within an overall strategic framework.

The 1983 reorganization was designed to make HP, over the next five years, a worldwide leader in providing integrated information solutions for medium to large companies.

HP believed that, in addition to an outstanding sales/support organization and commitment to R&D, the company had three other competitive advantages to help achieve its goals. First, HP was developing high-volume, low-cost manufacturing capabilities. Many of those state-of-the-art capabilities could be transferred to HP's customers as an added selling point. Second, HP produced nearly $200 million worth of integrated circuits for internal consumption. Second only to IBM, this captive production was several times larger than any other competitor. Last, and probably most important, HP had long provided computer systems for both technical and business applications, both of which would be needed to meet the integrated processing needs of manufacturers. DEC, HP's leading competitor in technical computers, had a limited business computer offering and did not even have a commercial-user sales force. IBM, traditionally a business computer supplier, had substantially less to offer the engineering and scientific markets than did HP.

SPECTRUM

Although HP enjoyed a reputation for highly reliable machines and consistently ranked first in customer satisfaction, by 1983 customers were showing signs of impatience with the failure to upgrade the HP3000. Some were defecting to other, more powerful machines. According to the *New York Times*, "Numerous projects were started to upgrade the 3000, beginning in 1974, but all were either cancelled or failed." A former HP manager complained, "Divisions were small and not allowed to do big things."[8] The problem was such that Young said, "We had to do something, or we'd sink."

HP decided to turn the 3000 into a hub for both its own personal computers and those of IBM. The 3000 was to be the ultimate departmental computer—a low-cost machine that could link personal computers and enable people to tap into information in bigger machines all over the country.

In addition, HP began promising an answer to its critics with Spectrum, a new project to unify HP's product line. Based on the relatively untested RISC technology, Spectrum sought to boost a computer's power by simplifying the complexity of its central processor. Young intended to launch the new family of Spectrum computers in the fall of 1985. He set up an 800-person group to develop every basic component of the Spectrum family. Young declared that the results of the Spectrum project would be the technological basis for every type of computer, and some instruments, sold by HP. He hoped to be able to ship significant quantities in 1986.

According to *Business Week*,

> Once Young developed the consensus he wanted to give Spectrum a final go-ahead in February 1983, he needed someone who could make sure that all the divisions agreed on the details of how the project would proceed. That job fell to Douglas C. Chance, general manager of HP's Information Systems Group. Young saw Chance as a strong strategist who could build a team and develop confidence. This was crucial because many technical decisions had to be made quickly before the machine could be handed over to a development team.
>
> Chance set up a committee of top officers and division managers that met monthly over dinner. As often as not, Chance learned, the issues that worried them most weren't technical. "The real concerns had to do with whether they could trust the others to do what we had all agreed to do," he recalls. Such fears "typically surfaced late at night after several bottles of wine."
>
> Eventually, as Spectrum grew, HP's divisions learned to cooperate under the new umbrella called the Information Technology Group. At its helm was veteran engineer George E. Bodway, a hearty, rumpled man with a knack for administration. "Nothing escapes him," an admirer says. Formed in May 1984, ITG quickly built a staff of 1,000 and for the first time brought into one group the people who develop such key elements of computers as operating systems, programming languages, and integrated-circuit designs. Some 20 divisions chipped in specialized software, peripheral devices, and other elements of Spectrum, with disagreements arbitrated by Bodway and a series of specialized councils.[9]

Spectrum was to be a powerful business minicomputer representing the first fruits of what was widely regarded as one of the most sweeping product transitions ever undertaken in the electronics industry. It also was the first product to reflect the new centralized approach. Spectrum eventually was to produce a common internal design for all the company's desktop and minicomputer product lines well into the 1990s.

According to Dean Morton, executive vice president in 1983, "We made a clear and unequivocal commitment and we expect that it will pay off. We don't have any alternative plans for the next-generation computers."[10]

THE 1984 REORGANIZATION[11]

On July 16, 1984, John Young announced a reorganization designed to accelerate the company's move toward a wider market and to compete more effectively with an increasingly aggressive IBM. The new structure (Exhibit 4) regrouped HP's dozens of product divisions under sectors focusing on markets rather than product lines. Two major sectors now would sell computers: one would concentrate on business customers, while the second would market computers and instruments to scientific and manufacturing customers. Young also closed down some computer-aided engineering (CAE) operations, lumping the remaining CAE activities under one executive, and authorized the licensing of software written by outsiders—an act verging on heresy.

A significant element of the reorganization was the shift of two of HP's top executives. Executive Vice President Ely, who had built the company's computer business from \$100 million a decade earlier to a \$2.4 billion in fiscal 1983, was "shunted aside, to a post where his relationship to the computer business will, by most accounts, be largely advisory. He will take charge of a smaller, more mature sector that includes medical and analytical products and the company's research laboratories."[12] The other move was the elevation of Executive Vice President Morton to the new post of chief operating officer, in line to become CEO. *Business Week* noted,

> The statesmanlike Morton is perceived as more akin in management style to Young and company founders William R. Hewlett and David Packard. Sources close to the company claim that Ely became increasingly difficult to work with during the 10 years that he built computers into HP's largest business. "He has been a disruptive force in the company—lecturing, browbeating, and intimidating people," complains one former executive.

In reacting to the changes, Ely commented that chief operating officer was "not high on my list of most-wanted jobs."

Young and the board had worried since 1978 that customers were demanding complete systems of computers and instruments for solving broad problems, such as factory automation, rather than individual instruments. As the dividing line between computer systems and test and measurement equipment blurred, different HP salespeople sometimes tried to sell the same customer different equipment for solving his or her problems, with different discounts and other conditions of sale. At one time, a customer might be offered any of 16 types of purchase agreements, depending on which salesperson was pitching.

Although Young insisted that the restructuring was a logical follow-up to the 1983 reorganization, outside observers thought it was a further reaction to the orders HP had been losing to IBM. Young cited the CAE failure as a reason for

EXHIBIT 4

Hewlett-Packard Corporate Organization, July 1984

Board of Directors Dave Packard, Chairman Bill Hewlett, Vice Chairman

Chief Executive Officer John Young, President
Chief Operating Officer Dean Morton, Executive Vice President

INTERNAL AUDIT
George Abbott, Manager

CORPORATE DEVELOPMENT
Tom Uhlman, Director

MARKETING AND INTERNATIONAL
Dick Alberding
Executive Vice President

U.S. FIELD OPERATIONS
Jim Arthur
Vice President and Director

Field Sales Regions: Eastern, Midwestern, Neely (Western), Southern

EUROPEAN OPERATIONS
Franco Mariotti
Vice President and Director

Field Sales Regions: France, Germany, Italy, Northern Europe, South/Eastern, United Kingdom
Manufacturing: France, Germany, United Kingdom

INTERCONTINENTAL OPERATIONS
Alan Bickell
Vice President and Director

Field Sales Regions: Australasia, Far East, Japan, Canada, Latin America
Manufacturing: Brazil, Canada, Japan, Korea, Malaysia, Mexico, Puerto Rico, Singapore

MAJOR ACCOUNTS MARKETING
Al Oliverio
Senior Vice President

CORPORATE MARKETING
Art Dauer
Director

Marketing Communications
Marketing Operations
Marketing Information Center
Finance and Remarketing Division
Computer Supplies Operation
Instrument Products Operation
Computer Support Division
Instrument Support Division
Corporate Parts Center

MEASUREMENT, DESIGN AND MANUFACTURING SYSTEMS
Bill Terry, Executive Vice President

MICROWAVE AND COMMUNICATIONS GROUP
Dick Anderson
General Manager

Stanford Park Division
Network Measurements Division
Signal Analysis Division
Spokane Division
Colorado Telecom Division
Queensferry Telecom Division
Microwave Technology Division
Queensferry Microwave Operation

ELECTRONIC INSTRUMENTS GROUP
Ned Barnhoff
General Manager

New Jersey Division
Santa Clara Division
Boblingen Instrument Division
YHP Instrument Division
  YHP Computer Operation
Integrated Circuits Division
  Santa Clara Tech Center
  Loveland Tech Center
  Colorado Springs Tech Center

DESIGN SYSTEMS GROUP
Bill Parzybok
Vice President and General Manager

Fort Collins Systems Division
Logic Systems Division
  Logic Design Operation
Colorado Springs Division
Boblingen Computer Division
Lake Stevens Instrument Division
  Boblingen Engineering Operation
Fort Collins Engineering Operation

MANUFACTURING SYSTEMS GROUP
Lew Platt
Vice President and General Manager

Data Systems Division
  Advanced Manufacturing Systems Operation
Manufacturing Productivity Division
Loveland Instrument Division
  Ponocorm Automation Operation
Manufacturing Test Division
Lyon Manufacturing Systems Operation

INFORMATION SYSTEMS AND NETWORKS
John Dyle, Executive Vice President

INFORMATION SYSTEMS GROUP
Doug Chance
Vice President and General Manager

Computer Systems Division
  CSY Roseville Operation
Boblingen General Systems Division
Office Productivity Division
Guadalajara Computer Operation
Administrative Productivity Division
  Information Resources Operation
  Administrative Productivity Operation
  Financial Systems Operation

PERSONAL COMPUTER GROUP
Cyril Yansouni
Vice President and General Manager

Roseville Terminals Division
Portable Computer Division
  Handheld Computer & Calculator Operation
Grenoble Personal Computer Division
Personal Office Computer Division
Personal Software Division
Puerto Rico Operation
Singapore Operation
Brazil Operation
Personal Computer Distribution Operation
Personal Computer Group Operation

PERIPHERALS GROUP
Dick Hackborn
Vice President and General Manager

Greeley Division
Computer Peripherals Bristol Division
Disc Memory Division
Boise Division
Vancouver Division
San Diego Division

INFORMATION NETWORKS GROUP
John Doyle (Interim)

Colorado Networks Operation
Grenoble Networks Division
Roseville Networks Division
Information Networks Division

INFORMATION TECHNOLOGY GROUP
George Bodway
General Manager

Cupertino IC Division
Fort Collins IC Division
Northwest IC Division
Information Hardware Operation
Information Software Operation

ANALYTICAL, COMPONENTS, MEDICAL AND TECHNOLOGY
Lew Platt

ANALYTICAL GROUP
Dieter Hoehn
General Manager

Avondale Division
  Lab Automation Systems Operation
Scientific Instruments Division
Waldbronn Division

COMPONENTS GROUP
John Blokker
Vice President and General Manager

Microwave Semiconductor Division
Optoelectronics Division
Optical Communication Division
Southeast Asia Operation

MEDICAL GROUP
Ben Holmes
General Manager

Andover Division
Boblingen Medical Division
McMinnville Division
Waltham Division
Medical Supplies Center
Health Care Productivity Operation

HP LABORATORIES
Joel Birnbaum
Vice President and Director

Manufacturing Research Center
Design and Measurement Research Center
Distributed Systems Center
Application Technology Center
Technology Research Center
Bristol Research Center

CORPORATE MANUFACTURING
Hal Edmondson
Vice President and Director

CORPORATE ENGINEERING
Chuck House
Director

ADMINISTRATION
Bob Boniface
Executive Vice President

CONTROLLER
Bob Wayman
Vice President

GENERAL COUNSEL AND SECRETARY
Jack Brigham
Vice President

TREASURY
George Newman
Treasurer

PATENTS AND LICENSES
Jean Chognard
Vice President

PERSONNEL
Bill Craven
Director

GOVERNMENT AFFAIRS
Bob Kirkwood
Director

PUBLIC RELATIONS
Dave Kirby
Director

(continued)

EXHIBIT 4 (CONTINUED)

Hewlett-Packard Corporate Organization, July 1984

HEWLETT-PACKARD CORPORATE ORGANIZATION — DECEMBER 1984

Hewlett-Packard is organized to provide its customers around the world with solutions to their increasingly complex measurement and computational needs.

Of the company's four business sectors, three offer a wide range of advanced electronic-based products. The fourth encompasses worldwide sales and marketing activities and integrates HP's diverse product lines. Giving the company common direction and cohesion are shared philosophies, practices and goals as well as technologies.

Within this context, the individual business units—called product divisions—are relatively small and self-sufficient so that decisions can be made at the level of the organization most responsible for putting them into action. Consistent with this approach, it has always been a practice at Hewlett-Packard to give each employee considerable freedom to implement methods and ideas that meet specific local organizational goals and broad corporate objectives.

Since its founding in 1939, the HP organization has grown to some 50 product divisions. To provide for effective overall management and coordination, the company has aligned these divisions into 12 product groups characterized by product and market focus.

HP's corporate structure is designed to foster small-business flexibility within its many individual operating units while supporting them with the strengths of a larger organization.

The accompanying chart provides a graphic view of the relationship of the various organizational elements. The organization has been structured to allow the groups and their divisions to concentrate on their product-development, manufacturing and marketing activities, while sharing common administrative systems for many of the tasks required of a company doing business worldwide. Normal and functional lines of responsibility and communication are indicated on the chart; however, direct and informal communication across lines and between levels is strongly encouraged.

Here is a closer look at the company's basic organizational units.

PRODUCT DIVISIONS/OPERATIONS
An HP division is a vertically integrated organization that conducts itself much like an independent business. Its fundamental responsibilities are to develop, manufacture and market products that are profitable and which make contributions in the marketplace by virtue of technological or economic advantage.

Each division has its own distinct family of products, for which it has worldwide marketing responsibility. A division also is responsible for its own accounting, personnel activities, quality assurance and support of its products in the field. In addition, it has important social and economic responsibilities in its local community.

Operations are organizational units dedicated to particular tasks, usually in support of a product group or various divisions within a group. They also are generally smaller in size than divisions.

PRODUCT GROUPS
Product groups are composed of divisions and operations having closely related product lines or market focus. Groups are responsible for coordinating the activities of their respective divisions. The management of each group has overall responsibility for the operations and financial performance of its members. Further, each group has worldwide responsibility for its manufacturing and marketing activities.

BUSINESS SECTORS
Reflecting its increased customer orientation and concentration on major markets, the company was realigned in August 1984 into four major sectors.

Measurement, Design and Manufacturing Systems

Information Systems and Networks

Analytical, Components, Medical and Technology

Marketing and International

These sectors provide the focal points for creating the common strategies needed in managing product lines that are increasingly interactive, and for developing overall HP solutions to the complex needs of customers.

By consolidating its worldwide field marketing and international manufacturing, the company is able to apply its unique range of computation and measurement solutions to the business and technical problems of customers around the world. Management staffs of the U.S. and international sales organizations assist the three product sectors in coordinating the sales and service functions.

The executive vice president in charge of each business sector is directly responsible to the chief operating officer for the performance of the sector's product groups.

CORPORATE ADMINISTRATION
The principal responsibility of Corporate Administration is to insure that the corporate staff offices provide the specialized policies, expertise and resources to support the field division and groups adequately on a worldwide basis. The executive vice president in charge of Corporate Administration also reports to the chief operating officer, providing an important upward channel of communication for the corporate staff activities.

CORPORATE RESEARCH AND DEVELOPMENT
HP Laboratories is the corporate research and development organization that provides a central source of technical support for the product-development efforts of HP operating divisions. In these efforts, the divisions make important use of the advanced technologies, materials, components and theoretical analyses researched or developed by HP Labs. Through endeavors in areas of science and technology, the corporate laboratories also help the company develop new areas of business.

CORPORATE MANUFACTURING
Corporate Manufacturing has responsibility for the coordination of manufacturing activities throughout HP, including the following functions: materials planning and procurement, manufacturing support and standards, quality improvement and assurance, manufacturing information systems, regulatory standards, environmental control, employee safety and health, and corporate physical-distribution systems.

CORPORATE ENGINEERING
Corporate Engineering is responsible for coordinating the company's engineering activities, with an emphasis on measures to increase engineering productivity through improved design tools, engineering processes, training and development programs and strategic coordination.

BOARD OF DIRECTORS
The Board of Directors and its chairman have ultimate responsibility for the legal and ethical conduct of the company and its officers. It is the board's duty to protect and advance the interests of the stockholders, to foster a continuing concern for fairness in the company's relations with employees, and to fulfill all requirements of the law with regard to the board's stewardship.

The board counsels management on general business matters and also reviews and evaluates the performance of management. To assist in discharging these responsibilities, the board has formed various committees to oversee the company's activities and programs in such areas as employees' benefits, compensation, financial auditing and investment.

CHIEF EXECUTIVE OFFICER/CHIEF OPERATING OFFICER
The chief executive officer is responsible for the direction and long range performance of the company, subject to the authority of the Board of Directors. Also, the chief executive officer serves as chairman of the Executive Committee. Reporting directly to the CEO are Corporate Development and Internal Audit.

The chief operating officer, who reports directly to the chief executive officer, has responsibility for the day-to-day operating performance of the company. Reporting directly to the chief operating officer are the four operating sectors of the company and Corporate Administration. The chief operating officer serves as chairman of the Management Council.

EXECUTIVE COMMITTEE
The Executive Committee is the company's primary policy-setting body. It reviews broad issues affecting the company and initiates strategies designed to maintain its direction and meet its goals. Members include the chief executive officer (who serves as committee chairman), chief operating officer, and the five executive vice presidents. Meetings are normally scheduled on a weekly basis.

MANAGEMENT COUNCIL
Primary responsibilities of this body are to review and formulate operating policies, and to turn policy decisions into corporate action. The council, chaired by the chief operating officer, also reviews performance expectations as reflected in the forward planning of the business sectors and monitors their operating results.

Council members serve variously on five committees charged with policy-setting responsibility for personnel, operations, marketing, computer architecture and networks and information systems. Each committee is chaired by an executive vice president; in addition, the 22 council members are all group and senior managers of the company.

hp HEWLETT PACKARD
Corporate Public Relations
3000 Hanover Street, Palo Alto, CA 94304

the reorganization. HP's 9000 series of computer workstations, intended to spearhead the company's drive into the CAE market—whose 30 percent growth rates prompted Young to call it "hotter even than personal computers"—had been announced in late 1982. However, the software needed to do computer-aided design and engineering would not come out until November 1985, and then it would be based heavily on software from two outside companies, one since bought by HP. *Business Week* believed that engineers who bought these kinds of computers to design integrated circuits had all but bypassed the 9000 in favor of products from small start-up companies, such as Calma Corporation. The reason HP was late in CAE was that CAE had fallen between the cracks of the company's two main businesses.

HP also floundered in its 1984 move into consumer markets with the HP 110 portable computer, introduced in May. Apart from the $3,000 price tag, major criticism of the 110 was its lack of the most-wanted software. Some expected it to perform like the first consumer PC, the HP 150, with the touch screen, but it sold better via direct sales to HP's loyal customers than in retail channels.

Even the continued 30 percent growth of the flagship 3000 series of minicomputers resulted largely from sales to the existing customer base. The 3000 series was trailing the growth rate of comparable machines from IBM and DEC.

Mounting Problems

1984 Results

In 1984 HP sales grew at a compound annual rate of 23.3 percent to more than $6 billion, compared with 20.8 percent for the prior seven years, but profit growth had slowed. Whereas between 1978 and 1982, profits grew at an annual rate of better than 25 percent, 1983 and 1984 saw growth of 19.5 percent.

Another area of concern for Young was management turnover. Not only did 38 of 750 managers quit the company in 1984 (nearly twice the number as in 1983), it was also reported that almost every upstart CAE venture now employed HP refugees. In January 1985 HP experienced its first departure of a top executive—Paul Ely, who left to head Convergent Technologies of San Jose, California.

According to *Fortune*,

> Ely's achievements are widely acknowledged. . . . By 1983 the workaholic Ely had helped boost sales to $2.4 billion, racking up a compound growth rate of 33 percent and pretax profits of $392 million. Despite recent problems with personal computers, he made computers Hewlett-Packard's biggest business.
>
> But Ely also cut up like a professional bad boy. Former subordinates say he believed that even a wrong decision was better than no decision at all, and that he would shoot from the hip, correcting his errors later. Although he was an inspiring manager, Ely didn't build strong teams, and he went on the warpath against the instruments side of Hewlett-Packard.
>
> Last July, after announcing a new organizational structure, Young named a chief operating officer. "Young made a presentation showing that as second in command, Dean O. Morton would do a better job inside the HP culture than Ely," recalls Antonie T. Knoppers, a director. "Ely was able but cocky. Within the parameters of HP's culture, he was just in bounds."[13]

1985 Results

By 1985, HP's share of the minicomputer market had slipped from 7 percent (in 1979) to 6 percent as competitors surpassed the HP3000, which processed 16 bits of information at a time, by offering much faster "superminis" that handled 32 bits. Despite spending more than $50 million between 1983 and 1985 to launch a line of personal computers, HP still had little visible market share, except with its innovative, low-cost printers.

Also, after investing at least $50 million, the company had yet to launch a competitive system into the booming market for CAE. Part of the problem was attributed to the fact that ten highly competitive divisions were responsible for developing different components of CAE systems. Young hoped to demonstrate some CAE systems at the Design Automation Conference in June of 1985, but several new firms had a long head start on HP.

By July 1985 Spectrum was long overdue. Originally the first of the new computers was to be announced before the end of 1985, but the date was postponed. It was now expected to be announced later in the year. HP acknowledged that it was having more difficulty than expected making the new machines capable of running software developed for its older computers. There also were reports that HP was behind in developing chips for the new machine. According to the *New York Times*, "Each time information is revealed, the project seems to be further off and less impressive than it once appeared."[14]

The most positive area for HP was the 3000. By mid-1985 20,000 HP3000s were in use—double the number three years previously—making it the most popular minicomputer after IBM's System/34 and System/36. It also had given HP 4 percent of the business departmental market. Its 23 percent increase in revenues over the previous six months accounted for virtually all of the company's 10 percent growth in sales (profits had declined by 12 percent). The spearhead of HP's new thrust was Series 37, the latest and smallest of the 3000 family. The size of a two-drawer file cabinet and starting at $20,000 (about half the previous lowest price for a 3000), "Mighty Mouse's" key selling point was its software, which went further than other makers in tying software applications on the large system to applications on the personal computer. By late 1985 the company had announced Vectra PC, the first HP computer compatible with an IBM model, PC-AT.

To sell its departmental concept, HP developed a two-pronged marketing strategy: it used its own sales force to reach big customers, and it sold to small businesses through third-party companies that wrote software geared to specific market niches and sold complete systems that met specific needs. For the first time, HP was selling to customers with revenues as low as $5 million.

By the end of the fiscal year, it was clear that 1985 would be the first year with an earnings decline since Young had become CEO—by 10 percent to $489 million. (See Exhibits 5–7 for financial statements.) HP's overall revenues grew only a modest 8 percent, to $6.5 billion. (The 3000 line accounted for about a third of 1985 revenues.) That figure had to be compared with double-digit growth rates for most other computer makers. HP's earnings in the same period fell for the first time since 1975, and HP's overall share of the worldwide minicomputer market had slipped to 5 percent from 5.5 percent in 1983. In the $37 billion market for commercial minis, it dropped from a 4.2 percent share in 1983 to 3.9 percent in 1985, while DEC moved from 5 percent to 7 percent. In the $15 billion market for technical minis, HP dropped to 7.8 percent from more than 12 percent five years earlier.

EXHIBIT 5

Hewlett-Packard Consolidated Statement of Earnings (millions)

	October 31	
ORDERS	1985	1984
Measurement, design, information, and manufacturing equipment and systems	$2,819	$3,135
Peripherals and network products	1,537	1,440
Service for equipment, systems, and peripherals	1,135	904
Medical electronic equipment and service	458	402
Analytical instrumentation and service	256	238
Electronic components	190	231
	$6,395*	$6,350*
NET REVENUE†		
Measurement, design, information, and manufacturing equipment and systems	$2,929	$2,879
Peripherals and network products	1,560	1,375
Service for equipment, systems, and peripherals	1,125	970
Medical electronic equipment and service	448	377
Analytical instrumentation and service	248	229
Electronic components	195	214
	$6,505	$6,044
Costs and expenses:		
Cost of goods sold	3,166	2,865
Research and development	685	592
Marketing	1,181	1,066
Administrative and general	715	661
	5,747	5,184
Earnings before taxes	758	860
Provision for taxes	269	313
Reversal of DISC taxes‡	—	(118)
Net earnings	$489	$665
Net earnings per share	$1.91	$2.59
Cash dividends per share	$.22	$.19

(continued)

For the years ended October 31	1985	1984	1983
Domestic orders	$3,662	$3,629	$2,901
International orders	2,733	2,721	2,021
*Total orders.	$6,395	$6,350	$4,922
Equipment	$5,204	$4,934	$3,862
Services	1,301	1,110	848
†Net revenue.	$6,505	$6,044	$4,710

‡Reversal of DISC taxes accrued prior to 1984 due to a change in U.S. tax law.

EXHIBIT 5 (CONTINUED)

Hewlett-Packard Consolidated Statement of Earnings (millions)

The company operates in a single industry segment: the design and manufacture of measurement and computation products and systems. The statement provides supplemental information showing orders and net revenue by groupings of similar products or services. The groupings are as follows:

- Measurement, design, information, and manufacturing equipment and systems: equipment and systems (hardware and software) used for design, manufacturing, office automation, and information processing; general-purpose instruments and computers; and handheld calculators.
- Peripherals and network products: printers, plotters, magnetic disc and tape drives, terminals, and network products.
- Service for equipment, systems, and peripherals: support and maintenance services, parts and supplies related to design and manufacturing systems, office and information systems, general-purpose instruments and computers, peripherals, and network products.
- Medical electronic equipment and service: products that perform patient monitoring, diagnostic, therapeutic, and data-management functions; application software; support and maintenance services; and hospital supplies.
- Analytical instrumentation and service: gas and liquid chromatographs, mass spectrometers and spectrophotometers used to analyze chemical compounds; support and maintenance services.
- Electronic components: microwave semiconductor and optoelectronic devices that are sold primarily to manufacturers for incorporation into electronic products.

DEC was a major reason, but so also were IBM and AT&T. In instrument sales, company revenues had dropped 3 percent over the previous year but provided more than one-third of revenues and regularly earned, before taxes, more than 20 cents on every dollar of sales.

1986 Results

On February 25, 1986, after spending an estimated $200 million, HP unveiled Spectrum. For the past three years, almost the entire company had been working on the project. Its cost in 1986 alone was expected to run in the hundreds of millions of dollars. Actually unveiled were two machines that would double and triple the power of the top model in the 3000 line. The smaller model, the Series 930, which was supposed to perform better than competing $450,000 minicomputers from DEC and IBM for about half the price, would be available by the end of 1986, and the larger Series 950 by the second half of 1987. To minimize risks, HP used well-proven chips instead of the latest available. Although the chips limited the speed of the machines, they were faster than most conventional ones. The

EXHIBIT 6

Hewlett-Packard Consolidated Balance Sheets (millions)

	October 31		
	1985	1984	1983
ASSETS			
Current assets:			
Cash and temporary cash investments	$ 1,020	$ 938	$ 880
Accounts and notes receivable	1,249	1,180	951
Inventories:			
Finished goods	401	373	279
Purchased parts and fabricated assemblies	592	650	469
Other current assets	80	60	53
Total current assets	$3,342	$3,201	$2,632
Property, plant, and equipment:			
Land	$ 230	$ 202	$ 167
Buildings and leasehold improvements	1,653	1,416	1,102
Machinery and equipment	1,400	1,173	888
Total P, P, and E	3,283	2,791	2,157
Accumulated depreciation and amortization	(1,134)	(923)	(726)
Net P, P, and E	2,149	1,868	1,431
Other assets	189	84	98
Total assets	$5,680	$5,153	$4,161
LIABILITIES AND SHAREHOLDERS' EQUITY			
Current liabilities:			
Notes payable	$ 260	$ 217	$ 148
Accounts payable	240	281	203
Employee compensation and benefits	397	398	300
Other accrued liabilities	302	162	103
Accrued taxes on earnings	111	203	112
Other accrued taxes	63	61	54
Total current liabilities	1,376	1,322	920
Long-term debt	102	81	71
Other liabilities	92	93	46
Deferred taxes on earnings	128	112	237
Total liabilities	$1,698	$1,608	$1,274
Shareholders' equity:			
Common stock and capital in excess of $1 par value	780	775	733
Retained earnings	3,202	2,770	2,154
Total shareholders' equity	3,982	3,545	2,887
Total liabilities and shareholders' equity	$5,680	$5,153	$4,161

company also introduced a 3000 series upgrade that did not use the new RISC technology.

By this time several small, start-up computer companies were offering products with RISC designs, and in January IBM had introduced a RISC-based engineering

EXHIBIT 7

Hewlett-Packard Consolidated Statement of Changes in Financial Position (millions)

	October 31		
	1985	1984	1983
Funds provided by operations:			
Net earnings	$489	$665	$432
Expenses not requiring an outlay of funds:			
Depreciation and amortization	299	237	191
Deferred taxes on earnings	97	(81)	105
Other, net	54	47	45
	939	868	773
Funds used by operations:			
Investment in property, plant, and equipment	632	661	466
Increase (decrease) in working capital, excluding net cash: Accounts and notes receivable	69	195	178
Inventories	(30)	256	89
Other current assets	20	(9)	(1)
Accounts payable and accrued liabilities	(22)	(179)	(104)
Accrued taxes on earnings	92	(78)	39
Other, net	19	(22)	2
	780	824	669
Nonoperating funds provided (used):			
Employee stock plans:			
Shares issued	156	112	108
Shares purchased	(240)	(142)	—
Dividends to shareholders	(57)	(49)	(40)
Other, net	21	24	32
	(120)	(55)	100
Increase (decrease) in net cash (cash and temporary cash investments, net of notes payable)	$ 39	$ (11)	$204
Net cash at beginning of year	721	732	528
Net cash at end of year	$760	$721	$732

workstation. Spectrum, however, represented by far the industry's biggest gamble on RISC to date. HP claimed that customers would have no difficulty converting software that was used on its current products.

For the quarter ended April 30 revenue was up 6 percent, but earnings had fallen 2 percent—the fifth such decline in a row. Although Young had been proclaiming that the computer slump had passed its low point and had predicted modest improvement for the year, he now admitted, "The fact is, our U.S. business has been essentially flat for nearly two years. It continues to be a difficult business environment." Nevertheless, in May HP lifted a 5 percent management salary cut it had imposed the previous summer. As a result, overhead grew, so tight hiring controls were maintained.

With a sharper-than-expected decline in European and other non-U.S. orders, net income for the third quarter (ended July 31) now was expected to decline by 13 percent, to $117 million—even lower than expected. Revenue would increase slightly, perhaps to $1.61 billion. This would mean that orders for the nine-month period would be essentially flat, rising 1 percent, with domestic orders declining 2 percent and international orders rising 4 percent.

On top of these developments, it was becoming clear that because of software snags, HP would have to delay shipping the 930 for at least six months, to mid-1987. Since two-thirds of the $100 million of orders for new Spectrum-technology computers were for the 930 machines, HP's 1987 computer sales might be lowered by about $200 million, or roughly half of anticipated revenue from the Spectrum-based product lines. When the news became public the company's stock, which was trading in the mid-$40 range, was likely to drop to its lowest point of the year. *Business Week* had recently raised the question: "Can Hewlett-Packard Put the Pieces Back Together?"

ENDNOTES

[1]Much of this section is based on Bro Uttal, "Mettle-Test Time for John Young," *Fortune*, April 29, 1985, pp. 242–248.

[2]John W. Wilson, Catherine L. Harris, and Gordon Block, "Can Hewlett-Packard Put the Pieces Back Together?" *Business Week*, March 10, 1986, p. 115.

[3]Uttal, "Mettle-Test Time," p. 244.

[4]"Can John Young Redesign Hewlett-Packard?" *Business Week*, December 6, 1982, pp. 74–76.

[5]Ibid., p. 74.

[6]Ibid., p. 78.

[7]Several earlier reorganizations had occurred in response to HP's growth into computers. The first major restructuring in 1969 established HP's first group structure. Further growth into several new markets led to a second major regrouping in 1974. The six product categories remained HP's basic lines into the mid-1980s: (1) electronic test and measuring instruments, (2) computers and computer-based systems, (3) calculators, (4) solid-state components, (5) medical electronic products, and (6) electronic instrumentation for chemical analysis. By 1976 HP had decided to refocus its computer strategy by separating technical/industrial systems from business/commercial systems, a strategy that had worked well to position HP as a strong player in both markets. In 1979 the Computer System Group had been reorganized into five groups: (1) Technical Computer, (2) Business Computer, (3) Computer Peripherals, (4) Terminals, and (5) Computer Marketing.

[8]Andrew Pollack, "Hewlett Bets the Store on Spectrum," *New York Times*, November 17, 1985, p. 28.

[9]Wilson, "Can Hewlett-Packard Put the Pieces Back Together?" p. 116.

[10]Pollack, "Hewlett Bets the Store."

[11]Most of this section is based on Uttal, "Mettle-Test Time," pp. 242–248, and "Why Hewlett-Packard Overhauled Its Management," *Business Week*, July 30, 1984, pp. 111–112.

[12]Ibid.

[13]Uttal, "Mettle-Test Time," p. 224.

[14]Pollack, "Hewlett Bets the Store," p. 28.

CASE 17

NEW ZEALAND DAIRY BOARD

> While milk is a raw material, milk is a thousand raw materials.
> John Murray, Company Secretary, New Zealand Dairy Board

> Producing commodities keeps you a peasant forever.
> John Parker, Deputy CEO, New Zealand Dairy Board

It was early January 1994, and Warren Larsen reread the Boston Consulting Group's recently released performance audit on the New Zealand Dairy Board (NZDB). The Boston Consulting Group (BCG) conducted its study to fulfill a requirement that NZDB's performance be audited every five years. Larsen, the recently appointed chief executive, was generally pleased with BCG's report, which compared NZDB with a variety of world best practices. However, in some areas NZDB departed significantly from best practice (see Exhibit 1). In addition, increasing global competition, volatility in commodity markets, oversupply of milk products, and foreign government subsidies would make continued performance in the world market a challenge. Larsen also counted shareholder (dairy producer) satisfaction among his chief priorities. The question the new CEO contemplated that January evening was how to crystalize NZDB's strategic direction while ensuring that the concerns of the BCG report and shareholders were addressed.

NZDB HISTORY

In 1993 dairy products accounted for 17 percent of the value of New Zealand's exports, similar to meat (17 percent), and followed by forestry (12 percent), metals/minerals/chemicals (12 percent), horticulture (7 percent), fishing (7 percent), and wool (5 percent). From the early days of the dairy industry in New Zealand, farmers had joined together to form cooperatives to collect, process, and market their members' milk. Traditionally, the members of each cooperative jointly owned the cooperative's assets (processing plants, collection and delivery vehicles, and so forth). The cooperatives retained a share of each year's profits for investment and financial reserves and distributed the remaining profits to the member farmers by way of increments to the basic milk price. The cooperative's net profits were divided by the total kilograms of milk solids (fat and nonfat components) received during the year to compute a payout per kilogram. Farmers were then paid according to the number of kilograms of milk solids they supplied during the year. Since all farmers in the cooperative received the same dollar payout per kilogram, the only way for an individual farmer to increase his or her payout was to add additional cows or to increase the volume of milk produced per cow. Individual cooperatives competed against one another, and the size of cooperatives was limited by the distance milk was able to be transported in half a day.

The case was prepared by Brad Webb, Darden 1995, under the supervision of Professor L. J. Bourgeois III. Research funding was provided by Ernst & Young, New Zealand.

EXHIBIT 1

Boston Consulting Group Report to New Zealand Dairy Board

Topic	Contrary to Best Practice	Some Significant Departures from Best Practice	In-line with Best Practice with Some Qualifications	In-line with Best Practice
1. Objectives				
2. Policy and Strategy Development				
3. Financial Management and Control				
4. Organizational Structure and Management				
5. Personnel				
6. Finance and Investment				
7. Marketing				
8. Research and Development				
9. Payment System				
10. Quality				
11. Communication				

7 out of 10 and improving

During World War II, the United Kingdom paid premium prices for more than 90 percent of New Zealand's dairy produce under a bulk marketing arrangement designed to counter wartime food shortages. This arrangement continued until 1954 when the United Kingdom released New Zealand from its obligation. Even after termination of the formal arrangement, the United Kingdom continued to buy the majority of New Zealand's dairy products, and New Zealand was referred to as "Britain's farm."

The New Zealand Dairy Board was formed as a statutory board under the Dairy Board Act of 1961. Under this act, NZDB was given the power to purchase, market, and control all dairy products manufactured in New Zealand for export. The act resulted in the formation of a single-desk export marketing organization which was required by statute to take all dairy products produced for export in New Zealand. Except for some coordinating activities, NZDB was not involved in the marketing of products within New Zealand, where the individual dairy cooperatives continued to compete freely with one another.

In the years immediately following its formation, NZDB participated in the commodity markets and became exceptionally skilled at exploiting the low-cost advantage of New Zealand's dairy farms. The majority of dairy farms in the United States, Japan, and parts of Europe fed cattle year-round with processed feed, which had to be grown, harvested, stored, and transported to the individual farms. The large amount of labor, equipment, handling, and transport involved resulted in high feed costs, which required higher milk prices to cover the costs of milk production. In contrast, New Zealand's dairy cattle grazed in lush pastures, which minimized the feed cost to the farmer. A comparison of the different costs of production by country is shown in Exhibit 2.

Although each cooperative contracted with selected farms to supply milk year-round for domestic consumption (also known as "town milk"), the great majority of New Zealand's dairies experienced seasonal production linked to the cycle of grass

EXHIBIT 2

Comparative Costs of Milk Production (cents per liter of milk in $ Australian)

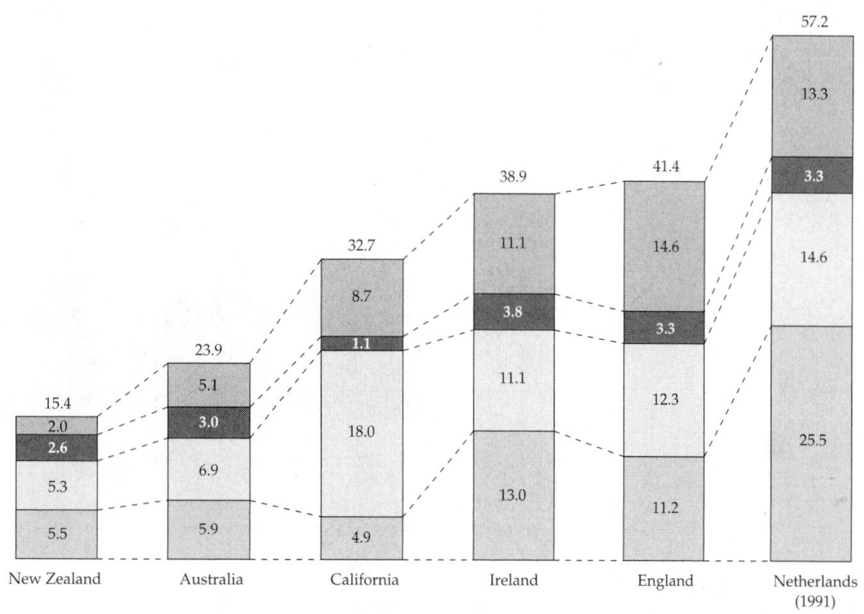

growth in pastures. The "milk curve" is shown in Exhibit 3. Weather conditions had tremendous influence on the volume of milk produced and caused total annual milk volumes to fluctuate as much as 10 percent.

INDUSTRY OVERVIEW

PRODUCTION

Virtually every country in the world has had some form of milk production. The export market for dairy products, however, was relatively small when compared to the total volume of milk produced globally. In 1993, only 8 percent, or 36 million tons, of the world's milk production from dairy cows entered export markets, while the other 92 percent was consumed domestically. Of that 36 million tons, only 27 million tons fell into the category of "accessible," or unrestricted, trade, while the remaining 9 million tons was traded bilaterally.

World milk production could be segmented on a national basis. New Zealand produced 2 percent of the world's milk annually but accounted for 17 percent of the world's trade in dairy exports in 1993 (see Exhibit 4). New Zealand's relatively small population base consumed only 5 percent of New Zealand's annual milk production, leaving the other 95 percent available for export. Other large producers of milk included the European Community, the United States, India, Australia, and Japan. With the exception of the liquid milk market, unprocessed milk had little value because it spoiled quickly. As a result, most dairy products were exported in processed form in products such as milk powder, cheese, protein concentrate, and butter.

EXHIBIT 3

Seasonal "Milk Curve"

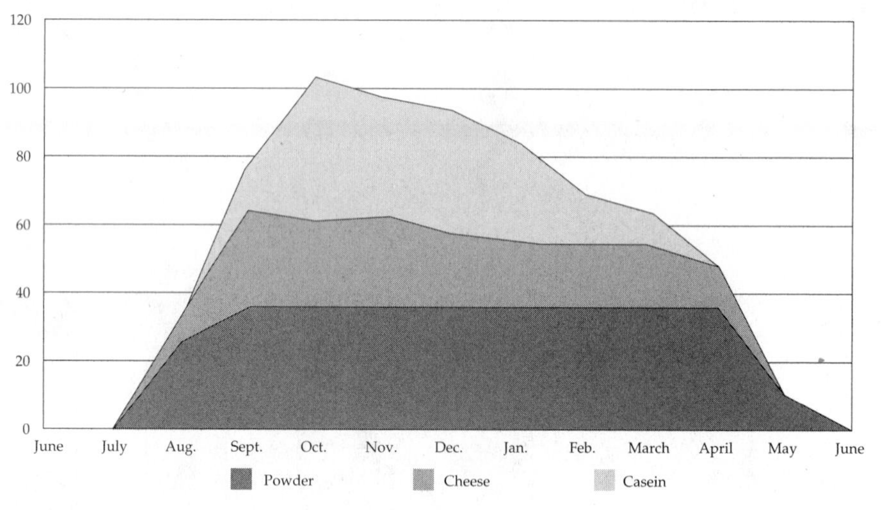

EXHIBIT 4

World Milk Production and Accessible Dairy Product Trade

Country	1993 Milk Production[a]	Total Share of Production	Exporter's Share of Accessible Trade
European Union	114.7 MMT	22%	49%
Former Soviet Union	79.0	15%	15
United States	69.0	13%	5
India	60.9	12%	—
Brazil	15.2	3%	—
Poland	11.9	2%	—
New Zealand	5.9	2%	22
Australia	0.4	.09%	8
Others	157.6	30%	6

[a]Total world production of 519 million metric tons (includes dairy cow, sheep, goat, and buffalo milk).

Market Segments

The world trade in dairy products could be separated into four broad product categories. In ascending order of complexity of processing, packaging, and marketing requirements, these were commodity products, ingredients, food service products, and branded consumer products. Competitors in the commodity business were primarily governmental export agencies or national cooperative marketing boards, while buyers tended to be government agricultural agencies who bought commodities in large volumes on a tender-offer basis. Players in the ingredients and food services sectors included national cooperative marketing organizations, government export agencies, and multinational food companies; buyers included large food manufacturing companies, multinational food service companies, and other manufacturing companies, such as pharmaceutical firms. The consumer products area was dominated by multinational food consumer products companies such as Philip Morris and Nestlé, with some limited participation from national export organizations. NZDB competed in all four categories.

Commodity Markets. Of the four primary dairy product segments, commodity markets grew the least and offered the lowest margins. World demand for dairy products was linked to population growth, and prices reflected supply and demand. (See Exhibits 5 and 6 for general production and price trends of skim

EXHIBIT 5

World Price Trends of Skim Milk Powder

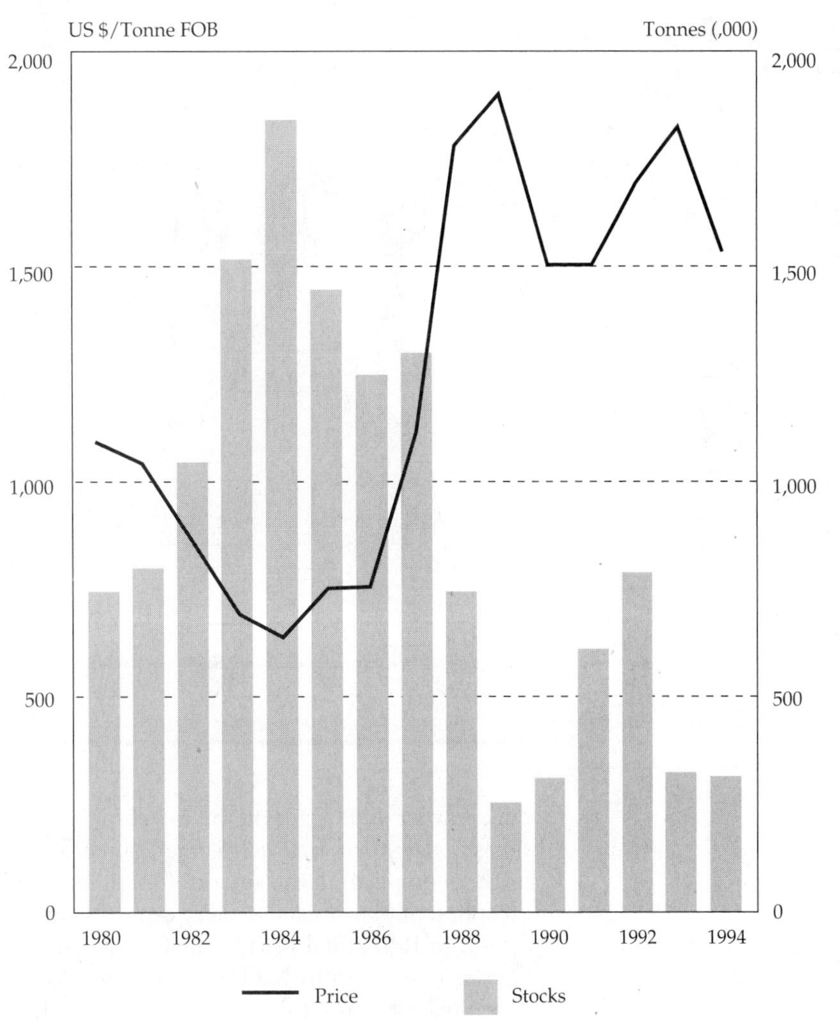

SOURCE: GATT.

EXHIBIT 6

World Price Trends of Butter

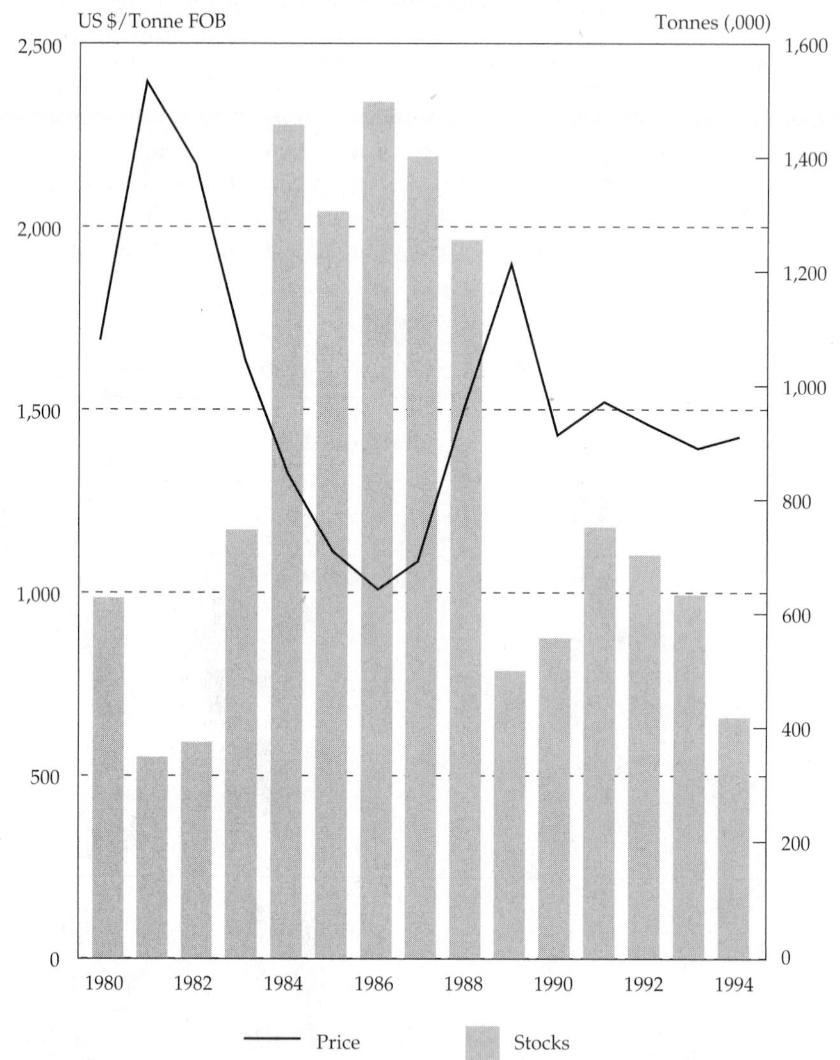

SOURCE: GATT.

milk powder and butter on the world markets for 1980 to 1994.) Government subsidies of dairy exports, such as the United States' Dairy Export Incentive Program, further complicated the smooth functioning of the commodity markets. With the exception of New Zealand, dairy exports from all countries were subsidized to some extent. In 1992, total worldwide dairy product export subsidies totaled US$6.0 billion, as compared to NZDB's total 1992 revenues of US$1.5 billion. Subsidies were greatest in the European Community, Japan, and the United States. In 1982, EEC export subsidies totaled US$2.2 billion and increased to US$4.5 billion in 1992. New Zealand was the only country that could profitably sell its products on the commodity markets at the world minimum prices established in the International Dairy Arrangement, a multicountry organization of dairy exporting nations.

Ingredients and Food Service Markets. Advances in technology and processes vastly expanded the number of dairy products traded internationally. The traded volume of both primary ingredients and specialized food service products increased significantly. Ingredient products included milk proteins such as caseinate, which were used in end products ranging from soft drinks to Cool Whip to pharmaceuticals. Food service products included such items as the cheese used by fast-food franchise operations and confectionery butter used by large food companies. These products were intermediates in the production process and were typically sold in bulk or large quantities to the manufacturer of the end product.

Consumer Markets. Branded consumer products included whole and skim milk powder, ice cream, spreadable butter, specialty cheeses, aerosol whipped cream, and short-shelf-life products such as fresh milk and cultured dairy products. (Exhibit 7 shows the range of products in the consumer segment.) These products were typically distributed via traditional retail distribution channels and required intensive advertising and promotion. Production of consumer dairy products was driven by high value-added processing with an emphasis on smaller quantities than other dairy product categories. Margins in the consumer segment were higher than in the other three segments. The profitability and additional margins captured through a branded consumer strategy are shown in Exhibit 8.

EXHIBIT 7

Product Range in Branded Consumer Dairy Products

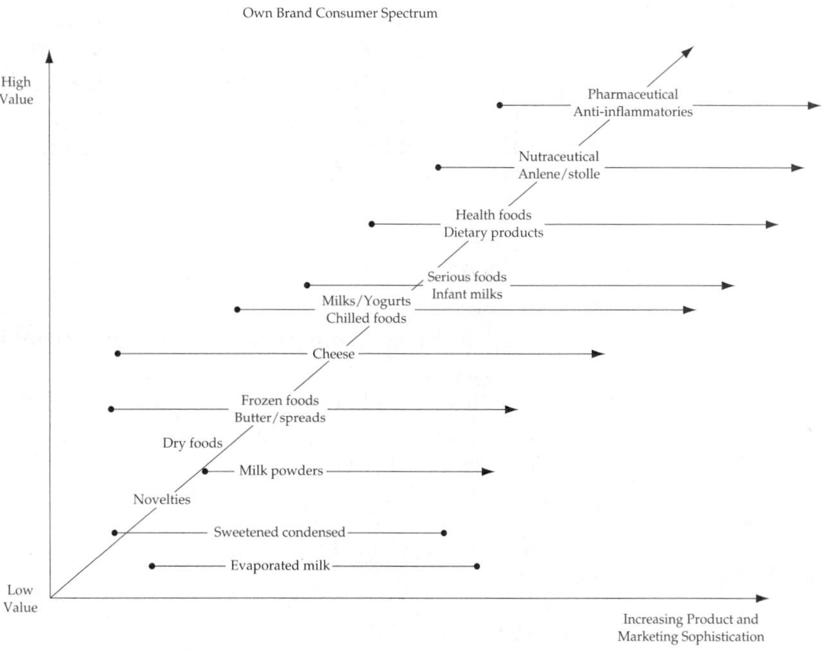

EXHIBIT 8

Analysis of In-Market Profits and Consumer Milk Powder Prices

			USD per Metric Tonne
Retail Price, Retailers' Costs and Profit	20%	Retail	5,000
Distribution, warehousing selling costs, and profit	15		4,000
Marketing costs and profit	20	Distribution price	3,250
Processing and packing costs and profit	10	Ex-factory	2,600
Freight and insurance	5	CIF price	1,900
Bulk FAS equivalent	30	FAS price	1,800

The following relationships also apply: a 1 percent net profit on commodity trading equates to US$18 per metric ton, a 5 percent net profit on an industrial ingredient sold in-market equates to US$100 per metric ton, and a 12.5 percent net profit from selling into retail after all costs, including advertising and promotion and return on in-market infrastructure, equates to US$500 per metric ton.

GATT Uruguay Round Results

On December 15, 1993, the GATT (General Agreement on Tariffs and Trade) Uruguay Round was successfully concluded after seven years of negotiations. The provisions of the agreement provided for significant changes in the world dairy product trade. Both the levels of subsidies and the volumes of products to which subsidies could be applied were reduced significantly. These changes promised to have a significant impact in the EC countries, which accounted for more than one-half of the world's traded dairy products. Under the new agreement, New Zealand received a 50 percent increase in its butter quota to the United Kingdom (from 52,000 MT to 76,600 MT) as well as improved access into the United States for its cheeses. The increase in the U.K. butter quota was significant for New Zealand, as the United Kingdom paid NZDB a premium price for a product that was becoming increasingly harder to sell due to global oversupply. New Zealand's U.K. butter quota was fixed at the increased level indefinitely. The effects of GATT would also increase the competitiveness of other dairy producers currently being subsidized to varying levels.

Capital Costs

Capital costs in the dairy industry were dependent upon the product sector in which an organization wished to compete and in which portion of the value chain the organization's involvement was focused. Investment requirements ranged from milk processing and recombining facilities to distribution infrastructure to brand building.

Producers of commodity products had to be able to separate milk into the desired constituents and produce bulk quantities of relatively unsophisticated finished products, such as whole milk powder (WMP), skim milk powder (SMP), butter, and cheese. Significant economies of scale could be realized in the commodities sector.

Given that the ingredients and food service sectors required further processing of the milk constituents, additional investment in both processes and technology was required. What was most crucial in the ingredient and food service sector was an organization's ability to produce consistently high-quality products delivered on time to the required specifications.

The consumer segment required significant investments in packaging, consumer research, distribution infrastructure, and advertising and promotion. Because fresh milk could not be shipped very far without spoiling, traded dairy products were transported in processed form. Shipping could represent a significant portion of a dairy exporting country's cost structure. Chris Kelly, NZDB's director of strategic planning, cited "the tyranny of distance" as being one competitive factor with which NZDB had to regularly contend.

SUPPLIERS

Milk was produced by dairy farmers whose farms varied in scale depending on the price paid for milk in the producing country (see Exhibit 9). Milk could be processed into fresh milk for drinking or manufactured into processed products, such as cheese, butter, and ice cream. The proportion of milk used in manufacturing also varied by country (see Exhibit 9). In general, milk was a commodity raw material, and excess production capacity existed globally as a result of dairy subsidies. Dairy farmers generally had little bargaining power with the organizations to whom they sold their milk.

In some countries, including New Zealand and Denmark, dairy farmers were organized into a cooperative structure in which the farmers themselves owned the processing facilities and exerted some influence over the way in which the milk products were manufactured and marketed. Farmers had the ability to change to whom they sold their milk. However, in reality, because of costs of transport of milk to the processing units, only those farmers on the borders between one processor and another could change their processor.

CUSTOMERS

The profile of dairy product buyers varied by product segment as follows:

- **Commodity.** These buyers were typically government or national-scale agencies who bought primarily on price through tender offers. These purchasers frequently had no loyalty to one seller, provided a competing seller could meet the same minimum quality standards. Sellers who participated in the commodity markets frequently worked through an agency structure and had little or no contact with the government issuing the tender. Buyers in this segment would purchase from as many sources as were necessary to obtain the required volume. Thus there were "world commodity prices" that varied with global supply and demand.
- **Ingredients.** Large regional, national, or multinational companies purchased these products and sought consistent taste, quality, and appearance from dairy

EXHIBIT 9

International Comparisions Herd Size[a] and Milk Production[b]

	Total Cows 000 Head	Average Herd Size	Milk Production[c] 000 Tonnes	Percent Used in Manufacturing[d]
New Zealand	2,357	169.6	7,873[d]	94.3
Australia	1,628	110.0	7,327[d]	75.7
United States	9,850	48.1	67,717	63.3
Canada	1,270	42.5	7,100	63.5
Japan	2,082	37.8	8,580	—
EEC—Total 12	21,900	19.6	97,799	73.2
Denmark	708	33.0	4,406	—
France	4,685	22.0	22,989	—
United Germany	5,382	17.3	25,610	—
Ireland	1,262	24.6	5,271	—
United Kingdom	2,747	68.2	13,884	—
Netherlands	1,821	40.5	10,504	—
C.I.S. (former USSR)	38,200	—	50,700[e]	—

[a]Latest available figures; all are 1991 figures, apart from New Zealand, Australia, and Japan, which are 1992 figures.

[b]Provisional figures for 1992, based on national statistics.

[c]Sales to factories and dairies (milk available for processing).

[d]1992/1993 season.

[e]State purchases.

Source: New Zealand Dairy Board documents.

products suppliers. In addition, these customers often required extensive technical assistance in tailoring a dairy ingredient to a product-specific application. Long-term partnerships were standard practice in this segment, a practice partially driven by necessity as many dairy ingredients had specific functional properties that were proprietary in nature.

- **Food Service.** These buyers were typically large national or regional food manufacturing or retail companies, including fast-food franchise operations like McDonald's and Pizza Hut. Because these companies stressed product consistency across their various outlets, they sought the same consistent quality that ingredients purchasers did, as well as on-time delivery. These customers were typically very loyal and also sought to form long-term, mutual trust relationships with their suppliers.

- **Consumer.** In industrialized Western countries, consumer products were distributed through extensive wholesale and retail structures, where large retail chains were increasing in size and geographic coverage. This phenomenon was less pronounced in developing countries.

The organizational infrastructure requirements needed to successfully compete in each segment were varied. For commodity products, the only requirements were "an agent, a phone, and a fax," according to John Parker, the current deputy chief executive and a 30-year veteran of NZDB. For in-market ingredient sales, marketing, sales, and technical capabilities were required. The food service segment required processing capabilities in addition to those skills needed for ingredient sales, while the consumer segment required distribution and brand marketing capabilities in addition to all the others.

Substitute Products

Two significant challenges to dairy products had arisen recently. The first involved health concerns about the consumption of animal fats, including those contained in dairy products such as cheese, ice cream, and butter. These concerns suggested a link between coronary disease and consumption of high levels of animal fat. The dairy industry responded by actively promoting the health benefits of dairy products, including osteoporosis prevention. The other significant challenge involved vegetable proteins in the ingredients segment. Vegetable proteins, including soy proteins, had many of the same performance characteristics of dairy proteins but were considerably cheaper to produce. (Depending on how soy proteins were produced, however, there could be hormonal traces that, if digested in large quantities, could harm consumers.)

Competition

Few companies competed across all segments of the dairy product business. However, some companies, like NZDB and MD-Foods of Denmark, had diversified into more than one segment.

Geography also defined competition in the dairy industry. The Irish Dairy Board competed in the European Community markets, and the Australian dairy companies targeted markets in Southeast Asia. When considered solely in terms of dairy products, NZDB competed in more product categories and regions than any of its major competitors.

Nestlé. Nestlé first entered the dairy products business in 1866 when it began producing condensed milk for the European market. In 1993, this Swiss multinational had total sales of US$39.1 billion, employed more than 209,000 personnel in 489 factories in 69 countries, and sold products in more than 100 countries. Nestlé's principal lines of business included beverages, prepared dishes and cooking aids, chocolate and confectionery, pharmaceuticals, and milk products and dietetics. The milk products and dietetics group generated US$10.85 billion in 1993, or 28 percent of Nestlé's sales. Nestlé's products, which were marketed globally under the umbrella of the Nestlé corporate logo, included sweetened and unsweetened condensed milk, yogurts, fresh cheese, powdered milk, vegetable-fat coffee creamer, infant nutrition formulas, slimming and weight control products, and ice cream.

In 1985, Nestlé acquired Carnation, a major dairy products company in the United States, and established a research center dedicated solely to human nutrition. In 1993, Nestlé further expanded its presence in the global ice cream business as it battled its arch rival, Unilever, for global dominance in this category. Nestlé also acquired Perrier and several milk companies in various locations. Nestlé competed with NZDB in the branded consumer products segment, especially in milk powders.

In Malaysia, Dumex, Dutch Lady, and two other marketers purchased milk powder from NZDB for repackaging and sale. Nestlé was disturbed by their success, but it reflected the tensions that were occurring between NZDB and some of its large business customers. NZDB supplied Nestlé with skim milk powder and anhydrous milk fat for recombining, and in 1993 it sold more than US$360 million of products to Nestlé. Nestlé tolerated NZDB's infringement of their consumer territory because NZDB's product quality and service were unsurpassed.

Kraft–General Foods. In 1988, Philip Morris acquired Kraft and merged it with General Foods to form a food industry giant. For decades, Kraft had been a significant force in the world cheese market, especially in the processed cheese category. In 1992, Philip Morris had total sales of US$59.13 billion and employed more than 161,000 people. Philip Morris's four principal lines of business included tobacco, beer, real estate and financial services, and food.

Kraft–General Foods served both the North American and international food markets and produced a wide range of food products in addition to cheese, including salad dressings, hot and cold instant beverages, lunch meats, frozen pasta, baked goods, cereals, ice cream, frozen dinners, and barbecue sauces. In the North American market, Kraft also had food service and food ingredients businesses. In 1992, Kraft held a greater than 40 percent share of the North American cheese market. Kraft's overall cheese sales volume increased in the international foods segment, accounting for US$1.48 billion in 1992. The company's research efforts focused on providing consumers with nutritional and healthy products, including reduced-fat and fat-free cheeses. In 1992, Philip Morris was still struggling to realize the synergies that drove the Kraft–General Foods merger. Several manufacturing operations were discontinued, and personnel reductions continued in the Kraft–General Foods division.

Australian Dairy Companies (ADC). The ADC was an export marketing organization formed by members of the Australian dairy industry to market the excess milk remaining after domestic consumer requirements had been met. Its 1993 revenues were $185 million Australian, and total volume sold was 440,000 tons. On a national level, Australia was the only country that approached New Zealand's ability to produce on a low-cost basis. However, exports of Australian dairy products were subsidized through the assessment of a levy on all dairy farmers. ADC was active in the commodity segments and did not have the same structure or export and manufacturing strategy as NZDB.

Irish Dairy Board (IDB). The IDB was a national export organization that marketed the export products of the Irish dairy industry. In 1993, IDB's total production was 519,000 tons, and total revenues were 1.214 billion Irish pounds. IDB was primarily involved in commodity trading of bulk products with a significant focus on exports to European Community members. With the results of the GATT

Uruguay Round, it was expected that IDB would focus its future efforts on selling more products within the European Community.

MD Foods. MD Foods, a cooperative formed by members of Denmark's dairy industry, controlled 86 percent of Denmark's milk production and produced products for both domestic and export consumption. Products included a wide range of specialty cheeses, whole milk powder, and casein and whey concentrates. Exports were handled by MD Foods–International, an affiliated company capitalized by market investors. MD Foods had a superior reputation for technical excellence in product development. Additionally, MD Foods had targeted many of the same markets and opportunities as NZDB, including the United States as a market for its casein and whey products. In 1992/1993, MD Foods had sales of US$2.01 billion, of which US$1.2 billion was from exports.

NZDB: 1973 to 1993

In 1973, the United Kingdom joined the Common Market. Not only were exports to the United Kingdom now governed by restrictive EC trade policies, but the EC also increased subsidies to support its own exports. With the new restrictions on its U.K. market, the Dairy Board was forced to scramble to sell its annual production. It was during this period that NZDB established its worldwide network of traders and agents, all of whom were dedicated to moving as much product as possible at the highest prices on the world's commodity markets. This network of agents and relationships would later prove crucial when NZDB branched out into value-added products in the late 1970s and the early 1980s. NZDB sold nearly all of its annual production on the world's commodity markets, suffering the volume and price swings so common to commodity goods. However, the NZDB staff became skilled at selling commodities and managing their effective market placement, even going so far as to purchase commodities from other nations' dairy marketing organizations for later placement into commodity markets when supply was short (and prices up). To NZDB, subsidized dairy producers from other countries did not seem to care about balancing supply with demand on the world markets. NZDB, however, saw an opportunity and became, in effect, a commodity manager and intermediary for other dairy producers.

After experiencing price swings and accompanying erratic payouts to farmers for several years, NZDB management decided in the late 1970s to vertically integrate the organization in order to capture the greatest returns for New Zealand dairy farmers. It was at this time that the agent network was leveraged. NZDB already had a presence, as described by Deputy CEO John Parker, "in the 80 least desirable countries in the world in which to do business," and these countries, with their underdeveloped or nonexistent dairy product markets, were not attractive to the major food industry giants like Nestlé and Kraft. NZDB saw an opportunity to build on its commodity-selling relationships by seeking out distribution partners through its agent network. Building on NZDB's limited experience in consumer goods from its days as the United Kingdom's primary dairy product supplier, the value-added aspect of NZDB was born.

Over time, NZDB shifted from being a heavily dependent trading body that focused on exports to a single market—the United Kingdom—to becoming a manufacturing and marketing organization offering a diverse range of products to customers and companies around the world. The rationale for changing the market

EXHIBIT 10

Development Profile for NZDB Offshore Company Network

INVESTMENT PROGRESSION	MANAGEMENT LABEL	RISK LEVEL
Sales to anyone ↓	Random shots	Very low
Sales to a few ↓	Aimed shots	
Agent appointed ↓	Bombardment	Low
Liaison ↓	Office infiltration	
Joint venture ↓	Pacification	Moderate
Buy out joint-venture partner ↓	Annexation	
Own company	Conquest	High

EXHIBIT 11

NZDB Business Line Segmentation 1994 and 2004 (Projected)

	1994	2004
Commodities	20.0%	15%
Ingredients	52.5	43
Food Service	5.0	7
Consumer	22.5	35
Total Volume (MTs)[a]	1,000,000	1,400,000

[a]Tons of *product* (as distinct from the tons of *liquid milk* reported in Exhibit 4); that is, minus water.

orientation was twofold: to capture a greater percentage of the total market value of each product produced and to increase the stability and security of returns to dairy farmers.

NZDB's shift to a marketing organization involved several key strategies, but according to John Parker, this shift was more "evolutionary than revolutionary." However, throughout this process, the emphasis remained focused on leveraging New Zealand's position as the world's low-cost milk producer. The primary strategic change was to minimize sales of commodities by shifting into producing and marketing products in all segments of the value chain. To achieve this end, NZDB invested in and developed a substantial offshore network of agents, joint ventures, and wholly owned subsidiaries. The model for building an offshore network is shown in Exhibit 10 and was followed by NZDB in nearly all of the countries in which it conducted business. To further emphasize the transition to a customer and marketing-driven organization, the senior managers of NZDB attempted to decentralize the organization and move its applied research closer to customers by opening five regional research and development centers and by managing the organization by region rather than as one global company.

The transition to competing in all four product segments was completed by 1993. Exhibit 11 shows NZDB 1994 sales by segment and projections for 2004.

Sourcing and Exporting

By early 1994, 15 dairy cooperatives existed in New Zealand, and the total investment in the industry exceeded NZ$15 billion. These cooperatives ranged in size from the huge New Zealand Cooperative Dairy Company (NZCDC), which produced nearly 44 percent of New Zealand's milk, to the tiny Kaikoura Dairy Cooperative, which produced only 0.3 percent of New Zealand's milk (see Exhibit 12). These 15 cooperatives represented the 14,000 dairy farmers who owned NZDB. The basic product flow was 8,000,000 tons of milk from 14,000 dairy farmers through 15 cooperative manufacturing dairy companies. These cooperatives produced more than 1 million metric tons of products, which were sold in more than 100 countries by NZDB's 80 offshore companies (see Exhibit 13). Exhibit 14 on page 16 shows New Zealand's top

Exhibit 12

Relative Dairy NZDB Company Milk Supply, 1992/1993

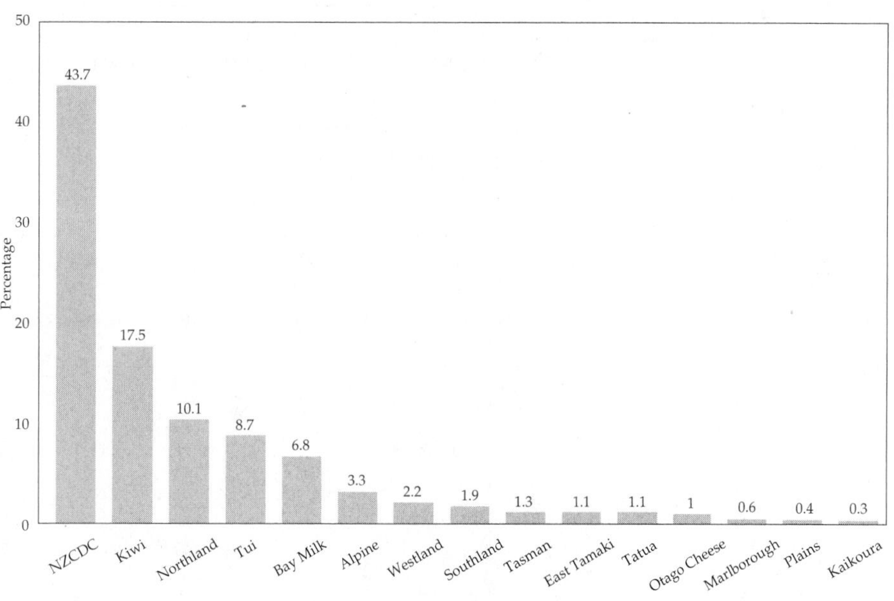

EXHIBIT 13

New Zealand Dairy Board Worldwide

OVERSEAS COMPANIES[a]	COUNTRIES REPRESENTED
Milk Products Holdings Australia Pty, Ltd.	Australia
Milk Products Holdings Europe, Ltd.	United Kingdom, Germany, Italy, Denmark, Egypt
Milk Products Holdings Latin America, Ltd.	Bermuda, Guatemala, Mexico, Peru, El Salvador, Venezuela, Chile, Jamaica
Milk Products Holdings Middle East EC	Bahrain
Milk Products Holdings North America, Inc.	United States, Canada
Milk Products Holdings South East Asia Pte, Ltd.	Singapore, Bangladesh, Mauritius, China, Hong Kong, Malaysia, South Africa, Taiwan, Sri Lanka, Thailand, Philippines
New Zealand Milk Products Japan, Ltd.	Japan, South Korea
New Zealand Milk Products CIS A.O.	Russia
Milk Products Holdings New Zealand, Ltd.	New Zealand
Finance Companies	New Zealand, Bermuda, Cayman Islands, United Kingdom

[a]Major subsidiaries and associate companies engaged in the marketing, distribution, processing, technology, or financing of the dairy industry and related products listed by country of incorporation.

EXHIBIT 14

New Zealand's Top Ten Dairy Trading Partners

	1987	1990	1992
Japan	7.3%	10.9%	13.2%
United Kingdom	16.1	13.4	12.6
United States	15.0	12.2	10.3
Mexico	1.6	9.1	5.5
Malaysia	5.1	5.9	6.9
Philippines	4.2	4.2	3.3
Algeria	1.5	3.1	2.5
Taiwan	1.9	2.5	3.4
Australia	1.7	2.7	3.3
Germany	1.6	3.3	2.6

EXHIBIT 15

New Zealand Dairy Board Sales by Region, Consumer Products (Tons)

Region	1991/1992 Actuals	1992/1993 Forecast	1993/1994 Planned
North America	100	100	120
North Asia	200	450	500
Southeast Asia	46,000	60,000	72,000
Central/South America	18,000	25,000	32,000
Africa/Europe	4,000	6,600	32,000
Middle East	9,800	10,500	12,000
Australia	6,500	10,000	12,000
Pacific	3,000	3,500	4,000
United Kingdom	65,000	65,000	65,000
C.I.S.	—	—	5,000
Totals	152,600	181,150	239,620

ten trading partners for dairy exports. Exhibit 15 shows NZDB's actual and forecasted totals by region for its own brand consumer products business.

Strategy

As defined in its mission statement, NZDB sought "to be the world's premier marketer of dairy products," with the accompanying goal of returning the highest possible payout to New Zealand's dairy farmers. To achieve these aims, NZDB committed itself to focusing solely on dairy products. Consequently, NZDB had no plans to diversify into or acquire nonrelated lines of business. Additionally, NZDB endeavored to sell all products within the year they were produced. Achieving a total sell-off of each year's production was becoming more difficult for two reasons: (1) herd sizes were increasing and (2) new entrants were converting to dairy farming from other types of pastoral farming due to the financial attractiveness of dairy farming (see Exhibit 16). Both of these events further increased the industry's capacity in New Zealand.

Traditionally, New Zealand dairy farmers considered their end customer to be NZDB in Wellington. NZDB provided the farmers with the bulk of their income and dealt with the cooperatives on production and financing issues. However, as NZDB moved offshore, decentralized, and emphasized a market-specific and customer-driven focus, NZDB's senior staff attempted to influence the management teams of cooperatives and, in turn, individual farmers to view its customers as being the offshore companies and specific in-market customers.

Products and Markets

Commodity. In its early stages, NZDB concentrated on the commodity markets, selling large volumes of products such as milk powders, butter, and cheese.

EXHIBIT 16

New Zealand Pastoral Farming Returns by Sector

Farming Sector	Return per Stock Unit[a] ($NZ)
Dairy	$103
Deer	$45
Beef	$36
Sheep	$30

[a]Per Stock Unit = per animal.

After the United Kingdom's admission to the Common Market in 1973, the Dairy Board began to provide commodity products differentiated by extra service and guaranteed quality. Customers in the commodity trade were typically government agencies, and business was conducted through tender offers in which an agency provided a set of product specifications—quality or nutritional—and sought to purchase a large volume of the product that met those specifications. Milk powder used for human nutrition in United Nations refugee camps is one example of such a product. However, because of the certified quality and higher level of service that NZDB offered to customers, the Dairy Board was really providing *ingredients* at commodity prices.

Ingredients. NZDB's wide variety of ingredient products included, for example, specialty fats for bakeries (used in Korea), rennet casein for imitation cheese (Italy), protein hydrolysates for medical applications (Japan), skim milk and whole milk powders for repackaging (Asia), and whey protein concentrate for use in meat (United States).

The ingredient area led to NZDB's success in the United States. Due to trade restrictions, NZDB was prohibited from bringing in large volumes of traditional ingredient products like milk powder and cheese. However, NZDB was able to bring in "obscure" dairy products like protein hydrolysate and caseinate, dairy products that had a wide variety of applications ranging from food service to pharmaceuticals. By and large, the subsidized U.S. dairy industry considered casein and whey, which was a by-product of cheese manufacturing, to be waste by-products of dairy production. NZDB approached and worked with numerous companies in the United States and elsewhere to develop specific products tailored to a customer's exact needs. For example, caseinate was used both in button manufacturing and in food manufacturing, where it was used to provide stiffness to Cool Whip. The vast majority of NZDB's ingredient formulations were proprietary. By 1994, NZDB's North American operations had revenues of US$400 million.

Food Service. In the food service segment, organizations like McDonald's, Pizza Hut, and Taco Bell were NZDB customers. Again, it was the outstanding quality of its products and stellar service reputation that led to NZDB's success here. NZDB targeted this segment as a key future area of focus for its sales force and was pushing its reputation for quality as its key selling point.

Business-to-Business Marketing and Sales. In its business marketing efforts, NZDB targeted technically sophisticated customers who had very specific applications in mind. As such, the NZDB sales force was well educated and typically had either a bachelor's or master's degree in a relevant discipline such as food science or industrial engineering. The sales force worked with specific large-account customers in an effort to meet current and future needs. In general, potential customers approached NZDB due to the outstanding reputation of its products. Typically, senior executives in Wellington were involved in transactions with key clients like Nestlé or Coca-Cola. The marketing staff was relatively lean for an organization of NZDB's size, and the members of the sales force had the power to make decisions in the field when it would help gain a new customer or satisfy an existing customer. Each sales rep was seen as one member of a customer service team, the other members coming from research and development, production, and finance.

Consumer Sector. NZDB had succeeded in shifting a significant share of volume from its commodity business into branded consumer products (see Exhibit 11). Several success stories resulted from a combination of marketing aggressiveness and research and development persistence and innovation, including Anchor-brand spreadable butter in the United Kingdom, Anlene milk powder in Southeast Asia, and Anchor-brand milk powders in Latin America.

Consumer Marketing and Sales. NZDB typically leveraged its existing market presence and contacts—agents and joint-venture partners—to establish its consumer business in a given country or region. Often, these relationships provided it with a distribution network, significant knowledge about consumer preferences, and insight into the positioning of competitors. NZDB's control of distribution ensured service and promptness for retailers and greater margins for the Dairy Board. NZDB generally entered consumer markets only where it could become the dominant brand or capture a strong second place. It also established a five-year, break-even profitability horizon by which time all brand investments had been recouped and the brand had achieved the targeted share. Entry into a specific market was generally viewed as a long-term commitment by the Dairy Board.

NZDB did not have an umbrella branding strategy. Instead, the Dairy Board used a variety of brands around the world, which posed challenges as the Board's global presence expanded. The Anchor brand was the most widely used and the most well known. NZDB relied heavily on New Zealand's "clean, green image" to appeal to consumers around the world. Television commercials presented images of cattle grazing on verdant pastures, firmly establishing in the consumer's mind the link between New Zealand's "clean and green" attributes and healthy, nutritious milk. NZDB also highlighted the "all-natural" composition of its products, especially Anlene, a calcium-fortified milk powder sold throughout Southeast Asia as a preventative for osteoporosis. Whereas the supplemental calcium in this milk powder had been recovered during milk processing operations, Anlene was positioned against similar products containing calcium extracted from chalk deposits. Consumers seemed to display a distinct preference for natural calcium.

In Malaysia, NZDB relied on the strength of "a mother's love" to sell milk powder for children. Although competing products touted nutritional and health benefits, NZDB believed that mothers already recognized that milk was good for their children and did not need to be told this. Instead, NZDB relied on a strong emotional appeal to suggest that mothers who really care about their children choose the New Zealand product.

NZDB was also able to leverage its role as an ingredient supplier in a Malaysian advertising campaign in the consumer milk powder category. In Malaysia, many of NZDB's milk powder competitors bought their bulk milk powder from NZDB, then recombined and packaged the milk powder for sale to consumers, competing directly against the Dairy Board's consumer milk powders. However, NZDB calculated that the volume of milk powder it sold in the combined ingredient and consumer product sectors made it the number-one supplier of milk powder in Malaysia, and an entire advertising and promotional campaign was designed around this theme. Although NZDB's product was not actually the leading consumer product, Malaysian consumers were bombarded with the message that New Zealand Dairy Board milk powders were the biggest and best-selling brand in Malaysia, resulting in NZDB's capturing the top spot in the consumer milk powder segment. According to Alistair Betts, group general manager of marketing, NZDB frequently relied on "guerrilla marketing" tactics like this milk powder campaign to capture share in new markets. This behavior sometimes drew criticism from its ingredient customers, Nestlé among them, who found themselves competing with the Dairy Board in the consumer segment while buying from it in the ingredients segment.

In many of its markets, NZDB had to educate consumers about the positive aspects of dairy products. In many Asian countries, including South Korea and Japan, cheese had not been a traditional food. However, the large populations in these countries made them attractive markets, and NZDB had frequently embarked on advertising campaigns that introduced and promoted dairy products. NZDB's overall advertising and promotion expenditures totaled NZ$55 million, $65 million, $83 million, and $102 million in 1991, 1992, 1993, and 1994, respectively.

Operations

Throughout its existence, NZDB's manufacturing philosophy had been threefold: to achieve a product mix that provided the maximum possible financial returns, to sell all products within the year they were produced, and to be a low-cost processor. The primary challenges were that NZDB had no control over the quantity of milk produced in a given year and that NZDB had to purchase all milk products offered for sale by the cooperatives. Given that weather could cause total annual milk volumes to vary by as much as 10 percent, defining the most profitable product mix was also a challenge. Additionally, because milk production was seasonal with a peak in November, dairy company facilities were designed to handle the peak production volumes, which often resulted in significant excess production capacity during the rest of the year.

At the beginning of each season, the product mix group forecasted milk production for the current season and for the next five years. As the season progressed, these forecasts were modified, and any necessary adjustments in the target product mix were made. Production of the various products was done by the individual dairy cooperatives. Although NZDB had an ideal product mix in mind each year, the Dairy Board was unable to mandate or otherwise assign production quotas to cooperatives. The only means by which the Dairy Board was able to influence the product mix of individual cooperatives was through the offer prices paid for various dairy products. For example, if market forecasts indicated that there would be an oversupply of skim milk powder on world markets in the coming year, then the price paid to New Zealand cooperatives for skim milk was adjusted downward to a point that the total skim milk volume from the cooperatives was close to the production target.

When additional manufacturing capacity was needed for existing or new products, interested dairy cooperatives submitted bids to NZDB prior to the construction or expansion of the new facilities. NZDB then awarded the construction right to the company that would be able to meet milk composition, product quality, and timely delivery standards at the lowest cost. The Dairy Board took into account the cost of capital employed and the interest costs associated with the new facilities. This production system was designed to be neutral. In other words, a dairy cooperative's profitability should be the same regardless of whether it produced bulk whole milk powder for the commodity markets, whey protein concentrate for the nutraceuticals markets, or cans of milk powder for the Malaysian consumer market.

The performance of all dairy companies was judged against standard cost models (one model for each of 500 products) developed by NZDB and approved by industry committees. The standard cost models were based on engineering principles and assigned costs based on the use of the latest process technology for a specified volume of milk and a given product type. When new technology became available, it was not integrated into the cost models until it had been in use for three years, at which time it was expected that cooperatives would have adopted the new technology. Dairy companies achieved profitability when they were able to produce at cost levels below those specified in the standard cost models. In early 1994, NZDB began using NZ$2.50 per kilogram as the "notional cost," or raw-materials price, of milk so that a profit-and-loss statement could be generated for manufacturing operations.

The use of standard cost models pushed the New Zealand dairy industry toward the lowest cost production possible. This was often reflected in manufacturing facilities which took full advantage of the economies of scale available. According to Dave Pilkington, group general manager of operations, "Dairy companies felt that the benefits of scale had been nearly maximized, and there were no longer any benefits to be gained by closing smaller plants in favor of larger ones. A new milk powder plant can easily cost NZ$100 million, and dairy companies were reluctant to continue investing in new facilities as they must be accountable to their individual members." For instance, Kiwi Milk Products installed the world's largest milk powder production facility in the world, a facility that was capable of processing 8 million liters of liquid milk per day. According to Pilkington, "this push for scale began to conflict with NZDB's marketing strategy, which emphasized more differentiated consumer products and a customer-oriented strategy. NZDB may need to offer financial incentives to reward dairy companies who consistently excelled in meeting quality and on-time delivery requirements."

The desired product mix prioritized products according to projected profitability and demand. Many possible combinations of products could be produced from a given volume of milk (see Exhibit 17). Standard New Zealand milk was composed of 11.5 percent cream and 88.5 percent skim milk by volume; and milk solids, including fat and protein, accounted for 8.1 percent of the total weight. The composition of

EXHIBIT 17

Typical Product Yields from 1,000 Litres of Milk

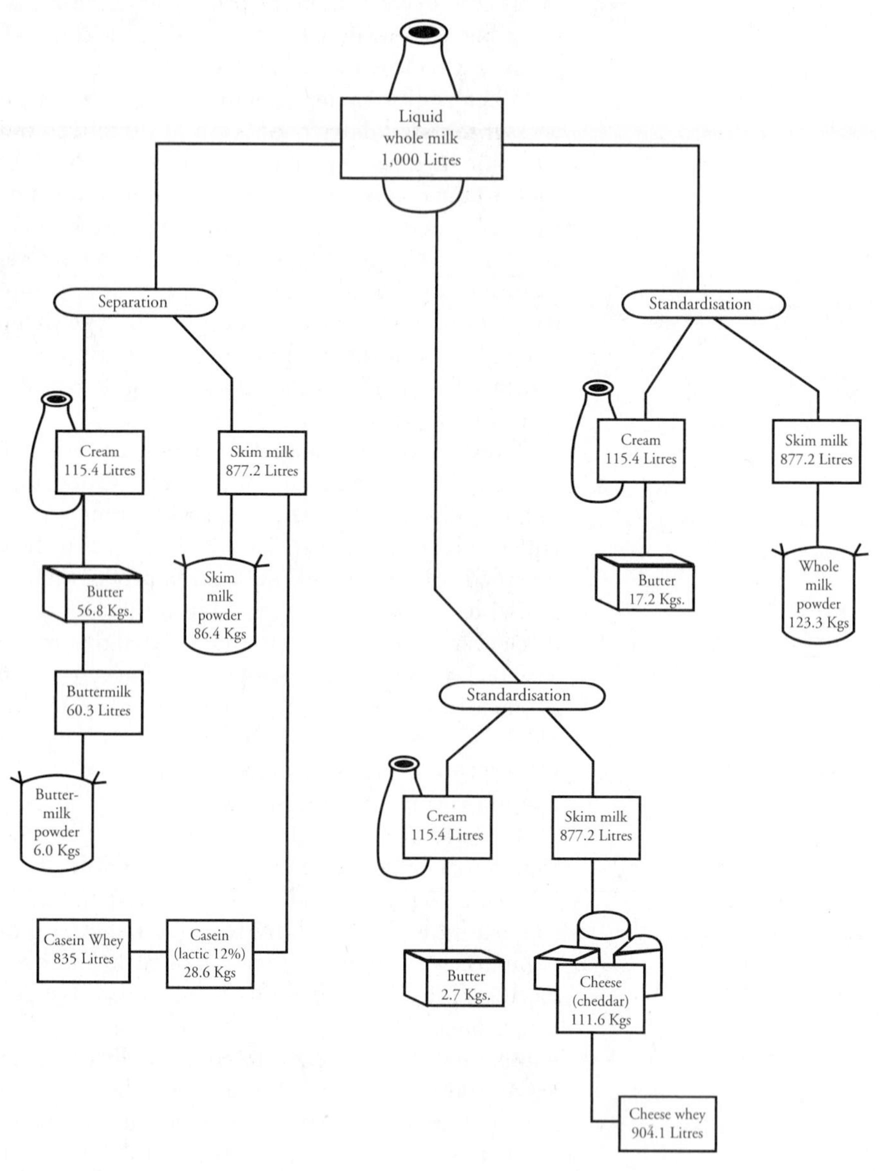

standard New Zealand milk is shown in Exhibit 18. Exhibit 19 shows the production volumes of whole milk products (including dry milk powder), skim milk products (SMP), cheese, cream products, casein, and buttermilk products (BMP) for the period from 1984 through 1993. From 1985 to 1990, the manufacturing cost of the New Zealand dairy industry steadily declined a total of 28.57 percent. From 1990 to 1993, the manufacturing cost slowly rose a total of 7.78 percent.

The production and manufacturing area was not without controversy. NZDB had come under fire from cooperatives when decisions were made about allocating new

EXHIBIT 18

Composition of Standard New Zealand Milk (on a weight % basis)

Fat	4.65%
Protein	3.43
Ash	0.67
Lactose	4.64
Water	86.61
Total	100.00%

EXHIBIT 19

Total New Zealand Dairy Production

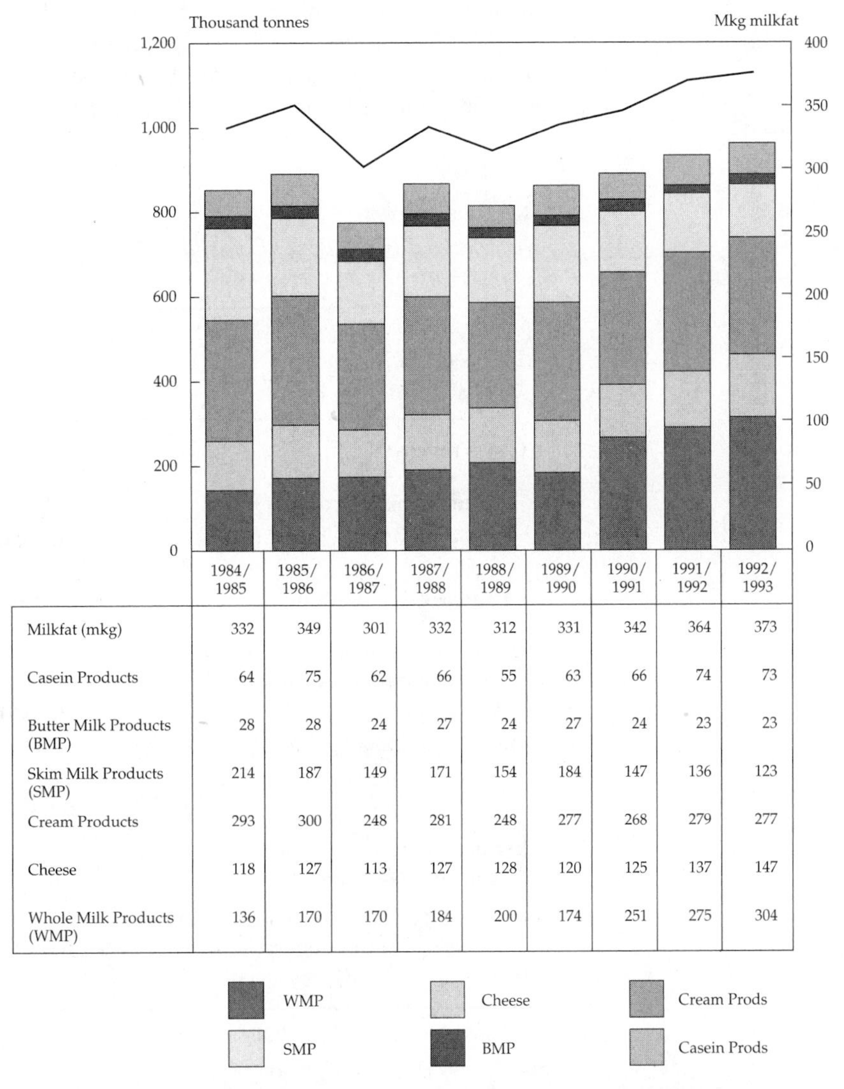

	1984/ 1985	1985/ 1986	1986/ 1987	1987/ 1988	1988/ 1989	1989/ 1990	1990/ 1991	1991/ 1992	1992/ 1993
Milkfat (mkg)	332	349	301	332	312	331	342	364	373
Casein Products	64	75	62	66	55	63	66	74	73
Butter Milk Products (BMP)	28	28	24	27	24	27	24	23	23
Skim Milk Products (SMP)	214	187	149	171	154	184	147	136	123
Cream Products	293	300	248	281	248	277	268	279	277
Cheese	118	127	113	127	128	120	125	137	147
Whole Milk Products (WMP)	136	170	170	184	200	174	251	275	304

production responsibilities as some cooperatives perceived this process to be political. Additionally, there were questions about whether the milk payment system was really neutral or whether or not it benefited some cooperatives more than others.

Finance and Treasury

Robin Golding, the group general manager of treasury, stated, "Both Standard & Poor's and Moody's gave NZDB an investment rating equivalent to that enjoyed by the New Zealand government. The Dairy Board was the first New Zealand corporation to receive a rating this high." Due to its creditworthiness, NZDB was able to secure financing at very favorable rates. The Dairy Board was also able to assist dairy companies with their financing needs—both seasonal cash flow requirements and long-term investment projects. NZDB's ability to finance dairy company investments resulted in a lower overall cost of borrowing to the industry because banks decreased interest rates in order to compete with the Dairy Board's internal rate and attract dairy company business. (See Exhibits 20, 21, and 22 for NZDB income statements and balance sheets.)

NZDB's treasury group was heavily involved in managing the foreign exchange risk associated with the offshore companies. Worldwide, dairy trade transactions were denominated primarily in U.S. dollars (80 percent), pound sterling (10 percent),

Exhibit 20

New Zealand Dairy Board Consolidated Revenue Statement for the Year Ended 31 May 1993

In Thousands of New Zealand Dollars	Group[a]		Board	
	1993	1992	**1993**	1992
Gross revenue	**$5,054,351**	$5,057,882	**$3,238,295**	$2,954,776
Earnings before taxation	**97,473**	159,722	**(91,331)**	57,449
Taxation charge	**(58,889)**	(62,845)	**(13,278)**	(23,495)
Earnings after taxation	**38,584**	96,877	**(104,609)**	33,954
Earnings attributable to minority shareholders in subsidiary companies	**(8,404)**	(8,761)	**0**	0
Share of retained earnings less losses of associate companies after taxation	**11,425**	7,580	**0**	0
Extraordinary gain arising from corporate restructuring	**0**	0	**19,576**	78,107
Earnings available for distribution transferred to the General Reserve	**$ 41,605**	$ 95,696	**$ (85,033)**	$ 112,061

[a]"Group" includes sales by NZDB subsidiaries.

Source: NZDB Annual Report.

EXHIBIT 21

New Zealand Dairy Board Consolidated Balance Sheet as of 31 May 1993 (In Thousands of New Zealand Dollars)

	GROUP		BOARD	
	1993	1992	**1993**	1992
Capital	**750,000**	0	**750,000**	0
Reserves	**708,694**	1,429,782	**685,062**	1,520,095
Total capital and reserves	**1,458,694**	1,429,782	**1,435,062**	1,520,095
Minority shareholders' interest in subsidiaries	**51,125**	47,719	**0**	0
Long-term liabilities	**150,766**	336,751	**81**	83
Deferred taxation	**9,635**	17,785	**417**	10,525
Current liabilities				
Bank overdrafts	**39,119**	37,456	**10,521**	340
Payables and accruals	**437,532**	555,080	**256,657**	297,793
Subsidiaries			**1,217,889**	758,932
Associates	**28,009**	20,235	**1,992**	17,702
Taxation	**18,752**	12,094	**22,901**	0
Short-term liabilities	**1,103,383**	851,492	**52,376**	153,330
Total current liabilities	**1,626,795**	1,476,357	**1,562,336**	1,228,097
Total capital, reserves, and liabilities	**$3,297,015**	$3,308,394	**$2,997,896**	$2,758,800
Fixed assets	**406,050**	409,394	**75,477**	84,864
Intangibles	**46,931**	37,079	**0**	0
Investments				
Subsidiaries			**659,843**	599,434
Associates	**85,471**	124,136	**13,646**	35,604
Share investments	**37,972**	40,296	**260**	242
Loans and advances	**58,287**	71,955	**54,022**	67,022
Total investments	**181,730**	236,387	**727,771**	702,302
Current assets				
Bank balances	**32,440**	69,001	**5,883**	22,060
Short-term deposits	**116,003**	50,185	**105,240**	29,162
Receivables and prepayments	**786,440**	978,303	**529,181**	615,574
Subsidiaries			**408,877**	267,500
Associates	**63,724**	63,582	**2,041**	49,708
Stocks	**1,642,931**	1,459,282	**1,143,426**	987,630
Taxation prepaid	**20,766**	5,181	**0**	0
Total current assets	**2,662,304**	2,625,534	**2,194,648**	1,971,634
Total assets	**$3,297,015**	$3,308,394	**$2,997,896**	$2,758,800

and a mixture of other currencies (10 percent). Because NZDB paid its shareholders, the dairy farmers, in New Zealand dollars, this created a transaction risk. In order to attract new customers and grow market share, NZDB subsidiaries conducted business in the local currencies of the many diverse markets in which the Dairy Board operated. This, too, posed a currency risk management challenge for NZDB. In 1993, the treasury group handled more than NZ$120 billion in settlements and

EXHIBIT **22**

New Zealand Dairy Board Consolidated Statement of Cash Flows for the Year Ended 31 May 1993 (In Thousands of New Zealand Dollars)

	Group			
		1993		1992
Opening cash balances				
Bank balances	**69,001**		53,076	
Short-term deposits	**49,948**		62,544	
Bank overdrafts	**(37,456)**		(55,136)	
Short-term and overnight borrowings	**(830,162)**		(779,886)	
		(748,669)		(719,402)
CASH FLOWS FROM OPERATING ACTIVITIES				
Cash was provided from:				
Receipts from customers	**5,803,071**		5,152,574	
Interest received	**48,866**		29,653	
Dividends received	**4,407**		7,621	
Cash was disbursed to:				
Payments to suppliers and employees	**(5,516,816)**		(4,970,510)	
Payment of interest	**(124,322)**		(122,155)	
Payment of taxes	**(119,118)**		(54,408)	
Net cash flows from operating activities	**96,088**		42,775	
CASH FLOWS FROM INVESTING ACTIVITIES				
Cash was provided from:				
Proceeds from sale of fixed assets	**51,894**		15,285	
Proceeds from sale of investments	**20,768**		50,960	
Collection of loans	**17,318**		0	
Cash was applied to:				
Acquisition of fixed assets	**(111,702)**		(51,066)	
Acquisition of investments	**(16,170)**		(16,932)	
Loans made	**0**		(3,173)	

(continued)

added more than NZ$200 million to the Board's bottom line through its foreign-exchange risk management program. Golding said, "The Dairy Board options desk is very innovative and operates on a 'best practice' level that is on a par with British Petroleum."

Developing the treasury group allowed NZDB to deal with customers in any country in any currency, and customers remarked quite favorably on the lack of foreign-exchange complications when doing business with the Dairy Board. In

EXHIBIT 22 (CONTINUED)

New Zealand Dairy Board Consolidated Statement of Cash Flows for the Year Ended 31 May 1993 (In Thousands of New Zealand Dollars)

	Group			
		1993		1992
Net cash flows used in investing activities	**(37,892)**		(4,926)	
CASH FLOWS FROM FINANCING ACTIVITIES				
Cash was provided from:				
Issue of shares	**1,550**		0	
Cash was applied to:				
Borrowings repaid	**(137,354)**		(75,642)	
Dividends paid	**(6,023)**		(2,416)	
Net cash flows used in financing activities	**(141,827)**		(78,058)	
EFFECT OF EXCHANGE RATE CHANGES	**15,736**		10,942	
CASH OF SUBSIDIARIES ACQUIRED/SOLD	**(2,809)**		0	
Net decreases in cash flows		**(70,704)**		(29,267)
Closing cash balances				
Bank balances	**32,440**		69,001	
Short-term deposits	**115,925**		49,948	
Bank overdrafts	**(39,119)**		(37,456)	
Short-term and overnight borrowings	**(928,619)**		(830,162)	
		($819,373)		($748,669)

essence, NZDB would tell customers, "Pay us in your local currency, and we'll take care of the rest."

R&D

NZDB had two primary research organizations, the Dairy Research Institute (DRI) and the Livestock Improvement Corporation (LIC). Both basic and applied research was conducted by these organizations. In 1993, DRI's budget was NZ$60 million, which was comparable on a percent-of-sales basis to the research budgets of NZDB's primary competitors (see Exhibit 23). LIC was recognized as a world leader in the development and application of breeding technology. Together, LIC and DRI combined their expertise to "engineer" milk, through breeding, to possess certain functional properties.

NZDB operated a regional research center in each of its five major markets (the United States, Southeast Asia, Europe, South Pacific, and the Middle East). This allowed the Dairy Board to tailor products to local customer needs and tastes. NZDB

EXHIBIT 23

R&D Spending in 1992 as a Percentage of Sales

Unilever	1.87%
NZDB	1.35
Nestlé	1.23
Kraft–General Foods	0.81

was successfully able to introduce dairy products in traditionally low-consumption areas like Asia and the Middle East. Previously, customer research and product development had been done at DRI in New Zealand, but NZDB discovered that its customers' needs and preferences varied significantly by region. Now, however, Dr. Kevin Marshall, NZDB's research and development manager, commented that "the independence of the individual research centers has not always allowed for synergies to be recognized in areas that are of mutual interest."

Marshall stated, "Included among NZDB's biggest research and development successes are Anlene milk powder, spreadable butter, whole milk powders, and protein hydrolysates. NZDB's future research priorities need to increase focus by spending more money on fewer products. For instance, although NZDB is comparable to competitors in R&D spending as a percent of sales, Nestlé has an entire research group focused solely on human nutrition. As the Dairy Board moves into more sophisticated products like nutraceuticals and pharmaceutical ingredients, it will eventually need to develop a capability to do clinical trials with humans."

ORGANIZATION AND LEADERSHIP

In early 1994, NZDB had more than 6,000 employees worldwide and was organized by function (treasury, external affairs, and so forth) and by product lines (milk powder, proteins, cheese, and cream products). The appendix that follows describes NZDB's organization and product lines. Throughout NZDB's history, the Wellington headquarters served as the nerve center of the organization. Most Dairy Board employees, including senior executives, were hired from within the New Zealand dairy industry.

In 1992, Warren Larsen became the NZDB chief executive and assumed oversight responsibilities for the Dairy Board's decentralization efforts. When Larsen took over NZDB's top job, the atmosphere at the Dairy Board seemed to Larsen to be that of a "New Zealand village, a provincial mentality. It was a real dues-paying, initiation-type atmosphere." Larsen found that "the existing power base was hard to shift because it was related to individual histories and personalities."

Larsen was preceded in his tenure by two chief executives who left their mark on the Dairy Board. Bernie Knowles served as CEO during NZDB's commodity market struggles and initial forays into value-added products during the 1970s. Marshall, NZDB's director of research and development, described Knowles as "a real seat-of-the-pants leader and a visionary who saw the need for offshore expansion. Bernie's goal was for NZDB to achieve excellence and leadership in commodity marketing because he felt it was where the future of the board lay." Murray Gough succeeded Knowles and remained as CEO for more than ten years. According to Marshall, Gough "systematized and further developed the offshore companies, and he foresaw the need for a push into consumer products. Murray still emphasized excellence in commodities, but he had worked in the United Kingdom so he recognized the value of a move into consumer products as well."

Larsen was very enthusiastic about his role as Dairy Board CEO. Larsen had set NZDB's becoming a bona-fide transnational as his primary goal. Attaining this status would require that NZDB move into consumer products to an even greater degree. Assisting Larsen in this transition was a veteran senior management team, many of whom had been with the Dairy Board since its early days, including:

- John Parker—deputy chief executive officer and a 30-year-plus veteran of the Dairy Board
- Peter Robertson—chief financial officer
- Alistair Betts—group general manager of marketing and a 25-year NZDB veteran
- Chris Kelly—a former veterinarian and a self-taught strategic planner who had recently assumed the role of manager of strategic planning
- Nigel Mitchell—director of external affairs and NZDB's "point man" on trade issues
- Chris Moller—manager of corporate development and finance who had previously headed the cheese division
- Robin Golding—a former merchant banker and manager of the treasury group
- John Murray—company secretary who had been with NZDB since its inception
- Dr. Kevin Marshall—manager of research and development and a multiyear veteran of NZDB

The Future

Chris Kelly, manager of strategic planning, felt the primary issue facing NZDB was how to allocate the organization's resources—financial, technical, and personnel—most effectively. According to Larsen, "Capital is an increasingly scarce resource because NZDB has to retain funds from farmers to obtain it. This required a shift from NZDB's practice of just getting into business wherever possible." Many of the other senior managers concurred with that assessment. The Dairy Board was now at a point where different organizational functions were competing with one another for financing. Larsen felt that "NZDB was vulnerable in its current position. NZDB can't be all things to all people and survive in its current form. NZDB needs to move up into short-shelf-life products for security, and this will require locally sourced milk for political reasons. NZDB will focus only on the global biggies in the food service market; we will try to link it to our consumer products through our distribution systems. The ingredient markets can never escape the commodity cycles, and NZDB can't survive on commodity placements, alone. The dilemma is, given that we are required to sell all the product within one year, do we sell it on the basis of volume, value, or both, and how should the performance of the marketing companies be measured?"

Larsen identified NZDB's future agenda as the following: "decentralize, which is the easy part, introduce better performance measurement systems, and then prioritize based on the results of performance measurement." Introduction of a new consumer brand required significant investment, funds that could otherwise be allocated to developing a new ingredient product. NZDB lacked internal product profitability measures, and deciding which project to fund was problematic. Compounding this problem was the Dairy Board's lack of a formal strategic planning process. Consequently, resource allocation was done on an "as available" rather than on an "as needed" basis.

As mentioned in the BCG report, NZDB was now wrestling with defining an industry vision, a process that would map out a path for the organization's future. Given the sheer volume of milk produced annually by New Zealand dairy farmers, NZDB management felt that commodities would always be one of the products marketed by the organization. Ideally, the Dairy Board would be able to control the amount of milk produced in New Zealand in order to better balance supply with product demand. However, NZDB was prohibited by statute from doing so. Individual cooperatives were considering imposing entry fees on new members in order to erect some barriers to entry and control industry capacity.

The measurement of NZDB's success had long been an issue in New Zealand, and it was an open question as to whether or not the Dairy Board was volume-driven or price-driven. There was great debate in New Zealand in early 1994 about whether or not NZDB did maximize returns to dairy farmers. Exhibit 24 shows

EXHIBIT 24

Trend in Prices Received for Milkfat since 1950/1951

	Dairy Board	Average Dairy Company Payout	
	Final Price	Total Actual	Inflation Adjusted
Season	$	Payout $	Payout ($ Dec. 1992)*
1950/51		0.63	12.70
1955/56		0.74	11.49
1960/61		0.69	9.20
1965/66		0.80	9.35
1970/71		0.85	7.59
1971/72		1.12	9.16
1972/73		1.11	8.61
1973/74		1.32	9.29
1974/75	1.36	1.30	8.13
1975/76	1.41	1.44	7.79
1976/77	1.53	1.52	7.11
1977/78	1.67	1.71	6.93
1978/79	1.73	1.79	6.59
1979/80	2.08	2.13	6.73
1980/81	2.65	2.64	7.18
1981/82	3.33	3.39	7.97
1982/83	3.61	3.67	7.49
1983/84	3.50	3.64	7.17
1984/85	3.96	4.06	7.31
1985/86	4.00	3.98	6.21
1986/87	3.31	3.54	4.67
1987/88	3.60	4.07	4.90
1988/89	5.30	5.70	6.56
1989/90	5.80	6.30	6.76
1990/91	3.70	4.23	4.33
1991/92	5.20	5.84	5.92
1992/93	5.65	6.38	6.38

*Weighted to give real dollar values (December 1992) using the Consumers Price Index.

EXHIBIT 25

New Zealand Dairy Board Relative Performance

COMPANY	CAPITALISATION MILLIONS	TOTAL SHARES SEPT. 1994 (000'S)	NPAT 1994 NZ$000	EPS 1994	RETURN ON EQUITY 1994	RETURN ON ASSETS 1994
Natural Gas	588	462,000	25,300	$0.150	41.2%	10.9%
Whitcoulls Group	460	121,000	24,300	0.201	25.7	17.7
Helicopter Line	211	44,000	13,000	0.306	23.5	21.2
Telecom Corp	9,563	1,890,000	528,100	0.279	23.6	19.0
NZDB— 1994/1995 forecast		**750,000**	**290,000**	**0.387**	**20.0**	**9.0**
Fernzcorp	791	140,000	38,300	0.301	18.9	11.8
Sanford	352	88,100	34,500	0.396	18.2	20.9
Air NZ	1,037	443,500	200,500	0.452	17.2	9.2
Skellerup	371	156,000	26,700	0.177	16.7	12.0
Independent Newspapers	642	129,000	44,200	0.383	11.2	10.7
F&P	440	104,800	27,000	0.258	10.4	11.6
Lion Nathan	1,520	547,700	185,400	0.363	9.4	9.5
Goodman Fielder	1,745	1,172,000	152,100	0.132	8.9	8.5
Carter Holt Harvey	6,338	1,690,000	325,300	0.192	8.2	7.0
Apple Fields	26	29,200	4,400	0.158	7.9	6.6
Fletcher Challenge Forests	807	757,000	58,500	0.077	7.8	6.2
DB Group	225	304,600	25,400	0.048	6.8	5.3
Fletcher Challenge Core Divisions	6,237	1,260,000	99,600	0.079	2.5	3.3

NZDB capital	750,000,000
NZDB reserves	700,597,000
Total Equity	1,450,597,000

NZDB NPAT based on SMV of $2.50/kg ms.

NZDB Total Assets (1994) 3,210,766,000

recent trends in payouts to dairy farmers. Exhibit 25 benchmarks NZDB's performance against other leading New Zealand companies.

Although NZDB was a cooperative, it was "run just like a corporate," according to Chris Moller, the group manager of finance and corporate development. NZDB tended to hire employees from within the dairy industry and to promote from within the Dairy Board, a practice that resulted in the Board culture becoming somewhat insulated from business realities. During the Dairy Board's commodity trading period, the typical employee possessed an entrepreneurial spirit and a high degree of technical competence. As the Board assumed more of a marketing role, it became apparent that a lack of marketing, financial performance measurement, and competitive analysis skills existed at NZDB. In addition, there was a real shortage of people with work experience in multinational organizations. An entrenched entrepreneurial spirit still persisted at the Dairy Board, and this sometimes complicated efforts to standardize and formalize board policies and procedures.

The Board's structure and decision making within New Zealand emphasized internal competition for resources (including milk and product supply) among product divisions. The challenge of ensuring appropriate internal competition processes in New Zealand to match the aggressive competition in overseas markets was an ongoing issue, and the chief executive wondered whether the existing product divisions were right for the future.

On a more fundamental level, the Dairy Board's expectations of its employees had changed. As the Dairy Board became more customer focused and less focused on doing business in Wellington, demands for employees to live and work overseas increased. Traditionally, board employees worked overseas for two- to three-year periods and then moved back to Wellington. Now, there was a need for people to remain overseas indefinitely in order to maintain strong customer relationships. Implementing effective succession planning for senior managers who had been with the Dairy Board since its inception was also a key concern, especially when considering that many of the Dairy Board's senior managers had been with the board since its infancy.

As he put down the BCG report, Larsen pondered the challenges that lay ahead for both the Dairy Board and himself. He wondered which ones to tackle first.

Appendix[1] to Case 17

The New Zealand Dairy Board and Its Structure

To undertake its chief function of purchasing all products for export and marketing them overseas, the Board has four main Product Divisions that are accountable for specific products (Cheese, Cream, Milkpowders, and Milkprotein). Two smaller divisions work with the other product divisions in carrying out their specialised activities: the Ingredients Division and the Consumer Products Division. (These divisions are supported by Secretariat, Services, Finance, External Policy and Planning, Group Personnel, Public Affairs, Corporate Investments, and the Computer Centre.)

Product Divisions

Milkpowders

This division is responsible for coordinating the production and worldwide marketing of milk powder products.

[1]Source: NZDB brochure.

EXHIBIT

NZDB Organisation Chart

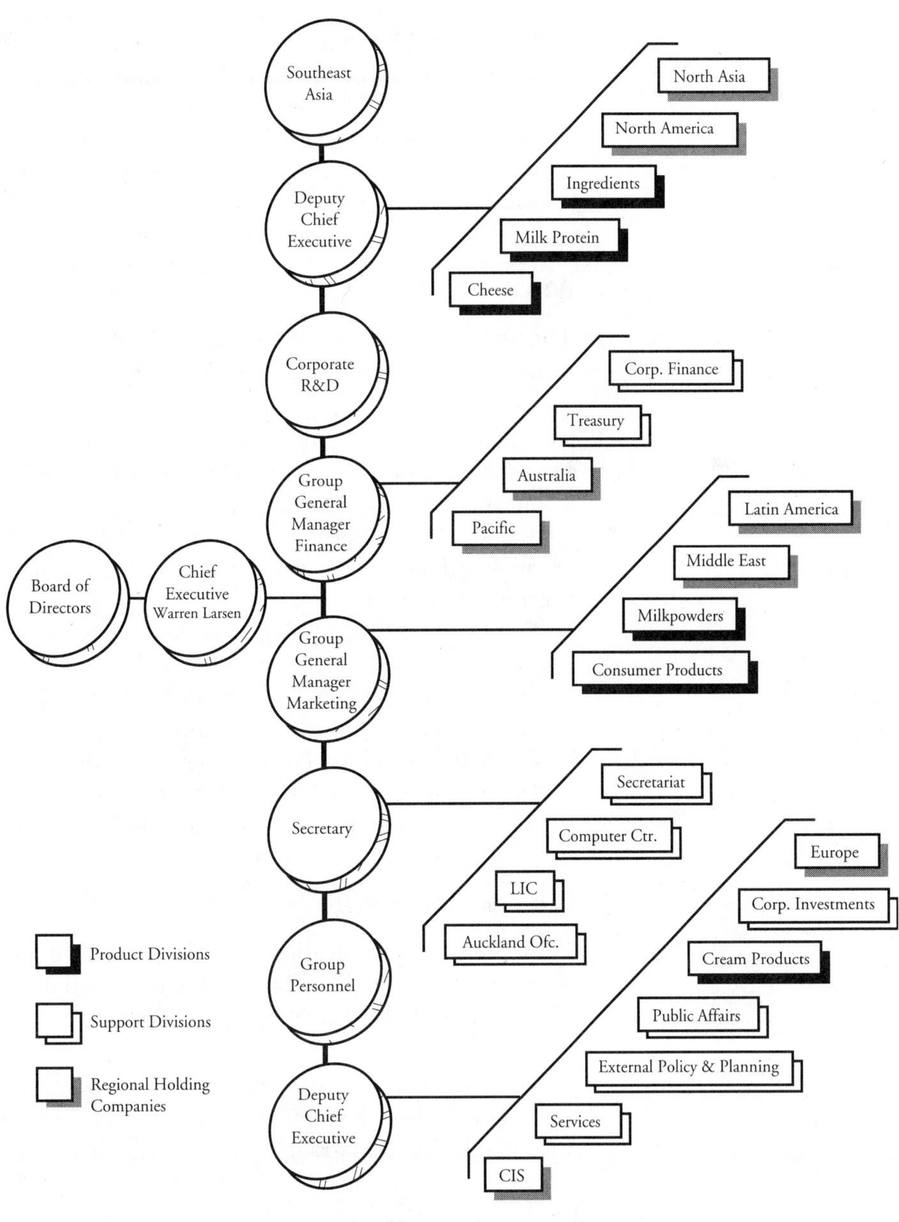

Key Features. Many tropical countries do not have a strong local dairy industry. For them, imported milk powders from countries such as New Zealand are the most important source of dairy products. The advantage of canned milk powder in tropical countries is that it will remain fresh for up to three years, whereas liquid milk starts to deteriorate after only a few hours.

The division has four main product groups:

- **Wholemilk Powder.** This powder is ordinary full cream milk that has been dried.
- **Skimmilk Powder.** Skimmilk is milk from which cream has been separated. It has a very low fat content.
- **Nutritional Products.** This group coordinates the production and marketing of nutritional products including infant formulae, health and sports food beverages, and Stolait™ Immune Milk.
- **Special Products.** This group is responsible for the development, production, and marketing of an increasing range of specialised products including cheese powder, UHT cream, and cream powders.

MILKPROTEIN

This division is responsible for coordinating the production and worldwide marketing of milk protein and whey products.

Key Features. Unlike butter, cheese, and milk powders, which are largely consumed in their original form, milk proteins are sold as industrial food ingredients or technical ingredients to industrial food manufacturers and technical users throughout the world. The division therefore has a different focus to other product divisions of the Board, being involved solely in industrial marketing, with no involvement in consumer marketing.

This division has two major operating groups:

- **Casein.** This section is responsible for coordinating the global production and marketing of all New Zealand casein products.
- **Whey Products for New Zealand Limited.** This subsidiary company of the Board is responsible for the global commercial exploitation of whey produced in New Zealand. It operates as an autonomous business unit of the Board.

CREAM PRODUCTS

This division is responsible for coordinating the production and export marketing of products containing a high level of milkfat-butter, anhydrous milkfat (AMF), fat mixes, and other fractionated cream products.

Key Features. A substantial proportion of the division's business is the large volume of salted butter shipped to Britain each year and repacked into Anchor pats. This highly lucrative trade is under threat from a reducing EC quota. As a result, this division is working hard to foster other large alternative markets, especially in the Middle East, North Africa, and Eastern Europe.

Development work is also underway on an increased range of consumer products for retail sale and specialised butter milkfat formulations for the international bakery and food ingredients sectors.

CHEESE

This division is responsible for coordinating the production and export marketing of cheese products and insuring that dairy companies generate the full potential of the local market.

Key Features. Cheese is showing an increase in consumption in most countries of the world but there is fierce competition among producing countries for a major share in this growth.

Cheese is sold in a wide range of forms, which necessitates a range of selling approaches from commodity trading, through brand management, to specialised industrial selling with a strong technical backup.

This division has three technical units:

- **Industrial Marketing.** This unit provides support for industrial export sales through stock procurement, inventory management, distribution logistics, technical service, and product development.
- **Food Service.** This unit covers the supply of cheese to organisations that perform another operation on the product before presenting it to the pubic, such as cooking, shredding, slicing, or melting.
- **Consumer.** This unit plans and supports the international consumer marketing of cheese products, the export logistics, and the procurement functions.

Ingredients

The purpose of this division is to drive the development of the Board's international dairy-based food ingredients business. The ingredients division

- provides specific functional performance attributes in its application
- is supported by a worldwide network with facilities and expertise encompassing research, development, production, product evaluation, and customer servicing

Application areas include:

- Bakery
- Confectionery
- Snack and convenience
- Cultured food products
- Ice cream

Alaco New Zealand. Alaco is a separate business unit within the Ingredients Division operating in the New Zealand market. Alaco acts as a commission agent for the four product divisions and other ingredient suppliers such as dairy companies.

Alaco was established to assist in the development of marketing specialised dairy-based ingredients on the New Zealand market as a basis for international development.

Consumer Products

This division was established to further the strategic thrust into marketing its own branded consumer products. With the advent of regional holding companies, the major day-to-day marketing thrust of the Board is offshore.

The primary functions of the Consumer Products Division are to

- provide a support function for the Board's objectives in consumer product development

- ensure commonality (where appropriate) in marketing approach, the variety of product types, and new product development
- measure overall progress in volume and returns for the consumer business
- administer the corporate brands policy
- build a corporate culture appropriate to the growth of the Board's international consumer business

Dairy Advisory Bureau. The Dairy Advisory Bureau is the advisory body of the New Zealand dairy industry that is responsible for food and health issues. The Bureau provides support for the Board's business developments offshore and has a role in nutrition promotion in the local market.

Three main areas of activity support development and marketing of consumer and ingredient products:

- **Nutrition information services.** Monitoring and advising on nutrition and health science, food regulations, media, product, and market developments.
- Coordinating of the Board's food health research programme.
- **Nutrition Programme.** In New Zealand the Bureau has a commitment to improving the knowledge and understanding of food and health issues and enhancing the value of dairy products in the diet.

CASE 18

DISNEY PRODUCTIONS: THE WALT YEARS

> I just want to leave you with this thought that it's just been sort of a dress rehearsal ...so if any of you start resting on your laurels, I mean, just forget it, because... we are just getting started.
>
> Walt Disney, quoted in *The Disney Management Style*

Almost 50 years after the company's founding, manicured lawns and ethereal quiet conveyed a campuslike atmosphere at Walt Disney Productions (WDP) in Burbank, California. Executives still arrived at work wearing Mickey Mouse polo shirts, animators still played the volleyball games Walt Disney encouraged on a studio lawn, Disney's favorite chili remained on the menu, and everyone still went by first names; but behind the facade was a very different company from the one Walt Disney left behind.

In early 1984, Raymond L. Watson, the new chairman of Walt Disney Productions, and Ronald Miller, the president, were faced with serious problems. Earnings had been sliding; for the company's fiscal six months ending March 31, although revenues had increased to $648.3 million, income declined 34 percent to $31.3 million. In the second quarter, the company's stock price, after reaching $84 the previous year—still a far cry from the heady days of the 1970s when it sold at 80 times earnings—had dropped to $51. In some brokerage houses, the stock had been downgraded from a "buy" to a "hold." To make matters worse, many prominent business and news publications were reporting the possibility of a takeover.

COMPANY HISTORY

Melville Bell Grosvenor, former editor of *National Geographic*, said in a 1966 edition,

> When future historians sit down to choose a Hall of Fame for our time, there will be trouble over the name of Walt Disney. Some judges will list him as an artist; others will call him an educator. Still others may insist that Disney belongs with the inventors, and some will argue that he was a naturalist. Each, in my view, will have a point, for Walt Disney is all these things. But on one question the historians are bound to agree: Walter Elias Disney was a genius who brought laughter and knowledge to the world in a distinctive American way.

ANIMATION

Walt Disney lived the American dream. Born in Chicago in 1901 and raised in rural Missouri, by the age of 10, he rose every morning at 3 A.M. to deliver newspapers

This case was revised by Jeanne M. Liedtka, Associate Professor of Business Administration. The original case was written by William E. Fulmer and Robert M. Fulmer. In addition to the publications mentioned in this case, a selected bibliography is given in the teaching note.

in the suburbs of Kansas City. At home, he drew pictures of animals, only to have his father tear them up. Later, while working as a cartoonist for the *Kansas City Tribune*, he used some of his free time to make a few short movies that combined live characters and animation. In 1923 he moved to Hollywood with $40 and a head full of ideas.

In the fall of 1927, Disney traveled to New York with his wife Lillian (called Lilly) to negotiate a new contract for an animated series called *Oswald the Rabbit.* The distributor stole the series and hired Disney animators away. It was a doleful trip back; Disney needed a whole staff of animators, and he also needed a new character—fast.

The idea for Mickey Mouse was born on that return train trip. "I've got it," Walt told Lilly. "I'll do a series about a mouse. I'm going to call him Mortimer Mouse." Lilly liked the idea but thought "Mortimer" sounded "too dignified for a mouse." Walt responded, "All right, we'll call him Mickey Mouse. Mickey has a good friendly sound."

In Hollywood, Walt, his brother Roy, and chief animator Ub Iwerks began work on Mickey Mouse. That first Mickey cartoon, *Plane Crazy*, was a bit of nonsense inspired by the Lindbergh flight. When Disney took the movie to New York, film distributors were not interested. Nor were they interested in a second Mickey film, produced while Disney was traveling.

About this time, sound was being introduced in films. So Disney and Iwerks rigged a homemade radio with a microphone, put up a white sheet as a screen, and with two helpers, stood at the mike behind it with noisemakers, a xylophone, and a harmonica played by Wilfred Jackson, a newly employed animator. For six hours, Roy projected a short bit of animation from *Steamboat Willie*, the third Mickey film. The "sound crew" watched the image and whanged away. The result was ragged, but Disney was convinced that sound was for cartoons.

He hurried to New York with the film to complete the *Steamboat Willie* sound track. During the process, he had to wire Roy for more money. To raise it, Roy sold, among other things, one of Walt's proudest possessions, his Moon Cabriolet, an automobile with red and green running lights. The additional capital, however, enabled Disney to add sound to the first two "mouse films."

Suddenly the talking mouse was the darling of distributors. Now they came to Disney, asking him what he wanted to do and what they could do to help him. They got only part of the answer they were hoping for. He did plan to go on making Mickey Mouse cartoons, but he did not want to sell the film outright. Remembering his earlier experiences, he insisted on retaining complete control of his product. He signed Pat Powers as exclusive distributor for the Mickey Mouse cartoons on a one-year contract with no guaranteed option for renewal.

By the time Disney left New York in 1929, he had a package of four Mickey Mouse films ready for release: *Plane Crazy*, *Gallopin' Gaucho*, *The Opry House*, and *Steamboat Willie.* The reception when these films went into national distribution was so positive that he decided to attempt an animated short without Mickey or Minnie. He created *The Skeleton Dance*, the first of the Silly Symphonies.

The Skeleton Dance had no story and no characters. It was set in a graveyard in the smallest hours of the night, when the skeletons emerged from their graves and vaults, danced together for a few minutes, and then, with the coming of dawn, climbed back into their resting places. One distributor told Disney it was simply too gruesome, and Pat Powers told him to stick to mice.

Disney was beginning to suspect that his deal with Pat Powers was not working out, however. Powers would send them occasional checks for $3,000 to $4,000 from

New York, which were enough to keep them going but not nearly what the Disneys believed they should be receiving for their widely acclaimed series. Walt and Roy were unable to get a full financial report on distribution revenues, and Powers, they discovered, had a somewhat shady business reputation. An even more disturbing rumor suggested that Powers was trying to make off with Ub Iwerks.

Roy and Walt casually mentioned to Powers that they needed additional cash. To indicate his goodwill, and in hopes of a tighter contract, Powers wrote a check for $5,000. Disney stalled him until the check cleared, then broke off contract negotiations. The Disneys made no attempt to retain the immensely talented Iwerks who, with Powers' backing, set up a new shop to produce a series called *Flip the Frog.* Flip did not catch on, because Iwerks lacked the one talent Disney had in abundance—that of story editor. Within a few years, Iwerks was back at work for Disney, on a strictly businesslike basis. Witnesses reported that, when passing Iwerks on the lot, Disney carefully looked the other way or, at best, spoke to him in monosyllables. Iwerks' technical genius was of enormous value to Disney, but his moment of disloyalty was never forgotten.

Disney continued to work with the Silly Symphonies because of their diversity and challenge. Because they were free of the script demands of Mickey and his gang, the Symphonies allowed more freedom to experiment with new concepts and techniques.

His next project involved Technicolor's new three-color process for film. Although a Silly Symphony called *Flowers and Trees* was already fully photographed in black and white, he decided to remake it in color. It was a gamble, because Technicolor was extraordinarily expensive, but the color version of this Silly Symphony caused a revolution in the animated-cartoon industry. In 1932 it became the first cartoon to win an Oscar.

Donald Duck made his first sputtering appearance in 1934. *The Wise Little Hen* made Donald an immediate hit. He went on to surpass Mickey as the star of the Disney stable. According to Disney,

> We're restricted with the mouse. He's become a little idol. The duck can blow his top and commit mayhem, but if I do anything like that with the mouse, I get letters from all over the world. "Mickey wouldn't act like that," they say.

As the pictures were cranked out, the art of animation progressed. Characters were given more dimension and perspective than the first, flat figures, but Disney was never satisfied with the status quo. "I knew locomotion was the key," he once said. "We had to learn to draw motion. We had to learn the way a graceful girl walks, how her dress moves, what happens when a mouse starts or stops running." Disney set up an elaborate school for his artists. "It was costly, but I had to have them ready for things we would eventually do." Even during financial difficulties, Disney maintained his commitment to the studio's extraordinary art school, where classic art and the old masters were studied.

His next dream was to make *Snow White and the Seven Dwarfs,* as the world's first feature-length cartoon. When word of this project got around Hollywood, many movie people said Disney was making his biggest mistake.

While his artists were training, Disney had technicians working on a new kind of camera he planned to use for *Snow White.* He was no longer satisfied with just round figures; now he wanted the illusion of depth in the scenes. To achieve it, he developed the radically different "multiplane" camera—and won an Academy Award for it. In photographing animated films, three separate drawings were usually involved, each done on a sheet of transparent celluloid. One showed the foreground, one the animated figures, and the last the background. Before the multiplane camera, the three celluloids were simply stacked together and the camera shot through them all, giving a flat image. With the multiplane, more than three celluloids could be used, and they could be placed in different planes, sometimes as much as three feet apart. The camera could focus in and out among these planes to give an effect of depth and motion.

Snow White cost $1.5 million. When the bankers became nervous about the costs, Disney reluctantly showed their representative the unfinished product to try to retain their confidence. He reported,

> We needed a quarter of a million dollars to finish the picture, so you can guess how I felt. He sat there and didn't say a word. Finally, the picture was over and he walked to his car, with me following him like a puppy dog. Then he said, "Well, so long. You'll make a lot of money on that picture." So we got the money.

Snow White and the Seven Dwarfs went on to make cinema history and brought many honors to Disney. In 1938, Yale gave him an honorary master of arts. The same year brought honors from Harvard and the University of Southern California.

The immediate manifestations of this euphoria were the studio at Burbank (which cost $3,800,000) and the animated films *Pinocchio* ($2,500,000), *Bambi* ($1,700,000), and *Fantasia* ($2,300,000). The Disneys were soon heavily in debt. According to Roy Disney, "Success is hard to take."

Walt's intensity in pursuit of quality reached into every aspect of the studio, and his animators were known for their talent as artists in the truest sense of the word. The great English political cartoonist, David Low, said of Disney,

> I do not know whether he draws a line himself. I hear that at his studios he employs hundreds of artists to do the work. But I assume that his is the direction, the constant aiming for improvement in the new expression, the tackling of its problems in an ascending scale and seemingly with aspirations over and above mere commercial success. It is the direction of a real artist. It makes Disney, not as a craftsman but as an artist who uses his brains, the most significant figure in graphic art since Leonardo.

The making of *Fantasia* was a perfect example of the Disney style: innovation and the "constant aiming for improvement." *Fantasia*, released in 1940, started out to be a kind of super Silly Symphony for Mickey Mouse, with Leopold Stokowski directing a full orchestra in "The Sorcerer's Apprentice." Disney built it into much more, a brilliant combination of animation and fine music—from Beethoven's "Pastoral Symphony" to Stravinsky's "Rite of Spring." *Fantasia* introduced stereophonic sound 15 years before it was generally used in motion pictures.

Fantasia was released at a time when Disney was losing much of his freedom to experiment. The company's heavy debts and the war in Europe, which knocked out the lucrative foreign market, had forced him to go public. In 1940 Walt Disney Productions issued 155,000 shares of 6 percent convertible preferred stock at $25 a share, raising $3,500,000. Walt and Roy received employment contracts with the company, but they were never again to run the firm with the same freedom and creativity as before. *Fantasia*, the high point of Disney's experimentalism, had to be released in an abbreviated version. "The bankers panicked," said Disney.

"*Fantasia* was never made to go out in regular release. I was asked to help cut it. I turned my back. Someone else cut it." It failed at the box office.

In the summer of 1941, the studio was hit by a jurisdictional strike, an event that so dismayed Walt Disney that he wept. With one catastrophe after another, the Disney stock slumped to $3 a share. According to Roy, "More than once I would have given up, had it not been for Walt's ornery faith that we would eventually succeed."

The crisis in the company was overshadowed over the next four years by war. The wartime public showed little interest in animated films. People wanted live action. Just before Pearl Harbor, Disney converted to war work, and soon about 94 percent of his efforts involved making training and propaganda films. There was little profit, but this war work helped reduce the company's bank loans to $500,000.

While Disney prints brought in some money and helped ease the company's debt problems, wartime production simply postponed the firm's other problems. "We had to start all over again," Walt said. The old free-wheeling, free-spending days were over. Roy commented, "When you go public it changes your life. Where you were free to do things, you are bound by a lot of conventions—bound to other owners."

True-Life Adventure Films

The nature films had begun with the animated *Bambi*, but after the war, Disney began looking for new kinds of films to make. He decided that "to get closer to nature we had to train our artists in animal locomotion and anatomy." He introduced live animals into the studio, deer and rabbits and skunks:

> But they were not good. They were just pets. So we sent the artists out to zoos, and all we got were animals in captivity. Finally I sent out some naturalist-cameramen to photograph the animals in their natural environment. We captured a lot of interesting things and I said, "Gee, if we really give these boys a chance, we might get something unique!"

Disney sent Alfred Milotte and his wife, Elma, to Alaska. They sent back miles of film. In reviewing it, Disney stumbled on one of the great stories of nature: the saga of the fur seals coming up from the sea to crowded island beaches in the Pribilofs to mate and calve. The film was *Seal Island*, which won an Oscar as 1948's best two-reel subject.

For another film, Disney kept cameraman-naturalist Milotte in the wild for more than a year, photographing the beaver's life habits. Out of Milotte's footage came an Oscar for *In Beaver Valley*. Other Oscar-winning films in the True Life Adventure series were *Nature's Half-Acre*, *Water Birds*, *The Alaskan Eskimo*, *The Living Desert*, *Bear Country*, *The Vanishing Prairie*, and *White Wilderness*. Between 1950 and 1960, more than a dozen films were produced in this series.

The True Life Adventures were sometimes criticized for being subjective and emotional. Because the producers anticipated the audience's tendency to identify with the animals on an emotional level, animal behavior was interpreted in human terms. The films were designed for the enjoyment of a mass audience—what Disney called the "big family."

Live-Action Films

Live-action feature-length films were a greater challenge than nature filming: "I had to grow with them," Disney said. "I couldn't make a live-action feature until I had experience." This came after the war as a result of money the company had impounded abroad. Disney went to England to use some of those funds and decided to experiment there with live action. "I struggled with it. I kept playing around. I couldn't decide what kind of live action I should do, what would please that big family." The format finally crystallized in the early 1950s with *Treasure Island, The Story of Robin Hood and His Merry Men, The Sword and the Rose,* and *Rob Roy, The Highland Rogue.* They were immensely popular films with the public, and Disney knew he could succeed with live action.

Meanwhile, he was working on another animated feature. It took him over two years to make it, but he hit the jackpot with it. *Cinderella* grossed more than $4 million domestically, and WDP, which had been in the red for two years, was solvent again.

The company's position was further strengthened in the 1950s by a rising tide of affluent youngsters and by further diversification, this time into ventures other than motion pictures. Roy Disney established a profitable film-distribution subsidiary in 1953, the Buena Vista project, which gave the company control of its film releases and reduced distribution costs from 30 percent of gross rentals to an estimated 15 percent.

Television

The motion picture industry had no clear notion of how to cope with television in the mid-1950s. Most studios were fearful. Roy Disney commented, "When the industry was cussing television and trying to ignore it, Walt moved in and worked with it and made it work for him."

Disney's strategy was simple enough. With the opening of Disneyland in the works, he started *The Wonderful World of Disney* in 1954. The series ran for two decades on NBC-TV. He also developed the *Mickey Mouse Club* television show. Television made a modest profit for Disney, but, more importantly, it provided free advertising for Disneyland, Disney motion pictures, and Disney himself. The TV productions went into the company's film library and were wholly owned by WDP.

Disney's ability to relate to his audiences was exemplified by the process of choosing kids for the *Mickey Mouse Club* show. Disney told producer Bill Walsh, "Don't get me those kids with the tightly curled hairdos—tap dancers—get me children who look like they're having fun. Then later we can teach them to tap dance or sing or whatever." He suggested going to ordinary schools and watching kids at recess, because "pretty soon there would be one we would watch—whether he was doing anything or not—because that would be the one we'd be interested in. And that would be the kid we'd want for the show." They used the technique and found Annette and Darlene and Cubby and the bunch—and they all became popular.

Along with launching *The Wonderful World of Disney* in 1954, the studio also released *20,000 Leagues Under the Sea,* the most ambitious live-action picture in company history. It was a big-budget movie using major Hollywood stars (Kirk Douglas, James Mason, Paul Lukas, and Peter Lorre) and spectacular special effects. The film combined fantasy and adventure with an excellent script and direction; it won two Oscars. It was followed by *Swiss Family Robinson, The Shaggy Dog, The Absent-Minded Professor, Son of Flubber, Pollyanna,* and *The Parent Trap.* In 1964 *Mary*

Poppins became one of the greatest hits in the history of the industry and captured five Academy Awards.

The studio was now enjoying success with a wide variety of live-action productions and animation. The outlook for Disney was bright, partly because of the decision to move into television rather than hoping it would not interfere with the movie business. Most other major studios experienced a sharp decline in their fortunes.

DISNEYLAND

Walt Disney had been thinking about Disneyland for 15 or 20 years before it became a physical reality. The idea of sinking millions of dollars into an amusement park, even Disney's kind of amusement park, seemed so preposterous that he did not mention it to anyone for a long time. He just quietly began planning. "I had all my drawing things laid out at home, and I'd work on plans for the park, as a hobby, at night."

He borrowed $100,000 against his life insurance policy to finance the planning of Disneyland. To find a proper site for it, Disney called in the Stanford Research Institute, which recommended three locations as alternatives. Disney picked Anaheim because it had five inches less rain a year than the San Gabriel or San Fernando Valley sites. It also happened to be in the population center of southern California and only 26 miles from Los Angeles. Disney purchased 244 acres of land, mostly orange groves, with his own money. To finance Disneyland, he brought in three investors: WDP, the American Broadcasting Company (ABC), and Western Printing and Lithographing Co.[1]

Disney wanted a park that adults could enjoy (adult guests outnumbered children three and a half to one). According to Dick Nunis, the boss of outdoor recreation, Disney believed, "Everyone's a kid at heart—all you have to do is let him find a way to be one." Disney people were also quick to point out the educational aspects of theme parks, but Disney had said, "I'd rather entertain and hope people learn than teach and hope they are entertained." He always maintained his audience was "honest adults."

In the park, Disney was a stickler for quality, authenticity, and attention to detail. There were 700 varieties of plants from all over the world. (It took 30 gardeners to care for them.) The trash bins cost $150 each to paint and were designed to be highly visible without clashing with their surroundings. Audio-Animatronic figures were so lifelike that they often invoked arguments as to whether they were real. An air jet was put in front of every porthole in the submarine, because fewer people suffered from claustrophobia if they had moving air and something to see.

The Matterhorn was 1⁄100 the height of the real one. It contained 500 tons of structural steel, and almost no two pieces were the same length, size, or weight. Disney designers studied hundreds of pictures of the rugged peak to create as close a copy as they could. Roy Disney opposed building the Matterhorn, because of the $7 million cost, but when Roy was away on a trip to Europe, Walt called an executive meeting. "We're going to build the Matterhorn and when Roy gets back from Europe, let him figure out how to pay for it." Walt had once commented, "The folks who win financially are the ones who don't worry about money."

Disneyland characters and entertainers underwent several days of training before meeting the public. They were to be neat, friendly, and courteous. No stone was to be left unturned to ensure people an enjoyable and hassle-free escape from the troubles of everyday life.

At the opening in July 1955, Disney said, "Disneyland will never be completed. It will grow as long as there is imagination left in the world."

Mineral King Project

"The fun is in always building something," Disney said. "After it's built, you play with it a little and then you're through. You see, we never do the same thing twice around here. We're always opening up new doors."

The next new door came out of Walt's personal interest in skiing. The Forest Service asked for bids to develop the Mineral King area into a year-round recreational area. An Alpine-like area, with its peaks rising as high as 12,400 feet in the Sequoia National Forest, Mineral King is about halfway between Los Angeles and San Francisco.

The most ambitious of the six bids submitted was by WDP. Disney's successful bid called for the construction of permanent housing with 2,400 beds plus temporary summer units with 4,800 beds; a 2,600-car parking area, and an Alpine Village from which cars would be excluded. Ski lifts would be designed to handle 15,000 to 20,000 skiers on the slopes at one time. A 25-mile road, part of it through the Sequoia National Park and over some of the most rugged terrain in the Sierra Nevada Mountains, was planned.

Disney's plan, and particularly the road, was opposed by the Sierra Club, a national organization of conservationists with considerable strength in California. Disney, surprised at the strength and tenacity of the Sierra Club, was ultimately forced to abandon the Mineral King project.

Walt Disney World

In October 1965 (approximately the same time as the Mineral King project was announced), Disney announced "the biggest thing we have ever tackled." The project (eventually, Walt Disney World and EPCOT) involved building two cities, one called "Yesterday" and one called "Tomorrow," in central Florida. These cities would include an airport, hotels, motels, convention facilities, industrial exhibits by U.S. corporations, shopping centers, camping grounds and facilities, curio and gift shops, service stations, golf, swimming, boating, a game refuge, power generators, and possibly even a movie studio. The project required seven years of planning and $600 million to build.

WDP firmly resolved to avoid repeating the principal business error made in the development of Disneyland: allowing hundreds of motels and other businesses to spring up around the periphery of the park. Calling them "honky-tonks," Disney believed they detracted from the park's image. Also, hotels in the vicinity of the park were grossing $300 million a year at a time when Disneyland grossed only $65 million. E. Cardon "Card" Walker, then executive vice president of WDP, said, "We were determined that if we ever did it again, we would buy enough land to control the complete environment."

In the early 1960s, the company's real estate agents purchased 27,443 acres in about 18 months at an average cost of just under $200 an acre under the company names of Tomahawk and Compass East. In October 1965, an announcement was made that the entire tract was owned by subsidiaries of Walt Disney.

Perhaps Disney's biggest coup in the project was the enabling legislation won from the state of Florida. It gave the company the powers of a county. It could establish its own building code and zoning regulations, form its own improvement district, and finance improvement with municipal bonds. It established two municipalities, Reedy Creek and Bay Lake, in which top Disney people were councilors. The company also got Florida to ban the use by others of any Disney characters in a business name anywhere in the state, and no business could advertise itself as being so many miles from Disney World.

Disney also worked out an impressive agreement with 17 building trade unions that contained no-strike, no-lockout clauses and provisions for handling grievances, including binding arbitration. When it became clear that the Florida management could not attract the number of attractive, personable young people it needed, the company decided to hire 1,200 students to rotate in 300 jobs. By working with colleges, they were able to hire 300 students each quarter in jobs related to their majors. Some colleges even gave credit for the experience. Although few inside opportunities to advance beyond entry-level positions existed, Disney created an outplacement program that brought employees who did not want to remain in park-related jobs together with corporations who did business in the park.

Work on the landscaping began three years before the park was built. The Jungle Cruise had to have real African flora, and Liberty Square had to have a 32-ton Liberty Oak. In all, 55,000 trees and shrubs were brought in from all over the world—not for planting but for testing.

Culture at the Theme Parks

The "service-through-people" theme at the Disney parks started with a special language. There was no such thing as a worker at Disney. The employees out front were "cast members," and the personnel department was "casting." Whenever someone worked with the public, he or she was "on stage." Red Pope (a long-time Disney observer and writer) noted this phenomenon when two of his children, aged 16 and 18, were hired by Disney World to take tickets. For this seemingly mundane job, four eight-hour days of instruction were required before they were allowed to go "on stage." They learned about Guests—not lowercase *c* customers, but uppercase *G* Guests.

When Pope asked his children why it had taken four days to learn how to take tickets, they replied,

> What happens if someone wants to know where the restrooms are, when the parade starts, what bus to take to get back to the campgrounds? We need to know the answers and where to get the answers quickly. After all, Dad, we're on stage and help produce the Show for our Guests. Our job every minute is to help Guests enjoy the party.[2]

People were brought into the Disney culture early. All of the parks had a grooming and behavior code. Men had to have their hair cut above their ears and collars and be clean-shaven. Women had to be "natural" and not wear large earrings, eye shadow, or noticeable makeup. Employees were to be pleasant and helpful at all times and not eat, drink, smoke, curse, or chew gum while working with the public. Everyone had to attend Disney University and pass "Traditions I" before going to specialized training. According to Red Pope,

> Traditions I is an all-day experience where the new hire gets a constant offering of Disney philosophy and operating methodology. No one is exempt from the course, from VP to entry-level part-timers. Disney expects the new CM (cast member) to know something about the company, its history and success, its management style before he actually goes to work. Every person is shown how each division relates to other divisions—Operations, Resorts, Food and Beverage, Marketing, Finance, Merchandising, Entertainment, etc. and how each division "relates to the show." In other words, "Here's how all of us work together to make things happen. Here's your part in the big picture."

Employees were well indoctrinated with the eleven characteristics of "The Disney Management Style": (1) we're a friendly, informal organization, (2) we work as a team, (3) it's all "our responsibility," (4) we're a Disney Democracy, (5) we communicate openly, (6) we make mistakes, because we're human, (7) we have a sense of humor, (8) we're creative people, (9) we're curious people, (10) we're businesspeople, and (11) we're not only dreamers, but doers.

The systems support for people on stage was also impressive. For example, hundreds of phones were hidden in the bushes as hot lines to a central question-answering service. The amount of effort put into the daily cleanup amazed even the most calloused outside observers.

Intense management involvement in the parks was highlighted at Disney by an annual week-long program called "cross-utilization." As Pope described it, this program entailed Disney executives leaving their desks and their usual business garb to "don a theme costume and head for the action." For a full week, the boss would sell tickets, popcorn, dishes of ice cream, or hot dogs, load and unload rides, park cars, drive the monorail or the trains, and take on any of the 100 on-stage jobs that made the entertainment parks come alive.

Transitions

In the midst of all this activity of the mid-1960s, Walt Disney was diagnosed as having cancer. According to Roy Disney, "I heard him refer to this cruel blow only once. 'Whatever it is I've got,' he told me, 'don't get it.'"

Having resigned all official positions in the company as early as 1960, Walt now was encouraging others to take on more responsibility. He claimed that his "greatest accomplishment was that I built an organization of people that enable me to do the things I wanted to do all my life." He had given his seven top producers an opportunity to share financially in the success or failure of their projects. He hoped that one of them would emerge as a clear successor. None had.

He was asked in 1963, "What happens when there is no more Walt Disney?"

> Every day I'm throwing more responsibility to other men. Every day I'm trying to organize them more strongly. But I'll probably outlive them all. I'm 61. I've got everything I started out with except my tonsils, and that's above average. I plan to be around for a while.

He died on December 15, 1966, two weeks after his 65th birthday.

Walt Disney's death left a creative void at Disney. Because he was such a catalyst for ideas, talented men and women had been willing to work for him. "When Walt was alive, he was the leader because he was a creative cyclone," said Roy.

Red Pope commented:

> How Disney looks upon people, internally and externally, handles them, communicates with them, rewards them, is in my view the basic foundation upon which five decades of success stand. I have come to observe closely and with reverence the theory and practice of selling satisfaction and serving millions of people on a daily basis successfully. It is what Disney does best.
>
> He was a genius, but a moody genius. If he liked an idea, he was lavish in his praise, but if he disliked an idea, he could be abrupt, curt, and bitingly critical. He had no patience with anyone who would settle for second best. As a result, Disney people sometimes worked with butterflies in their stomachs trying to come up with "what Walt wants."

Roy Disney, at age 74, tried to replace his brother's distinctive brand of creative leadership with management by committee. Working with Roy to carry on were William H. Anderson, production vice president; Donn B. Tatum, assistant to the president; Card Walker, marketing vice president; and Ronald W. Miller, Walt's son-in-law and a board member. Roy explained,

> I know a committee form is a lousy form in this business, but it's the best we've got until someone in the younger crowd shows he's got the stature to take over the leadership. If the chips are down, I've got the decisions. My way is to compromise, and I admit that that isn't a sound basis. But, I think I would do even more damage trying to make creative decisions the way Walt did.

Walt left a legacy of products. Five brand-new movies were all but in the can. Disneyland had just undergone an expansion, and Disney World was well along in the planning stages. Just weeks before his death, he first sketched EPCOT on a napkin and described it in a film as a model city, "a working community with employment for all." According to Roy,

> We've never before had this much product on hand. Walt died at the pinnacle of his producing career in every way. The big thing that is bugging American industry is planning ahead. We've got the most beautiful ten-year plan we could ask for.

As CEO, Roy Disney supervised the completion of Florida's Walt Disney World, which opened in October 1971, and later that year, he died at the age of 78.

Now the leadership passed to Card Walker. Walker, who had joined the company in 1938 as a mail clerk, possessed an encyclopedic knowledge of the business that had made him invaluable to the Disneys. He was very close to their families, a good friend, and an enthusiastic supporter. He tried to continue the Walt Disney spirit. He once remarked, "Walt's in this room. He'll always be in this room. We know what he would think is right or wrong, and that's good enough for us."

EPCOT

The immediate success of Walt Disney World spurred the decision in the mid-1970s to proceed with the Experimental Prototype Community of Tomorrow, EPCOT. Walt's original model-city concept, however, with a dome controlling the climate of the central city and office buildings that would be orbited by residences, schools, and green space, was too ambitious for even the most loyal Walt Disney followers. Disney management abandoned it as too expensive to keep technologically up to date and too difficult to control. Furthermore, the idea for 20,000 people to live and work in the community was scrapped. Instead, EPCOT evolved into two theme parks: Future World, to showcase past and future technologies and the expression of human imagination, and World Showcase, which simulated the cultures of nine nations (more to be added later) in a sort of permanent world's fair. It was a $1.2-billion project, and more than its predecessors, Disneyland and Disney World, EPCOT was aimed primarily at grown-ups.

As with all Disney endeavors, the logistics strained the imagination. Some 54 million tons of earth were moved; 16,000 tons of steel were used; and 500,000 board feet of lumber went into construction of the sets alone. Around the 40-acre man-made lagoon, 70 acres of sod were laid, 12,500 trees and 10,000 shrubs planted. More than l.5 million feet of film were shot in 30 different countries and edited for more than four hours of shows. An entire 3-D camera and projection system was invented for the 360-degree wraparound show in the Imagination pavilion.

Money from corporate tie-ins was crucial to Disney's ability to finance EPCOT, by generating more than one-third of the total cost. Large corporations paid up to $25 million each for the privilege of affixing their names to individual pavilions.

Just before EPCOT opened in the fall of 1982, Disney officials were surprised when Disney World characters voted 45 to 41 to be represented by the Teamsters. Although Disney had defeated earlier efforts by characters to join the stagehands' union, management accepted Teamster representation quietly. The Teamsters became the 17th union at Disney World and EPCOT. (Disneyland had 28 unions.) According to *Forbes*, "There had already been enough bad publicity from employees—evading the Disney ban on talking to the press—complaining anonymously to reporters about hot and dirty costumes, abusive child customers and low wages." (The wage base for Disney World employees, many of whom were food-and-beverage or sanitation workers, in 1983 was $4.60 to $6.00 per hour, resulting in a payroll of $4 million per week.)

Tokyo

In April 1983, after two years of construction involving 3,000 workers, the biggest Disneyland of them all at that time opened on 202 acres of landfill in Tokyo Bay. Oriental Land Company, the Japanese real-estate company that built and owned the park, had begun reclaiming the land almost 20 years earlier. For this desolate mud-flat land, it paid $70 per 3.3 square meters. By 1984 those 3.3-square-meter parcels were worth more than $2,000 each. With 300 acres still undeveloped, Oriental Lands stood to clear $740 million on resale, more than enough to cover the $673 million borrowed from Japanese banks to build this Disneyland.

Walt Disney Productions had started talks with Oriental Land in 1974, but a final agreement was not reached until 1979. Disney had zero cash investments in the project and, therefore, risked only its name. For the use of the name and the Disney know-how, Disney received 10 percent of the entrance gross and 5 percent on all food and souvenirs sold in the park. WDP retained "theme supervision" for the life of the project, which meant everything had to be done "Walt's way." Except for signs, which had Japanese subtitles under larger English words, there was little that was distinctly Japanese about the park. Only 2 of the park's 27 restaurants sold Japanese food, and they served only sushi and bento, basically an oriental box lunch. A weatherproof skylight covered the entire World Bazaar complex (Main Street

USA). Sheltered queue areas, walkways, and enclosed patios were also provided. Most of the electronic show and ride designs represented the latest in Disney technology and were more advanced than similar attractions at U.S. Disneyland and Disney World.

One-third of Japan's population lived within 90 minutes of the site, and first-year attendance was projected to be 10 million visitors, but the project was not without problems and risks. The weather was the most obvious difficulty. Tokyo averages 58.52 inches of rain and 108 rainy days every year. It snows every winter in Tokyo, and the park lies squarely in the path of the famous Pacific typhoons. This double threat obliged Disneyland's gardeners to provide gas heating for the park's 300,000 newly planted trees, and to tie every one down with four solid guy wires. Furthermore, Japanese children put in six, and sometimes seven, days per week at school, with only a week of vacation in May and two more in August.

Management Changes

Card Walker stepped down as chairman of WDP in May 1983 at the age of 68. He was succeeded by real-estate developer Raymond L. Watson, a long-time Disney board member. President of California's Irvine Company for 4 of his 17 years there, Watson was credited with much of the planning for the development of 60,000 acres that included the entire city of Irvine and sections of five adjacent cities.

The 57-year-old Watson was described as an "analytical planner with a conservative management track record" who was unlikely to tamper with the Disney heritage or "The Disney Way of Leadership" (Exhibit 1). According to Watson, "You don't come to a tradition-minded company and say, 'I'm going to change everything.' The employees would run you out of town."

Also in 1983 Ronald W. Miller, the 50-year-old one-time tight end for the Los Angeles Rams, was named president. Miller had joined the Disney studios three years after marrying Walt's eldest daughter in 1954. (They were separated in 1983.)

At least since the 1970s, company observers had voiced concern for the future of Walt Disney Productions. Some wondered whether the company had the creativity needed to capture new markets. Many of the "new" plans were leftover ideas of Walt Disney's. Top managers suggested that, if their plans seemed to fit a strategy of attracting older audiences, that was merely a coincidence. "What we are doing is intuitively based on a hell of a lot of experience," explained Card Walker. "More important than planning and research is the combination of experience we get from a lot of segments of the company." According to a former senior executive with Disney, "The company is creatively burned out. All those guys [top management] are so square you can't roll them downhill." A research analyst described current management as being "very businesslike and competent, but... squelching creativity."

A Review of Operations

Movie Division

The crisis facing Disney was most visible in the film division. In 1979 it had accounted for 20 percent of pretax earnings. In 1982 films lost $33 million. Part of the problem was demographics. Disney films had always appealed to a young (under

EXHIBIT 1

The Disney Way of Leadership

Human Relations Skills

Our ability to work positively with people lies in continually putting to practice some key points.

- Set the example...it starts with you.
- Encourage a positive attitude.
- Get to know your employees... treat them as individuals.
- Be with your team...provide encouragement and attention.
- Use empathy...look at the other person's point of view.
- Have respect for others.
- Be objective...be firm, fair, and consistent.
- Give recognition for a job well done.
- Maintain your sense of humor.
- All problems are not the same... treat each individually.
- If an employee has a problem... help solve it.
- If a promise is made...keep it.
- See that your employees have good working conditions.

Communications Skills

Since communication means getting ideas across and finding out what other people have to say, we stress the following points in the Disney Way of Leadership.

- Communicate clearly...get your message across.
- Let your employees know how they're doing.
- Encourage upward and downward communications.
- Listen to what employees have to say.
- Keep an open door and an open mind.
- Tell employees how they fit in... explain the big picture.
- Let your employees feel like they belong.
- Communication should be direct, open, and honest.

Training Skills

An efficient operation can never come about as the result of a "happy accident." Employees must have a clear-cut idea of what they are expected to accomplish and how to achieve it with the greatest proficiency.

Some key training points to remember:

- Be sure your employees receive the proper training which they need for doing their job.
- Provide for your employees' future growth and development.
- Give employees a chance to learn and participate.
- Encourage new ideas and creative contributions.

Other Leadership Skills

In addition to the aforementioned skills, the Disney Leader also needs to be aware of and skillful in areas of planning, organizing, directing, and controlling his/her team's efforts.

(continued)

SOURCE: *The Disney Management Style*, Walt Disney Productions (1977), pp. 32–34.

EXHIBIT 1 (CONTINUED)

The Disney Way of Leadership

Planning is really just looking ahead. Once objectives are understood, the means necessary to achieve them are presented in plans. Organizing is the process of putting all the resources together to carry out the plan. Directing involves the process of carrying out the plan using all the resources gathered. Controlling measures performance in relation to expected standards of performance.

The Disney Way of leadership stresses arranging work into a logical and workable manner to insure its successful completion. Keep in mind these helpful points.

- A plan of action is the best control to make sure we get there.
- Don't over-structure a plan... stay flexible.
- Set clearly defined priorities and completion schedules.
- Be realistic with target dates... but set them.
- Don't assume... follow-up on assignments and requests.
- Organize around jobs and people.
- Find the right person for the job.
- Issue effective and understandable instructions and directions.
- Establish effective controls to get things done in a timely manner and by priority.

In summary, the Disney Way of Leadership actually integrates all of these skills, applies them as appropriate at the point of action. For it is only through daily application and practice that we "fine tune" the essential skills of effective leadership.

---

14) audience. That group composed 14.7 percent of the population in 1950, 18.2 percent in 1960, 15 percent in 1970, and 13.6 percent in 1980.

The traditional Disney audience had indeed shrunk, but as Card Walker saw it, the problem ran even deeper: "Young adults today want a more sophisticated point of view, with more sex and violence. We don't ever want to go that far." Ron Miller, who served as executive producer throughout the decade of the 1970s, described the situation in personal terms. "We were not reaching that broad audience. I saw it with my own children. The moment they turned about 14 or 15, I would run a Disney film at home and they'd look and say, 'Oh God, not that corn again.'" Miller had been frustrated by being unable to bid for scripts like *Kramer vs. Kramer* and *Raiders of the Lost Ark* because of the Disney image.

The reluctance of freelance Hollywood talent to adapt to Disney's narrow range and stingy compensation deals had often kept Miller's instincts from bearing fruit. According to a former Disney executive, "Card [Walker] would listen but not hear. Ron would listen but not act." Reportedly, Miller had eagerly pursued Michael Eisner, president of Paramount Pictures (*Raiders of the Lost Ark*, *Saturday Night Fever*, *Flashdance*, *Terms of Endearment*, and the *Star Trek* movies) for the Disney studios, but *Business Week* reported,

> Industry experts assume that Eisner would have wanted more control than Disney was prepared to give. Says a key executive at a rival studio: "Disney's movie division

> is relatively small. Even though they are beefing up production, they will release only about 7 films a year. The majors each release more than 15. The movies are a small part of Disney's total business. Any heavy-weight would want some control of the theme-park operations. That would upset too many long-time Disneyites." And he adds: "People still doubt that Disney wants to—and can—change its image."

In recent years, there had been a talent drain, some of which was the result of the retirement of long-time animators. Don Bluth, a talented animator who produced the well-received film *The Secret of NIMH*, walked out of Disney in 1979 with 2 colleagues. They were soon followed by 14 more. As Bluth repeatedly told the press, his goal was to return to the "classic" Disney techniques of *Snow White* and *Pinocchio*.

Recent write-offs in the movie division included

Something Wicked This Way Comes	$21.0 million
Night Crossing	10.5 million
The Watcher in the Woods	6.8 million
Midnight Madness	4.5 million
Condorman	20.5 million

Not all of the movies in recent years had been losers. *The Rescuers*, an animated film, surpassed 1964's *Mary Poppins* in revenues. This fact escaped the attention of most Disney observers, however, because a large portion of the gross came from West Germany, where the movie was the biggest hit of all time. *The Fox and the Hound* cost $12 million to produce and earned $50 million. *The Black Hole* was disappointing but was expected to break even.

The Disney film library was another important company asset. Valued at $60 million and with annual amortization costs of approximately $66 million, it was estimated by some to be worth $400 million to $600 million. The library contained 650 titles ranging from classics such as *Mary Poppins* and *Snow White* to lesser films such as *The Shaggy D.A.* and *The Bootniks*. In 1983 *Snow White* was rereleased and brought in $20 million.

In 1981 Thomas Wilhite, who had been the company's publicity director, was given responsibility for all film production. Wilhite, then 27 and the company's youngest vice president, represented youth and a fresh approach. He was a film buff but had never produced a picture. Wilhite's first film, *Tron*, did not do well (a $10.4 million write-off) despite enormous advance publicity. Wilhite's next venture was *Tex*, a $5 million production about a teenager growing up in Oklahoma. It was favorably reviewed but drew small audiences.

In March 1983, Richard Berger, senior vice president for Worldwide Productions at 20th Century Fox, was made president of a new Disney subsidiary, Walt Disney Pictures. Eight months later, Wilhite quit, claiming "the film company is big enough for only one head of production." According to *Variety*,

> With unusual candor for a departing exec, Wilhite said that "Richard Berger and I didn't see things the same way. We disagreed on the viability of *Splash*, which he'd turned down at Fox. He never fulfilled his promise to bring staff salaries and titles up to industry standards. Everyone who came from the outside got the good salaries, but not those already here. I think my exit has been inevitable, one way or the other, for some time."

Consumer Products

The consumer products division was responsible for collecting royalties on the Disney name and characters. Every item that carried the name of Disney or any of its characters generated revenue—everything from Mickey Mouse ears, books, watches, and T-shirts to Tokyo dolls with Mickey wearing a kimono. On divisional assets of $37 million and revenues of $111 million, consumer products earned income of $57 million in 1983. In 1979 its pretax earnings were nearly a 200 percent return on assets. Some analysts had valued the consumer products division at $350 million.

Cable Television: The Disney Channel

TV revenues had declined from $44.4 million in 1982 to $27.9 million in 1983. The company that had produced *The Wonderful World of Disney* and *The Mickey Mouse Club* for network television no longer had any hit shows on the air.

To counter the decline, the Disney Channel was formed in April 1983, with an initial programming investment of $45 million. Offering a 16-hour-a-day schedule, seven days a week, the Disney Channel, six months later, had more than 532,000 basic subscriber homes and had signed agreements with 1,123 cable systems offering the service to 9.9 million homes in all 50 states. By March 31, 1984, the number of subscribers was 916,000. This record established the Disney Channel as the fastest growing and most successful new pay-television service in history and put it on target toward its projected breakeven of 2 million subscribers by the end of 1985.

Subscribers paid between $7 and $11 a month for Disney's family-oriented programming. The foundation for this service was the Disney library of feature films, cartoons, true-life adventures, educational shorts, and television shows. The Channel also acquired exclusive pay-television rights to 12 classic Charlie Chaplin features and purchased films such as *Can Can* and *Guys and Dolls* from other studios. In addition, Disney announced that 25 production crews were working on 658 shows (all half-hour and four-hour series) in Los Angeles, Orlando, and a dozen other sites throughout the United States.

If objectives were met, pay-TV services could generate profit margins of 25 percent. According to Jim Jimirro, president of Walt Disney Telecommunications, "The number of viewers who are interested in family entertainment has been very underestimated. There is every evidence that those people will reach vigorously for our type of product." More than 80 percent of the subscribers gave the channel high marks, and 21 percent of those surveyed never before had subscribed to any pay service (20 percent of the subscribers did not have children under the age of 13). Still, Jimirro admitted in 1984, "We have not yet reached our projected penetration levels." Only 7 percent of the homes that could get the channel were taking it. He had anticipated 15 percent.

In the first quarter of 1984, the Disney channel lost $11 million. The projected loss was cut from $15 million to $9 million in the second quarter by producing and acquiring less programming, cutting marketing expenditures, and amortizing some programming costs more slowly.

Some cable operations complained that management was too rigid in its marketing strategies. One reported, "They don't know the cable business, and they don't listen. We wanted to give the channel away free for two weeks to create a viewing habit among children so the parents would buy. But it was a tough struggle to finally convince Disney to do it."

Another complaint came from the National Coalition on Television Violence. After monitoring the channel for two weeks in 1984, the organization reported an average of 9 violent acts an hour on real-life programming and 18 an hour on cartoons, nearly as high as on the three networks. The Coalition described the level of violence as "quite troubling," and its chairman, a University of Illinois psychiatrist, claimed the violence could be harmful to children.

Theme Parks

In early 1984, concern also was being expressed about Disney's theme parks. Attendance had been virtually flat for the past decade. Disney World and Disneyland generated 87 percent of total 1983 income. EPCOT attendance rose in 1983 but fell 8 percent in the quarter ending December 31, 1983. Early 1984 attendance was off 19 percent. According to an analyst with Wertheim & Co., "The 19 percent drop was a big disappointment. It raises a real question about whether EPCOT Center has the growth potential the investors expected."

Some of the attendance drop could be attributed to the harsh eastern winter, but Disney World's decline was greater than neighboring attractions such as Cyprus Gardens and Sea World. According to Watson, "We think we may be losing the young marrieds, for example, because we are not marketing the resort and recreational aspects of the park."

According to one entertainment analyst, "The increment to the theme park's operating earnings from Disney's $1.2 billion investment probably did not exceed $80 million before taxes. After charging itself taxes, Disney is left with about $45 million. That represents less than a 4 percent return on EPCOT. If Disney had invested in Treasury bills, it could have done better." In 1983 depreciation on the amusement parks was $88 million. Total revenues were approximately $1 billion.

Attendance at California's Disneyland rose 10 percent in the first and second quarter of 1984 because of Disney's $45 million investment in rebuilding Fantasyland. Response to Tokyo Disneyland had been strong, with 1983 royalties estimated to be $10 million to $20 million.

Because of the Tokyo experience, top management was considering the desirability of building a Disneyland in Latin America or Europe. Another project being debated was a series of mini-Disney entertainment parks throughout the United States. If such projects were undertaken, some Disney executives thought the parks should be in urban centers; others championed suburban sites near popular shopping malls. Other executives feared such parks would cheapen the Disney name. According to Watson, "The idea has been around for years. I've told Ron [Miller, president] we should either decide on it or stop talking about it." Another option was to buy other amusement parks and add Disney's distinctive touch. Theme parks in North Carolina, Virginia, Texas, and Ohio recently had sold for just under two times revenue.

Real Estate

Outsiders expected Ray Watson to bring his expertise to Disney's real-estate holdings, including approximately 40 underdeveloped acres at the California Disneyland site. In Orlando, Disney owned 28,000 acres—a tract twice the size of Manhattan.

According to Watson, "If we've used up more than 3,000 acres of that I'm surprised." There had been talk about more hotels and Disney ventures such as shopping centers, residential housing, or industrial parks. Although some of the Florida property would be hard to develop, analysts estimated that its value would range from $1,000 to $1 million an acre. In addition to its central-Florida land, the company also owned about 40 acres of undeveloped Florida coastal property. Disney's total Florida land holdings were estimated to be worth $300 million to $700 million.

Conclusion

By February 1984, the personal shareholdings of Roy E. Disney (Walt's nephew) had dropped from $96 million in 1983 to $54 million because of the declining value of Disney stock. As Watson and Miller examined the latest financial reports for the company (Exhibits 2–6), they wondered what could be done to restore the value of the assets that the Disney brothers had built.

Endnotes

[1]Disneyland in 1989 was owned solely by Walt Disney Productions, which began buying out the other investors in 1957. For example, Disney bought out ABC's interest for $7.5 million and took over the food services as soon as the leases could be terminated.

[2]The comments by Red Pope are reported in Thomas J. Peters and Robert H. Waterman Jr., *In Search of Excellence* (New York: Harper & Row, 1982), pp. 167–68.

EXHIBIT 2

Walt Disney Productions Revenue by Major Groups (000)

	1983	1982	1981	1980	1979
ENTERTAINMENT AND RECREATION					
Walt Disney World					
Admissions and rides	**$ 278,320**	$153,504	$139,326	$130,144	$121,276
Merchandise sales	**172,324**	121,410	121,465	116,187	101,856
Food sales	**178,791**	121,329	114,951	106,404	95,203
Lodging	**98,105**	81,427	70,110	61,731	54,043
Disneyland					
Admissions and rides	**102,619**	98,273	92,065	87,066	75,758
Merchandise sales	**72,300**	76,684	79,146	72,140	60,235
Food sales	**45,699**	44,481	44,920	41,703	35,865
Participant Fees					
Walt Disney Travel Co., Tokyo Disneyland royalties and other	**83,044**	28,502	29,828	28,005	26,843
Total revenues	**$1,031,202**	$725,601	$691,811	$643,380	$571,079
Theme Park Attendance					
Walt Disney World	**22,712**	12,560	13,221	13,783	13,792
Disneyland	**9,980**	10,421	11,343	11,522	10,760
Total	**32,692**	22,981	24,564	25,305	24,552
MOTION PICTURES					
Theatrical					
Domestic	**$ 38,635**	$ 55,408	$ 54,624	$ 63,350	$ 49,594
Foreign	**43,825**	64,525	76,279	78,314	57,288
Television					
Worldwide	**27,992**	44,420	43,672	19,736	27,903
Home video and non-theatrical worldwide	**55,006**	37,749	22,231	10,565	9,273
Total revenues	**$165,458**	$202,102	$196,806	$171,965	$144,058
CONSUMER PRODUCTS AND OTHER					
Character merchandising	**$ 45,429**	$ 35,912	$ 30,555	$ 29,631	$ 24,787
Publications	**20,006**	20,821	24,658	22,284	18,985
Records and music publishing	**30,666**	26,884	27,358	23,432	16,129
Educational media	**10,259**	15,468	21,148	21,908	19,967
Other	**4,327**	3,453	12,704	1,905	1,768
Total revenues	**$110,697**	$102,538	$116,423	$ 99,160	$ 81,636

SOURCE: 1983 Annual Report.

EXHIBIT 3

Walt Disney Productions Consolidated Statements of Income (000)

	For the Year Ended September 30		
	1983	1982	1981
REVENUES			
Entertainment and recreation	$1,031,202	$ 725,610	$ 691,811
Motion pictures	165,458	202,102	196,806
Consumer products and other	110,697	102,538	116,423
Total revenues	1,307,357	1,030,250	1,005,040
COSTS AND EXPENSES OF OPERATIONS			
Entertainment and recreation	834,324	592,965	562,337
Motion pictures	198,843	182,463	162,180
Consumer products and other	53,815	54,706	65,859
Total costs and expenses of operations	1,086,982	830,134	790,376
OPERATING INCOME (LOSS) BEFORE CORPORATE EXPENSES			
Entertainment and recreation	196,878	132,645	129,474
Motion pictures	(33,385)	19,639	34,626
Consumer products and other	56,882	47,832	50,564
Total operating income before corporate expenses	220,375	200,116	214,664
CORPORATE EXPENSES (INCOME)			
General and administrative	35,554	30,957	26,216
Design projects abandoned	7,295	5,147	4,598
Interest expense (income), net	14,066	(14,781)	(33,130)
Total corporate expenses (income)	56,915	21,323	(2,316)
Income before taxes on income	163,460	178,793	216,980
Taxes on income	70,300	78,700	95,500
Net income	$ 93,160	$ 100,093	$ 121,480
Earnings per share	$2.70	$3.01	$3.72

SOURCE: 1983 Annual Report.

EXHIBIT 4

Walt Disney Productions Consolidated Balance Sheets (000)

	For the Year Ended September 30	
	1983	1982
ASSETS		
Current assets:		
Cash	$ 18,055	$ 13,652
Accounts receivable, net of allowances	102,847	78,968
Income taxes refundable	70,000	41,000
Inventories	77,945	66,717
Film production costs	44,412	43,850
Prepaid expenses	19,843	18,152
Total current assets	333,102	262,339
Film production costs—noncurrent	82,598	64,217
Property, plant, and equipment, at cost:		
Entertainment attractions, buildings, and equipment	2,251,297	1,916,617
Less: Accumulated depreciation	(504,365)	(419,944)
	1,746,932	1,496,673
Construction and design projects in progress		
EPCOT Center	70,331	120,585
Other	37,859	39,601
Land	16,687	16,379
	1,871,809	1,673,238
Other assets	93,686	103,022
	$2,381,195	$2,102,816
LIABILITIES AND STOCKHOLDERS' EQUITY		
Current liabilities:		
Accounts payable, payroll, and other accrued liabilities	$187,641	$ 210,753
Taxes on income	50,557	26,560
Total current liabilities	238,198	237,313
Long-term borrowings, including commercial paper of $118,200 and $200,000	346,325	315,000
Other long-term liabilities and noncurrent advances	110,874	94,739
Deferred taxes on income and investment credits	285,270	180,980
Stockholders' equity:		
Preferred shares, no par		
Authorized—5,000,000 shares, none issued		
Common shares, no par		
Authorized—75,000,000 shares		
Issued and outstanding—34,509,171 and 33,351,482 shares	661,934	588,250
Retained earnings	738,594	686,534
	1,400,528	1,274,784
	$2,381,195	$2,102,816

SOURCE: 1983 Annual Report.

EXHIBIT 5

Walt Disney Productions Consolidated Statements of Changes in Financial Position (000)

	For the Year Ended September 30		
	1983	1982	1981
Cash provided by operations before taxes on income (see below)	$308,369	$309,431	$316,949
Taxes paid (received) on income, net	(28,987)	34,649	106,144
Cash provided by operations	337,356	274,782	210,805
Cash dividends	41,100	39,742	32,406
	296,256	235,040	178,399
Investing activities:			
EPCOT Center, net of related payables	250,196	566,428	285,651
Other property, plant, and equipment	83,542	47,988	47,756
Film production and programming costs	83,750	52,295	55,454
Rights to the Walt Disney name	(3,640)	40,000	
EPCOT Center and The Disney Channel pre-opening and start-up costs	18,253	19,170	1,907
Long-term notes receivable and other	11,406	26,881	4,023
	443,507	752,762	394,791
	(147,251)	(517,722)	(216,392)
Financing activities:			
Long-term borrowings	137,500	205,000	110,000
Reduction of long-term borrowings	(99,925)		
Common-stock offering	70,883		
Common stock issued (returned) to acquire rights to the Walt Disney name and certain equipment	(3,640)	46,200	
Participation fees, net of related receivables	11,169	23,867	24,745
Collection of long-term notes receivable and other	35,667	2,030	7,646
	151,654	277,097	142,391
Increase (decrease) in cash and short-term investments	4,403	(240,625)	(74,001)
Cash and short-term investments, beginning of year	13,652	254,277	328,278
Cash and short-term investments, end of year	$ 18,055	$ 13,652	$254,277

The difference between income before taxes on income as shown on the "Consolidated Statements of Income" and cash provided by operations before taxes on income is explained as follows:

	1983	1982	1981
Income before taxes on income	$163,460	$178,793	$216,980
Charges to income not requiring cash outlays:			
Depreciation	90,184	41,917	38,886
Amortization of film production and programming costs	65,575	64,868	55,222
Other	15,526	9,950	9,449
Changes in:			
Accounts receivable	(25,863)	1,077	(18,591)
Inventories	(11,228)	(6,944)	(5,125)
Prepaid expenses	(1,691)	(2,754)	(3,960)
Accounts payable, payroll, and other accrued liabilities	12,406	22,524	24,088
	144,909	130,638	99,969
Cash provided by operations before taxes on income	$308,369	$309,431	$316,949

SOURCE: 1983 Annual Report.

EXHIBIT 6

Walt Disney Productions Selected Financial Data (000)

	1983	1982	1981	1980	1979
STATEMENTS OF INCOME					
Revenues	$1,307,357	$1,030,250	$1,005,040	$914,505	$796,773
Operating income before corporate expenses	220,375	200,116	214,664	231,300	205,695
Corporate expenses	42,849	36,104	30,814	25,424	20,220
Interest expense (income), net	14,066	(14,781)	(33,130)	(42,110)	(28,413)
Taxes on income	70,300	78,700	95,500	112,800	100,000
Net income	93,160	100,093	121,480	135,186	113,788
BALANCE SHEETS					
Current assets	333,102	262,339	457,829	506,202	484,141
Property, plant, and equipment, net of depreciation	1,871,809	1,673,238	1,069,369	762,546	648,447
Total assets	2,381,195	2,102,816	1,610,009	1,347,407	1,196,424
Current liabilities	238,198	237,313	181,573	145,291	119,768
Long-term obligations, including commercial paper of $118,200 (1983) and $200,000 (1982)	457,199	409,739	171,886	30,429	18,616
Total liabilities and deferred credits	980,667	828,032	442,891	272,609	235,362
Total net assets (stockholders' equity)	1,400,528	1,274,784	1,167,118	1,074,798	961,062
STATEMENTS OF CHANGES IN FINANCIAL POSITION					
Cash provided by operations	337,356	274,782	210,805	204,682	182,857
Cash dividends	41,100	39,742	32,406	23,280	15,496
Investment in property, plant, and equipment	333,738	614,416	333,407	149,674	56,629
Investment in film production and programming	83,750	52,295	55,454	68,409	44,436
PER SHARE					
Net income (earnings)	2.70	3.01	3.72	4.16	3.51
Cash dividends	1.20	1.20	1.00	.72	.48
Stockholders' equity	$40.58	$38.22	$35.99	$33.22	$29.76
Average number of common and common-equivalent shares outstanding during the year	34,481	33,225	32,629	32,513	32,426
OTHER					
Stockholders at close of year	60,000	61,000	60,000	62,000	65,000
Employees at close of year	30,000	28,000	25,000	24,000	21,000

SOURCE: 1983 Annual Report.

Case 19

Amer Group, LTD.

February 1986

A few hours earlier, Leif Ekstrom, 43, had phoned the headhunter who had placed him in his present position just two years ago, this time to tell him that he had decided to accept the offer to be president and chief operating officer of Amer Group, a dynamic and growing diversified corporation. In the quiet and relaxed confinement of his sauna, Leif now took time to reflect on his decision. As he felt the sweat begin to bead on his skin, he poured a little water from the bucket onto the heated rocks to add a bit of moisture to the dry heat. As he watched the steam rise, the warm sensation and sweet smell of pine relaxed him. He took a deep breath, and wondered how, as an outsider, he would be able to provide leadership and add value to the firm he would be heading as of April l.

Leif Ekstrom was at the time executive vice president of a forest products company in the midst of restructuring. The uncertainties presented by these changes, coupled with structural threats in the forest industry, gave him just enough reason to consider the Amer opportunity. In his mind, the consumer-oriented businesses at Amer Group had fascinating possibilities in terms of growth potential and international expansion, and, in spite of his strong financial background, he had always enjoyed the marketing aspects of business. He thought Amer Group had not been an outstanding company until the mid-1970s, but since Heikki O. Salonen had become president, it had undergone many transitions to become a highly successful and respected organization in the Finnish business community. Much of the company's success was a result of the corporate and divisional strategies that had been well defined in the last few years. Ekstrom liked the excitement of a changing organization, and he saw management freedom and the flexible decision-making policy at Amer Group as attractive challenges for his professional growth.

Amer Group was a multibusiness company, among the 30 largest in Finland, with corporate headquarters in Helsinki. The company was involved in motor vehicles, tobacco, communications, paper wholesaling, textiles and clothing, sporting goods, metals, and plastics. Its major international brand names included Toyota, Citroen, Suzuki, Marlboro, Belmont, Marimekko, Seiko, Casio, and After Eight. Amer had sales in North America, Europe, Scandinavia, Japan, and the Soviet Union.

Heikki Salonen had steered the company as president since 1972, and now, at 53 years of age, was taking the title of chairman and chief executive officer. Salonen stated that Amer's board members, investors, and outside analysts thought the company was "too much in one man's hands." He himself agreed with comments that, although his single-handed leadership of the firm had been effective, it was

This case was written by Ann Yungmeyer under the supervision of Associate Professor L. J. Bourgeois III. Revised February 1993.

no longer healthy for the future of the company. Amer's rapid growth, recent acquisitions, and the subsequent need to strengthen top management made some organizational changes necessary.

As COO, Ekstrom would be assuming the primary day-to-day leadership role in the firm. He felt confident in his abilities to handle the challenge ahead. "As foreign as these businesses are to me," he thought to himself, "it is not necessary to know the technical aspects of these products; rather, it is more important to know their roles and have vision about how to develop them in the marketplace."

Finnish History and Culture

Historians believe the Finns migrated north from near Hungary around 2,000 years ago, pushing the indigenous Lapps into more northern regions. Finland was incorporated into Sweden in the 12th century, in 1809 was conquered by Alexander I, and remained an autonomous grand duchy of the Russian Empire until 1917. Shortly after the Bolshevik Revolution, Finland declared independence. In 1918 it experienced a civil war that had colored domestic policies to the present. Finland fought the Soviet Union twice during World War II and was left with huge reparation debts. In 1948 an agreement was signed with the Soviet Union under which Finland was obligated to defend its own territory in the case of an armed attack against the Soviet Union via Finland.

Finland's active neutrality was reflected in its basic goal since 1944: to stay out of Great Power conflicts while building mutual confidence with the Soviet Union. Finland was culturally, politically, and socially Western, but the Finns realized they had to live in peace with their eastern neighbor.

Finland had a dynamic industrial economy as a result of technology and significant capital investment over the last two decades. Because industry expansion occurred later in Finland than in other industrialized countries, fixed assets, on the average, were modern and suited for volume production. In the early 1980s, the economic growth rate was among the highest in Europe. Exports amounted to roughly one-third of gross national product (GNP). Wood processing, metals manufacture, shipbuilding, foodstuff, and textiles were the main industries. Finland was self-sufficient in meat, dairy, grains, timber, and most minerals, while fruits, vegetables, nonwood raw materials, and energy were mainly imported.

The Finns held their history and nationalism, as well as traditions, in high regard. Important themes throughout their literature were humanity's unity with nature and an appreciation for the common people, the Finnish folk. The underlying appreciation for simplicity could be seen in artistic creations such as jewelry, textiles, glass, and furniture designs.

The most well-known feature of the Finnish way of life was the sauna. Most Finns took saunas at least once a week for cleansing and relaxation. Many corporate office buildings contained saunas for use at the end of the workday. Many Finns had a rustic cottage in the country where they went on weekends to enjoy peaceful relaxation and a sauna heated by natural wood fire. As one Finn put it, "This is our way to get back to nature and close to our traditions."

The Finns were very precise and punctual—in business, clean, neat, and orderly. Plans were usually well prepared and laid out, and good communication was stressed. They paid much attention to detail, even to the point of how they folded the napkins for coffee in a conference room. In short, Finns embodied Scandinavian values of simplicity, precision, tradition, pragmatism, and love of nature.

Background on Amer Group

Amer Group was founded in 1950 as a tobacco company by members of four major Finnish associations: the Engineering Society in Finland, the Association of Graduates of the Schools of Economics and Business Administration, the Student Union of the Helsinki School of Economics and Business Administration, and the Land and Water Technology Foundation. They had worked together successfully in fund-raising projects, and their aim was "to create a business from which the profits would be used to fund commercial and technical university education and research."[1] Industrial machinery was difficult to find after World War II, but they had an opportunity to purchase machinery for manufacturing cigarettes from a small liquidated company, and the association members saw a great future in new American-blend cigarettes, introduced to Europe by American soldiers during the war. They had an idea for a product that would later become the "Boston" brand. Thus the idea, product, and future plans led to development of the company and its original name, Amer-Tupakka.

In 1986 the four founding organizations still had representatives on the company's advisory board and remained principal shareholders. Amer Group (the company name that followed) had been listed on the Helsinki Stock Exchange since 1977 and on the London Stock Exchange since 1984, and by 1986 it had 16,330 shareholders, some of whom were foreign institutional investors.

Diversification from the tobacco industry began with a peat moss and shipping business; in the early 1970s, the company acquired a publishing and printing business. Later in the decade, it established a flower growing business, formed a division to import and market high-quality branded products such as watches and confectionery, and made acquisitions in the ice hockey equipment and paper wholesaling business. Amer Group continued expansion in the 1980s to auto imports, plastics and metals manufacture, textiles, and ready-to-wear clothing.

When Heikki Salonen arrived in 1972, the tobacco business was still small, and the peat moss and shipping companies were losing money. He immediately began to stabilize the businesses, turning around or divesting loss-making operations. In 1973 he reorganized by trimming representation on the board of directors and establishing the actual Amer Group as a holding company for the various independent business concerns. His vision for the company at that point was only "to diversify into areas where Amer Group could use proven strengths and well-developed skills." This process of strategy definition led to Amer Group's mission, "To market high-quality branded products." He reflected, "Many mistakes were made during this process of giving the company direction, but we managed to improve our overall result every year."

The four founding organizations could not provide the capital to finance further growth, so in 1977 when Salonen saw the company was in good financial condition, he decided to offer stock on the Helsinki Exchange. Shortly thereafter, Amer Group's independent companies were consolidated into a single corporate entity in order to improve its image to shareholders as well as for tax benefits. Although each division continued to operate more or less independently, in effect, Amer Group's central management was strengthened. Internationalization began with the acquisition of two hockey equipment businesses in North America. By 1984 Amer managers had been successful at balancing paying dividends with retaining enough earnings to finance growth and decided to list on the London Exchange. Management believed that foreign financing would improve Amer's investment alternatives and give the company higher visibility in the financial markets.

By this point, Amer had acquired or established nearly 30 businesses and made several divestments along the way. The company was gaining a reputation for being very fast paced. One veteran at Amer Group explained the active spirit: "It is the American influence; American firms tend to move fast, and our key management people in Amer Group have had training in the U.S. We have also learned quite a bit through our cooperative agreement with Philip Morris." Heikki Salonen summed it up: "Innovative, active spirit, even aggressiveness, have been and will be characteristic of our operations."

Amer had deliberately sought to invest in areas where marketing was the key factor and where management experience and understanding of markets could contribute to success. The mid-1980s' strategy was to find market vacuums that could be penetrated with the company's existing marketing expertise and to market, worldwide, products of superior quality. Amer Group concentrated in areas that were not particularly sensitive to economic fluctuations and did not require heavy investment in industrial fixed assets. Guiding principles for operations were high yield on capital employed, profitability, growth, and the safeguarding of operations. Amer Group's policy was to hold part of its capital in investment properties, with the aim of ensuring some stability in the long-term development of Amer Group's business.[2]

Heikki Salonen described Amer Group's philosophy:

> Our specialty is marketing know-how. It is the same for each division—to know how to plan and control the sales organization. It is a sophisticated yet very precise methodology. Each division develops its own specialized marketing and distribution skill and formulates its own strategy in terms of market share, positioning, and competitive factors. The aim is to establish or maintain a leading position in the domestic market while paving the way for international expansion. In a country the size of Finland, internationalization is a must for sustained market growth.

Salonen took pride in trying to recruit the best managers and encouraging them to come forward with new ideas. At the same time, he emphasized planning and tight financial control, as well as a certain conservatism. "I encourage my managers to reach for the stars while keeping their feet firmly on the ground" (which, he said, sounds better in Finnish). "We need creativity while taking reasonable risks. Small problems mean we are trying. If you have no loss-making operations, the shareholders will say you are not trying all possibilities enough."

Group Structure

Amer Group was organized into seven autonomous divisions (see Exhibit 1), plus the three headquarters departments of corporate planning, finance, and communications and public relations. All the divisions were part of the parent company, with the exception of Korpivaara (autos) and Marimekko (textiles), which had remained separate legal entities.

EXHIBIT 1

Amer Group Structure: Group Headquarters

Board of Directors
President
Finance and Administration
Corporate Planning
Communications and Public Relations

DIVISIONS

TOBACCO DIVISION

Amer-Tupakka
Amer-Brokers confectionary

COMMUNICATIONS DIVISION

Weilin+Goos publishing and printing
Finnreklama Oy printing
Kiviranta advertising services
Salomo Karvinen Oy direct marketing company
AmerInstitute, Amersoft education services

PAPER MERCHANTING AND CONVERTING DIVISION, AMERPAP SPORTS GOODS DIVISION

Amer Sport International, Inc., Canada, USA
Koho, Finland, Europe

MARKETING UNITS DIVISION

Golden Leaf consumer durables
Kukkameri cut flowers
Fionia Plant Export ApS, Denmark

KORPIVAARA

Toyota Group
Auto-Bon Citroyen, Suzuki
Kone-Diesel service and accessories
Metals
Konemuovi plastics
Trading furniture exports
Moottorialan Luotto financing

MARIMEKKO

Decembre Oy
Marimekko, Inc., USA
Marimekko GmbH, Fed. Rep. of Germany

SOURCE: 1984–1985 Annual Report.

EXHIBIT 2

Amer Group, Ltd. Five-Year Financial Summary (figures in FIM millions [mmk])

CONSOLIDATED STATEMENT OF INCOME[1]	1981	1982	1983	1984	1985
Gross sales	1,522	1,780	2,023	2,277	4,299
Net sales[2]	611	680	768	875	2,483
Foreign sales	138	87	109	155	246
Wages, salaries, and social expenses[3]	144	153	160	192	315
Operating profit before depreciation	100	93	101	121	297
Depreciation (statutory and IAS)[4]	18	22	22	26	168
Net interest expense	30	30	26	20	95
Profit before taxes and appropriations	57	49	60	81	132
Taxes	6	10	6	2	3
Net profit	4	9	9	16	32
CONSOLIDATED BALANCE SHEET					
Financial assets[5]	383	460	463	622	903
Inventory and finished goods	180	207	198	220	606
Fixed assets	228	230	266	295	955
Total assets	791	897	927	1,137	2,464
Current liabilities	362	382	368	407	1,035
Long-term liabilities	170	198	215	254	511
Untaxed reserves	157	195	200	252	652
Shareholders' funds	102	121	144	224	265
Total liabilities and equity	791	896	927	1,137	2,463
KEY INFORMATION					
Capital expenditures (mmk)	37	28	54	64	504
Return on capital employed	22%	17%	17%	18%	16%
Return on shareholder funds	37%	22%	19%	24%	18%
Debt-to-equity ratio	1.1	.9	1	.8	1
Dividend per share (mk)	1.3	1.8	2	2.7	3.4
Earnings per share (mk)	11.3	9.8	10.4	13.7	18.7
P/E ratio	2.2	5.1	7.6	8.6	5.2
Price of restricted "A" share (mk)	25	50	78.7	118	98
Average personnel	1,997	1,984	2,016	2,041	2,983

[1]The figures for 1985, 1984, and 1983 are for the 12 months to August 31; figures for 1982 to 1981 are for the calendar year. Consolidated statements include Finnish and foreign subsidiaries in which the parent company owns more than 50 percent voting rights. These statements were prepared in accordance with Finnish Accounting Standards. Because of differences with IAS standards in account classification, it is not possible to calculate ratios with the information given. Selected ratios are provided under Key Information.

[2]Net sales reflect adjustment to gross for excise duty, sales taxes, commissions, royalties, internal sales, and other adjustments.

[3]Social expenditures include statutory, contractual, and voluntary.

[4]The statutory portion of depreciation is charged as an appropriation.

[5]Financial assets include cash, A/R, advances, prepaid expenses, and other.

SOURCE: 1984–1985 Annual Report.

Finland was experiencing a strong trend toward decentralized management in the mid-1980s, and Amer Group was among those beginning to restructure their organizations. Objectives of the reorganization were to enhance the autonomy and efficiency of the operating divisions and to simplify Group management. Discussions about how to achieve these goals were taking place during the time the decision was made to hire a chief operating officer.

Major investment decisions and finance were Amer Group's principal centralized activities. Division presidents were consulting Salonen, however, whenever other types of decisions were necessary. Communication between the divisions and headquarters theoretically took place through the finance department. Management reporting was sketchy, however, and problems were not dealt with through normal organizational channels but in a "management by happening" manner (i.e., fires were put out as necessary). One corporate executive commented, "The administration was built around people and personalities, not structure."

Corporate planning conducted business development and personnel activities. Business development activities included procedural handling of acquisitions and divestitures, research of future business opportunities for Amer Group in areas outside the existing business divisions, as well as research support to the divisions for closely related businesses. The personnel department planned and coordinated in-house training and development programs in the areas of management and financial reporting for all of Amer Group. In addition to the training objective, these sessions provided an opportunity for division managers to come together to meet and have discussions in an educational environment.

Financial Structure

Amer Group's strong financial position was evident in net operating cash flow, which improved from negative 2 million FIM (Finn marks) in 1980 to positive 168 million FIM in 1984–1985.[3] Debt to equity came down from 1.1 in 1981 to .8 in 1984 and was at 1.0 after large acquisitions in 1984–1985. From 1981 to 1985, net sales grew at a 42 percent compound annual growth rate, profit before tax at 23 percent, and earnings per share at 13 percent. (See Exhibits 2 and 3 for financial statement highlights.)

Amer had 7.2 million shares outstanding and a total of 16,330 shareholders. Two types of shares were issued. All 1.5 million "K" shares were owned by the founder organizations of the company. Each "K" share had the right of ten votes, and every ten "A" shares had the right of one vote. "A" shares had been quoted on the Helsinki Stock Exchange since 1977 and on the London exchange since May 1984. "A" shares took precedence over "K" shares in receiving dividends and were always entitled to a dividend at least equal to that of "K" shares. New share issues were primarily for the purpose of financing acquisitions. For example, Amer Group acquired the majority holdings in Korpivaara and Marimekko in part with the issue of "A" shares.

The founding organizations owned more than 40 percent of total outstanding shares, representing 97 percent of the votes. In addition to all "K" shares, the founding organizations owned 28 percent (1.6 million) of the "A" shares.

The price of Amer Group shares had risen annually by an average of 30 percent during 1976–1985. During the same period, the prices on the Helsinki exchange rose an average of 11 percent a year. The corresponding rate of inflation was around 8 percent a year.

EXHIBIT 3

Amer Group, Ltd. Financial Statements in Accordance with International Accounting Standards (IAS)

Accounting principles in Finland differ in a number of ways from those in other countries. Financial statements of Finnish companies are significantly influenced by tax law, with the result that taxable profit can be reduced by appropriations to "untaxed reserves" and depreciation allowances. Because financial statements prepared according to Finnish standards may be unfamiliar to overseas readers, supplementary financial statements prepared in accordance with IAS are included here.

CONSOLIDATED STATEMENT OF INCOME SUMMARY	1984	1985
Gross sales	2,277	4,299
Net sales	875	2,483
Profit before tax and extraordinary items	88	132
Tax	(3)	(3)
Extraordinary items	—	17
Net profit	85	146
Transfer to/from untaxed reserves	(48)	(17)
	37	129

CONSOLIDATED BALANCE SHEET SUMMARY		
Current assets:		
Cash	122	112
Stock and work in progress	232	626
A/R and prepaid expenses	451	722
Total current assets	805	1,460
Fixed assets	247	745
Investments	44	56
Deposits	41	57
Goodwill	11	9
Total assets	1,148	2,327
Current liabilities:		
A/P and accrued liabilities	275	651
Current portion of long-term loan	45	78
Short-term loans	108	332
Total current liabilities	428	1,061
Long-term loans	232	485
Share capital	124	145
Share premium	73	183

(continued)

SOURCE: 1985 Annual Report.

EXHIBIT 3 (CONTINUED)

Amer Group, Ltd. Financial Statements in Accordance with International Accounting Standards (IAS)

Untaxed reserves	210	243
Retained earnings	81	207
Minority interest	0	3
Total liabilities and equity	1,148	2,327
SOURCE AND APPLICATION OF FUNDS		
Sources:		
Profit before tax and extraordinary items	88	132
Adjustment for depreciation	22	68
Sales of fixed assets	6	84
Issue of shares	72	131
Other increase in shareholder funds	0	33
Increase in long-term loans	64	331
	252	779
Application:		
Purchase of fixed assets	63	631
Purchase of investments	1	12
Repayment of long-term loans	47	45
Dividends paid	11	17
Taxes paid	3	3
Deposits	6	16
Other applications	1	0
Increase in working capital	120	55
	252	779

Amer Group's Businesses

A corporate document summarizing Amer's businesses is provided as Exhibit 4 (p. C19.10). Division performance figures are given in Exhibit 5 (p. C19.12).

Tobacco Division

Amer-Tupakka was Finland's leading distributor of tobacco products. It manufactured and sold primarily American-blend cigarettes such as Marlboro, Belmont, and L&M. The company's philosophy was to be "first on the market," and in 1955, Amer-Tupakka introduced the first filter-tipped cigarette in Finland, the "Boston Filter." In the opinion of Martti Santala, tobacco division president from 1972, "The success of this product was the real economic base of the company. We had gained 20 percent market share by the late '50s, and big volume with one product is very economical." A license agreement with Philip Morris Companies, Inc., began in 1961, which involved cooperation in product development, marketing, and manufacture, and in the procurement of raw tobacco. In Finland, Marlboro had the highest market share of any country in the world. Amer Group held a 59 percent

EXHIBIT 4

Amer Group Divisional Structure

Division	Division Segments/ Activities	Segment Companies/ Activities	Products	Trademarks/ Brand Names	Market Served
Tobacco	Amer-Tupakka	—	Tobacco products	Philip Morris Co.: "Marlboro," "Belmont," "L&M," "Multifilter" Others: "Clan," "Barres"	Consumer
	Amer-Brokers	—	Confectionary	Rountree Mackintosh pk: "After Eight," "Toffo,""Big Cat," Other: "Kit Kat"	Consumer
			Photographic products	Kodak	Consumer
Communi-cations	Weilin+Goos	—	Textbooks, encyclopedias	Otava	Educational institutions in Finland and other Western European countries
	Finnreklama	—	Books	Finnereklama	Soviet Union
	Kivranta, Kuva Oy	—	Lithography	Kivranta, Kuva Oy	Advertising agencies
	Amer Institute	—	Training pro-grams for sales management		Educational
	Amersoft	—	Microcomputer software	Amersoft	Consumer, business
	Salomo Karvinen Oy	—	Multivolume reference books, domestic appliances	Salomo Karvinen Oy	Consumer
Paper merchanting and converting	Amerpap	Paper merchanting	Special purpose papers for printing, art, commercial use	A. Ahlstrom Oy, Kymi Stromberg Oy, C.A. Serlachius Oy, United Paper Mills, and Others	Commercial, industrial, art
		Paper Con-verting	Postal wrappers, packaging materials, envelopes	—	Postal
		Other	Franking machines, mail handling machines, printing ink	Hasler	Postal, art

(continued)

Source: Company documents.

EXHIBIT 4 (CONTINUED)

Amer Group Divisional Structure

Division	Division Segments/ Activities	Segment Companies/ Activities	Products	Trademarks/ Brand Names	Market Served
Sporting goods	Amer Sport International, Inc.	—	Hockey equipment	"Koho," "Canadien"	North American sporting goods
	Koho	—	Hockey equipment	"Koho"	European and North American sporting goods
Marketing units	Golden Leaf	—	Watches, clocks, calculators, pens, cigarette papers	"Seiko," "Pulsar," "Lorus," "Casio," "Montblanc," "Zebra," "Rizla"	Consumer market in Western Europe
	Kukkameri	—	Flowers	—	Consumer market in Western Europe
	Fionia Plant Export ApS	—	Danish potted plants	—	Consumer market in Western Europe
Korpivaara	Vehicle business	Toyota Group, Auto-Bon	Cars, vans, trucks for sale and lease, spare parts	Toyota, Citroen, Suzuki	Consumer purchasers, dealers
		Trade school	Training for automotive salesmanship	—	Automotive dealerships
		Kone-Diesel	Automotive accessories	Kone-Diesel	Consumer purchasers
	Metal business	Hydor	Air and oil compressors	Hydor	Industrial customers
		Pemamek	Welding positioners, workpiece handlers	Pemamek	Industrial customers including metal fabricators
		Skavenir	Mechanical handling equipment	Skavenir	Industrial customers
	Plastics business	Konemuovi	Plastic sheets, ski boxes, partition walls, floor covers for vans, boats	Konemuovi	Automotive accessory purchasers, sporting goods purchasers, industrial customers

(continued)

EXHIBIT 4 (CONTINUED)

Amer Group Divisional Structure

Division	Division Segments/ Activities	Segment Companies/ Activities	Products	Trademarks/ Brand Names	Market Served
	Moottorialan Luotto	—	Financing of automotive purchasing and leasing	—	Automobile purchasers
Marimekko	—	—	Clothing, interior decoration, retail store operation	"Marimekko"	Consumer

EXHIBIT 5

Five-Year Division Highlights (sales in FIM millions)

Sales of the profit centers within each division are shown separately if products or markets are dissimilar.

	1981	1982	1983	1984	1985
TOBACCO					
Sales:					
Amer Brokers	—	—	—	7.2	11.5
Amer Tupakka	208.9	209.8	250.0	301.7	326.9
Division *total* sales	208.9	209.8	250.0	308.9	338.4
Share of Amer Group sales	34%	30%	32%	35%	13%
Personnel	357	338	335	355	352
Profit rating[a]	Good	Good	Good	Good	Good
COMMUNICATIONS					
Sales:					
Weilin+Goos	133.8	143.9	143.0	151.2	197.9
Advertising services	21.0	21.5	19.2	13.7	17.0
Finnreklama	—	—	—	—	34.6
Less internal sales	—	—	—	—	7.3
Division *total* sales	154.8	165.4	162.2	164.9	242.3
Share of Amer Group sales	25%	24%	21%	19%	9%
Personnel	696	675	637	641	828
Profit rating[a]	Good	Good	Good	Good	Good
PAPER					
Division *total* sales	101.5	148.4	167.4	180.7	199.5

(continued)

[a]Explanation of profit rating is given in Exhibit 6.

EXHIBIT 5 (CONTINUED)

Five-Year Division Highlights (sales in FIM millions)

	1981	1982	1983	1984	1985
Share of Amer Group sales	16%	21%	21%	20%	8%
Personnel	244	254	249	237	230
Profit rating[a]	Good	Good	Good	Good	Satis.
SPORTING GOODS					
Sales:					
Koho (Finland)	35.3	35.5	37.1	40.9	40.5
AmerSport International	44.6	51.1	60.7	70.6	69.8
AmerSport USA	15.2	16.9	25.6	43.4	38.0
Less internal sales	11.6	17.2	15.2	10.9	8.7
Division *total* sales	83.6	86.4	108.1	144.0	139.6
Share of Amer Group sales	14%	13%	14%	16%	5%
Personnel	471	375	646	542	433
Profit rating[a]	Fair	Loss	Loss	Fair	Loss
MARKETING UNITS					
Sales:					
Golden Leaf	8.1	32.3	37.1	42.0	39.3
Flowers and plants	22.2	24.6	26.8	34.4	44.1
Other	18.8	24.3	28.7	12.4	—
Division *total*	69.1	81.2	92.6	88.8	83.4
Share of Amer Group sales	11%	12%	12%	10%	3%
Personnel	118	123	131	101	107
Profit rating[a]	Fair	Fair	Fair	Good	Loss
KORPIVAARA					
Sales:					
Vehicles				1,149.1	1,389.7
Metals				45.7	51.1
Plastics				24.7	30.1
Other operations				12.2	41.0
Less internal sales					30.0
Division *total* sales				1,231.7	1,481.9
Share of Amer Group sales					57%
Personnel				745	816
Profit rating[a,b]				—	Good
MARIMEKKO					
Division *total* sales				109.2	102.1
Share of Amer Group sales					4%
Personnel				434	397
Profit rating[a,b]				—	Loss

[b]Marimekko and Korpivaara were acquired in 1984; profit rating is not applicable.

share in the total Finnish cigarette market, with Philip Morris products accounting for roughly 90 percent of sales.

Amer's chief competitors were Rettig, a Finnish company that held a license agreement with R. J. Reynolds, and British American Tobacco, a foreign-owned company. In 1970 Amer was the smallest tobacco company in Finland, but in 1974, after two strategic pricing moves to match prices with the competitive Rettig brand, Amer's market share jumped from 27 to 42 percent. Ever since, Amer had continued to gain on competitors.

A tobacco law passed in 1977 banned all cigarette advertising in Finland. Amer responded by increasing its sales force and, because of its already established high-market-share position, was not hurt by this legislation. "Big brands and brand groups advertise themselves," commented one tobacco executive. "In theory, the ban helps international brands, which continue to benefit from outside promotions, and it prevents competitors from successfully launching new products." Amer's cigarette prices increased whenever the government imposed a higher consumer sales tax, with no effect on the consumption level.

The total Finnish cigarette market had shown an increase of 8 percent since 1980, with a leveling off in 1984 and a slight decrease in 1985. Consumption was expected to remain the same in spite of a 5 percent price increase in January 1985. The trend toward quitting smoking had thus far not affected Amer's sales. Jukka Ant-Wuorinen, vice president of marketing, speculated that young smokers were replacing the "quitters," who tended to be over age 40.

The division also manufactured and sold Clan pipe tobacco and Rizla cigarette tobacco on a small scale, as well as filter cigars and cigarette filters for export.

Amer-Brokers was a small subsidiary unit that marketed confectionary and Kodak products under agreements with its principals. Products ranged from After Eight, Toffo, and KitKat chocolates, Swedish desserts and berry puddings to films and cameras sold in stores dealing in perishable goods. The unit planned to expand the sales organization to cover the entire country and to develop the product range by entering new cooperative agreements.

The tobacco division accounted for 13 percent of Amer Group's total net sales. Division net sales had been steadily increasing over the previous four years, and profit history had been rated "good." (See Exhibit 6 for an explanation of profit-rating terms.)

EXHIBIT 6

Amer Group Profitability Definitions

"Fair"—operating profit before depreciation is sufficient to cover the costs of the central administration, interest expense, taxes, and depreciation.

"Satisfactory"—operating profit before depreciation, in addition to the above, covers dividends, depreciation based on current cost, and the need for additional working capital caused by inflation.

"Good"—operating profit before depreciation, in addition to the above, is sufficient to cover the need for an increase in Amer Group's shareholders' funds.

"Loss making"—the criteria for fair profitability are not met.

SOURCE: Annual Reports.

The tobacco division contributed a high percentage of profit to Amer Group in proportion to sales volume. Whether Amer-Tupakka would be classified as a "cash cow" was disputed, because Amer Group was still investing in the business, market share was still gaining, and profits continued to increase.

Amer-Tupakka had increased its market share by an average of two percentage points each year since 1981 and expected to hold its current 59 percent share over the next year. Pipe- and cigarette-tobacco market share remained about the same at 4 percent.

The Amer corporate culture had changed as the company grew and more acquisitions were made. The family spirit of the 1970s eroded as each division cultivated its own, but the tobacco division continued to have the closest relationship "in spirit" with Amer Group because of strong ties to the company origins. Amer-Tupakka was located on the same premises as the Group headquarters. According to one tobacco executive, "As the climate gets 'colder' in the cigarette business, and if tobacco companies' social image becomes more negative, Amer-Tupakka employees are likely to associate themselves more closely with Amer Group than the tobacco operation."

Communications Division

Amer Group's communications division consisted of several units involved in graphics and education. The primary unit was Weilin+Goos, the third-largest publisher in Finland, acquired by Amer in 1970. Weilin+Goos specialized in publishing and printing textbooks and encyclopedias, multivolume books, and general literature, as well as diaries and calendars. For nearly 100 years, the company had held monopoly rights to publishing all almanacs and calendars in Finland, but in 1985, Weilin+Goos lost these rights to a competitor. Because this loss of a core business was to take effect in 1988, the division was in the process of redefining its strategies.

Another unit, Finnreklama, specialized in the printing of high-quality art books and other printed materials for the Soviet Union. Another business unit of the division, Kiviranta, was a leading service company in advertising copy materials. It produced copy material for newspaper and magazine advertisements and printed advertising. Other profit centers, added to the communications division in 1983–1984, included a direct marketing company of multivolume reference books, the Time/System time-management product, and domestic appliances.

In line with the electronic publishing trend, the division had entered the software business with the establishment of Amersoft, which produced and marketed Finnish-language software for home and business use. In the area of education, the division had established the Amer Institute to produce and market training programs for sales personnel and for PC-user training. The Amer Institute was the first training establishment in Europe to be authorized by Lotus Development Corporation of the United States.

The graphics industry in Finland was characterized mostly by small firms engaged in publishing, printing, binding, and photo and text processing. The ten largest companies controlled a major share of the market. The biggest customers were the government (which included schools), mass media, and industrial and wholesale organizations.

In book publishing and printing, Weilin+Goos had two main competitors, both of which specialized more in novels and general literature. Weilin+Goos held roughly a 20 percent market share in primary-school textbooks and a smaller share in the secondary-school and adult-education segments.

Printed advertising had increased significantly over the previous five years. As a proportion of GNP in 1983, total advertising expenditure in Finland was the fifth highest in the world.[4]

The printing industry was still quite labor intensive, although in the last decade major investments had been made in high-capacity machines capable of computerized phototypesetting and offset printing. Wages and salaries were the largest cost item, but raw-material costs (notably paper) were also sizable. Because printing technology was advancing rapidly, the industry had to reinvest an average of 10 percent of its annual turnover.

The Finnish graphic arts industry was largely based on the domestic market; exports accounted for only about 5 percent of total production in 1985. Industry exports had grown steadily over the previous few years, however, and prospects for increasing exports were quite good as a result of technological advances and added capacity. One drawback in international markets was price competition, but the strengths of Finland's leading printing exporters included state-of-the-art machinery, reliability, expertise, and good transport connections.

The communications division had been in a growing and experimental phase, becoming very diversified within its own widespread industry. Weilin+Goos accounted for 82 percent of division revenues in 1985, and its profits had been "good," whereas the other units reported either "losses" or "satisfactory" results for the year.

Top management was unclear about the division's future direction. Division managers had established that internationalization of markets was one opportunity for growth, but they had not defined their objectives in terms of products and services. The printing business would obviously change with the loss of monopoly rights on calendar printing, and the publishing business needed to move away from its arts and culture orientation toward a stronger profit orientation.

The communications division represented 9 percent of Amer Group's net sales. Seppo Saario, the president of the division, was a seasoned executive who had been in the company for many years and, as an executive vice president of Amer Group, worked closely with Heikki Salonen.

Paper Merchanting and Converting Division

Amer Group established its paper merchanting (wholesaling) and converting (manufacturing) division in 1979 by acquiring the largest paper wholesaler in Finland. Operating under the name Amerpap, the division held a domestic market share of more than 40 percent. Distributed products included coated and uncoated fine papers, high-quality art papers, self-adhesive papers and vinyls, carbonless copying papers, and office, household, and packaging papers. The converting unit produced envelopes and other packaging materials and sold related products such as mail-handling equipment and printing ink. Some 67 percent of division sales were from papers for printing, 14 percent from office and other paper products, and 19 percent from converted products.

Amerpap's major buyers included commercial printers and manufacturers of office supplies, art supplies, and commercial paper products. Amer's paper suppliers were generally large mills that manufactured only a few grades and, in general, did not stock ready-made products. The end customers that used printing paper, however, generally wanted smaller units, used several grades of paper, and required rapid deliveries. Thus the challenge for wholesalers was to buy paper in large quantities and deliver it rapidly in smaller, individual orders. Printing papers were supplied primarily by four large domestic suppliers supplemented by some special, imported art papers and self-adhesive materials. Amerpap had sole agency rights with its foreign suppliers and had relations with domestic suppliers, both of which were important factors to success.

In Finland's wholesale paper business, total consumption of printing papers grew by 3 percent in 1985 and was expected to continue at that rate. The consumption of high-quality art printing papers continued to grow faster than the overall market, whereas growth in the consumption of office papers, which had been rapid in previous years, leveled off during the year. For the third year in a row, prices of both printing and office papers had risen more slowly than inflation, partly because of intense price competition within the industry. In an industry where margins were already thin, profitability had lowered for most paper wholesalers. In the case of Amer, gross margin had remained steady as a result of rationalization of production.

There were five or six large competitors in printing-paper wholesaling. There was little product differentiation in the assortment offered to wholesalers, price competitiveness was characteristic, and barriers to entry were low. The situation was somewhat different in the office stationery trade, but competition was equally sharp.

Olli Laiho, president of the paper division, believed, "Service to the customer is a principal factor to success in this business." Amerpap's state-of-the-art computerized control system enabled it to keep track of product availability, offer quick delivery, and handle complaints and problems efficiently. To stay competitive, the sales force used techniques such as calling on customers' customers to influence graphic-design paper specification.

In the paper-converting market, total consumption of mail wrappers (envelopes and letter bags) had grown over the previous few years at about 3 percent annually because of growth in direct marketing and catalog selling. The circle of clients in this market was quite large, with small individual deliveries. Investment in fixed assets was light when compared with other areas in paper manufacturing.

The division's share of Amer Group net sales was 8 percent in 1985, and the profit report for the year was "satisfactory." The management team at Amerpap was fairly new, and the company had recently moved to a modern warehouse facility with large-volume capacity. Laiho had been in the company for six years and had run the operation independently; Salonen's interaction with the business had been minimal.

Sporting Goods Division

Amer Group's sporting goods division manufactured and sold ice hockey sticks and equipment under the Koho and Canadien trademarks, as well as motocross equipment. The division began with exports from a factory in Finland and developed an international sales network and overseas manufacturing, with several operations in Finland, another factory and management office in Quebec, and a sales and distribution company in New York. "It was a rough start with the North American operations, but we saw a great future in the leisure industry as free time was increasing," said Salonen. There were problems with Koho competing against its fellow product, Canadien, and with integrating the business. After the appointment of a new president and a reorganization, the business had started to recover, but excess capacity was a lingering problem.

During the 1984–1985 financial period, Amer Group was the largest manufacturer of ice hockey sticks in the world, with a 34 percent market share in Western countries. For ice hockey equipment, Amer Group was the largest manufacturer in Europe and the second largest in North America. Of the division's total sales, about 91 percent were outside Finland.

The market for ice hockey–related products was narrow and, of course, seasonal. Industry profitability was weak on the whole, and business conditions were further aggravated by tough price competition. To combat these difficulties, companies were moving toward increased use of subcontracted manufacture in low-cost labor countries and increasing the marketing of products used in summer sports. Many hockey-stick companies were owned by larger companies that could absorb the profit losses.

The principal market area for ice hockey sticks and equipment was North America, where 1985 sales fell below the level of the previous year. One Amer executive speculated that the hockey market was shrinking as competing leisure sports were gaining, and that would-be hockey players were losing interest because of increasing violence in the game.

Product development in sticks had been aimed at replacing the traditional wood structures with more durable and lighter plastic. Amer's Koho factory was progressing with this trend; 77 percent of its manufactured sticks contained a synthetic blade. Growth in sales of fully synthetic sticks continued, but the long-term effect of greater durability in sticks would lead to a reduction in total volume sold.

Sporting goods represented 5 percent of Amer Group net sales. The profit rating was "poor" for 1985. The division had been unprofitable throughout most of its history, but Amer Group was reluctant to retreat from its first step toward internationalization.

Marketing Units Division

In 1978, Amer's top management decided to consolidate several small profit centers into a separate import/marketing division, specializing in consumer goods. Of three marketing units in the division, the largest was Golden Leaf, which marketed consumer durables such as Seiko watches and clocks, Pulsar watches, Lorus alarm clocks, Casio calculators, and Montblanc and Zebra pens. The consumable product range included Rizla cigarette papers and cigarette machines and Ventti cigarette filters. Watches and clocks were distributed through watchmakers and jewelers, calculators and pens through bookshops and stationers, and consumable goods through nationwide wholesale chains.

Another business unit sold cut flowers, some of which were cultivated in Finland and the rest imported from various suppliers in the Netherlands, Italy, Spain, West Germany, Thailand, the United States, and Denmark, where Amer had a subsidiary company. In addition to cut flowers, this unit also sold pots, soil, plant nutrients, and flower-arrangement materials. A subsidiary export company, known as Fionia, was located on the isle of Fyn in Denmark and exported plants to continental Europe and Scandinavia.

Because of poorer-than-expected Christmas sales and consequent overstocking, 1985 sales of watches and clocks fell by 10 percent. Furthermore, consumers were favoring watches in the cheaper price range. Cigarette rolling was on the decline, which led to a 6 percent reduction in the total market for cigarette papers in 1985. Consumption of flowers was trending upwards, however, which was reflected in an

11 percent increase in wholesale purchases in 1985; but profitability in that industry was susceptible to energy-price fluctuations and high energy consumption during severe weather.

Marketing units accounted for 3 percent of Amer Group net sales and reported a loss in 1985. The division, primarily a distribution network, did not generate much discussion inside the Amer organization. One Amer executive simply referred to it as a "carousel," because three division presidents had been rotated through the unit over the 1982–1986 period.

Marimekko

Perhaps the best-known Finnish trademark internationally, Marimekko was a designer, manufacturer, and distributor of high-quality interior-decorating textiles, linens, other fabrics, and kitchenware, as well as ready-to-wear clothing and related accessories. The clothing line included cotton dresses, jersey and knitwear, shirts, canvas bags, and accessories, mostly for women. The products were frequently characterized by brightly colored, graphically forceful patterns and geometric designs (see Exhibit 7).

Amer Group acquired a majority holding in Marimekko at the beginning of 1985. Several Amer Group employees viewed the acquisition as "Heikki's baby." (Salonen had been a member of Marimekko's board of directors for several years prior to the acquisition).

Marimekko, once a family business, had been built on dreams, designs, ideology, and individuality. The public had an image of Marimekko as more of a "cultural phenomenon" than a business, yet Marimekko had been exposed to the harsh realities of the business world.

The company was established in the early 1950s, and the first ten years of operation were characterized by a growth and expansion so rapid that it gave rise to almost unlimited confidence in the future. Uncontrolled growth led to increasing debts and general costs, and the capital shortage turned into financial crisis by 1968. After a radical retrenchment and restructuring, the company was eventually restored to its health and went public in the mid-1970s.

Marimekko was very much a personal reflection of Armi Ratia, its artistic and creative founder. The culture she bred in the organization was still alive, even several years after her death. Her spirit was reflected in one of her memos to the staff, written in April 1975 (see Exhibit 8, p. 19.21).

The strengths on which Marimekko was built were also some of the weak threads in its unraveling. Armi Ratia stated from the beginning, "We would not court the public's favour by making the sort of garments we thought they wanted but by creating a totally new line, designed to our taste." One of the chief designers commented, "It is my job to educate the public's taste." Marimekko had constantly strived to keep its distance from international trends and popular fads. In one sense, this philosophy worked: the company set trends. In other ways, it was detrimental: Marimekko had products that could be easily imitated at far cheaper prices, albeit with a quality difference. In essence, Marimekko had been riding on its established trademark for many years and did not adopt the changes occurring throughout the industry—competitive price and product and low contract labor outside Finland.

Marimekko was a classic example of Finnish design and lifestyle, which was part of the "popular" Scandinavian look. Markets for this theme were well defined, but competitors were not so clearly identified. There were many specialty clothing

EXHIBIT 7

Example of Marimekko Garment

SOURCE: *Phenomenon Marimekko,* Amer Group, Finland, 1986.

and interior-design looks and many indirect competitors with varying themes. "It is difficult to formulate a general strategy, because the competitors are different in different markets. Our strategic problem is centered around the difficulty of finding a place in changing markets while maintaining the legendary Marimekko image," commented one executive.

EXHIBIT 8

Armi Ratia's Memo to Marimekko Staff

Marimekko Oy
Helsinki
21 April 1975

In order that we don't have to use our last shirt to sail through the threatening storms of this working life, I seriously suggest that each one of us at Marimekko reads this memo and STARTS ACTING ACCORDINGLY AND TAKES SOME INTELLIGENT MEASURES IN HIS OR HER OWN FIELD.

We are not in any immediate danger. We have time. And this we intend on using to dig our defenses. How is it these military terms creep in? Ha ha.

The matter about which I am talking sounds distressing, but we stand before it together, as a company, as individuals. We, like young upstarts, have been living beyond our means on all fronts; and savings, from money for food to the market in houses, have been scarce and battered by inflation. NOW WE MUST SAVE. The banks have closed their doors. The reserve fund is exhausted. We're running out of means. BUT NOT OUT OF TRICKS. OR FAITH. OR HOPE. WE'LL MANAGE AGAIN, BUT WE'LL HAVE TO PUT EVERYTHING BEHIND IT.

Everybody, try to save in the right way. From paper to electricity. From decorations to beauty. Photos to flowers and cloth to costs. Save time, not thoughts. Draw patterns, learn better the parts of the whole. So we'll survive and nobody will be crowing over our defeat.

With best wishes,
Armi Ratia

Source: *Phenomenon Marimekko*, Amer Group, Finland, 1986.

Marimekko owned several retail stores and also marketed through licenses and franchises (7 domestic and 13 overseas licensed manufacturers). A West German subsidiary, Marimekko GmbH, was a distribution agent in Germany and central Europe. Marimekko, Inc., was the U.S. subsidiary responsible for coordinating operations in the United States.

The world clothing industry was undergoing a structural change. Production of clothing was shifting to newly industrialized countries, and several developing countries were launching their industrialization with clothing production. Companies in industrialized countries were increasingly sending part of their production to countries with low-cost labor.

Consumer buying behavior was also changing. The seasonal concept and demand for variety in clothing put pressure on retailers and the industry to update collections frequently and to extend clothing lines. The trend toward constantly changing lines translated to shorter time between orders and deliveries and emphasis on punctual deliveries. Flexibility in clothing manufacturers' activities was becoming a more important competitive factor.

Because of their inability to be price competitive, Finnish clothing manufacturers had been losing market share in the European markets since 1981. They had not been able to control rising labor costs. Marimekko was no exception, and its clothing had always been perceived as expensive. The clothing industry was characterized by falling operating margins, evidenced by a drop in 1983 to an average of 6 percent, with no improvement in 1984 or 1985.

Marimekko's net sales, which were down 7 percent from the previous period, accounted for 4 percent of Amer Group's consolidated net sales in 1985. The company reported a loss during the financial year. Because of Salonen's representation on its board, and management and financial problems in the company, Marimekko was one of Amer's more closely monitored subsidiaries.

Korpivaara

Amer Group acquired a company larger than itself with the acquisition of Korpivaara, the oldest and largest importer of cars in Finland. Korpivaara, established in 1917, was a family-owned business until 1984, when Amer acquired 88 percent of the company. The company was the exclusive importer in Finland of Toyota, Citroen, and Suzuki cars and vans, as well as Toyota forklift trucks and Lotus sports cars. Vehicles were sold or leased either wholesale or at one of Korpivaara's two retail sales units.

A relaxed management style at Korpivaara had developed from family history and influence on the company. Only in 1976 were profit centers and the first five-year strategies introduced; the company gradually adopted a mixture of "family" and more structured, "hard profit" management.

When the three Korpivaara brothers reached retirement age and decided to sell to Amer, the change of ownership was not easily accepted by those who were part of the strong culture. Korpivaara's management felt pressure from Amer Group in the integration process, in areas such as modification of reporting systems and additional reporting requirements. Friction developed, and some people, "afraid to be swallowed," left the company—including Korpivaara's president. According to one long-standing employee, "The president was unwilling to listen to shareholder voice in a cooperative way." By 1986 the initial friction had subsided, but although Korpivaara executives recognized the value of the image association with Amer Group in commercial and financial markets, they preferred to continue their autonomous operation as a separate legal entity.

Automotive trade was very competitive in Finland because of the relatively small market of 5 million people. Finland's high personal income-tax structure and 50 percent excise and sales tax on automobiles made price elasticity high. Therefore, pricing was the number-one marketing factor. Mikko Ennevaara, Korpivaara's current president, explained, "It is difficult to maintain profit, especially in retail, as margins are thin and volume is the key."

The number of passenger cars and vans registered in Finland had increased over the previous five-year period because of a relaxation of monetary controls (which made credit easier to obtain), a reduction in motor vehicle tax, and a stable price level for cars.

Of Korpivaara's three major auto brands, Toyota was the leading make in passenger cars, vans, leased cars, and company cars and had been the leader in new-car registrations in Finland for several years. Citroen's market share was increasing in Finland, however, with the introduction of new models and favorable exchange rates. Suzuki marketed in the small-car range where price competition was keenest. Korpivaara held a 16.5 percent market share of Finland's total car and van market.

A separate unit of Korpivaara supplemented the auto-distribution lines by operating a countrywide service network and by selling imported car parts and accessories. About half the unit's sales were made through car dealers, with the remainder through car accessory and tire stores. "This service network has become an important competitive advantage for Korpivaara, as has our tire accessory line. We sell tires for all auto makes, and the margins are relatively high," commented Ennevaara.

Korpivaara also had the equivalent of a financing unit, which financed leasing operations for the company, its regional dealers, and customers.

Although roughly 93 percent of Korpivaara's revenues came from the motor-vehicle operations, there were several other profit units within the division, which included metals, plastics, and a trading department. (See Exhibit 5 for a sales breakdown.)

The metals unit (2.8 percent of Korpivaara sales) comprised three leading companies in Finland specializing in the manufacture of compressors, welding equipment, and mechanized materials-handling robots for use in engineering workshops. The Nordic countries and the Soviet Union were important markets.

Executives at Korpivaara questioned whether the metals unit would be able to find real opportunities in the high-tech metals market. The operation was relatively small, making competition against larger companies' R&D difficult. One executive expressed a preference for "only wanting to be in automotive."

The plastics unit (1.6 percent of Korpivaara sales) manufactured plastic sheet for its own finishing operations and for wholesale, mainly in Finland. It also produced vacuum-molded and rotation-molded products such as ski boxes, partition walls, and floor coverings for vans, as well as Terhi brand boats, sold through area dealers.

Korpivaara's trading department (1.0 percent of Korpivaara sales) exported Finnish furniture and Finnish-designed products to Japan.

Total net sales of the Korpivaara division accounted for 57 percent of Amer Group's net sales during the 1985 financial period. The division's sales had been increasing steadily over the previous five years, and profitability overall had been "good."

Corporate Culture

One of Amer Group's objectives, related to its stated strategy "to market well-established, high-quality, branded products," was "to build corporate managerial power through training and development." If Amer's businesses, although unrelated, were within the same "characteristic framework," then Amer Group would be able to train managers uniformly and interchange them as necessary. For example, when an international acquisition was made, the objective was to be able to draw from a corporate management pool, if necessary, to place a representative at the subsidiary post. The process involved building up a resource bank, sending managers out, and bringing them back. "In order to use this process," one executive noted, "the company must be expanding all the time."

The explicit mission statement had been questioned by several managers at Amer Group, who believed that the statement did not cover the full spectrum of business units and products within the divisions: "Right now the 'high-quality, branded-product' image does not fit for all products—like paper, metals, or plastics." The philosophy that marketing know-how was the Group's competitive specialty was also questioned; one young executive claimed, "Our area of expertise is really in financial control and insight."

These two challenges raised the questions of what the corporate umbrella actually represented and what direction it was taking. One manager answered,

> The Group needs to redefine its mission and stick to its strategy. Are we a holding company or something more? Growth in some of our product areas is very limited. Amer is a holding company today even if it doesn't admit it. It is a legal unit owning a portfolio. We should go more specialized in one direction or state that we are a holding company, but a holding company has no competitive edge.

Historically, divisional management had not been involved in strategy formulation for Amer Group, but some believed that the divisions should participate more actively in this process. The general feeling about corporate culture was summed up by one manager's comment that "there is no umbrella over Amer Group as far as culture; the businesses are so diverse, and each division has its own separate culture." Most thought this situation was proper: The divisions should be encouraged to have their own images. At corporate headquarters, the perception of a common culture was not uniform. One executive stated, "Theoretically, the corporate umbrella prevails through our business mission." But from another, "In principle, people are thinking positively together, but there is no real synergy or concrete direction." As described by another executive, "We have a dynamic image towards hard values; the culture is based on cold facts—profits."

According to one recently hired employee, Amer Group's public image was overall quite strong, especially in commercial and financial markets. Many young business and economics graduates saw Amer as a progressive, efficient, and profitable organization. The hard-line profit orientation was not, however, looked upon favorably by all. For example, when Amer acquired Marimekko, the press communicated some resentment that Marimekko might lose its refined artistic qualities by being swallowed up. Amer Group's association with the tobacco business also did not convey a popular social image.

Internally, conflicts and tensions had resulted from the organization's fast-paced growth. "No one was really controlling the environment," as one manager put it. The corporate planning and finance departments were "competing" in some areas, and the two groups seemed to have different chemistries. One manager described the situation as "new versus old schools" (young, talented financial juniors versus experienced, more conservative veterans). Kai Luotenon, head of corporate planning, had worked closely with Salonen and was "very much an action man; he initiated and implemented many changes in the Amer Group and hired lots of 'new schoolers.'" One of Amer's division managers believed strongly that, in order to resolve these conflicts within the Group, some changes in personnel were necessary.

Corporate Leadership

Heikki Salonen, wearing a blue-and-green-striped Marimekko shirt, showed his relaxed style as he sat on the couch in his office suite. He had a casual demeanor, yet commanded respect. He seemed to have an open and friendly relationship with his managers, at the same time carrying a certain mystique. Salonen was not visible around the office; he used a separate entrance and was often there at odd hours. Several people in the organization commented on his style: "He has a strong, colorful personality with a lot of charisma in Finnish business circles as well as at Amer Group." "He is a man of vision, a clever, quick decision maker and an action man." "He steers through the person-to-person approach." "He is a dominant leader, with many people reporting directly to him." "He has built an empire and it is hard for him to delegate." "His major hobby is work." Salonen described his own style of management as "more art than science." (See Exhibit 9 for a brief résumé.)

Salonen noted that, when he had decided more tactical management control was needed for Amer Group, he looked within the organization and also contracted with a headhunter. He said of the COO whom he would appoint, "He must be strong but not the same type as I am, to balance things." Necessary qualifications were management and an international business background, strong in economics; Salonen believed the marketing philosophy could be learned. Age was also a factor he considered: "You cannot have everyone retiring at the same time. On the other hand, they cannot be too young—the organization must accept them." It was a careful search process; Salonen believed, "We can make money only by our people."

Because the 1984–1985 acquisitions had more than doubled the size of the company, Amer Group's executives had fully anticipated Salonen's taking on a second person to handle operational issues. According to one manager, three or four insiders were considered or expected themselves to be considered for the position. Another manager commented, "There were two princes [internally]. Heikki took an outsider—typical for him." General speculation was that, from Salonen's point of view, the choice among internal candidates was not obvious, and potential conflicts could be avoided by looking outside the organization. The need for restructuring was not questioned, and the announcement of a COO and new president was apparently well received.

Leif Ekstrom was described as a "professional manager" who would bring strong organizational, financial, and leadership skills to Amer Group. At 43, he was known in Finnish business circles as one of Scandinavia's "rising young stars." (See Exhibit 10, p. 19.28, for résumé.)

In the process of evaluating the company he would soon be managing, Ekstrom thought that Amer Group was financially sound, but he wondered how long the group of businesses, as currently structured, would continue to meet shareholder objectives. Moreover, not only would he have to work out the corporate-divisional relationship, but also his role vis-à-vis Heikki Salonen. Ekstrom realized the necessity for separate tasks and the practical division of responsibilities between CEO and COO, but he saw the relationship as delicately entwined in terms of vision and leadership of the company. "In your thinking, you must consider things that are not your responsibility; you must work as if you had both roles," he thought to himself. "Now, how will I make my mark, come April l?"

Endnotes

[1]Company public relations bureau.

[2]Summary taken from Amer Group planning documents and annual reports.

[3]*Trade with Finland,* Helsinki School of Economics, 1986.

[4]*Graphic Arts in Finland,* industry publication, 1985.

EXHIBIT 9

Heikki O. Salonen

Chairman and Chief Executive Officer, Amer Group
Curriculum Vitae (Abbreviated)

Born:	May 12th, 1933, Joroinen
Marital Status:	Wife Kirsti; children Marju and Jyri
Education:	B.Sc. (Econ.) from the Helsinki School of Economics in 1958 M.Sc. (Econ.) from the Helsinki School of Economics in 1962
Military Rank:	Lieutenant

Following Books Published:

The Distribution Channels in the Foreign Trade and the Factors Affecting Their Structure (Helsinki Research Institute for Business Economics, 1962).

The Selection of the Export Organization (Ekonomia—series, 1977).

Previous Occupations:

Finnish Institute of Management	
—One of the First Course Administrators	1961–1967
The Finnish Institute of Export	
—The First President	1962–1967
Saastamoinen-Yhtyma Oy Teollisuus	
—Executive Vice President	1968
—President and Member of the Board	1969–1972
Main Occupation: Amer Group Ltd.	
—President and Chief Executive Officer	1972– 1986
—Chairman and Chief Executive Officer	1986–
—Chairman of all Amer Group company boards	

Outside Board Memberships (selected list):

Helsinki Research Institute for Business Economics	(Chairman, 1978–1985)
Finnish Employer's General Group	(1982–)
Confederation of Finnish Industries	(1984–)
Pohjola–yhtiot (Finland's biggest insurance company)	(1983–)
MTV Oy (Finnish commercial TV)	(1975–)
Foundation for Economic Education	(1983–)
The Finnish Heart Association	(1983–)

(continued)

EXHIBIT 9 (CONTINUED)

Helsinki School of Economics	(Advisory Board, 1979–)
Mannerheim League for Child Welfare	(1979–)
Medical Research Foundation	(1978–)
Scout Foundation	(1980–)
World Wildlife Fund Finland (Board of Trustees)	(1980–)
The Finnish Institute of Export	(1976–)
Kansallis Banking Group	(1986–)
Employer's Association of Food Industries	(1985–)

EXHIBIT 10

Leif Ekstrom

President, Amer Group
Curriculum Vitae

Born:	October 31, 1942, Vantaa
Marital Status:	Wife Heli; children Thomas and Niklas
Education:	B.S. (Econ.) from the Swedish School of Economics and Business Administration in 1966
Military Rank:	Second Lieutenant
Career:	Kone Oy Manager, Finance, 1966–1969
	Kone Hissar Ab Sweden Manager, Finance, 1969–1972
	Kone Oy Lift Group Controller, 1972–1978
	Kone Oy Lift Group Director, 1978–1980
	Oy Wilh. Schauman Ab Vice President, Finance, 1980–1984
	Rauma-Repola Oy Executive Vice President, 1984–1986
Other Commissions:	
	Karhu-Titan Oy —Member of the Board
	The Association of Finnish Advertizers —Member of the Board
	Midland Montagu Osakepankki —Member of the Supervisory Board
Hobbies:	Golf, tennis, slalom

Case 20

Arvin Industries, Inc.

To Jim Baker, president and CEO of Arvin Industries, the visit to the Far East had been a means to two useful ends: the inclusion of the entire board and all the division presidents was more than symbolic of Arvin's commitment to globalizing its business, and the November 1985 board meeting in Taiwan had been a good forum to communicate to the division presidents the firm's new emphasis on external acquisitions.

It had been a nice getaway. The smells, the colors, the crowded streets—in fact, the whole way of life—were a world away from the quiet of Columbus, Indiana, where Arvin was headquartered. The Orient seemed strange, and, although far from home, it was good for a change.

Now, on the day before the flight back to the United States, as he rode through downtown Taipei in a rickshaw, Baker reflected on the company's past and thought about how he would actually get his management team to buy into his vision for Arvin.

Arvin had been a conservative company for many, many years. Most division officers had come up through manufacturing and had generally been rewarded for being risk averse. "It was," Baker thought, "like pushing a noodle through a hole. You tell those people that 'cash is available, now do it,' but they have never done it before." So the issue was not simply one of implementing a new strategy. Baker believed a change of the culture of the company was needed. Arvin had to become more aggressive in the use of its plentiful resources.

"Easier said than done," he said to the rickshaw puller.

Company Background

In 1920 Richard H. Arvin invented the world's first automobile heater. Recognizing that he had a viable product but no resources to commercialize it, he formed a partnership with Indianapolis Air Pump, producer of hand-operated tire pumps, to gain access to its manufacturing and marketing facility. Within a few years, however, the pump maker bought the inventor's 50 percent share, ending Dick Arvin's association with the company.

Indianapolis Air Pump changed its name three times over the next 30 years before finally settling on Arvin Industries, Inc., in 1950. In the ensuing 20 years, Arvin solidified its position in the automotive market, entered the advanced electronics field with an acquisition, and established an overseas presence by building plants and offices in the Far East.

The Anderson Era

Gene Anderson joined Arvin in 1947. Born and bred in Indiana, Anderson worked his way up through manufacturing, became a plant manager in 1957, moved up to works manager of the automotive division in 1952, and then became vice president and general manager of that division in 1960. In 1961 Anderson was elected to the board of directors, was named one of the two executive vice presidents in 1968, and took over as the president and CEO in 1969. In December 1975, he was elected chairman of the board.

The most significant events during his tenure were (1) the decision to manufacture catalytic converters in an uncertain regulatory climate, (2) diversification beyond the core automotive business, and (3) changing the organization structure to a divisionalized form in 1973.

Catalytic Converters

In 1973, based on the rumors that Congress might mandate catalytic converters, Arvin took a gamble and invested more than $40 million to manufacture the new product. This move was significant; the previous annual capital investment had averaged about $5 million. Fortunately, the gamble paid off when the converters were mandated for 1975 model vehicles, positioning Arvin solidly into the automotive OEM market.

Diversification

At the beginning of the 1970s, more than 70 percent of the firm's revenues came from its core automotive OEM (original equipment manufacturer) business. This dependence on one business segment resulted in uneven financial performance but was not viewed as a significant threat to the firm until the Arab oil embargo of October 1973. The embargo led to a big slump in auto production, causing a major financial crisis for Arvin.

As a result of this experience, Arvin accelerated its efforts to diversify into businesses that were less cyclical but still offered opportunities that could be exploited with the firm's existing capabilities. Management decided to strengthen the firm's nonautomotive businesses through capital spending, internally developed new products, and acquisitions.

The success of the new corporate strategy was evident in the company's financial results between 1972 and 1977. During that period, revenues doubled, and the contribution of the nonautomotive groups to total operating profits went up from 4 percent to 28 percent.

By 1977 Arvin had become a leading supplier of original equipment to the Big Three in the auto industry and had a small presence in the replacement-parts market. Compact stereo was Arvin's flagship product in consumer electronics, and portable electric heaters gave it a good foothold in consumer housewares. The metals group provided the company with expertise in coating steel and aluminum coils and in sheet-metal stampings and assemblies. The applied technology group manufactured video equipment for adverse environmental conditions and special-purpose automated fabricating and assembly machinery; it also designed and installed security and process-control systems.

Divisionalization

During the course of diversifying, Arvin had begun to outgrow its centralized management structure. A need was felt to break the company into more manageable parts. Loren ("Chick") Evans, president of the North American automotive division, said, "The divisionalized approach to running the company had only really been put in place in about 1973. Those of us who were general managers before '73 really operated the business by running the engineering, the manufacturing, and the sales functions. All of the other support services were centralized. And, as we started growing in this period, we started having a lot of trouble because staff services could not keep pace. The staff would tend to give most attention to whoever made the most noise. So, naturally, the guys who ran the automotive business, the big business, got all the attention. We had to change that."

And changed it was. The staff functions devolved to the divisions so that the operating units could have more autonomy in conducting their businesses. In addition, Arvin continued the tradition of setting up plants of no more than 400 workers. While the new structure gave the impression of decentralization, in practice, most of the decision-making authority remained with the chief executive.

Other Management Concerns

In early 1977, in view of the heightened merger activity during the previous ten years, the board engaged White, Weld & Co. of New York to assess the vulnerability of Arvin to a hostile takeover. In a report to Anderson, the consultants pointed out that the firm's low price-to-earnings (P/E) ratio (five times), strong cash position, high return on equity (ROE), and highly fragmented shareholder base were some of the weaknesses that could lead to a hostile takeover attempt. On the other hand, the report suggested, the outstanding results of 1976, the relatively high financial leverage (44 percent at the end of 1976), the highly concentrated and cyclical nature of Arvin's business, the significant dollar value of its assets, the Indiana antitakeover statute, and the defensive measures in Arvin's corporate bylaws were significant deterrents to any unwelcome bid.

White, Weld urged Anderson to strengthen Arvin's defenses, however. The firm recommended that Arvin set up a defense unit consisting of internal management and outside professionals, strengthen its relationships with existing shareholders, improve earnings per share via an aggressive investment program, and consider creating a new series of preferred stock that, when issued, would give the holders a two-thirds class vote on any consolidation, merger, or sale of significant assets.

Baker, then executive vice president, said, "At that time the kinds of acquisitions that were going on were Harry Grey's [United Technologies'] unfriendly takeover of Otis and Carrier—the kind that seemed to be very logical business combinations. Even though they were unfriendly, they seemed to make a lot of sense. Yet, we did not want to be subject to one of those."

Subsequent to the report, Baker started to build the firm's expertise in takeover defense. The law firm of Wachtel, Lipton, Rosen & Katz was engaged to provide the legal perspective; Hill & Knowlton was engaged for financial public relations; and for investment banking services, White, Weld was retained. Merrill Lynch eventually replaced White, Weld after it acquired them.

The rationale for these moves was explained by Baker: "When the raider strikes, oftentimes it is what they call a Saturday Night Special or a Bear Hug—you have such a short period of time to respond and react and defend yourself that you have to do as many prior preparations as possible to put yourself in some kind of a balance with the guy that has his arms around you."

Late 1970s Operating Performance

In 1978 the business-segment classification was changed from one based on technology and product characteristics to one based on end markets. The new categories were automotive, appliances and hardware, government and utility, and commercial and industrial. The highlight of 1978 was the acquisition of Calspan for its research and development capabilities, which were to solidify Arvin's presence in the important government segment.

The year 1979 was tough for the company. Price competition intensified in the consumer electronics business, and a 60 percent capacity expansion in the coil-coating operation coincided with a decline in demand for automotive precoated metal as domestic production of light trucks and cars dropped 11 percent. Sales increased only slightly from $489 million to $493 million in 1979, and earnings dropped from $23.1 million to $20.4 million. Arvin's five largest customers accounted for approximately 70 percent of its total revenues for the year.

The depressed state of the automotive industry and continuing high inflation caused a carryover of pressure on margins into 1980. A 28 percent decrease in the North American production of cars and light trucks contributed to a 13 percent drop in sales to $428.8 million in 1980 and a decline in income to $7.6 million.

Arvin management decided that the automotive industry was experiencing not just the normal cyclical fluctuations but was, in fact, caught in a period of revolutionary economic and market changes. Rising gasoline prices and the poor state of the economy had shifted consumer preference toward smaller, fuel-efficient, imported cars. Foreign manufacturers, notably Japanese firms, had increased their market share from about 16 percent six years earlier to nearly 27 percent in 1980.

To deal with this industry realignment, Arvin recognized that, even as it consolidated its share of business on new models emerging from Detroit, it needed to develop supplier relationships with foreign automakers who established plants in the United States.

In 1981 Arvin put major cost-reduction programs in place as the firm tightened up its operations. Large numbers of people were laid off, and three automotive plants were closed. At the end of the year, each of the six operating divisions showed a profit, and corporate earnings had climbed to $12 million on a 15 percent increase in total sales. Revenues from the five largest customers were 62 percent of the total (see Exhibits 1 to 3 for financials).

Change of Guard

On April 1, 1981, the 12-year reign of Eugene Anderson came to an end as he retired from operations and Executive Vice President James K. Baker stepped up to become president. Baker became CEO of the company on November 1; Anderson retained his position as chairman of the board.

Baker was not the flamboyant personality one would expect to find in the rising star of a *Fortune* 500 company. He was a quiet man who shunned media attention

EXHIBIT 1

Arvin Industries, Inc. Income Statement (figures in thousands of dollars)

	1984	1983	1982	1981	1980	1979	1978
NET SALES	781,986	600,605	513,905	495,136	428,849	493,211	489,079
COSTS AND EXPENSES							
Costs of goods sold	663,085	508,265	434,890	421,560	363,129	410,562	397,315
Selling, general and administrative	62,624	59,437	58,482	51,406	48,615	45,570	40,383
Interest expense	7,801	7,960	8,356	7,684	7,861	9,075	9,088
Other income—net	(5,212)	(5,738)	(6,335)	(7,699)	(2,198)	(3,960)	(2,824)
	728,298	569,924	495,393	472,951	417,407	461,247	443,962
Earnings before income taxes	53,688	30,681	18,512	22,185	11,442	31,964	45,117
Income taxes	23,461	12,343	7,646	9,761	3,854	11,542	22,051
NET EARNINGS	30,227	18,338	10,866	12,424	7,588	20,422	23,066
Return on sales	3.87%	3.05%	2.11%	2.51%	1.77%	4.14%	4.72%
Return on equity	15.20%	10.01%	6.16%	7.15%	4.40%	12.26%	15.41%
Common shares outstanding	11,352	11,343	10,519	10,280	9,936	9,795	9,668
Primary EPS* ($)	2.59	1.58	0.93	1.09	0.61	1.92	2.24
Cash dividend per common share* ($)	0.75	0.74	0.75	0.75	0.75	0.68	0.66
Book value per share*	$ 17.84	$ 16.05	$ 15.61	$ 15.49	$ 15.30	$ 15.56	$ 14.44
Stock price at year end*	20.30	17.17	13.96	11.36	n/a	n/a	n/a

*NOTE: All per-share numbers are adjusted for a three-for-two stock split in 1984.

and believed in being effective by putting the pieces together behind the scenes. After getting a bachelor's degree in mathematics and physics from DePauw University in 1953 and serving in the U.S. Army for a few years, he had decided to get an MBA at Harvard in 1956. There his silent nature soon got him in trouble. He was pulled up by the first-year faculty for not participating in the class discussions and was told he might not get through the program. Recalling this experience, he said, "The classes were 90 in size. It was very easy for someone to hide behind the other 89 and not participate, and I was one of those. It was not very long before professors called you and said you had to participate."[1]

Baker's reserved style carried into his professional career at Arvin, which he joined upon graduation. Brooke Tuttle, director of the Columbus Economic Development Board and a close Baker friend, once said, "Jim Baker's perception of talking to the public is like Woody Hayes's perception of the forward pass. Three things can happen and two of them are bad."[2]

Success for Baker at Arvin was rapid, however. By 1960 he was general manager of Arvinyl and in 1966 was named a vice president. Two years later, he was named one of two executive vice presidents and elected to the board.

EXHIBIT 2

Arvin Industries, Inc. Balance Sheet (figures in thousands of dollars)

	1984	1983	1982	1981	1980	1979	1978
ASSETS							
Current assets:							
Cash and temporary investments	21,031	30,098	26,664	38,296	32,242	32,424	40,380
Accounts receivable—net	87,435	70,817	59,186	51,454	66,726	68,273	64,846
Inventories	81,545	66,570	65,108	64,053	72,021	68,669	80,482
Other current assets	10,337	9,164	9,760	8,693	2,595	2,748	2,608
Total current assets	200,348	176,649	160,718	162,496	173,584	172,114	188,316
Other noncurrent assets	17,860	20,527	20,753	17,702	10,752	10,871	8,889
Property, plant and equipment:							
Land	2,400	2,732	2,635	1,908	2,034	2,162	2,242
Buildings and leasehold improvements	66,997	70,743	68,061	62,037	61,510	59,804	54,905
Machinery and equipment	173,712	153,582	145,494	132,655	130,729	120,645	94,668
Construction in progress	4,871	2,820	1,371	1,270	1,482	3,620	14,642
	247,980	229,877	217,561	197,870	195,755	186,231	166,457
Less: Allowance for depreciation	116,115	103,978	93,585	86,556	77,656	67,839	59,058
	131,865	125,899	123,976	111,314	118,099	118,392	107,399
Special tools, etc.—net	4,382	4,980	4,764	1,890	2,164	1,749	3,444
Total noncurrent assets	136,247	130,879	128,740	113,204	120,263	120,141	110,843
Total assets	354,455	328,055	310,211	293,402	304,599	303,126	308,048
LIABILITIES AND SHAREHOLDERS' EQUITY							
Current liabilities:							
Short-term debt	4,716	6,485	6,646	5,258	5,471	5,262	4,636
Accounts payable	35,294	23,975	17,091	14,176	27,652	20,100	24,795
Accrued expenses	28,135	23,680	19,798	15,865	13,054	14,033	12,463
Income taxes payable	2,667	2,728	2,954	4,672	3,164	2,789	4,934
Total current liabilities	70,812	56,868	46,489	39,971	49,341	42,184	46,828
Noncurrent liabilities:							
Deferred income taxes	11,220	9,052	6,561	5,782	5,085	4,359	3,175
Long-term debt	63,773	73,105	79,949	72,165	78,197	83,684	97,887
Total noncurrent liabilities	74,993	82,157	86,510	77,947	83,282	88,043	101,062
Shareholder's equity:							
Capital stock:							
Preferred shares (no par value)	6,368	7,067	13,280	15,564	19,071	19,579	19,607
Common shares ($2.50 par value)	28,735	18,905	17,531	17,132	16,561	16,324	16,113
Capital in excess of par value	30,462	38,730	31,447	29,482	26,545	25,861	25,465
Retained earnings	145,779	124,679	115,276	113,306	109,799	111,135	98,973
Cumulative translation adjustments	(572)	(351)	(322)	none	none	none	none
Common shares in treasury (at cost)	(2,122)	none	none	none	none	none	none
Total shareholders' equity	208,650	189,030	177,212	175,484	171,976	172,899	160,158
Total liabilities and shareholders' equity	354,455	328,055	310,211	293,402	304,599	303,126	308,048

EXHIBIT 3

Arvin Industries, Inc. Financial Information by Business Segments

	1984	1983	1982	1981	1980	1979	1978
NET SALES							
Automotive	$408,269	$338,276	$281,178	$281,687	$258,133	$325,613	$340,722
Consumer	225,983	136,397	119,716	97,576	93,896	88,118	87,578
Government	94,512	84,069	77,800	75,400	41,205	44,326	32,910
Industrial	53,222	41,863	35,211	40,473	36,615	35,154	27,869
Total net sales	$781,986	$600,605	$513,905	$495,136	$429,849	$493,211	$489,079
INCOME FROM OPERATIONS							
Automotive	$41,392	$29,869	$17,602	$20,458	$13,844	$30,594	$42,017
Consumer	15,984	5,606	6,599	5,059	7,205	7,059	11,385
Government	4,986	3,245	1,476	2,754	704	1,866	1,281
Industrial	4,014	3,181	2,594	154	(760)	3,197	1,835
Total from operations	$66,376	$41,901	$28,271	$28,425	$20,993	$42,716	$56,518
Less:							
Interest	(7,801)	(7,960)	(8,356)	(7,684)	(7,861)	(9,075)	(9,088)
General corporation expense	(4,887)	(3,260)	(1,403)	1,444	(1,690)	(1,677)	(2,313)
Total EBT	$53,688	$30,681	$18,512	$22,185	$11,442	$31,964	$45,117
IDENTIFIABLE ASSETS							
Automotive	$167,653	$154,645	$152,118	$162,978	$176,722	$185,190	$176,373
Consumer	88,013	78,617	60,455	45,223	43,353	38,933	40,293
Government	20,549	18,474	18,644	20,590	23,189	24,118	16,344
Industrial	30,438	27,465	25,822	27,431	25,991	18,703	13,278
Total assets	$341,255	$319,133	$301,806	$299,000	$303,862	$305,587	$291,905
DEPRECIATION AND AMORTIZATION							
Automotive	$ 9,169	$ 8,816	$ 8,903	$ 9,430	$ 9,185	$10,554	$10,019
Consumer	5,450	4,579	3,243	1,942	1,954	1,524	1,292
Government	949	761	950	803	709	633	606
Industrial	1,487	1,254	976	990	925	652	495
General corporation	13	52	34	33	35	13	7
Total depreciation and amortization	$17,068	$15,462	$14,106	$13,198	$12,808	$13,376	$12,419
ADDITIONS TO PROPERTY, PLANT, AND EQUIPMENT							
Automotive	$18,375	$ 8,143	$ 4,460	$ 3,734	$ 8,466	$17,943	$19,105
Consumer	6,670	7,435	24,392	2,035	2,530	2,158	1,823
Government	1,363	1,376	1,002	652	1,045	1,257	4,764
Industrial	1,122	878	2,379	735	1,764	2,336	1,852
General corporation	43	241	5	24	0	0	0
Total capital additions	$27,573	$18,073	$32,238	$ 7,180	$13,805	$23,694	$27,544

Baker was active in Indiana community affairs. At the time of taking over the leadership of Arvin in 1981, he was the chairman of the Associated Colleges of Indiana, a trustee of DePauw University, and a director of the Columbus-area chambers of commerce. His business affiliations included directorships at Columbus Bank and Trust Company, Norlin Corporation, and Indiana National Corporation.

Arvin Game Plan for the 1980s

Baker's appointment as chief executive was viewed as a significant break from the past. Chuck Watson, president of Arvinyl division, noted, "Prior to Jim taking the head role in the company, Arvin had been run by the automotive people and by [the] manufacturing people. When Jim took over, he came from a broader background within the company and was probably more oriented towards finance and sales. That he came from the nonautomotive area must be considered a big change within the company."

Baker inherited difficult business conditions. The national economy, which had begun a downward slide almost three years earlier, was still laboring under the burden of unprecedented double-digit interest rates, and the third-quarter recovery in auto sales appeared to have stalled in the fourth.

In his first letter to the shareholders, Baker articulated the need for the firm to take the offensive. He outlined a three-pronged thrust for the 1980s: new products, meaningful presence in the global automotive market, and creative development of new businesses. With regard to new business development, he said, "We intend to acquire product lines that are compatible to our own. We want to find products with a satisfactory market share and high value added. Some of these additions may give us an expanded overseas presence."

One of Baker's first actions in his new role was to make, in his words, "a very hard-nosed assessment of how good we were and how weak we were in certain areas. We used that to build what we called the Arvin Game Plan, and we published it, much to the delight of the financial community. [See Exhibit 4.] We started publishing that in the 1982 annual report and have carried that almost unchanged ever since."

Chuck Watson recalled, "In addition to the outside world, it was the first time that everybody within the company had seen an articulated game plan, or set of objectives.... That would be representative of Jim Baker: setting some goals, setting some direction, and telling the world about it.

"One of the things that Jim did was just significant as the dickens. At one point, when the U.S. automotive industry was going down the tube, he made a strong statement that Arvin would be in the automotive OEM business. And that was really significant because many manufacturers were bailing out of the U.S. automotive OEM business, and he made a recommitment to stay."

Realignment at the Top

Once in the driver's seat, Baker decided that the reporting relationships of the senior executives ought to reflect his own management philosophy—that of more autonomy to the divisions. "April to November of 1981," Baker recalled, "I was the president but not CEO. I did some reorganizing and let go four top staff officers: the vice president of strategic planning, the treasurer, the controller, and house

EXHIBIT 4

The Arvin "Game Plan" for the 1980s

1. Maintain auto parts as the core business. Manage assets to proper capacity levels.
2. Increase exhaust replacement parts business through new products and acquisition.
3. Establish automotive presence in selected foreign countries.
4. Innovate new features and packaging concepts in home stereo products. Use electronics know-how to expand product lines into telecommunications, CATV, and energy areas.
5. Acquire new electronics product lines.
6. Continue Arvin leadership in portable electric heaters, and develop or acquire related products.
7. Fund aggressive research and product development in all operating divisions.
8. Manage metals group to provide cash for growth.
9. Manage advanced technology group in selected scientific areas, and provide technological support to other Arvin businesses.

SOURCE: 1982 Annual Report.

counsel. The controller was ready to retire, and I did not think that there was enough time to bring him up to speed with myself. Two of the four were not suitable team players and were not well regarded in the organization."

He then established the office of the president, which comprised three group vice presidents, the chief financial officer, the vice president of public affairs, and the vice president of administrative services. In essence, everybody reporting directly to the president was in this group.

Among the issues that the office of the president resolved were capital expenditures above threshold amounts, labor negotiations, and new product lines. These matters were routine, and the process was not new to the company; but Baker described it as "more regularly scheduled. The intention was to step up the pace. To do more things. To be more action oriented."

In addition, in order to have personal influence on the divisions, Baker created an executive staff, which was the office of the president plus the division presidents. "One of the important changes I made," he recalled, "was in the planning process. I never did feel that planning could be a staff function at the corporate level when you had so many divisions. That had to be done within the divisions and reviewed at the top level—note that I dismissed the vice president of strategic planning.

"One of the key elements in decentralized planning is that they [division executives] have to know what it is that you are looking for in the way of plans, what are the outside limits, how aggressive they should be. If they are too aggressive and it gets slapped down, they have wasted a lot of time in doing their plan. So you have to have a lot of discussion on what you as a CEO feel are the goals of the company in very specific terms, so that they know what their parameters are when they start their planning process." Executive staff meetings were a forum for these discussions.

Signs of Recovery

In 1982 prospects for a modest economic recovery appeared to be good. Short-term interest rates had dropped decisively in the middle of the year, and the accompanying rally in stock and bond prices was reassuring both as a precursor of improved economic performance and as evidence that the dramatic recovery made against inflation was viewed as durable. Arvin's annual sales increased slightly to break the $500 million mark. Net income, however, declined 12.5 percent to $10.9 million, reflecting carryover of the recessionary pressures from previous years.

About 10 percent of total 1982 sales came from new products, and this percentage was expected to increase during the remainder of the decade. Arvin introduced a whole new line of replacement exhaust parts manufactured in the United States for imported cars, whose growing industry segment accounted for a 28 percent market share in 1982. In addition, the firm entered the evaporative cooling business by purchasing the international metal products division from McGraw-Edison Company. The division's line of evaporative cooling products, said Baker, "shares a similar customer base, similar manufacturing processes, and energy-efficient characteristics with Arvin's existing heating and ventilating products." The new acquisition was renamed ArvinAir and formed the seventh operating division of the corporation.

The Jitters of Recession

Reflecting on his first year as the head of Arvin, Baker commented, "The thing that always escapes you, I think, is that the president's job looks much easier from even one chair away than it actually is. You are always surprised with how much responsibility you really feel when you step into that job. You realize that every person and every asset is essentially your responsibility, and the buck stops here....

"I was really shaken up by how difficult it was to operate in that '81–'82 time frame. We closed three plants quickly, while most of the other automotive suppliers waited for many months, and in some cases two or three years, before they adjusted their capacity to the new world of the 1980s.

"The major incentive for division presidents was cash generation—rather than cash being the responsibility of the treasurer. That gave all of us focus during a period of time. I didn't know what else to focus on. I wasn't bold enough to make any major moves.... It would have been wonderful to be able to do so, but I was not in the mood to make any major moves in 1981 or 1982.... It was a tough time and I was nervous, and I was not very bold, so cash management was the name of the game."

Chic Evans agreed: "It was not a period of growth but one of survival—being sure that we were being very wise."

Results of 1983

By the end of 1983, virtually all economic indicators were strongly positive, and most observers expected recovery to continue through 1985. Private housing starts had bottomed out more than a year earlier and had begun a strong upward surge in the July indicator. Automobile sales, another traditional end-of-recession leading indicator, had not yet given a clear upward signal, but there was considerable optimism based on lower interest rates and gasoline prices.

The year 1983 was good for Arvin. Sales increased 17 percent to cross $600 million, and net income shot up by $7.5 million to $18.3 million. Because of increasing raw-material prices and the inability of the company to pass on higher costs to the customers owing to intensifying competition, the 3 percent after-tax return on sales was far below the goal of 4.5 percent to 5 percent. The cash position, however, was strong at the end of the year, and the debt-to-capital ratio was less than 30 percent for the first time in ten years.

In the same year, Arvin solidified its presence in Brazil by restructuring COFAP, a joint venture to supply automotive parts in the Brazilian market. The expanded operations were to meet the needs of Arvin's two major U.S. OEM customers who were in the process of increasing their investments in Brazil.

Also in 1983, the board of directors gave approval for the formation of a joint venture with Belgium's Bosal International to manufacture tubular products from exotic materials. The new venture, with plants in West Germany, was to combine Arvin's catalytic-converter expertise with Bosal's manufacturing know-how and marketing expertise. This alliance would position Arvin against the day when Europe decided to mandate catalytic converters.

Clarifying his company's position regarding growth, Baker said at the annual shareholders' meeting, "While our long-range strategy is to use acquisitions and joint ventures to strengthen our business relative to competition, our diversification objective does not include assembling a group of businesses with an equal number of cyclical and contra-cyclical units... instead, it includes assembling a broad range of first-class customers who will ultimately provide us with the increased sales and profits we need to meet our goals."

Business Upturn

The accelerating economic expansion of 1984 helped Arvin set all-time records (see Exhibit 1). Each business segment expanded significantly, and the automotive proportion of sales declined to 52 percent. With sales as a measure, Arvin advanced from the 408th to the 355th place in the *Fortune* 500 ranking of the largest U.S. industrial corporations. Its ten largest customers accounted for 74 percent of total corporate revenues in 1984. Financially, Arvin was on a strong footing. Debt-to-capital dropped to less than 25 percent, and a healthy cash flow eliminated any need to borrow, despite significant working-capital outgo and capital expenditures to support higher sales.

To management, the year's performance was evidence of the success of its business strategies. While a favorable economic climate did help financial performance, the deliberate actions taken to contain costs, to improve productivity from investment in robotics and computerization, and to increase the flow of internally developed new products were beginning to pay off.

Internally developed new products remained the highest priority for the company. Sales of stainless-steel tubular manifolds (introduced in 1982), telecommunications products, newly designed compact stereo systems, and a larger number of fabricated metal parts for various industrial applications, to name only a few, accounted for more than $100 million of the 1984 sales volume.

In 1984 Arvin also made two additions to its business: the acquisition of AP de Mexico, S.A. de C.V., solidified its position as a supplier to automotive manufacturers and the aftermarket in Mexico, and the acquisition of Franklin Research Center strengthened the advanced research and testing business.

The Economic Landscape, 1980–1985

In addition to strengthening its business portfolio for a more secure future, in light of the merger wave that was gripping the U.S. financial markets during the 1980s, Arvin reinforced its position to ensure organizational independence. The latest merger activity was influenced by deregulation in certain industries, prevalence of divestiture transactions as conglomerates of earlier years rationalized their business portfolios, and an increasing frequency of leveraged buyouts facilitated by the availability of financing. In addition to the reinvigorating economy, other factors that contributed to the merger wave of the 1980s included (l) a changing political climate with the Reagan administration's stated policy of minimizing intervention in the free market; (2) stockmarket undervaluation of corporate assets coupled with financial innovations such as junk bonds; (3) the rise of arbitrageurs; and (4) the emergence of some very aggressive, financially astute deal makers.

The junk bond was created by Mike Milken of Drexel Burnham Lambert, Inc., to raise money for fledgling companies that did not have access to the traditional lending institutions. As Milken's idea gained acceptance among large institutional investors, he entered the takeover wars, providing empire builders with easy access to large sums of money. Drexel's power, according to one analyst, had been a "catalyst for a wave of large leveraged buyouts." He said, "Big companies used to worry only about takeover threats from other big companies. But with Drexel doing the financing, anybody long on ideas and short on capital is a threat."

A New Breed of Raiders

Sure enough, a handful of "takeover artists" began creating havoc in American board rooms. T. Boone Pickens was one such person. A sharp critic of senior managers of public corporations and a self-appointed champion of shareholders' rights with uncompromising ideas about how managers ought to run their corporations, Boone Pickens made a fortune buying oil companies for their undervalued assets and restructuring the assets of the acquired corporations. He believed in ownership for those in management positions, because, he claimed, professional managers often adopted a "me first, stockholder second" attitude. He boasted that he had played a large part in restructuring corporate America, which, he claimed, would make the country competitive again.

Carl Icahn was another raider who made managers nervous. He, too, scoffed at management ineptness and projected himself as a savior of stockholders' interests. His modus operandi was also to make hostile bids for companies he thought were undervalued because they were run by people he considered venal or nincompoops. At least some of his millions, however, came by greenmailing target companies.

Icahn's notable assault was on TWA in May 1985, when he was persuaded by the pilots' and machinists' unions to fight Frank Lorenzo of Texas Air, who, in turn, was lined up as a white knight by TWA's management. Lorenzo's higher bid was turned down by the board on August 20, and Icahn obtained a major piece of the airline.

While Pickens had a "mission" to protect the rights of the "little guy," and Icahn made similar altruistic claims, the Belzberg brothers of Canada made no bones about their intentions to make a quick buck. Controversial and wealthy, the Belzbergs were opportunistic acquisitors who regarded their capital as too risky to be invested in anything but the safest tangible assets. To assure a return on their investments, they usually controlled 4 percent to 8 percent of their target's stock before attempting a takeover. According to one report, "'Sam Belzberg' whispered over the phone is enough to send the managers of... North American companies into wild-eyed panic—and prompt... arbitrageurs to begin merrily snapping up shares of the next Belzberg victim."[3]

By 1984 the Belzberg brothers had built a huge conglomerate with interests in financial services, real estate, energy, and manufacturing. Most of their millions came from greenmailing their prey, such as their 1984 raid on Gulf Oil (jointly with Pickens), which earned them more than $50 million. In December of 1984, they threatened to take over Scovill Corporation on Christmas Eve. The investment community was surprised when, instead of greenmailing Scovill, they actually acquired it in January 1985.

"The Porcupine Defense"

In the face of this heightened takeover environment, Arvin decided that even as the company was being managed for survival during the 1981–1982 recession, a select group of company executives and outside consultants should meet occasionally to review Arvin's defenses. By 1985 the company had installed a range of barriers: a fair-price provision was in place to mitigate pressure on shareholders at the time of a tender offer; directors were elected to the board on staggered terms; stock was purchased and put in the savings and pension plans, to be voted by the (presumably friendly) trustees; and a supermajority provision, requiring approval of 80 percent of the board before change in control, was placed in the company charter. These defensive measures had evolved piecemeal over a decade, as the issue of defense was not at the top of management's agenda. However, these did represent the state of the art in takeover defense at the time.

Reacting to criticisms that each of these measures had inherent weaknesses, Fred Meyer, vice president of public affairs, said, "We are using what I call the Porcupine Theory. A porcupine with one quill, anybody can grab. A porcupine with hundreds of quills, however, causes some discomfort when grabbed. So the thing to do is to get [the defenses] all together, and that means that you have more items that a raider must deal with."

Arvin in 1985

The prospects for 1985 looked good. Automobile manufacturers were doing well, and the model mix was favorable to Arvin's applications. The industrial segment was experiencing a small increase in the shipment of precoated steel for pre-engineered buildings and in research and development activity for private industrial customers. The Department of Defense's increased emphasis in areas like the Strategic Defense Initiative (SDI) secured a favorable market for Calspan. Sales of brand-name products, comprising both automotive aftermarket and nonautomotive consumer businesses, were down, however, as a result of lack of anticipated market growth.

The numbers released for the first nine months of 1985 showed an increase in earnings to $24.7 million from $21.6 million during the corresponding period in 1984. Sales were up $32 million to $603 million over the same nine months.

At the end of 1985, eight operating divisions were serving the four broad market segments. Each operating division is briefly described below, and the division/segment matrix shown in Exhibit 5 gives a bird's-eye view of the various businesses of the corporation.

EXHIBIT 5

Operating Division and Business Segment Information

	Marketing and Distribution	Business Segments			
		Automotive	Consumer Appliances	Government and Utilities	Commercial and Industrial
ARVIN AUTOMOTIVE	Original equipment parts produced for Ford, General Motors, Chrysler, American Motors Corporation, and Volkswagen of America. Replacement parts marketed by Arvin and Supreme brands and private brand names.	Original equipment mufflers, exhaust and tail pipes; catalytic converters; tubular manifolds; fuel filler tubes; small diameter tubing; replacement exhaust system parts.			
ARVINYL	Fabricated parts and vinyl metal laminates are shipped to customers for a variety of end uses.	Decorative stampings of vinyl metal laminates; diesel engine oil pans and components; press-molded thermoplastics.	Vinyl metal laminate stampings.	Faceplates for telephone equipment; ship interior panels.	Vinyl metal laminate stampings.
ROLL COATER	Coils of steel and aluminum are prepainted and shipped to customers for fabrication into end use products.	Coil steel coated with zinc-rich primer for fabricating into automobile and track body parts.	Precoated coils of steel and aluminum for fabrication into products such as drapery hardware and refrigerator housings.		Precoated coils of steel and aluminum for pre-engineered buildings, motor homes, vending machines, and office furniture.

ARVIN *Consumer Housewares*	Distributed nationally to leading retailers. Marketed under the Arvin brand name and private brand names.		Portable electric heaters; fireplace heat exchangers; wind turbine home attic ventilators.		
ARVIN *Consumer Electronics*	Distributed to large retail chains and electronics manufacturers for marketing under private brand names.		Compact stereos and component systems; electronic assemblies; cable television converters; satellite receivers.		
ARVIN *ArvinAir*	Distributed through wholesale and national retail channels. Marketed under the Arvin brand name and trade names.		Evaporative coolers.		Evaporative coolers.
ARVIN CALSPAN	Contracted by U.S. government and private industry.	Comprehensive restraint testing; research and tire testing services; automotive accident research.		Research, development, and testing services.	Research, development, and testing services.
ARVIN DIAMOND	Contract basis			Security systems for power-generating plants.	Industrial video cameras.

North American Automotive

North American Automotive was a major supplier of original equipment exhaust systems for Ford, General Motors, and Chrysler; of catalytic converters for Ford and Chrysler; and of fuel filler tubes for General Motors, Volkswagen of America, and American Motors. In addition, through its Aftermarket Products Division, Arvin manufactured mufflers and a full line of exhaust-system replacement parts that were distributed through traditional channels under both the Arvin and Supreme brand names.

The rebound in automotive sales after the 1980–1982 recession enabled Arvin to have strong gains. The annual build rate in the North American auto industry increased 30 percent to 10.3 million units in 1983, and then again 19 percent to 12.25 million in 1984. Arvin's auto business had further success from new applications of its lightweight products, and it continued to gain from the cost-reduction and consolidation programs of the past few years.

Commenting on the direction of his division's business, Chick Evans said, "The heart of our aftermarket problem, besides the fact that we only had 4 or 5 percent market share, was that we never really had a business that stood out [on its own]." So in 1984 he decided to separate the production of replacement exhaust systems from the automotive plants and consolidate the manufacturing and distribution of the aftermarket business in one facility at Princeton, Kentucky.

The prospects for 1985 looked good. Segment sales were growing even faster than in the previous two years. A major factor was the rapid acceptance of the stainless-steel tubular manifold, whose growth in sales was expected to remain high for at least another year. In addition, a favorable industry model mix was helping an increase in market penetration for exhaust-system parts and decorative stampings of vinyl-on-metal laminate.

Consumer Electronics

Consumer Electronics was a major contract supplier of compact and component stereos to large retail chains and well-known U.S.-based manufacturers such as Radio Shack, Yorkx, and Sears. Arvin relied on low-cost manufacturing in Taiwan, supported by the engineering and distribution capability in the United States.

By 1980 the home audio industry had begun to show signs of maturing; industry shipments were down, and most manufacturers felt a squeeze in margins because of intensifying competition. Arvin reacted to these trends by emphasizing product innovation and extending its technological base in related areas. It became involved in the manufacture of cable television converters and satellite receivers as original equipment.

In 1985 sales for compact table and rack stereo systems were down from a record high of the previous year, mainly because of soft market conditions and inventory correction in the channels. The outlook for 1986 looked favorable, however, because of an acceptable level of inventory in the pipeline and a variety of new product introductions.

ArvinAir

In August 1985, Arvin announced the consolidation of the consumer housewares division with the ArvinAir division. Portable electric heaters and related products manufactured at Verona, Mississippi, and product engineering located in Columbus were scheduled to be merged into the ArvinAir facility in Phoenix, Arizona, where evaporative coolers were manufactured. The counter-seasonal nature of the markets for these products were expected to favor improved capacity utilization and operating efficiencies.

The consumer markets that this division served valued ready availability of products and competitive pricing. In addition to cutting costs at the manufacturing end, Arvin was meeting the saturated market conditions with a steady introduction of new products. By 1985 the cost-reduction initiatives had begun to pay off, and the new products, helped by expectations of market recovery, had begun to relieve the pressure on margins for the division.

Roll Coater

This capital-intensive, energy-guzzling division was the largest independent U.S. coater of coiled steel and aluminum for the automotive, appliance, construction, and agricultural markets. The key concerns of management included cost reduction, quality assurance, service, and maintenance of plant capacity utilization. New applications for coated metal strips were being developed to broaden the demand for the division's products.

The recession of 1981–1982 constrained demand for coated coils in automobiles and construction, but the division maintained its share in all its major markets with tight cost control and new product introductions. The resurgence of the automotive industry in 1983 boosted sales of coated coils to auto manufacturers. And because Roll Coater had expanded its nonautomotive businesses during the auto industry's four-year slump, the division was poised for growth in all the markets it served. In 1984 a new metal-embossing line was added so that the division could offer embossed designs in prepainted finishes applied to coils of steel.

Arvinyl

Arvinyl fabricated vinyl-on-metal laminates for a variety of end uses in consumer durables, commercial products, automotive applications, and office furniture. Product development for existing and new markets was a key to sustained leadership. In 1978 a decorative "soft touch" laminate was developed to give automotive stylists greater aesthetic freedom.

Another important product innovation was the development of damped metal, which consisted of a sheet of visco-elastic plastic laminated between two sheets of steel. This material offered opportunities to develop parts such as oil pans and valve covers for major engine manufacturers that would meet federal noise regulations for trucks.

The economic recession of the early 1980s derailed the anticipated growth in two of Arvinyl's major markets, microwave ovens and diesel engines, but the diversity of markets that Arvinyl served prevented its total collapse. Then, after two years of upbeat sales, the industrial slowdown of 1985 reduced the shipments of vinyl laminates and parts for industrial use, particularly formed parts supplied to diesel-engine manufacturers. With a more diversified customer base, however, Arvinyl was better positioned to handle another economic recession.

Advanced Technology Group

The advanced technology group consisted of Arvin/Calspan and Arvin/Diamond, which provided services and products to both private industry and the government.

Calspan offered scientific research, development, and testing capabilities through its seven regional technical centers. Diamond manufactured electronic products and systems for heavy industry, broadcast, CATV, and nuclear security markets. In addition, the technology group was a major contributor to the U.S. Department of Transportation's New Car Assessment Program and conducted extensive automotive crash tests.

Government regulation and defense policy were important variables that affected the business of these divisions. Regulations calling for improved communications and monitoring systems in nuclear power plants presented continuing growth opportunities for Arvin/Diamond. Also, the Reagan administration's avowed support of expanded defense investment promised an increased market for Arvin/Calspan's advanced technology services. For instance, by 1985 Calspan had approximately $10 million in contracts supporting the administration's Strategic Defense Initiative (Reagan's so-called Star Wars).

Project-management experience was a significant strength of this group, which helped the company win contracts from government and industry. One example was the three-year, $95.6 million contract to manage the wind-tunnel facilities for the U.S. Air Force at the Arnold Engineering Development Center in Tullahoma, Tennessee.

Calspan's technical skills and resources were enhanced by a joint venture formed in 1983 with The Research Foundation of the State University of New York, Buffalo, to conduct research on lasers, DNA molecules, and turbines. In September 1984, Franklin Research Center, a Philadelphia-based research and testing concern, was purchased for its technical expertise and new markets.

In 1985 Calspan won a five-year contract, valued at approximately $245 million, from the U.S. Air Force to operate aerospace flight-dynamics test facilities. In September of the same year, Calspan and the University of Tennessee arranged a nonprofit joint venture to conduct aerospace research.

The 1986 outlook for business with the government looked favorable, although the full impact of the new Gramm-Rudman-Hollings legislation on R&D funding was yet to be ascertained.

Strategy for Growth

Having successfully combated the economic downturn of 1981–1982, and confident that the healthy upward trend of the business in the last two years was based on the intrinsic strengths of the company, Jim Baker set out to grow Arvin through external acquisitions: "It had appeared that internal product development would neither generate enough growth nor absorb our cash flow. My attitude was: Let's do more. We have the resources, and if we don't use them, somebody else will. There is both the positive and also the threat."

Beginning in 1982, the operating divisions were encouraged to compile a working list of companies that were potential acquisitions, even if they were not up for sale. Baker said, "There was a possibility that those companies might come on the market for sale at some time. If we tracked them, we could move quickly.... We tried to establish a relationship with them. In some cases, we told the CEO, 'We are entirely friendly, and if you decide to sell, we would like to be first on your list.'" In order to guide the search for acquisition possibilities, Baker issued his "rules for success" for screening options (see Exhibit 6). The list of acquisition possibilities that had been compiled at headquarters is shown in Exhibit 7.

EXHIBIT 6

Arvin "Rules for Success"

The Arvin acquisition strategy is to acquire only those businesses that

- Are in subsegments of the industries where we now excel
- Maintain market leadership positions and low unit costs
- Compete with only "second-tier companies"
- Possess strong product development skills
- Bring products with high volume and steep cost curves
- Maintain a "culture" that is compatible with ours
- Retain good management

EXHIBIT 7

Acquisitions Possibilities, August 16, 1985

AUTOMOTIVE

Champion Spark Plug
Midwest Auto Distributors
NA-SA Auto Parts Distributors
Purolator-Stant
Champion Parts Rebuilders
Maremont
Midas
Trico
Moog
Parker-Hannefin
Echlin
Fram
Sealed Power
Dayco
Gates
Douglas & Lomason
Fatauba

ELECTRONICS

Tokheim
Lyall Electric

ARVINAIR

Bairuco
Scovill Divisions (Schrader)
W.P. Johnson

CALSPAN

Flightsafety International
Dynalectron
SPC
SRL
IITRI

OTHER

D & M
Standex International
Harmon-Motive
Mitsubishi Bank

SOURCE: Company documents.

Chick Evans agreed with the new philosophy. "Arvin had always correctly prided itself on finding growth internally—the catalytic converter, tubular manifold—you do better with those things than just going out and finding an acquisition. It was only really in this time frame that it became apparent that (a) we cannot invent everything internally, and (b) we cannot get larger market share in some products just because we might have a little better product or a little better strategy.

"Aftermarket was one of those that there was no way really to grow the business significantly without finding someone who had better distribution. And those were the steps that we started to take."

Ronald Rosin, president of ArvinAir, saw this new emphasis as an encouraging sign: "We, as one division, [were] already in the acquisition mode, [because] in a mature business such as ours, it is easier to grow through acquisitions. Our problem at this time is overcapacity, and we are trying to address that by finding product lines [that] will fill the excess capacity in our plants."

Chuck Watson's (Arvinyl) response was less enthusiastic. He said he did not think there was "a sense of urgency" but certainly encouragement that had not been there before. The stress had always been on developing products from within. "I guess my perception would be that acquisitions are not what we were really focusing on as a company. There have not been many made, and those we have made have not been all that wonderful. Roll Coater would have to be, from a pure profitability standpoint, the best acquisition we have made yet. And that was made in 1966."

James Smith, president of Roll Coater, also had a lukewarm response. "Since 1966," he said, "the production capacity at Roll Coater has been increased sixfold. So, our major emphasis has been on product diversification to maximize capacity utilization. Of course, we understand corporate priorities and are looking outside for acquisitions that fit our business. But, nothing is really coming out of it."

In preparation for a board meeting of August 29, 1985, Baker sent to each member a copy of an article on asset redeployment, with a memo highlighting the point: "It was recently said of Gulf & Western, 'They have to put their cash to work or somebody else will do it for them.' The theme of this board meeting will center on our management of financial resources."

The board agreed with Baker's statement that Arvin could be more aggressive than it had been, not only as a defense but also in a proactive manner. The board was very supportive in its own statements and gave a clear go-ahead to Baker: "Use the balance sheet to incur debt; look for acquisitions. You certainly can make cash acquisitions."

Implementing the decision, however, was not easy. According to Baker, "The way we were brought up at Arvin was available cash was what you brought in from operations. My charge to division presidents was, 'If you have a good deal, don't worry about where the cash comes from.'

"Acquisitions," he said, "are not easy for operating people, in that it is a high-risk action, [and] it takes a lot of time, both before and after the transaction. So, in spite of it being in the thinking, it just was not moving."

Evans said, "From the mid-1960s, when we stopped making acquisitions, to the mid-1980s, there had been few or no acquisitions. So we are not geared to making them."

Acquisition Options

Although the divisions themselves were not aggressively pursuing acquisitions, in November of 1985, Baker was looking closely at two acquisition possibilities:

Schrader Automotive, the world's leading manufacturer of tire valves for automobiles and trucks, and Lyall Electric, which specialized in high-quality wire assemblies for the heating, air-conditioning, appliance, and electronics industries. Schrader had originally been brought to Chick Evans's attention earlier that year, but at the suggested price of $60 million, he was uninterested. Arvin's information on these companies is given in Appendices I and II.

The Meeting in Taiwan

To reflect his commitment to an overseas presence, Baker had invited the board and all the division presidents to a visit to the company's Far East operations in November 1985. The scheduled board meeting was held in Taiwan during this visit, and the theme, again, was to use the firm's resources more aggressively to make external acquisitions.

To galvanize his division presidents into action, Baker told them, "You either grow your division by 12 percent a year, or, if you don't, you will be generating cash, and I will use that cash to make acquisitions so that the company will grow by 12 percent a year."

"In addition," he told the case writers, "incentive plans have always reflected corporate goals. Sales growth, in my view, is the key to the future. Our division presidents are so ingrained with profit making that my worry is not profits, but growth. Sales from acquisitions and joint ventures are included in their incentive plans. Sales growth from an expanding economy is given small credit."

Baker's 1985 incentive plan permitted division presidents to earn a bonus of up to 50 percent of base salary, with approximately 25 percent coming from growth in earnings per share, and up to 6 percent each from increases in share price, ROE, returns on sales, and "new sales" growth of more than $40 million. "New sales" included sales above threshold volumes of existing products, sales to new customers (e.g., heaters to Wal-Mart), sales in new countries, sales from new products, and sales from joint ventures and acquisitions completed in 1985.

"Now," thought Baker, "if I can only get them to go for it."

Endnotes

[1]Bill Koenig, "The Quiet Man," *The Indianapolis Star*, March 15, 1988, p. 1.
[2]Ibid.
[3]Gregory Miller, "What Does Sam Belzberg Really Want?" *Institutional Investor*, June 1986, p. 150.

Appendix I to Case 20

Lyall Electric, Inc.

Set up in 1952 by Lyall D. Morrill and Chester E. Dekko to make ready-made wiring assemblies for commercial refrigerators, Lyall Electric grew by expanding into a number of related businesses. By 1984 it was a privately held, multidivision company serving the appliance, automotive, and electronic industries with wire products. It was the most completely vertically integrated wire manufacturer in the United States.

The operations of the company were broken down into three categories: materials, with seven companies; assemblies, with three companies; and machinery and equipment, which comprised three more units. Transcending the entire organization was component sales, a separate group that handled the marketing of all corporate products. The products sold by the components group included wiring harnesses, connectors, service cords, flexible conductor assemblies, control boxes, and special electrical assemblies.

The firm's operating strategy was to keep the manufacturing units small and intimate. Seldom did a plant have more than 50 employees. In addition, almost all the plants were located in small towns, where not only did the employees know each other, but also a typical rural American work ethic prevailed.

The company's annual sales had risen sharply since 1982 and had reached $147 million in 1985. Management expected to maintain a 20-percent-per-year growth rate over the foreseeable future. Profit before taxes in 1985 was $13.658 million, and net profit was $7.658 million.

All the capital stock was owned by the directors and the estate trust of the late Lyall D. Morrill. No individual owned control, but the chairman, Chester Dekko, and secretary, Amy Morrill, the widow of Lyall Morrill, held a majority of the stock. Because Chester Dekko was emotionally tied to the company, any agreement would have to include his active role in running the firm after the merger/acquisition.

Lyall Electric, Inc., Its Consolidated Subsidiaries, and Its Operating Affiliated Companies Balance Sheet

ASSETS	October 25, 1984
Cash and cash equivalent	$ 3,811
Marketable securities	245
Notes, receivables, and affiliates	400
Accounts receivable	11,351
Inventories	15,881
Prepaid expenses	101
Refundable federal income taxes	529
Total current assets	$32,318
Land	$ 867
Buildings	11,282
Machinery and equipment	20,917
Construction in progress	1,021
Less accumulated depreciation	(13,398)
Net PP&E	$20,689
Other	128
Total assets	$53,135
LIABILITIES AND SHAREHOLDERS' EQUITY	
Short-term debt	$ 3,964
Current portion of LTD	879
Accounts payable	4,843
Accrued expenses	5,714
Federal income taxes payable	312
Customer deposits	96
Total current liabilities	$15,709
Net liability safe-harbor leases	510
Term debt, noncurrent portion	8,502
	24,721
Common stock, paid-in capital, and retained earnings	28,414
Total liabilities and shareholders' equity	$53,135

Appendix II to Case 20

Schrader Automotive

A division of Scovill Corporation, Schrader Automotive Group was the world's largest producer of valves for pneumatic tires and inner tubes. It had manufacturing operations in the United States, France, Brazil, Canada, South Africa, Australia, Mexico, and India. From those locations, Schrader served every major valve market except the Far East.

Schrader's market share in each area served was as follows:

Australia/Oceania	38%
Latin America	79
Europe/Africa	39
India/Eastern Asia	47
Mexico/Central America	96
South Africa/Southern Africa	85
USA/Canada	35

Schrader's overall worldwide market share was estimated to be 31 percent in 1984. An opportunity for the firm to grow its business was in the Far East market, which had good potential because many U.S. tube manufacturers had moved offshore, mainly to Korea and Taiwan. Tube production in the United States had dropped 40 percent in the first half of the 1980s. The total worldwide tire valve and accessories market was estimated at $260 million in 1984, with 60 percent going to OEMs and 40 percent to the aftermarket.

OEM customers included tube manufacturers, automobile manufacturers, and manufacturers of industrial products that used pneumatic valves. Aftermarket outlets were tire-equipment specialists, warehouse distributors, and mass merchandisers. Products sold in these two markets included valves for passenger and truck inner tubes, passenger and truck snap-in-tubeless valves, clamp-in valves for high performance, valve cores for automotive and industrial applications, caps and extensions, gauges, air chucks, and various other accessories. Products related through manufacturing processes or distribution included tire-repair materials and wheel weights.

The valve business was considered to be in the mature phase and was closely tied to automobile sales and tire-replacement rate. No significant growth was expected. Product innovations were rare, and whatever new products were introduced were basically a manufacturer's attempt to maintain its market position.

New products launched by Schrader in 1985 included (1) a Red Alert valve, which turned red when tire pressure was low, and (2) Visualizer, which equalized dual tires. Both were unsuccessful.

A potential product innovation that had strategic implications was the use of plastics to replace brass in valves. Prototype plastic valves with both brass and plastic cores had been produced in sample quantities, but none had been introduced as of the end of 1985.

In 1984 and 1985, Schrader consolidated its manufacturing operations. The facilities in the United Kingdom, Hong Kong, and Dickson, Tennessee, were closed, and a significant portion of production was shifted to France, Canada, and Brazil.

Because of the nonrecurrent expenses associated with plant closures, profitability had suffered over the last three years. The firm was expected to regain some of its operating margin in 1986, primarily from the gains in the U.S. market. Summary financial statistics for Schrader were as follows (figures in millions):

	1983	1984	1985	1986 Plan
Sales	$74.0	$81.9	$80.3	$82.6
Operating income	3.0	8.0	5.7	8.8
Net income	$ (2.2)	$ 1.6	$ 3.6	$ 3.2

Schrader's sales and assets broke down as follows:

Schrader Automotive, Inc. Financial Highlights ($ in millions)

	Net Sales			Net Income†			Net Controllable Assets		
	1984	1985	1986	1984	1985	1986	1984	1985	1986*
United States	34.5	29.7	31.6	(2.1)	.6‡	1.4	24.8	21.3	22.9
France	16.0	22.7	23.5	1.0	1.8	1.6	6.5	12.6	10.4
Brazil	11.6	14.1	14.4	1.4	1.2	(.2)	9.5	10.5	12.7
Canada	3.2	3.0	3.2	.2	.3	—	1.8	1.9	2.2
Mexico	5.6	4.7	3.4	.7	.2	.1	3.2	3.0	2.9
Australia	3.5	3.1	3.7	—	(.4)	(.1)	2.6	1.6	1.6
South Africa	3.5	2.4	2.8	.5	.4	.4	1.7	1.5	1.7
Other (closed operations)	4.0	.6	—	(.1)	(.5)	—	1.4	.1	—
Total	81.9	80.3	82.6	1.6	3.6‡	3.2	51.5	52.5	54.4

*Forecast.

†FIFO basis.

‡Excludes approximately $1.5 million Dickson closing expenses (pretax).

Case 21

Yamaha Corporation and the Electronic-Musical-Instruments Industry

> A change to a new type of music is something to beware of as a hazard of all our fortunes. For the modes of music are never disturbed without unsettling of the most fundamental political and social conventions.
>
> –Plato, *The Republic*

As Seisuke Ueshima, the newly appointed chairman and president of the Yamaha Corporation, looked down at the game of Go, he had an uneasy feeling that his stones controlling the center of the game board were vulnerable to being surrounded. Although Ueshima generally found playing Go relaxing, this game reminded him of the competitive position of the Yamaha Corporation.

The Yamaha board of directors expected Ueshima's strategic plan for Yamaha, the faltering giant of the musical-instruments industry, the next morning. The implications of his presentation would quickly be felt throughout the organization and among shareholders and would even be discussed in the gossip columns of the *Nikkei Weekly.*

Seisuke Ueshima, successor to three generations of the dynastic leadership of the Kawakami family, was something of an outsider because he came from Yamaha's sister company, Yamaha Motor Corporation. President Ueshima now had the tasks of improving the company's recent lackluster performance, strengthening morale, preserving Yamaha's positive brand reputation, maintaining the skills and competencies of the company, positioning the company for the impending market changes, and quickly developing the core capabilities needed to build Yamaha's future strategic position.

Company Background

In 1993, Yamaha Corporation was the world's largest manufacturer of musical instruments, accounting for almost half of the world's new musical-instrument sales. With a far more diversified product range than any of its competitors in the electronic-keyboard market, Yamaha had pursued a corporate strategy of sprawling conglomeration since World War II. While Yamaha's musical- and electronic-instruments businesses boomed during the 1950s–1970s, the profits from these core businesses were used to support other business divisions, such as the company's leisure, living, and sporting-goods divisions, which were financial losers. By 1993, the Yamaha Corporation owned a golf course, operated resort hotels, and produced furniture, kitchen sets, golf carts, computer chips, televisions, videocassette

This case was written by Andrew W. Spreadbury, MBA/J.D. 1994, under the supervision of Professor L. J. Bourgeois.

recorders (VCRs), and audio equipment, as well as virtually every type of musical instrument sold. All of these businesses were held loosely under the umbrella of the Nippon Gakki holding company, together with Yamaha Corporation's sister companies, Yamaha Motor Corporation—the world's second-largest motorcycle and snowmobile manufacturer—and the Yamaha Music Foundation, a network of music schools teaching millions of children around the world.

In the musical-instruments business, Yamaha Corporation had pursued a strategy of broader product, technology, and geographical scope than any of its competitors. Unlike any of its rivals, Yamaha produced musical instruments of all kinds—traditional acoustic as well as electric and electronic instruments—with products positioned at almost all price points. Yamaha was so large that it had a significant portion of almost every niche in the musical-instruments industry, and it was the clear leader in most niches. Struggling U.S. rivals accused Yamaha of emphasizing quantity over quality and of selling with advertising rather than with sound, but the strongest quality claims of those competitors was that their products were "every bit as good" as Yamaha's.[1]

Yamaha's broad-scoped business strategy and conglomerating corporate strategy were developed by three generations of the Kawakami family—who had presided over Yamaha since the mid-1930s, when Kaichi Kawakami rescued Yamaha from near bankruptcy—around what former Yamaha president Hiroshi Kawakami, grandson of Kaichi Kawakami, called the "bread-and-butter piano division."[2] Because the Japanese education system required every elementary-school child to learn to play at least one keyboard instrument and one wind instrument, Japan offered Yamaha a mass market for low-priced pianos that Yamaha came to dominate. Yamaha kept prices low by using, whenever possible, assembly-line techniques for its pianos, of which Yamaha produced 238,000 annually.[3]

Yamaha had made every effort however, not to sacrifice quality. The company openly declared its goal of catching up with Steinway, the world-renowned leader in sound quality. It tried to do so by concentrating on its vertical pianos—the pianos used in schools—in order to capture the loyalty of future virtuosi.[4] Yamaha used the same lumber to build its pianos that Steinway used. Yamaha carefully followed Steinway's research-and-development efforts and regularly purchased and disassembled Steinway pianos.[5] "We are chasing hard; we want to catch up with Steinway," Yamaha's managers declared in 1981.[6]

From its piano-making experience, Yamaha had developed capabilities in bending and laminating woods (for piano cabinets) and in marketing and distributing pianos. Yamaha subsequently applied these production, marketing, and distribution capabilities to guitars and drums. High production volume to meet local need strengthened Yamaha's skills in producing efficiently at low cost. Yamaha attained its position as world leader in musical-instrument sales by seizing markets for inexpensive beginners' instruments first, then conquering the middle-price range, and finally expanding into the top-of-the-line market.

With this expansion, Yamaha built large financial resources and brand-name recognition. Yamaha's annual income rose to a range of $60 million to $100 million by the early 1990s, and sales passed $4 billion (see Exhibit 1). This strong financial development allowed Yamaha Corporation an advertising budget that exceeded the annual sales of most of its niche competitors. Yamaha's ubiquitous product and price positioning, combined with its large advertising budget, made for extensive consumer recognition and loyalty, especially in Japan, the world's largest market for musical instruments.

EXHIBIT 1

Fact Sheet for Yamaha Corporation; Hamamatsu-shi, Shizuoka, Japan 430

Chairman: Hideto Eguchi
Chief executive officer: Seisuke Ueshima, president
Employees: 10,775

YAMAHA CORPORATION WORLDWIDE SALES (YEAR ENDING DECEMBER 31, 1991)

Electronic musical instruments (18% of total)	$ 736 million
Pianos (16%)	656
Conventional musical instruments excluding pianos (13%)	536
Home furniture and entertainment systems (13%)	533
Electronic equipment and metals (11%)	451
Other (29%)	1,192
Total sales of all products	$4,104 million

YAMAHA CORPORATION WORLDWIDE SALES BY REGION (1991)

Japan	71%
North America	10
Europe	11
Asia	5
Other	3
Total	100%

YAMAHA CORPORATION WORLDWIDE SALES

1983	$2,680 million	1988	$3,736 million
1984	3,256	1989	3,896
1985	3,408	1990	4,074
1986	3,304	1991	4,104
1987	3,488		

SOURCE: Worldscope, 1994; extrapolations from *Hoover's Handbook of World Business* and assorted periodicals.

Yamaha was also able to capitalize on its financial resources and knowledge of the musical-instruments industry to obtain patent rights to, and build on, its core of electronic-music-synthesis technology, enabling the company to capture its leading position of 30 percent to 35 percent of total market sales in electronic musical instruments. Yamaha built this leading position just as it had built its dominant position in the traditional-musical-instruments markets: beginning with low-price segments and moving up. This growth increased Yamaha's workforce to more than 12,000 skilled artisans and electronics experts. Yamaha had grown so large in relation to its many competitors that it had become largely insensitive to their activities.

Following its success in musical instruments, Yamaha began to diversify by making a multitude of sideline products that shared unique materials or manufacturing techniques with its "bread-and-butter" piano business, such as skis, tennis rackets, and furniture.[7] Similarly, from the relatively high-margin electronic-organ business, the company branched into the cutthroat competition of television, VCR, and audio-equipment production.[8] With only manufacturing-related capabilities supporting these businesses, Yamaha Corporation did not fare well with them. As Hiroshi Kawakami explained, top executives well versed in the musical-instruments market were not able to move aggressively on less familiar turf.[9] Yamaha's diversity of operations grew to be cumbersome because independent-minded divisions failed to pool resources and expertise.

Yamaha's earnings from the sale of its pianos and other traditional acoustic instruments had slowly declined from their peak in 1980 because world demand had fallen, stemming partly from the weak Japanese economy and partly from the declining birth rate in Japan and the rest of the developed world. In the United States, demand for pianos had fallen as a result of reduced birth rates, a drop in school and music programs, high interest rates, a decrease in disposable income, and sales-outlet closures.[10] Moreover, margins had narrowed because of price competition from Korean manufacturers. As a result of poor earnings from pianos, Yamaha took funds intended for other divisions to continue feeding the declining piano division.

Too much diversification, a lack of any major articulated goals or focus, and the resulting lackluster performance in all but the electronic-musical-instruments (EMI) businesses had produced a decline in employee morale and a loss of trust in the Kawakami dynasty that had guided the company for three generations. To the union, Hiroshi Kawakami appeared to be more interested in sports cars, skiing vacations, and concerts than in improving Yamaha's performance. In February 1992, the union joined with management to bring about a leadership coup, demanding that Hiroshi Kawakami resign as president and forcing him to relinquish his seat on the board in March 1993. (Kawakami was left—like his father, the president before him—with about 1 percent of Yamaha Corporation's stock.)

This dramatic move filled Yamaha Corporation and Japanese newspapers with tales of intrigue. It was a highly unusual display of Japanese labor-union power. Surveys taken in 1993 of Yamaha's union workers found that most would not recommend working at Yamaha to family or friends and that most would start working at another company if they could choose to start again—an unusually negative finding for a Japanese company.

The Development of Electronic Music

Technology helped make music a popular, mass-marketed product. Starting with nineteenth-century developments of various forms of player pianos, manufacturers provided reproductions of great musical performances to listeners who lacked access to the performers. In 1896, American inventor Thaddeus Cahill patented the first electric musical instrument, which generated sound with rotating electromechanical tone wheels.[11] In the 1920s and 1930s, several composers expressed dissatisfaction with conventional instrumental resources. The technological developments of the era provided amplifiers and speakers to change sonority.[12] In the late 1920s, optical-track recording, which converted electrical impulses from a microphone into photographic images on film that could then be read to another microphone for playback by an optical reader, was developed for sound film.[13] Around the same time, developments with electromagnets brought the ability to induce and sustain vibrations in piano strings.[14] By the 1930s electric pianos had been developed that replaced traditional-acoustic-piano soundboards with electrostatic pickups for amplification.[15]

The phonograph and the radio broadened popular access to, and interest in, music. With the U.S. postwar baby boom came a boom in interest in popular youth-oriented music such as rhythm and blues, rockabilly, rock 'n' roll, and heavy metal, as well as family-oriented varieties such as themes to popular films. In the United States, the largest and most influential market for recorded music since World War II, interest in music was driven by radio. As a result of local radio stations' delivering listeners to advertisers that wanted a specific, predictable audience, music styles and groups of consumers interested in those styles were highly segmented.[16] The increase in the number of radio stations and the market-targeting abilities of advertisers brought a more diverse range of musical styles.

At the same time recorded music was flourishing, play-it-yourself music was burgeoning. Although the total market for recorded music grew larger than that for play-it-yourself music, by 1993 more was spent each year in the United States on sheet music, music software, and instruments ($3.5 billion) than people under age 25 spent on records, cassettes, compact discs, and music videos ($3.2 billion).[17] The proliferation of high-quality stereo equipment, which, in turn, exposed listeners to the nuances of sound, increased consumer demand for high-quality sound from musical instruments.[18]

In the 1950s, musician-inventors such as Robert Moog and Donald Buchla developed synthesizers, which allowed all sound properties—pitch, envelope, amplitude, timbre, reverberation, modulation, and so forth—to be controlled by variations in voltage. Such instruments offered a great variety of sounds, far surpassing the scope of any mechanical instrument.[19]

MIDI

During the 1970s, the development of synthesizers paralleled that of the computer: The hardware was usually a pianolike keyboard and computer chips containing the synthesizer sounds and sound-controlling capabilities; the software was the operating system allowing the manipulation and storing of sounds and sound sequences. The storing of sound sequences in digital form was labeled "sequencing," a process similar, in principle, to storing analog sounds on a tape recorder. A sequencer, in contrast to a tape recorder, permitted the manipulation of individual digital signals, allowing, for example, the correction of errors with a single keystroke. It was, essentially, akin to a word processor. As with early computers, each manufacturer developed proprietary operating systems, thus making different keyboards (and the music sequences stored in them) incompatible with each other.

In the early 1980s, the invention and standardization of the electronic-musical-synthesis technology called MIDI introduced a great advance in music-making potential. MIDI (musical instrument digital interface) established a set of specifications that provided an efficient means of digitally conveying real-time musical-performance information, such as which sounds should be generated, which notes should be played, and how loud notes should be.[20] More important, MIDI was a universal digital interface that enabled instruments such as synthesizers, drum machines, sound samplers, and sequencers from any manufacturer to communicate with each other.[21] MIDI allowed for easy music editing and the ability to change the playback speeds and pitch or key of the sounds independently.[22] Since its introduction, MIDI had been applied to an increasingly diverse range of instruments and computer equipment.[23] It seemed to spark consumers' creativity, enabling a broad range of musical applications. The predicted trend of consumer demand was for products offering users an increased potential for expression and customization.

The Electronic-Musical-Instruments (EMI) Industry

The EMI market exploded from virtually ground zero in 1983 to almost $3 billion in sales worldwide in 1993. Roughly three-fourths of this market was for electronic keyboards. Although sales faltered during the 1990–1992 world recession, the general trend seemed to be up. Demand was historically linked to significant bursts of new-product technology, with demand subsiding in years in which product improvements were little more than cosmetic.

The EMI industry commanded margins roughly 10 percent to 12 percent higher than those in other consumer-electronic industries, primarily because it had built product differentiation with features that consumers wanted but found difficult to compare and value monetarily, such as musical "expressivity" and "voicing" (the recorded and copied sound of acoustic instruments).[24] Patents and talented design engineers gave the leading manufacturers the ability to predict what the competitors' next products would be like while keeping their own products different, which was the key to success in keyboard differentiation. Continual cost reductions also helped. Firms able to diversify by offering products in many price ranges tended to be the most profitable, as were the firms that scored a big hit with a very popular product.

The EMI industry was particularly influenced by Yamaha Corporation, which held and fiercely defended the rights to most of the patents essential to MIDI. Although competitors developed other technologies and purchased rights to or copied Yamaha's technologies, Yamaha's basic technological advantages, combined with its vast production, marketing, and distribution capabilities, made Yamaha's products the biggest sellers in the industry (see Exhibit 2). Yamaha's patents had long been the key to its success in the industry, and Yamaha defended them vigorously with ongoing patent-infringement litigation.

Popular products such as Yamaha's DX-7 and Clavinova organ were huge hits, and sales of electronic musical instruments and related MIDI products had grown to be about one-third of Yamaha's profits, making electronic musical instruments Yamaha's most successful business. Although some early, leading competitors like Moog Music and ARP had been forced out of the market, Yamaha had managed to keep a 30 to 35 percent share. Yamaha had built broad-based digital- and computer-technology capabilities, making it the leading producer of computer sound cards, the producer of the world's fastest 16-kilobyte SRAM chips, and the producer of 0.4 percent of the world's computer chips. As a result of these efforts, 78 percent of the consumers who owned one or more electronic keyboards owned one or more Yamahas—a level of brand penetration more than twice as high as that of any other competitor.[25]

EXHIBIT 2

Leading Manufacturers in the Electronic-Musical-Instruments Industry

Ultrapro Market | **Pro/Home Market** | **Home Market**

Retail Value $10,000 | Market Share and Position | Retail Value $300

10% | Yamaha 30%–35% | 30%

Roland 20%

Korg 20%

10% | Peavy 15%

Casio 5% | 50%

End Users

Stars who record mass-marketed popular music | Musicians, studios, bands, schools, churches, and amateur home players | Tinkerers and children

Products

Not portable | MIDI interface, CD-ROM, compatible with computer systems—portable, all self-contained | Portable keyboards

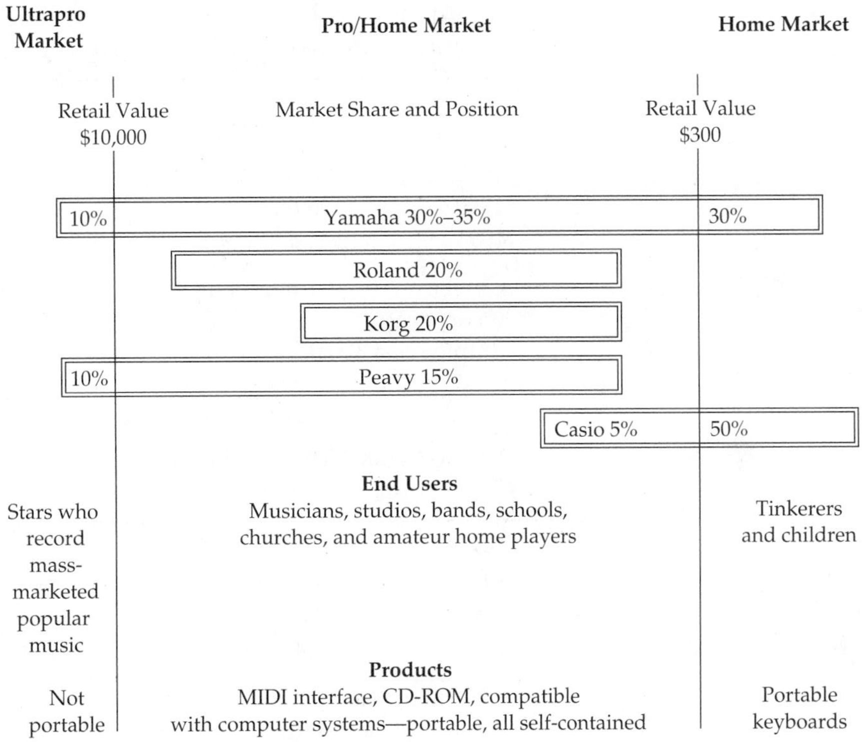

Yamaha's Major Competitors

The world's second-largest manufacturer of musical instruments in 1993 was the Kawai Musical Instruments Manufacturing Company (see Exhibit 3). Kawai sold pianos, electronic pianos, electronic organs, electronic musical instruments, formed-metal products, computers, software, and music lessons.[26]

The Young Chang Musical Instrument Company was the world's largest manufacturer of traditional acoustic pianos in 1993 (see Exhibit 3). Known for making high-quality pianos costing 20 percent less than comparable U.S. and Japanese models, the Korean firm had received training from Yamaha under a contractual agreement from 1967 to 1976.[27]

In 1993, Yamaha's most powerful competitors in the electronic-musical-instruments industry were primarily Japanese. Roland, with slightly more than 20 percent of the market, had almost as wide a range of MIDI instruments as Yamaha. It had a staff of capable musicians who gave Roland's electronic instruments what was probably the best voicing in the industry. Roland intended to expand into the amateur market, although its products were perceived as too expensive for most amateurs.

Korg had almost as much market share as Roland, and also had the advantage of exceptional voicing talent. Once owned by Yamaha, Korg was known for its

EXHIBIT 3

Yamaha's Competitors

KAWAI MUSICAL INSTRUMENTS MANUFACTURING CO., LTD.
Hamamatsu-shi, Shizuoka-ken 430, Japan

	Revenue
1988	¥85,628 million
1989	90,515
1990	96,603
1991	101,440

Chief executive officer: Hirotaka Kawai, president
Incorporation: 1951
Employees: 3,570

YOUNG CHANG MUSICAL INSTRUMENT CO., LTD.
Seo-ku, Inchon, South Korea

	Revenue
1989	US$55,787,000
1990	55,817,000
1991	54,929,000

Chairman: Jae-sup Kim
President: Sang-eun Nam
Employees: 4,597
Major shareholder: Jae-sup Kim, 17.2%
Business: Of 1991 revenues, upright pianos accounted for 78%; grand pianos, 10%; digital pianos, 3%; other, 9%.

ROLAND CORPORATION
Suminoe-ku, Osaka 559, Japan

	Revenue		
1988	¥30,000 million	1991	35,119
1989	31,818	1992	33,464
1990	33,803		

Chief executive officer: Ikutara Kakehashi, president
Incorporation: 1972
Employees: 695

(continued)

SOURCE: COMLINE Corporate Directory, COMLINE International Corporation, 1992; Teikoku Databank American, Inc., 1993; Worldscope, 1993.

EXHIBIT 3 (CONTINUED)

Yamaha's Competitors

KORG, INC.
Suginami-ku, Tokyo 168, Japan

	Revenue	Profits	Dividends
1992	¥14,177	¥18,560	50%
1993	12,883	11,044	284

Chief executive officer: Seiki Kato
Incorporation: 1964
Employees: 381

CASIO COMPUTER CO., LTD.
Shinjuku-ku, Tokyo 163, Japan

	Revenue
1991	¥304,826 million
1992	335,228
1993	383,423

workstation keyboards, sophisticated sound effects, drum machines, and sequencers. All Korg parts were custom-made. The company appeared to be planning a strong emphasis on software-synthesis machines that would be entirely programmable by the user.

Peavey, the one leading U.S. manufacturer, had a 15 percent share of the EMI market. It had strong relationships with U.S. dealers and offered the largest dealer margins. Peavey required its dealers to attend classes at Peavey University so they would understand and push Peavey products. In return, Peavey gave its dealers larger-than-average margins. The company did not allow the sale of its instruments via mail order. Peavey had a few strong products, including a sample playback box and a pianolike weighted keyboard (based on technology licensed from Yamaha). Peavey was suspected to be in trouble, however, because it had a poor image among professionals and was limited in software-based synthesis.

Smaller manufacturers included Akai, Ensoniq, and EMU. Akai produced mostly expensive products for professionals. Ensoniq, whose products appealed primarily to American rap musicians, was strong in cost cutting and software innovation, but its products had quality problems; its samplers had relatively low fidelity, its playback hardware was considered outdated and inefficient, and it cut corners on digital and analog hardware. EMU, based in California, focused on the professional market, had a polished image and a good marketing department, and was lowering its prices.

Casio, the Japanese consumer-electronics manufacturer, was the leader at the low end. Whenever consumers perceived innovation stagnation among the higher-end producers, Casio could be expected to increase its market share.

The threat of new entrants appeared low. Brand equity among leaders seemed high, entering the distribution chain was difficult, and substantial musical and engineering expertise and creativity—though not necessarily money—were required to develop products. Barriers to entry were raised as technology grew increasingly sophisticated. New players were entering the field of MIDI-based digitally recorded music, but there seemed to be little chance of their becoming manufacturers of synthesizer musical instruments. Only Matsushita, which had expressed interest in the EMI market, had the name and resources to do so successfully.

In 1993, the competition among suppliers to the EMI industry was high. Components used in making electronic keyboards were either commodities such as standard computer chips and plastics that were produced by many different suppliers and purchased for many different uses, or they were custom-made by the EMI manufacturers themselves. The largest EMI manufacturers were backward integrated.

Musical-instruments dealers were the direct buyers of electronic musical instruments. Although dealers could not force manufacturers to modify their products in order to carry them, they could threaten to drop product lines entirely. The applications of MIDI technology appeared to have reached a plateau, the marginal benefits of innovation were minor, and the products were becoming increasingly commoditylike. The likelihood of dealers increasing their strength through consolidation seemed small, however, because dealers were a diverse group. No single customer represented a significant portion of sales.

The same was true of consumers. Despite the diversity of musical tastes and desired product application, consumers could be placed in three categories (see Exhibit 2). The ultraprofessionals bought systems ranging from $10,000 to $250,000. Local professionals and high-end amateur consumers were interested in instruments priced from $300 to $10,000. The children's and tinkerers' market was for products priced below $300.

There seemed to be few identifiable market niches that had not been served. Consumer demand appeared to be relatively flat because the market had been saturated with MIDI products. Consumers who already owned MIDI products had little incentive to buy additional ones because they found that sound differences among products appeared to be minor. Although buyers were not overly price sensitive when paying for brand-new capability, they demanded lower prices for products without new capability.

Outlook for the Future

In the past five years, the gap between prices of high- and low-end MIDI instruments had narrowed. Consumer demand for production of high-quality sound samples programmed by manufacturers into MIDI instruments had increased. Consumers also wanted more miniaturization and self-containment. Consumers could now use computers to create initial sound signals to be entered into the memory of MIDI instruments. Products had grown more complicated and offered more features than before. Manufacturers offered improved customer services, such as speedy delivery and 800-number information. Producers had also tried to increase purchases with cosmetic differentiation, niche marketing with size and number of features, shortened product-life cycles to create the appearance of innovation, price imaging, and celebrity associations. The industry goal had traditionally been to "get an orchestra into a small box," but all advances to date had brought the industry no closer to attaining that goal.

Market conditions were changing. With the market saturated with the aging MIDI technology and products becoming increasingly commoditylike, prices and profit margins were dropping. Profit margins were also reduced because of falling consumer interest from a lack of significant product advances in recent years and the recent global economic downturn. Consumer desire for musical instruments that were simple and easy to understand put extra downward pressure on prices of higher-end models.

At the same time, the electronic-music industry was at the beginning of a new wave of technology. Engineers at Stanford University had developed computer hardware and software that modeled the physical vibrations of piano wires and the flow of air blown through wind instruments. Experts at Yamaha and its competitors believed this technology promised musical quality far superior to that of the MIDI-based synthetic musical instruments then available to consumers. The developers of this technology had promised to sell the rights to many manufacturers in the EMI industry rather than to Yamaha only. Some of Yamaha's executives believed this action would allow Yamaha's competitors to catch up with Yamaha in the EMI market. If the physical-modeling technology were licensed widely, they feared, the stable market positions of the leading manufacturers might be entirely upset.

The other major technological development in the electronic-music industry was the computer sound card, a computer chip or board of chips that generated audio output. Sound cards improved the capabilities of electronic musical instruments, added complex sound and voice simulation to video games, and turned personal computers into multimedia centers. The world market for sound cards was expected to grow from $112 million in 1992 to $436 million in 1996.[28] The market for sound cards in computers and a variety of home entertainment centers would be accompanied by a need for software to control the musical hardware. Because the manufacturers of home multimedia centers would be more likely than consumers to choose the brand of sound-card hardware and software to be used, strategic alliances were expected to be formed between electronic-musical-equipment companies and video-game and computer-multimedia-center manufacturers.

Yamaha at a Crossroads

Although Ueshima was experienced in managing international industrial operations, Yamaha Corporation's business seemed very different from the business of Yamaha Motor. He wondered what physical modeling and sound cards might mean to Yamaha in the future. He also wondered whether future consumer demand for simple, user-friendly instruments would increase. He had heard that music production was moving from a few big studios to many small studios tailored to individual artists. He had also heard that price pressure seemed likely to continue downward at all levels as a result of general advances in the computer industry. Consumer demand for sound-synthesizing technology might shift from the keyboard to other forms, such as the increasingly popular MIDI saxophone, guitar, bass, and drums.

Advances in other industries of which Ueshima had little knowledge also threatened to make an impact on Yamaha's market. For example, some experimenters had turned the "data-gloves" used in virtual-reality simulation games into prototype "hyperinstruments," which converted the movements of a musician mimicking the playing of an instrument—for example, a violin—into music.[29] Consumers had always sought new sounds, increased expressivity, and "better-feeling" instruments. Some in the industry also feared that the popularity of well-known stars' "unplugged" (acoustic instrument) recordings would cause consumers to lose interest in electronic musical instruments entirely.

Ueshima studied the Go board and tried to determine where his opponent's next moves would be and how he could position himself to remain on the offensive. He had the same task in managing Yamaha.

Endnotes

[1]"Here's How to Beat Japanese Firms: With a Drumstick!" *Kansas City Business Journal*, May 21, 1993, p. 1.

[2]"Yamaha Changes Management Tune," *Nikkei Weekly*, February 1, 1992, p. 9.

[3]"On Yamaha's Assembly Line," *New York Times*, February 22, 1981, p. 8E.

[4]David A. Garvin, "Steinway & Sons," Harvard Business School (9-682-025).

[5]Ibid.

[6]"On Yamaha's Assembly Line," *New York Times*, February 22, 1981, p. 8E.

[7]Brenton R. Schlender, "Yamaha: The Perils of Losing Focus," *Fortune*, May 17, 1993, p. 100.

[8]Ibid.

[9]"Yamaha Changes Management Tune," *Nikkei Weekly*, February 1, 1992, p. 9.

[10]"A Study on the Conditions of Competition between Imported and Domestically Produced Pianos," Report to the Subcommittee on Trade, Committee on Ways and Means, U.S. House of Representatives, on Investigation No. 332-159 under Section 332(b) of the Tariff Act of 1930, pp. 35–36.

[11]Richard Dobson, *A Dictionary of Electronic and Computer Music Technology* (New York: Oxford University Press, 1992), p. 150.

[12]*The New Grove Dictionary of Music and Musicians* (London: MacMillan Press Ltd., 1980), vol. 6, p. 107.

[13]*The New Grove Dictionary of American Music* (London: MacMillan Press Ltd., 1986), vol. 2, p. 30.

[14]Dobson, *Dictionary of Electronic and Computer Music Technology*, p. 124.

[15]*The New Grove Dictionary of American Music*, vol. 2, p. 29.

[16]"A Survey of the Music Business," *The Economist*, December 21, 1991, p. 12.

[17]Ibid., p. 18.

[18]"A Study on the Conditions of Competition between Imported and Domestically Produced Pianos," p. 36.

[19]*The New Grove Dictionary of Music and Musicians*, vol. 6, p. 108.

[20]"Crystal Semiconductor Demonstrates Family of New CD-Quality Wave-Table Synthesizer Chips," *Business Wire*, June 28, 1993.

[21]Dobson, *Dictionary of Electronic and Computer Music Technology*, 1992, p. 102.

[22]"Crystal Semiconductor."

[23]Dobson, *Dictionary of Electronic and Computer Music Technology*, p. 106.

[24]"Mass Merchants, Dealers Singing Profitable Tune from Keyboard Sales; Electronic Musical Keyboards," *Weekly Home Furnishings Newspaper*, © 1991.

[25]1991 *Keyboard* magazine survey.

[26]COMLINE Corporate Directory, COMLINE International Company, 1993.

[27]"Tacoma Strikes Right Chord for Korean Piano Maker," *Puget Sound Business Journal*, April 3, 1993.

[28]1992 study by Dataquest, Inc., a market-research firm.

[29]"A Survey of the Music Business," *Economist*, December 21, 1991, pp. 16–17.

Case 22

MacGregor Golf Company

Helsinki, September 1986

As they invited their American guests into the sauna at corporate headquarters, Leif Ekstrom, president of Amer Group, Heikki O. Salonen, chairman, and Kai Luotenon, head of corporate planning and development, wondered what price and terms they would have to offer to get MacGregor Golf Company.

At the same time, fatigued from their round of golf immediately following their arrival at Helsinki airport from Albany, Georgia, George Nichols, president of MacGregor, Nick Sarge, chief operating officer, and George Chane, representing Jack Nicklaus, owner, looked forward to heat-induced relaxation, a warm shower, and sleep.

As the unaccustomed whiff of heat hit him, Chane thought of Jack Nicklaus's lifelong association with MacGregor Golf, wondering if Jack could ever really part with it. Nichols leaned back and shut his eyes: "Ahh, this heat feels wonderful!" After working hard to turn the business around, he now dreamed of finally having enough cash to grow MacGregor to its full potential.

"Well, gentlemen, shall we begin?" said Salonen softly.

Amer Group, Spring 1986

Ekstrom, new president and chief operating officer of Amer Group, had studied much about Amer Group's businesses prior to his official appointment in April, so when Salonen decided to sell off the poorly performing ice hockey business, Ekstrom was in agreement. During and after the ice hockey spinoff, however, they considered other opportunities in the sports and leisure industries; in spite of the ice hockey failure, sporting goods seemed to fit Amer's strategy. Although segments of the sporting goods industry were highly competitive, especially since the entry of many Far East companies, and profits were generally not high, the general feeling among Amer's executives was that Amer, over the years, had learned many lessons about the industry and had created a strong image in commercial and financial markets. Interest in sports, leisure time, and sales of sports casual wear, which had been termed "an exploding fashion" by Ekstrom, were growing.

Salonen focused right away on the golf business and, to a lesser extent, tennis: "Tennis is the more competitive of the two segments, and the established brand names in tennis are very strong. Golf is a rapidly growing sport, more than 10 percent a year, especially in Europe and Japan." In comparing golf with ice hockey, he noted, "It is not so much a seasonal sport, except in Scandinavia. Golf markets are

This case was written by Ann Yungmeyer under the supervision of Professor L. J. Bourgeois III.

broader, and it can be a family sport, to include women, children, and retirees. You can play golf for 60 or 70 years of your life." As to the business, he continued, "Margins are higher, and golf companies are making money. Golf is a sport [that], at present, does not fluctuate with the economy, [because] golfers seem to be in good financial health."

Because Amer Group's business-development team was continuously researching many possibilities for growth, it was not unusual to have 20 projects going on at the same time. In addition, because Amer Group was well known for sporting goods among foreign investment bankers, at any given time there were literally "hundreds of choices" for acquisitions, as one Amer executive phrased it. In May 1986, one of Amer Group's U.S. institutional investors called and asked if Amer would be interested in contacting Jack Nicklaus, owner of MacGregor Golf Company, about a possible buyout. Amer's development team immediately began researching the golf business, MacGregor, and its competitors. Outside consultants were contracted to conduct two separate research studies of industry and competitive factors.

The Golf Equipment Industry

Historically, the number of golfers had correlated closely with the number of golf facilities. In the United States, golf had two explosions: one in the 1920s and one that began in the 1950s with a crescendo in the 1960s (see Exhibit 1). The number of golfers in the United States was projected to grow to between 18.5 million and 23.5 million by 1990. In the year 2000, the number of golfers would be 20 million to 41.5 million. (The lower numbers assumed the same historical percentage of

Exhibit 1

Growth of U.S. Golf Facilities

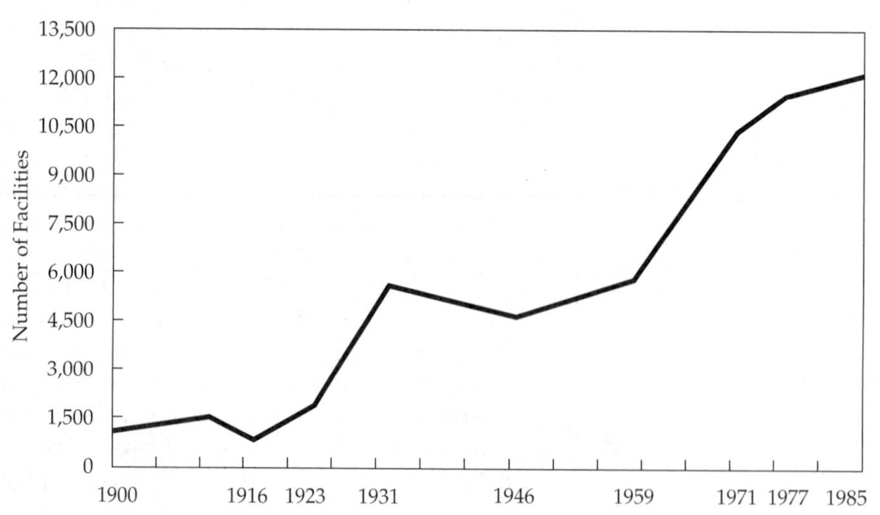

Source: G. Cornish and R. Whitten, *The Golf Course and NGF.*

players by age category. Higher numbers assumed a 5 percent additional increase in participation, which is 50 percent of the growth that golf experienced during the 1960s boom era.) The National Golf Foundation was projecting that by the year 1990, the average golfer would play 25 rounds per year. By the year 2000, the average number of rounds played was projected to be 29 per golfer.

Competitors selling to golfers in the United States could be divided into two segments: playing equipment and golf balls. In the equipment segment, MacGregor, Wilson, Ping, Spalding, and Hogan were the main competitors; while in the ball segment, Titleist and Spalding controlled the market. Internationally, the golf market was very fragmented, with MacGregor, Mizuno, Wilson, Dunlop-Slazinger, and Spalding serving roughly 25 percent of the market, and the remaining 75 percent being served by other companies.

The PIMS Study

As part of its research on MacGregor's position in June 1986, Amer Group engaged a PIMS program analysis, a consulting approach based on the 1960 General Electric project that studied the profit impact of market strategies (PIMS).[1] Amer Group made the results of the PIMS study available to MacGregor as well.

PIMS evaluated MacGregor in terms of its four business units: U.S. clubs and bags, international clubs and bags, soft goods, and golf balls. Among its conclusions were that MacGregor's 8 percent market-share position in golf clubs and bags was fifth behind Wilson (20 percent share), Ping (11 percent), Spalding, and Hogan (10 percent each). Internationally, its share was 6 percent, whereas no other company held more than 5 percent of the non-U.S. market. MacGregor's U.S. positions in golf balls (1 percent share) and soft goods (4 percent) were relatively minor.

MacGregor's 1986 total sales of $37.2 million and investment of $18.5 million were distributed as follows:

	Sales	Investment
U.S. clubs and bags	72%	67%
International clubs and bags	10	18
Soft goods	11	6
Golf balls	7	9

The company's actual return on investment compared with PAR ROI (see footnote 1) by segment for 1986 was as follows:

	Actual ROI	PAR ROI
U.S. clubs and bags	28%	14%
International clubs and bags	–7	6
Soft goods	35	16
Golf balls	–38	2

For the total operation, historical and projected ROI and PAR ROI were estimated to be as follows:

	Historical			Projected			
	1983	1984	1985	1986	1987	1988	1989
PAR ROI	17%	28	11	12	14	17	21
Actual/Planned ROI	21	−1	8	17	22	25	28

A financial forecast by PIMS is given in Exhibit 2. In general, PIMS concluded that MacGregor had a potential overall ROI of at least 15 percent if relative product quality were improved, investment intensity were reduced (by, say, reducing inventory), and capacity utilization increased.

MacGregor seemed to fit the Amer product image—high-quality, brand-recognized goods. MacGregor's products fell in line with Amer's strategy of obtaining a trademark and using brand development. It was an established company in an industry that offered growth opportunities, especially in international markets. Yet Amer Group

EXHIBIT 2

PIMS Projections (1986–1989) of MacGregor Financial Performance ($ millions)

	1983	1984	1985	1986	1987	1988	1989
INCOME STATEMENT							
Sales	49,9	52,3	34,0	37,2	43,3	47,0	50,5
Purchases	23,8	28,6	15,8	19,1	23,5	24,9	26,4
Value added	26,1	23,6	18,2	18,1	19,8	22,1	24,2
Manufacturing and distribution	10,9	11,2	8,9	8,3	8,1	9,1	10,2
Depreciation	0,1	0,3	0,4	0,5	0,5	0,5	0,5
Gross margin	15,1	12,1	8,9	9,3	11,3	12,5	13,5
Marketing	8,2	9,6	5,7	4,5	5,3	5,4	5,7
R&D	0,5	0,5	0,5	0,4	0,4	0,4	0,4
G&A	1,8	2,2	1,3	1,3	1,5	1,7	1,8
PBIT	4,6	−0,2	1,4	3,0	4,0	5,0	5,6
ROS (%)	9,2	−0,3	4,1	8,1	9,3	10,6	11,0
ROI (%)	21,0	−0,9	8,1	16,5	22,2	25,5	27,2
BALANCE SHEET							
Receivables	12,9	14,8	11,3	11,7	11,8	13,5	14,5
Inventories	16,8	15,6	8,6	8,3	8,9	8,3	8,3
Current liabilities	8,6	8,7	6,2	5,1	5,5	5,9	6,1
Working capital	21,0	21,8	13,7	14,9	15,3	15,9	16,8
GBV[a] of plant and equipment	0,8	2,0	2,6	2,7	2,9	3,6	4,1
Accumulated depreciation	0,1	0,2	0,7	0,8	1,1	1,7	2,1
NBV[b] of plant and equipment	0,7	1,8	2,1	1,9	1,8	1,9	2,0
Other assets	0,2	1,6	1,4	1,6	1,0	1,6	1,7
Investment	21,9	25,2	17,1	18,5	18,1	19,4	20,5

[a]Gross book value.

[b]Net book value.

SOURCE: PIMS report to Amer, June 1986.

had identified certain risks concerning the golf business and MacGregor specifically. According to Salonen, one concern was MacGregor's dependence on subcontractors in the Far East, where 80 percent of sporting goods were (at least partially) manufactured. One group of suppliers was supplying all of the major competitors with golf shafts and heads. A second area of concern was MacGregor's very dramatic history: It was a 90-year-old company that had been nearly bankrupt several times. A closer look at the company's history and management seemed wise.

History of MacGregor Golf Company

In 1874 a Scotsman named John MacGregor bought an interest in the Crawford Brothers shoe-last manufacturing operation founded in Dayton, Ohio. He introduced his partners to golf just as the United States was beginning to take to the game. Near the turn of the century, one year after A. G. Spalding Company became the first American company to sell its own clubs, MacGregor began making golf clubs with the same persimmon wood used in shoe lasts. In 1920 the shoe-last company was sold, and golf equipment became MacGregor's main business.

Following the Great Depression years in the 1930s, business suffered and the ailing MacGregor was sold to another sporting goods firm, P. Goldsmith Sons. Over the next few years, a revived MacGregor set most of the industry standards for quality and innovation. At the time, an established practice was for golf professionals (pros) to be under contract to specific equipment companies, but MacGregor saw a connection missing between club makers, the pros, and the best players. In order to bridge this void, MacGregor created customized clubs for pros and attracted stars such as Toney Penna, Ben Hogan, and Louise Suggs to the "MacGregor family" advisory staff. In addition to the technical expertise they brought to the company, these staff players also enhanced the firm's reputation and image.

The winning records and popularity of MacGregor's touring staff players contributed an important measure to the company's postwar success. Between 1937 and 1959, MacGregor's staff won 8 U.S. Open titles, 11 Masters, and 10 PGA championships—adding up to about 37 percent of all major championships during that period. In addition, impartial counts taken at tournaments during the postwar years consistently revealed that more than 50 percent of the fields in PGA events used MacGregor woods and irons.

Even as MacGregor was enhancing its image by contracting professional golfers, it continued to acknowledge and cultivate young talent. Players using MacGregor clubs captured British or U.S. amateur titles 12 times between 1946 and 1961.

Selling Strategy

MacGregor focused on selling high-end equipment. Because retailers were generally more price sensitive than quality conscious, MacGregor chose to distribute its premium equipment through the pro shops, which were more concerned with product attributes. "Don't just sell the most; sell the best," was the philosophy. Approximately 75 percent of company sales were made through pro shops, and 25 percent through retailers. As a result, MacGregor built a commanding position in the professional golf market, with about 40 percent share during the 1940s and 1950s. The company entered the apparel and accessories segment also, selling sportswear and shoes during World War II.

While tour staff players helped promote MacGregor equipment, sales came from the efforts of golf-club shop professionals. To make the pro policy work, MacGregor management needed direct salespeople who could gain the respect of golf professionals. Personal relationships were a key to success in such a business environment, so the company assembled a team of salespeople who understood golf and were themselves outstanding players. In addition, a common industry practice was to grant extended payment terms (up to five months, prior to the spring season). MacGregor often financed small pro shops until they made a sale. The result was that receivables represented up to 40 percent of total assets.

The Ball Controversy

Although MacGregor manufactured its own clubs, it subcontracted the production of a complete line of pro and dealer golf balls to the Worthington Ball Company of Elyria, Ohio. The pro ball "Tourney" sold well, and pros such as Ben Hogan, Demaret, and Nelson had used it regularly in all the major tournaments.

Following World War II, MacGregor decided to produce its own golf balls. The first run of balls was a disaster, however, because of MacGregor's lack of expertise in ball manufacturing and quality control. Every player who tried them decided to keep away from the "new" Tourney balls. This negative perception about the Tourney stuck in the minds of the golfing community, and the ball never recovered. "In golf," said an expert, "a ball becomes an old familiar friend. And even if it slices now and then, or betrays [a golfer] at the lips of cups, the player will not change to another brand unless there is a very severe circumstance." Even the firm's own contracted professionals resisted changing over to the Tourney. Tour players were required to play with the company ball, but most of them switched to other balls surreptitiously.

Changes in materials and production methods eventually rectified the ball problem. By 1953 MacGregor executives believed the new ball ranked at least equal with any other brand, but perceptions were hard to change. Players still refused to use the company ball. Management then tried to force the issue by passing a "play the Tourney, or else!" edict, an action that produced a lot of ill will. Ben Hogan was the first to leave as a result of this controversy, and he was soon followed by other professionals who would not use the MacGregor ball. Hogan founded a competing golf-equipment company shortly after. The exodus of top professionals tarnished the company's image and seemed to symbolize the decline of MacGregor Golf Company in a new, more competitive industry.

Change of Ownership

In 1958, after a few years of poor financial performance, MacGregor was sold to Brunswick-Balke-Collender Co. of Chicago for roughly $5 million. Brunswick, a respected company in the sporting goods industry, had significant presence in the bowling-equipment business.

Brunswick's management style deviated significantly from that of the former MacGregor leaders. Ted Bensinger, president of Brunswick, used sophisticated accounting methods and the most modern and efficient ways to increase production. The studied, impersonal culture of the new parent company began to replace the easygoing, family-style atmosphere at MacGregor. "To some of the older MacGregor workers, it was as if all of a sudden this big corporation waltzed in and changed MacGregor," said Nick Sarge, chief operating officer at MacGregor. "The core group of individuals now working for Brunswick were making more money and had better benefits than ever before, but they weren't as happy."

Bensinger had an ambition to make Brunswick the country's largest sporting goods conglomerate within five years. Naturally, MacGregor could not therefore keep serving just the pro market; extension into the retail market was imperative if it was to meet its goal of becoming *the* largest golf company owned by *the* largest sporting goods firm. Because the retail market demanded volume, not painstaking concern for the perfection of each club, in 1960 Brunswick expanded the golf division by adding a low-cost facility in Albany, Georgia, to service the retail golf equipment segment. The Ohio facility continued to produce the custom pro clubs.

MacGregor executives did not favor this redirection, which meant competing head-on with Wilson, a company that had dominated the retail market for 30 years. The market's reception was equally unenthusiastic: MacGregor posted a loss of $4 million in 1964. The company's share of the retail market remained at a low 3 percent, although it still commanded 30 percent of the pro market.

If there was a saving grace for MacGregor during the 1960s, it was the company's continued ability to recognize top golfing talent. Arnold Palmer began his career playing MacGregor clubs, as did Gene Littler. The best catch, made in the late 1950s, was a big kid with a crew cut whom the media called "Ohio Fats." His name was Jack Nicklaus.

The Nicklaus name began paying dividends for MacGregor early. In the first five years after signing his contract, the company used the Jack Nicklaus name exclusively on dealer-line equipment, and the name had significant impact in the retail arena as well.

Troubled financial times continued, however, throughout the 1960s and 1970s. In response, management closed the Ohio facility and consolidated all manufacturing in Albany, where the production of both custom and retail clubs was commingled. The new location had its problems, however. "The basic problem with the Albany plant was that retail clubs did not require the same care [that] pro-line clubs did," Sarge recalled. "A consulting firm recommended that we construct a wall to separate the manufacturing of custom and retail clubs. You couldn't craft pro clubs next to retail and not expect the quality of pro clubs to suffer."

In 1979 the Wickes Company purchased the MacGregor Golf division from Brunswick, while Equilink purchased all nongolf MacGregor sporting goods. Wickes provided temporary relief by pumping much-needed capital into the Albany factory but soon came into its own financial problems. In 1982, several weeks before declaring bankruptcy, Wickes looked for a buyer for MacGregor.

Jack Nicklaus, who had played with MacGregor clubs since he was 11 years old, had by 1982 been associated with the firm for more than 20 years through equipment contracts and his advisory role in golf-club design. Already the owner of a company called Golden Bear, Nicklaus decided he now wanted a stake in MacGregor.

A New Phase Begins

In 1982, leveraging the assets of MacGregor Golf, Golden Bear borrowed money from banks to acquire 80 percent of MacGregor stock, and Clark Johnson, senior vice president at Wickes, bought the rest. By January 1984, the original debt of $14.5 million had grown to $30 million, and the losses continued. Nicklaus thus sought the advice of George Chane, a friend and well-known "no-nonsense" consultant and troubleshooter, to identify problems at MacGregor.

On the advice of Chane, Nicklaus bought out Clark Johnson's 20 percent share of the company and began looking for a new president. "Our bank showed up with the attorneys wanting the keys to the front door and to liquidate the company," recalled one MacGregor executive. "George Chane requested several weeks to prepare a plan and began a massive program to streamline the company." He cut overhead by moving corporate offices from Atlanta to Albany. He implemented a hard asset-management program by reducing inventory through price reductions and by collecting receivables, and one "Black Friday" he reduced the workforce by one-third. "Chane did what he could on one end—cutting expenses and getting overhead down—but now it was time to turn to selling our way out."

In July 1984, Nicklaus hired George Nichols as the new president. Nichols had been president of Johnston and Murphy Shoe Company for ten years and, before joining MacGregor, was the president of the Bostonian Shoe Division of Clarke's of England, a company where Nicklaus had held a royalty contract for several years.

A study done by a consulting firm about this time identified the strengths and weaknesses of MacGregor. Brand recognition, credibility of Jack Nicklaus and his reputation in the market, inventory management, and expense control were the strong areas in the company. On the other hand, MacGregor needed to regain its reputation as an "innovator," consolidate its marketing and planning skills, revive the lackluster sales organization, and strengthen the distribution channels. Financial position, too, was weak, as net worth was negative, and working capital needs were being met by asset-based loans from Union Bank of California, which had attached severely restrictive covenants.

Nichols thus came into a bleak situation at MacGregor. "Morale was extremely low. Executives were working 12-hour days, seven days a week, trying to keep the company afloat," recalled John Baldwin, vice president of marketing and sales, who had been with MacGregor since the early Brunswick days. Earl Saxman, director of marketing, who came on board about the same time as George Nichols as a "hired gun," commented that he would never have taken the job if he had known how bad a shape MacGregor was in at the time: "There was no capital; the bank kept us in business and really did yeoman's work for us."

Besides financial woes, MacGregor also had product problems. As Nichols explained, "We were seen as a classic company [that] made traditional clubs; we were not regarded as innovators. We had a polarized product line which was big in the low-end and small in the high-end, with nothing in the middle range—at the price points where customers were willing to buy. MacGregor had relied on a manufacturing mentality, but in the highly competitive modern golf industry, a successful company needed a marketing mentality."

Over the next two years, Nichols implemented a strategic plan whose objective was to get the company profitable and attract an infusion of badly needed capital. He withdrew the company from the golf-ball business, where it had no meaningful market share. He then reorganized the sales function to cut the number of territory sales representatives and regional managers, and he improved the compensation plan.

The product line was segmented by price point and the development of "game improvement" clubs. MacGregor was moving away from its heritage of traditional woods and forged irons to the popular metal woods and a new casting process for irons. Several old-model clubs were dropped, and new designs were introduced—most notably, wedges and putters. The company adopted a "good, better, best" strategy with price/value, proven quality, and innovation being the respective key selling points. Other product lines such as golf bags, rain gear, and gloves were extended, a shirt and sweater line was introduced, and MacGregor entered the golf-shoe market.

Meanwhile, after a difficult period of tournament defeats, Jack Nicklaus began putting with the new Response ZT, which MacGregor had introduced at the 1986 PGA show in January. When the Masters rolled around at Augusta, Georgia, in April 1986, Nicklaus achieved his comeback victory. The morning after this victory, MacGregor received 5,000 orders for the Response ZT. MacGregor then increased its advertising budget from $300,000 to $1,000,000 and changed the message to both consumers and the trade to emphasize the following three points: (1) MacGregor makes products to help you play a better game and to enjoy the game; (2) the greatest player in the history of the game, Jack Nicklaus, is directly involved in the design, quality assurance, and performance of our products; and (3) MacGregor sets the quality standards for the golf industry.

The Nichols Management Style

George Nichols was described by his associates at MacGregor as "dictatorial, opinionated, and very demanding." Said one executive, "We had some loud meetings; he stepped forward and really ran the show. He was a taskmaster. George quickly identified weak links and weeded out several people."

Nichols's plan for MacGregor required improved communication throughout all levels of the management organization: "The plan specified that everyone in the organization must know what the company is trying to do and why; everyone must feel that [they are] accountable for results; everyone must truly believe that their contribution is meaningful; and everyone must be informed." The process of achieving those objectives included a weekly meeting of the key executives in each operative area—sales and marketing, administration, engineering, and manufacturing. The meetings examined business on the basis of the happenings of the previous week that would require greater coordination among the different functional areas, and they also served as an important communication device across the management layers.

The changes implemented by Nichols began to pay off in his first year. In 1984, MacGregor made a small operating profit but was still unable to service its debt. The loan was renegotiated at a more favorable interest rate. In the second year, the company made a small pretax profit, but it was insufficient for both debt service and funding additional growth. Nichols reflected, "Things were looking up because we now knew the company *could* produce a profit."

The recovery was given a boost by breakthroughs in new product development. Jack Nicklaus's success with the Response ZT putter in the 1986 Masters and Chi Chi Rodriguez's endorsement of CG 1800 woods and irons in the same year spurred the sales of MacGregor clubs. With these two successes, MacGregor reestablished its presence in the premium market segment. Confident that the business could be run profitably, Nichols laid out optimistic plans to grow and consolidate the firm's position in the industry. "Now that we had our act together," he affirmed, "we wanted to flex a little muscle." For that purpose, he estimated MacGregor had an immediate cash need of $10 million.

The high debt from the 1982 leveraged buyout ruled out borrowing from financial institutions, so the only option was an equity infusion. Nichols and Nicklaus considered taking the company public or forming a partnership with an individual or a group of investors, but neither option seemed feasible because Nicklaus wanted to retain majority interest to be able to run the company the way he wanted.

In March of 1986, in a telephone conversation with an old friend from his shoe business days, George Nichols was referred to a venture capitalist in Minneapolis. Although the venture capitalist turned out not to be interested in MacGregor, he knew a banker in Finland, who then introduced MacGregor to Amer Group.

A Merger Possibility

In May 1986, following an initial meeting with Kai Luotenon of Amer Group, George Nichols met with Jack Nicklaus's executive committee to ascertain the interests and needs of the three stakeholders in a merger: MacGregor, Jack Nicklaus (represented by Golden Bear), and Amer Group. The perspectives of the three players as they evaluated the option are briefly discussed in the following sections.

MacGregor

The real needs of MacGregor were clear: the company needed cash to pursue future opportunities, and it could not borrow any more. As an aid to Nichols's analysis, he prepared a financial forecast to 1990 for presentation to the Amer executives (see Exhibit 3).

Golden Bear

For Jack Nicklaus, the thought of selling MacGregor was an emotional issue. He had played with MacGregor clubs since childhood and had always wanted to "control the tools of my trade." He took a great deal of pride in having his peers praise his equipment on tour. He did not want to sell the business, but he knew he had no other choice. A key concern for Nicklaus was being able to liquidate the $4.5 million of MacGregor-related liabilities he had accumulated, as well as recouping the $1,009,000 in accrued royalties from MacGregor.

Amer Group

Having gone through the analyses of the golf industry and of MacGregor, Heikki Salonen wanted to get to know MacGregor's management; so he invited them to Helsinki in July for plant visits, golf, saunas, Russian dinners, and conversation. Following a full day of informal discussions, he began to feel confidence in MacGregor's management and optimism about the future outlook for the company.

The Deal: September 1986

George Nichols knew how to answer the question that Amer Group was asking, "What do you want for your company?" but as he and the Golden Bear executives traveled to Finland for the preliminary negotiations, he was anticipating a complicated twist to the proceedings because the three parties had different interests. He

EXHIBIT 3

Financial Data Summary: MacGregor Golf (1984–1986 actual; projected to 1990) ($ thousands)

	1984[a]	1985[b,c]	1986[c]	1987	1988	1989	1990
Net sales	52,583	34,292	38,615	44,641	48,754	52,212	55,320
Operating profit	−387	1,182	2,654	4,500	5,406	5,876	6,415
%	−0.7	3.4	6.9	10.1	11.1	11.3	11.6
Pretax profit	−4,543	−1,890	237	2,281	3,766	4,303	5,093
%	−8.6	−5.5	0.6	5.1	7.7	8.2	9.2
Net income	−5,206	−1,932	237	1,859	2,459	2,810	3,326
%	−9.9	−5.6	0.6	4.2	5.0	5.4	6.0
Average bank debt	23,576	18,681	19,035	15,667	12,967	11,461	9,756
Average net assets[c]	26,023	17,242	18,927	20,115	21,954	23,175	24,472
Ending equity	−3,228	−658	261	8,052	10,511	13,324	16,625
Average RONA %	−20.0	−11.2	1.3	8.9	11.2	12.1	13.6
Average ROI %	n/a	n/a	n/a	33.9	27.4	24.0	22.6
Asset turnover	1.49	1.45	1.59	1.69	1.77	1.79	1.81

Notes to Amer Management:

These pro forma financial data incorporate the fiscal year 1987 revised budget presented to the Union Bank on September 16, 1986, with the following additional assumptions:

1. Equity infusion of $5 million in November 1986
2. Royalty accrual of $1,009,000 reclassified to equity
3. Nicklaus royalty of $400,000 paid to Nicklaus semi-annually

Footnotes to Summary:

[a]Fiscal 1984 includes the results of operations for Japan for the entire year, while fiscal 1985 includes the results of operations for Japan for five months. Japan is now accounted for by the equity method of accounting.

[b]Fiscal 1985 net loss of $1,932 does not reflect a gain on sale of Japan of $4,273.

[c]Depreciation (not shown) = $346,000 in 1985; $339,000 in 1986.

knew he would be in a tough "middle position of the triangle," serving as both conduit and peacemaker. His challenge would be to "stay true to 'x' amount of cash infusion" for MacGregor.

ENDNOTES

[1]The PIMS approach used a detailed multiple regression analysis of the profit experiences for many businesses. The processed data were expected to answer, based on the experiences of other businesses operating under similar conditions, the following: (1) what profit rate is normal for a given business, (2) if the business continues on its current track, what will its future operating results be, (3) what strategic changes in the business have promise of improving these results, and (4) how will profitability or cash

flow change given a specific future strategy? The basic idea behind PIMS was to provide top managers with insight and information on expected profit performance of different kinds of businesses under different competitive conditions. Among the factors investigated and analyzed were market share, total marketing expenditures, product quality, R&D expenditures, and investment intensity. Thirty-five factors accounted for more than 80 percent of the variation in profit in the 600 business units analyzed in the PIMS database. Reports generated from the PIMS analysis included the PAR report, which specified the return on investment (ROI) that was normal (or par) for similar businesses. It also identified the major strengths and weaknesses of the particular business that accounted for the variation in PAR ROI when compared with all businesses in the PIMS database.

Case 23

Grupo Bacardi de Mexico, S.A.

The cold, blue eyes of Pepín Bosch stared down from the portrait on the wall of the boardroom. Bosch's gaze fell directly on Isaac Chertorivski, executive president of Bacardi y Cía, and his management team as they concluded their annual review of Grupo Bacardi's successes. It had been a good meeting, for 1991 had been yet another exceptional year. In this boardroom, whose walls were lined with a connoisseur's collection of Mexican art, Chertorivski felt the weight of four generations of management: Don Facundo Bacardi y Maso, who founded the company; Pepín Bosch, who had set the course for Bacardi Mexico 60 years earlier; Ernesto Robles Leon, the patrician dictator whose tenure had been marked by extremes of success and failure; and Juan Grau, the brilliant engineer whose strategy, management philosophy, and personal charisma had led to a rebirth of the operation.

Mexico had been one of the first foreign markets for Cuban-born Bacardi, and the site of many valuable lessons in managing the growth of the line of rum products invented by Don Facundo in 1862. The Mexican corporate headquarters, designed by the prominent Bauhaus architect Ludwig Mies van der Rohe in 1956, was one of Pepín Bosch's many monuments to his global strategy, a strategy that had increased the wealth of the family shareholders and had made BACARDI® rum the number-one-selling spirit in the world.

As he considered the experiences of his predecessors, Chertorivski was faced with the challenges of how to manage success and how to use the new management team structure to meet the opportunities and risks of the future. He warned the team, "We have fought our way to the top, yet we must be wary of complacency and arrogance. Do you know the saying '*Establo de vacas contentas*'?[1] I will never tolerate this."

The Bacardi Heritage

Meeting risks and challenges had always been a part of Bacardi's heritage. How these risks were met became focal points of corporate legends. These legends, passed down through the company, focused on the actions and work of individuals who had become tiles in the mosaic that was Bacardi. They served as illustrations of the spirit and culture that defined Bacardi: a culture held tightly together by the common bonds of friendship and loyalty and a spirit best described by the shared values of Bacardi people: quality, teamwork, creativity, long-term vision, productivity, high energy, and, most of all, family.

From its inception, Bacardi was a family affair. In 1862, Don Facundo Bacardi y Maso developed the secret formula and process that took the rough molasses made from sugarcane and transformed it into a pure, mellow, and dry light rum (Exhibit 1).

This case was prepared by Ted Forbes under the supervision of Lynn A. Isabella, Associate Professor of Business Administration.

Exhibit 1

How Rum Is Made

Rum is a spirit obtained from the distillation of fermented sugarcane products. Originally produced in the West Indies, rum is commonly made in all areas of the world where sugarcane grows. Sugarcane was introduced to the West Indies in the fifteenth century by Spain soon after Christopher Columbus opened up trade routes to the area. Rum was initially known as "kill devil," later referred to as "rumbullion," and eventually became the colloquial "rum." Early rums were known for their rough taste and were commonly cut with water. Most navies considered rum an essential ingredient in the well-being of their fleets. Differences in raw materials, fermentation processes, distillation, and aging methods now account for the wide variety of taste, color, and bouquet.

Rum is most commonly made from molasses, which is fermented through the introduction of yeast cultures. The fermentation takes from 2 to 12 days, depending on the process used; the fermented mixture is known as a "mash." Following fermentation, the mash is distilled; it is heated, and the evaporate is forced through a column, where the alcohol condenses out first. The resulting product is raw rum with a high alcohol content (at least 100 proof). The raw rum is stored in oak barrels, which add color and flavor and which mellow the distillate. After several years, the rum is charcoal filtered and blended to taste.

Various types and grades of rum are produced through combinations of filtering, aging, and blending. The clear, or white, rums are filtered both before and after aging. The darker rums are usually filtered before aging and often filtered after aging. All rums are combinations of different fermentation, distillation, and aging methods. Each of these phases directly influences the quality of the final product, which places a premium on the raw materials and yeasts, as well as the distiller's and blender's arts.

Rum is often consumed with fruit juices, colas, and other mixers, although the older, darker, premium blends are best enjoyed straight up or with tonic water and lime.

Word of the quality of Don Facundo's blend spread rapidly, and *ron BACARDI®* won gold medal after gold medal at world expositions; it was even credited with saving the life of the future king of Spain. While Don Facundo supervised the distilling, aging, and blending, his eldest son, Emilio, ran the office, and his two younger sons, Facundo and Jose, worked in the distillery and in sales and promotion.

From the humble beginnings of a small tin-roofed distillery, shared with a colony of fruit bats, BACARDI® rum became one of the world's most powerful brands—and *el murcielago* ("the bat") became its symbol. Currently, the descendants of Don Facundo still ran the company, maintained the culture, and answered each challenge with the same spirit as their ancestors. For almost a century after Don Facundo made his first bottle of rum, Cuba served as the base for a business that seemed to grow without limits. In 1958, because of the imminent danger of nationalization, Bacardi took the brand out of Cuba. Then, in 1960, the Bacardi spirit faced its ultimate challenge: Fidel Castro illegally confiscated the financial and physical assets of Bacardi and Company. There were other assets, however, he was not able to steal: the brand, the people, and their spirit. These assets were the foundation of all of Bacardi. These assets built Grupo Bacardi de Mexico.

The Era of Pepín Bosch

The Beginnings of Bacardi Mexico

Pepín Bosch was born in 1898 in Santiago de Cuba, the site of the tin-roofed building that housed the first Bacardi operation. Educated in the United States, Bosch returned to Cuba to work in his family's sugar mills. Bosch quickly worked his way into management and amassed a sizable fortune; nevertheless, the price of sugar collapsed in 1920, and Bosch soon found himself in Havana, working as a bookkeeper with First National City Bank, an American concern managed by a contact he had made in the sugar business. During his summers in Santiago, Bosch had fallen in love with a childhood friend, Enriqueta Schueg Bacardi, granddaughter of Don Facundo Bacardi. In 1922, they were married. In 1931, he began to work for Bacardi.

Hoping to expand internationally, Bacardi opened its first plant outside Cuba in Mexico in 1931. The man sent to open the Mexican operation was Jose Bacardi Fernandez. His business instincts, however, were not the best. When he died in May 1933 of pneumonia, the Mexican operation was in a shambles. Fearing a drain on an otherwise healthy business, Enrique Schueg asked Pepín Bosch to go to Mexico City to close down the operation. When Bosch got to Mexico, however, he sensed not an operation in disarray but a real business opportunity.

Observing that most Mexicans mixed their liquor with Coca-Cola, Bosch launched a marketing campaign linking the two. A bottle of Bacardi and a case of Coke made an instant *fiesta.* To differentiate BACARDI® rum from other liquors, Bosch had the product packaged in the same wicker-covered jugs that were used in Cuba. He increased the advertising budget, broadened distribution channels, and expanded production. Within a year, sales revenues had doubled, and by the end of 1934, all of the corporate debts were retired. Most important, the Mexican operation paid its first dividend to the Bacardi family shareholders.

Mexico was a formative experience for Bosch because it confirmed and solidified the management style he had set for himself. With his cold, blue eyes, soft speech, photographic memory, and clear sense of direction, Bosch could be an intimidating boss. He was always willing to reprimand a subordinate but was uncomfortable offering direct praise for a job well done. Bosch preferred to pass along congratulations indirectly, often telling a coworker how he had been pleased with someone's work, knowing that the word would eventually reach the right person.

The Legacy of Bosch

The Mexican turnaround proved to be the springboard for Bosch's career at Bacardi, a career that not only marked similar successes in other international markets but that also ultimately took him to the very top of the company. Immediately after reviving the Mexican market, Bosch went to Puerto Rico in 1936 to establish a facility to supply the U.S. market. Bosch finally returned to Santiago in 1947, with an unmistakable aura of success surrounding him as he took over as president.

From the top of the organization, Bosch began to leave his imprint on the whole company. Believing he needed to have his eyes and ears in all aspects of the company, he had the headquarters in Santiago gutted and redesigned so that all employees worked at their desks in one large room, Bosch included. A visitor to the facility would see a waiting room with swinging glass doors at the far end; through the glass doors was the single large office, and in the back left corner was Bosch's desk. He could see every employee, and every employee could see him. One executive recounted, "If you wanted to speak with Bosch, you would stand at the front of the room and wave to him. If he had time to meet with you, he would motion you over to his desk."

Bosch directed the careers of all Bacardi employees with a high degree of success. His instinctive approach to personnel decisions, however, sometimes led to mistakes; he often decided on new hires and promotions purely on the basis of people being *simpatico* to him. For example, Bosch selected the vice president of administration for the new plant in Recife, Brazil, based on an acquaintance he made at dinner. Once, the company plane was flying Bosch to Brazil on business. It was a 40-hour flight from Cuba, and the pilot had inadvertently forgotten to notify the Brazilian authorities of his flight plan. When the plane landed in Brazil to refuel, unannounced and unauthorized, Bosch, his wife, the pilot, and the copilot were thrown in jail. A friend of Bosch's, the president of Pan American Airlines in Brazil, helped clear up the misunderstanding, and they were soon on their way again. When they arrived at their destination in Recife, they were met by the district manager for Pan Am, who had set them up in the best suite in town and invited them out to dinner. Over dinner, it became clear to Bosch that he and the district manager saw things alike, and Bosch, who was there to initiate the opening of a new Bacardi distillery in Recife, appointed the man vice president of administration for the new plant. Unfortunately, the choice ultimately proved to be a bad one.

Bosch was a man who found it hard to admit he was wrong. When the sales manager for Brazil proved to be dishonest, lining his savings account with fictional expenses and paying for exotic family trips out of the company's treasury, Bosch obstinately refused to fire him. Despite the fact that all of the other vice presidents confronted Bosch with evidence and pushed for the man's removal, he would not give in. One of Bosch's key executives ultimately resigned over Bosch's handling of this dishonest manager. Three months after the loss of that key executive, Bosch finally let the sales manager go.

Despite his dictatorial mien and obstinate ways, Bosch had a soft side. He was known to pass out pesos to the poor in Santiago; several times he paid for the entire university education of complete strangers. He created harmony among the Bacardi labor force by paying better wages and offering better benefits than any other local company. As one executive commented: "Bosch controlled through an almost mystic process of terror, love, appreciation, and loyalty. You put it all together, and they don't sound right. But it worked."[2]

Bosch left Mexico in 1934, but he continued to run the operation from Cuba until the mid-1950s, when he hired Ernesto Robles Leon. Although Bosch had turned the organization around almost 20 years earlier, the personality and initiative of Robles Leon resulted in phenomenal success. Unfortunately, they also culminated in phenomenal failure that would once again jeopardize the future of Bacardi Mexico.

The Era of Ernesto Robles Leon

Bacardi Mexico Grows

Ernesto Robles Leon was a lawyer, "a tall, eloquent, charming, aristocratic figure with slicked-back hair and a pencil mustache. Like Bosch, he possessed the all-important quality of *presencia*."[3] Robles Leon had two crucial talents for the Mexican market: a flair for marketing and an adroit political hand. He took the strategy that Bosch had begun and built BACARDI® rum into the dominant brand in the spirits industry in Mexico. By marketing a tropical image of fun and popularity and by using a very successful and famous radio campaign *(Si hay BACARDI®, hay ambiente)*[4], Robles Leon increased sales every year. He kept prices competitive, while positioning the product as a premium brand. He built and solidified relationships with the Mexican government, which was a crucial component in running a successful business in Mexico.

Robles Leon ran his business as a family affair. At one point, he had four sons on the payroll. His style was decidedly authoritarian; he saw Bacardi as a personal empire. So strong was Robles Leon's need to control that he even fired his own son, Eduardo, in order to maintain his grip on the company.

Bacardi Mexico's Downhill Slide

Ultimately, Robles Leon was affected by his own pride and success. Because his income was based on a percentage of gross sales, he seemed interested only in increasing the number of cases sold, without regard to profitability or income stream. In addition, he enjoyed the trappings of power, most particularly the corporate plane, which he reserved for his own personal use. Robles Leon grew complacent and arrogant, as did many of his managers. The bar in the executive dining room was open from 1:00 P.M. until 6:00 P.M., and most of the managers were there as soon as it opened. Robles Leon reportedly said, "If you are going to sell rum, you have to drink rum."

These attitudes, coupled with strategic shortsightedness, finally brought Bacardi Mexico to the brink of destruction. In 1974, the price of sugarcane molasses tripled, and Robles Leon responded by raising the price of rum. Then, in an effort to boost gross sales, he introduced a line of cheaper rum, PALMAS®, and *aguardiente*, an inexpensive liquor, under the BACARDI® name and trademark. In order to maintain an uninterrupted dividend stream, he reduced advertising expenditures. These actions cheapened the BACARDI® brand image and identity and eroded rum's share of the liquor market.

Moreover, Robles Leon failed to realize the gravity of the market challenges coming from the Mexican brandy producers. The grape growers and the brandy industry successfully lobbied the Mexican government for preferred tax status, which resulted in the brandy industry's obtaining a $60 million operating-income advantage over Bacardi and the rest of the rum industry. The grape growers and brandy producers put this advantage to work by advertising heavily. Although marketing studies showed that brandy products were gaining ground, Robles Leon ignored them, refusing to believe that BACARDI® rum could lose share. These highly mixable brandies began to eat away steadily at Bacardi's market share, and by the mid-1970s, the brandy industry had captured 90 percent of the rum market.

The Mexican market, which Bacardi had turned from tequila to rum, had turned into brandy country.

Matters were made worse by a falling out with the Mexican government in the early 1970s that resulted in severe penalties for Bacardi. The government assessed Bacardi for taxes on spirits that the Mexican Treasury declared as sold, but which had actually evaporated during the aging process. The resulting audit led to a charge of $160 million, which exceeded the value of the entire company.

After the death of Robles Leon's wife in the mid-1970s, he became even more interested (aided by the company plane) in traveling and social pursuits than in running the company. As one employee recalled, "When Robles's wife died, there was no one to control him."

While Robles Leon was losing his grip in Mexico, major management changes were unfolding for Bacardi worldwide.

A New Management Philosophy for Bacardi

Top Management at Bacardi Changes

In 1976, changes in top management began to signal a new era for Bacardi worldwide. With the resignation of Pepín Bosch, the new top managers of Bacardi, Eddy Neilsen and Manuel Jorge Cutillas, both descendants of Don Facundo, split the responsibilities of overseeing the Bacardi empire. Power that was once wielded by a single individual, Bosch, was now shared by two executives: Neilsen ran Bacardi Imports (Miami, Florida), where he oversaw the U.S. market, while Cutillas served as chairman and chief executive officer (CEO) of Bacardi Mexico and also headed Bacardi & Co. (Nassau, Bahamas) and Bacardi International Ltd. (Bermuda) as shown in Exhibit 2. Together, they initiated a new style of management for Bacardi.

This new era would have a direct effect on the evolution of Bacardi Mexico. Mexico was Cutillas's first CEO position. He had previously been worldwide director of quality assurance, and a number of family members believed that Cutillas did not have the training for the job. However, as one executive stated, "The result was that he came to Mexico, he listened, he worked, and he began to believe in the country and its people."

In 1977, Eddie Neilsen and Manuel Jorge Cutillas chose Juan Grau to bring the new management philosophy to Mexico. According to Grau:

> When I came, Mexico was in big trouble. There was doubt as to whether we could continue the operation. Part of my charge was to make that assessment. Although Robles Leon had done a tremendous job from 1952 to 1960, he had taken it easy after that. He didn't realize what was happening and had not built an organization under him. That was not his style.

The Era of Juan Grau

Back to Mexico

Juan Grau has been described as charming, intelligent, conceptual, known for moments of explosive anger, confident in his authority and unafraid to use it—in short, a man with *presencia*. Grau grew up in Santiago de Cuba as childhood

EXHIBIT 2

Organization of the Bacardi Companies

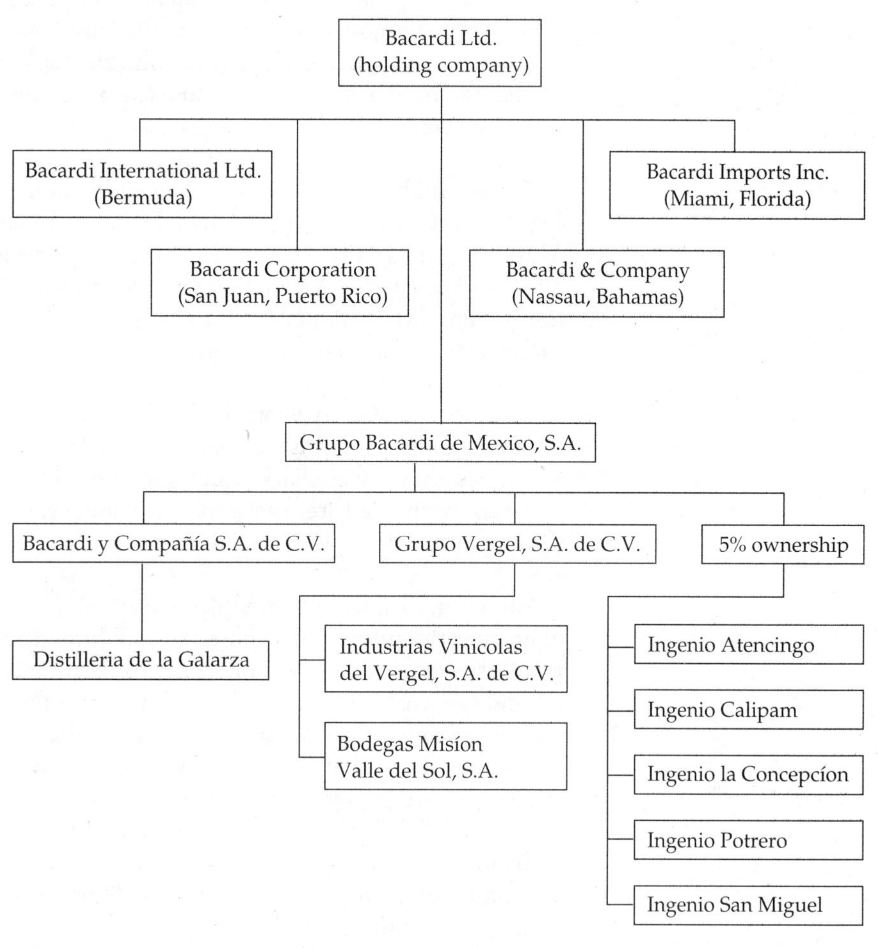

friend of Neilsen, Cutillas, and other Bacardi family members. Among his other friends was Fidel Castro. He received a degree in chemical engineering from the Massachusetts Institute of Technology in Cambridge, a prestigious engineering school in the United States. Unbeknownst to Grau, his father had secured him a job at the Bacardi-owned HATUEY® brewery in Havana. Upon graduation, however, he took a job with Procter & Gamble in Havana. He worked there for a year. When his father died in 1950, Grau accepted a position as technical director of the BACARDI® rum distillery in Santiago, a choice that would link his future to BACARDI® rum.

Grau's time at the distillery set the tone for his future experiences:

> We had a wonderful team at that plant. The distillery and the brewery were on the same premises, and Mr. Bosch was the president of both. He brought in a group of young engineers, including his son, George. There was tremendous

> team cooperation; it was really the best years of your life. It was a family. The guy in charge of the brewery, Joaquin Bacardi, Sr., was also an engineer. I talked with him every day in the brewery. My direct boss was Daniel Bacardi, and I had regular contact with him even though he was at the rum plant. In the afternoon, at 5 o'clock, Mr. Bosch would come to the lab to see what was happening. I was 22 years old and was in direct contact with the top guys in the company. They were your family and your friends. You felt that you belonged, that everyone wanted to help you.

Grau's analytical and engineering skills impressed Pepín Bosch, and in 1954, Bosch sent Grau to Mexico to help design and build a new distillery. The taste of Mexican rum had always been slightly different from the Cuban product. Soil variations in Mexico gave the molasses a different flavor, resulting in a slightly different-tasting rum. Bosch wanted Grau to design and build a new facility to rectify the taste variance as well as to increase capacity to meet sales forecasts. Grau recalled:

> I was sent to Mexico when I was 27 to design the distillery—I went by myself. I hired a couple of draftsmen, and I designed the thing myself. I wasn't too sure of the design, so I went back to Cuba and sat down with two of the engineers and asked for their advice. There was no hierarchy, no boss to clear this with . . . we were informal and very much a team.

Although the plant was completed in 1956, Grau stayed on in Mexico until 1959, operating the pilot plant where Bacardi honed its abilities to produce the same rum taste from different molasses grown in varying climatological conditions around the world. This expertise had become one of the core competencies of Bacardi worldwide. After Mexico, Bosch moved Grau to Puerto Rico to oversee the expansion of the plant in Catano. This plant had become the linchpin in Bosch's strategy for supplying the U.S. market.

In 1960, Bosch planned and executed a strategic move to Brazil and once again chose Grau to build the facility. The site chosen in Recife presented many problems and difficulties, but Grau solved the problems quickly and had the plant up and running in 11 months.

A difference of opinion between Grau and Bosch over the management of the BACARDI® rum plant in Recife was to interrupt Grau's steady rise within the Bacardi organization. In 1963, Grau left Bacardi at the age of 36. A dispute over the firing of a dishonest sales manager was for Grau "the straw that broke the camel's back." Grau resigned and returned to Mexico, intending to go into business on his own. He ran his own business for several years, noting, "This was when I discovered concepts such as cash flow!"

Grau's Management Philosophy Evolves

Grau's time in Mexico away from Bacardi was crucial to his development as a manager, for it taught him two important lessons. The first was cost consciousness:

> Very few people realize that the real reason for being in business is to create wealth. Most people say it is to make profit, but it is in fact to create wealth. And people often don't realize *where* you create wealth; it is in added value and in gross margin. This is when I learned about what I call the *critical resource.* I am a chemist,

> and the idea came to me from thinking about chemical reactions and their limiting reagents. There is always one resource in a company that is more scarce, and you have to optimize that. For example, when I was at Crane Valves, a U.S. company in Mexico, there were two large lathes making parts for valves and pumps. I realized that we could not make enough of both because we just didn't have the capacity. And then I saw that, per hour, when I was making pumps, I could get four times as much added value out of those two lathes as when I was making valves; I decided I had to choose—I decided that I would convert to being a pump manufacturer even though Crane was better known for making valves. The president of Crane in New York said to me, "But Juan, we are a valve company." I said, "Do you want to make money, or do you want to be a valve company? If you want to make money, we will be a pump company; if you want to be a valve company, buy a page in *Time* magazine; it is much cheaper." The president accepted that, and we took a company that had been losing money for five years and turned it around.

Grau's other seminal lesson came from his exposure to the concept of participative management. After turning Crane's operation around, Grau was looking for new challenges. During the early 1970s, with the Arab oil embargo in place, Mexico was in a boom period. One of Grau's competitors in the pump-and-valve business had bought an oil-field-equipment company and hired Juan Grau to run it.

> I [Grau] did not know anything about this business, and this company had tremendously good managers. They were excellent managers, except each one was concerned with his own function and they did not work together as a team. One was making parts, another was buying parts, another was in charge of quality . . . but each one was doing his own thing. It became a question of changing people or changing the attitudes of people.

One of the executives in the parent corporation of Grau's company introduced Grau to a fellow Cuban, Faustino Sotto, who was also an engineer. Sotto had become fascinated with the field of organizational development. Together, they began to plan the reorganization of the company, a reorganization that was to solidify Grau's participative style. Sotto recalled:

> One of the first things that happened with Mr. Grau took place in a management meeting . . . a meeting with two vice presidents. They decided to make big changes in the company. When they finished, Grau called me up and said, "Now we know what we are going to do." He explained everything to me, and I said, "That's fine, now how are you going to do it?" Juan replied, "Well, I'm going to summon all of the heads of the departments and tell them that this is how it is going to be." I said, "Juan, that is not going to work." He almost jumped out of his chair, saying "What do you mean it won't work? It is fine!" I replied, "Yes, it is fine, but people won't have any commitment, and if you want this to work, you have to involve the people. Let's go and give the people all of the data without making any conclusions and ask them what would be the ideal company." Grau initially rejected the idea, but he finally agreed with me. We had several meetings and then an executive retreat. Much to our surprise, the conclusion of the people was exactly what these three "geniuses" had already concluded. It was really dramatic because it all took place before vacation, and they restructured the company while all of the workers were gone. When they came back, it was a totally different company.

Back to Bacardi

After ten years on his own, Juan Grau could still not ignore the influence Bacardi had on him, and, in 1974, he accepted an offer from Manuel Jorge Cutillas to run the research-and-development laboratories in the new Jacksonville, Florida, facility:

> My heart was always with Bacardi. I choose my friends very carefully; I am very selective. For I have found that friendship is like money, easier made than kept. I believe that from a good enduring friendship comes a trust that binds forever and brings peace and enjoyment. The main reason I came back to Bacardi in 1974, to a much lesser position than I was holding, was to work again with my friends. The link between friendship and success is the climate for encouragement, for support, for enjoyment that trust creates. In this climate, the attributes of friendship, candor, and deep mutual concern become the attributes of a successful company.

In 1976, Grau, responding to Manuel Jorge Cutillas's challenge to evaluate the ongoing viability of the Mexican operation, returned to Mexico. Until Neilsen and Cutillas could convince Robles Leon to retire, Grau's title was controller, but his responsibilities were more in line with those of chief operating officer. Grau faced daily battles in bringing the company to profitability. As one employee recalled, "Every day was a fight between Robles Leon and Juan Grau." Grau himself recalled those early days:

> Before I came to Mexico, my office was used to house the information system. When it was converted to an office, Robles Leon told the chief engineer to shut off the air conditioning because the room had not been air conditioned before the computers were put in. That office is unbearable without air conditioning, so he had me suffering in there.

When Robles Leon finally retired after six months, Grau assumed the position of general manager. He had not fully realized, however, what a disastrous state of affairs awaited him. Relations with the Mexican government were at an all-time low. The workers were restless and talking with the unions. Some did not know what was happening, some did not care, and some were taking advantage of the situation. The sales force was demoralized; salespeople were paid on strict commission, and the decrease in sales volume did not leave them enough money to pay for traveling. As a result, they were not in the field and, thus, were not selling. Market share had eroded substantially, and the once premium image of BACARDI® rum was in a shambles. Bacardi Mexico was in a vicious downward spiral.

Bringing Mexico Back to Profitability

Grau's plan was simple in concept, yet complex in execution. The challenge was viewed as simultaneously external and internal: Improve the image of the brand and the morale of the people:

> I went to the records and found out what had happened to sales and gross profit, what was the gross profit, product by product, and what each one brought to the picture. Then we had a company meeting with everyone, including the workers.

> They had been kept in the dark so long that the first thing I had to do was to bring them into reality. Everyone had been talking in the halls, but I decided to bring it all into the open. I told them we were in really tough shape. I told them we had the support of the Bacardi family. I told them that we had this facility, we had the brand, and, most of all, we had them . . . and we had to fight together. I learned a long time ago that the most important thing that I could do was to get that feeling in the people. When you get that fighting spirit, you make ordinary people do extraordinary things.

The overall strategy for Mexico unfolded in distinct stages, which were reflected in the organizational structure (see Exhibit 3). Grau referred to the first stage as "The Turnaround":

> Robles Leon did not have an organization. He had everyone reporting directly to him. The gardener could not move a tree without talking to him. I had to build some structure, because there was none. The simplest thing was to go with a functional organization; I decided I needed a financial/administrative vice president, a marketing/sales vice president, and an industrial vice president. For the industrial position, which would be in charge of plant, equipment manufacturing, and unions, I chose Marco Antonio Delgadillo. He had been my partner in the construction business. For the financial position, I chose Ernesto Rodriguez Mellado, who had been chief accountant. For sales and marketing, I promoted Isaac Chertorivski, who had been in charge of advertising and coordinating the sales force.

Decisively and steadily, other changes were made. The compensation system for the sales force was changed so that the company reimbursed travel expenses and provided a base salary plus commission. The product line was pruned, eliminating *aguardiente* altogether and removing the BACARDI® name and trademark from PALMAS. Grau identified advertising as the critical resource and increased the budget; he also launched a new marketing strategy based on "*Carta de Oro . . . el Sabor Premiado.*"[5] When this campaign failed, he moved quickly to change the marketing strategy; Grau and Chertorivski fired the ad agency. After an extensive search and selection process, a new ad agency was hired; it launched a market-research project that revealed that BACARDI® Añejo had an unexpectedly strong image. The product line was segmented to reach two distinct target markets. Carta Blanca was aimed at the younger population, with the *Agarra la Jarra*[6] campaign, while Añejo was aimed at the older, more affluent population, with the *Añejo . . . la prueba*[7] campaign. Television advertising was used extensively.

Grau encouraged the sales force to create wealth rather than to increase sales volume; creating wealth was accomplished by increasing sales of those products that had the highest contribution margins. Because contribution per case varied across the product lines, Grau devised a new measurement system called margin-equivalent cases (MEC). MEC used the margins on *Carta Blanca* as a baseline and awarded sales commissions on the basis of margin returned by the sale. In order to increase sales of the high-margin products, the sales force had to be persuaded to focus on margin rather than volume. For example, Añejo produced five times the margin of *aguardiente.* In 1977, one-third of Bacardi's 900,000 cases in sales were *aguardiente.* Grau demonstrated to the sales force that the same commissions would be returned by selling only 60,000 cases of Añejo. The concept was simple, but change was not immediate:

EXHIBIT 3

Organizational Evolution of Bacardi Mexico

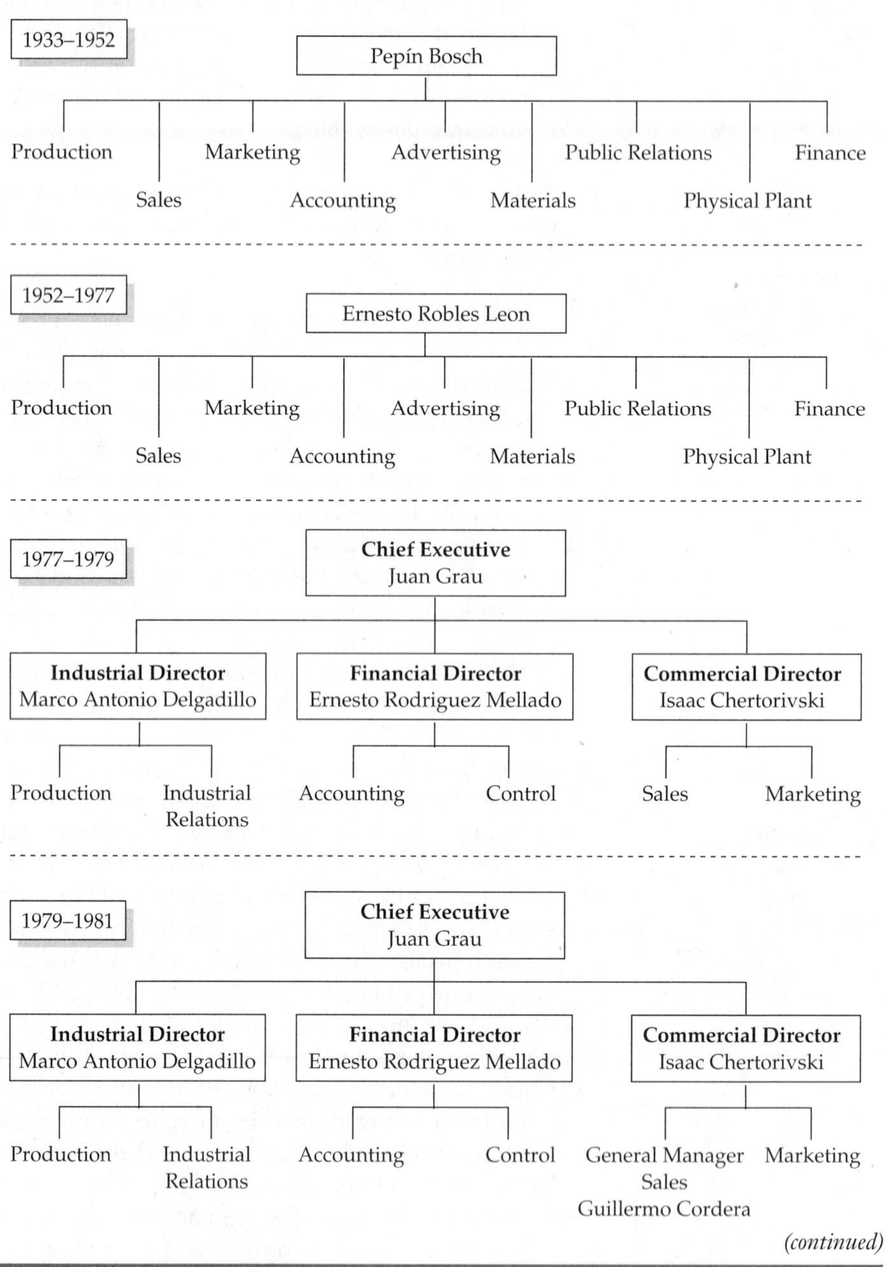

(continued)

It took years, and it took changing a lot of people. We had 60 salespeople. Sounds simple, but for people who were used to straight commission, it was a difficult transition. Isaac, who was very young at the time, and Guillermo Cordera, who came in later, both took that message very clearly to the people. They did it every time, at every sales convention.

EXHIBIT 3 (CONTINUED)

Organizational Evolution of Bacardi Mexico

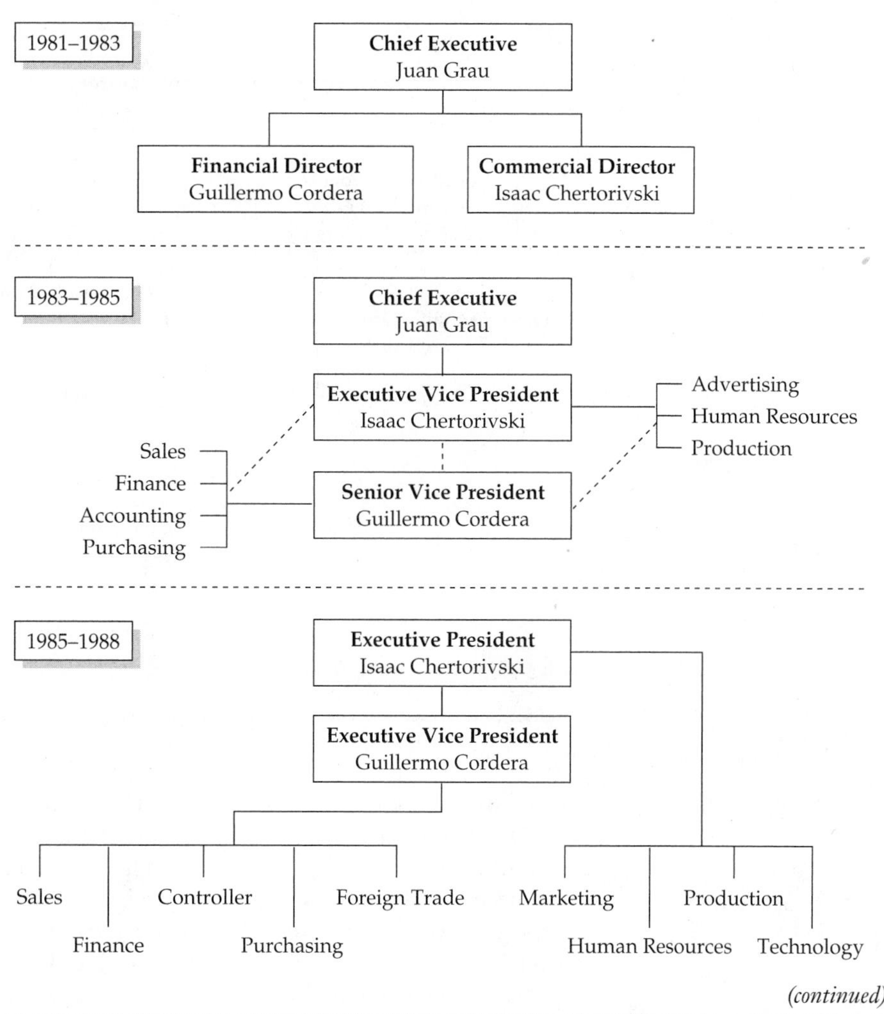

(continued)

Underpinning all of the changes Grau was implementing, there was a basic operating philosophy. To convey this message, Grau used the *el carrito* model:

> The company and each of its employees had to run on four wheels: hard work, enthusiasm, professionalism, and honesty. I didn't mind if the first three of these lost some air—we could blow them back up; but if one wheel, honesty, went down, you were out. And we had quite a few people leaving the company. We lost 10 percent of our sales force to the honesty wheel. People learned very quickly that there was no room for dishonesty.

Grau's initial changes during the turnaround put the company back on course. Sales and profits began to grow, and the precious brand image was improved. Not

EXHIBIT 3 (CONTINUED)

Organizational Evolution of Bacardi Mexico

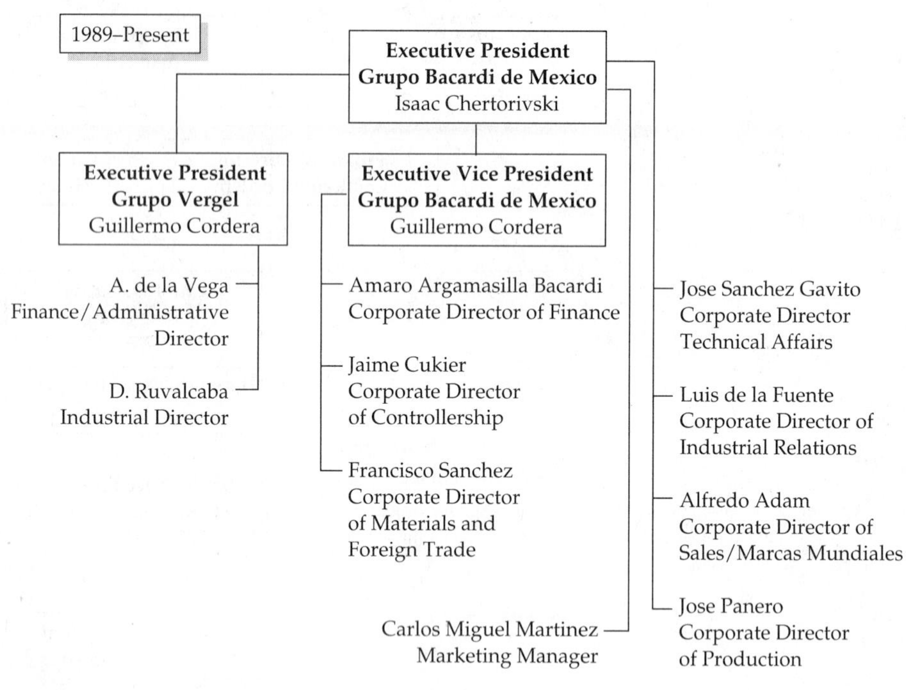

all of his actions, however, worked out. Delgadillo, the industrial director, proved to be less than adept at managing the unions; he antagonized their leadership and tried to intimidate the workers, and as a result the unions won control of the workforce. Grau's initial response was to reduce Delgadillo's areas of responsibility. When that action proved unsatisfactory, Delgadillo was let go. Chertorivski and Ernesto Rodriguez Mellado did not get along well, either. They were constantly fighting over the advertising budget, with Chertorivski wanting to spend and Mellado holding the purse strings tightly. Neither one was willing to concede the middle ground, and, finally, in 1980, Ernesto Rodriguez Mellado gave Grau an ultimatum: either Chertorivski left or he would. Grau fired Rodriguez Mellado and promoted Chertorivski to the position of executive director and chief operating officer (COO) with additional responsibility in human resources, production, acquisitions, and commercial activity.

Synergistic, Three-Headed CEO

With this new management team in place in 1981, Grau began the second phase of his Mexican adventure, what he referred to as the "synergistic, three-headed CEO" (Exhibit 3). Joining Grau at the top were Isaac Chertorivski and Guillermo Cordera:

> We had these two fairly old gentlemen as heads of the sales department. I let the older guy go and brought in a younger one, but he didn't make the grade.

> Guillermo Cordera had been in Venezuela with American Express; he was a manager there. I knew his family very well. He showed a lot of drive, to go work in Venezuela. He came back to Mexico and wanted to know if there was a job for him.
>
> Isaac and I decided to bring him into sales even though he had no experience in that area. He was 29 when he came to the group. We formed "the triumvirate"; that's what the staff called us. Eventually what we did was crisscross functions. Isaac was in charge of marketing, human resources, and technical/production. Cordera was in charge of sales and finance and responsible for accounting and purchasing. One was strong in advertising and marketing, and the other was strong in systems. Both were very bright. By crisscrossing functions and responsibilities, no one was all sales or all marketing or all production. We were so intertwined that we had to work together.

So well did they work together that their success was later immortalized in a three-branched *candelabro* that each kept in his office. The *candelabro* was given to them by the board of directors of Bacardi Mexico. Each branch was engraved with a name and an element: Fire—Isaac Chertorivski, Water—Guillermo Cordera, and Air—Juan Grau.

Fire—Isaac Chertorivski. Chertorivski was a second-generation Mexican; his grandparents emigrated from the Ukraine. He grew up "with limited resources, but with plenty of love, help, and strength." While still at the university, he opened an advertising agency with friends.

> It was a tremendously great experience. . . . I think it was one of my greatest experiences in the whole world because I learned how to build and grow a business. I learned how to deal with clients, how to run a business, how to build a team, and how a business goes broke!

Chertorivski was also involved in the student movements of the 1960s and later coordinated antigovernment activity at the university. After his own ad agency went broke, Chertorivski became media director for the Leo Burnett advertising agency in Mexico City. At 24, he made his first contact with the Bacardi Company.

> I was working at Leo Burnett, the advertising agency. BACARDI® rum was my account; and I made a relationship with Eduardo Robles Leon, the boss's son. Eduardo invited me to join Bacardi Mexico as their media manager—he said that they needed new blood. I was not at all sure about taking the job; Robles Leon was crazy . . . a dictator, a difficult person with no team. However, they offered me lots of money. I was thinking career management—it would be good to go to the client's side for a while—so I took the job.

Six months into his Bacardi Mexico position, Chertorivski decided to return to Leo Burnett. Three days before Chertorivski's departure, Robles Leon communicated how he felt about Chertorivski's upcoming departure. Chertorivski recalled: "He told me that if I left Bacardi, he would pull the BACARDI® rum account from Leo Burnett. I called the general manager of Burnett, and I told him that if I go with you, you will lose this account. And so I stayed with Bacardi."

It soon became clear to Chertorivski that Robles Leon was running the company into the ground.

> In the mid-seventies, I had developed a relationship with Manuel Jorge Cutillas, who was in charge of worldwide quality. He came to Mexico and once asked me how things were going; I told him the truth. I told him that things were very bad, we were going broke, and that Robles Leon was crazy. I told him I was looking for a new job. He asked me to wait—he said that things would change quickly. I kept looking for another job, but then Manuel Jorge became chairman of the board and brought Juan Grau to Mexico.

Chertorivski continued, his face breaking into a broad smile:

> And then I began to train Juan Grau! He trained me to be a manager, and I trained him in marketing! I became Juan's right hand. He was the quarterback, and I was the fullback. He says why don't we do this . . . and I get it done. He is very analytic and has a great strategic mentality; he is the great conceptualizer, the great operator—but I am the great doer. He knows how to put it on paper, and I know how to make it happen.

Four to five months into Grau's tenure in 1977, Chertorivski again almost left Bacardi. As Grau was reorganizing the company, he wanted to put Chertorivski in charge of marketing and hire a sales manager from outside the company.

> I [Chertorivski] said, "If you hire someone from outside, I'm going to leave." I was *hungry,* and even though I lacked the experience, I *wanted* this responsibility. Juan sent me away, but a week later he called me back. "I am going to make you commercial director," Grau told me, "with responsibility for both sales and marketing. But if we don't do well, the first head that will fall will be yours, Isaac." And so we shook hands and went to work. We worked together, we traveled together, and we built a good team.

Water—Guillermo Cordera. Cordera came on board in February 1979 as manager of the sales force. Trained as a certified public accountant, Cordera had risen rapidly through the ranks of IBM and American Express to a general manager's position in Venezuela. Guillermo did not like Venezuela, however, and wanted to return to Mexico. Cordera recalled expressing concern to Grau, when offered the position at Bacardi, about his lack of experience in managing a sales force:

> Grau's reply was, "Management doesn't make the sales; the salesmen make the sales. What we need is a *system* to manage the salesmen; just think of sales as a system, Guillermo." I took the job because I wanted to return to Mexico, because of the prestige of Bacardi, and because of the great challenge it presented to me. They were in bad financial shape, and I could bring financial knowledge. And I had the utmost respect for Juan Grau . . . he was a very strong man, and this was a chance to work for him.

The changes Cordera made quickly were instrumental to Grau's turnaround plan. He reorganized the structure of the sales force and eliminated redundancies in the territories and tasks. He also demanded that the sales force begin to polish Bacardi's tarnished image:

> On a trip to Guadalajara, Grau, Chertorivski, and I visited a store where the BACARDI® rum display was a shambles. Juan asked, "How can we sell with such a

> bad image?" We launched Operation *Escoba* (broom), which removed old, damaged products from the store shelves and spruced up the shelf displays.

The salesmen were provided with new labels, and every single bottle of BACARDI® rum in Mexico was dusted, polished, and relabeled. Cordera instilled cost consciousness in all the sales force, introducing forms to fill out for product giveaways. Soon the sales force became aware of the cost of their generosity.

> We were operating under the motto, "We have not a single peso to waste, but we have millions to invest." This was not an easy job. The average salesman had 18 years with Bacardi and was 50 years old. I was 28. I worked with a 50-year-old sales manager; people were set in their ways; they thought their way was the only way. It was hard to be accepted by them.

At the 1979 sales convention in Acapulco, MEC was used for the first time in the corporate sales contests. The top three sales teams, measured by MEC, won a trip to Rio de Janeiro. Sales goals were posted on the walls of the factory in "alliterative" steps: 2,222,222 liters sold; 3,333,333 liters sold; 4,444,444 liters sold. The plan began to work, and the target grew ever higher.

Bacardi Mexico established a reputation with its wholesalers as a professional company, tough but fair. Cordera shortened credit terms and offered an extra 1 percent discount to wholesalers who attached a check to their order. Although Bacardi demanded much from its distributors, it gave good discounts to those who followed the plan. Cordera remembered having to revoke the account of one of Bacardi's biggest wholesalers in Guadalajara because of late payments: "We had to send a message to the trade that this was the way it was going to be with Bacardi. If you play it our way, we will take very good care of you, but if you don't . . ."

Organizational Schizophrenia Creates a Management Team

Grau, Chertorivski, and Cordera each had offices in a corner of the large, rectilinear building that was the headquarters of Bacardi Mexico. While the "holy trinity" made tremendous strides in furthering the profitability of Bacardi Mexico, Grau was aware of the difficulties the arrangement caused other managers:

> Isaac and Guillermo were more or less at the same level. We found two things; there was a big gap between the triumvirate and the managers, and the company was beginning to split into the Isaac group and the Cordera group. So we decided that we had to change that organization. We were very flexible and found it easy to change it in response to how people were behaving and to the maturity of the people. Instead of forcing a structure, we adapted the structure to the people.
>
> We decided that we could not have two people here at the same level. Manuel Jorge Cutillas and I decided to make Isaac executive vice president—this was in 1983–84—second to me, and Cordera, senior VP; then we had a group of functional directors, but they were really vice presidents.

At this point (1983), Mexico had arrived at the third phase, the "management team" (Exhibit 3).

With the turmoil of the late 1970s behind them, Grau and his team began to show significant growth in the Mexican liquor market. The BACARDI® brand had been rehabilitated to the point where a superpremium rum, Solera, was launched successfully. Gains were made in the political arena as well. Bacardi Mexico succeeded in convincing the Mexican government to rescind the favorable excise-tax status it had granted to brandy producers. Bacardi found a level playing field on which to compete with Domecq, Mexico's leading brandy producer.

When Grau took over in 1977, sales were 750,000 cases per year; in 1983, sales hit 2 million cases. With the spotlight of the Mexican business community shining on Grau, he saw a chance to send a message about the role young managers played and the values he had learned earlier in his career.

> We were approached by a prestigious organization called the Association for Sales and Marketing Executives. Every year they chose an "executive of the year." In late 1983, they came to see me and decided that I would be named "Distinguished Executive of the Year for 1984." I was delighted, but I didn't think they could honor me alone. The young men who had worked with me were just as responsible. So I told them that I would not accept unless they honored all three of us. This was important, to show what the team could do. To have three people named as executives of the year was a first in Mexico, and it has not happened again. It was important to send a signal in Mexico that you could work as a team and have very young people. In my speech I said that we were a synergistic executive body, to which each brings our special talents, and, together, we become a very strong executive. Isaac and Guillermo bring youth and enthusiasm, and I bring my international experience.

By 1985, sales in Mexico had reached 3.3 million cases. At that time, Grau was asked to head the U.S. operation, Bacardi Imports. After consulting with Manual Jorge Cutillas and the board of directors, Grau asked Isaac Chertorivski, one of those young executives who had been instrumental in accomplishing the turnaround, to come to his office. "Isaac, I think it's the moment . . . we have decided to appoint you president."

The Era of Isaac Chertorivski

Isaac Chertorivski was a large man, six feet tall and very fit. Although his wide face broke rapidly into a smile, there was an underlying intensity to his gaze—and to his opinions. Chertorivski's desk sat at one end of a large suite. To his left was a floor-to-ceiling window that ran the length of the room. At 1:00 P.M. every day in the summer, he looked out to see 500 children in Bacardi hats and T-shirts—sons and daughters of Bacardi workers—waiting for their mothers to take them home from the company-sponsored day camp. On the walls were photographs of Chertorivski with former Mexican president Miguel de la Madrid; with current president Carlos Salinas de Gortari; with his wife, son, and daughter; and with Juan Grau. Behind him was a bookcase with more photographs, assorted books and binders, and more than a dozen bottles of BACARDI® rums. At his left side was a table with five telephones and a pair of interesting sculptures. His desk chair was missing the casters on two legs, and he rocked back and forth as he talked. He picked up one of the sculptures.

> As a child, I always knew I wanted to be a leader of something. I studied business administration at the University of Mexico because I wanted to be a leader. I get a

lot of satisfaction working in a big position in a big company, and I want to make Bacardi the best company in Mexico. This sculpture . . . every year a survey is made of the top 20 companies in Mexico, and Bacardi has been first in each category for the last eight years in a row—with a 10 to 20 percent lead. This one [sculpture] is for the best human resources company in the country. This other one is for the best marketing company; we also have the award for the best work environment. I am proud of these awards because of the competition from very highly structured companies like Unilever, Procter & Gamble, and Coca-Cola. We are not so structured. We are very free here, totally professional, and unencumbered by rigid structures.

At 44, Isaac Chertorivski was one of the most successful and influential executives in Mexico. In his wallet, Chertorivski carried two business cards, one engraved "Executive Presidente, Grupo Bacardi," the other engraved, "Asesor del Presidente de la Republica."[8]

Grupo Bacardi de Mexico's expanding sales base helped push worldwide BACARDI® rum sales to new heights in the late 1980s. In 1987, BACARDI® rum sold 20 million cases worldwide, with 25 percent of those sales in Mexico; in 1988, 21 million cases worldwide, with 27 percent in Mexico; and in 1989, 22 million cases worldwide, with 28 percent in Mexico; in 1989, Grupo Bacardi sold 6.1 million cases in Mexico and became the third-largest producer of beverage alcohol in the world. Between 1981 and 1991, sales increased 539 percent. In 1991, sales exceeded 7.7 million cases, and Bacardi held a 90 percent share of the Mexican rum market and 34 percent of the total Mexican spirits market. (See Exhibit 4 for products and Exhibits 5, 6, and 7 for sales and market-share information.)

Chertorivski's Current Management Team

The combination of business success and management camaraderie heavily influenced the organization that Chertorivski built for Grupo Bacardi. The corporate ethic was built around results, quality, and teamwork. When he gained the presidency in 1985, Chertorivski began to build.

My first challenge was to build a strong executive team. Everything is a continuing process, and I often talked with Juan during this phase. I began by looking at the team that was in place at that moment, then I considered what kind of team we were going to need.

I had a different idea from other companies. For example, most companies want their financial area under one director; I put two—one in finance and one controller. Why? In finance was Amaro Argamasilla Bacardi, with 20 years in the company. I wanted to reinforce this area so I brought in a man from IBM, Jaime Cukier. He was their corporate controller for all of Mexico, and he had 22 years' experience. This combination gives me a solid "A" team in finance.

In the operations area, we had three people. First was Jose Panero, who had built six Bacardi plants yet never worked for Bacardi; he's a lone wolf, never before worked on a team. I made him VP for production. As VP for technical affairs, I put in Jose Sanchez Gavito; he is in charge of the distillery and quality control. And in materials we have a man who has been with us 25 years, who has earned our confidence, Francisco Sanchez. The way this all works is that when one guy is not in Mexico, the other can cover for him. They each get along very well, and they can visit our various plants interchangeably.

EXHIBIT 4

Products Manufactured by Grupo Bacardi

RUMS

Bacardi Solera 1873

A super-premium product positioned at the top of the Bacardi line.

Bacardi Añejo

A premium product that helped Bacardi Mexico recover its position in the spirits market.

Bacardi Carta de Oro

An amber rum that is similar to the white rum.

Bacardi Carta Blanca

This white Bacardi rum sets the standard for the company's products.

Ron Palmas Oscuro

Less expensive than the Bacardi brand rums, Ron Palmas targets the middle of the rum market.

BACARDI COCKTAILS

Planter's Punch

A fruit-based Bacardi rum cocktail.

Piña Colada

A popular cocktail made with Bacardi rum, pineapple juice, and coconut milk.

Mango Colada

Similar to the Piña Colada, except mango is substituted for pineapple.

Daiquiri

One of the oldest rum drinks, using lime juice as a base.

Fraesi Colada

Similar to the Piña Colada, except strawberry is substituted for pineapple.

BRANDIES

Viejo Vergel

Vergel's premium brandy.

Gran Vergel

Vergel's basic brandy.

(continued)

EXHIBIT 4 (CONTINUED)

Products Manufactured by Grupo Bacardi

WINES

Chateau Avignon
A classic red wine.

Tannhauser
A white table wine.

Cordianne—Vino Tinto
A red wine cooler.

Cordianne—Vino Blanco
A white wine cooler.

> Then we have human resources. When Juan Grau named me executive vice president of the company, he put me in charge of HR. I said, "Well, Juan, I need someone I can trust." So I brought in a friend of mine, an old college pal, who had been my political rival. He had many years of HR experience with Kimberly-Clark, Bimbo [a very large Mexican baked-goods company], and Unilever. This is Luis de la Fuente, and he has been with us 12 years now.
>
> Next is sales; today Cordera looks at sales. In marketing, we don't have a VP, but we have three managers. Marketing is my area. It is the key in this type of company. I work with the managers and I see *everything* that goes on in marketing.
>
> This is the group. [See Exhibit 8.]. We are nine people—first-class people, very willing—a great team. We have a special kind of organization that can handle any situation. No one is stuck in one particular area, and this is how we like to work. This team, our average time working with Bacardi is 14 years, and our average work experience is 25 years. All are professionals, and we are all friends. All have worked in other companies, and we all bring a wide variety of experiences.

When asked what he looked for in a team member, Chertorivski replied:

> First of all, we like to have friends: honest, loyal builders who work to help the team. These people who are on the team, they have been VPs since August 1985. We try to get people who will be happy with this group, this company, and themselves. We are not like Procter & Gamble. I tell people if they want to change titles, go to P&G, but if they want to enjoy their work and grow personally, Bacardi is the place to be.
>
> And we are a tight team. For example, we once had a general sales manager. One November day he came in and said, "Isaac, I'm going to leave the company in January." Cordera and I talked it over, and we went back to him and said, "You won't be leaving in two months; you'll be leaving in two minutes."

CORDERA AND CHERTORIVSKI

Cordera believed that he and Chertorivski had developed a strong working relationship:

EXHIBIT 5

Bacardi y Cia S.A. Rum and Brandy Sales Growth

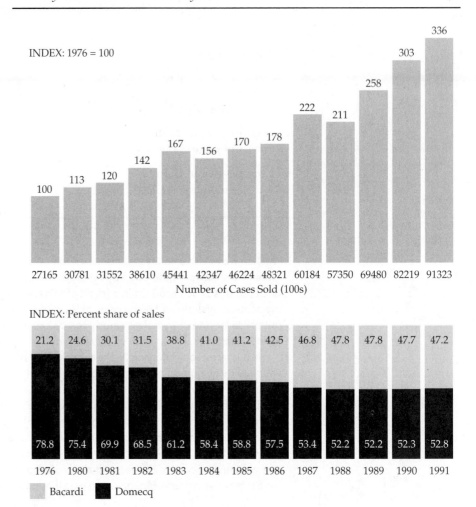

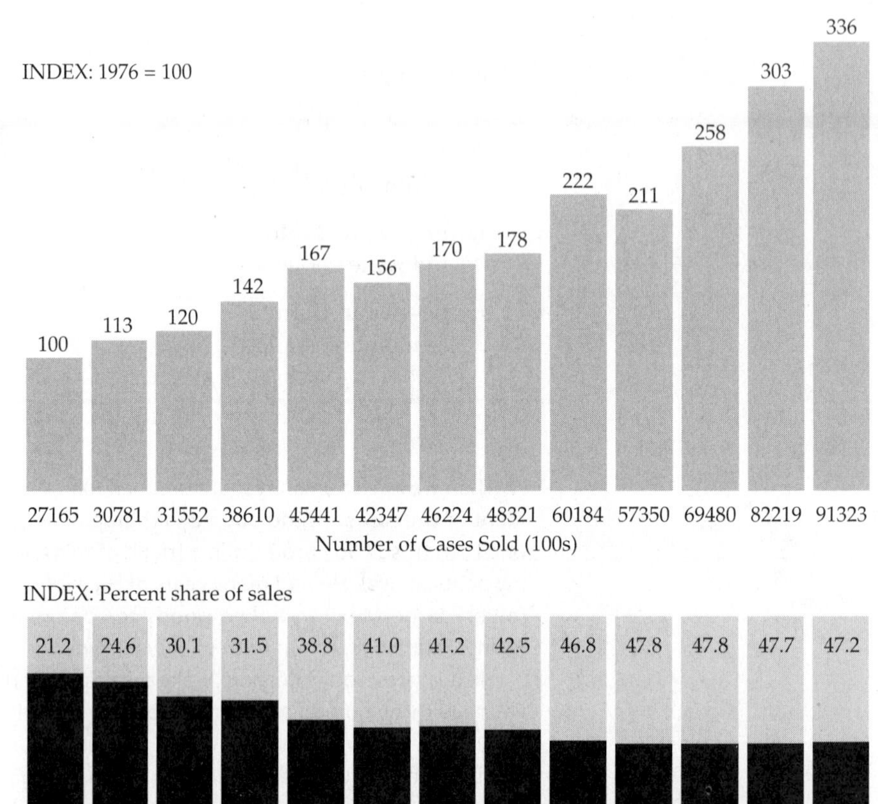

Isaac treats me as his equal. I always consult with him, and he always consults with me. I listen to him; he listens to me. That is part of the success; we are able to talk, to see what is good and what is bad. His expertise is marketing, and I listen to him; my expertise is finance, and he listens to me. I think that is the key.

And we work out our differences well. For example, Isaac was concerned about the sales force, and that is my responsibility. He felt that they were having problems as a result of how we paid them. We pay a lot—five or six months' salary—at a time. Isaac wanted to increase their purchasing power so they would spend more time selling. So he called me in and says, "Let's give them a raise in pesos and an advance against their profit sharing."

I said, "Let me take a look at it." So I got together with the sales managers and came to the conclusion that this was not the real problem. The problem was that 30 percent or more of their salary was commission, and, for some people, all of

EXHIBIT 6

Bacardi y Cia S.A. Evolution of Liquor Sales by Category

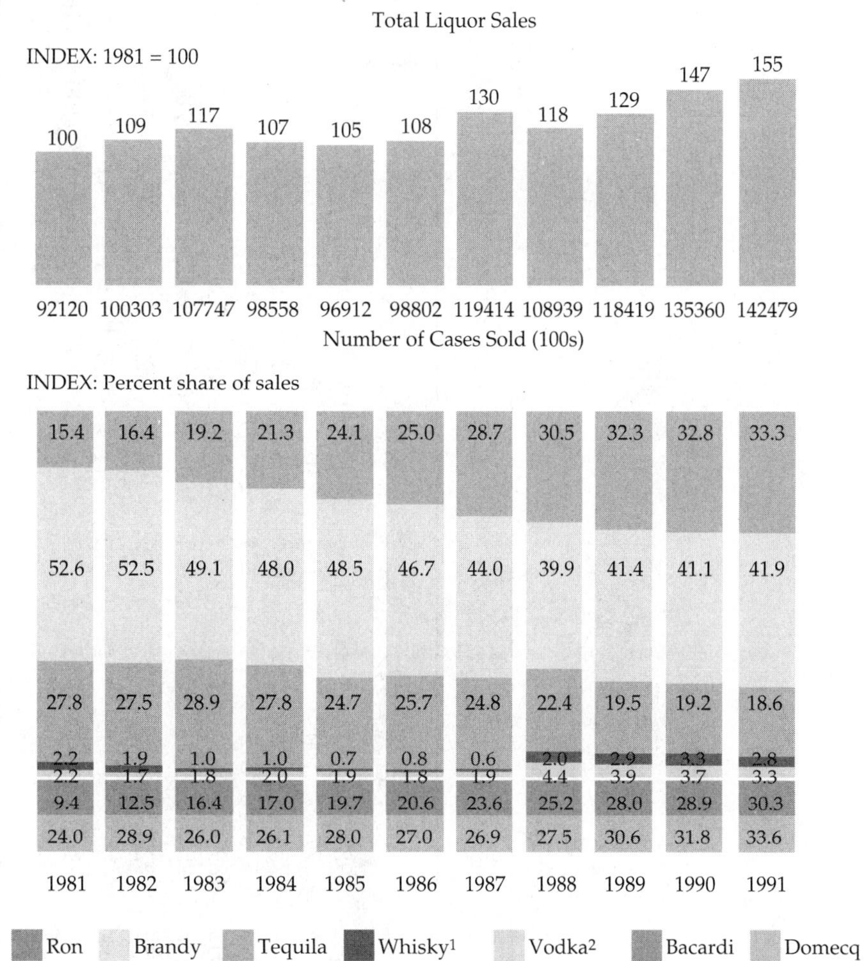

[1]A partir de 1984 solo whisky nacional, a partir de 1988 whisky nacional y importado.

[2]A partir de 1983 solo Valle de Mexico, a partir de 1988 total Mexico.

their annual sales come at the end of the year. They make very little money during the year, but at the end of the year there is a lot of money.

I suggested to Isaac that we change the whole concept. Let's forget about commissions and keep them on a good steady salary for 12 months; then we can give them a performance bonus every three months. Isaac was totally against it. He said, "A salesman without a commission is not a salesman! I don't want this system."

So we started looking for ways to resolve the issue. We talked a lot. We argued a lot. But we are working together for the company, and we are looking out for the goals of the company. In the end, we created the best possible solution to the problem.

EXHIBIT 7

Bacardi y Compañía, S.A. de C.V. Sales per Calendar Year

000 9-LITER CASES

	1981	1982	1983	1984	1985	1986	1987	1988	1989	1990	1991	% 91/90
Solera	30	55	77	100	136	158	210	257	430	660	937	42
Añejo	495	677	754	936	979	1074	1185	1562	2037	2656	3179	20
Carta Oro	277	399	526	315	243	234	246	267	210	297	258	(13)
Carta Blanca	629	1045	1895	2223	2031	2389	3246	3519	3395	3993	3332	(17)
	1431	2176	3252	3574	3389	3855	4887	5605	6072	7606	7706	1
Index	100	152	227	250	237	269	342	392	424	532	539	
Palmas	77	86	55	47	45	31	44	43	43	64	109	71
Cocktails	—	—	18	63	62	33	35	89	104	130	109	(16)
Martini & Rossi	—	—	—	—	—	—	17	14	15	18	9	(51)

EXHIBIT 8

The Bacardi Management Team

JAIME CUKIER
VICE PRESIDENT, CONTROLLERSHIP, GRUPO BACARDI

Birthdate:	15 March 1936
Citizenship:	Mexican
Education:	B.S., Chemical Engineering, 1960 M.B.A., 1982
Experience:	Joined Bacardi in 1986 as director of controllership, Bacardi y Cia. Twenty-two years with IBM de Mexico in sales, planning, and marketing and as general controller. In present position since 1988 (September).

JOSE SANCHEZ GAVITO
VICE PRESIDENT, TECHNICAL AND RUM BLENDING, GRUPO BACARDI

Birthdate:	28 March 1948
Citizenship:	Mexican
Education:	B.S., Chemical Engineering, 1972 Advanced Management Skills, 1982, 1987
Experience:	Joined Bacardi in 1978 as a supervisor of Tequilena, after he was manager, planning and control. In present position since 1989.

LUIS DE LA FUENTE
VICE PRESIDENT, INDUSTRIAL RELATIONS

Birthdate:	8 October 1948
Citizenship:	Mexican
Education:	B.A., Business Administration, 1971 Advanced Management Skills, 1984
Experience:	Joined Bacardi in 1981 as industrial relations manager. In present position since 1988. Ten years' experience in human resources with Kimberly Clark, Grupo Industrial Bimbo, and Unilever.

JOSE PANERO
VICE PRESIDENT, PRODUCTION

Birthdate:	17 August 1932
Citizenship:	Argentine
Education:	B.D., Engineering, 1959 Advanced Management Skills, 1986, 1987
Experience:	Originally joined Bacardi in 1964. Rejoined Bacardi in 1972. Supervised construction of various Bacardi facilities,

(continued)

EXHIBIT 8 (CONTINUED)

The Bacardi Management Team

including Recife, Brazil (with fellow Cuban Juan Grau); Mexico; Martinique; Spain; Venezuela; and Puerto Rico. In present position since 1988 (September).

AMARO ARGAMASILLA BACARDI
VICE PRESIDENT, FINANCE

Birthdate: 20 May 1952
Citizenship: Mexican
Education: C.P.A., 1976
Advanced Management Skills, 1987
Experience: Joined Bacardi as clerk in 1971. Progressed through finance department. In present position since 1988 (September). He is a member of the board of Bacardi, Ltd.

FRANCISCO SANCHEZ
VICE PRESIDENT, MATERIAL AND FOREIGN TRADE

Birthdate: 9 March 1939
Citizenship: Mexican
Education: C.P.A., 1964
M.B.A., 1978
Experience: Joined Bacardi in 1971 as accountant and progressed through comptroller's office. In present position since 1989. Previously with IBM and Pfizer Mexico in financial positions.

ALFREDO ADAM
VICE PRESIDENT, SALES, VERGEL

Birthdate: 25 January 1943
Citizenship: Mexican
Education: B.A., Accounting, 1968
C.P.A., 1970
Experience: Joined Bacardi in 1990 at current level. Previously worked as public accountant; worked in the Mexican government, and was dean of accounting and business school of the National University of Mexico for eight years.

For the seven vice presidents, the team was a major part of their lives. Regular meetings were held every other Monday. Meetings began with lunch in the executive dining room and ran until about 6:00 P.M. A typical agenda would have 10 to 18 items; the agenda for a recent meeting included the following items:

- A review of the semester's (six months) business results
- Sales goals for the next semester
- An analysis of the new company mission statement
- A review of the total-quality plan for the Vergel plant

When asked what it was like to be part of the team, several of the vice presidents compared it to a marriage. One noted: "Sometimes it is good, and sometimes it is not. There is always the potential for conflict, yet we are able to work through that because we share a common bond. Overall, we feel we are very successful, but we often hear that we are in a crisis."

Managing the team was not always easy for Isaac Chertorivski:

> It depends on the day. Some days I hear very clearly and discuss things, but there are other days when I don't. I try to be very participative; I try very hard. My style of leadership is to work in a team, but it is not always easy. Sometimes I am very explosive.

Every January, a three-day meeting of the executive team took place at *La Galarza*, the converted *hacienda* that housed both a distillery and the company retreat facility. The strategy sessions began with discussions among the men of the things that were important to them. "We begin with the human side to reinforce the team. Each man takes a few minutes to talk with his colleagues about how the year has been for him personally, his friends, his family, his ups, his downs, and how he feels about being part of the team." Then, for the next two to three days, the team put in 14- to 16-hour days planning.

When asked if everyone had an equal voice, all the vice presidents laughed, but Chertorivski laughed loudest. "They try to influence me, but none has been successful!" There was also a sharing of expertise: "When we discuss difficult issues, highly conceptual things, we help each other. We don't want to let the team down . . . to be the one who drags the team down. And if we make a mistake, we correct it."

To which Cordera replied, "Depends on how big a mistake it is!"

Each man had a particular point of view that was respected and synthesized. "We have room to grow in this team; we can make our own decisions, and there is no one looking over our shoulder." The company was poised to face its challenges, both personal and strategic.

Guillermo Cordera was currently facing one of the biggest challenges. The acquisition of Grupo Vergel in 1989 gave Bacardi a position in the Mexican brandy market and an opportunity to take on Domecq in its own backyard. VERGEL® brandy ran a distant third to Domecq's Presidente and Don Pedro brands. The acquisition was not easy for Grupo Bacardi. Some found it difficult to accept Bacardi Mexico's entry into the brandy business. As executive president of the Vergel division, Cordera found himself in an unaccustomed position as regards a Bacardi product—being in back of the pack, rather than in front:

> My challenge is to put Vergel on the map. We have volume but no profit. We need to grow Vergel more. We have extra capacity that we need to use, and we have to fight for shelf space. It is tough. I am impatient, impulsive, and ambitious. It is frustrating to move slowly; sometimes it is hard to accept that Bacardi Mexico is a company with stable growth.

Chertorivski faced a different challenge. Flush with the success of sales in Mexico, Chertorivski was concerned that complacency and arrogance were lurking:

> Today I think I need to create a crisis to make my people work more. There are two kinds of crisis, real and fabricated. Perhaps our people are a little complacent. Yesterday when talking with Cordera, I said it is time to create a crisis. How to do this? Tell them that we are not growing, that we must work harder. Be very upset, very gruff, and talk hard. We will hold a lot of analysis sessions to find out what is wrong. And there will be specific examples of what must be corrected. And three or four months later, they have things fixed. And then I will take them out to lunch and tell them how well they have done.

Behind Chertorivski's desk was a credenza, on which a gray phone sat. There was an identical phone in Cordera's office. They were connected to a private line that only Chertorivski and Cordera shared. The two executives were in constant contact. Chertorivski, with his marketing and public-relations skills, supplied the perspective of growth and expansion; Cordera, with his financial and systems background, supplied the long-range financial perspective. According to Grau, "Neither one could run the company on his own, but together they are unbeatable."

ENDNOTES

[1]Spanish for "stable of content cows."
[2]Peter Foster, *Family Spirits: The Bacardi Saga* (Toronto: MacFarlane, Walter & Ross, 1990), p. 66.
[3]Ibid., p. 116.
[4]Spanish for "If there is Bacardi, there is atmosphere."
[5]"Gold Medal . . . the Premium Flavor."
[6]"Grab the Jug."
[7]"Aged . . . the proof (or test)."
[8]"Advisor to the President of the Republic."

Case 24

Bennett Association (A)

In mid-October 1981, as Michael Silva reviewed his management plans for the Bennett Association, he wondered about all he needed to accomplish. Having been CEO for less than two weeks, he felt he needed to make some significant changes in the companies that formed the Bennett Association. He wanted to have a clear picture of his strategy before he began, because he would need to implement the changes as quickly as possible. Despite having worked with the company for six months as a consultant, Silva was unsure whether the actions he was considering would be sufficient to turn the company around. Developing suggestions as a consultant and implementing them as a CEO were two entirely different things.

Part of the problem, he believed, was the very nature of the company he now ran. A group of traditional, family-owned companies, the Bennett Association had developed a strong, conservative, even paternalistic culture, which could make it resist adapting to changing situations. Several members of the Bennett family still worked at the various Bennett companies, including three as presidents of the paint and glass business, the leasing company, and the car rental agency. Perhaps Silva's most important concern was Wallace F. Bennett, for 24 years the U.S. senator from Utah and current chairman of the Bennett board. Although "the senator" had pledged his support to Silva, clearly the senator's primary allegiance was to the company he had guided for 50 years and to the 200 family members for whom it provided a source of income.

The Bennett Association needed change, however. The banks had made that much evident when they demanded that an outside president be brought in to manage it. For the last four years, the Bennett companies had lost money, and this trend was continuing in 1981. Silva's major concern was whether the tradition-bound Bennett family would accept the fundamental changes necessary to save the company.

Another consideration was how many of the changes he should implement before his six-week vacation began on December 1. A three-month delay might result in even larger losses. On the other hand, if he wasn't there to push for the changes, staff resistance could undermine implementation of his strategy.

History of the Bennett Association

The Bennett Association was organized in 1917 as a Massachusetts trust to function as a holding company responsible for the financial interests of the trust beneficiaries—the descendants of John F. Bennett. The descendants received income from the trust according to the number of shares they held, which were similar to stock certificates. The decision-making authority rested with a board of trustees composed of family members. No nonfamily member could own shares.

Bennett's Paint and Glass, originally a grain and feed store known as Sears and Liddle (which dated from 1882), had always been the primary source of the Bennett Association's income. In 1884, John F. Bennett joined the company, and, in 1900, he bought out the owners to save the store from bankruptcy and changed the name to Bennett's.

The company soon became profitable, and it began to manufacture paint in 1904. As profitability continued, the physical plant doubled over the next 20 years. In 1920, John F.'s son, Wallace, a graduate of the University of Utah, joined the growing company. In that year, Bennett's also entered the retail glass business.

Wallace was given increasing responsibility for the store's operations. By the mid-1920s, he was running the entire manufacturing and sales functions. His brother Harold, two years his junior, saw little opportunity for himself in the family business and began a career at ZCMI, a large department-store chain in Utah. Harold, however, retained a seat on the board of directors.

In 1932, a struggle for control of the company after the death of one of John F. Bennett's brothers ended with John F. narrowly retaining control. However, he became increasingly dependent on his son Wallace to make day-to-day decisions. Although John F. Bennett remained president until his death in 1938, Wallace effectively ran the company.

During the next ten years, under Wallace's guidance, the company not only survived the Great Depression but also opened four new branches. During that period, Wallace developed a process that radically changed the paint industry. Until that time, all paint was tinted in the factory, with only 8 to 12 colors available to consumers. Dealers carried large inventories of the few colors in a variety of sizes. Although some experiments had been made with premeasured tubes of tint that could be added to basic white paint by the dealers to create varied colors, the process had met with limited acceptance.

Expanding on this idea, however, Wallace hired an interior decorator who created 3,000 distinct colors of paint by mixing tints. In 1935, Wallace decided to distribute 1,320 colors, launching Colorizer—the nation's first controlled tinting system. With this new system, paint dealers could carry much lower inventories. Using white paint as a base, dealers could add specific amounts of pigment to create a previously unavailable spectrum of colors. In 1949, Bennett organized Colorizer Associates as a group of regional paint manufacturers to promote the system nationally. These companies paid Bennett's royalties in exchange for tints and color cards. In 1981, Bennett's still owned and operated Colorizer Associates, although it represented a small stream of income.

In the late 1930s, Wallace expanded and diversified the association by acquiring a local Ford franchise—Bennett Motor Company—of which he became president.

In 1949, when he became president of the National Association of Manufacturers (NAM) headquartered in New York, Wallace turned the business over to his brother Richard (12 years younger than Wallace), who had worked in the company for some time. In 1950, after his stint as NAM president, Wallace returned to Utah to reassume control of Bennett's. Because Richard was reluctant to step down, Wallace, at the urging of several friends, chose to run for the U.S. Senate. He won and held the seat for four terms. (A more complete biography of Senator Bennett can be found in the Case Appendix on page C24.17.)

Under Richard's leadership, the Bennett Association continued to grow in profits and revenues. Although the Ford franchise was sold in 1967, the Bennett Association retained two spin-off businesses: Bennett Leasing, which was involved in all types of automotive, truck, and equipment leasing, and a National Car Rental franchise at the Salt Lake City airport. In 1976, an advertising company, Admix, was created to meet the promotional requirements of the Bennett Association and other Salt Lake City businesses.

After Richard's unexpected death in 1976, operating control of the Bennett companies fell to Wallace (Wally) G. Bennett, the senator's oldest son. Although Richard had been formally president only of Bennett's Paint and Glass, he had exercised strong, if informal, control over the other companies. When Wally assumed control, he focused all his attention on Bennett's Paint and Glass, allowing the other company presidents freedom to manage their own operations. Although they still shared a common board of directors, the companies became increasingly independent, and each maintained control of its own finances. (See Exhibit 1 for a partial family tree.)

Serving with the Senator on the board of directors in 1981 were his brother Harold, by then chairman of the board of ZCMI, nephews Richard K. Winters and Kenneth Smith, and nephew-in-law Donald Penny. Voting power was unequally distributed, with the senator having three votes; Harold, two; and the others, one each.

Financial Situation

Many internal and external factors contributed to the financial problems that the Bennett companies had faced since 1976. The Arab oil embargo and unprecedented levels of inflation had driven material costs higher and higher. However, to remain

Exhibit 1

Family Members in the Bennett Association

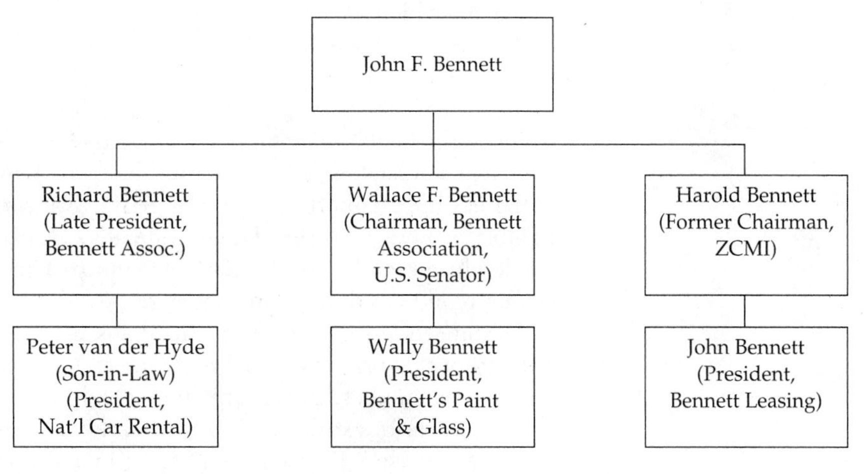

EXHIBIT 2

Organization Chart of Bennett Association

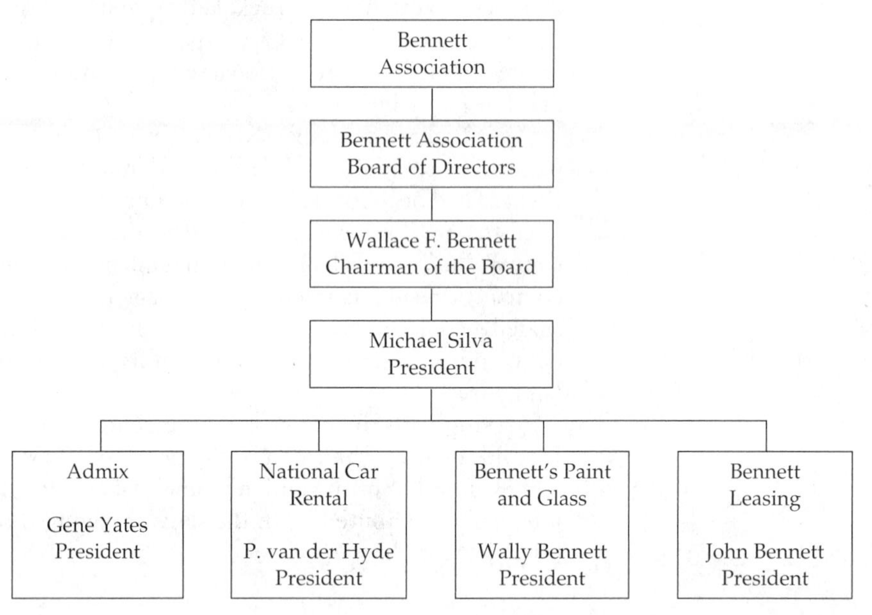

competitive, the paint company could not raise prices at a rate that would compensate for these increases. Compounding this problem was the lack of strong, central financial controls. Richard had been familiar with the financial needs of the various businesses and had relied on his experience to notice any expenses that appeared out of line. The weakness of this piecemeal control system and lack of centralized budget became painfully apparent, however, when Wally assumed control. He was inexperienced with financial controls and could not convince his managers to institute a companywide budget.

As a result of these and other factors, in 1976 the Bennett Association suffered its first loss in over 50 years, and it continued to lose increasing amounts in successive years. In 1981, the anticipation of a $3.2 million loss on revenues of $28 million precipitated the bank's demand that an outside CEO be hired.

When Michael Silva became president, the Bennett Association included Bennett Leasing, Bennett's Paint and Glass, National Car Rental, and Admix (see Exhibit 2). The first three of these generated the majority of revenues and were each headed by a member of the Bennett family. The four were in different markets, however, and faced different challenges.

Despite the five years of operating losses, the Bennett financial situation was not without its bright spots. The Bennett Association owned more than $12 million in unencumbered assets, including eight acres of prime industrial land in Salt Lake City; various stocks and securities; the buildings and manufacturing facilities; and stores in Utah, Nevada, and Idaho. In addition, the Bennett name was recognized and respected throughout the region.

The Bennett Companies: Industry and Company Background

Bennett's Paint and Glass

In 1981, the U.S. paint and coatings industry was widely dispersed and included nearly 1,200 producers. Half of all the paints, varnishes, and lacquers sold covered buildings, predominantly houses. The second-largest primary market was automobile and other original equipment manufacturers, which used a third of the coatings produced. The remaining share of the market went to special-purpose coatings, which were high-performance coverings used to prolong equipment life in such industries as petroleum and chemicals. Forecasts over the next ten years indicated that this segment would be the fastest growing in the coatings industry.

Building-paint sales were seasonal, peaking in the spring and summer, and closely tied to the construction industry. Since 1979, the depressed housing and automobile markets had caused a slump in paint sales (see Exhibit 3, U.S. paint shipments). In addition to the decline in new home construction, the recession had hurt sales in the large repainting market as people put off painting their homes. Recovery in the paint industry lagged that of the construction industry, because coatings are applied toward the end of home building.

Employing a total of 345 people, Bennett's Paint and Glass was the most well known of the Bennett companies and traditionally the most successful. Since the advent of the Colorizer concept in the 1930s, Bennett's had dominated the paint business in Utah and Idaho. Bennett's original store on 23rd South Street was well remembered by Salt Lake City residents even though it had long since changed hands and now housed a dress shop. Although it was a well-established and prominent Salt Lake City business, Bennett's high visibility within the community nevertheless seemed disproportionate to its size.

Exhibit 3

Paint, Varnish, and Lacquer Trade Sales, 1971–1981 (millions of gallons)

Year	Sales
1971	431.0
1972	451.5
1973	424.0
1974	474.7
1975	451.5
1976	473.5
1977	486.2
1978	512.3
1979	571.3
1980	529.5
1981	504.9

Sources: U.S. Department of Commerce, Bureau of the Census; *Kline Guide to the Paint Industry*, 1981.

As elsewhere, the paint and coatings market in Utah was fragmented and competitive. Neither Bennett's nor any of its major competitors (Fuller-O'Brien, Howells, Pittsburgh Paint & Glass, and Sears) had much more than a 10 percent share of commercial and consumer sales. Estimates indicated that Bennett's, with more than $1 million in consumer sales, outsold Sears in this area.

The manufacturing, warehousing, distribution, and leasing operations of the paint and glass business were located on an eight-acre parcel of land on 23rd South in Salt Lake City. Topped by the Colorizer trademark, a bold spectrum of colors, Bennett's light green, nine-story warehouse dwarfed all other buildings in the area and was easily visible from the nearby freeway. Under the same roof were the paint-manufacturing and the glass-tempering operations and one of Bennett's 14 retail outlets.

Representative of all the Bennett's stores, the Salt Lake City outlet carried a complete line of Bennett's paints, along with painting supplies, bathroom and lighting fixtures, and a variety of sample windows. Windows were made to order for both walk-in customers and private contractors. Bennett's also bid on window contracts offered by large, national construction companies, although it had recently had difficulty securing contracts.

Branch and Outlet Sales. Each Bennett retail outlet in Utah, Nevada, and Idaho employed between 10 and 20 people. Dealers reported to an area manager, who then reported to a sales vice president in Salt Lake City. In addition to the Bennett-owned branches, salespeople visited 200 to 300 independent hardware stores that stocked Bennett's paint. Only about 20 percent of these stores generated the majority of all sales made through this channel. Salespeople were assigned to a specific geographical district, received a car and an expense account, and were paid on a commission basis.

Captive dealers purchased paint from Bennett's at cost and then used a 50 percent markup to determine retail price. The dealers either sold the paint to customers at full price or applied a variety of trade discounts. For example, depending on the volume of business, contractors purchased supplies for as little as 10 percent above dealer cost. Each dealer's performance was evaluated by sales volume.

Manufacturing. Bennett's manufactured a whole line of paints, including both latex and oil-based brands. The manufacturing facility included a research department (experimenting with different additives to improve product quality) and a maintenance staff of three full-time and two part-time people who kept the operation running smoothly. Productivity for the facility was 1,969 gallons per person per month in 1981, well below the industry average (see Exhibit 4).

As president, Wally Bennett had added both the huge new warehouse and a modern tempering that gave Bennett's state-of-the-art technology. The warehouse on 23rd South measured 80' × 80' × 80'. Merchandise was arranged along high corridors serviced by modern forklifts that moved both vertically and horizontally.

Thirty-nine employees working in three shifts staffed the warehouse. The morning shift filled the "will call" orders from the previous day, the afternoon shift stored the morning's paint production, and the night shift filled dealer orders.

Three unions represented workers in the plant: the Glaziers, the Allied Glass Workers, and the Steel Workers. In June 1981, the unions called a strike for a wage increase. For several weeks, management successfully ran the plant, and many felt that

EXHIBIT 4

Paint Industry Productivity, 1970–1980

YEAR	AVERAGE GALLONS PRODUCED PER PERSON PER MONTH
1970	1,737
1971	1,931
1972	1,946
1973	1,959
1974	2,030
1975	2,154
1976	2,132
1977	2,184
1978	2,144
1979	2,371
1980	2,260

SOURCE: *Kline Guide to the Paint Industry*, 1981.

Bennett's was on the verge of winning, but the unions compromised on a contract that provided a 5 percent wage increase each year for three years. Although some managers wanted to hold out, Wally Bennett decided to accept the compromise.

Management. Years of profitability had lulled most of Bennett's highly tenured employees into a strong sense of security. Both the managerial and production staffs seemed unresponsive to calls for financial improvement and appeared unaware of the toll the economy was taking on the company's income statement.

A particular problem had been the attitude of Jack Nielson, former executive vice president of Bennett's. Jack Stevens, vice president of finance for the Bennett Association, commented on how Nielson's recent retirement had solved some of the problems:

> Jack was a VP of production, and he had been something of a favored son of Richard. He was quite egotistical and difficult to work with at times. Anyone who opposed him created a lot of problems, since this guy would always lose his temper. Because of that and Wally's style, he seemed to exercise more dominance over Wally than any of the other people. Wally always appeared to be rather cautious with this guy and would listen to him more than anyone else. Unfortunately, this guy didn't always have the best business insights. He was an engineer by trade and had been running the production operation, but he was promoted to executive vice president and began to have a bigger say in the way the rest of the business was run. As a result, it was often very hard to get new ideas into motion.

Jack Stevens had also wanted to get the company to use some form of budgeting:

> I know that budgeting is an excellent tool for management, but to others at Bennett's it is just an irritating accounting system. I provide each cost center with a history of their expenses for the current year, so all they have to do is put in a new number. The whole thing falls on deaf ears. When DeVon Johnson [currently VP of marketing] came on board, he had an interest in it, but he can't implement it. Wally, in fact, came to me one day with a figure that represented the expenses that we would have for the coming year and asked me to calculate the amount of sales we would have to generate to cover those expenses. Jack O'Brien had said that we couldn't cut expenses without adversely affecting our sales function, so that number became our sales target for the year.

Bennett Leasing

The equipment-leasing industry dated from the 1950s, when tax credits and accelerated depreciation incentives for investment enhanced the popularity of equipment leasing. The industry experienced explosive growth in the 1960s, particularly in the transportation area (trucks, autos, airplanes, railroad cars), office and information-processing equipment, and industrial equipment and facilities. In 1981, leasing remained one of the fastest-growing industries in the United States with more than 1,800 firms writing agreements for billions of dollars of equipment. Not only the number, but also the value of transactions had increased substantially, facilitated in part by the development of leveraged leasing. (Exhibit 5 describes leasing trends.) Inflation, risky business cycles, and high interest rates had forced firms of all sizes to turn to leasing.

Firms leased equipment for a variety of reasons, primarily to take advantage of tax credits and to have more flexible financing. Many small firms leased because they lacked sufficient capital to support debt financing of equipment purchases. Leasing companies could take advantage of certain tax benefits resulting from accelerated depreciation and investment tax credits and pass the benefits on, through reduced rates, to firms that could not. Differences in capital costs to a leasing company and an operating company encouraged leasing. Operating companies also gained more financial flexibility, because leasing extended the length of financing, allowed constant-cost financing, and conserved working capital. Leases could be tailored to the needs of lessees, such as those in seasonal businesses, and because few or no restrictive covenants were required, as with debt financing, firms could conserve existing lines of credit.

EXHIBIT 5

Equipment-Leasing Growth

YEAR	EQUIPMENT COST ADDED (000S)
1979	8,039,000
1980	10,214,400
1981	13,374,700

SOURCES: American Association of Equipment Lessors; *1982 Survey of Accounting and Business Practices; World Leasing Yearbook*, 1982.

In addition to the numerous quantifiable benefits, leasing reduced the risk of equipment obsolescence, particularly important in an era of rapid technological change, and often was simply more convenient than borrow-and-purchase options. The convenience factor was particularly influential in automobile leasing. While automobile purchases were down throughout the country in 1981, the leasing population remained stable and was expected to grow. Projections indicated that, by 1985, more than 40 percent of cars purchased would be lease financed, double the 1981 lease base.

With the growing acceptance of the equipment-leasing concept, there arose increasing demand for specialized leases and fast, low-cost maintenance plans. These trends, along with inflationary pressures, were forcing small leasing companies to tighten and streamline operations in order to compete in this highly competitive marketplace.

The Bennett Leasing Company was a holdover from the Bennett Association's expansion into the automobile industry in the 1930s. Senator Bennett retained his role as president of the franchise throughout his presidency of NAM and his Senate terms. He had turned over operating control, however, to a resident manager. In 1967, when Ford announced that it didn't want absentee franchise owners, Bennett decided to sell. Although it could have resisted Ford's demands, the Bennett Association sold the franchise, retaining car and truck leasing and truck maintenance. These operations, headed by John Bennett, Harold's son, constituted the leasing company when Michael Silva arrived.

Management. Tall, laconic, and thoughtful, John Bennett bore a strong physical resemblance to other members of the family, especially his cousin Wally. John liked to explore thoroughly each business decision made by the company. His analytical style and careful consideration of each issue led many around him to observe that he might have been a good college professor. He enjoyed the people with whom he worked and felt that his organization was strong, stable, and customer oriented.

By 1981, Bennett Leasing had 35 employees and had had as many as 40 at one time. Although it was willing to lease nearly any type of equipment, automotive and truck leases to major fleet customers, small businesses, and individuals provided the bulk of the revenues. In 1981, 1,800 autos and light trucks were under lease.

Like many leasing companies using floating-rate leases, Bennett Leasing lost money between 1979 and 1981 because of sustained high-interest-note levels. Despite the increasing losses, neither the sales staff nor management appeared to be concerned. John Bennett commented:

> When Mike (Silva) took over the business, I realized that several changes needed to be made. I know that Michael is looking at the trucking business because it has lost money for us over the past several years, but I have some misgivings about that. I've been here since 1954, and I've noticed that the trucking business is the least interest-sensitive business that we have.

About half of the leasing company's employees worked in the trucking side of the business. The truck-leasing segment was growing along with the rest of the leasing industry, increasing the number of units in service by 31 percent and revenues by 22 percent in ten years.

At Bennett Leasing, many of the employees were experienced mechanics, involved in the maintenance operation. John added:

Mike is wondering what to do with the people in our company. He just doesn't know them as well as I do. There are some of them who might be a bit mediocre, but they have some skills and experience that would be very hard to replace. Many of these people are good friends of mine, and some of them have been here longer than I. We probably need some change in the climate, but you also need stability, experience, and knowledge. We don't want to get rid of expertise.

National Car Rental

The car rental industry began in 1916, but the most rapid growth had occurred since 1960. Although 8 to 12 corporate systems could be considered the leading national firms in the business, as many as 5,000 independent firms and system licensees operated on a local or regional basis. By 1981, 40 million car rental transactions generated more than $3 billion in revenues. The current 19 percent rate of growth (see Exhibit 6) was predicted to continue through 1981 because of the high cost of car ownership, the price of gasoline, and increasing reliance on "fly/drive" forms of business and vacation travel.

The overwhelming majority of rental-car service consumers were business travelers, and between 75 percent and 85 percent of rental car revenues were generated through rentals made at airports. More than 90 percent of car rental fleets were rented to commercial users.

The National Car Rental franchise at the Salt Lake City Airport became part of the Bennett Motor Company in 1959. The franchise had nearly 400 cars, and in a good week all were rented. Closely tied to tourism and business travel, the business was somewhat cyclical. In 1981, the winter snowfall in the Salt Lake City area had not been plentiful, and there was some concern throughout the area about the impact of this situation on the local economy. In addition, after Budget Rent-A-Car started a premium giveaway to increase business in October 1981, the other major rental companies, including National, became involved in a premium war. As a result, National Car Rental Corporation eventually lost $15 million, and the local Bennett-owned franchise dropped from third to fourth in its share of the Salt Lake–area market.

On the other hand, Salt Lake City had been tabbed the second-fastest-growing city of the 1980s in the United States, and Western Airlines had plans to make Salt Lake City its new hub of operations, which would result in expansion of the

Exhibit 6

Car Rental Growth—Selected Years

Year	Units in Service	Revenues (millions)
1970	319,000	$ 936
1972	341,000	1,048
1978	448,000	2,303
1980	512,000	3,349

Source: American Car Rental Association, 1983.

airport. Many corporations were moving there, which increased the level of business travel. All these developments boded well for the local car rental franchise and the local economy.

Management. Peter van der Hyde, president of the company, had run the franchise for many years. Born in Holland, he had married one of Richard Bennett's daughters and then came to work for the Bennett Motor Company before it was sold. Van der Hyde worked closely with Richard until the latter's death, and many felt that, if Richard had outlived his brothers, van der Hyde might have been his successor. Tall and tanned, he still spoke with a slight Dutch accent:

> I try to run a tight ship here. I feel a moral obligation to the stockholders, and I think it's paid off. Our profit has gone up every year since I took over in 1976. In this business, it's very easy to lose customers and hard to get them back. I think you need three things to be successful here: good financing, good luck, and common sense.

Van der Hyde operated a lean, efficient business with no intermediate levels of supervision. Although concerned about the company as a whole, van der Hyde was proudest of his own operation. Even when the other Bennett companies were losing money, the National franchise was always in the black. As one observer noted, "That company does nothing but generate cash. The nature of the work is relatively routine, so they can pay low wages, and all transactions are in cash or by credit cards."

Admix

Admix, employing only five people, was the smallest of the Bennett companies. Most of its business was in developing commercials, and the operation stayed small by contracting out much of the work. Before coming to Admix, President Gene Yates had worked for several ad agencies managing large accounts, including Western Airlines and Rockwell International. Under his leadership, Admix had been profitable since its founding—unaffected by the depressed economy. It was not generally known that Bennett owned Admix; the company had deemphasized the relationship so as not to reduce the number of potential clients.

There was little interaction between Admix and the other companies owned by the Bennett Association. Michael Silva noted, "No one has paid much attention to Gene. He was making money before I came, and he seems to be doing okay now."

Bennett Association: Key Management Personnel (see Exhibit 7)

Wally Bennett: Paint and Glass

The eldest son of the senator, Wally Bennett, after serving in the military for three and one-half years, had spent his entire career with Bennett's. Like his father, he attended the University of Utah and then held a variety of positions at Bennett's Paint and Glass (most recently, director of personnel) before taking control of the company in 1976. As were many family members, he was active in church and civic affairs.

Wally was tall, with graying hair, and had a patrician air about him. Now in his mid-50s, he was popular around the Salt Lake area; most people who met him found

EXHIBIT 7

Key Management Personnel

	POSITION	YEARS WITH COMPANY	APPROXIMATE AGE
John Bennett	President, Bennett Leasing	20+	55
Wallace F. Bennett	Chairman, Bennett Association	50+	82
Wallace G. Bennett	President, Bennett's Paint and Glass	25+	55
DeVon Johnson	Executive Vice President, Bennett's Paint and Glass	1	57
Michael Silva	CEO, Bennett Association	0	30
Jack Stevens	Controller, Bennett's Paint and Glass	5	52
Peter van der Hyde	President, National Car Rental	20+	53

him very agreeable and enjoyed his company. Extremely sensitive to the needs and feelings of others in the business, he would often postpone decisions that might upset his staff until he could contact all the parties involved. He would gather his staff together to try to resolve many of the problems facing the company through consensus decision making. If the group could not arrive at a decision, he would often put the issue off until a later meeting, where it could be discussed more thoroughly.

He had inherited from his father a strong concern for the welfare of the company's employees, and he always tried to act in a way that reflected that concern. Although he maintained a high regard and respect for his father, Wally tended not to consult him on most business decisions. He relied mostly on his 25 years of experience in the company and the expertise of his staff. Although he could have exercised more control over the other Bennett companies, as did Richard before him, he chose to devote himself almost exclusively to the paint and glass business.

DeVon Johnson: Executive Vice President, Paint and Glass

DeVon Johnson was relatively new to the company. Immaculately and elegantly dressed, he tended to speak rapidly and directly, generating tremendous energy. Before coming to Bennett's, he spent 35 years in the paint business with Fuller-O'Brien, where he rose from stockboy to vice president of the company. Adhering to the management philosophy of "putting in a little more than you expect to get back," Johnson dramatically improved Fuller's sales and profits in each position he had held. He was the youngest branch manager in the history of the company.

Eventually, because of the breadth of his sales and operations experience, Fuller began to depend on him to turn around problem areas.

Johnson resigned from Fuller-O'Brien for family reasons and contacted Bennett's about a job shortly thereafter. He was hired as vice president of marketing, and, by September 1981, he replaced Jack Nielson, who retired, as executive vice president of the company.

Johnson had a full slate of objectives for the company. First, he felt it should become more customer oriented, particularly in responding to complaints more quickly. Second, he was concerned about plant productivity. Although fully staffed, the plant's output was below industry average. Third, Johnson wanted to increase Bennett's market share:

> I'd love to run a company ten times this size. I don't like to sit still. I can't wait to get to work in the morning. I know that I'm impatient, but I've never been a flash in the pan. We're still learning here, and some of the people don't know what they can do yet. In the morning, I get here before 7:30, and I work through the day. I usually don't even leave the office for lunch because I bring along a bag lunch that I can eat right here at my desk. I got used to that in other jobs, and I don't want to change now.

Johnson was concerned about the constraints he felt in meeting the challenges facing the company. Because it was a family-owned, traditional business, led by the son of the chairman, implementing major changes would probably mean repeatedly going back to the board.

The lack of concern shown by others in the company about the growing losses also puzzled him. Despite all the problems, he did not believe people were changing their approaches to the problems. Also, although he liked Wally and enjoyed working with him, he wasn't sure whether Wally's deliberate, consensus-oriented style was what Bennett's needed to pull it out of this slide.

The Senator

Senator Wallace F. Bennett was an active board chairman. Known throughout the company and the family as "the senator," he provided continuity to a company that had had three presidents in five years. His energy, creativity, and leadership skills served him well, not only in running the companies but also in his successful careers as president of NAM and as a U.S. senator. Throughout his terms in Congress, the senator had kept his post as chairman of the board and had kept abreast of company activities.

Eighty-two at the time Michael Silva became president, the senator remained physically and mentally active. His daily routine included long walks (up to six and a half miles) and a full schedule of activities at his office on the second story of the original Bennett's building on First South. He was a prominent and respected figure in the city, involved in civic and church affairs.

The senator was ordinarily modest about his many accomplishments but exhibited a justifiable pride about Bennett's early years under his presidency:

> We were bold then. We dominated the paint business in Utah. When we developed the Colorizer concept, everyone told us it wouldn't work. But overnight, we revolutionized the paint business.

I feel very close to Mike because we can give each other ideas. I think I have been able to suggest a few things that Mike has agreed with, and I know that he has come up with a lot of ideas on his own that I thought were great. I think we can be a good team.

I wonder about the future of the Bennett Association. Within the company, there has been a real political struggle for power since Richard's death. I think we needed an outsider.

Michael Silva

Michael Silva grew up in Hawaii and attended Brigham Young University (BYU), where he was active in school politics and competed successfully in several intercollegiate and national debate tournaments. Upon graduation, he enrolled in a master's program in organizational behavior at BYU, where his quick, analytical mind and remarkable verbal abilities soon distinguished him. In an argument or discussion, Silva's debating prowess made him an intimidating opponent. Generally, Silva had gotten along well with the faculty and peers but at times appeared impatient and aloof. Although he had completed 95 percent of the degree requirements and had grades well above the class average, several confrontations with faculty members caused him to leave the program shortly before graduation.

Silva was 30 years old when he took over as president of the Bennett Association, but he had a wealth of experience behind him. After leaving BYU, he had been through a series of remarkable job changes, each of which gave him more responsibility. He began as an assistant to the president of Skaggs Foods but, after a year, moved back to Hawaii to take a staff job as a corporate planner at State Savings and Loan, a large Hawaiian operation with assets of $500 million, 16 branches, and more than 300 employees. At the S&L, he worked his way up to a position as assistant to the chairman of the board. After two years with State, he returned to the Intermountain West area as manager of Peat, Marwick, Mitchell's bank consulting unit. While Silva was in this position, Warren Pugh, owner of Cummins Intermountain Diesel Company, asked Silva to come straighten out his banking problems, which were costing the company tens of millions of dollars. He was able to put Cummins on a sound financial footing, but only by laying off 70 percent of the workforce. Silva then moved to Arthur Young, Inc., as manager of consulting services for the Salt Lake City office.

Silva began to work with the Bennett Association when it engaged the services of Arthur Young in late February 1981. In June 1981, the banks informed Bennett that, because of continued losses, they were going to call in their loans unless the company would agree to an outside CEO—a first in the history of the Bennett Association. Bennett then asked Arthur Young to help them find someone who could make the company profitable once again.

Several candidates with impressive credentials were interviewed by the senator and the board. Although each candidate felt that he could improve Bennett's position, they all agreed a complete turnaround would take at least five years. The board members (in particular, the senator) were not impressed with the applicants. Wallace finally said, "Gentlemen, I don't think we need to go outside and look for people to help us. I think we have the man right here who is best suited for the job."

In August 1981, Silva was offered the job and, after some negotiation, signed a three-year contract as CEO of what would be called Bennett Enterprises, a central management company that would control the various companies owned by the Bennett Association. He would begin his duties as CEO in early October 1981.

Management Style. Silva's office, located in the Bennett Leasing Company building, was pleasantly, if sparsely, decorated. His office and his secretary's office were separated from the leasing operation by a heavy, black swinging door, referred to as the "Iron Curtain." Relatively small by executive standards, the office had few of the trappings that one might associate with a CEO. He did have a small computer, one of two he owned. A small, framed quotation (from Machiavelli) immediately caught the eye of any visitor:

> There is nothing more difficult to carry out, or more doubtful to success, or more dangerous to handle, than to initiate a new order of things. For the reformer has enemies in all those who profit by the old order, and lukewarm supporters in all those who would profit by the new order.

The existence of the Iron Curtain was significant. Silva was explicit about his non-open-door policy. He was protective of his office time and went out of his way to make it difficult for people to find him. He believed that if people knew his time was valuable and he was difficult to find, they were better prepared than otherwise when they did catch him. Besides, he felt his lack of availability often encouraged people to solve problems themselves.

He managed telephone calls with the same spirit. His secretary, Dixie Clark, screened all calls. Only those from his family or the senator were allowed to come through immediately. For all other calls, he was "out of the office" or "in a meeting." Periodically during the day, Silva would sort through the messages and return the calls that seemed important. By the end of the day, message slips littered his desk.

When he entered the building, he would greet everyone cheerfully, at times almost playfully. He seemed genuinely pleased with those in the company who would banter with him:

> That is something that I encourage. I like the atmosphere of mild sarcasm that we have created here. I encourage people to tease me because I get better information about how people are feeling. It's a type of informal communication.

Schedule. Silva's daily routine as CEO followed one of two patterns. In the first, he arose early and arrived at the office at 5:00 or 6:00 A.M. He wrote, dictated correspondence, and planned until 8:00 or 9:00, when he began to see people and make calls. After lunch he went home to enjoy the rest of the day with his family. In the second pattern, Silva stayed home in the morning and helped prepare the children for school. He then arrived at the office around 10:00 A.M. and worked until lunch. After lunch he would remain at the office until around 3:00, when he went home to be with his family.

In the evenings, his schedule was less variable. He helped with dinner (he was an accomplished cook) and afterward put the children to bed. Often he worked (usually on his own writing) from 10:00 P.M. until 1:00 or 2:00 A.M. He seldom needed more than four or five hours of sleep:

> I have never worked one Saturday or one Sunday in my career. I don't think I have ever worked an eight-hour day. I made a decision when I started to work that my family was always going to come first in my life. This is the first job that has offered me real flexibility. I found that I could easily become too involved with my work, but I don't want to. I work hard at keeping my family number one. I don't want my

work to become my life. I really like the freedom that this job could offer me now. I like both the freedom and the money, but I probably wouldn't give up the freedom for the money. I want time to be with my family. Time, in fact, probably drives everything I do. I'm something of a time fanatic. Everything is driven by my time resource. I won't take on anything that will require any more of my time than I already give.

I don't think that it is any big deal to be a good manager. Most anyone could probably be a reasonable manager. The real question is whether you can do it differently. Can you do it in a way that doesn't eat up your life? Can you have an impact in your job and still maintain a family life?

I think that there are three roles that have to be mastered in management. You need to know strategy, the culture, and the numbers. The problem that you generally find is that few people who are sensitive to issues like culture enjoy working with numbers. You can usually find people who like to do two of those roles, but not all three.

Michael Silva Discusses the Company Situation

After assuming control of Bennett Association on October 1, 1981, Silva felt that he had a good understanding of how the company operated but was unclear about which problems to attack first, which managers were reliable, and which approach he should take to making changes. He also knew that the six-week vacation he negotiated as a part of his contract was to begin soon, and he was unsure about initiating any major change only to have it sputter and die in his absence. Silva interviewed the key managers from each of the businesses and spent a considerable amount of time with the senator. He wanted to have as much input as possible before he began to implement a plan.

He talked at length about the situation he faced:

When the company brought in all of the outside applicants for the job, they all took a strictly financial approach and said it would take at least five years to turn the company around. I don't think we have that much time, and I think we can do it in less than that. All of the other people they interviewed for this job said that it was a financial problem. I think the problem is as much cultural as it is financial.

Silva noted that employees at Bennett's seemed to have an unwritten expectation that if they had a job with Bennett's, they would never be laid off. Even during the Great Depression, no one in Bennett's had been let go. Perhaps for this reason, even though the company was having severe financial troubles, there was a noticeable lack of concern among employees and managers about losing their jobs. They had made no special efforts to improve performance or productivity, or even to attract new customers. Some pressure had been put on the sales districts, but with limited response.

Commenting on his goals, Silva stated:

We're going to have a difficult time turning this around. Our biggest businesses are tied directly to the housing and automobile markets, and so we are going to have a hard time if this recession gets any worse.

We need to stress excellence and making a profit in the long run. It's important to remember that all the variables that insure a profit in the long run are

> human resource variables. I want people to think they are the best. I will not stand for mediocrity. We should demand the absolute best from our people, but then pay them accordingly. Many companies try to pay their people the least amount possible and still keep them. I think that's crazy. I think you should pay them as much as possible to still make a profit. It makes a big difference in the way they think about themselves. More than anything, I think we should be strategy driven. We want to have revenues of $100 million by 1990.
>
> I want to be a leader here. The difference between a leader and a manager is that a manager manages systems and a leader manages values. We need to stress new values, those that emphasize performance. I need to have the confidence of the people here, because when an organization doesn't sense that their leader can get them through a crisis, they lose their incentive.

One factor Silva worried about particularly was the reaction of members of the Bennett family to any changes he might make:

> Part of my contract states that the board cannot counteract my decisions. They can cancel my contract at any time, but I don't have to get their approval for any of my decisions, and they can't counteract what I decide. I don't think I have time for an educational process each time I make a decision. Decisions will have to be made in a hurry, and I don't have the time to go back and forth with the board. I do stay in close contact with the senator, though. He has been very helpful so far. I probably see him two times a week, but I talk to him at least once a day.
>
> I like to define culture as the personality of a company, and so I think there are two ways to change that personality. The first is by long-term change, where you gradually work at some of the problem areas in the culture. The second is trauma, where you massively address the company problems.

Given Bennett's unique history and his goals, Silva was not sure what exactly he should do.

Appendix to Case 24

Senator Wallace Foster Bennett's Biographical Sketch

The first of five children of John Foster Rosetta (Wallace) Bennett, Wallace Foster Bennett was born November 13, 1898, in Salt Lake City, Utah. Both his parents were of English ancestry and of the Mormon faith. At the time of Wallace's birth, his father, who had crossed the plains in a covered wagon at the age of three, was occupied in establishing the paint and glass concern his son now heads. Bennett has quoted with approval his father's dictum that "no transaction of any sort is good unless both sides profit from it."

Young Bennett attended the Salt Lake City public schools and the church high school known as the Latter-Day Saints University, where he took part in debating and choral singing (he says he has an "ordinary bass voice"). Graduated in 1916, he entered the University of Utah, where he majored in English and won a varsity letter in debating. A member of the university's ROTC, 19-year-old Wallace Bennett was commissioned a second lieutenant of infantry in September 1918 and was assigned to Colorado College as an instructor. His own college education completed and the B.A. from Utah having been awarded to him in 1919, Bennett returned to Colorado as principal of a Mormon school, the San Luis State Academy at Manassa. "It was always my understanding," he has stated, "that I would come into the family business, in which I had spent most of my summers during high school and college. I returned to the business June 1, 1920, and have been with it ever since."

Beginning as an office clerk in the family's business, Bennett soon advanced to cashier, then production manager, then sales manager. He became secretary-treasurer by 1929, the year he also assumed the same post in the Jordan Valley Investment Company of Salt Lake City. Three years later Wallace Bennett took over the general management of the Bennett Paint and Glass Company, his father retaining the presidency. In that year, too, Bennett embarked on a one-hour daily broadcast series, called "The Observatory Hour," over station KSL.

During the depression of the 1930s, Bennett recounted, none of his firm's employees was discharged, though this meant cutting wages. At his father's death in 1928, the eldest son became president and general manager, with one brother, Harold, serving as vice president, and the other, Richard, as secretary-treasurer.

In 1939, he and several friends organized the Bennett Motor Company, a Ford dealership, with him as president. During the next eight years, the Bennett Paint and Glass Company went through an expansion phase: in 1949 it had warehouses and seven retail stores to handle its stock of paints, enamels, polishes, cleansers, mirrors, and other "decorator and household specialties." What its president described as the most modern paint manufacturing plant in the West was completed in 1948, two years after he shortened the firm name to "Bennett's." To illustrate his labor-relations program to a NAM audience in 1948, Bennett told them, "The man who sweeps out our retail store calls me Wallace."

While retaining the presidency of the paint and glass company, in 1947 Bennett turned the management over to his brother Richard. Another business association of Wallace Bennett's was with Zion's Savings Bank and Trust Company, of which he was a director and executive committee member. The Utah manufacturer also served on the boards of the Utah Home Fire Insurance Company, the Utah Oil Refining Company, and the Bannock Hotel Corporation. He was a former president of the National Glass Distributors Association, a former vice president of the National Paint, Varnish and Lacquer Association, and a director and former chairman of the public relations committee of the Utah Manufacturers Association. These business interests were to result in his selection as a vice president and director of the National Association of Manufacturers.

In December 1948, Bennett addressed about two thousand people at a session on labor-management teamwork, declaring: "If we can give these people [employees] satisfaction as well as wages, we can overcome the philosophy of the class struggle. If we do not give them a feeling of partnership and achievement, then forces that would tear us apart will take over. Time is running out." Bennett was elected by the NAM board in December to succeed Morris Sayre as president. One statement Bennett made was: "My selection is a recognition of the growing importance of Western industry and of the importance of small business. This is the first time the presidency of NAM has gone west of Chicago."

At his first press conference, the Utah businessman told reporters that he intended to spend his presidential year traveling throughout the United States, preaching "the partnership of the men who put up the money, and the men who do the work, and the men who tie the whole thing together" and the responsiblity of management to convey this to the workers. He urged NAM not to serve the interests of free industry alone, but of all freedom, because "if any part of freedom falls, the whole thing falls." Bennett said that in his business he accepted the AFL glaziers' closed shop, despite his personal disapproval, because the closed shop was "traditional in the building trades." The new NAM president also stated that his strongest competition came not from larger but from smaller firms, and he recommended that the government deal with inflation by shifting its bonds from the hands of banks into those of private investors.

Case 25

Charlottesville-Albemarle Legal Aid Society

Alex Gulotta, newly appointed director of the Charlottesville-Albemarle Legal Aid Society, was in the midst of drafting his first director's report. He wrote:

> As the program's new director, I have been overwhelmed by the warm welcome extended to me by the legal community, the social services community, and the client community. From my discussions with community leaders, it is clear that the Charlottesville-Albemarle Legal Aid Society is well respected for its advocacy on behalf of those in need.
>
> The unfortunate reality, however, is that the need for Legal Aid services continues to outstrip our ability to respond. The program's attempt to provide some level of individual service to all income-eligible clients increasingly limits the time available to respond to each problem. As resources are taxed, the program's advocates are forced to react to client dilemmas rather than to actively work toward long-term solutions.
>
> Legal Aid is approaching the new fiscal year with the hope and energy occasioned by change. Our goal is to turn a very good legal services program into one of the very best.

As he considered how to get that process under way, Gulotta thought about the changes that the organization had experienced in its 28-year history and the challenges that he faced in setting its strategic direction for the future.

History

The Charlottesville-Albemarle Legal Aid Society provided free legal advice and representation to low-income households in six jurisdictions, including Albemarle, Fluvanna, Greene, Louisa, and Nelson Counties and the city of Charlottesville (see area map, Exhibit 1). The Legal Aid Society provided these services to clients with civil (rather than criminal) legal problems, especially those involving housing, employment, consumer protection, domestic relations, health care, and public benefits. According to the 1990 census, approximately 21,000 people in the areas served by the Legal Aid Society lived at or below the poverty line and were, therefore, financially eligible for free legal services.

The Legal Aid Society was incorporated in 1967 as a nonprofit Virginia corporation by a committee of the Charlottesville-Albemarle Bar Association in cooperation with a group from the University of Virginia School of Law. The Legal Aid

This case was written by Jeanne M. Liedtka, Associate Professor of Business Administration.

EXHIBIT 1

Charlottesville-Albemarle Legal Aid Society Area Map

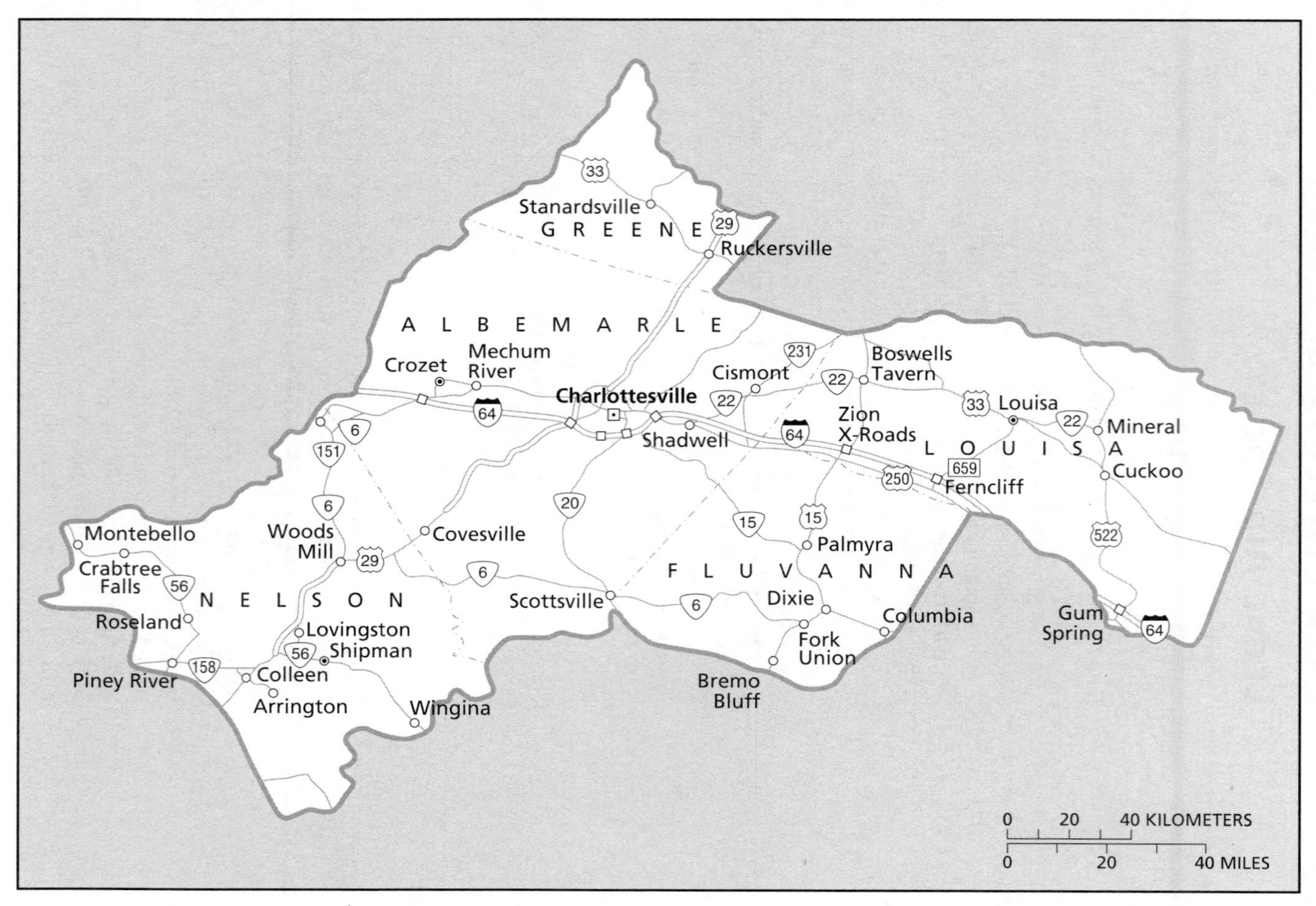

Society originally operated in a borrowed space. Law students interviewed new clients and volunteer attorneys took the cases.

This wholly volunteer concept continued until the first funding was received from the federal Office of Economic Opportunity in 1971. The first paid Legal Aid Society staff members were hired that year. The program consisted of one full-time attorney and two support staff.

During the period from 1971 to 1981, increased funding allowed the program to gradually expand its staff and caseload. By 1980, there were 15 staff members, including six attorneys and four paralegals. Ninety-three percent of revenues were provided by the federal government through the Legal Services Corporation, which replaced the Office of Economic Opportunity in 1974.

The increases in federal funding ended abruptly in the early 1980s. In 1981 and 1982, federal legal services funding was reduced by 25 percent. In addition, the Legal Services Corporation required that 12.5 percent of the grant be diverted away from direct services to clients. Instead, the Legal Aid Society was required to use this 12.5 percent of the grant to encourage private attorneys to help them with their work. For the rest of the 1980s, the Legal Aid Society received either no additional federal funding or very small increases. Taking inflation into account, the level of federal funding dropped by 40 percent during these years. The result was a significant reduction in office staff. During the 1980s the total number of staff dropped from 15 to 8 and the number of staff attorneys dropped from 6 to 4. Except for one new paralegal position, the staff had remained at this reduced level. Exhibit 2 summarizes fiscal year 1993–94 sources of funding (revenues) and expenses.

These reductions forced changes in the way the program provided its services. During the 1970s, all eligible clients with legal problems were assigned to attorneys or paralegals, who provided whatever legal services the client needed. In the early 1980s, this changed. All clients continued to receive advice about their legal problems, but most received nothing more. Attorneys were able to provide additional services, such as in-court representation, in only a small percentage of cases.

Another change involved contact with the rural counties within the area. In the 1970s, the Legal Aid Society staff had regular office hours in Fluvanna, Greene, Louisa, and Nelson Counties, and staff attorneys traveled to these counties to meet with new clients. However, due to diminishing resources, this practice was abandoned. Instead, a toll-free 800 number was installed to allow these clients to contact the office directly.

One significant positive change was the increased involvement of local private attorneys in the Legal Aid Society's work through pro bono volunteer projects and reduced-fee arrangements. In 1991, the Charlottesville-Albemarle Bar Association enacted a Pro Bono Policy under which each member engaged in the private practice of law agreed to donate a minimum of 25 hours per year to pro bono legal services. The bar also created a Pro Bono Committee to administer the program in cooperation with the Legal Aid Society. More than 100 local attorneys provided legal services to Legal Aid Society clients. Without this assistance, the Legal Aid Society would have been forced to further restrict the services provided to low-income residents.

Although federal funding remained stagnant during the 1980s, the program was successful in getting funding from other sources. In cooperation with other legal services programs in Virginia, the Society obtained funding from new state government sources. In addition, the Virginia State Bar established a statewide Interest on Lawyer Trust Accounts (IOLTA) program, which earmarked the interest

EXHIBIT 2

Charlottesville-Albemarle Legal Aid Society Revenues and Expenses, FY 1993–94

REVENUES	
Legal Services Corp.	$ 210,318
State of Virginia	58,251
IOLTA (Virginia Law Foundation)	36,915
Albemarle County	12,775
Charlottesville	21,793
Charlottesville CDBG	7,907
Fluvanna County	2,680
Jefferson Area Board for Aging (JABA)	5,300
Interest	1,394
Other[1]	27,061
Total revenues	$ 384,394
Fund balance from previous year's operations	$ 2,687
Total funds available for year	$ 387,081
EXPENSES	
Personnel	$ 296,340
Nonpersonnel	74,811
Equipment purchase transfer	2,225
Total expenses	$ 373,376
Fund balance, end of year:	$ 13,705

[1]Other revenue sources include the Thomas Jefferson Area United Way, the Charlottesville-Albemarle Bar Association, fees from the Lawyer Referral Service, and other donations.

earned on these trust accounts for Legal Aid's use. In 1993, the Bar mandated participation in this program by all Virginia attorneys, giving the Legal Aid Society a significant increase in its revenues.

During the same time, the Legal Aid Society obtained additional funding from local sources, including the city of Charlottesville and the counties of Albemarle and Fluvanna. In 1992, it also began receiving funding as part of the Thomas Jefferson Area United Way Campaign. In addition, the Legal Aid Society sometimes received funding for special projects (an example was the Community Development Block Grant from the city of Charlottesville, which funded legal services for victims of domestic violence from 1992 until 1994).

The Legal Aid Society Client Base

The number of clients contacting the Legal Aid Society for help had expanded dramatically during the previous few years. For much of its history, the Legal Aid Society kept its income eligibility level at 125 percent of the federal poverty level, the maximum permitted by the Legal Services Corporation. However, between 1988 and 1992, the number of eligible clients contacting the Legal Aid Society increased by more than 68 percent. The dramatic increase in eligible clients led the Legal Aid Society Board of Directors in 1992 to reduce the eligibility limit to 100 percent of the poverty level.

The funding available to the Legal Aid Society was not sufficient to allow the staff to accept all cases in which legal services were requested, even with the new income eligibility criteria. Because of this reality, the Legal Aid Society Board of Directors was required to amend a "Statement of Priorities," which was used to determine which cases would be accepted and which would be turned away. For many years one of the priorities of the Legal Aid Society had been to provide legal advice to every eligible client. All of the approximately 2,600 eligible clients who called the Legal Aid Society during FY 1993–94 received, at a minimum, the chance to discuss their case with a lawyer or a skilled paralegal.

Advice was all that many clients needed, but others required further legal services. In the past, these services included the drafting of documents, negotiation with adverse parties, and representation in court. The Society used the Statement of Priorities to determine which clients could receive these additional services. In general, the factors that determined eligibility for full representation included

- the importance of the case for the client
- the likelihood that the legal representation would be successful
- whether alternative legal services were available
- whether the client could obtain the remedy sought without legal representation
- the resources and expertise of the Legal Aid Society staff
- whether the problem affected a large number of people in the low-income community

Under the current policy, the following categories of cases were given priority in receiving legal services:

1. Basic human needs cases
   a. income maintenance
   b. shelter
   c. health care
   d. safety
2. Domestic relations cases
3. Problems of elderly cases

It was felt that the time had come to review the program's priorities again. As Gulotta lamented, "We can't help everyone all the way. Our system was premised on the fact that we know we don't have enough funds so we must prioritize."

Exhibit 3 lists the main categories of cases handled by the Legal Aid Society during FY 1993–94, based on cases closed during the year. "Advice only" cases were

EXHIBIT 3

Cases Handled by the Legal Aid Society, FY 1993–94

PROBLEM TYPE	ADVICE ONLY	% OF TOTAL	FULL REPRESENTATION	% OF TOTAL
Consumer/ finance	379	16.9	57	12.7
Education	8	0.4	0	0
Employment	103	4.6	12	2.7
Family	1,005	44.7	184	41.2
Juvenile	13	0.6	1	0.2
Health	34	1.5	21	4.7
Housing	339	15.1	94	21.0
Income support	183	8.1	56	12.6
Individual rights	35	1.6	13	2.9
Miscellaneous	147	6.5	9	2.0
Totals	2,246	100.0	447	100.0

cases in which a client received legal advice or brief follow-up service, but a case file was not formally opened. "Full representation" cases referred to cases that fell within the priority areas identified by the board. These cases were formally opened and assigned to a staff person, who provided whatever services were necessary, including in-court representation where appropriate.

The Charlottesville-Albemarle Bar Association

Through its pro bono efforts, the local bar association also provided a number of services. (See Exhibit 4.) These services included work in the following areas:

Advice and consultation project. Under this project, attorneys came to the Legal Aid Society office to provide consultation and advice. Three attorneys came each week and spent a half day interviewing approximately six to eight clients. During FY 1993–94, a total of 131 attorneys participated in this project, donating 477 hours and providing legal services to approximately 775 clients.

Divorce panel. Prior to 1991, attorneys accepted referrals of no-fault divorces for a reduced fee of $100 per case. During 1991, the Legal Aid Society changed its practice to make use of the tax credit program set up by the Virginia Neighborhood Assistance Act. Under this program, attorneys donated their services without a fee,

EXHIBIT 4

Pro Bono Projects of Bar Association, FY 1993-94

PROJECT	# OF ATTORNEYS	# OF CASES
Advice and Consultation	131	775
Full Representation		
Divorce panel	22	63
Custody panel	17	18
Bankruptcy panel	21	62
Wills panel	20	27
Total Full Representation	80	170

and they received a tax credit of the value of the donated services. In FY 1993–94, 63 divorce cases were referred.

Custody panel. The Neighborhood Assistance Act program was also extended to referrals of contested custody cases. During FY 1993–94, 18 contested custody cases were referred.

Bankruptcy panel. The bankruptcy panel was formed in the spring of 1992 at the suggestion of the Bankruptcy Committee of the Charlottesville-Albemarle Bar Association. Approximately 21 attorneys participated on this panel, receiving tax credits under the Neighborhood Assistance Act for their work. Of the 62 bankruptcy cases referred to the panel during FY 1993–94, 30 resulted in discharges and 10 were still pending at the end of the year. In the remainder of the cases, the clients failed to follow through, often due to their inability to raise the $160 non-waivable fee necessary to file a Chapter 7 petition with the bankruptcy court.

Wills panel. In the fall of 1992 a panel was formed to assist low-income elderly individuals with wills, powers-of-attorney, living wills, and simple estates. Twenty-one Charlottesville attorneys participated on this panel, providing their work without charge. In FY 1993–94, 27 clients received assistance from this panel.

THE LEGAL AID SOCIETY'S SITUATION IN EARLY 1995

As Gulotta took on his new responsibilities as director in July 1994, he knew that the Legal Aid Society was well regarded in the community for the quality of its legal work and its relationships with its clients. Joy Johnson, a client of the Legal Aid Society who had worked with them through her tenant association, described her initial interactions with Legal Aid staff:

> In my case . . . I don't know if I can say where I was living at the time. But it was a real bad drug area. Every night, there was gunshots out there. I would call the police and let them know that, you know, it's a lot of people out here. They're making noise, I cannot sleep or whatever. They would come run them away. As soon as the police leave, they'd be right back. So, I went to management to let them know what was going on. Nothing seemed to have been done until somebody actually shot at my house and the bullet just missed my cousin. . . . So, I went to management again and nothing was done. So I went to Legal Aid. And I said, "This is what's happening. We need some help here." So they came in, got the ball rolling, so that area is no longer the worst area anymore. On the personal level, I've felt comfortable in dealing with them because they were very sensitive to whatever issue it is that you brought before them. They wasn't snobbish, they were just down to earth and so you could really talk openly to them. They don't look down, you know, on you or anything. They help you any kind of way . . . any kind of way you need their services. If people knew more about the Legal Aid Society, then they would go in and get help. It's just getting the people to realize that the Legal Aid Society is there for them.

Johnson believed that the Legal Aid Society could increase its impact by moving out into the community on a more regular basis:

> One of the things we're trying to do is to be in the community to let people know their rights or to work with people if they have any problems. So being on-site, once or twice a week, could be a help to people who have whatever issues, just to go in and talk to them and see. I tell a lot of people and I always have, you know. If you feel that you have rights, and something is not right, then go to the Legal Aid Society. See if you can get the help. And that's what they basically need to know, that the Legal Aid Society is there to help them. A lot of people are afraid to speak up against what's happening to them in public housing because they're afraid that if they say something, then they're going to be evicted anyway. So, the Legal Aid Society will come into the community and tell them, you have a right to voice your opinion, you know, you can't be evicted for it.

Despite the ever increasing need for services, Gulotta was mindful of the strains that the current situation was placing on his staff. "During my interviews here, it was clear that some feeling existed that people were overtaxed. We needed to find a structure where people could do their work without being ground up in the process."

One tension created for his staff was caused by the volume of clients who needed more than advice, but who had to be turned away because no one was available to help them. Another tension was created by the kinds of cases the Legal Aid Society took on. The organization's current stated objective was for an attorney to consult with all eligible clients concerning their legal problems. Theoretically, the Legal Aid Society staff concurred. However, in practice the staff attorneys felt that too much of their time was devoted to providing advice and handling "routine casework," and not enough time was devoted to "impact" advocacy. The high volume of individually-focused routine casework was seen by staff as putting "Band-aids" on the serious problems that the poor community faced, at the expense of pursuing solutions that would address the root causes of the problems they faced. "Impact" work was seen as challenging the system itself in a way intended to have a broader impact than individual casework. It consisted of a strategy with a concerted focus to respond in a more proactive way to taking certain kinds of cases, combined with a highly visible, public relations-oriented stance. As Gulotta explained:

> Impact work doesn't have to be a case—it can involve strategies like opening up previous cases of a certain type. It involves looking at problems, finding a common thread, and creating an advocacy strategy that attempts to get at the *causes* of these problems, rather than just the symptoms. . . . I came here from a program (the Appalachian Research and Defense Fund of Kentucky) whose mandate was broader. My former director was very involved in the civil rights movement. We worked with that kind of big vision—an organization that can change poor people's lives and make their lives better. Do you help everybody with their will or divorce or do you challenge the way the system reacts to that? Lawyers and paralegals need the time, creativity, and drive to do that kind of work. Some people are better suited to a larger volume of routine case activity.

The attorneys and paralegals at the Legal Aid Society agreed with Gulotta and emphasized that the high volume of cases they now accepted represented "quantity versus quality." They expressed a strong desire to take cases that would have a greater impact on the indigent community, such as class action suits and civil rights cases. They had a concern over the increasing number of domestic cases, almost 50 percent of casework at present, and felt that these cases did little for the community as a whole, were extremely time consuming, yet rarely resolved.

The staff felt that the high proportion of domestic cases probably stemmed from previous clients referring new clients. Because the majority of the cases involved domestic issues, it was not surprising that clients with similar domestic problems encouraged one another to seek help from the Legal Aid Society. The staff felt that they needed to alter this trend. Domestic cases absorbed too much of their time and prevented them from doing other meaningful work. Furthermore, if the staff could find other means to reach eligible customers rather than rely on "word-of-mouth," then they would be able to attract different cases that would benefit a greater number of poor people.

Client composition determined the issues that the Legal Aid Society currently addressed; however, it was difficult to determine how clients were actually referred. Other social service agencies referred a small number of clients. Other clients had attended educational seminars promoted by the Legal Aid Society or read informational material produced by them.

The recent decline in the number of clients from the surrounding counties further frustrated the staff. Unfortunately, these numbers dropped when the Society discontinued in-person appointments in surrounding counties. This concerned several of the staff attorneys, who felt that rural poverty interests were often neglected and should be addressed. The staff members who had been involved in appointment times in the rural counties emphasized their importance and suggested that efforts should be made to restore this service.

The Screening Process

Traditionally, individuals contacted the Legal Aid Society by telephone and were immediately screened by the receptionist and assigned a phone interview with a Legal Aid Society paralegal to determine if the client was financially eligible for services, and, if so, how the case would be pursued. During the scheduled phone conversation, the paralegal's objective was to determine if the case was "advice only" or would actually necessitate litigation. The cases that required litigation were turned over to a Legal Aid Society lawyer. The "advice only" cases were scheduled with a volunteer lawyer. If the "advice only" problem was simple enough, the paralegal would actually provide the advice during the phone call.

This process was complicated by the fact that many clients lacked telephones, making call-backs difficult. It was also complicated by clients returning with the same problems, even though the Legal Aid Society had previously declined to represent them. Recently, a client had come through for the fourth time with the same legal problem, explaining, "I thought that if it got bad enough you'd help me." Gulotta felt that this process could be improved.

The current system for using pro bono lawyers was another potential area for improvement. Gulotta wondered whether the volunteer lawyers might be better utilized if they handled more ongoing litigation, rather than just giving advice. Gulotta believed that cases such as routine evictions and protective custody and restraining orders would require about a half day's work, no more time than the lawyers were already donating. He had also thought about whether more aggressive recruiting of volunteers and some additional fund-raising efforts might help.

Legal Aid Society's Constituencies

In addition to the above issues, Gulotta found the balancing act of managing the Society's relationships with its different constituencies a challenge. Clients wanted their individual cases handled. Staff lawyers were anxious to do less casework and more impact work. Additionally, two other constituencies played an important role.

One constituency was the local bar association and the local attorneys in private practice whom it represented. The Society relied on this group for the majority of the members of its governing board, for a significant level of financial support, and for encouraging pro bono work among its membership. An impending change in state law would soon allow local law firms to decide whether the interest on their IOLTA funds would be assigned to the Legal Aid Society or not.

The Legal Aid Society had a history of working well with the local bar association. As a former bar association president commented:

> I think one thing that the Legal Aid Society does well is to place its leadership inside the local bar association. For example, the head of the Legal Aid Society has attended every meeting that I've ever attended of the board of directors of the Charlottesville-Albemarle Bar Association. I think that there's a close working relationship between the Bar and the Legal Aid Society. And I think that, as a starting point, that's important when you're looking to the members of our profession to make individual contributions to Legal Aid.

Individually, local attorneys involved with the Legal Aid Society had a variety of opinions about how to increase its effectiveness. Some felt that the visibility of its work needed to be increased. One attorney commented:

> The Legal Aid Society is the voice for the poor community. They are the foremost advocate for the working poor and poor people in our community. . . . If I have a

criticism, it's that I think the voice needs to be louder. I think that there are important issues affecting poor people which are not being addressed in a loud enough fashion. . . I think that advocates for poor people, especially lawyers, have two arenas that they need to function in. One is the legal arena, and the other is the political arena. And, there are a lot of decisions that are made by our governments which affect the clientele who use the Legal Aid Society. I don't know if, politically, there was a fear on the part of directors of the past going after the hand that feeds them because a lot of the funding comes locally, as well as from the state. But, it seems to me that they need to be louder, that they need to bring attention to problems with the particular legislation, with ordinances that affect their clients.

The other area, being a louder advocate in the legal arena, is that I think that the Legal Aid Society needs to do more high-profile cases that have impact on the client community. That taking individual cases sometimes can have that kind of impact . . . taking collective cases can have even a bigger impact. There are many parts of our community that are extremely poor that don't get services at all, and part of it is due to Congress' own restrictions, but some of it is due to the priorities that the Legal Aid Society sets.

And so, I know that there are limitations. There have always been dedicated, loyal lawyers at Legal Aid. But I guess I am critical about some of the priorities and feel that more needs to be done in a louder fashion.

Others felt that education was a critical area. Another local attorney noted:

We see a steady stream of young, healthy, intelligent people going off to jail for extensive periods of time, and they don't see that they [the Legal Aid Society] are able to help these people. It's not simply a matter of the Legal Aid Society, or of the attorneys, but it's a real societal problem. . . . I'd like to see something in our schools that helps people stay out of the legal system by teaching them to read, by teaching them to do mathematics, by teaching them to balance a checkbook, by teaching them the importance of saving, and of training them with skills to get jobs. It seems to me somebody's falling down there, and the legal system is there to address problems that arise, but a lot of the problems arise because the people don't have the basic skills to begin with. I'm not sure that it's the Bar's problem. I think that the problem lies deeper in our society. We deal with the problems that arise, but how can we help prevent those problems from arising in the first place?

Another lawyer disagreed:

I don't think the Legal Aid Society ought to spend its time in the schools. I think that there are tenant associations that devote a good portion of their time working primarily on housing issues which are very major concerns to people. That's where I think the Legal Aid Society attorneys ought to be spending their time.

Others argued for education with a different focus:

What they do is they schedule an attorney for, say, an afternoon a week. You're scheduled to come in and you interview clients who have preset appointments. The areas applied just run the gamut. I tend to get a lot of bankruptcy and domestic relations because that's what I do. But the people who come in need more education about the legal system. They need some easy way to learn more about their rights, their obligations. They need some basic training in leases. They need some basic training in used-car sales. They come in and talk to an attorney. The attorney has maybe anywhere from 20 to 30 minutes per client. So you can't give them a lot of real information in that time. You're busy listening to what they have to say, but you don't have the time to give them all the information they might need. It seems to me that if we had some kind of teaching tool here, that we might help the Legal Aid Society clients from getting into some of the fixes that they get into, and learning how to cope with those fixes once they get into them. So, I see the Legal Aid Society as a teaching organization as well as a legal organization.

Still others felt that local attorneys, as well as clients, needed education:

If it's a paying client, you will make yourself aware of whatever law needs to be addressed and you will take care of all of that client's problems. I think that whether we're working on a pro bono case or a paying case, we need to have that same attitude. Attorneys are, and I will make a broad generalization, ivory tower babies. We're very privileged. We have telephones, and we have good incomes. And we have transportation. We don't face a lot of the problems that these clients are facing every day. I had a case of a landlord/tenant dispute. The client was being sued for the remainder of the lease and she didn't show up in court on the day that it was to be heard by the judge. Well, she said she had forgotten. But I think that the problem was that she didn't have transportation to the court. She had two small children, and no one to take care of those children. The attorney has to be aware of these situations and sort of troubleshoot, I think, because there are ways to solve this. Now this particular single mom didn't have a place to live, and she'd been kicked out on the street repeatedly. I worked very closely with the social worker to get her subsidized housing, which is almost nonexistent at this point. I mean, the waiting lists are forever. I think that there are ways that attorneys can work with social service agencies to benefit people. But I think some education for the attorneys is also important, because we don't know what these people are facing. We don't live this life. And until you've been involved with it for a good period of time, you don't know how to react to these situations.

One lawyer commented on the need to encourage more pro bono work and the difficulty that she had encountered in doing so:

I was working for a firm that did not approve of its associates working for the Legal Aid Society, which was a real struggle, because I have always been committed to that. I think it's a privilege to practice law, and I think that we owe something to the community and this is my way of paying back, so to speak. So, I think that, in some respects, more attorneys would be involved if there was a concerted effort to deal with the partners of established firms who are reluctant at this time to permit their associates to assist.

Others felt strongly that more staff lawyers rather than volunteers were needed:

I think we need more Legal Aid attorneys. I don't anticipate this is a good political climate to be asking Congress, the state, or even local governments for more money. But, I don't think that anything beats having an actual full-time staff attorney as opposed to relying on some wonderful attorneys who volunteer their time. It's much more efficient, and I think a higher quality of practice, to have more lawyers who are specialized and who know this area of law. I think that more important cases could be brought because you would have additional resources in allowing the attorneys time to work on a more complex case than they do now.

There are just certain areas in the law that people in private practice don't have a lot of experience in. I'm thinking about Medicaid or federally subsidized housing, where people of low income tend to have issues come up that people in private practice don't handle. So they tend to do that well. They tend to develop expertise in those areas, and they provide a really needed resource there. It's not lawyers like myself that are really going to ultimately help representation of the poor, it's going to be the lawyers who specialize and are trained in this area.

Some thought that more attention to fund-raising would be useful:

Charlottesville is somewhat stratified, so to speak. There's the inner city, and we have a much higher concentration of poor people in the city of Charlottesville than we do, say, in the county of Albemarle. There's also a very wealthy group of people whose daily lives are not touched by these people. They don't see them, they don't know what they're facing, they don't know what they're going through, they don't know their problems. I think that a fund-raising effort, even if it is not ultimately successful in terms of generating additional funds, might bring these issues to the public awareness, which I think is important.

A second Legal Aid Society constituency was the social work community, who were often involved with the same clients as the Legal Aid Society. Exhibit 5 describes a number of the area social service agencies that worked with the Legal Aid Society. The social work community saw the Legal Aid Society's role as critical and the quality of service provided as excellent. One noted:

I can see, as a social worker going into court, a huge difference in what my clients get going into court going with an attorney and what they get going into court without one. It's dramatic. I think part of the problem is that people don't understand the need to have an attorney when they're dealing with these issues. I see people all the time who want to do it on their own, or have been told they can do it on their own, and don't even know what happens when they go in there. I get a lot of resistance from clients about contacting the Legal Aid Society from time to time, too. It's not a lack of understanding that there are lawyers out there, it's a lack of understanding about the need for representation—that it's vital.

A second social worker commented:

I think they provide outstanding representation. I think they go the extra mile. They do research, case preparation, I think that's head and shoulders above, or equal to, any attorney in town or any law office in town. I think the frustration is that of the hundreds of clients who come through whose case they're not able to accept and assign a particular attorney to where they offer some kind of limited service or advice-only kind of a thing.

EXHIBIT 5

Charlottesville-Albemarle Selected Social-Service Groups

Monticello Area Community Action Agency: Administers Head Start, job-training programs, housing programs, and a variety of other community-development activities. Started as part of the War on Poverty's community-empowerment initiatives.

Mediation Center: Provides mediation services and training, including a large program in the Charlottesville schools. Also receives referrals from the local courts.

Jefferson Area Board for Aging: Serves clients 60 and older and their care-givers. Programs include nutrition, home-delivered meals, case management, home-care services, and an adult day-care center.

Department of Social Services (Albemarle, Fluvanna, Greene, Louisa, and Nelson Counties): Provides welfare benefits, child-protective services, adult-protection services, foster care, adoption, and custody studies.

Virginia Citizens Consumer Council: Works to improve the laws that affect consumers in Virginia, through lobbying and education.

Independence Resource Center: Operates independent-living centers for disabled individuals, providing counseling, advocacy, and skills training.

Other organizations that the Legal Aid Society works with include the local AIDS Services Group, the Association of Retarded Citizens, the Focus Women's Resource Center, and the Shelter for Help in Emergency.

Another added:

> My impression's been that the people who have been on the staff the last few years who I've known are highly professional. They are there because they want to be serving low-income people. They are not there because it was the only job in town or it was a fallback or anything else. They are committed to the people they are serving and to doing the best for their clients. I also think that they provide a valuable service, even when they can't accept a case, because they bring enough information about the service areas in which they're involved to at least provide information for social service providers about where to get help or how to provide access to the bureaucratic system for the social worker or for the client to work for him- or herself. There are a lot of lawyers, I think, who are only interested in doing things that are what I call strictly "lawyer's work," and where they will be able to see things through from the beginning to the end. And I think that Legal Aid lawyers, like a lot of people who serve the same client base, are realistic. They can't do everything, but if they can be part of the bigger picture of service provider, they take that role and fit into the jigsaw puzzle of service providers.

Social workers raised a concern about the extent to which the complexity of clients' situations made it difficult to draw the boundaries between their role and the Legal Aid Society's. One commented:

> Our clients don't have just a legal problem. You know, getting your custody settled is probably not going to settle all the issues you have in your life as a single parent: a bad divorce, your income has changed, your housing has changed. So, as a social worker and as a case manager, I make that Legal Aid Society referral. . . . Okay, that's done. She or he is going to take care of that one, then I'm going to go in another direction to look for the housing issues or whatever. It's a piece of the puzzle. You depend on your specialist to handle the specialized issues. When you do social work, you learn a lot about law, but not nearly enough to handle giving someone advice.

Another added:

> I think that maybe we could get more bang for our buck here if we viewed them more as legal technicians and people who need to rely on maybe other systems to do some of the hand holding and supportive role so that they can have more time available to be giving legal advice, doing cases, getting out to the community to provide legal services to people who can't come in or have other barriers to the Legal Aid Society. I really think that because the type of people who go into the Legal Aid Society are so committed, they very easily can get sucked right under and spend hours and hours and hours doing things that a qualified social worker could do as well or better, which is taking time away from their being legal advocates.

She offered an example:

> A lawyer has to drive 45 minutes to Lovingston to juvenile court on a custody case. And, due to whatever circumstances cause it—either forgetting, car breaking down, driver not showing up for transportation, child being sick needing to stay at home—I mean, there's a zillion things that can go wrong and the client doesn't end up in court. Those kinds of issues come up constantly in terms of people getting to the office to get advice or to prepare for cases, in getting to court to go into their case. I, personally, don't think it's a good use of a lawyer's time to go drive to pick up a client to take him or her to a case—this happens. A lawyer should be spending their time lawyering, in my opinion. And I think that many of the clients involved have huge gaps in their support systems, in available resources. But I don't think it's a good use of time for the lawyers to try to fill those gaps when things are not going to go back to a staff of 15 or whatever we had at Legal Aid before, where we did go out to the guy. We're not going back to that.

Others disagreed:

> When I try to think about being able to provide services for my clients, I really try to think of how we're going to be able to keep that person from getting sucked down that black hole to where they just don't come back. I'm an educator and I spend way too much of my time doing things that are not education because I'm trying to build up support systems. I end up doing tons of those other things

because, darn it, I said I was going to get this person this service and I will get them transportation and I will get them translation and I will get them child care and I will do whatever it takes to follow this through. And it's not an effective use of my time, but it's really reality for my clients. And I really appreciate the fact of Legal Aid's going the extra mile.

Some social workers were skeptical about the increased use of volunteers:

I think volunteers, while that's a great concept, there's so much accountability in being a case manager and you've got to stick to it. You can't bail out when the going gets rough. And volunteers, they're wonderful folks. We have a huge, great program. But you need to pay the people. They need to know that they've got to stick with it. Volunteers show up, but then they don't show up again unless somebody keeps on them—unless you can find a really wonderful volunteer coordinator. I don't think Legal Aid could afford to divert resources to pay a volunteer coordinator. And I don't think they should. I think that salary would be better served with even a part-time extra attorney.

Others questioned the policy changes that had been made concerning income criteria and service to the outlying counties:

In the good old days, someone from the Legal Aid Society used to come out to Fluvanna County like once a week or once a month, whatever it was. And it was always the same person, and so we not only had someone in the community that we could count on, but we then knew who it was going to be. We could call them or get them out there. Now, they're so limited, you know, "We do these things, and these are all that we can do." And I think their income guidelines are too strict. I work with a lot of folks who are barely making it, but they make too much money to get the Legal Aid Society. And legal services are some of the most expensive things to purchase imaginable.

One suggested better ways of reaching potential clients:

I think Legal Aid—and a lot of other organizations that are service providers that have to reach a client population that don't necessarily know about the availability of services—have to market themselves. Not through mass-media advertising, not through the social-service agencies, because I think the social-service agencies know about Legal Services. But getting word out through other community-based networks, like the churches. In this area, churches are probably one of the best means of communicating the availability of events and services. And maybe Legal Aid just has to figure out where its target populations are and get more information out through that network.

Some expressed a concern at what they saw as an impending scramble for funds:

One thing that I'm always concerned about—and I think, I hope, everybody here has the same concern—is that even though Charlottesville is a very generous community, we're all competing for the same donors. And to the extent that anyone else races into the fund-raising market, we'll be spreading the dollars more thinly. And I don't know how we deal with that. But it's going to be a critical issue for everybody.

One social worker voiced her frustration at the failure of the larger social-service community, including the Legal Aid Society, to work more closely together:

> With all the budget cuts, it's not business as usual. It can't be. It can never be, to be honest. I'm trying to take this negative thing that has happened and turn it around and make it positive. For this population, we have, believe it or not, over 200 funded human-service organizations in this little town. It's amazing. God, we've got all these services and we need to coordinate and cooperate. That's our problem in this city. Everybody's very turf oriented. I mean, I can understand to some extent, but it doesn't make any sense for the client.

In reviewing the diverse views of his various constituencies, Gulotta saw at least one thing on which all agreed: The Legal Aid Society's resources were insufficient to meet the demand for its services. He wondered how to move the Legal Aid Society forward in this increasingly complicated and resource-constrained environment. (See Exhibit 6 for Gulotta's résumé.)

> I'm new to the organization and new to the role of director of a program. It's become very obvious to me that our having a strategy is now *my* job as opposed to being part of an organization and fitting into someone else's plan.

EXHIBIT 6

Résumé of Alex R. Gulotta

Qualifications

Bar Admissions:	Virginia, Kentucky, Wisconsin
J.D.:	Marquette University Law School, 1984 Cum Laude
B.A.:	Marquette University, 1981 Major: Theology Minor: Math/Computing

Professional Experience

CHARLOTTESVILLE-ALBEMARLE LEGAL AID SOCIETY, INC.—Charlottesville, Virginia

Executive Director—June 1994 to Present

Directly responsible for overall management of low-income civil legal services program serving over 2,200 clients per year in the City of Charlottesville and Albemarle, Greene, Louisa, and Nelson Counties in central Virginia; supervision of three attorneys, two paralegals, and three support persons; development and implementation of the program's litigation strategies and priorities; development and maintenance of numerous funding sources for a total annual budget of approximately $400,000.

APPALACHIAN RESEARCH AND DEFENSE FUND OF KENTUCKY, INC.—Columbia, Kentucky

Senior Attorney—February 1991 to 1994

Staff Attorney—June 1985 to July 1988

(continued)

EXHIBIT 6 (CONTINUED)

Résumé of Alex R. Gulotta

Responsible for direct-service caseload and development of major law-reform litigation. Participated in complex litigation in a wide variety of substantive areas, including adversary proceedings in bankruptcy court involving complex student-loan issues; defense of FmHA federal-mortgage foreclosures; TILA, FDCPA, UCC, and related consumer actions; civil-rights actions involving excessive use of force and deliberate indifference to obvious medical need; Title VII cases involving sex and race discrimination; actions to review the denial, reduction, or termination of public benefits such as Social Security, food stamps, AFDC, Medicaid, and unemployment insurance; NLRB-contested unfair labor-practice proceedings; environmental torts; and a wide variety of federally subsidized housing matters. Successfully negotiated with Kentucky officials on behalf of a large class of food stamp recipients to correct constitutionally defective practices relating to termination of benefits for alleged intentional violation of program rules.

LINDSEY WILSON COLLEGE—Columbia, Kentucky

Part-time Faculty Member—March 1992 to July 1993

Responsible for developing and teaching courses in business ethics, business law (contracts and UCC), and advanced business law (consumer protection, governmental regulation, and business formation) in a four-year business-degree program.

LEGAL SERVICES OF NORTHEASTERN WISCONSIN, INC.—
Green Bay, Wisconsin

Managing Attorney and Staff Attorney—July 1988 to February 1991

As a Staff Attorney in the program's Oshkosh branch office, responsible for representing low-income households in the areas of public benefits, housing, family, and consumer protection. As Managing Attorney of the program's main office, responsible for overall operation of legal-services office serving over 1,600 clients per year; supervision of three attorneys, five paralegals, and three support persons; litigation of cases in state and federal courts. Successfully negotiated with Wisconsin officials on behalf of a large class of AFDC and food stamp recipients to correct constitutionally defective notices proposing benefit reduction to recoup alleged overpayments. Coordinated services with other agencies serving the client community with emphasis on the special needs of Southeast Asian immigrants and Native Americans. Appointed by the Board of Directors during the summer of 1990 to serve as Acting Executive Director of the three-office, 15-county program with an annual budget of $800,000.

ADVISORY BOARD MEMBER—Adair County Adult Day Health Center

CLIENT ADVOCATE—Lake Cumberland Area Welfare Reform Council

CASE 26

LOUISIANA-PACIFIC CORPORATION

I've gotten used to being called a first.

— Bonnie Guiton Hill

Gazing out her vast office window overlooking the Grounds at the University of Virginia, Bonnie Guiton Hill pondered the uncertain future of Louisiana-Pacific Corporation (LP) and the role she would or *should* play in it. Hill, a recently appointed LP director, found the latest turn of events at this building-materials concern quite troubling. During the early 1990s, LP had been a darling of Wall Street, nearly doubling sales in three years (from $1.7 billion in 1991 to $3.0 billion in 1994) and reaching record profits of $347 million in 1994 (Exhibit 1). All of that had changed, however, by July 27, 1995. The company now found itself facing numerous problems: consumer class-action suits stemming from the failure of LP's most profitable product, a 56-count criminal indictment from the U.S. Justice Department due to environmental violations, and several shareholder lawsuits as a result of the company's plunging stock price (Exhibit 2).

After contemplating LP's recent troubles, Hill took the measure of the task in front of her. In two hours, she would board a plane to Chicago, where the next morning the outside directors of LP's board would conduct a special meeting. Although the stated topic of discussion was the future of the company, Hill knew the real reason for the meeting was to discuss the fate of Harry Merlo and his two loyal executive vice presidents, James Eisses and Ronald Paul, both of whom were also board members. As Hill pondered what she would say at the meeting, she reflected on the events leading up to LP's current situation.

INDUSTRY OVERVIEW

The forest-products industry was one of the most intensely competitive industries because of its highly cyclical nature, low growth prospects, capital-intensive operations, and commodity products. The fortunes of the industry depended heavily on macroeconomic trends, such as interest rates and housing starts. Competition was based primarily on cost. Because scale economies were crucial for achieving low costs in this industry, the largest firms, such as International Paper and Georgia-Pacific, also tended to be the most profitable. Most additions to capacity were of an expensive, quantum, and irreversible nature. This combination of scale economies and significant fixed costs resulted in the industry's maintaining not only

This case was written by Scott Mall, MBA 1996, under the supervision of L. J. Bourgeois, Professor of Business Administration.

EXHIBIT 1

Louisiana-Pacific Corporation Summary Financial Statements (dollar amounts in millions except per-share data)

	1994	1993	1992	1991	1990
INCOME STATEMENTS					
Net sales	$3,039.5	$2,511.3	$2,184.7	$1,702.1	$1,793.3
Gross profit	558.6	423.6	297.5	106.3	144.6
Interest, net	(1.0)	5.0	14.4	18.9	7.6
Provision (benefit) for income taxes	209.8	173.2	106.2	31.5	45.9
Income (loss)	346.9	254.4	176.9	55.9	91.1
Income (loss) per share	3.15	2.32	1.63	0.52	0.82
Cash dividends per share	$0.49	$0.43	$0.39	$0.36	$0.35
BALANCE SHEETS					
Current assets	$721.9	$614.1	$539.1	$461.4	$509.1
Timber and timberlands	693.5	673.5	531.2	532.7	518.3
Property, plant, and equipment, net	1,273.2	1,145.9	1,070.3	1,066.1	1,036.8
Other assets	55.1	32.8	65.4	46.9	39.9
Total assets	2,743.7	2,466.3	2,206.0	2,107.1	2,104.1
Current liabilities	344.8	317.2	295.5	259.5	195.5
Long-term debt, net of current portion	209.8	288.6	386.3	492.7	588.7
Deferred income taxes and other	339.7	289.1	163.2	151.3	153.2
Stockholders' equity	1,849.4	1,571.4	1,361.0	1,203.6	1,166.7
Total liabilities and stockholders' equity	$2,743.7	$2,466.3	$2,206.0	$2,107.1	$2,104.1
KEY FINANCIAL TRENDS					
Working capital	$377.1	$296.9	$243.6	$201.9	$313.6
Plant and logging-road additions	286.0	208.4	161.4	152.3	330.4
Timber additions, net	66.0	81.5	40.1	49.6	44.4
Total capital additions	$352.0	$289.9	$201.5	$201.9	$374.8
Long-term debt as a percentage of total capitalization	10%	16%	22%	29%	34%
Income as a percentage of average equity	20%	17%	14%	5%	8%

high entry barriers, but also high exit barriers. As a result, industry firms frequently faced significant price pressures due to excess capacity. Management practices within the industry were highly conservative and somewhat reactive.

EXHIBIT 2

Louisiana-Pacific Corporation Stock-Price History

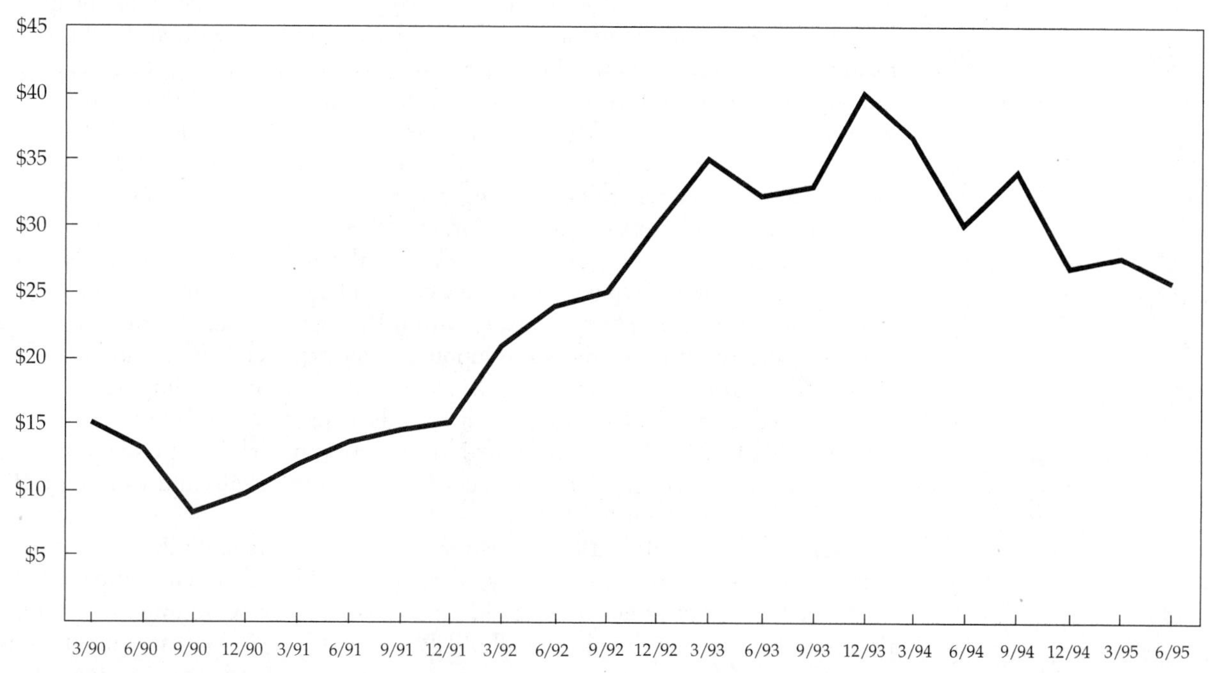

COMPANY BACKGROUND

LP was a *Fortune* 500 company based in Portland, Oregon, principally engaged in the manufacture of wood-based products, and to a lesser extent, wood-based pulp. It owned approximately 1.6 million acres of timberland in Louisiana, northern California, and Texas. Most of the company's trees were fast-growing southern pine. The company was created in 1973 when the Federal Trade Commission pressured Georgia-Pacific Corporation (GP) to spin off its southern-pine operations. After the spin-off, LP tapped Harry Merlo, a former GP executive vice president, as its chief executive officer (CEO). In 1980, Merlo championed the development of oriented strand board (OSB), an inexpensive plywood substitute made from plentiful younger trees that most companies considered waste timber. By the mid-1980s, OSB had become the company's best-selling product, and LP was experiencing tremendous growth. The forest-products industry, not known for innovative product development, began touting Merlo as a visionary of engineered forest products.

By 1995, LP was the world's largest OSB producer, accounting for 30 percent of total North American OSB production. OSB sales accounted for 40 percent of LP's revenues and 35 percent of its operating profits. In early 1994, LP announced plans to build two new OSB manufacturing plants, which would increase the company's OSB production capacity by 35 percent. Several of LP's competitors were also planning to bring new OSB capacity on-line during the following two years. Merlo, now 70 years old, continued to lead this $3 billion forest-products giant as chairman and CEO.

Harry A. Merlo

Harry Angelo Merlo began his life dirt poor, but idea rich. In 1937, as a 12-year-old working in a northern California grocery store, Merlo would carry home the hearts and brains discarded by butchers, and his Italian-immigrant mother would transform them into savory stews. Three years later, at the age of 15, Merlo began his lifelong romance with forest products by taking a job in a local lumberyard. During these formative years, Merlo came to revere his mother, who made tremendous sacrifices to save money for his college education. In 1949, after a brief stint in the U.S. Marines (where he was a light-heavyweight boxing champion), Merlo graduated from the University of California at Berkeley.

After college, Merlo took an entry-level job with California-based Rounds Lumber Company, where he quickly became vice president and part owner. In addition to being recognized as a "fast-tracker" within Rounds Lumber, Merlo also began to gain notoriety with customers and suppliers. One supplier, GP, was so impressed with Merlo that it offered him a job. Merlo turned GP down, saying he was loyal to his own company. Undeterred, GP effectively acquired Merlo's services by buying Rounds Lumber. Merlo continued his meteoric professional rise by leading GP's western lumber operations to record profits in the 1960s and winning GP's Man of the Year award in 1969.

After the LP spin-off in 1973, Merlo was charged with making the $400 million company competitive in an industry dominated by billion-dollar companies. In 1978, the U.S. government added to Merlo's challenges by expanding the National Redwood Forest, thereby placing all of LP's old-growth timber off-limits to logging. Viewing this government move as a precursor to even more stringent logging restrictions, Merlo set out to develop an alternative way to make his company's products. Taking his cue from his exploits as a youngster in the town market, Merlo bet the future of his company on his vision of using small, fast-growing "trash" trees to make reconstituted panel products such as OSB, a plywood substitute made by bonding wood fibers together with resin. Merlo bet right. Sales of the new products soared, and OSB began to steal significant market share from plywood. Industry veterans watched in amazement as LP made profitable products from timber that they had theretofore treated as refuse.

During the following 15 years, Merlo extended the highly successful OSB product line and continued to bet correctly on risky new products, such as using recycled newspaper to make insulation and turning wastepaper into wallboard. By 1995, OSB was the company's premier product line, and Merlo had built the once-modest LP into a $3 billion empire by making silk purses out of sows' ears.

Management Style

From the start, Merlo began to mold LP into his own lean and quick-footed image. Exhibiting strong entrepreneurial instincts, he encouraged creativity via a "shoot-from-the-hip" style of product development. Merlo's unconventional methods paid off in 1980 when OSB became a huge success. During the 1970s and 1980s, Merlo made most of the key company decisions himself and focused on instilling a performance-driven corporate culture in the rank and file. Employees were encouraged with a "Yes We Can!" corporate campaign as Merlo pushed for lower costs and higher profits. Plant managers, who enjoyed unparalleled autonomy when it came to local management, were constantly encouraged to push more tons out the door. The managers responded to this approach: The company was recognized as having some of the highest capacity-utilization rates in the industry. Employees were highly compensated, and Merlo had managed to boost employee ownership to one of the highest rates in the industry. Promotions were rare, however, as Merlo believed in keeping the ranks of middle managers sparse. Merlo's aversion to bloated organizational charts carried over to Portland headquarters, where the CEO maintained a very light corporate staff.

During the 1990s, Merlo began to include two other executives—James Eisses, head of LP's Northern Division, and Ronald Paul, head of LP's Southern Division—in making key decisions. Merlo also continued to cultivate LP's "can-do" attitude by setting aggressive goals for plant managers. Finally, Merlo maintained his visionary practices by acting as the main generator of new-product ideas.

Personal Style

By 1995, Merlo had parlayed his tremendous business success into an opulent lifestyle filled with possessions, beautiful women, and famous friends. Indeed, Merlo's personal life was practically inseparable from his business career. For example, Merlo's 1994 salary and bonus hit $5 million even as the company was providing him with such perks as a company jet, a 107-foot yacht, and a 7,300-square-foot Portland estate complete with cook, housekeeper, and an annual budget of $300,000. Also, Merlo's fetish for "tall attractive blondes" had allegedly been made part of the informal screening process for new hires at Portland headquarters. Finally, the chairman of the board's Nominating Committee was Merlo's longtime hunting buddy, the legendary test pilot Chuck Yeager (Exhibit 3).

One of Portland's most controversial figures, Merlo was called the "extravagant red carnation in the gray flannel lapel of Portland business." The same probably could be said of Merlo's status within the forest-products industry. Merlo had long rankled the insular Portland business community by avoiding the country-club set. Instead of doing what was expected of a 70-year-old CEO, this perennial (twice-divorced) bachelor threw lavish parties at his company-owned estate and used LP's private jets to fly in celebrity performers, such as tenor Luciano Pavarotti.

Merlo appeared to bask in his celebrity status and did much to keep the dream alive. At an age when most corporate CEOs had been retired for five years, Merlo kept going strong because of a regimented exercise and nutrition schedule. Youthful in appearance even at 70, Merlo had tried to turn back the hand of time through several cosmetic surgeries to tighten his sagging skin, straighten his once-crooked nose, and thicken his thinning hair. Highly fashion conscious, Merlo regularly sported Italian suits with cowboy boots and hammered-gold jewelry.

But by the 1990s, accusations that Merlo had crossed the line of decorum in the workplace began to arise. In August 1993, Merlo was sued by a former employee alleging sexual harassment. In her complaint, the 22-year LP veteran said that women who tolerated Merlo's alleged behavior were granted "large stock options." Merlo and the company refused to comment, and the suit was still pending in July 1995. In a separate suit filed in January 1995, a former LP receptionist alleged sexual discrimination against two LP employees. Although Merlo was not named in the suit, the CEO's behavior was mentioned in a deposition given by the plaintiff, who described Merlo's behavior as "physically and verbally offensive." This suit was also pending in July 1995.

EXHIBIT 3

Louisiana-Pacific Corporation Board of Directors

MANAGEMENT DIRECTORS

Harry Merlo

Merlo is chairman of the board and president of LP and has been the company's chief executive officer since LP was incorporated in 1972. He serves as chairman of the board's Executive Committee and serves on the Nominating Committee.

James Eisses

Eisses is LP's executive vice president and had previously been the company's vice president, Operations. He has been a director since February 1991 and serves on the board's Executive Committee. He is also the general manager of LP's Northern Division.

Ronald Paul

Paul is LP's vice president, Operations. He has been a director since January 1994 and is also the general manager of LP's Southern Division.

OUTSIDE DIRECTORS

Pierre du Pont IV

Governor du Pont is the former governor of Delaware and a former member of the U.S. House of Representatives. He is a partner in the law firm of Richards, Layton & Finger of Wilmington, Delaware. He joined the board in 1991 and serves on the Compensation, Environmental Affairs, Audit, and Nominating Committees.

Donald Kayser

Kayser is a retired director and executive vice president of Morrison Knudsen Corporation, a construction and engineering firm. He joined LP's board in 1972 and serves as chairman of the board's Audit Committee and as a member of the Compensation, Environmental Affairs, and Nominating Committees.

Francine Neff

Neff, a former treasurer of the United States, is vice president of Net, Inc., a private investment company. She joined LP's board in 1984 and serves as chairman of the board's Compensation Committee and as a member of the Nominating, Environmental Affairs, and Audit Committees.

Bonnie Guiton Hill

Hill is dean of the McIntire School of Commerce at the University of Virginia. She was formerly secretary of the California State and Consumer Services Agency and director of the U.S. Office of Consumer Affairs. She joined LP's board in April 1993 and serves as chairman of the board's Environmental Affairs Committee and as a member of the Audit, Compensation, and Nominating Committees.

Charles Yeager

General Yeager is a retired brigadier general of the United States Air Force and was the first person to fly faster than the speed of sound. He has been a member of LP's board since 1984 and serves as chairman of the board's Nominating Committee and as a member of the Compensation, Environmental Affairs, Executive, and Audit Committees.

Bonnie Guiton Hill

Henrietta F. (Bonnie) Guiton Hill's earliest memories were of poverty and survival. Raised as an only child by an alcoholic mother, in later years Hill remembered trying to survive on her mother's pay as a maid. Hill viewed her high-school education as merely a means of finding a job in order to stay off welfare. In 1966, at the age of 25, Hill married and continued to work her way through a series of low-paying jobs in San Francisco. In 1971, Hill's young husband suffered a debilitating heart attack, which caused Hill to go through a period of critical self-evaluation. Hill concluded that a college education was necessary if she was to keep her family above the poverty level. At the age of 30 and caring for both her weakened husband and her 1-year-old daughter, Nichele, Hill enrolled at Mills College in Oakland, California, where she had been working as a secretary.

Working as a counselor at Mills and caring for her husband and daughter, Hill still was able to earn close to a 4.0 GPA in her undergraduate studies. After receiving her bachelor's degree in 1975 and serving as Mills' assistant dean of students from 1975 to 1976, Hill never again needed to look for a job. Hill's experience at Mills College shot her straight up the ladder of success as corporations and governments sought her out. After becoming a corporate executive with Kaiser Aluminum & Chemical Corporation, Hill was appointed by President Reagan in 1984 to the U.S. Postal Rate Commission, where she quickly rose to the vice chairman position in 1986. During the early part of her professional career, Hill somehow continued to indulge her newfound appetite for knowledge by first earning a master's degree from California State University at Hayward and then a doctorate in education from the University of California at Berkeley.

In 1989, Hill achieved her greatest promotion to date when President Bush appointed her as his principal advisor for consumer affairs. During her two years serving President Bush, Hill earned significant amounts of praise, even from groups not always enthusiastic about Bush's appointees. One such group said that they were "thrilled" about Hill's work, and did not "expect this level of concern and involvement." By the time Hill had completed her work for President Bush in 1991, she was one of the highest-ranking African American women in the administration.

Hill's star continued to rise in 1991, when she was named California's Secretary for State and Consumer Services. Hill was the first African American woman to serve in the cabinet of a California governor. In July 1992, Hill continued to welcome new challenges as she accepted the position of dean of the McIntire School of Commerce at the University of Virginia. Hill was the first African American dean in the 78-year history of the school, and only the seventh woman to head one of the nation's 245 accredited schools of business. In March 1993, Hill was named to LP's board of directors, where she served as chairperson of the Environmental Affairs Committee and as a member of the Audit, Compensation, and Nominating Committees. By 1995, Hill was serving as a director on several boards, including AK Steel, Crestar Bank, Hershey Foods, and Niagara Mohawk Power.

Company Problems

During the 1980s, LP was faced with the enviable challenge of adding enough capacity for the growing demand for its hottest product, OSB. As a result, Merlo built plants at a breakneck rate and pushed existing plants to increase productivity. As LP became a billion-dollar company, Merlo continued to keep middle-management ranks thin. Merlo had cultivated a bottom-line culture that focused primarily on quantity. Plant managers, who enjoyed virtual autonomy as long as they produced profits, began to scrimp on materials, avoid product testing, and build plants without environmental permits. This culture and these practices were reinforced by LP's growing profitability, which was fueled primarily by OSB sales. During the early 1990s, however, LP's aggressive operating style began to show signs of weakness.

Because of the inherent nature of operations in the forest-products industry, many firms were frequently cited by government officials and special-interest groups as "threats" to the environment. Therefore, when LP's problems began to surface in the early 1990s, Merlo was able to rationalize them as the "cost of doing business" in an environmentally unfriendly industry. As more and more lawsuits were filed, however, it became increasingly difficult for the tough-talking CEO to blame the industry as a whole.

The first external indication of serious problems arose in 1990, when LP was fined $3 million for dumping millions of gallons of untreated waste daily into the Pacific Ocean. In July 1993, soon after Vice President Gore announced his campaign to protect the environment, the Environmental Protection Agency levied an $11 million fine against LP for falsely reporting emissions at 14 plants. This was the largest civil penalty ever imposed under the Clean Air Act. That same month, LP earned the dubious distinction of being named by *Fortune* magazine as one of the ten least environmentally aware companies in America.

During this period, LP also discovered that its cash cow, OSB, was having performance problems in the residential market. OSB consumers in warm-weather areas began observing a rapid deterioration of their OSB siding during the most humid months. Most disturbingly, consumers everywhere were exclaiming that *mushrooms* were growing out of their OSB-sided houses. As a result, several class-action suits were filed against LP. In 1992, the Minnesota attorney general sued LP over defective siding, and the company agreed to pay for repairs. From 1990 to 1994, thousands of homeowners in Florida joined together in three separate class-action suits. One was settled and two were still pending in July 1995. By the mid-1990s, LP's out-of-pocket expenses for these consumer-related suits ran into the tens of millions of dollars.

In 1995, the company's environmental problems continued. An LP pulp plant in Alaska was fined $6 million for Clean Water Act violations, and the *Oregonian* (a Portland newspaper) reported that LP managers at an Idaho OSB plant knowingly manufactured substandard products and then deceived the American Plywood Association into certifying the panels. Finally, in April 1995, a news report indicated that LP would be indicted in Colorado for environmental violations and fraud involving its OSB manufacturing processes. This news sparked a dozen shareholder lawsuits and even caused Merlo to offer his resignation to the board of directors. The board, apparently calmed by Merlo's promises of improved production practices, insisted Merlo stay.

In June 1995, the Colorado grand jury did indict LP and two plant managers for environmental violations and fraud at the company's Montrose, Colorado, OSB plant. Amidst this backdrop of environmental violations, consumer-warranty claims, and shareholder lawsuits, the company found it more and more difficult to account for its actions. On July 24, 1995, just one week after having released second-quarter earnings of $42 million, LP was forced to restate these figures *down* by $16 million because of the company's growing legal problems. This move prompted several more shareholder suits and further decreased LP's credibility with the capital markets.

The Chicago Meeting

The importance of Hill's role in the board of directors' meeting could not be overstated. First of all, Hill had recently spearheaded a board-led internal investigation of the company's affairs, which revealed a lack of management controls as a result of Merlo's "personalized and entrepreneurial" leadership style. Moreover, Hill was keenly aware of the increased media attention surrounding corporate boards' fulfilling their fiduciary responsibilities to shareholders. This trend, in fact, was part of the reason Hill had pushed for Friday's special board meeting. Finally, Hill was, presumably, the most objective of the outside board members because of her brief association with LP and Merlo. Merlo had handpicked all of his board members, most of whom were unequivocally loyal to him, as evidenced by their refusal even to consider his offer of resignation earlier in the year.

As Hill began to leave her University of Virginia office to head for the airport, she reflected on her trailblazing tendencies in the past and wondered what actions were called for given LP's current dilemma.

CASE 27

STRATEGIC PLANNING AT THE NEW YORK BOTANICAL GARDEN (A)

Start a major job of institutional planning and change, and you will find there are all of these different stakeholders. My experience in institutional life has been that you might as well find ways to make them happy at the outset. You might as well just take it on up-front and get consensus because otherwise you are going to do it in a piecemeal way. This way you don't dissipate all of your time and energy trying to make everyone happy later on; because basically you have to make them happy, especially in a troubled institution. You've got to get everyone smoothed out and online. If you don't do it up-front, you're doing constantly—and I find that very draining. You can't get anything done—every day you wait for the phone calls from all of the unhappy people. That is the way a lot of people run an institution—they let it come up every day, they wait, they get exhausted spending so much time and energy dealing with people who aren't on board.

—Gregory Long

Gregory Long, president of the New York Botanical Garden, walked slowly to the podium at Sotheby's Auction House.[1] The date was April 21, 1993, and assembled before him were 400 of the Garden's most influential stakeholders—the board, current and potential donors, heads of government agencies and other nonprofit organizations, Garden members, and business executives. All of these listeners had an important potential role in the plan for the Garden's future that Long was about to unveil.

The Sotheby location, like the guest list, had been selected with care. Here in Manhattan, Long reasoned, even marginally interested individuals could easily drop by for the one-hour presentation, with cocktails to follow—unlikely if the presentation had been held in the north central Bronx, the Garden's home. He thought of tonight as the kind of theatrical event for which New York was well known. Carefully written, orchestrated, and rehearsed, the presentation shared with the public, for the first time, the view of the Garden's future that had emerged during its extensive and inclusive planning process. It presented the "collated results of collective thinking" that had been going on for two years, as Long described it.

This case was written by Jeanne M. Liedtka, associate professor of Business Administration. This case was written as a basis for class discussion rather than to illustrate effective or ineffective handling of an administrative situation.

He felt that he had been working toward this presentation since his arrival at the Garden as president in 1989. The wording on the Sotheby invitation (contained in Exhibit 1) reflected his conviction: "This is not just a beloved New York City institution getting a facelift; rather the transformation of an institution."

As he prepared to outline the strategic plan and the master plan for the facility that had been two years in the making, Long was concerned—could he create the level of excitement in this community necessary to accomplish the ambitious aims for institutional change that the plan set out? Would these important constituents see the plan as unattainable, given the Garden's current circumstances?

An Overview of the New York Botanical Garden[2]

The story of the creation of the New York Botanical Garden began with a belated honeymoon visit to England in 1888, taken by a New York City couple, Elizabeth and Nathaniel Lord Britton, both dedicated botanists. Upon visiting the Royal Botanic Gardens at Kew, the couple resolved that New York should have a garden "just like that" at Kew, and embarked on an ambitious, and ultimately successful, campaign to convince politicians and wealthy New Yorkers of the desirability of establishing such a botanical garden.

The New York Botanical Garden was incorporated by a special act of the New York State Legislature in 1891 for the purpose of establishing and maintaining a botanical garden, museum, and arboretum "for the collection and culture of plants, flowers, shrubs and trees; the advancement of botanical science and knowledge and the prosecution of original researches therein and in kindred subjects; for affording instruction in the same; for the prosecution and exhibition of ornamental and decorative horticulture and gardening; and for the entertainment, recreation, and instruction of the people."

The 1891 Act directed the Board of Commissioners of the New York City Department of Parks to set aside up to 250 acres of the Bronx Park for the Garden, once the Garden had raised \$250,000. The \$250,000 was successfully raised; the 250 acres were set aside in the northern half of the Bronx Park; and the City agreed to underwrite a bond issue of \$500,000 for buildings and improvements. The Garden opened to the public in 1895.

The 1891 Act remained the Garden's corporate charter. The Garden had pursued its tripartite mission—science, education, and horticulture—for over 100 years and still operated on the basis of a partnership between the private and public sectors. The Garden was a museum accredited by the American Association of Museums and was widely recognized as one of the world's leading research and educational institutions in the plant sciences, with extensive programs in plant exploration and systematics, economic botany, and scientific publishing. The Garden's Herbarium, a collection of 6,000,000 preserved plant specimens, was the largest in the Western Hemisphere. The Garden's Library housed one of the world's largest botanical and horticultural research collections.

The Garden's grounds in the Bronx also constituted one of America's most famous public gardens. Designated a National Historic Landmark in 1967, the Garden contained an unusual variety of natural topography, a 40-acre tract of virgin forest, historic specialty gardens and living plant collections, and several architecturally significant structures, including the Enid A. Haupt Conservatory.

The Garden was a private not-for-profit corporation under New York law and a tax-exempt organization under section 501(c)(3) of the Internal Revenue Code.

EXHIBIT 1

The Sotheby Invitation

The New York Botanical Garden recently completed an intensive planning process which has resulted in consensus on commitments and priorities through the end of the decade. You are cordially invited to attend, on Wednesday evening, April 21, 1993, a special presentation announcing plans for the future of this venerable New York City institution as it strives to move forward toward the new century with vitality and meaningful work from the neighborhoods of the Bronx to the rainforests of Brazil. We hope you will join us.

The Host Committee

YOU ARE CORDIALLY INVITED TO
ATTEND
A SPECIAL PRESENTATION
HERALDING THE RENAISSANCE
OF
THE NEW YORK BOTANICAL GARDEN
WEDNESDAY, APRIL 21, 1993
FROM 6:00 TO 8:00 P.M.
AT
SOTHEBY'S
1334 YORK AVENUE AT 72ND STREET
NEW YORK CITY
PROGRAM BEGINS AT 6:30 P.M.

(continued)

EXHIBIT 1 (CONTINUED)

The Sotheby Invitation

THE GARDEN PLAN FOR
THE NEW YORK BOTANICAL GARDEN

GREGORY LONG
President

MRS. DONALD B. STRAUS
Senior Vice Chairman

LYNDEN B. MILLER
Landscape and Garden Designer

SHEILA GRINELL
Author, *A New Place for Learning Science*

THOMAS J. HUBBARD
Chairman

RECEPTION IN THE GALLERY

ON DISPLAY, FINE ENGLISH AND CONTINENTAL SILVER AND WORKS OF BOTANICAL INTEREST

THE HOST COMMITTEE

NORMA KETAY ASNES

MR. & MRS. MORTIMER BERKOWITZ III

DIANA D. BROOKS

JOAN K. DAVIDSON

MR. & MRS. MARQUETTE DEBARY

BETH RUDIN DEWOODY

MR. & MRS. EUGENE P. GRISANTI

MRS. ANDREW HEISKELL

MR. & MRS. THOMAS J. HUBBARD

PEGGY ROCKEFELLER

SHELBY WHITE & LEON LEVY

The New York Botanical Garden gratefully acknowledges Sotheby's generosity in hosting this event.

The Garden owned the contents of its facilities and collections, and managed and operated its premises and buildings, title to which remained with the City. In this corporate structure, the Garden was similar to other City cultural institutions that occupied City land and structures, including The Metropolitan Museum of Art, The American Museum of Natural History, and Lincoln Center for the Performing Arts. Like those institutions, the Garden came within the jurisdiction of the New York City Department of Cultural Affairs.

The Garden's Scientific Programs

The Garden was one of the world's leading centers for research in plant systematics and economic botany. The main purposes of the Garden's research were to discover and document plant diversity; to provide the taxonomic system for plants (the nomenclature by which all knowledge about plants is organized and transmitted); and to elucidate the evolutionary biology of plants through modern analysis techniques.

The Garden's Institute of Economic Botany researched the use of plants by human cultures. The Institute's work had been to identify little-known or underutilized plants with medicinal, nutritional, or economic value. Scientists working within the Institute investigated tropical deforestation, medicinal plants, nutrition, disease, sustainable development, and the importance of indigenous knowledge.

The Garden published nine scientific journals and monographic series and approximately 30 nonserial titles each year. Garden scientists taught courses at The City University of New York, Cornell University, Yale University, Fordham University, Lehman College, and other colleges and universities.

The Garden's Educational Programs

The Garden's educational programs, both formal and informal, focused on plants and the environment and were designed to meet the educational needs of various constituencies ranging from preschool children to graduate students. The Garden was the only nonacademic institution in the New York City area to offer formal training in botany. The Garden offered over 400 adult education courses each year. Bronx Green-Up was an outreach program that helped communities create gardens in vacant lots in the Bronx. Plant Information and Reference Library Services provided information to the public, staff, and students at the Garden.

Significant Structures at the Garden

The focal point of the Garden's physical premises was the late-Victorian glass building known today as the Enid A. Haupt Conservatory. Completed in May 1902, it was one of the earliest greenhouses built in America. It was also considered by many architects and historians to be the nation's greatest glass house, and was the largest conservatory for public display in the United States.

Another major edifice at the Garden was the museum building, designed by Robert W. Gibson and completed in 1905. The museum building housed the Herbarium, the Library (in the contiguous Pratt Library Building), other science facilities, an exhibition of living orchids, a retail shop, public reception, visitor information, restrooms, and an auditorium.

A New Team Arrives

Despite its proud history, assets, and significance in its field, the Garden was an institution much in need of rejuvenation—both physically and financially—when Gregory Long arrived to assume the presidency in 1989.

Thomas Hubbard, previously a board member, elected chairman of the Garden's 45-member Board of Managers in June 1991, recalled the circumstances surrounding Gregory Long's selection:

> I was on the Committee that selected Gregory. When he interviewed, he already knew more about the Garden than anyone—more than we did. When that meeting was over, we looked at each other and said, "He's it." . . . He recognized, from day one, that we needed to get the Garden into the mainstream of New York cultural institutions—and he knew where every dollar in New York was.

The organization, at that time, was "adrift," as one senior manager described it. The Garden had received no major capital spending from the City in years; even maintenance needs had been inadequately met. Because of its parklike landscape and because it charged no admission, the Garden had become, in the perception of many of its users, a public park—a place to bicycle, picnic, walk the dog, throw a frisbee, or take a leisurely (or less than leisurely) drive through. Long had different ideas:

> There was a perception, because this institution was headed by scientists, that this was a campus for those scientists, and the public came and used the campus for passive recreation. We wanted to end the perception of the Garden as a public park. What we wanted users to see in the future was a botanical garden, a museum of plants, and not a public park.

The living plants, so vital to the Garden's mission, could not be properly displayed or cared for in a park-usage environment. Thus, one of Long's early actions, as president, was to fence the Garden, and to ban dogs and cars, a move that was met with dismay on the part of some of the Garden's neighbors:

> They were a core group of customers, and we didn't want to lose them. This has been a very difficult issue for us throughout. There was a core group of users who used the Garden in ways that didn't relate to our primary function as a museum, ways that weren't really appropriate, but we needed them anyway.

Resources at the Garden were also severely limited. Richard Schnall, vice president for horticulture, explained: "Staff didn't have the resources to do what they needed to—staff had to fight for a telephone, there was not enough propagation space, and there were too few visitor amenities, like restrooms—it was pretty fundamental stuff."

Several of the Garden's historic structures, the Conservatory, in particular, were known to be in dire need of costly renovations.

The Garden's operating finances were another major cause for concern. Exhibit 2 contains financial statements for the New York Botanical Garden for fiscal years 1991 and 1992. Sources of funds included gifts and grants from individuals, foundations, and corporations; appropriations from New York City, New York State, and federal government agencies; membership revenues; tuition and publication income;

EXHIBIT 2

Statement of Changes in Fund Balances (fiscal years ending June 30)

	1991	1992
Fund balance, beginning of year	$ 408,702	$ 458,820
Revenues and other additions		
Appropriations—City of New York	5,170,899	4,096,232
Grants and contracts:		
Federal	93,505	127,900
State	1,126,087	1,131,065
Private contracts	42,123	108,078
Private gifts and grants	3,041,993	2,355,407
Special events	1,662,379	2,037,085
Investment income and realized gains	232,298	200,308
Other earned income	2,581,929	2,654,464
Auxiliary enterprises	1,313,925	1,430,952
Total revenues and other additions	$15,265,138	$14,141,491
Expenses and other deductions		
Program Services	$ 4,816,772	$ 4,034,805
Support Services	8,251,231	9,015,242
Auxiliary Enterprises	1,260,618	1,340,718
Total expenditures and other deductions	14,328,621	14,390,765
Transfers among funds—additions (deductions)		
Land, buildings, and equipment	(311,160)	N/A
Other transfers	(575,239)	N/A
Total transfers among funds	(886,399)	277,102
Net change to the fund balance	50,118	27,828
Fund balance, end of year	$ 458,820	$ 486,648

SOURCE: Morgan Stanley prospectus.

income from retail operations; and income earned on its endowment. In 1991, for instance, the Garden earned just over $500,000 from parking, food, and admissions. Across the street, the Bronx Zoo earned more than $11 million from these operations during the same period. Market value of the endowment at June 30, 1992, was approximately $22 million, with the annual draw on the endowment averaging approximately 6.5 percent. This endowment was seen as inadequate, relative to the size of the Garden's annual operating budget. The Garden's financial dependence on annual appropriations from the City of New York, in particular, left it vulnerable, Long felt, to the vagaries of the City's finances and politics.

This set of serious concerns prompted Long and his executive vice president and chief financial officer, John Rorer, to pursue the idea of embarking on a comprehensive planning process. In explaining their rationale, Long elaborated:

> Although the Garden's work was of a high caliber, and demands for its services locally, nationally, and internationally had never been greater, the Garden had a serious and potentially deeply damaging problem. It had grown to be an institution with an operating budget of nearly $21 million and only a precarious, underendowed revenue base in place to support its major commitments. In fiscal year 1992, income from endowment funded only 9 percent of the operating costs. The Garden itself and its public programs and activities funded only another 33 percent of operating costs. The remaining 67 percent of operating income was derived from contributions by the private sector to the Garden's Annual Fund and from government grants. These two sources are the two least dependable of all not-for-profit revenue sources, especially in today's era of governmental financial crisis and economic recession.

Throughout this period, the Garden was committed to achieving a balanced budget. This had been accomplished only through a combination of aggressive new fund-raising efforts and significant reductions in staff and operating expenses. At the same time, it was the strong opinion of the Garden's leadership that further cuts or additional staff reductions would signal a downward spiral in reputation

EXHIBIT 3

Sources of Operating Support, Fiscal Years 1984 to 1992

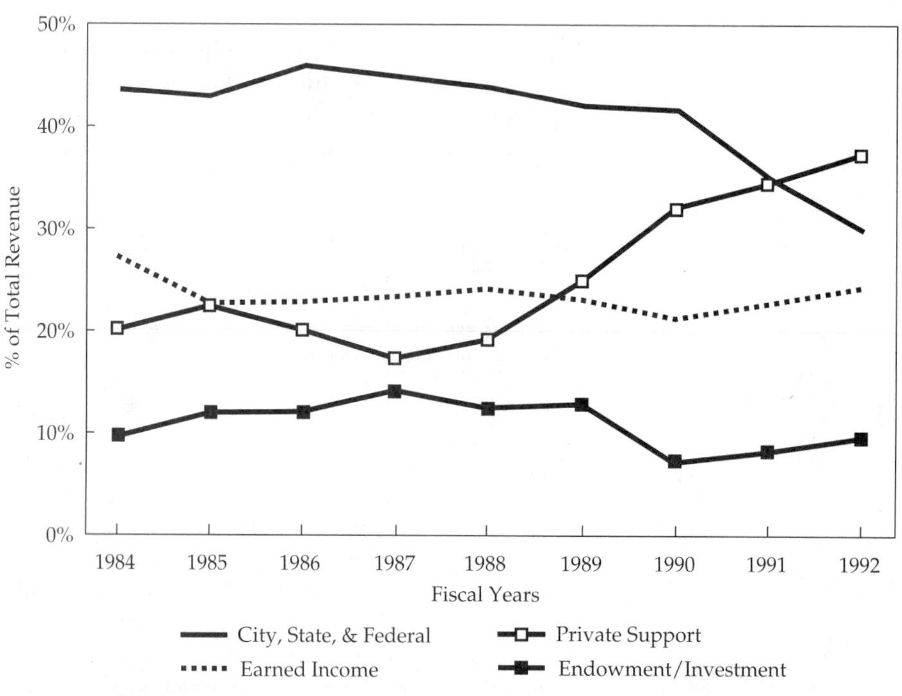

NOTE: Increases in endowment income for FY '87, '88, '89 resulted from the extensive use of realized capital gains.

from which it would be impossible to recover. Exhibits 3, 4, and 5 contain a more detailed look at sources of operating support, trends in city and state funding, and changes in full-time positions, over a multiyear period.

Paula Kascel, a professional planner, joined New York Botanical Garden as director of Long-Range Planning in January 1990, and explained what she saw as Long and Rorer's motivation:

> Both saw the significance and value of an institutional exercise that brought sort of new understanding to the organization in terms of where it was headed. Both

EXHIBIT 4

Trends in City and State Funding, FY1987–FY1992

	Total City and State Support	% of Total Revenue
1987	$6,321,000	40.4%
1988	6,474,000	39.4
1989	6,681,000	36.0
1990	6,964,000	35.0
1991	6,335,000	32.0
1992	5,251,000	25.3

EXHIBIT 5

Summary of Net Change in Full-Time Positions from FY1989 to FY1992

	Total FT Positions, FY1989	FT Positions Reduced, FY1989–92	FT Positions Added FY1989–92	Net Change	% Change
Security	43	13.0	0.0	–13.0	–30.2
Operations	48	9.0	0.0	–9.0	–18.8
Horticulture	55	7.0	2.0	–5.0	–9.1
Finance and Administration	35	7.0	5.5	–1.5	4.3
Education	21	4.5	0.0	–4.5	–21.4
Science	51	5.0	0.0	–5.0	–9.8
Retail Sales	10	4.0	0.0	–4.0	–40.0
External Relations/ Visitor Services	9	3.0	5.0	2.0	22.2
Garden Magazine	3	3.0	0.0	–3.0	–100.0
Library	16	2.5	0.0	–2.5	–15.6
Development	10	2.0	4.0	2.0	20.0
Rental Marketing	3	0.0	0.0	0.0	—
Total	304	60.0	16.5	–43.5	–14.3

> understood the value of unearthing a large organization and examining it and its old ways and then making decisions based on that familiarity. There was a lot of vestigial behavior, lots of balkanization at the Garden. Gregory and John informed one another in terms of their own experiences and decided together that to really move the Garden forward in terms of its financial stability but also programmatically, it really needed to be examined and then a whole new funding base had to be developed for the institution.

A seven-year time frame was selected for the plan. In explaining his rationale for the choice of such a long time horizon, Long noted: "We had so much to do—there was more than could be done in the usual five-year time frame."

The Planning Process

The planning process that Long and Rorer set in motion consisted of three overlapping phases: (1) the preparation of an early "protoplan," a kind of miniplan written by the senior staff that allowed them to begin the process of fund-raising; (2) the

Exhibit 6

The New York Botanical Garden Master Planning Process: Making a New Garden, 1989–99

A. The Proto Plan: 1989–91

1. cars and dogs out
2. the museum concept
3. a garden not a park
4. outdoor cafe
5. Rock Garden restoration
6. Forest restoration
7. Beth's Maze and Children's Corner
8. Family Garden upgrade
9. perimeter fence and Metro North Station upgrade
10. interpretation and maps

B. The Program Plan: 1990–92

1. strategic plan for institution
2. Science Plan
3. Horticulture Plan
4. Education Plan
5. Financial Plan

C. Master Planning: 1991–92

1. visitor experience
2. restoration of buildings and landscapes
3. exhibition facilities
4. education facilities
5. infrastructure survey
6. topographic maps
7. circulation and transportation

program plan, created in a widely inclusive process that involved managers at every level, that set out the Garden's strategy for the future in the key programmatic areas, and incorporated a financial plan of their implications; and (3) the master plan, which detailed the capital projects necessary to achieve the program plan. Exhibit 6 details the components of each of these stages.

The planning process that Long and Rorer devised and implemented was an ambitious one in terms of who it involved, how they worked together, and what they produced.

Who Was Involved

Long and Rorer decided that the planning process should involve everyone at the Garden with responsibility for program implementation. In the Botanical Science Research Division, this included all of the individual scientists; in horticulture, it included all curators and head gardeners. Also included were custodial and physical plant managers, as well as those in the finance area. In total, the expanded planning group included about 85 participants, including 12 invited members of the board. In selecting board members, Long and Rorer looked for level of interest, time availability, and people with potentially challenging views. "You don't want to avoid those kinds of ideas until the end of the process; you need to get them integrated early on," Long believed.

Planning-group members participated at four levels. At level one, frontline program managers offered their input. At level two, the directors to whom those managers reported synthesized their managers' input and used it to formulate their own recommendations. At level three, the vice presidents—Long's direct reports (see Exhibit 7)—synthesized the inputs from level two and made their recommendations to Long himself. At each level, presenters reported their recommendations to the entire planning group of 85, for comment and questions.

Long then synthesized these recommendations into a final plan that he brought to the board for their approval. It was this plan that he would present tonight at Sotheby's.

How They Worked Together

The emphasis on creating an open forum of discussion prevailed at each level in the planning process. The expanded planning group met once every three weeks in the Snuff Mill, for several hours, for two years. Over this time period, the entire group was invited to listen to presentations from all other managers involved. Each presentation was followed by a question-and-answer session. Attendance at the meetings was high—averaging no less than 60 participants throughout.

The presentations began at level one with the scientists—the science mission was seen as central and the scientists, as a group, were generally comfortable presenting their work to large audiences. Each scientist was asked to speak about his or her work, its contribution to the Garden, and his or her hopes for their ideal future. Each was asked to describe the kind of resources that would be needed to help him or her achieve their professional vision. Brian Boom, vice president for Science, offered a typical example. The scientists would say things like, "I'm 50 years old, I have another 15 years of active career, this is what I think I can accomplish, given these resources." In horticulture, for example, the curator of the Rock Garden presented his view of what the Rock Garden could be. The emphasis, throughout, was on "blue-sky thinking." All planning members listened to all presentations—security

EXHIBIT 7

New York Botanical Garden Senior Management

The following are summaries of the professional and educational backgrounds of the president and the vice presidents.

Gregory R. Long, President and Chief Executive Officer. Mr. Long has worked in the management of cultural institutions in New York City for 25 years. Born and raised in Kansas City, Missouri, Mr. Long moved to New York City in 1965, where he attended New York University and received a Bachelor of Arts degree in Art History in 1969. He began his career at The Metropolitan Museum of Art in 1969. He worked in development and public affairs at The American Museum of Natural History from 1972 to 1975 and the New York Zoological Society from 1975 to 1982. From 1982 to 1989 Mr. Long served as vice president for Public Affairs of The New York Public Library, where he played a leading role in a long-range planning process for the Library's 86 constituent libraries and directed private fund-raising in the $307,000,000 Campaign for the Library. Mr. Long was appointed president of the Garden in 1989.

John E. Rorer, Executive Vice President and Chief Financial Officer. Mr. Rorer came to the Garden as chief financial officer in 1989. Before joining the Garden, from 1976 to 1989, Mr. Rorer served in several management positions at Polytechnic University in Brooklyn, New York. His last position there was as vice president for Finance and Administration and chief financial officer. At Polytechnic, Mr. Rorer also participated in the creation, planning, and development of Metrotech, a $1 billion, 16-acre commercial/academic complex in downtown Brooklyn, adjacent to the University's campus. He held a series of increasingly responsible positions in New York City government from 1969 to 1976. Mr. Rorer is a graduate of Harvard College and holds a master's degree in Public Administration from New York University.

Dr. Brian M. Boom, Vice President for Botanical Science. Dr. Boom is the vice president for Botanical Science and the Pfizer Curator of Botany. Dr. Boom, who came to the Garden in 1983 as a research associate, is responsible for setting policy and guiding research efforts for the Garden's programs in basic and applied botany. Prior to his appointment as vice president for Botanical Science, Dr. Boom served as the Garden's director of Science Development. Dr. Boom received his Ph.D. in Biology from the City University of New York in 1983. He is also an adjunct assistant professor of Biology at the City University of New York, an adjunct associate professor of Tropical Dendrology at the School of Forestry and Environment Studies of Yale University, a visiting research professor at New York University, and an adjunct professor at Columbia University.

Rosemarie Garipoli, Vice President for Development. Ms. Garipoli joined the Garden in August 1989. As vice president for Development she had primary responsibility for the Garden's fund-raising. Her previous employment included teaching art history as well as several positions of increasing responsibility in the not-for-profit sector. Prior to joining the Garden she

(continued)

EXHIBIT 7 (CONTINUED)

New York Botanical Garden Senior Management

worked for the Bank Street College of Education as director of Development and Public Affairs and the Jewish Museum as assistant director. She holds a BA and an MFA from New York University.

John F. Reed, Vice President for Education. Mr. Reed first came to the Garden in 1965 as an assistant librarian. He took on increasing responsibilities, including the combined position of vice president for Education and director of the Library. During his tenure at the Library he completed many important tasks, notably the 25-year effort to recatalog the entire collection and make it available on computer. He is a graduate of the University of New Hampshire and has an AMLS from the University of Michigan.

Richard A. Schnall, Vice President for Horticulture. As the vice president for Horticulture, Mr. Schnall is responsible for planning and budgeting the Garden's horticulture program. Mr. Schnall came to the Garden in 1986. He has also served as the Garden's arboretum and grounds manager and the director of Horticulture. Before joining the Garden, Mr. Schnall was a horticulturist at Haywood Technical College in North Carolina and at the Donald M. Kendall Sculpture Gardens in Purchase, New York.

Marie Sexton, Vice President for External Relations. Ms. Sexton joined the Garden in October 1989. As vice president for External Relations she oversaw the departments of Public Relations, Special Events, Membership, and Retail Operations. Her previous employment included 10 years with the New York Zoological Society and six years with the New York Public Library as manager of Public Affairs. She is a graduate of Brown University.

and operations managers listened and presented to the scientists and gardeners and vice versa.

The director of Planning, Paula Kascel, played a significant role in the articulation and presentation of each individual's ideas. She worked individually with each presenter beforehand. As she described her role in the "public-performance component": "I didn't guide—I had no agenda. I was there to hear what they did and help them articulate it as best they could, so that their work was presented in the best possible light."

Paula found that her background in theater was often as helpful as her planning expertise in these discussions. "We really worked to make the presentations entertaining," she noted. "Performance values mattered."

The open dialogue after the presentations was sometimes lively, especially as the process progressed and managers at the next level, having listened to their people's presentations, began the process of prioritizing and making decisions as to what would or would not go into the next planning level. Throughout the process, budgeting staff worked with each presenter to develop spending estimates. Exhibit 8 contains a memo outlining the questions to be answered at level two.

Level three began the most difficult phase of prioritization and sequencing. The price tag for the blue-sky thinking was totaled and estimated to be about $235 million. Fund-raising consultants estimated that the maximum fund-raising capacity of the

EXHIBIT 8

The New York Botanical Garden Memorandum

TO: Level II Planning Participants
FR: Paula Kascel
RE: Revised Level II Planning Summary
DT: September 20, 1990

==

Attached is a revised edition of Planning Our Own Future, Level II.

A draft of the narrative questions designed to facilitate your thinking about the future of your department was circulated to you on June 18, 1990. The narrative questions in this revised version remain the same, with two minor changes which are underlined in the following samples:

> Page 2 E. How would increased <u>inter</u>departmental interaction and collaboration better serve the Garden institutionally?"
>
> Page 3 A. In ideal terms, how would you like to see your department develop over the next five-year period beginning <u>7/1/92</u> (Cancel; reorganize/redirect; develop further.) Please describe in detail.

As you know, in addition to completing all of the information in this summary, Level II presenters are asked to summarize their thinking on a departmental basis for Fiscal Years 1993–1997 in a ten-minute presentation to the members of the Expanded Planning Group.

In these planning presentations, Department Heads are asked to give a clear and concise overview of the goals of their departments, and the actions and resources which will be required to achieve those goals for Fiscal Years 1993–1997. The questions on Pages 3 and 4 of the written summary should serve, in part, as a guide for your planning presentations, although specific questions on Pages 1 and 2 may also be incorporated, based on your individual approach.

(continued)

Garden was no more than \$165 million. So the senior staff took on the challenging role of bringing the "pie-in-the-sky thinking back down to earth," as one described it. Each area was allocated a portion of the \$165 million and asked to adhere to this figure in making their choices about what would remain in the plan moving forward. They were then asked to sequence these initiatives and spending across the seven-year planning horizon.

New York's Fiscal Crisis

Approximately nine months into the Garden's planning process, the City of New York began to experience severe financial trouble. This situation had a significant impact on the planning process itself. As CFO John Rorer described the situation:

EXHIBIT 8 (CONTINUED)

The New York Botanical Garden Memorandum

THE NEW YORK BOTANICAL GARDEN

SEPT. 1990

PLANNING OUR OWN FUTURE LEVEL II

Name__________________________Title__________________Date_________

I. ASSESSMENT OF CURRENT PROGRAM(S)

A. Please give a general description of your department as it currently exists.

B. The programs and activities of your department are designed to reach/serve whom?

C. How does the work of your department relate to and support the overall purposes of the Garden?

D. Please describe how your department supports and reinforces activities of other departments.

E. How would increased interdepartmental interaction and collaboration better serve the Garden institutionally?

F. What are the criteria used to evaluate your department?

G. What are the strengths and weaknesses of your department as it is currently designed?

H. How has your department changed since inception?

I. Please name and describe programs, activities or attitudes by other organizations which have influenced your thinking about the future of your department and which could serve as models for NYBG.

(continued)

New York's financial crisis got translated into financial trouble for the New York Botanical Garden as well as other similarly situated institutions around New York City. So we started looking at our financials, saying "What does this mean?" Indeed, if the shape of our funding is changing, how do we ensure survival? So we shifted a bit in our focal point in the planning process and said, "Let's talk about how we structure what we do so that not only can we realize our dreams and visions of the organization, but also so that we can survive financially, because we're going to lose some of our government support and that's clear." We had a small endowment, we didn't generate much money from visitors, and we knew there was a limit to increased private fund-raising. So that was a bit of a shift midstream. We did projections and presented them to the whole planning group and everybody saw the disaster coming, the big deficits, if we didn't change the funding trends that were emerging.

EXHIBIT 8 (CONTINUED)

The New York Botanical Garden Memorandum

II. PROGRAM DIRECTIONS/NEW INITIATIVES
OVER FIVE-YEAR PERIOD

A. In ideal terms, how would you like to see your department develop over the five-year period beginning 7/1/92? (Cancel; reorganize/redirect; develop further.) Please describe in detail.

B. Please describe, in order of priority, what specific actions could be taken to more fully develop your department over this five-year period.

C. In order of priority, what new initiatives(s) would you like the Garden to undertake in your department in the future? What are the arguments in support of these new initiatives, e.g., benefits to the Garden, etc.?

D. Describe and estimate what current department expenses could be saved to help fund these new initiatives.

E. Describe and estimate what new or expanded sources of revenue could be identified to support these initiatives.

F. Please highlight any collaborative professional efforts which would be integral to new program initiatives.

G. What are the significant trends which you feel will influence the future direction of your department (both negatively and positively) and which should be considered by the Garden as it plans for the future?

H. Please relate these trends to the specific recommendations and new program initiatives identified by you and by members of your staff.

As a result of these discussions, the focus became a blended plan that combined a baseline operational plan for current operations with the more future-focused set of new aspirations for the Garden. The newly configured plan would not be an "add-on wish list," in Long's terms, but a comprehensive blueprint that would "run the Garden" on a day-to-day basis.

This also led to a focus on revenue generation as an important component of the early phases of the plan. Earned-income goals were established for the restaurant and catering facilities, retail operations, and membership. By early 1993, with the strategic plan completed, detailed business plans were being written in each of these areas. These included business-development activities, marketing plans, and pro-forma financial projections, all of which fed into the overall financial plan.

Long and Rorer chose not to wait until the completion of the planning process before acting on several of the issues that arose during planning discussions. One of the initiatives that they undertook immediately was to begin the process of amending the Garden's charter to permit the charging of admission fees. This required an act of the New York State Legislature in Albany, which was successfully passed in July 1991.

Another area where they chose to act immediately was in the realm of computerization. Paula Kascel describes the evolution of this issue:

> Everyone was really struggling with technology and doing it at their own pace. This ranged from legal pads and number-two pencils to people who were fairly sophisticated on the Internet (in 1990!). We heard concerns from the Library, from Administration, from Education—we saw that this was a strategic issue, an institutional issue. Gregory and John chose to lift it out, put the resources toward it, put it on fast forward. They created information-service programs and started to deal with the issue of information management on an institutional basis. That, to me, is an example of how planning is not a linear process—you can't stop reacting or moving forward just because planning is under way.

Board Involvement

In addition to including board members as part of the planning team, the board was briefed at each meeting on the progress of the planning process. The board's confidence in Hubbard and Long facilitated the entire board's support for the process. "Besides," Hubbard commented, "we had tried a standard boiler-plate approach to strategic planning several years before, with outside help, and nothing ever came of it," so the board was open to trying a different approach. In addition, the New York Public Library, under Long and Vartan Gregorian's leadership, had previously used a process very similar to the one that Long and Rorer now proposed to accomplish a major institutional turnaround that had received international attention.

Paula Kascel, who worked extensively with the board in her role as director of Long-Range Planning, recalled two important points in the planning process when the board raised concerns that required addressing. The first related to the state of the economy.

As Gregory described the situation in the 1990–91 time frame:

> The economy was very bad—the country's, the City's, in general, and we were not a strong enough competitor for the private funding that we would need. There were times when looking at our needs just got overwhelming. We were having tremendous problems just balancing our current budget—we had reduced staff by almost 15 percent between 1989 and 1992—yet everybody seemed to want so much. How would we ever satisfy them? These were the dark days.

Long responded by inviting an economist to speak at a board retreat on the topic of cycles in the economy in relation to philanthropic giving. This talk demonstrated to the board that, at no point since the 1950s, had the bottom fallen out of philanthropic giving. The economist also suggested that the economy would likely be coming out of recession by the time the fund-raising campaign would be ready to launch. This reassured the board of the financial feasibility of implementing the plan.

The second issue of concern to the board related to what Paula Kascel described as "talking in details":

> We kept talking to the board in detail. I need computers, I need secretaries, I need more vehicles. Now, going into this level of detail was absolutely necessary, but

> the board was starting to drown in the details—the minutiae was starting to drown us all—especially the board. In November 1991, Gregory began to talk about how all of these little pieces of individual staff-member needs, at every level of detail, actually advanced a small set of major mission components. Everything fit into one of these three categories that emerged: (1) giving new vigor to Botanical Science research, (2) the public aspect of the museum, and (3) financial stability. If you took all of these individual visions to their natural conclusion, this is the story they told.

The board came to understand how each new vehicle or computer supported a larger vision. In the process, they became more comfortable with the plan's detailed focus, having seen its connection with an emerging view of the Garden's future.

Community Relations

Throughout the planning process, the opinions and feedback of community members were solicited as input to the plan. As Long described his view of the role of the community: "Seeking the community's opinion and acting on it are essential elements in maintaining good relations, in generating enthusiasm for new developments, and in obtaining community support when it is needed."

An important job of the Garden's Community Relations Committee had been to work with the small group of neighbors in the Bronx who did not want to bring more people into the Garden, to help them to understand that the institution's survival depended upon making the changes contained in the plan.

The Outcomes of the Planning Process

By April 1993, when Long took the podium at Sotheby's, the strategic-planning process had produced a comprehensive set of program, master, and financial plans.

The program plan outlined three objectives:

Part I: *Give new vigor and focus to botanical research.*

Part II: *Bring more visitors to the Garden and enrich their experience.*

Part III: *Achieve financial and managerial stability.*

All new initiatives were placed within the context of the larger vision outlined by these objectives. The elements of the master plan for the development of the grounds and facilities were incorporated within each of these program areas.

Part I: Give New Vigor and Focus to Botanical Research

The scientific mission of the Garden would remain central to its purpose of moving forward. In fact, the ongoing habitat destruction, and attendant erosion of plant-genetic diversity, that accompanied tropical-forest destruction made the Garden's historical focus on botanical research even more prominent and vital, the plan argued. In rededicating and escalating the Garden's commitment to collect, verify, and disseminate information on the plant species of the world, the plan made the construction of a new library/herbarium building and the upgrading of laboratory facilities top priorities. It created a new Institute of Systematic Botany to complement the existing Institute of Economic Botany, formed in 1981. Staffing and endowing the new institute was a plan priority, as was endowing two additional positions in economic botany. Upgrading the library resource base, through computerization, acquisitions, and conversions, was also included.

Part II: Bring More Visitors to the Garden and Enrich Their Experience

This part of the plan focused on the public aspect of the Garden and centered on the restoration of the Garden as a living museum. The plan argued that the Garden's distinguished scientific-research programs could never be made to be fully self-supporting, nor could initiatives around environmental education, programs for children, or urban revitalization initiatives like Bronx Green-Up, it was essential that the Garden increase visitor volume and attendant revenues. Accomplishing this required the renovation of the Enid A. Haupt Conservatory as a top priority, establishing a horticulture endowment, and completing a plant inventory. The restoration would require the closing of the Conservatory, the Garden's most popular visitor attraction, for a period of four years. Priorities also included broadening opportunities for learning through the creation of additional programming and a Children's Adventure Garden, and improving the visitor's experience by the addition of more parking, restrooms, and public programming, along with the renovation of the Garden's auditorium, and the construction of a visitor orientation center, and the creation of a new main entrance.

Part III: Achieve Financial and Managerial Stability

This portion of the plan focused on ensuring the Garden's future financial health by increasing revenue on three fronts—annual giving, endowment, and earned income. Exhibit 9 details the revenue growth required, by area, in the plan. The construction

Exhibit 9

Revenue Growth Required FY1992–99

Revenue Source	Percentage Growth, FY1992–FY1999
Conservatory admissions/parking/voluntary contributions	213.0%
Indirect costs recovered	200.8
Tour income	193.8
Tuition and fees	109.0
Gross membership income	96.8
Scientific publications	93.9
Auxiliary enterprises	82.6
Miscellaneous income	76.0
Endowment income	51.5
Grants and contracts	43.5
Appropriation—city of New York	43.2
Annual fund	40.4
State appropriation	37.2
Total operating revenues	58.5

of a new restaurant and catering facility was an important priority, as was expanding marketing. Advancing institutional management, especially in the area of computers, along with restoring security staff positions, and upgrading maintenance and operations, were also important initiatives.

THE MASTER PLAN

To implement these programmatic priorities, the master plan for the grounds and facilities described the concept of the "Garden within the Garden." The Garden identified the location, in the western portion of the grounds, where institutional investment would be focused and where public activities and horticultural programming would be concentrated. This concept called for restoring existing structures, investing in new buildings and gardens, and providing new amenities to enhance the visitor's experience. Exhibit 10 contains the details of the master plan.

EXHIBIT 10

Renovating the New York Botanical Garden: The Master Plan

GREEN SPACES

Renovating the Botanical Garden

A planned renovation of the New York Botanical Garden will take seven years and cost an estimated $165 million. So far, which relies on a mixture of public and private funds, has raised $60 million.

1. New library and herbarium
2. Renovated lecture hall
3. Restoration of museum exterior
4. New restaurant and catering area
5. Extensive $21 million renovation to the Enid A. Haupt Conservatory, also called the Crystal Palace. The greenhouse will be closed for two years.
6. New visitor center
7. Expanded parking
8. New main entrance
9. New children's garden
10. Redesigned native plants garden
11. Expanded education project in 40-acre virgin hemlock forest
12. New plant nursery

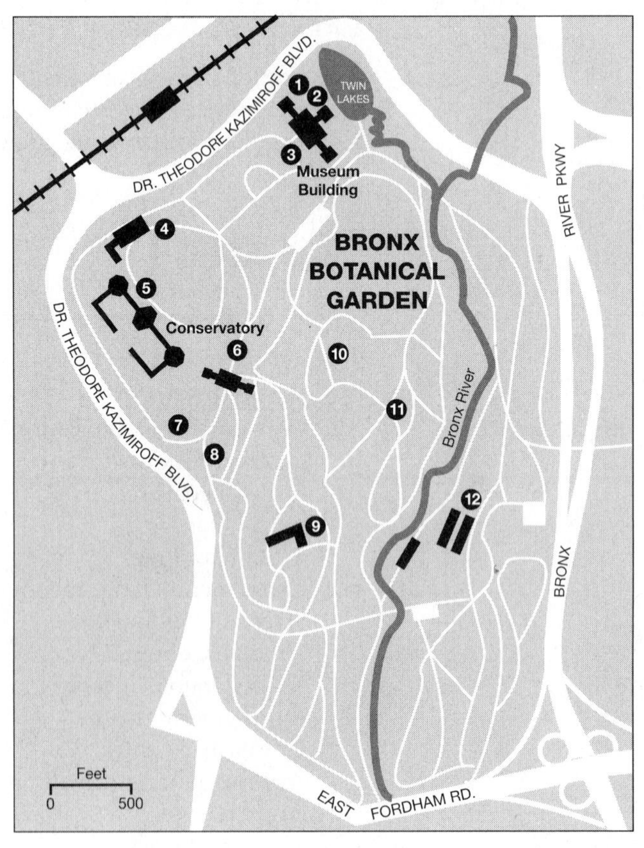

EXHIBIT 11

Summary of Campaign Needs: Operating, Endowment, and Capital

OPERATING NEEDS

Supporting the Growth of the Annual Fund, 1993–99

1993	$6,300,000
1994	6,800,000
1995	7,200,000
1996	7,500,000
1997	8,000,000
1998	8,400,000
1999	$9,000,000

New Vigor and Focus for Botanical Science, 1993–99

Herbarium Computerization	$1,761,000
Staffing the Institutes of Systematic and Economic Botany	1,120,000
Library Catalog Computerization	1,025,000
Forest Research	842,000
Improving Access to Herbarium Collections	675,000
Building Library Staff	479,000
Conserving Library Collections	376,000
Marketing Scientific Publications	240,000
Library Acquisitions	$ 126,000

An American Horticultural Showcase, 1993–99

Building Horticulture Staff	$ 749,000
Stewardship of the Forest	683,000
Horticulture Computerization	467,000
Turfgrass Improvements	226,000
Completing the Plant Inventory	160,000
Restoring the Montgomery Conifer Collection	100,000
Demonstration Gardens	$ 82,000

Environmental Education, 1993–99

Children's Adventure Project	$ 3,285,000
Environmental Education in the Forest	651,000
Graduate Program Coordinator	437,000
Marketing for Continuing Education	210,000
Continuing Education Facilities	55,000
Recertifying the Continuing Education Program	$ 45,000

The Visitor's Experience, 1993–99

New Public Programs	$ 895,000
New Signage and Interpretation	425,000
Audience Research	$ 115,000

Financial and Managerial Stability, 1993–99

Conducting a Capital Campaign	$3,300,000
Advertising and Marketing	1,025,000
New Institutional Computer Initiative	872,000
Expanding Maintenance and Operations Staff	680,000
Membership Promotion	593,000
Restoring Security Staff	471,000
Financial Analysis and Planning	360,000
Capital Projects Management	354,000
Retail Operations	300,000
Volunteer Program	296,000
Community Relations Program	280,000
Inventory Controls	145,000
Marketing of Rental Events	$ 105,000

(continued)

EXHIBIT 11 (CONTINUED)

Summary of Campaign Needs: Operating, Endowment, and Capital

ENDOWMENT NEEDS

Botanical Science Endowments

Science Fund	$9,525,000
Vice Presidency for Botanical Science	1,250,000
Chair in Institute of Economic Botany	1,250,000
Chair in Institute of Economic Botany	1,250,000
Chair in Institute of Systematic Botany	1,250,000
Chair in Institute of Systematic Botany	1,250,000
Chair in Institute of Systematic Botany	1,250,000

Horticulture Endowments

Horticulture Fund	5,000,000
Rock and Native Plant Garden Curator or Rose Garden Curator	800,000
Horticulture Taxonomist	800,000
Demonstration Gardens	400,000

Endowment to Support New Facilities

Plant Studies Center for the Library and Herbarium	4,975,000
Children's Adventure Garden	2,000,000

CAPITAL NEEDS

Plant Studies Center for the Library and Herbarium	$28,590,000
Enid A. Haupt Conservatory Restoration and Exhibits	24,860,000
Garden Cafe and Terrace Room	7,500,000
Main Building Facade Restoration	6,200,000
Children's Adventure Garden	4,847,000
Parking and Rest Rooms at the West Gate Entry	2,900,000
The Arthur and Janet Ross Lecture Hall	1,080,000
Snuff Mill Redevelopment and Related Site Improvements	923,000
Satellite Horticulture Facility and Propagation Range Upgrades	800,000
Master Planning	668,000
Miscellaneous Capital Projects	558,000
Replacing Equipment: Horticulture/Operations/Security	475,000
Visitor Center/Entry Plaza at the West Gate	350,000
Relocating the Shop	300,000
Renovating the Laboratories	300,000
Demonstration Gardens Complex	118,000
Woody Plant Nursery	72,000
New Irrigation Systems	60,000

N.B. The total cost of restoring the Enid A. Haupt Conservatory and installing new exhibits includes more than $11,000,000 provided by the city of New York prior to the initiation of The Campaign for the Garden.

The Campaign for the Garden, 1993–99

Taken together, the comprehensive set of plans created in the strategic-planning process set the stage for the launch of the most ambitious fund-raising campaign in the Garden's history, and one of the most ambitious ever undertaken by any New York City cultural institution. Its goal was $165 million, more than twice the Garden's previous fund-raising goal of $63 million. Exhibit 11 details the operating, capital, and endowment needs outlined for the campaign.

The $165 million campaign had been broken down into goals for the different sources of support, both government and private. Private sources included corporations, foundations, board members, and other individuals. Present in the Sotheby's audience that night were many of the people who could be most influential in helping the Garden meet these goals.

As Long reached the podium at Sotheby's, the audience became quiet, waiting for the presentation to begin. Some of them, Long conjectured, might be thinking that they had already waited too long for the unveiling of the Garden's hoped-for future—that two years was too long for a planning process to take. Long disagreed:

> I suppose that you could think of it as a two-year planning process followed by a seven-year implementation period, but that is not how I look at it. We gave ourselves nine years, in total, to get a lot done. I think of our first two years as an investment in reaching consensus among a lot of people about what this institution would become—without which, we could not go on to accomplish significant things. I consider it time well spent.

Endnotes

[1]Sotheby's Auction House made its auditorium available for use, free of charge, to nonprofit institutions in the New York City area.

[2]Much of the following history is excerpted from a Morgan Stanley prospectus, dated July 18, 1996, for revenue bonds for the Trust for Cultural Resources of the City of New York.

CASE 28

STRATEGIC PLANNING AT THE NEW YORK BOTANICAL GARDEN (B)

In a word, it is magnificent. A landmark glasshouse of superb design and construction, the Enid A. Haupt Conservatory of the New York Botanical Garden stands as testimony to the consummate invention and skill applied to every aspect of its regenesis into one of the most splendid exhibitions of botanical life in the world.[1]

With these words, *Landscape Architecture* magazine began its May 1997 cover story devoted to the reopening of the Enid A. Haupt Conservatory at the New York Botanical Garden. The *New York Times* proclaimed it "a newly opalescent jewel in New York City's crown."

> Re-opening to the public after a four-year, $25 million rehabilitation, the Conservatory is the centerpiece of the Garden's seven-year plan for renovation and renewal. The huge plant collection, now numbering 3,000, in this museum of horticulture, has also been re-installed, with some new plants and new settings, and a spacious cafe now stands in the spruce grove near the Conservatory. . . . From the Garden's new entrance at the Conservatory Gate with its "lollipop" standing clock, the visitor is now led through a triangular circuit described as "the garden within the Garden."[2]

The Garden's grand reopening celebration on May 1, 1997, was considered by some to be the most important day in the history of the Garden. In addition to the reopening of the Conservatory and the opening of the Garden's new entrance, restaurant, and a host of other visitor amenities, the announcement was made that fund-raising had been completed for the construction of the new Library and Herbarium. Scheduled to break ground in late 1997, the Library/Herbarium complex completion, along with the opening of the Children's Adventure Garden, in 1998, would largely bring to fruition the ambitious goals set out in the Garden's master plan, completed in 1993. The Garden's fund-raising campaign, set at $165 million in 1993, was extended to $175 million in February 1995, and had raised $146 million as of April 30, 1997. The vice president of Botanical Science described his emotions at seeing the entire staff of the Garden come together to celebrate: "The scientists with the gardeners with the employees who washed the floors—it was a very moving moment."

This case was written by Jeanne M. Liedtka, Associate Professor of Business Administration. This case was written as a basis for class discussion rather than to illustrate effective or ineffective handling of an administrative situation.

But Gregory Long, president of the Garden since 1989, was calm amid the media hoopla:

> The whole city was moved—which is hard to do in New York—and the Garden is back in a powerful way. But at the celebration, I felt very calm—the hard part was four or five years back figuring out how hard it would be to accomplish all of this and going ahead anyway. Putting the Conservatory re-opening in context, we figured it all out years ago.

The Garden's extraordinary success at creating and implementing a strategic plan that skeptics had seen as overly ambitious in 1993 earned Long much praise at the celebration. He demurred: "I got a lot of congratulations, but I don't think that a process like this is ever about a single person. Four hundred people had been working for eight years—this was a victory for the *process* itself and all of the people who worked on it."

Reflections on the Planning Process at the Garden

"Democracy" at Work

When asked for their assessment of why the Garden's strategic-planning process, undertaken between 1990 and 1992, had succeeded so well, participants almost always began with an acknowledgment of the contribution of the "democratic nature" of the process. Richard Schnall, vice president of Horticulture, remarked:

> The remarkable part of the process was that it was as democratic as it was—members of every area, at every level, were involved. Gardeners and curators stood up in a room full of peers, senior management, and board members and said, "I have to fight for a telephone, there's not enough growing space." It was all stuff that we had been saying for years among ourselves—but we'd never said it out loud before.

The word "democratic" was repeated by many others who described the process. Bruce Riggs, manager of Plant Interpretation and Records, went on to remark:

> We presented our beliefs of what should happen from our point of view so that everyone got to hear it. It was an open, almost a democratic presentation. Some of them were humorous and some of them were—well, you know, some people can talk better than others. . . . But everyone had a vested interest in their area . . . it was a "no-holds-barred" opportunity to give your opinion.

Schnall noted that "the process was never meant to say that everything was perfect. People didn't have the resources to do what they needed to do. The process was very educational—you came to realize that you were not the only one suffering from a lack of resources."

The word "educational" was also repeated by many participants when they described key features of the planning process. Opinions as to who received the education varied. Some talked about the opportunity for employees outside of the research area to listen, for the first time, to the scientists actually describe their work and its impact on the field of botany. Employees from other areas were amazed and proud of the Garden's contributions. "People were surprised at the depth of the talent," one participant noted. "There were extraordinary people at all levels." "I worked here for 25 years and never really understood what those other people did," another commented.

Others felt that it was the scientists themselves who received the education. Brian Boom, vice president of Botanical Science, commented:

> During the process, we all began to see that earned income needed to be pursued aggressively. We saw that making a visitor's experience richer made money and that money brought value to the sciences. Most of the scientists didn't see this before. They were oblivious to how many people even visited the Garden. The planning process helped them to see that there was more to the work of the Garden than just them describing their species and working on their new book.

Still others felt that it was senior management and the board who received an education. One member of the horticulture area noted: "I'd like to think that the process was educational enough that some things happened that wouldn't have happened otherwise. We educated Gregory and the Board—because gardeners saw things that they couldn't."

Long himself believed that the democratic and educational aspects of the planning process succeeded in "unbalkanizing the organization" by "giving people a broader perspective and an increased respect and love for the organization as a whole that defused historic tensions between departments." CFO John Rorer agreed:

> In the end, we accomplished three things—first, we had the raw material, through the presentations, to write the plan; second, we had a pretty good idea what people's priorities were; and the third thing, just as important in my view, is that we educated the whole staff about what was going on in the institution.

The process also resulted in a sense of personal commitment to the plan's priorities. This outcome evolved from both the broadened institutional perspective and also from employees' evident commitment to their work. Paula Kascel, director of Long-Range Planning from 1990 to 1994, talked about the enormous individual pride that she encountered in her work with managers on their planning presentations:

> As Studs Terkel said, "Everybody works" and then you find people with deep personal connection to their work, and you just can't know in advance where you'll find it. We had really good people in finance and accounting—not just stars in science and horticulture. I remember Lenny Williams, one of our security supervisors, reminding people about how important the interface between security and the public was—he also reminded us how each individual's different talents contribute to an organization.

A frontline manager echoed similar thoughts:

> One really good thing about the planning process was that everyone who was here for the long haul got to put their input in and, therefore, they were vested in the plan. They understood the process of how priorities were determined and felt like what they said was heard and appreciated—and they felt more valuable. If you had not felt like you participated and you were told what to do, rather than being creative, you wouldn't feel like you were vested. We're all professionals and have

> all been doing this for a long time, and we hope we're doing this for the good of people—I mean, this institution isn't here to just benefit itself. . . . So we all want people to sign on to what we believe in, so we really put an extra effort in—everybody does. You feel it. Before, there was the heart of people who wanted to do good things, but they didn't have the means. The means have arrived because the plan is in place and people can see there's a plan and they know what game we are playing and what our goals are.

Involvement in the planning process also gave participants a longer-term perspective and patience. John Bernstein, vice president for Finance, noted:

> In this sort of broad bottom-up approach, you get a lot more buy-in, a lot more understanding. I mean, the planning book says, in 1993, that in 1998 I'm going to get another scientist. That's a big leap of faith for a manager of research staff to believe—but I also see that the plan said in 1994 there would be an extra lawn mower on the grounds. And, what do you know, I just saw that shiny new lawn mower arrive. In that respect, the education of the entire staff allowed the arrival of the new lawn mower to give *everybody* the belief that the plan might actually work.

Bringing Along the "Doubting Thomases"

The sense of involvement evident in these comments was not present at the start of the process. Paula Kascel recalled the difficulty of getting the process under way:

> I used to joke that, early on, I once asked one of the scientists what a word meant and he yelled the word back at me. I said, "This isn't botany for the hard of hearing—I *heard* it, I just don't know what it means." So they are not generally a warm and lovable group. . . . One of the scientists—I'll call him Bill—was my first appointment; his specialty was mosses, I think, and he'd been here his whole career. He'd seen people come and go. A more cynical soul you cannot imagine facing. I think for the most part cynical on all levels, including what could *you* possibly have to contribute to this institution. He asked me why this planning process would be different than all of the other ones. "Because, this time," I said, "you'll know *why* you don't get what you want."

Brian Boom described the changes in attitude that the scientists experienced as the process went on:

> In the beginning, it was a period of mixed feelings—the euphoria of being asked about what we needed without a ceiling, confounded by the doubt that this would go anywhere. Some felt that this was just the administration's way of making work that kept us from our real work and was just for the greater glory of the administration—to justify their existence. I became less of a doubter when I was appointed director of Science Development early in the process—I got more of an institutional perspective. But for the other scientists, it happened slower. I think for many it was when we had a formal presentation on the results of Level Two. They started to realize—oh gosh, it hasn't gone away—they are still thinking about the ideas that I gave them.

Kascel argued that starting with the scientists had been key to the success of the process, for several reasons:

> Part of it had to do with respect for the scientists and the significance of their work. I think it was also a strategic choice in that this was the place where the complaints were going to be most likely. Also, they were the most performance ready. They're scholars, they're teachers, they're accustomed to public speaking.

The scientists set a high standard in their presentations, one that subsequent presenters in horticulture, finance, and operations worked hard to maintain.

As John Rorer noted:

> The scientists were so strictly professional, they set the standards. You didn't get a lot of people showing up ad-libbing. We had charts, slides, we had complete presentations all the way through. I think that the scientists setting that tone at the beginning did more to professionalize the process than anything we could have designed.

Although many managers in other areas found the process of presenting to the large group nerve-racking and intimidating ("We had people outside of science who got physically sick before presenting," one staff member recalled), most came away with a renewed sense of self-confidence in their role and their value to the institution.

Attendance at the presentations remained high throughout the two years they went on. "Everyone, even the scientists, continued to come to the meetings because there was a sense of excitement," Brian Boom remarked. "The blue-sky thinking at the outset was key—it was uplifting, it got people *hooked*."

The Role of Leadership

The attendance of Gregory Long, Tom Hubbard (chairman of the board), and John Rorer at the meetings was important as well. As Paula Kascel noted:

> People had to be sure that they were not going to be penalized in the present tense. They were being asked to figure out how to put a lot of extra effort into a planning process while still doing a good job at what they were doing. I think what allowed people to do that was how much attention Gregory, in particular, paid to this. They knew that it was as important to Gregory—and John and Tom—that they were participating in this effort as it was that they were getting their present-tense work taken care of.

Another vice president noted: "People started to look at our leadership and say, 'Maybe they're serious this time. This time, we've got charismatic leadership that might actually pull it off'—and the enthusiasm just grew."

In reflecting on the role that Gregory Long, as president, played in the process, Tom Hubbard remarked: "As CEO, Gregory Long, and as CFO, John Rorer, were the catalyst for the whole resurgence. Yet the process, once rolling, was almost independent of Gregory and John—they made everybody feel that 'this is your life.'"

Paula Kascel, in her role as director of the planning process, was also seen as central to the plan's success. Anna Ferrigno, director of Budget and Planning, noted:

> There was some resentment—people felt overwhelmed with what they had to do in their normal daily routine and then they had to plan, as well. But Paula was able to get them to do it. She worked very well with people and helped them throughout the process. That was a big accomplishment—with the wrong person, it would not have worked as smoothly.

Brian Boom concurred:

> She was so well organized and persistent, she gained credibility with even the scientists. We really appreciated her administrative abilities. She respected what program people said and shaped it to be more coherent. She helped us put it into the context of the plan, with dollar amounts attached. With her, it was almost like going out on a military maneuver—she got our preparations in order and insisted on rehearsals.

The continuity of leadership, both among top management and on the board, during the postplanning period was also seen as key. The consistent commitment to the plan itself and the detailed knowledge of why the different elements of the plan were essential to the Garden's future development ensured that the plan was not "shelved." John Rorer noted: "The people who conceived the plan are all, for the most part, still here, both senior management and board leadership—that has allowed us to stay the course in the implementation process."

Measuring and Monitoring Plan Progress

John Rorer and his staff also played a decisive role in the implementation of the plan. His staff developed a tracking model, using the plan as a road map. Parallel-tracking mechanisms monitored operating financials, program spending, and capital funds. Goals and benchmarks were clearly laid out. Funds were monitored as they were raised and spent, and the timing of decisions was adjusted, as necessary. Anna Ferrigno noted:

> What we have done subsequent to 1993 is to use the plan as a road map as we start our budget process for each fiscal year. We always return back to that original document as we make decisions about where we're going, what we can afford to do, how we are doing with funders, and what is most reasonable to assume for the upcoming fiscal years. . . . So we know where we are right on target, where we thought we would be, which initiatives we need to intentionally lag behind on because some of the original timing decisions in the plan did not work out. . . . We just went through a very thorough review of where we are to date from inception of the campaign that we presented to the expanded planning group about two months ago.

These bimonthly updates to the expanded planning group were an important element of the monitoring process. The different areas took turns reporting on their progress vis-à-vis the plan. As one participant observed: "It's the opportunity for a member of the group to stand up and say to senior management, 'You've reneged on your plan commitments.'"

In the early days following the presentation of the plan, the term *NIP*—not in plan—was coined by Rosemarie Garipoli, then vice president for Development.

When Tim Landi succeeded her, he also took on her role as "plan police." He commented:

> I came in during the very first days of implementing the plan. When I came on, I was called the "plan police" because we actually tied our development system to an accounting system. I can find that $33,000 in the plan for the direct-mail-campaign component of your gift. With our tracking report, I can look up a donor and I can track their gift to the plan and see where it matches. . . . It's been interesting to have this guideline and actually follow it when a gift comes in and to see where it fit into the plan, develop financial reports that tie to the general ledger to see that we aren't spending more—to make sure that we don't raise $175 million but have $120 million of the right dollars and $55 million of the wrong ones. So it's been extremely helpful in keeping the institution in sync with the plan developed by all of these people four years ago. Any other institution I've been with, we always made our goal in terms of the dollars in the capital campaign—but not necessarily for the same purpose that we set out with. Here, I can talk with authority about implementing a plan that did cover the aspects that we thought it should. To a funder, that says that "I'm not going to give you money now and in four years you're coming back to me for the exact same thing."

Exhibit 1 contains an example of one of Landi's tracking reports. Under the NIP philosophy, you had to take something out of the plan to put something in, or find additional funding.

In addition to tracking the progress of the plan's implementation and the Garden's fund-raising campaign, the Garden extended the strategic-planning process by undertaking business planning for revenue-producing activities. These business plans set income goals for each revenue-generating activity and detailed the set of action steps required to realize the dollar goals. Business plans were created for areas such as Continuing Education, Group Tours, Membership, and the Children's Adventure Garden. A feasibility study was done for catering and food service that resulted in the decision to build the new Garden Cafe and Terrace Room.

Once developed, these business plans were reviewed and updated, usually annually. This action enabled each revenue area to measure its progress against income goals and to make adjustments in its business plans, as necessary, on an ongoing basis.

Convergence on Priorities

One of the things that facilitated the success of the NIP control mechanism was the degree of consensus that existed in support of the plan's priorities. As Gregory Long described it, "When the day came in the process to set priorities, they just fell out," in a way that was apparent to all planning-group members.

Paula Kascel offered an example:

> An interesting common theme that sort of emerged in the areas of education and visitor services was serving families and children. In the past, we had mostly been concerned with how to restrain that child. You know—don't pick, don't climb, don't roll, jump, or swim. Here, we had two areas of the Garden that didn't normally have a lot of interaction beginning, more or less, to identify the same issue. You had the education department talking about the need for more public programming for children and the whole visitor-services area talking about how

Exhibit 1

"Give New Vigor and Focus to Botanical Research"—Funds Raised/Pledged as of 9/20/94

Funding Priorities for Botanical Research	Goal	Raised/Pledged to Date	Balance Needed
Build and endow a new library/herbarium building	$33,565,000	$23,077,500	$10,487,500
Laboratory renovation and upgrade	300,000	0	300,000
Staffing the ISB/expanding research staff/grad. coord.	1,532,444	929,965	602,479
Library computerization	1,024,595	846,225	178,370
Strengthen the collections through acquisitions	125,731	0	125,731
Build staff to provide critical information services	479,387	56,098	423,289
Conservation	376,110	13,045	363,065
Strengthen Herbarium management	675,000	478,432	196,568
Expand science computerization	1,489,342	951,430	537,912
Strengthen scientific publications	40,000	40,000	0
Research initiatives for NYBG Forest Project	2,019,760	588,361	1,431,399
Endowment (ISB, IEB, library)	17,025,000	14,525,000	2,500,000
Subtotal	**$58,652,369**	**$41,506,056**	**$17,146,313**
Total amount raised for Science Annual Fund over 7–year period	7,732,631	3,332,097	4,400,534
Total	**$66,385,000**	**$44,838,153**	**$21,546,847**

> important this demographic segment was. From two entirely different sides of the world we saw starting to emerge a common theme that had not really been talked about before. That, to me, was one of the most interesting parts of this whole planning process—that this has become sort of a united goal of this institution—to develop and to put new emphasis on the involvement of children and family audiences at the Garden.

Another area where a new priority emerged and a consensus developed around it concerned the idea of the new entrance. "A department head in visitor services came up with the idea of a new entrance. Education endorsed it and, in time, it just became *obvious* to us all that we needed a new entrance," Long explained.

One of the attendant weaknesses of the planning process, however, became evident as implementation progressed. As John Rorer noted, "In a process like this, you build the weaknesses of your frontline people into the plan." The native-plant garden offered an example of this phenomenon that was widely discussed. "The curator of that garden didn't convince us that it was a high priority for development," Rorer explained. "That curator did not have a large, expansive vision." Richard Schnall continued, "The person who succeeded them did, but the plan was set by then and it's been tough to work their new ideas in. Opportunities were missed."

This reluctance to alter the plan—to invoke NIP—was largely seen as a strength, however. "We haven't said that we won't change something in the plan—but somebody has really got to make a case for it. The value of the plan is that it gives us the discipline to make those choices," Long remarked.

The Value of Focus and Flexibility

Brian Boom echoed a similar thought: "The plan drove us to focus, to tight and dogged persistence to a set of goals. . . . Yet it also allowed for a degree of flexibility. It kept you from getting too opportunistic without stifling important new ideas."

The situation with molecular systematics provided a case in point. Molecular systematics emerged as a new area of study that was not anticipated in the plan. Brought to the Garden's attention by a board member, it became a new initiative pursued outside of the plan, for two reasons. First, it was in an important area that was complementary to the plan, which had gotten cut at Level Three in the planning process. Second, the interested board member stepped forward to provide additional funding, so that the initiative did not detract financially from pursuit of the plan's priorities.

Another situation that tested the flexibility of the plan and its planners arose in late 1994, when it became apparent that the costs of the primary capital projects included in the master plan would exceed the estimates upon which the plan was based. In the Conservatory, for instance, the use of an expensive deleading technique that added several million dollars to the total cost of the renovation became necessary. The decision was made to increase the budgets of the capital projects deemed to be of most importance, such as the Conservatory; to remove from the current plan the construction of another major project, the new Visitor Center, which was seen to be of lower priority; and to increase the goal for the fund-raising campaign from $165 million to $175 million.

In considering the focus/flexibility tension, Long remarked: "I think a well-crafted plan has to be flexible enough to tolerate change and focused enough to define the course. It should be the baseline against which progress and changing circumstances are evaluated."

WORKING WITH EXTERNAL STAKEHOLDERS

The Garden used the plan to redefine its relationships with a variety of important external stakeholders. Hubbard and Long unveiled the plan to the larger public with much fanfare at Sotheby's Auction House in 1993. In 1995, they organized a more detailed presentation of the Garden's progress, delivered at Christie's Auction House. Rorer described what he saw as the effect of these public discussions:

> At the time it was created, the plan was better than the institution—it was a view of what we *wanted* to be. As people came to understand and accept the plan, they came to embrace the Garden that they saw through the plan, rather than the Garden as it actually was, even though not much had actually been accomplished yet. The net result was that we had almost instant credibility. That credibility facilitated the fund-raising process.

Tim Landi, arriving after the planning process had been completed, recalled his initial reaction to the plan from the perspective of a professional fund-raiser:

> What I found remarkable about the plan was that it was an extremely complicated affair from a programmatic view, and from a development view it was both programmatic and financial—with endowment and earned-revenue portions in addition to the strict philanthropy part. Put that all together and you have a sort of narrative and numbers crashing into each other. . . . I think that justifies and professionalizes a type of fund-raising that has not been done before. . . . We've all seen a lot of plans in our lives, but this one is different. . . . Now, it's "Look at our plan, look at what we've accomplished and let the numbers speak for themselves." Then it becomes a management tool and a fund-raising tool, in a sense. We don't have to invent a list of accomplishments. Instead, it's "Here's the case study—I'll show you the new Conservatory, I'll show you the online computer system. In fact, let's sit in your office and dial into the Library." That's pretty powerful stuff.

Landi noted, in particular, the way that the plan facilitated his ability to manage upward—to keep both Long and the board focused on the agreed-upon priorities. He offered an example:

> There are many times when Gregory might go out and have an idea—he's got more of these than anybody we know—and let's say we are going to see the Mellon Foundation today. I can pull out the plan and say, "No—we don't want them to do that. That will not help us at all! You could give me a million dollars and it doesn't help the institution at all. Remember the plan—we've got three scientists who are supported by soft money and we need to get them three endowments." A corporation might say to us, "We're really interested in *this*." And we could take out our plan and be very specific about what we're trying to accomplish and say, "But look at what you can plug into here instead! Help me work with this so you can be a big player in implementing this plan!"

The plan facilitated the ability to "manage upward" in other ways as well, as Tom Hubbard noted: "The atmosphere of the board has changed dramatically. We have added 25 new members during the last four years. . . . We thought small and it took Gregory to teach us to think big."

Another important constituency that valued the plan was the investment community. In August of 1996, the Garden became the first botanical garden in the United States to go into the bond market, issuing $30 million in bonds. Bond insurers and investment bankers cited three reasons behind their willingness to do the deal at favorable rates: (1) the strength of the plan itself and the Garden's successful track record in implementing it, (2) the strength of Gregory Long's reputation as a fund-raiser, and (3) the Garden's ability to balance its budget from 1989 onward.

Paula Kascel summed up her views on the planning process:

> One of the things that I've come to understand about planning is that it is mostly about giving people the ability to recognize change, and to understand it when it happens to you. The planning process gave people a common vocabulary, a way to talk about change. To talk about the difference—the before and the after. It established a common language here among colleagues who didn't share a common professional language. . . . This is about strategic thinking. We exist in a world right now where people are barraged by issues of the environment. What does it all really mean? How do we make sense of it? Does my individual action matter at all? We believed that people—employees, members, and donors alike—wanted to attach themselves to an extraordinary mission—they want to be attached to a vision and to have a sense of their contribution to something of lasting significance.

Looking Ahead

As the end of the original strategic-planning period, December 31, 1999, drew near, Gregory Long prepared to begin the process anew:

> There is still a lot left to do—all of our priorities have not been realized—infrastructure, endowment, a new visitor-center building—all remain to be accomplished. I'm not worried about a lack of new ideas in the next round—I'm worried about paying for all of the new ideas that we'll come up with and still securing the base.

Endnotes

[1]L. Koebner, "Green House," *Landscape Architecture* 87, 5 (May 1997): 60.
[2]P. Deitz, "A Victorian Gem Restored," *New York Times* (Sunday, April 27, 1997): 8–9.

Case 29

Dollar General Corporation (A) Abridged

In February 1984, Cal Turner, Jr., 44-year-old president of Dollar General Corporation, was finally looking forward to returning to business as usual after the hectic pace of the past few months. The company had been understaffed even before the 1983 acquisition of 280 Hirsch stores from Interco, Inc. Now, just as the conversion of these stores to DG stores was on schedule, Interco was offering to sell DG another chain.

Company Background

Dollar General's roots stretched back to when J.L. Turner, Cal Jr.'s grandfather, quit school at age 11 to help support his widowed mother and three younger siblings living on a small, mortgaged farm. In his mid-20s, J.L. began running a local general store. Later he bought two stores of his own, only to see them fail, and he then went to work for a grocery and dry-goods wholesaler.

As J.L. traveled the small towns of Tennessee and Kentucky during a time "when everybody's belly was flat up against their backbone," a fellow merchant suggested to him that the depression was forcing near-bankrupt retailers to sell their inventories for next to nothing. So J.L. began taking out short-term bank loans of $2,000 or $3,000 and buying complete inventories from hard-up merchants. He would sell the merchandise as quickly as possible and repay the bank, usually within 30 days. Financing was easy because depression-era banks were starved for good loans.

According to Cal Jr., "My grandfather was a keen observer of people and what they needed." On one occasion, J.L. noticed in a cold tobacco barn that tobacco farmers were paid by produce companies once a year by check, not cash. To attract them to his store, Turner had a boy distribute right-hand gloves with a message pinned to them: "If you let us cash your check, we'll give you the left glove free." Cal Jr. described his grandfather as one "who would buy anything he could turn around for a profit." Cal Sr., chairman of DG, added, "My father really was a trader."

A February 2, 1968, article on Cal Sr. in *The Louisville Courier-Journal* noted that, before he had graduated from Scottsville High School, he was already a storekeeper:

> Merchandising is all he ever wanted to do, he admitted. A crack basketball player, he played on the Vanderbilt freshman team before dropping out of college [in 1931] to take a job with a Nashville wholesale firm.

This case was abridged by L. J. Bourgeois III, professor of Business Administration. The original was written by Jim Kennedy and William E. Fulmer.

In 1936, Cal Sr. opened a "bargain store" in Old Hickory, Tennessee. In a short time, he had opened stores in Gainesboro and Manchester, Tennessee, and bought a small store in Scottsville. Three years later he and J.L. sold their stores and established J.L. Turner & Son, Wholesalers, based in Scottsville. Both partners went on the road, and in their first year sold $65,000 worth of goods.

Turner & Son were not picky about what they purchased. Although buying primarily soft goods, they once bought a tomato cannery. "We got into retailing [in 1946]," claimed Cal Jr., "when my Dad got stuck in ladies' panties." After World War II, Cal Sr. found himself trying to sell thousands of dozens of ladies' panties. He had purchased them at $7.50/dozen, but because so much merchandise hit the market after the war, Cal Sr. lowered his price and went from retailer to retailer trying to convince them to buy his stock at $4.50 and average the cost in with their more expensive merchandise. The merchants all told him the same thing: They couldn't buy his cheaper stock until they sold the more expensive stock that they previously had bought from him. "I came home and told my father we were going to have to do something to protect ourselves," related Cal Sr. So they decided to go directly to the consumer by opening a retail store in Albany, Kentucky, and buying 50 percent interests in various bargain stores in the area that bought merchandise from Turner & Son.

By 1955, Turner & Son had 35 self-service dry-goods stores and sales of $2 million. Observing that larger department stores occasionally held dollar-day sales where all items were priced at one dollar or less, Cal Sr. decided that "with low overhead and volume buying, we should be able to have dollar days the year around in smaller towns. That's the way we figured, but, frankly, I was very uncertain about the response when we opened our first dollar store more or less as an experiment at Springfield, Kentucky, in May of 1956." The store sold $8,000 of its $13,800 stock in the first two days. Later a Knoxville store moved $42,000 the first week, a Memphis store sold $1 million during the first ten months, and a Bowling Green store dispensed with half of its stock in the first two days.

The Turners discovered that, as volume increased, more companies became interested in selling merchandise to Turner & Son. According to Cal Sr.:

> When a manufacturer has an item he wants to clean out, we'll buy all he has on hand, if it's quality merchandise, and then try to sell it quickly in our dollar stores. I remember very well that around that time the color pink in men's clothes was the fashion. Well, pretty soon we ran hundreds and hundreds of dozens of pink corduroy pants for a dollar. People driving through these little towns saw nearly every man on the street was wearing pink pants.

After several stores were operating, Cal Sr. said,

> People were chasing down our Dollar General trucks, trying to find out where they could buy the goods. People came looking for us. This is really how the franchise end of our business started. In the beginning . . . we called them associate stores. They would be called Sam's Dollar Store, or whatever the associate wanted to call it, but they would buy the goods from us.

In 1957, with his father's health declining, Cal Sr. was almost single-handedly running a company that had sales of over $5 million from its 14 self-service dry-goods stores (no item above $10) and 15 Dollar General stores (no item above $1). During the 1960s, the associate stores were converted to franchise stores. In return for accepting more centralized control of merchandise allocations and agreeing to use the name "Dollar General" on their stores, associate owners were offered higher discounts on merchandise.

Even after prices in the stores rose above one dollar, DG insisted that pricing be in even dollars, which eliminated the need for adding machines at the register. A small card showing tax amounts for each price level was taped onto the cash register. A store manager plus a couple of clerks could run the stores, and, because of the small-town locations, rent was reasonable.

By 1966, the company consisted of 255 stores with sales of $25.8 million. In 1968, with sales of $40.5 million, the company went public with a 300,000 share offering at $16.50 a share, and changed its name to Dollar General Corporation. A year later, the chain consisted of 345 stores, and stores with the Dollar General sign accounted for 88 percent of revenues.

When DG's stock price rose to over $50 per share and split two for one, a second public offering was undertaken at $33.50 a share. These funds were used in 1973 to finance the acquisition of 70 Silco store sites.

In 1973, the family showed they were in Scottsville to stay by constructing a distribution warehouse and office complex with the help of a Scottsville bond issue. The structure tied together three freestanding warehouses into a total warehouse about the size of five football fields. They also converted the old office building—a former warehouse—into a fixture factory where all the display tables in Dollar General stores were made.

In 1977, Cal Turner, Jr., was named president of a company with 680 stores—418 company owned and 262 franchised—in 22 states. The previous year, sales had reached $109 million, with 80 percent from retail sales and 20 percent from sales to franchisees. Return on sales was 3.9 percent, up from 3.7 percent and 3.1 percent in the prior two years, respectively.

Company Headquarters: Scottsville

Although the place was an unlikely home for a $500 million retailer, Cal Jr. made no apologies for headquartering in Scottsville, Kentucky: "I feel sorry for anybody who doesn't live in Scottsville. The culture of our company largely emanates from Scottsville." Population "4,500 and growing," Scottsville was the county seat for Allen County, deep in southern Kentucky, about an hour north of Nashville and 20 miles from the nearest interstate.

A visitor to the town would probably stay in one of the motels in Bowling Green, Kentucky—some 30 miles away. Driving into town, one's first stop would most likely be at one of the town's two traffic lights. Then a left turn, a drive past establishments like the "Sonic Drive-In Restaurant" and the local "Chainsaw World," and the visitor eventually would arrive at the town square.

The square was typical "Small Town America," with a mixture of old and new buildings, one of which was, of course, a bank. On one corner, attached to an old but well-kept red-brick storefront, was a huge black-and-yellow Dollar General sign. This store—like most Dollar General outlets—was immune to architectural classification. Dollar General didn't care, however, and neither did their customers, which was the important thing to the company.

Although the building was plain, it wasn't uninviting. Neatly stacked bargain items outside the store spoke of better buys inside. The interior was brightly lit, with merchandise displayed in an orderly fashion—shirts stacked on sturdy wooden tables, jeans hung on racks in the center of the store, and overalls somewhere in between. Along the walls of the air-conditioned store were long rows of toothpaste, shampoo, and laundry bleach and assorted other "health and beauty aids." Piles of disposable diapers rose nearly to the ceiling. Every few feet, large red signs proclaimed ground-floor prices: jeans for $8; shirts at two for $7, or $5 apiece; men's leather deck-shoes for $15. Customers could also buy Dollar General motor oil or Dollar General grape soda by the 2-liter bottle. Ninety percent of the goods were priced under $10, and nothing was above $30.

At each table, clothes were stacked smallest to largest, left to right. A browse through the store revealed such labels as Van Heusen and Sedgefield. On hangers, pants were spaced about two finger widths apart to prevent overcrowding. Shoes were in the rear right-hand corner, displayed by size. The "impulse" rack stood by the cash register and contained items like batteries, razor blades, and Goo-Goo cluster candy bars. Clerks smiled and offered to help. Every DG customer had to be greeted, and some came in every day to see if new merchandise had arrived.

About one-half mile west of the square on U.S. Highway 31 was DG's carpentry shop, where the company made most of its own fixtures at a 50 percent cost saving. This building was the previous site of the warehouse and offices of Turner & Son. When the new corporate headquarters opened in 1973, the shop moved here from a converted chicken coop. Inside, 18 workers busily manufactured tables, wall units, checkout counters, auxiliary checkouts, flats, circles for the wooden racks, and end caps for the shoe racks. (Only metal racks and a few specialty containers were purchased.)

Corporate headquarters was located one-half mile past the carpentry shop. A three-story administration building adjoined a huge silver warehouse that connected three smaller warehouses, formerly tobacco barns, by underground passage. Next to the warehouse, on the first level, trailers nestled close by as they were loaded. The three warehouses were on a slight elevation above the main building, which was said to be "down in the holler."

Space was cramped inside the office building—a testament to DG's rapid growth. On the third floor were executive offices and a bullpen where 28 bookkeepers busily fed weekly store results into computer terminals. People chatted and laughed, but all seemed to be working diligently.

Cal Turner, Jr.

After graduating from Vanderbilt University in 1962 with a major in business and economics, and a three-year tour in the navy, Cal Jr. wrestled with whether to go into the ministry or business:

> I decided to do both, by joining Dollar General. I know this is going to sound corny, but I really believe that running this company and practicing the Protestant work ethic are my calling. Dollar General is more to me than a job—it's a mission and a responsibility. There are givers and takers in this world, and I want to make sure I end up on the right side of the fence.

In 1966, he was made executive vice president (at the time there were only two officers: president and secretary/treasurer), and assumed the presidency in 1977.

According to Cal Jr., Dollar General's "people-centeredness and tight-fisted control of overhead" have always been hallmarks of the company, and the real values traced back to J.L. Turner, whose portrait hung on the wall outside the executive suite. In addition, Cal Sr. was the "ultimate entrepreneur," with a "tight, hands-on control of the business. He was a dynamo who worked so hard you didn't dare not work as hard." But, he added, "when he was running the company, the organization chart was a circle." In Cal Jr.'s view, "I was the only one who could undertake the mission of bringing in professional management. [Dad] saw the need to let go of some things, to manage the company differently, but he couldn't have let go of things to just anyone."

Cal Jr. saw his job as primarily one of perpetuating the long history of success his family had experienced in retailing:

> The test of anyone under God is stewardship of their God-given resources. The scripture that says "unto him to whom much is given, much is required" is a driving force for me. I don't consider the stock in my name to be mine. You pass it on.

In 1977, in its largest acquisition to date, the company acquired the bankrupt $30 million (sales) United Dollar Stores (UDS), an Arkansas-based chain of 89 company-owned and 61 franchised stores, as well as 176 Dollar General franchised units operated by Rankin Co. of Columbia, Mississippi. According to Cal Jr., the $6 million purchase of UDS was made in part because of potential liquidation values. In the first 11 days of liquidation sales, the company grossed more than $3 million. Moreover, Dollar General acquired the UDS warehouse in Dumas, Arkansas, which provided the company a second warehouse of 350,000 square feet. Obtaining the warehouse made the repurchase of the Rankin franchises particularly attractive. Not only could the warehouse be operated rent-free until 1980, when the company would buy it for $1.4 million, but the Dumas warehouse, because of its location, would be able to serve the Rankin stores more efficiently than had been possible in the past. Management also hoped that the second warehouse would allow the company to achieve its goal of reducing store delivery times from every three and one-half weeks to every two weeks. The acquisition took longer to digest than the Turners had hoped, however—two years—because almost three-fourths of the stores had been unprofitable at the time of purchase.

After the acquisition, Cal Jr. quickly decided that the company was growing too rapidly to permit "seat-of-the-pants" management. He therefore hired several experienced managers, including Ed Burke, manager of operating analysis of National Industries, as vice president of finance, and Bobby Carpenter, marketing officer and assistant general counsel for First American Corporation, as general counsel and vice president of administration, and he promoted his younger brother Steve Turner to executive vice president of merchandise.

Perhaps the biggest change wrought by Cal Jr. was the introduction of formal strategic planning. He had become convinced of the need for it at a management conference in the late 1970s. Dollar General did not even have a budget, so Cal Jr. was unsure what his father's reaction to his decision would be:

> I went straight into my father's office, shut the door, and said, "Dad, we have a decision. Do we start doing this now or wait until you die?" I didn't know if he'd

like the idea or not, but he looked at me and said, "Would you tell me what it is?" Then he said, "Not only do I support you, I think it's the only way to go. I can't do it, but I'm behind you."

Soon, Dollar General had a strategic plan and better training for employees—partly because of Cal Jr.'s own ideas and partly because of his willingness to go outside the company for managerial talent when necessary. According to Cal Jr., "I'm a generalist. I've been exposed to the entrepreneurial feel of my Dad, but I see the trap of it, and the need for systems and structure. Yet I have a strong desire to keep it simple."

Recent Company History

During the early 1980s, DG's strategy was gradual growth in existing regions:

Year	Beginning of Year	Stores Opened	Stores Closed	Stores at End of Year
1979	632	88	32	688
1980	688	65	31	722
1981	722	79	40	761
1982	761	98	36	823

Cal Jr. explained that there was plenty of room for geographical expansion doing just what the company had been doing; all of Pennsylvania, for example, had only 21 Dollar General stores.

The recession of that period seemed to work to the company's advantage. When other retailers were struggling, DG was, according to Cal Jr., "grinning like a mule eating briars." Simply put, recession increases demand for our stores. People out there are looking for bargains." Steve Turner believed that recessions created "opportunities to buy" and referred to hundreds of thousands of children's apparel batches purchased at 50 percent off and dress shirts at 10 percent of retail prices.

In 1983, Interco, a St. Louis–based manufacturing and retailing conglomerate, offered to sell its poorly performing P.N. Hirsch chain (annualized 1983 sales of $135 million) to Dollar General. Hirsch consisted of about 280 stores in 11 midwestern and southern states (70 in towns with DG stores), plus a modern but union-represented warehouse. Although the acquisition did not fit with current strategy, and DG had no unions, Cal Jr. had been interested: "We just use a good ol' common-sense approach, [but] we also believe in breaking the rules for the right reason."

He had been concerned that the average Hirsch unit, 7,700 square feet, had sales per square foot of only $50, compared with $75 for Dollar General. To learn more about Hirsch's performance, at Hirsch management's suggestion, he had Dollar General employees posing as insurance inspectors visit 90 percent of Hirsch's stores. "That's a great way to observe employees at work when they're not putting on airs," he said. "Who wants to impress an insurance man, for crying out loud?"

"What we really wanted," he explained, "was Interco's Eagle chain down in Florida." Nevertheless, he found the whole Hirsch deal attractive, because it increased the number of stores by 30 percent and the total selling space by 50 percent. "With [Hirsch]...we obtained favorable leases in locations...that are often better than those of our own stores," he noted. "The $50 million purchase represents about three years of normal store growth for us." The acquisition also allowed additional efficiencies from the company's warehouses. Both the Dumas and Scottsville facilities added second shifts, and the Scottsville warehouse was expanded by 100,000 square feet to 430,000 square feet. The company also added 86 new trailers and 17 tractors to its fleet to help service all the new stores.

Dollar General wasted no time in converting the Hirsch units. By sending large numbers of DG employees and managers to the store locations and working long, hard hours, nearly 100 of the 250 stores were converted from November 1983 to March 1984, and the rest were expected to be opened in time for the back-to-school selling season. The Hirsch acquisition and regular growth resulted in a net gain of 304 stores—338 new stores and 34 closed—for 1983. (See Exhibit 1 for locations of DG stores in 1983.)

EXHIBIT 1

Location of Company-Owned Dollar General Stores (as of December 31, 1983)

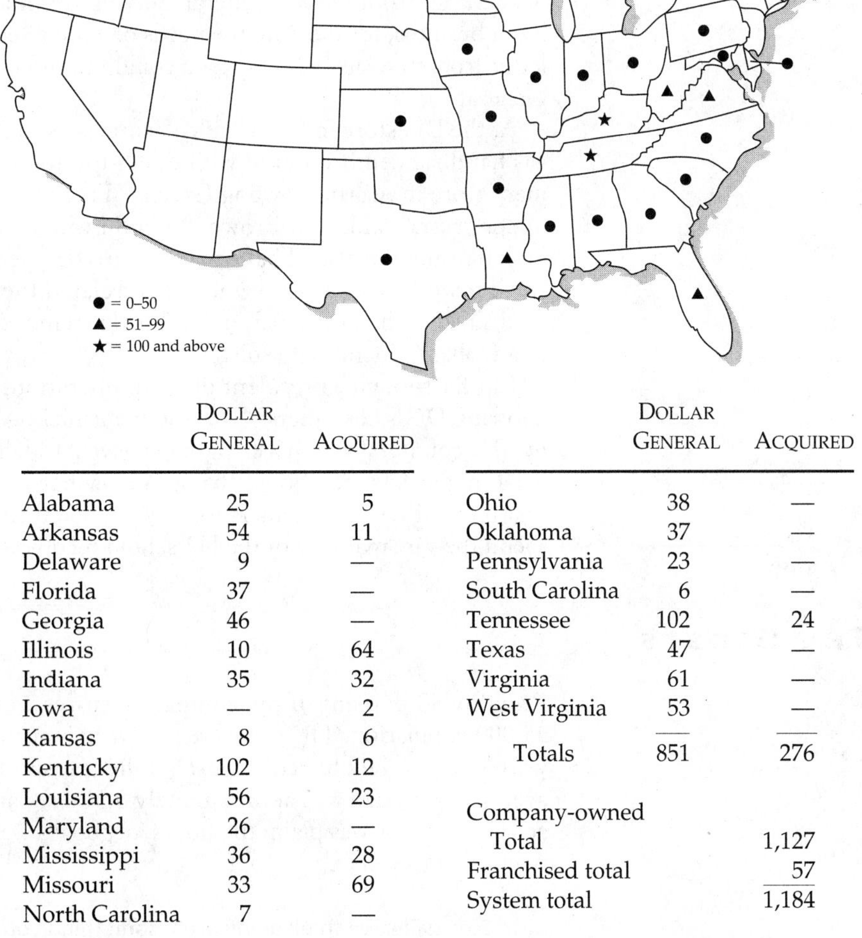

	Dollar General	Acquired		Dollar General	Acquired
Alabama	25	5	Ohio	38	—
Arkansas	54	11	Oklahoma	37	—
Delaware	9	—	Pennsylvania	23	—
Florida	37	—	South Carolina	6	—
Georgia	46	—	Tennessee	102	24
Illinois	10	64	Texas	47	—
Indiana	35	32	Virginia	61	—
Iowa	—	2	West Virginia	53	—
Kansas	8	6	Totals	851	276
Kentucky	102	12			
Louisiana	56	23	Company-owned Total		1,127
Maryland	26	—	Franchised total		57
Mississippi	36	28	System total		1,184
Missouri	33	69			
North Carolina	7	—			

In the wake of the Hirsch acquisition, Dollar General hired Jim Barton, 26-year veteran and former regional director of retail operations for Ben Franklin Stores, as vice president of retail operations, and added two outside directors: the former president of Kmart and the former president of the American Management Association.

Current Operations

By the start of 1984, Dollar General had 5,500 employees (3,500 full-time), annual sales of $350 million, and 2,200 shareholders (45 percent of the common stock was held by the Turner family). See Exhibit 2 for a ten-year summary of financial operations of the company and Exhibits 3 and 4 for current consolidated income statements and balance sheets, respectively.

The company's stated mission was "to serve, better than anyone else does, our customer's needs for quality, basic merchandise at the lowest everyday price." In Cal Jr.'s words, "We are renegade retailers. We operate in markets other retailers don't want. We occupy buildings other retailers don't want. We buy merchandise other retailers don't want. And we serve customers other retailers don't want." He was proud of such things as a DG television ad that showed a little boy, wearing jeans and a jacket, getting on the school bus. His "whole outfit from the skin out cost $22.52," all from Dollar General. Serving this market was, to Turner, "more than just a business; it's meeting the needs of a huge segment of the population. I have a letter from one lady who says she couldn't send her child to school without Dollar General."

At the DG store in Russellville, Kentucky, store manager Melba Brown sold canvas handbags embroidered with ducks for about $2, $5 less than a large department store in nearby Bowling Green. "These kids can carry handbags just like the upper crust," said Mrs. Brown. "A child who comes from a poor family wants to look like anyone else. That peer pressure they feel is so enormous, especially in a small town." In a similar vein, Cal Jr. related the story of a lady whose son loved Izod shirts. "She buys a pair of Izod socks, removes the alligator, and sews them on to a Dollar General polo shirt."

Jim Barton, vice president of retail operations, emphasized the importance of knowing DG's customers: "We know our niche—the low-to-middle-income family. [Discounters] who have upgraded have left their customers behind. [This leaves us] a bigger base to choose from. We try hard not to upgrade." He pointed out that most of DG's customers were women and cited statistics that showed women spend the vast majority of the household income.

The Stores

Roughly 80 percent of the company's stores were located in towns of less than 25,000 population. The rest were mainly in inner-city urban areas where customers were likely to be blue collar, use public transportation, and live downtown. The average store size was approximately 5,500 square feet—about one-eighth of an acre. The decor was plain: tile floors, pegboard walls, and bright fluorescent lights. According to Cal Jr.,

> In Scottsville, we think ambience is something you ride to the hospital in. It's hard to convince the customer he's getting a bargain if he sees carpeting and a boutique

EXHIBIT 2

Dollar General Corporation Financial Information, 1974–1984 (dollars in thousands except per-share amounts)

	1974	1975	1976	1977	1978	1979	1980	1981	1982	1983	1984
Net sales	$ 74,201	$ 87,844	$109,132	$129,559	$161,694	$177,774	$209,753	$245,453	$290,069	$346,655	$480,514
Net income	2,317	3,261	4,223	4,805	4,881	6,259	5,852	7,208	11,333	15,126	20,598
Net income per share	$.15	$.21	$.27	$.31	$.31	$.40	$.37	$.46	$.73	$.97	$1.32
Cash dividends per share	—	$.01	$.02	$.03	$.04	$.05	$.07	$.11	$.13	$.16	$ .20
Weighted-average shares outstanding (000)	15,462	15,744	15,720	15,720	15,721	15,721	15,721	15,699	15,620	15,628	15,654
Return on average assets (%)	6.35	8.12	9.46	8.87	7.32	8.35	7.26	8.29	11.56	11.61	12.55
Return on average equity (%)	9.90	12.88	14.70	14.64	13.15	14.92	12.44	13.87	19.14	21.54	24.16
Total assets	38,455	41,872	47,165	60,863	72,439	77,402	83,905	89,971	106,223	154,299	173,963
Stockholders' equity	23,854	26,777	30,660	34,986	39,233	44,677	49,375	54,580	63,825	76,582	93,916
Long-term obligations	4,260	3,383	2,563	6,938	16,964	15,574	14,428	13,276	12,118	35,720	26,950
Company-owned stores	402	410	418	761	632	688	722	761	823	1,127	1,080
Franchised stores	242	246	262	90	101	59	63	65	60	57	48
Inventory turnover	3.0	3.1	3.2	2.6	3.0	2.9	3.2	3.6	3.5	3.0	3.4

SOURCE: 1984 Annual Report.

EXHIBIT 3

Dollar General Corporation Consolidated Statement of Income, 1982–1984 (in thousands except per-share amounts)

	1984	Percentage of Net Sales	1983	Percentage of Net Sales	1982	Percentage of Net Sales
Net sales	$480,514	100.0	$346,655	100.0	$290,069	$100.0
Cost of goods sold	337,029	70.1	244,094	70.4	205,837	71.0
Gross profit	143,485	29.9	102,561	29.6	84,232	29.0
Operating expenses	99,341	20.7	71,077	20.5	60,834	21.0
Operating profit	44,144	9.2	31,484	9.1	23,398	8.0
Interest expense	4,146	.9	1,808	.5	1,665	.5
Income before taxes on income	39,998	8.3	29,676	8.6	21,733	7.5
Provision for taxes on income	19,400	4.0	14,550	4.2	10,400	3.6
Net income	$20,598	4.3	$ 15,126	4.4	$ 11,333	3.9
Net income per share	$1.32		$0.97		$0.73	
Weighted-average number of shares outstanding	15,654		15,628		15,620	

SOURCE: 1984 Annual Report.

EXHIBIT 4

Dollar General Corporation Consolidated Balance Sheet, 1983–1984 (in thousands)

ASSETS	1984	1983
Current assets:		
Cash and cash equivalents	$ 4,681	$ 15,863
Merchandise inventories	142,264	113,903
Other current assets	2,530	5,430
Total current assets	149,475	135,196
Property and equipment, at cost:		
Land	93	93
Buildings	5,319	3,834
Furniture and fixtures	24,772	20,767
	30,184	24,694
Less accumulated depreciation	11,675	9,368
	18,509	15,326
Other assets	5,979	3,777
Total assets	$173,963	$154,299
LIABILITIES AND STOCKHOLDERS' EQUITY		
Current liabilities:		
Current portion of long-term obligations	$ 875	$ 5,346
Accounts payable, trade	33,040	18,996
Accrued expenses	9,610	8,001
Income taxes	5,760	7,858
Total current liabilities	49,285	40,219
Long-term obligations	26,950	35,720
Deferred income taxes	3,812	1,778
Total liabilities	$80,047	$77,717
Stockholders' equity:		
Common stock, shares outstanding 1984—15,651 1983—15,655	9,226	9,226
Additional paid-in capital	22,250	22,236
Retained earnings	64,760	47,293
	96,236	78,755
Less treasury stock, at cost	2,320	2,173
Total stockholders' equity	93,916	76,582
Total liabilities and stockholders' equity	$173,963	$154,299

setting. We deliberately avoid frou-frou. Besides, you can cover a lot of sins with some paint and some paneling.

Dollar General didn't buy real estate; they leased it for $1.70 per square foot on the average. The company generally preferred downtown locations that other stores had abandoned long ago in favor of suburban malls (where rents typically were $14–$35 per square foot). On the other hand, an increasing number of Dollar General stores—currently 50 percent—were located in suburban "strip" malls. (Nationally, such locations rented for $4–$15 a square foot.) The stores were open six days a week, at least one evening, and, where possible, on Sundays.

About 35 percent of the merchandise for a typical store was ordered at the store manager's discretion from the "want list"—made up from a corporate checklist of merchandise available for sale. The remaining 65 percent came from specials and other merchandise dictated by headquarters. All merchandise was divided into four categories: soft goods, such as clothes (47 percent); health and beauty aids (21 percent); hardware, such as motor oil (24 percent); and shoes (8 percent).

Pricing was simplified because many of the items had "price points," which meant they would always sell for the same price, or never above a given price (for example, jeans never sold for more than $10). The stores did not accept credit cards, only cash or a personal check, and there was no layaway program.

Ninety percent of store managers were women. Barton claimed that the key in small towns was "local people," and it just so happened that there were many more women than men to choose from. According to another manager, women "do a better job of minding the store. Men have something in their hormones that makes them want to go out and see what's happening over at the barber shop or post office." A store manager could expect to earn about $12,000 plus a bonus of 10 percent pretax profits, which would typically be a second income for a "working wife" in a small town, according to Barton. Medical benefits were available to the entire family of the store manager; full-time clerks paid $5–$10 a week for the coverage.

A major task for each manager was to hire a chief clerk and one or two other clerks and train them. Also, at the end of each week, the manager paid each clerk in cash and deposited the remaining money in the bank.

The DG People

Dollar General's 1,080 stores were divided into 15 areas and 84 districts. Gene Cartwright, director of recruiting/training, was charged with the task of developing the district managers (DMs) and store managers (SMs). The entry level for college graduates was usually district manager, although most DM slots were filled by promotion of successful store managers. In general, the company preferred to recruit DMs at small, regional colleges and universities like Western Kentucky in Bowling Green.

In recruiting DMs, Cartwright looked for "commitment to excellence" and the "willingness to work hard"—qualities Cartwright called "want to." Cartwright also looked for a "people orientation." "We're a people business. Our two most important assets are people and merchandise, in that order."

In reflecting on his involvement in recruiting, Cal Jr. observed,

> I want a leader who has our style, but I don't want a clone. When everybody wears the same suit, you don't have a company, you have an army. I want people who have skill and expertise, but my discussion is always of values: What are your goals? How will you reach them? Tell me about your kids, and your dad. Being a manager is being both a teacher and a parent in a different setting.

Linda Nelson was typical of the people DG liked to hire:

> On March 11, 1982, Dollar General had their grand opening in Portageville, Missouri. I worked at Fred's (a discount store) across the street as a sales clerk. At 8:30 A.M. people were lined up in front of the store waiting for the doors to open. We had very little business that day, so at lunch time I went across the street to see what Dollar General had to offer. Once I got inside, I was surprised at the low prices. I liked what I saw. The merchandise and the prices were great.

Four months later, she became a clerk at DG, and, in less than a year, she was promoted to store manager. In her first year as manager, the store recorded sales of $252,883 and profits of $8,545.90; one year later, sales were $285,564 and profits $19,185.12. Nelson, like many employees, did most of her shopping at DG, even though employees received no discounts.

Although selection of people was usually by "gut instinct," the company had moved toward such techniques as written profiles designed to measure "intrinsic, extrinsic, and systemic values." Consultants hired by Dollar General to interpret test results had explained that the test showed how honest and hard working a person was and what made him or her "tick."

Jim Barton cited several reasons for his decision to join the company, the main one being the "phenomenal growth" of Dollar General. Having come from a retailer that "was opening new stores, but closing even more of them," Barton had experienced first-hand the atrophy that can accompany stagnation. Barton also noted that Dollar General had been remarkably consistent in executing its strategy of delivering the basics at the lowest price, and he was enthusiastic about both the management team and the participative style of Cal Jr.:

> Dollar General is a company, but it also is a feeling. There is a sense of excitement. The staff works six days a week; it's a work-oriented place. We all have titles, but we don't talk about them. We don't wear our titles—we're on a first-name basis.

Training

Cal Turner, Jr., described the old training system for store managers as follows:

> We'd go into a new town, hire some local help, and spend several days opening a new store. After the store was stocked, we'd look over the local crew and pick the one who seemed the brightest and most hard working. We'd give her the keys, show her how to fill out a deposit slip, and in a couple of weeks a truck would come to bring some more merchandise.

The results were not always as the company hoped. Some stores were energetically and enthusiastically managed—neat and clean. In another you could find a manager with "a cigarette hanging out of the side of her mouth." The store would be dirty, and customers could be in there 15 minutes before a clerk would even know they were there.

Consequently, the company began training store managers in all the fine points of successfully running a Dollar General store. The training included instruction on ordering, stocking, filling out the operations reports, and dealing effectively with customers. The DG wisdom was summarized in the operations manual—a comprehensive looseleaf notebook that told managers where to display merchandise, how to rotate stock, when to post advertisements, how to dress, and always to greet customers—even if only to say hello. Every employee, including clerks, was required to read the manual and agree to live within its provisions. Although each store was different, procedures were standardized as much as possible. Cartwright explained, "We want everybody to be singing out of the same hymn book."

As part of this effort, in 1984 the company began holding one-day regional sales manager meetings. Small groups of store managers would be exposed to the latest management techniques and given the chance to air their complaints and to cavort with fellow employees. In 1985, at least 500 managers would be so trained. Jim Barton attended all of the meetings, and Cal Jr. either opened or closed them. He liked to "dare employees to reach their highest capabilities" and to challenge them to "be a bigger person than you are now." Several participants had written the company to comment on the usefulness of the meetings.

Training for new district managers involved a six-month program (although only three months were conducted at any one time) that included stocking and displaying merchandise, and becoming intimately familiar with DG's "way of doing things." Trainees also practiced opening and closing stores at the full-size, "mock" store in Scottsville, and spent substantial time in the field gaining hands-on experience with a veteran store manager in a district different from the one they would run.

Information Systems

Operational reporting from the stores filled 75 mailbags each week. These simple forms, prepared by hand by each store manager, essentially totaled the accompanying cash-register tapes into a net sales figure and summarized weekly expenses. After the forms were received in Scottsville, 28 bookkeepers computerized the data. Each bookkeeper was responsible for about 35–40 stores. The information was consolidated into operations reports by district, area, and store, returned to the appropriate managers, and sent to Barton. Turnaround was roughly one week.

When Barton received area reports, the first figures he checked were weekly sales, weekly sales versus the budget, and year-to-date sales versus the budget. He also checked salary figures particularly closely if a store was in trouble.

In addition to the standard reports, a "watch list" showing the stores that were performing below expectations was also prepared. Most of the stores on the watch list were new stores that were not as profitable as expected. Stores generally moved into the black within 30 to 60 days, but if the store was still losing money after six to nine months, the company began to reevaluate the decision to be in that market. Although it took four days to open a store, it took only one to close a "sour store." According to Cal Jr., "We're going to close a store that doesn't work. Shucks, that's just simple redeployment of assets."

Barton liked to stick with a store as long as possible: "Quite often the problems are correctable; poor promotion or even a bad attitude on the part of clerks can reduce a store's sales." To check out the situation, Barton used "designated shoppers," who were unknown to store personnel, to report on the attitude displayed to customers.

Barton spent approximately half of each week visiting stores, occasionally accompanied by Cal Sr. After strolling around the store and observing employees at work, Barton would introduce himself to the entire crew. He encouraged employees to air their complaints and was not reluctant to hand out compliments if appropriate. He would discuss matters privately with the store manager and leave it to him or her to inform the crew and implement corrective action. He preferred to give the manager a chance to talk and then cover any negative findings discreetly and positively, in what he called "corrective conversation."

Barton was quick to point to a six-inch stack of suggestions on his desk as evidence that the company listened to ideas from store personnel. "We're always challenging the store managers for new ideas," he said.

In 1984, Dollar General started a companywide newsletter that contained a column from the president, articles about how to improve store operations, special-interest articles about employees—both senior managers and clerks—and letters from employees or retirees.

The Merchandise

According to Cal Jr., "The fun part of this business is haggling. First you haggle on the price. Then you haggle on the terms." He added, "A Turner will buy just about anything if it's at half-price.... And my grandfather always said, 'If it's bought right, it's half sold.'" Although there was a staff of eight buyers, headed by Steve Turner, Cal Sr. still enjoyed trading. "He's so smooth on the phone," said Cal Jr., "that you get to liking him so much that before long you're giving him a better deal." Cal Jr. was convinced that many sellers came to Scottsville because of the long-established relationships built by his father. "Salesmen can't buy us lunch," he emphasized. "We buy. We're also very loyal. If you're selling to us, we'll stick with you unless you get out of line."

According to Cal Jr., "Too many people think we just sell junk. We're in the business of giving value to our customers. We cut our teeth in Kentucky and Tennessee towns serving the farmer—a very demanding consumer who has to have something that holds up well." The majority of Dollar General's soft goods were irregulars (IRs) or closeouts (a garment that the manufacturer had overproduced or was discontinuing). An irregular garment, usually 3 percent of a manufacturer's production, was one that for some reason failed to meet the standards of a manufacturer, but one often could not tell the difference between IRs and normal merchandise. For example, as a highly successful ploy to get analysts to come to Dollar General's financial presentations, Cal Jr. used to give away free IR golf shirts to all attendees—just to show how good irregulars could be. Cal Jr. occasionally bought his own clothes at DG. After describing a sports jacket he bought for 30 percent of its original price, Steve Turner commented, "It was a great buy, but we made a bundle." (The average cost for the jackets was approximately 11 percent of the original retail price.)

Twenty manufacturers, under contract to DG, sent in a steady stream of irregulars in almost every clothing category. The company agreed to buy all of the goods a manufacturer wanted to ship, so long as they met Dollar General's standards. In return, the prenegotiated prices usually ran 40–50 percent less than normal. No single supplier accounted for more than 6 percent of total purchases. Labels were unimportant, because the company never advertised brand names, even when they were available in the store.

Closeouts provided about one-third of the soft goods sold by Dollar General. For example, DG had recently bought 15,000 dozen pairs of discontinued girls knee-high socks for 23 cents a pair and sold them for 75 cents a pair. Dollar General would not buy closeouts or fashion errors under contract, because it preferred to negotiate each deal separately.

DG drove a hard bargain. In the words of one salesman who had dealt with the company for a long time:

> My advice for those wanting to sell to Dollar General: If the price isn't lower than low, don't even go! I had 700,000 pairs of panties that had a retail price of $4.50 each and a wholesale cost of $25.08 per dozen. Mr. Turner Sr. offered me $5.50 per dozen, claiming he only charges 75 cents per pair in his stores no matter how good they are! Ultimately, I accepted his offer.
>
> I enjoy sitting in the waiting room and observing first-time salesmen come out of the office. Often their faces are pale. They've just realized that they have been picked clean of everything but the fillings in their teeth, and now they have to go back to New York and explain why they gave the merchandise away.

But fairness was important. According to Cal Jr., "My father and grandfather always preached that you can't deny the seller his profit, that you have to treat him fairly."

If an item would sell, the company was willing to buy whatever was available. "If somebody will let us help set the price, we'll let them help set the quantity," said Cal Sr.

Even though closeouts and IRs made up most of the soft-goods inventory, the company did not hesitate to complete certain irregular lines by buying "the gaps" at full price or by purchasing "fill-ins" Thus a shipment of Rustler jeans IRs with three sizes missing would be rounded out by jeans bought at full price. Fill-ins were one of two things: staple merchandise such as socks or underwear that were often unavailable as closeouts or IRs, or seasonal garments such as winter jackets. While most items of this type were purchased through importers, the company had purchasing agreements with many domestic manufacturers as well.

The company also did not ignore fashion trends and had opened a buying office in New York City in late 1983. "There's no point in buying something unless the consumer wants it," said Cal Jr. "[And] clothing no longer is simply something to cover one's nakedness. Even people living on welfare buy according to fashion."

To buy health and beauty aids, DG usually waited for manufacturers' price promotions and then bought as much as possible at the promotion price—whether they needed it or not. Also, for instance, if a shampoo maker changed the package or formula, truckloads of the old product could be expected to arrive at the DG warehouses.

Not every purchase was successful. The August 19, 1980, issue of *The Wall Street Journal* reported:

> Steve Turner thought he had pulled off a real coup last Christmas, buying 100,000 silk scarves for 85 cents apiece. "Not much happened," he says, "so I figured . . . people didn't realize what a good buy this was." So, he says, "in a brilliant move," he raised the price to $8.50 from $2.00. The result? "Still nothing," he says. "Now they're selling for $1.00, and I hope I'm getting down to about 50,000. Maybe we tried to sell a Rolls Royce out of a Chevy dealership."

Dollar General's Future

As Cal Jr. reflected on the future of the company and his role, he thought that the company would have to continue its emphasis on "tight-fisted control" of overhead.

And he thought they would have to communicate better, which meant "letting employees know what's expected of who by whom." He added:

> The workplace is the primary instiller of values in a person and can help meet a person's need for self-esteem. Most people spend more time at work than they do with their families, their church, or themselves. All gripes boil down to "I don't understand my mission; what's expected of me?"

Cal Jr. believed that hard work was important "not just because the extra productivity will make more money for the company." He felt that a lot of work and responsibility increased employee commitment: "We'd rather someone have too much to do than not enough." He recognized the inherent difficulties in motivating people and providing a challenging and rewarding work environment, while at the same time being a penny-pincher about expenses. "It's tough," he admitted. "The question is 'How do you be Scrooge and Santa Claus at the same time?'"

He believed that he had brought down considerable hardship on his employees by asking them to convert all 280 Hirsch stores to Dollar Generals in an eight-month period: "People will walk off a cliff for a company, but our people walked through the fire of hell."

Although he thought the stores were a good buy, the company's strategy was to build sales in existing stores, not by acquisition: "There's really too much growth in our existing markets to worry too much about acquisition. Besides, we don't need the ego trip of being a national retailer." (Exhibit 5 gives information on recent industry performance. Exhibit 6 presents information on DG's three major competitors.)

Cal Jr. discounted any serious competitive threats to Dollar General: "We're our own worst enemy. In the past, we've had poor training, poor delivery, and an absence of systems. We've executed poorly." He was optimistic that Dollar General "could recognize and correct its mistakes," however, and still maintain its "unique ability to laugh at itself."

EXHIBIT 5

Industry Data

OPERATING RESULTS OF SELF-SERVICE DISCOUNT DEPARTMENT STORES (PERCENTAGE OF SALES)

ITEM	26 Chains 1981–1982	28 Chains 1982–1983	Range for Middle 50%
Gross margin	28.70	28.26	26.67 – 31.48
Leased department income	.45	.41	.00 – .64
Gross income	29.14	28.87	27.06 – 32.04
Total expense	24.88	24.74	23.64 – 29.83
Net operating profit	4.26	3.93	1.32 – 5.03
Other income or deduct	−1.05	−.68	−1.50 – .45
Earnings before income taxes	3.21	2.93	1.14 – 4.58
Federal and state income taxes	1.45	1.28	.31 – 1.87
Net earnings after taxes	1.76	1.66	.58 – 2.50

(continued)

SOURCE: Annual Mass Retailing Institute. All data have been revised.

EXHIBIT 5 (CONTINUED)

Industry Data

DISCOUNT STORE SALES BY CATEGORY

	Volume (bil. $)	Sales per Store (mil. $)	Annual Sales per sq. ft. ($)	Annual Turns	Initial Markup (%)	Gross Margin (%)
Women's apparel	13.3	1,644	164	5.2	46.5	36.0
Men's and boys' apparel	7.4	915	120	3.2	45.1	35.3
Housewares	5.9	729	127	3.4	40.0	31.5
Health and beauty aids	5.2	642	282	4.2	25.4	18.8
Automotive	4.8	593	259	3.2	36.6	28.3
Hardware	4.5	556	173	2.3	41.3	32.9
Sporting goods	3.4	420	168	2.5	38.0	28.2

SOURCE: Standard & Poor's Industry Surveys.

EXHIBIT 6

Competitor Financial Data, 1981–1984

KMART

	1981	1982	1983	1984
Sales (millions)	$16,527	$16,772	$18,598	$21,096
Net income (millions)	220.3	261.8	492.3	499.1
Inventory turnover	5.3	5.1	5.2	4.6
Long-term debt (millions)	2,167.0	2,420.4	2,533.5	2,887.0
Net worth (millions)	2,455.6	2,601.3	2,940.1	3,233.8
Payout ratio	53%	47%	27%	30%
Shares outstanding (millions)	123.98	124.49	125.91	125.02
ROE	9.0	10.0	16.7	15.4
ROS	1.36	1.56	2.65	2.36

Kmart was the nation's second-largest retail chain with 2,174 stores in 48 states, the District of Columbia, Puerto Rico, and Canada, plus 15 Builders Square home improvement stores, 898 Walden bookstores, 52 Designer Depot off-price retail outlets, 178 Jupiter and Kresge stores, and 155 cafeterias. Some of the more recent projects had met with mixed results. For example, the off-price chain Designer Depot was losing money, the video pizza parlors were closed after 18 months, and the jury was still out on the company's attempt to open financial centers in 110 of its stores. In addition to acquisitions, Kmart was trying to increase sales from its existing stores by renovating store appearance, adding specialty departments, and upgrading label merchandise—especially apparel. By the end of 1984, 435 stores had received complete renovation to "the Kmart of the 1980s" and were showing 50 percent volume gains. The company planned to have all stores finished by 1986.

(continued)

SOURCES: *Value Line; Fortune*, May 27, 1985; *Business Week*, October 14, 1985; *Forbes*, January 28, 1985; *Dun's Business Month*, March 1985.

EXHIBIT 6 (CONTINUED)

Competitor Financial Data, 1981–1984

WAL-MART

	1981	1982	1983	1984
Sales (millions)	$2,455.0	$3,376.3	$4,666.9	$6,400.9
Net income (millions)	82.8	124.1	196.2	270.8
Inventory turnover	5.0	6.1	6.4	5.8
Long-term debt	258.8	329.1	380.8	491.1
Net worth	331.4	495.0	743.9	990.6
Payout ratio	10%	10%	10%	11%
Shares outstanding (millions)	129.68	134.42	139.92	140.22
ROE	25.0	25.1	26.4	27.3
ROS	3.37	3.68	4.20	4.23

Started in 1962, Wal-Mart had opened 800 stores in 20 southeastern and south-central states, most within a 450-mile radius of corporate offices in Bentonville, Arkansas, or one of five other regional warehouses. Most Wal-Mart stores were located in towns of 10,000–15,000 people and were comparable in size to Kmart, averaging about 40,000 square feet. Each store had 36 merchandise departments that marketed 60,000 items in both hard- and soft-goods categories, although hard goods made up about 65 percent of the merchandise. Most goods were name brand. The store boasted convenience with plenty of parking, speedy checkout lines, layaway, and credit. All stores were fully computerized with registers that fed information to the company's central computer. Same-store sales growth had averaged 12–15 percent in the past few years, and new stores were being opened at a rate of approximately 115 a year. Wal-Mart was expected to continue growing much faster than the projected 2.4 percent rate for department stores and chains. Recently the company had begun upscaling somewhat in order to compete more effectively with Kmart. In addition, it had recently started a wholesale chain, Sam's Wholesale Club.

FAMILY DOLLAR

	1981	1982	1983	1984
Sales (millions)	$181.7	$207.4	$264.4	$340.9
Net income (millions)	9.1	10.7	15.7	23.6
Inventory turnover	4.1	4.0	4.3	4.9
Long-term debt	0	0	0	0
Net worth	46.4	55.0	70.0	91.0
Payout ratio	21%	21%	17%	14%
Shares outstanding (millions)	28.2	28.24	23.53	28.64
ROE	19.6	19.5	27.4	25.9
ROS	5.01	5.16	5.94	6.92

This Charlotte, North Carolina, company, started in 1960, operated 889 stores in 20 states. Located primarily in shopping malls in small southeastern towns of fewer than 15,000 people, Family Dollar also had stores in metropolitan

(continued)

EXHIBIT 6 (CONTINUED)

Competitor Financial Data, 1981–1984

areas, such as Atlanta, New Orleans, and Pittsburgh. The heaviest concentrations were in North and South Carolina, but Family Dollar had recently spread to Texas, Missouri, Indiana, and New Jersey and hoped to go nationwide with 1,000 stores in 1985. All growth was financed through internal earnings, and Family Dollar carried no long-term debt. It had only closed 22 stores over the past 15 years. Most of Family Dollar's growth came from new stores, as same-store sales growth hovered in the 7–9 percent range. The stores offered a wide variety of goods, and 95 percent of the prices were less than $17, with the average shopper spending $6 on each trip. The average store was a leased, 6,000–8,000-square-foot "cookie cutter" that could be stocked in 12 days. The stores were self-service, and all purchases were in cash. Name-brand merchandise accounted for about 30 percent of the total, with the balance in unlabeled or manufacturer-label products. Irregulars and seconds accounted for less than 4 percent of store merchandise. Sales were divided equally between soft and hard goods, including toys, toothpaste, bleach, and motor oil. Most stores were run by women, who earned $15,000 to $20,000 a year for a workweek that often reached 70 hours. The average store grossed about $500,000 to $550,000 a year, with a few grossing more than $1,000,000. Headquarters, with 12 buyers who worked with more than 1,000 suppliers, forced about 60 percent of the goods on each store, but even items left to the store manager's discretion were carefully limited by management. In addition, headquarters set all prices and markdowns and shipped from a single warehouse. Computerized shelf labels indicated the maximum and minimum that was to be stocked at any one time. Theft, or "shrinkage," was kept at 1.5 percent, comparable with the industry. Inventories were counted at 5 percent of the stores each week, and lie-detector tests were administered annually to every employee.

For the future, Cal Jr. thought he personally should

> place a great deal of emphasis on doing those things that are unique to me—planning and people. I'm responsible for determining the direction of the company, articulating it to the constituents, and preserving the culture. As I have to delegate more, I find I hold on to the people-intensive activities—communicating, recruiting, etc. I also need to remember that my name is Turner and get into the warehouse and stores. No one wants to work for a bureaucracy.

Cal Jr. also hoped to be able to devote more time to some of his personal interests, like preaching an occasional sermon at the Scottsville Methodist Church, taking a more active role in his church's music program ("a lot of little ol' ladies want me to sing at their funerals"), getting his golf and tennis games back in shape, and maybe even spending some time with his family on the ski slopes.

THE EAGLE PROPOSAL

Such was the situation when, in February 1984, the chief executive officer and the executive vice president of Interco arrived in Scottsville on short notice, ostensibly for a friendly visit and a tour of the facilities. At the conclusion of the visit, however, as the guests took a seat in Cal Turner, Jr.'s, office, the Interco CEO remarked, "We didn't just come for the fun of it. We're ready to sell the Eagle stores." "When?" asked Cal Jr. "By the end of the year," was the reply. The asking price was $50 million (including a substantial amount of goodwill). Although the chain was described as "marginally profitable," with estimated sales of $90–$100 million, Interco was unwilling to release operating statements on it.

Eagle Family Discount Stores consisted of over 206 leased stores of about 6,000–8,000 square feet each, in prime locations all over Florida, plus a warehouse near Miami. Some stores were in small towns, but most were in cities of considerable size, such as Miami, Jacksonville, and Tampa–St. Petersburg. Most were also in strip shopping centers, anchored by Winn-Dixie grocery stores and Eckerd drugstores, and had rental rates twice DG's average. Among their major products were sporting, automotive, electrical, and plumbing goods, and swimming pool chemicals and accessories; 40 percent of the stores' sales were cigarettes.

As Cal Jr. considered the pros and cons of the offer, he thought about how nervous his father had been about the recent growth. Cal Sr. felt that the new Hirsch stores needed "tender loving care" and that Dollar General needed to "settle down, sell some merchandise, and let growth take care of itself."

Besides, management was on record with the stockholders as opposing one acquisition on the heels of another and had stressed in the company's recent annual report that the company's primary strategy was to "[build] sales in existing stores." The secondary growth strategy was "to increase the number of stores in operation in an orderly and profitable manner."

Furthermore, the company was already understaffed, with ten vacant district manager positions. The Eagle deal would create a need for at least another ten district managers.

Ed Burke (VP Finance) repeatedly pointed out to Cal Jr. that the current financial statements would take a beating and that few of the Hirsch stores were yet profitable. Inventory turnover and return on assets would be especially affected. Furthermore, previously planned improvements in distribution facilities for 1984 (including a third warehouse) could cost $5 million, and advertising expenses were scheduled to increase by $3.4 million over the 1983 level of $6.8 million. He only half-jokingly pointed out that this acquisition, combined with the Hirsch acquisition, would require Dollar General to acquire more debt than the company had had in sales a few years earlier.

According to Cal Jr., "I was in turmoil. Our people had gone through hell with the Hirsch acquisition. Yet here was the opportunity I had wanted in 1983." He decided to call a meeting of the planning group (the vice presidents of retail operations, finance, and administration, the executive vice president of merchandise, and the general merchandise manager) to discuss the offer. He wanted a consensus on the decision. He also hoped the quote on the wall plaque just outside his office would remain true: "Things work out best for those who make the best of how things work out."

CASE 30

BIG SKY, INC.: THE MAGASCO PAPER MILL (A)

BIG SKY, INC.

Big Sky was an integrated forest-products company headquartered in the Northwest with operations throughout the United States and Canada. Founded when two well-established lumber companies merged operations, Big Sky was a young organization by industry standards. The company manufactured and distributed paper and paper products, office products, and building products and owned and managed timberland to support its operations. In 1990 Big Sky reported sales of $4.5 billion and earnings of $275 million. Paper and paper products accounted for $2.5 billion in sales and represented 70 percent of the company's operating income and 55 percent of its revenue. Office and building products accounted for the balance.

During the fiscal year 1990, Big Sky invested a company record $750 million in the expansion, modernization, and improvement of its plant and facilities. The majority of these improvements were made at the company's paper-manufacturing facilities. Most of these operations were located in the Pacific Northwest, the Southeast, and the Northeast. Because papermaking required vast amounts of lumber, the majority of Big Sky's paper mills were located in rural timberlands. Big Sky manufactured a broad range of products, including uncoated white papers for printing and general business use, newsprint and uncoated groundwood paper for the manufacture of such products as paperback books, coated paper for magazines and catalogs, containerboard used in the construction of corrugated containers, and market pulp that was sold to other manufacturers.

Paper operations at Big Sky were divided into two primary groups: P-Three and Plain Paper. The P-Three division was responsible for producing three primary paper products: newsprint for publishing, linerboard for packaging, and marketable pulp. The Plain Paper division was responsible for producing all other products, including business forms, envelopes, and carbonless and copier papers.

THE PAPER INDUSTRY

The practice of papermaking dated back to at least the third millennium B.C. when the Egyptians first recorded their activities on pounded papyrus stalks. Although not as ancient as papyrus, the basic process of changing wood chips into pulp and then drying and pressing the pulp into paper sheets had not changed much over the past several hundred years. By 1990, however, papermaking had evolved into a highly capital-intensive and technology-driven industry. As a result of the introduction of modern information systems and computer-aided manufacturing, papermaking was an increasingly efficient and sophisticated process.

Prepared by F. B. Brake, Jr., under the supervision of Alexander B. Horniman, Professor of Business Administration. Revised September 1995.

Because of the nature of the extensive plant and equipment required to operate a modern paper mill, the cost structure of papermaking was heavily weighted toward fixed costs. In 1990 a single paper machine capable of producing 500 tons of paper a day was estimated to cost in excess of $500 million. The raw-material cost of timber and labor costs—the two primary variable costs—had traditionally received little attention.

Historically, the papermaking industry had close ties to the lumber industry. In fact, many companies such as Big Sky were direct descendants of lumber companies. Because of the paper industry's dependence on timber as a raw material, most paper companies were vertically integrated and owned or were closely affiliated with timber operations in order to reduce their exposure to commodity price fluctuations. Culturally, the paper industry shared the Paul Bunyan mystique of the timber industry. Papermakers, like lumberjacks, were often characterized as "macho" and "tough, rugged individualists." Because of the manual nature of the work, both industries were known for their high incidence of injury. The Occupational Safety and Health Act (OSHA), passed by Congress in the 1960s, cited the forest-products industry, including papermaking activities, along with more celebrated industries such as meat packing, as the focus of OSHA's early efforts to reduce work-related injuries and deaths.

Large organized labor groups, such as the United Paper Workers International, represented much of the industry's workforce. At some mills, workers in different industry trade groups represented workers in various functional areas—the machinists, who were responsible for performing the maintenance function, or the paper-machine operators. Over the years, these groups had negotiated lucrative contracts for their members. In addition to wages that were comparable to those paid in the steel industry, the industry trade representatives had negotiated for a number of concessions that were commonly found in the timber industry. For example, lumber companies and the saw mills they owned typically operated on a 40-hour workweek, closing on weekends and holidays. Because these operations were so labor intensive, this was considered an acceptable practice. Many union representatives at paper mills had successfully negotiated similar "cold shutdowns" at their locations. Because of the high fixed costs associated with running a paper mill, this practice was, however, extremely costly to the paper companies. One mill manager estimated that a cold shutdown for a three-day holiday weekend had cost his mill almost $6 million.

In addition to wage and benefit concessions, the unions had been very successful in negotiating for restrictive work practices that specifically defined individual work practices and job assignments. Restrictive work practices often precluded qualified personnel from performing tasks at different locations within the mill or on different mill machinery, regardless of the employee's ability to perform the job. Management was often unable to deploy its workforce efficiently as a result of these work practices. Mill managers regularly compensated for the inflexible nature of their labor agreements by simply hiring additional employees. Many of the restrictive work practices and spiraling wage costs were tolerated by management because the industry had traditionally considered wage costs to be just a fraction of the total manufacturing cost.

Throughout much of the 1970s, demand exceeded supply in the industry, and papermakers were reluctant to close their mills over strikes for wage concessions they knew they would not have to absorb. A company executive addressing an industry gathering explained this logic:

> From the mid-'60s to the mid-'70s, we found it much easier to simply let union representatives dictate conditions to us without offering much resistance, perhaps believing—or hoping—that things would correct themselves. . . . Often we were fairly certain that many of the conditions demanded—whether they related to work practices or wage and benefit rates—were not in the best interests of our operations or our employees long term, but it was simply easier, less hassle, to acquiesce to union demands and then simply pass on increased costs to the customer. We had a business environment that allowed us to do that.

By the late 1970s, however, the situation had clearly gotten out of control. "We found ourselves in a fight for the very lives of our companies—and the jobs of our employees," said another executive. The industry was facing increasingly stiff competition from foreign manufacturers, particularly from Scandinavia and South America. Most foreign manufacturers had substantially lower labor costs than U.S. papermakers and were receiving assistance from their home governments in the form of subsidies and import restrictions.

Because demand for domestically manufactured paper products had historically exceeded supply, most U.S. manufacturers had traditionally operated at, or near, capacity. Many consumers would accept virtually any product shipped from the mill, so most manufacturers had adopted a manufacturing philosophy based on quantity as opposed to quality. As a direct result of encroaching foreign competition, however, capacity throughout the United States was on the rise. For the first time in recent memory, supply exceeded demand. At the same time, foreign manufacturers were also introducing higher quality products. Consequently, domestic consumers of paper products were increasingly demanding in terms of the quality they expected from U.S. manufacturers. As a result of increased industry capacity and the relatively low rate of annual inflation during the early 1970s, however, manufacturers were unable to pass along cost increases associated with the quality programs they needed to initiate in order to remain competitive. Industry profitability thus declined throughout the late 1970s.

In order to increase efficiency and productivity, in the late 1970s and early 1980s, many companies attempted to introduce new, more relaxed work practices when bargaining with unions. As one industry executive stated, "We needed to be substituting more flexible work practices for antiquated work rules that, over the years, had virtually immobilized many of our operations in a web of inefficiency and lowered productivity." Many industry observers were convinced that fierce foreign competition, increasing customer demands, rising labor costs, and restrictive labor practices would force many mills out of business.

In response to dwindling profits, more and more companies were willing to operate mills during strikes, a practice long avoided by the industry. In some extreme cases, when striking employees refused to return to work, they were replaced. Despite these apparent hardball tactics, most experts agreed that concessions would be required of everyone; something serious had to be done. In response to critics who claimed that the paper companies were just trying to drive out the unions, one industry veteran offered the following response: "None of these tactics were meant to bust the union as some would suggest. Rather, they demonstrated our increased willingness to maintain commitments to our customers and to the communities who depend on the successful operation of our facilities."

The Magasco Mill

The Magasco Mill, a member of Big Sky's Alpine Division, was located in an area commonly known as Texarkana, where the borders of Texas, Arkansas, and Louisiana converge. Because of the proximity of vast pine groves and a temperate climate that accommodated accelerated tree-growing cycles, the area was ideal for papermaking. Opened in the early 1970s, Magasco was one of the first mills actually built by Big Sky. Most of the company's other papermaking operations had been acquired through various mergers and acquisitions. The mill was equipped with the latest technological innovations, including three cutting-edge paper machines capable of producing in excess of 1,500 tons of newsprint and linerboard a day.

When plans for the Magasco Mill were originally announced, Big Sky stated that it intended to introduce state-of-the-art management practices at the new facility. The hope was that the de novo effort would enable managers to introduce new work practices free from the influence of established cultures found at facilities purchased by Big Sky. The company hoped Magasco would serve as a model for other company mills as well as the rest of the industry.

While many other new mills in the South were discouraging the formation of unions at their mills, Big Sky actually invited organized labor into the Magasco Mill. They anticipated that this action would foster a cooperative environment and reduce the possibility of future conflicts between labor and management.

None of the approximately 500 skilled laborers, all of whom were represented by the Amalgamated Paperworkers Union (APU), or 150 managers and engineers was required to use a time clock. Management perceived the absence of a time clock, a symbolic gesture, to be a token of the trust between management and labor. The concept of "multicraft" was also introduced to provide flexibility in the maintenance functions. Multicraft required each employee to be skilled in and to perform multiple tasks rather than discretely defined job functions. At the time, these practices were considered revolutionary by industry standards.

Magasco, like most other papermaking operations at the time—with demand exceeding supply—was profitable even in the start-up years. The fact that the mill opened in the middle of a recession had little bearing on its initial performance. Despite early financial success, little headway was made, however, with management's attempt to to institute what some observers considered to be the most progressive work practices in the industry. After five years of Magasco operation, it was clear that, despite a contractual agreement between the APU and management, a functional craft distinction had evolved and the multicraft initiative had failed. Time clocks also appeared, at the APU's request. The union claimed that without time clocks its members were not being equitably compensated for overtime.

As was the case at many other mills, management found complying with labor's demands easier than following through on its own initiatives. Despite hopes for a mutually cooperative work environment, an adversarial relationship between labor and management soon established itself at Magasco. The mill quickly developed a reputation throughout the industry as a labor-relations hotbed. Part of the reason for this reputation stemmed from a much publicized strike at Magasco in the early 1970s.

The primary catalyst for the strike was management's unwillingness to grant further concessions in the area of restrictive work practices. The strike involved so much violence at the mill that a judge issued a permanent restraining order restricting picketing activities from anywhere within sight of the mill gate. As one employee said, "This place had a reputation in the industry as the Alamo. . . . It was a place you were sentenced to." Another employee related an incident in which, when he was introduced to a group of executives from competing mills at an industry gathering, and it was announced that he worked at Magasco, the group erupted in laughter.

In addition to continued labor strife, the Magasco Mill faced a number of other challenges during the late 1970s. As a company, Big Sky, like many other major corporations, had adopted a corporate strategy of diversification during the 1960s. Before long, the company found itself managing operations ranging from South American cattle ranches to Caribbean cruise lines, in addition to its core businesses, the paper operations. Operations at Magasco were largely ignored by the corporate staff throughout this period, as more attention and resources were directed toward the company's other businesses.

As a result of the declining profitability of the paper industry (as well as a number of its diversified holdings), Big Sky experienced dire financial problems in the mid- to late 1970s. In an attempt to save the company from financial ruin, executives at corporate headquarters began to exert significant pressure on individual operating units. As a result, mill managers throughout the company were forced to surrender much of their autonomy.

Not surprisingly, Magasco experienced a tremendous amount of management turnover during this time. Some Magasco veterans claimed that the only constant at the mill was the union representatives who sat down at the bargaining table every three years to negotiate a new contract. As one longtime employee said, "There are a lot of management teams buried in this mill." The high attrition rate in the managerial ranks at the Magasco location was widely acknowledged not to be necessarily attributable to the quality of mill managers. "It was," as one employee said, "as if they were facing insurmountable odds."

Throughout the late 1970s and early 1980s, management attempted to introduce a number of new initiatives and mandates. The APU, however, was extremely reluctant to comply with any of management's change initiatives, because the union had come to understand the short-lived nature of most of management's proposals. Many employees shared the following story: No sooner would a change be initiated at the mill than a Big Sky corporate jet would fly over the plant with a representative from headquarters on board and land at the small municipal airport outside of town. Before the plane took off at the end of the day, the change would be reversed.

The mill's problems during the late 1970s and early 1980s were not solely financial. Despite the presence of safety procedures—warning signs and posters located throughout the facility promoting safe work practices—the mill had a dismal safety record. Two people were killed at Magasco in industrial accidents during one year, and every year a number of others were disabled so badly they could not return to work. As one employee said, "It wasn't a big deal for any number of people to be so severely injured that they never came back to the mill after being hurt on the job." In addition to the tremendous pain and suffering incurred by the injured employee and his or her family, these accidents directly influenced the mill's financial performance. Under state worker's compensation regulations, Big Sky could be required to set aside as much as $300,000 immediately following an accident for future payment to a disabled employee.

"Times, They Are A-Changing"

Jock Duncan joined Big Sky as the director of human resources at Magasco a few months before the mill management was set to negotiate its three-year contract with the APU in the summer of 1983. Duncan came from the chemical industry, where he had nearly two decades of experience in human resources. Initially, he was surprised by the restrictive nature of the work practices in the paper industry. He quickly concluded that relations between management and the union employees at Magasco were adversarial at best. "The workforce here at the mill was much more compliant than those in the chemical or petroleum industries at that time," Duncan later recalled.

Duncan was disturbed by the assumptions made by management and labor about the role hourly employees should play in the workplace. He knew these assumptions were the result of years of behavioral observation and reinforcement. As illustrated in Exhibit 1, in a mutual compliance organization such as Magasco, management, based on behavioral observations, assumed employees were antagonistic and apathetic. Systems and work technologies were eventually developed on the basis of these assumptions. This approach often resulted in fragmented work assignments and constant supervision by management. Employees, perceiving management as adversarial and nontrusting because of the work practices instituted, often responded by exhibiting apathetic and antagonistic behavior, thereby reinforcing management's original perception.

Despite Big Sky's original expectations, by the time of Duncan's arrival, the Magasco Mill, along with most of the company's other facilities, was characterized by poor labor relations and hazardous working conditions. The mill was also losing nearly $35 million a year. Magasco's newsprint machines were operating at just over 80 percent capacity, and the linerboard machines were producing at just over 90 percent of total capacity. As a result of increased competition and increasing capacity, the market price of the mill's paper was falling at a rate of 9 percent a year, while its total manufacturing cost per ton was increasing by 9 percent. Duncan and the other senior members of the mill's management team believed that the mill's survival hinged on the successful introduction of significant changes at the upcoming labor negotiations.

The discrete work assignments that had developed over the years as a result of various managements' reluctance to aggravate labor had put a choke hold on the

Exhibit 1

Mutual Compliance Model

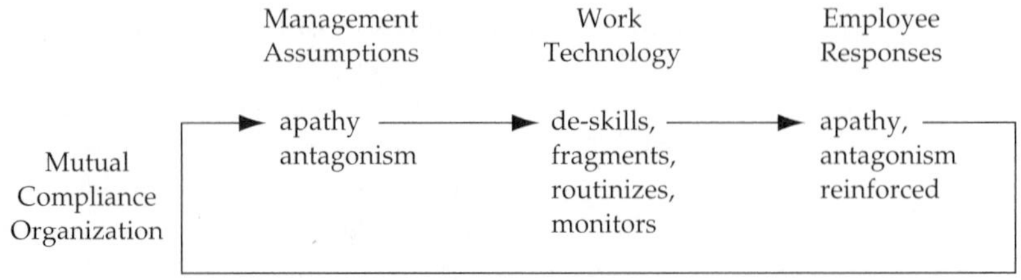

	Management Assumptions	Work Technology	Employee Responses
Mutual Compliance Organization	→ apathy antagonism →	de-skills, fragments, routinizes, monitors →	apathy, antagonism reinforced (loops back)

mill's ability to produce paper efficiently and affordably, particularly in the face of foreign competition. Management concluded that more flexible work practices had to be introduced. Although recent labor agreements had clearly defined step-by-step job descriptions and work assignments for the APU members at the mill, Duncan and the other managers proposed new language that would provide management with greater discretion in defining and assigning work. Duncan knew from past negotiations that a change in the wording from one contract to another of this magnitude was serious enough to instigate a walkout.

In order to facilitate the change to a more flexible work environment, management planned to introduce the team concept. This approach represented a radical departure from the mill's traditional work assignments and was reminiscent of the multicraft concept originally introduced at the mill nearly a decade earlier. In the team approach, the mill would be divided into three primary functional areas: the paper machines, the pulp mill, and the wood yard. Whereas each area might have previously had anywhere from 10 to 15 individual jobs, it was proposed that these jobs be divided into three or four clusters or teams consisting of 3 to 4 jobs. Teams of employees would be assigned to a particular cluster, and each employee would be expected to perform every job in the cluster on a rotating basis. This process would broaden the skill base of every employee and provide management with greater flexibility in developing work assignments.

The rationale for introducing the team concept was described in the proposed contract as follows:

> The team concept is designed to improve the efficiency and competitive position of the mill [by] providing for the flexible utilization of production and storeroom personnel. The elements of the Team Concept are considered essential to the survival of the mill.

Mill management was acutely aware of the sensitivity of the proposed changes but believed that a crisis situation had developed and that without tremendous change the mill might go under. As Duncan noted, "We knew we were introducing a tremendous amount of change, but it had to be done."

In an attempt to alleviate some of the anxiety regarding the proposed changes, management assured the APU that no union jobs would be threatened as a result of the introduction of the team concept. In the preamble to the proposed labor agreement, management included the following statement: "No current employee will lose his employment or suffer a reduction in his wage rate due to the implementation of the team concept."

The Walkout

Unfortunately, it came as no surprise when the APU representatives recommended a walkout at the beginning of the talks. "Change requires loss," said Duncan, a key figure in the negotiations, "and the union representatives realized that they were being asked to make sacrifices—sacrifices they felt they could not make." While the union members walked out of the mill, management was determined to keep the mill up and running. For what may have been the first time in industry history, the salaried staff of a paper mill actually took over running the paper machines.

In the weeks leading up to the contract negotiations, Duncan and the other members of the staff had been preparing for the logistical nightmare that would follow in the wake of a walkout. In order to keep the mill operating, Big Sky was prepared to keep the production facilities fully staffed. A camp was set up on the mill property, and salaried employees from throughout the company were ferried on commercial airlines as needed in order to meet the mill's production schedule. One participant likened the experience to a military airlift.

In another break with tradition, management made every effort to keep all employees, including those on strike, as well as the community, abreast of the ongoing negotiation. In the past, Magasco had left it up to the union to keep its members informed. This time, however, management wanted to ensure that everyone knew what was happening. In addition to establishing a hotline that any employee could call to get daily updates, mill management worked closely with the press to keep the community informed. As managers of the largest employer in the surrounding three-county area, Magasco Mill management also met regularly with community and business leaders to keep them up to date on the situation.

About a month into the strike, when little progress was being made and both parties appeared to be deadlocked over the proposed changes in the contract, the federal mediators who had been called in to oversee the negotiations announced that the talks were at an impasse. Management developed a replacement strategy.

In accordance with its contingency plan, mill management began interviewing prospective applicants to replace the striking workers. Because the country was still recovering from a recession, Big Sky had no shortage of qualified applicants from which to choose. Unemployed papermakers drove in from as far away as Ohio and Maine to be processed. Throughout this time, tensions continued to rise as some of the striking employees realized that they might soon be replaced. Acts of violence and harassment, including instances of gunfire, were reported at several of the assessment centers Big Sky had established around Magasco for the processing of applicants. Several of the incidents were captured on videotape. The situation became so charged and received so much attention that the site was visited by the FBI and the Bureau of Alcohol, Tobacco and Firearms.

Despite these incidents, management was determined to keep the mill running and continued to process applicants. Finally, Big Sky announced that it would implement all changes outlined in its proposed labor agreement during the first week of November, two months after the contract had originally been proposed, and any striking employee who wished to return to work at that time would be welcomed; those who didn't would be replaced.

The day before the changes were scheduled to go into effect, the mill was contacted by the office of the governor-elect, who had strong ties to labor and felt a moral obligation to lend his assistance. He asked Big Sky to delay action for 24 hours while he personally attempted to resolve the situation. Big Sky agreed to postpone its initiative but informed the governor-elect that it would agree to no concessions and would institute the changes as outlined in its original proposal regardless of the outcome of his discussions. To the surprise of many observers, the governor-elect was able to reach an accord with the union and informed Big Sky that the striking employees would come back to work with no conditions. They would accept the originally proposed labor agreement, including the contested team concept.

Despite the governor-elect's assurances, when Duncan and the rest of the negotiating team met with the APU representatives to ratify the contract, the APU suddenly demanded a condition. Specifically, the union asked for amnesty for those employees captured on videotape during the conflicts that erupted at the processing centers. The mill manager was furious with the APU's lack of good faith. He was not about to begin bargaining at that point, and he informed the governor-elect that the union representatives had not followed through on his promise. The governor-elect responded with tremendous disappointment and told management to do what it had to do.

During the strike, a phone bank had been established at the mill to inform applicants of Big Sky's decision to hire them as replacements in the event an agreement between Big Sky and the APU could not be reached. As the meeting broke up in downtown Magasco, Duncan prepared to drive out to the mill to initiate the replacement process. When he arrived at the mill and began to gather the team to phone, he was informed that the union representatives had changed their minds and would not request any concessions.

The news hit Duncan like nothing he had ever experienced. Now what would he and the mill manager do? Was it possible to really create a "new Magasco mill"? Was it possible to transform all the negative energy that had been focused on the strike to building a totally different organization? These questions and what seemed like hundreds of other ideas flooded his mind. What was possible? How should the journey start?

Case 31

The Public Communications Department at New York Telephone

There is no organization in the whole telephone company that is held in higher esteem.

Doug Mello, Group Vice President
Manhattan, August 1992

According to Bob Bellhouse, former general manager of the $300 million public communications department of New York Telephone (PubComm), "A few years ago, the public telephone business in the New York Telephone Company was generally considered to be a backwater, leave-it-alone, laissez-faire operation." Under his leadership, however, the department had been transformed into a model of organizational effectiveness. Furthermore, since his move to the corporate engineering department in October 1991, the team he left behind had continued to chart a course of improvement and success. Donna Torres, who had taken over as general manager when Bellhouse left, said in August 1992:

> There isn't any task or any job that is too difficult for these people. You just give them a problem and they solve it. I guess part of the magic of what happened was not only a lot of good, creative, solid technical innovation but also the building of a team [that] is without peer.

Company Background

In 1982, AT&T signed a consent decree with the U.S. Justice Department agreeing to divest its local communications networks by January 1, 1984. The divestiture spawned seven new regional Bell operating companies (RBOCs), which were independent but held joint and equal ownership in Bell Communications Research (Bellcore), AT&T's former laboratory research division. NYNEX Corporation, one of the seven new RBOCs, provided local service and access to long-distance carriers in the New York and New England regions. Within its area, independent companies that had not been part of the AT&T system, such as Southern New England Telephone Company (SNET), also continued to operate.

In 1992, NYNEX was organized into 11 principal subsidiaries. New York Telephone Company provided telecommunications services within the state of New

---

This case was written by William F. Allen, Darden MBA 1992, under the supervision of Alexander B. Horniman, professor of Business Administration, and Robert D. Landel, The Henry E. McWane Professor of Business Administration, Darden School, University of Virginia.

York; New England Telephone and Telegraph served New England. Other major groups included NYNEX Science & Technology, NYNEX Worldwide Services, and NYNEX Mobile Communications. For financial reporting purposes, revenue and expenses were grouped into five segments. Exhibit 1 contains segment descriptions and selected segment financial data for the 1989–1991 period.

EXHIBIT 1

NYNEX Financial Data (in millions)

SEGMENT REVENUES

	1991	1990	1989
Telecommunications	$11,138.1	$11,076.2	$11,029.9
Cellular	324.1	310.4	237.4
Publishing	849.2	850.8	815.6
Financial/Real estate	78.9	83.8	57.0
Other operations	838.4	1,260.9	1,055.5
	$13,228.8	$13,582.1	$13,195.4

SEGMENT OPERATING INCOME

	1991	1990	1989
Telecommunications	$1,978.3	$2,407.0	$1,939.5
Cellular	48.5	60.2	48.2
Publishing	47.4	118.1	115.4
Financial/Real estate	27.0	75.7	50.9
Other operations	(169.3)	(374.0)	(120.9)
	$1,608.4	$2,105.3	$1,756.7

SEGMENT DESCRIPTIONS

Telecommunications
Local telephone service, network access to long-distance services, materials management, technical and support services, Bellcore, product development, and marketing.

Cellular
Wireless telecommunications services and products.

Publishing
White and Yellow Pages, telemarketing products and services.

Financial/Real estate
Financial products and services.

Other operations
Information delivery, software, and consulting services.

SOURCE: 1991 NYNEX Annual Report.

The Public Communications Department

Prior to the divestiture of AT&T, the pay-telephone business was a "regulated stepchild" of the former Bell System companies, according to John Chichester, a PubComm District Manager. Chichester explained:

> The word *profitability* never came [across] the lips of anyone. That's the way AT&T worked. They just poured money into us as they did the many other units within the Bell System. They took it from their profitable entities and put it into the non-profitable entities. They would just force-feed you with money. . . . It was something in those days they felt they had to do; they had to provide the public with pay telephones. Most regulatory agencies would have crucified them if they ever attempted to stop [providing pay telephones].

At that time, public telephone stations and booths were placed without regard to any strategic implications or profitability. Key telephone operations were divided among other larger departments, which operated basically without any budget constraints.

PubComm was not formally organized as a unified department until late 1978. According to Staff Manager Susie Satran, "One of the problems in the beginning was getting other groups, even within the telephone company, to recognize our existence and our worth." In particular, technical assistance from other departments was difficult to obtain.

Looking back on that period, Bellhouse said he believed

> Morale suffered because the department had been neglected in terms of the resources provided to it. There had been no formal training curriculum for public telephone operations in almost twenty years. We had to completely reinvent training.

Introduction of Competition

In 1985 the Federal Communications Commission (FCC) decided to allow private ownership of public telephone stations. Later that year, the Public Service Commission of New York State passed an enabling act that cleared the way for competition in the public telephone business beginning in 1986. A number of competitors quickly entered the business.

By 1988, these competitors, which serviced customer-owned, coin-operated telephones (COCOTs), had captured roughly 14 percent of the New York public telephone market. In many instances, these companies promised to proprietors higher commissions than New York Telephone. The COCOT vendors also generally enjoyed a cost advantage by employing nonunion labor and using cheaper phone equipment. At the same time, COCOT vendors were experimenting with state-of-the-art technology in a few of their stations and offered many features unavailable at New York Telephone stations.

The COCOT vendors were only forced by regulation to maintain the basic 25-cent local call. Unlike New York Telephone, the COCOT vendors could set their own rates for such classes of phone calls as cross-city and long-distance overtime and operator-handled calls. In addition, the COCOT vendors aggressively pursued new locations, often finding very profitable spots that had been neglected by New York Telephone.

At first, New York Telephone simply continued its past practices. According to Chichester:

> We handled competition in those early stages very poorly. We had the Bell mentality that said "No one can come in and take this over from us. We're too good. We know what we're doing. We're the best."

Bellhouse stated later, "We knew competition was occurring, and we didn't know what to do about it."

Because of the lack of information on revenues and expenses, PubComm had no idea how much it earned or spent. The department focused mainly on repairing and installing phones. The sales effort consisted of sitting back and waiting for the phone to ring with new orders.

The COCOT vendors made significant inroads into the business in the first few years of competition, but New York Telephone then stopped the hemorrhaging. By 1992, it was losing only about 1 percent of market share a year. However, Chichester noted that the COCOT vendors "were here to stay and have made our lives very interesting."

The Bellhouse Task Force

In June 1986, George Barletta, New York Telephone's vice president of customer services, assembled a six-person task force to examine the feasibility of creating a divested, lightly regulated public telephone subsidiary. Bob Bellhouse was brought in to lead the team, which included three people on loan from other departments and two permanent PubComm assignees.

For more than a year, the team conducted an iterative business case analysis of the public telephone business. The team consistently concluded that the cost of taking the business out on its own was too high and that the public telephone business was too tightly entwined with the New York Telephone network to separate it. In performing the study, however, the team introduced a very powerful notion. Bellhouse stated:

> We discovered how to run that department as a business. In other words, we adopted a mindset that said you don't really have to legally set up a separate subsidiary. You can close your eyes and pretend that you are a separate subsidiary and run it like a business. And that's what we did.

The next two years were spent developing the mindset and tools necessary to compete.

In February 1988, Bellhouse was promoted to general manager of PubComm. At the time, PubComm was losing money, and it was mired in service problems that left New York Telephone highly vulnerable to its competitors. Bellhouse was given three years to make the business profitable and to fix the service problems. Two of the most pressing problems were vandalism and fraud. As Chichester noted, "We happen to have New York City, which is the most difficult place in the country to do business in pay telephones."

Taking On the Vandals and Thieves

These days, New Yorkers who want to use a pay phone to reach out and touch someone usually end up wanting to punch someone.

Don Broderick
New York Post, April 18, 1990

The temptation posed by millions of dollars worth of quarters sitting on the streets of New York had proved to be irresistible to New York's highly creative criminal element. Chichester estimated that between 150,000 and 200,000 acts of pay-telephone vandalism were committed each year, with roughly 15,000 stations accounting for most of the damage. Thousands of phone stations were blown up beyond recognition. According to Bellhouse,

> The deteriorating service of public telephones wasn't because New York Telephone was not fulfilling its responsibilities. It was largely because there was an organized group of people who were vandalizing the phones to get the money out of them or to keep our phones in poor working condition.

As the crippling combination of vandalism and the service repair crisis threatened the PubComm business, New York Telephone established a campaign to increase awareness of the vandalism problem among city officials, community boards, and law enforcement agencies. The company's efforts were aided by the media, with which NYNEX's department of external affairs enjoyed a very good relationship. In addition, newspaper and television organizations were willing to cover the stories, because the vandalism and fraud made for good copy. Bellhouse noted that the coverage "served our purpose because it enabled us to get the attention of the police department, the judicial system, [and] the courts." Bellhouse also met with local community boards and the district attorney's office to increase the pressure on the courts to hand out stiff, meaningful sentences to phone vandals.

In addition, PubComm redirected its own security unit to catching vandals. Previously, PubComm had relied on the corporate security group, but it was not in a position to deal with public telephone vandalism. The department also engaged a professional security agency to focus on increasing the number of arrests and convictions. The security group used contacts in local precincts to aid its effort. The in-house security group proved very effective, snaring an average of about 90 people per month.

PubComm also used technology to attack the constantly evolving stream of vandalism and fraud engendered by the very creative and adaptive thieves of New York. For example, after the 1987 release of a popular movie that included a scene showing people how to make free calls by grounding the phone with a pin pushed through the transmitter, New York Telephone found itself replacing 190,000 handsets per year at $30 per piece. To solve the problem, Pubcomm developed a stainless-steel cover for the transmitter unit. The thieves responded by breaking the steel cord and inserting a straight pin into the cord to ground the phone. Moreover, the vandals quickly discovered that the pay telephone stored the coins inserted while the pin was in the cable, and, when the pin was removed, all the change was released into the coin-return bucket. The PubComm Department eventually developed a $30 circuit isolator that eliminated the grounding vulnerability.

PubComm tackled the problem of long-distance phone fraud by working directly with its pay-telephone equipment manufacturer. Enterprising thieves were making up to $2,000 a day stealing calling-card numbers and selling time to people who wanted to make international calls. Places such as Grand Central Station and Port Authority bus terminals were ideal for the operation because they were air conditioned, well equipped with phones, and experienced transient traffic. Some people would bring their families to these locations and spend the day making illegal calls to relatives overseas at well below market rates. Other criminals discovered how to dial into the switchboards of large New York City businesses and then get an outside line to make long-distance calls.

PubComm used an electronic device to monitor these locations and gather the data necessary to solve the problems. Armed with the dialing sequences and routines being used by the criminals, PubComm approached the supplier of the electronic phones and requested that the software be changed to block certain dialing sequences. Within 60 days, the company had successfully installed the new software.

Committing to Quality

Quality is not a program or a buzzword at NYNEX. It is a way of life. It is the key to achieving sustained excellence over time in satisfying customers, share owners, and fellow employees.

William C. Ferguson
Chairman of the Board and Chief Executive Officer
NYNEX, March 6, 1991

The executives of New York Telephone's parent believed in the importance of quality. The challenge in 1990 was to spread that belief to all levels of the organization. NYNEX Chairman Ferguson approached this challenge by sending a letter in Spring 1990 to NYNEX managers introducing the Malcolm Baldridge Award as an award worthy of pursuit by the company and its employees. In time, the company began to focus on the components within the Baldridge Award.

The turning point for PubComm came in the fall of 1990 when New York Telephone conducted a "Strategic Quality Planning Seminar" (SQPS). Because of their unique synergies, the public communications and operator services departments were selected for the coordinated pilot run of the seminar. According to Bellhouse, the seminar "gave us an opportunity to get away for a few days and focus in on quality in a way that had not been done before at New York Telephone."

The managers spent a lot of time talking about processes. New York Telephone had traditionally focused on internal results, without recognizing the importance of work and social processes. Managers also learned about quality management tools, such as Pareto analysis and fish-bone diagrams. As Bellhouse observed:

> During the post-SQPS period, our language changed. We were ready for it, and it occurred just at the right time. We started talking among ourselves using the words that you find in a quality pamphlet. It was natural. . . . It didn't feel artificial.

He also noted:

> A crucially important block of time in this seminar was delivered by a consultant to Florida Power & Light. This module was called "Voice of the Customer." We talked about all the different ways that you should be listening to your customer—ranging from measurements, technical systems, what you read in the newspaper, [to] what your employees can discern—and that became a major change for us. We started asking customers in a different way than we had before.

This new approach led to increases in customer satisfaction. For example, PubComm established a system of calling its proprietary customers and informing them that their phones were fixed. At the same time, these customers were asked if they were satisfied with the repair and the service in general. When the program was first started, the satisfaction rate was only about 70 percent. The customer satisfaction rate in 1992 was more than 97 percent.

Several steps were taken to increase customer satisfaction. Technical training was provided to the technicians. In addition, the dispatch system was improved so that the technicians had more information about the problems when they arrived at the location. Previously, technicians conducted rudimentary tests but often found nothing wrong. Only after subsequent calls from the customer were the problems properly diagnosed. The PubComm department also worked with the purchasing organization to improve or replace substandard phone parts.

Bellhouse considered the focus on training vital to PubComm's quality improvement.

> The Strategic Quality Planning Seminar was so important. We were so enthused about it. We quickly put every management person in the department through that training. We didn't bring in trainers. We trained ourselves. We rolled the training down. So my directors and I conducted the training for the next group, and then they trained their people, so we had a sense of shared understanding throughout the department.

Bellhouse summed up the success story of the quality movement by stating:

> There was no golden relay, no magic bullet, no one thing that fixed it. It was all of those things—managed not from the top but from the middle—and empowerment of those people—just giving them broad goals and a lot of training and coaching.

Embracing Technology

Right now, I believe that New York Telephone is on the leading edge of technology in the pay-telephone industry across the country.

John Chichester
August 1992

In addition to dealing with the vandalism and service problems, Bellhouse had recognized early in his appointment that PubComm needed to decrease costs and position itself to move quickly as new customer requirements arose. PubComm decided that it needed new technology to compete against the product offerings of the COCOT vendors in 1987, but it took three years for New York Telephone to master the technology it envisioned.

Collecting the Right Data

Prior to the Bellhouse era, the public communications department had little useful data to guide its planning and decision making. Chichester recalled:

> We used to manage the business without ever having data. It's not that we didn't want to use data. I don't think we had the systems. We didn't have the people.

PubComm significantly improved its analysis of maintenance data by taking advantage of a corporate system that had been originally intended for marketing analysis and modifying it for a specialized maintenance application. The Strategic Quality Planning Seminar reinforced this notion of managing from data. Chichester noted that "when we started basing our decisions on factual data, it was a big improvement. You can't fix something unless you know what's broken and how bad it's broken."

One of the first requests to Bellhouse by the sales organization was to develop a system to track profitability. After several frustrating false starts with consultants, PubComm developed a successful partnership with the corporate comptroller's office. Together, they developed the coin contribution model to capture revenue, expenses, and profitability along several different dimensions, including by phone station, group, building, and account. The model, an activity-based costing system, focused on cost drivers as a more accurate means of allocating overhead costs.

According to the sales manager, Jay Ruiz, without the coin contribution model, "we could not operate in today's environment." In the past, PubComm had offered standard commission rates to proprietors. The advent of competition, which opened commission rates up for negotiation, added a complexity that could only be tackled with relevant and reliable data. PubComm had to seek stable, long-term sources of revenue and profit. From 1990 to 1992, approximately 2,300 phones were identified as unprofitable, and half of them were taken out of service. The remainder were left operative primarily because of public safety concerns. The New York Telephone Company recognized the value of the coin contribution model by selecting it as a winner in its Technical Excellence Program.

Retrofitting Phones

Technological improvements were also made on the phones themselves. Virtually all of New York Telephone's public telephones were Western Electric 1C/2C electromechanical sets, which were equipped with mechanical coin chutes. These chutes were highly susceptible to both failure and vandalism. New York Telephone could not afford the investment necessary to replace the Western Electric sets entirely with the new technology offered by the COCOT vendors. Unfortunately, no off-the-shelf technology existed to upgrade the New York Telephone pay phones.

To solve this problem, a cross-functional team of managers from New York Telephone and New England Telephone assembled in 1987. This team spent two days designing the current equipment into the public telephone of the future. The team divided technical requirements for transforming the current phones into two categories. The first contained the minimum requirements for improving internal components. Key requirements were a free-fall electronic coin chute, remote self-diagnostics, automatic trouble reporting to a host computer, remote programmability, coin-box accounting to allow collection scheduling, fraud prevention, and receiver amplification.[1] The new phone also had to operate with the standard central office line and without any external power source.

The second category of requirements called for a modular design to allow for the offering of new high-end customer features as the market demanded them. The final design used a bus architecture to allow for this addition of features.

After the meeting, a request for information was sent to 50 vendors, asking them to submit a set of detailed functional and technical specifications to match the team's design. At the time, an industry journal commented, "NYNEX has asked for the impossible." Several vendors responded, however, and Mars Electronics International (MEI), a vending equipment division of M&M/Mars Company, was chosen because of its reputation for quality and experience in developing custom applications.

The retrofit project progressed slowly. The prototypes received in 1988 did not work properly, and, in early 1989, a trial of 200 stations was also unsuccessful. Senior management grew increasingly impatient with the lack of improvement in the "customer trouble report rate," a common telephone service measurement. Bellhouse and his team were under great pressure to cancel or downsize the project, but by the end of 1989, management decided the technology was ready for large-scale deployment. Unfortunately, the deployment came at a very difficult time for New York Telephone.

In August 1989, the International Brotherhood of Electrical Workers and the Communication Workers of America, which represented approximately 35,000 New York Telephone craftspeople, had staged a walkout. The main stumbling block in the negotiations had involved employee contributions to medical benefit plans. The company was gripped by a bitter and divisive four-month strike. Many incidents of violence and vandalism punctuated the growing rift between management and craftspeople. In response to the service crisis that ensued, management personnel worked 12- to 16-hour shifts as they assumed the maintenance and collection responsibilities.

The 1989 strike generated a serious morale problem for the Bellhouse organization. The bitter nature of the strike, combined with the deepening service crisis and long working hours, created a stressful working environment. The logjam was finally broken in December, but management morale sank at the news of concessions. Although NYNEX Chairman William Ferguson maintained that, overall, the company had actually got more than it had sought, some managers believed they had been abandoned by senior management.

Because of the labor strike, the new retrofit technology was installed by inexperienced management people, and the installation of the 10,000 retrofit units exacerbated the service crisis. Chichester noted:

> There was a key word that was missing from our perspective—*patience*. We were attempting to fix a service crisis by deploying this technology quickly as opposed to sitting back and making sure it was right.

When the striking technicians returned to work in December, they were confronted with service problems involving a technology they had never seen. The department immediately conducted a mass training campaign to educate the workforce about the new technology. In the wake of the settlement, craftspeople and management held many meetings and conferences to clear the air, resolve differences, and reopen lines of communication. In the summer of 1991, a full year ahead of schedule, the unions and NYNEX negotiated a four-year extension of the labor contract.

By the end of 1991, New York Telephone had installed 23,000 retrofit kits and another 24,000 stand-alone chutes.[2] The breakthrough in limiting vandalism and improving customer service as a result of the deployment was extraordinary. On the retrofitted stations, vandals were no longer able to ground the transmitter leads. The self-diagnostics feature allowed PubComm to solve problems before they were reported. The average collection amount per station increased 18 percent because of improvements in collection scheduling, which resulted in substantial reduction of the collection expenses.

Key internal signs of the improved quality of customer service included the following:

- Total troubles cleared reduced by 30 percent.
- Number of full coin boxes decreased by 40 percent.[3]
- Number of stations out of service longer than 24 hours dropped by 38 percent.
- False alarm dispatches reduced by 32 percent.[4]

Quality Confidence Agreements

During the retrofit operation, PubComm discovered the importance of holding its suppliers accountable for the quality of equipment shipments. Although the new technology was improving customer service, the failure rate was generating some concern among management. The failure rate for the stand-alone chute reached 40 percent during the first developmental trials. PubComm negotiated a quality confidence agreement with its supplier to help curb the chute quality problem.

The agreement, the first of its kind at NYNEX, required the supplier to replace defective parts and to remit a $75 rebate for each defect above a 4 percent acceptable failure rate. The rebate amount represented an estimate of the total handling costs incurred by PubComm as a result of a defective component. Chichester noted:

> When people at NYNEX first hear about this arrangement, they focus on the money aspect, but the money is only a device, a way to put teeth in the program. We'd prefer that our suppliers not have to pay us anything—that they always would meet our quality goals.[5]

After the quality confidence agreement was signed in July 1991, the failure rate for the stand-alone chute decreased 87 percent and remained close to the acceptable 4 percent rate outlined in the agreement. Future agreements were to focus on cutting the failure rate even further.

Other Technological Innovations

In 1989 PubComm received another Technical Excellence Program citation for its development of a robotic key system. The robot prepared a shackle of keys for each technician based on the collection schedule for the day. The introduction of the robotic system eliminated many labor-intensive positions.

In 1992, the department was testing a new electronic lock system that would allow technicians to carry a small handheld computer device. The necessary codes for opening the locks would be downloaded from the host computer back at the collection center.

PubComm also used technology to change the way the customer pays for service. The first effort was coinless, or "charge-a-call," stations. The number of coinless phones deployed throughout the state had been level at 4,400 for several years. In 1989, however, PubComm replaced 700 coin telephones on the New York City sidewalks with the coinless variety. Bellhouse observed that the coinless phone was

> the first significant shift in our product mix. Up until that point, we had basically said, like the Model T Ford, "you can have any kind of phone you want as long as it's this one." We began an evolution to change the product mix away from coins.

The change-card phones represented the second phase of that evolution. This new type of station accepted only small credit-card-like cards that had been purchased in advance in $5 denominations. PubComm was hoping to deploy 3,000 change-card phones a year. Donna Torres, who estimated that at some point half of all pay phones would be change-card phones, commented:

> This whole business is changing very drastically. Change card is a technology three years ago we thought we'd never do. It's all over Europe and it's all over Japan; everyone has it. We are the first company in the United States to have it. That's something that could change the face of the way public communications looks in the streets of New York over the course of the next five years.

"Catchballing" the Business Plan

Our Department Business Plan is the sum of the ideas of all of our people. We hoped that a "top down" vision would couple with "bottoms up" practical knowledge and creativity. And that's what happened.

Public Communications Business Unit Plan 1991–95
September 18, 1991

The 1991 business plan for PubComm was developed through a "catchball" approach. First, Bellhouse and his four district managers discussed the NYNEX vision statement, mission statement, and corporate strategy. Next, the planning team focused on the New York Telephone mission, vision, and values statements contained in Exhibit 2. PubComm then chose to concentrate on four of New York Telephone's ten corporate strategies: "Employee Communications and Trust," "Meet Customer Requirements," "Manage Down the Costs," and "Make Quality a Strategic Tool." In addition, a fifth corporate strategy, "Improving Earnings Growth," was addressed as a result of implementing the other four strategies.

A planning team next created a mission statement for PubComm to serve as a framework for pursuing the strategies. PubComm dedicated itself to becoming the premier public telephone service in the State of New York. The department had already developed an extensive understanding of what customers required from public telephones. Thus, the 1991 business plan concluded, "simply stated, the public

EXHIBIT 2

New York Telephone's Business and Goals

Mission Statement

New York Telephone will provide quality communication services at prices viewed as reasonable by our customers, with competitive earnings, in a corporate environment that encourages employee excellence and development, making our company, in the eyes of its employees, the greatest company to work for in America.

Vision Statement

New York Telephone is a member of the NYNEX family of companies, a leader in the information industry through the combined efforts and skills of all employees.

- Quality is our hallmark. We profitably market quality products and services and anticipate opportunities to serve our customers better.
- The heart of our business is an information network driven by highly sophisticated technology.
- We are financially strong. Each segment of our business makes a profitable contribution to the competitive earnings essential for our long-term success.
- Individual leadership is manifest throughout our company, inspiring excellence based on mutual trust and respect.
- We have a common commitment to our corporate mission, goals, and objectives, and achieve them through individual and team initiatives which are recognized and rewarded on the basis of performance.
- We rely on open communication and teamwork as our style of management and foster individual growth and opportunity.
- We demand integrity of ourselves in all that we do.
- Through the day-to-day efforts of every employee, we constantly earn our corporate reputation for responsible leadership in the eyes of our customers, our investors, and the communities we serve.
- We have transitioned into a company that has learned to adapt and flourish in a competitive environment.

Values

New York Telephone's values embrace the highest levels of customer satisfaction, quality, integrity, respect for our people, and commitment to communities in which we operate.

wants convenient, low-cost, clean, simple to use, working phones; and agents want commissions and hassle-free service."

The planning team defined "premier" in terms of the achievement of "future state objectives" congruent with the four corporate strategic goals and the identified customer requirements. These objectives, presented in Exhibit 3, guided the development of detailed action plans to move the department to where it wanted to be.

Once the core strategies and future state objectives were identified, the district managers were allowed considerable flexibility in developing their own business plans. Each district contained different organizational functions. As the planning team observed:

> There are now four separate but interrelated district business plans. Together, they form a mosaic which, as it is completed, will bring us much closer to our objectives.

The district plans were the product of the inputs of every level of management. The district managers built on the ideas of the people closest to their customers.

EXHIBIT 3

Public Communications Department Objectives

Mission Statement

We pledge to be the premier Public Telephone Company in New York State no matter who enters the field.... We're here to stay.

Future State Objectives

When benchmarked against customer requirements and other public telephone operations, New York Telephone Public Communications will:

1. employ at every level and in every position the most professional and valued employees.
2. have the best understanding of customers' needs, anticipate their requirements, and provide solutions [that] exceed their expectations.
3. utilize the best data and analysis to guide our decisions.
4. provide the most reliable station equipment and network.
5. provide the fastest repair service with perfect customer satisfaction.
6. provide the quickest installation service with perfect customer satisfaction.
7. operate with the lowest material costs.
8. benefit from the highest degree of brand recognition and customer/agent satisfaction.
9. ensure that Public Communications employees are the most enthusiastic, valued, and satisfied employees.

More than 200 individual action plans supported the overall business plan. Each plan represented a proposal and commitment from a specific management person. All managers were held accountable for the implementation of those plans, through the performance appraisal process.

Operation Desert Storm

In April 1991, an interruption in Bellhouse's stewardship threatened the momentum of the PubComm organization. Bellhouse, a lieutenant colonel in the U.S. Army Reserve, was summoned to active duty to participate in the protection of Kurdish refugees in northern Iraq following the conclusion of Operation Desert Storm. Chichester stated that, by the time Bellhouse departed, "Things were on the move back into the right direction." Nevertheless, some uncertainty arose over how the department would operate in Bellhouse's absence. He had been able to gain the support and respect of upper management and was able to accomplish many things by virtue of his contacts and power. Rich Chapman, an area operations manager, said, for instance, "I lost a lot. I relied a lot on Bob to use his name to push things, to get things done. I lost my hook."

Speaking for his district organization, Chichester said, "We kind of thought we were going to head downhill." Susie Satran, staff manager, on the other hand, observed that "because [Bellhouse] had structured the organization as such a team, there wasn't any kind of fear that everything was going to fall apart." Chichester added that "Bellhouse had a lot of confidence in us. He stated that many, many times."

Jim Parla, one of the district managers, was chosen to be the acting general manager in Bellhouse's absence. Chichester noted:

> Parla was very open-minded. He listened to the people that did know, that did have the answers. He wasn't one to shove things down our throat. He left us kind of alone. We did what we had to do. We had some fears, but they went away quickly.

In the words of Jay Ruiz, sales manager, "everything moved smoothly" while Bellhouse was gone.

Bellhouse returned in July and was thrown a big welcome-home party by his department. In recognition of their performance in building the team and sustaining the process of continuous improvement, all of the district managers received on-the-spot awards.

Reflections on Success

Bellhouse cited three important approaches that guided his success in turning around the Public Communications business: gathering the right information, exploiting technology, and taking care of his people.

Bellhouse asserted:

> Information that we needed was initially almost nonexistent. The information that we could get had little credibility. So improving the quality of the information

and designing that information in a way that it was not a stick—not something that we used to beat up on each other about, but the information was designed and delivered in a way that management at each level got the information that they could use.

Since they knew what the goal was and now they had information and they had been trained how to use information—what kind of steps to take—it worked. It took a long, long time to build the information systems to do that. Some of it was trial and error. Sometimes you thought you had good information and it ended up you didn't, so that was really a struggle.

Bellhouse noted that he had

an intrinsic belief that we could achieve a great deal through an integrated system of technological improvements. There was a school of thought in the company that said, "Don't do that! The way you should manage that department is with labor and leave everything plain and simple. Don't overcomplicate things." I don't believe that is the right answer. So we advanced the state of technology on a whole host of things. And we did this in a way, while it's not complete and it's not perfect, that these technological mechanizations and data improvements were all interconnected. We didn't do a coin contribution model just because we wanted to understand profitability. We did it because it gave you a whole host of activity-based cost information. For example, it gave you a new way of looking at maintenance costs you couldn't see the old way. On the other hand, we chose not to do bar coding—we postponed it—because we didn't understand how it would fit in. We didn't understand how it would connect into all the other things, so we decided we were not ready to deploy that yet.

Bellhouse had recognized that he had a tremendous employee morale problem on his hands:

Morale in the department had suffered greatly over the years. It was poor when I arrived because of isolation, stagnation, and weak leadership at the upper levels of the department. Only two of the top eight managers in the department then were still in their positions in 1991. On the other hand, we promoted a record number of excellent people throughout the department and brought in people with fresh perspectives from the outside.

Morale also suffered because the department had been neglected corporately in terms of the resources provided to it. There had been no formal coin-telephone training curriculum for that business in almost 20 years. We had to completely reinvent training.

We had to find ways to make people feel better about their jobs [and to] feel better about their successes. We had to proclaim success to ourselves as well as to upper management to restore that vitality that is in our department now. We did this by local recognition programs and by successfully competing for corporate excellence awards.

During the difficult times, the New York Telephone Company was extremely critical of the department, threatening to go out of the business or threatening to downsize it to an absolute minimum number of phones that they could get by with in terms of the Public Service Commission. We reported results on a monthly basis, and every month when the numbers weren't right, it was crucifixion time again. And it was hard to maintain the long view. Some of the things we did had a fairly shallow learning curve. You had to achieve a critical mass of technology out in the field in order to gain the benefits.

At the time Bellhouse was orchestrating the turnaround, several anonymous allegations of wrongdoing by members of his department were submitted to the Office of Ethics and Business Conduct. Bellhouse noted how important it was to protect his people:

> There were a lot of investigations going on at that time—really unpleasant stuff. While we were trying to fix the service and improve the department, others were making anonymous accusations that could quite literally destroy people's careers. My philosophy was: I believe in you; I will do everything in my power, to extreme lengths, to protect you—not to protect you because you've done something wrong, but because I know you, and I know you haven't done anything wrong. And what I need you to do, because you are the expert, is to equip me with information so that I can then go and do what I need to do with my supervisors.

Reflections on Leadership

PubComm's district manager, John Chichester, a highly decorated Vietnam veteran, believed that Bellhouse's military background helped him as a leader. Chichester stated, "I think it teaches leadership better than anything in the world."

Commenting on his military background, Bellhouse said:

> Some people misread that. A lot of people think I went to West Point. I did not. I graduated from Hofstra's ROTC[6] program. My military background does have a big part, but in a way that a lot of people don't know, because I don't talk about it very much. When I was a second lieutenant in Germany, I was a platoon leader in an armored cavalry division. I made a lot of really big mistakes; no one got hurt, but I made a lot of mistakes that, when I look back on them now, I feel ashamed. I can put it in perspective. My college education did not equip me for that, so I made mistakes and as a result was transferred out of that unit to a headquarters organization. At headquarters, I did very, very well. I stayed in the Reserve program and have had a great military career. It was a good learning environment, because while I made mistakes there, I was allowed to get past them and grow. I didn't have to carry them with me. Aside from that, I think my military experience keeps my head clear, because it gives me a separate organizational environment in which to participate.

Summing up his experience at PubComm, Bellhouse stated, "In my career, I have never been as fully engaged as I was when I was there." He believed that he gained much insight into his roles as leader and manager:

> You can learn from everybody around here, but you've got to have that trust; you've got to have that communication. You've got to think of each other as real people, not just an empty suit or "the boss." You've got to feel comfortable with being wrong and letting people tell you when you are wrong.

You've got to have ears, and then you have to respond to what you see, not just react to what the numbers say. One of the nice things about that department is that you get to see your customers all the time. You could see if people were happy with the product or not. You get a different set of eyes. Believe me, when the phones are not working, you see people slamming down handsets.

You've got to have fun at work. You've got to somehow not get bogged down in a defensive behavior of finger pointing. My philosophy is to force ourselves to fully discuss those things and then make a decision and move on. People are not permitted to attack others. It's just not in the acceptable set of behaviors. If you have a good idea—great. If you have a problem—you folks had better talk about that and get it resolved, because that's what is needed to solve the problem.

You've got to have a real clear vision. You have to have this burning passion of the way you want it to be. You have to test everything out against that. It's all got to fit together. It has to be internally consistent. All the pieces have to fit.

Endnotes

[1]John Bonczek and John Chichester, "New Tricks for Old Telephones," *Telephone Engineer & Management*, July 15, 1992, p. 25.

[2]A stand-alone chute was a modification of the pay station that, while improving service, did not contain the full complement of features deployed with the retrofit kits.

[3]Phone stations automatically become inoperative when the coin box is full.

[4] Bonczek and Chichester, "New Tricks for Old Telephones," p. 26.

[5]"Supplier to NYNEX: 'We'll Put Our Money Where Our Mouth Is,'" *Impact*, Summer 1992, p. 6.

[6]Reserve Officers Training Corps.

CASE 32

OSIM CORPORATION (A)

On Thursday, June 9, 1983, Tom Stark was walking toward the office of Bob Cedarholm, OSIM's chairman of the board, contemplating the alleged internal "revolt" to overthrow Dave Wright, the president. Stark was wondering what and how much to say to Cedarholm during their impending meeting.

Stark had returned to work at OSIM just three days earlier, following a one-year in-residence Executive Management Program at a prestigious eastern business school. Prior to this time, Stark had earned a Ph.D. in industrial engineering from MIT and had spent nine years at OSIM. Now, at age 37, he was OSIM's first director of strategic planning and had the task of introducing strategic planning to the company. From the first day, however, in addition to the technical task of strategic planning, Stark had also been confronted with this highly charged political situation. It was made even more complicated for Stark because Dave Wright had acted as Stark's mentor during much of Stark's time at OSIM and had sponsored him in the Management Program. The situation had implications for the future of the firm, Stark's relationship with Wright, his career, and his personal ethics.

In his mind, Stark was going over his first days back at OSIM:

> I came back to work on June 6, a Monday, and I had a conversation with the president about start-up tasks and priorities. Then on Wednesday, Frank Lewisburg, the marketing director, invited me out to lunch. We spent about two and one-half hours together. During this lunch period, he brought up a number of points rather forcefully. The first one was that there is a conspiracy going on in the company. Frank and other members of the group feel that company goals are not being achieved because of Dave Wright's ineffective leadership, and they are meeting nightly, essentially to discuss how to remove Dave or to make him ineffective so that the company can move ahead on its growth plans. He announced, in essence, that he was lined up with Bob, the chairman of the board; that they had pressured Bob in the past into making some organizational changes (some of which would increase Frank's responsibilities); that the chairman of the board was himself lined up with management at Shilo [OSIM's parent company] in New York; and that there was an impending reorganization, at which time these problems would be taken care of. He predicted the reorganization would take place around the first of August and advised me to state my preferences and alliances now, because when that reorganization took place, things were going to be different. He said if I wanted to be on the right side of things, I'd better get on the chairman's team.
>
> My initial reaction was disbelief. I knew Frank was prone to hyperbole, and I felt maybe this was a combination of that characteristic and two glasses of wine. And then my next reaction was, "Wow, these guys are playing hardball, and they seem

This case was written by L. J. Bourgeois III, assistant professor of Business Policy, and Clare Swanger, research associate, Stanford Graduate School of Business.

to be playing for keeps." This is not a nice, cozy academic problem you can ponder for awhile but something in the middle of the swirl of events. I was sort of resenting this—being placed in such a position so quickly. And damn it, I hardly have my feet on the ground. I don't even know where my office is, and here I am being invited to join a palace revolt.

Then Frank ended up by saying that he would make an appointment for me with the chairman of the board; he would talk to the chairman before I went to see him and would tell him that he had had this conversation with me. Then he told me that I should go in and pledge my allegiance if I knew what was good for me. I agreed to talk to the chairman, because I was already committed to meet with him that week.

History of OSIM Corporation

OSIM Corporation was a medium-sized consulting firm located in Sunnyvale, California. Founded in the 1930s following the Great Depression, OSIM had prospered and grown slowly but steadily by providing engineering services to local businesses. In the 1950s, OSIM entered the commercial real-estate business to capitalize on the beginning westward population migration. During the 1960s, OSIM's growth accelerated as the economy in Silicon Valley, based on high-technology businesses, boomed. To service the new companies, OSIM instituted financial advisory services and combined business services, which provided small and emerging companies with a wide range of services. Finally, OSIM began providing specialized litigation support in response to existing client demand for such services. By 1982, OSIM had revenues of $75 million, although both revenues and profits had fluctuated in the previous few years as the nature of the consulting business changed (see Exhibit 1).

OSIM Corporation had five basic services areas, with many types of subservices (see organization chart in Exhibit 2):

- *Engineering.* The engineering services division provided a broad range of services to a wide variety of client organizations, both industrial and governmental. The division's distinctive competence lay in developing and implementing innovative approaches to engineering problems through the use of operations research, process control, network analysis, information processing, and computer system development. OSIM bid almost solely on

Exhibit 1

OSIM Corporation Financial Highlights ($ in millions)

	1982	1981	1980	1979
Revenue	$75.2	$65.9	$60.3	$45.0
Net income	.4	1.8	1.5	1.1
Total assets	46.8	34.9	27.6	24.4
Shareholders' equity	$ 9.1	$ 8.7	$ 6.9	$ 5.4
Number of employees at year-end	1,322	1,230	1,206	1,056

EXHIBIT 2

OSIM Corporation Organizational Structure

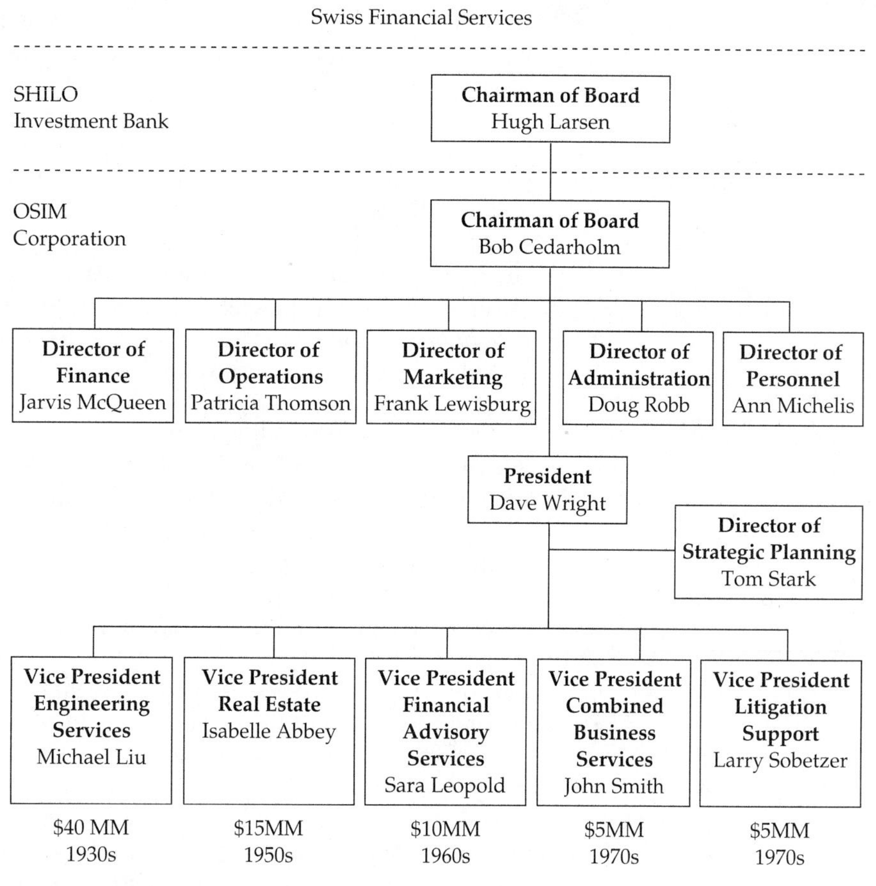

"one-off" type projects that required sophisticated technical competence and creativity—the staff's "power alleys." Engineering services accounted for approximately 55 percent of OSIM revenues in 1982 and exerted substantial influence on the company as a whole, partly because it was the oldest business within the company and partly because it was the largest.

- ***Real Estate.*** The real-estate division developed and managed commercial real estate, particularly shopping centers and industrial parks. OSIM entered the real-estate business during the 1950s when commercial and industrial growth began to accelerate throughout Silicon Valley. Having operated in Sunnyvale since the 1930s, OSIM had developed a strong reputation for high-quality work and had accumulated a great deal of knowledge about the local area, which aided the real-estate division immeasurably.
- ***Financial.*** The financial advisory services division provided financial consulting, investment banking services, and seed capital to local firms. It originated in the 1960s as a follow-on to the engineering and real-estate

businesses, since financing was a central element in both. Having the financial services capability in addition to engineering and real-estate expertise allowed OSIM to meet a substantial portion of many organizations' outside consulting-service needs.

- ***Combined Business Services.*** The CBS division provided a full range of financial and consulting services to small, privately held businesses. Although these companies did not require major investment banks or accounting firms, they did need professional advice across a wide spectrum of their activities. The CBS group employed CPAs, MBAs, financial analysts, and lawyers. OSIM was well positioned to serve the small company market in Silicon Valley because it was so well known and respected in the area. OSIM's strategy was to develop strong relationships with emerging companies, with the idea of providing additional services as the companies expanded. CBS grew rapidly during the 1970s as small companies flourished in the Sunnyvale area.
- ***Litigation Support.*** OSIM also had consultants who worked solely on providing litigation support to firms needing expert testimony and witnesses. Most of this business arose through San Francisco Bay area law firms that drew on OSIM's expertise and reputation in the engineering area. Client development was particularly haphazard in this group, although litigation support was both OSIM's fastest-growing and most profitable (per hour) service area. Because many consulting firms appeared to be ready to enter this business within the next couple of years, a group of people at OSIM wanted to invest in the litigation support division and rationalize client development in order to capitalize on the field's apparent attractiveness.

OSIM's work was project oriented and technical in nature. Each project involved delivering a service, but the services varied greatly among divisions and types of clients. OSIM's revenue was usually generated by one-off types of projects, with little follow-on work.

OSIM's customers could include almost any organization. Business clients ranged from small start-ups to large, established *Fortune* 500 firms. Most industries were represented, including electronics and other high-technology areas, chemicals, construction, defense, and agriculture. OSIM also worked for nonprofit organizations, especially hospitals, and some local governments.

The kind of people OSIM believed would succeed at consulting, and whom OSIM had to hire and retain, were highly skilled, professional, energetic, willing to work long hours, and independent and entrepreneurial on the one hand but able to work as a member of a team on the other. Most of the professional staff were attracted to OSIM because of the intellectual stimulation, financial compensation, and flexibility it offered. Virtually everyone had an advanced degree, either in a technical or engineering specialty or from a business school. Many could have worked independently, but they benefited from OSIM's reputation, from contact with other talented people, and from the financial resources OSIM could apply to support their work. After a few years at OSIM, they could expect to be able to choose their own work.

The culture at OSIM strongly reflected the characteristics of the consulting profession and the types of people attracted to it. It was a loosely coordinated corporation that had had virtually no central planning. The name of the game was "chargeable hours." Projects were bid on the basis of "total revenue" or "hourly billing rate," but, in either case, hours were closely tracked. An hour not billed was an hour's revenues lost forever. Compensation and advancement at OSIM were linked to chargeable hours, although technical competence, ability to generate new business, and ability to get along with people also entered into the picture.

Exhibit 2 shows OSIM's organizational structure. Below the vice presidents, who were heads of divisions, were project managers, senior associates, and junior associates. Background information on the primary protagonists with Stark in this situation is given in the case appendix. The VPs and the project managers were accustomed to choosing the type of work they wanted to do and to structuring it themselves in order to complete it. Not much corporate focus characterized this approach, but the professional staff enjoyed their independence.

History of Swiss Financial Services/Shilo Investment Bank and the Acquisition of OSIM

Shilo Investment Bank, based in New York, was a wholly owned subsidiary of the huge international financial conglomerate, Swiss Financial Services (SFS). SFS owned several dozen companies in just about as many countries, which gave it a strong worldwide presence in the expanding financial services arena. With Switzerland as a base, SFS could provide clients with a broad array of services and make the most of increasing global interdependence and easing regulatory restrictions.

Shilo was SFS's North American investment banking arm. It was one of the dominant U.S. investment banks and provided a full range of financial services. At SFS's request, and consistent with its own objectives, Shilo embarked on a plan of acquisitions during the late 1970s and early 1980s. Shilo intended to secure and bolster its position in the U.S. market, where financial service and consulting competition was fierce, mergers were occurring, and inefficient firms were starting to disappear.

The decision to sell OSIM to Shilo was made in January 1983 and announced in March. Stark was at the Executive Management Program but learned of the decision sometime during February. Although OSIM was a corporation, four people maintained most of the control: Chairman Cedarholm, President Wright, Michael Liu (vice president, engineering services), and Isabelle Abbey (vice president, real estate). These four people benefited financially from the acquisition, while the other vice presidents and the directors of OSIM did not. The result was some bad feelings, particularly from officers who had spent many years at OSIM and felt they had not been adequately compensated for their time and efforts.

Most people within OSIM realized that being part of Shilo—and even more significantly, SFS—would provide OSIM with financial resources to compete effectively in the changing world of consulting and financial services. Some also worried, however, that Shilo and SFS would impose additional structure and control on OSIM, thus detracting from its independence. In addition, some people were contemplating the potentially lucrative move of leveraging the investment made in previous R&D work by selling "solutions" over and over again. Such a step could lead to two groups within OSIM: Those who would design and create solutions to client problems and those who would be charged with merely repeatedly implementing already-developed, cookie-cutter products.

OSIM Strategy Evolution to Date

OSIM's strategy had evolved over time to include provision of a wide range of services to an ever-wider range of clients. The majority of OSIM's business came from small and middle-sized companies and some government agencies, and the company had developed some specialization in electronics and construction.

In general, OSIM's strategy evolved implicitly rather than through any explicit, centrally planned process. Basically, whatever technical problem, real-estate project, or deal-making opportunity any officer wanted to pursue, he or she could. The expansion of services arose from several factors: (l) OSIM's high level of technical competence, (2) the industry trend toward an increasing overlap of consulting and financial service suppliers, (3) the independent, entrepreneurial characteristics of the staff, and, probably most importantly, (4) the desire on the part of OSIM's staff for intellectual and creative challenge, which was more likely to occur with new types of services, projects, and client industries than with repetitive projects.

OSIM had also been influenced by Dave Wright's management style. As Stark described it,

> The management style of the president could be characterized as decentralized management over the years. He's an inspirational-type leader but not at all an operations manager. He had let the organization run—the divisions run—independently and autonomously.

Some of the officers who were upset about the terms of OSIM's acquisition by Shilo were also unhappy with Dave Wright's objectives and style. Again, according to Stark,

> Frank Lewisburg [the marketing director] told me that a good company is one where there's structure and discipline and a style of each person playing his role, a team approach, and so on; whereas this company has really been run on an entrepreneurial basis, very informal communications, lack of decision making, delegation of everything to the divisions, and a resulting protective, highly autonomous behavior on the part of the divisions. Frank found that bothersome, and he didn't think it was going to work in the long run. He felt a company couldn't develop to any size with that, and I think that's absolutely right. He comes from a very-large-company background, so he's very familiar with that culture. He doesn't understand a small-company, entrepreneurial culture and found it very uncomfortable to work with the lack of structure and lack of rules; he just had a general uneasiness about who is he and what role is he playing. The only disagreement that I have with Frank is that Dave Wright brought the company to where it is today, and it's kind of hard to argue with the fact that it's been very successful. It doesn't mean that we don't have growth problems and challenges from here on out, but let's not ignore the strength of the approach that Dave used. It may have outlived its usefulness, but it did work up to this point.

Strategic planning had been tried on occasion in the past at OSIM, but to no avail. Stark explained,

> In our case, planning is viewed as a nuisance task that is separate from management, and there has been no breakthrough on the several attempts that have been made. In fact, the very title or term *strategic planner* has been contaminated.

The Outlook for Strategic Planning and Strategic Change at OSIM

Stark had to consider several key factors in initiating strategic planning at OSIM. The first was the attitudes toward planning, which varied at different levels of the firm. Stark recalled,

> The general attitude that I got from talking to any vice president was, "Oh, you want to know about what we're doing and what kind of business we're in? Ask me anything you want to know, and I'll tell you, but don't bother my people." It's the autonomy and "chargeable hours" business again. There was a definite crust in the organization at the vice president level through which it was difficult to move. Whereas if I talked to managers or senior associates, they were all enthusiastic about planning, talked about what they were doing, saw a critical need for planning in the organization, and were willing to support it. This was generally true, firmwide. There may have been pockets of resistance, but generally there was a lot of energy and enthusiasm at the lower levels.

The second factor was the degree and form of support from top management. Stark explained,

> The president, Dave Wright, may be intellectually committed to the process but may not actually give firm backing to the planning sequence as we go through it. The chairman, Bob Cedarholm, will be bottom up and pragmatic. This affects my posture regarding the division heads and other officers: in particular, it defines the level of formal or implicit authority that I have. The view is that, if the chairman and president publicly endorse and support this effort and are willing to make it happen, it makes my job easier and I have more implicit and formal authority. If they are not going to back it up, if they are just going to *talk* strategic planning, then I've got to do much more persuasion, particularly of the division heads and other officers.
>
> I think I designed my own job to a large extent. When I was in the Management Program and learning of the acquisition, I was having discussions with the president about playing some sort of planning role when I got back. We talked extensively about that because, under the acquisition, the planning function was even more important and more complex, especially with the interaction with the other parts of the SFS group. Through a series of discussions at the end of May, we shaped plans for a strategic-planning staff position which I would move into when I came back to OSIM. During that time, I also had one conversation with the chairman of the board. He was very enthusiastic about this role and thought it was very important for OSIM. I guess I contributed most of the initiative in terms of defining it.

A third factor was Stark's own credibility as a planner with OSIM:

> On the positive side, I come from the ranks and have had experience with different parts of the company, so I understand their problems. The extent to which I appear to be using this position for my advantage is important, so I am very careful to present the image of putting OSIM first, that planning isn't everything, and that no one should get the idea that this could come out big for me in the short run. That is

what I need to be sensitive to, I believe. The planner's own personal style will influence his acceptability also, whether he is directive in nature or more of a facilitator.

Another part is my detachment from previous associations. If they think I'm partial to the engineering services VP, I will lose credibility, and I have to be careful about that. My previous job was manager in the engineering services division, and I reported to the vice president.

Finally, and very important I think, is the credibility of my formal education, and whether or not they believe there is something to that. But I'm not going to explain to them the full scope and extent of what I know, because that always remains a competitive advantage in promoting and implementing strategic planning.

The fourth issue was the integration with Shilo planning:

To the question, "Are OSIM's changes being dictated by New York?" I would say that, in an implicit way, the perception is that if we don't get our act together, New York will get it together for us, and so it's our chance to do it on our own. There's a definite influence, but it's indirect.

One factor in this is the conscious attempt on our part to use to our advantage in planning the fact that nobody knows what Shilo expects from us. So we'd better get our act together before Shilo comes swooping in and lays goals on us, and the way to get our act together is through planning. Nobody can say, "Well, I've talked to those guys; I know what they want, and they are not going to do any planning for five years and forget it." It is the anxiety about what the new owners are going to do to us that can be used to our advantage. The director of operations and I will consciously be using that anxiety as we go through the budgeting cycle and then into the planning cycle with the VPs. You might go to them and say that we need to get our act together; we need to put our plans together. Shilo will probably require that from us, so we better design our own system. Some of that may be true or not, but we can use that as part of the internal selling process on the stick end. Another uncertainty is whether or not our system is compatible with the Shilo planning process. I know that it is, because Shilo doesn't have a planning process, so that's no problem. And another political factor is Shilo's belief in the effectiveness of planning. Particularly, the chairman of the board of Shilo is an ex-planner and believes in it; so we've got his support and it helps.

The fifth issue was OSIM's previous experience with planning, mentioned earlier. Because most people viewed planning as nonsense and didn't believe anything would happen, Stark had to deal with this bias:

There was the whole set of issues having to do with how to sell this process to the vice presidents and the use of "small wins" early on to overcome their concern about what's going to happen to them when you start planning. Are we going to plan them out of a job? Are we going to cut up their organization and give parts to someone else? And just the cultural inertia against planning and the focus on operations—the general resistance to change.

Personal Challenges and Risks

Stark's intellectual challenge involved the technical issues of instituting strategic planning at OSIM. To begin, he organized his thoughts and asked a series of questions:

> How am I going to plan my attack on my firm? Is an incremental strategy right for the organization, or a so-called synoptic strategy? Do we start with a set or statement of corporate goals, or do we start with a business definition? How do we organize people into planning groups in the company, and at what level? Implicit in that question is how to get around the vice presidents—this crust level I was encountering. What portfolio-analysis tools are appropriate for our kind of business? How should competitor analysis be done? How about industry analysis? At what levels do you do portfolio analysis in the organization? How do you organize into business units? Is the current organization appropriate? Are charters well enough defined? And there are other specific issues having to do with the planning relationship between us and Shilo and the planning relation between us and the rest of SFS. Then we get into issues like performance measurement, computer-based support systems for monitoring progress, reporting systems, and so on.

Stark was looking forward to his position at OSIM:

> Coming into the job, it looked like an ideal set-up. I'd been with the company for nine years; I knew the style of business, the customers, the people. I had watched it grow over the years. As part of a network in the company, I had a lot of contacts. I had been working in the technical areas and had a technical background similar to the people in the company. On the other hand, going through the Management Program and seeing how things *might* be done, I could see a lot of payoff in bringing some of the strategic management techniques to this company. Also, the president and the chairman, but particularly the president, were talking strategic management strongly. The acquisition had provided capitalization and the potential for working toward a world-class international consulting and financial services firm. So, it was all very exciting and timely and fortuitous.

However, Stark

> saw the problem of dealing with a consulting-type culture and moving that into a planning mode as a significant implementation problem, as well as a significant challenge in the area of how you define businesses, how you think about planning in the consulting and financial services industries, how you might structure a rational planning process. That part was to be a challenge. It was further complicated by the passive management style of the president.
>
> So already there was substantial challenge requiring a good deal of clear-headed thinking. But then things were further complicated by the political intrigue that I walked into in the first week. Here I was, with a formidable technical task, and now I had to deal with politics as well. My reaction was, "Oh, s—t. I thought this was going to be fun. Now it's going to be work."

Then there were the calculations of personal risk:

> There was discussion on several levels. One was with the marketing director at lunch my first week back at OSIM. He said, "You know, if we don't get our act together, this place could fail. You and I can't be hired by A. D. Little or others, because we're too old. If we don't make it here . . . We can sit around five years from now and laugh about this, but now's the time to take action. We all want to get rich" and that kind of thing. And, "You've got a family to support; you'd

better think about *them.*" Talking later to my wife Janet, I said, "I have to think about you and the kids."

So you know there's self-preservation there. I don't know to what extent that enters in—maybe at an unconscious level. I did not sit down and calculate what the odds are. Another concern is that I'm possibly going to be thrown out on my ass, and therefore I had better go talk to the chairman.

During the lunch with Frank Lewisburg, Stark was startled to learn that Patricia Thompson, director of operations, and Doug Robb, director of administration, were Lewisburg's coconspirators. "My general reaction to this whole thing was disbelief. Like, oh come on, this can't be real."

These thoughts, and the ones described previously, were running through Stark's mind as he headed for his meeting with Bob Cedarholm.

Stark's Meeting with the Chairman

Stark went in to see the chairman on Thursday, June 9, the morning after his discussion with Lewisburg. The meeting started out interestingly; Cedarholm closed the door and said, "Well, Tom, how candid do you want to be?"

Appendix to Case 32

Histories of Key Players in OSIM

- ***Hugh Larsen.*** Chairman of the board of Shilo Investment Bank, OSIM's parent company. Larsen had extensive consulting and financial analysis experience and had been a strategic planner. As such, he believed in the process of strategic planning and could be expected to encourage and push it at OSIM.
- ***Bob Cedarholm.*** Chairman of the board of OSIM Corporation. Cedarholm was a financial wheeler-dealer and a "business" type of person. He was beginning to talk strategic management.
- ***Dave Wright.*** President of OSIM Corporation. Wright held a Ph.D. and was very technically oriented. He had been with OSIM for many years and had risen through the engineering services division. Wright was Tom Stark's mentor.
- ***Patricia Thompson.*** Director of operations.
- ***Doug Robb.*** Director of administration.

  Thompson and Robb had been with OSIM Corporation for many years, including the high-growth years of the 1970s. Because of the length of their terms with OSIM, they were unhappy not to have benefited financially from the acquisition. They performed staff functions and were administrative, nontechnical types who were more naturally inclined to work with the chairman than the president.
- ***Frank Lewisburg.*** Director of marketing. Lewisburg was an administrative, nontechnical, big-company, business-type person. He believed he could lead

OSIM to higher growth but felt held back by OSIM's president and the president's unstructured management style.

- ***Michael Liu.*** Vice president, engineering services. Liu had worked for OSIM for more than 20 years and was a major financial beneficiary of OSIM's acquisition by Shilo. His power in the organization stemmed from his long tenure and his competent control of OSIM's largest division.
- ***Isabelle Abbey.*** Vice president, real estate. Abbey joined OSIM in the mid-1960s and was responsible for solidifying and expanding OSIM's real-estate division. As a result, she exercised substantial influence within the company and was rewarded financially for her achievements at the time of the acquisition.

CASE 33

PENINSULAR INSURANCE (A)

Patrick Wale stood in the conference room staring in amazement at the chairman, Tan Sri Ibrahim Nassan. Ibrahim Nassan, the titular head of Peninsular Insurance, had just taken charge of Wale's planning meeting with an interruption that Wale saw as an attempt to subvert his authority with his managers. By the looks on their faces, Wale surmised that his managers were just as surprised as he by such an overt power play. With the 1985 Malaysian economy in recession, and company revenues sliding, now was not the time to play politics. As his adrenaline began to flow, Wale was at a loss as to how to regain control of the meeting and, by implication, of his Malaysian insurance organization. As his mind raced, he thought, "All I know is that, whatever I do next, it's going to have to be played by the Malay rules: respect for elders and 'saving face.' The question is whether I can show one without losing the other."

BACKGROUND

Patrick Wale had arrived in Kuala Lumpur ("KL," capital of Malaysia) almost three years previously to oversee the merger of the wholly owned Malaysian subsidiary of New Zealand Insurance Corporation (NZI) with the Malaysian-majority-owned Peninsular Insurance. He should have been finished within the first 12 months. In fact, however, after the first two years, he had barely scratched the surface of a project that was becoming more Byzantine by the week.

Wale considered himself good at adapting and working with other cultures. His work for NZI had taken him to Nigeria, South Africa, India, and, in his last position as branch manager, to Hong Kong, NZI's largest branch in Asia ($8 million in annual sales). (See Exhibit 1 for a profile of Wale and other key executives.)

Wale had felt at home in the freewheeling, business-first culture of Hong Kong. The absence of political barriers allowed him to concentrate on "getting on with business" without the worry of government regulations. But when NZI's then general manager of international operations called to offer him the position of chief executive officer of the Malaysian joint venture, Wale jumped at the opportunity.

The combination of NZI's $12 million subsidiary with its 49 percent owned, $4 million Peninsular would be double the size of the Hong Kong division in staff and sales. The task was an unusual one, because Wale would actually be wearing two hats: as the head of the NZI subsidiary reporting to the home office in New Zealand and as general manager of Peninsular reporting to the local board. That situation would change, however, when the merger went through and the combined ($16 million) entity would be 74 percent owned by NZI and working under a single management.

This case was prepared by James M. Berger, Darden MBA 1992, under the supervision of Professor L. J. Bourgeois III.

EXHIBIT 1

Peninsular Insurance Central Characters

PATRICK WALE: AGE 42

After dropping out of high school in New Zealand, 16-year-old Patrick Wale began work in 1961 as an office boy with NZI. He studied in night school for three years to complete the insurance exams and began to move up the corporate hierachy. In 1966, he was offered a position with the overseas staff.

A self-described adventurer, Wale accepted transfers to offices around the world, including Nigeria, India, South Africa, and Hong Kong. Each move improved his position within the corporation and finally led to his present appointment as CEO of the NZI joint venture with a Malaysian partner.

Married in 1969, Wale met his wife in Calcutta, where she was working for the British High Commission. Their two children, a 14-year-old son and a 13-year-old daughter, had been recently sent to boarding schools in England.

NIGEL FISHER: AGE 57

Fisher had been employed by NZ since 1942; he was appointed to a senior position with the home office in 1960 after a series of international transfers. His progress within the company appeared stalled after the 1981 merger produced a surfeit of middle managers, but he was appointed general manager of the international group in 1985 after its previous two years of results fell well below corporate expectations for the Asian operations. Fisher was due to retire in June of 1986.

Fisher was described by a colleague as possessing strong analytical but weak interpersonal skills and having a dour personality.

TAN SRI HAJI IBRAHIM NASSAN: AGE 73

Tan Sri Haji Ibrahim Nassan Bin Haji Ibrahim Siddiq[1] (his full name) had a prominent civil-servant career with the Malaysian government, culminating in his role as secretary general of Internal Affairs, responsible for the police, justice, and immigration. Retired at age 55, he was quickly invited to sit on several company boards and had been Peninsular Insurance's chairman since 1967. He had been required to retire from all but Peninsular's board at age 70.

Nassan was known as a man who paid strong attention to detail and required a high level of protocol at all times. He was married and had five sons.

[1]A convention in Malaysian names and titles conveyed social and political rank, lineage, and Muslim pilgrimage: "Datuk" was a title conveyed on men of accomplishment. "Tan Sri" was a higher honor, fewer in number. It was given by the sultan, usually for public servants of high rank. "Tan" was the highest honor possible in Malaysia, short of royalty. "Haji" indicated that the individual had made the pilgrimage to Mecca. "Bin" meant "son of."

NZI, Ltd.

New Zealanders pride themselves on their self reliance ... it's called kiwi ingenuity.
Annemarie Orange, Darden 1992, native of New Zealand

NZI was a diversified financial services company based in Auckland, New Zealand. One of the country's largest companies, NZI was formed in 1981 from the merger of New Zealand Insurance (founded 1859) and South British Insurance Company (founded 1872). The result was a multinational corporation operating in 24 countries through hundreds of offices.

Revenues of the merged company had reached $630 million in 1982, with a reported net income of $28 million. The international divisions of NZI's General Insurance Group contributed 35 percent of divisional income. (See Exhibit 2 for organization of NZI.) Each of the seven divisions of the company was run as a profit center.

NZI had concentrated its foreign business in the Pacific Rim and Africa and adopted a strategy of growth through local offices in order to gain a balance in both operations and the product mix offered by the company.

NZI had recently been riding a tremendous wave of new business brought about by booming regional economies and an aggressive new corporate style of management that expanded the company's business into previously unconventional areas.

Exhibit 2

NZI Organization in 1985

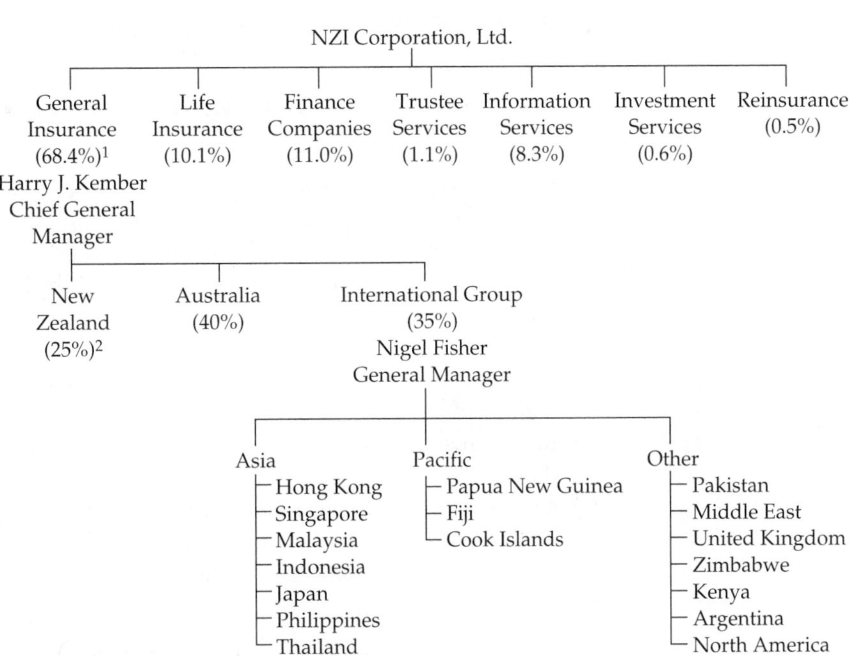

[1]Percent of total NZI revenues.

[2]Percent of total general insurance revenues.

NZI had also concentrated on shifting power to the local offices in order to encourage growth, and the new strategy called for equally aggressive management by NZI's field managers, who were afforded a large degree of autonomy by the home office. Within the financial services industries of the Pacific and Asia, NZI was considered to be one of the most aggressive in its mix of markets, products, and technologies.

NZI held interests in two key Malaysian operations. NZI Malaysia was a branch network offering the full range of insurance services and accounting for $12 million in revenues. Peninsular Insurance Company, with $4 million in revenues, was 49 percent owned by NZI, with the remainder owned by Malaysian nationals. Peninsular had been formed by NZI in 1967 with the ultimate aim of controlling all its business interests in Malaysia, in line with government policy of local incorporation of foreign branches.

Weak profits in an otherwise growing economy had led to a decision in 1982 to consolidate all Malaysian operations in order to reduce costs and provide for a more coherent strategy. An agreement was reached that Peninsular Insurance would merge with NZI Malaysia in a pooling-of-interests transaction.

MALAYSIA

The Federation of Malaysia was a peninsular country located at the southern tip of Thailand, with two Malaysian states located several hundred miles across the South China Sea on the island of Borneo. Following independence from the United Kingdom in 1957, the federation was established in 1963. Malaysia was a constitutional monarchy whose king (the Yang di Pertuan Agong) was elected for a five-year period by a council of nine ruling sultans from the federated states.

NATURAL RESOURCES AND THE ECONOMY

Malaysia had a population of 14 million people, with the capital of Kuala Lumpur housing 938,000. The country held a dominant world position in rubber, palm oil, pepper, tin, and tropical hardwoods; these and other abundant natural resources had given Malaysia one of the highest annual growth rates per capita in the world: growth at 4.5 percent per year since 1965 and per-capita gross national product of more than $1,555 by 1985.

The government had been aggressively pushing the economy toward a manufacturing base since the 1970s. Emphasis was on building the travel and communication infrastructure necessary for industrial growth, and the government maintained a policy of encouraging rapid population growth in order to stimulate domestic demand. The policy appeared to be working: Manufacturing began to overtake agriculture as a percentage of gross domestic product and, by the 1980s, was the main source of economic growth. The unemployment rate was 5.6 percent in 1985 and the inflation rate was 3.7 percent.

POLITICAL ASPECTS AND THE NEP

It's not a law, it's a government policy, and it is really like shadow boxing because you never really know quite where the target is.

Patrick Wale

Because Malaysia was a multiracial society, friction generated by the different cultures was the most important aspect of Malaysian politics. Political parties were based primarily on racial lines; the United Malays National Organization was the largest but shared power in a broad-based coalition with the Malaysian Chinese Association, the Malaysian Indian Congress, and several other, smaller parties.

After a violent anti-Chinese race riot in 1969, the Malaysian government established the "mitigation of inequity between races" as the overriding goal for the government. As a response to this goal, the New Economic Policy (NEP) was established in 1970 to help the "bumiputra" (Malay for "son of the soil"), which refers to native Malays, who were considered the main beneficiaries of the policies. One way the NEP attempted to reach its goals was through increased spending on education and basic services. Public enterprises such as the Trust Council for Indigenous Peoples were chartered to finance native Malay businesses and to provide advice to prospective Malay businesspeople.

The government had also set a goal of increasing native Malay ownership in the corporate sector to 30 percent by 1990. All other Malays were designated 40 percent corporate ownership, and foreign-owned stakes were to fall to the remaining 30 percent. In addition, foreign-owned companies were required to restructure equity so at least 70 percent was held by Malaysian investors.

According to Wale, at the time of his arrival in 1982 the government was putting extra pressure on foreign firms to "domesticate" their firms and to increase their local share holdings. One way of applying this pressure was to grant very limited term work permits. Government regulations in 1982 required all foreign nationals to apply for a visitor's work visa, usually for 12 months. But when pressure on a company was desired, only 3 or 6 months were given, and the threat was always present that a visa would not be renewed. As Wale described this threat, "I had no idea whether I would be here for the full five years of my assignment or I would be on the plane in a month's time. They were playing the game with all insurance companies here that the best way to make foreign companies take on local partners was to mess around with their work permits."

Another important factor in the Malaysian political structure was the presence of the military. In the early years of the federation, in a period known locally as "the emergency," the country was plagued by civil war. Not until the middle 1970s did the threat from the Communist insurgents greatly lessen. The product of the civil war was a virulently anti-Communist government that retained full constitutional control of the professional military force.

The NZI Malaysian Staff

Well it's all very much tied into the Asian face thing, that you don't just say what's on your mind to the guy in case you offend him.

Patrick Wale

Not long after taking over as general manager of Peninsular, Wale established good working relationships with the management and board. (Wale was appointed to the board in March 1983, as an alternate for Harry Kember, a board member based in New Zealand.) The foremost figure of the company was the local chairman of the board, Tan Sri Ibrahim Nassan, a prominent citizen in Malaysia who had once served as a high-level government official in the Interior Department (see Exhibit 1).

Wale soon realized that the chairman was remote from any real decision making for Peninsular; he served in a mostly ceremonial role. The chairman would show up at board meetings, start the occasion with a brief speech (usually written for him), and then leave management to discuss the mundane operational issues. Wale found the chairman to be a supportive gentleman; he allowed Wale to go about the business of modernizing the company's operation and organizing the mechanics of the merger, and he was particularly helpful in the area of smoothing over potential problems with the government. Immigration had been one of the departments under the chairman's supervision, and he expedited Wale's reapplication for a work permit several times.

The 73-year-old chairman, at 5'7", was quite a contrast with Wale who, at 42, was 6'4" and weighed 250 pounds. Recently, Nassan had been forced to leave most of his other board positions because of the mandatory retirement age written into most public companies' bylaws. Peninsular, as a private company, did not have such a rule. The chairman was thought to be quite well off financially, although Wale had also heard that he had recently been involved in some rather unfortunate investments, probably in the volatile Malaysian stock market.

Since the early, supportive days, Wale had found himself on occasion becoming annoyed by the chairman's tendency to bypass Wale and call the corporate secretary, Goh Lai King, when he wished to check on the business or consult with a manager. King had been with Peninsular for almost 15 years, and the chairman had formed a separate line of communication with him. Wale believed that, as a matter of protocol, the CEO should be the first to be consulted for advice or questions, but he had also recognized how petty it would be to try to cut off this communication. (See Exhibit 3 for Peninsular organization.)

EXHIBIT 3

Peninsular Organization in 1985

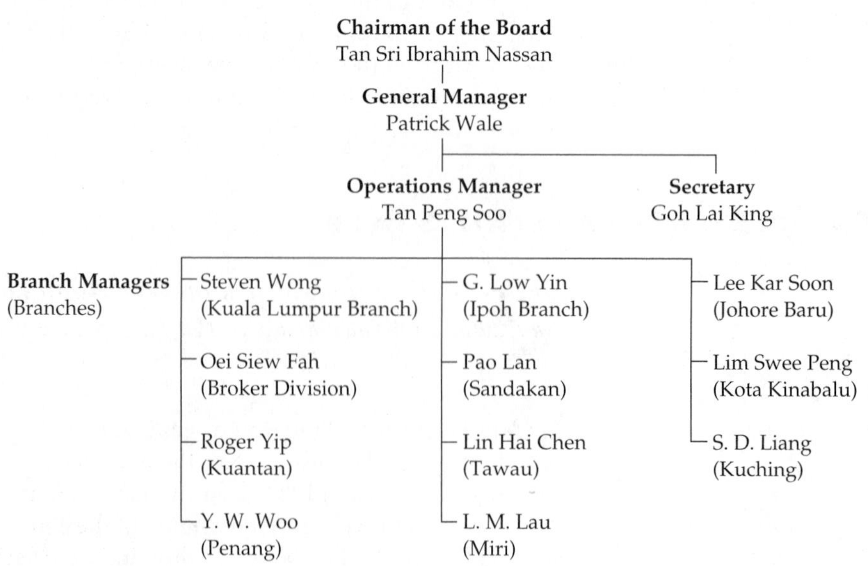

Wale had also quickly formed a close working relationship with the Malaysian operations manager, Tan Peng Soo. Soo was particularly knowledgeable about the daily workings of Peninsular, and Wale relied on his judgment about how best to implement the new training and computerization programs that would bring Peninsular's operations up with the rest of the NZI organization. Because Wale expected to move on when the merger was consummated, he began grooming Tan Peng Soo for the CEO position. Wale understood that Soo's strong business acumen and Malaysian nationality would make him a natural choice to run the merged company.

Meeting with the Chairman

The question was whether the merger would ever come to fruition. Wale had become increasingly frustrated by the tortuously slow nature of Malaysian business dealings, particularly those with the vast government bureaucracy. Two years had already passed, and almost nothing had been accomplished. He spent most of his time waiting months for written replies from government officials, replies that would have taken days in Hong Kong.

During this first two years in Malaysia, Wale occasionally visited the chairman at his home in a wealthy KL neighborhood to update him on the progress of the merger and discuss how the business was doing in general. Wale had arranged such a meeting to discuss the slow replies of the government and an upcoming board meeting with the visiting directors from New Zealand.

As a courtesy, Wale had always visited the chairman at home, but he was becoming increasingly uncomfortable with the practice. He had noticed that, while they were seated in the chairman's sitting room discussing business, the chairman's wife would be sitting in the adjacent room apparently listening in on their conversation. She would often make an excuse to come in and interrupt and would then linger on during the discussion. The chairman's wife was quite a bit younger than he, probably 15 or 20 years. Wale recognized that she was a strong-willed woman, and perhaps this trait, combined with her ability to make her presence felt and known, was what made Wale uncomfortable.

On this humid July 1984 day, the chairman seemed to have little to offer in regard to the government delays. Wale then asked, "Well, sir, do you have any suggestions on where we may want to host the dinner for our visiting board members? I thought that your club did a superior job on the last occasion."

The chairman leaned forward, "Yes, well, I believe . . ."

"The club? Certainly not the club!" His wife suddenly emerged into the room. "Why don't we try the Rasa Sayang for a change? I think the gentlemen from the home office would much prefer that."

Wale observed the chairman as his wife continued telling them where the meeting should be and what should be on the menu. The chairman was obviously a bit taken aback, and Wale realized that he probably had the same expression on his own face.

Driving back to his office that afternoon, Wale decided to discontinue the practice of going to the chairman's house to talk business. Perhaps he was being silly, but the wife's interference was bothersome.

Nigel Fisher Visits

Several months later (February 1985), Wale received a call from Nigel Fisher in the New Zealand office telling him that Fisher would be visiting the Malaysia office in two weeks. Fisher was the newly appointed general manager in charge of international operations, the third general manager in as many years. Fisher had worked with Wale before, and Wale looked forward to being able to discuss with him the reasons for the merger's slow going. Wale hoped to receive the level of support from the home office necessary to accelerate the merger.

A few days before Fisher's arrival, the chairman called Wale to his office. He requested that Wale arrange for King, the company secretary, to be present at Nassan's meeting with Fisher "just in case there is anything that I would like to put on the record." Wale checked with King later that day to arrange for him to attend the meeting.

The day before the meeting, King approached Wale and asked whether it was really necessary for him to attend. King said, "I am very sorry, but I realized that I have a prior appointment with the Tax Department and think that it oughtn't be broken." Wale readily agreed that the appointment was important and promised that, if necessary, he would take notes. Wale assured King that the chairman would not mind.

"Well, the chairman did bloody well mind," Wale recounted later. Before the meeting with Fisher, Wale went to the chairman's office and asked whether he would like for Wale to sit in and take notes on the meeting. "No, I would prefer this meeting to be one on one," the chairman responded. The meeting lasted almost an hour, and, immediately afterward, the chairman called Wale into his office. "Where is Mr. King?" he asked as Wale took a seat. "I instructed you to have him here to take notes."

"Yes, he came to me yesterday and informed me that he had a previous engagement with the tax office. I told him to carry on with his meeting and that I would take any notes if you wanted. But obviously you . . ."

"This is very upsetting, Patrick. Why did you countermand my specific instructions for the secretary?"

Wale had never heard this kind of tone from the chairman, who was always scrupulously polite. "I must apologize if it seems that way. It was a genuine misunderstanding on my part. I had thought that under the circumstances he should carry on with his meeting and I could take notes."

"The circumstances were that I gave specific orders, and you saw fit to ignore them. If you ever countermand my instructions again, I will call the home office to have you removed from Malaysia."

Wale left the office feeling confused and a bit angry at the chairman's behavior. It was becoming apparent that he would have to start keeping his eyes open to what was a changing situation at Peninsular.

Soon thereafter, Wale asked Fisher about what had transpired during the meeting. Although Wale had never particularly got on with Fisher, finding Fisher's style too aloof for his tastes, he was confident that Fisher was sufficiently loyal to him not to discuss things with a local chairman behind Wale's back. Fisher said, "Oh, we mostly discussed the mechanics of the merger, the pricing of the shares, and that sort of thing. I told Tan Sri Nassan that NZI believes in keeping an arm's-length relationship with our foreign offices. Said we would act as corporate advisers and assured him that we wouldn't steamroll the minority stockholders." When Wale brought up the timing of the merger and his troubles with the bureaucracy, however, he was frustrated by Fisher's lack of support.

"I'm sure you will get things moving along. You're just going to have to stop spending so much time dealing with the politics," Fisher said, smiling weakly.

Wale understood that his point was not getting through. If he had learned one thing from his two and a half years in Malaysia, it was that business *was* politics here.

The Annual Planning Meeting

I guess I was fairly stunned.

Patrick Wale

In the next six months, the two companies made some real progress toward the merger. Wale met with the corporate attorneys, who calculated that, at the negotiated pricing, NZI should control 76 percent of the new entity, which would afford the company similar representation on the board. The company planned to keep the present four-to-four ratio of NZI representatives and local board members, however, to keep up the appearance of a joint venture.

For the moment, Wale was concerned with the annual planning meeting scheduled for the end of September. During the meeting, the managers of each of Peninsular's 12 regional branches would present their individual financial plans and their strategies, staffing, and support needs for the coming year. As Wale described it, "We would put all these into the melting pot at this workshop and then come back about a month later with a finalized plan on a countrywide basis. This was the start of that cycle—asking each territory to stand up for 15 to 20 minutes and give a rundown on their major objectives for the year, their strategies, and where their strengths and weaknesses were. Normally, it would be the practice of two or three of us at the KL office to ask probing questions of the branch manager." The managers were encouraged to try out new ideas and to question each other or Wale about operational practices. Wale saw this open forum as serving two purposes: It encouraged branch managers to think beyond their own office's needs, and it could anticipate many of the questions that would come from the home office when budget requests were reviewed.

This year, Wale was particularly concerned about the downturn in the Malaysian economy and wanted to keep the next year's costs to a minimum. (Peninsular was projecting a small loss for the year—see Exhibit 4.) As he always did, Wale asked the chairman if he would like to address the meeting before morning tea. The chairman agreed and accepted Wale's offer to write a brief speech on the state of the company.

The meeting was held in the board room; the large, adjustable table was that day configured in an open square, at which sat the 12 branch managers, the corporate secretary, the technology manager, Tan (the operations manager), Wale, and the chairman (seated next to each other). The morning started normally enough. The chairman offered his welcome to the branch managers and read Wale's opening statement. After the morning tea, Wale called the meeting to order. To his surprise, the chairman had not slipped out as he normally did but had come back to his seat next to Wale.

During the second presentation by a branch manager, Wale interrupted to question the manager's figures:

> Wale: "Mr. Lan, I'm not sure I see the basis for your staffing requirements. What are the growth projections that you are using for your figures?"
>
> Branch Manager: "We are forecasting a 15 percent growth in sales and revenues."
>
> Wale: "From what I have seen of your present operations, I would say that you already have the excess staffing necessary to support even a 15 percent growth,

EXHIBIT 4

Peninsular Insurance Financial History

NEW ZEALAND INSURANCE, LTD.
(NZ $ MILLIONS)

	1982	1983	1984
Revenues	630	752	805
Net income	28	18	49

PENINSULAR INSURANCE
(NZ $ MILLIONS)[1]

	1982	1983	1984	1985(e)
Revenues	5.6	4.9	4.8	4.2
Net income	.3	.6	.4	(.04)

[1]Converted at NZ $1.00 = 1.17 Malaysian ringitt. In 1985, NZ $1.00 = US $0.468.

which is certainly aggressive. From a cost basis, I do not see how you can justify that many more people. Do you suppose..."

Chairman: "Hold on, Patrick. It is very easy for you managers in the central office to look at numbers and question them. But this man is dealing with the reality of working in the field and seems to have very good reasons for his staffing numbers. You always expect these poor chaps in the branch to meet the targets, but then they never get the proper support from you. Now they cannot even get the staff they require to do their job correctly."

Wale (after pausing for a moment): "Mr. Chairman, perhaps we should take a look at this situation after the meeting. I'm sure we can discuss this and have it sorted out very quickly."

Chairman: "The issue is certainly an important one. I believe that all of the branch managers would like clarity about the signals they are getting from the central office in Kuala Lumpur. Mr. Lan's projections seem perfectly reasonable, and I know from my long association with Peninsular Insurance that his office is one of the finest in this organization. Mr. Lan, please continue with your excellent presentation. And Patrick, I will be happy to discuss this with yourself and Mr. Soo at the end of these proceedings."

The chairman waved his hand at Lan as a signal for him to continue. The branch manager stammered to a start and quickly moved on to a new topic.

Wale did not hear a word of it. The chairman's outburst had come as a complete shock, and Wale was trying to gather his wits and consider what his next move should be. He scanned the faces around the table as the managers quickly switched their eyes from him and back to the speaker. Soo returned his gaze with a look that was both stunned and quizzical, and Wale knew that they were thinking the same thing: "What is the old bugger up to?"

Wale was not about to stand aside. For the rest of the day, he continued to facilitate the meeting, but there was almost no free exchange of ideas from the managers from that point on. Everyone seemed to be concerned about saying something that might lead to another controversy. Meanwhile, the chairman continued to chime in, making it perfectly clear who he thought was in charge of the proceedings.

Wale wondered what his next move should be. He wondered what the chairman's next move would be. The man did have connections, and the merger was six months, at least, from completion. Having a retired bureaucrat who knew nothing about business attempting to run the show certainly was not going to help things along. And what about the other managers? Wale had never considered questioning their loyalty, but this episode put everything in a new light.

Case 34

Dollar General Corporation (B)

Part of the fun of being the leader is being able to set the pace of values your company has. You have to trust people. A lot of companies are held back by leaders who are not trusting. People know [when] they are not trusted, and those who know they are not trusted are going to wind up being less trustworthy. . . .

Cal Turner, Jr.
Advantage, November 1987

December 1987

As he skied down the slopes of the Rocky Mountains in Utah, Cal Turner, Jr., was trying to sort out the happenings in Dollar General over the previous 34 months, which had culminated in disastrous financials, a company in turmoil, and the deterioration in his relationship with his chief operating officer (his younger brother, Steve). He needed the solitude and cold air to clear his head.

A tremendous amount of change had occurred in Dollar General since the acquisition of Eagle Stores in early 1985, and Cal Jr. now had to provide decisive leadership to arrest the downward trend in the performance of his company. The year 1985 had been bad, 1986 was worse, and, even though there were signs of slight recovery in 1987, the company was still a long way from the good health it had enjoyed in the early 1980s. (See Exhibit 1 for financials.)

The Deal with Interco

Eagle Family Discount Stores, Inc., bought from Interco in February 1985, were the stores Cal Jr. had always wanted, because of their locations in a high-potential region. Florida was a state with dense populations of low-, middle-, and fixed-income families—according to Cal Jr., "a lot of our kind of customers who want the basic consumables." Other benefits of Eagle were the attractive store locations, many of which were in busy, strip shopping centers. In addition, Interco had been persistent with its efforts to make a deal with Dollar General (DG).

Dollar General turned Interco down twice, in April and in July 1984, on the grounds that DG field management was still in the early stages of managing the Hirsch acquisition. Interco came back with a sweetened offer in October 1984. This time serious discussions were initiated.

On February 11, 1985, DG acquired certain assets and assumed leasehold liabilities of the 206 Eagle retail stores for approximately $35 million. The acquisition

This case was written by Anrug Sharma, MBA 1988, and Associate Professor L. J. Bourgeois III, with the research assistance of Rafael Villanueva, MBA 1988. Revised 7/93.

EXHIBIT 1

Dollar General Corporation Financial Data 1982–1986

Financial Highlights
(dollars in thousands except per share amounts)

	1986	1985	1984	1983	1982
Net sales	$564,782	$584,437	$480,514	$346,655	$290,069
Cost of goods sold	409,416	411,904	337,029	244,094	205,837
Operating expenses	140,885	130,413	99,341	71,077	60,834
Interest expense	6,852	7,341	4,146	1,808	1,665
Income taxes	3,311	16,950	19,400	14,550	10,400
Net income	$ 4,318	$ 17,829	$ 20,598	$ 15,126	$ 11,333
Weighted-average shares outstanding (000)	18,793	18,791	18,785	18,754	18,744
Net income per share	$.23	$.95	$1.10	$.81	$.60
Cash dividends per share	$.20	$.20	$.17	$.13	$.11
Return on average assets	1.88%	8.88%	12.55%	11.61%	11.55%
Return on average equity	3.98%	17.66%	24.16%	21.54%	19.14%
Total assets	$232,388	$227,566	$173,963	$154,299	$106,223
Stockholders' equity	108,789	107,955	93,916	76,582	63,825
Long-term obligations	$ 52,258	$ 64,265	$ 26,950	$ 35,720	$ 12,118
Company-owned stores	1,303	1,278	1,080	1,127	823

Stock Prices by Quarter

	1985		1986	
	High bid	Low bid	High bid	Low bid
1st Q	27 ½	20 ¾	24 ⅛	18 ¾
2nd Q	29 ⅜	19 ¼	21 ½	18 ¼
3rd Q	28 ⅞	19 ¼	21 ¼	12 ⅛
4th Q	23 ¾	18	15 ¾	12 ¼

was accounted for as a purchase and funded through internally generated funds, installment notes payable to Interco, and a revolving term loan with the banks.

A Year of Adjustment

While the price was right, and the deal made sense from a broad, strategic perspective, the acquisition was hardly an off-the-shelf fit with the Dollar General organization. One problem was Eagle's warehouse complex in southern Florida. It consisted of several dilapidated World War II hangar buildings and had a chemical manufacturing plant on the premises.

DG decided, however, to keep the warehouse buildings until the following February (1986), because there was a one-year lease remaining with the Dade Airport Authority, and management believed it would take about a year to find a subsitute. "The first time we could see it [working]," said Cal Jr., "was after we bought it."

According to Cal Jr., "The culture there was totally different." Eagle appeared to have no systems, and management discipline was lacking. The employees were mostly non-English-speaking Cubans, so there was a communication problem to start with. Reflecting on his first official visit to the warehouse, Cal Jr. said, "I remember my first talk—I stood up and told them about our company and everything, and introduced Steve [Turner] who would have a more direct role down there. Then after about five minutes, they sort of announced, 'Now an interpreter will give them your message.' Only then did I realize they did not speak English!... The two words we got from them were 'no problem, no problem.' I would say, 'This is what I would like you to do: Take this box up there.' 'No problem, no problem.' And they would not do it either.... They were picking merchandise from all levels of racks, and they had soft goods on the top shelf. If someone needed blouses, he would pull with a long stick, and two dozen would fall down. He would pick up the six that he wanted and leave the rest there. That is the kind of way that place was. Man, I couldn't get out of there soon enough."

In addition, the merchandise in the warehouse was not the same as that supplied to the DG stores outside Florida. Eagle customers were predominantly males purchasing pool supplies, cigarettes, and automotive equipment. "So, here we are," said Cal Jr., "with all these stores to convert, without our kind of warehousing, without our kind of employees, without our kind of merchandise, yet in a market that has a lot of potential."

Tom Holsted, who was the assistant warehouse manager with Eagle at the time of the merger, maintained a diary of events on the job. In it, he described the premerger scene this way: "During the last few months of 1984, Eagle had begun to turn around. Gene Howenstein, the new president since August 1, was intrumental in changing the morale of the employees, and everyone was optimistic about the future. Store sales were encouraging, buyers were busy planning their overseas trips, and exciting new goods were rolling into the distribution center.

"One day in October, Ron Aylward of Interco and Gene Howenstein arrived unannounced at the warehouse at 7:30 in the morning. This was an unusual visit because of the early hour, and because they were accompanied by a stranger who was casually dressed. Neither Aylward nor Howenstein bothered to introduce the stranger.

"Then, towards the end of the year, rumors began to circulate that the company was going to be sold. No one, however, paid attention to it because such rumors had been around for years.

"Around the middle of January 1985, two buyers said that their Orient trip had been cancelled. This reignited the speculation that we were being sold. From then on it was a guessing game about who the new owners would be.

"On Friday the 1st of February, management was asked to attend a meeting in the president's office at 4 P.M. There, Gene announced that Interco had contracted to sell all of the stores and related assets of Eagle Family Discount Stores, Inc., to Dollar General Corporation, of Scottsville, Kentucky. He informed us that our employment would terminate upon closing of the sale, which would be toward the end of the month. He said that Dollar General intended to operate the stores and the distribution center, and wished to consider some of us for employment.

"On Tuesday, the 5th, we were called into a meeting with Howenstein and Aylward. Also present was the stranger from October, but this time he was introduced as Cal Turner, Jr., president of Dollar General. Mr. Turner introduced his brother, Steve, the executive vice president of the company, and they told us about their plans for Eagle. The meeting then moved to the distribution center, where the Turners visited with warehouse employees.

"On Monday, the 11th, DG representatives from Scottsville and Dumas, Arkansas, arrived to begin the transformation of Eagle to Dollar General. The predominantly Cuban staff in the distribution center was somewhat bewildered, and, at times, amused by these strangers with funny accents. We all had to take a P.E.P (pre-employment profile) test before being officially deemed employees of Dollar General. These were very stressful times for many of our people who did not speak English and could not understand the test, even with the aid of an interpreter. But we made it, and were officially Dollar General employees on the 22nd of February."

To assimilate Eagle into the parent organization, DG reinstituted the exhausting process they had used with the P. N. Hirsch acquisition. Physical conversions, from one set of fixtures and physical inventory to another, took substantial dollar investments and taxed the field management to its limits.

An important component of the strategy was to screen current Eagle employees and rehire the ones that fit the bill. A consulting psychologist was sent down to Florida to conduct a management inventory. He came back with a report that "the district managers there are just about average to your existing ones, nothing great, but I don't see anything quite great among your existing managers either."

Perhaps because of the culture shock, perhaps because of the uncertainty that comes along with a merger, the first few months after the acquisition saw a tremendous amount of turnover among Eagle employees. DG decided to close the office portion of Eagle and run the operations from Scottsville. Steve Turner, at 40 the youngest of the Turners, took charge of merchandising and operations in Florida. He retained only two members of the Eagle management team: Bill Bragg, district manager with Eagle, was assigned to be the area manager in charge of Florida, and Tom Holsted was taken in as the Florida warehouse manager.

The main problem in assimilating the Eagle Stores, however, was the difference between the two company cultures. While Dollar General Corporation prided itself on the strong work ethic and honest character of its employees, and believed that lack of complicated systems and procedures was its major strength, the old Eagle management had established control through rules, regulations, and (as perceived by some employees) manipulation, intimidation, and coercion. According to Bob Carpenter, Dollar General's vice president of administration at the time, "Our system was so much more lax than what they were used to, they thought no one cared."

RESULTS AND ANALYSIS OF THE FIRST YEAR

Considering the additional tax of the Eagle merger on company resources, DG's weak financial results for the year were not totally unexpected. Even though corporate sales increased by over $100 million to $584.4 million (over 80 percent of this increase from the acquired Florida stores), high conversion and operating expenses resulted in a 13 percent drop in net income.

The average P. N. Hirsch store cost 17.1 percent more to operate than an old Dollar General store but produced only 2.4 percent more in sales. The cost of operating an average Eagle store was also high, but whether the costs reflected any chronic problems was not clear because of the distortions from liquidations, conversions, and grand-opening activities.

Total corporate inventory shrinkage (the year-end difference between inventory on the books and inventory as counted) was $18.45 million, which represented 3.2 percent of annual sales. (The industry average was about 1.5 to 2 percent.) Because approximately half of this figure came from the new Florida stores, management believed that it reflected the strain on operations arising from the first phase of settling down. The shrinkage was expected to be substantially reduced in the following year.

Contrast between the Hirsch and Eagle Acquisitions

While 1984 also had been a year of transition for DG as the 850-store company assimilated the 280 Hirsch stores, there were significant differences between the Hirsch and Eagle acquisitions. The Hirsch stores increased DG's presence in its immediate marketplace, particularly Illinois and Missouri. Lease costs of the acquired locations were slightly lower than those of the existing Dollar General leases. The merchandise and target customers were about the same. Liquidation sales coincided with the high-volume Christmas shopping season, and conversion of stores began in January, a slack retailing month. Also, the stores were in good condition, so they required a modest conversion investment. From an operational standpoint, the geographical proximity of the Hirsch stores made it relatively easy for the field management to keep an eye on existing Dollar General stores while they brought Hirsch into the fold.

The Eagle acquisition, coming just 15 months after the Hirsch one, caught middle managers just as they were recovering from the exhausting first bout. The timing was also a drawback, in that the peak Christmas selling season had passed, and with it the chance to unload unwanted inventory profitably. Furthermore, Eagle did not offer the product and market synergies that Hirsch had.

DG's weak performance in 1985 raised some immediate operational concerns. All the functions in the company had been stretched to their limits as a result of the two acquisitions, and a need was perceived for developing systems that would satisfy the control necessary in a larger organization. "While all this conversion of the stores was going on," wrote Tom Holsted, "we were getting calls in the distribution center from Store Managers, asking us what they were to do with completed credit requests books. Books completed months earlier were being found under the tables and in backrooms. They were not processed by the Scottsville office. We were receiving such calls up until the closing of our warehouse for repair in January [1986]."

In keeping with its philosophy of low overhead, DG had always operated with a thin staff at the senior-management and corporate-office level. The 280 Hirsch stores had added responsibilities to an already thinly staffed company, and the addition of another 206 Eagle stores stretched the management resources immensely.

Events of 1986

Distribution in Miami

DG allowed the lease on the Miami warehouse to expire on February 5, 1986. In fact, the warehouse ceased functioning at the end of 1985, because certain repairs had to be performed before the buildings were handed over to the owners. Noting the events leading up to the closing, Tom Holsted wrote, "In the middle of August, Steve Turner arrived and met with the supervisors individually and explained the closing to them. I was already aware of this from my earlier conversations with Steve and Sammy Allen, Director of Warehousing and Distribution.

"Steve offered them incentive pay if they would stay until the phase-out was complete. Every supervisor pledged his support till the end. I went out along with an interpreter and met with each department one by one, and every employee said that they appreciated our not waiting till Christmas to tell them.

"During the next four months everything was just routine. We continued serving our stores and preparing them for the Christmas selling season. December consisted of pulling and shipping final orders to the stores, preparing and taking the year-end inventory, and, sadly for me, the final Christmas luncheon with these employees, who endured so much this year.

"During January our maintenance department completed the repairs on the buildings. On the evening of February 4, 1986, Steve Turner called and instructed me to cease operation, close the division and liquidate."

The firm was building a 250,000-square-foot, highly automated distribution center in Homerville, Georgia, that was to become fully operative in September 1986. In the interim, the Florida stores were to be served from the Scottsville and Dumas distribution centers. However, this process was costly and disruptive. The personnel in the Arkansas warehouse strained under this additional load, and, as a result, even this warehouse began to experience high employee turnover. Problems in the quality of delivery arose, and the normal two-week delivery cycle stretched to three weeks. The merchandise mix reaching Florida stores was inconsistent with the demand, even with the climate. For example, the clothing shipped was meant for young people, while the demographics in Florida were skewed toward older folks. In one instance, chocolate bars shipped to the stores all melted in the Florida heat.

To overcome an increasingly acute problem of shortage of merchandise in Florida stores, Steve Turner, who was then DG's chief operating officer, established an independent company called ADS (Advanced Distribution Services). ADS leased 15 satellite warehouses, located in metropolitan areas among DG's 23 states (two in Florida), to distribute merchandise (especially high-bulk items such as pillows and diapers) to the DG stores through contracts with local freight companies. As part of a general overhaul of control systems, the company also put in place in 1986 a computerized system for tracking merchandise, although bugs in the software prevented it from being totally effective. In March of 1986, in an effort to address the control problem, DG hired Mike Haggard, an attorney, to head internal security and management information systems (MIS).

Management Restructuring

During this period, Cal Jr. began to feel that the company was losing its edge in opportunistic buying and that indecisive leadership in merchandising was one of the reasons. He had significant differences with Steve, in management style and philosophy, which surfaced as the two brothers disagreed on how the systematic problems in merchandising were to be tackled.

For example, earlier (late 1984), Steve had been having his own problems with the general merchandising manager (in charge of buyers), who worked almost independently. He would not take direction from Steve and was busy building his own empire in the critical merchandising department. But, in spite of Cal Jr.'s urging, Steve could not bring himself to fire him. Finally, Cal Jr. had to fire him. Steve then promoted a personal friend, Ron Humphrey, as the new general merchandising manager.

The management group recognized that merchandising had been, for perhaps too long, the core function in the company, and the nine buyers making purchasing decisions for the entire firm were, essentially, directing the course of the business. According to one executive, "To be a buyer, you have 'arrived' in this company." Cal Jr. said, "We had a culture of being great buyers. We believed our customer needed to come in and see what we had bought—kind of a buying culture, not a selling culture. We needed to change that.... I felt that, if we got better in touch with the customer and competition, we could bring about that change (away) from merchandising."

To accomplish this goal, Cal Jr. restructured the company in the fall of 1986 (see Exhibit 2). In September, Carol Harris was brought in as vice president of marketing, a newly created function to infuse a marketing orientation in the "buy low/sell low" organization. Advertising was shifted from Steve Turner and, along with store development, put under Carol. Steve was given the key portfolios of merchandising (buying), store operations, and distribution. Ed Burke (secretary) retained finance; data processing was transferred to Mike Haggard in administration; and Bob Carpenter was assigned human resources.

Two further steps were considered to deal with the changing character of the company. One was a move of headquarters to Nashville, Tennessee, and the other was an increased emphasis on formal planning sessions.

The Move to Nashville

The issue of moving corporate headquarters was a ticklish one. Steve and Cal Jr. agreed that a move from Scottsville was necessary if the company was to attract management talent to run an increasingly complex organization. Moreover, the distribution center in Scottsville had made it a hub of activity, and it was common practice for line managers to come to the corporate office for help in making operating decisions. This phenomenon distracted senior management from cultivating a more strategic view of the business. Moving away from Scottsville, the corporate staff believed, would enable it to concentrate on larger issues facing the company.

On the other hand, the company had its roots in Scottsville. The firm's public relations line was: We are a small-town company, operating small stores in small towns, and keeping close to our customer. When Cal Jr. took the proposal to Cal Turner, Sr., the startled founder and chairman of the board said, "Son, I must admit that I am not rational, I am emotional about this. However, I know it is absolutely the wrong thing to do."

Cal Jr. was not able to convince Cal Sr. about the value of this change. Although upset, Cal Jr.'s father respected him enough not to resist the move actively, and the corporate functions were finally transferred to Nashville in November 1986.

EXHIBIT 2

Dollar General Corporation Organization Structures

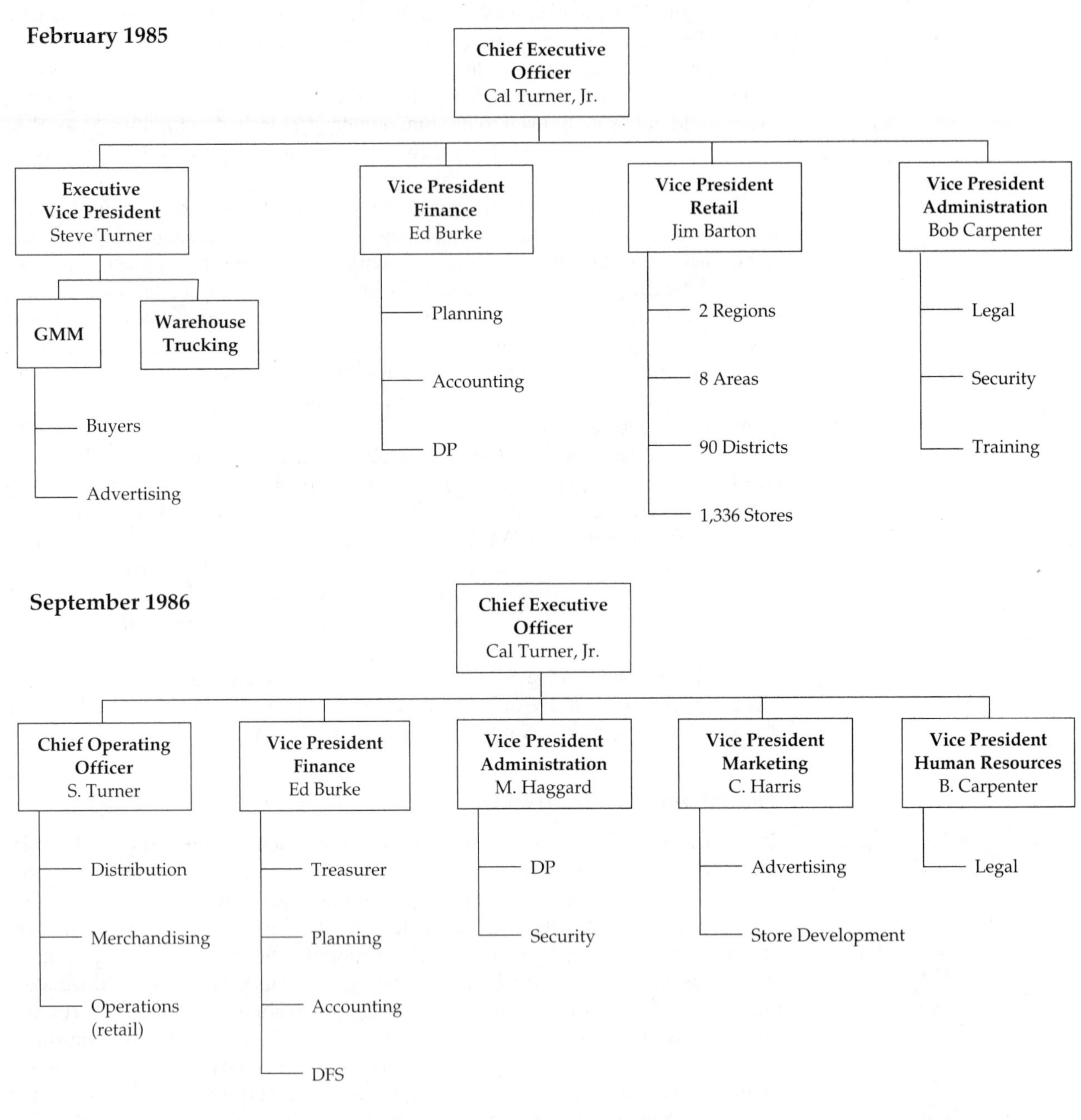

"I still had to deal with the rest of the Scottsville society," Cal Jr. said long after the move. "I had to explain to them that we were only moving headquarters staff, not the warehouse operations, and that the guts of DG would remain in Scottsville. I stated this in a speech to the Rotary Club." Cal Sr., however, remained upset for a long time.

PLANNING

The need for strategic planning, unlike the move, was something everyone agreed on. The process had been initiated in the late 1970s, was abandoned somewhat during the acquisition period, but was resumed with vigor in February 1986 in response to the high inventory shrinkage and employee turnover of the previous year.

A week-long planning session in September 1986 brought all the senior executives together in Hamilton, New York, to chart a course for the ailing organization. In attendance were the Turner brothers, Ed Burke (finance), Bob Carpenter (human resources), Jim Barton (operations), and Mike Haggard (administration). Also present was Carol Harris, vice president of marketing, on her first day with the company.

The agenda for this meeting included a reexamination of the business strategy and development of mission statements for the company. "We worked very, very hard for two, two-and-a-half days on the mission statement," recalled Carol, "and were about brain-dead by the middle of the week." The remainder of the week was spent setting operating goals for 1987. The charge at the end of the week was for each executive to develop operating plans to achieve his or her department's goals. These plans were to be shared at the December meeting.

Carol found the lack of planning after Hamilton to be very frustrating. As Bob Carpenter recalled, "After returning to work, we all got caught up in putting out fires." The meeting, according to Carol, "was followed up in December 1986 with what was supposed to be an update on where everybody was relative to the actual plans that had been formulated. But there was no sense of an operating plan, no accountability systems in place; there were no budget responsibilities. Here we are in December, and all we have done is set targets. There was a retail sales goal, but we did not get to the operating plans for 1987 until we were well into the second quarter (of 1987). So it was a feeling of business just sort of slipping away from you.

"We started out with the intent to devote two full days a month to planning, and we did not do that. We did not review the financials. Ed Burke was proprietary about the financial data." Bob Carpenter corroborated: "Ed had the philosophy of 'let me worry about the figures, the rest of you go out and operate.' Ed would not allow others to research data from his department."

"I had a $17 million budget out there," Carol continued, "working on its own with a mediocre general ledger system to keep track of it. It was a matter of trying to hold the thing together with chewing gum and paper clips.... So what I was experiencing was a combination of frustration and curiosity as to how you could run a business with 1,300 stores and not be in the stores. It was obvious that the personnel needed training and that no one had talked to them in a long time. We'd show up in the hinterlands of Pennsylvania and you would think we were the long lost relatives from Paducah. There had been some erosion of the customer base, and we were not asking the questions that you would expect in a corporation this size."

EVENTS OF 1987

Just before the 1986 numbers were to be released, Ed Burke walked into Cal Jr.'s office with financials in hand, and said, "Coopers and Lybrand suggest that we check with our lenders before we release these."

"Oh? Well, what do *you* say, Ed?" asked Cal Jr.

"Well." Pause. "We do have some covenant violations."

"We can handle those, but I don't know why we need to hold on to the financials."

"Look," Ed said, "we have some covenant violations, which if the lenders don't waive, can be a basis for their calling the loan." Ed took a deep breath. "And we cannot cover the loan."

For Cal, this news was emotionally devastating: "Look at this company! Look at its history! And look at its profitability!... We did one acquisition which was good. We have a few problems with the second one, and now the CFO comes in and talks Chapter 11!"

When the 1986 numbers came out, everybody was shocked. For the first time in the firm's history, sales had dropped—from $584 million in 1985 to $564 million in 1986. Net income had shrunk from $17 million in 1985 to just $4 million in 1986, and the inventory shrinkage had shot up sharply to about $22 million.

The results implied to Cal Jr. that he was not in complete control of the company. Steve wasn't either, even though Cal Jr. had delegated to him responsibility for merchandising, distribution, store operations—for the most part, the guts of the business. Cal had mostly kept close ties with human resources, the people end of the business.

Management Response

Initial management response to this first clear sign of deterioration in the company was to step up internal security, because the high shrinkage figure—3.9 percent of sales as opposed to the anticipated 2.6 percent—was particularly troublesome. Moreover, of the $21.6 million reported in shrinkage losses for 1986, only $7.4 million came from Florida stores; the rest came from the older stores!

Shoplifting and pilferage alone could not explain the large numbers: It was awfully hard for somebody to walk off with merchandise worth thousands of dollars, because the stores carried cheap and bulky items. The indication was that something big was going on in the company and that management was not even aware of it. The only way so much money could be diverted was to have truckloads of merchandise never making their way to the stores. "So," said Cal Jr., "we decided to staff a real internal security department and have investigators go out ... and stop the hemorrhage."

A director of loss prevention was hired in May, with specific responsibilities for security protection and auditing of company records. Steve made a request for five additional investigators, but Cal Jr. believed that a slow buildup was important to avoid mishandling of the situation. He approved two investigators in the new department before he took off for a vacation in August.

Focus Groups

Although they did not account for the bulk of shrinkage, the Florida shrinkage numbers were bad enough that in January 1987 Carol Harris and Bob Carpenter each visited 10 stores and conducted focus group interviews among the field managers in Miami, Tampa, and Jacksonville to get a handle on what was going on in Florida. The results were disturbing: Nobody was concerned about the massive shortfall in inventory.

In her notes on the meeting with Marty McGrath, a district manager in the Jacksonville area, Carol wrote, "Marty was unable to present a clear profile of the typical Dollar General customer in his district. He did not know the population of

Jacksonville, nor was he prepared to give me any kind of specific information which would help me better understand the other markets within his district. He merely described his customers as people looking for a bargain.... In all honesty I cannot fault Marty for not better understanding his market and his customer. I have yet to ask this question of any district manager and get a clear, succinct description. It is not surprising that when emphasis from management is placed on retail operations that a market-driven orientation is absent.

"He doesn't know. This should not be surprising, given that Marty received no formal training.... He began his career with Dollar General as part of the conversion team. He said that someone gave him the key, said he could do it, and hit the road.

"He made a very interesting comment: He said that he thought Dollar General was nothing more than repackaged Eagle, that Dollar General was Eagle with a new name. When you get right down to it, he said, Dollar General is the same old chain of old, nasty, ugly stores. ... The former Eagle managers feel as if they were 'conquered.'"

Bob Carpenter's notes indicated that "there is a great deal of resentment toward the Scottsville operations group. There is an 'us versus them' attitude throughout the area. The feeling is that 'we don't need country bumpkins telling us how to run a store in Florida. If you leave us alone we'll show you.'"

The "us versus them" attitude was found in all three cities. Bill Bragg, the Florida area manager, fostered it by telling Eagle district managers (DMs) not to call Scottsville for anything but to go through him. The DMs told their store managers not to contact their Scottsville bookkeepers, the warehouse, or anyone else, without going through the DM first. In effect, Florida was isolating itself from its new owners.

In retrospect, at least one executive believed that the conversion was attempted too quickly: "We threw up a (Dollar General) sign and expected the consumer to beat the doors down." Some experienced DG area and district managers were sent down from better areas and districts in the country to do the conversion, and they reported to Scottsville that they were doing the conversions as fast as possible. With the Hirsch experience behind them, they wanted to get this over with. They were working furiously—going from store to store—hoping to be able to return to their homes soon. As it was, many of them were away (in Florida) for six months.

Another executive recalled, "It was not uncommon for a store manager to be recruited and, in a period of a week or two weeks, to be given the keys to the store and be told by the district manager, 'I'll be back.' Well, six months roll around and the DM shows up again, and here's the poor person he trusted with a quarter of a million dollars worth of inventory who has never been told how to order, what to do with the inventory when she does receive it, how to calculate a daily rate of sales, how to hire and fire and train and develop those employees."

Finally, Bob Carpenter commented, "Our wage structure, which was based on a rural Kentucky standard, was very different from the urban pay structure in our Florida stores. No reliable people were available at our wage structure in urban areas. So Jim Barton, vice president of retail operations, worked out a policy to account for the pay differences between our rural and urban stores. He, however, had a difficult time doing this because he dealt on a store-by-store basis, and if you have 1,300 stores to work on, it is impossible to do a good job."

It became clear from the focus groups that Bill Bragg (Florida area manager) was working against Scottsville management. He was fired in January 1987. In addition,

Jim Barton's ability to manage the increased number of stores came into question. In May he was demoted to administrator of Florida stores and subsequently reassigned as an area manager for Orlando, North Florida. In the same month, Philip Wright was brought into the corporate office to fill the position left by Barton.

The Turmoil of 1987

Almost immediately after the focus groups in February, DG sent a team, a hit squad of sorts, to assess the situation in Florida. A large number of district and store managers were polygraphed, drug screened, and interviewed by psychologists. Those suspected of being involved in individual theft at the store level, or organized theft, were fired. The idea was to root out the cancer quickly and go on with assimilating Eagle employees into the DG culture—something that had been neglected as the management focused on physical conversions.

As a first attempt at putting together a corporate culture program in Florida, at Carol Harris's suggestion, a series of meetings called "Camp Dollar General" was started in May 1987. The series was a combination of meetings for two-and-a-half days, in four different sessions, to bring every store and district manager in Florida up-to-date in terms of the firm's plans in the state and to outline DG's corporate history and culture; it was also a forum for people to get together and exchange ideas. This program was completed within a month.

The director of loss prevention had begun to snoop around in Florida at about the same time as Camp Dollar General was introduced. From May through July 20, 1987, he worked on 45 cases. Then, as he got deeper into the situation, he recognized that the problem was more serious than it appeared. In the next month, when the two special investigators were added, the security department really started cranking.

Theft was uncovered at every level of the organization—in the field, at the store-manager level, at the clerk level, the DM level, and the area-manager level. Eventually, it was also uncovered at the buyer level. The investigation uncovered three buyers accepting cash payments and/or gifts from vendors. This much could be verified, although other allegations had been made as well. In addition, two buyers were found to be having a love affair. As Bob Carpenter recalled, "We noticed a change in the lifestyles of (some of) our merchandisers."

The firing started about mid-1987, and the numbers increased as the momentum built up. About 400 people were terminated as a result of investigations; criminal proceedings were initiated against a large number of employees; and nearly 150 arrests were made. The turnover among store managers and clerks reached over 200 percent during this period. "Where does it end?" Cal Jr. thought, "Where will it stop? I mean, how much of the iceberg has been exposed?"

He realized that DG's problems went beyond the pervasive stealing. The 1984 bookkeeping system was adequate for 850 stores, but they now had 480 more stores to crank out weekly reports on. So the load of stores per bookkeeper had gone up by a third.

Cal Jr. had an interesting analogy for the state of the company after Eagle was purchased: "Look, we were used to growth, and we were like a teenager who has his jeans too short because he is growing so rapidly. He will be used to that, as that growth is normal. But if he really had a spurt of growth, he would burst the rear end out of his jeans. And that is what happened to us. Our ass was showing."

In Cal Jr.'s mind, a major problem was the CFO. Ed Burke, unable to demonstrate that he could take charge of the problem, fell from grace. As one executive put it, "Ed Burke was capable, but he was not capable of handling a bigger company." He was let go in July 1987. Bob Carpenter was named secretary and was asked to fill the CFO spot for about two months until Bruce Quinnell was hired as CFO and treasurer in September.

Meanwhile, Steve had allowed three more of the requested additional investigators to be hired while Cal Jr. was away on vacation in August. When Cal returned, he was upset at what he considered an impulsive decision, and he did not appreciate not being consulted by Steve on the padding of the security department.

Fall Restructuring

Cal Jr. described his brother as "more emotional, whereas I am more practical." As one executive put it, "Steve studied philosophy; Cal studied business administration. Steve is more of a procrastinator who will ponder over a decision—unlike Cal, who is more of a decision maker." Cal Jr. recalled, "Steve is seven years younger than I, and early in life he was determined to be different from me. Growing up, Steve said, 'Cal Jr., I wish you'd go on and decide what you want to do, so I know what I am not going to do. I don't want you to be my boss.' It's tough on him. I came into the company under one shadow (Cal Sr.); Steve came in under two, trying to become a shadow generator himself."

Now Cal Jr. had become disenchanted with his brother's role in the business; he felt Steve did not have the capability to provide meaningful direction to merchandising and operations, let alone run the company in the event something were to happen to Cal Jr. Consequently, he hired Jim Holland in September as an executive vice president with the express responsibility of leading the strategic-planning effort in the company, but with Cal intending to groom him as a possible successor.

The company was restructured into three broad areas: operations, finance, and development. Steve's portfolio remained untouched, but Bruce Quinnell came in as CFO, and Jim Holland was given (in addition to planning) responsibilities in marketing, MIS, and human resources.

Jim Holland's first responsibilities were to get the team ready for the fall planning session in Hamilton, develop an operating plan for 1988, and begin thinking about a long-range plan for the next five years. When his plans were revealed at the meeting, however, he was a disaster. Unable to adapt to the culture and the human dynamic in the company, he recommended remedies that were totally out of sync with the realities of the situation. His personality and planning procedures were too rigid and inflexible. Carol Harris noted, "The company was not ready (for Jim). He came with a ... planning process ... that was too much, too soon, too radical, and too much of a departure from what people were used to. They rejected it totally." When asked to modify his process to fit DG's culture, Jim said, "Absolutely not. I'm in charge of planning. We will do it my way." Steve could not stand him, and threatened to resign. So Jim Holland was gone in five weeks.

Post-Planning Struggle

After the meeting, Cal Jr. decided he needed to get personally involved in the running of the business if he was to revive his ailing company. Operations and merchandising were both in disarray, and he had certain ideas about how he wanted to go about fixing them.

After Jim Holland left, Cal said to Steve, "Now we've got to get our stuff together, you and I, because merchandising and operations are both broke."

Steve said, "Merchandising is okay. I can handle it. You take operations and run it the way you want."

Cal responded, "I want to divide the two and bring in experienced people from other retailers to run them. Why don't you become the vice chairman of the board? That way you can influence the strategic direction of the business and still be involved in the affairs of the firm."

Steve realized that Cal was trying to move him away from the mainstream; he said, "If I can't be actively involved in the running of the business, I am not going to do it."

Cal said, "Okay, then *act* like a chief operating officer. Let's agree upon an agenda for the development of this company. I just want to see what your budget is going to be for the next year, what sales are. Let us talk about that."

Steve replied, "Well, give me some time. I will get the group together and work it out, and then get back to you."

Steve convened his group and put together an action plan for the following year. That plan was completely unacceptable to Cal Jr., however, because "it contained no action. It consisted of items such as, 'Consider doing an analysis of . . .' or 'conduct a study of. . . .' The line items did not add up to the sales target, and the sales goals which the whole executive team set in September had been reduced, unilaterally, by Steve." To Cal Jr., this was just further evidence that Steve did not want to take direction from him.

So Cal Jr. faced a dilemma: On the one hand, the business was faring badly, and on the other, his brother, who had the responsibility for merchandising and operations, was resisting the changes Cal wanted to implement. For the first time in his long career, Cal Jr. was feeling frustrated: He just did not know what to do.

In addition, he was beginning to get the word that Steve was politicking among the management group, trying to draw people into his camp and have them swear allegiance to him. Cal had stumbled on this situation quite accidentally. One morning in November, an executive was sitting in Cal Jr.'s office, and the two were discussing plans for the coming year. The conversation shifted to the plan figures that Steve had turned in, and Cal Jr. said, "There probably isn't agreement on these numbers."

The executive replied, "Well, there is more disagreement going on than you may realize."

"You mean within the company?"

The executive leaned forward in his chair and said emphatically, "*Yes*, in this company."

Cal inferred that the executive wanted him to ask more, so he said, "Somebody has been talking to you about this, and I guess it is Steve."

"Yes."

As the executive later recounted, "Steve had talked to me about his feelings for his brother, and he was lining us all up. All of us who worked for him were going to have to make a choice. It was coming down to camp A and camp B, and he wanted to get a bunch of us who reported to him firmly entrenched in his camp."

Another executive recalled, "Steve would tell me about the conversations that he and his brother would have, and he would share with me how frustrated he was with his brother and would go back to what it was like when they were growing up. He would reference Cal's management style and his ability to run the company, and he would cast a great deal of doubt on whether or not, he thought, Cal could run the company.

"Steve was forcing Cal's hand. What he told me he wanted to do was to force Cal into making a decision about him, and that if Cal fired him, he was going to call for a meeting of the board and a special vote of the shareholders. He wanted Cal to make a decision to leave the company. The message I was getting from Steve was: Both of us cannot be here; one of us is going to have to make a choice."

The Ski Trip of December 1987

The events of the previous three years had resulted in a major cultural and moral transformation in Dollar General. Once a company with essentially a rural character, the retailer had encountered major problems in extending itself into the unknown by going into urban Florida, where the way of life was not in tune with the values of small-town America. In an effort to overcome these problems, Cal had restructured management two times in less than two years, and the turnover at the senior-executive level had been more than he anticipated. Consequently, operational performance and morale in the company were way down. It was a clear case of indigestion, and Cal was wondering whether, for once, he had bitten off more than he could chew. (See Exhibit 3 for the 1987 third quarter results.)

In addition to all these changes, Cal could not take charge with the chief operating officer of the company resisting every move he wanted to make.

What Cal had to resolve before he got off the ski slopes was: "How do I take charge and turn this company around without adversely affecting the matrix of relationships—particularly with the family and with Steve—that I have to manage?"

EXHIBIT 3

Dollar General Corporation Third-Quarter Report 1987[1]
(dollars in thousands except per share amounts)

For the periods ended September 30:

	Three Months	
	1987	1986
Net sales	$136,879	$133,966
Income before taxes	1,332	1,302
Taxes on income	583	565
Net income	749	737
Net income per share	$.04	$.04
Weighted-average shares outstanding	18,876	18,792

	Nine Months	
	1987	1986
Net sales	$398,863	$378,632
Income before taxes	2,179	1,088
Taxes on income	954	472
Net income	1,225	616
Net income per share	$.07	$.03
Weighted-average shares outstanding	18,839	18,788

[1]Subject to year-end audit and adjustments.

CASE 35

THE WALT DISNEY COMPANY: THE ARRIVAL OF EISNER AND WELLS

In the fall of 1984, Walt Disney Productions announced the selection of a new executive team:

> Michael D. Eisner was elected Chairman and Chief Executive Officer of Walt Disney Productions in September 1984.
>
> Formerly President and Chief Operating Officer of Paramount Pictures Corporation for eight years, Mr. Eisner was closely involved in that studio's major motion picture successes during his tenure, including *Saturday Night Fever, Grease, Raiders of the Lost Ark, Indiana Jones and the Temple of Doom* and *Terms of Endearment.* He also was instrumental in Paramount's lineup of hit television series, including *Happy Days, Taxi* and *Cheers.* During Mr. Eisner's tenure, Paramount Pictures Corporation enjoyed unprecedented success, achieving six consecutive fiscal year records for revenues and earnings.
>
> Prior to joining Paramount, Mr. Eisner was Senior Vice President, Prime Time Production and Development, for ABC Entertainment. Under his leadership, ABC became the No. 1 prime time network through development of series, limited series and motion picture programming. Earlier, ABC gained network leadership in daytime, early morning and children's programming under Mr. Eisner's direction.
>
> Mr. Eisner began his career in the entertainment industry at CBS Television with the network's programming department.
>
> A native of New York City, Mr. Eisner attended Lawrenceville School and graduated from Denison University of Granville, Ohio.
>
> Frank G. Wells was elected President and Chief Operating Officer of Walt Disney Productions in September 1984.
>
> Previously, Mr. Wells was Vice Chairman of Warner Bros., Inc., the motion picture subsidiary of Warner Communications. During 15 years with Warner Bros., Mr. Wells also served as Vice President—West Coast (1969), President (1973) and as Co-Chief Executive Officer (1977).
>
> Before his association with Warner Bros., Mr. Wells was a partner in the Hollywood Law firm of Gang, Tyre and Brown, practicing in the field of entertainment industry law for 10 years.
>
> A Phi Beta Kappa graduate of Pomona College at Claremont, California, Mr. Wells attended Oxford University as a Rhodes Scholar and later earned an LLB degree from Stanford University.
>
> The son of a career U.S. Navy officer, Mr. Wells is a native of Coronado, California. He served two years in the U.S. Army, earning the rank of first lieutenant.
>
> Mr. Wells has had the personal goal of scaling the summits of the highest mountains on each of the seven continents. With the exception of Mt. Everest, from

This case was prepared by Jeanne M. Liedtka, associate professor of Business Administration.

which he was forced to turn back a day away from the top, he achieved his objective during 1983.[1]

Eisner and Wells arrived to find in decline the firm that had captured a unique place in American culture. Profits had fallen for three consecutive years. Theme park attendance was similarly eroding. Disney's market share of box office revenues had dropped to 4 percent, placing it last among the major studios. Furthermore, the takeover battle waged against Saul Steinberg in spring of 1984 had diverted management attention away from repairing the ills in company operations while increasing debt burden dramatically. Although previous CEO Ron Miller had been in the job only 19 months, the Disney board of directors believed that decisive new management was needed from the outside to revitalize the firm. In making its selection, the board hoped that the combination of Eisner's creativity and Wells's business acumen, both legendary in Hollywood, would restore the luster of the firm's unique assets.

In their first annual report, produced two months later, Eisner and Wells addressed their letter to "Our Owners and fellow Disney employees":

> We joined Disney at the culmination of the most difficult period in the company's 61 year history. . . . On September 22, we joined 28,000 other dedicated employees who are eager to build and create value through excellence. As the newest "cast members" of Walt Disney Productions, we are both enthusiastic and respectful in becoming a part of a corporate culture that is unparalleled in American industry. As we approach our task of building Disney excellence around the world, we do so with a sense of pride and humility in following previous management successes in producing animated classic motion pictures, imaginative theme parks and entertainment magic. . . .[2]
>
> Our job, essentially, is to accelerate Disney even further into the mainstream of American entertainment. We will do this by emphasizing creativity in every aspect of the company's business. This challenge requires that we give great latitude, within pre-set financial boundaries, to the resources at hand while at the same time carefully managing Disney's largely untapped measure of assets. . . . The first objective in our new business plan calls for a dedicated effort to improve performance in *every* area. We intend to achieve a greater degree of balance between the various sectors in order to avoid substantial swings in income due to possible adverse effects on a single line of business.
>
> Among our corporate goals is assuring the success of The Disney Channel, returning Disney to an industry leadership role in motion pictures and network television, expanding film distribution in both under-utilized and untapped ancillary markets, accelerating land development, and extending our important Consumer Products business.[3]

Upon his arrival, Eisner settled into Walt's old office, hired his former secretary, and, over a six-month period, fired more than 400 Disney people. The new "Disney team" embarked immediately on an ambitious series of moves in each of the firm's major lines of business.

The Movie Business

Given the backgrounds of Eisner and Wells, it was no surprise that they focused immediate attention on the live-action portion of the movie business. Within a week of their arrival, they had hired Jeffrey Katzenberg, former production chief at Paramount, to head the movie division. Within six months, he had been joined by 30 more former Paramount executives. They set course on a new strategy of film making that "combined Hollywood's creative chutzpah and strict financial self-discipline."[4] Their goal was to make movies having broad audience appeal at below-average costs. To accomplish this, they utilized both performers whose careers had gone into decline (Bette Midler, Richard Dreyfuss, Robin Williams) and television actors (Ted Danson, Tom Selleck) for starring roles. To protect them on the downside, they set up a risk-sharing arrangement with Silver Screen Pictures that pumped new funds into the business and reduced potential losses on flops. Katzenberg, with a reputation for scheduling staff meetings at 10:00 P.M. and expecting seven-day work weeks, quickly geared up production to meet Eisner's stated goal of 10 to 15 live-action features annually.

The new team's commitment to the animation business was equally evident, though more of a surprise to many. Rumors circulated at the time of their arrival that Eisner and Wells would shut down the animation unit. Its animator corps had already fallen from a high of 400 to 200, with the public loss of several prominent talents (Don Bluth and Tim Burton) especially painful. Instead, Roy Disney asked to head the unit himself and called the entire group together in late 1984, and challenged the animators to "show them [Eisner and Wells] that we can contribute." Within six months, Eisner set a goal of producing a new animated film every 18 months, versus the four- to five-year norm at Disney. He launched a new intern program and authorized the purchase of $12 million in computer equipment—a request made more than three years before but rejected by Walker and Miller as too expensive.

Equally important, Eisner launched the search for a new animated character worthy of joining the ranks of Mickey and Donald. He thought that he had found one in the person (or animal) of Roger Rabbit and began producing a film of the same name in late 1986. An ambitious combination of live action and animation, it was intended to push the state-of-the-art to new boundaries in the old Disney tradition. Eisner hired Steven Spielberg, veteran of *E.T.* and *An American Tail*, to direct. Spielberg felt that Disney animators were not up to the task. As part of a compromise, a joint animation unit was set up—for every new animator hired, a Disney animator would also be used. When the film opened, *Newsweek* noted:

> In a marriage made in Hollywood heaven, Disney brings marketing savvy and a proud tradition of animation back to the ground-breaking days of Walt Disney himself.[5]

Eisner's search for successful new characters continued with the decision to produce *The Little Mermaid.* Disney's first classic fairytale since *Sleeping Beauty* almost 30 years before, *The Little Mermaid* was meant to be, Roy Disney recalled, "the kind of movie that Walt would have made."[6]

Eisner and Wells also made the decision to release, on a gradual basis, the entire set of Disney classic films, a film archive that analysts had valued at $400 million, for sale to the home market on videocassette. The first offering was *Pinocchio.* This reversed a long-standing policy created by Walt Disney himself, who had been vehemently opposed to the frequent showing of his classics.

Television

Shortly after their arrival, Eisner and Wells stated publicly that they viewed the Disney Channel's current losses as "excellent long-term investments in a business that represents a cornerstone of our future." Within a month, they had negotiated a ten-year contract with Cablevision Systems of New York, setting a precedent for the type of long-term pacts they hoped to establish with other multiple systems operators. Investment in the Disney Channel continued as new rates were negotiated to increase the channel's attractiveness to cable system operators, and new shows, such as the new Mickey Mouse Club, were added.

The new team also expanded Disney's network exposure, producing a series of weekly shows *(The Golden Girls)* and Saturday morning cartoons. The *Magical World of Disney* was resurrected on Sunday nights, with Eisner acting as host.

The Theme Park Division

Eisner, Wells, and their families spent three days in Orlando, Florida, riding every ride and sampling every restaurant at Disney World in the first two weeks after taking their new jobs. Impressed, they decided that the theme park operation would be left largely untouched. "I couldn't understand *how* a company that was this badly mismanaged at the top could be so fantastic at the middle management level. The executives at the park remembered how Walt had done it," Eisner commented after his visit.[7]

Nevertheless, they felt, the parks were suffering from under-investment and a lack of new attractions. Eisner and Wells committed to doubling park spending, financed via a $5 increase in daily ticket prices (from $18 to $23), implemented gradually over a two-year period. They also authorized the first major marketing campaign in the company's history. By 1985, seven major attractions had been added in Orlando (including the Disney-MGM Theme Park, Typhoon Lagoon, and the Living Seas Pavilion at Epcot), and four each were added at Disneyland in California and Tokyo. Euro-Disneyland was scheduled to open in 1992. They hired renowned architects, such as Michael Graves and Robert Stern, to design new luxury hotels. Within five years, nearly 3,800 rooms had been added in Orlando.

Merchandising

The new team brought, for the first time, top management support for aggressive marketing. The first Disney retail store opened in March of 1987. Two years later, 50 stores were in operation, with 50 more planned. Disney began partnering with major corporations, such as McDonald's and Coca-Cola for joint promotion of products. The *Disney Catalog* was launched in 1985, and the *Childcraft* catalog firm was acquired soon after.

Real Estate

Arvida Corporation was sold for $404 million in 1987.

Conclusion

Throughout these changes, Eisner's and Wells's personal styles were a pervasive influence. "Wells knows the details of every budgetary dispute, contract negotiation, legal problem, or personnel issue," *Fortune* noted in profiling Wells as one of the "great second bananas."[8] Eisner was known for orchestrating frequent "Gong Shows," in which executives were expected to present new ideas that were then gonged if deemed unappealing. *Fortune* observed:

> Eisner is a CEO who is more hands-on than Mother Teresa. His chief duty at Disney is to lead creatively, to be a thinker, inventor, and cheerleader for new ideas—in founder Walt's own words, to be an Imagineer. Says Eisner: "Every CEO has to spend an enormous amount of time shuffling papers. The question is, how much of your time can you leave free to think about ideas? To me, the pursuit of ideas is the only thing that matters. You can always find capable people to do almost everything else. . . . My problem is not too few ideas; my problem is too many *bad* ideas. . . . When I hear a bad idea coming out of my mouth, I've got to stop before it gets to somebody who's going to spend money."

Endnotes

[1]Walt Disney Company press release, September 22, 1984.
[2]Walt Disney Productions Annual Report, 1984, p. 1.
[3]Ibid., p. 2.
[4]"How Disney Keeps the Magic Going," *Fortune*, December 4, 1989, p. 112.
[5]Michael Reese, "The Making of Roger Rabbit," *Newsweek*, June 27, 1988, p. 54.
[6]"How Disney Keeps the Magic Going," p. 111.
[7]Ron Grover, *The Disney Touch*, Homewood, IL: Richard D. Irwin, Inc., 1991.
[8]John Huey, "Secrets of Great Second Bananas," *Fortune*, May 6, 1991.

Case 36

Big Sky, Inc.: The Magasco Paper Mill (B)

As Jock Duncan, director of human relations at the Magasco Mill, later reflected, "It couldn't have come any closer. We were within 10 minutes of replacing those guys." The mill had experienced over 200 days of strike in the last 10 years. Most of the mill's employees had become accustomed to returning to the mill the morning after a settlement had been reached and going directly to their jobs. "It had become a tradition," said Duncan, "the way it was done—that people would go right back out onto the floor."

This time, however, they would not go directly back to their jobs. Duncan and the other mill managers were determined to make a change at the mill, and they believed the first day would be critical in setting the tone for the future. "The climate for change had to be established the very first day. We were going to start things off differently," Duncan said. As the mill continued to operate under the efforts of the salaried staff, each returning employee went through an eight-hour orientation before returning to his or her post. Big Sky had erected classroom trailers on the mill property and scheduled each employee to participate in a one-day seminar to ensure that everyone fully understood the proposed changes. Nobody at Magasco had ever experienced anything remotely comparable to the type of training Duncan and the other managers planned. As Duncan later noted, "Just the orientation itself was a significant variable, not to mention the changes we planned to introduce."

The actual orientation consisted of a number of modules: introductions to the team concept, new disciplinary procedures, and the new safety initiative. The safety initiative received more attention than any other segment; in fact, three hours were dedicated to safety. In addition to the training, each employee was issued a hard hat, safety glasses, safety shoes, and ear plugs. Duncan and the others knew they were taking a risk by promoting safety; only three years earlier, following the work-related deaths of two mill employees, mill management had initiated a safety drive that met with tremendous resistance. In fact, the mill union representative at the time was reportedly seen drop-kicking his newly acquired hard hat across the plant floor.

"They couldn't have faced much more trauma those first few weeks. They were being asked to accept things they didn't want. It was a tremendously emotional process, introducing these changes," said Duncan. "There was a tremendous amount of loss and anger. We could see it in their faces."

The Safety Initiative

As Duncan explained the drive for safety,

> We decided we were going to have a cause—a vision that could be articulated and a plan that could be communicated so that everyone could understand it. We

---

This case was prepared by S. B. Brake, Jr., under the supervision of Professor Alexander Horniman.

> were going to be the safest paper mill in the world. There was a mind-set in place that if you were going to make paper you had to get hurt. We wanted people to know that they didn't have to get hurt to do their jobs.

Mill management was convinced that its cause was one every employee could adopt. For Duncan, creating a safe working environment did more than just help prevent injuries and reduce workmen's compensation expense. "If you want people to know that you love them," said Duncan, "you have to convince them. By making this mill a safer place to work, we thought we might help people see that we really loved them."

Management recognized that the systems and structures at the mill had to be mutually complementary for the mill actually to become the safest paper mill in the world. This meant ensuring that the proper processes and systems were in place. Duncan later commented,

> We aligned ourselves as management and focused specifically on that cause. Safety came first in all of our managers' goal documents. And even though they [the managers] might have been very effective in other traditional areas of management—like efficiency, cost, and the environment—if they weren't effective in safety, that wouldn't have reflected well on what we were trying to do.

LISTENING

As part of the change process, Duncan and Dan Stevenson, the mill manager who was transferred to Magasco shortly after the strike, initiated a practice they called "Listening." Once a week, for two hours, they were committed to meeting with mill employees at an open forum. In the first year following the strike, they held a total of 54 such meetings. Hoping to establish a nonthreatening environment, Duncan and Stevenson told employees they could say whatever they wanted, and they were assured that their names would not be used later. Duncan described the process:

> We started with the managers and we asked them a very simple question, "What can we do to make this a better place to work? And that covers any area you want to talk about; it's your meeting." After we went through the managers, then we met with the superintendents and then the foremen. You can understand that the managers were somewhat threatened when we had the meetings with their subordinates. . . . When we finished with a manager's set of superintendents, we gave the manager a set of our notes. . . . We sat down with him, and we said, "Some of these we've already said 'no' to, and some of them we don't know the answer to and you can better solve them." The manager was then to take our notes, research the issues, and have a follow-up meeting.

After experiencing some early success with the salaried employees, Duncan and Stevenson then approached the hourly employees. They always met with individual teams, typically ranging from 5 to 15 people. In order to foster a communicative forum, the managers, supervisors, and foremen for these particular groups were never present. And, as was the case with the earlier meetings, names were never used when reports were prepared. Duncan explained,

> We were aiming for the hourly workers all along. At first they were very hostile. We had just come back from the strike, and they were extremely hostile. But we

> told them everything was fair game; if they wanted to, they could call us SOBs. Some did! But they also talked about things that needed to be fixed—machines, tools, and management styles.
>
> It took us a while to convince them that their names wouldn't be used, but they were so primed at first they didn't care. Whenever we finished with a group, we would give a set of notes to the manager for that area, not the foreman or the superintendent. The manager was to have a feedback session within three weeks. The answer might be "I'm still working on that," but something had better have been corrected. The manager should respond to something that can be fixed, can be changed; or tell them that cannot or will not happen. He might tell them, "We don't have the money" or "It's against company policy," like if somebody would say, "Let's quit wearing hard hats."

While the listening sessions brought many issues to management's attention that required lengthy study, management was immediately and regularly challenged to fulfill its commitment to make the mill a better place to work. Commenting on the need to follow through on this promise, Duncan said,

> You have to respond if there is a broken window and the wind is blowing into the machine shop. You better have that fixed the next day. There is no excuse for not having that fixed when the manager goes back to that next feedback meeting. Now, that's a simple example and there are more complex examples (some so complex that you and they know the manager can't respond within three weeks), but the manager better address each point that can be fixed easily and have done something about those.

Duncan and Stevenson considered the meetings to be an absolutely essential part of the change process. Not only did the listening provide management with insight, but the sessions provided management with an opportunity to prove itself. Duncan commented,

> These meetings were a big element in developing trust, showing that we "walked our talk" and did what we said, responding to their needs. . . . This tool has proven to be so powerful that I would never try to manage anything again without it. You have to know what is going on out there in the operation. It's a living survey instrument that is going on all the time. Soon, everyone was having listening meetings, not just me and the mill manager. Foremen and supervisors had their own, too. It's just so powerful.

The Assimilation Process

Level I

Not long after the changes were introduced at Magasco, Duncan and some of the other mill managers attended a seminar on individual and organizational change at a southeastern business school. Referring to the various levels of organizational culture (illustrated in Exhibit 1) discussed in the course, Duncan said of his experience at Magasco, "At the beginning, we had a hard time achieving even level I changes. We had a long way to go before we got to the core of the 'onion.' We were struggling with the outer layers. Just getting them to wear the safety equipment

EXHIBIT 1

Cultural Levels

The Cultural Assimilation Process

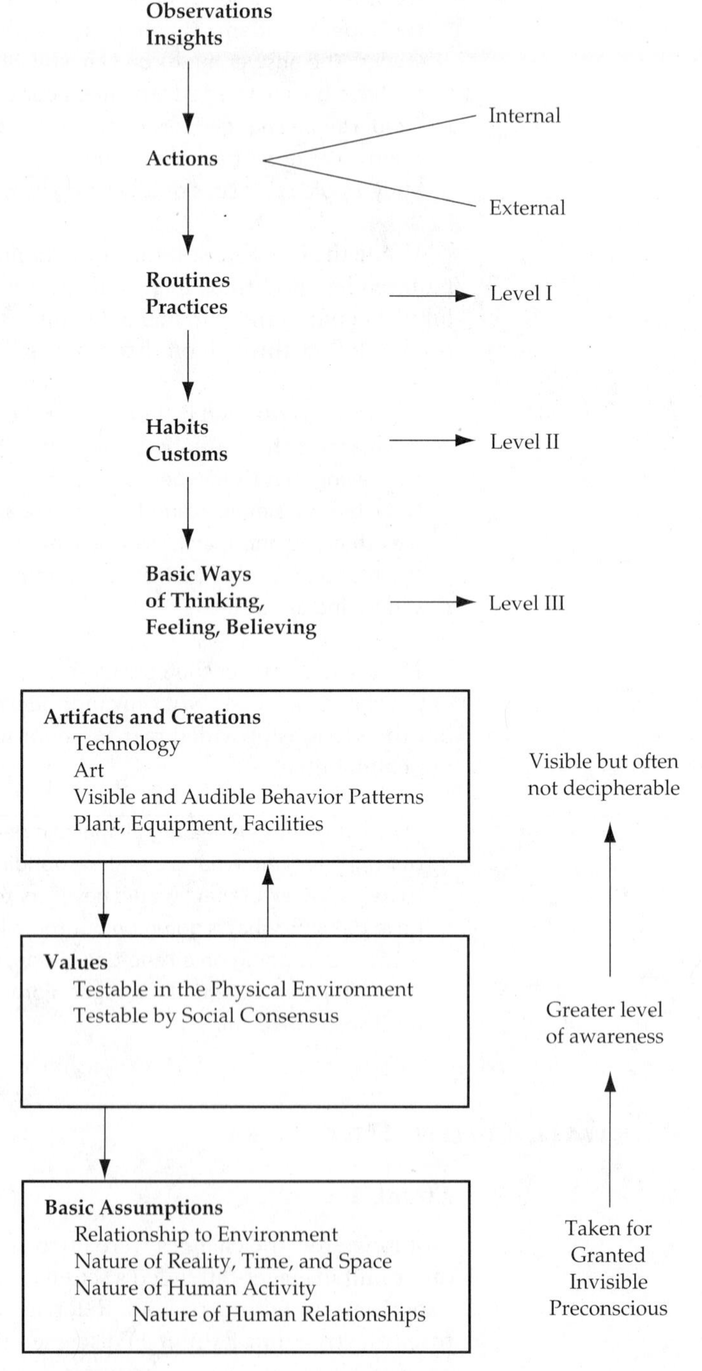

Adapted from E. Schein, *Organization Culture and Leadership.* (San Francisco: Jossey-Bass, 1980, 1989).

was tough enough." Level I refers to cultural artifacts and behaviors that are observable through visible and audible behavior patterns.

At first, change took place only in small pockets, at the periphery of the organization. "It was amazing, though," said Duncan, "how quickly some groups caught on." For example, one 40-member team, responsible for the grinding of wood chips, experienced early success with the team concept and the safety initiative. "They were an isolated group," recalled Duncan. "They had a good change manager who understood the process. They went through the steps to integrate change faster than anyone else. Within four months, they were there! We were amazed. They were rotating themselves through the team concept, learning the jobs, and seeing how much fun it could actually be."

Gradually, employees in other areas of the mill heard about these early successes and they too began to integrate many of the team concepts and safety practices into their daily regimens. As Duncan said, "At first, a lot of our people would glance over the shoulders of employees who were actually using team concepts and the safety procedures and say, 'Hey, those guys are doing weird stuff.' But pretty soon they started to see how well it worked and all of a sudden it wasn't so weird anymore."

The mill continued to reinforce the safety initiative through regular safety training and safety meetings. Management had also established what was known as an implementation team. Duncan described their role:

> They acted as consultants. They understood the team concept and the safety concept and what we were trying to do and were actually consultants on the floor. They were managers we picked from our workforce and were assigned areas of the mill where they consulted. They checked every day. They said, "How are you rotating? How are you getting the team concept started? How are you assigning the work?" And they would answer questions, serve as coaches, and observe behavior.

Throughout the first year following the strike, the change initiatives continued to be challenged at all levels of the organization, not just by the hourly staff. Some managers and supervisors did not openly embrace all of the changes. As Duncan recalled,

> We actually didn't give some merit increases to people whose safety performance in their area was significantly behind everyone else's. This was one way we tried to align ourselves to the cause. We even had to suspend some managers and supervisors, along with some hourly people, without pay for outright poor judgment in a safety matter. . . . We had to walk our talk. We had to show them that we cared about this.

Despite resistance, Duncan continued to look for a success, and the managers set a goal of breaking the record for hours worked without a safety accident: "They hadn't ever done very well here before, but it was the first step." About eight months were needed to reach the first milestone. Duncan described what happened next:

> We celebrated! Man, did we celebrate—crazier than anyone's ever celebrated before! We, the managers, actually cooked breakfast for every employee at the mill. . . . We waited tables, we poured coffee, and we thanked them. We did everything we could to mark the occasion. They thought we were crazy—wearing little white jackets and chef hats. They just couldn't believe it.

Not long after meeting the mill's first objective, in the fall of 1984, Duncan and his staff distributed a survey in order to gauge systematically the response of the mill's hourly employees to the recently introduced changes. While some of the responses were surprisingly positive, the survey also indicated that management had a long way to go before some of the well-ingrained belief systems would change. As shown by the results in Exhibit 2, despite management's efforts to promote the

EXHIBIT 2

1984 Employee Survey

STATEMENT	% FAVORABLE THIS REPORT
25 I really care about the future of the company.	72
03 I enjoy working with the people here.	86
24 We are encouraged to reduce costs and increase production.	30
12 I am paid fairly for the kind of work I do.	68
06 My OCC pay is comparable to other companies in the area.	74
33 Management at this location is committed to a safe workplace.	0
36 Employees in my work area work well together as a team.	0
07 My performance is evaluated periodically.	53
01 I am satisfied with my job.	47
28 Supervisor gives clear understanding of job responsibilities.	51
15 I have not looked for a job with another company recently.	54
21 I feel free to tell my supervisor what I think.	48
17 My supervisor is fair in dealing with me.	52
18 When I have a complaint, I feel free to express it.	50
09 My supervisor maintains high standards of performance.	47
14 I know where I stand in my job performance.	48
35 Training is available to help me do my job more effectively.	0
05 I am proud to work for the company.	39
27 Our company has good working conditions.	39
06 My benefits are as good as those of other companies in the area.	49
02 My job makes good use of my skills.	41
04 I get recognition when I do good work.	32
11 My job allows me to improve my skills.	39
23 Opportunities to let location management know our feelings.	35
30 Suggestions I make to improve area are considered.	32
26 We are told why changes are made that affect our jobs.	24
20 Policies, procedures and work rules are fair.	27
31 I receive enough information about how well company is doing.	34
22 Policies, procedures, work rules consistently administered.	38
10 I am satisfied with my benefits.	33
19 Favoritism is not a problem in my area.	35
16 Opportunities in the company for those who want to get ahead.	26
29 Corporate management communicates conditions accurately.	18
13 I have confidence in the fairness of management.	14
12 I feel action will be taken as a result of this survey.	12
34 Retirement benefits are as good as those of other companies.	0
Average percent favorable:	43

safety program and to increase training opportunities, specifically through the team concept, one year after the introduction of these programs, few respondents strongly agreed with the statements relating to these subjects.

Level II

Nevertheless, proof of the mill's progress was evidenced by its improved financial performance: By 1985 the mill was earning over $26 million dollars, which represented a $60 million turnaround in two years. Monthly production had increased from 53,000 tons a month in 1983 to 55,000 in 1985. Grievances filed on behalf of hourly employees by the Amalgamated Paperworkers Union had declined from 80 to just 3 a month in the same period. After two or three years, the team concept and the safety initiative had gained a foothold throughout most areas of the mill. Prescribed safety routines and practices were being followed, and the mill had begun to receive recognition within the company and from industry groups for its improved safety record. By 1989 Magasco had achieved such success with its safety training that it was recognized by the Pulp and Paper Association and Big Sky's Pulp and Paper Division for its safety performance.

Evidence of the cultural changes taking place during this time could be seen in the declining injury rate and heard in the daily language used at the mill. "Papermaking has always been considered a quantity business," said Duncan. "At the change of shifts, you've always been able to hear somebody ask how many tons were made on the outgoing shift. But after a couple of years, we started to hear employees asking if anyone had been hurt on the prior shift. That was something new."

In 1986 Duncan distributed the same survey that had been distributed in 1984. In just two years, the change in responses was tremendous. As illustrated by Exhibit 3, without exception, the favorable response rate to every question had increased over the 1984 survey and, in some cases, significantly. Where no favorable responses had been recorded in 1984 to a statement regarding safety, this time 82 percent of the respondents said management was committed to making the mill a safe place to work. Similar responses were recorded with reference to teamwork and training.

Throughout this period, the mill was gradually transforming from what Duncan had earlier described as a "mutually compliant" organization characterized by apathetic and antagonistic relations between management and employees to a state of mutual commitment. Management and labor had both demonstrated their commitment to change. Gradually, management's perception of employees changed, and employees began to believe more in what management was doing. Fragmented work practices based on outmoded assumptions were replaced by upgraded work technologies. In the kind of process illustrated in Exhibit 4, as a result of employee responses to the changes introduced by management, combined with management's ability to follow through on its commitment to make the mill a safer and better place to work, new behaviors, assumptions, and perceptions were reinforced.

By 1986 management believed that enough progress had been made at the mill that the time had come to increase the amount of autonomy available to the mill's hourly staff. Management and labor at Magasco had long followed a traditional model of management/labor relations. Through an adversarial bargaining process, management and the union determined how much control managers and employees would have over the work process. In the model shown in Exhibit 5, management was proposing to move from quadrant IV to quadrant III by increasing the degree to which employees could act without managerial direction. The expansion of employee empowerment not only signaled a change in management/labor

EXHIBIT 3

1986 Employee Survey

STATEMENT	% FAVORABLE THIS REPORT
25 I really care about the future of the company.	91
03 I enjoy working with the people here.	87
24 We are encouraged to reduce costs and increase production.	86
12 I am paid fairly for the kind of work I do.	83
06 My OCC pay is comparable to other companies in the area.	82
33 Management at this location is committed to a safe workplace.	82
36 Employees in my work area work well together as a team.	79
07 My performance is evaluated periodically.	78
01 I am satisfied with my job.	77
28 Supervisor gives clear understanding of job responsibilities.	75
15 I have not looked for a job with another company recently.	74
21 I feel free to tell my supervisor what I think.	74
17 My supervisor is fair in dealing with me.	73
18 When I have a complaint, I feel free to express it.	73
09 My supervisor maintains high standards of performance.	69
14 I know where I stand in my job performance.	69
35 Training is available to help me do my job more effectively.	68
05 I am proud to work for the company.	66
27 Our company has good working conditions.	66
06 My benefits are as good as those of other companies in the area.	63
02 My job makes good use of my skills.	62
04 I get recognition when I do good work.	62
11 My job allows me to improve my skills.	61
23 Opportunities to let location management know our feelings.	55
30 Suggestions I make to improve area are considered.	53
26 We are told why changes are made that affect our jobs.	51
20 Policies, procedures and work rules are fair.	48
31 I receive enough information about how well company is doing.	48
22 Policies, procedures, work rules consistently administered.	46
10 I am satisfied with my benefits.	45
19 Favoritism is not a problem in my area.	43
16 Opportunities in the company for those who want to get ahead.	40
29 Corporate management communicates conditions accurately.	29
13 I have confidence in the fairness of management.	27
12 I feel action will be taken as a result of this survey.	18
34 Retirement benefits are as good as those of other companies.	18
Average percent favorable:	62

relations at Magasco from the adversial past, it also illustrated management's willingness to surrender more of its control over work practices at the mill.

In order to increase employee autonomy, management planned to turn over all training functions to the hourly employees. Management had traditionally

EXHIBIT 4

Mutual Commitment Model

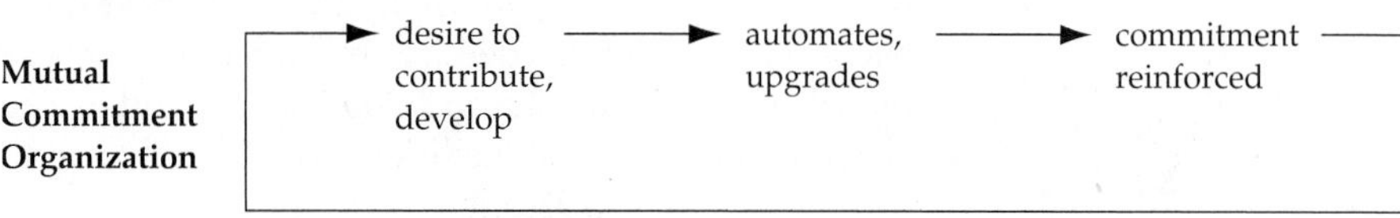

EXHIBIT 5

Management/Labor Model Conceptual Design

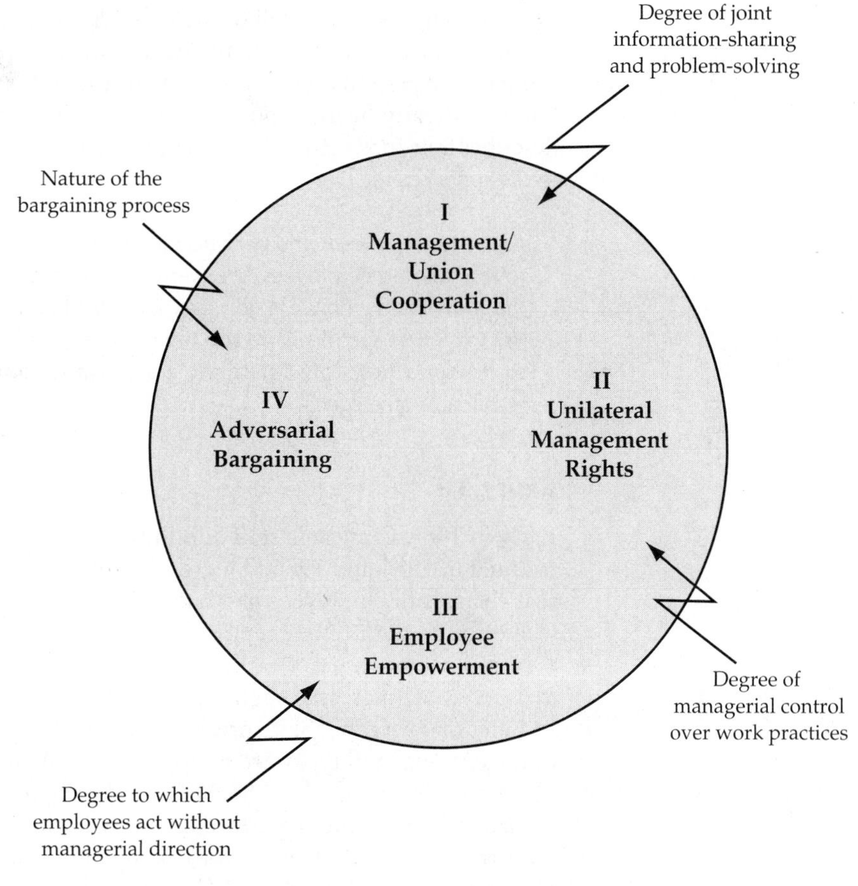

considered training to be one of its primary responsibilities. Thus, by relinquishing this function, management was consciously reducing its authority to dictate future events at the mill.

With the consent of the hourly employees, management developed and initiated a peer-training program in which a select group of employees with strong performance records were relieved of their line duties for up to 18 months in order to design training programs. "The idea," said Duncan, "was to have the hourly employees develop training systems and materials written in their own language, for them and by them." Duncan and the others at the mill strongly believed that the peer-training team needed its own office space, separate from the executive offices, in order to feel truly autonomous, but no funds were available in the capital budget to build additional facilities. "We literally had to bootleg the supplies to build the place," Duncan recalled.

Once established, the center provided skills assessments for new and veteran operators. The center also administered post tests immediately following training and retention tests at later stages to test for recall and training effectiveness. All grading and testing were conducted on a peer basis. Eventually, the training center was expanded and equipped with modern training equipment, including interactive video systems and a video-production facility. The training center also became the site of a fitness center, stocked with weight machines and other exercise equipment, which was open to all of the mill's employees.

Management's desire to increase the amount of employee involvement ultimately reduced the responsibilities of some of the mill's salaried staff. The supervisors had historically been responsible for the training function at the mill. Duncan describes how management had to define a new role and new responsibilities for the mill's supervisors.

> As the team concept and peer training began to take form, there was a real threat to the salaried employees. We were cutting into our chunk of the pie, and it was the supervisors who were going to lose. Like I said, with change, somebody always has to make a sacrifice, and this time it was management, the supervisors. We had to design a new role for them, a very important role, as an observer and as resource, a true coach.

Level III

Early in 1988, Duncan's staff administered the same employee survey it had distributed in 1984 and 1986. The results confirmed management's perceptions that real changes in employees had taken place over the last five years. As can be seen in Exhibit 6, with few exceptions, employee responses were just as favorable as they had been two years earlier. In fact, the aggregate favorable response rate to the survey had increased slightly, from 62 percent in 1986 to 63 percent in 1988.

Later that year, Big Sky's president accepted the American Paper Institute's prestigious Annual Safety Award at New York's Waldorf Astoria on behalf of all the Magasco mill employees. The API award recognized Magasco as the safest mill of its size in North America. Moreover, it was widely acknowledged throughout the industry that North American working conditions were superior to those found anywhere else in the world. To Duncan and the other employees at the mill, therefore, this award, in effect, recognized Magasco as the safest mill of its size in the world. In addition to the API award, the mill set a company record by accumulating 2.4 million work hours without an accident. Exhibit 7 provides a list of all of the mill's safety awards as of 1990 and the criteria for each award.

By 1990 Duncan believed that the team concept and the safety initiative were firmly embedded in the mill's culture: "We've reached the core of the onion where safety and the team concept are concerned." In a period of just over five years, the

EXHIBIT 6

1988 Employee Survey

Statement		% Favorable This Report
25	I really care about the future of the company.	90
03	I enjoy working with the people here.	87
24	We are encouraged to reduce costs and increase production.	86
12	I am paid fairly for the kind of work I do.	86
06	My OCC pay is comparable to other companies in the area.	85
33	Management at this location is committed to a safe workplace.	83
36	Employees in my work area work well together as a team.	82
07	My performance is evaluated periodically.	80
01	I am satisfied with my job.	74
28	Supervisor gives clear understanding of job responsibilities.	73
15	I have not looked for a job with another company recently.	73
21	I feel free to tell my supervisor what I think.	72
17	My supervisor is fair in dealing with me.	72
18	When I have a complaint, I feel free to express it.	70
09	My supervisor maintains high standards of performance.	68
14	I know where I stand in my job performance.	67
35	Training is available to help me do my job more effectively.	66
05	I am proud to work for the company.	64
27	Our company has good working conditions.	64
06	My benefits are as good as those of other companies in the area.	64
02	My job makes good use of my skills.	63
04	I get recognition when I do good work.	63
11	My job allows me to improve my skills.	60
23	Opportunities to let location management know our feelings.	60
30	Suggestions I make to improve area are considered.	56
26	We are told why changes are made that affect our jobs.	53
20	Policies, procedures and work rules are fair.	52
31	I receive enough information about how well company is doing.	50
22	Policies, procedures, work rules consistently administered.	48
10	I am satisfied with my benefits.	47
19	Favoritism is not a problem in my area.	45
16	Opportunities in the company for those who want to get ahead.	38
29	Corporate management communicates conditions accurately.	36
13	I have confidence in the fairness of management.	32
12	I feel action will be taken as a result of this survey.	23
34	Retirement benefits are as good as those of other companies.	22
	Average percent favorable:	63

mill had gone from losing $35 million a year to making over $110 million a year. As presented in Exhibit 8, productivity and efficiency had skyrocketed. The mill was expected to produce 91,000 tons of paper a month by 1990, as compared with

EXHIBIT 7

Magasco Safety Awards

	American Paper Institute Awards	
1990	Safety Excellence Award	1 million Safe Hours
1988	Annual Safety Award	
1986	Safety Excellence Award	1.875 million Safe Hours
1986	Safety Excellence Award	1.5 million Safe Hours
1985	Safety Excellence Award	1 million Safe Hours
	National Safety Council	
1990	Award of Merit	
1988	2nd Place, Safety and Health Contest (Annual)	
1988	Award of Honor	
1987	Award of Merit	
1986	Award of Merit	
1985	Award of Honor	
	Southern Pulp and Paper Association	
1988	Achievement Award	
1985	Safety Award	
	Big Sky, Inc.	
May 1989	Corporate Safety Record Established	
1988	President's Award[1]	
1987	President's Award[1]	
1987	Pulp and Paper Mill's Safety Award	
1986	President's Award[1]	
1986	Division Safety Award	
1985	Vice President's Award[2]	
1985	Pulp and Paper Mill's Safety Award	

[1]Earned by accumulating 12 months, *and* 1 million work hours, without a lost work day case.

[2]Earned by accumulating 12 months, *or* 1 million work hours, without a lost work day case.

API SAFETY AWARD PROGRAM FOR PRIMARY OPERATIONS

SAFETY EXCELLENCE AWARDS

Recognition for outstanding safety performance will be given to primary operations of API member companies that achieve any of the following work-hour totals *without a Lost Work Day Case*[3] (provided there are no fatalities or permanent and total disability injuries during the period involved).

- 1,000,000 Work Hours OR Calendar Years[4]
- 1,500,000 Work Hours
- 2,000,000 Work Hours
- 2,500,000 Work Hours

Work-Hour thresholds continue at intervals of 500,000.

[3](As reported on OSHA Form 200)

[4](January 1st through December 31st)

(continued)

EXHIBIT 7 (CONTINUED)

Magasco Safety Awards

Upon written notification by the company to the API Employee Relations Department (specifying the number of safe work hours and the dates when the record began and was completed), API will have the appropriate plaque prepared and forwarded.

ANNUAL SAFETY AWARDS

Once a year, API will present Safety Awards to five primary mills based on each mill's safety performance during the previous five years (i.e., awards to be presented in 1990 will cover the period January 1, 1985, through December 31, 1989). Winners will represent five different work-hour classifications reflecting mill size, as follows:

- Mills accumulating more than 2,500,000 work hours annually.
- Mills accumulating 1,500,000 to 2,500,000 work hours annually.
- Mills accumulating 1,000,000 to 1,500,000 work hours annually.
- Mills accumulating 500,000 to 1,000,000 work hours annually.
- Mills accumulating fewer than 500,000 work hours annually.

The winners must meet three criteria:

1. There must be no fatalities or permanent and total disability injuries during the five-year period.
2. The mill's OSHA Total Cases Incidence Rate for the most recent year must be lower than that of the year immediately preceding (i.e., the 1989 rate must be lower than the 1988 rate).
3. The mill must have the lowest cumulative five-year Total Cases Incidence Rate in its work-hour classification.

At the end of each calendar year, individual mills will submit to the American Paper Institute the necessary five-year data on the "Summary of Occupational Injuries and Illnesses" forms furnished. Complete information must reach API on or before the deadline specified on the form. These awards will be presented by API in March of each year during Paper Week.

FACTS ABOUT THE NATIONAL SAFETY COUNCIL's OCCUPATIONAL SAFETY/HEALTH AWARD PROGRAM

The Occupational Safety/Health Award Program is a noncompetitive safety incentive and recognition award program designed to promote the reduction and elimination of occupational injuries and illnesses. The program is available to all employer members of the National Safety Council.

There are currently over 8,000 organizations participating annually in this program, representing 42 principal industries throughout the United States.

Records submitted for evaluation are required to be kept according to the Recordkeeping Requirements under the Occupational Safety and Health Act of 1970 (Revised 1978) by the U.S. Department of Labor. All information submitted to the council is kept strictly confidential.

(continued)

EXHIBIT 7 (CONTINUED)

Magasco Safety Awards

The program provides for giving recognition to every organization that completes a calendar year with a perfect record (without a case involving days away from work or death). Organizations with nonperfect records may also earn recognition if they meet certain criteria. There are five levels of recognition under this program.

DISTINGUISHED ACHIEVEMENT IN OCCUPATIONAL SAFETY AND HEALTH AWARD: Only three of these awards are given out each year. They are presented to the small, medium, and large company that has attained the BEST occupational safety performance of those records submitted to the Council for evaluation. This is the highest honor presented to an industrial organization by the National Safety Council.

AWARD OF HONOR: There are three different ways an organization may earn this award: (1) By accumulating 3,000,000 or more perfect employee-hours, (2) by establishing the Best Record in a specific Standard Industrial Classification (SIC), (3) by reducing the incidence rates as required.

AWARD OF MERIT: This award may be earned by accumulating between 1,000,000 and 2,999,999 perfect employee-hours or by reducing the incidence rates as required.

AWARD OF COMMENDATION: Any organization that accumulates between 200,000 and 999,999 perfect employee-hours may earn this award.

PRESIDENT'S CITATION AWARD: Any organization that has attained a perfect record of less than 200,000 employee-hours may earn this award.

INTERIM AWARDS: The program also provides an award for safety achievements that are attained within a given year. An organization must have a minimum of 1,000,000 perfect employee-hours and meet other specific requirements. Awards must be applied for on an "Interim Award Application Form." (Special provisions are made for the construction industry.)

WORK INJURY AND ILLNESS RATES: This is an annual publication that is a summary of all occupational injury and illness data submitted to the Council by companies participating in the Occupational Safety/Health Award Program. These statistics are broken down by SIC code and details rates, trends, and changes in occupational injury and illness for current and past years.

86,000 in 1983, with basically the same number of employees. This increase was the equivalent of adding a new $500 million machine with a daily capacity of 500 tons. In the area of grievances filed by the union on behalf of its membership, filings had declined by 1990 from an average of 80 a month immediately following the strike to 2 a month. Operating capacity on all of the mill's paper machines was near 100 percent.

Duncan attributed all of these improvements to the changes initiated in the early 1980s:

EXHIBIT 8

Big Sky, Inc. Operating Statistics (monthly averages in constant 1989 $)

	1982	1983	1984	1985	1986	1987	1988	1989	KB-1990
Manhours	88,118	88,086	86,030	86,636	85,829	90,234	90,061	91,136	91,909
Production	45,414	52,621	51,542	55,181	57,421	60,936	64,634	67,806	66,039
Production/Manhour	0.52	0.61	0.80	0.64	0.67	0.68	0.71	0.74	0.73
Headcount	488	492	486	499	506	513	509	513	513
Permanent			472	486	487	492	496	513	
Temporary			13	13	19	21	11		
Unheeded Payroll—Operations	850,167	1,056,349	1,020,790	1,116,332	1,142,482	1,156,421	1,249,333	1,189,977	1,224,729
Per Ton	18.40	19.91	19.81	20.23	19.90	18.96	19.55	17.55	18.55
Unheeded Payroll—Maintenance	721,027	574,109	546,220	547,630	574,376	581.196	542,014	570,473	587,061
Per Ton	15.81	10.91	11.02	10.29	10.00	9.54	8.39	8.41	8.89
Contract Maintenance	790,067	610,636	1,219,302	1,119,783	1,112,992	1,288,540	1,449,560	1,362,250	1,122,448
Per Ton	17.32	11.60	23.66	20.29	19.38	20.82	22.43	19.94	17.00
Total Maintenance	2,482,028	2,122,301	3,119,211	2,917,791	3,007,473	3,269,265	3,529,496	3,262,916	3,180,750
Per Ton	54.41	40.33	50.52	52.88	52.38	53.65	54.41	43,12	48.16
Attitudes									
Grievances		80	3	3	3	2	3	2	
Absentee Rate		210	1.45	1.19	0.99	1.04	1.09	0.85	

> Our progress so far has been a direct result of our safety program, our team concept, peer training and increased employee involvement. We've let the employees get involved, focused on a few important things, been able, as leaders, to articulate what's going on and what's in it for everyone, and last but not least, we've celebrated and recognized. We focused, we had a cause, and we approached it with passion.

Despite the obvious success of the programs initiated in 1983, Duncan believed that the mill would continue to improve. Commenting on the mill's most recent progress in the targeted areas, he said,

> We've gone to the next plateau. We have developed what we call a critical observation program in safety. We have defined our own critical behaviors in areas of safe and unsafe behavior. It's been proven that 96 percent of all accidents occur because of behavior, not conditions. All the teams have defined their own critical behaviors. Again, we are trying to align people differently on the task so they are not just wearing safety equipment and following rules, but they are designing a process and defining critical behavior. Now they've trained each other to look for those behaviors and coach and counsel their peers on what they saw.

Quality

At a time when many mills were initiating quality programs, Magasco had chosen to follow through on its commitment to the team concept and its goal to be the safest paper mill in the world. Management considered these issues to be critical to the survival of the mill. With increasing capacity and foreign products of superior quality, however, quality had become an increasingly important factor in sales. Mills located in the south such as Magasco were at a significant disadvantage when it came to quality. While trees grew faster in the south, the fibers from the slower growing trees in the north were superior and made a significantly better sheet of paper. Duncan noted, "We've got one customer who's told us to send him paper from one of our Canadian mills for the time being until we can get our quality up."

In response to increasing customer demands and the influx of superior foreign products, management initiated a quality program at the mill in the late 1980s. Like the earlier changes at Magasco, this initiative demanded a realignment in the way employees approached their jobs. Whereas previously management had preached quantity at the expense of quality in order to meet demand, with this initiative, most employees were trained in formal brainstorming and other classic problem-solving techniques, and while computers actually monitored production quality, all of the mill's machine operators were trained to read process-control charts. In 1986, the mill began publishing a daily quality index, which summarized quality in paper production, pulp, and wood chips—all deemed critical to generating superior products. As seen in Exhibit 9, the mill gradually increased the quality of its products as measured by these quality indexes.

Commenting on the progress of the mill's quality effort, Duncan made the following statement:

> We make a significantly better sheet in 1990 than we did five years ago, but I'd say we're still tinkering around with levels I and II changes, and not far into level II where quality is concerned. When I can say that our culture is a pattern that

EXHIBIT 9

Quality Index[1]

	1985	1986	1987	1988	1989	1990
Newsprint	604	640	775	800	817	804
Linerboard	443	689	721	764	881	933

[1]Perfect score = 1,000

results in behavior that clearly means quality—the tradition to make a quality sheet rather than a whole lot of paper—then we'll be getting to level III. You still see operators coming in at shift changes and seeing how many tons were made and asking if anyone got hurt. Quantity, tons—it's still in their blood.

The Future

Back at his office, after returning from his walk through the mill, Duncan wondered about the challenges ahead. Most of the mills in the Plain Paper Division were well behind Magasco when it came to labor relations, employee involvement, and safety. Duncan and Stevenson had been through a lot together, and it looked like there were many more challenges to come. He wondered if the same tactics used at Magasco would be successful at other mills.

Of more immediate importance, however, was the future of the Magasco mill. So much progress had been made over the last seven years; it almost seemed too good to be true. But Duncan also remembered how hard it had been to institute change. Many battles had been fought since he first arrived at Magasco. Duncan wondered what would happen after he and Stevenson were no longer around to put out the fires and fight for the cause. Would the mill continue to improve with new management? Had change really taken place?

A figure in the doorway brought Duncan back to the present. It was one of the hourly employees who had recently been assigned to the training center. In addition to designing and implementing peer-training programs, he had been asked to prepare and deliver a presentation on the team concept for some visiting human resource executives from other Big Sky paper mills. "How many people will be coming in next week for the seminar, Jock? I've got to put this presentation together for them."

"Yes," Duncan thought, "this place sure has come a long way since that morning when we all came back from that strike."

CASE 37

RODALE PRESS (A)

Maria hung up the telephone with a look of concern on her face. It was April 15, 1996, and she was one month into her developmental leave from her family's company, Rodale Press. She had just been speaking to John Griffin about her first "Letter from Main Street," a monthly communication that she planned to continue over the coming year to update senior management and her family on her progress, status, and ideas (see Appendix). John Griffin was the head of Rodale's magazine division, and he had told her that her letter "scared him." It was "too abstract" and he was worried that Maria was going to insist that the company go back to its "hippie ways," thereby driving away advertisers and hurting the business.

Concerned that he had missed the point, Maria explained that she was not trying to recreate the past, but rather position the company for an uncertain and rapidly changing future. She was not trying to tell him what to do, just to get people thinking. "Sometimes it is scary to think too much," she thought to herself. She had a lot to prepare for in the coming months, and she wondered if she would be ready to lead the company from its recent success into the challenges that lay ahead.

COMPANY HISTORY

The humble beginnings of Rodale Press can be traced back to 1931, when J. I. Rodale published his first magazine, *The Humorous Scrapbook*. J. I. had started a manufacturing business with his brother in 1923. In an effort to reduce operating costs, the brothers had decided to move the business to Emmaus, Pennsylvania, from New York City in 1930. The subsequent success of the manufacturing business enabled J. I. to pursue his dream of publishing a magazine. This first attempt was priced at $0.25 per copy, and J. I. delivered the first issue himself. Unfortunately, the magazine folded after the first issue, but J. I. persevered in the pursuit of his dream.

Between 1931 and 1940, J. I. published several other magazines, many of which targeted health and nutrition, and most of these were unsuccessful. In 1940, he purchased a 60-acre farm near Emmaus to pursue his interest in organic farming, an agricultural method considered radical at the time. His farming activities led to the 1942 launch of a new magazine, *Organic Farming and Gardening*. In 1950, the first issue of *Prevention* magazine was published. These two magazines became the cornerstones of Rodale's publishing business through the 1950s and 1960s. By 1937, Rodale had also entered into direct-mail book publishing.

In 1951, J. I.'s son, Robert, was named president of Rodale Press. Robert Rodale was an advocate for organic gardening, and had interests in nutrition, fitness, health, and sports. These interests drove the focus of Rodale's businesses. For example,

This case was written by Catherine Elliott (Darden 1998); Marcien Jenckes (Darden 1998) and Daren Samuels (Darden 1998) under the supervision of L. J. Bourgeois, professor of Business Administration.

Rodale's 1977 purchase of *Bicycling* magazine was directly tied to Bob Rodale's interest in the sport.

When J. I. Rodale died in 1971, Bob Rodale became chairman and CEO of Rodale Press, and the company grew considerably under his guidance. Rodale Books was established as a separate division in 1975, and in 1981, *Prevention* magazine launched national distribution. While the number of internally created magazines grew throughout this period, the company took advantage of opportunistic acquisitions that included *Runner's World* (1985), *American Woodworker* (1987), and *Backpacker* (1988).

Bob Rodale was killed in an auto accident while visiting the Soviet Union in 1990. He was working in Russia on a project to assist in the development of organic farming practices. Following his untimely death, his wife Ardath (Ardie) Rodale assumed leadership of the company as chairman and CEO. Ardie Rodale had been active in managing the Rodale Press's physical facilities, but had not previously been involved in the day-to-day management of the publishing business.

Rodale Press in the 1990s

By 1990, Rodale Press had evolved into a large publishing house, which was organized into two divisions: magazines and books. Rodale managed seven magazines with a total circulation of 5.5 million readers and revenues of $72.9 million. The book division generated $92.0 million in sales and was subdivided into five groups: one-shots, book clubs, continuity series, retail trade, and annuals.[1] The company's return on sales varied significantly from year to year, ranging between 1 percent and 12 percent, with an average of about 5 percent. Throughout the first half of the decade, Rodale's revenues had grown at a compound rate of 12 percent, and were projected to total $316.1 million by year-end 1996 (Exhibit 1).

By almost any measure, Rodale was financially successful under Ardie's leadership. This success was based on several aspects of Rodale's business. A major contributor had been the company's specialization in health and fitness, which grew in popularity in the 1980s and 1990s. (The company's stated mission was "to inspire, motivate and enable people to improve their lives and the world around them." Rodale's tag line, which showed up on many of its magazines, was, "You can do it—How to do it.") In addition, Rodale possessed special capabilities in product development and marketing directly to readers through the mail. Product development was important in establishing new magazines and building the book business. Marketing was important to the book division because the cost of direct-mail marketing activities was about $15 per copy sold. Rodale's book division managers viewed marketing as a core competency. Rodale had also succeeded in recruiting a talented core of professional management to run the magazine and book divisions.

[1] Definitions:
one-shots—single titles published as a stand alone product
book clubs—books within a single editorial category offered at slight discounts through membership clubs, e.g. Men's Health Book Club
continuity series—sets of books sold in volumes
retail trade—book stores (about 10% of Rodale's book volume)
annuals—once per year series with seasonal editorial content

EXHIBIT 1

Financial Information

TABLE 1: REVENUES, 1990–1996 ($000S)*

Year	Magazine Division	Book Division	Return on Sales
1990	72,180	91,980	5.0%
1991	76,886	115,651	2.5%
1992	74,637	139,840	2.1%
1993	98,188	152,535	12.0%
1994	118,051	146,574	6.3%
1995	128,750	142,281	4.4%
1996 (est.)	151,350	164,719	2.7%

*Data have been disguised.

TABLE 2: RODALE'S MAGAZINE PROPERTIES: GROWTH IN CIRCULATION

Magazine	Origination	Circulation 1990	Circulation 1997	CAGR
Prevention	1950	3,022,108	3,250,000	1.0%
Organic Gardening	1979	1,034,842	800,000	–3.6%
Bicycling	1977, acquired	375,490	300,000	–3.2%
Runner's World	1985, acquired	447,600	440,000	–2.4%
Men's Health	1986	249,815	1,450,000	28.6%
Rodale's Scuba Diving	1991		200,000	
Mountain Bike	1993 spin-off from *Bicycling*		140,000	
American Woodworker	1987, acquired	175,287	300,000	8.0%
Backpacker	1988, acquired	196,373	240,000	2.9%
Heart & Soul	1993		260,000	
Fitness Swimmer	1995		60,000	
New Woman	1997, planning to acquire		1,300,000	
Total		5,501,515	8,740,000	6.8%

TABLE 3: EMPLOYMENT

Year	Number of Employees
1980	725
1983	791
1986	923
1989	1,087
1992	1,051
1995	1,266
1997 (plan)	1,300

Among the company's most distinctive skills were its ability to generate editorial content for mass consumption from esoteric medical journals and scientific research, and its ability to manage a large database of customer names for direct marketing of books.

FUTURE CHALLENGES

Despite its solid financial performance, Rodale faced several new challenges in 1996, ranging from an identity crisis and confusion about strategic direction to a rapidly changing industry. The first formidable challenge was the preservation of the company's traditional culture and values. The company was becoming fragmented as the individual magazine and book brands were being emphasized above the corporate brand. Together with very different management styles between the two divisions of the company and a number of acquisitions that were operated separately, the emphasis on individual brands had contributed to the erosion of a single corporate culture.

A second major challenge facing Rodale was the company's rapidly changing business environment. Paper and postage were very significant costs that had been increasing rapidly, but were beyond Rodale's control. (In 1996 alone, the price of printing paper had risen 40 percent.) The Internet, the so-called "new media," presented a new, yet-to-be-understood competitive challenge. In magazines, Rodale competed with large media companies, such as Time-Life, Advance (publishers of *Condé Nast Traveler*), Primedia, McGraw-Hill, and Hearst Corporation (Exhibit 2). Several of these firms were either private or closely held, but were all much larger and diversified than Rodale Press. Rodale's main competition in books was the Reader's Digest Company and Time-Life. However, in books, Amazon.com was emerging as a force in online book retailing. In the "trade," or traditional retail book channel of distribution, consolidation was under way, with Border's and Barnes & Noble leading the way in large-scale book retailing. As a result of these trends, management found itself competing not only with traditional publishers, but against an entire set of new competitors, which were attempting to use a new and growing portfolio of media to deliver their product. As the company looked for growth opportunities, it lacked a clear strategic vision or framework to guide new-product development. A balance needed to be forged between imposing a centralized or uniform corporate direction and maintaining an environment that fostered innovation and risk taking.

Furthermore, how would the company measure its growth? Should it be in terms of sales and profits, or would it be more appropriate to measure growth in terms of readership? Rodale's mission, after all, was to positively influence peoples' lives, rather than primarily to create shareholder value. Nonetheless, the continued financial success of the business was very important to the Rodale family. Furthermore, employment, creative opportunities, employee benefits[2], and healthy senior management compensation were all dependent on the financial success of Rodale Press.

---

[2]Company perks included "Energy House," the company health & fitness club and running track, and company cafeterias with healthy foods labeled according to their nutritional value.

EXHIBIT 2

Rodale Magazines' Competitive Universe

Rodale Magazines	Competes With	Total Circulation	Total Paid Subscriptions	Newsstand Sales	1-year Sub Price	2-year Sub Price
Bicycling (BI)	—	276,434	181,897	94,537	15.97	29.97
Runner's World (RW)	—	451,512	365,773	85,739	19.95	36.95
Men's Health (MH)	—	44,722	None	44,722	8.85	N/A
Backpacker (BP)	—	175,992	139,692	36,300	18.00	32.00
Scuba Diving (SD)	—	Not established	—	—	—	—
American Woodworker (AW)	—	91,456	84,469	6,987	12	22
Prevention (PR)	—	2,876,609	2,656,000	220,609	13.97	24.97
Organic Gardening (OG)	—	1,047,658	1,041,199	6,459	12.97	23.97
Competitors						
Outside	BP/BI/RW	276,264	211,989	64,275	18.00	28.00
Sierra	BP	334,316	326,725	7,591	12.00	20.00
Outdoor Photographer	BP	101,634	65,140	36,494	21.95	43.9
Flower & Garden	OG	634,511	623,223	11,288	6.00	11.00
Horticulture	OG	195,521	184,437	11,084	18.00	32.00
Harrowsmith	OG	202,155	189,752	12,403	20.00	40.00
Mother Earth News	OG	718,924	595,694	123,230	18.00	33.00
National Gardening	OG	N/A	—	—	—	—
Running Times	RW	41,600	14,100	27,500	17.50	34.00
Track & Field News	RW	30,510	25,398	5,112	22.00	42.00
Triathlete	RW	109,448	41,792	67,656	19.95	35.95
Esquire	MH	705,278	587,723	117,555	17.94	34.00
GQ	MH	686,842	305,709	381,133	18.16	34.33
Rolling Stone	MH	1,176,690	856,682	320,008	23.95	35.95
Fine Woodworking	AW	275,169	224,294	50,875	18.00	34.00
Wood	AW	400,075	328,147	71,928	25.00	48.00
Workbench	AW	911,962	876,641	35,321	6.00	12.00
Woodworker's Journal	AW	125,831	123,320	2,511	12.00	24.00
Shop Notes	AW	—	—	—	—	—
Woodsmith	AW	—	—	—	—	—
American Health	PR	811,235	735,574	75,661	14.95	28.00
Health	PR	1,025,351	1,015,351	10,000	22.00	44.00
Reader's Digest	PR	16,566,650	15,636,050	930,600	14.47	N/A
Good Housekeeping	PR	5,202,526	3,521,736	1,680,790	15.97	27.97
TV Guide	PR	16,969,260	8,832,670	8,136,590	29.90	59.80
Soap Opera Digest	PR	1,017,635	290,518	727,117	39.00	70.00
Redbook	PR	4,088,739	3,208,442	880,297	11.97	21.97
Woman's Day	PR	6,021,136	98,143	5,922,993	15.13	N/A
Family Circle	PR	5,773,484	1,146,591	4,626,893	16.15	N/A

(continued)

EXHIBIT 2 (CONTINUED)

Rodale Magazines' Competitive Universe

Rodale Competitors	Competes With	Total Circulation	Total Paid Subscriptions	Newsstand Sales	1-year Sub Price	2-year Sub Price
Ladies Home Journal	PR	5,125,052	4,086,417	1,038,635	19.95	39.90
McCall's	PR	5,353,595	4,590,558	763,037	12.95	N/A
Better Homes & Gardens	PR	8,012,659	7,392,159	620,500	14.00	26.00
People	PR	3,311,793	1,418,170	1,893,623	58.50	117.00
Modern Maturity	PR	16,734,801	16,734,801	none	2.40	N/A
Bicycle Guide	BI	242,652	202,504	40,148	14.90	None
Mountain Bike Action	BI	37,606	7,227	30,378	17.98	31.95
Velo News	BI	13,507	13,022	485	18.00	36.00
Mountain & City Biking	BI	—	—	—	—	—
Winning	BI	107,044	27,623	79,421	22.50	None
Skin Diver	SD	221,737	180,345	41,392	19.94	34.94
Underwater USA	SD	28,248	25,583	2,665	9.95	17.95
Scuba Times	SD	27,312	13,660	13,652	16.00	N/A
Discover Diving	SD	—	—	—	—	—
Dive Training	SD	—	—	—	—	—
Sports Illustrated	MH	3,154,018	3,032,486	121,532	61.88	113.36
Golf Digest	RW	1,239,100	1,117,728	121,372	19.94	29.94
Golf	RW	912,157	808,127	104,030	15.94	27.97
Tennis	RW	528,975	479,349	49,626	17.94	26.94
Muscle & Fitness	—	578,150	110,658	467,492	35.00	65.00
Playboy	MH	3,732,948	2,415,917	1,317,031	24.00	38.00
Field & Stream	—	2,004,465	1,897,948	106,517	15.94	27.94
Ski	RW	464,794	366,277	98,517	9.94	19.94
Outdoor Life	—	1,513,389	1,366,361	147,028	13.94	24.97
Skiing	RW	456,040	352,590	103,450	11.94	22.97
Sports Afield	—	521,164	428,106	93,058	13.97	24.97
Sport	—	930,565	771,767	158,798	12.00	18.00
Penthouse	—	2,251,491	227,934	2,023,557	36.00	65.00
Sporting News	—	733,343	688,832	44,511	59.95	119.90
Golf World	—	104,438	64,888	39,550	22.00	44.00
Golf Illustrated	—	265,649	234,059	31,590	15.00	30.00
World Tennis	—	388,754	362,938	25,816	15.94	29.94

GOVERNANCE ISSUES

After Bob Rodale's death in 1990, day-to-day management and decision making remained with the COO and President, Bob Teufel, and the heads of the book and magazine divisions, Pat Corpora and John Griffin, respectively. The CEO/Chairman of the Board position passed on to Ardie Rodale, Maria's mother, a personality very different from the visionary dreamer that her husband was. The Board of

Directors consisted of Ardie Rodale and her four living children, the three managers mentioned above, and Paul Wessell, the chief financial officer. Although the whole family had input into the management of the company, Bob Rodale's will had stipulated that the voting shares of the company would be given to Maria Rodale upon Ardie's retirement.

MANAGEMENT

The three top executives of Rodale Press, Teufel, Corpora, and Griffin, were highly qualified and loyal professionals who maintained the traditions and family values that had defined the company under Bob Rodale's leadership. Those values constituted Rodale's corporate brand, which had little recognition outside the company, but was well defined. "We have found that people think the family lives on a farm and writes the magazines and books. That's our brand image: family owned and environmentally concerned." And Teufel, aged 54, believed that image had become the culture of the company and that the culture was integrated enough to survive Bob Rodale's departure. "You can remove almost anyone from a business that has a culture and the culture remains. There are no changes in the business part of the business." However, it was becoming apparent that the business was changing and that the centralized culture of the company was slowly being eroded without the visionary leadership of Bob Rodale.

One of the family values that Teufel maintained was the reluctance to dispose of properties prematurely. An example of this was *Rodale's Scuba Diving*, a magazine that had not met the internal milestones required to continue with publication. Maria questioned Teufel's reluctance to terminate or sell that magazine, but in spite of voicing her concerns, nothing changed. The final decision still rested with Ardie, who took her guidance from Bob. Overall, Bob Teufel was a talented executive with strong industry connections and valuable skills. He had known Maria since she was born, and had watched her grow into a rebellious teenager and creative young adult. However, the current incarnation of Maria Rodale as "leader-in-waiting" was new, and her ascension to power could significantly change the way the company was run.

Similar to the decision concerning *Scuba Diving*, many of Ardie Rodale's decisions as chairman of the board were made with Teufel's guidance and counsel. Typically, Teufel ran the board meetings and set the agendas for them.

Pat Corpora, head of the book division, was known as a talented, hard-driving, even brilliant executive who produced consistently strong results for the company. It was said he could turn a profit out of anything. Yet many felt that Corpora's success had come to some extent at the expense of his people. There was the feeling that the division's short-term success may have damaged the long-term creativity of the employees. His tendency to control every detail was commonly discussed within the company. Corpora had recently returned from a six-week senior executive program at the University of Virginia.

In early 1996 a discussion between Corpora, Teufel, and Maria Rodale revealed Corpora's ambition to take the COO position of a proposed, newly organized Rodale that would divide the company by thematic areas (Health, Home and Garden, and Active Sports). Corpora's memo to Teufel read:

> I think you're a great CEO and I'd rather work for no one else. However, managing a major reorganization and the day-to-day operations of this new structure, in addition to your other responsibilities (family matters, company representation, strategic

issues) would be excessive. I believe you need a strong COO who can manage the day-to-day decision making and have responsibility for implementing and executing the potential benefits of this new structure. You need someone that will insure consistency throughout the organization.

John Griffin, head of the magazine division, was cut from different cloth. A very well liked, personable executive, he fostered a creative, flexible environment. Whereas Corpora ran a centralized operation, Griffin ran magazines as decentralized, quasi-independent business units. As Maria noted: "What is best about the magazine division is that they have created an environment where highly talented and mature people have a chance to try new things, fail often and learn from their mistakes, and grow and develop with a lot of freedom." As Griffin himself put it: "In addition to being the quantitative leader, we want to be the qualitative leader."

Maria Rodale, now 32 years old, started working at Rodale in 1987, under Teufel, Griffin, and Corpora at different times in her career. She had held positions in the circulation area of several titles and, more recently, as creative director (Exhibit 3).

FAMILY

Bob and Ardie Rodale had five children. The oldest son, David, had passed away in 1985, but the others were all involved with the family business in some work capacity, as well as having seats on the board.

Heather Stoneback, at age 44 the oldest daughter, was a level-headed woman who, as a girl, had helped her mother raise the younger children. She had joined Rodale after a career as a schoolteacher. Heather's first responsibility in Rodale was managing training programs. Eventually, she had advanced to director of Human Resources. Although she lacked formal managerial training, she was active in enhancing her professional development. Her husband, Tom Stoneback, was VP of Administration. Tom held a Ph.D. in environmental science. He had held several positions within the company, including work on a variety of environmental projects with Bob Rodale. Clearly, his skills were better suited for some of the company's more scientific work, but in his current position he could not explore those opportunities. Moreover, he felt some frustration with his lack of influence in the company.

The next daughter in line, Heidi, age 42, had also worked in several areas of the company, including the start-up of the child-care center and several newsletters. She was married to a doctor who was also a world-class competitive swimmer. Currently, Heidi ran *Fitness Swimmer Magazine*. The magazine and the newsletters had not been financially successful. There was tension between Maria and Heidi; Heidi felt she could/should have been chosen for the future CEO position.

Anthony, at age 31, was the youngest. He ran the Rodale Institute, a nonprofit experimental organic farm primarily supported by the business. The Institute reflected the roots of the organization and Bob Rodale's commitment to organic farming. It was the type of position for which Tom Stoneback would have been well qualified because of his educational background and experience. Anthony's real passion was photography, so he traveled extensively, pursuing this interest and documenting the work of the Institute abroad.

Exhibit 3

Maria Rodale's Resume—1995

Maria Rodale
209 Main Street
Emmaus, PA 18049

EXPERIENCE

1994 to Present
Vice President, Corporate Creative Director, Rodale Press
Overall management of $4.5 million budget, 80-person group that includes Creative Department, Photography and Video Departments.

Continually take on projects that cross the boundaries of the corporation, including: Book Cover Design and Approval Process Analysis, New Media Task Force, Photo Rights Database, Technology Task Force, and Corporate Strategic Planning Process.

1991 to 1994
Creative Director, Rodale Press
Responsible for a $3 million, 65-person staff department that creates and produces all of the direct-response promotions for Rodale Press books and magazines.

1989 to 1991
Assistant Circulation Manager, *Backpacker Magazine*, Rodale Press
Fully responsible for the circulation management and profitability of *Backpacker Magazine,* including budgeting, promotion planning, and fulfillment.

1987 to 1989
Promotion Coordinator, Circulation Department
***Prevention Magazine*, Rodale Press**
Worked on the circulation launch of *Men's Health* and *Backpacker Magazine.* Managed "Source 4 and 6" of *Prevention Magazine.* Was responsible for testing the first sweepstakes blow-in, which is now the standard for all Rodale magazines.

1986 to 1987
Coordinator of Regenerative Psychology and Spirituality, Rodale Press
Assisted Robert Rodale in the development of his theory of Regeneration as it concerned the mind and spirit. Wrote the "Seven Tendencies of Regeneration." Wrote a column in the *Regeneration Newsletter* on Inner Fitness.

1985 to 1986
Assistant, Fenton Communications
Washington, DC
Coordinated press conferences, wrote press releases, and managed the office of a progressive public relations company. Worked on the campaign that broke the "Iran-Contra" story.

(continued)

EXHIBIT **3**

Maria Rodale's Resume—1995

1981 to 1982
Technical Artist, Creative Department, Rodale Press
Performed basic design and paste-up in the pre-computer era.

EDUCATION

BA in Communications Theory and Art
Muhlenberg College, Allentown, PA
Graduated December 1985, GPA 3.5

OTHER

Places I have traveled: France, Germany, Austria, England, Scotland, Italy, Alaska, Hawaii, Caribbean, Canada and most of the US
Personal: Married, with one daughter, age 13
Hobbies: Painting, writing, reading, organic gardening and landscaping, gourmet cooking, exercising, music, home decorating, continuing my education.
Boards: Served on the Board of the Rodale Institute from 1986 to 1991
Currently serve on the Board of Directors of Rodale Press

Ardie Rodale, chairman of the Board and matriarch of this family, was a warm, outgoing, intensely spiritual person who was given to hugging people and delivering inspirational speeches. She was passionate about her family and her causes, and championed them both inside and outside the firm. Before and after her husband's death, she had been the director of Environmental Resources. She was responsible for the physical surroundings of the company, and her presence was evident throughout Rodale's facilities. Ardie loved art, and she decorated the offices extensively. Walking through the administrative office at Rodale Press was similar to a museum tour. Ardie selected works from Asia, Africa, and Appalachia. There were also Native American pieces on display. She retained her environmental role along with her CEO responsibilities.

Ardie had no business background, although she had extensive and varied experience in volunteer work. She therefore received significant guidance from Bob Teufel. To her, board meetings were venues for her children to display their accomplishments. The board contained no outside members, and among the family members there was little financial training. Recently a Darden accounting professor had given a seminar for family board members on financial training for the nonfinancial manager.

Maria's succession to a position of influence at Rodale would involve assuaging the fears and egos of the family members involved, sorting out an effective working relationship with her mother, and gaining enough confidence from Teufel, Griffin, and Corpora that she could provide leadership.

Maria Rodale

As she sat in her home office on the morning of April 15, Maria reflected on what she considered to be the major turning point in her life, and she considered her next move. In 1985, after graduating from college, she had decided to leave Pennsylvania for Washington, D.C. The decision to move was made difficult, because her brother had just died of AIDS and her tearful father had pleaded with her to stay and carry on his vision. Her response at the time was that she would be of more use in Washington than if she stayed at home. "I was right," she remembered. Among other accomplishments during her time in Washington as a single parent at 20, she was able to demonstrate that she could make a living independently of Rodale Press. She also gained perspective on Rodale and began to think about a vision for making positive change. Most importantly, she learned that she possessed the power to "reinvent herself" through the process of going away from the family and the business, gaining a new perspective, then returning home.

During the following 10 years, Maria had continued to learn about Rodale's businesses through her various positions within the company. These jobs ranged from Technical Artist to Corporate Creative Director. Now at age 35, she spent most of her time thinking about her continuing role in the company. Maria had known since her father's death in 1990 that she would be assuming the position of chairman and CEO of Rodale Press. Also, Bob Rodale's will had specified that Maria alone would inherit the right to vote the company's voting shares. However, to achieve success as chairman and CEO, she faced the challenge of changing her relationships with the nonfamily, professional managers within Rodale, who had successfully managed the operations of the company even before her father's death. Indeed, Bob Teufel, John Griffin, and Pat Corpora had been instrumental in managing the company during most of Maria's life. In addition, she felt competing pressures between her business goals and the interests of her family members.

There were many things that gave her confidence about her skills as a business leader. She was proud of her success at Rodale to this point and had recently proved that she was capable of making difficult business decisions. Under her guidance, the company outsourced video production in order to achieve lower costs and higher efficiency, while bolstering production expertise. In implementing that change, she discharged an employee whom she had known and worked with for 20 years. The consequences of the decision had given her pause, but she knew that it was in the best interest of Rodale. Through actions such as that one, Maria believed that she had demonstrated her abilities to upper management and had built credibility to make the next move in her career.

The decision that Maria had to help Ardie make was when and how would Maria assume leadership of Rodale Press. Should she replace her mother as chairman and CEO simultaneously, or assume these roles separately, and at different times? Should she create a new position for herself? She realized that whatever was decided, it would be difficult for the organization to accept. Already, she had floated these issues and had heard reservations from upper management and her family. She saw what was happening in the company's business environment and knew that Rodale needed strong leadership to thrive in the future—she could provide that leadership, but not without the support of the family and current management. She was inheriting a successful organization that was facing new challenges and could not afford to become a victim of her father's success. Throughout her entire career she had fought against having people discount her accomplishments and ability because they attributed her position to nepotism.

All of Maria's experience had been in sales instead of product development, where most of the other upper management had spent significant amounts of time. In addition, she had never run a profit center and had only limited experience outside of Rodale. These items concerned her and had been highlighted by some of the comments that she elicited from the company's leadership team about her role within Rodale. Many of the managers had seen her grow up, and they were reluctant to have her move into a senior leadership position within the company at this time.

Pat Corpora often talked about her needing "a bit more seasoning before she can take over a key leadership role." John Griffin, who offered that he was "not sure Maria is ready yet, she has not run a profit and loss organization," echoed this sentiment.

In addition, Bob Teufel recognized that the Rodale family dynamics could also create a challenge for Maria. He was "not sure that she should take a coleadership role with her mother because people might try to split the two and play a favorite. They'll go to the person they think they can get the best ear from. So I wouldn't recommend that kind of position."

Despite this feedback, Maria believed that she was ready to assume a greater role in the company. Changes needed to take place, and she wanted to play a significant role in making them. In fact, that is what her father had wanted her to do. Accordingly, she had decided to take a 12-month sabbatical (which was extended to 18 months when Maria became pregnant with her daughter Eve) to prepare, develop herself, and set an agenda, but mainly to "reinvent" herself. In creating the position to which she would return, Maria had to be cautious against alienating her family. What role should she craft for herself? Was she really ready to assume more responsibility? How would the others react to her assertion of power? These were all things that she would consider over the next 17 months during her leave and issues that troubled her now after she finished speaking to John. She clearly had a lot of work in front of her.

APPENDIX

Letter from Main Street

To: Ardie Rodale
Bob Teufel
John Griffin
Pat Corpora
Heather Stoneback
Heidi Rodale
Anthony Rodale
Mike Sincavage
Peter Spiers
Barb Newton
Lou Cinquino
Debbie Lindtner

March 4, 1996

From: Maria Rodale

Month One
The Journey

One of the greatest things about working from home is being able to listen to the radio all day. The best stations are WXPN (104.9) which comes out of the University of Pennsylvania, WMUH (91.7) from Muhlenberg, and the various National Public Radio Stations at the bottom of the dial. Being all-listener supported, there are no commercials (I hate commercials). So the day becomes a continuous stream of music and intelligent talking, like a journey where you never know where you are going or will end up. Kind of like this year for me!

The other day there was an interview on the radio with Houston Smith, professor emeritus of philosophy and religion at Syracuse University. He is also the author of the just released *Illustrated Guide to the World's Religions*. It's an excellent book that I had just finished reading, so I wanted to hear what he had to say.

He told a story about when, as a young man, he had spent time in a Zen Monastery studying koans. His first koan was this:

> A monk asked Jo Shu (a famous Chinese master),
> "Does a dog have a Buddha-nature?," to which
> Jo Shu replied, "Mu."
> (To recognize the seeming contradiction here, we need to know that the Buddha had said that even grass has a Buddha-nature, and the word "Mu" means no.)

A koan is a saying that is not possible to answer rationally. The challenge is even not to answer it, but to cause you to go beyond your normal response to things.

So off Houston went to try to find the answer. At Zen monasteries one is not permitted to sleep for more than three hours at a time and the schedule is very rigorous and difficult. After three weeks of trying to answer and failing, he started to get very angry. He was getting sick and feeling very sorry for himself. Finally, he had had it and stormed in to the monk, on purpose

(continued)

APPENDIX (CONTINUED)

Letter from Main Street

ignoring the traditional respectful bowing rituals. The monk, rather than his usual formal introduction, asked him:

"What's the matter? How are you doing? Are you feeling O.K.?"

Disarmed, Houston replied, "No, I am feeling really sick and I have had it with this stupid exercise."

The monk changed his demeanor back to his "formal self" and said to him, "**What is sickness or health, but a distraction?**"

Although health is a desirable state, it is not the point of life. The point of life is the journey itself, and what you learn while you are traveling.

For a company that considers itself a health company, the idea that health is a distraction is a pretty powerful message, which, to me, supports our careful entry into spiritual publishing. One can be quite healthy but still miserable and negative. And in sickness one can find a meaning that didn't exist before. Illness can become a transformative, regenerative experience. If we are truly to inspire, motivate, and enable people to improve their lives and the world around them, we need to look beyond our current definition of health. We need to think of ourselves as guides on the journey to healing.

Now, I know Main Street, Emmaus, is not California—but I still think there is a hotbed of trends being born right under our noses. That's why I'm going to make a prediction. A brief preface is in order, however, to assure you that no occult tools were used in the development of this prediction. The only tool used was my own experience and the "brain in my stomach," which was just proven to exist in everyone and reported about in the *New York Times* a few weeks ago. I predict that the next BIG trend in fitness is going to be Spiritual Fitness.

What is Spiritual Fitness? It is using both traditional religious forms of exercise (Yoga, T'ai Chi, Aikido, etc.) and modern forms of exercise to find inner peace and meaning as well as outward health. (Multitasking exercise, if you will.) As the teachings of yoga tell, the outward body is the manifestation of the inward mind. It also includes using your body to expand and teach your mind.

Debbie Yost just informed me that she will be putting my book idea on this subject on the next survey. The title is *Your Complete Guide to Spiritual Fitness*. That makes two ideas I've got on the surveys! The other one is the book I plan on writing this year: *Your Beautiful and Delicious Organic Garden—Maria Rodale's Seasonal Guide to Designing, Planting, and Enjoying Your Home Landscape* (ahh the land of long subtitles!). I've also submitted a cookbook idea. But no word yet as to whether it will make it on the survey or not.

Speaking of Spiritual Fitness, I've been taking the Yoga class at the energy center and it's amazing. (And, let me assure you, there are very normal people in the class. People you might consider friends… lots of them!) I didn't realize how tight I was until I stretched. *Allure Magazine* recently reported that the top four most elite fitness activities in Los Angeles are Yoga, Spinning ("If you have to ask what it is, you're not cool enough to know"), Kick-Boxing, and Pilates. Pilates is some strange stretching machine thing. Spinning involves special stationary bikes in a classroom experience. Nothing like spinning your wheels and not getting anywhere! What kind of journey is that?!

As with most journeys, the hardest part is deciding to go and getting ready to go. Now that my journey has begun, it's delightful! I will keep you posted each month in these letters from Main Street. But you also know, I'm not very far away.

Case 38

Rodale Press (B)

Seventeen months after the phone call from John Griffin, Maria was excited about returning to work. During her time off, she had developed a 90-day plan that outlined both her visible and "invisible" (nonobservable) actions and how they might be interpreted by those around her (Exhibit 1). With the feedback and buy-in of her family, she had crafted a position for herself as vice chairman of the board and director of strategy (Exhibits 2 and 3). Finally, she penned the speech she intended to deliver at a meeting of Rodale's top 50 executives and board members on the eve of her return on Monday, September 22, 1997 (Exhibit 4).

As Maria polished off her speech and rehearsed it for the final time, she received Rodale's quarterly financial report for the first nine months of 1997 (Exhibit 5).

This case was written by Catherine Elliott (Darden 1998); Marcien Jenckes (Darden 1998) and Daren Samuels (Darden 1998) under the supervision of L. J. Bourgeois, professor of Business Administration.

EXHIBIT 1

Maria Rodale's 90-Day Plan

THE SCENARIO:

Major Business Issues (as culled from facilitator interviews, survey and observation):

- Future direction of growth (what media, what products, what scope)
- Leadership and the ability and willingness to make tough decisions about people, products, and the future
- Structure—brand-based, corporate versus product areas, centralized versus decentralized
- Compensation—tying bonuses to actual results we want to see and competitiveness with industry and community
- Accountability—Holding people accountable for their business and management actions and results
- Bench strength—having the people trained and ready to grow as we need them
- People—inspiring, motivating, rewarding, and retaining them
- Creativity, innovation, and risk taking and open communication

Major Employee Issues (as culled from the recent employee satisfaction survey):

- Dissatisfaction with salaries, especially low—and especially the discrepancy between high and low and the seeming unfairness of bonuses
- The discordance between our stated mission and our actual practices and profit/budget focus—distrust of upper management
- Communication and working together between books, magazines, service groups, brands. Communication from the top down not clear and consistent
- Book division—overworked, underappreciated, burnt out
- Little guys—underpaid, underappreciated, ignored
- Sadness over Bob's death and the emptiness left in his absence

(continued)

EXHIBIT 1 (CONTINUED)

Maria Rodale's 90-Day Plan

Job Title:
Vice Chairman of Rodale Press
Key Job Responsibilities:
The Board of Directors
Strategic Planning and Implementation
Family Business Issues
New Business Opportunities
Announcement Date:
July 4, 1997
Return Date:
September 1997

THE ANNOUNCEMENT:

Visible:

- A memo to all employees explaining my new job, plans and hopes for the future. Memo will include date for strategic planning session and my plan to visit and talk with every group within the company over the next year. Acknowledge the major issues we need to face together.

Interpretation:
Positive: There is hope for the future, and she's coming to see "me" personally to talk about it. The next generation of the family is finally taking control.
Negative: Nepotism at work again. Does she really deserve it? What if she changes things I don't want to see changed? Spoiled brat. She's never run a profit center. What does she know?

- A press release with the facts to major media

Interpretation:
Positive: Next generation finally comes out—Rodale retains its independent, privately owned status.
Negative: Nepotism—who is this woman and what has she done to prove herself? Will my background look substantial enough in *The Wall Street Journal*?

Invisible:

- Meet with family to discuss my plans and answer questions
- Meet with Bob Teufel to make sure he is clear and on-board
- Have a full organizational chart created
- Find an office

Interpretation:
Positive: Finally she is taking action, and the future is on track—perhaps we can resolve some of these long-standing issues now.
Negative: Where does this leave "me"? Will she take all my power away? How will I look to the employees and the public now?

Response: The key is to position myself as the "family representative," not as the "heir." With Bob, the key will be to not threaten his dignity, position, and respect within the industry and company—to be perceived as his partner, rather than his "boss."

(continued)

EXHIBIT 1 (CONTINUED)

Maria Rodale's 90-Day Plan

THE PRE-RETURN

Visible:

- Hold strategic planning session

Interpretation:
Positive: She's taking action right away, maybe something will actually happen this time.
Negative: She doesn't waste time taking over. Poor Bob.

Invisible:

- Start looking for a secretary/assistant

THE RETURN
SEPTEMBER

Visible:

- Catch up on what's been going on: Meet with VPs and key employees. Attend executive staff meetings. Hold twice-monthly meetings with Pat, Bob, John, and Paul individually. Meet weekly with Ardie. Clarify with all of them what they would like from me and what they expect from me. Spend a day listening to customer service calls.
- Sign up for and attend the orientation program to see how new employees are introduced to the company.
- Hold strategic planning session and start making things happen.
- Run the first board meeting. Review our progress from the last board retreat, identify a list of current board issues, and discuss strategic plan.
- Set up a systematic schedule and plan for the family meetings and for addressing family business issues. Hire lawyer for our generation. Set up communication strategy and list of things they want to be involved with.
- Set up "world tour" to all buildings and offices to report on strategic plan, provide hope and information for the future, and LISTEN to their concerns.

Interpretation:
Positive: She is really involved and getting out to talk and see people (from the top to the bottom). It feels good to be paid attention to and listened to. Finally someone is taking charge.
Negative: Who does she think she is, "Miss take over the world"?! Anybody can talk. Let's see what she really DOES. She thinks she's funny but she's not. Am I going to have a job when this whole thing is over and done with?

OCTOBER

Invisible:

- Digest the results of the strategic planning session, meetings, and board meeting and develop action plan.

(continued)

EXHIBIT 1 (CONTINUED)

Maria Rodale's 90-Day Plan

- Take the organizational chart and rework. Identify weak links and strong points. Make my reorganizational plan.
- Create my own 1998 budget.
- Review all company salaries with Ardie to see where the problems are. Have industry comparison figures available. Decide on what approach we want to take to make corrections.
- Decide on my communication chain with employees (use of company newsletter, memos, meetings, etc.).

Interpretation:
Positive: Gee, she's rather quiet this month. What's she thinking? What's going to happen? Will she still have a Halloween Parade Party?
Negative: This is going to be scary, crazy, and stupid. Still haven't seen any real changes. Higher-ups might feel that some of their freedom, independence, and compensation might be taken away.

Visible:

- Send out communication to whole company regarding the results of the strategic planning session and what the next steps are (to squelch rumors and build anticipation). List the major issues that will be addressed.
- Discuss weak-link areas and salary discrepancies with managers and ask for action and correction plan.
- Actively review, analyze, and approve the '98 Budget. Incorporate compensation changes in the budget.
- Ask for volunteers for a "Corporate Conscience Committee" to regularly audit what we say we do with what we actually do.
- Meet with family (including extended) and kids (separately) to talk about the future of Rodale Press. Get their ideas, feedback, and visions. Get ideas for family trips and how they want to be involved. Review the history with the kids. Finish the two- or three-day process with a big family picnic with fun, games, and food that reflect our new future together. Perhaps pick one or two volunteers to assist in the planning of future events and programs. Share my goals with them.

Interpretation:
Positive: Managers might begin to feel the heat of changes. Some will like it. Some won't. Most employees will start to feel a part of the regular communication chain—feel "in the know." Family might start to feel like a cohesive group with hope for the future.
Negative: Managers might not like changes. Some may even get probationary warnings (i.e., dead wood might get burnt for fuel). People may think changes are stupid and unnecessary. Kids and family might feel that they don't want to be involved or all they want is money. I have to be careful not to diminish their parents' role in anything—to include them. I also have to be careful not to show too much favoritism to Maya [Maria's 16-year-old daughter].

(continued)

EXHIBIT 1 (CONTINUED)

Maria Rodale's 90-Day Plan

NOVEMBER

Visible:

- Start implementing organizational changes: Teufel's role, COO role, corporate and divisional structures.
- Set up and sponsor Brand Synergy meetings and retreats. First meetings should be to identify issues, barriers to working together, and possible solutions. Assign teams to solve problems and correct. Review strategic planning results and ideas and check for workability. Involve everyone in the implementation. Ask each group for their future growth plans and ideas.
- Ask for volunteers for a "benefits review task force." Let people from all areas of the company identify the benefit changes they would like to see.

Interpretations:
Positive: Wow, she is really making things happen now. The people changes are long overdue. We've been talking about brand building for four years. Finally someone is doing something about it!
Negative: I can't believe she is so cruel and heartless by getting rid of or changing the jobs of certain people. More freaking meetings to attend to. I don't like it here anymore. I quit.

Invisible:

- Have Filomena [a human resources consultant] or someone independent conduct a "how is she doing" check amongst key employees, including my mother and family. Also ask people directly how I am doing and what else I could be doing to meet their needs.
- Begin plans for the first meeting pavilion. Start working with a permaculture designer on reforming the landscape to grow more of our own food, provide more environmental energy benefits, and create more outdoor spaces for people to enjoy and regenerate in. (Have raspberry bushes lining some of the walkways, create an herb garden for the food kitchen, create outdoor picnic areas with shade right outside each cafeteria). Will be visible by spring.
- Ask Florence [sister-in-law] and some of the kids to put together the Rodale History archives and museum. Turn Fitness House into the home base for it (including a meeting room for the board of directors and other meetings, dining areas, and "library/lounge"). But start with a traveling exhibit to all the buildings and offices. Will be visible by spring.
- Based on all interviews, meetings, strategy sessions, and information, create action plan and goals for 1998.

Interpretation:
Positive: She is doing things that are grounding us in our heritage again. We are being reconnected to our history, but with a new twist. She seems to be willing to hear and accept feedback.
Negative: She's crazy. And paranoid.

(continued)

EXHIBIT 1 (CONTINUED)

Maria Rodale's 90-Day Plan

Major signals I want to send based on the above actions:

- I have a long-term vision and plan and am willing to make it happen.
- I care about people—what they think, what they are paid, and how they are managed.
- I care about my family and am willing to make time to include everyone and bring us all together.
- I am willing to take risks and support creativity and innovation.
- I understand and value the history of what Rodale Press was founded on.

EXHIBIT 2

Questions for Maria Rodale's Family

In order to put together a job description for my return, it would be very helpful to me to get your input. Mom, Bob Teufel, and I have been discussing my return as vice chairman and director of Corporate Strategy (or something similar). In order for me to best represent the owners' concerns and needs in that position, please take a few minutes to answer the following questions in writing.

1. What roles and responsibilities would you want to see from a vice chairman at Rodale Press?

2. What are the most critical issues at Rodale Press that you would want me to deal with on my return?

3. What are your major concerns about me taking the role of vice chairman and how would you like me to address them?

4. Looking ahead five or ten years, what roles and responsibilities would you like the vice chairman and chairman of Rodale Press to have?

EXHIBIT 3

Maria Rodale's Proposed Job Description

JOB DESCRIPTION
VICE CHAIRMAN – DIRECTOR OF STRATEGY

For Public/Company Information:

STRATEGIC PLANNING AND IMPLEMENTATION

- Be responsible for coordinating and developing a corporate strategy (on an ongoing basis) and ensuring effective implementation with the help, support, and cooperation of the leaders of the company.
- Attend major divisional and product strategic planning sessions in order to contribute the big picture corporate strategic vision to their efforts.
- Be a champion for visual excellence in all of our products.
- Seek and communicate innovative new ways of looking at our business, our products, and our customers so that we stay successful into the future.

THE BOARD OF DIRECTORS

- Work with the family and nonfamily managers to set the agenda for board meetings.
- Identify and implement ways for our board to continually be more effective.

ASSIST CHAIRMAN

- Serve as a link between the chairman and the company by regularly visiting all buildings and departments in order to communicate corporate information, get feedback, answer questions, and keep in touch with employees at all levels.

MANAGE FAMILY BUSINESS ISSUES

- Help family to develop policies, guidelines, and skills for our and future generations.
- Be responsible for managing the experts for legal, estate, and tax issues facing the company as a result of being a family business (i.e., "S corporation"–type issues)

Not for public information (behind the scenes):

ASSIST CHAIRMAN

- ***Assist chairman on a day-to-day basis in developing and communicating corporate, family, and environmental mission and vision to employees and the public.***
- ***Assist chairman in analyzing and making major business decisions.***

(continued)

EXHIBIT 3 (CONTINUED)

Maria Rodale's Proposed Job Description

- *Assist chairman by: attending monthly building meetings, scanning all of our publications and products, review outside proposals for books and magazines, and route to the right people.*

STRATEGIC PLANNING AND IMPLEMENTATION

- *Help to identify and mentor new leaders within the company.*
- *Constantly strive to align our corporate actions with our ideals and vision in our business, our corporate culture, the environment, and in my own actions.*

MANAGE FAMILY BUSINESS ISSUES

- *Serve as representative to the family within the business by coordinating family meetings, communicating important information to everyone, and organizing our efforts so that we are moving forward in a positive way.*
- *Be a communication interface between the family and nonfamily managers to make sure that we all know what is going on about the business and the family business issues (this is not meant to take the place of one-on-one communication between each family member and the nonfamily managers).*
- *Coordinate family business retreats, meetings, and events.*

MANAGE THE BOARD OF DIRECTORS

- *Organize an annual or biannual board retreat.*

EXHIBIT 4

Maria Rodale's "Reentry Speech" September 22, 1997

When I left a year and a half ago, I wasn't sure what my destination was, and how I could make my best contribution to Rodale Press when I returned. But as I read in a *Men's Health* article once in a story about an eighty-year-old adventurer—it's not a real adventure unless you *don't* know where you are going.

So I traveled, I read, I explored the history of this company, I took courses on business and on gardening, I talked to all sorts of people, I rested, I had a baby, and I am still learning, from the inside out, about our book editorial process by writing a book. I also kept the corporate strategic planning process moving forward. And gradually it became more and more clear that what I could do best, and what this company needed most from me, was strategy: strategic thinking, planning, and doing.

Rodale Press has had the good fortune over the years of having tremendous growth and success, much of it due to the hard work and skills of all of you.

But with growth and success comes complexity and a certain sense of satisfaction. Yes, we are successful, yes, we are leaders, yes, we are good and we try to do the right things.

But are we good enough?

Is there more we can do?

How can we continue to lead in a world that seems to be moving faster than we are?

How can we align our strategy and business with our mission and our values?

These questions need to be asked and need to be answered—not only as I am sure you are all doing for your product areas, but for the company as a whole. Each of our products and divisions have done well on their own, but I think we can do even better if we connect everything and look at it all together and find some synchronicity and synergy.

But still the question remains... why do we need to grow? Why do we need to be profitable?

Traditionally the answer has been to maximize shareholder value. But that's not why the Rodale family is here and what matters most to us (although it does matter).

The family—my mother, Heather, Heidi, Anthony, and I are firmly committed to remaining a privately owned family business. We are here for three main reasons:

1. We are here because we believe that Rodale Press can make the world a better place—for the health of people, the health of the environment, and the health of our employees.
2. We are here because we believe that being privately owned gives all of us —including you—unique and exciting opportunities to take big risks, be innovative, and try things that may be shocking or strange at first, but can eventually lead to great things.

(continued)

EXHIBIT 4

Maria Rodale's "Re-Entry Speech" September 22, 1997

3. We are also here because we love what this company stands for, we believe in it and are excited about what the possibilities for the future are.

Success, growth, and profits can be seen as a sign that our message is being embraced and accepted by more people and that we are making a positive difference in people's lives... as long as those profits and growth are gained honestly and in accordance with what we believe.

But first, we all have a lot of questions to answer about our future. Where are we going? How will we get there? What do we need to do to position ourselves for future growth? And most importantly, how can we accomplish our business goals while being committed to our integrity and our values?

It is a lot harder to take a half-billion-dollar company with over a thousand employees on an adventure than it is to do on your own.... We need to at least attempt to know where we are going, and have plans to guide us... including knowing where the rest stops are (that welcome buses). But hopefully we will always be open to adventures along the way.

That's why we are here today with [strategy consultant] and launching the corporate planning process.

And that's what I'll be working on in the next few years.

I am truly excited to be here in this time and in this place. We are on the verge of a new millennium and facing a dynamic new environment of change and growth in our industry and in the world. The global changes in technology, cultures, markets, and lifestyles are creating a world where new rules are being written every day, and huge opportunities exist for those who have the speed, flexibility, and creativity to make bold moves.

We are fortunate. We have a terrific heritage. We have been lucky to have the strong and knowledgeable leadership of my mother, Bob, Pat, and John. We have a company filled with talented and motivated people. We are operating from a position of financial strength. We are in the thrilling position of being able to create our own future and create a better world. We can change the world—in fact, we are doing it every day.

As Margaret Mead said, "Never doubt that a small group of thoughtful, committed citizens can change the world. Indeed, it is the only thing that ever has."

I look forward to working with all of you and welcome your ideas, feedback, and partnership. But I have to confess—I was tempted to stay on leave for longer. I hate wearing shoes and my book still isn't done. But I also have to say—it's great to be back.

Thanks.

EXHIBIT 5

Rodale Press Most Recent Financial Data (disguised) ($000s)

NET INCOME DETAIL

	Nine months ended: 9/30/97	Budget	9/30/96
One Shot	9,751.5	2,315.8	4,949.1
Trade	2,112.4	2,263.8	2,137.1
Book Clubs	(44.0)	747.0	769.7
Continuity Series	364.8	(437.6)	(474.2)
Annuals	(647.7)	(935.8)	(1,714.9)
International	282.8	31.3	405.5
Book Division Total	11,819.9	3,984.7	6,072.4
Previews	3,257.6	2,659.3	2,626.6
Specials	234.1	(314.2)	(502.3)
Organic Gardening	155.4	(118.7)	(508.9)
American Woodworker	3.3	(589.0)	(418.2)
Runner's World	2,501.3	938.5	1,516.8
Bicycling	348.2	(39.4)	72.7
Mountain Bike	414.9	112.7	160.1
Backpacker	859.8	1,105.9	889.1
Men's Health	8,706.4	3,969.3	3,050.2
Scuba Diving	(506.9)	(700.4)	(803.1)
Heart & Soul	(1,137.2)	(1,394.7)	(1,776.9)
Fitness Swimmer	(411.5)	(386.9)	(311.5)
Men's Confidential	(12.7)	(14.7)	(94.7)
Magazines: USA	14,412.5	5,227.9	3,899.9
Runner's World Int'l	16.0	(39.4)	(180.1)
MB Germany	(117.4)	(93.4)	(386.9)
Men's Health Int'l	(530.9)	(1,311.3)	(2,403.9)
Russian Venture	(63.4)	(68.0)	(86.7)
Int'l Development	(119.4)	(399.5)	–
Magazines Int'l	(815.1)	(1,911.6)	(3,057.5)
Magazines Total	13,597.5	3,316.3	842.4
Health Promotions	(120.7)	(10.0)	100.1
Rodale Interactive	(773.1)	(1,173.9)	(427.5)
New Woman	(611.6)	–	–
Pub. Svcs Over/Under	901.8	–	45.4
Operating Divisions	24,813.7	6,117.1	6,632.6
Other Operations	(2,678.7)	(2,728.0)	(2,572.0)
Research	(735.0)	(975.8)	(906.5)
Rodale Corporate Total	21,400.0	2,413.2	3,154.2

Credits List

Chapter no.	Credit
CHAPTER 1	
Management Focus Box	*senior management "Grand Plans" from the Wall Street Journal* Reprinted with permission of The Wall Street Journal © 1988 Dow Jones & Company, Inc. All rights reserved worldwide.
Management Focus Box:	*letter to the editor from the Wall Street Journal* Reprinted with permission of The Wall Street Journal © 1988 Dow Jones & Company, Inc. All rights reserved.
Exhibit 1.1	From INVESTOR CAPITALISM by MICHAEL USEEM. Copyright © 1996 by Michael Useem. Reprinted by permission of Perseus Books LLC.
Exhibit 1.3	Reprinted by permission, H. Mintzberg, "Patterns in Strategic Formation," Management Science, Volume 24, Number 9, May 1979, p. 945. Copyright 1979, The Institute of Management Sciences (currently INFORMS), 901 Elkridge Landing Road, Suite 400, Linthicum, Maryland 21090-2909 USA.
CHAPTER 2	
Exhibit 2.3	From A. L. Glass & K. J. Holyoak, Cognition, 1986, pp. 142, 143, Random House. Reproduced with permission of The McGraw-Hill Companies.
CHAPTER 3	
Exhibit 3.7	Reprinted with the permission of Rawson Associates/Scribner, a Division of Simon & Schuster from The Machine That Changed The World by James P. Womack, Daniel T. Jones, Daniel Roos. Copyright © 1990 James P. Womack, Daniel T. Jones, Daniel Roos and Donna Sammons Carpenter.
Exhibit 3.8a	Reprinted with the permission of Rawson Associates/Scribner, a Division of Simon & Schuster from The Machine That Changed The World by James P. Womack, Daniel T. Jones, Daniel Roos. Copyright © 1990 James P. Womack, Daniel T. Jones, Daniel Roos and Donna Sammons Carpenter.
Exhibit 3.8b	Reprinted with the permission of Rawson Associates/Scribner, a Division of Simon & Schuster from The Machine That Changed The World by James P. Womack, Daniel T. Jones, Daniel Roos. Copyright © 1990 James P. Womack, Daniel T. Jones, Daniel Roos and Donna Sammons Carpenter.

CHAPTER 4

Exhibit 4.8	Adapted with the permission of The Free Press, A Division of Simon & Schuster from Competitive Strategy: Techniques for Analyzing Industries and Competitors by Michael E. Porter. Copyright © 1980 by The Free Press.
Exhibit 4.10	F. M. Scherer and David Ross, Industrial Market Structure and Economic Performance, Second Edition. Copyright © 1980 by Houghton Mifflin Company. Used with permission.
Exhibit 4.11	R. Barnes. Motion and Time Study: Design & Measurement of Work, 7th edition. Copyright ©1980. New York. Wiley. Reprinted by permission of John Wiley & Sons, Inc.
Exhibit 4.12	Reprinted by permission of Harvard Business Review. Exhibit 1, Price of the Model T, 1909-1923. From "Limits of the learning curve" by William J. Abernathy and Kenneth Wayne, Sept.-Oct. 1974. Copyright © 1974 by the President and Fellows of Harvard College; all rights reserved.
Exhibit 4.13	Reprinted by permission of Wall Street Journal. © 1997 Dow Jones & Company, Inc. All rights reserved worldwide.
Exhibit 4.14	Reprinted by permission of Wall Street Journal. © 1996 Dow Jones & Company, Inc. All rights reserved worldwide.
Exhibit 4.16	Reprinted by permission of Wall Street Journal. © 1992 Dow Jones & Company, Inc. All rights reserved worldwide.
Exhibit 4.17	Reprinted by permission of Wall Street Journal. © 1991 Dow Jones & Company, Inc. All rights reserved worldwide.
Exhibit 4.18	Reprinted by permission of Wall Street Journal. © 1997-1998 Dow Jones & Company, Inc. All rights reserved worldwide.

CHAPTER 5

Exhibit 5.03	Peapod, Inc. Reprinted by permission.

CHAPTER 6

Exhibit 6.9	Reprinted by permission of Wall Street Journal. © 1995 Dow Jones & Company, Inc. All rights reserved worldwide.

CHAPTER 7

Exhibit 7.2	Adapted with the permission of The Free Press, A Division of Simon & Schuster from Competitive Strategy: Techniques for Analyzing Industries and Competitors by Michael E. Porter. Copyright © 1980 by The Free Press.
Exhibit 7.8	Source: Michael E. Porter and Pankaj Ghemawat, General Electric vs. Westinghouse in Large Turbine Generators (A), case no. 9-380-128. Boston: Harvard Business School, 1980. Copyright © 1980 by the President and Fellows of Harvard College.

Exhibit 7.9 — From The Fifth Discipline by Peter M. Senge. Copyright © 1990 by Peter M. Senge. Used by permission of Doubleday, a division of Bantam Doubleday Dell Publishing Group, Inc.

Exhibit 7.10 — From The Fifth Discipline by Peter M. Senge. Copyright © 1990 by Peter M. Senge. Used by permission of Doubleday, a division of Bantam Doubleday Dell Publishing Group, Inc.

Exhibit 7.11 — Reprinted from the July 8, 1991 issue of Business Week by permission. Copyright 1991 by The McGraw-Hill Companies.

Exhibit 7.12 — Reprinted by permission of Wall Street Journal. © 1993 Dow Jones & Company, Inc. All rights reserved worldwide.

CHAPTER 8

Exhibit 8.5 — Benchmarking: A Continuous Learning Process. From Benchmarking for Success. Presentation by E. Pappacena, partner, Arthur Andersen.

Exhibit 8.7 — Reprinted from the November 30,1992 issue of Business Week by permission. Copyright 1992 by The McGraw-Hill Companies.

Exhibit 8.8 — From Restoring our Competitive Edge: Competing Through Manufacturing. R. H. Hayes & S. C. Wheelwright. Copyright ©1984, John Wiley & Sons, Inc. Reprinted by permission of John Wiley & Sons, Inc.

Exhibit 8.11 — GE Dishwashers: Several Models, All Based on a Common Platform. From R. Sanchez & D. Sudharshan. 1993. Real-time market research. Marketing Intelligence and Planning, 11(7): 29-38. p. 33. Reprinted by permission.

Exhibit 8.12 — Adapted with the permission of The Free Press, A Division of Simon & Schuster from World Class Manufacturing: The Next Decade by Richard J. Shonberger. Copyright © 1996 by Richard J. Shonberger.

Exhibit 8.13 — Adapted with the permission of The Free Press, A Division of Simon & Schuster from World Class Manufacturing: The Next Decade by Richard J. Shonberger. Copyright © 1996 by Richard J. Shonberger.

Exhibit 8.15 — Adapted with the permission of The Free Press, A Division of Simon & Schuster from Intelligent Enterprise: A Knowledge and Service Based Paradigm For Industry by James Brian Quinn. Copyright © 1992 by James Brian Quinn.

Exhibit 8.16 — Adapted with the permission of The Free Press, A Division of Simon & Schuster from Intelligent Enterprise: A Knowledge and Service Based Paradigm For Industry by James Brian Quinn. Copyright © 1992 by James Brian Quinn.

Exhibit 8.17 — Reprinted by permission of Harvard Business Review. How Productivity Varies in the Insurance Industry. From "Managing our way to higher service-sector productivity" by Michael van Biema and Bruce Greenwald, July-Aug. 1997. Copyright © 1997 by the President and Fellows of Harvard College; all rights reserved.

CHAPTER 9

Exhibit 9.7	Reprinted by permission of Wall Street Journal. © 1997 Dow Jones & Company, Inc. All rights reserved worldwide.
Exhibit 9.11	Reprinted by permission of Wall Street Journal. © 1996 Dow Jones & Company, Inc. All rights reserved worldwide.

CHAPTER 10

Exhibit 10.5	Reprinted by permission of Harvard Business School Press. From Strategy, Structure and Economic Performance by Richard P. Rumelt. Boston MA 1986, p. 66. Copyright © 1986 by the President and Fellows of Harvard College; all rights reserved.
Exhibit 10.8	Source: Christopher A. Bartlett and Michael Y. Yoshino, Corning Glass Works International (B-1), case no. 38-161. Boston: Harvard Business School, 1981. Copyright 1981 by the President and Fellows of Harvard College.

CHAPTER 11

Exhibit 11.3	From INVESTOR CAPITALISM by MICHAEL USEEM. Copyright © 1996 by Michael Useem. Reprinted by permission of Perseus Books LLC.
Exhibit 11.8	From The Fifth Discipline by Peter M. Senge. Copyright © 1990 by Peter M. Senge. Used by permission of Doubleday, a division of Bantam Doubleday Dell Publishing Group, Inc.
Exhibit 11.9	From The Fifth Discipline by Peter M. Senge. Copyright © 1990 by Peter M. Senge. Used by permission of Doubleday, a division of Bantam Doubleday Dell Publishing Group, Inc.
Exhibit 11.10 (Management Focus Box)	Letter by Sister Doris Gormley OSF reprinted by permission.
Exhibit 11.11 (Management Focus Box)	Excerpts of letter from Cypress Semiconductor CEO T. J. Rodgers reprinted by permission.

CHAPTER 12

Exhibit 12.4	The Attraction-Selection-Attrition Cycle. Adapted from "An interactionist perspective on organizational effectiveness," Fig. 2.1, p. 35, by B. Schneider in Organizational Effectiveness, edited by K. S. Cameron and D. S. Whetten, 1983. New York. Academic Press. Reprinted by permission.

INDEX

Page numbers that are preceded by another number and period refer to case studies. For example, 12.3 refers to page 3 of Case 12. The case studies are found in the second half of the book.